1
BASKETBALL ALMANAC

Contributing Writers

Marty Strasen
Matt Marsom
Nick Rousso
Michael Bradley
Mike Sheridan

Pete Palmer
David Korus
Bruce Herman
Murray Rubenfeld

Marty Strasen is a freelance sports writer who has covered both pro and college basketball. He is a sports writer for the *Waterloo (Iowa) Courier* and has also written for several major newspapers, including the *Detroit Free Press*. He is the former assistant editor of *Basketball Weekly*.

Matt Marsom is an editor for *NBA Inside Stuff*. He is a contributor, consultant, and former managing editor of *Basketball Weekly*. Marsom is a contributing writer for *Street & Smith* magazines.

Nick Rousso is editor of *Ultimate Sports Basketball* and is also a freelance writer and editor. He is the former editor of *Dick Vitale's Basketball* and *Don Heinrich's College Football*, and he was an associate editor for *Bill Mazeroski's Baseball, The Show*, and *Don Heinrich's Pro Review*.

Michael Bradley is a freelance writer whose work has appeared in *The Sporting News, The Philadelphia Inquirer*, and a variety of national sports publications.

Mike Sheridan is managing editor of *Basketball Times* and *Eastern Basketball*.

Pete Palmer edited both *Total Baseball* and *The Hidden Game of Baseball* with John Thorn. He was the statistician for the *1994 Baseball Almanac* and *1992 Fantasy League Baseball*. Palmer is a member of the Society for American Baseball Research (SABR).

David Korus is a freelance sports statistician who lives in Massachusetts.

Bruce Herman is a freelance writer who has contributed to *Sports Illustrated, Inside Sports*, and *USA TODAY Baseball Weekly*. He is also the managing editor of the *New York Mets Official Yearbook*.

Murray Rubenfeld is Executive Producer of "The Sports Card Report Radio Show" and has written extensively on basketball for several hobby publications. He is a basketball card price-guide analyst for *The Sports Card News*.

Statistics in the College Basketball Review section were provided by the National Collegiate Athletic Association.

Cover Photo Credit: Duomo

CONTENTS

CONTENTS

CONTENTS

6 CONTENTS

NBA Veterans and Rookies

In this section, you'll find scouting reports on 300 NBA veterans and 60 NBA rookies (plus a recap of the 1994 college draft on page 308). The NBA will tip off the 1994-95 season with 324 players, so this section is sure to include most every player on each NBA roster.

Each player's scouting report begins with his vital stats: team, position, height, weight, etc. Next comes a four-part evaluation of the player. "Background" reviews the player's career, starting with college and continuing up through the 1993-94 season. "Strengths" examines his best assets, including such traits as character and leadership. "Weaknesses" assesses the player's significant flaws, including things like attitude and off-court behavior. And "analysis" tries to put the player's game into perspective.

For a quick run-down on each player, you'll find a "player summary" box. The box also includes a "fantasy value" figure, which suggests a draft price for any of the fantasy basketball games that have mushroomed throughout the country. The price range is a guide based on $260 for a 15-player roster. Some players are valued at $0, meaning they are not worth drafting. Finally, the box contains a "card value" figure, which is a suggested buying price for a mint 1993-94 basketball card of that player. The values do not reflect cards from premium sets, such as Fleer Ultra.

The scouting reports of the NBA veterans include their college and NBA statistics. The college stats include games (G), field goal percentage (FGP), free throw percentage (FTP), rebounds per game (RPG), and points per game (PPG). The veterans' NBA stats include the following:

- games (G)
- minutes (MIN)
- field goals made (FGs/FG)
- field goal percentage (FGs/PCT)
- 3-point field goals made (3-PT FGs/FG)
- 3-point field goal percentage (3-PT FGs/PCT)
- free throws made (FTs/FT)
- free throw percentage (FTs/PCT)
- offensive rebounds (Rebounds/OFF)
- total rebounds (Rebounds/TOT)
- assists (AST)
- steals (STL)
- blocked shots (BLK)
- points (PTS)
- points per game (PPG)

The 60 NBA rookies are divided into two categories. The 27 first-round draft picks receive one-page write-ups, while the 27 second-rounders—as well as a half-dozen top nondrafted players—receive half-page write-ups. Second-rounders' stats include rebounds per game (RPG), assists per game (APG), steals per game (SPG), and blocks per game (BPG).

ALAA ABDELNABY

Team: Boston Celtics
Position: Forward
Height: 6'10" **Weight:** 240
Birthdate: June 24, 1968

NBA Experience: 4 years
College: Duke
Acquired: Traded from Bucks for draft rights to Jon Barry, 12/92

Background: Abdelnaby, who was born in Egypt and moved to the United States in 1971, led Duke to three Final Fours and established a school record for career field goal percentage (.599). His playing time as a Trail Blazer rookie was limited, but he doubled his scoring average in 1991-92 before trades to Milwaukee and Boston. Abdelnaby was an early disappointment as a Celtic until he found a comfort zone as a role-player off the bench. Injuries limited him to less than half a season in 1993-94.

Strengths: Abdelnaby will not lead a team in scoring but is capable of hitting double figures when called upon. He possesses good offensive skills around the basket and will not force bad shots. He is a solid rebounder and gets many of his points off the offensive glass. He has good hands and works hard. Abdelnaby is willing to play defense.

Weaknesses: Abdelnaby's perimeter game has a long way to go, especially in the areas of passing and ball-handling. His defensive repertoire does not include shot-blocking, despite his size. He had problems gaining confidence early in his career and showed signs of the same last season.

Analysis: Abdelnaby has not approached his potential as an NBA player. He has the physical skills to be a decent low-post scorer who helps his team by chasing loose balls and keeping his man off the glass. To date, he has not done those things consistently for a Boston team that's been in need of some added fire. With the Celtics adding Dominique Wilkins and Pervis Ellison over the summer, Abdelnaby's playing time will likely be limited.

PLAYER SUMMARY	
Will	hit the boards
Can't	hit jumper consistently
Expect	reserve minutes
Don't Expect	an enforcer
Fantasy Value	$1
Card Value	5-8¢

COLLEGE STATISTICS

		G	FGP	FTP	RPG	PPG
86-87	DUKE	29	.580	.522	1.7	3.7
87-88	DUKE	34	.496	.698	2.0	4.9
88-89	DUKE	33	.634	.701	3.8	8.9
89-90	DUKE	38	.620	.775	6.6	15.1
Totals		134	.599	.728	3.7	8.5

NBA REGULAR-SEASON STATISTICS

		G	MIN	FGs FG	FGs PCT	3-PT FGs FG	3-PT FGs PCT	FTs FT	FTs PCT	Rebounds OFF	Rebounds TOT	AST	STL	BLK	PTS	PPG
90-91	POR	43	290	55	.474	0	.000	25	.568	27	89	12	4	12	135	3.1
91-92	POR	71	934	178	.493	0	.000	76	.752	81	260	30	25	16	432	6.1
92-93	MIL/BOS	75	1311	245	.518	0	.000	88	.759	126	337	27	25	26	578	7.7
93-94	BOS	13	159	24	.436	0	.000	16	.640	12	46	3	2	3	64	4.9
Totals		202	2694	502	.500	0	.000	205	.717	246	732	72	56	57	1209	6.0

MAHMOUD ABDUL-RAUF

Team: Denver Nuggets
Position: Guard
Height: 6'1" **Weight:** 168
Birthdate: March 9, 1969

NBA Experience: 4 years
College: Louisiana St.
Acquired: 1st-round pick in 1990 draft (3rd overall)

Background: In two seasons at LSU, the former Chris Jackson accomplished things most four-year players will never approach. He broke three NCAA freshman records: most points in a game against a Division I opponent (55), most in a season (965), and highest scoring average (30.2 PPG). After two lackluster NBA seasons, he won the 1992-93 Most Improved Player Award as he led the Nuggets in scoring and assists. He maintained his team leadership and impressive numbers after converting to Muslim before the 1993-94 campaign.

Strengths: A great athlete who is extremely quick, Abdul-Rauf is blessed with big-time talent. He can score by getting to the hoop, with his long-range shooting, or in the open court. He does not use strings, but somehow the ball is attached to his hand. A crossover dribble and quick release make him tough to defend. He made 219 of 229 free throws last year—the second-best conversion rate of all time, behind Calvin Murphy.

Weaknesses: Abdul-Rauf should be a better thief and assist man than he is. He has the quickness to penetrate and dish, but he looks to score himself first. He could also be a defensive nuisance if he decided to devote himself to that aspect of the game.

Analysis: A neurological disorder called Tourette's Syndrome and a great deal of scrutiny since his college days have not prevented Abdul-Rauf from becoming a fine NBA guard. He has displayed a much higher level of dedication in the past two years, which has helped him shake some of his many detractors. He says his religious conversion has helped him put less pressure on himself, and it shows.

PLAYER SUMMARY

Will ....get his points
Can't..................dominate on defense
Expect ....18-20 PPG
Don't Expect.....................missed FTs
Fantasy Value $12-15
Card Value.............................12-20¢

COLLEGE STATISTICS

		G	FGP	FTP	APG	PPG
88-89	LSU	32	.486	.815	4.1	30.2
89-90	LSU	32	.461	.910	3.2	27.8
Totals		64	.474	.863	3.6	29.0

NBA REGULAR-SEASON STATISTICS

				FGs		3-PT FGs		FTs		Rebounds						
		G	MIN	FG	PCT	FG	PCT	FT	PCT	OFF	TOT	AST	STL	BLK	PTS	PPG
90-91	DEN	67	1505	417	.413	24	.240	84	.857	34	121	206	55	4	942	14.1
91-92	DEN	81	1538	356	.421	31	.330	94	.870	22	114	192	44	4	837	10.3
92-93	DEN	81	2710	633	.450	70	.355	217	.935	51	225	344	84	8	1553	19.2
93-94	DEN	80	2617	588	.460	42	.316	219	.956	27	168	362	82	10	1437	18.0
Totals		309	8370	1994	.439	167	.319	614	.921	134	628	1104	265	26	4769	15.4

MICHAEL ADAMS

Team: Charlotte Hornets
Position: Guard
Height: 5'10" **Weight:** 175
Birthdate: January 19, 1963

NBA Experience: 9 years
College: Boston College
Acquired: Traded from Bullets for
1996 and 1997 2nd-round picks, 8/94

Background: Adams was named second-team All-Big East three straight years at Boston College. The former CBA Rookie of the Year (1986) holds or has held numerous NBA 3-point records and, in 1993-94, he became only the third player in league history to hit 900 career treys. He played in the 1992 All-Star Game. Adams ran the point in Washington for the past three seasons but was traded to Charlotte over the summer.

Strengths: Adams has two primary weapons: his quickness and his 3-point shooting. He is, quite literally, a threat to score from anywhere on the court. He can penetrate almost at will and still races the ball to the offensive end. Opponents don't like to see him at the line.

Weaknesses: Although he shoots 3-pointers like there's no tomorrow, he converts less than one-third of them. His field goal percentage is traditionally brutal. As quick as he is, he should be more of a defensive thief. Naturally, he's a prime post-up target because of his stature.

Analysis: The Bullets discarded Adams again after cutting him twice and trading him once earlier in his career. A separated shoulder hampered him last season, and his career seems on the decline. In Charlotte, he'll battle another mighty mite, Muggsy Bogues, for playing time at the point.

PLAYER SUMMARY	
Will	fire when open
Can't	block shots
Expect	good quickness
Don't Expect	50-percent shooting
Fantasy Value	$1-3
Card Value	5-10¢

COLLEGE STATISTICS

		G	FGP	FTP	APG	PPG
81-82	BC	26	.495	.590	1.5	5.3
82-83	BC	32	.481	.809	5.3	16.2
83-84	BC	30	.455	.756	3.5	17.3
84-85	BC	31	.467	.748	3.2	15.3
Totals		119	.470	.750	3.5	13.9

NBA REGULAR-SEASON STATISTICS

		G	MIN	FGs FG	FGs PCT	3-PT FGs FG	3-PT FGs PCT	FTs FT	FTs PCT	Rebounds OFF	Rebounds TOT	AST	STL	BLK	PTS	PPG
85-86	SAC	18	139	16	.364	0	.000	8	.667	2	6	22	9	1	40	2.2
86-87	WAS	63	1303	160	.407	28	.275	105	.847	38	123	244	85	6	453	7.2
87-88	DEN	82	2778	416	.449	139	.367	166	.834	40	223	503	168	16	1137	13.9
88-89	DEN	77	2787	468	.433	166	.356	322	.819	71	283	490	166	11	1424	18.5
89-90	DEN	79	2690	398	.402	158	.366	267	.850	49	225	495	121	3	1221	15.5
90-91	DEN	66	2346	560	.394	167	.296	465	.879	58	256	693	147	6	1752	26.5
91-92	WAS	78	2795	485	.393	125	.324	313	.869	58	310	594	145	9	1408	18.1
92-93	WAS	70	2499	365	.439	68	.321	237	.856	52	240	526	100	4	1035	14.8
93-94	WAS	70	2337	285	.408	55	.288	224	.830	37	183	480	96	6	849	12.1
Totals		603	19674	3153	.414	906	.331	2107	.850	405	1849	4047	1037	62	9319	15.5

DANNY AINGE

Team: Phoenix Suns
Position: Guard
Height: 6'5" **Weight:** 185
Birthdate: March 17, 1959

NBA Experience: 13 years
College: Brigham Young
Acquired: Signed as a free agent, 7/92

Background: Ainge was a multi-sport star at Brigham Young and played two years of professional baseball with the Toronto Blue Jays, primarily as an infielder. He batted .220. He has enjoyed much greater success in the NBA, where he was an All-Star in 1988 and won two championship rings with the Boston Celtics. He has spent his last two years as an important reserve with a strong Phoenix team.

Strengths: Ainge remains one of the better 3-point shooters in the league. He is also a fierce competitor with championship experience and tremendous leadership skills. When games are on the line, he's capable of winning them.

Weaknesses: Ainge is not a first-rate defender and he's not getting any quicker—though he is feisty. On offense, he is not much of a creator. His shooting percentage is nothing to boast about.

Analysis: Once a superbrat, Ainge has become a steadying influence. He has had much to do with Phoenix's rise to annual league title contender. Last season, he became only the second player in NBA history to reach 900 career 3-pointers.

PLAYER SUMMARY	
Will	stick 3-pointers
Can't	shut down a star
Expect	veteran leadership
Don't Expect	20 PPG
Fantasy Value	$2-4
Card Value	5-12¢

COLLEGE STATISTICS

		G	FGP	FTP	RPG	PPG
77-78	BYU	30	.514	.864	5.8	21.1
78-79	BYU	27	.548	.768	3.8	18.4
79-80	BYU	29	.533	.782	3.9	19.1
80-81	BYU	32	.518	.824	4.8	24.4
Totals		118	.526	.816	4.6	20.9

NBA REGULAR-SEASON STATISTICS

		G	MIN	FGs FG	FGs PCT	3-PT FGs FG	3-PT FGs PCT	FTs FT	FTs PCT	Rebounds OFF	Rebounds TOT	AST	STL	BLK	PTS	PPG
81-82	BOS	53	564	79	.357	5	.294	56	.862	25	56	87	37	3	219	4.1
82-83	BOS	80	2048	357	.496	5	.172	72	.742	83	214	251	109	6	791	9.9
83-84	BOS	71	1154	166	.460	6	.273	46	.821	29	116	162	41	4	384	5.4
84-85	BOS	75	2564	419	.529	15	.268	118	.868	76	268	399	122	6	971	12.9
85-86	BOS	80	2407	353	.504	26	.356	123	.904	47	235	405	94	7	855	10.7
86-87	BOS	71	2499	410	.486	85	.443	148	.897	49	242	400	101	14	1053	14.8
87-88	BOS	81	3018	482	.491	148	.415	158	.878	59	249	503	115	17	1270	15.7
88-89	BOS/SAC	73	2377	480	.457	116	.380	205	.854	71	255	402	93	8	1281	17.5
89-90	SAC	75	2727	506	.438	108	.374	222	.831	69	326	453	113	18	1342	17.9
90-91	POR	80	1710	337	.472	102	.406	114	.826	45	205	285	63	13	890	11.1
91-92	POR	81	1595	299	.442	78	.339	108	.824	40	148	202	73	13	784	9.7
92-93	PHO	80	2163	337	.462	150	.403	123	.848	49	214	260	69	8	947	11.8
93-94	PHO	68	1555	224	.417	80	.328	78	.830	28	131	180	57	8	606	8.9
Totals		968	26381	4449	.469	924	.379	1571	.849	670	2659	3989	1087	125	11393	11.8

VICTOR ALEXANDER

Team: Golden State Warriors   **NBA Experience:** 3 years
Position: Center/Forward   **College:** Iowa St.
Height: 6'9" **Weight:** 265   **Acquired:** 1st-round pick in 1991 draft
Birthdate: August 31, 1969   (17th overall)

Background: Alexander weighed nearly 300 pounds as an Iowa State freshman but exploded as a sophomore, finishing third in the Big Eight in scoring and rebounding. He had an outstanding senior season, was drafted in the first round, and has played a prominent role in his three seasons with Golden State. Alexander has been a part-time starter in each of the last two seasons, although last year his scoring average dropped after peaking at 11.2 PPG in 1992-93.

Strengths: Alexander is a highly skilled offensive player. He has surprising mobility, good post-up skills, a soft shooting touch, and tremendous hands. He knows what to do with the ball near the basket and can amaze people with some of the shots he'll pull off in traffic. He shoots better than 50 percent from the floor. He is also a pretty solid rebounder when he sets his mind to it.

Weaknesses: Defense has never been a high priority with Alexander, whose weight can also still be a problem. Questionable commitment comes into play in both areas. He'll impress everyone in the house one game, then disappear the next. Passing is one of the weaker aspects of his game and he too often relies on offensive finesse rather than power. He's a poor free throw shooter.

Analysis: It's clear Alexander will never be a chiseled, Karl Malone type. But he has done a better job of conditioning himself since his rookie season and the Warriors can look inside when he's on the floor. Alexander is a very polished offensive player who, with more assertiveness, could give his team a man-sized boost in the paint.

PLAYER SUMMARY

Will ....score in traffic
Can't ....hit his FTs
Expect ....impressive spurts
Don't Expect ....blazing speed
Fantasy Value $2-4
Card Value ....7-12¢

COLLEGE STATISTICS

		G	FGP	FTP	RPG	PPG
87-88	ISU	23	.600	.500	1.4	1.7
88-89	ISU	29	.583	.651	8.8	19.9
89-90	ISU	28	.585	.578	8.7	19.7
90-91	ISU	31	.659	.677	9.0	23.4
Totals		111	.538	.635	7.3	17.0

NBA REGULAR-SEASON STATISTICS

		G	MIN	FGs FG	FGs PCT	3-PT FGs FG	3-PT FGs PCT	FTs FT	FTs PCT	Rebounds OFF	Rebounds TOT	AST	STL	BLK	PTS	PPG
91-92	GS	80	1350	243	.529	0	.000	103	.691	106	336	32	45	62	589	7.4
92-93	GS	72	1753	344	.516	10	.455	111	.685	132	420	93	34	53	809	11.2
93-94	GS	69	1318	266	.530	2	.154	68	.527	114	308	66	28	32	602	8.7
Totals		221	4421	853	.524	12	.333	282	.641	352	1064	191	107	147	2000	9.0

GREG ANDERSON

Team: Detroit Pistons
Position: Forward/Center
Height: 6'10" **Weight:** 230
Birthdate: June 22, 1964

NBA Experience: 6 years
College: Houston
Acquired: Signed as a free agent, 9/93

Background: Anderson played behind Hakeem Olajuwon as a freshman at the University of Houston before emerging as one of the premier rebounders in Southwest Conference history. He was named NBA All-Rookie with San Antonio and played two promising years there. Since undergoing knee surgery in 1989, however, he has played with four NBA teams and in Europe. He averaged 6.4 PPG and 7.4 RPG for Detroit last season.

Strengths: "Cadillac" is first and foremost a rebounder. Opponents find it tough to manuever around his big body and he uses his strength to his advantage. He also can be a capable low-post scorer with some power moves around the basket. He shoots for a high percentage and will block some shots.

Weaknesses: Anderson has done very little consistently since the knee injury, although his decline as a player is due to a lot more than that. His desire to be a top NBA player has been legitimately questioned. His offensive range is limited, he does not handle the ball well, and he is a terrible passer. He shoots less than 60 percent from the free throw line and sends opponents there often.

Analysis: The fact that Anderson started more than half the season for the Pistons last year says less about him than it does about Detroit's struggles on the front line. Cadillac did have his moments, like the night he scored 23 points, and he contributed as a rebounder for the entire season. Ideally, however, you would like to have this journeyman coming off the bench.

PLAYER SUMMARY	
Will	crash the boards
Can't	shoot FTs
Expect	good size
Don't Expect	crisp passes
Fantasy Value	$1
Card Value	5-10¢

COLLEGE STATISTICS

		G	FGP	FTP	RPG	PPG
83-84	HOU	35	.485	.528	3.5	3.3
84-85	HOU	30	.573	.535	8.1	15.4
85-86	HOU	28	.572	.586	12.9	19.1
86-87	HOU	30	.526	.604	10.6	18.2
Totals		123	.550	.576	8.5	13.5

NBA REGULAR-SEASON STATISTICS

		G	MIN	FGs FG	FGs PCT	3-PT FGs FG	3-PT FGs PCT	FTs FT	FTs PCT	Rebounds OFF	Rebounds TOT	AST	STL	BLK	PTS	PPG
87-88	SA	82	1984	379	.501	1	.200	198	.604	161	513	79	54	122	957	11.7
88-89	SA	82	2401	460	.503	0	.000	207	.514	255	676	61	102	103	1127	13.7
89-90	MIL	60	1291	219	.507	0	.000	91	.535	112	373	24	32	54	529	8.8
90-91	MIL/NJ/DEN															
		68	924	116	.430	0	.000	60	.522	97	318	16	35	45	292	4.3
91-92	DEN	82	2793	389	.456	0	.000	167	.623	337	941	78	88	65	945	11.5
93-94	DET	77	1624	201	.543	1	.333	88	.571	183	571	51	55	68	491	6.4
Totals		451	11017	1764	.491	2	.125	811	.564	1145	3392	309	366	457	4341	9.6

KENNY ANDERSON

Team: New Jersey Nets
Position: Guard
Height: 6'11" **Weight:** 170
Birthdate: October 9, 1970

NBA Experience: 3 years
College: Georgia Tech
Acquired: 1st-round pick in 1991 draft (2nd overall)

Background: A legend at New York City's Archbishop Malloy High, Anderson was an instant hit at Georgia Tech. He led the ACC in assists as a freshman. When teammates Dennis Scott and Brian Oliver left for the NBA, Anderson tried to carry the team for a year and then turned pro at the end of his sophomore season. After a contract holdout and disappointing rookie year, Anderson has thrived as the Nets' point guard the past two seasons. He has finished among the NBA assist leaders each of the last two years and made his All-Star debut last February.

Strengths: Anderson is a classic point guard with a scorer's mentality. He is a terrific ball-handler, passer, and penetrator with a special ability to see the floor. He can create plays and finish them and has 3-point range with his awkward-looking jumper. Defensively, he relies on quick hands and superior anticipation. He has become respected for his leadership as well.

Weaknesses: Sometimes Anderson still tends to go for the spectacular play instead of the logical one. Bigger guards can post him up, although he has grown somewhat stronger. He is still not a consistent perimeter shooter, which begs defenders to sag.

Analysis: Anderson's breakthrough year of 1992-93 was cut short when John Starks took him out with a flagrant foul, but Anderson came back with a vengeance last season. The former prep and college All-American is on his way to becoming one of the best in the pro game as well. Other point guards enjoy watching him play, and so will NBA fans as he continues his rise to the top.

PLAYER SUMMARY	
Will	display dazzling skills
Can't	post up
Expect	more All-Star showings
Don't Expect	a gunner
Fantasy Value	$25-30
Card Value	20-35¢

COLLEGE STATISTICS

		G	FGP	FTP	APG	PPG
89-90	GT	35	.515	.733	5.3	20.6
90-91	GT	30	.437	.829	5.6	25.9
Totals		65	.473	.787	5.4	23.0

NBA REGULAR-SEASON STATISTICS

				FGs		3-PT FGs		FTs		Rebounds						
		G	MIN	FG	PCT	FG	PCT	FT	PCT	OFF	TOT	AST	STL	BLK	PTS	PPG
91-92	NJ	64	1086	187	.390	3	.231	73	.745	38	127	203	67	9	450	7.0
92-93	NJ	55	2010	370	.435	7	.280	180	.776	51	226	449	96	11	927	16.9
93-94	NJ	82	3135	576	.417	40	.303	346	.818	89	322	784	158	15	1538	18.8
Totals		201	6231	1133	.418	50	.294	599	.795	178	675	1436	321	35	2915	14.5

NICK ANDERSON

Team: Orlando Magic
Position: Forward/Guard
Height: 6'6" **Weight:** 205
Birthdate: January 20, 1968

NBA Experience: 5 years
College: Illinois
Acquired: 1st-round pick in 1989 draft (11th overall)

Background: Anderson was a unanimous All-Big Ten selection on the "Flying Illini" Final Four team of 1988-89 and was an instant starter and double-figure scorer in the NBA with Orlando. He led the Magic in scoring in 1991-92, the year before Shaquille O'Neal joined the team. His scoring numbers dipped during the 1993-94 season, which coincided with Anfernee Hardaway's rookie campaign.

Strengths: Anderson can put the ball in the basket. He shoots with 3-point range and is able to get to the hoop with his tremendous quickness and leaping ability. At his offensive best when aggressive, he's strong enough to attack the hoop through traffic and draw fouls. He can play two positions and is a fine backcourt rebounder. He has a great feel for the game and can be dominant at times.

Weaknesses: Anderson's most significant weakness is his on-the-ball defense. He does, however, hit the defensive glass. Offensively, he has been lost in the shuffle more in the last two years than he was early in his career. His free throw and 3-point accuracy are causes for concern.

Analysis: Anderson has seemed on the verge of NBA stardom within the past two years, but youngsters O'Neal and Hardaway have grabbed the spotlight in Orlando and will keep it for years to come. Anderson remains capable of taking over games and continues to raise his level of play in areas other than scoring. He may never be a marquee name in the league, but his game is respected by players and coaches alike.

PLAYER SUMMARY	
Will	score in spurts
Can't	overshadow O'Neal
Expect	clutch 3-pointers
Don't Expect	20 PPG
Fantasy Value	$25-30
Card Value	8-15¢

COLLEGE STATISTICS

		G	FGP	FTP	RPG	PPG
87-88	ILL	33	.572	.642	6.6	15.9
88-89	ILL	36	.538	.669	7.9	18.0
Totals		69	.553	.657	7.3	17.0

NBA REGULAR-SEASON STATISTICS

		G	MIN	FGs FG	FGs PCT	3-PT FGs FG	3-PT FGs PCT	FTs FT	FTs PCT	Rebounds OFF	Rebounds TOT	AST	STL	BLK	PTS	PPG
89-90	ORL	81	1785	372	.494	1	.059	186	.705	107	316	124	69	34	931	11.5
90-91	ORL	70	1971	400	.467	17	.293	173	.668	92	386	106	74	44	990	14.1
91-92	ORL	60	2203	482	.463	30	.353	202	.667	98	384	163	97	33	1196	19.9
92-93	ORL	79	2920	594	.449	88	.353	298	.741	122	477	265	128	56	1574	19.9
93-94	ORL	81	2811	504	.478	101	.322	168	.672	113	476	294	134	33	1277	15.8
Totals		371	11690	2352	.468	237	.328	1027	.695	532	2039	952	502	200	5968	16.1

WILLIE ANDERSON

Team: San Antonio Spurs
Position: Guard/Forward
Height: 6'8" **Weight:** 200
Birthdate: January 8, 1967

NBA Experience: 6 years
College: Georgia
Acquired: 1st-round pick in 1988 draft
(10th overall)

Background: Anderson finished eighth on Georgia's all-time scoring list, competed on the United States Olympic team in 1988, and played in the 1987 Pan-Am Games. After he averaged 18.6 PPG as a rookie with San Antonio, his scoring average declined for four straight years while leg injuries limited his playing time. The 1993-94 season was a comeback year for Anderson, who rejoined the starting lineup and returned to double-figure scoring.

Strengths: Anderson, who in his early years drew comparisons to former Spurs scoring great George Gervin, is one of the more versatile players in the league. He plays both the two and three spots with equal success. He can penetrate and is a good passer. Though lean in build, he is not afraid to challenge with drives to the hoop. He is a fine free throw shooter and has 3-point range with his jumper.

Weaknesses: Anderson has never been among the league's top marksmen. The leg injuries and his declining scoring average seemed to take their toll on his confidence, and he may never return to the high-scoring days he enjoyed as a rookie. His first step may also have taken a mild hit because of the injuries.

Analysis: Anderson answered a lot of doubters with his successful return last year, helping the Spurs contend in the Western Conference and finishing among the team's leaders in several categories. He probably will never score like he did early in his career, but San Antonio is clearly a better team with this versatile player on the floor.

PLAYER SUMMARY	
Will	play two positions
Can't	rely on jumpers
Expect	great versatility
Don't Expect	return to 18 PPG
Fantasy Value	$6-8
Card Value	5-10¢

COLLEGE STATISTICS

		G	FGP	FTP	RPG	PPG
84-85	GA	13	.487	.625	1.5	3.3
85-86	GA	29	.503	.787	3.4	8.5
86-87	GA	30	.500	.794	4.1	15.9
87-88	GA	35	.500	.784	5.1	16.7
Totals		107	.500	.784	3.9	12.6

NBA REGULAR-SEASON STATISTICS

			FGs		3-PT FGs		FTs		Rebounds						
	G	MIN	FG	PCT	FG	PCT	FT	PCT	OFF	TOT	AST	STL	BLK	PTS	PPG
88-89 SA	81	2738	640	.498	4	.190	224	.775	152	417	372	150	62	1508	18.6
89-90 SA	82	2788	532	.492	7	.269	217	.748	115	372	364	111	58	1288	15.7
90-91 SA	75	2592	453	.457	7	.200	170	.798	68	351	358	79	46	1083	14.4
91-92 SA	57	1889	312	.455	13	.232	107	.775	62	300	302	54	51	744	13.1
92-93 SA	38	560	80	.430	1	.125	22	.786	7	57	79	14	6	183	4.8
93-94 SA	80	2488	394	.471	22	.324	145	.848	68	242	347	71	46	955	11.9
Totals	413	13055	2411	.476	54	.252	885	.784	472	1739	1822	479	269	5761	13.9

GREG ANTHONY

Team: New York Knicks
Position: Guard
Height: 6'2" **Weight:** 185
Birthdate: November 15, 1967

NBA Experience: 3 years
College: Portland; Nevada-Las Vegas
Acquired: 1st-round pick in 1991 draft (12th overall)

Background: Anthony spent his first college season at Portland, where he played shooting guard. Jerry Tarkanian moved him to point guard at UNLV, where Anthony directed the Rebels to the national title in 1990 and to the Final Four in 1991. He has demonstrated glimpses of great play in his three NBA seasons but also has made his share of mistakes. He was a part-time starter for the Knicks last season but wound up the year in a reserve role.

Strengths: Anthony is a take-charge type, although some would use less flattering words to describe his demeanor. He loves to compete and is extremely confident, especially in his ball-handling. He is adept at the running game and can thread the needle with his passing. He has a natural ability to create and keeps his eyes peeled for the open man.

Weaknesses: Anthony's shooting is the reason he's never become a full-time starter. It's a safe bet he'll be left wide open in favor of double-teams elsewhere, and his miserable percentages show why. He tends to gamble too much on defense, a habit picked up in college, and he's an easy post-up victim for bigger guards. Erratic play has characterized his early years.

Analysis: Anthony thrives in the open court, yet the Knicks are not a run-and-gun team. His gritty competitiveness and hustle on defense do fit the New York style, but he simply does not shoot well enough to be a productive NBA scorer. His decision-making has improved to the point where there are much worse back-up point guards in the league.

PLAYER SUMMARY

Will ....run the court
Can't ....stick as a starter
Expect......................competitiveness
Don't Expect ....good shooting
Fantasy Value $1-3
Card Value..................................7-12¢

COLLEGE STATISTICS

		G	FGP	FTP	APG	PPG
86-87	PORT	28	.398	.694	4.0	15.3
88-89	UNLV	36	.443	.699	6.6	12.9
89-90	UNLV	39	.457	.682	7.4	11.2
90-91	UNLV	35	.456	.775	8.9	11.6
Totals		138	.437	.707	6.9	12.6

NBA REGULAR-SEASON STATISTICS

				FGs		3-PT FGs		FTs		Rebounds						
		G	MIN	FG	PCT	FG	PCT	FT	PCT	OFF	TOT	AST	STL	BLK	PTS	PPG
91-92	NY	82	1510	161	.370	8	.145	117	.741	33	136	314	59	9	447	5.5
92-93	NY	70	1699	174	.415	4	.133	107	.673	42	170	398	113	12	459	6.6
93-94	NY	80	1994	225	.394	48	.300	130	.774	43	189	365	114	13	628	7.8
Totals		232	5203	560	.393	60	.245	354	.730	118	495	1077	286	34	1534	6.6

B.J. ARMSTRONG

Team: Chicago Bulls
Position: Guard
Height: 6'2" **Weight:** 185
Birthdate: September 9, 1967

NBA Experience: 5 years
College: Iowa
Acquired: 1st-round pick in 1989 draft
(18th overall)

Background: After becoming Iowa's all-time leader in assists, Armstrong was plucked by the Bulls in the 1989 draft. He saw early action and was Chicago's top bench player during the team's 1991 and 1992 NBA championship seasons. The baby-faced guard came into his own in 1992-93, leading the NBA in 3-point accuracy, and he was honored with his first All-Star Game appearance during another fine effort in 1993-94.

Strengths: Armstrong has made himself one of the most dangerous and confident jump-shooters in the game. Leave him open and he'll kill you, from both inside and behind the 3-point arc. He possesses the quickness to trigger Chicago's running game and defend quick point guards. He's bright, works hard, and does what is asked of him. He's also a steady free throw shooter.

Weaknesses: Armstrong still tries to force things from time to time. His passing skills are perhaps not of the caliber of other point guards. He leads the Bulls in neither steals nor assists, although having a teammate like Scottie Pippen has a lot to do with that. He's a better spot-up shooter than creator.

Analysis: It took him a while to win full-time starting duties from John Paxson, but once he did he raised his game to All-Star level. He is supremely confident with his jump shot, and for good reason. Few are more reliable from outside. He has also become a team leader since the retirement of Michael Jordan and has performed well in that role.

PLAYER SUMMARY

Will ....bury 3-pointers
Can't ....top Pippen in assists
Expect ....clutch shooting
Don't Expect ....reserve stints
Fantasy Value $10-13
Card Value ....12-25¢

COLLEGE STATISTICS

		G	FGP	FTP	APG	PPG
85-86	IOWA	29	.485	.905	1.4	2.9
86-87	IOWA	35	.519	.794	4.2	12.4
87-88	IOWA	34	.482	.849	4.6	17.4
88-89	IOWA	32	.484	.833	5.4	18.6
Totals		130	.492	.831	4.0	13.1

NBA REGULAR-SEASON STATISTICS

			FGs		3-PT FGs		FTs		Rebounds						
	G	MIN	FG	PCT	FG	PCT	FT	PCT	OFF	TOT	AST	STL	BLK	PTS	PPG
89-90 CHI	81	1291	190	.485	3	.500	69	.885	19	102	199	46	6	452	5.6
90-91 CHI	82	1731	304	.481	15	.500	97	.874	25	149	301	70	4	720	8.8
91-92 CHI	82	1875	335	.481	35	.402	104	.806	19	145	266	46	5	809	9.9
92-93 CHI	82	2492	408	.499	63	.453	130	.861	27	149	330	66	6	1009	12.3
93-94 CHI	82	2770	479	.476	60	.444	194	.855	28	170	323	80	9	1212	14.8
Totals	409	10159	1716	.484	176	.443	594	.853	118	715	1419	308	30	4202	10.3

VINCENT ASKEW

Team: Seattle SuperSonics
Position: Guard
Height: 6'6" **Weight:** 226
Birthdate: February 28, 1966

NBA Experience: 5 years
College: Memphis St.
Acquired: Traded from Kings for a 1993 2nd-round pick, 11/92

Background: After a three-year career at Memphis State, Askew entered the NBA draft early and found the going rough. He was selected 39th overall by Philadelphia in 1987 but was waived after 14 games. He played in Italy and in the World Basketball League and was twice MVP of the Continental Basketball Association, where he set the single-season scoring record in 1989-90 (26.5 PPG). Askew has since played for Golden State, Sacramento, and Seattle. He was a valuable reserve with the Sonics last season.

Strengths: Askew is a survivor who has paid his dues. He does not specialize in anything, but he'll give you quality minutes and shoot for a high percentage. He proved to be a fine complementary player last year. He has more than enough size to bang with big guards.

Weaknesses: His journeys through four pro leagues indicate that his game is not suited for every team. He has yet to prove he can score bushels of points in the NBA. Askew has the style of a small forward and the size of a big guard. His range is limited.

Analysis: Askew has a lot of heart and has solidified his place in the NBA. He was a key ingredient off the bench in Seattle's mix last season and helped the Sonics become one of the top teams in the league. His toughness and ability to perform several roles well has put him a cut above some of the league's other ex-CBA players.

PLAYER SUMMARY

Will ....find a role
Can't ....score like in CBA
Expect.................................toughness
Don't Expect....................many starts
Fantasy Value $2-4
Card Value ....5-10¢

COLLEGE STATISTICS

		G	FGP	FTP	RPG	PPG
84-85	MSU	35	.511	.634	3.3	8.3
85-86	MSU	34	.490	.814	6.7	10.9
86-87	MSU	34	.483	.787	5.0	15.1
Totals		103	.492	.751	5.0	11.4

NBA REGULAR-SEASON STATISTICS

		G	MIN	FGs FG	FGs PCT	3-PT FGs FG	3-PT FGs PCT	FTs FT	FTs PCT	Rebounds OFF	Rebounds TOT	AST	STL	BLK	PTS	PPG
87-88	PHI	14	234	22	.297	0	.000	8	.727	6	22	33	10	6	52	3.7
90-91	GS	7	85	12	.480	0	.000	9	.818	7	11	13	2	0	33	4.7
91-92	GS	80	1496	193	.509	1	.100	111	.694	89	233	188	47	23	498	6.2
92-93	SAC/SEA	73	1129	152	.492	2	.333	105	.705	62	161	122	40	19	411	5.6
93-94	SEA	80	1690	273	.481	6	.194	175	.829	60	184	194	73	19	727	9.1
Totals		254	4634	652	.482	9	.191	408	.753	224	611	550	172	67	1721	6.8

STACEY AUGMON

Team: Atlanta Hawks
Position: Guard/Forward
Height: 6'8" **Weight:** 205
Birthdate: August 1, 1968

NBA Experience: 3 years
College: Nevada-Las Vegas
Acquired: 1st-round pick in 1991 draft (9th overall)

Background: Augmon, who played four positions for UNLV, established a reputation as the nation's finest college defensive player. He played on the U.S. Olympic team in 1988 and was a key player in UNLV's run to the national title in 1990. He was drafted No. 9 by Atlanta, became a starter in his first year, and made the NBA All-Rookie first team. He has improved his numbers in virtually every category in each of the last two seasons and now averages about 15 points per game.

Strengths: Augmon has lived up to his defensive billing while also proving to be a vastly underrated and productive offensive player. He gets to the basket, runs the floor, and is a superb finisher. He has worked to improve his free throw and field goal percentages. His post-up game is strong. He has great instincts for the ball, a long wingspan, and the ability to get to the boards.

Weaknesses: Augmon has improved his jump-shooting but has limited range and is still a much better slasher than shooter. His only other glaring offensive deficiency is his ball-handling against pressure. He's tough, but his slight build gives stronger opponents an edge on the blocks.

Analysis: Augmon has turned out to be much more than a stopper. Yes, he remains a tremendous defensive player, but he also scores his share of points and his leadership has helped the Hawks become one of the better teams in the league. Few expected Augmon to become the wonderfully complete player he is, and he continues to improve virtually by the game.

PLAYER SUMMARY

Will	get in the passing lane
Can't	shoot with range
Expect	spark at both ends
Don't Expect	3-pointers
Fantasy Value	$17-20
Card Value	8-15¢

COLLEGE STATISTICS

		G	FGP	FTP	RPG	PPG
87-88	UNLV	34	.574	.647	6.1	9.2
88-89	UNLV	37	.519	.663	7.4	15.3
89-90	UNLV	39	.553	.671	6.9	14.2
90-91	UNLV	35	.587	.727	7.3	16.5
Totals		145	.555	.677	6.9	13.7

NBA REGULAR-SEASON STATISTICS

				FGs		3-PT FGs		FTs		Rebounds						
		G	MIN	FG	PCT	FG	PCT	FT	PCT	OFF	TOT	AST	STL	BLK	PTS	PPG
91-92	ATL	82	2505	440	.489	1	.167	213	.666	191	420	201	124	27	1094	13.3
92-93	ATL	73	2112	397	.501	0	.000	227	.739	141	287	170	91	18	1021	14.0
93-94	ATL	82	2605	439	.510	1	.143	333	.764	178	394	187	149	45	1212	14.8
Totals		237	7222	1276	.500	2	.118	773	.727	510	1101	558	364	90	3327	14.0

ANTHONY AVENT

Team: Orlando Magic
Position: Forward
Height: 6'10" **Weight:** 235
Birthdate: October 18, 1969
NBA Experience: 2 years

College: Seton Hall
Acquired: Traded from Bucks for
Anthony Cook and a 1994 1st-round
pick, 1/94

Background: Avent was considered one of the best prep centers in the country while at Shabazz High School in Newark, New Jersey. He averaged 17.8 points and 9.9 rebounds per game during his senior year at Seton Hall and became the highest draft choice ever out of that school when Atlanta selected him 15th overall in 1991. He spent his first pro season in Italy before joining Milwaukee in 1992-93. The Bucks traded Avent to Orlando in January 1994 and he was a part-time starter for each team last year.

Strengths: The strong-bodied Avent is on the floor for two reasons—defense and rebounding. A good athlete, he runs the floor and hustles on both ends. He's blessed with a great work ethic and a team-first attitude. A natural on the offensive glass, Avent uses his instincts to get points on putbacks. He is one of the better offensive rebounders in the league.

Weaknesses: Avent is not a productive offensive player. He thinks too much about his moves instead of using his strength to pull them off, and his scoring average declined drastically last season. He was once demoted to a lesser league in Italy, where defense often goes unappreciated. His shooting is nightmarish and it's reflected in his percentages.

Analysis: Avent was Milwaukee's best rebounder before his trade to Orlando for Anthony Cook and a first-round pick in 1994. The trade itself attests to the value the Magic placed on his rebounding and defensive ability. Until he develops a consistent offensive game, however, Avent will probably struggle for playing time. His work ethic makes his future promising.

PLAYER SUMMARY	
Will	pound the glass
Can't	shoot with range
Expect	rebounding, defense
Don't Expect	much offense
Fantasy Value	$0
Card Value	7-10¢

COLLEGE STATISTICS

		G	FGP	FTP	RPG	PPG
88-89	SH	38	.456	.653	3.0	4.4
89-90	SH	28	.488	.618	9.4	10.5
90-91	SH	34	.577	.750	9.9	17.8
Totals		100	.531	.701	7.1	10.7

NBA REGULAR-SEASON STATISTICS

		G	MIN	FGs FG	PCT	3-PT FGs FG	PCT	FTs FT	PCT	Rebounds OFF	TOT	AST	STL	BLK	PTS	PPG
92-93	MIL	82	2285	347	.433	0	.000	112	.651	180	512	91	57	73	806	9.8
93-94	MIL/ORL	74	1371	150	.377	0	.000	89	.724	144	338	65	33	31	389	5.3
Totals		156	3656	497	.414	0	.000	201	.681	324	850	156	90	104	1195	7.7

THURL BAILEY

Unrestricted Free Agent
Last Team: Minnesota Timberwolves
Position: Forward
Height: 6'11" **Weight:** 247
Birthdate: April 7, 1961

NBA Experience: 11 years
College: North Carolina St.
Acquired: Traded from Jazz with a
1992 2nd-round pick for Tyrone
Corbin, 11/91

Background: Bailey starred for the 1983 N.C. State national championship team and hit the critical shot versus UNLV to send the Wolfpack to the Final Four. With Utah, he twice finished second in the voting for the NBA's Sixth Man Award. He was traded to Minnesota in 1991-92 and has not enjoyed as much success. He has failed to score in double figures the last two years.

Strengths: No one in the league has an unkind word to say about Bailey, a soft-spoken leader. He is a well-schooled low-post player and a quick turnaround shooter with decent range. He's a good free throw shooter. He is also a record-cutting vocalist, trombone player, and avid charity worker.

Weaknesses: Bailey's skills have diminished somewhat over the last several years. His moves are not as crisp as they used to be and his numbers not as impressive. He does not do much defensively, and his leadership has not turned the Timberwolves around.

Analysis: Bailey is still capable of contributing on both ends of the court, but not like he once could. An unrestricted free agent, he may wind up on another team this winter. Bailey is the kind of guy you root for.

PLAYER SUMMARY	
Will	lead by example
Can't	regain old form
Expect	a team player
Don't Expect	a title ring
Fantasy Value	$0
Card Value	5-8¢

COLLEGE STATISTICS

		G	FGP	FTP	RPG	PPG
79-80	NCST	28	.436	.673	3.6	4.5
80-81	NCST	27	.525	.736	6.1	12.3
81-82	NCST	32	.548	.814	6.8	13.7
82-83	NCST	36	.501	.717	7.7	16.7
Totals		123	.513	.745	6.2	12.2

NBA REGULAR-SEASON STATISTICS

				FGs		3-PT FGs		FTs		Rebounds						
		G	MIN	FG	PCT	FG	PCT	FT	PCT	OFF	TOT	AST	STL	BLK	PTS	PPG
83-84	UTA	81	2009	302	.512	0	.000	88	.752	115	464	129	38	122	692	8.5
84-85	UTA	80	2481	507	.490	1	1.000	197	.842	153	525	138	51	105	1212	15.1
85-86	UTA	82	2358	483	.448	0	.000	230	.830	148	493	153	42	114	1196	14.6
86-87	UTA	81	2155	463	.447	0	.000	145	.805	145	432	102	38	88	1116	13.8
87-88	UTA	82	2804	633	.492	1	.333	337	.826	134	531	158	49	125	1604	19.6
88-89	UTA	82	2777	615	.483	2	.400	363	.825	115	447	138	48	91	1595	19.5
89-90	UTA	82	2583	470	.481	0	.000	222	.779	116	410	137	32	100	1162	14.2
90-91	UTA	82	2486	399	.458	0	.000	219	.808	101	407	124	53	91	1017	12.4
91-92	UTA/MIN	84	2104	368	.440	0	.000	215	.796	122	485	78	35	117	951	11.3
92-93	MIN	70	1276	203	.455	0	.000	119	.838	53	215	61	20	47	525	7.5
93-94	MIN	79	1297	232	.510	0	.000	119	.799	66	215	54	20	58	583	7.4
Totals		885	24330	4675	.473	4	.121	2299	.813	1268	4624	1272	426	1058	11653	13.2

VIN BAKER

Team: Milwaukee Bucks
Position: Forward
Height: 6'11" **Weight:** 232
Birthdate: November 23, 1971

NBA Experience: 1 year
College: Hartford
Acquired: 1st-round pick in 1993 draft (8th overall)

Background: Baker toiled in obscurity for Hartford, but he caught the eye of NBA scouts when he finished second in scoring in Division I as a junior. Baker ranked fourth in the nation in scoring and 17th in rebounding as a senior and set school records in career scoring, field goals, free throws, and blocked shots. Drafted eighth overall by Milwaukee, Baker proved to be one of the more surprising 1993-94 rookies. He led the Bucks in rebounding and blocked shots and was among their top scorers.

Strengths: Baker has good size and a polished finesse game to go with it. Likened by some to Danny Manning upon entering the draft, he has panned out to be a productive player around the basket. He is quick, is a good ball-handler for his size, and runs the court smoothly. Baker can play at least two frontcourt positions, and some feel his perimeter game is strong enough for a third. He also adds a shot-blocking dimension.

Weaknesses: Baker made some of the typical rookie mistakes. He put up horrible numbers from the free throw line and tried to swat everything at the defensive end. He is not an overly physical player in the low post yet lacks the consistent jump shot to thrive on the perimeter.

Analysis: Most expected Baker to struggle during his early career in the NBA. After all, it was a hefty jump in competition from the lowly North Atlantic Conference. But Baker came through with flying colors, earning NBA Rookie of the Month honors in February after averaging 16.6 PPG and 9.6 RPG. He and frontcourt mate Glenn Robinson are two of the young players around whom Milwaukee hopes to build a team.

PLAYER SUMMARY	
Will	score, rebound
Can't	shoot 3-pointers
Expect	a fine career
Don't Expect	muscle
Fantasy Value	$19-22
Card Value	25-50¢

COLLEGE STATISTICS

		G	FGP	FTP	RPG	PPG
89-90	HART	28	.617	.390	2.9	4.7
90-91	HART	29	.491	.678	10.4	19.6
91-92	HART	27	.440	.657	9.9	27.6
92-93	HART	28	.477	.625	10.7	28.3
Totals		112	.475	.637	8.5	20.0

NBA REGULAR-SEASON STATISTICS

			FGs		3-PT FGs		FTs		Rebounds						
	G	MIN	FG	PCT	FG	PCT	FT	PCT	OFF	TOT	AST	STL	BLK	PTS	PPG
93-94 MIL	82	2560	435	.501	1	.200	234	.569	277	621	163	60	114	1105	13.5
Totals	82	2560	435	.501	1	.200	234	.569	277	621	163	60	114	1105	13.5

CHARLES BARKLEY

Team: Phoenix Suns
Position: Forward
Height: 6'6" **Weight:** 252
Birthdate: February 20, 1963
NBA Experience: 10 years

College: Auburn
Acquired: Traded from 76ers for Jeff Hornacek, Tim Perry, and Andrew Lang, 6/92

Background: Barkley was known as the "Round Mound of Rebound" at Auburn, where he starred at nearly 270 pounds. He was named SEC Player of the Year as a junior and then entered the NBA draft. In just his second season, he developed into a 20-PPG, 12-RPG player. He has since played at a level few can match. He won Olympic gold in 1992 and was named MVP of the 1992-93 season, his first with Phoenix. He surpassed 17,000 career points last year.

Strengths: Barkley's game features the complete package. He is among the top rebounders and scorers in the league. He shoots with range, muscles inside against seven-footers, and gets to the line. His strength and demeanor make him intimidating at both ends. He's capable of dominating, yet he has also shown great leadership on a strong team.

Weaknesses: Barkley's controversial past includes late-night bar fights and courtside spitting. He seems to have toned down his act but remains an outspoken figure. Leg and back injuries have nagged him of late.

Analysis: Barkley said last season that he may retire soon. When he does, the NBA will lose a true superstar and one of its most colorful players. Barkley is the kind of talent that comes along once in a great while. He still craves a championship ring.

PLAYER SUMMARY

Will....................................dominate
Can't ....hide his feelings
Expect ....20 PPG, 12 RPG
Don't Expect ....timid play
Fantasy Value $65-70
Card Value ....25-40¢

COLLEGE STATISTICS

		G	FGP	FTP	RPG	PPG
81-82	AUB	28	.595	.636	9.8	12.7
82-83	AUB	28	.644	.631	9.5	14.4
83-84	AUB	28	.638	.683	9.5	15.1
Totals		84	.626	.652	9.6	14.1

NBA REGULAR-SEASON STATISTICS

				FGs		3-PT FGs		FTs		Rebounds						
		G	MIN	FG	PCT	FG	PCT	FT	PCT	OFF	TOT	AST	STL	BLK	PTS	PPG
84-85	PHI	82	2347	427	.545	1	.167	293	.733	266	703	155	95	80	1148	14.0
85-86	PHI	80	2952	595	.572	17	.227	396	.685	354	1026	312	173	125	1603	20.0
86-87	PHI	68	2740	557	.594	21	.202	429	.761	390	994	331	119	104	1564	23.0
87-88	PHI	80	3170	753	.587	44	.280	714	.751	385	951	254	100	103	2264	28.3
88-89	PHI	79	3088	700	.579	35	.216	602	.753	403	986	325	126	67	2037	25.8
89-90	PHI	70	3085	706	.600	20	.217	557	.749	361	909	307	148	50	1989	28.4
90-91	PHI	67	2498	665	.570	44	.284	475	.722	258	680	284	110	33	1849	27.6
91-92	PHI	75	2881	622	.552	32	.234	454	.695	271	830	308	136	44	1730	23.1
92-93	PHO	76	2859	716	.520	67	.305	445	.765	237	928	385	119	74	1944	25.6
93-94	PHO	65	2298	518	.495	48	.270	318	.704	198	727	296	101	37	1402	21.6
Totals		742	27918	6259	.562	329	.256	4683	.734	3123	8734	2957	1227	717	17530	23.6

DANA BARROS

Team: Philadelphia 76ers
Position: Guard
Height: 5'11" **Weight:** 165
Birthdate: April 13, 1967
NBA Experience: 5 years

College: Boston College
Acquired: Traded from Hornets with Sidney Green, draft rights to Greg Graham, and a 1994 1st-round pick for Hersey Hawkins, 9/93

Background: Barros, who finished his career as the all-time scoring leader at Boston College, became the first player in Big East history to lead the conference in scoring in back-to-back years. He served mostly as a reserve in his four years in Seattle, and his .446 3-point average in 1991-92 was tops in the NBA. A trade to Philadelphia made him a starter in 1993-94 and he posted career highs in most categories.

Strengths: Barros is a very good 3-point shooter and is not shy about putting them up. He ranked among the league leaders in 3-pointers made and 3-point percentage last season. Small and extremely quick, he is also adept at getting to the hole. Barros possesses loads of confidence.

Weaknesses: Barros is not as polished a playmaker as most point guards, possessing the mentality of a two guard. His assist-to-turnover ratio will not lead the league and he is too content to settle for the long-range jumper. He is suspect on defense because of his size and does not come up with as many steals as a player with his quickness should.

Analysis: Barros came to the 76ers in a three-way deal that sent Kendall Gill to Seattle and Hersey Hawkins to Charlotte. Philadelphia got a fine shooter and Barros got the chance to escape from the shadow of Gary Payton. It's premature to call him one of the better guards in the NBA, but his long-range shooting and desire to be a standout bode well.

PLAYER SUMMARY	
Will	shoot when open
Can't	post up
Expect	high 3-point pct.
Don't Expect	10 APG
Fantasy Value	$7-9
Card Value	5-10¢

COLLEGE STATISTICS

		G	FGP	FTP	APG	PPG
85-86	BC	28	.479	.791	3.5	13.7
86-87	BC	29	.458	.850	3.8	18.7
87-88	BC	33	.480	.850	4.1	21.9
88-89	BC	29	.475	.857	3.3	23.9
Totals		119	.473	.841	3.7	19.7

NBA REGULAR-SEASON STATISTICS

		G	MIN	FGs FG	FGs PCT	3-PT FGs FG	3-PT FGs PCT	FTs FT	FTs PCT	Rebounds OFF	Rebounds TOT	AST	STL	BLK	PTS	PPG
89-90	SEA	81	1630	299	.405	95	.399	89	.809	35	132	205	53	1	782	9.7
90-91	SEA	66	750	154	.495	32	.395	78	.918	17	71	111	23	1	418	6.3
91-92	SEA	75	1331	238	.483	83	.446	60	.759	17	81	125	51	4	619	8.3
92-93	SEA	69	1243	214	.451	64	.379	49	.831	18	107	151	63	3	541	7.8
93-94	PHI	81	2519	412	.469	135	.381	116	.800	28	196	424	107	5	1075	13.3
Totals		372	7473	1317	.455	409	.398	392	.820	115	587	1016	297	14	3435	9.2

JON BARRY

Team: Milwaukee Bucks
Position: Guard
Height: 6'5" **Weight:** 195
Birthdate: July 25, 1969

NBA Experience: 2 years
College: Pacific; Paris; Georgia Tech
Acquired: Draft rights traded from
Celtics for Alaa Abdelnaby, 12/92

Background: One of four sons of Hall of Famer Rick Barry to play Division I basketball, the younger Barry began his college career at Pacific, sat out a year, and played a season at Paris (Texas) Junior College before settling down at Georgia Tech. He led the Yellow Jackets in 3-point field goals as a senior. He was drafted by Boston in 1992 and, after not being able to agree on a contract, was traded to Milwaukee. After struggling as a rookie, Barry improved to 6.2 PPG during the 1993-94 season.

Strengths: Barry knows the game, hustles, and displays a tremendous court sense. He is a splendid passer, perhaps from having to give up the ball while teamed with his father during pick-up games, and he handles the ball very well. He owns 3-point range with his jumper and will lead the break. He also works hard on the defensive end and comes up with his share of steals.

Weaknesses: Barry was known as a good shooter in college, but he has yet to make shots in the NBA with any kind of consistency. His field goal percentage over the last two years was awful, although he does seem to be improving. He does not offer much help on the boards and he is not built to be a strong NBA defensive player.

Analysis: Don't give up on Barry. If there's one trait that characterizes him, it's his willingness to do whatever it takes to make it. His shooting is improving and should continue to do so with more minutes. There are several other parts of the game he needs to hone to become a productive player at this level, however. He will put in the work, and Dad's a great off-season coach.

PLAYER SUMMARY	
Will	shoot with range
Can't	outscore his dad
Expect	further improvement
Don't Expect	new family records
Fantasy Value	$2-4
Card Value	5-8¢

COLLEGE STATISTICS

		G	FGP	FTP	RPG	PPG
87-88	PAC	29	.372	.746	2.6	9.5
90-91	GT	30	.444	.732	3.7	15.9
91-92	GT	35	.429	.697	4.3	17.2
Totals		**94**	**.421**	**.717**	**3.6**	**14.4**

NBA REGULAR-SEASON STATISTICS

				FGs		3-PT FGs		FTs		Rebounds						
		G	MIN	FG	PCT	FG	PCT	FT	PCT	OFF	TOT	AST	STL	BLK	PTS	PPG
92-93	MIL	47	552	76	.369	21	.333	33	.673	10	43	68	35	3	206	4.4
93-94	MIL	72	1242	158	.414	32	.278	97	.795	36	146	168	102	17	445	6.2
Totals		119	1794	234	.398	53	.298	130	.760	46	189	236	137	20	651	5.5

JOHN BATTLE

Team: Cleveland Cavaliers
Position: Guard
Height: 6'2" **Weight:** 190
Birthdate: November 9, 1962

NBA Experience: 9 years
College: Rutgers
Acquired: Signed as a free agent, 7/91

Background: Battle led the Atlantic 10 in scoring in his last two years at Rutgers. He demonstrated both shooting and scoring ability in six years with Atlanta, where he averaged about ten PPG and his field goal percentage was always around 45 or 46. He has spent the last three seasons in Cleveland, where he has struggled since a fine 1991-92 campaign.

Strengths: Battle is known as a shooter. He knocks down the mid-range jumper, gets his shot off in the paint, uses screens to get open, and is a strong leaper. He's been a steady free throw shooter during his career and is well-liked by his teammates.

Weaknesses: Battle seemed to lose some confidence during a dismal 1992-93 and has not regained his form. He is not a great threat from beyond the 3-point line and he no longer offers much on defense. He is not very effective as a playmaker or backcourt rebounder.

Analysis: Battle, who signed a six-year, multi-million-dollar contract with the Cavs in 1991, has been a solid reserve guard for most of his career. But his days with the Cavaliers have not been his best. A dislocated elbow cost him some time last season, and one has to wonder if he can regain the form that made him a double-figure scorer annually.

PLAYER SUMMARY

Will	score off the bench
Can't	regain old form
Expect	streak shooting
Don't Expect	many starts
Fantasy Value	$0
Card Value	5-8¢

COLLEGE STATISTICS

		G	FGP	FTP	APG	PPG
81-82	RUT	29	.433	.429	0.8	2.4
82-83	RUT	31	.489	.725	1.3	5.9
83-84	RUT	25	.493	.725	1.4	21.0
84-85	RUT	29	.491	.729	2.6	21.0
Totals		114	.488	.707	1.5	12.1

NBA REGULAR-SEASON STATISTICS

		G	MIN	FGs FG	FGs PCT	3-PT FGs FG	3-PT FGs PCT	FTs FT	FTs PCT	Rebounds OFF	Rebounds TOT	AST	STL	BLK	PTS	PPG
85-86	ATL	64	639	101	.455	0	.000	75	.728	12	62	74	23	3	277	4.3
86-87	ATL	64	804	144	.457	0	.000	93	.738	16	60	124	29	5	381	6.0
87-88	ATL	67	1227	278	.454	16	.390	141	.750	26	113	158	31	5	713	10.6
88-89	ATL	82	1672	287	.457	11	.324	194	.815	30	140	197	42	9	779	9.5
89-90	ATL	60	1477	275	.506	2	.154	102	.756	27	99	154	28	3	654	10.9
90-91	ATL	79	1863	397	.461	14	.286	270	.854	34	159	217	45	6	1078	13.6
91-92	CLE	76	1637	316	.480	2	.118	145	.848	19	112	159	36	5	779	10.3
92-93	CLE	41	497	83	.415	1	.167	56	.778	4	29	54	9	5	223	5.4
93-94	CLE	51	814	130	.476	5	.263	73	.753	7	39	83	22	1	338	6.6
Totals		584	10630	2011	.466	51	.260	1149	.795	175	813	1220	265	42	5222	8.9

BENOIT BENJAMIN

Team: New Jersey Nets
Position: Center
Height: 7'0" **Weight:** 265
Birthdate: November 22, 1964

NBA Experience: 9 years
College: Creighton
Acquired: Traded from Lakers for Sam Bowie, 6/93

Background: Benjamin played for Creighton and led the nation in blocked shots (5.1 BPG) as a junior. He gave up his final year of college eligibility to enter the NBA draft and played five-plus years with the Los Angeles Clippers. Benjamin has played with four different teams during the last four years, most recently starting in the middle for New Jersey during the 1993-94 campaign.

Strengths: Benjamin has always been a good defensive rebounder and shot-blocker. He has a soft touch on offense and very refined passing skills for a big man. He still has nights when he makes you think he can be one of the better centers in basketball.

Weaknesses: The word "enigma" should be stitched on the back of Benjamin's extra-large jersey. For reasons mostly unknown, he has never displayed the desire or consistency to raise his game to the next level. He has not shot 50 percent from the field in four years.

Analysis: It appears to be too late for Benjamin to become a prominent NBA center despite his considerable natural ability. Each of the past two years has seen him score below double figures. He starts, gets his rebounds, and enjoys an occasional hot night, but he is not the center a contending team wants on the floor for very long.

PLAYER SUMMARY	
Will	get his rebounds
Can't	shake his inconsistency
Expect	the unexpected
Don't Expect	leadership
Fantasy Value	$2-4
Card Value	5-8¢

COLLEGE STATISTICS

		G	FGP	FTP	RPG	PPG
82-83	CRE	27	.555	.655	9.6	14.8
83-84	CRE	30	.543	.743	9.8	16.2
84-85	CRE	32	.582	.738	14.1	21.5
Totals		89	.562	.720	11.3	17.7

NBA REGULAR-SEASON STATISTICS

				FGs		3-PT FGs		FTs		Rebounds						
		G	MIN	FG	PCT	FG	PCT	FT	PCT	OF	TOT	AST	STL	BLK	PTS	PPG
85-86	LAC	79	2088	324	.490	1	.333	229	.746	161	600	79	64	206	878	11.1
86-87	LAC	72	2230	320	.449	0	.000	188	.715	134	586	135	60	187	828	11.5
87-88	LAC	66	2171	340	.491	0	.000	180	.706	112	530	172	50	225	860	13.0
88-89	LAC	79	2585	491	.541	0	.000	317	.744	164	696	157	57	221	1299	16.4
89-90	LAC	71	2313	362	.526	0	.000	235	.732	156	657	159	59	187	959	13.5
90-91	LAC/SEA	70	2236	386	.496	0	.000	210	.712	157	723	119	54	145	982	14.0
91-92	SEA	63	1941	354	.478	0	.000	171	.687	130	513	76	39	118	879	14.0
92-93	SEA/LAL	59	754	133	.491	0	.000	69	.663	51	209	22	31	48	335	5.7
93-94	NJ	77	1817	283	.480	0	.000	152	.710	135	499	44	35	90	718	9.3
Totals		636	18135	2993	.496	1	.056	1751	.719	1200	5013	963	449	1427	7738	12.2

TONY BENNETT

Team: Charlotte Hornets
Position: Guard
Height: 6'0" **Weight:** 175
Birthdate: June 1, 1969

NBA Experience: 2 years
College: Wisconsin-Green Bay
Acquired: 2nd-round pick in 1992 draft (35th overall)

Background: Bennett finished his career at the University of Wisconsin-Green Bay as the Mid-Continent Conference's all-time scoring and assist leader as well as the NCAA's all-time leader in 3-point field goal percentage (.497). He broke or tied 22 school records at UWGB, where he was coached by his father, Dick Bennett. Drafted in the second round by Charlotte in 1992, he has served as a reserve point guard and 3-point shooting threat in limited playing time.

Strengths: Like many coaches' sons, Bennett displays a keen understanding of the game. He plays within himself, sees the court well, distributes the ball to the right people, and handles pressure. He has the makings of a fine shooter with range beyond the NBA 3-point arc, but his field goal percentage has been dismal in his first two seasons.

Weaknesses: Bennett is a step slower than most NBA point guards, a fact that emerged during pre-draft camps and dropped his stock a bit. It gives him a lot of trouble on defense, where he generally is a target of the opposition. His assist-to-turnover ratio is outstanding, but he does not create like the better point guards in the league. He has not been a big NBA scorer and his percentage from the field is a concern.

Analysis: Compared to Charlotte teammate Muggsy Bogues, Bennett looks like he's standing still. Throw in the fact that he has not shot for a high percentage, and you have the reason why Bennett has not seen extended action on a consistent basis. He gives you solid minutes as a reserve point guard, but he is not adept at creating much momentum on either end of the floor.

PLAYER SUMMARY

Will .... shoot the trey
Can't .... out-race Muggsy
Expect .... few turnovers
Don't Expect .... flashy playmaking
Fantasy Value $0
Card Value .... 5-10¢

COLLEGE STATISTICS

		G	FGP	FTP	APG	PPG
88-89	WGB	27	.522	.847	5.1	19.1
89-90	WGB	30	.504	.859	5.2	16.6
90-91	WGB	31	.547	.836	5.0	21.5
91-92	WGB	30	.534	.826	5.1	20.2
Totals		118	.528	.840	5.1	19.4

NBA REGULAR-SEASON STATISTICS

			FGs		3-PT FGs		FTs		Rebounds						
		G	MIN	FG	PCT	FG	PCT	FT	PCT	OFF	TOT	AST	STL	BLK	PTS	PPG
92-93	CHA	75	857	110	.423	26	.325	30	.732	12	63	136	30	0	276	3.7
93-94	CHA	74	983	105	.399	27	.360	11	.733	16	90	163	39	1	248	3.4
Totals		149	1840	215	.411	53	.342	41	.732	28	153	299	69	1	524	3.5

DAVID BENOIT

Team: Utah Jazz
Position: Forward
Height: 6'8" **Weight:** 220
Birthdate: May 9, 1968

NBA Experience: 3 years
College: Tyler; Alabama
Acquired: Signed as a free agent, 8/91

Background: Benoit started playing basketball in high school and began his college career at Tyler Junior College before transferring to Alabama. He started in both of his years there and led the Tide to two NCAA tourney berths. Benoit was the Rookie of the Year in the Spanish League in 1990-91 after averaging 22 PPG and ten RPG. He has spent most of his three years in Utah as a reserve at small forward.

Strengths: Benoit is at his best when blocking shots and crashing the boards. He can jump out of the gym and has long arms that help him play above his man. Benoit can provide offense in a number of ways. He runs the court, finishes on the break, and even shoots from beyond the 3-point arc from time to time.

Weaknesses: Benoit struggles to overcome his inconsistency. He has his problems handling the ball and passing, and over the last two years his jump shot has abandoned him, which is reflected in his field goal percentage. He turns the ball over more often than he gets credit for an assist. He tends to play too fast for his own good. Although aggressive on defense, he's often caught out of position and can be pushed around.

Analysis: Expected to take over the starting small-forward role after Utah traded Blue Edwards two years ago, Benoit did not rise to the challenge. He is still learning the game and is horribly inconsistent. Benoit spent the first part of last year on the injured list and never did find a rhythm after returning to action in late December. He needs a breakthrough campaign.

PLAYER SUMMARY	
Will	run the court
Can't	find his touch
Expect	leaping ability
Don't Expect	consistency
Fantasy Value	$1
Card Value	5-10¢

COLLEGE STATISTICS

		G	FGP	FTP	RPG	PPG
88-89	ALA	31	.507	.738	8.0	10.8
89-90	ALA	35	.515	.767	6.1	10.5
Totals		66	.511	.752	7.0	10.6

NBA REGULAR-SEASON STATISTICS

		G	MIN	FGs FG	FGs PCT	3-PT FGs FG	3-PT FGs PCT	FTs FT	FTs PCT	Rebounds OFF	Rebounds TOT	AST	STL	BLK	PTS	PPG
91-92	UTA	77	1161	175	.467	3	.214	81	.810	105	296	34	19	44	434	5.6
92-93	UTA	82	1712	258	.436	34	.347	114	.750	116	392	43	45	43	664	8.1
93-94	UTA	55	1070	139	.385	12	.203	68	.773	89	260	23	23	37	358	6.5
Totals		214	3943	572	.431	49	.287	263	.774	310	948	100	87	124	1456	6.8

MOOKIE BLAYLOCK

Team: Atlanta Hawks
Position: Guard
Height: 6'1" **Weight:** 185
Birthdate: March 20, 1967

NBA Experience: 5 years
College: Midland; Oklahoma
Acquired: Traded from Nets with Roy Hinson for Rumeal Robinson, 11/92

Background: Mookie, born Daron Oshay Blaylock, earned All-America recognition at Oklahoma and was the first NCAA player to collect 200 assists and 100 steals in back-to-back seasons. Blaylock was selected 12th by New Jersey in 1989 and became the Nets' starting point guard. He was acquired by Atlanta in a 1992 trade for Rumeal Robinson and has since enjoyed his two finest seasons. He made his All-Star debut in 1994.

Strengths: Blaylock is one of the best defensive point guards in the game. His quickness and instincts help him rank among the league leaders in steals annually. Offensively, he's a prototypical point guard with sharp passing skills who can score on drives through the lane and with his jumper. He has 3-point range, handles the ball capably against pressure, and has become a team leader.

Weaknesses: Blaylock does not shoot for a high percentage and is still prone to ice-cold nights. There are times he should stick to driving and dishing instead of firing 3-point bombs. Concerns about his decision-making no longer exist.

Analysis: Blaylock made the jump to All-Star status last season and many feel he can be even better. "He has a chance to be one of the top point guards in the league," coach Lenny Wilkens said last season. He sets a great tempo for the talented Hawks, plays splendid defense, and creates at the offensive end. With a more consistent jumper, he could easily become an All-Star regular.

PLAYER SUMMARY

Will	pick your pocket
Can't	shoot 50 percent
Expect	steady leadership
Don't Expect	defensive lapses
Fantasy Value	$16-19
Card Value	7-12¢

COLLEGE STATISTICS

		G	FGP	FTP	APG	PPG
85-86	MID	34	.566	.738	—	16.8
86-87	MID	33	.516	.723	—	19.6
87-88	OKLA	39	.460	.684	5.9	16.4
88-89	OKLA	35	.455	.650	6.7	20.0
Totals		141	.495	.696	6.3	18.1

NBA REGULAR-SEASON STATISTICS

				FGs		3-PT FGs		FTs		Rebounds						
		G	MIN	FG	PCT	FG	PCT	FT	PCT	OFF	TOT	AST	STL	BLK	PTS	PPG
89-90	NJ	50	1267	212	.371	18	.225	63	.778	42	140	210	82	14	505	10.1
90-91	NJ	72	2585	432	.416	14	.154	139	.790	67	249	441	169	40	1017	14.1
91-92	NJ	72	2548	429	.432	12	.222	126	.712	101	269	492	170	40	996	13.8
92-93	ATL	80	2820	414	.429	118	.375	123	.728	89	280	671	203	23	1069	13.4
93-94	ATL	81	2915	444	.411	114	.334	116	.730	117	424	789	212	44	1118	13.8
Totals		355	12135	1931	.416	276	.313	567	.744	416	1362	2603	836	161	4705	13.3

CORIE BLOUNT

Team: Chicago Bulls
Position: Forward
Height: 6'10" **Weight:** 242
Birthdate: January 4, 1969

NBA Experience: 1 year
College: Rancho Santiago; Cincinnati
Acquired: 1st-round pick in 1993 draft
(25th overall)

Background: Standing only 6'5" when he finished high school, Blount enrolled at Rancho Santiago C.C. in California and was selected Junior College Player of the Year by *Basketball Times* before transferring to Cincinnati. He averaged 9.4 PPG and blocked 85 shots in two years with the Bearcats, helping the team to seven NCAA Tournament wins. Chicago drafted Blount 25th overall in 1993 and he averaged about three PPG last year in limited playing time.

Strengths: Blount possesses great athletic ability and uses it best on the defensive end. He's wiry-strong, gets up and down the court like a guard, and swats shots instinctively. Blount shows the potential to be a productive rebounder at the NBA level, although he never dominated the boards in college. He has been compared favorably to John Salley but enjoys the game more.

Weaknesses: For offense, don't dial Blount. He has no perimeter game to speak of and opponents will give him open jumpers all night. Blount never made a 3-pointer in four years of college and is no threat at all from 18 feet and beyond. Moreover, even his offensive skills in the paint are sub-standard. He is a poor free throw shooter.

Analysis: The Bulls did not need an immediate presence at the power-forward slot and drafted a player they hoped would emerge down the road. "Down the road" is now, as power forwards Horace Grant and Scott Williams have left as free agents. Blount is never going to lead the team in scoring, but he does run the floor, play defense, and block shots well enough to stick. If he could add a few more pounds of muscle, continue his improvement in shot-blocking and rebounding, and develop a short-range jumper, Blount would be a solid NBA player.

PLAYER SUMMARY	
Will	run, swat shots
Can't	rely on jumper
Expect	athletic prowess
Don't Expect	much offense
Fantasy Value	$1
Card Value	7-10¢

COLLEGE STATISTICS

		G	FGP	FTP	RPG	PPG
91-92	CINC	34	.479	.556	6.3	8.2
92-93	CINC	21	.550	.566	8.1	11.3
Totals		55	.511	.559	7.0	9.4

NBA REGULAR-SEASON STATISTICS

			FGs		3-PT FGs		FTs		Rebounds						
	G	MIN	FG	PCT	FG	PCT	FT	PCT	OFF	TOT	AST	STL	BLK	PTS	PPG
93-94 CHI	67	690	76	.437	0	.000	46	.613	76	194	56	19	33	198	3.0
Totals	67	690	76	.437	0	.000	46	.613	76	194	56	19	33	198	3.0

MUGGSY BOGUES

Team: Charlotte Hornets
Position: Guard
Height: 5'3" **Weight:** 140
Birthdate: January 9, 1965

NBA Experience: 7 years
College: Wake Forest
Acquired: Selected from Bullets in 1988 expansion draft

Background: Bogues learned the game at famed Dunbar High School in Baltimore, where he teamed with Reggie Lewis and Reggie Williams. At Wake Forest, he terrorized ACC guards with his intimidating quickness, and he set ACC career records for assists and steals. His pro career took off after Charlotte plucked him from the Bullets in the 1988 expansion draft. He has ranked among the league leaders in assists each of the last three seasons.

Strengths: Bogues makes the league's so-called quick playmakers look as though they're standing still. Always moving, he's a pest on both ends. Few can stop him from driving past his man and dishing off, and he's always a threat to swipe your dribble. He is among the assist-to-turnover ratio leaders annually and is an accurate free throw shooter.

Weaknesses: His most obvious drawback is his size. He can't shoot over anyone and Spud Webb can post him up. His shooting has improved but he is not a huge scorer and is no threat to beat you from 3-point range.

Analysis: His team has shopped for a starting point guard but has never found one to replace Bogues, although newcomer Michael Adams will try his luck this year. The last two years have been Bogues's best in the scoring column and he continues to burn opponents with his quickness and playmaking. A video was released last season entitled, "They Don't Tell Me No: The Muggsy Bogues Story." That says it all.

PLAYER SUMMARY	
Will	get past his man
Can't	dunk
Expect	constant movement
Don't Expect	3-pointers
Fantasy Value	$8-10
Card Value	5-10¢

COLLEGE STATISTICS

		G	FGP	FTP	APG	PPG
83-84	WF	32	.304	.692	1.7	1.2
84-85	WF	29	.500	.682	7.1	6.6
85-86	WF	29	.455	.730	8.4	11.3
86-87	WF	29	.500	.806	9.5	14.8
Totals		119	.473	.749	6.6	8.3

NBA REGULAR-SEASON STATISTICS

		G	MIN	FGs FG	FGs PCT	3-PT FGs FG	3-PT FGs PCT	FTs FT	FTs PCT	Rebounds OFF	Rebounds TOT	AST	STL	BLK	PTS	PPG
87-88	WAS	79	1628	166	.390	3	.188	58	.784	35	136	404	127	3	393	5.0
88-89	CHA	79	1755	178	.426	1	.077	66	.750	53	165	620	111	7	423	5.4
89-90	CHA	81	2743	326	.491	5	.192	106	.791	48	207	867	166	3	763	9.4
90-91	CHA	81	2299	241	.460	0	.000	86	.796	58	216	669	137	3	568	7.0
91-92	CHA	82	2790	317	.472	2	.074	94	.783	58	235	743	170	6	730	8.9
92-93	CHA	81	2833	331	.453	6	.231	140	.833	51	298	711	161	5	808	10.0
93-94	CHA	77	2746	354	.471	2	.167	125	.806	78	313	780	133	2	835	10.8
Totals		560	16794	1913	.457	19	.144	675	.797	381	1570	4794	1005	29	4520	8.1

MANUTE BOL

Unrestricted Free Agent
Last Team: Philadelphia 76ers
Position: Center
Height: 7'7"   **Weight:** 225

Birthdate: October 16, 1962
NBA Experience: 9 years
College: Bridgeport
Acquired: Signed as a free agent, 3/94

Background: A member of the Dinka Tribe, Bol was discovered in the Sudan and imported to Bridgeport College, where he was more a novelty than anything. He speaks four languages and once killed a lion with a spear in an African tribal ritual. He has never averaged four PPG but has blocked more than 2,000 shots in nine seasons. He played in 14 games with three different teams in 1993-94.

Strengths: The tallest man in NBA history does one thing well—block shots. He led the league in that category in 1985-86 and 1988-89 despite limited playing time. He was named to the second-team All-Defensive Team in 1986. He forces even the best leapers to alter their shots.

Weaknesses: Everything other than shot-blocking falls into this category. Bol can't shoot at all and has no post-up skills to speak of. He can't dribble, pass, or run the floor effectively. When he scores, it's accidental. No NBA team wants to make a commitment to him.

Analysis: Bol, who once made a staggering six 3-pointers in a game, served brief stints last season with Miami and Washington before winding up back with the 76ers, who had earlier released him. He scored only eight points all season. Expect Bol to continue his NBA travels, only because he's virtually impossible to shoot over.

PLAYER SUMMARY

Will ....block shots
Can't ....do much else
Expect............a league-wide curiosity
Don't Expect .....long-term contracts
Fantasy Value...................................$0
Card Value ....5-10¢

COLLEGE STATISTICS

		G	FGP	FTP	RPG	PPG
84-85	BPT	31	.611	.595	13.5	22.5
Totals		31	.611	.595	13.5	22.5

NBA REGULAR-SEASON STATISTICS

				FGs		3-PT FGs		FTs		Rebounds						
		G	MIN	FG	PCT	FG	PCT	FT	PCT	OFF	TOT	AST	STL	BLK	PTS	PPG
85-86	WAS	80	2090	128	.460	0	.000	42	.488	123	477	23	28	397	298	3.7
86-87	WAS	82	1552	103	.446	0	.000	45	.672	84	362	11	20	302	251	3.1
87-88	WAS	77	1136	75	.455	0	.000	26	.531	72	275	13	11	208	176	2.3
88-89	GS	80	1769	127	.369	20	.220	40	.606	116	462	27	11	345	314	3.9
89-90	GS	75	1310	56	.331	9	.188	25	.510	33	276	36	13	238	146	1.9
90-91	PHI	82	1522	65	.396	1	.071	24	.585	66	350	20	16	247	155	1.9
91-92	PHI	71	1267	49	.383	0	.000	12	.462	54	222	22	11	205	110	1.5
92-93	PHI	58	855	52	.409	10	.313	12	.632	44	193	18	14	119	126	2.2
93-94	MIA/WAS/PHI	14	116	4	.211	0	.000	0	.000	3	18	1	2	16	8	0.6
Totals		619	11617	659	.406	40	.200	226	.561	595	2635	171	126	2077	1584	2.6

WALTER BOND

Team: Utah Jazz
Position: Guard
Height: 6'5" **Weight:** 200
Birthdate: February 1, 1969

NBA Experience: 2 years
College: Minnesota
Acquired: Signed as a free agent, 10/93

Background: After a standout career at Collins High School in south Chicago, Bond saw action in all 26 games as a freshman at the University of Minnesota and starred as both a junior and senior. Overlooked in the 1991 NBA draft, Bond made the CBA All-Rookie Team in Wichita Falls. Dallas signed him before the 1992-93 season and he averaged eight PPG in the Mavericks' backcourt. Utah picked him up before the 1993-94 campaign and his scoring and minutes plunged.

Strengths: Bond does a little bit of everything. He is a solid rebounder for a guard and is willing to stick with his man. He can also score points by posting up smaller defenders and by nailing 3-point shots. He once hit nine 3-pointers in a CBA playoff game and he made 19 of his 54 long-distance attempts last season. He works hard and wants to make it.

Weaknesses: Bond has been horribly inconsistent as a pro. His shooting percentage has hovered around the .400 mark and has been a large reason for his time on the bench. He is not very quick, which was probably the biggest factor in his being bypassed in the draft. It takes away options at the offensive end and causes him to draw a lot of whistles on defense. He does not have a great feel for the game.

Analysis: Bond, who gives teammates free haircuts, enjoyed a decent NBA debut with the Mavericks two years ago but crashed to reality last season. With a talented Utah team, he was resigned to a reserve role in which he averaged only ten minutes per game. It will require much more than that for Bond to develop some consistency in his play.

PLAYER SUMMARY

Will	convert treys
Can't	burn his man
Expect	free haircuts
Don't Expect	many starts
Fantasy Value	$0
Card Value	5-8¢

COLLEGE STATISTICS

		G	FGP	FTP	RPG	PPG
87-88	MINN	26	.527	.500	1.4	2.4
88-89	MINN	30	.531	.556	3.7	6.0
89-90	MINN	32	.510	.678	4.2	10.5
90-91	MINN	15	.381	.657	4.5	11.6
Totals		103	.480	.635	3.4	7.3

NBA REGULAR-SEASON STATISTICS

		G	MIN	FGs FG	FGs PCT	3-PT FGs FG	3-PT FGs PCT	FTs FT	FTs PCT	Rebounds OFF	Rebounds TOT	AST	STL	BLK	PTS	PPG
92-93	DAL	74	1578	227	.402	7	.167	129	.772	52	196	122	75	18	590	8.0
93-94	UTA	56	559	63	.404	19	.352	31	.775	20	61	31	16	12	176	3.1
Totals		130	2137	290	.402	26	.271	160	.773	72	257	153	91	30	766	5.9

ANTHONY BONNER

Team: New York Knicks
Position: Forward
Height: 6'8" **Weight:** 225
Birthdate: June 8, 1968

NBA Experience: 4 years
College: St. Louis
Acquired: Signed as a free agent, 10/93

Background: Bonner led all Division I players in rebounding as a senior at St. Louis University. He finished his career as the school's all-time leader in points, rebounds, steals, and games played. He was a sixth man and part-time starter for the Kings before the team renounced his rights in September 1993. The Knicks signed him before the 1993-94 season and Bonner became a key role-player off the bench.

Strengths: Bonner is a typical Knick—a bruising rebounder who is willing to sacrifice his body. He shows a great work ethic and mixes it up at both ends of the floor. He's especially strong on defense, where he lacks power-forward size but can match up with them. He's downright fearless. Bonner knows his limitations and rarely takes a bad shot.

Weaknesses: Offense is not on Bonner's resume. Though he shoots for a high percentage and can knock down a mid-range jumper, he has no business putting up a lot of them. He's a dismal free throw shooter. His dribbling and passing are sub-par and he's prone to turnovers when he tries to do too much. He would be prone to fouling out if he played starter's minutes.

Analysis: Bonner is a workhorse, the kind Knicks coach Pat Riley loves to use to wear down the opposition. Bonner is a force on the boards and plays the kind of defense no NBA player wants to contend with. His offensive skills are limited, but he knows his role and sticks to it with a great attitude. Just don't have him on the line in a tight game.

PLAYER SUMMARY	
Will	defend, rebound
Can't	shoot FTs
Expect	bumps and bruises
Don't Expect	a scoring machine
Fantasy Value	$0
Card Value	7-12¢

COLLEGE STATISTICS

		G	FGP	FTP	RPG	PPG
86-87	STL	35	.592	.661	9.6	10.3
87-88	STL	28	.537	.597	8.8	13.8
88-89	STL	37	.560	.582	10.4	15.5
89-90	STL	33	.500	.693	13.8	19.8
Totals		133	.539	.634	10.7	14.8

NBA REGULAR-SEASON STATISTICS

				FGs		3-PT FGs		FTs		Rebounds						
		G	MIN	FG	PCT	FG	PCT	FT	PCT	OFF	TOT	AST	STL	BLK	PTS	PPG
90-91	SAC	34	750	103	.448	0	.000	44	.579	59	161	49	39	5	250	7.4
91-92	SAC	79	2287	294	.447	1	.250	151	.627	192	485	125	94	26	740	9.4
92-93	SAC	70	1764	229	.461	0	.000	143	.593	188	455	96	86	17	601	8.6
93-94	NY	73	1402	162	.563	0	.000	50	.476	150	344	88	76	13	374	5.1
Totals		256	6203	788	.471	1	.091	388	.585	589	1445	358	295	61	1965	7.7

ANTHONY BOWIE

Team: Orlando Magic
Position: Guard
Height: 6'6" **Weight:** 200
Birthdate: November 9, 1963

NBA Experience: 5 years
College: Seminole; Oklahoma
Acquired: Signed as a free agent, 12/91

Background: Bowie played college ball at Oklahoma, where he learned to play at a breakneck pace. He was drafted by Houston in 1986, but he played his first NBA ball with San Antonio in 1988-89. He was picked up by the Rockets in '89 but was let go the following year. Bowie has played some of his best ball since being picked up by Orlando from the CBA during the 1991-92 campaign. He saw action in 70 games as a reserve last season.

Strengths: Bowie is a versatile player who can be used at three positions, though shooting guard is his primary position. He glides up and down the court and can shoot the lights out in streaks. He can also get to the basket and is a very good free throw shooter. Bowie plays hard off the bench and can start when called upon. He averaged 14.6 PPG in 1991-92.

Weaknesses: Bowie is vulnerable against quicker guards and bigger forwards. He tends to play out of control at times, trying to do too much. He's not a great ball-handler. Bowie is at his best in transition and coming off screens rather than creating offense on his own. He did not shoot well from long range last season, making only one 3-pointer.

Analysis: Bowie's attitude, effort, and ability to fill in where needed have earned him a spot on the Orlando roster for the last three seasons. He scored only 4.6 PPG during the 1993-94 campaign, largely because the rest of the team stayed pretty healthy. The versatile Bowie accepts his job as a role-player.

PLAYER SUMMARY	
Will	play three positions
Can't	dribble expertly
Expect	versatility
Don't Expect	great control
Fantasy Value	$0
Card Value	5-10¢

COLLEGE STATISTICS

		G	FGP	FTP	RPG	PPG
84-85	OKLA	37	.515	.773	5.8	13.4
85-86	OKLA	35	.502	.808	4.6	13.3
Totals		72	.509	.787	5.2	13.4

NBA REGULAR-SEASON STATISTICS

		G	MIN	FGs FG	FGs PCT	3-PT FGs FG	3-PT FGs PCT	FTs FT	FTs PCT	Rebounds OFF	Rebounds TOT	AST	STL	BLK	PTS	PPG
88-89	SA	18	438	72	.500	1	.200	10	.667	25	56	29	18	4	155	8.6
89-90	HOU	66	918	119	.406	6	.286	40	.741	36	118	96	42	5	284	4.3
91-92	ORL	52	1721	312	.493	17	.386	117	.860	70	245	163	55	38	758	14.6
92-93	ORL	77	1761	268	.471	15	.313	67	.798	36	194	175	54	14	618	8.0
93-94	ORL	70	948	139	.481	1	.056	41	.837	29	120	102	32	12	320	4.6
Totals		283	5786	910	.472	40	.294	275	.814	196	733	565	201	73	2135	7.5

SAM BOWIE

Team: Los Angeles Lakers
Position: Center
Height: 7'1" **Weight:** 263
Birthdate: March 17, 1961

NBA Experience: 9 years
College: Kentucky
Acquired: Traded from Nets for Benoit Benjamin, 6/93

Background: Bowie and Ralph Sampson came out of high school in the same year as perhaps the most heralded tandem of big men ever. Bowie was on his way to becoming a star at Kentucky when serious leg injuries forced him to miss two seasons. Portland drafted him ahead of Michael Jordan. His career has been plagued by injuries, including knee surgery that cost him much of his 1993-94 campaign with the Lakers.

Strengths: Bowie has a soft touch and is a fine passer for a big man. He hits the 18-footer, sticks free throws, and does a decent job on the glass. He has always been able to block shots despite his chronic leg injuries.

Weaknesses: The biggest weakness with Bowie is his health, as he's lost more than six seasons to injury. The word "soft" has been used to describe Bowie's overall game. He has never become adept at attacking the hoop with power. His field goal percentage is low for a center.

Analysis: Bowie is not considered one of the top centers in the league, and one has to wonder how much longer he can be effective on legs that spend more time in the operating room than on the floor. When healthy, he is capable of contributing with soft jumpers, blocked shots, and precise passing. However, he will never live up to his draft status.

PLAYER SUMMARY	
Will	hit his FTs
Can't	stay healthy
Expect	a soft touch
Don't Expect	much power
Fantasy Value	$3-5
Card Value	5-10¢

COLLEGE STATISTICS

		G	FGP	FTP	RPG	PPG
79-80	KEN	34	.531	.764	8.1	12.9
80-81	KEN	28	.520	.720	9.1	17.4
83-84	KEN	34	.516	.722	9.2	10.5
Totals		96	.522	.735	8.8	13.4

NBA REGULAR-SEASON STATISTICS

		G	MIN	FGs FG	FGs PCT	3-PT FGs FG	3-PT FGs PCT	FTs FT	FTs PCT	Rebounds OFF	Rebounds TOT	AST	STL	BLK	PTS	PPG
84-85	POR	76	2216	299	.537	0	.000	160	.711	207	656	215	55	203	758	10.0
85-86	POR	38	1132	167	.484	0	.000	114	.708	93	327	99	21	96	448	11.8
86-87	POR	5	163	30	.455	0	.000	20	.667	14	33	9	1	10	80	16.0
88-89	POR	20	412	69	.451	5	.714	28	.571	36	106	36	7	33	171	8.6
89-90	NJ	68	2207	347	.416	10	.323	294	.776	206	690	91	38	121	998	14.7
90-91	NJ	62	1916	314	.434	4	.182	169	.732	176	480	147	43	90	801	12.9
91-92	NJ	71	2179	421	.445	8	.320	212	.757	203	578	186	41	120	1062	15.0
92-93	NJ	79	2092	287	.450	2	.333	141	.779	158	556	127	32	128	717	9.1
93-94	LAL	25	556	75	.436	1	.250	72	.867	27	131	47	4	28	223	8.9
Totals		444	12873	2009	.453	30	.316	1210	.747	1120	3557	957	242	829	5258	11.8

SHAWN BRADLEY

Team: Philadelphia 76ers
Position: Center
Height: 7'6" **Weight:** 245
Birthdate: March 22, 1972

NBA Experience: 1 year
College: Brigham Young
Acquired: 1st-round pick in 1993 draft (2nd overall)

Background: From tiny Castle Dale, Utah, Bradley stayed close to home as a collegian. He played just one season at Brigham Young (as a freshman in 1990-91) and blocked 177 shots that year—the second-highest figure in NCAA history. He once swatted 14 in a game. Bradley spent two years in Australia on a Mormon mission, then entered the draft and was taken second overall by Philadelphia. He averaged 10.3 PPG and 3.0 BPG before a dislocated kneecap against Portland ended his season on February 18.

Strengths: Bradley has considerable skills for a player his size. His wide wingspan and good timing make him a shot-blocking force, and he is not afraid to pound the boards. He has an array of offensive moves, including a mid-range jump shot. Unlike some of the other giants, Bradley has real athletic skills: He was a star baseball player in high school. He wants to be a top-notch pivot and has the work habits to help him get there.

Weaknesses: Bradley's body still has a ways to go. He needs to continue hitting the weights, not to mention the refrigerator. His body could stand another 30 or so pounds of muscle. His field goal percentage is horrible for a big man, he gets in foul trouble, and he needs to develop a better feel for the game.

Analysis: Philadelphia expected it would take Bradley a few years to develop, so any judgement of his progress may be premature. He has displayed signs of becoming a well-rounded player with the ability to dominate on defense. However, there were also several nights when you wondered why he was a lottery pick. Bradley should be a much better player in a year or two.

PLAYER SUMMARY

Will......................................block shots
Can't ....absorb a pounding
Expect ....steady improvement
Don't Expect ....tons of points
Fantasy Value $6-8
Card Value ....20-50¢

COLLEGE STATISTICS

		G	FGP	FTP	RPG	PPG
90-91	BYU	34	.518	.692	7.7	14.8
Totals		34	.518	.692	7.7	14.8

NBA REGULAR-SEASON STATISTICS

			FGs		3-PT FGs		FTs		Rebounds					
	G	MIN	FG	PCT	FG	PCT	FT	PCT	OFF	TOT	AST	STL	BLK	PTS	PPG
93-94 PHI	49	1385	201	.409	0	.000	102	.607	98	306	98	45	147	504	10.3
Totals	49	1385	201	.409	0	.000	102	.607	98	306	98	45	147	504	10.3

TERRELL BRANDON

Team: Cleveland Cavaliers
Position: Guard
Height: 5'11" **Weight:** 180
Birthdate: May 20, 1970

NBA Experience: 3 years
College: Oregon
Acquired: 1st-round pick in 1991 draft
(11th overall)

Background: After sitting out his freshman year at Oregon under Prop 40, Brandon had two terrific seasons at point guard, leading the Pac-10 in scoring and steals as a junior. He entered the NBA draft early and was selected 11th overall by Cleveland. He has been a critical performer when Mark Price has been injured but has served primarily as a reserve in his three years with the Cavaliers. Brandon has averaged between seven and nine PPG every season.

Strengths: Brandon has good vision and court sense, is an excellent leaper, and is explosive with the ball. He was a terrific offensive player in college and has demonstrated an ability to put the ball in NBA buckets as well. He has a quick release and a pull-up jump shot. He gives the Cavs a spark with his energy off the bench.

Weaknesses: Brandon did not play much defense in college and it is not his strength at the NBA level. He has quickness and gets back in transition but needs to muscle up against his man in halfcourt play. His shooting percentage has been up and down, and it suffered a drastic drop last year after a fine 1992-93. He's not automatic when open and is no 3-point ace.

Analysis: Brandon has struggled with defense and shooting but has made great strides in other aspects of the game. His ball-handling and decision-making are reliable and he gives the Cavaliers a lift off the bench. With Mark Price ahead of him, however, the prospects are not good for Brandon becoming any more than a role-player in Cleveland.

PLAYER SUMMARY	
Will	provide a spark
Can't	shoot like Price
Expect	7-plus PPG
Don't Expect	3-pointers
Fantasy Value	$2-4
Card Value	7-10¢

COLLEGE STATISTICS

		G	FGP	FTP	APG	PPG
89-90	ORE	29	.474	.752	6.0	17.9
90-91	ORE	28	.491	.850	5.0	26.6
Totals		57	.484	.810	5.5	22.2

NBA REGULAR-SEASON STATISTICS

				FGs	3-PT FGs		FTs		Rebounds						
		G	MIN	FG	PCT	FG	PCT	FT	PCT	OFF	TOT	AST	STL	BLK	PTS	PPG
91-92	CLE	82	1605	252	.419	1	.043	100	.806	49	162	316	81	22	605	7.4
92-93	CLE	82	1622	297	.478	13	.310	118	.825	37	179	302	79	27	725	8.8
93-94	CLE	73	1548	230	.420	7	.219	139	.858	38	159	277	84	16	605	8.3
Totals		237	4775	779	.440	21	.216	357	.832	124	500	895	244	65	1936	8.2

FRANK BRICKOWSKI

Team: Sacramento Kings
Position: Forward/Center
Height: 6'10" **Weight:** 248
Birthdate: August 14, 1959

NBA Experience: 10 years
College: Penn St.
Acquired: Signed as a free agent, 8/94

Background: Brickowski led Penn State in scoring his junior and senior years. After being drafted in the third round by the Knicks, he played overseas for three years in Italy, France, and Israel. Brickowski played for the Sonics, Lakers, Spurs, and Bucks before a February 1994 trade sent him from Milwaukee to Charlotte. The Hornets let him go in the off-season and he signed a free-agent contract with Sacramento.

Strengths: Brickowski possesses good size and quickness around the basket and is effective as a low-post scorer. He is a reliable shooter when open and can also muscle inside. He has averaged double figures in the scoring column six of the last seven years and is strong on the defensive end.

Weaknesses: Brickowski is not the athletic power forward who thrives in an open-court game. Nagging injuries over the last three years have slowed him, including a rib injury early last season. He is not a good ball-handler or passer.

Analysis: The Hornets lost big men Larry Johnson and Alonzo Mourning for a long stretch last season and felt Brickowski's ability to score and play interior defense would help fill the void. He works hard and is surprisingly adept in several aspects of the game. He's good for about a dozen points and will do his best to keep his man from getting away.

PLAYER SUMMARY	
Will	work on both ends
Can't	shoot treys
Expect	double-figure scoring
Don't Expect	ball-handling
Fantasy Value	$10-13
Card Value	5-8¢

COLLEGE STATISTICS

		G	FGP	FTP	RPG	PPG
77-78	PSU	25	.457	.840	2.6	3.8
78-79	PSU	24	.495	.792	4.5	5.7
79-80	PSU	27	.521	.781	7.5	11.3
80-81	PSU	24	.601	.778	6.3	13.0
Totals		100	.537	.788	5.3	8.5

NBA REGULAR-SEASON STATISTICS

		G	MIN	FGs FG	FGs PCT	3-PT FGs FG	3-PT FGs PCT	FTs FT	FTs PCT	Rebounds OFF	Rebounds TOT	AST	STL	BLK	PTS	PPG
84-85	SEA	78	1115	150	.492	0	.000	85	.669	76	260	100	34	15	385	4.9
85-86	SEA	40	311	30	.517	0	.000	18	.667	16	54	21	11	7	78	2.0
86-87	LA/SA	44	487	63	.508	0	.000	50	.714	48	116	17	20	6	176	4.0
87-88	SA	70	2227	425	.528	1	.200	268	.768	167	483	266	74	36	1119	16.0
88-89	SA	64	1822	337	.515	0	.000	201	.715	148	406	131	102	35	875	13.7
89-90	SA	78	1438	211	.545	0	.000	95	.674	89	327	105	66	37	517	6.6
90-91	MIL	75	1912	372	.527	0	.000	198	.798	129	426	131	86	43	942	12.6
91-92	MIL	65	1556	306	.524	3	.500	125	.767	97	344	122	60	23	740	11.4
92-93	MIL	66	2075	456	.545	8	.308	195	.728	120	405	196	80	44	1115	16.9
93-94	MIL/CHA	71	2094	368	.488	4	.200	195	.768	85	404	222	80	27	935	13.2
Totals		651	15037	2718	.521	16	.225	1430	.742	975	3225	1311	613	273	6882	10.6

SCOTT BROOKS

Team: Houston Rockets
Position: Guard
Height: 5'11" **Weight:** 165
Birthdate: July 31, 1965
NBA Experience: 6 years

College: Texas Christian; San Joaquin Delta; Cal.-Irvine
Acquired: Traded from Timberwolves for a 1995 2nd-round pick, 9/92

Background: Brooks divided his college career among Texas Christian, San Joaquin Delta Junior College, and finally Cal.-Irvine, where he led the Pacific Coast Athletic Association in scoring, steals, and free throw percentage. Despite being passed up in the NBA draft, he emerged from the CBA and has spent two years apiece in Philadelphia, Minnesota, and Houston. His last two years have been his best.

Strengths: Brooks is a tireless worker who loves to pressure the ball from one end of the court to the other. His quickness, great hands, and ability to handle the ball make him the consummate point guard and a nice sparkplug off the bench. He's pesky, is a good penetrator, hits the 3, and rarely misses a free throw.

Weaknesses: Most of his offense comes when nothing else is available for Brooks, who is a passer first and scorer second. His size works against him on the defensive end, where bigger guards shoot over him or post him up. He almost never gets a rebound and is best used as a reserve.

Analysis: Brooks, a California surfer type, simply loves to play the game and has contributed everywhere he has unpacked his bags. He shows the floor leadership coaches love and his attitude off the bench has helped Houston become one of the top few teams in the NBA. He rarely does anything to hurt the team and his overall numbers the last two years indicate that he's still improving.

PLAYER SUMMARY

Will	distribute the ball
Can't	rebound
Expect	floor leadership
Don't Expect	10 PPG
Fantasy Value	$0
Card Value	5-10¢

COLLEGE STATISTICS

		G	FGP	FTP	APG	PPG
83-84	TCU	27	.529	.714	1.4	3.8
84-85	SJD	31	.525	.882	—	13.1
85-86	C-I	30	.448	.886	3.2	10.3
86-87	C-I	28	.478	.845	3.8	23.8
Totals		116	.489	.860	2.8	12.8

NBA REGULAR-SEASON STATISTICS

			FGs		3-PT FGs		FTs		Rebounds						
	G	MIN	FG	PCT	FG	PCT	FT	PCT	OFF	TOT	AST	STL	BLK	PTS	PPG
88-89 PHI	82	1372	156	.420	55	.359	61	.884	19	94	306	69	3	428	5.2
89-90 PHI	72	975	119	.431	31	.392	50	.877	15	64	207	47	0	319	4.4
90-91 MIN	80	980	159	.430	45	.333	61	.847	28	72	204	53	5	424	5.3
91-92 MIN	82	1082	167	.447	32	.356	51	.810	27	99	205	66	7	417	5.1
92-93 HOU	82	1516	183	.475	41	.414	112	.830	22	99	243	79	3	519	6.3
93-94 HOU	73	1225	142	.491	23	.377	74	.871	10	102	149	51	2	381	5.2
Totals	471	7150	926	.448	227	.368	409	.850	121	530	1314	365	20	2488	5.3

DEE BROWN

Team: Boston Celtics
Position: Guard
Height: 6'1" **Weight:** 161
Birthdate: November 29, 1968

NBA Experience: 4 years
College: Jacksonville
Acquired: 1st-round pick in 1990 draft
(19th overall)

Background: Brown was Jacksonville's main man as a junior, leading the Dolphins in scoring, rebounding, and steals while splitting time between big guard and small forward. He helped solidify the Celtics' backcourt as a first-team All-Rookie performer, then missed more than half of the 1991-92 season following arthroscopic knee surgery. He has started for most of the last two years and posted career highs in most statistical categories in 1993-94.

Strengths: Brown has played both guard positions well. He has a tremendous vertical leap that he displayed while winning the NBA's Slam Dunk Contest in 1991. He has lightning-quick speed and is especially dangerous on the fastbreak, where he can dish off or finish the play himself. He's a good on-the-ball defender and is a very good free throw shooter.

Weaknesses: Brown has become a much better two guard thanks to an improved jump shot, but defenders are still best advised to give him an extra step and take their chances with him on the perimeter. He is not a great 3-point shooter. He needs to learn to take advantage of screens.

Analysis: After dividing the point-guard role between Brown and Sherman Douglas, Boston's brass decided it was best to keep both on the floor. That will change this year because of the arrival of Blue Edwards, who will likely play two guard and steal minutes from both players. Brown is not among the best in the league at either position, but his versatility and athletic ability have helped him become a fine pro player.

PLAYER SUMMARY

Will	play above the rim
Can't	live by the trey
Expect	versatility, athleticism
Don't Expect	20 PPG
Fantasy Value	$20-25
Card Value	8-20¢

COLLEGE STATISTICS

		G	FGP	FTP	APG	PPG
86-87	JACK	21	.431	.591	0.8	3.4
87-88	JACK	28	.452	.818	2.0	10.1
88-89	JACK	30	.490	.824	3.7	19.6
89-90	JACK	29	.496	.683	5.2	19.3
Totals		108	.482	.762	3.1	13.9

NBA REGULAR-SEASON STATISTICS

				FGs		3-PT FGs		FTs		Rebounds						
		G	MIN	FG	PCT	FG	PCT	FT	PCT	OFF	TOT	AST	STL	BLK	PTS	PPG
90-91	BOS	82	1945	284	.464	7	.206	137	.873	41	182	344	83	14	712	8.7
91-92	BOS	31	883	149	.426	5	.227	60	.769	15	79	164	33	7	363	11.7
92-93	BOS	80	2254	328	.468	26	.317	192	.793	45	246	461	138	32	874	10.9
93-94	BOS	77	2867	490	.480	30	.313	182	.831	63	300	347	156	47	1192	15.5
Totals		270	7949	1251	.466	68	.291	571	.820	164	807	1316	410	100	3141	11.6

MIKE BROWN

Team: Minnesota Timberwolves
Position: Forward/Center
Height: 6'10" **Weight:** 260
Birthdate: July 19, 1963

NBA Experience: 8 years
College: George Washington
Acquired: Traded from Jazz for Felton Spencer, 6/93

Background: Brown went from Atlantic 10 Freshman of the Year to George Washington University's second all-time leading scorer and rebounder. He began his pro career in Italy before moving to Chicago, Utah, and most recently Minnesota after a 1993 draft-day trade. Brown has played in every game over the last five seasons, although 1993-94 was not among his better ones.

Strengths: Strength and size are Brown's biggest attributes. He's got enough power in his frame to push around even the strongest big men. He can play power forward or center. He is most valuable as a rebounder and defender, where his physical style irritates opponents. He's a workhorse.

Weaknesses: Brown has never been much of a scorer and last season was no exception. He does not show much touch from the perimeter and his field goal percentage has been down the last two years. Quicker players can beat him to the spot and Brown does not block many shots for a man his size. Foul trouble has also plagued him.

Analysis: Brown has been a reliable role-player and part-time starter during his career. He rebounds, wears opponents down with his bulk, and gets every penny's worth out of his fouls. Minnesota hoped to see some of the scoring punch he had shown in flashes early in his career, but on that count Brown draws low marks. His offense seems to be slipping.

PLAYER SUMMARY	
Will	bang the boards
Can't	torch the nets
Expect	physical defense
Don't Expect	sweet shooting
Fantasy Value	$0
Card Value	5-10¢

COLLEGE STATISTICS

		G	FGP	FTP	RPG	PPG
81-82	GW	27	.497	.518	8.5	15.6
82-83	GW	29	.520	.655	10.3	17.1
83-84	GW	29	.535	.730	12.1	19.6
84-85	GW	26	.480	.649	11.0	16.6
Totals		111	.509	.653	10.5	17.3

NBA REGULAR-SEASON STATISTICS

				FGs		3-PT FGs		FTs		Rebounds						
		G	MIN	FG	PCT	FG	PCT	FT	PCT	OFF	TOT	AST	STL	BLK	PTS	PPG
86-87	CHI	62	818	106	.527	0	.000	46	.639	71	214	24	20	7	258	4.2
87-88	CHI	46	591	78	.448	0	.000	41	.577	66	159	28	11	4	197	4.3
88-89	UTA	66	1051	104	.419	0	.000	92	.708	92	258	41	25	17	300	4.5
89-90	UTA	82	1397	177	.515	1	.500	157	.789	111	373	47	32	28	512	6.2
90-91	UTA	82	1391	129	.454	0	.000	132	.742	109	337	49	29	24	390	4.8
91-92	UTA	82	1783	221	.453	0	.000	190	.667	187	476	81	42	34	632	7.7
92-93	UTA	82	1551	176	.430	0	.000	113	.689	147	391	64	32	23	465	5.7
93-94	MIN	82	1921	111	.427	0	.000	77	.653	119	447	72	51	29	299	3.6
Totals		584	10503	1102	.458	1	.143	848	.697	902	2655	406	242	166	3053	5.2

P.J. BROWN

Team: New Jersey Nets
Position: Forward/Center
Height: 6'11" **Weight:** 240
Birthdate: October 14, 1968

NBA Experience: 1 year
College: Louisiana Tech
Acquired: 2nd-round pick in 1992 draft (29th overall)

Background: Brown, drafted 29th overall by New Jersey in 1992, spent his first professional season in Greece after making contract demands the Nets were not prepared to meet. He averaged 17.0 PPG and 13.7 RPG overseas. New Jersey signed the former Louisiana Tech shot-blocking standout and first-team All-Sun Belt Conference player before the 1993-94 season. Last year, Brown started more than half the team's games.

Strengths: Brown is a relentless rebounder and defensive specialist who can play both center and power forward. He has long arms and good timing to block shots and gets his hands on his share of steals. Opposing big men hate to see Brown as their match-up because they know it means a night of wear and tear. A physical presence, Brown also gets up and down the court swiftly for a big man.

Weaknesses: Though his offensive game improved by leaps and bounds during his year overseas, putting the ball in the basket is not Brown's specialty and likely never will be. He has nothing to offer on the perimeter and his shooting percentage is awful for an inside player. You don't want him handling the ball, as he'll turn it over almost as often as he'll get an assist.

Analysis: The Nets have benefitted greatly from the addition of Brown, who finished among the rookie leaders in several categories and was chosen to play in the Schick Rookie Game on All-Star Weekend. He recorded games with as many as 14 rebounds and five blocked shots and has the potential to be a defensive cornerstone for the Nets. He has a long way to go offensively, but his coaches did not seem too concerned.

PLAYER SUMMARY	
Will	bang on defense
Can't	set up the offense
Expect	blocks, rebounds
Don't Expect	50-percent shooting
Fantasy Value	$1
Card Value	5-10¢

COLLEGE STATISTICS

		G	FGP	FTP	RPG	PPG
88-89	LT	32	.415	.568	5.6	4.7
89-90	LT	27	.461	.593	8.5	8.9
90-91	LT	31	.540	.653	9.7	14.4
91-92	LT	31	.489	.730	9.9	12.7
Totals		121	.488	.654	8.4	10.1

NBA REGULAR-SEASON STATISTICS

			FGs		3-PT FGs		FTs		Rebounds						
	G	MIN	FG	PCT	FG	PCT	FT	PCT	OFF	TOT	AST	STL	BLK	PTS	PPG
93-94 NJ	79	1950	167	.415	1	.167	115	.757	188	493	93	71	93	450	5.7
Totals	79	1950	167	.415	1	.167	115	.757	188	493	93	71	93	450	5.7

RANDY BROWN

Team: Sacramento Kings
Position: Guard
Height: 6'3" **Weight:** 190
Birthdate: May 22, 1968

NBA Experience: 3 years
College: Houston; New Mexico St.
Acquired: 2nd-round pick in 1991 draft (31st overall)

Background: Brown played at Collins High School in Chicago before starting his college career at Houston. He transferred to New Mexico State after his sophomore year and set school records for assists and steals while twice earning first-team All-Big West honors. A second-round choice by Sacramento, Brown has played mostly in a reserve role for three seasons. His scoring dropped to 4.5 PPG last season.

Strengths: Known as a defensive whiz at up-tempo New Mexico State, Brown has backed up his reputation as a pro. He's quick, is tough, has good hands, and is not afraid to challenge opponents. He also rebounds very well from the backcourt. He showed during his second year that he is capable of filling in as a starter. He has improved his decision-making.

Weaknesses: Brown will not score a lot of points at the NBA level. His jump shot is sporadic, he has trouble from the free throw line, and he's not a 3-point threat. As well, his playmaking does not put him in a class with the average NBA point guard. His assist-to-turnover ratio is less than two. He goes for every ball on defense and gets called for reaching fouls.

Analysis: Brown has potential as a disruptive defensive player who can also set up the offense when called upon. His quick hands and feet are a lot for opposing guards to handle. Brown's offensive game remains unrefined, however. He is neither an accomplished shooter nor a top-notch playmaker who can make teammates look better. You could find worse in terms of a back-up point guard.

PLAYER SUMMARY

Will	go for steals
Can't	rely on jump shot
Expect	quick hands, feet
Don't Expect	winning playmaking
Fantasy Value	$1
Card Value	5-10¢

COLLEGE STATISTICS

		G	FGP	FTP	APG	PPG
86-87	HOU	28	.506	.583	2.9	3.8
87-88	HOU	29	.451	.750	5.6	7.0
89-90	NMST	31	.446	.712	3.5	13.2
90-91	NMST	29	.399	.691	6.4	12.1
Totals		117	.436	.703	4.6	9.1

NBA REGULAR-SEASON STATISTICS

				FGs		3-PT FGs		FTs		Rebounds						
		G	MIN	FG	PCT	FG	PCT	FT	PCT	OFF	TOT	AST	STL	BLK	PTS	PPG
91-92	SAC	56	535	77	.456	0	.000	38	.655	26	69	59	35	12	192	3.4
92-93	SAC	75	1726	225	.463	2	.333	115	.732	75	212	196	108	34	567	7.6
93-94	SAC	61	1041	110	.438	0	.000	53	.609	40	112	133	63	14	273	4.5
Totals		192	3302	412	.455	2	.125	206	.682	141	393	388	206	60	1032	5.4

MARK BRYANT

Team: Portland Trail Blazers
Position: Forward
Height: 6'9" **Weight:** 245
Birthdate: April 25, 1965

NBA Experience: 6 years
College: Seton Hall
Acquired: 1st-round pick in 1988 draft
(21st overall)

Background: As a senior, Bryant helped take Seton Hall to its first NCAA Tournament and was an All-Big East selection. He started 32 of his first 34 games as a pro but then encountered injury problems over his first few years, including two broken bones. He has spent all six pro seasons with Portland and has seen considerable reserve playing time each of the past two years.

Strengths: Bryant is physically impressive and plays tough defense. He's willing to throw his weight around and battle inside with the league's big men. He's a good rebounder, runs the floor well, and owns a decent short-range jumper. He does not take many bad shots. He has stepped in and done an adequate job when asked to start.

Weaknesses: Bryant will never score a lot of points. His offensive repertoire is limited and he is not a good ball-handler or passer. He is easy to overlook in a boxscore. Bryant is not the kind of player who comes into the game and ignites his team. His range is limited and his free throw shooting is sub-par.

Analysis: A valuable banger and role-player because of his size and strength, Bryant is not a power forward who will dazzle you with his skills. His last two seasons have been his best, yet he is hardly one of the league's household names. Bryant is best suited for a reserve role, but his unselfish approach to the game clearly has aided the Blazers.

PLAYER SUMMARY

Will	bang on defense
Can't	shoot with range
Expect	physical play
Don't Expect	much offense
Fantasy Value	$0
Card Value	5-8¢

COLLEGE STATISTICS

		G	FGP	FTP	RPG	PPG
84-85	SH	26	.475	.649	6.8	12.2
85-86	SH	30	.523	.678	7.5	14.0
86-87	SH	28	.496	.706	7.1	16.8
87-88	SH	34	.564	.748	9.1	20.5
Totals		118	.521	.705	7.7	16.2

NBA REGULAR-SEASON STATISTICS

		G	MIN	FGs FG	FGs PCT	3-PT FGs FG	3-PT FGs PCT	FTs FT	FTs PCT	Rebounds OFF	Rebounds TOT	AST	STL	BLK	PTS	PPG
88-89	POR	56	803	120	.486	0	.000	40	.580	65	179	33	20	7	280	5.0
89-90	POR	58	562	70	.458	0	.000	28	.560	54	146	13	18	9	168	2.9
90-91	POR	53	781	99	.488	0	.000	74	.733	65	190	27	15	12	272	5.1
91-92	POR	56	800	95	.480	0	.000	40	.667	87	201	41	26	8	230	4.1
92-93	POR	80	1396	186	.503	0	.000	104	.703	132	324	41	37	23	476	5.9
93-94	POR	79	1441	185	.482	0	.000	72	.692	117	315	37	32	29	442	5.6
Totals		382	5783	755	.486	0	.000	358	.673	520	1355	192	148	88	1868	4.9

MATT BULLARD

Unrestricted Free Agent
Last Team: Houston Rockets
Position: Forward
Height: 6'10" **Weight:** 235

Birthdate: June 5, 1967
NBA Experience: 4 years
College: Colorado; Iowa
Acquired: Signed as a free agent, 8/90

Background: Bullard played two years at Colorado, led the team in scoring as a sophomore, and then transferred to Iowa, where he once connected on six 3-pointers in a game. He was not drafted but played well enough in the 1990 Los Angeles summer league to earn a spot with the Rockets. He was a regular reserve in his second and third years but did not see as much action during a strange 1993-94 campaign.

Strengths: Bullard's game is built around long-range shooting. He owns a sweet jumper and will kill you from behind the arc if you leave him open. He's made more than 200 treys in the last three years. He can also shoot over most defenders and is an accurate free throw shooter. Bullard plays within himself and makes the right pass.

Weaknesses: Bullard does not create with the dribble. He needs open jumpers or screens to be effective. He's not a good rebounder, and low-post offense is not a solid part of his game despite his good size. Seemingly everything he threw up last year was a 3. He lacks the quickness to defend small forwards.

Analysis: Bullard encountered one of the most wacky 1993-94 seasons of anyone. He boarded a plane after an alleged midseason trade from Houston to Detroit, yet he arrived in the Motor City to discover he had not been traded at all. So he played out the year in Houston, where he saw more time on the bench than he had the previous seasons. His long-range shooting alone will keep him in someone's plans.

PLAYER SUMMARY

Will	...................................can the trey
Can't	.........................thrive in the paint
Expect	...........................instant offense
Don't Expect	...................playmaking
Fantasy Value	..................................$0
Card Value	...................................5-8¢

COLLEGE STATISTICS

		G	FGP	FTP	RPG	PPG
85-86	COLO	28	.604	.818	6.4	12.7
86-87	COLO	28	.521	.742	10.0	16.6
88-89	IOWA	20	.564	.800	6.2	9.1
89-90	IOWA	18	.434	.720	2.9	11.4
Totals		94	.533	.768	6.8	12.8

NBA REGULAR-SEASON STATISTICS

			FGs		3-PT FGs		FTs		Rebounds						
	G	MIN	FG	PCT	FG	PCT	FT	PCT	OFF	TOT	AST	STL	BLK	PTS	PPG
90-91 HOU	18	63	14	.452	0	.000	11	.647	6	14	2	3	0	39	2.2
91-92 HOU	80	1278	205	.459	64	.386	38	.760	73	223	75	26	21	512	6.4
92-93 HOU	79	1356	213	.431	91	.374	58	.784	66	222	110	30	11	575	7.3
93-94 HOU	65	725	78	.345	50	.325	20	.769	23	84	64	14	6	226	3.5
Totals	242	3422	510	.426	205	.362	127	.760	168	543	251	73	38	1352	5.6

SCOTT BURRELL

Team: Charlotte Hornets
Position: Forward
Height: 6'7" **Weight:** 218
Birthdate: January 12, 1971

NBA Experience: 1 year
College: Connecticut
Acquired: 1st-round pick in 1993 draft (20th overall)

Background: A defensive star at Connecticut, Burrell became the only player in NCAA Division I history to amass 1,500 points, 750 rebounds, 300 steals, and 275 assists. He doubled as a baseball pitcher in the Toronto Blue Jays' farm system for three seasons, but he gave up baseball to play in the NBA. He was drafted 20th overall by Charlotte and was a part-time rookie starter. He missed over a month with a strained Achilles tendon.

Strengths: Burrell is an accomplished defender and a fantastic athlete. He uses his wingspan and quick hands to anticipate his opponent's moves and has also shown some shot-blocking potential. He gets up and down the floor quickly and has an offensive game built for transition. Burrell rebounds well and is not afraid to throw his weight into bigger people.

Weaknesses: Burrell was never a consistent shooter in college and his jump shot did not seem to improve much in his first pro season. For much of the year, he hovered around the 40-percent mark from the field. He also did not contribute much in the way of steals despite being known as a defensive standout. He is not a great ball-handler or distributor. While he does several things fairly well, he does not dominate any aspect of the game.

Analysis: Burrell did an admirable job as a starter when the Hornets were without frontcourt stars Larry Johnson and Alonzo Mourning. For most of his rookie year, however, he struggled to find consistent minutes and his play was up-and-down. NBA eyes see him as a potentially disruptive defender who will also contribute on the boards and in transition. He'll see more action as his offense improves.

PLAYER SUMMARY	
Will	run the floor
Can't	hit half his shots
Expect	defensive potential
Don't Expect	perimeter prowess
Fantasy Value	$1
Card Value	8-15¢

COLLEGE STATISTICS

		G	FGP	FTP	RPG	PPG
89-90	CONN	32	.386	.623	5.5	8.2
90-91	CONN	31	.440	.592	7.5	12.7
91-92	CONN	30	.453	.611	6.1	16.3
92-93	CONN	26	.411	.760	6.0	16.1
Totals		119	.426	.640	6.3	13.1

NBA REGULAR-SEASON STATISTICS

				FGs		3-PT FGs		FTs		Rebounds						
		G	MIN	FG	PCT	FG	PCT	FT	PCT	OFF	TOT	AST	STL	BLK	PTS	PPG
93-94	CHA	51	767	98	.419	2	.333	46	.657	46	132	62	37	16	244	4.8
Totals		51	767	98	.419	2	.333	46	.657	46	132	62	37	16	244	4.8

WILLIE BURTON

Team: Miami Heat
Position: Guard/Forward
Height: 6'8" **Weight:** 217
Birthdate: May 26, 1968

NBA Experience: 4 years
College: Minnesota
Acquired: 1st-round pick in 1990 draft
(9th overall)

Background: Burton became the University of Minnesota's No. 2 career scorer (behind Mychal Thompson) and led the Gophers into the Southeast Regional finals as a senior. Miami chose him ninth in the 1990 draft and he started late in his rookie year, but knee injuries, a bout with depression, and a foot injury have cost him significant playing time in the three seasons since. He spent over a month on the injured list last season.

Strengths: The versatile Burton can play either big guard or small forward and possesses a scorer's mentality. Although his scoring numbers have been down the last two years, he'll have games in the high 20s. Slashing to the hoop is his bread and butter. He has good range with a hot-and-cold jumper and good athletic ability.

Weaknesses: Burton is not one to distribute. He has never been a good or willing passer, dating back to his college days. Another reason you want to limit his ball-handling time is that he commits a lot of turnovers. Inconsistency is the biggest drawback with Burton, and it shows up on both ends of the court.

Analysis: Burton returned to a healthier number of games played last season, but his playing time has still been limited and his scoring is not what it was during his first two seasons in the league. Injuries have contributed to his troubles, but so has inconsistent play. He thinks like a scorer, but he is not a talented enough player to get away with ignoring other aspects of the game. Better passing would be a start.

PLAYER SUMMARY

Will ....slash to the hoop
Can't ....find open men
Expect ....points off the bench
Don't Expect ....great defense
Fantasy Value $0
Card Value ....10-20¢

COLLEGE STATISTICS

		G	FGP	FTP	RPG	PPG
86-87	MINN	28	.455	.649	4.2	8.7
87-88	MINN	28	.516	.713	5.6	13.7
88-89	MINN	30	.529	.797	7.5	18.6
89-90	MINN	32	.519	.770	6.4	19.3
Totals		118	.511	.749	6.0	15.3

NBA REGULAR-SEASON STATISTICS

			FGs		3-PT FGs		FTs		Rebounds						
		G	MIN	FG	PCT	FG	PCT	FT	PCT	OFF	TOT	AST	STL	BLK	PTS	PPG
90-91	MIA	76	1928	341	.441	4	.133	229	.782	111	262	107	72	24	915	12.0
91-92	MIA	68	1585	280	.450	6	.400	196	.800	76	244	123	46	37	762	11.2
92-93	MIA	26	451	54	.383	5	.333	91	.717	22	70	16	13	16	204	7.8
93-94	MIA	53	697	124	.438	3	.200	120	.759	50	136	39	18	20	371	7.0
Totals		223	4661	799	.439	18	.240	636	.773	259	712	285	149	97	2252	10.1

MITCHELL BUTLER

Team: Washington Bullets
Position: Guard
Height: 6'5" **Weight:** 210
Birthdate: December 15, 1970

NBA Experience: 1 year
College: UCLA
Acquired: Signed as a free agent, 10/93

Background: Butler was a standout on a UCLA team that also included current NBA players Don MacLean and Tracy Murray. Though he helped the Bruins back to national prominence while playing as many as four different positions in college, Butler was bypassed in the 1993 NBA draft. He made Washington's roster as a free agent in training camp last year and wound up averaging 6.9 PPG and shooting nearly 50 percent from the field.

Strengths: Butler is blessed with both athletic ability and versatility. He can play both guard and forward. He is a pretty accurate mid-range shooter and can also score with his back to the basket against smaller defenders. Butler is at his best in an up-tempo game, where he can pull up for jumpers, finish with jams, or find the open man. He helps out on the boards, especially the offensive, and has shown a great work ethic.

Weaknesses: In a halfcourt game, Butler is not nearly as effective as he is in transition. He does not have the ball-handling skills to act as a set-up man and his offensive range is limited. He committed more turnovers last season than he dished out assists. While he puts forth the effort, Butler still has a lot to learn about NBA defense. He is a horrible free throw shooter.

Analysis: Butler was one of Washington's more pleasant surprises last season. Considered a marginal talent coming out of college, he worked his way onto the Bullets' roster and played a significant role off the bench. He saw action in 75 games and made 19 starts. While he would not have made that kind of impact on a better team, Butler must be commended for his drive.

PLAYER SUMMARY	
Will	thrive at fast pace
Can't	shoot FTs
Expect	versatility
Don't Expect	defensive skills
Fantasy Value	$0
Card Value	5-10¢

COLLEGE STATISTICS

		G	FGP	FTP	RPG	PPG
89-90	UCLA	33	.538	.625	2.8	6.2
90-91	UCLA	32	.548	.513	4.2	7.9
91-92	UCLA	33	.489	.451	4.2	8.0
92-93	UCLA	32	.512	.526	5.3	9.5
Totals		130	.519	.528	4.1	7.9

NBA REGULAR-SEASON STATISTICS

			FGs		3-PT FGs		FTs		Rebounds						
	G	MIN	FG	PCT	FG	PCT	FT	PCT	OFF	TOT	AST	STL	BLK	PTS	PPG
93-94 WAS	75	1321	207	.495	0	.000	104	.578	106	225	77	54	20	518	6.9
Totals	75	1321	207	.495	0	.000	104	.578	106	225	77	54	20	518	6.9

MICHAEL CAGE

Team: Cleveland Cavaliers
Position: Forward/Center
Height: 6'9" **Weight:** 230
Birthdate: January 28, 1962

NBA Experience: 10 years
College: San Diego St.
Acquired: Signed as a free agent, 8/94

Background: Cage was voted Western Athletic Conference Player of the Year as a senior at San Diego State. He finished as the school's career leader in scoring, rebounding, and games played. He won the NBA rebounding title by grabbing 30 boards on the final night of the 1987-88 season as a Clipper. He has shot better than 50 percent while playing every game in each of the last five seasons. Cage signed a three-year deal with Cleveland in August.

Strengths: The tough, muscular Cage has made his living off the backboard. While he no longer starts regularly or rates among the league leaders, he still gets the job done. He shoots a high percentage, plays defense, and does whatever it takes to help the team.

Weaknesses: Cage has never been known for his offense. His low-post moves are predictable, yet he has spent a large portion of his career playing out of position at center. He's not a reliable ball-handler or passer and is a downright lousy free throw shooter.

Analysis: Cage is the kind of guy you want on your side. He comes to work ready to mix it up and keep his man off the boards. If it will help the team win, he will do it. His offensive abilities are very limited and his playing time has decreased somewhat, but you can always rely on Cage.

PLAYER SUMMARY	
Will	mix it up
Can't	make his FTs
Expect	defense, rebounds
Don't Expect	a lot of points
Fantasy Value	$0
Card Value	5-10¢

COLLEGE STATISTICS

		G	FGP	FTP	RPG	PPG
80-81	SDS	27	.558	.756	13.1	10.9
81-82	SDS	29	.488	.661	8.8	11.0
82-83	SDS	28	.570	.747	12.6	19.5
83-84	SDS	28	.562	.741	12.6	24.5
Totals		112	.548	.732	11.8	16.5

NBA REGULAR-SEASON STATISTICS

				FGs		3-PT FGs		FTs		Rebounds						
		G	MIN	FG	PCT	FG	PCT	FT	PCT	OFF	TOT	AST	STL	BLK	PTS	PPG
84-85	LAC	75	1610	216	.543	0	.000	101	.737	126	392	51	41	32	533	7.1
85-86	LAC	78	1566	204	.479	0	.000	113	.649	168	417	81	62	34	521	6.7
86-87	LAC	80	2922	457	.521	0	.000	341	.730	354	922	131	99	67	1255	15.7
87-88	LAC	72	2660	360	.470	0	.000	326	.689	371	938	110	91	58	1046	14.5
88-89	SEA	80	2536	314	.498	0	.000	197	.743	276	765	126	92	52	825	10.3
89-90	SEA	82	2595	325	.504	0	.000	148	.698	306	821	70	79	45	798	9.7
90-91	SEA	82	2141	226	.508	0	.000	70	.625	177	558	89	85	58	522	6.4
91-92	SEA	82	2461	307	.566	0	.000	106	.620	266	728	92	99	55	720	8.8
92-93	SEA	82	2156	219	.526	0	.000	61	.469	268	659	69	76	46	499	6.1
93-94	SEA	82	1708	171	.545	0	.000	36	.486	164	444	45	77	38	378	4.6
Totals		795	22355	2799	.513	0	.000	1499	.676	2476	6644	864	801	485	7097	8.9

ELDEN CAMPBELL

Team: Los Angeles Lakers
Position: Forward/Center
Height: 6'11" **Weight:** 235
Birthdate: July 23, 1968

NBA Experience: 4 years
College: Clemson
Acquired: 1st-round pick in 1990 draft
(27th overall)

Background: Campbell led the Atlantic Coast Conference in blocked shots three straight years and became Clemson's career scoring leader. He scored 21 points in an NBA Finals game as a Laker rookie and finished 13th in the league in blocks per game in 1991-92. The 1993-94 campaign was his first full year as a starter and he averaged career highs in most statistical categories.

Strengths: Best known for his shot-blocking and defensive intimidation, Campbell has great instincts for the ball, has a huge wingspan, and is a superb athlete and leaper. He was again among the league leaders in blocks last year, finishing 11th overall. He gets up and down the floor and finishes with flair. He has made himself a better inside scorer and worked himself into a more prominent role.

Weaknesses: Campbell is still not a solid halfcourt offensive player. His jump shot has improved but remains unreliable, and he does not own a vast repertoire of low-post moves. Campbell does not spot open men and he commits a lot of fouls by trying to block every shot. He is best suited for an open-court game.

Analysis: Campbell finally held onto a starting role for a full season and the reviews were mixed. He had some dazzling nights, but there were still too many games in which he failed to have an impact. A slow pace is not to his liking. Magic Johnson was named Laker coach late in the season and had the team running more than it had in recent years. Campbell hopes new coach Del Harris will retain the up-tempo approach in 1994-95.

PLAYER SUMMARY	
Will	...run the court
Can't	...take it slow
Expect	...2 BPG
Don't Expect	...low-post mastery
Fantasy Value	...$8-10
Card Value	...7-12¢

COLLEGE STATISTICS

		G	FGP	FTP	RPG	PPG
86-87	CLEM	31	.554	.702	4.1	8.8
87-88	CLEM	28	.629	.619	7.4	18.8
88-89	CLEM	29	.550	.688	7.7	17.5
89-90	CLEM	35	.522	.599	8.0	16.4
Totals		123	.562	.641	6.8	15.3

NBA REGULAR-SEASON STATISTICS

				FGs		3-PT FGs		FTs		Rebounds						
		G	MIN	FG	PCT	FG	PCT	FT	PCT	OFF	TOT	AST	STL	BLK	PTS	PPG
90-91	LAL	52	380	56	.455	0	.000	32	.653	40	96	10	11	38	144	2.8
91-92	LAL	81	1876	220	.448	0	.000	138	.619	155	423	59	53	159	578	7.1
92-93	LAL	79	1551	238	.458	0	.000	130	.637	127	332	48	59	100	606	7.7
93-94	LAL	76	2253	373	.462	0	.000	188	.689	167	519	86	64	146	934	12.3
Totals		288	6060	887	.457	0	.000	488	.652	489	1370	203	187	443	2262	7.9

TONY CAMPBELL

Unrestricted Free Agent
Last Team: Dallas Mavericks
Position: Guard/Forward
Height: 6'7" **Weight:** 215
Birthdate: May 7, 1962

NBA Experience: 10 years
College: Ohio St.
Acquired: Traded from Knicks with a
1997 1st-round pick for Derek Harper,
1/94

Background: Campbell was selected Big Ten Player of the Year after leading
Ohio State as a senior. His pro career started on the Detroit bench and in the
CBA, but he exploded onto the scene with the Lakers in the 1989 playoffs. He
was Minnesota's leading scorer in its first three years of existence before
becoming a reserve with the Knicks, who traded him to Dallas in January 1994.

Strengths: Putting the ball in the basket is Campbell's specialty. He gets to the
hoop, draws fouls, and is not afraid to take clutch shots. He is able to play both
small forward and big guard. He has tons of confidence, has nice moves, and will
torch the nets when he gets loose.

Weaknesses: Campbell is not the kind of player who makes those around him
better. He'll get his points, but they're not accompanied by many assists.
Campbell is a below-average rebounder, and many of his struggles in New York
stemmed from his allergies to defense.

Analysis: Scoring is Campbell's game. He learned about passing and defense
from the Knicks and became a more frequently used player until his trade. He
returned to a scoring role in Dallas, but he will not take top billing on a team led
by high-scoring youngsters Jamal Mashburn and Jim Jackson. Actually, it's
uncertain whether the Mavs will re-sign him for 1994-95.

PLAYER SUMMARY	
Will	get to the hoop
Can't	rack up assists
Expect	high-scoring spurts
Don't Expect	great defense
Fantasy Value	$1
Card Value	5-10¢

COLLEGE STATISTICS

		G	FGP	FTP	RPG	PPG
80-81	OSU	14	.417	.500	0.6	1.6
81-82	OSU	31	.424	.798	5.0	12.8
82-83	OSU	30	.503	.799	8.3	19.0
83-84	OSU	29	.513	.807	7.4	18.6
Totals		104	.482	.798	6.0	14.7

NBA REGULAR-SEASON STATISTICS

				FGs		3-PT FGs		FTs		Rebounds						
		G	MIN	FG	PCT	FG	PCT	FT	PCT	OFF	TOT	AST	STL	BLK	PTS	PPG
84-85	DET	56	625	130	.496	0	.000	56	.800	41	89	24	28	3	316	5.6
85-86	DET	82	1292	294	.484	2	.222	58	.795	83	236	45	62	7	648	7.9
86-87	DET	40	332	57	.393	0	.000	24	.615	21	58	19	12	1	138	3.5
87-88	LAL	13	242	57	.564	1	.333	28	.718	8	27	15	11	2	143	11.0
88-89	LAL	63	787	158	.458	2	.095	70	.843	53	130	47	37	6	388	6.2
89-90	MIN	82	3164	723	.457	9	.167	448	.787	209	451	213	111	31	1903	23.2
90-91	MIN	77	2893	652	.434	16	.262	358	.803	161	346	214	121	48	1678	21.8
91-92	MIN	78	2441	527	.464	13	.351	240	.803	141	286	229	84	31	1307	16.8
92-93	NY	58	1062	194	.490	2	.400	59	.678	59	155	62	34	5	449	7.7
93-94	NY/DAL	63	1214	227	.443	7	.250	94	.783	76	186	82	50	15	555	8.8
Totals		612	14052	3019	.458	52	.234	1435	.786	852	1964	950	550	149	7525	12.3

ANTOINE CARR

Unrestricted Free Agent
Last Team: San Antonio Spurs
Position: Forward
Height: 6'9" **Weight:** 255
Birthdate: July 23, 1961

NBA Experience: 10 years
College: Wichita St.
Acquired: Traded from Kings for Dwayne Schintzius and a 1994 2nd-round pick, 9/91

Background: Carr played with Cliff Levingston and Xavier McDaniel at Wichita State, where his No. 35 was retired after an All-America career. He played five-plus years in Atlanta with varying degrees of success before becoming a big scorer in Sacramento. He has served as both a starter and reserve in three years with San Antonio. An ankle injury sidelined him for much of last season.

Strengths: Carr can play both power forward and center because of his strong low-post game at both ends of the floor. He holds his position in the lane, loves to put his body on opposing players, and can put the ball in the hole. He's a fierce finisher, once shattering a backboard in warm-ups with the Hawks.

Weaknesses: When pushed away from the paint, Carr becomes largely ineffective. Most of his rebounding and scoring comes as a result of superior positioning rather than hustle. This notorious bruiser has always picked up a lot of fouls.

Analysis: Carr was invaluable to the Spurs when regular power forward Terry Cummings was sidelined for the 1992-93 season. Over the past two seasons, however, injuries and age have diminished his own effectiveness. A free agent, he'll likely wind up on another team this season.

PLAYER SUMMARY	
Will	deliver bruises
Can't	play on the perimeter
Expect	a reserve enforcer
Don't Expect	much touch
Fantasy Value	$1-3
Card Value	5-10¢

COLLEGE STATISTICS

		G	FGP	FTP	RPG	PPG
79-80	WSU	29	.501	.667	5.9	15.2
80-81	WSU	33	.586	.765	7.3	15.8
81-82	WSU	28	.566	.791	7.0	16.0
82-83	WSU	22	.575	.765	7.6	22.6
Totals		112	.557	.746	6.9	17.1

NBA REGULAR-SEASON STATISTICS

				FGs		3-PT FGs		FTs		Rebounds						
		G	MIN	FG	PCT	FG	PCT	FT	PCT	OFF	TOT	AST	STL	BLK	PTS	PPG
84-85	ATL	62	1195	198	.528	2	.333	101	.789	79	232	80	29	78	499	8.0
85-86	ATL	17	258	49	.527	0	.000	18	.667	16	52	14	7	15	116	6.8
86-87	ATL	65	695	134	.506	1	.333	73	.709	60	156	34	14	48	342	5.3
87-88	ATL	80	1483	281	.544	1	.250	142	.780	94	289	103	38	85	705	8.8
88-89	ATL	78	1488	226	.480	0	.000	130	.855	106	274	91	31	62	582	7.5
89-90	ATL/SAC	77	1727	356	.494	0	.000	237	.795	115	322	119	30	68	949	12.3
90-91	SAC	77	2527	628	.511	0	.000	295	.758	163	420	191	45	101	1551	20.1
91-92	SA	81	1867	359	.490	1	.200	162	.764	128	346	63	32	96	881	10.9
92-93	SA	71	1947	379	.538	0	.000	174	.777	107	388	97	35	87	932	13.1
93-94	SA	34	465	78	.488	0	.000	42	.724	12	51	15	9	22	198	5.8
Totals		642	13652	2688	.510	5	.143	1374	.775	880	2530	807	270	660	6755	10.5

BILL CARTWRIGHT

Unrestricted Free Agent
Last Team: Chicago Bulls
Position: Center
Height: 7'1" **Weight:** 245
Birthdate: July 30, 1957
NBA Experience: 14 years

College: San Francisco
Acquired: Traded from Knicks with
1988 1st- and 3rd-round picks for
Charles Oakley and 1988 1st- and 3rd-
round picks, 6/88

Background: Cartwright was an All-American at San Francisco, and the Knicks chose him third overall in the 1979 draft. He had an up-and-down career in New York, twice averaging 20-plus PPG but then languishing because of injuries. He caught his second wind in Chicago, where he started on the Bulls' three world championship teams. Recurring knee and back problems now plague him.

Strengths: Cartwright is an old-fashioned low-post scorer who uses his size well on the blocks. His gangly, over-the-head shot somehow goes in often enough to make him an offensive threat away from the paint, and he still plays above-average interior defense.

Weaknesses: Mr. Bill has a faulty pair of hands, has very little athletic ability, and is not a good rebounder. Age and injuries are wearing down his body.

Analysis: Cartwright quite literally is on his last leg. He spent three separate stints on the injured list last season with back and knee ailments as the Bulls tried to save him for the playoffs. Retirement is not far off.

PLAYER SUMMARY

Will	defend top centers
Can't	trade in his knees
Expect	impending retirement
Don't Expect	82-game seasons
Fantasy Value	$0
Card Value	5-10¢

COLLEGE STATISTICS

		G	FGP	FTP	RPG	PPG
75-76	SF	30	.530	.735	6.9	12.5
76-77	SF	31	.566	.733	8.5	19.4
77-78	SF	21	.667	.733	10.1	20.6
78-79	SF	29	.605	.734	15.7	24.5
Totals		111	.589	.734	10.2	19.1

NBA REGULAR-SEASON STATISTICS

		G	MIN	FG	FGs PCT	FG	3-PT FGs PCT	FT	FTs PCT	OFF	Rebounds TOT	AST	STL	BLK	PTS	PPG
79-80	NY	82	3150	665	.547	0	.000	451	.797	194	726	165	48	101	1781	21.7
80-81	NY	82	2925	619	.554	0	.000	408	.788	161	613	111	48	83	1646	20.1
81-82	NY	72	2060	390	.562	0	.000	257	.763	116	421	87	48	65	1037	14.4
82-83	NY	82	2468	455	.566	0	.000	380	.744	185	590	136	41	127	1290	15.7
83-84	NY	77	2487	453	.561	0	.000	404	.805	195	649	107	44	97	1310	17.0
85-86	NY	2	36	3	.429	0	.000	6	.600	2	10	5	1	1	12	6.0
86-87	NY	58	1989	335	.531	0	.000	346	.790	132	445	96	40	26	1016	17.5
87-88	NY	82	1676	287	.544	0	.000	340	.798	127	384	85	43	43	914	11.1
88-89	CHI	78	2333	365	.475	0	.000	236	.766	152	521	90	21	41	966	12.4
89-90	CHI	71	2160	292	.488	0	.000	227	.811	137	465	145	38	34	811	11.4
90-91	CHI	79	2273	318	.490	0	.000	124	.697	167	486	126	32	15	760	9.6
91-92	CHI	64	1471	208	.467	0	.000	96	.604	93	324	87	22	14	512	8.0
92-93	CHI	63	1253	141	.411	0	.000	72	.735	83	233	83	20	10	354	5.6
93-94	CHI	42	780	98	.513	0	.000	39	.684	43	152	57	8	8	235	5.6
Totals		934	27061	4629	.526	0	.000	3386	.772	1787	6019	1380	454	665	12644	13.5

SAM CASSELL

Team: Houston Rockets
Position: Guard
Height: 6'3" **Weight:** 195
Birthdate: November 18, 1969

NBA Experience: 1 year
College: Florida St.
Acquired: 1st-round pick in 1993 draft (24th overall)

Background: From legendary Dunbar High School in Baltimore, Cassell had two sensational seasons at San Jacinto J.C. in Texas before transferring to Florida State. He prospered on a talented Seminole unit, leading the Atlantic Coast Conference in steals and scoring 30 or more points four times as a senior. Drafted 24th overall by Houston in 1993, Cassell spent his rookie year primarily as a reserve guard for one of the better backcourts in the league.

Strengths: Cassell has great quickness, agility, and hands, and has shown an aptitude for taking the ball to the basket. He was compared to Sedale Threatt as a pro prospect, and there are many similarities between the two. Three-point range and the ability to play both guard positions are among them. Cassell is a very good free throw shooter. Coaches also love his defensive potential.

Weaknesses: Like most rookies, Cassell needs to develop more consistency. He'll turn the ball over while trying to make the spectacular play, and his field goal percentage needs a boost. Better decision-making is a must. The consensus is he will eventually be a very good defender; however, he is still prone to lapses on that end of the court and his man often takes advantage of them. He's not much of a rebounder.

Analysis: Considering he was a late first-round pick, Cassell enjoyed a fine rookie season. He shot the 3-pointer better than most rookie guards, was chosen to play in the Schick Rookie Game, and joined Scott Brooks as frequently used guards off the Houston bench. Moreover, he was a key playoff contributor as the Rockets marched to the NBA championship. He'll only get better as he sees more action.

PLAYER SUMMARY	
Will	shoot the trey
Can't	shoot 50 percent
Expect	continued improvement
Don't Expect	many rebounds
Fantasy Value	$5-7
Card Value	25-50¢

COLLEGE STATISTICS

		G	FGP	FTP	APG	PPG
91-92	FSU	31	.454	.704	3.8	18.4
92-93	FSU	35	.502	.759	4.9	18.3
Totals		66	.478	.733	4.4	18.3

NBA REGULAR-SEASON STATISTICS

			FGs		3-PT FGs		FTs		Rebounds						
	G	MIN	FG	PCT	FG	PCT	FT	PCT	OFF	TOT	AST	STL	BLK	PTS	PPG
93-94 HOU	66	1122	162	.418	26	.295	90	.841	25	134	192	59	7	440	6.7
Totals	66	1122	162	.418	26	.295	90	.841	25	134	192	59	7	440	6.7

DUANE CAUSWELL

Team: Sacramento Kings
Position: Center
Height: 7'0" **Weight:** 240
Birthdate: May 31, 1968

NBA Experience: 4 years
College: Temple
Acquired: 1st-round pick in 1990 draft (18th overall)

Background: Causwell's college career at Temple was cut a semester short because of academic ineligibility, but he finished second in the nation in blocked shots as a junior (4.1 BPG). Projected as a back-up center, Causwell started 55 games as a rookie and finished 15th in the league in blocked shots. He improved his total during his second season but has since been slowed by injuries. He spent about half of the 1993-94 campaign on the injured list with a bad left foot, and he played only 674 minutes altogether.

Strengths: With his quick leaping ability and long wingspan, Causwell is a fine shot-blocker. He gets up and down the floor better than most of the league's centers and is a fine overall athlete. In addition, he does not take bad shots. Causwell annually leads the Kings in field goal percentage.

Weaknesses: Causwell tends to leave the dirty work for others while he lunges to block every shot. He could also stand to be a lot more physical on offense. Passing the ball is not in his repertoire. He's a dismal outside shooter, as reflected in his free throw percentage, which is in the low 60s for his career. His left foot remains a big concern.

Analysis: Considered a project coming out of college, Causwell surprised a lot of people with his ability to block shots in the NBA and score a little around the basket. However, his game remains soft in most other areas and a bum left foot has not held up in either of the last two seasons. Causwell is the kind of player who needs to stay in the lineup if he hopes to raise his game.

PLAYER SUMMARY	
Will	block shots
Can't	shoot from outside
Expect	athletic ability
Don't Expect	triple-doubles
Fantasy Value	$1
Card Value	5-10¢

COLLEGE STATISTICS

		G	FGP	FTP	RPG	PPG
87-88	TEMP	33	.491	.433	2.6	2.0
88-89	TEMP	30	.514	.683	8.9	11.3
89-90	TEMP	12	.486	.596	8.3	11.3
Totals		75	.504	.624	6.0	7.2

NBA REGULAR-SEASON STATISTICS

				FGs		3-PT FGs		FTs		Rebounds						
		G	MIN	FG	PCT	FG	PCT	FT	PCT	OFF	TOT	AST	STL	BLK	PTS	PPG
90-91	SAC	76	1719	210	.508	0	.000	105	.636	141	391	69	49	148	525	6.9
91-92	SAC	80	2291	250	.549	0	.000	136	.613	196	580	59	47	215	636	7.9
92-93	SAC	55	1211	175	.545	0	.000	103	.624	112	303	35	32	87	453	8.2
93-94	SAC	41	674	71	.518	0	.000	40	.588	68	186	11	19	49	182	4.4
Totals		252	5895	706	.532	0	.000	384	.619	517	1460	174	147	499	1796	7.1

CEDRIC CEBALLOS

Team: Phoenix Suns
Position: Forward
Height: 6'7" **Weight:** 225
Birthdate: August 2, 1969

NBA Experience: 4 years
College: Cal. St. Fullerton
Acquired: 2nd-round pick in 1990 draft (48th overall)

Background: Ceballos, a Hawaii native, played just one year of varsity basketball in high school before going on to lead the Big West in scoring as a junior and senior at Cal. State Fullerton. His rookie season in the NBA came as a pleasant surprise to the Suns and he has since become the team's starting small forward. Ceballos led the NBA in field goal percentage in 1992-93. He fractured his left foot during the 1993-94 preseason but came back in January and enjoyed his most productive season.

Strengths: Ceballos is an energetic, athletic player who can flat-out score. He plays above the rim, gets to the basket, and shoots a high percentage from the field. His outside shooting has improved greatly. He runs the floor, loves working the baseline, and has great hands. Ceballos is a flashy performer who won the NBA's Slam Dunk Contest in 1992 with a blindfolded jam. He also rebounds well.

Weaknesses: His biggest flaw remains his lack of defensive intensity. Ceballos often perceives stopping his man as a chore. His leaping ability gives him tremendous potential as a shot-blocker, yet he has not put up big numbers in that category. He does not own a deft touch from 3-point range.

Analysis: Ceballos is one of the NBA's rising stars. He scored 40 points in a game last season and became one of the top three scorers for the Suns, along with Charles Barkley and Kevin Johnson. He has always had flair. Now he has shown he can put the team on his shoulders and carry it offensively. In a shootout, you want him on your side.

PLAYER SUMMARY	
Will	get to the basket
Can't	dominate on defense
Expect	scoring, rebounding
Don't Expect	a block a game
Fantasy Value	$5-7
Card Value	8-15¢

COLLEGE STATISTICS

		G	FGP	FTP	RPG	PPG
88-89	CSF	29	.442	.672	8.8	21.2
89-90	CSF	29	.485	.670	12.5	23.1
Totals		58	.463	.671	10.7	22.1

NBA REGULAR-SEASON STATISTICS

		G	MIN	FGs FG	FGs PCT	3-PT FGs FG	3-PT FGs PCT	FTs FT	FTs PCT	Rebounds OFF	Rebounds TOT	AST	STL	BLK	PTS	PPG
90-91	PHO	63	730	204	.487	1	.167	110	.663	77	150	35	22	5	519	8.2
91-92	PHO	64	725	176	.482	1	.167	109	.736	60	152	50	16	11	462	7.2
92-93	PHO	74	1607	381	.576	0	.000	187	.725	172	408	77	54	28	949	12.8
93-94	PHO	53	1602	425	.535	0	.000	160	.724	153	344	91	59	23	1010	19.1
Totals		254	4664	1186	.529	2	.087	566	.714	462	1054	253	151	67	2940	11.6

TOM CHAMBERS

Unrestricted Free Agent
Last Team: Utah Jazz
Position: Forward
Height: 6'10" **Weight:** 230

Birthdate: June 21, 1959
NBA Experience: 13 years
College: Utah
Acquired: Signed as a free agent, 8/93

Background: Chambers earned All-America recognition at the University of Utah before moving on to become one of the NBA's most productive scorers. He has played in four All-Star Games in 13 years, winning MVP honors in 1987. He went to the Suns in 1988 as the first unrestricted free agent in NBA history. Utah signed him before the 1993-94 campaign but did not re-sign him after it.

Strengths: A double-figure scorer in every one of his 13 seasons, Chambers can shoot from outside or go strong to the hoop with either hand. He provides stable leadership, hits the boards, and plays an intelligent brand of basketball.

Weaknesses: Chambers has lost a step and is therefore not the match-up problem he once was. He was never a top-notch defender and still isn't. His field goal percentage has been sub-par for four straight seasons.

Analysis: Chambers is winding down his high-scoring career as a veteran reserve, and an effective one at that. He played in 80 games for the Jazz during the 1993-94 season and, while not the player he once was, he contributed greatly to their success. He went over the 19,000-point mark for his career.

PLAYER SUMMARY	
Will	score from anywhere
Can't	match his previous level
Expect	10-plus PPG
Don't Expect	quickness
Fantasy Value	$0
Card Value	5-10¢

COLLEGE STATISTICS

		G	FGP	FTP	RPG	PPG
77-78	UTA	28	.496	.625	3.7	6.4
78-79	UTA	30	.544	.543	8.9	16.0
79-80	UTA	28	.543	.713	8.7	17.2
80-81	UTA	30	.594	.742	8.7	18.6
Totals		116	.553	.665	7.6	14.6

NBA REGULAR-SEASON STATISTICS

				FGs		3-PT FGs		FTs		Rebounds						
	G	MIN	FG	PCT	FG	PCT	FT	PCT	OFF	TOT	AST	STL	BLK	PTS	PPG
81-82 SD	81	2682	554	.525	0	.000	284	.620	211	561	146	58	46	1392	17.2
82-83 SD	79	2665	519	.472	0	.000	353	.723	218	519	192	79	57	1391	17.6
83-84 SEA	82	2570	554	.499	0	.000	375	.800	219	532	133	47	51	1483	18.1
84-85 SEA	81	2923	629	.483	6	.273	475	.832	164	579	209	70	57	1739	21.5
85-86 SEA	66	2019	432	.466	13	.271	346	.836	126	431	132	55	37	1223	18.5
86-87 SEA	82	3018	660	.456	54	.372	535	.849	163	545	245	81	50	1909	23.3
87-88 SEA	82	2680	611	.448	33	.303	419	.807	135	490	212	87	53	1674	20.4
88-89 PHO	81	3002	774	.471	28	.326	509	.851	143	684	231	87	55	2085	25.7
89-90 PHO	81	3046	810	.501	24	.279	557	.861	190	571	190	88	47	2201	27.2
90-91 PHO	76	2475	556	.437	20	.274	379	.826	104	490	194	65	52	1511	19.9
91-92 PHO	69	1948	426	.431	18	.367	258	.830	86	401	142	57	37	1128	16.3
92-93 PHO	73	1723	320	.447	11	.393	241	.837	96	345	101	43	23	892	12.2
93-94 UTA	80	1838	329	.440	14	.311	221	.786	87	326	79	40	32	893	11.2
Totals	1013	32589	7174	.469	221	.310	4952	.807	1873	6474	2206	857	597	19521	19.3

REX CHAPMAN

Team: Washington Bullets
Position: Guard
Height: 6'4" **Weight:** 205
Birthdate: October 5, 1967

NBA Experience: 6 years
College: Kentucky
Acquired: Traded from Hornets for Tom Hammonds, 2/92

Background: At Kentucky, Chapman became the first freshman to lead the Wildcats in scoring and the third Kentucky player to score 1,000 points in his first two years. He left school after his sophomore year and was a 15-plus PPG scorer for Charlotte in his first three pro years. He was acquired by Washington in 1991-92 but his career has been slowed somewhat by injuries since. He missed over a month with a dislocated ankle last season but enjoyed his best scoring year as a pro.

Strengths: Chapman is a great athlete who can sky. His vertical leap has been measured at 42 inches. Yet lay off him in fear of the drive and he can burn you from outside with 3-point range. His shooting reached a career-high level last season and he is solid from the free throw line. He has become a better all-around player.

Weaknesses: Poor shot selection has been the knock on Chapman throughout his career, although he certainly has improved. He has a tendency to try to do it all himself rather than getting his teammates involved. He remains somewhat suspect on defense. His history of injuries is a concern.

Analysis: Chapman came into the 1993-94 season 20 pounds lighter than he did the year before and enjoyed perhaps his best season. His leaping ability seemed to be restored by the weight loss and he made strides in several other key areas. His shooting and defensive awareness were a lot better. Chapman may still make a good name for himself as a pro.

PLAYER SUMMARY	
Will	play above the rim
Can't	stay healthy
Expect.	a scoring bent
Don't Expect	great defense
Fantasy Value	$12-15
Card Value	5-10¢

COLLEGE STATISTICS

		G	FGP	FTP	RPG	PPG
86-87	KEN	29	.444	.735	2.3	16.0
87-88	KEN	32	.501	.794	2.9	19.0
Totals		61	.475	.771	2.6	17.6

NBA REGULAR-SEASON STATISTICS

		G	MIN	FGs FG	FGs PCT	3-PT FGs FG	3-PT FGs PCT	FTs FT	FTs PCT	Rebounds OFF	Rebounds TOT	AST	STL	BLK	PTS	PPG
88-89	CHA	75	2219	526	.414	60	.314	155	.795	74	187	176	70	25	1267	16.9
89-90	CHA	54	1762	377	.408	47	.331	144	.750	52	179	132	46	6	945	17.5
90-91	CHA	70	2100	410	.445	48	.324	234	.830	45	191	250	73	16	1102	15.7
91-92	CHA/WAS	22	567	113	.448	8	.276	36	.679	10	58	89	15	8	270	12.3
92-93	WAS	60	1300	287	.477	43	.371	132	.810	19	88	116	38	10	749	12.5
93-94	WAS	60	2025	431	.498	64	.388	168	.816	57	146	185	59	8	1094	18.2
Totals		341	9973	2144	.443	270	.341	869	.797	257	849	948	301	73	5427	15.9

CALBERT CHEANEY

Team: Washington Bullets
Position: Forward
Height: 6'7" **Weight:** 209
Birthdate: July 17, 1971

NBA Experience: 1 year
College: Indiana
Acquired: 1st-round pick in 1993 draft (6th overall)

Background: Though not highly recruited out of high school in Evansville, Indiana, Cheaney received a scholarship from Indiana and developed into one of the best players in Hoosier history. He set a Big Ten record for total points and scored in double figures in 58 of his final 59 games. The John Wooden and James Naismith Award winner as Player of the Year, he was drafted sixth overall by Washington in 1993 and was one of the Bullets' five double-figure scorers as a rookie small forward.

Strengths: Cheaney is a silky-smooth player with a variety of skills. He slithers to the basket, can get his own shot, and is an accurate jump-shooter within about 20 feet. Some called him the best pure shooter of the 1993 draft class. Cheaney is quick, agile, and effective in transition. He also rebounds, passes, plays defense, and is a gritty competitor. He does not shy away from the big shots.

Weaknesses: Cheaney's biggest weakness is perhaps his inability to connect from the NBA 3-point line. That takes away some of his versatility because you'd like to have a shooting guard with at least a capable long-range stroke. He's prone to the turnover, but so is just about every rookie. Cheaney's best defensive days are ahead of him.

Analysis: Cheaney landed in the NBA running. He scored 20 points against the Celtics in the season opener. A competitor in the Schick Rookie Game, he started most of Washington's outings after the All-Star break except for a stretch in March when a foot injury sidelined him. Cheaney gives the Bullets a well-rounded and hard-working player who will continue to improve with playing time. He may one day become a 3-point threat.

PLAYER SUMMARY	
Will	get his shot off
Can't	hit the NBA 3
Expect	smooth moves
Don't Expect	fear of pressure
Fantasy Value	$7-9
Card Value	20-40¢

COLLEGE STATISTICS

		G	FGP	FTP	RPG	PPG
89-90	IND	29	.572	.750	4.6	17.1
90-91	IND	34	.596	.801	5.5	21.6
91-92	IND	34	.522	.800	4.9	17.6
92-93	IND	35	.549	.795	6.4	22.4
Totals		132	.559	.790	5.4	19.8

NBA REGULAR-SEASON STATISTICS

			FGs		3-PT FGs		FTs		Rebounds						
	G	MIN	FG	PCT	FG	PCT	FT	PCT	OFF	TOT	AST	STL	BLK	PTS	PPG
93-94 WAS	65	1604	327	.470	1	.043	124	.770	88	190	126	63	10	779	12.0
Totals	65	1604	327	.470	1	.043	124	.770	88	190	126	63	10	779	12.0

PETE CHILCUTT

Team: Detroit Pistons
Position: Forward/Center
Height: 6'10" **Weight:** 232
Birthdate: September 14, 1968
NBA Experience: 3 years

College: North Carolina
Acquired: Traded from Kings with a conditional 1st-round pick and a 1994 2nd-round pick for Olden Polynice, 2/94

Background: A solid complementary player for coach Dean Smith at North Carolina, Chilcutt was never named first- or second-team All-ACC, but he played every game during his four years with the Tar Heels. He was drafted 27th overall by Sacramento in 1991 and played mostly as a reserve in two-plus years with the Kings, although he did start some. He was traded to Detroit last February in a deal that sent Olden Polynice to Sacramento.

Strengths: Chilcutt has a very soft shooting touch with good range for a big man. He has the potential to pose a match-up problem for power forwards and centers who like to stay near the bucket. He's fundamentally sound in most areas and hits the boards. He works hard at both ends and shows a nice feel for the game.

Weaknesses: Chilcutt doesn't possess exceptional speed, quickness, jumping ability, or any other athletic skill. In fact, nothing about his game is awe-inspiring. He's not able to create his own shot or set up others, although he is a skilled high-post passer. He tends to play soft at both ends. Physical defense and post-up offense are not his style. He rarely gets to the line and his accuracy there dipped last season.

Analysis: The Pistons got two draft choices and Chilcutt for Polynice, and their hope is that the picks will be more helpful than the player. Chilcutt does possess some offensive skills and had worked his way into the starting lineup with the Kings. However, he is best used to provide a few points and rebounds off the bench.

PLAYER SUMMARY	
Will	pull centers outside
Can't	dominate physically
Expect	perimeter touch
Don't Expect	a regular starter
Fantasy Value	$0
Card Value	5-10¢

COLLEGE STATISTICS

		G	FGP	FTP	RPG	PPG
87-88	NC	34	.564	.706	3.2	4.9
88-89	NC	37	.537	.623	5.4	6.9
89-90	NC	34	.514	.714	6.6	9.0
90-91	NC	35	.538	.765	6.6	12.0
Totals		140	.536	.710	5.5	8.2

NBA REGULAR-SEASON STATISTICS

				FGs		3-PT FGs		FTs		Rebounds						
		G	MIN	FG	PCT	FG	PCT	FT	PCT	OFF	TOT	AST	STL	BLK	PTS	PPG
91-92	SAC	69	817	113	.452	2	1.000	23	.821	78	187	38	32	17	251	3.6
92-93	SAC	59	834	165	.485	0	.000	32	.696	80	194	64	22	21	362	6.1
93-94	SAC/DET	76	1365	203	.453	3	.200	41	.631	129	371	86	53	39	450	5.9
Totals		204	3016	481	.463	5	.294	96	.691	287	752	188	107	77	1063	5.2

DOUG CHRISTIE

Team: Los Angeles Lakers
Position: Guard/Forward
Height: 6'6" **Weight:** 205
Birthdate: May 9, 1970
NBA Experience: 2 years

College: Pepperdine
Acquired: Draft rights traded from SuperSonics with Benoit Benjamin for Sam Perkins, 2/93

Background: Christie became Pepperdine's best player since Dennis Johnson. He led the Waves to the NCAA Tournament in 1991 and 1992, was MVP and slam-dunk champion at the NABC All-Star Game, and was drafted 17th overall by the Sonics in 1992. Unable to sign him after a prolonged holdout, Seattle traded his rights and Benoit Benjamin to the Lakers for Sam Perkins. After a rookie year cut to 23 games, Christie fared better in 1993-94, posting a double-figure scoring average and becoming a starter.

Strengths: Christie, a great athlete, is versatile and super-smooth. Despite his surgically repaired knee, he plays above the rim and can fit in at multiple positions. He slashes to the hoop, shoots with 3-point range, and is a gifted passer who never averaged less than four APG in college. He plays with a high energy level and is capable of huge offensive games.

Weaknesses: Christie is still learning a lot about the game. His field goal percentage is nothing to write home about, although he does show potential as a 3-point threat if he can gain some consistency. His defense also shows signs of life but not much regularity. Christie often tries to make great plays when none are available and turns the ball over far too often.

Analysis: Christie is capable of playing both guard positions or small forward. That versatility and his tremendous raw ability make him a valuable player for the Lakers in the immediate future. Look for Christie to become a player who can score points in bunches with long-distance shooting and drives to the bucket. With more consistency and fewer mistakes, he would become a fine pro player.

PLAYER SUMMARY	
Will	play three positions
Can't	eliminate turnovers
Expect	further improvement
Don't Expect	veteran decisions
Fantasy Value	$5-7
Card Value	15-30¢

COLLEGE STATISTICS

		G	FGP	FTP	RPG	PPG
89-90	PEP	28	.503	.714	4.1	8.9
90-91	PEP	28	.469	.765	5.2	19.1
91-92	PEP	31	.466	.746	5.9	19.5
Totals		87	.473	.747	5.1	16.0

NBA REGULAR-SEASON STATISTICS

		G	MIN	FGs FG	FGs PCT	3-PT FGs FG	3-PT FGs PCT	FTs FT	FTs PCT	Rebounds OFF	Rebounds TOT	AST	STL	BLK	PTS	PPG
92-93	LAL	23	332	45	.425	2	.167	50	.758	24	51	53	22	5	142	6.2
93-94	LAL	65	1515	244	.434	39	.328	145	.697	93	235	136	89	28	672	10.3
Totals		88	1847	289	.433	41	.313	195	.712	117	286	189	111	33	814	9.3

DERRICK COLEMAN

Team: New Jersey Nets
Position: Forward
Height: 6'10" **Weight:** 240
Birthdate: June 21, 1967

NBA Experience: 4 years
College: Syracuse
Acquired: 1st-round pick in 1990 draft
(1st overall)

Background: Teamed with Billy Owens and Sherman Douglas, Coleman played on one of Syracuse's most talented squads ever. He averaged 17.9 PPG and 12.1 RPG and earned several college Player of the Year awards as a senior. New Jersey selected him as the No. 1 pick in the 1990 draft and he won the NBA Rookie of the Year Award. He has been one of the league's best power forwards. Last season, he made his first All-Star Game appearance and was named to Dream Team II, the U.S. national squad.

Strengths: Coleman hurts you in a number of ways. He can kill you with his jump shot, his moves to the bucket, or his post-up repertoire. He's supremely confident, having learned the game on the Detroit playgrounds. He can either start or finish the break and has 3-point range. He blocks shots and is one of the better rebounding forwards in the league.

Weaknesses: There are those who say Coleman does not work hard enough night after night to reach his limitless potential. Charles Barkley said as much last year, although Coleman disagrees. His shooting percentage is sub-par and his turnover total high. His brash attitude has rubbed people the wrong way.

Analysis: Expect Coleman to be an All-Star regular in years to come after being voted a starter last season. Although he has his critics, some have also called him the best overall power forward in the game today. He certainly rates among the top players in basketball and shows signs of becoming even better. When he's hot, he can flat-out dominate the opposition.

PLAYER SUMMARY	
Will	score, rebound
Can't	shake his critics
Expect	an All-Star regular
Don't Expect	few turnovers
Fantasy Value	$45-50
Card Value	15-30¢

COLLEGE STATISTICS

		G	FGP	FTP	RPG	PPG
86-87	SYR	38	.560	.686	8.8	11.9
87-88	SYR	35	.587	.630	11.0	13.5
88-89	SYR	37	.575	.692	11.4	16.9
89-90	SYR	33	.551	.715	12.1	17.9
Totals		143	.568	.684	10.7	15.0

NBA REGULAR-SEASON STATISTICS

				FGs		3-PT FGs		FTs		Rebounds						
		G	MIN	FG	PCT	FG	PCT	FT	PCT	OFF	TOT	AST	STL	BLK	PTS	PPG
90-91	NJ	74	2602	514	.467	13	.342	323	.731	269	759	163	71	99	1364	18.4
91-92	NJ	65	2207	483	.504	23	.303	300	.763	203	618	205	54	98	1289	19.8
92-93	NJ	76	2759	564	.460	23	.232	421	.808	247	852	276	92	126	1572	20.7
93-94	NJ	77	2778	541	.447	38	.314	439	.774	262	870	262	68	142	1559	20.2
Totals		292	10346	2102	.468	97	.290	1483	.771	981	3099	906	285	465	5784	19.8

BIMBO COLES

Team: Miami Heat
Position: Guard
Height: 6'2" **Weight:** 185
Birthdate: April 22, 1968

NBA Experience: 4 years
College: Virginia Tech
Acquired: Draft rights traded from Kings for Rory Sparrow, 6/90

Background: Coles left Virginia Tech as the first player to lead the Metro Conference in scoring three straight years. He also set a school record for assists and was a member of the 1988 United States Olympic team. Drafted by Miami, he missed a total of just two games in his first three NBA seasons and averaged double figures in scoring twice. That total, along with his playing time, dropped somewhat during 1993-94.

Strengths: Coles is extremely quick and can get to the hoop against virtually anyone. He has been a productive distributor off the bench for the Heat. After shooting 40 percent as a college senior, he has raised his accuracy to the 45-percent range as a pro. Defense has never been a problem, thanks to his fleet feet. Coles loves to play the game.

Weaknesses: His perimeter shooting remains inconsistent, and Coles should not be launching as many NBA 3-pointers as he does. He makes well under 30 percent of them, prompting defenders to back off and let him fire. Coles will rush plays at times. He is not much of a rebounding force and will never be a big scorer in the NBA.

Analysis: Coles, who has been called a shooting guard in the body of a point guard, has become a pretty capable back-up at the point. In fact, his ability to handle and distribute the ball is more valuable to Miami than any other part of his game. His shooting is sporadic and he did not score last season like he did the previous two. Added consistency would help keep him in the rotation.

PLAYER SUMMARY	
Will	distribute
Can't	shoot consistently
Expect	good quickness
Don't Expect	50-percent shooting
Fantasy Value	$4-6
Card Value	5-10¢

COLLEGE STATISTICS

		G	FGP	FTP	APG	PPG
86-87	VT	28	.412	.716	4.0	10.0
87-88	VT	29	.443	.741	5.9	24.2
88-89	VT	27	.455	.785	5.2	26.6
89-90	VT	31	.404	.738	3.9	25.3
Totals		115	.429	.748	4.8	21.6

NBA REGULAR-SEASON STATISTICS

		G	MIN	FGs FG	FGs PCT	3-PT FGs FG	3-PT FGs PCT	FTs FT	FTs PCT	Rebounds OFF	Rebounds TOT	AST	STL	BLK	PTS	PPG
90-91	MIA	82	1355	162	.412	6	.176	71	.747	56	153	232	65	12	401	4.9
91-92	MIA	81	1976	295	.455	10	.192	216	.824	69	189	366	73	13	816	10.1
92-93	MIA	81	2232	318	.464	42	.307	177	.805	58	166	373	80	11	855	10.6
93-94	MIA	76	1726	233	.449	20	.202	102	.779	50	159	263	75	12	588	7.7
Totals		320	7289	1008	.449	78	.242	566	.799	233	667	1234	293	48	2660	8.3

TYRONE CORBIN

Team: Utah Jazz
Position: Forward
Height: 6'6" **Weight:** 222
Birthdate: December 31, 1962
NBA Experience: 9 years

College: DePaul
Acquired: Traded from Timberwolves for Thurl Bailey and a 1992 2nd-round pick, 11/91

Background: After leading DePaul in both scoring and rebounding as a junior and senior, Corbin made his NBA debut with San Antonio. He played for Cleveland, Phoenix, and Minnesota before the Timberwolves traded him to Utah in 1991-92. Corbin, a reserve small forward with the Jazz, has played in at least 80 games each of the last five years.

Strengths: Corbin has rightfully earned his reputation as a hard worker and physical player. He fights for rebounds, gets good inside position, comes up with steals and loose balls, and plays strong defense on men his size or bigger. Corbin is able to stick the mid-range jumper with regularity. He's a workaholic and a class act.

Weaknesses: The bumping and grinding inside are necessary because Corbin does not own the silky-smooth game that many of the league's premier small forwards possess. He does not create much off the dribble for either himself or his teammates. He does not shoot well from beyond 18 feet.

Analysis: Corbin is the kind of player a coach loves. On a Minnesota team that needed scoring, he was a scorer. On a Utah team that needs his grit, he provides it. He works hard either starting or off the bench. Last season was not one of his best, however.

PLAYER SUMMARY	
Will	get on the floor
Can't	thrive on treys
Expect	maximum effort
Don't Expect	a scoring machine
Fantasy Value	$1
Card Value	5-10¢

COLLEGE STATISTICS

		G	FGP	FTP	RPG	PPG
81-82	DeP	28	.417	.718	6.1	5.1
82-83	DeP	33	.471	.773	7.9	10.6
83-84	DeP	30	.525	.744	7.4	14.2
84-85	DeP	29	.534	.814	8.1	15.9
Totals		120	.504	.764	7.4	11.5

NBA REGULAR-SEASON STATISTICS

		G	MIN	FGs FG	FGs PCT	3-PT FGs FG	3-PT FGs PCT	FTs FT	FTs PCT	Rebounds OFF	Rebounds TOT	AST	STL	BLK	PTS	PPG
85-86	SA	16	174	27	.422	0	.000	10	.714	11	25	11	11	2	64	4.0
86-87	SA/CLE	63	1170	156	.409	1	.250	91	.734	88	215	97	55	5	404	6.4
87-88	CLE/PHO	84	1739	257	.490	1	.167	110	.797	127	350	115	72	18	625	7.4
88-89	PHO	77	1655	245	.540	0	.000	141	.788	176	398	118	82	13	631	8.2
89-90	MIN	82	3011	521	.481	0	.000	161	.770	219	604	216	175	41	1203	14.7
90-91	MIN	82	3196	587	.448	2	.200	296	.798	185	589	347	162	53	1472	18.0
91-92	MIN/UTA	80	2207	303	.481	0	.000	174	.866	163	472	140	82	20	780	9.8
92-93	UTA	82	2555	385	.503	0	.000	180	.826	194	519	173	108	32	950	11.6
93-94	UTA	82	2149	268	.456	6	.207	117	.813	150	389	122	99	24	659	8.0
Totals		648	17856	2749	.474	10	.139	1280	.801	1313	3561	1339	846	208	6788	10.5

CHRIS CORCHIANI

Team: Boston Celtics
Position: Guard
Height: 6'1" **Weight:** 185
Birthdate: March 28, 1968

NBA Experience: 3 years
College: North Carolina St.
Acquired: Signed as a free agent, 9/93

Background: Corchiani, Florida's two-time Mr. Basketball, was the fire in N.C. State's "Fire and Ice" backcourt tandem that also included Rodney Monroe. He became the first player in NCAA history to amass 1,000 career assists. Corchiani was drafted in the second round by Orlando in 1991 but was cut in training camp and spent some time in the Global Basketball Association. After playing in 61 NBA games over his first two years, he signed with Boston before last season and saw reserve action in 51 games.

Strengths: Corchiani is a true point guard who can direct an offense and get the ball in the right hands. He will hand out almost as many assists as he scores points. He handles the ball and passes well, has 3-point range on his jumper, and plays sound position defense. He helps out on the defensive glass and has a keen understanding of the game.

Weaknesses: Corchiani is not an offensive-minded pro player. He scored only one point for every four minutes he was on the floor last season. He does not shoot the ball consistently and rarely looks for a chance to do so. He does not bring great quickness to the floor, although he hustles. He tends to over-pass, which shows in the turnover column.

Analysis: Don't look for Corchiani to show up among your nightly scoring leaders. He does not possess the offensive skills or confidence to do much besides set up his teammates. Defenders can back off and dare him to shoot. He does play with a lot of heart on both ends of the floor and works hard enough to keep a roster spot.

PLAYER SUMMARY	
Will	direct the offense
Can't	score at will
Expect	crisp passes
Don't Expect	10 PPG
Fantasy Value	$0
Card Value	5-10¢

COLLEGE STATISTICS

		G	FGP	FTP	APG	PPG
87-88	NCST	32	.508	.833	7.3	6.3
88-89	NCST	31	.495	.805	8.6	10.5
89-90	NCST	30	.421	.832	7.9	13.1
90-91	NCST	31	.466	.822	9.6	16.3
Totals		124	.463	.822	8.4	11.5

NBA REGULAR-SEASON STATISTICS

				FGs		3-PT FGs		FTs		Rebounds						
		G	MIN	FG	PCT	FG	PCT	FT	PCT	OFF	TOT	AST	STL	BLK	PTS	PPG
91-92	ORL	51	741	77	.399	10	.270	91	.875	18	78	141	45	2	255	5.0
92-93	ORL/WAS	10	105	14	.583	0	.000	16	.762	1	7	16	6	0	44	4.4
93-94	BOS	51	467	40	.426	11	.289	26	.684	8	44	86	22	2	117	2.3
Totals		112	1313	131	.421	21	.269	133	.816	27	129	243	73	4	416	3.7

TERRY CUMMINGS

Team: San Antonio Spurs
Position: Forward
Height: 6'9" **Weight:** 245
Birthdate: March 15, 1961

NBA Experience: 12 years
College: DePaul
Acquired: Traded from Bucks for Alvin Robertson and Greg Anderson, 5/89

Background: Cummings led DePaul in rebounding in each of his three seasons. He was drafted second overall by San Diego in 1982 and became the first rookie since Kareem Abdul-Jabbar to rank in the top ten in scoring and rebounding. Cummings played in two All-Star Games with Milwaukee and excelled with San Antonio before undergoing reconstructive knee surgery in 1992.

Strengths: Cummings was once one of the top scoring and rebounding forwards in basketball. He has a large array of post-up moves and can still stick the occasional jump shot. Few can match his smarts. He still shows flashes of his game-breaking form.

Weaknesses: Cummings seems to have lost his edge since the knee injury. He's a step slower and his offensive effectiveness has declined. Defense has always been a knock on Cummings, but that seems to go with the territory when you're a scorer.

Analysis: Cummings has always played the game like he's been called to war. He still does. He returned to the court earlier than expected after his knee surgery but has not matched his previous level of play. He should be remembered as one of the premier power forwards to play the game.

PLAYER SUMMARY	
Will	crash the boards
Can't	regain his quickness
Expect	17,000 career points
Don't Expect	dominant defense
Fantasy Value	$0
Card Value	5-10¢

COLLEGE STATISTICS

		G	FGP	FTP	RPG	PPG
79-80	DeP	28	.508	.832	9.4	14.2
80-81	DeP	29	.498	.750	9.0	13.0
81-82	DeP	28	.567	.756	11.9	22.3
Totals		85	.530	.775	10.1	16.4

NBA REGULAR-SEASON STATISTICS

		G	MIN	FGs FG	FGs PCT	3-PT FGs FG	3-PT FGs PCT	FTs FT	FTs PCT	Rebounds OFF	Rebounds TOT	AST	STL	BLK	PTS	PPG
82-83	SD	70	2531	684	.523	0	.000	292	.709	303	744	177	129	62	1660	23.7
83-84	SD	81	2907	737	.494	0	.000	380	.720	323	777	139	92	57	1854	22.9
84-85	MIL	79	2722	759	.495	0	.000	343	.741	244	716	228	117	67	1861	23.6
85-86	MIL	82	2669	681	.474	0	.000	265	.656	222	694	193	121	51	1627	19.8
86-87	MIL	82	2770	729	.511	0	.000	249	.662	214	700	229	129	81	1707	20.8
87-88	MIL	76	2629	675	.485	1	.333	270	.665	184	553	181	78	46	1621	21.3
88-89	MIL	80	2824	730	.467	7	.467	362	.787	281	650	198	106	72	1829	22.9
89-90	SA	81	2821	728	.475	19	.322	343	.780	226	677	219	110	52	1818	22.4
90-91	SA	67	2195	503	.484	7	.212	164	.683	194	521	157	61	30	1177	17.6
91-92	SA	70	2149	514	.488	5	.385	177	.711	247	631	102	58	34	1210	17.3
92-93	SA	8	76	11	.379	0	.000	5	.500	6	19	4	1	1	27	3.4
93-94	SA	59	1133	183	.428	0	.000	132	.589	132	297	50	31	13	429	7.3
Totals		835	27426	6934	.487	39	.289	2913	.711	2576	6979	1877	1033	566	16820	20.1

DELL CURRY

Team: Charlotte Hornets
Position: Guard
Height: 6'5" **Weight:** 208
Birthdate: June 25, 1964

NBA Experience: 8 years
College: Virginia Tech
Acquired: Selected from Cavaliers in 1988 expansion draft

Background: Curry, the Metro Conference Player of the Year as a senior, became the league's second-leading career scorer. He was a successful college pitcher and was drafted by the Baltimore Orioles. Curry was also drafted by the Utah Jazz, traded to Cleveland, and picked up by Charlotte in the expansion draft. He has averaged double figures in each of the last seven years and won the NBA's Sixth Man Award in 1993-94.

Strengths: Curry has the ability to light up the scoreboard in a hurry with a dangerous outside shot, particularly from 3-point land. He ranks among the most accurate 3-point and free throw shooters in the game. Former Timberwolves coach Bill Musselman once described him as one of the five best pure shooters in the NBA.

Weaknesses: Perhaps too congenial in his approach, Curry is not a willing or able defender. He's not physical with players his size or larger and lacks the quickness and desire to keep up with smaller ones. Curry is not a gifted passer and would rather shoot anyway.

Analysis: Curry's stroke is a thing of beauty. When he is hot, you want the ball to touch his hands every time down the floor. Few can match his perimeter prowess and range. Curry also offers a willingness to do his job in a reserve role. He has provided 15-16 PPG for the Hornets the last three years.

PLAYER SUMMARY	
Will	hit from long range
Can't	bang on defense
Expect	points in bunches
Don't Expect	many assists
Fantasy Value	$7-9
Card Value	5-10¢

COLLEGE STATISTICS

		G	FGP	FTP	RPG	PPG
82-83	VT	32	.475	.850	3.0	14.5
83-84	VT	35	.522	.759	4.1	19.3
84-85	VT	29	.482	.758	5.8	18.2
85-86	VT	30	.529	.789	6.8	24.1
Totals		126	.505	.785	4.8	19.0

NBA REGULAR-SEASON STATISTICS

		G	MIN	FGs FG	FGs PCT	3-PT FGs FG	3-PT FGs PCT	FTs FT	FTs PCT	Rebounds OFF	Rebounds TOT	AST	STL	BLK	PTS	PPG
86-87	UTA	67	636	139	.426	17	.283	30	.789	30	78	58	27	4	325	4.9
87-88	CLE	79	1499	340	.458	28	.346	79	.782	43	166	149	94	22	787	10.0
88-89	CHA	48	813	256	.491	19	.345	40	.870	26	104	50	42	4	571	11.9
89-90	CHA	67	1860	461	.466	52	.354	96	.923	31	168	159	98	26	1070	16.0
90-91	CHA	76	1515	337	.471	32	.372	96	.842	47	199	166	75	25	802	10.6
91-92	CHA	77	2020	504	.486	74	.404	127	.836	57	259	177	93	20	1209	15.7
92-93	CHA	80	2094	498	.452	95	.401	136	.866	51	286	180	87	23	1227	15.3
93-94	CHA	82	2173	533	.455	152	.402	117	.873	71	262	221	98	27	1335	16.3
Totals		576	12610	3068	.464	469	.382	721	.852	356	1522	1160	614	151	7326	12.7

LLOYD DANIELS

Team: San Antonio Spurs
Position: Guard
Height: 6'7" **Weight:** 210
Birthdate: September 4, 1967

NBA Experience: 2 years
College: None
Acquired: Signed as a free agent, 7/92

Background: A New York City playground legend, Daniels dropped out of three high schools. He never played college basketball after his recruitment to UNLV resulted in an NCAA investigation. He was also arrested on drug charges. He has played in the CBA, the GBA, the USBL, and New Zealand. He credits John Lucas for helping him overcome drug and alcohol problems. Daniels finally reached the NBA in 1992-93 with San Antonio and has finished second on the team in 3-pointers in each of his two seasons.

Strengths: Once considered the top prep player in the nation, Daniels still brings a lot of natural ability to the floor. He owns great range with his jump shot, fine offensive post-up moves, and a nice feel for the game. His passing skills have always drawn rave reviews and he can play either shooting guard or point guard despite his 6'7" size.

Weaknesses: Daniels lacks consistency in most phases of the game. His shooting is sporadic and his field goal percentage ugly. He spends too much time in bitter cold spells. He is not much help on defense, due both to a lack of interest and a lack of quickness. He can match up with big guards but quicker point guards give him trouble. His biggest weaknesses in the past came off the court.

Analysis: "Swee' Pea" has more stories to tell than your average two-year NBA player. There are times when you watch him on the court and can see flashes of the player everyone thought he would be. More often, however, you see a player struggling to regain the touch that made him one of the most revered playground stars in Big Apple history. You pull for him to stay clean.

PLAYER SUMMARY	
Will	hit the 3
Can't	rediscover his legend
Expect	flashes of brilliance
Don't Expect	consistency
Fantasy Value	$1
Card Value	10-20¢

COLLEGE STATISTICS

—DID NOT PLAY—

NBA REGULAR-SEASON STATISTICS

			FGs		3-PT FGs		FTs		Rebounds						
	G	MIN	FG	PCT	FG	PCT	FT	PCT	OFF	TOT	AST	STL	BLK	PTS	PPG
92-93 SA	77	1573	285	.443	59	.333	72	.727	86	216	148	38	30	701	9.1
93-94 SA	65	980	140	.376	44	.352	46	.719	45	111	94	29	16	370	5.7
Totals	142	2553	425	.418	103	.341	118	.724	131	327	242	67	46	1071	7.5

BRAD DAUGHERTY

Team: Cleveland Cavaliers
Position: Center
Height: 7'0" **Weight:** 263
Birthdate: October 19, 1965

NBA Experience: 8 years
College: North Carolina
Acquired: 1st-round pick in 1986 draft
(1st overall)

Background: Daugherty performed in the McDonald's High School All-Star Game as a 16-year-old senior. At North Carolina, he led the Atlantic Coast Conference in rebounding as a junior and led the country in field goal percentage as a senior. He has appeared in the NBA All-Star Game in five of the last seven years. He surpassed 10,000 career points last season but was limited by dizziness and a back injury.

Strengths: Daugherty can hurt you inside or out. He has the power to muscle underneath for baskets and also has the touch to make precision passes from the high post. Rivals have called him the best passing center in the league. Of his many offensive weapons, the best is a jump hook.

Weaknesses: Daugherty is not as physical as some of the other centers in the league and he won't block as many shots as you'd like—less than one per game. His shooting percentage and scoring average both dropped last season. His back is a concern.

Analysis: Daugherty is a complete player with one of the best attitudes you'll find among pro athletes. He has never drawn the acclaim of some of the marquee big men like Ewing, Olajuwon, and O'Neal, and last year he did not join them in the All-Star Game. When he is healthy, however, Daugherty is every bit as valuable to his team.

PLAYER SUMMARY

Will..............................score, rebound
Can't ....dominate on defense
Expect......................18 PPG, 10 RPG
Don't Expect ....2 BPG
Fantasy Value.........................$40-45
Card Value ....10-20¢

COLLEGE STATISTICS

		G	FGP	FTP	RPG	PPG
82-83	NC	35	.558	.663	5.2	8.2
83-84	NC	30	.610	.678	5.6	10.5
84-85	NC	36	.625	.742	9.7	17.3
85-86	NC	34	.648	.684	9.0	20.2
Totals		135	.620	.700	7.4	14.2

NBA REGULAR-SEASON STATISTICS

			FGs		3-PT FGs		FTs		Rebounds							
		G	MIN	FG	PCT	FG	PCT	FT	PCT	OFF	TOT	AST	STL	BLK	PTS	PPG
86-87 CLE	80	2695	487	.538	0	.000	279	.696	152	647	304	49	63	1253	15.7
87-88 CLE	79	2957	551	.510	0	.000	378	.716	151	665	333	48	56	1480	18.7
88-89 CLE	78	2821	544	.538	1	.333	386	.737	167	718	285	63	40	1475	18.9
89-90 CLE	41	1438	244	.479	0	.000	202	.704	77	373	130	29	22	690	16.8
90-91 CLE	76	2946	605	.524	0	.000	435	.751	177	830	253	74	46	1645	21.6
91-92 CLE	73	2643	576	.570	0	.000	414	.777	191	760	262	65	78	1566	21.5
92-93 CLE	71	2691	520	.571	1	.500	391	.795	164	726	312	53	56	1432	20.2
93-94 CLE	50	1838	296	.488	0	.000	256	.785	128	508	149	41	36	848	17.0
Totals	548	20029	3823	.532	2	.143	2741	.747	1207	5227	2028	422	397	10389	19.0

ANTONIO DAVIS

Team: Indiana Pacers
Position: Forward
Height: 6'9" **Weight:** 230
Birthdate: October 31, 1968

NBA Experience: 1 year
College: Texas-El Paso
Acquired: 2nd-round pick in 1990 draft (45th overall)

Background: Davis finished his career at Texas-El Paso No. 5 on the all-time rebounding chart and was named to the WAC All-Defensive Team as a senior. A second-round draft pick of Indiana in 1990, he spent his first two pro seasons in Greece and averaged 11.1 PPG and 9.9 RPG with Philips Milan of the Italian League in 1992-93. Davis returned to America for his rookie season last year and averaged 7.7 PPG and 6.2 RPG for the Pacers.

Strengths: Davis is an exceptional leaper who is capable of controlling both the offensive and defensive glass. He also plays solid defense and blocked more than a shot per outing last season. He works tirelessly on that end of the floor. Davis has improved his offensive game by leaps and bounds since his college career. He converts a high percentage of his shots.

Weaknesses: Davis does not own a vast offensive repertoire. Once asked to list his weaknesses as a potential pro player, he answered: "My offensive skills." He did score more than expected as an NBA rookie, but his range is limited and his low-post moves are nothing special. He is a poor free throw shooter and passer who is uncomfortable on the perimeter.

Analysis: If anyone needed a few years overseas to develop his skills, it was Davis. He came back a much better and more well-rounded player than when he left, and he proved to be invaluable to the Pacers down the regular-season stretch and during the playoffs last year. A fine rebounder and defender who never stops hustling, he played in the Schick Rookie Game and has a bright future in the big league.

PLAYER SUMMARY

Will ....work on defense
Can't ....shoot with range
Expect ....rebounds, blocks
Don't Expect........impressive moves
Fantasy Value..............................$1-3
Card Value ....7-12¢

COLLEGE STATISTICS

		G	FGP	FTP	RPG	PPG
86-87	UTEP	28	.344	.433	1.8	1.3
87-88	UTEP	30	.590	.548	6.5	9.3
88-89	UTEP	32	.544	.619	8.0	14.3
89-90	UTEP	32	.522	.642	7.6	10.8
Totals		122	.540	.600	6.1	9.2

NBA REGULAR-SEASON STATISTICS

				FGs		3-PT FGs		FTs		Rebounds						
		G	MIN	FG	PCT	FG	PCT	FT	PCT	OFF	TOT	AST	STL	BLK	PTS	PPG
93-94	IND	81	1732	216	.508	0	.000	194	.642	190	505	55	45	84	626	7.7
Totals		81	1732	216	.508	0	.000	194	.642	190	505	55	45	84	626	7.7

DALE DAVIS

Team: Indiana Pacers
Position: Forward
Height: 6'11" **Weight:** 230
Birthdate: March 25, 1969

NBA Experience: 3 years
College: Clemson
Acquired: 1st-round pick in 1991 draft
(13th overall)

Background: At Clemson, Davis teamed with Elden Campbell for three seasons to form the "Duo of Doom." As a senior, Davis led the ACC in rebounding for a third consecutive season and became the third ACC player with more than 1,500 points, 1,200 rebounds, and 200 blocked shots. The 13th pick in 1991, he has started for the Pacers in the last two of his three seasons and enjoyed his best year in 1993-94 despite breaking a bone in his left wrist.

Strengths: Davis has a great body and solid instincts. He is the aggressive, hard-working type who loves a challenge. His long arms and fine athletic ability make him a force as a rebounder and shot-blocker. A fan favorite in Indianapolis, he maintains a high percentage from the field because he does not put up ill-advised shots. He runs the floor like a smaller man and has become a better scorer.

Weaknesses: Davis's range is limited and his low-post moves are too often predictable. However, he knows his limitations on the offensive end and plays within them. Many of his non-transition points follow offensive rebounds. When it comes to free throw shooting and passing prowess, Davis is hardly your man.

Analysis: A self-proclaimed rebounding and defensive force, Davis was expected to have his best year after the Pacers traded Detlef Schrempf to Seattle. He did. He posted career highs in most offensive categories while continuing to alter opponents' game plans on the other end of the floor. Coaches and fans alike enjoy his skills and enthusiasm for the game.

PLAYER SUMMARY

Will ....attack shots
Can't ....shoot with range
Expect ....defense, rebounding
Don't Expect ....high scoring
Fantasy Value..........................$12-15
Card Value ....7-12¢

COLLEGE STATISTICS

		G	FGP	FTP	RPG	PPG
87-88	CLEM	29	.532	.506	7.7	7.8
88-89	CLEM	29	.670	.646	8.9	13.3
89-90	CLEM	35	.625	.596	11.3	15.3
90-91	CLEM	28	.532	.580	12.1	17.9
Totals		121	.588	.589	10.0	13.6

NBA REGULAR-SEASON STATISTICS

			FGs		3-PT FGs		FTs		Rebounds						
		G	MIN	FG	PCT	FG	PCT	FT	PCT	OFF	TOT	AST	STL	BLK	PTS	PPG
91-92	IND	64	1301	154	.552	0	.000	87	.572	158	410	30	27	74	395	6.2
92-93	IND	82	2264	304	.568	0	.000	119	.529	291	723	69	63	148	727	8.9
93-94	IND	66	2292	308	.529	0	.000	155	.527	280	718	100	48	106	771	11.7
Totals		212	5857	766	.549	0	.000	361	.538	729	1851	199	138	328	1893	8.9

HUBERT DAVIS

Team: New York Knicks
Position: Guard
Height: 6'5" **Weight:** 183
Birthdate: May 17, 1970

NBA Experience: 2 years
College: North Carolina
Acquired: 1st-round pick in 1992 draft (20th overall)

Background: A nephew of former North Carolina and NBA great Walter Davis, Hubert Davis gradually developed into a star at North Carolina, leading the Atlantic Coast Conference in 3-point field goal percentage as a junior and his team in scoring as a senior. He was drafted by the Knicks with the 20th pick in 1992 but saw little playing time as a rookie. He started some games last season despite sitting out more than a month with a fractured bone in his right hand.

Strengths: Walter Davis was one of the greatest shooters in NBA history, and his nephew has a sweet stroke as well. Hubert has range beyond the 3-point line, boasts an accurate pull-up jumper, and can be deadly when he squares up to the basket. He moves well without the ball and uses screens. He runs the floor, makes sound choices, and is a better passer than most notice. He's also a deadly free throw shooter.

Weaknesses: Davis is slight in build and can be shoved around by some of the league's bigger guards. His lack of muscle hurts him on the defensive end, where he also does not have the raw quickness to keep his man from getting past him. He does not contribute much on the boards and must get better at creating his own shot.

Analysis: People were impressed with Davis as a rookie, even though he didn't play much. Last season, Davis won over even more fans. He sank a very high percentage of his treys, raised his overall shooting accuracy greatly, and played himself into a much more prominent role with one of the best teams in basketball. He has the look of a double-figure scorer for years to come.

PLAYER SUMMARY	
Will	fill the net
Can't	muscle his man
Expect	10-plus PPG
Don't Expect	rebounds
Fantasy Value	$3-5
Card Value	8-15¢

COLLEGE STATISTICS

		G	FGP	FTP	RPG	PPG
88-89	NC	35	.512	.774	0.8	3.3
89-90	NC	34	.446	.797	1.8	9.6
90-91	NC	35	.521	.835	2.4	13.3
91-92	NC	33	.508	.828	2.3	21.4
Totals		137	.498	.819	1.8	11.8

NBA REGULAR-SEASON STATISTICS

				FGs		3-PT FGs		FTs		Rebounds						
		G	MIN	FG	PCT	FG	PCT	FT	PCT	OFF	TOT	AST	STL	BLK	PTS	PPG
92-93	NY	50	815	110	.438	6	.316	43	.796	13	56	83	22	4	269	5.4
93-94	NY	56	1333	238	.471	53	.402	85	.825	23	67	165	40	4	614	11.0
Totals		106	2148	348	.460	59	.391	128	.815	36	123	248	62	8	883	8.3

TERRY DAVIS

Team: Dallas Mavericks
Position: Forward/Center
Height: 6'10" **Weight:** 250
Birthdate: June 17, 1967

NBA Experience: 5 years
College: Virginia Union
Acquired: Signed as a free agent, 8/91

Background: From tiny Virginia Union, Davis made headlines as a two-time Central Intercollegiate Athletic Association Player of the Year. Though he wasn't drafted, he signed with Miami in 1989 and was a bench player for two years. He signed with Dallas in 1991 and enjoyed his two most productive seasons before shattering his left elbow in a gruesome car accident in the spring of 1993. He returned for 15 games last season.

Strengths: Davis emerged as a full-time starter, big-time board man, and tough defender during his first two years in Dallas. He plays with fire in his eyes and provides a good combination of strength and agility. He is capable of playing both forward and center and has demonstrated the ability to be a double-figure scorer.

Weaknesses: The biggest question mark, of course, remains his left elbow. He made his return last January but was back on the injured list one month later. Davis has a modest offensive game. He does not possess good ball-handling or passing skills and does not make consistently wise decisions with the ball. He's a terrible free throw shooter.

Analysis: Davis has to overcome an injury that shattered his elbow into 15 pieces. There was a time when he was just hoping to move his arm again. A friend of his was killed in the accident. Davis has maintained a positive attitude and his one-month comeback was rather remarkable considering the extent of the injury. He's hoping for more.

PLAYER SUMMARY

Will ....play with heart
Can't...................................shoot FTs
Expect.....another comeback attempt
Don't Expect ....an easy haul
Fantasy Value $1
Card Value ....5-10¢

COLLEGE STATISTICS

		G	FGP	FTP	RPG	PPG
85-86	VU	27	.462	.605	4.3	4.1
86-87	VU	32	.521	.690	11.3	11.5
87-88	VU	31	.566	.715	10.9	22.7
88-89	VU	31	.615	.682	11.9	22.3
Totals		121	.567	.692	9.8	15.5

NBA REGULAR-SEASON STATISTICS

				FGs		3-PT FGs		FTs		Rebounds						
		G	MIN	FG	PCT	FG	PCT	FT	PCT	OFF	TOT	AST	STL	BLK	PTS	PPG
89-90	MIA	63	884	122	.466	0	.000	54	.621	93	229	25	25	28	298	4.7
90-91	MIA	55	996	115	.487	1	.500	69	.556	107	266	39	18	28	300	5.5
91-92	DAL	68	2149	256	.482	0	.000	181	.635	228	672	57	26	29	693	10.2
92-93	DAL	75	2462	393	.455	2	.250	167	.594	259	701	68	36	28	955	12.7
93-94	DAL	15	286	24	.407	0	.000	8	.667	30	74	6	9	1	56	3.7
Totals		276	6777	910	.466	3	.188	479	.607	717	1942	195	114	114	2302	8.3

JOHNNY DAWKINS

Team: Philadelphia 76ers
Position: Guard
Height: 6'2" **Weight:** 170
Birthdate: September 28, 1963
NBA Experience: 8 years

College: Duke
Acquired: Traded from Spurs with Jay Vincent for Maurice Cheeks, Chris Welp, and David Wingate, 8/89

Background: Dawkins finished his college career No. 1 on Duke's all-time scoring list. He was the first ACC player to collect 2,000 points, 500 assists, and 500 rebounds. San Antonio took him with the No. 10 pick in 1987 but he missed most of 1988-89 with a leg injury and nearly all of 1990-91 with a torn anterior cruciate ligament. He returned to lead Philadelphia in assists in 1991-92 but has not been a regular starter since.

Strengths: Dawkins is at his best when slashing to the basket. He can score himself or drive and dish. He generally makes wise choices with the ball and handles it well against pressure. He is a reliable free throw shooter, has 3-point range, and has displayed fine leadership ability and court sense.

Weaknesses: Dawkins has been more tentative about taking the ball to the bucket since missing the season with the knee injury. His field goal percentage is low, as he is too content to settle for 3-pointers or outside jumpers. Bigger guards give him problems on the defensive end. He's not much of a rebounder.

Analysis: Dawkins once looked like a future star point guard. But Jeff Hornacek took his starting spot from him two years ago and Dana Barros stole it away last season, both on non-playoff teams. Dawkins seems to have lost a little something, perhaps because of his knee troubles, although a team could do worse than having him start at the point.

PLAYER SUMMARY	
Will	handle the ball
Can't	win starting job
Expect	good FT shooting
Don't Expect	stardom
Fantasy Value	$0
Card Value	5-10¢

COLLEGE STATISTICS

		G	FGP	FTP	APG	PPG
82-83	DUKE	28	.500	.682	4.8	18.1
83-84	DUKE	34	.481	.831	4.1	19.4
84-85	DUKE	31	.495	.795	5.0	18.8
85-86	DUKE	40	.549	.812	3.2	20.2
Totals		133	.508	.790	4.2	19.2

NBA REGULAR-SEASON STATISTICS

		G	MIN	FGs FG	FGs PCT	3-PT FGs FG	3-PT FGs PCT	FTs FT	FTs PCT	Rebounds OFF	Rebounds TOT	AST	STL	BLK	PTS	PPG
86-87	SA	81	1682	334	.437	14	.298	153	.801	56	169	290	67	3	835	10.3
87-88	SA	65	2179	405	.485	19	.311	198	.896	66	204	480	88	2	1027	15.8
88-89	SA	32	1083	177	.443	0	.000	100	.893	32	101	224	55	0	454	14.2
89-90	PHI	81	2865	465	.489	22	.333	210	.861	48	247	601	121	9	1162	14.3
90-91	PHI	4	124	26	.634	1	.250	10	.909	0	16	28	3	0	63	15.8
91-92	PHI	82	2815	394	.437	36	.356	164	.882	42	227	567	89	5	988	12.0
92-93	PHI	74	1598	258	.437	26	.410	113	.796	33	136	339	80	4	655	8.9
93-94	PHI	72	1343	177	.418	37	.352	84	.840	28	123	263	63	5	475	6.6
Totals		491	13689	2236	.456	155	.328	1032	.855	305	1223	2792	566	28	5659	11.5

TODD DAY

Team: Milwaukee Bucks
Position: Guard
Height: 6'7" **Weight:** 200
Birthdate: January 7, 1970

NBA Experience: 2 years
College: Arkansas
Acquired: 1st-round pick in 1992 draft
(8th overall)

Background: The 1988 prep Player of the Year in Memphis, Day signed with Arkansas and teamed in the backcourt with Lee Mayberry. Day led Arkansas to a 115-24 record in four seasons and earned several All-America honors as a junior and senior. Off the court, he had his share of problems. Day was drafted eighth overall by Milwaukee in 1992 and has been one of the team's top four scorers in each of his two pro seasons.

Strengths: Day does a little bit of everything. He shoots with range, can put the ball on the floor, gets up and down the court quickly, and is a fine finisher. His quick feet, long arms, and ability to leap out of the gym make him a potentially dominant defensive player. He also rebounds well. The feisty and athletic Day will not back down from a challenge.

Weaknesses: Day is a streaky player in almost all respects. That goes for his shooting, his control of the basketball, and his defense. His head is not always in the game at both ends and he picks up his share of fouls. A scorer, he'll continue launching ill-advised shots even when ice-cold. He takes far too many 3-pointers for the rate at which he hits them.

Analysis: Day is a splendid athlete and one of the central figures in Milwaukee's plan to rebuild. He has been a half-time starter in each of his first two years, but that will become a full-time job in the seasons ahead. Though capable of bringing a crowd to its feet and winning games with great plays, Day is also capable of getting himself yanked with ill-advised decisions. His inconsistency can no longer be blamed on inexperience.

PLAYER SUMMARY	
Will	run all day
Can't	avoid cold spells
Expect	scoring sprees
Don't Expect	total control
Fantasy Value	$8-10
Card Value	15-30¢

COLLEGE STATISTICS

		G	FGP	FTP	RPG	PPG
88-89	ARK	32	.451	.715	4.0	13.3
89-90	ARK	35	.491	.760	5.4	19.5
90-91	ARK	38	.473	.747	5.3	20.7
91-92	ARK	22	.499	.764	7.0	22.7
Totals		127	.479	.747	5.3	18.9

NBA REGULAR-SEASON STATISTICS

				FGs		3-PT FGs		FTs		Rebounds						
		G	MIN	FG	PCT	FG	PCT	FT	PCT	OFF	TOT	AST	STL	BLK	PTS	PPG
92-93	MIL	71	1931	358	.432	54	.293	213	.717	144	291	117	75	48	983	13.8
93-94	MIL	76	2127	351	.415	33	.223	231	.698	115	310	138	103	52	966	12.7
Totals		147	4058	709	.424	87	.262	444	.707	259	601	255	178	100	1949	13.3

TERRY DEHERE

Team: Los Angeles Clippers
Position: Guard
Height: 6'3" **Weight:** 190
Birthdate: September 12, 1971

NBA Experience: 1 year
College: Seton Hall
Acquired: 1st-round pick in 1993 draft (13th overall)

Background: A prep teammate of Bobby Hurley, Dehere was slow to develop in high school but became a star at Seton Hall. He was the Pirates' primary offensive weapon for four years, during which he surpassed Chris Mullin to become the Big East's all-time leading scorer. He was named first-team all-conference three times and league Player of the Year as a senior. He was drafted 13th by the Clippers in 1993 and averaged just over ten minutes per game as a rookie.

Strengths: Dehere can get his own shot in halfcourt situations and is dangerous in transition. He was known for his offense in college and has had some degree of success in limited pro playing time. He has 3-point range and a very quick release. He is smart, knows how to win, and will not back down from a challenge.

Weaknesses: Dehere struggled in his first pro season. He buried his shots only slightly better than a third of the time and thus was not on the floor for many extended periods. Even free throws gave him trouble despite hitting at an 82-percent clip in college. He is a bit small for shooting guard and does not possess great ball-handling and passing skills.

Analysis: Most everyone thought it would take a year or two for Dehere to become a solid pro player, and that forecast appears to be right on the money. His rookie year was a shooter's nightmare, although it is difficult to develop consistency in a couple of five-minute stretches per game. Dehere is a hard worker who will bust his tail to become a better contributor. He has much work to do, but he'll get his chance with the rebuilding Clippers.

PLAYER SUMMARY

Will	get his shots
Can't	find his touch
Expect	more practice
Don't Expect	instant results
Fantasy Value	$3-5
Card Value	8-15¢

COLLEGE STATISTICS

		G	FGP	FTP	RPG	PPG
89-90	SH	28	.402	.797	3.4	16.1
90-91	SH	34	.463	.839	3.0	19.8
91-92	SH	31	.427	.830	3.7	19.4
92-93	SH	35	.461	.818	3.0	22.0
Totals		128	.442	.822	3.2	19.5

NBA REGULAR-SEASON STATISTICS

			FGs		3-PT FGs		FTs		Rebounds						
	G	MIN	FG	PCT	FG	PCT	FT	PCT	OFF	TOT	AST	STL	BLK	PTS	PPG
93-94 LAC	64	759	129	.377	23	.404	61	.753	25	68	78	28	3	342	5.3
Totals	64	759	129	.377	23	.404	61	.753	25	68	78	28	3	342	5.3

VINNY DEL NEGRO

Team: San Antonio Spurs
Position: Guard
Height: 6′4″ **Weight:** 200
Birthdate: August 9, 1966

NBA Experience: 4 years
College: North Carolina St.
Acquired: Signed as a free agent, 7/92

Background: Sinking nearly 45 percent of his 3-point shots as a collegian at North Carolina State, Del Negro was an All-ACC pick as a senior. He played two pro seasons with Sacramento before putting in a two-year stint in Italy. He led his team to the Italian A League title in 1992 and was named league MVP after averaging 26.0 PPG. He returned to the NBA with San Antonio two seasons ago and started more than half the time in 1993-94.

Strengths: Del Negro is sound in most aspects of the game. He is a very accurate jump-shooter with range, can get his own shots, handles the ball expertly, and makes the right passes. He rarely misses a free throw and rarely makes a mistake with the ball in his hands. He's a fine defensive rebounder for a guard thanks to superior positioning.

Weaknesses: What Del Negro offers in fundamentals he lacks in sheer explosiveness. He is not quick enough to create havoc off the dribble or to enjoy much success defensively against speedy point guards, although he is a better athlete than his body indicates. The Spurs have looked for other starters at the point, but without much success.

Analysis: Del Negro is not flashy and certainly not among the game's top point guards, but no one could beat him out in San Antonio for most of last year. He enjoyed his best NBA season and proved he could handle the wheel of a winner. He scored about ten points a game. Heavily involved in charity work, he is a class act on and off the court.

PLAYER SUMMARY	
Will	run the offense
Can't	dazzle a crowd
Expect	solid leadership
Don't Expect	All-Star votes
Fantasy Value	$1
Card Value	5-8¢

COLLEGE STATISTICS

		G	FGP	FTP	RPG	PPG
84-85	NCST	19	.571	.652	0.7	2.1
85-86	NCST	17	.367	.636	0.8	1.7
86-87	NCST	35	.494	.887	3.3	10.4
87-88	NCST	32	.515	.839	4.9	15.9
Totals		103	.502	.825	2.9	9.1

NBA REGULAR-SEASON STATISTICS

			FGs		3-PT FGs		FTs		Rebounds						
	G	MIN	FG	PCT	FG	PCT	FT	PCT	OFF	TOT	AST	STL	BLK	PTS	PPG
88-89 SAC	80	1556	239	.475	6	.300	85	.850	48	123	206	65	14	569	7.1
89-90 SAC	76	1858	643	.462	10	.313	135	.871	39	198	250	64	10	739	9.7
92-93 SA	73	1526	218	.507	6	.250	101	.863	19	163	291	44	1	543	7.4
93-94 SA	77	1949	309	.487	15	.349	140	.824	27	161	320	64	1	773	10.0
Totals	306	6889	1063	.481	37	.311	461	.851	133	693	1067	237	26	2624	8.6

VLADE DIVAC

Team: Los Angeles Lakers
Position: Center
Height: 7'1" **Weight:** 260
Birthdate: February 3, 1968

NBA Experience: 5 years
College: None
Acquired: 1st-round pick in 1989 draft
(26th overall)

Background: Divac was a national sports hero in the former Yugoslavia before being drafted by the Lakers in 1989. His wedding was televised nationally. He led Partizan to the European club championship in 1988 and averaged 20 points and 11 rebounds in his three years there. He was named to the 1990 NBA All-Rookie Team and has been the Lakers' starting center ever since. Last season was his statistical best.

Strengths: Divac is a very skilled player in most respects. He is a gifted passer and ball-handler for a big man and his low-post offense has come a long way since he crossed the ocean. He has always been a good outside shooter with range. Divac provides both shot-blocking and rebounding and runs the floor well for a big man.

Weaknesses: Divac has never been the consistently dominant player some expected he would be. When he plays aggressively, he can be a force. He does not do so all the time, although last year he improved on that count. Divac can rely too much on finesse when he has the ball in the paint. He must assert himself nightly.

Analysis: Divac provides most of the things you want from a starting center. He scores, rebounds, and blocks shots, and he brings the added dimensions of good passing and perimeter touch. He is inspired by Magic Johnson and was one of the happiest men in L.A. when his former teammate returned as head coach. Inconsistency is his biggest hurdle.

PLAYER SUMMARY	
Will	rebound, block shots
Can't	dominate physically
Expect.	impressive skills
Don't Expect	stardom
Fantasy Value	$35-40
Card Value	8-12¢

COLLEGE STATISTICS

—DID NOT PLAY—

NBA REGULAR-SEASON STATISTICS

			FGs		3-PT FGs		FTs		Rebounds						
		G	MIN	FG	PCT	FG	PCT	FT	PCT	OFF	TOT	AST	STL	BLK	PTS	PPG
89-90	LAL	82	1611	274	.499	0	.000	153	.708	167	512	75	79	114	701	8.5
90-91	LAL	82	2310	360	.565	5	.357	196	.703	205	666	92	106	127	921	11.2
91-92	LAL	36	979	157	.495	5	.263	86	.768	87	247	60	55	35	405	11.3
92-93	LAL	82	2525	397	.485	21	.280	235	.689	220	729	232	128	140	1050	12.8
93-94	LAL	79	2685	453	.506	9	.191	208	.686	282	851	307	92	112	1123	14.2
Totals		361	10110	1641	.510	40	.250	878	.702	961	3005	766	460	528	4200	11.6

SHERMAN DOUGLAS

Team: Boston Celtics
Position: Guard
Height: 6'0" **Weight:** 180
Birthdate: September 15, 1966

NBA Experience: 5 years
College: Syracuse
Acquired: Traded from Heat for Brian Shaw, 1/92

Background: Douglas was the catalyst on a Syracuse team that included Billy Owens and Derrick Coleman. As a senior, he became the NCAA career assists leader and a first-team All-American. Despite being drafted in the second round, he made the NBA All-Rookie Team with Miami in 1989-90. Douglas was traded to Boston during the 1991-92 season and has overcome some personal problems to become the Celtics' starting point guard.

Strengths: A nifty ball-handler with deceptive moves to the hoop, Douglas is a tremendous penetrator and shows strong leadership skills. He takes care of the ball and knows where to dish it. He amassed 22 assists against the 76ers last April. He is an above-average scorer from the point-guard position. He once led the Heat in scoring and has rejoined the double-figure ranks.

Weaknesses: Douglas is not a pure shooter from the perimeter and has big trouble from the foul line and 3-point arc. He also does not rate among the best defensive lead guards in the NBA. Douglas does not have great quickness and comes up with few steals.

Analysis: Douglas displaced Dee Brown as Boston's point guard two years ago and kept his starting job last season. Although he scored more points with Miami, the last year and a half has seen the former Syracuse star play some of the best basketball of his career. He has earned respect league-wide for his leadership and ability to create.

PLAYER SUMMARY	
Will	drive and dish
Can't	rely on jumper
Expect	9 APG
Don't Expect	a FT ace
Fantasy Value	$8-10
Card Value	7-12¢

COLLEGE STATISTICS

		G	FGP	FTP	APG	PPG
85-86	SYR	27	.613	.727	2.1	5.4
86-87	SYR	38	.531	.744	7.6	17.3
87-88	SYR	35	.519	.693	8.2	16.1
88-89	SYR	38	.546	.632	8.6	18.2
Totals		138	.538	.695	7.0	14.9

NBA REGULAR-SEASON STATISTICS

				FGs		3-PT FGs		FTs		Rebounds						
		G	MIN	FG	PCT	FG	PCT	FT	PCT	OFF	TOT	AST	STL	BLK	PTS	PPG
89-90	MIA	81	2470	463	.494	5	.161	224	.687	70	206	619	145	10	1155	14.3
90-91	MIA	73	2562	532	.504	4	.129	284	.686	78	209	624	121	5	1352	18.5
91-92	MIA/BOS	42	752	117	.462	1	.100	73	.682	13	63	172	25	9	308	7.3
92-93	BOS	79	1932	264	.498	6	.207	84	.560	65	162	508	49	10	618	7.8
93-94	BOS	78	2789	425	.462	13	.232	177	.641	70	193	683	89	11	1040	13.3
Totals		353	10505	1801	.487	29	.185	842	.661	296	833	2606	429	45	4473	12.7

CLYDE DREXLER

Team: Portland Trail Blazers
Position: Guard
Height: 6'7" **Weight:** 222
Birthdate: June 22, 1962

NBA Experience: 11 years
College: Houston
Acquired: 1st-round pick in 1983 draft (14th overall)

Background: Drexler gained notoriety at the University of Houston, where he played in two Final Fours, for his breathtaking dunks. He has maintained that reputation as a pro and has led Portland in scoring average six of the past seven years. Drexler is the Blazers' all-time leader in several categories, including scoring. Drexler played in his eighth All-Star Game last season.

Strengths: Phenomenal leaping ability and hang time have helped "Clyde the Glide" establish himself as a superstar. Few can make things happen in the open court or finish like he can. Drexler shoots with 3-point range and his post-up moves give small guards fits. He rebounds well and has been a team leader.

Weaknesses: Drexler has been slowed by injuries the last two years. Last season, a severely sprained ankle kept him out of some early-season games. His shooting accuracy and scoring have declined in the last two years.

Analysis: Drexler has been one of the premier attractions in the NBA over the last several seasons, but he appears to be past his prime. He failed to lead the team in scoring last season and he is no longer always the first option on offense. He remains an All-Star-caliber player.

PLAYER SUMMARY

Will ....excite a crowd
Can't ....win a ring
Expect............................about 20 PPG
Don't Expect ....a stopper
Fantasy Value............................$14-17
Card Value ....15-25¢

COLLEGE STATISTICS

		G	FGP	FTP	RPG	PPG
80-81	HOU	30	.505	.588	10.5	11.9
81-82	HOU	32	.569	.608	10.5	15.2
82-83	HOU	34	.536	.737	8.8	15.9
Totals		96	.538	.643	9.9	14.4

NBA REGULAR-SEASON STATISTICS

		G	MIN	FGs FG	FGs PCT	3-PT FGs FG	3-PT FGs PCT	FTs FT	FTs PCT	Rebounds OFF	Rebounds TOT	AST	STL	BLK	PTS	PPG
83-84	POR	82	1408	252	.451	1	.250	123	.728	112	235	153	107	29	628	7.7
84-85	POR	80	2555	573	.494	8	.216	223	.759	217	476	441	177	68	1377	17.2
85-86	POR	75	2576	542	.475	12	.200	293	.769	171	421	600	197	46	1389	18.5
86-87	POR	82	3114	707	.502	11	.234	357	.760	227	518	566	204	71	1782	21.7
87-88	POR	81	3060	849	.506	11	.212	476	.811	261	533	467	203	52	2185	27.0
88-89	POR	78	3064	829	.496	27	.260	438	.799	289	615	450	213	54	2123	27.2
89-90	POR	73	2683	670	.494	30	.283	333	.774	208	507	432	145	51	1703	23.3
90-91	POR	82	2852	645	.482	61	.319	416	.794	212	546	493	144	60	1767	21.5
91-92	POR	76	2751	694	.470	114	.337	401	.794	166	500	512	138	70	1903	25.0
92-93	POR	49	1671	350	.429	31	.233	245	.839	126	309	278	95	37	976	19.9
93-94	POR	68	2334	473	.428	71	.324	286	.777	154	445	333	98	34	1303	19.2
Totals		826	28068	6584	.480	377	.292	3591	.786	2143	5105	4725	1721	572	17136	20.7

KEVIN DUCKWORTH

Team: Washington Bullets
Position: Center
Height: 7'0" **Weight:** 280
Birthdate: April 1, 1964

NBA Experience: 8 years
College: Eastern Illinois
Acquired: Traded from Trail Blazers for Harvey Grant, 6/93

Background: Duckworth established a career rebounding record at Eastern Illinois, where he posted a .631 field goal percentage as a senior. His pro career started slowly in San Antonio, but he was voted the NBA's Most Improved Player for 1987-88 with Portland and played in the 1989 All-Star Game. He was traded to Washington before the 1993-94 season and had his worst year since his rookie campaign.

Strengths: Duckworth is agile and possesses a soft touch for a man of his size. His low-post game can be potent and polished, featuring hooks and turnaround jumpers. His range is pretty good and he is capable of big scoring nights.

Weaknesses: Duckworth has simply lost it over the past three seasons. Weight and foul problems have always followed him, but his troubles have stretched to all aspects of his game. He's never been a great rebounder, shot-blocker, or defender, and offense also has become a struggle. His shooting percentages from the field and the line have become embarrassing, and he no longer scores in double figures.

Analysis: Duckworth has gone from All-Star to liability in just a few years, and many would contend that his demeanor and attitude have had a lot to do with his declining play. A change of scenery did not help him and another change is probably in his future. He is overmatched by many of the league's centers.

PLAYER SUMMARY

Will.............................take up space
Can't ....regain old form
Expect ....soft touch
Don't Expect ....a rebirth
Fantasy Value.............................$0
Card Value ....5-10¢

COLLEGE STATISTICS

		G	FGP	FTP	RPG	PPG
82-83	EILL	30	.528	.674	6.0	9.6
83-84	EILL	28	.597	.685	6.8	11.6
84-85	EILL	28	.516	.657	7.5	19.0
85-86	EILL	32	.631	.762	9.1	19.5
Totals		118	.577	.705	7.4	15.0

NBA REGULAR-SEASON STATISTICS

				FGs		3-PT FGs		FTs		Rebounds							
		G	MIN	FG	PCT	FG	PCT	FT	PCT	OFF	TOT	AST	STL	BLK	PTS	PPG
86-87	SA/POR	65	875	130	.476	0	.000	92	.687	76	223	29	21	21	352	5.4
87-88	POR	78	2223	450	.496	0	.000	331	.770	224	576	66	31	32	1231	15.8
88-89	POR	79	2662	554	.477	0	.000	324	.757	246	635	60	56	49	1432	18.1
89-90	POR	82	2462	548	.478	0	.000	231	.740	184	509	91	36	34	1327	16.2
90-91	POR	81	2511	521	.481	0	.000	240	.772	177	531	89	33	34	1282	15.8
91-92	POR	82	2222	362	.461	0	.000	156	.690	151	497	99	38	37	880	10.7
92-93	POR	74	1762	301	.438	0	.000	127	.730	118	387	70	45	39	729	9.9
93-94	WAS	69	1485	184	.417	0	.000	88	.667	103	325	56	37	35	456	6.6
Totals		610	16202	3050	.470	0	.000	1589	.740	1279	3683	560	297	281	7689	12.6

CHRIS DUDLEY

Unrestricted Free Agent
Last Team: Portland Trail Blazers
Position: Center
Height: 6'11" **Weight:** 240

Birthdate: February 22, 1965
NBA Experience: 7 years
College: Yale
Acquired: Signed as a free agent, 8/93

Background: A Yale graduate, Dudley was second in the nation in rebounding as a senior. Cleveland drafted him in 1987, but the Cavs sent him to New Jersey in 1989-90. He averaged a career-high 7.1 PPG in 1990-91. Before the 1993-94 season, he turned down a $21 million, seven-year offer from the Nets for an $11 million, seven-year deal in Portland. He then broke his ankle in the third game of the season.

Strengths: Dudley attacks the glass and opposing players with equal abandon. He knows how to use his large frame inside to wall off opponents from the backboards. He has an aggressive, forceful approach to everything he does. Dudley is a smart, tough defender who blocks a lot of shots.

Weaknesses: Dudley has proven that brains have nothing to do with free throw shooting. In fact, his offensive game in general, including his field goal shooting and passing, is very weak. He commits a lot of fouls.

Analysis: Not many pro players are content to pound the daylights out of people and chase every rebound without scoring, but that's how Dudley makes his living. He challenged the league salary cap last season, accepting a lesser offer from the Blazers thinking that he would opt for free agency after one year in Portland and re-sign for more money. The broken ankle caused his plan to backfire and may have cost him a bundle.

PLAYER SUMMARY	
Will	chase rebounds
Can't	hit FTs
Expect	hard fouls
Don't Expect	10 PPG
Fantasy Value	$1
Card Value	5-10¢

COLLEGE STATISTICS

		G	FGP	FTP	RPG	PPG
83-84	YALE	26	.464	.467	5.1	4.5
84-85	YALE	26	.446	.533	10.2	12.6
85-86	YALE	26	.539	.482	9.8	16.2
86-87	YALE	24	.569	.542	13.3	17.8
Totals		102	.513	.512	9.5	12.7

NBA REGULAR-SEASON STATISTICS

		G	MIN	FGs FG	FGs PCT	3-PT FGs FG	3-PT FGs PCT	FTs FT	FTs PCT	Rebounds OFF	Rebounds TOT	AST	STL	BLK	PTS	PPG
87-88	CLE	55	513	65	.474	0	.000	40	.563	74	144	23	13	19	170	3.1
88-89	CLE	61	544	73	.435	0	.000	39	.364	72	157	21	9	23	185	3.0
89-90	CLE/NJ	64	1356	146	.411	0	.000	58	.319	174	423	39	41	72	350	5.5
90-91	NJ	61	1560	170	.408	0	.000	94	.534	229	511	37	39	153	434	7.1
91-92	NJ	82	1902	190	.403	0	.000	80	.468	343	739	58	38	179	460	5.6
92-93	NJ	71	1398	94	.353	0	.000	57	.518	215	513	16	17	103	245	3.5
93-94	POR	6	86	6	.240	0	.000	2	.500	16	24	5	4	3	14	2.3
Totals		400	7359	744	.404	0	.000	370	.451	1123	2511	199	161	552	1858	4.6

JOE DUMARS

Team: Detroit Pistons
Position: Guard
Height: 6'3" **Weight:** 195
Birthdate: May 23, 1963

NBA Experience: 9 years
College: McNeese St.
Acquired: 1st-round pick in 1985 draft
(18th overall)

Background: Dumars led the Southland Conference in scoring three times and averaged 26.4 PPG his junior year at McNeese State. In Detroit, he got pegged early as all-defense, no-offense. He has increased his scoring steadily, however, and now tallies a team-leading 20-plus points per game. He was named MVP of the 1989 NBA Finals, remains an all-defensive performer, and has played in four All-Star Games.

Strengths: Michael Jordan will vouch for the one-on-one defensive prowess of Joe D. He is a modest, unassuming leader who is also a deadly shooter with great range. Moreover, he can penetrate and pass like a point guard when asked to fill that role. He's one of the premier clutch shooters and class players in the league.

Weaknesses: Dumars is not a strong rebounder at all, and his field goal percentage took a dip last season. He has played through nagging injuries over the last couple of years.

Analysis: There are still very few big guards in the league you'd take over this guy. That's why Dumars was selected to play with Dream Team II, the 1994 U.S. national team. He remains a premier defender and big-time scorer from the backcourt who can burn you in a variety of ways.

PLAYER SUMMARY	
Will	hit clutch shots
Can't	revive the Pistons
Expect	defense, 20 PPG
Don't Expect	a third ring
Fantasy Value	$13-16
Card Value	10-15¢

COLLEGE STATISTICS

		G	FGP	FTP	RPG	PPG
81-82	MSU	29	.444	.719	2.2	18.2
82-83	MSU	29	.435	.711	4.4	19.6
83-84	MSU	31	.471	.824	5.3	26.4
84-85	MSU	27	.495	.852	4.9	25.8
Totals		116	.462	.788	4.2	22.5

NBA REGULAR-SEASON STATISTICS

		G	MIN	FGs FG	FGs PCT	3-PT FGs FG	3-PT FGs PCT	FTs FT	FTs PCT	Rebounds OFF	Rebounds TOT	AST	STL	BLK	PTS	PPG
85-86	DET	82	1957	287	.481	5	.313	190	.798	60	119	390	66	11	769	9.4
86-87	DET	79	2439	369	.493	9	.409	184	.748	50	167	352	83	5	931	11.8
87-88	DET	82	2732	453	.472	4	.211	251	.815	63	200	387	87	15	1161	14.2
88-89	DET	69	2408	456	.505	14	.483	260	.850	57	172	390	63	5	1186	17.2
89-90	DET	75	2578	508	.480	22	.400	297	.900	60	212	368	63	2	1335	17.8
90-91	DET	80	3046	622	.481	14	.311	371	.890	62	187	443	89	7	1629	20.4
91-92	DET	82	3192	587	.448	49	.408	412	.867	82	188	375	71	12	1635	19.9
92-93	DET	77	3094	677	.466	112	.375	343	.864	63	148	308	78	7	1809	23.5
93-94	DET	69	2591	505	.452	124	.387	276	.836	35	151	261	63	4	1410	20.4
Totals		695	24037	4464	.473	353	.382	2584	.848	532	1544	3274	663	68	11865	17.1

RICHARD DUMAS

Team: Phoenix Suns
Position: Forward
Height: 6'7" **Weight:** 210
Birthdate: May 19, 1969

NBA Experience: 1 year
College: Oklahoma St.
Acquired: 2nd-round pick in 1991 draft (46th overall)

Background: Dumas made an instant splash at Oklahoma State, leading the Cowboys in scoring as a sophomore. Chased by academic and alcohol troubles, however, he was forced to take his career to Israel. He was drafted in the second round by the Suns in 1991 but suspended before the 1991-92 season for failing a random drug test. He played in the USBL and CBA, completed a drug treatment program, and then exploded onto the NBA scene with Phoenix in 1992-93. He was suspended again for drugs for the entire 1993-94 season.

Strengths: Dumas is a flashy, exciting, and tremendously talented player. He slashes to the hoop as well as anyone in the league and is a splendid finisher. He thrives in the open court but also has a steady mid-range jumper. He also knows how to put the ball in the hole and can hold his own defensively. Dumas is good off the dribble with both hands.

Weaknesses: There is obviously a checkered history with Dumas, who is now one drug suspension away from blowing it. It appeared as though he had overcome his troubles as a rookie, but that was not the case. On the court, Dumas is not always a willing passer. He racked up more turnovers than he did assists as a rookie, and he does not have 3-point range.

Analysis: Sixers coach John Lucas, who helped Dumas rehabilitate from his drug problem the first time, says Dumas has "Dr. J.-type ability." Phoenix coach Paul Westphal calls him a potential Dream Team player. But similar compliments have been heaped on others who have messed up their careers with drugs. Dumas has all the ability in the world. Can he keep his head on straight?

PLAYER SUMMARY

Will	slash to the hoop
Can't	shake drug habit
Expect	double-digit scoring
Don't Expect	an instant cure
Fantasy Value	$9-11
Card Value	10-25¢

COLLEGE STATISTICS

		G	FGP	FTP	RPG	PPG
87-88	OSU	30	.548	.747	6.4	17.4
88-89	OSU	28	.448	.617	7.0	15.7
Totals		58	.494	.694	6.7	16.6

NBA REGULAR-SEASON STATISTICS

			FGs		3-PT FGs		FTs		Rebounds						
	G	MIN	FG	PCT	FG	PCT	FT	PCT	OFF	TOT	AST	STL	BLK	PTS	PPG
92-93 PHO	48	1320	302	.524	1	.333	152	.707	100	223	60	85	39	757	15.8
Totals	48	1320	302	.524	1	.333	152	.707	100	223	60	85	39	757	15.8

ACIE EARL

Team: Boston Celtics
Position: Center/Forward
Height: 6'11" **Weight:** 240
Birthdate: June 23, 1970

NBA Experience: 1 year
College: Iowa
Acquired: 1st-round pick in 1993 draft
(19th overall)

Background: After redshirting his first year at Iowa, Earl led the Big Ten in blocks as a freshman and finished his career with 365 swats—seventh best in NCAA annals. He finished his career ranked in the top five in Hawkeye history in points, rebounds, and blocks. He was chosen as a finalist for the Wooden Award as a senior. Earl was drafted 19th overall by the Celtics in 1993 and averaged about 5.5 PPG in reserve playing time behind veteran center Robert Parish.

Strengths: Earl's greatest asset is his ability to block shots. He has a body the Boston brass loves and good timing when attacking the ball. He catches the basketball well and has been able to put the ball in the hole, although he looks awkward doing so. He has pretty good touch from outside, though not much range. He takes well to coaching.

Weaknesses: Earl is not among the better athletes at his position. He does not explode off the floor, which could hurt his production as an NBA rebounder and shot-blocker. He is slow-footed and lacks quickness to the ball. Earl needs to develop a low-post repertoire if he hopes to become Boston's big man of the future. His field goal and free throw percentages need boosts.

Analysis: Now that Parish has said his farewells to Boston, Earl, Pervis Ellison, and rookie Eric Montross will battle for playing time in the pivot. Earl is a little bit like the Chief. Neither is able to fly down the court or provide much in the way of acrobatic drives to the hoop. But if Earl can take something from the way Parish works in the low post and comes to play night after night, he could become a solid NBA center.

PLAYER SUMMARY	
Will	block shots
Can't	explode off the floor
Expect	steady improvement
Don't Expect	another Parish
Fantasy Value	$1-3
Card Value	8-15¢

COLLEGE STATISTICS

		G	FGP	FTP	RPG	PPG
89-90	IOWA	22	.440	.739	3.5	6.0
90-91	IOWA	32	.503	.665	6.7	16.3
91-92	IOWA	30	.533	.667	7.8	19.5
92-93	IOWA	32	.505	.701	8.9	16.9
Totals		116	.508	.680	7.0	15.3

NBA REGULAR-SEASON STATISTICS

			FGs		3-PT FGs		FTs		Rebounds						
	G	MIN	FG	PCT	FG	PCT	FT	PCT	OFF	TOT	AST	STL	BLK	PTS	PPG
93-94 BOS	74	1149	151	.406	0	.000	108	.675	85	247	12	24	53	410	5.5
Totals	74	1149	151	.406	0	.000	108	.675	85	247	12	24	53	410	5.5

BLUE EDWARDS

Team: Boston Celtics
Position: Forward/Guard
Height: 6'5" **Weight:** 200
Birthdate: October 31, 1965
NBA Experience: 5 years

College: Louisburg; East Carolina
Acquired: Traded from Bucks with Derek Strong for Ed Pinckney and draft rights to Andrei Fetisov, 6/94

Background: Edwards was a junior college All-American before his two-year career at East Carolina. As a senior, he led the Pirates in scoring, rebounds, steals, assists, blocked shots, 3-point percentage, and field goals. He spent three seasons with Utah and started at small forward his last two years there. He was traded to Milwaukee before the 1992-93 season, started with the Bucks for two years, and then was dealt to the Celtics last June.

Strengths: Edwards presents a rare combination of speed and strength, and you'd be pressed to find a better pure athlete. He's a tremendous finisher on the break, can post up, and is blessed with a nice outside jumper with 3-point range. Edwards had increased his scoring average every year in the league before last season. He can play big guard and small forward.

Weaknesses: Edwards turns the ball over almost as often as he gets credit for an assist. He's not one of his team's better ball-handlers. Edwards gets broken down off the dribble by guards yet lacks the size to defend forwards well. His shooting accuracy and scoring average declined last season.

Analysis: The Bucks picked up Edwards in an effort to become a more athletic team, and the Celtics apparently had the same intentions. He can be a very exciting player to watch, and also a productive one. His offensive numbers took a dive last season as opponents realized they could no longer ignore him from the outside. He'll have to work harder for his points.

PLAYER SUMMARY	
Will	make exciting plays
Can't	avoid fouling
Expect	athletic versatility
Don't Expect	20 PPG
Fantasy Value	$3-5
Card Value	5-10¢

COLLEGE STATISTICS

		G	FGP	FTP	RPG	PPG
84-85	LOU	29	.636	.645	6.1	17.8
85-86	LOU	31	.700	.658	6.0	22.3
86-87	ECAR	28	.561	.739	5.6	14.4
88-89	ECAR	29	.551	.755	6.9	26.7
Totals		117	.612	.701	6.2	20.4

NBA REGULAR-SEASON STATISTICS

				FGs		3-PT FGs		FTs		Rebounds						
		G	MIN	FG	PCT	FG	PCT	FT	PCT	OFF	TOT	AST	STL	BLK	PTS	PPG
89-90	UTA	82	1889	286	.507	9	.300	146	.719	69	251	145	76	36	727	8.9
90-91	UTA	62	1611	244	.526	6	.250	82	.701	51	201	108	57	29	576	9.3
91-92	UTA	81	2283	433	.522	39	.379	113	.774	86	298	137	81	46	1018	12.6
92-93	MIL	82	2729	554	.512	37	.349	237	.790	123	382	214	129	45	1382	16.9
93-94	MIL	82	2322	382	.477	38	.358	151	.799	104	329	171	83	27	953	11.6
Totals		389	10834	1899	.508	129	.350	729	.763	433	1461	775	426	183	4656	12.0

DOUG EDWARDS

Team: Atlanta Hawks
Position: Forward
Height: 6'7" **Weight:** 235
Birthdate: January 21, 1971

NBA Experience: 1 year
College: Florida St.
Acquired: 1st-round pick in 1993 draft (15th overall)

Background: One of the nation's top recruits in 1989, Edwards was once considered the best player in Florida high school history. He recorded 16 double-doubles as a senior at Florida State and was among the ACC's top ten in six categories. Though listed at 6'9" in college, he measured 6'7" at the Chicago pre-draft camp. He was drafted 15th by Atlanta but started the 1993-94 season on the injured list after undergoing right calf surgery.

Strengths: Edwards is a good all-around player but not great in any area. He can be a decent shooter facing the basket, rebounds, and plays the game with a general toughness about him. He was a big-time scorer in college, and some feel he has the potential to reach double figures as a pro. He has some natural ability and a pretty good feel for the game.

Weaknesses: Some NBA people insisted that Edwards was vastly overrated coming out of college. He lacks quickness and end-to-end speed. His low-post offensive game is not up to big-league standards, and he is not a consistent enough outside shooter to make a living on the perimeter. He lacks the explosiveness to be a starting small forward and the size to start at the power-forward spot.

Analysis: The Hawks reached for Edwards in the middle of the first round, and he played only 107 minutes as a rookie while the team posted the best record in the Eastern Conference. There were not many minutes available at forward with Atlanta, and Edwards's calf injury did not help his standing. He needs to become either a better shooter or a more creative inside scorer to earn more minutes. Both would be ideal.

PLAYER SUMMARY

Will ....play with toughness
Can't. ....shoot with range
Expect. ....improvement
Don't Expect ....starts
Fantasy Value. $0
Card Value ....10-15¢

COLLEGE STATISTICS

		G	FGP	FTP	RPG	PPG
90-91	FSU	32	.519	.709	7.1	16.4
91-92	FSU	30	.512	.747	9.0	17.1
92-93	FSU	31	.528	.722	9.4	18.3
Totals		93	.520	.725	8.4	17.2

NBA REGULAR-SEASON STATISTICS

		G	MIN	FGs FG	FGs PCT	3-PT FGs FG	3-PT FGs PCT	FTs FT	FTs PCT	Rebounds OFF	Rebounds TOT	AST	STL	BLK	PTS	PPG
93-94	ATL	16	107	17	.347	0	.000	9	.563	7	18	8	2	5	43	2.7
Totals		16	107	17	.347	0	.000	9	.563	7	18	8	2	5	43	2.7

KEVIN EDWARDS

Team: New Jersey Nets
Position: Guard
Height: 6'3" **Weight:** 202
Birthdate: October 30, 1965

NBA Experience: 6 years
College: Lakewood; DePaul
Acquired: Signed as a free agent, 7/93

Background: Edwards finished his college career with the best shooting percentage (.534) ever by a DePaul guard and became known as a high-flying dunker. He played in nearly every game in his first four years with the Heat, but he rarely saw action after the 1993 All-Star break and New Jersey picked him up after the season. His 1993-94 campaign with the Nets saw him finish third on the team in scoring.

Strengths: Edwards has a quick first step to the basket and isn't bashful about putting it up on his drives. He is capable of posting big-time scoring numbers and has 3-point range with his jumper. He puts out a good effort on the defensive end and comes up with a lot of steals.

Weaknesses: Because of his inconsistency, Edwards was out of the Heat's rotation for more than half of the 1992-93 season. His jump shot is streaky and he has never posted great shooting percentages. Edwards is not a reliable playmaker and he's had a history of being turnover-prone.

Analysis: The death of Drazen Petrovic before the 1993-94 season thrust Edwards into a starting role with his new team, and it's a role he relishes. He is no Petrovic, however, especially in his perimeter shooting. Edwards had one of the better years of his career, but he is not built to knock down long jumpers or score an All-Star's share of points. The job he has done goes less noticed, yet the Nets have been fairly pleased.

PLAYER SUMMARY	
Will	drive the lane
Can't	replace Petrovic
Expect	double-figure scoring
Don't Expect	5 APG
Fantasy Value	$8-10
Card Value	5-10¢

COLLEGE STATISTICS

		G	FGP	FTP	RPG	PPG
84-85	LAKE	33	.589	.715	5.4	18.6
85-86	LAKE	32	.626	.761	7.5	24.1
86-87	DeP	31	.536	.808	5.0	14.4
87-88	DeP	30	.533	.783	5.3	18.3
Totals		126	.576	.760	5.8	18.9

NBA REGULAR-SEASON STATISTICS

		G	MIN	FGs FG	FGs PCT	3-PT FGs FG	3-PT FGs PCT	FTs FT	FTs PCT	Rebounds OFF	Rebounds TOT	AST	STL	BLK	PTS	PPG
88-89	MIA	79	2349	470	.425	10	.270	144	.746	85	262	349	139	27	1094	13.8
89-90	MIA	78	2211	395	.412	9	.300	139	.760	77	282	252	125	33	938	12.0
90-91	MIA	79	2000	380	.410	24	.286	171	.803	80	205	240	130	46	955	12.1
91-92	MIA	81	1840	325	.454	7	.219	162	.848	56	211	170	99	20	819	10.1
92-93	MIA	40	1134	216	.468	5	.294	119	.844	48	121	120	68	12	556	13.9
93-94	NJ	82	2727	471	.458	35	.354	167	.770	94	281	232	120	34	1144	14.0
Totals		439	12261	2257	.434	90	.301	902	.793	440	1362	1363	681	172	5506	12.5

CRAIG EHLO

Team: Atlanta Hawks
Position: Guard
Height: 6'7" **Weight:** 205
Birthdate: August 11, 1961

NBA Experience: 11 years
College: Odessa; Washington St.
Acquired: Signed as a free agent, 7/93

Background: As a senior, Ehlo set a Pac-10 record for assists at Washington State. He was a reserve for Houston before spending some time in the CBA. He spent seven years in Cleveland as both a starter and reserve before signing as a free agent with Atlanta before the 1993-94 season. He averaged about ten PPG off the bench last year.

Strengths: Ehlo can do a little of everything. He is a tough defender who throws his body around for the team. He is an underrated scorer and shooter with great range. He was second on the Hawks last season in 3-pointers made and attempted. He also rebounds and keeps the ball moving.

Weaknesses: "A step slow" is the knock on Ehlo. He does not possess the quickness or athletic ability to stick with faster players one-on-one. He does not create much on offense, but rather feeds off teammates.

Analysis: Ehlo is a fine complementary player on a good team, and he has played with two of those. He'll beat you if you leave him open and he rarely does anything to hurt his own team. He's had a large hand in coach Lenny Wilkens's 900 NBA victories.

PLAYER SUMMARY	
Will	knock down treys
Can't	outrace quick guards
Expect	a team player
Don't Expect	great athleticism
Fantasy Value	$4-6
Card Value	5-10¢

COLLEGE STATISTICS

		G	FGP	FTP	RPG	PPG
79-80	ODES	28	.487	.714	5.1	12.6
80-81	ODES	30	.500	.772	6.8	20.7
81-82	WSU	30	.479	.600	2.2	5.1
82-83	WSU	30	.547	.633	3.2	12.0
Totals		118	.505	.701	4.3	12.6

NBA REGULAR-SEASON STATISTICS

		G	MIN	FGs FG	FGs PCT	3-PT FGs FG	3-PT FGs PCT	FTs FT	FTs PCT	Rebounds OFF	Rebounds TOT	AST	STL	BLK	PTS	PPG
83-84	HOU	7	63	11	.407	0	.000	1	1.000	6	9	6	3	0	23	3.3
84-85	HOU	45	189	34	.493	0	.000	19	.633	8	25	26	11	3	87	1.9
85-86	HOU	36	199	36	.429	3	.333	23	.793	17	46	29	11	4	98	2.7
86-87	CLE	44	890	99	.414	5	.172	70	.707	55	161	92	40	30	273	6.2
87-88	CLE	79	1709	226	.466	22	.344	89	.674	86	274	206	82	30	563	7.1
88-89	CLE	82	1867	249	.475	39	.390	71	.607	100	295	266	110	19	608	7.4
89-90	CLE	81	2894	436	.464	104	.419	126	.681	147	439	371	126	23	1102	13.6
90-91	CLE	82	2766	344	.445	49	.329	95	.679	142	388	376	121	34	832	10.1
91-92	CLE	63	2016	310	.453	69	.413	87	.707	94	307	238	78	22	776	12.3
92-93	CLE	82	2559	385	.490	93	.381	86	.717	113	403	254	104	22	949	11.6
93-94	ATL	82	2147	316	.446	77	.348	112	.727	71	279	273	136	26	821	10.0
Totals		683	17299	2446	.460	461	.374	779	.689	837	2626	2137	822	213	6132	9.0

MARIO ELIE

Team: Houston Rockets
Position: Guard
Height: 6'5" **Weight:** 210
Birthdate: November 26, 1963

NBA Experience: 4 years
College: American International
Acquired: Traded from Trail Blazers for a 1995 2nd-round pick, 8/93

Background: A world traveler, Elie played in Portugal, Argentina, Ireland, and Miami (of the USBL) after his college career at American International. He speaks four languages. He was drafted by Milwaukee in 1985 but released before the season. Elie joined Albany of the CBA during 1989-90 and saw his first NBA action in 1990-91 with Philadelphia (three games). He has since played key roles with Golden State, Portland, and most recently Houston.

Strengths: Elie is one of the top defensive stalwarts in the league. He holds his own against big scorers on a nightly basis. He can play just about any position except center. Offensively, Elie shoots his unorthodox jump shot with 3-point range. He is a very good ball-handler and passer and is rock-solid from the free throw line. He has been underrated at most of his stops.

Weaknesses: Elie has an inconsistent and funny-looking outside shot and does not maintain a high percentage from the field. He is not a dominant athlete, nor is he overpowering in any one area. He lacks quickness and does nothing that would be noticed by a casual fan. Speedy opponents give him trouble defensively.

Analysis: Elie is a rare player who works tirelessly to keep playing in the NBA. He has performed well for his last three teams and was the best reserve on a talented Rockets team for most of 1993-94. He averaged career highs in most categories, including scoring, although a broken right hand in late March sidelined him. One of these days, someone will hang onto this underappreciated journeyman. Houston, perhaps?

PLAYER SUMMARY

Will ....work tirelessly
Can't ....unpack his bags
Expect ....great defense
Don't Expect ....regular starts
Fantasy Value.............................$1-3
Card Value ....7-12¢

COLLEGE STATISTICS

		G	FGP	FTP	RPG	PPG
81-82	AI	25	.586	.742	8.3	15.4
82-83	AI	31	.527	.739	7.7	15.9
83-84	AI	31	.565	.794	8.6	18.9
84-85	AI	33	.549	.777	9.0	20.1
Totals		120	.555	.767	8.4	17.7

NBA REGULAR-SEASON STATISTICS

		G	MIN	FGs FG	FGs PCT	3-PT FGs FG	3-PT FGs PCT	FTs FT	FTs PCT	Rebounds OFF	Rebounds TOT	AST	STL	BLK	PTS	PPG
90-91	PHI/GS	33	644	79	.497	4	.400	75	.843	46	110	45	19	10	237	7.2
91-92	GS	79	1677	221	.521	23	.329	155	.852	69	227	174	68	15	620	7.8
92-93	POR	82	1757	240	.458	45	.349	183	.855	59	216	177	74	20	708	8.6
93-94	HOU	67	1606	208	.446	56	.335	154	.860	28	181	208	50	8	626	9.3
Totals		261	5684	748	.476	128	.340	567	.854	202	734	604	211	53	2191	8.4

SEAN ELLIOTT

Team: San Antonio Spurs
Position: Forward
Height: 6'8" **Weight:** 215
Birthdate: February 2, 1968
NBA Experience: 5 years

College: Arizona
Acquired: Traded from Pistons for draft rights to Bill Curley and a 1997 2nd-round pick, 7/94

Background: Elliott was college basketball's 1989 Player of the Year at Arizona, where he broke Lew Alcindor's Pac-10 record with 2,555 career points. He started 69 games as a rookie for San Antonio and was an 82-game starter the next two years. He was traded to Detroit in the October 1993 deal that sent Dennis Rodman to the Spurs. Detroit tried to trade him to Houston in midseason, but the trade was nixed when Elliott failed a physical (kidney disorder). He was dealt back to the Spurs in July.

Strengths: Elliott has a diverse offensive arsenal. He can shoot from the perimeter, drive to the hoop, handle the ball, and make crisp passes. Despite his lack of bulk, he is capable of big rebounding numbers and plays standout defense. His versatility allows him to play big guard in addition to small forward.

Weaknesses: Elliott does not thrive in the halfcourt game. Also, stronger players can wear him down on defense and render him less effective at the offensive end. He shot poorly from the field last year, turned the ball over, and did not rebound like he can. Doctors disagree on the seriousness of his kidney disorder.

Analysis: Elliott had the look of an All-Star during his final year in San Antonio, but his trade to Detroit did nothing to make an All-Star appearance a reality. He was overshadowed by Isiah Thomas and Joe Dumars on a poor team, while the Pistons' style of play was not suited to his open-court skills. The return to San Antonio could be just what he needs.

PLAYER SUMMARY	
Will	work the baseline
Can't	bang in halfcourt game
Expect	better scoring
Don't Expect	bulk
Fantasy Value	$8-10
Card Value	8-15¢

COLLEGE STATISTICS

		G	FGP	FTP	RPG	PPG
85-86	ARIZ	32	.486	.749	5.3	15.6
86-87	ARIZ	30	.510	.770	6.0	19.3
87-88	ARIZ	38	.570	.793	5.8	19.6
88-89	ARIZ	33	.480	.841	7.2	22.3
Totals		133	.512	.793	6.1	19.2

NBA REGULAR-SEASON STATISTICS

			FGs		3-PT FGs		FTs		Rebounds						
	G	MIN	FG	PCT	FG	PCT	FT	PCT	OFF	TOT	AST	STL	BLK	PTS	PPG
89-90 SA	81	2032	311	.481	1	.111	187	.866	127	297	154	45	14	810	10.0
90-91 SA	82	3044	478	.490	20	.313	325	.808	142	456	238	69	33	1301	15.9
91-92 SA	82	3120	514	.494	25	.305	285	.861	143	439	214	84	29	1338	16.3
92-93 SA	70	2604	451	.491	37	.356	268	.795	85	322	265	68	28	1207	17.2
93-94 DET	73	2409	360	.455	26	.299	139	.803	68	263	197	54	27	885	12.1
Totals	388	13209	2114	.484	109	.315	1204	.825	565	1777	1068	320	131	5541	14.3

DALE ELLIS

Team: San Antonio Spurs
Position: Guard/Forward
Height: 6'7" **Weight:** 215
Birthdate: August 6, 1960
NBA Experience: 11 years

College: Tennessee
Acquired: Traded from Bucks via the Trail Blazers; Blazers sent Alaa Abdelnaby to Bucks, and Spurs sent rights to Tracy Murray to Blazers, 7/92

Background: Ellis was an All-American at Tennessee, where his shooting accuracy enabled him to average 22.6 PPG his senior year. He was a faceless reserve for Dallas for three years, but the infamous trade for Al Wood brought him to Seattle and stardom. Ellis has since played for Milwaukee and San Antonio, and last March he became the first player in NBA history to make 1,000 career 3-pointers.

Strengths: Ellis has one of the prettiest—and one of the deadliest—jumpers in the league. He is particularly effective coming off screens and shooting from 3-point land. He was once one of the game's greatest offensive weapons, and he can still fill it up from anywhere.

Weaknesses: Ellis is not a great defensive player, rebounder, or ball-handler, but he does not claim to be. He has also encountered some off-the-court problems during his career.

Analysis: Ellis can still light up the scoreboard after 11 years of pro gunning. He has averaged at least 15 PPG over the last eight seasons and still shoots the 3 as accurately and as often as virtually anyone in the NBA. Still a starter, he will someday be remembered as one of the best long-range shooters in history.

PLAYER SUMMARY

Will ....score from anywhere
Can't ....be left open
Expect ....100-plus treys
Don't Expect.......a defensive stopper
Fantasy Value................................$6-8
Card Value ....5-10¢

COLLEGE STATISTICS

		G	FGP	FTP	RPG	PPG
79-80	TENN	27	.445	.775	3.6	7.1
80-81	TENN	29	.597	.748	6.4	17.7
81-82	TENN	30	.654	.720	6.3	21.2
82-83	TENN	21	.601	.751	10.0	22.6
Totals		107	.595	.765	6.3	19.3

NBA REGULAR-SEASON STATISTICS

				FGs		3-PT FGs		FTs		Rebounds							
		G	MIN	FG	PCT	FG	PCT	FT	PCT	OFF	TOT	AST	STL	BLK	PTS	PPG	
83-84	DAL	67	1059	225	.456	12	.414	87	.719	106	250	56	41	9	549	8.2	
84-85	DAL	72	1314	274	.454	42	.385	77	.740	100	238	56	46	7	667	9.3	
85-86	DAL	72	1086	193	.411	63	.364	59	.720	86	168	37	40	9	508	7.1	
86-87	SEA	82	3073	785	.516	86	.358	385	.787	187	447	238	104	32	2041	24.9	
87-88	SEA	75	2790	764	.503	107	.413	303	.767	167	340	197	74	11	1938	25.8	
88-89	SEA	82	3190	857	.501	162	.478	377	.816	156	342	164	108	22	2253	27.5	
89-90	SEA	55	2033	502	.497	96	.375	193	.818	90	238	110	59	7	1293	23.5	
90-91	SEA/MIL	51	1424	340	.474	57	.363	120	.723	66	173	95	49	8	857	16.8	
91-92	MIL	81	2191	485	.469	138	.419	164	.774	92	253	104	57	18	1272	15.7	
92-93	SA	82	2731	545	.499	119	.401	157	.797	81	312	107	78	18	1366	16.7	
93-94	SA	77	2590	478	.494	131	.395	83	.776	70	255	80	66	11	1170	15.2	
Totals		796	23481	5448	.489	1013	.402	2005	.780	1201	3016	1244	722	152	13914	17.5	

HAROLD ELLIS

Team: Los Angeles Clippers
Position: Guard
Height: 6'5" **Weight:** 200
Birthdate: October 7, 1970

NBA Experience: 1 year
College: Morehouse
Acquired: Signed as a free agent, 1/94

Background: Ellis was named conference Player of the Year during his last three seasons at tiny Morehouse College in Atlanta, and he started his pro career with Quad City of the CBA in 1992-93. He averaged 23.3 PPG in the USBL in the summer of 1993 and 21.4 PPG with Quad City for 21 outings last year before latching on with the Clippers. He played in 49 games, started 16, and averaged 8.7 PPG with L.A.

Strengths: There was never a doubt about the athletic ability of Ellis, who at 6'5" can play above the bucket. He is a scorer who runs the floor like the wind and can finish with high-flying jams. Moreover, he also plays scrappy defense. Versatile, he is capable of filling in at small forward in addition to his normal role as a shooting guard.

Weaknesses: Ellis was considered a "tweener" coming out of college. Some feel he is not a good enough perimeter shooter and ball-handler to thrive at guard yet is too small to be a productive forward in the NBA. He must learn to recognize open teammates and get them the ball. He could stand to improve his consistency in all aspects.

Analysis: What a ride it has been for Ellis in two pro years. His strong play in the CBA and USBL earned him a shot with the Clippers, and he promptly jumped on it. He was fined $3,500 for tossing an elbow at the Knicks' Eric Anderson in his very first NBA game, and later lit up the Celtics for 29 points on national television. He is an exciting player who should get a chance with the Clippers, who seem to be going with a youth movement.

PLAYER SUMMARY	
Will	play above the rim
Can't	spot open men
Expect	finishes with style
Don't Expect	great consistency
Fantasy Value	$1-3
Card Value	5-10¢

COLLEGE STATISTICS

		G	FGP	FTP	RPG	PPG
88-89	MORE	29	.630	.607	8.5	23.0
89-90	MORE	33	.543	.696	7.9	23.6
90-91	MORE	32	.531	.610	7.2	24.0
91-92	MORE	26	.560	.581	8.7	25.6
Totals		120	.562	.627	8.0	24.0

NBA REGULAR-SEASON STATISTICS

			FGs		3-PT FGs		FTs		Rebounds						
	G	MIN	FG	PCT	FG	PCT	FT	PCT	OFF	TOT	AST	STL	BLK	PTS	PPG
93-94 LAC	49	923	159	.545	0	.000	106	.711	94	153	31	73	2	424	8.7
Totals	49	923	159	.545	0	.000	106	.711	94	153	31	73	2	424	8.7

LaPHONSO ELLIS

Team: Denver Nuggets
Position: Forward
Height: 6'8" **Weight:** 240
Birthdate: May 5, 1970

NBA Experience: 2 years
College: Notre Dame
Acquired: 1st-round pick in 1992 draft (5th overall)

Background: Ellis finished his college career as one of only four Notre Dame players to score 1,000 points and grab 1,000 rebounds. He became the all-time Fighting Irish leader in blocked shots despite missing parts of his sophomore and junior seasons because of academics. He was drafted fifth overall by Denver in 1992 and was a first-team All-Rookie selection after starting all 82 games and rating among rookie leaders in blocked shots, rebounding, and scoring. He has averaged about 15 PPG in his first two seasons.

Strengths: Ellis and center Dikembe Mutombo form one of the best shot-blocking tandems in the league. He has great natural instincts and is an outstanding athlete who plays above the rim. He also gives the Nuggets another big-time rebounder, and he produces on the offensive end. Ellis possesses a nice shooting touch both facing the basket and in the post.

Weaknesses: Ellis needs to improve his position defense. He tends to rely too much on the blocked shot as a weapon instead of muscling his man away from the hoop. He is not overly forceful on the offensive end either, instead getting by on his skills and touch around the basket. His free throw shooting and passing out of double-teams both need work.

Analysis: Ellis is a confident performer who has been invaluable to the Nuggets in his first two years. A skilled and productive offensive player, he also provides intimidation with his ability to alter shots. As he continues to learn the ins and outs of NBA defense and becomes more assertive, he will grow in stature. He has all the natural tools to be a star.

PLAYER SUMMARY

Will	attack shots
Can't	apply bruises
Expect	15-plus PPG
Don't Expect	high FT pct.
Fantasy Value	$25-30
Card Value	15-30¢

COLLEGE STATISTICS

		G	FGP	FTP	RPG	PPG
88-89	ND	27	.563	.684	9.4	13.5
89-90	ND	22	.511	.675	12.6	14.0
90-91	ND	15	.573	.716	10.5	16.4
91-92	ND	33	.631	.655	11.7	17.7
Totals		97	.577	.675	11.1	15.5

NBA REGULAR-SEASON STATISTICS

		G	MIN	FGs FG	FGs PCT	3-PT FGs FG	3-PT FGs PCT	FTs FT	FTs PCT	Rebounds OFF	Rebounds TOT	AST	STL	BLK	PTS	PPG
92-93	DEN	82	2749	483	.504	2	.154	237	.748	274	744	151	72	111	1205	14.7
93-94	DEN	79	2699	483	.502	7	.304	242	.674	220	682	167	63	80	1215	15.4
Totals		161	5448	966	.503	9	.250	479	.709	494	1426	318	135	191	2420	15.0

LeRON ELLIS

Team: Charlotte Hornets
Position: Forward/Center
Height: 6'10" **Weight:** 240
Birthdate: April 28, 1969

NBA Experience: 2 years
College: Kentucky; Syracuse
Acquired: Signed as a free agent, 9/93

Background: Ellis was a rising star at Kentucky, but he left the program after it was placed on probation in 1989. He transferred to Syracuse, where he was forced to take a back seat to Derrick Coleman and Billy Owens. He averaged 11.1 PPG during his senior season and was drafted 22nd by the Clippers. He played in only 29 games as a rookie and did not make an NBA roster in 1992-93. Charlotte signed him for 1993-94 and he saw action in 50 outings.

Strengths: Ellis has above-average athletic ability for his size. He is quick off his feet, runs the floor well, and has good agility. Ellis also has a fine pair of hands. He looks to score yet does not shy away from defense. He has potential as a quality shot-blocker and rebounder and was once considered a defensive specialist.

Weaknesses: Ellis was labeled an underachiever in college and the tag has followed him to the pros. Despite some natural ability, he does not always apply himself. His offensive game is nothing to write home about. He has a limited and predictable low-post game and lacks the consistency to make a living on the perimeter. He's a four but he thinks like a three. He's a poor free throw shooter and poses little threat from the perimeter.

Analysis: Ellis, whose father Leroy played 14 seasons with the Lakers, 76ers, and Bullets, will not last as long as Dad did in the NBA. He got off to a slow start and has not progressed rapidly. He had a few decent games as a Hornet last season, but were it not for a rash of injuries, he'd have spent much more time on the bench. There are a truckload of question marks about his game.

PLAYER SUMMARY	
Will	get off his feet
Can't	meet expectations
Expect	shot-blocking
Don't Expect	10 PPG
Fantasy Value	$0
Card Value	10-20¢

COLLEGE STATISTICS

		G	FGP	FTP	RPG	PPG
87-88	KEN	28	.462	.524	3.0	4.3
88-89	KEN	32	.519	.677	5.5	16.0
89-90	SYR	32	.451	.519	4.0	6.0
90-91	SYR	32	.507	.605	7.7	11.1
Totals		124	.497	.615	5.1	9.5

NBA REGULAR-SEASON STATISTICS

			FGs		3-PT FGs		FTs		Rebounds						
	G	MIN	FG	PCT	FG	PCT	FT	PCT	OFF	TOT	AST	STL	BLK	PTS	PPG
91-92 LAC	29	103	17	.340	0	.000	9	.474	12	24	1	6	9	43	1.5
93-94 CHA	50	680	88	.484	0	.000	45	.662	70	188	24	17	25	221	4.4
Totals	79	783	105	.453	0	.000	54	.621	82	212	25	23	34	264	3.3

PERVIS ELLISON

Team: Boston Celtics
Position: Forward/Center
Height: 6'10" **Weight:** 225
Birthdate: April 3, 1967

NBA Experience: 5 years
College: Louisville
Acquired: Signed as a free agent, 7/94

Background: As a freshman, Ellison was the MVP of the 1986 NCAA Tournament after lifting Louisville past Duke for the title. He recorded 2,000 points and 1,000 rebounds in college and closed his career among the Division I all-time leaders in blocked shots. The No. 1 pick in the 1989 draft, he struggled with Sacramento for a season and was traded to Washington. He won the Most Improved Player Award in 1991-92, scoring a team-leading 20 PPG. Knee injuries sliced time from his last two seasons, and he wound up signing a free-agent contract with Boston over the summer.

Strengths: Ellison has long arms and good athletic skills. He can be an effective shot-blocker and rebounder. In fact, he led his team in blocks two years ago despite missing 33 games. He possesses potent moves around the basket and is good with both hands. He has been a productive scorer in past years.

Weaknesses: Injuries played a key role in Ellison's slow NBA start and continue to hinder him. Last season was his worst since his forgettable rookie year in Sacramento. He is not very physical for a center and his shooting percentage took a plunge last season. He seems to have lost confidence.

Analysis: Ellison had been written off as a big-time bust, came back with a great year in 1991-92, and has since taken three steps back. He has made a living on the injured list during his career, and it has clearly hampered his progress. It will probably take a healthy season to restore some of his effectiveness. His knees are the key to his future.

PLAYER SUMMARY	
Will	block shots
Can't	stay healthy
Expect	inside scoring
Don't Expect	physical play
Fantasy Value	$5-7
Card Value	8-15¢

COLLEGE STATISTICS

		G	FGP	FTP	RPG	PPG
85-86	LOU	39	.554	.682	8.2	13.1
86-87	LOU	31	.533	.719	8.7	15.2
87-88	LOU	35	.601	.692	8.3	17.6
88-89	LOU	31	.615	.652	8.7	17.6
Totals		136	.577	.687	8.4	15.8

NBA REGULAR-SEASON STATISTICS

		G	MIN	FGs FG	FGs PCT	3-PT FGs FG	3-PT FGs PCT	FTs FT	FTs PCT	Rebounds OFF	Rebounds TOT	AST	STL	BLK	PTS	PPG
89-90	SAC	34	866	111	.442	0	.000	49	.628	64	196	65	16	57	271	8.0
90-91	WAS	76	1942	326	.513	0	.000	139	.650	224	585	102	49	157	791	10.4
91-92	WAS	66	2511	547	.539	1	.333	227	.728	217	740	190	62	177	1322	20.0
92-93	WAS	49	1701	341	.521	0	.000	170	.702	138	433	117	45	108	852	17.4
93-94	WAS	47	1178	137	.469	0	.000	70	.722	77	242	70	25	50	344	7.3
Totals		272	8198	1462	.513	1	.056	655	.695	720	2196	544	197	549	3580	13.2

JO JO ENGLISH

Team: Chicago Bulls
Position: Guard
Height: 6'4" **Weight:** 195
Birthdate: February 4, 1970

NBA Experience: 2 years
College: South Carolina
Acquired: Traded from Timberwolves for a future draft pick, 11/93

Background: English averaged better than 15 PPG in each of his final three seasons at South Carolina, leading the Gamecocks in scoring and 3-pointers each time. He was ignored in the 1992 draft, however, and failed to make the Rockets in training camp. He averaged 14.5 PPG in the CBA during the 1992-93 season and played 31 minutes for the Bulls. Chicago gave him another chance last season and English wound up averaging 3.6 PPG during 36 contests.

Strengths: First and foremost, English is a scorer. He possesses very good quickness and can use it to get his shot off against the majority of defenders. He is also not afraid to take it to the basket and can finish his drives with dunks. The NBA 3-pointer is easily within his range, and he is a talented enough athlete to handle himself on defense.

Weaknesses: English is a marginal player who needs to keep working on most aspects of his game. His shooting was horribly inconsistent last season and he made less than half of his free throw attempts. Better shot selection would be a start. He is a below-average ball-handler and assists man, preferring to finish plays instead of starting them. His defense, like the rest of his game, lacks the crucial element of consistency.

Analysis: English survived two ten-day contracts and went about his first real NBA season in relative obscurity until the playoffs, where he gained notoriety (as well as a one-game suspension) for a benches-clearing scuffle with Derek Harper of the Knicks. English is a scorer, but he has yet to tally double figures in an NBA game. He'll need every ounce of his fine work ethic to continue playing in the NBA.

PLAYER SUMMARY	
Will	get his shots
Can't	shoot FTs
Expect	athletic ability
Don't Expect	consistency
Fantasy Value	$0
Card Value	8-15¢

COLLEGE STATISTICS

		G	FGP	FTP	RPG	PPG
88-89	SCAR	28	.422	.586	1.1	3.8
89-90	SCAR	27	.489	.626	4.8	15.3
90-91	SCAR	33	.462	.736	3.3	15.0
91-92	SCAR	27	.430	.620	3.6	15.8
Totals		115	.455	.659	3.2	12.5

NBA REGULAR-SEASON STATISTICS

			FGs		3-PT FGs		FTs		Rebounds						
	G	MIN	FG	PCT	FG	PCT	FT	PCT	OFF	TOT	AST	STL	BLK	PTS	PPG
92-93 CHI	6	31	3	.300	0	.000	0	.000	2	6	1	3	2	6	1.0
93-94 CHI	36	419	56	.434	8	.471	10	.476	9	45	38	8	10	130	3.6
Totals	42	450	59	.424	8	.400	10	.435	11	51	39	11	12	136	3.2

PATRICK EWING

Team: New York Knicks
Position: Center
Height: 7'0" **Weight:** 240
Birthdate: August 5, 1962

NBA Experience: 9 years
College: Georgetown
Acquired: 1st-round pick in 1985 draft
(1st overall)

Background: Ewing led Georgetown to three NCAA finals, including the championship in 1984, and was the consensus Player of the Year as a senior while setting records across the board. He starred on the 1984 and 1992 gold-medal-winning Olympic teams. He was named NBA Rookie of the Year with the Knicks in 1986 and has been a perennial All-Star. He has been at the top of his game in leading the Knicks to back-to-back division titles.

Strengths: A franchise player, Ewing is the complete package in the pivot. He intimidates on defense, swats shots, hoards boards, and is virtually unstoppable one-on-one when he gets the ball in the post. He has developed a dangerous jump shot that no one can challenge, and he gets his points despite double- and triple-teams. He's flat-out dominant.

Weaknesses: There is very little Ewing can't do outside of shooting 3-pointers. He commits a lot of turnovers, but that goes with the territory when you're surrounded at all times. He struggled in last year's NBA Finals.

Analysis: Ewing has been considered one of the premier centers in the league for several years, and his last two years have drawn him serious MVP consideration. He became New York's all-time scoring leader last December, bypassing the great Walt Frazier, and reached 15,000 career points last January.

PLAYER SUMMARY

Will ....dominate games
Can't ....be stopped solo
Expect............Hall of Fame induction
Don't Expect.....................open shots
Fantasy Value...........................$70-75
Card Value ....20-35¢

COLLEGE STATISTICS

		G	FGP	FTP	RPG	PPG
81-82	GEOR	37	.631	.617	7.5	12.7
82-83	GEOR	32	.570	.629	10.2	17.7
83-84	GEOR	37	.658	.656	10.0	16.4
84-85	GEOR	37	.625	.637	9.2	14.6
Totals		143	.620	.635	9.2	15.3

NBA REGULAR-SEASON STATISTICS

				FGs		3-PT FGs		FTs		Rebounds						
		G	MIN	FG	PCT	FG	PCT	FT	PCT	OFF	TOT	AST	STL	BLK	PTS	PPG
85-86	NY	50	1771	386	.474	0	.000	226	.739	124	451	102	54	103	998	20.0
86-87	NY	63	2206	530	.503	0	.000	296	.713	157	555	104	89	147	1356	21.5
87-88	NY	82	2546	656	.555	0	.000	341	.716	245	676	125	104	245	1653	20.2
88-89	NY	80	2896	727	.567	0	.000	361	.746	213	740	188	117	281	1815	22.7
89-90	NY	82	3165	922	.551	1	.250	502	.775	235	893	182	78	327	2347	28.6
90-91	NY	81	3104	845	.514	0	.000	464	.745	194	905	244	80	258	2154	26.6
91-92	NY	82	3150	796	.522	1	.167	377	.738	228	921	156	88	245	1970	24.0
92-93	NY	81	3003	779	.503	1	.143	400	.719	191	980	151	74	161	1959	24.2
93-94	NY	79	2972	745	.496	4	.286	445	.765	219	885	179	90	217	1939	24.5
Totals		680	24813	6386	.522	7	.121	3412	.742	1806	7006	1431	774	1984	16191	23.8

DUANE FERRELL

Unrestricted Free Agent
Last Team: Atlanta Hawks
Position: Forward
Height: 6'7" **Weight:** 209
Birthdate: February 28, 1965

NBA Experience: 6 years
College: Georgia Tech
Acquired: Signed as a free agent, 11/90

Background: At Georgia Tech, Ferrell pumped in more than 1,800 points in his four years but was not drafted by an NBA team. He signed with Atlanta as a free agent, was cut after one season, and then re-signed with the Hawks four months later. Ferrell averaged double figures in scoring in his fourth and fifth years in the league before dipping back into single digits last season.

Strengths: Ferrell appreciates his job and shows it with all-out effort. He's got a quick first step and gets to the hoop with scoring in mind. He has developed his mid-range jumper to the point where defenders have to respect it. His defense is solid if unspectacular. He will not take many ill-advised shots.

Weaknesses: Ferrell is not a dynamite offensive player. His range is limited and his shooting is still not the best part of his game. He does not create much for teammates and he's not a big help on the boards. Ferrell will commit a turnover about as often as he gets an assist. His athletic skills are marginal at best.

Analysis: Ferrell takes nothing for granted, especially his job. His CBA days have taught him that much. He played very well at times for Atlanta, especially when injuries to regulars thrust him into the starting lineup. Last season, however, his playing time sank below 20 minutes per game for the first time in three seasons. Ferrell will keep battling for his chance, but it doesn't look like he'll ever have a prominent role with an NBA club.

PLAYER SUMMARY

Will	go to the hoop
Can't	keep starting job
Expect	hard work
Don't Expect	spectacular play
Fantasy Value	$0
Card Value	5-10¢

COLLEGE STATISTICS

		G	FGP	FTP	RPG	PPG
84-85	GT	32	.504	.571	4.1	9.1
85-86	GT	34	.595	.758	4.9	12.1
86-87	GT	29	.519	.812	5.9	17.9
87-88	GT	32	.532	.749	6.6	18.6
Totals		127	.537	.733	5.4	14.3

NBA REGULAR-SEASON STATISTICS

		G	MIN	FGs FG	FGs PCT	3-PT FGs FG	3-PT FGs PCT	FTs FT	FTs PCT	Rebounds OFF	Rebounds TOT	AST	STL	BLK	PTS	PPG
88-89	ATL	41	231	35	.422	0	.000	30	.682	19	41	10	7	6	100	2.4
89-90	ATL	14	29	5	.357	0	.000	2	.333	3	7	2	1	0	12	0.9
90-91	ATL	78	1165	174	.489	2	.667	125	.801	97	179	55	33	27	475	6.1
91-92	ATL	66	1598	331	.524	11	.333	166	.761	105	210	92	49	17	839	12.7
92-93	ATL	82	1736	327	.470	9	.250	176	.779	97	191	132	59	17	839	10.2
93-94	ATL	72	1155	184	.485	1	.111	144	.783	62	129	65	44	16	513	7.1
Totals		353	5914	1056	.489	23	.280	643	.771	383	757	356	193	83	2778	7.9

DANNY FERRY

Team: Cleveland Cavaliers
Position: Forward
Height: 6'10" **Weight:** 245
Birthdate: October 17, 1966
NBA Experience: 4 years
College: Duke

Acquired: Draft rights traded from Clippers with Reggie Williams for Ron Harper, 1990 and 1992 1st-round picks, and a 1991 2nd-round pick, 11/89

Background: After an illustrious career at Duke, in which he was named the nation's Player of the Year as a senior, Ferry snubbed the NBA and spent a year in Italy to avoid playing with the L.A. Clippers. When his rights were traded to Cleveland for Ron Harper, he came home and was a big disappointment. He has come off the bench for four years with the Cavs and his best scoring output was 8.6 PPG. He averaged about five per outing last season.

Strengths: Ferry is at his best on the perimeter despite his 6'10" size. He knows where to spot up and can hit from 3-point land. Having grown up the son of former NBA player Bob Ferry, Danny has shown decent instincts and court sense. He is a precise passer and you won't find many who shoot free throws more accurately.

Weaknesses: It looks like Ferry will never translate his college potential into NBA success. He is slow and can't work for his own shot. He feeds off others instead of making things happen. He's not much help on defense, where small forwards blow by him. He has not been able to hit consistently from the field.

Analysis: Ferry is a 3-point threat off the bench and a guy you want in to preserve a fourth-quarter lead because of his touch from the free throw line. But the former college Player of the Year is far from being the kind of multi-talented player he was expected to be. He's a role-player who has a hard time staying on the floor with the talented Cavaliers.

PLAYER SUMMARY

Will ....spot up for 3
Can't ....achieve expectations
Expect..............................high FT pct.
Don't Expect ....many starts
Fantasy Value $0
Card Value ....5-10¢

COLLEGE STATISTICS

		G	FGP	FTP	RPG	PPG
85-86	DUKE	40	.460	.628	5.5	5.9
86-87	DUKE	33	.449	.844	7.8	14.0
87-88	DUKE	35	.476	.828	7.6	19.1
88-89	DUKE	35	.522	.756	7.4	22.6
Totals		143	.484	.775	7.0	15.1

NBA REGULAR-SEASON STATISTICS

				FGs		3-PT FGs		FTs		Rebounds						
		G	MIN	FG	PCT	FG	PCT	FT	PCT	OFF	TOT	AST	STL	BLK	PTS	PPG
90-91	CLE	81	1661	275	.428	23	.299	124	.816	99	286	142	43	25	697	8.6
91-92	CLE	68	937	134	.409	17	.354	61	.836	53	213	75	22	15	346	5.1
92-93	CLE	76	1461	220	.479	34	.415	99	.876	81	279	137	29	49	573	7.5
93-94	CLE	70	965	149	.446	14	.275	38	.884	47	141	74	28	22	350	5.0
Totals		295	5024	778	.441	88	.341	322	.845	280	919	428	122	111	1966	6.7

VERN FLEMING

Team: Indiana Pacers
Position: Guard
Height: 6'5" **Weight:** 185
Birthdate: February 4, 1962

NBA Experience: 10 years
College: Georgia
Acquired: 1st-round pick in 1984 draft (18th overall)

Background: Fleming teamed with Dominique Wilkins at Georgia and, as a senior, led the SEC in scoring. He played on the 1984 Olympic team and was credited by Michael Jordan as providing his toughest defense in practices. The last three seasons were the only ones in his ten with the Pacers in which he did not average double figures in scoring, as he has been used in a reserve role.

Strengths: Fleming is a savvy player who can play either shooting or point guard. He has a height advantage over most playmakers. Fleming is the Pacers' all-time assists leader. He plays defense and makes very few mistakes. He can still get to the hoop and is approaching 10,000 career points.

Weaknesses: The reason the Pacers searched for several years to find a better point guard than Fleming is his sub-par creative ability. Indiana feels his scorer's mentality is better suited to a spot on the second unit. Fleming does not possess great quickness and is no threat from the 3-point arc.

Analysis: Fleming has gone from productive starting point guard to a reserve who sees about 18-20 minutes per night. He is still a valuable man to have around because he can give you leadership off the bench without making mistakes. He is well-respected around the league for his work ethic.

PLAYER SUMMARY	
Will	play defense
Can't	regain starting spot
Expect	10,000 career points
Don't Expect	10 PPG
Fantasy Value	$0
Card Value	5-10¢

COLLEGE STATISTICS

		G	FGP	FTP	RPG	PPG
80-81	GEOR	30	.480	.697	2.7	10.0
81-82	GEOR	31	.496	.640	3.9	9.9
82-83	GEOR	34	.535	.716	4.6	16.9
83-84	GEOR	30	.503	.754	4.0	19.8
Totals		125	.508	.705	3.8	14.2

NBA REGULAR-SEASON STATISTICS

				FGs		3-PT FGs		FTs		Rebounds						
		G	MIN	FG	PCT	FG	PCT	FT	PCT	OFF	TOT	AST	STL	BLK	PTS	PPG
84-85	IND	80	2486	433	.470	0	.000	260	.767	148	323	247	99	8	1126	14.1
85-86	IND	80	2870	436	.506	1	.167	263	.745	102	386	505	131	5	1136	14.2
86-87	IND	82	2549	370	.509	2	.200	238	.788	109	334	473	109	18	980	12.0
87-88	IND	80	2733	442	.523	0	.000	227	.802	106	364	568	115	11	1111	13.9
88-89	IND	76	2552	419	.515	3	.130	243	.799	85	310	494	77	12	1084	14.3
89-90	IND	82	2876	467	.508	12	.353	230	.782	118	322	610	92	10	1176	14.3
90-91	IND	69	1929	356	.531	4	.222	161	.729	83	214	369	76	13	877	12.7
91-92	IND	82	1737	294	.482	6	.222	132	.737	69	209	266	56	7	726	8.9
92-93	IND	75	1503	280	.505	7	.194	143	.726	63	169	224	63	9	710	9.5
93-94	IND	55	1053	147	.462	0	.000	64	.736	27	123	173	40	6	358	6.5
Totals		761	22288	3644	.503	35	.200	1961	.766	910	2754	3929	858	99	9284	12.2

RICK FOX

Team: Boston Celtics
Position: Guard/Forward
Height: 6'7" **Weight:** 231
Birthdate: July 24, 1969

NBA Experience: 3 years
College: North Carolina
Acquired: 1st-round pick in 1991 draft
(24th overall)

Background: Born in Canada, Fox moved to the Bahamas when he was two years old. He had a very limited basketball background before playing high school ball in Warsaw, Indiana. Though he was never a marquee player at North Carolina, he was drafted late in the first round by the Celtics in 1991. He spent two-and-a-half years primarily as a reserve before working his way into the starting lineup midway through last season. He averaged 11 PPG, setting a career high.

Strengths: Fox is a well-rounded player with good skills in most phases of the game and a great feel for what to do with the ball. He owns a strong body and is not afraid to challenge. He's an excellent passer and a solid defender. He has 3-point range, works hard, and has improved his perimeter game.

Weaknesses: Outside shooting has been the biggest thorn in the side of Fox, who is a very good athlete. Opponents still cut off his drive to the bucket and force him to shoot from the perimeter, although he has become more reliable. Fox commits too many turnovers and fouls and should be a better rebounder than he is.

Analysis: Fox looks to have a bright future after an up-and-down three years in Boston. He was a rookie smash, tailed off in his second year, and gave the Celtics a lift when he was inserted into the starting rotation last February. His defense, court sense, and athletic ability are assets. As his perimeter game improves, this hard-working athlete will begin to draw more notice. His biggest problem this year is that the Celtics' guard and small-forward positions are awfully crowded.

PLAYER SUMMARY

Will ....challenge his man
Can't ....thrive from long range
Expect ....all-around skills
Don't Expect ....a sweet stroke
Fantasy Value...............................$4-6
Card Value ....8-15¢

COLLEGE STATISTICS

		G	FGP	FTP	RPG	PPG
87-88	NC	34	.628	.500	1.9	4.0
88-89	NC	37	.583	.790	3.8	11.5
89-90	NC	34	.522	.735	4.6	16.2
90-91	NC	35	.453	.804	6.6	16.9
Totals		140	.518	.757	4.2	12.2

NBA REGULAR-SEASON STATISTICS

				FGs		3-PT FGs		FTs		Rebounds					
		G	MIN	FG	PCT	FG	PCT	FT	PCT	OFF	TOT	AST	STL	BLK	PTS	PPG
91-92	BOS	81	1535	241	.459	23	.329	139	.755	73	220	126	78	30	644	8.0
92-93	BOS	71	1082	184	.484	4	.174	81	.802	55	159	113	61	21	453	6.4
93-94	BOS	82	2096	340	.467	33	.330	174	.757	105	355	217	81	52	887	10.8
Totals		234	4713	765	.468	60	.311	394	.765	233	734	456	220	103	1984	8.5

KEVIN GAMBLE

Unrestricted Free Agent
Last Team: Boston Celtics
Position: Guard/Forward
Height: 6'5"　**Weight:** 210
Birthdate: November 13, 1965

NBA Experience: 7 years
College: Lincoln; Iowa
Acquired: Signed as a free agent, 12/88

Background: After an unspectacular college career at Lincoln College and Iowa, Gamble was drafted by Portland in the third round. He wound up playing in the CBA and the Philippines. Gamble was given one last NBA chance in 1988-89 with a rebuilding Celtics team. He made the most of it, becoming the team's top perimeter marksman. He scored in double figures four years in a row, but he left Boston as a free agent after last season.

Strengths: Gamble is a reliable outside shooter who connected at better than 50 percent from the field in four of his six Celtic years. He is a 3-point threat and solid free throw shooter who also gets out on the break and finishes with either hand. He is a scrappy, hungry ballplayer who appreciates his job.

Weaknesses: Gamble, who can play both big guard and small forward, is not a strong defender or rebounder. Those deficiencies, however, were not the worst of his problems last season. Pushed into a reserve role for most of the year, he struggled from the perimeter and connected on a disturbing percentage of his 3-point efforts.

Analysis: Gamble was arguably Boston's best player two years ago, but last season several of his teammates surpassed him. Drawing more attention from defenders, his shooting became sporadic and his rebounding and defense showed little improvement. He needs to bounce back with a strong year.

PLAYER SUMMARY
Will ....shoot when open
Can't ....star on defense
Expect ....10-plus PPG
Don't Expect ....rebounding
Fantasy Value..............................$1-3
Card Value ....5-10¢

COLLEGE STATISTICS

		G	FGP	FTP	RPG	PPG
83-84	LINC	30	.559	.777	9.2	21.3
84-85	LINC	31	.579	.817	9.7	20.5
85-86	IOWA	30	.474	.700	1.7	2.6
86-87	IOWA	35	.544	.697	4.5	11.9
Totals		126	.558	.768	6.2	14.1

NBA REGULAR-SEASON STATISTICS

		G	MIN	FG	FG PCT	3-PT FG	3-PT PCT	FT	FT PCT	OFF	TOT	AST	STL	BLK	PTS	PPG
87-88	POR	9	19	0	.000	0	.000	0	.000	2	3	1	2	0	0	0.0
88-89	BOS	44	375	75	.551	2	.182	35	.636	11	42	34	14	3	187	4.3
89-90	BOS	71	990	137	.455	3	.167	85	.794	42	112	119	28	8	362	5.1
90-91	BOS	82	2706	548	.587	0	.000	185	.815	85	267	256	100	34	1281	15.6
91-92	BOS	82	2496	480	.529	9	.290	139	.885	80	286	219	75	37	1108	13.5
92-93	BOS	82	2541	459	.507	52	.374	123	.826	46	246	226	86	37	1093	13.3
93-94	BOS	75	1880	368	.458	25	.243	103	.817	41	159	149	57	22	864	11.5
Totals		445	11007	2067	.518	91	.294	670	.816	307	1115	1004	362	141	4895	11.0

CHRIS GATLING

Team: Golden State Warriors
Position: Forward
Height: 6'10" **Weight:** 220
Birthdate: September 3, 1967

NBA Experience: 3 years
College: Old Dominion
Acquired: 1st-round pick in 1991 draft (16th overall)

Background: Gatling did not play during his first two years in college. He originally signed with Pittsburgh but sat out the 1986-87 season because of Prop 48 restrictions. He then transferred to Old Dominion, where NCAA rules required him to sit out the 1987-88 season. He was a two-time Sun Belt Conference Player of the Year, however, scoring over 20 PPG all three seasons. He has become a key reserve for Golden State over the last two of his three pro seasons and has also made several starts.

Strengths: Gatling is an explosive leaper who blocks shots and gets to the offensive and defensive glass. He possesses very good agility and runs the floor like a guard. He is quick to the basket with a soft touch and good hands. He shoots well over 50 percent from the field and has displayed a scoring bent.

Weaknesses: Gatling, a post player in college, is not at his best while facing the basket. He does not dominate physically but rather with his leaping ability and long arms. He's been called soft, especially on defense. His outside shooting is streaky and his range limited. Gatling is not the man you want at the free throw line late in a close game.

Analysis: Gatling is an impressive athlete who has shown a great deal of promise. The Warriors pressed him into starting duty earlier than expected because of injuries over the past two years, and for the most part Gatling has responded. While his scoring average fell last season, he raised his rebounding and shot-blocking contributions. He has the look of a solid contributor and has the confidence to match.

PLAYER SUMMARY

Will	run the floor
Can't	shoot treys
Expect	rebounds, blocks
Don't Expect	ill-advised shots
Fantasy Value	$2-4
Card Value	7-12¢

COLLEGE STATISTICS

		G	FGP	FTP	RPG	PPG
88-89	OD	27	.616	.704	9.0	22.4
89-90	OD	26	.580	.670	10.0	20.5
90-91	OD	32	.620	.692	11.1	21.0
Totals		85	.606	.689	10.1	21.3

NBA REGULAR-SEASON STATISTICS

		G	MIN	FGs FG	FGs PCT	3-PT FGs FG	3-PT FGs PCT	FTs FT	FTs PCT	Rebounds OFF	Rebounds TOT	AST	STL	BLK	PTS	PPG
91-92	GS	54	612	117	.568	0	.000	72	.661	75	182	16	31	36	306	5.7
92-93	GS	70	1248	249	.539	0	.000	150	.725	129	320	40	44	53	648	9.3
93-94	GS	82	1296	271	.588	0	.000	129	.620	143	397	41	40	63	671	8.2
Totals		206	3156	637	.564	0	.000	351	.670	347	899	97	115	152	1625	7.9

KENNY GATTISON

Team: Charlotte Hornets
Position: Forward/Center
Height: 6'8" **Weight:** 246
Birthdate: May 23, 1964

NBA Experience: 7 years
College: Old Dominion
Acquired: Signed as a free agent, 12/89

Background: The Sun Belt Conference Player of the Year in 1986, Gattison finished his career as the league's all-time leading rebounder. He also garnered All-America consideration as a senior at Old Dominion, ranking third nationally in field goal percentage at .637. Gattison played with Phoenix for a year before tearing the anterior cruciate ligament in his left knee. He spent part of 1988-89 in Italy and has been with Charlotte since 1989-90. He scored a career-high 12.7 PPG in 1991-92.

Strengths: Gattison is super-intense, the kind of player who will do whatever is asked, no matter the consequences. He sets screens, blocks out, and bangs the boards. He is versatile and can perform a number of functions, including strong inside scoring. He can play both center and power forward.

Weaknesses: Gattison has virtually no touch from beyond 12 feet, as his poor free throw shooting indicates. His reckless, physical style of play often puts him in foul trouble. He is just too small to guard centers effectively despite all the time he has spent trying to do so. Charlotte's recent addition of Robert Parish relieves Garrison of that burden.

Analysis: Gattison, who consistently shoots over 50 percent from the field, fits in well as a reserve role-player. The addition of Alonzo Mourning by the Hornets two years ago has allowed him to fill that role instead of starting. You can count on Gattison for rebounding, scoring in the paint, and physical play off the bench.

PLAYER SUMMARY	
Will	do what's asked
Can't	shoot with range
Expect	reserve minutes
Don't Expect	bad shots
Fantasy Value	$1
Card Value	5-10¢

COLLEGE STATISTICS

		G	FGP	FTP	RPG	PPG
82-83	OD	29	.503	.705	7.5	8.4
83-84	OD	31	.494	.650	7.1	11.1
84-85	OD	31	.538	.610	9.2	16.1
85-86	OD	31	.637	.673	7.8	17.4
Totals		122	.552	.650	7.9	13.3

NBA REGULAR-SEASON STATISTICS

		G	MIN	FGs FG	FGs PCT	3-PT FGs FG	3-PT FGs PCT	FTs FT	FTs PCT	Rebounds OFF	Rebounds TOT	AST	STL	BLK	PTS	PPG
86-87	PHO	77	1104	148	.476	0	.000	108	.632	87	270	36	24	33	404	5.2
88-89	PHO	2	9	0	.000	0	.000	1	.500	0	1	0	0	0	1	0.5
89-90	CHA	63	941	148	.550	1	1.000	75	.682	75	197	39	35	31	372	5.9
90-91	CHA	72	1552	243	.532	0	.000	164	.661	136	379	44	48	67	650	9.0
91-92	CHA	82	2223	423	.529	0	.000	196	.688	177	580	131	59	69	1042	12.7
92-93	CHA	75	1475	203	.529	0	.000	102	.604	108	353	68	48	55	508	6.8
93-94	CHA	77	1644	233	.524	0	.000	126	.646	105	358	95	59	46	592	7.7
Totals		448	8948	1398	.524	1	.091	772	.654	688	2138	413	273	301	3569	8.0

MATT GEIGER

Team: Miami Heat
Position: Center
Height: 7'0" **Weight:** 245
Birthdate: September 10, 1969

NBA Experience: 2 years
College: Auburn; Georgia Tech
Acquired: 2nd-round pick in 1992 draft (42nd overall)

Background: Geiger made the SEC All-Freshman team and started all 28 games as a sophomore at Auburn. He transferred to Georgia Tech, where his 65 blocked shots as a senior ranked second to John Salley in the school history books. Once considered a lottery-type talent, Geiger slipped to 42nd in the 1992 draft. He played little as a rookie but broke into the team's rotation last season and averaged more than seven points per game.

Strengths: Geiger shoots the ball well for a big man, as reflected in his percentages, and has the ability to put it on the floor when called to do so. His 7'0", 245-pound body was what most attracted scouts, and he is learning to use it a little better in the post. He is willing to bang at both ends of the floor. His size allows him to block shots, although he has not swatted many as a pro. He will rarely take a shot he can't make.

Weaknesses: Geiger does not rebound as well as he should for a player who's seven feet tall. In fact, his rookie year saw him collect more personal fouls than boards. Although he has improved his coordination, he still does not have great control over his massive body. Geiger does not pass well at all from either the low or high post. His awareness of teammates needs work.

Analysis: Geiger seems to be developing nicely for an NBA project. He improved in virtually every category in his second year in the league and his coaches showed more confidence in him by giving him more minutes. He still does not make a whole lot happen, but he cut down on some of the mistakes in his game.

PLAYER SUMMARY

Will ....bang in the post
Can't ....control the glass
Expect ....few bad shots
Don't Expect..................court sense
Fantasy Value $1
Card Value ....5-8¢

COLLEGE STATISTICS

		G	FGP	FTP	RPG	PPG
87-88	AUB	30	.513	.660	4.1	6.4
88-89	AUB	28	.504	.688	6.6	15.9
90-91	GT	27	.549	.671	6.4	11.4
91-92	GT	35	.611	.706	7.3	11.8
Totals		120	.545	.687	6.1	11.4

NBA REGULAR-SEASON STATISTICS

		G	MIN	FGs FG	FGs PCT	3-PT FGs FG	3-PT FGs PCT	FTs FT	FTs PCT	Rebounds OFF	Rebounds TOT	AST	STL	BLK	PTS	PPG
92-93	MIA	48	554	76	.524	0	.000	62	.674	46	120	14	15	18	214	4.5
93-94	MIA	72	1199	202	.574	1	.200	116	.779	119	303	32	36	29	521	7.2
Totals		120	1753	278	.559	1	.111	178	.739	165	423	46	51	47	735	6.1

KENDALL GILL

Team: Seattle SuperSonics
Position: Guard
Height: 6'5" **Weight:** 210
Birthdate: May 25, 1968

NBA Experience: 4 years
College: Illinois
Acquired: Traded from Hornets for
Eddie Johnson and Dana Barros, 9/93

Background: Gill was considered one of the top college guards in the country at
Illinois. He helped the Illini to the Final Four as a junior and the following year
was named a first-team All-Big Ten selection and a UPI first-team All-American.
Gill played in all 82 games as a Charlotte rookie and led the Hornets in scoring
with 20.5 PPG during his second season. He requested a trade in his third year,
and before the 1993-94 season he was shipped to Seattle, where he helped lead
the Sonics to one of their most successful seasons.

Strengths: Gill is a great leaper who plays bigger than his 6'5" height. His
versatility allows him to play both guard slots and he has become a solid leader.
Gill is not afraid to take clutch jumpers and he can shoot them with 3-point range.
He's a well-rounded athlete who plays defense and crashes the boards. He hates
losing.

Weaknesses: Gill is not one of the better outside shooters in the league. His
3-point and free throw percentages are average at best for a guard and he hits
only about 45 percent from the field. He has been known to place a premium on
individual recognition.

Analysis: Gill got what he wanted when he was dealt to Seattle in a deal that
landed Dana Barros in Philadelphia and Hersey Hawkins in Charlotte. The
Sonics made out well too, acquiring a versatile guard who plays to win and
thrives in an up-tempo game. Gill provides scoring, ball-handling, distributing,
rebounding. . . you name it. Better outside shooting could make him a star.

PLAYER SUMMARY

Will ....thrive in transition
Can't ....shoot the lights out
Expect ....backcourt versatility
Don't Expect ....a steady stroke
Fantasy Value............................$14-17
Card Value ....10-20¢

COLLEGE STATISTICS

		G	FGP	FTP	RPG	PPG
86-87	ILL	31	.482	.642	1.4	3.7
87-88	ILL	33	.471	.753	2.2	10.4
88-89	ILL	24	.542	.793	2.9	15.4
89-90	ILL	29	.500	.777	4.9	20.0
Totals		117	.501	.755	2.8	12.0

NBA REGULAR-SEASON STATISTICS

				FGs		3-PT FGs		FTs		Rebounds						
		G	MIN	FG	PCT	FG	PCT	FT	PCT	OFF	TOT	AST	STL	BLK	PTS	PPG
90-91	CHA	82	1944	376	.450	2	.143	152	.835	105	263	303	104	39	906	11.0
91-92	CHA	79	2906	666	.467	6	.240	284	.745	165	402	329	154	46	1622	20.5
92-93	CHA	69	2430	463	.449	17	.274	224	.772	120	340	268	98	36	1167	16.9
93-94	SEA	79	2435	429	.443	38	.317	215	.782	91	268	275	151	32	1111	14.1
Totals		309	9715	1934	.454	63	.285	875	.776	481	1273	1175	507	153	4806	15.6

ARMON GILLIAM

Team: New Jersey Nets
Position: Forward/Center
Height: 6'9" **Weight:** 245
Birthdate: May 28, 1964

NBA Experience: 7 years
College: Independence; UNLV
Acquired: Signed as a free agent, 8/93

Background: As a college senior, Gilliam was a consensus second-team All-American while leading UNLV to the Final Four and averaging 23.2 points and 9.3 rebounds per game. Phoenix took him No. 2 in the 1987 draft and he was an All-Rookie choice. He was traded to Charlotte and then Philadelphia, where he enjoyed a career year in 1991-92. New Jersey signed him after the 1992-93 campaign, and Gilliam averaged about 12 points and six boards per outing last season.

Strengths: A versatile player, Gilliam can play both center and power forward. Nicknamed "The Hammer" for his physical style, he can be unstoppable when he gets the ball in the low post, where he beats opponents with accurate hook shots and turnaround jumpers. He has stretched his shooting range.

Weaknesses: Gilliam is a scorer first and everything else second. Despite his size and strength, he is not a good defender. The knock has always been lack of interest in that phase of the game. He's a poor ball-handler and no better as a passer. He is not among the more consistent big men in the game.

Analysis: Gilliam is an above-average talent who has helped the Nets in a reserve role. He hoisted his shooting accuracy back to the 50-percent range and did a decent job scoring, rebounding, and even playing a little defense. He's been a reliable player in recent years, having seen action in 80 or more games for three straight seasons.

PLAYER SUMMARY	
Will	look to score
Can't	handle the ball
Expect	about 12 PPG
Don't Expect	great defense
Fantasy Value	$5-7
Card Value	5-10¢

COLLEGE STATISTICS

		G	FGP	FTP	RPG	PPG
82-83	IND	38	.621	.632	8.3	16.9
84-85	UNLV	31	.621	.653	6.8	11.9
85-86	UNLV	37	.529	.737	8.5	15.7
86-87	UNLV	39	.600	.728	9.3	23.2
Totals		145	.590	.693	8.3	17.2

NBA REGULAR-SEASON STATISTICS

				FGs		3-PT FGs		FTs		Rebounds						
		G	MIN	FG	PCT	FG	PCT	FT	PCT	OFF	TOT	AST	STL	BLK	PTS	PPG
87-88	PHO	55	1807	342	.475	0	.000	131	.679	134	434	72	58	29	815	14.8
88-89	PHO	74	2120	468	.503	0	.000	240	.743	165	541	52	54	27	1176	15.9
89-90	PHO/CHA	76	2426	484	.515	0	.000	303	.723	211	599	99	69	51	1271	16.7
90-91	CHA/PHI	75	2644	487	.487	0	.000	268	.815	220	598	105	69	53	1242	16.6
91-92	PHI	81	2771	512	.511	0	.000	343	.807	234	660	118	51	85	1367	16.9
92-93	PHI	80	1742	359	.464	0	.000	274	.843	136	472	116	37	54	992	12.4
93-94	NJ	82	1969	348	.510	0	.000	274	.759	197	500	69	38	61	970	11.8
Totals		523	15479	3000	.496	0	.000	1833	.772	1297	3804	631	376	360	7833	15.0

GREG GRAHAM

Team: Philadelphia 76ers
Position: Guard
Height: 6'4" **Weight:** 183
Birthdate: November 26, 1970
NBA Experience: 1 year

College: Indiana
Acquired: Draft rights traded from Hornets with Dana Barros and Sidney Green for Hersey Hawkins, 9/93

Background: A high-profile recruit for Bob Knight, Graham took a couple years to become a dependable player. He helped Indiana to the Final Four as a junior and hit an amazing 51 percent from 3-point land (57 of 111) as a senior. His draft stock shot up with good postseason camps. He was taken 17th by Charlotte, then dealt to Philadelphia before his rookie season. He played in 70 games last season, averaging 4.8 PPG.

Strengths: Graham can trap and press with the best guards and is tough to shake as a one-on-one defensive player. He has come a long way as an offensive player too. He has the quickness to get open for shots and shows potential as a fine long-range shooter. Graham rarely misses from the free throw line. He improved every year in college and has not yet approached his limits.

Weaknesses: Graham is undersized for the NBA and it hurts him in several areas. He gets out-muscled defensively and must work twice as hard at the offensive end to overcome stronger opponents. He's especially small for the off-guard post, yet he lacks the distributing skills to thrive at the point. Graham has not brought his accurate perimeter shot to the pro ranks, making only two of 25 3-point tries last season.

Analysis: The 76ers obtained Graham in the deal that sent Hersey Hawkins to Charlotte before the 1993-94 season. While he is no Hawkins to be sure, Graham did enjoy some fine games despite seeing limited action most of the time. He has the makings of an outstanding up-tempo defender, as he racked up almost as many steals as assists. However, that also says something about his offensive feel.

PLAYER SUMMARY	
Will	pick your pocket
Can't	out-muscle his man
Expect	3-point attempts
Don't Expect	a natural passer
Fantasy Value	$1
Card Value	7-12¢

COLLEGE STATISTICS

		G	FGP	FTP	RPG	PPG
89-90	IND	29	.471	.778	2.6	9.7
90-91	IND	34	.510	.694	2.6	8.7
91-92	IND	34	.502	.741	4.0	12.8
92-93	IND	35	.551	.825	3.2	16.5
Totals		132	.514	.766	3.1	12.0

NBA REGULAR-SEASON STATISTICS

			FGs		3-PT FGs		FTs		Rebounds						
	G	MIN	FG	PCT	FG	PCT	FT	PCT	OFF	TOT	AST	STL	BLK	PTS	PPG
93-94 PHI	70	889	122	.400	2	.080	92	.836	21	86	66	61	4	338	4.8
Totals	70	889	122	.400	2	.080	92	.836	21	86	66	61	4	338	4.8

SNOOPY GRAHAM

Team: Atlanta Hawks
Position: Forward
Height: 6'6" **Weight:** 200
Birthdate: November 28, 1967

NBA Experience: 3 years
College: Ohio
Acquired: Signed as a free agent, 11/91

Background: Paul "Snoopy" Graham led Ohio University in scoring with 22.2 PPG during his final year with the Bobcats. Before the 1991-92 season, he played for the Philadelphia Spirit of the USBL. He has also played in Australia and in the CBA. Atlanta signed him in 1991 and Graham spent his first two years among the team's top six scorers. Last season, however, he played only 128 minutes over 21 games.

Strengths: The unorthodox Graham is capable of putting the ball in the hole. He can be a dangerous outside shooter with 3-point range and can also get to the basket. Graham owns a nice post-up repertoire, largely because he played with his back to the bucket for some of his college career. He spots open men and gets them the ball.

Weaknesses: Graham is a below-average defender who tends to use his hands more than his feet. His wheels simply aren't up to the task of handling the quicker guards. He's also not much help on the boards. Graham does not rank among the better athletes in the league, and you don't want him handling the ball too often against pressure. He's been inconsistent in his play.

Analysis: Graham was waived by the Hawks on Halloween of 1991 only to re-sign a week later. Since then, he has served as both a starter and a bench-warmer during his three years in Atlanta. He played more of the latter role last season, averaging only about six minutes per outing and scoring a career-low 2.8 PPG. He does know how to score and will stick in the NBA for that reason.

PLAYER SUMMARY	
Will	look to score
Can't	shut down his man
Expect	3-point shots
Don't Expect	super speed
Fantasy Value	$0
Card Value	5-10¢

COLLEGE STATISTICS

		G	FGP	FTP	RPG	PPG
85-86	OHIO	29	.480	.773	4.7	15.9
86-87	OHIO	22	.478	.743	5.4	21.1
87-88	OHIO	30	.550	.770	5.1	20.0
88-89	OHIO	29	.520	.811	7.0	22.2
Totals		110	.508	.780	5.5	19.7

NBA REGULAR-SEASON STATISTICS

				FGs		3-PT FGs		FTs		Rebounds						
		G	MIN	FG	PCT	FG	PCT	FT	PCT	OFF	TOT	AST	STL	BLK	PTS	PPG
91-92	ATL	78	1718	305	.447	55	.390	126	.741	72	231	175	96	21	791	10.1
92-93	ATL	80	1508	256	.457	42	.298	96	.733	61	190	164	86	6	650	8.1
93-94	ATL	21	128	21	.368	3	.231	13	.765	4	12	13	4	5	58	2.8
Totals		179	3354	582	.448	100	.339	235	.739	137	433	352	186	32	1499	8.4

GARY GRANT

Team: Los Angeles Clippers
Position: Guard
Height: 6'3" **Weight:** 195
Birthdate: April 21, 1965
NBA Experience: 6 years

College: Michigan
Acquired: Draft rights traded from SuperSonics with a 1989 1st-round pick for Michael Cage, 6/88

Background: A consensus All-American at Michigan, Grant concluded his career as the school's all-time leader in assists and earned Big Ten Defensive Player of the Year honors as a junior. He led all NBA rookies in steals and assists before spending two years in and out of a starting job with the Clippers. Grant spent most of the last two seasons as a back-up to Mark Jackson at the point-guard position.

Strengths: Grant is known as a solid on-the-ball defender with good quickness and instincts. He overcame ankle surgery in 1990 and knee surgery in 1991 with his athletic skills intact. He also has good size, handles the ball well, and is effective in transition. He's reliable on the free throw line.

Weaknesses: Grant's decision-making has long been questioned. Offensively, he does not do enough to warrant starting. He does not penetrate consistently, he rarely gets to the line, and he is not a good enough shooter to justify staying on the perimeter. His 3-point shooting is poor and his field goal accuracy is sub-standard as well.

Analysis: Grant is a fine reserve point guard as a defender and athlete. However, there does not seem to be much chance that he will fulfill the potential he displayed early in his career. He has not enjoyed a double-figure scoring season since his second year in the league and has not improved his shooting much. He does just enough to keep playing in L.A.

PLAYER SUMMARY	
Will	play strong defense
Can't	shoot straight
Expect	reserve minutes
Don't Expect	3-point accuracy
Fantasy Value	$1
Card Value	5-10¢

COLLEGE STATISTICS

		G	FGP	FTP	APG	PPG
84-85	MICH	30	.550	.817	4.7	12.9
85-86	MICH	33	.494	.744	5.6	12.2
86-87	MICH	32	.537	.782	5.4	22.4
87-88	MICH	34	.530	.808	6.9	21.1
Totals		129	.528	.790	5.7	17.2

NBA REGULAR-SEASON STATISTICS

				FGs		3-PT FGs		FTs		Rebounds						
		G	MIN	FG	PCT	FG	PCT	FT	PCT	OFF	TOT	AST	STL	BLK	PTS	PPG
88-89	LAC	71	1924	361	.435	5	.227	119	.735	80	238	506	144	9	846	11.9
89-90	LAC	44	1529	241	.466	5	.238	88	.779	59	195	442	108	5	575	13.1
90-91	LAC	68	2105	265	.451	9	.231	51	.689	69	209	587	103	12	590	8.7
91-92	LAC	78	2049	275	.462	15	.294	44	.815	34	184	538	138	14	609	7.8
92-93	LAC	74	1624	210	.441	11	.262	55	.743	27	139	353	106	15	486	6.6
93-94	LAC	78	1533	253	.449	17	.274	65	.855	42	142	291	119	12	588	7.5
Totals		413	10764	1605	.450	62	.262	422	.763	311	1107	2717	718	61	3694	8.9

HARVEY GRANT

Team: Portland Trail Blazers
Position: Forward
Height: 6'9" **Weight:** 225
Birthdate: July 4, 1965
NBA Experience: 6 years

College: Clemson; Independence; Oklahoma
Acquired: Traded from Bullets for Kevin Duckworth, 6/93

Background: Harvey is the identical twin brother of the Bulls' Horace Grant. The two enrolled together at Clemson, but they were competing for the same spot and Harvey transferred to Oklahoma. He led the Sooners to the NCAA title game in 1988. He was a disappointment with Washington in his first two seasons but he totaled 18-plus PPG in his next three years. A trade sent Grant to Portland in 1993-94 and his scoring slipped to 10.4 PPG.

Strengths: Grant is one of the hardest-working and most coachable players you'll encounter. He possesses a good outside shot with range up to 20 feet, and his lean, wiry body is perfect for running the court. He's a fine passer from his forward slot. Grant has good lateral quickness on defense and works hard at that end of the floor.

Weaknesses: Harvey is not as muscular as Horace and not as effective in the paint. His low-post offense is not nearly as refined. He has been accused of playing soft and staying away from the boards. Off-season surgery on his right wrist may hamper him early this season.

Analysis: Harvey has not received the notoriety of his brother, and with the Blazers he is not likely to stand out as he did with the less-talented Bullets. Expect him to improve on last season's numbers, however, as his style is a perfect fit for the up-tempo Western Conference. Portland made out well on a trade that helped them unload an unproductive Kevin Duckworth.

PLAYER SUMMARY

Will	get out on the break
Can't	dominate the boards
Expect	all-out effort
Don't Expect	Horace's acclaim
Fantasy Value	$5-7
Card Value	7-12¢

COLLEGE STATISTICS

		G	FGP	FTP	RPG	PPG
84-85	CLEM	28	.496	.585	4.5	5.1
85-86	IND	33	.586	.707	11.8	22.4
86-87	OKLA	34	.534	.730	9.9	16.9
87-88	OKLA	39	.547	.729	9.4	20.9
Totals		134	.553	.712	9.1	17.0

NBA REGULAR-SEASON STATISTICS

		G	MIN	FGs FG	FGs PCT	3-PT FGs FG	3-PT FGs PCT	FTs FT	FTs PCT	Rebounds OFF	Rebounds TOT	AST	STL	BLK	PTS	PPG
88-89	WAS	71	1193	181	.464	0	.000	34	.596	75	163	79	35	29	396	5.6
89-90	WAS	81	1846	284	.473	0	.000	96	.701	138	342	131	52	43	664	8.2
90-91	WAS	77	2842	609	.498	2	.133	185	.743	179	557	204	91	61	1405	18.2
91-92	WAS	64	2388	489	.478	1	.125	176	.800	157	432	170	74	27	1155	18.0
92-93	WAS	72	2667	560	.487	1	.100	218	.727	133	412	205	72	44	1339	18.6
93-94	POR	77	2112	356	.460	2	.286	84	.641	109	351	107	70	49	798	10.4
Totals		442	13048	2479	.480	6	.122	793	.725	791	2257	896	394	253	5757	13.0

HORACE GRANT

Team: Orlando Magic
Position: Forward
Height: 6'10" **Weight:** 235
Birthdate: July 4, 1965

NBA Experience: 7 years
College: Clemson
Acquired: Signed as a free agent, 7/94

Background: In his senior season at Clemson, Grant was the ACC Player of the Year after averaging 21.0 PPG. The Bulls were fortunate in getting Scottie Pippen (fifth) and Grant (tenth) in the 1987 draft. Grant played a key role on Chicago's three straight NBA championship teams, annually ranking among the league leaders in field goal percentage. Grant played in his first NBA All-Star Game last season and scored at a career-high clip. He signed a free-agent deal with Orlando in July.

Strengths: Grant stands among the most talented and athletic power forwards in the game. He's a quick leaper who can outrun most power forwards while still holding his own in the strength department. He's in his element in the open court, and he has become a fine post scorer and passer. He's a stellar defender who will block shots.

Weaknesses: Grant has limited range and he is a poor free throw shooter. He questioned his role in Chicago's offense in past seasons, and last year he openly campaigned for another team to sign him away from the Bulls.

Analysis: Grant is one of the hardest-working players in basketball, and his talents are appreciated by teammates, fans, and opponents alike. He did not feel the Bulls appreciated him, however, in delaying contract negotiations and he became an unrestricted free agent. Grant will help take Orlando to another level and will likely make another All-Star appearance or two.

PLAYER SUMMARY

Will	work his tail off
Can't	shoot FTs
Expect	15 PPG
Don't Expect	bad shots
Fantasy Value	$20-25
Card Value	8-15¢

COLLEGE STATISTICS

		G	FGP	FTP	RPG	PPG
83-84	CLEM	28	.533	.744	4.6	5.7
84-85	CLEM	29	.555	.637	6.8	11.3
85-86	CLEM	34	.584	.725	10.5	16.4
86-87	CLEM	31	.656	.708	9.6	21.0
Totals		122	.598	.704	8.0	13.9

NBA REGULAR-SEASON STATISTICS

				FGs		3-PT FGs		FTs		Rebounds						
		G	MIN	FG	PCT	FG	PCT	FT	PCT	OFF	TOT	AST	STL	BLK	PTS	PPG
87-88	CHI	81	1827	254	.501	0	.000	114	.626	155	447	89	51	53	622	7.7
88-89	CHI	79	2809	405	.519	0	.000	140	.704	240	681	168	86	62	950	12.0
89-90	CHI	80	2753	446	.523	0	.000	179	.699	236	629	227	92	84	1071	13.4
90-91	CHI	78	2641	401	.547	1	.167	197	.711	266	659	178	95	69	1000	12.8
91-92	CHI	81	2859	457	.578	0	.000	235	.741	344	807	217	100	131	1149	14.2
92-93	CHI	77	2745	421	.508	1	.200	174	.619	341	729	201	89	96	1017	13.2
93-94	CHI	70	2570	460	.524	0	.000	137	.596	306	769	236	74	84	1057	15.1
Totals		546	18204	2844	.530	2	.077	1176	.675	1888	4721	1316	587	579	6866	12.6

JEFF GRAYER

Team: Golden State Warriors
Position: Guard/Forward
Height: 6'5" **Weight:** 210
Birthdate: December 17, 1965

NBA Experience: 6 years
College: Iowa St.
Acquired: Signed as a free agent, 7/92

Background: This second-team All-American became Iowa State's all-time leading scorer and played on the 1988 U.S. Olympic team. Milwaukee drafted Grayer in the first round in 1988, but he missed most of his first year with a knee injury and never averaged double figures in four years with the Bucks. Golden State signed him in July 1992, but left knee surgery cut his 1992-93 season in half. He returned to play in 67 games last year.

Strengths: Grayer brings good defensive ability, athletic skills, and versatility to the court. He knows how to shake free and go to the hoop with a variety of moves. He's also a decent ball-handler and can rack up points posting up. He hit a career-high .526 from the field last season because he improved his shot selection.

Weaknesses: Grayer's outside jumper is awkward-looking and inconsistent. His free throw shooting is also sub-par and he's no threat from 3-point range. Grayer penetrates but will not be mistaken for a point guard because of his passing. He's turnover-prone and has never reached his scoring potential.

Analysis: Grayer is a role-player who is ideally suited to coming off the bench. He can defend at multiple positions and will not hurt his team offensively. Even though his 6.8 PPG last season was the second-lowest average of his career, Golden State's coaches were thrilled to see his shooting percentage top the .500 mark for the first time.

PLAYER SUMMARY

Will..................................play defense
Can't.................................shoot FTs
Expect..............................versatility
Don't Expect..................10-plus PPG
Fantasy Value..........................$0
Card Value...........................5-8¢

COLLEGE STATISTICS

		G	FGP	FTP	RPG	PPG
84-85	ISU	33	.529	.653	6.5	12.2
85-86	ISU	33	.547	.629	6.3	20.7
86-87	ISU	27	.504	.740	7.0	22.4
87-88	ISU	32	.523	.711	9.4	25.3
Totals		125	.526	.686	7.3	20.0

NBA REGULAR-SEASON STATISTICS

		G	MIN	FGs FG	FGs PCT	3-PT FGs FG	3-PT FGs PCT	FTs FT	FTs PCT	Rebounds OFF	Rebounds TOT	AST	STL	BLK	PTS	PPG
88-89	MIL	11	200	32	.438	0	.000	17	.850	14	35	22	10	1	81	7.4
89-90	MIL	71	1427	224	.460	1	.125	99	.651	94	217	107	48	10	548	7.7
90-91	MIL	82	1422	210	.433	0	.000	101	.687	111	246	123	48	9	521	6.4
91-92	MIL	82	1659	309	.448	19	.288	102	.667	129	257	150	64	13	739	9.0
92-93	GS	48	1025	165	.467	2	.143	91	.669	71	157	70	31	8	423	8.8
93-94	GS	67	1096	191	.526	2	.167	71	.602	76	191	62	33	13	455	6.8
Totals		361	6829	1131	.462	24	.229	481	.663	495	1103	534	234	54	2767	7.7

A.C. GREEN

Team: Phoenix Suns
Position: Forward
Height: 6'9" **Weight:** 225
Birthdate: October 4, 1963

NBA Experience: 9 years
College: Oregon St.
Acquired: Signed as a free agent, 9/93

Background: Green was named Pac-10 Player of the Year as a junior at Oregon State and wound up his career as the school's second-leading rebounder and third-leading scorer. He led the Lakers in rebounding four straight years from 1986-90, and he was voted a starter in the 1989-90 All-Star Game. He was signed as a free agent by Phoenix in September 1993 and scored at a career-high pace last season.

Strengths: A hard-working player, Green rebounds, scores, and gets to the line. He is a fine outside shooter and is not afraid to go inside. He's an aggressive defender, runs the floor, and provides great durability. He has played all 82 games in eight of his nine seasons.

Weaknesses: Green does not create as much as he feeds off his teammates. A lot of his points come on putbacks and "garbage" buckets. He doesn't have great shooting range.

Analysis: Green probably will never play in another All-Star Game, but his play has been extremely valuable to the Lakers and now the Suns. He is a coach's dream, the kind of player who will go all-out in whatever role he's placed. He has not missed a game in more than seven years. He's a spokesman for the community group "Athletes for Abstinence."

PLAYER SUMMARY	
Will	crash the boards
Can't	stick 3-pointers
Expect	all-out hustle
Don't Expect	creativity
Fantasy Value	$12-15
Card Value	5-10¢

COLLEGE STATISTICS

		G	FGP	FTP	RPG	PPG
81-82	OSU	30	.615	.610	5.3	8.6
82-83	OSU	31	.559	.689	7.6	14.0
83-84	OSU	23	.657	.770	8.7	17.8
84-85	OSU	31	.599	.680	9.2	19.1
Totals		115	.602	.696	7.7	14.7

NBA REGULAR-SEASON STATISTICS

				FGs		3-PT FGs		FTs		Rebounds						
		G	MIN	FG	PCT	FG	PCT	FT	PCT	OFF	TOT	AST	STL	BLK	PTS	PPG
85-86	LAL	82	1542	209	.539	1	.167	102	.611	160	381	54	49	49	521	6.4
86-87	LAL	79	2240	316	.538	0	.000	220	.780	210	615	84	70	80	852	10.8
87-88	LAL	82	2636	322	.503	0	.000	293	.773	245	710	93	87	45	937	11.4
88-89	LAL	82	2510	401	.529	4	.235	282	.786	258	739	103	94	55	1088	13.3
89-90	LAL	82	2709	385	.478	13	.283	278	.751	262	712	90	66	50	1061	12.9
90-91	LAL	82	2164	258	.476	11	.200	223	.738	201	516	71	59	23	750	9.1
91-92	LAL	82	2902	382	.476	12	.214	340	.744	306	762	117	91	36	1116	13.6
92-93	LAL	82	2819	379	.537	16	.348	277	.739	287	711	116	88	39	1051	12.8
93-94	PHO	82	2825	465	.502	8	.229	266	.735	275	753	137	70	38	1204	14.7
Totals		735	22347	3117	.506	65	.243	2281	.747	2204	5899	865	674	415	8580	11.7

TOM GUGLIOTTA

Team: Washington Bullets
Position: Forward
Height: 6'10" **Weight:** 240
Birthdate: December 19, 1969

NBA Experience: 2 years
College: North Carolina St.
Acquired: 1st-round pick in 1992 draft (6th overall)

Background: "Googs" started 92 games during his North Carolina State career and became the third Wolfpack player to record 1,500 points and 800 rebounds in a career. He led the ACC in rebounding and 3-pointers per game as a senior. His father was a high school coach and two of his brothers played professionally in Europe. There was some groaning when the Bullets drafted him sixth overall, but he was a first-team All-Rookie performer and improved on his first-year numbers in 1993-94.

Strengths: Gugliotta has been compared to Larry Bird by none other than Michael Jordan and Pat Riley. That's because he does a little bit of everything. He shoots with range, finds open men, rebounds, handles the ball, plays tough defense, and runs the floor. He has started at guard, forward, and center and is a natural leader. Gugliotta led the Bullets in boards by a wide margin last season.

Weaknesses: Gugliotta does not have a great arsenal of inside moves. His skills are better suited to the role of small forward than any of the other positions he's asked to play. He needs to develop a power game and hoist his field goal and free throw percentages. He takes far too many 3-point attempts for his conversion rate. He turns the ball over frequently.

Analysis: Gugliotta followed up his surprising rookie year with an even more productive season in 1993-94. He has become a team leader in a flash, and why not? His array of skills can be matched by few others in the league. The Bird comparisons remain premature, but the Bullets appear to have a future franchise-type player in this hard-working youngster. His teammates respect him, as do his opponents.

PLAYER SUMMARY

Will ....score, rebound
Can't..............thrive from long range
Expect ....leadership, versatility
Don't Expect ....high percentages
Fantasy Value...........................$40-45
Card Value ....20-40¢

COLLEGE STATISTICS

		G	FGP	FTP	RPG	PPG
88-89	NCST	21	.429	.655	1.7	2.7
89-90	NCST	30	.504	.672	7.0	11.1
90-91	NCST	31	.500	.644	9.1	15.2
91-92	NCST	30	.449	.685	9.8	22.5
Totals		112	.476	.668	7.3	13.7

NBA REGULAR-SEASON STATISTICS

		G	MIN	FGs FG	FGs PCT	3-PT FGs FG	3-PT FGs PCT	FTs FT	FTs PCT	Rebounds OFF	Rebounds TOT	AST	STL	BLK	PTS	PPG
92-93	WAS	81	2795	484	.426	38	.281	181	.644	219	781	306	134	35	1187	14.7
93-94	WAS	78	2795	540	.466	40	.270	213	.685	189	728	276	172	51	1333	17.1
Totals		159	5590	1024	.446	78	.276	394	.666	408	1509	582	306	86	2520	15.8

TOM HAMMONDS

Team: Denver Nuggets
Position: Forward
Height: 6'9" **Weight:** 225
Birthdate: March 27, 1967

NBA Experience: 5 years
College: Georgia Tech
Acquired: Signed as a free agent, 2/93

Background: Hammonds was a third-team All-American as a senior at Georgia Tech. Though taken No. 9 by Washington in the 1989 draft, Hammonds has played sparingly in his five NBA years. His best year was with the Bullets and Hornets in 1991-92, and he signed with Denver during the 1992-93 season. He averaged only about four PPG with the Nuggets last season.

Strengths: Hammonds has a weight room-sculpted, NBA body. He showed flashes of scoring and rebounding ability early in 1991-92, before he was traded for Rex Chapman and subsequently suffered a season-ending groin injury. He hits the defensive glass and is capable of blocking shots. He won't throw up many bad shots.

Weaknesses: Hammonds is a classic "tweener." He is not wide or strong enough to thrive at power forward, yet his skills facing the basket are not where they need to be for the three spot. He has not shown an ability to put the ball on the floor, nor does he pass the ball well. He's often a victim of match-up problems on defense. He tends to be lost in the shuffle.

Analysis: Inconsistent play and a lot of time on the bench have characterized the career of Hammonds, who was considered one of the best talents to come out of the Atlantic Coast Conference. Now he is easily overlooked. Injuries have helped slow his progress, but his biggest problem has been his inability to establish himself at a position. He continues to play spot roles where needed, but not much more.

PLAYER SUMMARY

Will..............show promising flashes
Can't ....gain steady minutes
Expect.....................inconsistent play
Don't Expect ....10 PPG
Fantasy Value $0
Card Value ....5-8¢

COLLEGE STATISTICS

		G	FGP	FTP	RPG	PPG
85-86	GT	34	.609	.816	6.4	12.2
86-87	GT	29	.569	.797	7.2	16.2
87-88	GT	30	.568	.826	7.2	18.9
88-89	GT	30	.538	.773	8.1	20.9
Totals		123	.566	.801	7.2	16.9

NBA REGULAR-SEASON STATISTICS

				FGs		3-PT FGs		FTs		Rebounds						
		G	MIN	FG	PCT	FG	PCT	FT	PCT	OFF	TOT	AST	STL	BLK	PTS	PPG
89-90	WAS	61	805	129	.437	0	.000	63	.643	61	168	51	11	14	321	5.3
90-91	WAS	70	1023	155	.461	0	.000	57	.722	58	206	43	15	7	367	5.2
91-92	WAS/CHA	37	984	195	.488	0	.000	50	.610	49	185	36	22	13	440	11.9
92-93	CHA/DEN	54	713	105	.475	0	.000	38	.613	38	127	24	18	12	248	4.6
93-94	DEN	74	877	115	.500	0	.000	71	.683	62	199	34	20	12	301	4.1
Totals		296	4402	699	.472	0	.000	279	.656	268	885	188	86	58	1677	5.7

ANFERNEE HARDAWAY

Team: Orlando Magic
Position: Guard
Height: 6'7" **Weight:** 195
Birthdate: July 18, 1972
NBA Experience: 1 year

College: Memphis St.
Acquired: Draft rights traded from Warriors with 1996, 1998, and 2000 1st-round picks for draft rights to Chris Webber, 6/93

Background: Hardaway was *Parade's* 1989-90 national High School Player of the Year, after averaging nearly 37 PPG at Memphis Treadwell. However, he sat out his freshman year at Memphis State under Prop 48 requirements, then suffered a gunshot wound in his right foot in the summer of 1991. He recovered and became his conference's Player of the Year in 1991-92 and 1992-93. He was drafted No. 3 by Golden State but was immediately dealt to Orlando, where he was among the premier NBA rookies last season.

Strengths: "Penny" has been compared to Magic Johnson, and not without reason. He has great size for a point guard, which allows him to see the floor and spot open men. He directs the fastbreak with authority, handles the ball deftly, and knows how to get off his shot in traffic. He can also post up and has superior defensive quickness. He is a more productive pro scorer than some expected. "Pennies for Penny's Pals" raises money for charity.

Weaknesses: Hardaway coughed up the ball far too often last season, but that's a mistake that plagues most rookies. He also did not convert a high percentage of his 3-point attempts. His perimeter shooting needs to become more consistent. He could also stand to add some muscle.

Analysis: In one season, Hardaway has shown signs of superstardom. He finished the 1993-94 campaign among rookie leaders in virtually every category, helped Orlando reach the playoffs for the first time, and sold tickets with his exciting brand of basketball. You can tell in just a few minutes of viewing that he's grown up with a basketball in his hands. With Hardaway and Shaquille O'Neal, Orlando has one of the best inside-outside combinations in the league.

PLAYER SUMMARY	
Will	trigger the break
Can't	push people around
Expect	an All-Star future
Don't Expect	a slow pace
Fantasy Value	$45-50
Card Value	$1.00-3.00

COLLEGE STATISTICS

		G	FGP	FTP	APG	PPG
91-92	MSU	34	.433	.652	5.5	17.4
92-93	MSU	32	.477	.767	6.4	22.8
Totals		66	.456	.717	5.9	20.0

NBA REGULAR-SEASON STATISTICS

			FGs		3-PT FGs		FTs		Rebounds						
	G	MIN	FG	PCT	FG	PCT	FT	PCT	OFF	TOT	AST	STL	BLK	PTS	PPG
93-94 ORL	82	3015	509	.466	50	.267	245	.742	192	439	544	190	51	1313	16.0
Totals	82	3015	509	.466	50	.267	245	.742	192	439	544	190	51	1313	16.0

TIM HARDAWAY

Team: Golden State Warriors
Position: Guard
Height: 6'0" **Weight:** 195
Birthdate: September 12, 1966

NBA Experience: 4 years
College: Texas-El Paso
Acquired: 1st-round pick in 1989 draft
(14th overall)

Background: Hardaway surpassed Nate Archibald as the all-time scoring leader at the University of Texas-El Paso. In 1989-90, he led all rookies in assists and steals while directing the high-powered Golden State offense. Hardaway has since appeared in three All-Star Games. He sat out the entire 1993-94 campaign after surgery to his left knee. He was earlier selected to play internationally with Dream Team II.

Strengths: Few can handle the ball like Hardaway. His between-the-legs crossover dribble, dubbed the "UTEP two-step," mesmerizes even the best of defenders and usually opens a clear lane to the basket. His long-range shot is unorthodox but he shoots it with 3-point range. Hardaway is a quick, effective floor leader who gets the ball into the right hands, which are often his own. He is also solid on defense.

Weaknesses: Knee injuries have put a halt to Hardaway's heroics recently. When healthy, his small frame makes him vulnerable against bigger guards, especially on defense. His shooting percentage is not great and he takes a few too many chances defensively.

Analysis: Hardaway is a bona fide superstar. Without him, the Warriors are nowhere near the team they are when he's healthy. The king of the crossover dribble certainly ranks among the best and most explosive point guards in the game. The ball is attached to his hand. Doctors expect him to bounce back from his knee problems, although it may take a while to shake the rust off.

PLAYER SUMMARY

Will	control the ball
Can't	trade in his knees
Expect	court savvy
Don't Expect	a slow tempo
Fantasy Value	$20-25
Card Value	15-30¢

COLLEGE STATISTICS

		G	FGP	FTP	APG	PPG
85-86	UTEP	28	.521	.651	1.9	4.1
86-87	UTEP	31	.490	.663	4.8	10.0
87-88	UTEP	32	.449	.754	5.7	13.6
88-89	UTEP	33	.501	.741	5.4	22.0
Totals		124	.484	.718	4.5	12.8

NBA REGULAR-SEASON STATISTICS

				FGs		3-PT FGs		FTs		Rebounds						
		G	MIN	FG	PCT	FG	PCT	FT	PCT	OFF	TOT	AST	STL	BLK	PTS	PPG
89-90	GS	79	2663	464	.471	23	.274	211	.764	57	310	689	165	12	1162	14.7
90-91	GS	82	3215	739	.476	97	.385	306	.803	87	332	793	214	12	1881	22.9
91-92	GS	81	3332	734	.461	127	.338	298	.766	81	310	807	164	13	1893	23.4
92-93	GS	66	2609	522	.447	102	.330	273	.744	60	263	699	116	12	1419	21.5
Totals		308	11819	2459	.464	349	.342	1088	.770	285	1215	2988	659	49	6355	20.6

DEREK HARPER

Team: New York Knicks
Position: Guard
Height: 6'4" **Weight:** 206
Birthdate: October 13, 1961
NBA Experience: 11 years

College: Illinois
Acquired: Traded from Mavericks for Tony Campbell and a 1997 1st-round pick, 1/94

Background: Harper led the Big Ten in steals for two straight years, then declared for the NBA draft after his junior season. He was the first player in league history to improve his scoring average in each of his first eight years. He was traded to New York in January 1994 and was a part-time starter for the Atlantic Division champs last season.

Strengths: A respected all-around talent who plays both guard spots, Harper has good quickness and great reach and is willing to play belly-up defense. He is a solid 3-point shooter and a veteran leader who gives all he's got every night. He is not afraid to take the clutch shots.

Weaknesses: Carrying the hapless Mavs wore Harper down. His shooting has not been steady in the last two years and he was not among New York's first scoring options after the trade.

Analysis: The Knicks dealt Tony Campbell and a No. 1 pick for Harper because they thought he could help them contend for the title. That says something about the respect Harper and his all-around abilities have earned. He is not the player he once was, but he still provides some outside punch and a competitive spirit.

PLAYER SUMMARY	
Will	take clutch shots
Can't	score like in Dallas
Expect	veteran leadership
Don't Expect	huge numbers
Fantasy Value	$2-4
Card Value	7-12¢

COLLEGE STATISTICS

		G	FGP	FTP	APG	PPG
80-81	ILL	29	.413	.717	5.4	8.3
81-82	ILL	29	.457	.756	5.0	8.4
82-83	ILL	32	.537	.675	3.7	15.4
Totals		90	.478	.701	4.7	10.9

NBA REGULAR-SEASON STATISTICS

				FGs		3-PT FGs		FTs		Rebounds						
		G	MIN	FG	PCT	FG	PCT	FT	PCT	OFF	TOT	AST	STL	BLK	PTS	PPG
83-84	DAL	82	1712	200	.443	3	.115	66	.673	53	172	239	95	21	469	5.7
84-85	DAL	82	2218	329	.520	21	.344	111	.721	47	199	360	144	37	790	9.6
85-86	DAL	79	2150	390	.534	12	.235	171	.747	75	226	416	153	23	963	12.2
86-87	DAL	77	2556	497	.501	76	.358	160	.684	51	199	609	167	25	1230	16.0
87-88	DAL	82	3032	536	.459	60	.313	261	.759	71	246	634	168	35	1404	17.0
88-89	DAL	81	2968	538	.477	99	.356	229	.806	46	228	570	172	41	1404	17.3
89-90	DAL	82	3007	567	.488	89	.371	250	.794	54	244	609	187	26	1473	18.0
90-91	DAL	77	2879	572	.467	89	.362	286	.731	59	233	548	147	14	1519	19.7
91-92	DAL	65	2252	448	.443	58	.312	198	.759	49	170	373	101	17	1152	17.7
92-93	DAL	62	2108	393	.419	101	.393	239	.756	42	123	334	80	16	1126	18.2
93-94	DAL/NY	82	2204	303	.407	73	.360	112	.687	20	141	334	125	8	791	9.6
Totals		851	27086	4773	.469	681	.349	2083	.747	567	2181	5026	1539	263	12310	14.5

RON HARPER

Unrestricted Free Agent
Last Team: Los Angeles Clippers
Position: Guard
Height: 6'6" **Weight:** 198
Birthdate: January 20, 1964
NBA Experience: 8 years

College: Miami (OH)
Acquired: Traded from Cavaliers with 1990 and 1992 1st-round picks and a 1991 2nd-round pick for Reggie Williams and draft rights to Danny Ferry, 11/89

Background: Harper left Miami of Ohio with the all-time Mid-American Conference scoring record and finished second in Rookie of the Year voting with Cleveland. He was traded to the Clippers in November 1989, but his first campaign there was cut short when he tore the anterior cruciate ligament in his right knee. Harper returned for the second half of the 1990-91 season and has regained his form. He left the Clippers as a free agent after last season.

Strengths: Harper is a big-time scorer who can excite a crowd. He is a dominant open-court player with slashing moves to the hoop and tremendous finishing ability. He's a nifty passer and a natural leader with supreme confidence. He rebounds and even blocks shots.

Weaknesses: Poor shot selection has been a career-long knock on Harper, who does not shoot for a high percentage. He is more a scorer than a shooter. Harper, like others before him, expressed discontent with the Clippers.

Analysis: Harper was one of the main reasons the Clippers reached the playoffs two of the last three years. He averaged 20 PPG for the third time in his career last season. With a more consistent outside shot and a steadier hand, Harper could be a marquee player.

PLAYER SUMMARY	
Will	get to the hoop
Can't	make Clips contenders
Expect	18-20 PPG
Don't Expect	great shooting
Fantasy Value	$35-40
Card Value	5-10¢

COLLEGE STATISTICS

		G	FGP	FTP	RPG	PPG
82-83	MIA	28	.497	.674	7.0	12.9
83-84	MIA	30	.537	.570	7.6	14.9
84-85	MIA	31	.541	.661	10.7	24.9
85-86	MIA	31	.545	.665	11.7	24.4
Totals		120	.534	.642	9.3	19.5

NBA REGULAR-SEASON STATISTICS

		G	MIN	FGs FG	FGs PCT	3-PT FGs FG	3-PT FGs PCT	FTs FT	FTs PCT	Rebounds OFF	Rebounds TOT	AST	STL	BLK	PTS	PPG
86-87	CLE	82	3064	734	.455	20	.213	386	.684	169	392	394	209	84	1874	22.9
87-88	CLE	57	1830	340	.464	3	.150	196	.705	64	223	281	122	52	879	15.4
88-89	CLE	82	2851	587	.511	29	.250	323	.751	122	409	434	185	74	1526	18.6
89-90	CLE/LAC	35	1367	301	.473	14	.275	182	.788	74	206	182	81	41	798	22.8
90-91	LAC	39	1383	285	.391	48	.324	145	.668	58	188	209	66	35	763	19.6
91-92	LAC	82	3144	569	.440	64	.303	293	.736	120	447	417	152	72	1495	18.2
92-93	LAC	80	2970	542	.451	52	.280	307	.769	117	425	360	177	73	1443	18.0
93-94	LAC	75	2856	569	.426	71	.301	299	.715	129	460	344	144	54	1508	20.1
Totals		532	19465	3927	.452	301	.283	2131	.726	853	2750	2621	1136	485	10286	19.3

LUCIOUS HARRIS

Team: Dallas Mavericks
Position: Guard
Height: 6'5" **Weight:** 190
Birthdate: December 18, 1970

NBA Experience: 1 year
College: Long Beach St.
Acquired: 2nd-round pick in 1993 draft (28th overall)

Background: Harris completed his four years at Long Beach State as the leading scorer in Big West history. He averaged 23.1 PPG as a senior and earned all-conference first-team honors in each of his last two seasons. He was the first pick in the second round of the 1993 draft, ahead of college teammate Bryon Russell (Utah). Harris came off the bench in 77 games with Dallas and averaged 5.4 PPG.

Strengths: Harris is known for his long-range shooting skills. He has range beyond the NBA 3-point arc and a quick release. He can be deadly when coming off a screen or pulling up in transition. Harris has good size for a guard and is not afraid to help out on the boards. He's a willing passer and has worked on his defense. His work habits have drawn compliments.

Weaknesses: Besides shooting, nothing about Harris truly grabs your attention. He does not have great quickness and is not able to get his shot off with a defender in front of him. He's more the catch-and-shoot type. Though he has the range, he couldn't hit from downtown consistently last year. Harris also lacks the ball-handling and passing abilities of most NBA guards, and thus will rarely be asked to play the point. He has much to learn about man-to-man defense.

Analysis: Harris did a nice job at times off the Dallas bench, once scoring 16 points in a game and averaging more than two boards per game from the backcourt. His size and shooting ability have Dallas brass optimistic that he will develop into a first round-type talent. There are several holes in his game, but at least with the struggling Mavericks he'll be able to earn time to work on his deficiencies.

PLAYER SUMMARY	
Will	hit the trey
Can't	handle the point
Expect	backcourt rebounds
Don't Expect	great defense
Fantasy Value	$0
Card Value	8-12¢

COLLEGE STATISTICS

		G	FGP	FTP	RPG	PPG
89-90	LBS	32	.430	.694	4.8	14.3
90-91	LBS	28	.396	.700	4.7	19.7
91-92	LBS	30	.471	.734	4.3	18.8
92-93	LBS	32	.525	.774	5.3	23.1
Totals		122	.458	.727	4.8	19.0

NBA REGULAR-SEASON STATISTICS

			FGs		3-PT FGs		FTs		Rebounds						
	G	MIN	FG	PCT	FG	PCT	FT	PCT	OFF	TOT	AST	STL	BLK	PTS	PPG
93-94 DAL	77	1165	162	.421	7	.212	87	.731	45	157	106	49	10	418	5.4
Totals	77	1165	162	.421	7	.212	87	.731	45	157	106	49	10	418	5.4

SCOTT HASKIN

Team: Indiana Pacers
Position: Forward/Center
Height: 6'11" **Weight:** 250
Birthdate: September 19, 1970

NBA Experience: 1 year
College: Oregon St.
Acquired: 1st-round pick in 1993 draft
(14th overall)

Background: Stashed in Corvallis, Oregon, Haskin enjoyed a nice college career without any fanfare. He wasn't much as a freshman or sophomore, and he missed the 1990-91 season because of a back injury that required surgery. However, he made the All-Pac-10 team and led the league in blocked shots his last two years. He was drafted 14th by the Pacers but missed much of his rookie year with a knee injury.

Strengths: A general manager once called Haskin a poor man's Kevin McHale. He is an agile athlete who can help a team on both ends. He can face the basket and score or back in and hook with either hand. Quick feet and good timing serve him well as a shot-blocker, and he runs the court efficiently. He has good size and has demonstrated some toughness.

Weaknesses: Some question whether Haskin is physically strong enough to bang with NBA centers on a nightly basis. There's no telling from a rookie year in which he played only 186 minutes. He will not be a big scorer unless he vastly expands both his low-post moves and his shooting range. He's a poor free throw shooter, passer, and ball-handler. He's seen his share of the bench.

Analysis: Haskin is hardly an impact player and was probably drafted too high. Even before tearing ligaments in his right knee in February, he was not earning much playing time with an Indiana team that featured a lot of young frontcourt talent. The biggest thing Haskin has going for him is the ability to block shots, and he will likely serve that role as a back-up at both center and power forward. The rest of his game, however, needs a lot of work.

PLAYER SUMMARY

Will.............................block shots
Can't.....................get off the bench
Expect............................limited action
Don't Expect ....much scoring
Fantasy Value $0
Card Value ....8-12¢

COLLEGE STATISTICS

		G	FGP	FTP	RPG	PPG
88-89	OSU	24	.492	.571	2.5	3.1
89-90	OSU	29	.497	.785	4.8	8.2
91-92	OSU	31	.613	.779	6.5	18.0
92-93	OSU	27	.521	.645	8.1	16.7
Totals		111	.550	.711	5.6	11.9

NBA REGULAR-SEASON STATISTICS

				FGs		3-PT FGs		FTs		Rebounds						
		G	MIN	FG	PCT	FG	PCT	FT	PCT	OFF	TOT	AST	STL	BLK	PTS	PPG
93-94	IND	27	186	21	.467	0	.000	13	.684	17	55	6	2	15	55	2.0
Totals		27	186	21	.467	0	.000	13	.684	17	55	6	2	15	55	2.0

HERSEY HAWKINS

Team: Charlotte Hornets
Position: Guard
Height: 6'3" **Weight:** 190
Birthdate: September 29, 1966
NBA Experience: 6 years

College: Bradley
Acquired: Traded from 76ers for Dana Barros, Sidney Green, draft rights to Greg Graham, and a 1994 1st-round pick, 9/93

Background: Hawkins went from being a 6'3", all-city center at Westinghouse High School in Chicago to an outside gunner at Bradley. As a senior, he led the nation in scoring and was named the nation's Player of the Year. He left college as the fourth-leading scorer in NCAA history. After three years among the NBA's top 25 in scoring, the former All-Star was traded last year from Philadelphia to Charlotte in a three-way swap also involving Seattle.

Strengths: Hawkins is one of the more dangerous 3-point shooters in the league. He can dishearten the opposition by landing his bombs in rapid succession. He knows how to get to the hoop and has improved his overall floor game. He is close to automatic from the free throw line. Hawkins does not slack off on defense and also grabs some rebounds.

Weaknesses: Hawkins is probably not an All-Star player on a good team. He is overshadowed in Charlotte by stars like Alonzo Mourning and Larry Johnson. His scoring average has declined on his new team. Hawkins is not among the better passing and ball-handling guards in the league.

Analysis: Hawkins plays hard and can kill you with his jump shot. Leave him open for an instant and the former Sixer will drill shots with range up to 25 feet. His average dipped on a Charlotte team already stocked with scorers, but Hawkins helped out as a defender and backcourt rebounder almost as much as he did as a shooter.

PLAYER SUMMARY	
Will	shoot with range
Can't	be the star in Charlotte
Expect	hustle at both ends
Don't Expect	5 APG
Fantasy Value.	$25-30
Card Value	7-12¢

COLLEGE STATISTICS

		G	FGP	FTP	RPG	PPG
84-85	BRAD	30	.581	.771	6.1	14.6
85-86	BRAD	35	.542	.768	5.7	18.7
86-87	BRAD	29	.533	.793	6.7	27.2
87-88	BRAD	31	.524	.848	7.8	36.3
Totals		125	.539	.806	6.5	24.1

NBA REGULAR-SEASON STATISTICS

			FGs		3-PT FGs		FTs		Rebounds						
	G	MIN	FG	PCT	FG	PCT	FT	PCT	OFF	TOT	AST	STL	BLK	PTS	PPG
88-89 PHI	79	2577	442	.455	71	.428	241	.831	51	225	239	120	37	1196	15.1
89-90 PHI	82	2856	522	.460	84	.420	387	.888	85	304	261	130	28	1515	18.5
90-91 PHI	80	3110	590	.472	108	.400	479	.871	48	310	299	178	39	1767	22.1
91-92 PHI	81	3013	521	.462	91	.397	403	.874	53	271	248	157	43	1536	19.0
92-93 PHI	81	2977	551	.470	122	.397	419	.860	91	346	317	137	30	1643	20.3
93-94 CHA	82	2648	395	.460	78	.332	312	.862	89	377	216	135	22	1180	14.4
Totals	485	17181	3021	.464	554	.394	2241	.867	417	1833	1580	857	199	8837	18.2

CARL HERRERA

Team: Houston Rockets
Position: Forward
Height: 6'9"　**Weight:** 220
Birthdate: December 14, 1966
NBA Experience: 3 years

College: Jacksonville; Houston
Acquired: Draft rights traded from Heat with draft rights to Dave Jamerson for draft rights to Alec Kessler, 6/90

Background: Born in Trinidad and raised in Venezuela, Herrera did not play basketball until the age of 13. He was noticed by colleges for his play as a 16-year-old point guard on the Venezuelan national team in the Pan-Am Games. He spent two years at Jacksonville (Texas) Junior College and one at the University of Houston. After starting his professional career in Spain, Herrera has spent three years with the Rockets, mostly as a reserve.

Strengths: Herrera is a magnificent athlete who was a volleyball star as a teenager. It's not difficult to see what made him a standout in that sport—tremendous leaping ability. He also possesses a great pair of hands. He can play both forward spots and gets up and down the floor like a guard. He handles the ball and can be a force on the boards.

Weaknesses: Herrera does not have the basketball skills of the average NBA small forward. His offensive range is not good, and last year his shooting percentage tumbled as he tried to do more from the perimeter. He is also a sub-par free throw shooter. Herrera does not make anything happen via the pass and lacks court sense.

Analysis: Herrera has a power forward's game and a small forward's body. He is at his best while cleaning the glass and scoring on putbacks. His great athletic ability and the fact he is still learning the game make him a worthwhile player to have on the roster. His playing time was cut on a strong Houston team last year, largely because his perimeter skills needed work.

PLAYER SUMMARY	
Will	jump out of the gym
Can't	hit from outside
Expect	athletic ability
Don't Expect	crisp passes
Fantasy Value	$0
Card Value	8-15¢

COLLEGE STATISTICS

		G	FGP	FTP	RPG	PPG
89-90	HOU	33	.565	.804	9.2	16.7
Totals		33	.565	.804	9.2	16.7

NBA REGULAR-SEASON STATISTICS

				FGs		3-PT FGs		FTs		Rebounds						
		G	MIN	FG	PCT	FG	PCT	FT	PCT	OFF	TOT	AST	STL	BLK	PTS	PPG
91-92	HOU	43	566	83	.516	0	.000	25	.568	33	99	27	16	25	191	4.4
92-93	HOU	81	1800	240	.541	0	.000	125	.710	148	454	61	47	35	605	7.5
93-94	HOU	75	1292	142	.458	0	.000	69	.711	101	285	37	32	26	353	4.7
Totals		199	3658	465	.508	0	.000	219	.691	282	838	125	95	86	1149	5.8

ROD HIGGINS

Unrestricted Free Agent
Last Team: Cleveland Cavaliers
Position: Forward
Height: 6'7" **Weight:** 215
Birthdate: January 31, 1960

NBA Experience: 12 years
College: Fresno St.
Acquired: Signed as a free agent, 12/93

Background: Higgins led Fresno State in scoring in each of his final three years. He overcame his journeyman label in the NBA (he was with four different teams in 1985-86) by playing for six years with Golden State from 1986-92. He has since played single seasons with Sacramento and Cleveland. He averaged only 5.4 PPG in 36 games with the Cavs last year.

Strengths: Though he plays both forward spots and has even filled in at center, Higgins is at his best from 3-point land. He made 44 percent of his long-range attempts last season. He works hard, is a team player, and has shown a remarkable ability to adjust.

Weaknesses: Higgins prefers to catch and shoot; he is not a great threat off the dribble. He is also no great defensive threat, although he does work at that end of the floor. Nagging injuries have slowed him in recent seasons.

Analysis: Higgins is a consummate pro. Team first, Higgins second. His 3-point shooting can turn games around, and his versatility is likely to keep him in the league for a couple more seasons despite the fact that he has seen his most productive days.

PLAYER SUMMARY	
Will	shoot the trey
Can't	blow past defenders
Expect	a team player
Don't Expect	many starts
Fantasy Value	$0
Card Value	5-8¢

COLLEGE STATISTICS

		G	FGP	FTP	RPG	PPG
78-79	FSU	22	.516	.742	5.8	9.4
79-80	FSU	24	.506	.724	5.7	12.9
80-81	FSU	29	.558	.852	5.4	15.4
81-82	FSU	29	.531	.771	6.3	15.1
Totals		104	.532	.805	5.8	13.5

NBA REGULAR-SEASON STATISTICS

			FGs		3-PT FGs		FTs		Rebounds						
	G	MIN	FG	PCT	FG	PCT	FT	PCT	OFF	TOT	AST	STL	BLK	PTS	PPG
82-83 CHI	82	2196	313	.448	13	.317	209	.792	159	366	175	66	65	848	10.3
83-84 CHI	78	1577	193	.447	1	.045	113	.724	87	206	116	49	29	500	6.4
84-85 CHI	68	942	119	.441	10	.270	60	.667	55	147	73	21	13	308	4.5
85-86 SEA/SA/NJ/CHI	30	332	39	.368	1	.111	19	.704	14	51	24	9	11	98	3.3
86-87 GS	73	1497	214	.519	3	.176	200	.833	72	237	96	40	21	631	8.6
87-88 GS	68	2188	381	.526	19	.487	273	.848	94	293	188	70	31	1054	15.5
88-89 GS	81	1887	301	.476	66	.393	188	.821	111	376	160	39	42	856	10.6
89-90 GS	82	1993	304	.481	67	.347	234	.821	120	422	129	47	53	909	11.1
90-91 GS	82	2024	259	.463	73	.332	185	.819	109	354	113	52	37	776	9.5
91-92 GS	25	535	87	.412	33	.347	48	.814	30	85	22	15	13	255	10.2
92-93 SAC	69	1425	199	.412	43	.323	130	.861	66	193	119	51	29	571	8.3
93-94 CLE	36	547	71	.436	22	.440	31	.738	25	82	36	25	14	195	5.4
Totals	774	17143	2480	.466	351	.343	1690	.808	942	2812	1251	484	358	7001	9.0

TYRONE HILL

Team: Cleveland Cavaliers
Position: Forward
Height: 6'9" **Weight:** 243
Birthdate: March 17, 1968

NBA Experience: 4 years
College: Xavier (OH)
Acquired: Signed as a free agent, 7/93

Background: Hill joined an exclusive group of college players to score 2,000 points and grab 1,000 rebounds in a career. He was among the top three nationally in rebounding as a junior and senior at Xavier. He led Golden State in offensive rebounds as a rookie, in defensive boards in his second year, and in both categories his third. He packed for Cleveland after 1992-93 and averaged about 10 PPG and 8.5 RPG with the Cavaliers last season.

Strengths: Rebounding has always been Hill's forte, and he has shown he can dominate the glass at the NBA level. He has a muscular body and uses it to get inside position. He snares boards with great instincts, leaping ability, and hard work. Hill is an adequate defender and can score on the low blocks. He also runs the floor well for a big man.

Weaknesses: Hill does not have a diverse offensive arsenal in the low post. He has been called mechanical and is most effective on putbacks. Hill is a poor outside shooter and is ineffective from the free throw line. He annually finished among the league leaders in personal fouls when he was starting. A sprained thumb limited him somewhat last season.

Analysis: Hill can be compared to monster rebounders Dennis Rodman and Larry Smith, although he has not yet reached their level. Like those two veterans, he offers much more in terms of physical play and rebounding than he does on the offensive end, although he scored at a career-high clip last season. Hill also has the potential to be a strong defensive player.

PLAYER SUMMARY

Will..........................crash the boards
Can't ....make 3-pointers
Expect ....improving defense
Don't Expect...............flashy offense
Fantasy Value..............................$5-7
Card Value ....8-15¢

COLLEGE STATISTICS

		G	FGP	FTP	RPG	PPG
86-87	XAV	31	.552	.672	8.4	8.8
87-88	XAV	30	.557	.745	10.5	15.3
88-89	XAV	33	.606	.701	12.2	18.9
89-90	XAV	32	.581	.658	12.6	20.2
Totals		126	.579	.692	11.0	15.9

NBA REGULAR-SEASON STATISTICS

		G	MIN	FGs		3-PT FGs		FTs		Rebounds		AST	STL	BLK	PTS	PPG
				FG	PCT	FG	PCT	FT	PCT	OFF	TOT					
90-91	GS	74	1192	147	.492	0	.000	96	.632	157	383	19	33	30	390	5.3
91-92	GS	82	1886	254	.522	0	.000	163	.694	182	593	47	73	43	671	8.2
92-93	GS	74	2070	251	.508	0	.000	138	.624	255	754	68	41	40	640	8.6
93-94	CLE	57	1447	216	.543	0	.000	171	.668	184	499	46	53	35	603	10.6
Totals		287	6595	868	.517	0	.000	568	.657	778	2229	180	200	148	2304	8.0

DONALD HODGE

Team: Dallas Mavericks
Position: Center
Height: 7'0" **Weight:** 235
Birthdate: February 25, 1969

NBA Experience: 3 years
College: Temple
Acquired: 2nd-round pick in 1991 draft (33rd overall)

Background: Hodge had a brief college career at Temple. He sat out his freshman year because of Prop 48 restrictions and forfeited his senior year to enter the NBA draft. As a sophomore, he led the Owls in rebounding and field goal percentage. A second-round choice of Dallas, Hodge averaged 8.4 PPG as a rookie. His scoring has dropped in the two years since, bottoming out at 2.7 PPG last season.

Strengths: Hodge has excellent size, great hands, and a soft touch around the basket. His range is better than expected, and it helped him surprise some of the better centers in the league as a rookie. Hodge has become a better free throw shooter. He also passes and runs the floor well for a big man and hits the offensive glass.

Weaknesses: There is virtually no power in Hodge's game. He's a finesse player in all respects. He lacks the bulk to be considered a potentially dominant rebounder, and he does not assert himself on the defensive glass. He has a long way to go with his defensive know-how in general. He's not the shot-blocking force he can be and he has not converted with consistency at the offensive end.

Analysis: Hodge had a surprising rookie year, but over the last two seasons he has reverted to the form that got him labeled a project coming into the league. What he really needs is a stronger body that he can use to challenge opponents rather than trying to get cute with the ball. When you can't find minutes with the Mavs, something's wrong.

PLAYER SUMMARY	
Will	use finesse
Can't	out-muscle his man
Expect	good hands
Don't Expect	20 minutes
Fantasy Value	$0
Card Value	5-10¢

COLLEGE STATISTICS

		G	FGP	FTP	RPG	PPG
89-90	TEMP	31	.541	.713	8.2	15.1
90-91	TEMP	34	.535	.716	6.9	11.6
Totals		65	.538	.714	7.5	13.3

NBA REGULAR-SEASON STATISTICS

		G	MIN	FGs FG	FGs PCT	3-PT FGs FG	3-PT FGs PCT	FTs FT	FTs PCT	Rebounds OFF	Rebounds TOT	AST	STL	BLK	PTS	PPG
91-92	DAL	51	1058	163	.497	0	.000	100	.667	118	275	39	25	23	426	8.4
92-93	DAL	79	1267	161	.403	0	.000	71	.683	93	294	75	33	37	393	5.0
93-94	DAL	50	428	46	.455	0	.000	44	.846	46	95	32	15	13	136	2.7
Totals		180	2753	370	.446	0	.000	215	.703	257	664	146	73	73	955	5.3

JEFF HORNACEK

Team: Utah Jazz
Position: Guard
Height: 6'4" **Weight:** 190
Birthdate: May 3, 1963
NBA Experience: 8 years

College: Iowa St.
Acquired: Traded from 76ers with Sean Green and a conditional 2nd-round pick for Jeff Malone and a conditional 1st-round pick, 2/94

Background: Hornacek walked on at Iowa State, earned a scholarship, and wound up setting a Big Eight career assist record with 665. His pro career has evolved in a similar pattern—from unheralded to highly respected. He increased his scoring average each year through 1989-90 and led the Suns in 1991-92 with 20.1 PPG. He earned a spot in the 1992 All-Star Game. Hornacek was traded to the 76ers in 1992 and to Utah in February 1994.

Strengths: A dead-eye gunner, Hornacek will kill you if you leave him open from anywhere on the court—inside or outside the 3-point line. He rarely misses a free throw. He makes few mistakes, is good with both hands, and approaches the game with a great work ethic. He can handle both guard spots.

Weaknesses: The fact that Hornacek is not a great athlete has not stopped him from achieving at every level. He has not shot the ball as accurately over the past two seasons. His size (or lack of it) works against him on defense.

Analysis: A coach's son, Hornacek has a thorough understanding of the game and plays it at a high level. Utah used him primarily as a third guard, but he is more than capable of being an above-average starter at either the one or two slot. His sub-50-percent shooting can be written off to having played with three teams in the last three years.

PLAYER SUMMARY

Will	hit when open
Can't	enter dunk contest
Expect	court savvy
Don't Expect	blocked shots
Fantasy Value	$25-30
Card Value	7-12¢

COLLEGE STATISTICS

		G	FGP	FTP	RPG	PPG
82-83	ISU	27	.422	.711	2.3	5.4
83-84	ISU	29	.500	.790	3.5	10.0
84-85	ISU	34	.521	.844	3.6	12.5
85-86	ISU	33	.478	.776	3.8	13.7
Totals		123	.489	.790	3.3	10.7

NBA REGULAR-SEASON STATISTICS

		G	MIN	FGs FG	FG PCT	3-PT FGs FG	FG PCT	FTs FT	FT PCT	Rebounds OFF	TOT	AST	STL	BLK	PTS	PPG
86-87	PHO	80	1561	159	.454	12	.279	94	.777	41	184	361	70	5	424	5.3
87-88	PHO	82	2243	306	.506	17	.293	152	.822	71	262	540	107	10	781	9.5
88-89	PHO	78	2487	440	.495	27	.333	147	.826	75	266	465	129	8	1054	13.5
89-90	PHO	67	2278	483	.536	40	.408	173	.856	86	313	337	117	14	1179	17.6
90-91	PHO	80	2733	544	.518	61	.418	201	.897	74	321	409	111	16	1350	16.9
91-92	PHO	81	3078	635	.512	83	.439	279	.886	106	407	411	158	31	1632	20.1
92-93	PHI	79	2860	582	.470	97	.390	250	.865	84	342	548	131	21	1511	19.1
93-94	PHI/UTA	80	2820	472	.470	70	.337	260	.878	60	279	419	127	13	1274	15.9
Totals		627	20060	3621	.497	407	.380	1556	.860	597	2374	3490	950	118	9205	14.7

ROBERT HORRY

Team: Houston Rockets
Position: Forward
Height: 6'10" **Weight:** 220
Birthdate: August 25, 1970

NBA Experience: 2 years
College: Alabama
Acquired: 1st-round pick in 1992 draft
(11th overall)

Background: Named Alabama prep Player of the Year at Andalusia High, Horry stayed at home to play his college ball with the Crimson Tide. He helped the Tide to the final 16 of the NCAA Tournament twice and finished his career as the all-time school leader in blocked shots. The 11th pick in the 1992 draft, Horry has been a two-year starter for Houston at small forward. He was third on the team in rebounds and steals and second in blocks last season after a fine rookie campaign.

Strengths: Horry is a splendid athlete who loves to challenge shots. In addition to being All-SEC in college, he also made the all-league defensive team and has brought his nose for the ball and strong rebounding to the pros. He's also a decent scorer who creates his own shots and has a quick first step. He can shoot with 3-point range, moves well without the ball, and finds open men. He oozes confidence, and with reason.

Weaknesses: Horry is not the scoring machine many starting small forwards are. He gets many of his points with transition dunks. He is not a great ball-handler. Gaining night-to-night consistency should be his next step in becoming a better player. He converts under one-third of his 3-point attempts.

Analysis: Not many players step into the NBA and start from Day One, especially on a contending team. That tells you what kind of talent Horry is. The former Alabama star pumps life into the Rockets with his energetic play, and he had a large hand in the team's run to the 1994 NBA championship. His biggest asset is probably his ability to perform many aspects of the game at a high level.

PLAYER SUMMARY	
Will	block shots
Can't	handle like a guard
Expect	energetic play
Don't Expect	glaring weaknesses
Fantasy Value	$13-16
Card Value	20-40¢

COLLEGE STATISTICS

		G	FGP	FTP	RPG	PPG
88-89	ALA	31	.427	.644	5.0	6.5
89-90	ALA	35	.467	.760	6.2	13.1
90-91	ALA	32	.449	.804	8.1	11.9
91-92	ALA	35	.470	.727	8.5	15.8
Totals		133	.458	.742	7.0	12.0

NBA REGULAR-SEASON STATISTICS

| | | G | MIN | FGs | | 3-PT FGs | | FTs | | Rebounds | | AST | STL | BLK | PTS | PPG |
				FG	PCT	FG	PCT	FT	PCT	OFF	TOT					
92-93	HOU	79	2330	323	.474	12	.255	143	.715	113	392	191	80	83	801	10.1
93-94	HOU	81	2370	322	.459	44	.324	115	.732	128	440	231	119	75	803	9.9
Totals		160	4700	645	.466	56	.306	258	.723	241	832	422	199	158	1604	10.0

ALLAN HOUSTON

Team: Detroit Pistons
Position: Guard
Height: 6'6" **Weight:** 200
Birthdate: April 4, 1971

NBA Experience: 1 year
College: Tennessee
Acquired: 1st-round pick in 1993 draft
(11th overall)

Background: Kentucky's Mr. Basketball as a prep, Houston was headed to the University of Louisville, where his father Wade was one of Denny Crum's assistants. Plans changed when the elder Houston was offered the head-coaching job at Tennessee. Allan enjoyed a bang-up career with the Vols, amassing 2,801 points—second in SEC history to Pete Maravich. Houston was drafted 11th by the Pistons and was the sixth-leading scorer on the team in 1993-94.

Strengths: Houston is considered a pure shooter with excellent mechanics. He can score on pull-up jumpers or after spotting up behind a screen. He converted a high percentage from long distance in college and has NBA 3-point range. He is a very good free throw shooter. The son of a coach, he knows the game inside and out.

Weaknesses: Most rookies have shooting troubles, and Houston's first-year shooting was nightmarish at times. He spent much of the year fighting to reach the .400 mark from the field, mostly a result of his inability to score with defenders in his face. The open jumper is not as great a problem. Houston needs a lot of work defensively. On the lean side, he does not play with much intensity or physical abandon.

Analysis: Houston was not nearly the smash Lindsey Hunter was among Detroit's rookie guards, but give him time. It's a rare player who steps into the big leagues and continues to score in bushels, especially when you're backing up a player like Joe Dumars. Houston must learn to get good shots despite NBA defense, and he could stand some defensive tips himself. Dumars is a great teacher, and Houston's willing to learn.

PLAYER SUMMARY	
Will	shoot with range
Can't	score like in college
Expect	some improvement
Don't Expect	defensive stardom
Fantasy Value	$6-8
Card Value	12-20¢

COLLEGE STATISTICS

		G	FGP	FTP	RPG	PPG
89-90	TENN	30	.437	.805	2.9	20.3
90-91	TENN	34	.482	.863	3.1	23.7
91-92	TENN	34	.453	.840	5.3	21.1
92-93	TENN	30	.465	.878	4.8	22.3
Totals		128	.460	.849	4.0	21.9

NBA REGULAR-SEASON STATISTICS

			FGs		3-PT FGs		FTs		Rebounds						
	G	MIN	FG	PCT	FG	PCT	FT	PCT	OFF	TOT	AST	STL	BLK	PTS	PPG
93-94 DET	79	1519	272	.405	35	.299	89	.824	19	120	100	34	13	668	8.5
Totals	79	1519	272	.405	35	.299	89	.824	19	120	100	34	13	668	8.5

BYRON HOUSTON

Team: Seattle SuperSonics
Position: Forward
Height: 6'5" **Weight:** 250
Birthdate: November 22, 1969
NBA Experience: 2 years

College: Oklahoma St.
Acquired: Traded from Warriors with Sarunas Marciulionis for Ricky Pierce, draft rights to Carlos Rogers, and two 1995 2nd-round picks, 7/94

Background: Houston was an All-American at Oklahoma State, finishing his career as the school's all-time leader in nine statistical categories, including scoring, rebounding, and blocked shots. He joined Danny Manning and Wayman Tisdale as the only Big Eight players with 2,000 points, 1,000 rebounds, and 200 blocks. Houston was taken 27th in the 1992 draft by Chicago, then traded to Golden State. He finished second on the Warriors in rebounds as a rookie but saw less action last season. He was traded to Seattle in July.

Strengths: Owner of a body that's been sculpted in the weight room, Houston is extremely strong. He is not afraid to bump and bruise and usually comes out on the better end of such physical play. Houston also possesses good quickness and is a strong rebounder considering his height. In that sense, he has been compared to Charles Barkley.

Weaknesses: That whistle you hear is a referee nailing Houston for yet another personal foul. He was among the most guilty foulers in the league in his first season, and has been disqualified from 16 games to date. He tends to use his frame rather than his feet on defense. Houston is not nearly the scorer he was at the college level. He's a poor free throw shooter and jump-shooter.

Analysis: Houston has a long way to go before he can be compared to Barkley or Larry Johnson. Yes, he's physical. No, he does not possess their ability to score. Houston's nice rookie contributions were largely the result of a rash of injuries in the Golden State camp. He played just over 12 minutes per game last year and has some talented players in front of him in Seattle.

PLAYER SUMMARY

Will ....get physical
Can't ....avoid fouling
Expect ....strong rebounding
Don't Expect ....10 PPG
Fantasy Value...........................$0
Card Value ....8-15¢

COLLEGE STATISTICS

		G	FGP	FTP	RPG	PPG
88-89	OSU	30	.583	.745	8.4	13.0
89-90	OSU	31	.528	.731	10.0	18.5
90-91	OSU	32	.573	.743	10.5	22.7
91-92	OSU	34	.533	.700	8.6	20.2
Totals		127	.552	.729	9.4	18.7

NBA REGULAR-SEASON STATISTICS

		G	MIN	FGs FG	FGs PCT	3-PT FGs FG	3-PT FGs PCT	FTs FT	FTs PCT	Rebounds OFF	Rebounds TOT	AST	STL	BLK	PTS	PPG
92-93	GS	79	1274	145	.446	2	.286	129	.665	119	315	69	44	43	421	5.3
93-94	GS	71	866	81	.458	1	.143	33	.611	67	194	32	33	31	196	2.8
Totals		150	2140	226	.450	3	.214	162	.653	186	509	101	77	74	617	4.1

JAY HUMPHRIES

Team: Utah Jazz
Position: Guard
Height: 6'3" **Weight:** 195
Birthdate: October 17, 1962
NBA Experience: 10 years

College: Colorado
Acquired: Traded from Bucks with Larry Krystkowiak for Blue Edwards, Eric Murdock, and a 1992 1st-round pick, 6/92

Background: An All-Big Eight selection as a senior at Colorado, Humphries set 16 school records, including career assists, steals, and games played. He was drafted by Phoenix, where he started all 82 games in his second and third seasons. A 1988 trade brought him to Milwaukee, and he led the Bucks in assists in his last three seasons there. He was dealt to Utah before the 1992-93 season and has seen most of his minutes as a reserve.

Strengths: Humphries is a versatile veteran who can play both guard positions, and he has. His all-around abilities include scoring, handling the ball, solid passing, and above-average defense. He's good with both hands. He was once Milwaukee's captain and is respected for his leadership.

Weaknesses: Humphries lacks the creativity of the league's more spectacular playmakers and does not shoot consistently enough to be a top-tier shooting guard. He plays conservatively. His poor shooting percentage is a concern.

Analysis: Humphries appears to be past his double-figure scoring days, unless he lands with a team that could offer more minutes. It is unlikely he will be any better than the No. 3 guard on a Utah team that boasts John Stockton and Jeff Hornacek. Humphries still has much to offer in terms of a steadying hand.

PLAYER SUMMARY	
Will	run the offense
Can't	create like Stockton
Expect	versatility
Don't Expect	10 PPG
Fantasy Value	$0
Card Value	5-10¢

COLLEGE STATISTICS

		G	FGP	FTP	APG	PPG
80-81	COLO	28	.517	.660	3.5	6.4
81-82	COLO	27	.467	.639	4.3	10.3
82-83	COLO	28	.501	.632	6.2	14.3
83-84	COLO	29	.509	.788	6.0	15.4
Totals		112	.498	.696	5.0	11.7

NBA REGULAR-SEASON STATISTICS

				FGs		3-PT FGs		FTs		Rebounds						
		G	MIN	FG	PCT	FG	PCT	FT	PCT	OFF	TOT	AST	STL	BLK	PTS	PPG
84-85	PHO	80	2062	279	.446	4	.200	141	.829	32	164	350	107	8	703	8.8
85-86	PHO	82	2733	352	.479	4	.138	197	.767	56	260	526	132	9	905	11.0
86-87	PHO	82	2579	359	.477	5	.185	200	.769	62	260	632	112	9	923	11.3
87-88	PHO/MIL	68	1809	284	.528	3	.167	112	.732	49	174	395	81	5	683	10.0
88-89	MIL	73	2220	345	.483	25	.266	129	.816	70	189	405	142	5	844	11.6
89-90	MIL	81	2818	496	.494	21	.300	224	.786	80	269	472	156	11	1237	15.3
90-91	MIL	80	2726	482	.502	60	.373	191	.799	57	220	538	129	7	1215	15.2
91-92	MIL	71	2261	377	.469	42	.292	195	.783	44	184	466	119	13	991	14.0
92-93	UTA	78	2034	287	.436	15	.200	101	.777	40	143	317	101	11	690	8.8
93-94	UTA	75	1619	233	.436	38	.396	57	.750	35	127	219	65	11	561	7.5
Totals		770	22861	3494	.477	217	.296	1547	.782	525	1990	4320	1144	89	8752	11.4

LINDSEY HUNTER

Team: Detroit Pistons
Position: Guard
Height: 6'2" **Weight:** 180
Birthdate: December 3, 1970

NBA Experience: 1 year
College: Alcorn St.; Jackson St.
Acquired: 1st-round pick in 1993 draft (10th overall)

Background: After playing high school ball in Jackson, Mississippi, Hunter played a year at Alcorn State but transferred to Jackson State for the 1990-91 season. He was an immediate success at JSU, reaching double figures in 29 of 30 games during his first year there. He averaged 26.7 PPG as a senior, fifth highest in the nation. The tenth overall draft choice in 1993, Hunter was a popular rookie in Detroit and one of five Pistons to average double figures in scoring last season.

Strengths: Hunter is a lightning-quick point guard who can get his shot off against virtually anybody one-on-one. He also has a quick release and outstanding range. A great athlete, Hunter is lethal in the open court and explosive taking the ball to the rim. He knows how to find open men. He has the makings of a fine defensive player and led the Pistons in steals by a wide margin during the 1993-94 campaign.

Weaknesses: Hunter was successful from the 3-point arc but dismal from closer to the basket. He found it much more difficult to finish his drives to the hoop against NBA defenders. He shot well below 40 percent from the field. Hunter does not always play under great control and is still learning the point-guard position. He was strictly a shooting guard in college.

Analysis: Hunter is a key to Detroit's future. Isiah Thomas and Joe Dumars have brought plenty of backcourt thrills to the Motor City, and the electrifying Hunter will try to pick up where his tutors left off. He's a promising player both offensively and defensively because of his great quickness and feel for the game. Expect his scoring to soar in years to come when he develops better consistency.

PLAYER SUMMARY	
Will	get shots off
Can't	shoot for high pct.
Expect	a bright future
Don't Expect	slow wheels
Fantasy Value	$9-11
Card Value	15-30¢

COLLEGE STATISTICS

		G	FGP	FTP	APG	PPG
88-89	ASU	28	.393	.719	3.5	6.0
90-91	JSU	30	.409	.695	3.5	20.9
91-92	JSU	28	.412	.637	4.3	24.8
92-93	JSU	34	.412	.771	3.4	26.7
Totals		120	.409	.709	3.7	19.9

NBA REGULAR-SEASON STATISTICS

				FGs		3-PT FGs		FTs		Rebounds						
	G	MIN	FG	PCT	FG	PCT	FT	PCT	OFF	TOT	AST	STL	BLK	PTS	PPG
93-94 DET	82	2172	335	.375	69	.333	104	.732	47	189	390	121	10	843	10.3
Totals	82	2172	335	.375	69	.333	104	.732	47	189	390	121	10	843	10.3

BOBBY HURLEY

Team: Sacramento Kings
Position: Guard
Height: 6'0" **Weight:** 165
Birthdate: June 28, 1971

NBA Experience: 1 year
College: Duke
Acquired: 1st-round pick in 1993 draft (7th overall)

Background: One of many quality players from St. Anthony's, a prep powerhouse in New Jersey, Hurley went to Duke and did nothing but win. The Blue Devils went to three Final Fours and won two national championships (1991 and 1992) with Hurley, who owns the NCAA career assists record (1,076) and set a Duke standard for career 3-pointers (264). A fine rookie year with Sacramento ended on December 12, 1993, when Hurley suffered life-threatening injuries in an auto accident.

Strengths: Hurley is the prototypical point guard. He's quick, anticipates well in transition, and can break down a defense with his dribble. He runs a precise offense and knows where teammates like the ball delivered. He can shoot with range, though perhaps not past the NBA 3-point line, and craves the ball when the game is on the line. Defensively, he plays the passing lanes well and has a nose for steals. He's tough.

Weaknesses: Lack of size is Hurley's biggest liability. It puts him at a disadvantage against most NBA guards defensively and forces him to be creative at the offensive end. He is not able to get his shot off whenever he wants, as he could in college. His shooting percentage will suffer for it. Hurley's injuries have provided a huge hurdle for him to clear.

Analysis: Hurley has been compared to the likes of Bob Cousy and John Stockton. The NBA's original Dream Team got a glimpse of his talents during pre-Olympic practice sessions and he became an instant starter for the Kings. The basketball world stood still when his life was threatened last December, and it marveled at the way Hurley began his recovery. He has started to play basketball again, and no one is betting against his return.

PLAYER SUMMARY

Will ....distribute
Can't ....out-muscle his man
Expect ....gruelling rehab
Don't Expect ....a quitter
Fantasy Value..............................$1-3
Card Value ....20-40¢

COLLEGE STATISTICS

		G	FGP	FTP	APG	PPG
89-90	DUKE	38	.351	.769	7.6	8.8
90-91	DUKE	39	.423	.728	7.4	11.3
91-92	DUKE	31	.433	.789	7.6	13.2
92-93	DUKE	32	.421	.803	8.2	17.0
Totals		140	.410	.776	7.7	12.4

NBA REGULAR-SEASON STATISTICS

			FGs		3-PT FGs		FTs		Rebounds						
		G	MIN	FG	PCT	FG	PCT	FT	PCT	OFF	TOT	AST	STL	BLK	PTS	PPG
93-94	SAC	19	499	54	.370	2	.125	24	.800	6	34	115	13	1	134	7.1
Totals		19	499	54	.370	2	.125	24	.800	6	34	115	13	1	134	7.1

JIM JACKSON

Team: Dallas Mavericks
Position: Guard
Height: 6'6" **Weight:** 220
Birthdate: October 14, 1970

NBA Experience: 2 years
College: Ohio St.
Acquired: 1st-round pick in 1992 draft
(4th overall)

Background: A rare two-time Mr. Basketball in Ohio, Jackson led Toledo Macomber to a state championship as a senior. He started all 93 games the Buckeyes played in his three years at Ohio State. Jackson was named Big Ten Freshman of the Year and was a consensus All-American as a junior. The fourth player taken in the 1992 draft, he went through a bitter contract holdout with Dallas before finally signing a deal worth $20 million. The 1993-94 campaign was his first full one as a pro and he finished at about 19 PPG.

Strengths: Jackson is a tremendous talent and a big-time scorer. He is blessed with the ability to post up, drive to the hoop, or hit from the perimeter. He's also the kind of player who can make those around him look better, which is quite a feat with the Mavericks. His passing skills are highly advanced and he crashes the boards. Jackson's a gym rat who keeps himself in first-rate condition.

Weaknesses: Jackson has made a habit of trying to do too much, which is an easy habit to fall into with the Mavs. He turns the ball over a staggering number of times—more than four per game. His perimeter shooting is not as consistent as it will be down the road, and he does not convert a high percentage of his 3-point attempts.

Analysis: Jackson has started every game for the Mavericks since joining the team with 28 games left in the 1992-93 season. He, Jamal Mashburn, and Jason Kidd are three young franchise players who will ensure that lowly Dallas enjoys better days ahead. Until then, however, Jackson will earn praise from the opposition for his court sense and ability to score.

PLAYER SUMMARY	
Will	become a standout
Can't	avoid turnovers
Expect	18-20 PPG
Don't Expect	a Dallas title
Fantasy Value	$20-25
Card Value	25-50¢

COLLEGE STATISTICS

		G	FGP	FTP	RPG	PPG
89-90	OSU	30	.499	.785	5.5	16.1
90-91	OSU	31	.517	.752	5.5	18.9
91-92	OSU	32	.493	.811	6.8	22.4
Totals		93	.503	.784	5.9	19.2

NBA REGULAR-SEASON STATISTICS

		G	MIN	FGs FG	FGs PCT	3-PT FGs FG	3-PT FGs PCT	FTs FT	FTs PCT	Rebounds OFF	Rebounds TOT	AST	STL	BLK	PTS	PPG
92-93	DAL	28	938	184	.395	21	.288	68	.739	42	122	131	40	11	457	16.3
93-94	DAL	82	3066	637	.445	17	.283	285	.821	169	388	374	87	25	1576	19.2
Totals		110	4004	821	.433	38	.286	353	.804	211	510	505	127	36	2033	18.5

MARK JACKSON

Team: Indiana Pacers
Position: Guard
Height: 6'3" **Weight:** 185
Birthdate: April 1, 1965
NBA Experience: 7 years

College: St. John's
Acquired: Traded from Clippers with draft rights to Greg Minor for Pooh Richardson, Malik Sealy, and draft rights to Eric Piatkowski, 6/94

Background: Jackson was a second-team All-American as a senior at St. John's and finished his career with the school's all-time assists record. With the Knicks, he earned the unanimous vote for NBA Rookie of the Year in 1987-88 and won a trip to the All-Star Game the following season. He has finished among the league's assist leaders three years in a row, including the last two with the Clippers. In June, he was dealt to the Pacers.

Strengths: Jackson is an explosive playmaker with big-time penetrating ability. He cuts through the lane and can either find the open man or make acrobatic shots. His court vision is superb. He's a capable outside shooter with 3-point range. Jackson thrives in transition and helps out on the boards.

Weaknesses: During Jackson's roller-coaster NBA history, the down times have been largely mental. His play deteriorated when fans in New York got on him and he was once suspended for ripping the Knicks organization. He is not a great defender and his shooting percentage was down last season.

Analysis: Jackson became the mainstay at point guard for the Clippers and turned in two fine seasons in L.A. The Pacers, searching for a steady hand to run the team, found the right man in Jackson. When allowed to run the court with some talent around him, Jackson is an above-average playmaker.

PLAYER SUMMARY	
Will	distribute
Can't	shut down his man
Expect	8 APG
Don't Expect	more All-Star trips
Fantasy Value	$14-17
Card Value	5-10¢

COLLEGE STATISTICS

		G	FGP	FTP	APG	PPG
83-84	STJ	30	.575	.688	3.6	5.8
84-85	STJ	35	.564	.725	3.1	5.1
85-86	STJ	36	.478	.739	9.1	11.3
86-87	STJ	30	.504	.806	6.4	18.9
Totals		131	.510	.751	5.6	10.1

NBA REGULAR-SEASON STATISTICS

		G	MIN	FGs FG	FGs PCT	3-PT FGs FG	3-PT FGs PCT	FTs FT	FTs PCT	Rebounds OFF	Rebounds TOT	AST	STL	BLK	PTS	PPG
87-88	NY	82	3249	438	.432	32	.254	206	.774	120	396	868	205	6	1114	13.6
88-89	NY	72	2477	479	.467	81	.338	180	.698	106	341	619	139	7	1219	16.9
89-90	NY	82	2428	327	.437	35	.267	120	.727	106	318	604	109	4	809	9.9
90-91	NY	72	1595	250	.492	13	.255	117	.731	62	197	452	60	9	630	8.8
91-92	NY	81	2461	367	.491	11	.256	171	.770	95	305	694	112	13	916	11.3
92-93	LAC	82	3117	459	.486	22	.268	241	.803	129	388	724	136	12	1181	14.4
93-94	LAC	79	2711	331	.452	36	.283	167	.791	107	348	678	120	6	865	10.9
Totals		550	18038	2651	.464	230	.287	1202	.760	725	2293	4639	881	57	6734	12.2

KEITH JENNINGS

Team: Golden State Warriors
Position: Guard
Height: 5'7" **Weight:** 160
Birthdate: November 2, 1968

NBA Experience: 2 years
College: East Tennessee St.
Acquired: Signed as a free agent, 7/92

Background: Nicknamed "Mister," the 5'7" Jennings was named Southern Conference Most Valuable Player as a junior and senior at East Tennessee State and finished his career as the all-time NCAA leader in 3-point percentage (.493). However, he went undrafted and spent the 1991-92 season in Germany. Golden State signed him in 1992 but major knee surgery limited his NBA debut to eight games. He returned to play in 76 games last season.

Strengths: Jennings is quick as lightning and the ball is attached to his hand. He's creative with his passing and can also get through the trees himself. He brings a scoring mentality to the point-guard position and has NBA 3-point range. He made more treys (56) than teammate Chris Mullin last season. He's also an accurate free throw shooter and a promising defensive pick-pocket because of his speed.

Weaknesses: Size is the obvious drawback, and it's the main reason Jennings was bypassed by everyone in the 1991 draft. Opponents can post him up and shoot over him at will. He's not a high-flying, dunker type like Spud Webb. For all his quickness, Jennings has been a more adept scorer than a defender. He's not much help on the boards for obvious reasons, and he can play out of control.

Analysis: Jennings is a talented little man who zips around the floor like Muggsy Bogues. Though he has not reached Muggsy's level of consistency, Jennings possesses a better jump shot and more range than Charlotte's mighty mite and has some of the same defensive potential. He overcame what was considered a serious injury to his right knee and played some quality minutes as a Golden State reserve last season.

PLAYER SUMMARY	
Will	drill the trey
Can't	block shots
Expect	superior quickness
Don't Expect	slam dunks
Fantasy Value	$1
Card Value	7-12¢

COLLEGE STATISTICS

		G	FGP	FTP	APG	PPG
87-88	ETST	29	.489	.826	6.3	12.9
88-89	ETST	31	.510	.847	6.5	14.5
89-90	ETST	34	.575	.877	8.7	14.8
90-91	ETST	33	.596	.895	9.1	20.1
Totals		127	.549	.861	7.7	15.7

NBA REGULAR-SEASON STATISTICS

		G	MIN	FGs		3-PT FGs		FTs		Rebounds		AST	STL	BLK	PTS	PPG
				FG	PCT	FG	PCT	FT	PCT	OFF	TOT					
92-93	GS	8	136	25	.595	5	.556	14	.778	2	11	23	4	0	69	8.6
93-94	GS	76	1097	138	.404	56	.371	100	.833	16	89	218	65	0	432	5.7
Totals		84	1233	163	.424	61	.381	114	.826	18	100	241	69	0	501	6.0

AVERY JOHNSON

Team: San Antonio Spurs
Position: Guard
Height: 5'11" **Weight:** 175
Birthdate: March 25, 1965

NBA Experience: 6 years
College: Cameron; Southern
Acquired: Signed as a free agent, 7/94

Background: Johnson led the nation in assists as a junior and senior at Southern University, where he was a two-time Southwestern Athletic Conference Player of the Year. He was not drafted but he latched on in Seattle as a free agent and played two years there. He has since seen action for Denver, San Antonio (twice), Houston, and Golden State. The younger brother of former Piston star Vinnie Johnson, Avery had a career year with the Warriors last season. The Spurs signed him for a third time over the summer.

Strengths: A pure point guard, Johnson covers the court like a pinball. His quickness allows him to penetrate and show off his crafty passing skills. A willing distributor, he has a knack for finding the open man and he sees the court better than most. For his small stature, Johnson displays the toughness and leadership coaches love.

Weaknesses: The younger Johnson is not the shooting machine his older brother once was for the Pistons. Avery prefers creating to finishing, although he averaged double figures in scoring for the first time last season. His range does not extend to the 3-point line. He's not a physical force.

Analysis: Teams keep cutting Johnson, and he simply latches on somewhere else and proves to be a valuable addition. The Warriors needed a replacement for the injured Tim Hardaway, so they signed Johnson last October and the well-traveled guard ran the offense virtually from start to finish. He's got a great heart that makes him tough to keep out of the lineup.

PLAYER SUMMARY

Will ....work for his minutes
Can't ....shoot like Vinnie
Expect ....playmaking, heart
Don't Expect ....high scoring
Fantasy Value................................$3-5
Card Value ....5-10¢

COLLEGE STATISTICS

		G	FGP	FTP	APG	PPG
84-85	CAM	33	.509	.618	3.2	4.3
86-87	SU	31	.439	.615	10.7	7.1
87-88	SU	30	.537	.688	13.3	11.4
Totals		94	.497	.641	8.9	7.5

NBA REGULAR-SEASON STATISTICS

		G	MIN	FGs FG	FGs PCT	3-PT FGs FG	3-PT FGs PCT	FTs FT	FTs PCT	Rebounds OFF	Rebounds TOT	AST	STL	BLK	PTS	PPG
88-89	SEA	43	291	29	.349	1	.111	9	.563	11	24	73	21	3	68	1.6
89-90	SEA	53	575	55	.387	1	.250	29	.725	21	43	162	26	1	140	2.6
90-91	DEN/SA	68	959	130	.469	1	.111	59	.678	22	77	230	47	4	320	4.7
91-92	SA/HOU	69	1235	158	.479	4	.267	66	.653	13	80	266	61	9	386	5.6
92-93	SA	75	2030	256	.502	0	.000	144	.791	20	146	561	85	16	656	8.7
93-94	GS	82	2332	356	.492	0	.000	178	.704	41	176	433	113	8	890	10.9
Totals		390	7422	984	.476	7	.123	485	.714	128	546	1725	353	41	2460	6.3

EDDIE JOHNSON

Unrestricted Free Agent
Last Team: Charlotte Hornets
Position: Forward/Guard
Height: 6'7" **Weight:** 215
Birthdate: May 1, 1959

NBA Experience: 13 years
College: Illinois
Acquired: Traded from SuperSonics with Dana Barros for Kendall Gill, 9/93

Background: In college, Johnson set Illinois career records for scoring, rebounding, and field goals. He was a standout with the Kings before winning the NBA's Sixth Man Award in 1988-89 with Phoenix. He spent two-plus years as a great sixth man in Seattle before a September 1993 trade brought him to Charlotte. He became a free agent after last season.

Strengths: One of the best off-the-bench shooters in recent history, Johnson releases the ball quickly and possesses great range. He topped the 17,000-point mark last December. He rates among the better 3-point threats in the league.

Weaknesses: Johnson struggles when his jump shot is taken away. He does not go to the hoop with confidence and is not known for his passing. Defense is not his forte either. He was unhappy playing for Charlotte.

Analysis: The veteran Johnson remains one of the best at what he does—shooting quick jumpers from long distance and providing leadership off the bench. You don't want to leave him open. Last season, however, was his lowest scoring effort since his rookie campaign.

PLAYER SUMMARY

Will	hit from long range
Can't	star on defense
Expect	reserve leadership
Don't Expect	20 PPG
Fantasy Value	$1
Card Value	5-10¢

COLLEGE STATISTICS

		G	FGP	FTP	RPG	PPG
77-78	ILL	27	.427	.741	3.1	8.1
78-79	ILL	30	.415	.531	5.7	12.1
79-80	ILL	35	.462	.655	8.9	17.4
80-81	ILL	29	.494	.756	9.2	17.2
Totals		121	.454	.671	6.9	14.0

NBA REGULAR-SEASON STATISTICS

		G	MIN	FGs FG	FGs PCT	3-PT FGs FG	3-PT FGs PCT	FTs FT	FTs PCT	Rebounds OFF	Rebounds TOT	AST	STL	BLK	PTS	PPG
81-82	KC	74	1517	295	.459	1	.091	99	.664	128	322	109	50	14	690	9.3
82-83	KC	82	2933	677	.494	20	.282	247	.779	191	501	216	70	20	1621	19.8
83-84	KC	82	2920	753	.485	20	.313	268	.810	165	455	296	76	21	1794	21.9
84-85	KC	82	3029	769	.491	13	.241	325	.871	151	407	273	83	22	1876	22.9
85-86	SAC	82	2514	623	.475	4	.200	280	.816	173	419	214	54	17	1530	18.7
86-87	SAC	81	2457	606	.463	37	.314	267	.829	146	353	251	42	19	1516	18.7
87-88	PHO	73	2177	533	.480	24	.255	204	.850	121	318	180	33	9	1294	17.7
88-89	PHO	70	2043	608	.497	71	.413	217	.868	91	306	162	47	7	1504	21.5
89-90	PHO	64	1811	411	.453	70	.380	188	.917	69	246	107	32	10	1080	16.9
90-91	PHO/SEA	81	2085	543	.484	39	.325	229	.891	107	271	111	58	9	1354	16.7
91-92	SEA	81	2366	534	.459	27	.252	291	.861	118	292	161	55	11	1386	17.1
92-93	SEA	82	1869	463	.467	17	.304	234	.911	124	272	135	36	4	1177	14.4
93-94	CHA	73	1460	339	.459	59	.393	99	.780	80	224	125	36	8	836	11.5
Totals		1007	29181	7154	.477	402	.329	2948	.840	1664	4386	2340	672	171	17658	17.5

ERVIN JOHNSON

Team: Seattle SuperSonics
Position: Center
Height: 6'11" **Weight:** 245
Birthdate: December 21, 1967

NBA Experience: 1 year
College: New Orleans
Acquired: 1st-round pick in 1993 draft
(23rd overall)

Background: Johnson didn't play high school ball and nearly passed on college too. He bagged groceries in a Baton Rouge, Louisiana, store for nearly three years before soliciting a scholarship from New Orleans. He ranked in the nation's top 20 in rebounding, blocked shots, and field goal percentage as a senior and set several school records. He was drafted 23rd by Seattle last season but played only about six minutes per game in 45 contests.

Strengths: Johnson is from Block High School, and blocks are what he does best. He averaged about one every 12 minutes as a rookie last season. E.J. was a defensive specialist in college who has potential as a fine NBA rebounder. He hits the offensive glass with abandon. Johnson gives maximum effort, makes his fouls count, and gets up and down the floor.

Weaknesses: For offense, Johnson is not your man. He is very limited with the ball in his hands, capable of scoring only on tips and simple plays. One problem is his hands; they're small and stiff and prevent him from catching the ball surely. Last year, he was a 26-year-old rookie and there are some doubts as to how much he can improve over his next several years in the league. He did not show much last season.

Analysis: Johnson was not expected to come in and play right away with the talented Sonics, who posted the best record in the NBA. He did not. When he did get a look, however, he displayed flashes of promise as a shot-blocker and rebounder. The other nuances of NBA defense will need to be learned, and he will not become a first-rate offensive player at this level.

PLAYER SUMMARY	
Will	block shots
Can't	shine on offense
Expect	reserve minutes
Don't Expect	sweet shooting
Fantasy Value	$2-4
Card Value	10-15¢

COLLEGE STATISTICS

		G	FGP	FTP	RPG	PPG
89-90	NO	32	.579	.561	6.8	6.3
90-91	NO	30	.572	.537	12.2	12.7
91-92	NO	32	.584	.714	11.1	15.4
92-93	NO	29	.619	.674	11.9	18.4
Totals		123	.591	.646	10.5	13.1

NBA REGULAR-SEASON STATISTICS

			FGs		3-PT FGs		FTs		Rebounds						
	G	MIN	FG	PCT	FG	PCT	FT	PCT	OFF	TOT	AST	STL	BLK	PTS	PPG
93-94 SEA	45	280	44	.415	0	.000	29	.630	48	118	7	10	22	117	2.6
Totals	45	280	44	.415	0	.000	29	.630	48	118	7	10	22	117	2.6

FRANK JOHNSON

Unrestricted Free Agent
Last Team: Phoenix Suns
Position: Guard
Height: 6'1" **Weight:** 180
Birthdate: November 23, 1958

NBA Experience: 10 years
College: Wake Forest
Acquired: Signed as a free agent, 10/92

Background: The brother of Eddie Johnson (a former All-Star guard with Atlanta), Frank Johnson was a first-round pick of Washington out of Wake Forest. He spent seven relatively quiet years with the Bullets and one with Houston before playing three years in Italy. Phoenix cut him during the 1992 training camp but called him back early in the 1992-93 season. He became a free agent after the 1993-94 campaign.

Strengths: Johnson is very strong for his 180-pound frame and is an aggressive, fearless defender. He makes the right play at the right time and does not try to exceed his bounds. Johnson isn't one to squawk about playing time.

Weaknesses: The Suns tried to get Johnson to shoot more, but he is not a particularly offensive-minded player. He is not likely to return to his second-year numbers, when he averaged 12.5 PPG and 8.1 APG. He won't dazzle anyone with his creativity and is no Kevin Johnson when it comes to quickness.

Analysis: The Suns were looking for a veteran guard and they found their man almost by accident. Though overshadowed from a sheer talent standpoint, Frank Johnson was extremely valuable when K.J. was injured. Ankle and hamstring injuries nagged Frank last season.

PLAYER SUMMARY

Will.............................run the offense
Can't ....beat out K.J.
Expect ....a veteran reserve
Don't Expect.....................complaints
Fantasy Value..................................$0
Card Value ....5-10¢

COLLEGE STATISTICS

		G	FGP	FTP	RPG	PPG
76-77	WF	30	.457	.696	2.8	11.6
77-78	WF	29	.492	.689	3.1	16.2
78-79	WF	27	.477	.768	2.3	16.1
79-80	WF	5	.281	1.00	1.8	5.6
80-81	WF	29	.521	.819	2.1	16.2
Totals		120	.483	.753	2.6	14.6

NBA REGULAR-SEASON STATISTICS

				FGs		3-PT FGs		FTs		Rebounds							
		G	MIN	FG	PCT	FG	PCT	FT	PCT	OFF	TOT	AST	STL	BLK	PTS	PPG
81-82	WAS	79	2027	336	.414	17	.215	153	.750	34	147	380	76	7	842	10.7
82-83	WAS	68	2324	321	.408	14	.230	196	.751	46	178	549	110	6	852	12.5
83-84	WAS	82	2686	392	.467	11	.256	187	.742	58	184	567	96	6	982	12.0
84-85	WAS	46	925	175	.489	6	.353	72	.750	23	63	143	43	3	428	9.3
85-86	WAS	14	402	69	.448	0	.000	38	.704	7	28	76	11	1	176	12.6
86-87	WAS	18	399	59	.461	0	.000	35	.714	10	30	58	21	0	153	8.5
87-88	WAS	75	1258	216	.434	1	.111	121	.812	39	121	188	70	4	554	7.4
88-89	HOU	67	879	109	.443	1	.167	75	.806	22	79	181	42	0	294	4.4
92-93	PHO	77	1122	136	.436	1	.083	59	.776	41	113	186	60	7	332	4.3
93-94	PHO	70	875	134	.448	2	.167	54	.783	29	82	148	41	1	324	4.6
Totals		596	12897	1947	.439	53	.218	990	.760	309	1025	2476	570	35	4937	8.3

KEVIN JOHNSON

Team: Phoenix Suns
Position: Guard
Height: 6'1" **Weight:** 190
Birthdate: March 4, 1966
NBA Experience: 7 years
College: California

Acquired: Traded from Cavaliers with Mark West, Tyrone Corbin, 1988 1st- and 2nd-round picks, and a 1989 2nd-round pick for Larry Nance, Mike Sanders, and a 1988 1st-round pick, 2/88

Background: Johnson concluded his college career as California's all-time leader in scoring, assists, and steals. He averaged more than 21 points and 11 assists per game in his first four full seasons with Phoenix. He won the league's Most Improved Player Award in 1988-89. Groin, hamstring, and knee injuries limited him during the 1992-93 season, but he bounced back last year for his third All-Star appearance.

Strengths: One frightening gift runs through Johnson—unbelievable quickness. There is virtually no one capable of stopping his one-on-one penetration. Leave him open from outside and he will bury jumpers up to 20 feet. His passing skills are made more devastating because he draws multiple defenders when he goes to the hoop. He'll pick your pocket with his defensive quickness.

Weaknesses: Injuries have become a concern over the last two years. Without him in the lineup, Phoenix is simply not the same team. Johnson does not possess 3-point range and he is not much help on the boards.

Analysis: Johnson is the kind of point guard you love to have as a teammate. Because of his supreme quickness and ability to score, defenses collapse on him and lanes to the basket open up for his teammates. When playing at 100 percent, he is clearly one of the dominant lead guards in the NBA and is bound for more All-Star showings.

PLAYER SUMMARY

Will ....penetrate at will
Can't ....take health for granted
Expect ....18-20 PPG
Don't Expect ....many treys
Fantasy Value...........................$45-50
Card Value ....12-25¢

COLLEGE STATISTICS

		G	FGP	FTP	APG	PPG
83-84	CAL	28	.510	.721	2.3	9.7
84-85	CAL	27	.450	.662	4.1	12.9
85-86	CAL	29	.490	.815	6.0	15.6
86-87	CAL	34	.471	.819	5.0	17.2
Totals		118	.477	.757	4.4	14.0

NBA REGULAR-SEASON STATISTICS

		G	MIN	FGs FG	PCT	3-PT FGs FG	PCT	FTs FT	PCT	Rebounds OFF	TOT	AST	STL	BLK	PTS	PPG
87-88	CLE/PHO	80	1917	275	.461	5	.208	177	.839	36	191	437	103	24	732	9.1
88-89	PHO	81	3179	570	.505	2	.091	508	.882	46	340	991	135	24	1650	20.4
89-90	PHO	74	2782	578	.499	8	.195	501	.838	42	270	846	95	14	1665	22.5
90-91	PHO	77	2772	591	.516	9	.205	519	.843	54	271	781	163	11	1710	22.2
91-92	PHO	78	2899	539	.479	10	.217	448	.807	61	292	836	116	23	1536	19.7
92-93	PHO	49	1643	282	.499	1	.125	226	.819	30	104	384	85	20	791	16.1
93-94	PHO	67	2449	477	.487	6	.222	380	.819	55	167	637	125	10	1340	20.0
Totals		506	17641	3312	.494	41	.193	2759	.837	324	1635	4912	822	126	9424	18.6

LARRY JOHNSON

Team: Charlotte Hornets
Position: Forward
Height: 6'7" **Weight:** 250
Birthdate: March 14, 1969

NBA Experience: 3 years
College: Odessa; Nevada-Las Vegas
Acquired: 1st-round pick in 1991 draft
(1st overall)

Background: L.J. originally signed with Southern Methodist, but he ended up at Odessa (Texas) Junior College after SMU officials questioned his retake of the SAT. UNLV won the national title in Johnson's first season and he was the nation's consensus Player of the Year in 1990-91. He was selected No. 1 overall by Charlotte in the 1991 draft and won Rookie of the Year honors. He made his first All-Star appearance in 1993 but missed the 1994 All-Star Game and much of last season with a strained back.

Strengths: Johnson possesses incredible strength that carries over into virtually every aspect of the game. He can't be moved once he gets position on the low blocks. He has advanced post-up scoring skills, is a superb passer, rebounds with a vengeance, and is a tough defensive player. He can score from inside and out. He is one of the game's most popular personalities.

Weaknesses: About the only big concern with Johnson is a back that kept him on the injured list for two months last season. Johnson is a physical player, but defense would not be considered his strength. He is not a productive shot-blocker nor much of a theft at that end of the court.

Analysis: Johnson underwent back surgery in the summer of 1993, but he could not weather the wear and tear of a full season last year. His absence probably cost the Hornets a playoff berth. When healthy, L.J. is one of the most dominant power players in basketball. He is also one of the league's most marketable young stars and has a bright future ahead of him.

PLAYER SUMMARY

Will ....score, rebound
Can't..........................trade in his back
Expect ....an All-Star regular
Don't Expect ....soft play
Fantasy Value..........................$25-30
Card Value ....20-50¢

COLLEGE STATISTICS

		G	FGP	FTP	RPG	PPG
87-88	ODE	35	.649	.794	12.3	22.3
88-89	ODE	35	.653	.760	10.9	29.8
89-90	UNLV	40	.624	.767	11.4	20.6
90-91	UNLV	35	.662	.818	10.9	22.7
Totals		145	.648	.780	11.4	23.7

NBA REGULAR-SEASON STATISTICS

				FGs		3-PT FGs		FTs		Rebounds						
		G	MIN	FG	PCT	FG	PCT	FT	PCT	OFF	TOT	AST	STL	BLK	PTS	PPG
91-92	CHA	82	3047	616	.490	5	.227	339	.829	323	899	292	81	51	1576	19.2
92-93	CHA	82	3323	728	.526	18	.254	336	.767	281	864	353	53	27	1810	22.1
93-94	CHA	51	1757	346	.515	5	.238	137	.695	143	448	184	29	14	834	16.4
Totals		215	8127	1690	.510	28	.246	812	.778	747	2211	829	163	92	4220	19.6

POPEYE JONES

Team: Dallas Mavericks
Position: Forward
Height: 6'8" **Weight:** 250
Birthdate: June 17, 1970
NBA Experience: 1 year

College: Murray St.
Acquired: Draft rights traded from
Rockets for draft rights to Eric Riley,
6/93

Background: A two-time Ohio Valley Conference Player of the Year and an NCAA Tournament regular at Murray State, Jones was drafted by Houston in the second round in 1992. He spent his first professional season in the Italian A2 League, averaging 21.1 points and 13.3 rebounds a game. His rights were traded to Dallas on draft day of 1993 and he started more than half of the Mavericks' games as an NBA rookie. He led Dallas in rebounds.

Strengths: He's Popeye the rebounding man. Jones has a massive frame and knows how to get to the boards. No other Maverick was within 200 rebounds of his total. Jones also has some skills with the ball. His footwork and back-to-the-basket game are fundamentally sound and he owns a great set of hands. Also, he shoots with a soft touch and is an outstanding passer. He uses his big rear end to back into the paint.

Weaknesses: Weight problems have held Jones back throughout his career. It's something he will have to watch. Although he scored a ton of points in college and in Italy, Jones does not own a vast offensive repertoire. His range is limited and he tries to rely too much on finesse when he gets the ball inside. He does not block many shots and he picks up a lot of fouls.

Analysis: Jones enjoyed a fairly successful first season in the NBA. He honed his offensive skills during the year overseas and was a more effective player than many expected. He displayed a pretty nice touch around the basket. He would not have seen as much floor time on a team with more talent than the Mavs, however. He could stand to use more power on both ends of the court.

PLAYER SUMMARY	
Will	work the boards
Can't	avoid fouls
Expect	inside touch
Don't Expect	a power player
Fantasy Value	$1
Card Value	10-20¢

COLLEGE STATISTICS

		G	FGP	FTP	RPG	PPG
88-89	MSU	30	.489	.754	4.6	5.8
89-90	MSU	30	.500	.757	11.2	19.5
90-91	MSU	33	.493	.711	14.2	20.2
91-92	MSU	30	.488	.778	14.4	21.1
Totals		123	.493	.751	11.2	16.7

NBA REGULAR-SEASON STATISTICS

			FGs		3-PT FGs		FTs		Rebounds						
	G	MIN	FG	PCT	FG	PCT	FT	PCT	OFF	TOT	AST	STL	BLK	PTS	PPG
93-94 DAL	81	1773	195	.479	0	.000	78	.729	299	605	99	61	31	468	5.8
Totals	81	1773	195	.479	0	.000	78	.729	299	605	99	61	31	468	5.8

ADAM KEEFE

Team: Atlanta Hawks
Position: Forward
Height: 6'9" **Weight:** 240
Birthdate: February 22, 1970

NBA Experience: 2 years
College: Stanford
Acquired: 1st-round pick in 1992 draft
(10th overall)

Background: Keefe was Stanford's rock in the middle, a three-time Pac-10 rebounding champion. The MVP of the NIT as a junior, Keefe was also a world-class volleyball player who had to de-emphasize the sport because of his basketball commitment. He was the tenth pick in the 1992 draft and played in all 82 games for Atlanta as a rookie. His numbers and playing time were cut rather dramatically last season.

Strengths: Keefe is big, strong, and smart. He plays within himself and is unselfish, almost to a fault. He bangs the boards aggressively, is not afraid of contact, and gets to the free throw line. He is also a pretty good face-up shooter within his limited range. He takes to coaching, wants to learn, and is a team player all the way.

Weaknesses: Most of Keefe's skills are in the unpolished stage. He is very limited in his back-to-the-basket moves and is a step slow when he goes to the hoop. He often struggles to convert in traffic and is not much of a finisher. Keefe is a willing passer, but he needs to develop a sense of where and when to deliver the ball. He does not intimidate defensively. In fact, he is not a standout at any aspect of the sport.

Analysis: The big redhead is clearly not one of the ten best players in his draft class. He's a big man who finds it hard to score inside and is not quick enough to pull his game out to the perimeter. The minutes were simply not there on a much-improved Atlanta team last season, so he did not get much of a chance to improve on his first season.

PLAYER SUMMARY

Will ....work his tail off
Can't ....blow past defenders
Expect........................reserve minutes
Don't Expect..............anything flashy
Fantasy Value...............................$0
Card Value ....7-12¢

COLLEGE STATISTICS

		G	FGP	FTP	RPG	PPG
88-89	STAN	33	.633	.689	5.4	8.4
89-90	STAN	30	.627	.725	9.1	20.0
90-91	STAN	33	.609	.760	9.5	21.5
91-92	STAN	29	.564	.746	12.2	25.3
Totals		125	.600	.736	9.0	18.6

NBA REGULAR-SEASON STATISTICS

				FGs		3-PT FGs		FTs		Rebounds						
		G	MIN	FG	PCT	FG	PCT	FT	PCT	OFF	TOT	AST	STL	BLK	PTS	PPG
92-93	ATL	82	1549	188	.500	0	.000	166	.700	171	432	80	57	16	542	6.6
93-94	ATL	63	763	96	.451	0	.000	81	.730	77	201	34	20	9	273	4.3
Totals		145	2312	284	.482	0	.000	247	.710	248	633	114	77	25	815	5.6

SHAWN KEMP

Team: Seattle SuperSonics
Position: Forward
Height: 6'10" **Weight:** 245
Birthdate: November 26, 1969

NBA Experience: 5 years
College: None
Acquired: 1st-round pick in 1989 draft (17th overall)

Background: Kemp never played a minute of college basketball. He was a Prop 48 casualty at Kentucky, transferred to Trinity Junior College amid scrutiny, then opted for the draft. His athletic dunks caught immediate attention during his rookie year and he became a starter for the Sonics in his second season. He has played in back-to-back All-Star Games and is among the league leaders in rebounding, field goal percentage, and shot-blocking.

Strengths: Kemp's dunks are almost a nightly feature on the TV sports highlights. He is blessed with great quickness to the hoop and dominating physical ability. He is strong, has a great vertical leap, and knows his way around the court. Kemp also plays physical defense and blocks shots with the best of forwards. He leads a talented team in scoring, rebounding, blocks, and several other categories.

Weaknesses: Kemp is not a great outside shooter, although he has improved, and his range is limited. His biggest weakness is in the area of fouling. He fouled out of no less than ten games last season. He also commits an inordinate number of turnovers from trying to do too much.

Analysis: Kemp was a crowd-pleaser from the moment he stepped onto the NBA hardwood. He has since raised his overall game to the stage where he is capable of dominating the opposition on any given night. Kemp was chosen to play with Dream Team II and will be an All-Star regular for years to come. He's a franchise player.

PLAYER SUMMARY	
Will	score, rebound, block
Can't	be stuffed on dunks
Expect	highlight reels
Don't Expect	3-pointers
Fantasy Value	$65-70
Card Value	20-40¢

COLLEGE STATISTICS

—DID NOT PLAY—

NBA REGULAR-SEASON STATISTICS

		G	MIN	FGs FG	FGs PCT	3-PT FGs FG	3-PT FGs PCT	FTs FT	FTs PCT	Rebounds OFF	Rebounds TOT	AST	STL	BLK	PTS	PPG
89-90	SEA	81	1120	203	.479	2	.167	117	.736	146	346	26	47	70	525	6.5
90-91	SEA	81	2442	462	.508	2	.167	288	.661	267	679	144	77	123	1214	15.0
91-92	SEA	64	1808	362	.504	0	.000	270	.748	264	665	86	70	124	994	15.5
92-93	SEA	78	2582	515	.492	0	.000	358	.712	287	833	155	119	146	1388	17.8
93-94	SEA	79	2597	533	.538	1	.250	364	.741	312	851	207	142	166	1431	18.1
Totals		383	10549	2075	.508	5	.143	1397	.716	1276	3374	618	455	629	5552	14.5

STEVE KERR

Unrestricted Free Agent
Last Team: Chicago Bulls
Position: Guard
Height: 6'3" **Weight:** 180

Birthdate: September 27, 1965
NBA Experience: 6 years
College: Arizona
Acquired: Signed as a free agent, 9/93

Background: Kerr was a second-team All-American as a senior at Arizona, where he set a Pac-10 record in 1987-88 by shooting .573 from 3-point range. He is the NBA's all-time leader in 3-point field goal percentage, although he has served mostly in a reserve role with Phoenix, Cleveland, Orlando, and Chicago. The Bulls signed him in September 1993 and he enjoyed his best campaign to date in 1993-94. Though a free agent, he was expected to re-sign with the Bulls.

Strengths: From just about anywhere, Kerr can flat-out shoot the ball. In 1989-90, he became one of two players in NBA history to shoot better than 50 percent from 3-point range over a season. Kerr is also a great free throw shooter and has boosted his scoring output. He works hard and plays with smarts.

Weaknesses: Kerr does very little off the dribble, largely because he is a step slower than the average NBA guard. He does not create much for himself or his teammates. He hustles defensively but again is limited by his lack of speed. He has never been quite good enough to start.

Analysis: No one has hit long-range jumpers at a better rate than Kerr during his career. The Bulls decided to take a chance with him after his dismal 1992-93 campaign and it paid big dividends. Kerr came off the Chicago bench firing and, along with B.J. Armstrong, gave the team a one-two 3-point punch that few clubs could match. Kerr will work his way into the rotation.

PLAYER SUMMARY

Will ....knock down treys
Can't.................................block shots
Expect ....long-range offense
Don't Expect.............creative genius
Fantasy Value...............................$1
Card Value ....5-10¢

COLLEGE STATISTICS

		G	FGP	FTP	RPG	PPG
83-84	ARIZ	28	.516	.692	1.2	7.1
84-85	ARIZ	31	.568	.803	2.4	10.0
85-86	ARIZ	32	.540	.899	3.2	14.4
87-88	ARIZ	38	.559	.824	2.0	12.6
Totals		129	.548	.815	2.2	11.2

NBA REGULAR-SEASON STATISTICS

		G	MIN	FGs FG	FG PCT	3-PT FGs FG	FG PCT	FTs FT	FT PCT	Rebounds OFF	TOT	AST	STL	BLK	PTS	PPG
88-89	PHO	26	157	20	.435	8	.471	6	.667	3	17	24	7	0	54	2.1
89-90	CLE	78	1664	192	.444	73	.507	63	.863	12	98	248	45	7	520	6.7
90-91	CLE	57	905	99	.444	28	.452	45	.849	5	37	131	29	4	271	4.8
91-92	CLE	48	847	121	.511	32	.432	45	.833	14	78	110	27	10	319	6.6
92-93	CLE/ORL	52	481	53	.434	6	.231	22	.917	5	45	70	10	1	134	2.6
93-94	CHI	82	2036	287	.497	52	.419	83	.856	26	131	210	75	3	709	8.6
Totals		343	6090	772	.472	199	.445	264	.852	65	406	793	193	25	2007	5.9

JEROME KERSEY

Team: Portland Trail Blazers
Position: Forward
Height: 6'7" **Weight:** 225
Birthdate: June 26, 1962

NBA Experience: 10 years
College: Longwood College
Acquired: 2nd-round pick in 1984 draft (46th overall)

Background: Kersey rewrote the record books at NAIA Longwood College, where he became the all-time leader in points, rebounds, steals, and blocked shots. He started his pro career modestly before receiving consideration for the league's Most Improved Player Award in 1987-88, when he averaged 19.2 PPG. Since then, however, his scoring average has dipped in six consecutive years.

Strengths: Kersey runs the floor and punctuates the fastbreak for many of his points. He owns great athletic ability and mixes it with hustle. He is an above-average rebounder for a small forward and loves to challenge opponents' lay-ups on the break.

Weaknesses: Kersey has always struggled with shot selection, and his field goal percentage reflects it. His conversion rate continues to decline. He is horribly inconsistent, gets called for a lot of fouls, and does not know when to give up the ball. His days as a double-figure scorer, at least in Portland, are probably done.

Analysis: Kersey was once expected to develop into a dominant player, but not anymore. He seems to decline season by season and cannot reverse the trend. Cliff Robinson stole his starting job two years ago and led the Blazers in scoring last season. Perhaps a change of scenery would do Kersey good. Something has got to change.

PLAYER SUMMARY	
Will	run the floor
Can't	regain old form
Expect	rebounding
Don't Expect	good shooting
Fantasy Value	$2-4
Card Value	7-10¢

COLLEGE STATISTICS

		G	FGP	FTP	RPG	PPG
80-81	LONG	28	.629	.586	8.9	16.9
81-82	LONG	23	.585	.633	11.3	17.0
82-83	LONG	25	.560	.608	10.8	14.6
83-84	LONG	27	.521	.606	14.2	19.6
Totals		103	.570	.607	11.3	17.0

NBA REGULAR-SEASON STATISTICS

				FGs		3-PT FGs		FTs		Rebounds						
		G	MIN	FG	PCT	FG	PCT	FT	PCT	OFF	TOT	AST	STL	BLK	PTS	PPG
84-85	POR	77	958	178	.478	0	.000	117	.646	95	206	63	49	29	473	6.1
85-86	POR	79	1217	258	.549	0	.000	156	.681	137	293	83	85	32	672	8.5
86-87	POR	82	2088	373	.509	1	.043	262	.720	201	496	194	122	77	1009	12.3
87-88	POR	79	2888	611	.499	3	.200	291	.735	211	657	243	127	65	1516	19.2
88-89	POR	76	2716	533	.469	6	.286	258	.694	246	629	243	137	84	1330	17.5
89-90	POR	82	2843	519	.478	3	.150	269	.690	251	690	188	121	63	1310	16.0
90-91	POR	73	2359	424	.478	4	.308	232	.709	169	481	227	101	76	1084	14.8
91-92	POR	77	2553	398	.467	1	.125	174	.664	241	633	243	114	71	971	12.6
92-93	POR	65	1719	281	.438	8	.286	116	.634	126	406	121	80	41	686	10.6
93-94	POR	78	1276	203	.433	1	.125	101	.748	130	331	75	71	49	508	6.5
Totals		768	20617	3778	.480	27	.186	1976	.696	1807	4822	1680	1007	587	9559	12.4

WARREN KIDD

Unrestricted Free Agent
Last Team: Philadelphia 76ers
Position: Forward
Height: 6'9" **Weight:** 235
Birthdate: September 9, 1970

NBA Experience: 1 year
College: Middle Tennessee St.
Acquired: Signed as a free agent, 10/93

Background: Kidd, from Harpersville, Alabama, led the nation in rebounding as a senior at Middle Tennessee State and shot a blistering .664 from the field during his career. He was named first-team All-Ohio Valley Conference for three consecutive years. He went undrafted in 1993 but was signed by Philadelphia and was in the starting lineup on opening day. He spent most of his rookie season coming off the bench. When the Sixers signed Scott Williams in July, they renounced their rights to Kidd.

Strengths: Kidd earned a reputation as a big-time rebounder in college and has demonstrated that same potential as a pro. Though he averaged less than four boards per game last year, he did enjoy some fine outings on the glass. He also displayed an offensive game that was better than expected. He shoots for a high percentage, even from mid-range, and does little to hurt his team on offense.

Weaknesses: Kidd did not rebound as well as expected last season, which ultimately kept him in a reserve role. He also has a lot to learn on the defensive end of the court. He won't hurt his team on offense, but at the same time he does not have the look of a scorer. He played exclusively under the basket in college and needs to expand his perimeter game considerably.

Analysis: Kidd beat out Tim Perry for the starting power-forward spot during the 1993-94 preseason, but he eventually backed up Perry for most of the year. For some reason, Kidd seemed to hit the proverbial wall after a surprising start, then played his way back into favor as the season progressed. Philly preferred Williams over Kidd, but the youngster does have a future in the NBA.

PLAYER SUMMARY	
Will	rebound
Can't	play the perimeter
Expect	high FG pct.
Don't Expect	a lot of offense
Fantasy Value	$0
Card Value	5-10¢

COLLEGE STATISTICS

		G	FGP	FTP	RPG	PPG
90-91	MTS	30	.700	.534	12.3	13.4
91-92	MTS	27	.664	.585	10.8	13.9
92-93	MTS	26	.630	.571	14.8	15.0
Totals		83	.664	.564	12.6	14.0

NBA REGULAR-SEASON STATISTICS

				FGs		3-PT FGs		FTs		Rebounds						
		G	MIN	FG	PCT	FG	PCT	FT	PCT	OFF	TOT	AST	STL	BLK	PTS	PPG
93-94	PHI	68	884	100	.592	0	.000	47	.547	76	233	19	19	23	247	3.6
Totals		68	884	100	.592	0	.000	47	.547	76	233	19	19	23	247	3.6

STACEY KING

Team: Minnesota Timberwolves
Position: Forward/Center
Height: 6'11" **Weight:** 250
Birthdate: January 29, 1967

NBA Experience: 5 years
College: Oklahoma
Acquired: Traded from Bulls for Luc
Longley, 2/94

Background: King earned All-America and Big Eight Player of the Year
accolades as a senior at Oklahoma, where he led the conference in scoring and
rebounding as a senior. He was named second-team All-Rookie with Chicago in
1989-90. He was inconsistent with the Bulls but was a member of three straight
NBA title teams. He was traded in February 1994 to Minnesota, and King fared
better as a starter for the T'Wolves.

Strengths: King runs the floor well for a big man and has shown some promise
offensively. He looks to score whenever he touches the ball. He possesses a
decent hook shot and a turnaround jumper in the post. While not a banger on
defense, King does a decent job pressuring the ball and has the makings of a
fine shot-blocker.

Weaknesses: King is not a great rebounder, and that is probably the biggest
reason the Bulls shipped him north. He is not physical in the post on either end of
the court and gets murdered on the glass by opposing centers. His glaring
weakness has simply been his inconsistency. He takes some bad shots and
misses most of them.

Analysis: The trade to Minnesota for Luc Longley was probably the best thing
that could have happened to King. It gave him a chance to start, and he put up
some pretty decent numbers over the final quarter of the season. If he would
make a commitment to rebounding and take better shots, King could still surprise
some people.

PLAYER SUMMARY	
Will	look to score
Can't	dominate physically
Expect	Minnesota starts
Don't Expect	All-Star play
Fantasy Value	$3-5
Card Value	5-10¢

COLLEGE STATISTICS

		G	FGP	FTP	RPG	PPG
85-86	OKLA	14	.388	.744	3.8	6.0
86-87	OKLA	28	.438	.621	3.9	7.0
87-88	OKLA	39	.543	.675	8.5	22.3
88-89	OKLA	33	.524	.718	10.1	26.0
Totals		114	.516	.690	7.2	17.6

NBA REGULAR-SEASON STATISTICS

		G	MIN	FGs FG	FGs PCT	3-PT FGs FG	3-PT FGs PCT	FTs FT	FTs PCT	Rebounds OFF	Rebounds TOT	AST	STL	BLK	PTS	PPG
89-90	CHI	82	1777	267	.504	0	.000	194	.727	169	384	87	38	58	728	8.9
90-91	CHI	76	1198	156	.467	0	.000	107	.704	72	208	65	24	42	419	5.5
91-92	CHI	79	1268	215	.506	2	.400	119	.753	87	205	77	21	25	551	7.0
92-93	CHI	76	1059	160	.471	2	.333	86	.705	105	207	71	26	20	408	5.4
93-94	CHI/MIN	49	1053	146	.428	0	.000	93	.684	90	241	58	31	42	385	7.9
Totals		362	6355	944	.479	4	.250	599	.717	523	1245	358	140	187	2491	6.9

GREG KITE

Team: Orlando Magic
Position: Center
Height: 6'11" **Weight:** 260
Birthdate: August 5, 1961

NBA Experience: 11 years
College: Brigham Young
Acquired: Signed as a free agent, 8/90

Background: Kite helped Danny Ainge rally BYU into the 1981 NCAA East Regional finals and finished his career ranked third on the school's rebounding charts. He was mostly a reserve center with Boston, the L.A. Clippers, and Charlotte before Sacramento picked him up in 1989-90. Kite started 173 games over the next three years with the Kings and Magic, but he has since been glued to the bench.

Strengths: Kite is a physical defender who gets under the skin of other centers. Some call him dirty. He bangs the body defensively, takes hard fouls, and knows his limitations on offense. His hard work has been rewarded with playing time on poor teams. Injuries limited him even further last year.

Weaknesses: Kite could not be an offensive force in an empty gym. He averages less than a bucket per game these days and has a career mark below three PPG. He cannot capably dribble the ball, find open men, or hit shots from anywhere. Injuries limited him even further last year.

Analysis: The addition of Shaquille O'Neal two years ago moved Kite to the position he ought to be in—reserve center. He spent more time on the injured list and the bench than he did on the court last season. He deserves credit for lasting this long in the NBA.

PLAYER SUMMARY	
Will	irritate his man
Can't	make a shot
Expect	numbered days
Don't Expect	a bucket a game
Fantasy Value	$0
Card Value	5-10¢

COLLEGE STATISTICS

		G	FGP	FTP	RPG	PPG
79-80	BYU	21	.292	.480	4.1	1.9
80-81	BYU	32	.489	.495	8.5	8.3
81-82	BYU	30	.467	.446	7.8	6.2
82-83	BYU	29	.437	.571	8.8	7.7
Totals		112	.452	.504	7.6	6.4

NBA REGULAR-SEASON STATISTICS

				FGs		3-PT FGs		FTs		Rebounds						
		G	MIN	FG	PCT	FG	PCT	FT	PCT	OFF	TOT	AST	STL	BLK	PTS	PPG
83-84	BOS	35	197	30	.455	0	.000	5	.313	27	62	7	1	5	65	1.9
84-85	BOS	55	424	33	.375	0	.000	22	.688	38	89	17	3	10	88	1.6
85-86	BOS	64	464	34	.374	0	.000	15	.385	35	128	17	3	28	83	1.3
86-87	BOS	74	745	47	.427	0	.000	29	.382	61	169	27	17	46	123	1.7
87-88	BOS/LAC	53	1063	92	.449	0	.000	40	.506	85	264	47	19	58	224	4.2
88-89	LAC/CHA	70	942	65	.430	0	.000	20	.488	81	243	36	27	54	150	2.1
89-90	SAC	71	1515	101	.432	1	1.000	27	.500	131	377	76	31	51	230	3.2
90-91	ORL	82	2225	166	.491	0	.000	63	.512	189	588	59	25	81	395	4.8
91-92	ORL	72	1479	94	.437	0	.000	40	.588	156	402	44	30	57	228	3.2
92-93	ORL	64	640	38	.452	0	.000	13	.542	66	193	10	13	12	89	1.4
93-94	ORL	29	309	13	.371	0	.000	8	.364	22	70	4	2	12	34	1.2
Totals		669	10003	713	.441	1	.167	282	.491	891	2585	344	171	414	1709	2.6

JOE KLEINE

Team: Phoenix Suns
Position: Center
Height: 7'0" **Weight:** 271
Birthdate: January 4, 1962

NBA Experience: 9 years
College: Notre Dame; Arkansas
Acquired: Signed as a free agent,
8/93

Background: Kleine, who transferred to Arkansas after a year at Notre Dame, led the Razorbacks in scoring as a junior and senior and was a member of the gold-medal-winning 1984 U.S. Olympic team. He started 60 games and averaged 9.8 PPG with Sacramento in 1987-88, his best statistical year. He backed up Robert Parish for four years in Boston and played in 74 games for Phoenix last season.

Strengths: Opponents cringe when Kleine checks into the game. He uses his huge body to put the hurt on people. He rebounds, sets hard picks, and plays a style of defense that could get him arrested for assault. His fouls result in bruises. His work ethic is exemplary.

Weaknesses: Finesse has no place in Kleine's game. He possesses poor hands, should be forbidden to dribble the ball, and is a below-average passer. His only real role in the offense is as a screen-setter and rebounder. Foul trouble would be a problem if he saw more than 12 minutes per game.

Analysis: As a back-up center who doesn't play a lot of minutes, Kleine does what is asked of him. He rebounds, plays defense, throws his weight around, and gets the most out of his fouls. He simply does not possess the offensive game to be a productive starter on a decent team.

PLAYER SUMMARY	
Will	cause bruises
Can't	play with finesse
Expect	a physical presence
Don't Expect	starts
Fantasy Value	$0
Card Value	5-8¢

COLLEGE STATISTICS

		G	FGP	FTP	RPG	PPG
80-81	ND	29	.640	.750	2.4	2.6
82-83	ARK	30	.537	.633	7.3	13.3
83-84	ARK	32	.595	.773	9.2	18.2
84-85	ARK	35	.607	.720	8.4	22.1
Totals		126	.587	.723	7.0	14.5

NBA REGULAR-SEASON STATISTICS

			FGs		3-PT FGs		FTs		Rebounds						
	G	MIN	FG	PCT	FG	PCT	FT	PCT	OFF	TOT	AST	STL	BLK	PTS	PPG
85-86 SAC	80	1180	160	.465	0	.000	94	.723	113	373	46	24	34	414	5.2
86-87 SAC	79	1658	256	.471	0	.000	110	.786	173	483	71	35	30	622	7.9
87-88 SAC	82	1999	324	.472	0	.000	153	.814	179	579	93	28	59	801	9.8
88-89 SAC/BOS	75	1411	175	.405	0	.000	134	.882	124	378	67	33	23	484	6.5
89-90 BOS	81	1365	176	.480	0	.000	83	.830	117	355	46	15	27	435	5.4
90-91 BOS	72	850	102	.468	0	.000	54	.783	71	244	21	15	14	258	3.6
91-92 BOS	70	991	144	.491	4	.500	34	.708	94	296	32	23	14	326	4.7
92-93 BOS	78	1129	108	.404	0	.000	41	.707	113	346	39	17	17	257	3.3
93-94 PHO	74	848	125	.488	5	.455	30	.769	50	193	45	14	19	285	3.9
Totals	691	11431	1570	.461	9	.265	733	.793	1034	3247	460	204	237	3882	5.6

NEGELE KNIGHT

Team: San Antonio Spurs
Position: Guard
Height: 6'1" **Weight:** 182
Birthdate: March 6, 1967

NBA Experience: 4 years
College: Dayton
Acquired: Traded from Suns for a future 2nd-round pick, 11/93

Background: Knight left Dayton as the school's all-time assists leader and was sixth on the career scoring list. As a rookie with Phoenix during the 1990-91 season, he emerged as a reliable back-up to Kevin Johnson at the point. He served in that role for three seasons with Phoenix before a trade in November 1993 brought him to San Antonio for a second-round draft choice. He set a career high in scoring in 1993-94.

Strengths: Knight does well in an open-court game, pushing the ball up-court and making good decisions at high speed. He is extremely confident with the ball and is a hard-nosed defender who will not back down. He has proven to be a capable starter but accepts his reserve role and comes ready to play. He has shown a knack for scoring and has a decent stroke.

Weaknesses: Knight has not displayed the playmaking that made him highly sought-after during his first two seasons in Phoenix. In fact, he was only fourth on the Spurs in assists last season. He does not possess NBA 3-point range. Defensively, he plays tough but does not force a lot of turnovers.

Analysis: Knight was once a hot prospect who had teams ready to trade a great deal for his services. "A second-round steal," he was called. As it turned out, he was traded only for a second-round draft choice. His shooting has improved and he is capable of filling in as a starter when called upon. Now he could stand to brush up on his playmaking and his overall consistency.

PLAYER SUMMARY

Will	...........................fill in as starter
Can't	..................star as a playmaker
Expect	...............................confidence
Don't Expect	...........loads of assists
Fantasy Value	..................................$1
Card Value	...............................5-12¢

COLLEGE STATISTICS

		G	FGP	FTP	APG	PPG
85-86	DAY	30	.379	.670	4.3	7.1
87-88	DAY	31	.472	.713	4.9	14.8
88-89	DAY	29	.366	.735	5.2	13.9
89-90	DAY	32	.503	.800	6.8	22.8
Totals		122	.440	.746	5.4	14.8

NBA REGULAR-SEASON STATISTICS

			MIN	FGs		3-PT FGs		FTs		Rebounds						
		G	MIN	FG	PCT	FG	PCT	FT	PCT	OFF	TOT	AST	STL	BLK	PTS	PPG
90-91	PHO	64	792	131	.425	6	.240	71	.602	20	71	191	20	7	339	5.3
91-92	PHO	42	631	103	.475	4	.308	33	.688	16	46	112	24	3	243	5.8
92-93	PHO	52	888	124	.391	0	.000	67	.779	28	64	145	23	4	315	6.1
93-94	PHO/SA	65	1438	225	.474	4	.190	141	.810	28	103	197	34	11	595	9.2
Totals		223	3749	583	.443	14	.212	312	.732	92	284	645	101	25	1492	6.7

JON KONCAK

Team: Atlanta Hawks
Position: Center
Height: 7'0" **Weight:** 250
Birthdate: May 17, 1963

NBA Experience: 9 years
College: Southern Methodist
Acquired: 1st-round pick in 1985 draft
(5th overall)

Background: Koncak concluded his career at Southern Methodist as the school's all-time leader in rebounds, blocked shots, and field goal percentage. He played for the gold-medal-winning U.S. Olympic team in 1984. He served most of his first seven seasons with Atlanta as a reserve, but he signed a six-year, $13.2 million contract in 1989. He has led the Hawks in blocks as a starter in each of the last two years.

Strengths: The reason the Hawks were forced to match Detroit's contract offer five years ago was Koncak's value at the defensive end of the court. He bangs, plays sound position defense, and blocks shots. He brings good size to the middle and is unselfish on offense.

Weaknesses: Koncak offers next to nothing offensively, which is why Atlanta fans have viewed him as a big-league bust. He hasn't averaged more than six PPG since his rookie year and he shoots a poor percentage from the field. He's a horrible ball-handler and passer.

Analysis: Koncak is a defensive role-player who has improved his game in areas most fans don't notice. He starts for a strong Atlanta team because he blocks shots, sets picks, defends, and does not require many shots. His contract becomes less of an issue as others rake in multi-million-dollar pacts.

PLAYER SUMMARY	
Will	work on defense
Can't	gain offensive notice
Expect	blocked shots
Don't Expect	athletic ability
Fantasy Value	$0
Card Value	5-8¢

COLLEGE STATISTICS

		G	FGP	FTP	RPG	PPG
81-82	SMU	27	.461	.620	5.7	10.0
82-83	SMU	30	.527	.691	9.4	14.6
83-84	SMU	33	.621	.607	11.5	15.5
84-85	SMU	33	.592	.667	10.7	17.2
Totals		123	.559	.649	9.5	14.5

NBA REGULAR-SEASON STATISTICS

		G	MIN	FGs FG	FGs PCT	3-PT FGs FG	3-PT FGs PCT	FTs FT	FTs PCT	Rebounds OFF	Rebounds TOT	AST	STL	BLK	PTS	PPG
85-86	ATL	82	1695	263	.507	0	.000	156	.607	171	467	55	37	69	682	8.3
86-87	ATL	82	1684	169	.480	0	.000	125	.654	153	493	31	52	76	463	5.6
87-88	ATL	49	1073	98	.483	0	.000	83	.610	103	333	19	36	56	279	5.7
88-89	ATL	74	1531	141	.524	0	.000	63	.553	147	453	56	54	98	345	4.7
89-90	ATL	54	977	78	.614	0	.000	42	.532	58	226	23	38	34	198	3.7
90-91	ATL	77	1931	140	.436	1	.125	32	.593	101	375	124	74	76	313	4.1
91-92	ATL	77	1489	111	.391	0	.000	19	.655	62	261	132	50	67	241	3.1
92-93	ATL	78	1975	124	.464	3	.375	24	.480	100	427	140	75	100	275	3.5
93-94	ATL	82	1823	159	.431	0	.000	24	.667	83	365	102	63	125	342	4.2
Totals		655	14178	1283	.473	4	.103	568	.600	978	3400	682	479	701	3138	4.8

LARRY KRYSTKOWIAK

Unrestricted Free Agent
Last Team: Orlando Magic
Position: Forward
Height: 6'9" **Weight:** 240
Birthdate: September 23, 1964

NBA Experience: 8 years
College: Montana
Acquired: Signed as a free agent, 9/93

Background: At Montana, Krystkowiak was named Big Sky Conference MVP three times and Academic All-American twice, finishing his career as the school's all-time scoring leader. He played with San Antonio as a rookie and became a starter in his second year with Milwaukee, but a serious knee injury in the 1989 playoffs eventually required reconstructive surgery. He was traded to Utah in 1992 but returned to the injured list for most of last season, which he spent in Orlando. He left the Magic as a free agent after the season.

Strengths: Krystkowiak knows his limits and plays within them. His game is founded on heart and hustle and he is not afraid to sacrifice his body. His work ethic during his grueling rehab mirrored his style on the court. He can be a decent medium-range shooter and is not shy about going to the glass.

Weaknesses: "Krysto" admits that his torn-up knee has taken something from his game, and he continues to be plagued by injury problems. He doesn't have much range on his jumper. His slow-footedness hurts him most on the defensive end. He has averaged double figures just once in his career.

Analysis: Krystkowiak showed what he's made of by recovering from a serious knee injury—the now-famous torn anterior cruciate ligament. Hard work is second nature to him. He can be a very good complementary player who does what he's asked and gives his all, but he has to be on the court first.

PLAYER SUMMARY	
Will	hustle at both ends
Can't	stay healthy
Expect	a solid role-player
Don't Expect	a full season
Fantasy Value	$0
Card Value	5-8¢

COLLEGE STATISTICS

		G	FGP	FTP	RPG	PPG
82-83	MONT	28	.433	.688	4.3	4.9
83-84	MONT	30	.547	.805	10.5	18.0
84-85	MONT	80	.585	.840	10.2	21.1
85-86	MONT	32	.578	.760	11.4	22.2
Totals		120	.561	.790	9.2	16.8

NBA REGULAR-SEASON STATISTICS

		G	MIN	FGs FG	FGs PCT	3-PT FGs FG	3-PT FGs PCT	FTs FT	FTs PCT	Rebounds OFF	Rebounds TOT	AST	STL	BLK	PTS	PPG
86-87	SA	68	1004	170	.456	1	.083	110	.743	77	239	85	22	12	451	6.6
87-88	MIL	50	1050	128	.481	0	.000	103	.811	88	231	50	18	8	359	7.2
88-89	MIL	80	2472	362	.473	4	.333	289	.823	198	610	107	93	9	1017	12.7
89-90	MIL	16	381	43	.364	0	.000	26	.788	16	76	25	10	2	112	7.0
91-92	MIL	79	1848	293	.444	0	.000	128	.757	131	429	114	54	12	714	9.0
92-93	UTA	71	1362	198	.466	0	.000	117	.796	74	279	68	42	13	513	7.2
93-94	ORL	34	682	71	.480	0	.000	31	.795	38	123	35	14	4	173	5.1
Totals		398	8799	1265	.459	5	.139	804	.793	622	1987	484	253	60	3339	8.4

TONI KUKOC

Team: Chicago Bulls
Position: Forward
Height: 6'10" **Weight:** 230
Birthdate: September 18, 1968

NBA Experience: 1 year
College: None
Acquired: 2nd-round pick in 1990 draft (29th overall)

Background: Kukoc was considered one of the greatest players ever to play in Europe, starring for Benetton Treviso of the Italian 1A League and earning several Player of the Year honors. He was compared to Magic Johnson. He averaged 19 points, six rebounds, and five assists a game in his final year overseas. His NBA rights have belonged to the Bulls since 1990, when they drafted him in the second round, and the team finally lured him to America last season. He was one of four Bulls to score in double figures.

Strengths: Kukoc is a tremendous all-around talent whose best assets are his court vision and unselfishness. He does a little bit of everything, including shooting with 3-point range, handling the ball, and finding the open man. He finished among rookie leaders in scoring, assists, rebounding, and steals. He is a veteran of top-notch competition and hit a number of clutch, game-winning shots in his first NBA season.

Weaknesses: Kukoc is not a physically strong player, and he could use some added muscle for the grinding style of defense required in the NBA. He was accustomed to playing zone in Europe and is still learning man-to-man defense. His shooting was streaky last year and he turned the ball over better than twice a game on average.

Analysis: Kukoc was first seen by many American basketball fans on Croatia's silver-medal-winning Olympic team in 1992. He was hardly a letdown in his first NBA season, playing confidently against the best players in the world and holding his own. He fit in nicely with veterans like Scottie Pippen and Horace Grant and will eventually become a starter before his American career is complete.

PLAYER SUMMARY	
Will	spot open men
Can't	dominate physically
Expect	all-around ability
Don't Expect	fear in the clutch
Fantasy Value	$5-7
Card Value	20-50¢

COLLEGE STATISTICS

—DID NOT PLAY—

NBA REGULAR-SEASON STATISTICS

			FGs		3-PT FGs		FTs		Rebounds						
	G	MIN	FG	PCT	FG	PCT	FT	PCT	OFF	TOT	AST	STL	BLK	PTS	PPG
93-94 CHI	75	1808	313	.431	32	.271	156	.743	98	297	252	81	33	814	10.9
Totals	75	1808	313	.431	32	.271	156	.743	98	297	252	81	33	814	10.9

CHRISTIAN LAETTNER

Team: Minnesota Timberwolves
Position: Forward
Height: 6'11" **Weight:** 235
Birthdate: August 17, 1969

NBA Experience: 2 years
College: Duke
Acquired: 1st-round pick in 1992 draft
(3rd overall)

Background: The only collegiate player on the 1992 Olympic Dream Team, Laettner was named national Player of the Year as a senior and was the catalyst behind Duke's back-to-back national championships in 1991 and 1992. He became the only player in history to start in four Final Fours. The third choice overall in the 1992 draft, he has led the Timberwolves in rebounds and blocked shots both seasons and in scoring last year.

Strengths: Laettner can score from inside and out. He has good range with his jumper, yet is strong enough to muscle inside for short bank shots and dunks. He is solid fundamentally. Mentally tough, Laettner has never been afraid to take clutch shots and likes to have the ball in his hands. He's a strong rebounder and is not afraid to muscle up on defense. He owns team records for rebounds and free throws in a season.

Weaknesses: Abrasive. Annoying. Cocky. All have been used to describe Laettner, a difficult personality to size up. Teammates have called him selfish, although he has racked up the assists in his two seasons. He turns the ball over far too often, draws a lot of whistles, and does not shoot for a high percentage.

Analysis: Minnesota G.M. Jack McCloskey may have hit the nail on the head when he offered of a rookie Laettner: "He's going to become the player he already thinks he is." Say what you will about him, but Laettner is a big-league talent. While his supreme confidence has caused some to resent him, it also helps him play above the level that most can achieve. He deserves recognition for what he does on the court.

PLAYER SUMMARY

Will	make headlines
Can't	be easily figured
Expect	scoring, rebounding
Don't Expect	universal respect
Fantasy Value	$40-45
Card Value	10-25¢

COLLEGE STATISTICS

		G	FGP	FTP	RPG	PPG
88-89	DUKE	36	.723	.717	4.7	8.9
89-90	DUKE	38	.511	.836	9.6	16.3
90-91	DUKE	39	.575	.802	8.7	19.8
91-92	DUKE	35	.575	.815	7.9	21.5
Totals		148	.574	.806	7.8	16.6

NBA REGULAR-SEASON STATISTICS

				FGs		3-PT FGs		FTs		Rebounds						
		G	MIN	FG	PCT	FG	PCT	FT	PCT	OFF	TOT	AST	STL	BLK	PTS	PPG
92-93	MIN	81	2823	503	.474	4	.100	462	.835	171	708	223	105	83	1472	18.2
93-94	MIN	70	2428	396	.448	6	.240	375	.783	160	602	307	87	86	1173	16.8
Totals		151	5251	899	.462	10	.154	837	.811	331	1310	530	192	169	2645	17.5

ANDREW LANG

Team: Atlanta Hawks
Position: Center
Height: 6'11" **Weight:** 250
Birthdate: June 28, 1966

NBA Experience: 6 years
College: Arkansas
Acquired: Signed as a free agent, 9/93

Background: Lang completed his collegiate career at Arkansas as the school's all-time leader in blocked shots. His playing time increased in each of his four years with Phoenix and he blocked 201 shots in 1991-92. He went to Philadelphia in the 1992 trade that sent Charles Barkley to Phoenix, but the 76ers renounced his rights after the 1992-93 season. Atlanta signed him in September 1993 and used him as a reserve.

Strengths: When it comes to defensive middle men, Lang is a good one. He has blocked more than 700 shots in his career and is capable of holding his own on the glass. He's blessed with great lateral quickness for his size. His instincts are first-rate and he runs the floor well for a center. He hustles at both ends.

Weaknesses: Lang will never be a big scorer. Most of his points come from within a few feet of the hoop. After four years of shooting better than 50 percent with the Suns, he has dropped off the last two years. He does not handle the ball well, even in the pivot, and he does not own a vast array of moves. He also draws a lot of fouls.

Analysis: Defensively, Lang can be a factor because of his quickness and shot-blocking. However, he failed to block 100 shots last season for the first time since his rookie year. Offensively, Lang remains a liability. He does work hard and he knows his limitations. He is best used as a reserve and will likely continue in that role for the rest of his career.

PLAYER SUMMARY

Will	.....................swat shots
Can't	..........................handle the ball
Expect	..........defensive intimidation
Don't Expect	............full-time starting
Fantasy Value.	...............................$0
Card Value	..................................5-10¢

COLLEGE STATISTICS

		G	FGP	FTP	RPG	PPG
84-85	ARK	33	.405	.563	2.0	2.6
85-86	ARK	26	.466	.607	6.5	8.1
86-87	ARK	32	.500	.644	7.5	8.1
87-88	ARK	30	.527	.450	7.3	9.3
Totals		121	.489	.575	5.7	6.9

NBA REGULAR-SEASON STATISTICS

			FGs		3-PT FGs		FTs		Rebounds						
	G	MIN	FG	PCT	FG	PCT	FT	PCT	OFF	TOT	AST	STL	BLK	PTS	PPG
88-89 PHO	62	526	60	.513	0	.000	39	.650	54	147	9	17	48	159	2.6
89-90 PHO	74	1011	97	.557	0	.000	64	.653	83	271	21	22	133	258	3.5
90-91 PHO	63	1152	109	.577	0	.000	93	.715	113	303	27	17	127	311	4.9
91-92 PHO	81	1965	248	.522	0	.000	126	.768	170	546	43	48	201	622	7.7
92-93 PHI	73	1861	149	.425	1	.200	87	.763	136	436	79	46	141	386	5.3
93-94 ATL	82	1608	215	.469	1	.250	73	.689	126	313	51	38	87	504	6.1
Totals	435	8123	878	.498	2	.182	482	.717	682	2016	230	188	737	2240	5.1

ERIC LECKNER

Team: Detroit Pistons
Position: Center/Forward
Height: 6'11" **Weight:** 265
Birthdate: May 27, 1966

NBA Experience: 5 years
College: Wyoming
Acquired: Traded from 76ers for a future 2nd-round pick, 7/94

Background: Leckner was named Most Valuable Player of the Western Athletic Conference Tournament for three straight years at Wyoming, where he ranked among NCAA leaders in field goal percentage as a senior. He labored as a reserve during most of his first four NBA seasons in Utah, Sacramento, and Charlotte. He was signed by the 76ers before the 1993-94 campaign and traded to Detroit after it.

Strengths: Leckner has some pretty good moves in the post and a decent jumper when squared to the hoop. He rebounds, sets hard picks, works hard on defense, and does not try to play above and beyond his capabilities. Leckner is well-liked for his personality and his willingness to play the game with all he's got.

Weaknesses: Leckner is a marginal talent at best. He's been a back-up center for most of his career because he possesses neither the game skills nor the athletic ability to score a lot of points. He is not an impact player in any phase of the game. He's a step slow, has "hard hands," and can be outrebounded by smaller, quicker opponents. He draws a lot of fouls.

Analysis: Leckner will not pop up in conversations about athletic ability among centers. He is a third-teamer for a lot of clubs, but he wound up starting for the 76ers during the 1993-94 season after Shawn Bradley was lost for the year. The team lost virtually every game with him in the pivot. Leckner will earn more minutes by default with the pivot-poor Pistons.

PLAYER SUMMARY	
Will	use his body
Can't	burn his man
Expect	maximum effort
Don't Expect	great ability
Fantasy Value	$0
Card Value	5-10¢

COLLEGE STATISTICS

		G	FGP	FTP	RPG	PPG
84-85	WYO	29	.583	.615	3.9	8.4
85-86	WYO	36	.582	.612	5.8	15.8
86-87	WYO	34	.631	.706	7.2	18.6
87-88	WYO	32	.644	.756	6.6	15.4
Totals		131	.612	.681	5.9	14.8

NBA REGULAR-SEASON STATISTICS

			FGs		3-PT FGs		FTs		Rebounds						
		G	MIN	FG	PCT	FG	PCT	FT	PCT	OFF	TOT	AST	STL	BLK	PTS	PPG
88-89	UTA	75	779	120	.545	0	.000	79	.699	48	199	16	8	22	319	4.3
89-90	UTA	77	764	125	.563	0	.000	81	.743	48	192	19	15	23	331	4.3
90-91	SAC/CHA	72	1122	131	.446	0	.000	62	.559	82	295	39	14	22	324	4.5
91-92	CHA	59	716	79	.513	0	.000	38	.745	49	206	31	9	18	196	3.3
93-94	PHI	71	1163	139	.486	0	.000	84	.646	75	282	86	18	34	362	5.1
Totals		354	4544	594	.505	0	.000	344	.669	302	1174	191	64	119	1532	4.3

TIM LEGLER

Team: Dallas Mavericks
Position: Guard
Height: 6'4"　**Weight:** 210
Birthdate: December 26, 1966

NBA Experience: 4 years
College: La Salle
Acquired: Signed as a free agent, 3/93

Background: Legler enjoyed a hot-shooting career at La Salle before starting a transient career in the Continental Basketball Association. He shot a blistering .465 from 3-point range for the Omaha Racers in 1991-92. Before playing with Utah and ultimately landing with Dallas in 1992-93, he saw brief stints in Phoenix and Denver. He played a career-high 79 games with the Mavericks last season.

Strengths: Long-range shooting is the calling card of Legler, who canned 52 of 139 treys during the 1993-94 campaign. He's also a great shooter from the free throw line, can handle the ball when asked to do so, and does not shy away from defense. He has paid his dues in pro basketball and became an 8.3-PPG scorer with Dallas last year.

Weaknesses: The main reason it took Legler so long to find an NBA home for a full season is his marginal athletic ability. He lacks the speed and quickness required to get to the basket regularly and play tough defense against some of the better two guards in the league. He is not an offensive creator. All in all, Legler is not outstanding in any area of the game but shooting.

Analysis: Finally, Legler seems to have drawn enough NBA interest to stick with someone. He landed with Dallas midway through the 1992-93 season and saw his first full slate of action last year. He gave the Mavericks a shooting threat with great range off the bench and displayed a fine work ethic. Nevertheless, Legler remains a one-dimensional player who would struggle for playing time on a more talented NBA team.

PLAYER SUMMARY	
Will	shoot with range
Can't	create on offense
Expect	a 3-point specialist
Don't Expect	multiple talents
Fantasy Value	$0
Card Value	5-10¢

COLLEGE STATISTICS

		G	FGP	FTP	RPG	PPG
84-85	LaS	26	.469	.708	2.8	6.0
85-86	LaS	28	.502	.833	3.9	12.9
86-87	LaS	33	.478	.782	4.5	18.7
87-88	LaS	34	.502	.803	4.1	16.7
Totals		121	.490	.791	3.9	14.0

NBA REGULAR-SEASON STATISTICS

		G	MIN	FGs FG	FGs PCT	3-PT FGs FG	3-PT FGs PCT	FTs FT	FTs PCT	Rebounds OFF	Rebounds TOT	AST	STL	BLK	PTS	PPG
89-90	PHO	11	83	11	.379	0	.000	6	1.00	4	8	6	2	0	28	2.5
90-91	DEN	10	148	25	.347	3	.250	5	.833	8	18	12	2	0	58	5.8
92-93	UTA/DAL	33	635	105	.436	22	.338	25	.803	25	59	46	24	6	289	8.8
93-94	DAL	79	1322	231	.438	52	.374	142	.840	36	128	120	52	13	656	8.3
Totals		133	2188	372	.428	77	.355	210	.833	73	213	184	80	19	1031	7.8

LAFAYETTE LEVER

Unrestricted Free Agent
Last Team: Dallas Mavericks
Position: Guard
Height: 6'3" **Weight:** 175
Birthdate: August 18, 1960

NBA Experience: 11 years
College: Arizona St.
Acquired: Traded from Nuggets for 1990 and 1991 1st-round picks, 6/90

Background: Lever led Arizona State in scoring, assists, and steals as a senior. He emerged as one of the top rebounding guards in NBA history, grabbing a staggering 734 boards in 1989-90. The two-time All-Star underwent arthroscopic surgery on his right knee four games into the 1990-91 campaign and has also had left knee surgery. He saw his first action in nearly two years last season—54 starts and 81 games. Lever was a free agent this summer.

Strengths: Lever was once one of the league's best and most complete guards. He still rebounds well from the backcourt, handles the ball, and runs the offense. He has 3-point range. His comeback is a testament to his work habits.

Weaknesses: Health is still a concern with Lever, who missed a full 211 games because of injury in the three seasons preceding the 1993-94 campaign. On two surgically repaired knees, he is only a shadow of the player he once was.

Analysis: Lever has made an improbable comeback from major knee surgery, but it would be false to say he has come back completely. He is mostly used as a point guard now, where he once rated among the most versatile and talented guards in basketball. He surpassed 10,000 career points last season.

PLAYER SUMMARY	
Will	rebound
Can't	return to All-Star form
Expect	veteran leadership
Don't Expect	loads of points
Fantasy Value	$1
Card Value	5-10¢

COLLEGE STATISTICS

		G	FGP	FTP	RPG	PPG
78-79	ASU	29	.413	.737	1.5	3.6
79-80	ASU	29	.445	.699	4.3	9.2
80-81	ASU	28	.463	.724	4.9	11.6
81-82	ASU	27	.454	.818	5.4	16.3
Totals		113	.450	.753	4.0	10.1

NBA REGULAR-SEASON STATISTICS

		G	MIN	FGs FG	FGs PCT	3-PT FGs FG	3-PT FGs PCT	FTs FT	FTs PCT	Rebounds OFF	Rebounds TOT	AST	STL	BLK	PTS	PPG
82-83	POR	81	2020	256	.431	5	.333	116	.730	85	225	426	153	15	633	7.8
83-84	POR	81	2010	313	.447	3	.200	159	.743	96	218	372	135	31	788	9.7
84-85	DEN	82	2559	424	.430	6	.250	197	.770	147	411	613	202	30	1051	12.8
85-86	DEN	78	2616	468	.441	12	.316	132	.725	136	420	584	178	15	1080	13.8
86-87	DEN	82	3054	643	.469	22	.239	244	.782	216	729	654	201	34	1552	18.9
87-88	DEN	82	3061	643	.473	12	.211	248	.785	203	665	639	223	21	1546	18.9
88-89	DEN	71	2745	558	.457	23	.348	270	.785	187	662	559	195	20	1409	19.8
89-90	DEN	79	2832	568	.443	36	.414	271	.804	230	734	517	168	13	1443	18.3
90-91	DAL	4	86	9	.391	0	.000	11	.786	3	15	12	6	3	29	7.3
91-92	DAL	31	884	135	.387	17	.327	56	.750	56	161	107	46	12	347	11.2
93-94	DAL	81	1947	227	.408	26	.351	75	.765	83	283	213	159	15	555	6.9
Totals		752	23814	4244	.447	162	.310	1783	.771	1442	4523	4696	1666	209	10433	13.9

BRAD LOHAUS

Team: Milwaukee Bucks
Position: Forward/Center
Height: 7'0" **Weight:** 235
Birthdate: September 29, 1964
NBA Experience: 7 years

College: Iowa
Acquired: Traded from Timberwolves for Randy Breuer and a conditional exchange of 1991 or 1992 2nd-round picks, 1/90

Background: In his senior year at Iowa, Lohaus increased his scoring average by nearly eight points per game and shot 54 percent from the field. He has played with four NBA teams in seven years, his best numbers coming with expansion Minnesota in 1989. Lohaus was traded to Milwaukee in the middle of 1989-90. He scored a career-low four PPG in the 1993-94 season after tying a career high the year before.

Strengths: Lohaus is loaded with perimeter punch. He shoots with unlimited range and has a quick release. He's hit about 34 percent of his career 3-pointers and has made more than 270. Lohaus also blocks shots and gets up and down the court quickly for a seven-footer.

Weaknesses: If ever there was a guard in a center's body, Lohaus is the man. Despite his height, he possesses virtually no inside game. His back-to-the-basket skills are forgettable. He is prone to cold spells from the outside and does not create his own shots with the dribble like he catches and fires. He plays soft.

Analysis: At his best, Lohaus is the definition of a match-up problem. What seven-footer wants to defend beyond the 3-point line? On the flip side, Lohaus does not stack up with opposing big men in the paint on either end of the court. What's worse, he posted career lows in both shooting and scoring last season.

PLAYER SUMMARY	
Will	shoot treys
Can't	thrive inside
Expect	a guard's mentality
Don't Expect	10 PPG
Fantasy Value	$0
Card Value	5-8¢

COLLEGE STATISTICS

		G	FGP	FTP	RPG	PPG
82-83	IOWA	20	.310	.538	0.6	1.3
83-84	IOWA	28	.404	.673	5.2	6.8
85-86	IOWA	32	.431	.794	3.2	3.6
86-87	IOWA	35	.540	.692	7.7	11.3
Totals		115	.467	.695	4.6	6.3

NBA REGULAR-SEASON STATISTICS

				FGs		3-PT FGs		FTs		Rebounds						
		G	MIN	FG	PCT	FG	PCT	FT	PCT	OFF	TOT	AST	STL	BLK	PTS	PPG
87-88	BOS	70	718	122	.496	3	.231	50	.806	46	138	49	20	41	297	4.2
88-89	BOS/SAC	77	1214	210	.432	1	.091	81	.786	84	256	66	30	56	502	6.5
89-90	MIN/MIL	80	1943	305	.460	47	.343	75	.728	98	398	168	58	88	732	9.1
90-91	MIL	81	1219	179	.431	33	.277	37	.685	59	217	75	50	74	428	5.3
91-92	MIL	70	1081	162	.450	57	.396	27	.659	65	249	74	40	71	408	5.8
92-93	MIL	80	1766	283	.461	85	.370	73	.723	59	276	127	47	74	724	9.1
93-94	MIL	67	962	102	.363	46	.343	20	.690	33	150	62	30	55	270	4.0
Totals		525	8903	1363	.445	272	.345	363	.736	444	1684	621	275	459	3361	6.4

GRANT LONG

Team: Miami Heat
Position: Forward
Height: 6'8" **Weight:** 230
Birthdate: March 12, 1966

NBA Experience: 6 years
College: Eastern Michigan
Acquired: 2nd-round pick in 1988 draft (33rd overall)

Background: As a senior at Eastern Michigan, Long was named Mid-American Conference Player of the Year and MVP of the MAC Tournament. He became a full-time Miami starter in December 1990 and was one of the league's most improved players during the 1991-92 campaign. Long scored in double figures for the third consecutive season in 1993-94, despite missing a month with a broken hand.

Strengths: Long is a hard-working player who attacks the boards, runs the floor, plays go-get-'em defense, and can also score. Coaches love his attitude and his willingness to give 100 percent every night. He is a decent medium-range jump-shooter and ranks among the league's top thieves from the power-forward position.

Weaknesses: Long is not a finesse player. He's not a smooth driver and his skills with the ball are nothing to boast about. He was among the league leaders in fouls early in his career and still draws his share of six-foul nights. His shooting accuracy has tailed off over the last two seasons—a cause for some concern.

Analysis: Long will never be a superstar, but his work ethic and durability have made him invaluable to the Miami ballclub. Coaches appreciate a guy who comes to work with a lunch pail and hard hat and gets after it. The underrated Long will rebound and play tough defense with the best of them. Look for him in the weight room and on the practice floor, not in the All-Star Game.

PLAYER SUMMARY

Will ....come to play
Can't...............................avoid fouling
Expect ....rebounds, defense
Don't Expect............................finesse
Fantasy Value...........................$8-10
Card Value ....5-10¢

COLLEGE STATISTICS

		G	FGP	FTP	RPG	PPG
84-85	EMU	28	.564	.609	4.0	4.1
85-86	EMU	27	.526	.644	6.6	8.6
86-87	EMU	29	.549	.725	9.0	14.9
87-88	EMU	30	.555	.765	10.4	23.0
Totals		114	.549	.725	7.6	12.9

NBA REGULAR-SEASON STATISTICS

				FGs		3-PT FGs		FTs		Rebounds						
		G	MIN	FG	PCT	FG	PCT	FT	PCT	OFF	TOT	AST	STL	BLK	PTS	PPG
88-89	MIA	82	2435	336	.486	0	.000	304	.749	240	546	149	122	48	976	11.9
89-90	MIA	81	1856	257	.483	0	.000	172	.714	156	402	96	91	38	686	8.5
90-91	MIA	80	2514	276	.492	1	.167	181	.787	225	568	176	119	43	734	9.2
91-92	MIA	82	3063	440	.494	6	.273	326	.807	259	691	225	139	40	1212	14.8
92-93	MIA	76	2728	397	.469	6	.231	261	.765	197	568	182	104	31	1061	14.0
93-94	MIA	69	2201	300	.446	1	.167	187	.786	190	495	170	89	26	788	11.4
Totals		470	14797	2006	.478	14	.206	1431	.769	1267	3270	998	664	226	5457	11.6

LUC LONGLEY

Team: Chicago Bulls
Position: Center
Height: 7'2" **Weight:** 265
Birthdate: January 19, 1969

NBA Experience: 3 years
College: New Mexico
Acquired: Traded from Kings for Stacey King, 2/94

Background: Originally from Perth, Australia, Longley was coveted by pro scouts from the day he set foot on the New Mexico campus. He never emerged as a consistent force for the Lobos despite becoming the school's all-time leading scorer and rebounder. Longley was drafted seventh by Minnesota in 1991 but struggled with the Timberwolves. He was dealt to Chicago for Stacey King in February 1994 and started some for the Bulls.

Strengths: Longley has refined skills for a big man. He is a very good passer, moves pretty well, and can occasionally score in the paint. His primary weapon, of course, is his size. But along with it, Longley owns a nice touch. He also rebounds and blocks shots. He did his best pro scoring late last season with the Bulls and displayed a better willingness to play hard.

Weaknesses: The big Aussie has always struggled to find consistency. He lacked it as a collegian and his first three pro seasons have not helped him dispel the rap. His intensity, desire, and ability to take the game seriously have been questioned. Longley has never applied himself physically to reach his potential. His low-post offense needs to become much stronger.

Analysis: Longley has clearly been a disappointment when you consider where he was drafted. He should have been able to contribute with the lowly Timberwolves, but could not. The Bulls, searching for their starting center of the future, took a chance with Longley and he played very well at times. If those times become more regular, perhaps there is still hope for a player once considered a natural.

PLAYER SUMMARY	
Will	block shots
Can't	reach his potential
Expect	good touch
Don't Expect	consistency
Fantasy Value	$1
Card Value	7-10¢

COLLEGE STATISTICS

		G	FGP	FTP	RPG	PPG
87-88	NM	35	.500	.392	2.7	4.0
88-89	NM	33	.578	.769	6.8	13.0
89-90	NM	34	.559	.821	9.7	18.4
90-91	NM	30	.656	.716	9.2	19.1
Totals		132	.586	.735	7.0	13.4

NBA REGULAR-SEASON STATISTICS

		G	MIN	FGs		3-PT FGs		FTs		Rebounds		AST	STL	BLK	PTS	PPG
				FG	PCT	FG	PCT	FT	PCT	OFF	TOT					
91-92	MIN	66	991	114	.458	0	.000	53	.663	67	257	53	35	64	281	4.3
92-93	MIN	55	1045	133	.455	0	.000	53	.716	71	240	51	47	77	319	5.8
93-94	MIN/CHI	76	1502	219	.471	0	.000	90	.720	129	433	109	45	79	528	6.9
Totals		197	3538	466	.463	0	.000	196	.703	267	930	213	127	220	1128	5.7

GEORGE LYNCH

Team: Los Angeles Lakers
Position: Forward
Height: 6'8" **Weight:** 223
Birthdate: September 3, 1970

NBA Experience: 1 year
College: North Carolina
Acquired: 1st-round pick in 1993 draft
(12th overall)

Background: Lynch never became the college superstar that some thought he would be, but he found a niche and flourished in Dean Smith's North Carolina system. He set a school record with 241 career steals and became the second-leading rebounder in Tar Heels history. After winning a national title as a senior, he was drafted 12th by the Lakers. He averaged 9.6 PPG and was second on the team in steals as a rookie.

Strengths: Lynch goes after every loose ball, plays aggressive defense, and is not afraid to throw his body around. He can play both forward positions because he makes up in heart what he lacks in size. Lynch is a fine rebounder who finished third on the Lakers in that category last season. He's well-schooled fundamentally, which goes back to his Carolina days. He hustles for steals and is a better-than-expected scorer.

Weaknesses: Poor ball-handling and perimeter-shooting skills kept Lynch from being a lottery pick and could decide how far he progresses as a pro. Mainly a power forward in college, he's undersized at that position in the NBA. He has limited range on his jump shot and is a very poor free throw shooter. Many of his points come after steals or offensive rebounds, not after great moves.

Analysis: Lynch was drafted much sooner than expected, but the results after one year seem to justify the Lakers' decision. He received votes for the All-Rookie first team but did not make either squad. Lynch did not play in 11 of his first 28 games, but he came on after being named a starter in January and enjoyed a fine second half of the 1993-94 season. His energy is contagious, and he will continue to grow on a young Laker squad.

PLAYER SUMMARY	
Will	chase loose balls
Can't	shoot FTs
Expect	steals
Don't Expect	3-point range
Fantasy Value	$5-7
Card Value	20-40¢

COLLEGE STATISTICS

		G	FGP	FTP	RPG	PPG
89-90	NC	34	.521	.663	5.4	8.6
90-91	NC	35	.523	.630	7.4	12.5
91-92	NC	33	.539	.649	8.8	13.9
92-93	NC	38	.501	.667	9.6	14.7
Totals		140	.519	.651	7.8	12.5

NBA REGULAR-SEASON STATISTICS

			FGs		3-PT FGs		FTs		Rebounds						
	G	MIN	FG	PCT	FG	PCT	FT	PCT	OFF	TOT	AST	STL	BLK	PTS	PPG
93-94 LAL	71	1762	291	.508	0	.000	99	.596	220	410	96	102	27	681	9.6
Totals	71	1762	291	.508	0	.000	99	.596	220	410	96	102	27	681	9.6

DON MacLEAN

Team: Washington Bullets
Position: Forward
Height: 6'10" **Weight:** 235
Birthdate: January 16, 1970
NBA Experience: 2 years

College: UCLA
Acquired: Draft rights traded from
Clippers with William Bedford for John
Williams, 10/92

Background: MacLean finished his UCLA career as the leading scorer in school
and Pac-10 history. He led all Division I players in free throw percentage as a
senior and was a first-team all-conference selection three years in a row. Detroit
drafted MacLean 19th overall in 1992 and traded him to the Clippers, but he
wound up in Washington via another deal. He averaged 6.6 PPG in 62 rookie
outings before enjoying a tremendous second season, winning the league's Most
Improved Player Award.

Strengths: MacLean has a scorer's mind-set and a game to match. He knows
how to put the ball in the hole. He is a deadly perimeter marksman with a quick
release and is a reliable free throw shooter. MacLean, who improved his shooting
percentage by about 70 points last season, also helps out on the boards. He
possesses leadership qualities and boundless confidence.

Weaknesses: Spotting up, MacLean gets the job done. But get in his face and
force him to use the dribble and he is not nearly as effective. His accuracy tapers
off significantly beyond about 18-20 feet. The NBA 3-pointer is not his specialty.
MacLean turns the ball over as frequently as he records an assist. He is not a
defensive stalwart. He needs to expend more energy on that end of the court.

Analysis: MacLean was one of the biggest surprises in the league last year. He
hoisted his scoring average by a dozen points and drew league-wide praise for
his improved shooting. He attributed his success to off-season weight training
that greatly improved his strength. With his confidence at an all-time high, there
is no telling how productive MacLean will become.

PLAYER SUMMARY

Will.....................spot up for jumpers
Can't ....star on defense
Expect ....a scoring bent
Don't Expect ....many assists
Fantasy Value.............................$16-19
Card Value ....10-20¢

COLLEGE STATISTICS

		G	FGP	FTP	RPG	PPG
88-89	UCLA	31	.555	.816	7.5	18.6
89-90	UCLA	33	.516	.848	8.7	19.9
90-91	UCLA	31	.551	.846	7.3	23.0
91-92	UCLA	32	.504	.921	7.8	20.7
Totals		127	.531	.860	7.8	20.5

NBA REGULAR-SEASON STATISTICS

		G	MIN	FGs FG	FGs PCT	3-PT FGs FG	3-PT FGs PCT	FTs FT	FTs PCT	Rebounds OFF	Rebounds TOT	AST	STL	BLK	PTS	PPG
92-93	WAS	62	674	157	.435	3	.500	90	.811	33	122	39	11	4	407	6.6
93-94	WAS	75	2487	517	.502	3	.143	328	.824	140	467	160	47	22	1365	18.2
Totals		137	3161	674	.485	6	.222	418	.821	173	589	199	58	26	1772	12.9

MARK MACON

Team: Detroit Pistons
Position: Guard
Height: 6'5" **Weight:** 185
Birthdate: April 14, 1969
NBA Experience: 3 years

College: Temple
Acquired: Traded from Nuggets with Marcus Liberty for Alvin Robertson and a 1995 2nd-round pick, 11/93

Background: Macon was a superstar from Day One at Temple. He was the nation's leading freshman scorer and led the Owls to a 32-2 record. He struggled after that but still finished as the school's career scoring leader. As a rookie with Denver, his field goal percentage of 37.5 was the lowest of any starter in the league. A November 1993 trade sent him to Detroit, where he struggled to get off the bench.

Strengths: Macon was considered the best defensive guard in the 1991 draft, and he has backed it up with intense combativeness. He has excellent lateral quickness and is a good leaper, although injuries have set him back. He brings good size to the backcourt and comes up with his share of steals. He looks to score at the offensive end.

Weaknesses: Macon simply cannot shoot the basketball with any consistency. He has converted at less than 40 percent from the field in two of his three years. He has no 3-point ability to speak of, he takes poor shots, and he turns the ball over too often. Some thought he could play the point, but his poor assist-to-turnover ratio says otherwise.

Analysis: Macon is a scrapper, the kind of defensive player you want on your team. He gets in his man's face and refuses to back down. That explains why he has done so much starting despite his dismal numbers. He does have potential at that end, as long as he does not try to make a living as a shooter. Unless he develops consistency, however, he'll spend a lot of time on the bench.

PLAYER SUMMARY

Will ....hustle on defense
Can't ....shoot straight
Expect ....combativeness
Don't Expect ....consistency
Fantasy Value...............................$0
Card Value...............................8-12¢

COLLEGE STATISTICS

		G	FGP	FTP	RPG	PPG
87-88	TEMP	34	.454	.771	5.6	20.6
88-89	TEMP	30	.407	.776	5.6	18.3
89-90	TEMP	31	.389	.798	6.0	21.9
90-91	TEMP	31	.440	.766	4.9	22.0
Totals		126	.423	.780	5.6	20.7

NBA REGULAR-SEASON STATISTICS

				FGs		3-PT FGs		FTs		Rebounds						
		G	MIN	FG	PCT	FG	PCT	FT	PCT	OFF	TOT	AST	STL	BLK	PTS	PPG
91-92	DEN	76	2304	333	.375	4	.133	135	.730	80	220	168	154	14	805	10.6
92-93	DEN	48	1141	158	.415	0	.000	42	.700	33	103	126	69	3	358	7.5
93-94	DEN/DET	42	496	69	.375	2	.200	23	.676	18	41	51	39	1	163	3.9
Totals		166	3941	560	.385	6	.130	200	.717	131	364	345	262	18	1326	8.0

DAN MAJERLE

Team: Phoenix Suns
Position: Guard/Forward
Height: 6'6" **Weight:** 220
Birthdate: September 9, 1965

NBA Experience: 6 years
College: Central Michigan
Acquired: 1st-round pick in 1988 draft (14th overall)

Background: Majerle was a three-time All-Mid-American Conference selection at Central Michigan, where he ranked second on the all-time scoring, steals, and field goal-percentage lists. He totaled 27 points and six steals in his pro debut and has since emerged as one of the NBA's premier all-around players. Majerle has played in two All-Star Games, and he has led the league in 3-pointers made and attempted each of the last two seasons.

Strengths: Majerle is one of the most versatile stars in the game. He handles the ball with confidence, rebounds well, plays relentless defense, and scores from both inside and outside. "Thunder Dan" possesses tremendous leaping ability and uses it to his full advantage, yet he also has become a dangerous 3-point shooter (he made eight in a game last year). His work ethic, all-out hustle, and physical style are contagious.

Weaknesses: Now that Majerle is an accomplished long-distance shooter, he must avoid the temptation to make a living on the perimeter. He is still one of the best at getting the ball to the hoop off the dribble.

Analysis: Formerly recognized as one of the league's outstanding reserves, Majerle is now one of its more recognizable starters. Whatever his team needs—offense, defense, speed, leadership—Majerle provides. His 3-point numbers don't begin to describe his all-around ability. His restaurant in Phoenix opened to rave reviews and his game draws the same. He was selected to play internationally on Dream Team II.

PLAYER SUMMARY	
Will	hustle every minute
Can't	be left open
Expect	two treys per game
Don't Expect	50-percent shooting
Fantasy Value	$18-21
Card Value	8-15¢

COLLEGE STATISTICS

		G	FGP	FTP	RPG	PPG
84-85	CMU	12	.568	.582	6.7	18.6
85-86	CMU	27	.527	.718	7.9	21.4
86-87	CMU	23	.555	.552	8.5	21.1
87-88	CMU	32	.521	.645	10.8	23.7
Totals		94	.536	.631	8.9	21.8

NBA REGULAR-SEASON STATISTICS

		G	MIN	FGs FG	FGs PCT	3-PT FGs FG	3-PT FGs PCT	FTs FT	FTs PCT	Rebounds OFF	Rebounds TOT	AST	STL	BLK	PTS	PPG
88-89	PHO	54	1354	181	.419	27	.329	78	.614	62	209	130	63	14	467	8.6
89-90	PHO	73	2244	296	.424	19	.237	198	.762	144	430	188	100	32	809	11.1
90-91	PHO	77	2281	397	.484	30	.349	227	.762	168	418	216	106	40	1051	13.6
91-92	PHO	82	2853	551	.478	87	.382	229	.756	148	483	274	131	43	1418	17.3
92-93	PHO	82	3199	509	.464	167	.381	203	.778	120	383	311	138	33	1388	16.9
93-94	PHO	80	3207	476	.418	192	.382	176	.739	120	349	275	129	43	1320	16.5
Totals		448	15138	2410	.451	522	.368	1111	.747	762	2272	1394	667	205	6453	14.4

JEFF MALONE

Team: Philadelphia 76ers
Position: Guard
Height: 6'4" **Weight:** 205
Birthdate: June 28, 1961
NBA Experience: 11 years

College: Mississippi St.
Acquired: Traded from Jazz with a conditional 1st-round pick for Jeff Hornacek, Sean Green, and a conditional 2nd-round pick, 2/94

Background: Malone broke Bailey Howell's career scoring record as a four-year starter at Mississippi State. He spent his first seven pro seasons with the Washington Bullets and played in two All-Star Games. Malone continued as one of the league's best pure shooters in three-plus years with Utah. He was traded by the Jazz to Philadelphia in February 1994.

Strengths: You'll have to search to find a better pure shooter than Malone, who annually hovers around 50 percent from the perimeter and rarely misses from the free throw line. Malone can simply fill the basket from anywhere inside the 3-point arc.

Weaknesses: Amazingly, Malone does not possess 3-point range. He does not run the floor well for a guard, nor does he create. He will not provide assists, steals, rebounds, or blocked shots. Defense has never been his forte.

Analysis: His scoring numbers have dipped somewhat in each of the last two seasons, but Malone remains an accomplished and productive shooter. For that reason, you can't keep him out of the starting lineup. Malone will likely surpass 17,000 career points in 1994-95, his 12th year in the league.

PLAYER SUMMARY	
Will	bury his jumper
Can't	hit from 3-point range
Expect	16-18 PPG
Don't Expect	defense
Fantasy Value	$3-5
Card Value	5-10¢

COLLEGE STATISTICS

		G	FGP	FTP	RPG	PPG
79-80	MSU	27	.459	.824	3.3	11.9
80-81	MSU	27	.490	.820	4.2	20.1
81-82	MSU	27	.549	.743	4.1	18.6
82-83	MSU	29	.531	.824	3.7	26.8
Totals		110	.512	.809	3.8	19.5

NBA REGULAR-SEASON STATISTICS

				FGs		3-PT FGs		FTs		Rebounds						
		G	MIN	FG	PCT	FG	PCT	FT	PCT	OFF	TOT	AST	STL	BLK	PTS	PPG
83-84	WAS	81	1976	408	.444	24	.324	142	.826	57	155	151	23	13	982	12.1
84-85	WAS	76	2613	605	.499	15	.208	211	.844	60	206	184	52	9	1436	18.9
85-86	WAS	80	2992	735	.483	3	.176	322	.868	66	288	191	70	12	1795	22.4
86-87	WAS	80	2763	689	.457	4	.154	376	.885	50	218	298	75	13	1758	22.0
87-88	WAS	80	2655	648	.476	10	.417	335	.882	44	206	237	51	13	1641	20.5
88-89	WAS	76	2418	677	.480	1	.053	296	.871	55	179	219	39	14	1651	21.7
89-90	WAS	75	2567	781	.491	1	.167	257	.877	54	206	243	48	6	1820	24.3
90-91	UTA	69	2466	525	.508	1	.167	231	.917	36	206	143	50	6	1282	18.6
91-92	UTA	81	2922	691	.511	1	.083	256	.898	49	233	180	56	5	1639	20.2
92-93	UTA	79	2558	595	.494	3	.333	236	.852	31	173	128	42	4	1429	18.1
93-94	UTA/PHI	77	2560	525	.486	7	.583	205	.830	51	199	125	40	5	1262	16.4
Totals		854	28490	6879	.485	70	.253	2867	.871	553	2269	2099	546	100	16695	19.5

KARL MALONE

Team: Utah Jazz
Position: Forward
Height: 6'9" **Weight:** 256
Birthdate: July 24, 1963

NBA Experience: 9 years
College: Louisiana Tech
Acquired: 1st-round pick in 1985 draft
(13th overall)

Background: Malone finished third on the all-time scoring list at Louisiana Tech despite playing just three years. In nine years with Utah, he has missed only four games. Malone was third in the voting for 1986 Rookie of the Year and has played in seven All-Star Games, winning MVP honors in 1989 and 1993. He finished second to Michael Jordan in scoring four times and is annually in the top five. He won gold in the 1992 Olympics.

Strengths: Nicknamed "The Mailman" because he delivers, Malone is virtually impossible for one man to stop. He is big, quick, and incredibly strong. If he fails to score, he almost always draws a foul. He has gone to the line more than anyone in the NBA in five of the last six years. He plays defense and owns the boards. His shot-blocking improved considerably last year.

Weaknesses: Malone commits a lot of turnovers, largely because defenders swarm him almost every time he touches the ball. He has not delivered much playoff success to the Jazz.

Analysis: The Mailman has established himself as one of the premier forwards basketball has seen in recent years. Get him the ball in the post, and no one in the game is going to stop him from scoring or getting to the line. He has racked up 19,000 career points and 8,000 career rebounds.

PLAYER SUMMARY	
Will	score in the post
Can't	be stopped by one
Expect	25 PPG, 12 RPG
Don't Expect	soft play
Fantasy Value	$70-75
Card Value	20-40¢

COLLEGE STATISTICS

		G	FGP	FTP	RPG	PPG
82-83	LAT	28	.582	.623	10.3	20.9
83-84	LAT	32	.576	.682	8.8	18.8
84-85	LAT	32	.541	.571	9.0	16.5
Totals		92	.566	.631	9.3	18.7

NBA REGULAR-SEASON STATISTICS

		G	MIN	FGs FG	FGs PCT	3-PT FGs FG	3-PT FGs PCT	FTs FT	FTs PCT	Rebounds OFF	Rebounds TOT	AST	STL	BLK	PTS	PPG
85-86	UTA	81	2475	504	.496	0	.000	195	.481	174	718	236	105	44	1203	14.9
86-87	UTA	82	2857	728	.512	0	.000	323	.598	278	855	158	104	60	1779	21.7
87-88	UTA	82	3198	858	.520	0	.000	552	.700	277	986	199	117	50	2268	27.7
88-89	UTA	80	3126	809	.519	5	.313	703	.766	259	853	219	144	70	2326	29.1
89-90	UTA	82	3122	914	.562	16	.372	696	.762	232	911	226	121	50	2540	31.0
90-91	UTA	82	3302	847	.527	4	.286	684	.770	236	967	270	89	79	2382	29.0
91-92	UTA	81	3054	798	.526	3	.176	673	.778	225	909	241	108	51	2272	28.0
92-93	UTA	82	3099	797	.552	4	.200	619	.740	227	919	308	124	85	2217	27.0
93-94	UTA	82	3329	772	.497	8	.250	511	.694	235	940	328	125	126	2063	25.2
Totals		734	27562	7027	.525	40	.256	4956	.719	2143	8058	2185	1037	615	19050	26.0

DANNY MANNING

Team: Phoenix Suns
Position: Forward
Height: 6'10" **Weight:** 235
Birthdate: May 17, 1966

NBA Experience: 6 years
College: Kansas
Acquired: Signed as a free agent, 8/94

Background: Manning was voted college Player of the Year in 1988, when he led Kansas to the NCAA championship. He ended his college career with more than three dozen school, conference, and NCAA records. His early NBA years were slowed by a tear of the anterior cruciate in his right knee. He played in two All-Star Games before a February 1994 trade sent him to Atlanta. Manning stunned fans over the summer when he signed a low-figure contract with Phoenix.

Strengths: Manning is a big-time scorer who has averaged more than 20 PPG each of the last two years. He drills his quick-release jumper and owns a deadly half-hook that he throws in from all angles. He moves well without the ball. He has been called a point guard in the body of a forward—a tribute to his passing skills. He makes those around him better.

Weaknesses: Manning commits a truckload of fouls. He is only an average rebounding forward. Manning encountered some off-court problems with the Clippers, asking for a trade that eventually came last season. He does not possess 3-point range.

Analysis: Though Phoenix had little room under the salary cap, Manning signed with the Suns anyway, trusting that they would "take care of him" in future years. He'll now team with Charles Barkley, Cedric Ceballos, and A.C. Green in one of the most talented forward units in NBA history. Manning will likely start at small forward.

PLAYER SUMMARY	
Will	make teammates better
Can't	drill treys
Expect	20 PPG
Don't Expect	selfish play
Fantasy Value	$50-55
Card Value	12-20¢

COLLEGE STATISTICS

		G	FGP	FTP	RPG	PPG
84-85	KAN	34	.566	.765	7.6	14.6
85-86	KAN	39	.600	.748	6.3	16.7
86-87	KAN	36	.617	.730	9.5	23.9
87-88	KAN	38	.583	.734	9.0	24.8
Totals		147	.593	.740	8.1	20.1

NBA REGULAR-SEASON STATISTICS

		G	MIN	FGs FG	FGs PCT	3-PT FGs FG	3-PT FGs PCT	FTs FT	FTs PCT	Rebounds OFF	Rebounds TOT	AST	STL	BLK	PTS	PPG
88-89	LAC	26	950	177	.494	1	.200	79	.767	70	171	81	44	25	434	16.7
89-90	LAC	71	2269	440	.533	0	.000	274	.741	142	422	187	91	39	1154	16.3
90-91	LAC	73	2197	470	.519	0	.000	219	.716	169	426	196	117	62	1159	15.9
91-92	LAC	82	2904	650	.542	0	.000	279	.725	229	564	285	135	122	1579	19.3
92-93	LAC	79	2761	702	.509	8	.267	388	.802	198	520	207	108	101	1800	22.8
93-94	LAC/ATL	68	2520	586	.488	3	.176	228	.669	131	465	261	99	82	1403	20.6
Totals		399	13601	3025	.516	12	.185	1467	.738	939	2568	1217	594	431	7529	18.9

SARUNAS MARCIULIONIS

Team: Seattle SuperSonics
Position: Guard
Height: 6'5" **Weight:** 215
Birthdate: June 13, 1964
NBA Experience: 4 years

College: Vilnius St.
Acquired: Traded from Warriors with Byron Houston for Ricky Pierce, draft rights to Carlos Rogers, and two 1995 2nd-round picks, 7/94

Background: The Lithuanian Marciulionis was the leading scorer on the Soviet Union's 1988 Olympic gold-medal-winning team in Seoul, South Korea, and played for Lithuania in the 1992 Games. He became the first Soviet player in the NBA when he signed in 1989, and finished sixth among rookies in scoring in 1989-90. He led all non-starters in scoring (18.9 PPG) and all guards in field goal percentage (.538) in 1991-92. He spent the 1993-94 season on the injured list following surgery on his right knee, then was dealt to Seattle after the season.

Strengths: Although he plays left-handed, Marciulionis is ambidextrous. Anyone unconvinced should watch him handle the ball. He has a nice jumper but prefers driving inside, where he uses his strength. He's capable of scoring in traffic, racking up the assists, and going to the free throw line. His work habits are exceptional.

Weaknesses: Injuries are a huge concern. His chronic leg problems led to knee surgery after the 1992-93 campaign and he did not play last season. When healthy, Marciulionis does not have as much confidence in his jumper as he has in his ability to get to the basket, and he struggles from beyond the 3-point line. Defense and rebounding are not strengths.

Analysis: Marciulionis is a multi-talented player. He scores, handles the ball, distributes, and gets to the line with his uncanny penetration. The one thing he has not been able to do is stay off the injured list. It will probably take some time for him to reach his previous level of play, assuming he can at all.

PLAYER SUMMARY	
Will	get to the hoop
Can't	stay healthy
Expect	solid ball-handling
Don't Expect	a speedy recovery
Fantasy Value	$6-8
Card Value	8-15¢

COLLEGE STATISTICS

—DID NOT PLAY—

NBA REGULAR-SEASON STATISTICS

			FGs		3-PT FGs		FTs		Rebounds						
	G	MIN	FG	PCT	FG	PCT	FT	PCT	OFF	TOT	AST	STL	BLK	PTS	PPG
89-90 GS	75	1695	289	.519	10	.256	317	.787	84	221	121	94	7	905	12.1
90-91 GS	50	987	183	.501	1	.167	178	.724	51	118	85	62	4	545	10.9
91-92 GS	72	2117	491	.538	3	.300	376	.788	68	208	243	116	10	1361	18.9
92-93 GS	30	836	178	.543	3	.200	162	.761	40	97	105	51	2	521	17.4
Totals	227	5635	1141	.528	17	.243	1033	.771	243	644	554	323	23	3332	14.7

JAMAL MASHBURN

Team: Dallas Mavericks
Position: Forward
Height: 6'8" **Weight:** 240
Birthdate: November 29, 1972

NBA Experience: 1 year
College: Kentucky
Acquired: 1st-round pick in 1993 draft
(4th overall)

Background: Dan Issel, Kenny Walker, and Jack Givens are the only Kentucky players to score more points than Mashburn, who started every game in his three years in Lexington. As a senior, he finished second to Indiana's Calbert Cheaney in balloting for the Wooden Award as the national Player of the Year. Mashburn forfeited a year's eligibility to enter the draft, was chosen fourth overall by Dallas, and led all rookies in scoring last season.

Strengths: Mashburn is a fine athlete who can muscle in the paint or stretch a defense with his NBA 3-point shooting. His "Monster Mash" dunks and fluid style make him a favorite with fans. He runs the floor, finds open men, handles the ball, and can put the ball in the hole with the best of them. He has the athleticism to defend small forwards and can swing to power forward if need be. He has a nice feel for the game.

Weaknesses: Mashburn came up with his share of steals but cannot yet be called an accomplished defender. He does not swat many shots and gets lit up on occasion. He is a good rebounder, but he has the potential to be a much better one. His shot selection is bound to improve in future years, which will help his field goal percentage.

Analysis: Mashburn was an instant starter with Dallas, the worst team in the NBA over the last two years. His play did not help the team much in the win column last season, but it bodes well for the future of the franchise. Mashburn might be the best all-around talent in his draft class. He scores, shoots, passes, rebounds, and works hard on defense. He's also the kind of player you'd pay money to watch.

PLAYER SUMMARY

Will ....shoot, score
Can't ....swat many shots
Expect ....a franchise player
Don't Expect ....an early title
Fantasy Value.........................$19-22
Card Value ....35-75¢

COLLEGE STATISTICS

		G	FGP	FTP	RPG	PPG
90-91	KEN	28	.474	.727	7.0	12.9
91-92	KEN	36	.567	.709	7.8	21.3
92-93	KEN	34	.492	.670	8.4	21.0
Totals		98	.516	.697	7.8	18.8

NBA REGULAR-SEASON STATISTICS

			FGs		3-PT FGs		FTs		Rebounds						
	G	MIN	FG	PCT	FG	PCT	FT	PCT	OFF	TOT	AST	STL	BLK	PTS	PPG
93-94 DAL	79	2896	561	.406	85	.284	306	.699	107	353	266	89	14	1513	19.2
Totals	79	2896	561	.406	85	.284	306	.699	107	353	266	89	14	1513	19.2

ANTHONY MASON

Team: New York Knicks
Position: Forward
Height: 6'7" **Weight:** 250
Birthdate: December 14, 1966

NBA Experience: 5 years
College: Tennessee St.
Acquired: Signed as a free agent, 7/91

Background: Mason finished his career at Tennessee State with more than 2,000 career points. He was drafted by Portland in the third round in 1988 but spent his first pro season in Turkey. He was signed by New Jersey in 1989 and played 21 games for the Nets. He spent the 1990-91 campaign in the CBA, though he played three games with Denver. Mason was a free-agent signee of the Knicks in 1991 and has been one of their top players off the bench over the last three seasons.

Strengths: Mason is a menace to opponents who have the misfortune of running into him. He owns a bruising body and uses it to establish a physical presence. He bangs, plays defense, is a tremendous rebounder, and runs the court. He handles the ball well and can bring it up the floor to beat pressure. He works hard and is determined.

Weaknesses: Mason, a former 20-PPG scorer in the CBA, will not score a ton of points in the NBA. He's not a pure outside shooter, he struggles from the free throw line, and his lack of height puts him at a disadvantage as a post-up scorer. Mason has earned a reputation as a complainer.

Analysis: Mason lives up to his name in that he's built like a brick wall. He gives the Knicks another physical presence, along with a productive rebounder who will score points through his hustle. He does not take kindly to time on the bench, which is both a plus and a minus. When he's happy, Mason is a tough match-up.

PLAYER SUMMARY	
Will	handle the ball
Can't	shoot FTs
Expect	a physical presence
Don't Expect	Mr. Congeniality
Fantasy Value	$1
Card Value	8-12¢

COLLEGE STATISTICS

		G	FGP	FTP	RPG	PPG
84-85	TSU	28	.469	.648	5.3	10.0
85-86	TSU	28	.482	.715	6.9	18.0
86-87	TSU	27	.448	.659	9.7	18.8
87-88	TSU	28	.454	.773	10.4	28.0
Totals		111	.461	.713	8.1	18.7

NBA REGULAR-SEASON STATISTICS

				FGs		3-PT FGs		FTs		Rebounds						
		G	MIN	FG	PCT	FG	PCT	FT	PCT	OFF	TOT	AST	STL	BLK	PTS	PPG
89-90	NJ	21	108	14	.350	0	.000	9	.600	11	34	7	2	2	37	1.8
90-91	DEN	3	21	2	.500	0	.000	6	.750	3	5	0	1	0	10	3.3
91-92	NY	82	2198	203	.509	0	.000	167	.642	216	573	106	46	20	573	7.0
92-93	NY	81	2482	316	.502	0	.000	199	.682	231	640	170	43	19	831	10.3
93-94	NY	73	1903	206	.476	0	.000	116	.720	158	427	151	31	9	528	7.2
Totals		260	6712	741	.492	0	.000	497	.675	619	1679	434	123	50	1979	7.6

MARLON MAXEY

Team: Minnesota Timberwolves
Position: Forward
Height: 6'8" **Weight:** 250
Birthdate: February 19, 1969

NBA Experience: 2 years
College: Minnesota; Texas-El Paso
Acquired: 2nd-round pick in 1992 draft (28th overall)

Background: Maxey played sparingly as a freshman at Minnesota, then transferred to Texas-El Paso and led the Miners in scoring in each of his three seasons. He was twice sidelined by knee injuries but was impressive in post-college camps and was the first pick in the second round of the 1992 draft. Maxey played in 43 games as a rookie and in 55 last season, averaging 4.5 points and almost four rebounds per contest.

Strengths: Maxey is a tough, Chicago-schooled player who can dunk in traffic and has a pretty nice feel for what to do around the basket. He is capable of playing above-average defense and faring well on the boards. He uses a mix of strength and quickness inside and will block some shots. Maxey does not put up many bad shots and converts at a high percentage.

Weaknesses: Maxey is still a little raw offensively, possessing a limited array of moves on the blocks and getting a fair share of his points from running the floor and hitting the boards. He does not have good range at all. Maxey rates well below average as a ball-handler and is a horrible passer, as his assist totals can attest. He is not the most fundamentally sound player.

Analysis: Maxey was once thought to be a first-round talent, so Minnesota was glad to get him in the second round two years ago. However, he has not become the player the Timberwolves thought he would become by this time in his young career. Maxey will rebound, defend, and run the court, but his poor passing skills and limited offensive arsenal hamper his effectiveness and have relegated him to a reserve role.

PLAYER SUMMARY

Will..........................dunk over people
Can't ....shoot with range
Expect ....toughness
Don't Expect ....10 PPG
Fantasy Value................................$0
Card Value ....8-12¢

COLLEGE STATISTICS

		G	FGP	FTP	RPG	PPG
87-88	MINN	13	.281	.619	3.2	2.4
89-90	UTEP	30	.547	.692	7.8	12.4
90-91	UTEP	17	.513	.719	7.1	14.4
91-92	UTEP	25	.521	.727	7.4	15.2
Totals		85	.518	.708	6.8	12.1

NBA REGULAR-SEASON STATISTICS

				FGs		3-PT FGs		FTs		Rebounds						
		G	MIN	FG	PCT	FG	PCT	FT	PCT	OFF	TOT	AST	STL	BLK	PTS	PPG
92-93	MIN	43	520	93	.550	0	.000	45	.643	66	164	12	11	18	231	5.4
93-94	MIN	55	626	89	.533	0	.000	70	.714	75	199	10	16	33	248	4.5
Totals		98	1146	182	.542	0	.000	115	.685	141	363	22	27	51	479	4.9

VERNON MAXWELL

Team: Houston Rockets
Position: Guard
Height: 6'5" **Weight:** 190
Birthdate: September 12, 1965

NBA Experience: 6 years
College: Florida
Acquired: Acquired from Spurs for cash, 2/90

Background: Maxwell's past is cluttered with accomplishment and controversy. He broke Florida's all-time scoring record, but later admitted to using cocaine and accepting cash payments. He has been in and out of trouble as a pro as well, but since San Antonio sold his rights to Houston, he has made more news on the court than off. He has made more 3-pointers than anyone since the 1990-91 season, and he helped the Rockets to the 1994 NBA championship.

Strengths: Maxwell throws his weight around on defense and he backs down from no one. He can match up effectively with big guards and smaller point men. He is a long-range force on offense but can also get to the hoop with his athletic ability and acrobatics. He talks a big game and plays it with exuberance.

Weaknesses: "Mad Max" has been called the "Mad Bomber." Although he is annually among the most frequent 3-point shooters in the league, he has never been among the most accurate. Overall, he has not shot better than 41.3 percent from the field in any of his last four seasons. He's something of a loose cannon. He was arrested on a weapons charge last season.

Analysis: Maxwell is a huge reason the Rockets have become one of the top teams in the NBA. His defense is exemplary and his offensive skills explosive. His shooting percentage is awful, but that's part of the Maxwell mystique. He is capable of striking at any instant, either with a barrage of treys or a verbal onslaught toward the opposition.

PLAYER SUMMARY	
Will	fire from anywhere
Can't	shoot for percentage
Expect	hard-nosed defense
Don't Expect	the silent type
Fantasy Value	$9-11
Card Value	8-15¢

COLLEGE STATISTICS

		G	FGP	FTP	RPG	PPG
84-85	FLA	30	.445	.686	2.4	13.3
85-86	FLA	33	.463	.701	4.5	19.6
86-87	FLA	34	.485	.742	3.7	21.7
87-88	FLA	33	.447	.715	4.2	20.2
Totals		130	.462	.715	3.7	18.8

NBA REGULAR-SEASON STATISTICS

		G	MIN	FGs FG	FGs PCT	3-PT FGs FG	3-PT FGs PCT	FTs FT	FTs PCT	Rebounds OFF	Rebounds TOT	AST	STL	BLK	PTS	PPG
88-89	SA	79	2065	357	.432	32	.248	181	.745	49	202	301	86	8	927	11.7
89-90	SA/HOU	79	1987	275	.439	28	.267	136	.645	50	228	296	84	10	714	9.0
90-91	HOU	82	2870	504	.404	172	.337	217	.733	41	238	303	127	15	1397	17.0
91-92	HOU	80	2700	502	.413	162	.342	206	.772	37	243	326	104	28	1372	17.1
92-93	HOU	71	2251	349	.407	120	.332	164	.719	29	221	297	86	8	982	13.8
93-94	HOU	75	2571	380	.389	120	.298	143	.749	42	229	380	125	20	1023	13.6
Totals		466	14444	2367	.412	634	.320	1047	.729	248	1361	1903	612	89	6415	13.8

LEE MAYBERRY

Team: Milwaukee Bucks
Position: Guard
Height: 6'2" **Weight:** 175
Birthdate: June 12, 1970

NBA Experience: 2 years
College: Arkansas
Acquired: 1st-round pick in 1992 draft (23rd overall)

Background: Mayberry grew up in Tulsa, where Nolan Richardson coached before going to Arkansas, and eventually played for Richardson with the Razorbacks. He led them to nine NCAA Tournament wins in four years and finished as the school's career leader in assists, steals, and 3-point field goal percentage. A first-round draft choice of the Bucks, he has not missed a game in his two seasons.

Strengths: Mayberry is a point guard who can score from the perimeter, forcing defenses to account for him. He possesses 3-point range and can get his shot off in spite of his size. He has fine leadership qualities, is durable, takes care of the ball, and runs the offense. He loves the transition game and does not commit a lot of turnovers. He has potential as a defensive nuisance, a role he played well in college.

Weaknesses: Mayberry is not nearly as effective in the pro game as he was in college, mostly because it is harder to make up for his slight build at this level. He gets posted up on the defensive end and struggles when screened. He lacks the lightning quickness to get past defenders and does not have the moves to score a lot of points. Mayberry has struggled from the free throw line.

Analysis: Mayberry has been a capable reserve point guard in his two years, but nothing spectacular. He handles the ball well and makes pretty good decisions. His potential to become a starter depends a lot on his outside shot, because he simply lacks the size to pose much of a threat on his moves to the hoop. He'll improve defensively with more experience.

PLAYER SUMMARY	
Will	handle the ball
Can't	crack starting lineup
Expect	defensive improvement
Don't Expect	post-up offense
Fantasy Value	$1
Card Value	10-20¢

COLLEGE STATISTICS

		G	FGP	FTP	APG	PPG
88-89	ARK	32	.500	.736	4.2	12.9
89-90	ARK	35	.507	.792	5.2	14.5
90-91	ARK	38	.484	.634	5.5	13.2
91-92	ARK	34	.492	.744	5.9	15.2
Totals		139	.495	.724	5.2	14.0

NBA REGULAR-SEASON STATISTICS

			MIN	FGs		3-PT FGs		FTs		Rebounds						
		G		FG	PCT	FG	PCT	FT	PCT	OFF	TOT	AST	STL	BLK	PTS	PPG
92-93	MIL	82	1503	171	.456	43	.391	39	.574	26	118	273	59	7	424	5.2
93-94	MIL	82	1472	167	.415	41	.345	58	.690	26	101	215	46	4	433	5.3
Totals		164	2975	338	.435	84	.367	97	.638	52	219	488	105	11	857	5.2

XAVIER McDANIEL

Team: Boston Celtics
Position: Forward
Height: 6'7" **Weight:** 205
Birthdate: June 4, 1963

NBA Experience: 9 years
College: Wichita St.
Acquired: Signed as a free agent, 9/92

Background: McDaniel led Wichita State in scoring, rebounding, and field goal percentage as a junior and senior and was an All-American in 1985. He earned All-Rookie honors with Seattle and scored more than 20 PPG in each of his next four years, making the All-Star Game in 1988. He has since played with Phoenix, New York, and Boston.

Strengths: At his best, McDaniel has what you look for in a small forward. He puts points on the board with a turnaround jump shot and is a fine finisher. He also rebounds and can play physical defense. McDaniel backs down from no one. He's been known as a big-game player.

Weaknesses: McDaniel has seen his better days. He seems to go through frequent lapses these days and his numbers reflect it. He is not a pure shooter, nor is he a polished or willing passer. He has been resigned to reserve duty in the past couple of years and seems to have lost a step.

Analysis: The "X-Man" has been one of the more explosive forwards in the league during his career. Over the last few years, however, he has not been nearly as effective. Last season saw his shooting and scoring numbers tumble to career lows on a Celtic team that did not make the playoffs. It just seems like he's playing out the string.

PLAYER SUMMARY	
Will	hit the boards
Can't	regain starting job
Expect	a physical presence
Don't Expect	20 PPG
Fantasy Value	$1
Card Value	5-10¢

COLLEGE STATISTICS

		G	FGP	FTP	RPG	PPG
81-82	WSU	28	.504	.628	3.7	5.8
82-83	WSU	28	.593	.541	14.4	18.8
83-84	WSU	30	.564	.680	13.1	20.6
84-85	WSU	31	.559	.634	14.8	27.2
Totals		117	.564	.624	11.6	18.4

NBA REGULAR-SEASON STATISTICS

		G	MIN	FGs FG	FGs PCT	3-PT FGs FG	3-PT FGs PCT	FTs FT	FTs PCT	Rebounds OFF	Rebounds TOT	AST	STL	BLK	PTS	PPG
85-86	SEA	82	2706	576	.490	2	.200	250	.687	307	655	193	101	37	1404*	17.1
86-87	SEA	82	3031	806	.509	3	.214	275	.696	338	705	207	115	52	1890	23.0
87-88	SEA	78	2803	687	.488	14	.280	281	.715	206	518	263	96	52	1669	21.4
88-89	SEA	82	2385	677	.489	11	.306	312	.732	177	433	134	84	40	1677	20.5
89-90	SEA	69	2432	611	.496	5	.294	244	.733	165	447	171	73	36	1471	21.3
90-91	SEA/PHO	81	2634	590	.497	0	.000	193	.723	173	557	187	76	46	1373	17.0
91-92	NY	82	2344	488	.478	12	.308	137	.714	176	460	149	57	24	1125	13.7
92-93	BOS	82	2215	457	.495	6	.273	191	.793	168	489	163	72	51	1111	13.5
93-94	BOS	82	1971	387	.461	10	.244	144	.676	142	400	126	48	39	928	11.3
Totals		720	22521	5279	.491	63	.266	2027	.718	1852	4664	1593	722	377	12648	17.6

DERRICK McKEY

Team: Indiana Pacers
Position: Forward
Height: 6'10" **Weight:** 220
Birthdate: October 10, 1966
NBA Experience: 7 years

College: Alabama
Acquired: Traded from SuperSonics
with Gerald Paddio for Detlef
Schrempf, 11/93

Background: McKey earned Southeastern Conference Player of the Year accolades after leading Alabama to a conference title as a junior. He entered the draft a year early, was named to the 1987-88 All-Rookie Team, and became a starter the next year. McKey has averaged 12-16 PPG every season since. He was traded from Seattle to Indiana before the 1993-94 season and his scoring dipped for the fifth straight year.

Strengths: All the athletic skills are at McKey's disposal. He has great leaping ability and handles the ball like a big guard. He drives to the hoop, passes well, and uses both hands effectively. He's a pure scorer who shoots well, has 3-point range, and helps out on defense. He is a fine complementary player.

Weaknesses: The knock on McKey has been his inability to remain focused and play with intensity on a nightly basis. He'll score 20 points one night and take four shots the next. He tends to play passively on offense, is slight in build, and is an average rebounder at best. He seems too content with a supporting role.

Analysis: McKey was a budding star in his early years but has never fulfilled his expectations. Last year's trade for Detlef Schrempf drew all sorts of criticism from the Indianapolis media. Although McKey played well at times, you never knew what to expect out of him from one night to the next. It's a rap he can't shake.

PLAYER SUMMARY	
Will	spot open men
Can't	fulfill potential
Expect	high-scoring nights
Don't Expect	consistency
Fantasy Value	$11-14
Card Value	7-12¢

COLLEGE STATISTICS

		G	FGP	FTP	RPG	PPG
84-85	ALA	33	.477	.606	4.1	5.1
85-86	ALA	33	.636	.786	7.9	13.6
86-87	ALA	33	.581	.862	7.5	18.6
Totals		99	.580	.797	6.5	12.4

NBA REGULAR-SEASON STATISTICS

				FGs		3-PT FGs		FTs		Rebounds						
		G	MIN	FG	PCT	FG	PCT	FT	PCT	OFF	TOT	AST	STL	BLK	PTS	PPG
87-88	SEA	82	1706	255	.491	11	.367	173	.772	115	328	107	70	63	694	8.5
88-89	SEA	82	2804	487	.502	30	.337	301	.803	167	464	219	105	70	1305	15.9
89-90	SEA	80	2748	468	.493	3	.130	315	.782	170	489	187	87	81	1254	15.7
90-91	SEA	73	2503	438	.517	4	.211	235	.845	172	423	169	91	56	1115	15.3
91-92	SEA	52	1757	285	.472	19	.380	188	.847	95	268	120	61	47	777	14.9
92-93	SEA	77	2439	387	.496	40	.492	220	.741	121	327	197	105	58	1034	13.4
93-94	IND	76	2613	355	.500	9	.290	192	.756	129	402	327	111	49	911	12.0
Totals		522	16570	2675	.497	116	.328	1624	.791	969	2701	1326	630	424	7090	13.6

NATE McMILLAN

Team: Seattle SuperSonics
Position: Guard/Forward
Height: 6'5" **Weight:** 190
Birthdate: August 3, 1964

NBA Experience: 8 years
College: Chowan; North Carolina St.
Acquired: 2nd-round pick in 1986 draft (30th overall)

Background: McMillan was a junior college All-American before transferring to North Carolina State and averaging nearly seven assists per game as a senior. As a pro, he finished among the NBA's top ten in assists in each of his first three years. He has never averaged more than 7.6 PPG, but he is Seattle's career assists leader and led the league in steals with almost three per game during the 1993-94 season.

Strengths: McMillan is known for his defense, rebounding, and passing. His good size, deceiving quickness, and relentless effort help him shut down opponents ranging from point guards to small forwards. Few are better pick-pockets. McMillan is a steady ball-handler and an unselfish leader. He has become a dangerous long-range shooter.

Weaknesses: McMillan has never been much of a scorer despite his ability to penetrate and now shoot. The last time he averaged double figures in scoring was his second year of junior college. McMillan is brutal from the free throw line, an oddity considering his long-range stroke.

Analysis: McMillan was one of the best sixth men in the league last season because of his leadership and defensive ability. He was one of the big reasons Seattle finished with the best record in the NBA. He has carved a productive career out of doing less glamorous things than scoring, and he is still near the top of his game.

PLAYER SUMMARY	
Will	pick your pocket
Can't	hit his FTs
Expect	defense, leadership
Don't Expect	8 PPG
Fantasy Value	$5-7
Card Value	5-10¢

COLLEGE STATISTICS

		G	FGP	FTP	RPG	PPG
82-83	CHOW	27	.580	.696	5.0	9.9
83-84	CHOW	35	.544	.769	9.8	13.1
84-85	NCST	33	.454	.674	5.7	7.6
85-86	NCST	34	.485	.733	4.6	9.4
Totals		129	.515	.722	6.4	10.1

NBA REGULAR-SEASON STATISTICS

		G	MIN	FGs FG	FGs PCT	3-PT FGs FG	3-PT FGs PCT	FTs FT	FTs PCT	Rebounds OFF	Rebounds TOT	AST	STL	BLK	PTS	PPG
86-87	SEA	71	1972	143	.475	0	.000	87	.617	101	331	583	125	45	373	5.3
87-88	SEA	82	2453	235	.474	9	.375	145	.707	117	338	702	169	47	624	7.6
88-89	SEA	75	2341	199	.410	15	.214	119	.630	143	388	696	156	42	532	7.1
89-90	SEA	82	2338	207	.473	11	.355	98	.641	127	403	598	140	37	523	6.4
90-91	SEA	78	1434	132	.433	17	.354	57	.613	71	251	371	104	20	338	4.3
91-92	SEA	72	1652	177	.437	27	.276	54	.643	92	252	359	129	29	435	6.0
92-93	SEA	73	1977	213	.464	25	.385	95	.709	84	306	384	173	33	546	7.5
93-94	SEA	73	1887	177	.447	52	.391	31	.564	50	283	387	216	22	437	6.0
Totals		606	16054	1483	.451	156	.328	686	.651	785	2552	4080	1212	275	3808	6.3

OLIVER MILLER

Team: Phoenix Suns
Position: Center
Height: 6'9" **Weight:** 285
Birthdate: April 6, 1970

NBA Experience: 2 years
College: Arkansas
Acquired: 1st-round pick in 1992 draft
(22nd overall)

Background: Miller never gained as much attention as Arkansas teammates Todd Day and Lee Mayberry, yet he finished as the school's career leader in blocked shots (345) and field goal percentage (.636) while ranking second in career rebounds (886). A late first-round choice by Phoenix in 1992, Miller spent time on the injured list because his 300-plus pounds were bothering his legs and feet. He shed some 45 pounds and has since been a key contributor as both a starter and reserve center.

Strengths: Miller is a tremendous all-around talent when in the 280-pound range. He is a phenomenal outlet passer, owns a great pair of hands, and is very agile for a man his size. His touch with the basketball is extraordinary. Miller knows how to score on the interior, is a good short-range shooter, blocks shots, and seals his man off the boards. He shoots for a great percentage.

Weaknesses: Though his weight has been under 300 pounds of late, it will always have to be monitored. His legs give him trouble when he puts on a few extra pounds. He has trouble guarding centers who are quick and agile. Miller is a dismal free throw shooter and picks up too many fouls. His range is only about 12-14 feet.

Analysis: Miller continues to grow (no pun intended) as a surprising NBA player. He spent more than a third of last season in the Phoenix starting lineup, shot better than 60 percent from the field, and pushed his scoring average toward the double-figure range. Miller will likely become the Suns' full-time starting center this year, and he has given indications that he can be a very good one if he maintains his commitment.

PLAYER SUMMARY	
Will	convert inside
Can't	make FTs
Expect	extraordinary touch
Don't Expect	a lean machine
Fantasy Value.	$7-9
Card Value	10-25¢

COLLEGE STATISTICS

		G	FGP	FTP	RPG	PPG
88-89	ARK	30	.547	.641	3.7	7.7
89-90	ARK	35	.639	.652	6.3	11.1
90-91	ARK	38	.704	.644	7.7	15.7
91-92	ARK	34	.602	.647	7.7	13.5
Totals		137	.636	.646	6.5	12.2

NBA REGULAR-SEASON STATISTICS

			FGs		3-PT FGs		FTs		Rebounds						
	G	MIN	FG	PCT	FG	PCT	FT	PCT	OFF	TOT	AST	STL	BLK	PTS	PPG
92-93 PHO	56	1069	121	.475	0	.000	71	.710	70	275	118	38	100	313	5.6
93-94 PHO	69	1786	277	.609	2	.222	80	.584	140	476	244	83	156	636	9.2
Totals	125	2855	398	.561	2	.167	151	.637	210	751	362	121	256	949	7.6

REGGIE MILLER

Team: Indiana Pacers
Position: Guard
Height: 6'7" **Weight:** 185
Birthdate: August 24, 1965

NBA Experience: 7 years
College: UCLA
Acquired: 1st-round pick in 1987 draft (11th overall)

Background: Miller was an All-Pac-10 selection as a senior and left UCLA ranked second to Lew Alcindor on the school's career scoring list. He established himself as a 3-point shooter during his first two years with Indiana, then improved his all-around game and earned a trip to the All-Star Game in 1989-90. His 91.8-percent free throw accuracy led the NBA in 1990-91. He topped 10,000 career points last season and put on a shooting clinic in the Eastern Conference finals against the Knicks.

Strengths: Miller is not only one of the league's premier shooters, but also one of its best offensive players. He's virtually automatic from the line and deadly from long range. He has elevated his play to the star level, and there is no longer doubt about his ability to create his own shots and get to the basket. He works hard and moves well without the ball.

Weaknesses: Miller is rail thin and unable to play physical defense. He's not always the most willing defender anyway. He has the potential to be a much better rebounder and shot-blocker.

Analysis: Miller became the Pacers' career scoring leader last season and has led the team in that category in each of the last five years. You won't find a more hard-working or durable player in the NBA. His string of 345 consecutive starts was snapped last year. Miller is a franchise player who was chosen to play internationally with Dream Team II.

PLAYER SUMMARY	
Will	drill the trey
Can't	play punishing defense
Expect	20 PPG
Don't Expect	missed FTs
Fantasy Value	$40-45
Card Value	12-20¢

COLLEGE STATISTICS

		G	FGP	FTP	RPG	PPG
83-84	UCLA	28	.509	.643	1.5	4.6
84-85	UCLA	33	.553	.804	4.3	15.2
85-86	UCLA	29	.556	.882	5.3	25.9
86-87	UCLA	32	.543	.832	5.4	22.3
Totals		122	.547	.836	4.2	17.2

NBA REGULAR-SEASON STATISTICS

				FGs		3-PT FGs		FTs		Rebounds						
		G	MIN	FG	PCT	FG	PCT	FT	PCT	OFF	TOT	AST	STL	BLK	PTS	PPG
87-88	IND	82	1840	306	.488	61	.355	149	.801	95	190	132	53	19	822	10.0
88-89	IND	74	2536	398	.479	98	.402	287	.844	73	292	227	93	29	1181	16.0
89-90	IND	82	3192	661	.514	150	.414	544	.868	95	295	311	110	13	2016	24.6
90-91	IND	82	2972	596	.512	112	.348	551	.918	81	281	331	109	13	1855	22.6
91-92	IND	82	3120	562	.501	129	.378	442	.858	82	318	314	105	26	1695	20.7
92-93	IND	82	2954	571	.479	167	.399	427	.880	67	258	262	120	26	1736	21.2
93-94	IND	79	2638	524	.503	123	.421	403	.908	30	212	248	119	24	1574	19.9
Totals		563	19252	3618	.498	840	.390	2803	.877	523	1846	1825	709	155	10879	19.3

CHRIS MILLS

Team: Cleveland Cavaliers   **NBA Experience:** 1 year
Position: Forward/Guard   **College:** Kentucky; Arizona
Height: 6'6" **Weight:** 216   **Acquired:** 1st-round pick in 1993 draft
Birthdate: January 25, 1970   (22nd overall)

Background: Though he started every college game he played and won Pac-10 Player of the Year honors, Mills had a star-crossed career. He played one year at Kentucky but was forced to leave because of an illegal-payments scandal. Mills transferred to Arizona, where he was called an underachiever despite two strong seasons and one outstanding season. He dipped to 22nd in the 1993 draft but enjoyed a fine rookie campaign with Cleveland, starting 18 games and scoring 9.4 points per contest.

Strengths: Mills is an accomplished perimeter shooter. He has outstanding mechanics with NBA 3-point range, and he can fill it up in a hurry if you leave him open. He's also a fine finisher. Mills is a decent rebounder, a capable shot-blocker, and a good passer with court sense. He started some last season and played in the Schick Rookie Game.

Weaknesses: Mills is a cross between a big guard and a small forward, although he spent most of his time as the latter during his rookie year. He lacks the size to shut down the league's high-scoring forwards and the explosiveness to stay with the guards. He is not as adept at getting to the hole as he is at spotting up. He draws a lot of whistles for reaching.

Analysis: Mills proved to be a wise choice late in the first round. Only three Cavaliers earned more minutes than he did during a rookie season that surprised some of his critics. Mills missed two games after experiencing an irregular heartbeat in December but extensive testing determined that he has no underlying heart condition. Look for him to play a significant role in the future for the Cavaliers.

PLAYER SUMMARY	
Will	spot up for jumpers
Can't	muscle against forwards
Expect	good court sense
Don't Expect	explosiveness
Fantasy Value	$10-13
Card Value	15-25¢

COLLEGE STATISTICS

		G	FGP	FTP	RPG	PPG
88-89	KEN	32	.484	.713	8.7	14.3
90-91	ARIZ	35	.519	.746	6.2	15.6
91-92	ARIZ	31	.506	.777	7.9	16.3
92-93	ARIZ	28	.520	.836	7.9	20.4
Totals		126	.508	.767	7.6	16.5

NBA REGULAR-SEASON STATISTICS

			FGs		3-PT FGs		FTs		Rebounds						
	G	MIN	FG	PCT	FG	PCT	FT	PCT	OFF	TOT	AST	STL	BLK	PTS	PPG
93-94 CLE	79	2022	284	.419	38	.311	137	.778	134	401	128	54	50	743	9.4
Totals	79	2022	284	.419	38	.311	137	.778	134	401	128	54	50	743	9.4

TERRY MILLS

Team: Detroit Pistons
Position: Forward
Height: 6'10" **Weight:** 250
Birthdate: December 21, 1967

NBA Experience: 4 years
College: Michigan
Acquired: Signed as a free agent, 10/92

Background: Mills helped lead Michigan to the 1989 NCAA championship as a junior, then earned honorable-mention All-America status as a senior. He was drafted by Milwaukee, traded, and spent his rookie year with Denver and New Jersey. Detroit signed him as a free agent before the 1992-93 campaign and Mills has since had his two most productive years. He led the troubled Pistons in rebounding and was second in scoring last season.

Strengths: Mills possesses loads of offensive talent. He has extraordinary touch and good range on his jumper for a big man. He buries the turnaround and keeps his defender away with his backside. He shoots for a high percentage and has become a big scorer. Mills is a very good rebounder who also blocks a few shots and knows how to play the game.

Weaknesses: Mills has struggled through weight problems, although they appear to be behind him. Despite the fact he is not a physical defender, foul trouble has plagued him in each of the last two years. He ranks among league leaders in that category. As indicated, he should be a much better defender. He does not possess great quickness.

Analysis: Mills has returned home and found the Pistons much more to his liking. He was considered by some to be an underachiever after becoming a big-name high school player, but he has turned things around over the last two years and thrived as a scorer, rebounder, and accurate shooter from inside and out. Detroit's leaders have retired, and the talented Mills will be expected to compensate.

PLAYER SUMMARY

Will ....shoot with range
Can't ....abandon his diet
Expect ....scoring, rebounding
Don't Expect ....punishing defense
Fantasy Value.....................$20-25
Card Value ....5-10¢

COLLEGE STATISTICS

		G	FGP	FTP	RPG	PPG
87-88	MICH	34	.531	.729	6.4	12.1
88-89	MICH	37	.564	.769	5.9	11.6
89-90	MICH	31	.585	.759	8.0	18.1
Totals		102	.562	.755	6.7	13.8

NBA REGULAR-SEASON STATISTICS

		G	MIN	FGs FG	FGs PCT	3-PT FGs FG	3-PT FGs PCT	FTs FT	FTs PCT	Rebounds OFF	Rebounds TOT	AST	STL	BLK	PTS	PPG
90-91	DEN/NJ	55	819	134	.465	0	.000	47	.712	82	229	33	35	29	315	5.7
91-92	NJ	82	1714	310	.463	8	.348	114	.750	187	453	84	48	41	742	9.0
92-93	DET	81	2183	494	.461	10	.278	201	.791	176	472	111	44	50	1199	14.8
93-94	DET	80	2773	588	.511	24	.329	181	.797	193	672	177	64	62	1381	17.3
Totals		298	7489	1526	.480	42	.309	543	.777	638	1826	405	191	182	3637	12.2

HAROLD MINER

Team: Miami Heat
Position: Guard
Height: 6'4" **Weight:** 220
Birthdate: May 5, 1971

NBA Experience: 2 years
College: Southern California
Acquired: 1st-round pick in 1992 draft
(12th overall)

Background: A prized recruit of George Raveling at Southern Cal., Miner led the previously woeful Trojans to the NCAA Tournament in 1991 and 1992. He joined Lew Alcindor as the only players in Pac-10 history to score more than 2,000 points in three seasons. Miner, a left-hander, is nicknamed "Baby Jordan" for his similarities to Michael in appearance and style. Miami took him 12th overall in the 1992 draft and he won the NBA's 1993 Slam Dunk Contest. He has averaged about ten PPG each season.

Strengths: Miner has charisma. His great hang time and explosive dunks often send crowds into a frenzy, and he is very creative with the ball. A remarkable athlete, he is capable of going either around people or over them as he attacks the basket. He can get his shot whenever he wants to and will seldom lose a game of one-on-one.

Weaknesses: Probably the biggest reason Miner has not earned more playing time with the Heat is his reluctance to pass the ball. He tries to do too much and does not have a great concept of creating for others. He turns the ball over as often as he gets an assist. In addition, Miner does not qualify for comparisons to Jordan when it comes to defense. The range on his jump shot does not extend to the 3-point arc.

Analysis: Miner, a half-time starter last season, would warrant several more minutes if he could learn a little about defense and giving up the ball. The athletic potential is there for him to become a stopper, but passing might be a tougher skill to learn. As a scorer, few can match the explosiveness of Baby Jordan. He can simply sky.

PLAYER SUMMARY

Will ....play above the rim
Can't ....spot open men
Expect......................acrobatic dunks
Don't Expect ...Jordanesque defense
Fantasy Value...............................$4-6
Card Value ....20-50¢

COLLEGE STATISTICS

		G	FGP	FTP	RPG	PPG
89-90	USC	28	.473	.841	3.6	20.8
90-91	USC	29	.453	.800	5.5	23.5
91-92	USC	30	.438	.811	7.0	26.3
Totals		87	.453	.814	5.4	23.6

NBA REGULAR-SEASON STATISTICS

				FGs		3-PT FGs		FTs		Rebounds						
		G	MIN	FG	PCT	FG	PCT	FT	PCT	OFF	TOT	AST	STL	BLK	PTS	PPG
92-93	MIA	73	1383	292	.475	3	.333	163	.762	74	147	73	34	8	750	10.3
93-94	MIA	63	1358	254	.477	4	.667	149	.828	75	156	95	31	13	661	10.5
Totals		136	2741	546	.476	7	.467	312	.792	149	303	168	65	21	1411	10.4

SAM MITCHELL

Team: Indiana Pacers
Position: Forward
Height: 6'7" **Weight:** 210
Birthdate: September 2, 1963
NBA Experience: 5 years

College: Mercer
Acquired: Traded from Timberwolves with Pooh Richardson for Chuck Person and Micheal Williams, 9/92

Background: Mitchell finished his career as the all-time leading scorer at Mercer, but he got a late start as a pro. After being drafted and cut by Houston in 1985, he began a teaching career. His comeback carried him to the USBL, to the CBA, and on a two-year stint in France before he became the NBA's oldest rookie (26) in 1989-90. Mitchell was a double-figure scorer for three years in Minnesota before a 1992 trade made him an Indiana reserve.

Strengths: Mitchell is a versatile forward who plays with intensity and smarts. He is tough, both mentally and physically, and has a great work ethic. On offense, Mitchell is best at driving and getting to the line. He also rebounds at both ends of the court and bangs on defense.

Weaknesses: Mitchell is an inconsistent outside shooter who sometimes tries to do too much. His shooting range is limited yet he will still launch the 3-pointer from time to time. He also sends opponents to the line too often. He led the league with 338 fouls during his second season. Mitchell is a below-average ball-handler and passer.

Analysis: As many expected during his Minnesota days, Mitchell is not a double-figure scorer on a decent team. That has become apparent in Indiana, where he was used mainly as a reserve last season and saw his playing time reduced during the Pacers' postseason run. Mitchell has averaged career lows in scoring each of his two years with Indiana.

PLAYER SUMMARY

Will ....get to the line
Can't ....avoid fouling
Expect..................a versatile reserve
Don't Expect ....10 PPG
Fantasy Value $0
Card Value ....7-12¢

COLLEGE STATISTICS

		G	FGP	FTP	RPG	PPG
81-82	MER	27	.497	.717	3.7	7.1
82-83	MER	28	.519	.784	5.9	16.5
83-84	MER	26	.507	.781	7.1	21.5
84-85	MER	31	.516	.750	8.2	25.0
Totals		112	.512	.763	6.3	17.7

NBA REGULAR-SEASON STATISTICS

			FGs		3-PT FGs		FTs		Rebounds					
		G	MIN	FG	PCT	FG	PCT	FT	PCT	OFF	TOT	AST	STL	BLK	PTS	PPG
89-90	MIN	80	2414	372	.446	0	.000	268	.768	180	462	89	66	54	1012	12.6
90-91	MIN	82	3121	445	.441	0	.000	307	.775	188	520	133	66	57	1197	14.6
91-92	MIN	82	2151	307	.423	2	.182	209	.786	158	473	94	53	39	825	10.1
92-93	IND	81	1402	215	.445	4	.174	150	.811	93	248	76	23	10	584	7.2
93-94	IND	75	1084	140	.458	0	.000	82	.745	71	190	65	33	9	362	4.8
Totals		400	10172	1479	.440	6	.105	1016	.778	690	1893	457	241	169	3980	9.9

CHRIS MORRIS

Team: New Jersey Nets
Position: Forward
Height: 6'8" **Weight:** 210
Birthdate: January 20, 1966

NBA Experience: 6 years
College: Auburn
Acquired: 1st-round pick in 1988 draft
(4th overall)

Background: Following in the footsteps of past Auburn greats Charles Barkley and Chuck Person, Morris was the fourth player selected in the 1988 NBA draft. After season No. 1, the Nets looked like geniuses for taking him when they did. An All-Rookie second-team selection, Morris was New Jersey's top all-around performer. He leveled off after two strong years but has averaged 10-15 PPG in each of his six NBA seasons.

Strengths: Morris matches up athletically with just about any small forward in the NBA. He runs the floor, can handle the ball, drives to the hoop, and has become a reliable 3-point shooter. In short, he can be a pretty decent scorer in a position known for big scorers. He's also a solid defender and rebounder who loves a challenge.

Weaknesses: Morris has a well-known history as a troublemaker. He once refused to re-enter a game after then-coach Bill Fitch had pulled him. Inconsistency and poor shot selection have also plagued him. The focus is not always there. He has yet to match the scoring production of his second season in the league.

Analysis: Morris has been hampered by inconsistency throughout his career, but last year it was mostly injuries that held him back, including a broken right thumb during the season's second half. He might never match the 14.8 PPG he scored as an NBA sophomore, but the Nets brass likes his defense. That should be enough to keep him on the floor.

PLAYER SUMMARY

Will ....run the floor
Can't..............................maintain focus
Expect. ....solid defense
Don't Expect ....15 PPG
Fantasy Value..............................$9-11
Card Value ....5-10¢

COLLEGE STATISTICS

		G	FGP	FTP	RPG	PPG
84-85	AUB	34	.477	.620	5.0	10.4
85-86	AUB	33	.500	.670	5.2	9.8
86-87	AUB	31	.559	.711	7.3	13.5
87-88	AUB	30	.481	.795	9.8	20.7
Totals		128	.501	.712	6.7	13.4

NBA REGULAR-SEASON STATISTICS

				FGs		3-PT FGs		FTs		Rebounds						
		G	MIN	FG	PCT	FG	PCT	FT	PCT	OFF	TOT	AST	STL	BLK	PTS	PPG
88-89	NJ	76	2096	414	.457	64	.366	182	.717	188	397	119	102	60	1074	14.1
89-90	NJ	80	2449	449	.422	61	.316	228	.722	194	422	143	130	79	1187	14.8
90-91	NJ	79	2553	409	.425	45	.251	179	.734	210	521	220	138	96	1042	13.2
91-92	NJ	77	2394	346	.477	22	.200	165	.714	199	494	197	129	81	879	11.4
92-93	NJ	77	2302	436	.481	17	.224	197	.794	227	454	106	144	52	1086	14.1
93-94	NJ	50	1349	203	.447	53	.361	85	.720	91	228	83	55	49	544	10.9
Totals		439	13143	2257	.450	262	.298	1036	.734	1109	2516	868	698	417	5812	13.2

ALONZO MOURNING

Team: Charlotte Hornets
Position: Center
Height: 6'10" **Weight:** 240
Birthdate: February 8, 1970

NBA Experience: 2 years
College: Georgetown
Acquired: 1st-round pick in 1992 draft
(2nd overall)

Background: From Chesapeake, Virginia, Mourning was one of the country's best high school players ever, rating ahead of Shawn Kemp, Chris Jackson, and Billy Owens in the class of 1988. He set the NCAA record for career blocks (453), and as a senior he became the first player to be named Big East Player of the Year and Defensive Player of the Year in the same season. A No. 2 overall draft pick, he earned NBA All-Rookie honors in 1992-93 and has averaged about 21 PPG and 10 RPG in each of his two pro seasons.

Strengths: Mourning is already a dominant NBA big man. He scores, rebounds, blocks three shots a night, and is a ferocious competitor who loves contact and hates to lose. Mourning is a polished and productive offensive player, possessing a vast array of low-post moves and the ability to score from the perimeter. He gets to the line several times a night. Mourning made the All-Star Game for the first time last season.

Weaknesses: Mourning often seems to go it alone. He turns the ball over too frequently and does not dish out much more than one assist per game. In his very first NBA game, he either shot or committed a turnover the first 12 times he touched the ball. Mourning plays with a combative style that leads to a lot of personal fouls.

Analysis: Like former college teammate Dikembe Mutombo and like Patrick Ewing before him, Mourning is yet another dominant Georgetown center. Many felt he was a better player than Shaquille O'Neal in his draft class. He spent much of the second half of last season on the injured list, which was costly to the Hornets. Mourning was chosen to play with Dream Team II internationally.

PLAYER SUMMARY

Will ....swat shots
Can't ....pass like Mr. Robinson
Expect......................21 PPG, 10 RPG
Don't Expect ....3 APG
Fantasy Value...........................$50-55
Card Value ....30-75¢

COLLEGE STATISTICS

		G	FGP	FTP	RPG	PPG
88-89	GEOR	34	.603	.667	7.3	13.1
89-90	GEOR	31	.525	.783	8.5	16.5
90-91	GEOR	23	.522	.793	7.7	15.8
91-92	GEOR	32	.595	.758	10.7	21.3
Totals		120	.566	.754	8.6	16.7

NBA REGULAR-SEASON STATISTICS

			FGs		3-PT FGs		FTs		Rebounds						
	G	MIN	FG	PCT	FG	PCT	FT	PCT	OFF	TOT	AST	STL	BLK	PTS	PPG
92-93 CHA	78	2644	572	.511	0	.000	495	.781	263	805	76	27	271	1639	21.0
93-94 CHA	60	2018	427	.505	0	.000	433	.762	177	610	86	27	188	1287	21.5
Totals	138	4662	999	.509	0	.000	928	.772	440	1415	162	54	459	2926	21.2

CHRIS MULLIN

Team: Golden State Warriors
Position: Forward
Height: 6'7" **Weight:** 215
Birthdate: July 30, 1963

NBA Experience: 9 years
College: St. John's
Acquired: 1st-round pick in 1985 draft
(7th overall)

Background: Mullin made every All-America team as a senior and virtually every one as a junior at St. John's. He graduated as the Big East's all-time scoring leader. His pro career began with two good years, but since he voluntarily entered alcohol rehab in 1987-88, he has gotten better. He has played in four All-Star Games and the 1992 Olympics.

Strengths: Mullin possesses a wonderful overall game. He shoots with great touch and 3-point range, and he can kill you even with a hand in his face. He is a superb passer, is an above-average rebounder, and plays heads-up defense. He's among the best free throw shooters in NBA history. Mullin is a leader with a great feel for the game.

Weaknesses: Mullin will never win any awards for his athletic ability, though he is actually quicker than he looks. Finger and thumb injuries have kept him on the injured list for parts of the last two seasons.

Analysis: Mullin was likened to Larry Bird coming out of college, and after a so-so start he has lived up to such high billing. When healthy, he is one of the premier players and scorers in the league. In his first game back after a torn ligament kept him out early last season, Mullin poured in 23 points. Expect him to return to his 20-PPG days.

PLAYER SUMMARY	
Will	score from anywhere
Can't	dunk like Jordan
Expect	nearly 20 PPG
Don't Expect	selfishness
Fantasy Value	$45-50
Card Value	12-25¢

COLLEGE STATISTICS

		G	FGP	FTP	RPG	PPG
81-82	STJ	30	.534	.791	3.2	16.6
82-83	STJ	33	.577	.878	3.7	19.1
83-84	STJ	27	.571	.904	4.4	22.9
84-85	STJ	35	.521	.824	4.8	19.8
Totals		125	.550	.848	4.1	19.5

NBA REGULAR-SEASON STATISTICS

		G	MIN	FGs FG	PCT	3-PT FGs FG	PCT	FTs FT	PCT	Rebounds OFF	TOT	AST	STL	BLK	PTS	PPG
85-86	GS	55	1391	287	.463	5	.185	189	.896	42	115	105	70	23	768	14.0
86-87	GS	82	2377	477	.514	19	.302	269	.825	39	181	261	98	36	1242	15.1
87-88	GS	60	2033	470	.508	34	.351	239	.885	58	205	290	113	32	1213	20.2
88-89	GS	82	3093	830	.509	23	.230	493	.892	152	483	415	176	39	2176	26.5
89-90	GS	78	2830	682	.536	87	.372	505	.889	130	463	319	123	45	1956	25.1
90-91	GS	82	3315	777	.536	40	.301	513	.884	141	443	329	173	63	2107	25.7
91-92	GS	81	3346	830	.524	64	.366	350	.833	127	450	286	173	62	2074	25.6
92-93	GS	46	1902	474	.510	60	.451	183	.810	42	232	166	68	41	1191	25.9
93-94	GS	62	2324	410	.472	55	.364	165	.753	64	345	315	107	53	1040	16.8
Totals		628	22611	5237	.513	387	.348	2906	.862	795	2917	2486	1101	394	13767	21.9

ERIC MURDOCK

Team: Milwaukee Bucks
Position: Guard
Height: 6'1" **Weight:** 190
Birthdate: June 14, 1968
NBA Experience: 3 years

College: Providence
Acquired: Traded from Jazz with Blue Edwards and a 1992 1st-round pick for Jay Humphries and Larry Krystkowiak, 6/92

Background: As a junior at Providence, Murdock suffered a stress fracture in his leg and was hospitalized with an irregular heartbeat. He followed it up with a terrific senior season, however, and set an NCAA record with 376 career steals. He played in 50 games as a rookie with Utah, was traded to Milwaukee, and emerged as one of the most improved players in the league in 1992-93. He has tallied about 15 PPG in two years with the Bucks, leading the team last season.

Strengths: The versatile Murdock can flat-out play as an NBA point guard. He is quick to the hoop and can either finish the play himself or dish to open teammates after drawing traffic. His jump shot has become more reliable and he can make it from the 3-point arc. His quick hands make him an expert thief and fine overall defender. He's young and full of energy.

Weaknesses: Murdock has erased several of the elements in this category over the last two years. He must make sure he does not abandon his drives to the hoop simply because his jumper is better. He is prone to the turnover against pressure, although his ball-handling has improved greatly.

Analysis: Getting out of Utah allowed Murdock to escape John Stockton's shadow and develop at the pro level. His play with the Bucks has kept the highly touted Lee Mayberry in a reserve role. Murdock has rated among the league leaders in steals and assists the past two seasons and is his team's best scorer, all of which says a lot about his desire to achieve.

PLAYER SUMMARY	
Will	pick your pocket
Can't	avoid turnovers
Expect	energetic leadership
Don't Expect	reserve minutes
Fantasy Value	$18-21
Card Value	7-10¢

COLLEGE STATISTICS

		G	FGP	FTP	APG	PPG
87-88	PROV	28	.413	.738	3.8	10.7
88-89	PROV	29	.457	.762	4.9	16.2
89-90	PROV	28	.419	.762	3.3	15.4
90-91	PROV	32	.445	.812	4.6	25.6
Totals		117	.436	.783	4.2	17.3

NBA REGULAR-SEASON STATISTICS

				FGs		3-PT FGs		FTs		Rebounds						
		G	MIN	FG	PCT	FG	PCT	FT	PCT	OFF	TOT	AST	STL	BLK	PTS	PPG
91-92	UTA	50	478	76	.415	5	.192	46	.754	21	54	92	30	7	203	4.1
92-93	MIL	79	2437	438	.468	31	.261	231	.780	95	284	603	174	7	1138	14.4
93-94	MIL	82	2533	477	.468	69	.411	234	.813	91	261	546	197	12	1257	15.3
Totals		211	5448	991	.464	105	.335	511	.792	207	599	1241	401	26	2598	12.3

GHEORGHE MURESAN

Team: Washington Bullets
Position: Center
Height: 7'7" **Weight:** 330
Birthdate: February 14, 1971

NBA Experience: 1 year
College: Cluj University
Acquired: 2nd-round pick in 1993 draft (30th overall)

Background: Muresan is a 23-year-old giant who is taller than even Shawn Bradley and weighs more by a lot. He is, in fact, the largest player in the history of the NBA. He played well for Pau Orthez, a professional team in France, averaging 18.7 points and 10.3 rebounds per game before being drafted in the second round by the Washington Bullets in 1993. He overcame his leg injuries and averaged 5.6 PPG during his 1993-94 rookie season.

Strengths: Muresan is a mountain of a man. His massive bulk is his most obvious and clearly his greatest attribute. He takes up space on defense, blocks about a shot per game despite limited minutes, and can score when he gets the ball on the blocks. He shoots for a high percentage because he rarely takes a shot from outside a few feet. Muresan has soft hands and has potential as a rebounder and defender.

Weaknesses: Athletic ability does not show up on Muresan's resume. He is slow on his feet and cannot get off the floor at all. He has a history of ankle and knee injuries that have caused him to fail several physical exams. He's not a good passer and you don't want him dribbling the ball. He should contribute a lot more on the boards, considering his size.

Analysis: The Bullets took a gamble on Muresan, who came to America on a one-year visa, and it worked out pretty well. G.M. John Nash was pleased with the physical presence provided by the Romanian's 7'7", 330-pound frame. Denver guard Robert Pack may have said it best, noting that getting around a Muresan pick is like running around the block. His skills are limited, but his body never ends.

PLAYER SUMMARY	
Will	eat up space
Can't	win a footrace
Expect	impossible screens
Don't Expect	grace
Fantasy Value	$3-5
Card Value	10-20¢

COLLEGE STATISTICS

—DID NOT PLAY—

NBA REGULAR-SEASON STATISTICS

	G	MIN	FGs FG	FGs PCT	3-PT FGs FG	3-PT FGs PCT	FTs FT	FTs PCT	Rebounds OFF	Rebounds TOT	AST	STL	BLK	PTS	PPG
93-94 WAS	54	650	128	.545	0	.000	48	.676	66	192	18	28	48	304	5.6
Totals	54	650	128	.545	0	.000	48	.676	66	192	18	28	48	304	5.6

TRACY MURRAY

Team: Portland Trail Blazers
Position: Forward
Height: 6'8" **Weight:** 220
Birthdate: July 25, 1971
NBA Experience: 2 years

College: UCLA
Acquired: Draft rights traded from Spurs via the Bucks; Blazers sent Alaa Abdelnaby to Bucks, and Bucks sent Dale Ellis to Spurs, 7/92

Background: Murray was the highest-scoring player in California prep history when he signed to play at UCLA. While sharing the ball with Don MacLean, Murray finished his college career second in Pac-10 history in 3-point field goals (197) and hit them at a 50-percent clip as a junior. Drafted 18th by San Antonio in 1992, he soon went to Portland in a three-way deal. He led the league in 3-point percentage during the 1993-94 season.

Strengths: Murray can flat-out shoot the ball. There was no better 3-point shooter in the NBA last season than Murray, who buried 50 of his 109 long-range attempts. Murray creates match-up problems because big men are forced to play him outside the arc. He has also shown glimpses of ability to score in the post. Murray has good passing instincts.

Weaknesses: Murray faces match-up problems on defense. When he plays the perimeter, his opponents are too quick for him. When he's inside, they're too tough. He does not have a body made for physical play. While he can shoot the lights out when open, he does not do much off the dribble. He's a very poor rebounder for his size and does little other than shoot.

Analysis: Murray made a name for himself with his 3-point shooting last season, but being a league leader does not make you a premier player. While he gave the Blazers a spark with his touch off the bench, he needs to improve his defense drastically and become a more versatile and physical player offensively. What he does during the off-season will dictate how prominent a player Murray will be.

PLAYER SUMMARY

Will	.drain the trey
Can't	.pound his man
Expect	.a sweet stroke
Don't Expect	.rebounds
Fantasy Value	.$2-4
Card Value	.8-15¢

COLLEGE STATISTICS

		G	FGP	FTP	RPG	PPG
89-90	UCLA	33	.442	.767	5.5	12.3
90-91	UCLA	32	.503	.794	6.7	21.2
91-92	UCLA	33	.538	.800	7.0	21.4
Totals		98	.500	.791	6.4	18.3

NBA REGULAR-SEASON STATISTICS

		G	MIN	FGs FG	FGs PCT	3-PT FGs FG	3-PT FGs PCT	FTs FT	FTs PCT	Rebounds OFF	Rebounds TOT	AST	STL	BLK	PTS	PPG
92-93	POR	48	495	108	.415	21	.300	35	.875	40	83	11	8	5	272	5.7
93-94	POR	66	820	167	.470	50	.459	50	.694	43	111	31	21	20	434	6.6
Totals		114	1315	275	.447	71	.397	85	.759	83	194	42	29	25	706	6.2

DIKEMBE MUTOMBO

Team: Denver Nuggets
Position: Center
Height: 7'2" **Weight:** 245
Birthdate: June 25, 1966

NBA Experience: 3 years
College: Georgetown
Acquired: 1st-round pick in 1991 draft (4th overall)

Background: Mutombo was raised in Zaire, a French-speaking African nation, and was forced to sit out his freshman season at Georgetown because the SAT was not offered in French. His college scoring was modest but his shot-blocking helped earn him Big East Defensive Player of the Year honors in 1990 and 1991. He was the only rookie to appear in the 1992 All-Star Game. Mutombo led the league with 4.1 blocked shots per game last season.

Strengths: Great size, a giant wingspan, and underrated quickness make Mutombo a force to be reckoned with. He blocked 39 more shots than anyone last season and is annually among the top rebounders also. Considered a below-average offensive player out of college, Mutombo has silenced his critics with accurate hook shots and inside conversions. He does not take shots he can't make, as his field goal percentage indicates.

Weaknesses: Mutombo does not have the shooting range of a Patrick Ewing, David Robinson, or Hakeem Olajuwon. He also lags behind those post men in terms of knowledge of the game, especially where and when to deliver his passes. Poor free throw shooting is Mutombo's biggest problem. His scoring average dropped off in his sophomore season.

Analysis: Mutombo is one of the most dominant defensive centers in the game and is better offensively than most expected he would be. He works hard, longs to learn, and can rebound and block shots with the best of them. An international spokesman for CARE, his No. 1 off-season priority is visiting and helping the poverty-stricken people of his homeland. He's a class act and a fine player.

PLAYER SUMMARY

Will.................................intimidate
Can't ....shoot with range
Expect. ....interior defense
Don't Expect ....passive offense
Fantasy Value............................$20-25
Card Value ....20-40¢

COLLEGE STATISTICS

		G	FGP	FTP	RPG	PPG
88-89	GEOR	33	.707	.479	3.3	3.9
89-90	GEOR	31	.709	.598	10.5	10.7
90-91	GEOR	32	.586	.703	12.2	15.2
Totals		96	.644	.641	8.6	9.9

NBA REGULAR-SEASON STATISTICS

				FGs		3-PT FGs		FTs		Rebounds						
		G	MIN	FG	PCT	FG	PCT	FT	PCT	OFF	TOT	AST	STL	BLK	PTS	PPG
91-92	DEN	71	2716	428	.493	0	.000	321	.642	316	870	156	43	210	1177	16.6
92-93	DEN	82	3029	398	.510	0	.000	335	.681	344	1070	147	43	287	1131	13.8
93-94	DEN	82	2853	365	.569	0	.000	256	.583	286	971	127	59	336	986	12.0
Totals		235	8598	1191	.520	0	.000	912	.637	946	2911	430	145	833	3294	14.0

PETE MYERS

Unrestricted Free Agent
Last Team: Chicago Bulls
Position: Guard
Height: 6'6"　**Weight:** 180
Birthdate: September 15, 1963

NBA Experience: 6 years
College: Faulkner St.; Arkansas-Little Rock
Acquired: Signed as a free agent, 10/92

Background: Myers, who played in relative obscurity at Arkansas-Little Rock, has been the definition of a journeyman since leaving college. He saw action with five different teams in his first five years, including two stints with the Spurs, and also played in the CBA and Europe. Myers was signed by Chicago before the 1993-94 season and started 81 games for the Bulls. Though a free agent this summer, he was expected to re-sign with Chicago.

Strengths: Myers turned out to be a valuable player who does a little bit of everything. He runs the court, passes, and plays aggressive defense on just about anyone. His offensive game turned out to be far better than expected after the Bulls signed him. Myers is at his best in transition.

Weaknesses: The reason Myers bounced around for so long was his lack of a consistent offensive strength. While he gets his points, he is not a great pure shooter or a dominant attack-the-basket type. He needs a go-to move. Myers also seemed to be lost between about three positions before last season, when he developed as a big guard.

Analysis: All Myers was asked to do last season was take over Michael Jordan's starting big-guard spot. Clearly, he does not approach the level of His Airness. But the fact that Myers drew more praise than criticism for his play says a lot. He gave coach Phil Jackson quality minutes all season and during the playoffs while surprising a lot of people with his 7.9 PPG. He was an excellent acquisition.

PLAYER SUMMARY	
Will	run the floor
Can't	dominate
Expect	good versatility
Don't Expect	another Jordan
Fantasy Value	$1
Card Value	5-10¢

COLLEGE STATISTICS

		G	FGP	FTP	RPG	PPG
81-82	FAUL	26	.548	.743	5.1	12.4
82-83	FAUL	26	.578	.627	7.5	15.2
84-85	ALR	30	.451	.719	7.1	14.8
85-86	ALR	34	.534	.747	7.9	19.2
Totals		116	.521	.712	7.0	15.6

NBA REGULAR-SEASON STATISTICS

				FGs		3-PT FGs		FTs		Rebounds						
		G	MIN	FG	PCT	FG	PCT	FT	PCT	OFF	TOT	AST	STL	BLK	PTS	PPG
86-87	CHI	29	155	19	.365	0	.000	28	.651	8	17	21	14	2	66	2.3
87-88	SA	22	328	43	.453	0	.000	26	.667	11	37	48	17	6	112	5.1
88-89	PH/NJ	33	270	31	.425	0	.000	33	.688	15	33	48	20	2	95	2.9
89-90	NY/NJ	52	751	89	.396	0	.000	66	.660	33	96	135	35	11	244	4.7
90-91	SA	8	103	10	.435	0	.000	9	.818	2	18	14	3	3	29	3.6
93-94	CHI	82	2030	253	.455	8	.276	136	.701	54	181	245	78	20	650	7.9
Totals		226	3637	445	.435	8	.163	298	.685	123	382	511	167	44	1196	5.3

LARRY NANCE

Unrestricted Free Agent
Last Team: Cleveland Cavaliers
Position: Forward/Center
Height: 6'10" **Weight:** 235
Birthdate: February 12, 1959
NBA Experience: 13 years

College: Clemson
Acquired: Traded from Suns with
Mike Sanders and a 1988 1st-round
pick for Tyrone Corbin, Kevin Johnson,
Mark West, 1988 1st- and 2nd-round
picks, and a 1989 2nd-round pick, 2/88

Background: Nance, Clemson's leading rebounder for three consecutive
seasons, joined the Suns 13 years ago. His trade to the Cavs for Kevin Johnson
and others was, at the time, the biggest in Suns history. Nance, a former All-
Defensive Team member and three-time All-Star, was hobbled by injuries last
season. He became a free agent after the campaign.

Strengths: A healthy Nance was the best shot-blocking forward in the league for
a long time. He is still capable of turning games around on the defensive end. He
can still score and rebound and has always been a good passer.

Weaknesses: Injuries. He underwent surgery on his right knee in November
1993 but it did not hold up for even half a season. Nance has never been a great
perimeter shooter.

Analysis: Nance is a consummate pro and a team player through and through.
Most of his assets on the court involve hard work and athletic ability, although
one has to wonder how he will fare on a reconstructed knee in his final years.
You can't beat his leadership.

PLAYER SUMMARY

Will ....come to play
Can't ....regain young legs
Expect ....veteran leadership
Don't Expect ....the Nance of old
Fantasy Value..............................$6-8
Card Value ....5-10¢

COLLEGE STATISTICS

		G	FGP	FTP	RPG	PPG
77-78	CLEM	25	.467	.471	3.1	3.1
78-79	CLEM	29	.519	.636	7.2	11.1
79-80	CLEM	32	.515	.598	8.1	13.9
80-81	CLEM	31	.575	.690	7.6	15.9
Totals		117	.533	.628	6.7	11.5

NBA REGULAR-SEASON STATISTICS

		G	MIN	FGs FG	FGs PCT	3-PT FGs FG	3-PT FGs PCT	FTs FT	FTs PCT	Rebounds OFF	Rebounds TOT	AST	STL	BLK	PTS	PPG
81-82	PHO	80	1186	227	.521	0	.000	75	.641	95	256	82	42	71	529	6.6
82-83	PHO	82	2914	588	.550	1	.333	193	.672	239	710	197	99	217	1370	16.7
83-84	PHO	82	2899	601	.576	0	.000	249	.707	227	678	214	86	174	1451	17.7
84-85	PHO	61	2202	515	.587	1	.500	180	.709	195	536	159	88	104	1211	19.9
85-86	PHO	73	2484	582	.581	0	.000	310	.698	169	618	240	70	130	1474	20.2
86-87	PHO	69	2569	585	.551	1	.200	381	.773	188	599	233	86	148	1552	22.5
87-88	PHO/CLE	67	2383	487	.529	2	.333	304	.779	193	607	207	63	159	1280	19.1
88-89	CLE	73	2526	496	.539	0	.000	267	.799	156	581	159	57	206	1259	17.2
89-90	CLE	62	2065	412	.511	1	1.000	186	.778	162	516	161	54	122	1011	16.3
90-91	CLE	80	2927	635	.524	2	.250	265	.803	201	686	237	66	200	1537	19.2
91-92	CLE	81	2880	556	.539	0	.000	263	.822	213	670	232	80	243	1375	17.0
92-93	CLE	77	2753	533	.549	0	.000	202	.818	184	668	223	54	198	1268	16.5
93-94	CLE	33	909	153	.487	0	.000	64	.753	77	227	49	27	55	370	11.2
Totals		920	30697	6370	.546	8	.145	2939	.755	2299	7352	2393	872	2027	15687	17.1

JOHNNY NEWMAN

Unrestricted Free Agent
Last Team: New Jersey Nets
Position: Forward
Height: 6'7" **Weight:** 205
Birthdate: November 28, 1963

NBA Experience: 8 years
College: Richmond
Acquired: Traded from Hornets for Rumeal Robinson, 12/93

Background: Newman, who set a career scoring record at Richmond, spent one season with the Cavs before being waived. The Knicks picked him up and moved him from big guard to small forward. Signed by the Hornets as a restricted free agent four summers ago, Newman enjoyed his best pro season in Charlotte in 1990-91. He was traded to New Jersey for Rumeal Robinson last December, then became a free agent after the season.

Strengths: Newman is the definition of a slasher. He'll get to the hoop for finishes or trips to the line, where he is an 80-percent shooter. He has scored in double figures every season except his first. He is an impressive athlete who is not afraid to challenge defenses.

Weaknesses: Newman is streaky and prone to dismal nights. He has been called a selfish offensive player, and he dished out less than one assist a night last season. Newman is also not much help as a stopper or rebounder. He makes only about a quarter of his 3-point shots.

Analysis: An All-Star one night, a dog the next. That has been the book on Newman, who has the athletic ability to be a fine all-around player but hasn't made the necessary commitment. He has been shuffled in and out of the starting lineup over the last several years. He is probably best used as a scorer off the bench who is capable of scoring points in bunches.

PLAYER SUMMARY	
Will	look for the rim
Can't	spot open teammates
Expect	streak shooting
Don't Expect	consistency
Fantasy Value	$2-4
Card Value	5-8¢

COLLEGE STATISTICS

		G	FGP	FTP	RPG	PPG
82-83	RICH	28	.529	.719	3.1	12.3
83-84	RICH	32	.528	.787	6.1	21.9
84-85	RICH	32	.551	.773	5.2	21.3
85-86	RICH	30	.517	.890	7.3	22.0
Totals		122	.532	.800	5.5	19.5

NBA REGULAR-SEASON STATISTICS

				FGs		3-PT FGs		FTs		Rebounds						
		G	MIN	FG	PCT	FG	PCT	FT	PCT	OFF	TOT	AST	STL	BLK	PTS	PPG
86-87	CLE	59	630	113	.411	1	.045	66	.868	36	70	27	20	7	293	5.0
87-88	NY	77	1589	270	.435	26	.280	207	.841	87	159	62	72	11	773	10.0
88-89	NY	81	2336	455	.475	97	.338	286	.815	93	206	162	111	23	1293	16.0
89-90	NY	80	2277	374	.476	45	.317	239	.799	60	191	180	95	22	1032	12.9
90-91	CHA	81	2477	478	.470	30	.357	385	.809	94	254	188	100	17	1371	16.9
91-92	CHA	55	1651	295	.477	13	.283	236	.766	71	179	146	70	14	839	15.3
92-93	CHA	64	1471	279	.522	12	.267	194	.808	72	143	117	45	19	764	11.9
93-94	CHA/NJ	81	1697	313	.471	24	.267	182	.809	86	180	72	69	27	832	10.3
Totals		578	14128	2577	.471	248	.307	1795	.808	599	1382	954	582	140	7197	12.5

KEN NORMAN

Team: Atlanta Hawks
Position: Forward
Height: 6'8" **Weight:** 223
Birthdate: September 5, 1964

NBA Experience: 7 years
College: Wabash Valley; Illinois
Acquired: Traded from Bucks for Roy Hinson, 6/94

Background: Norman was a two-time All-Big Ten selection at Illinois, where he set a school record for field goal percentage. He became a starter for the Clippers late in his rookie season, then increased his scoring average by nearly ten points in 1988-89. He has not improved on that season since. Norman signed as a free agent with Milwaukee before the 1993-94 season and was the Bucks' No. 2 rebounder. He was traded to Atlanta in June.

Strengths: Norman considers himself a banger and loves to rebound and play defense. Nicknamed "Snake" for his slithering moves around the basket, he can score points in bunches and thrives in an open-court game. Big for a small forward, Norman also puts up a reliable mid-range jumper and has surprised people with his range.

Weaknesses: The glaring weakness in Norman's game is his horrendous free throw shooting, which stands at less than 60 percent for his career. It's perplexing because he's a fine shooter from 15 feet and even further out. Norman is not the kind of forward who can break down his defender off the dribble. He was unhappy playing for the Clips and the Bucks.

Analysis: Teammates, coaches, and opponents alike respect Norman for his toughness. He comes to battle, does the dirty work, and is also a dangerous offensive player when he gets on a roll. Norman commands respect on the court and off—he owns several dogs, attack rottweilers among them.

PLAYER SUMMARY

Will	bang on defense
Can't	sink his FTs
Expect	12-plus PPG
Don't Expect	snazzy dribbling
Fantasy Value	$7-9
Card Value	7-10¢

COLLEGE STATISTICS

		G	FGP	FTP	RPG	PPG
82-83	WAB	35	.605	.673	10.3	20.4
84-85	ILL	29	.632	.663	3.7	7.8
85-86	ILL	32	.641	.802	7.1	16.4
86-87	ILL	31	.578	.727	9.8	20.7
Totals		127	.608	.717	7.9	16.6

NBA REGULAR-SEASON STATISTICS

		G	MIN	FGs FG	FGs PCT	3-PT FGs FG	3-PT FGs PCT	FTs FT	FTs PCT	Rebounds OFF	Rebounds TOT	AST	STL	BLK	PTS	PPG
87-88	LAC	66	1435	241	.482	0	.000	87	.512	100	263	78	44	34	569	8.6
88-89	LAC	80	3020	638	.502	4	.190	170	.630	245	667	277	106	66	1450	18.1
89-90	LAC	70	2334	484	.510	7	.438	153	.632	143	470	160	78	59	1128	16.1
90-91	LAC	70	2309	520	.501	6	.188	173	.629	177	497	159	63	63	1219	17.4
91-92	LAC	77	2009	402	.490	4	.143	121	.535	158	448	125	53	66	929	12.1
92-93	LAC	76	2477	498	.511	10	.263	131	.595	209	571	165	59	58	1137	15.0
93-94	MIL	82	2539	412	.448	63	.333	92	.503	169	500	222	58	46	979	11.9
Totals		521	16123	3195	.494	94	.281	927	.584	1201	3416	1186	461	392	7411	14.2

CHARLES OAKLEY

Team: New York Knicks
Position: Forward
Height: 6'9" **Weight:** 245
Birthdate: December 18, 1963
NBA Experience: 9 years

College: Virginia Union
Acquired: Traded from Bulls with 1988 1st- and 3rd-round picks for Bill Cartwright and 1988 1st- and 3rd-round picks, 6/88

Background: The top Division II rebounder in the country in 1984-85, Oakley grabbed more than 17 per game at tiny Virginia Union. He made the NBA All-Rookie Team with Chicago the following season. Oakley was second in the league in rebounding in 1986-87 and 1987-88 but was shipped to New York in 1988 in exchange for Bill Cartwright. Last season, he was third on the Knicks in scoring and first in rebounding.

Strengths: Oakley rebounds and plays punishing defense. Once the NBA's "Chairman of the Boards," Oakley still uses his wide body around the glass. It requires great courage to drive toward him. He has been a key for the Knicks in setting a physical tone and becoming a title contender.

Weaknesses: Oakley is prone to launching bad shots from the perimeter, although he has made himself a better shooter. He does not jump well, relying more on brute strength. He commits a lot of fouls and is not the most popular guy in the league.

Analysis: Oakley is an enforcer and a rock-solid complement to Patrick Ewing. Pat Riley has built his team around physical defense and rebounding, and Oakley is a proven star in those categories. He is probably the biggest reason the Knicks have earned their reputation as the toughest team in the league.

PLAYER SUMMARY

Will	bruise the opposition
Can't	avoid fouls
Expect	rebounds, defense
Don't Expect	soft play
Fantasy Value	$7-9
Card Value	8-15¢

COLLEGE STATISTICS

		G	FGP	FTP	RPG	PPG
81-82	VU	28	.620	.610	12.5	15.9
82-83	VU	28	.582	.588	13.0	19.3
83-84	VU	30	.612	.621	13.1	21.7
84-85	VU	31	.625	.669	17.3	24.0
Totals		117	.611	.626	14.0	20.3

NBA REGULAR-SEASON STATISTICS

				FGs		3-PT FGs		FTs		Rebounds						
		G	MIN	FG	PCT	FG	PCT	FT	PCT	OFF	TOT	AST	STL	BLK	PTS	PPG
85-86	CHI	77	1772	281	.519	0	.000	178	.662	255	664	133	68	30	740	9.6
86-87	CHI	82	2980	468	.445	11	.367	245	.686	299	1074	296	85	36	1192	14.5
87-88	CHI	82	2816	375	.483	3	.250	261	.727	326	1066	248	68	28	1014	12.4
88-89	NY	82	2604	426	.510	12	.250	197	.773	343	861	187	104	14	1061	12.9
89-90	NY	61	2196	336	.524	0	.000	217	.761	258	727	146	64	16	889	14.6
90-91	NY	76	2739	307	.516	0	.000	239	.784	305	920	204	62	17	853	11.2
91-92	NY	82	2309	210	.522	0	.000	86	.735	256	700	133	67	15	506	6.2
92-93	NY	82	2230	219	.508	0	.000	127	.722	288	708	126	85	15	565	6.9
93-94	NY	82	2932	363	.478	0	.000	243	.776	349	965	218	110	18	969	11.8
Totals		706	22578	2985	.495	26	.248	1793	.736	2679	7685	1691	713	189	7789	11.0

HAKEEM OLAJUWON

Team: Houston Rockets
Position: Center
Height: 7'0" **Weight:** 255
Birthdate: January 21, 1963

NBA Experience: 10 years
College: Houston
Acquired: 1st-round pick in 1984 draft
(1st overall)

Background: Olajuwon led Houston to the Final Four three consecutive years, and he led the nation in rebounding and field goal accuracy as a senior. He was selected Southwest Conference Player of the 1980s by media and coaches. The former soccer goalie in Nigeria has made nine All-Star trips in ten seasons and has won three shot-blocking and two rebounding titles. Last year, he was the NBA's MVP and Defensive Player of the Year while leading the Rockets to the NBA championship.

Strengths: Olajuwon is one of the most talented and versatile centers ever. He is one of the best scorers, rebounders, and shot-blockers in the game. He has an amazing touch for a center, is an excellent passer, and is the leader of a talented team. Few play with his intensity and effectiveness on a nightly basis.

Weaknesses: Olajuwon piles up a lot of fouls and turnovers, but that's because he's always in the middle of everything. His squabbles with management are a thing of the past.

Analysis: With Michael Jordan retired, Olajuwan now reigns as the greatest player in the NBA. Last season, he scored a career-high 27.3 PPG while continuing to dominate as a rebounder and shot-blocker. He has over 17,000 career points and is still going strong. He's simply a force.

PLAYER SUMMARY	
Will	dominate regularly
Can't	be stopped by one
Expect	Hall of Fame induction
Don't Expect	poor outings
Fantasy Value	$85-90
Card Value	20-50¢

COLLEGE STATISTICS

		G	FGP	FTP	RPG	PPG
81-82	HOU	29	.607	.563	6.2	8.3
82-83	HOU	34	.611	.595	11.4	13.9
83-84	HOU	37	.675	.526	13.5	16.8
Totals		100	.639	.555	10.7	13.3

NBA REGULAR-SEASON STATISTICS

		G	MIN	FGs FG	FG PCT	3-PT FGs FG	PCT	FTs FT	FT PCT	Rebounds OFF	TOT	AST	STL	BLK	PTS	PPG
84-85	HOU	82	2914	677	.538	0	.000	338	.613	440	974	111	99	220	1692	20.6
85-86	HOU	68	2467	625	.526	0	.000	347	.645	333	781	137	134	231	1597	23.5
86-87	HOU	75	2760	677	.508	1	.200	400	.702	315	858	220	140	254	1755	23.4
87-88	HOU	79	2825	712	.514	0	.000	381	.695	302	959	163	162	214	1805	22.8
88-89	HOU	82	3024	790	.508	0	.000	454	.696	338	1105	149	213	282	2034	24.8
89-90	HOU	82	3124	806	.501	1	.167	382	.713	299	1149	234	174	376	1995	24.3
90-91	HOU	56	2062	487	.508	0	.000	213	.769	219	770	131	121	221	1187	21.2
91-92	HOU	70	2636	591	.502	0	.000	328	.766	246	845	157	127	304	1510	21.6
92-93	HOU	82	3242	848	.529	0	.000	444	.779	283	1068	291	150	342	2140	26.1
93-94	HOU	80	3277	894	.528	8	.421	388	.716	229	955	287	128	297	2184	27.3
Totals		756	28331	7107	.516	10	.175	3675	.705	3004	9464	1880	1448	2741	17899	23.7

JIMMY OLIVER

Team: Boston Celtics
Position: Guard/Forward
Height: 6'6" **Weight:** 208
Birthdate: July 12, 1969

NBA Experience: 2 years
College: Purdue
Acquired: Signed as a free agent, 10/93

Background: Oliver averaged 19.2 PPG during his senior season at Purdue, won the Big Ten free throw title, and was named first-team all-conference. He was drafted in the second round by Cleveland and played 27 games for the Cavaliers in 1991-92 before being released. He led Sioux Falls of the CBA during the 1992-93 season before Boston signed him in October 1993. He played in 44 games for the Celtics last season.

Strengths: Oliver fashions himself a scorer. He has good range on his jumper and can shoot the lights out when he's hot. He also goes to the hoop, can draw fouls, and has always been a steady free throw shooter. Oliver is versatile, having the ability to play both big guard and small forward. He possesses good athletic ability and is not afraid to challenge the best players in basketball.

Weaknesses: Typical of many players who bounce between the CBA and the big leagues, Oliver falls squarely between two positions. He is not big or strong enough to compete with the league's better forwards and lacks the sheer quickness to be a big-time backcourt player. He's inconsistent on both ends of the court, prone to prolonged cold spells offensively, and not well-schooled in defensive fundamentals.

Analysis: Oliver is either a great CBA player or a below-average NBA talent. He averaged 17.3 PPG during his season with the Sioux Falls Skyforce after failing with Cleveland and getting cut by Detroit in the 1992 preseason. He made six starts with the Celtics last season and averaged about five points and 12 minutes per game. He needs to become more consistent if he hopes for a breakthrough year at the NBA level.

PLAYER SUMMARY	
Will	challenge his man
Can't	bang with forwards
Expect	streak shooting
Don't Expect	a stopper
Fantasy Value	$0
Card Value	5-10¢

COLLEGE STATISTICS

		G	FGP	FTP	APG	PPG
88-89	PURD	31	.435	.581	2.4	5.3
89-90	PURD	30	.489	.642	2.5	8.0
90-91	PURD	29	.466	.861	4.6	19.2
Totals		90	.465	.751	3.1	10.7

NBA REGULAR-SEASON STATISTICS

			FGs		3-PT FGs		FTs		Rebounds						
	G	MIN	FG	PCT	FG	PCT	FT	PCT	OFF	TOT	AST	STL	BLK	PTS	PPG
91-92 CLE	27	252	39	.398	1	.111	17	.773	9	27	20	9	2	96	3.6
93-94 BOS	44	540	89	.416	13	.406	25	.758	8	46	33	16	1	216	4.9
Totals	71	792	128	.410	14	.341	42	.764	17	73	53	25	3	312	4.4

SHAQUILLE O'NEAL

Team: Orlando Magic
Position: Center
Height: 7'1" **Weight:** 303
Birthdate: March 6, 1972

NBA Experience: 2 years
College: Louisiana St.
Acquired: 1st-round pick in 1992 draft
(1st overall)

Background: Shaq was a two-time All-American in his three years at Louisiana State and earned a handful of Player of the Year honors after his sophomore campaign. Few NBA Rookie of the Year winners have ever made as big an impact as Shaq did. He was the first rookie to start an All-Star Game since Michael Jordan. He made his second All-Star start last season and lost the league scoring title on the final day of the season.

Strengths: O'Neal is as powerful as any player in the game. He has torn down two backboards on slam dunks and is virtually unstoppable when he gets the ball in the paint and heads for the hoop. He scores, rebounds, and swats shots with the best of them. He led the league in field goal percentage last season and also led Orlando to its first playoff appearance. He has become the game's most popular fan attraction.

Weaknesses: Critics say O'Neal does not have a go-to move other than the monster dunk, although he clearly expanded his repertoire last season. His biggest struggles come from the free throw line, and he gets there more than any player. Like many big men, foul trouble hurts him. O'Neal has a big ego, which irritates other NBA stars.

Analysis: O'Neal has turned out to be worth every penny of the $40 million the team will pay him over his first seven years. He has resurrected the Magic in just two years, and he has done so with charisma. Off the court, he has cut a successful rap album, has starred in a movie (*Blue Chips*), and has become one of the biggest names in the entire entertainment industry.

PLAYER SUMMARY	
Will	dominate the middle
Can't	hit his FTs
Expect	MVP consideration
Don't Expect	single-teams
Fantasy Value	$70-75
Card Value	75¢-$5.00

COLLEGE STATISTICS

		G	FGP	FTP	RPG	PPG
89-90	LSU	32	.573	.556	12.0	13.9
90-91	LSU	28	.628	.638	14.7	27.6
91-92	LSU	30	.615	.528	14.0	24.1
Totals		90	.610	.575	13.5	21.6

NBA REGULAR-SEASON STATISTICS

		G	MIN	FGs FG	FGs PCT	3-PT FGs FG	3-PT FGs PCT	FTs FT	FTs PCT	Rebounds OFF	Rebounds TOT	AST	STL	BLK	PTS	PPG
92-93	ORL	81	3071	733	.562	0	.000	427	.592	342	1122	152	60	286	1893	23.4
93-94	ORL	81	3224	953	.599	0	.000	471	.554	384	1072	195	76	231	2377	29.3
Totals		162	6295	1686	.582	0	.000	898	.572	726	2194	347	136	517	4270	26.4

BO OUTLAW

Team: Los Angeles Clippers
Position: Forward
Height: 6'8" **Weight:** 210
Birthdate: April 13, 1971

NBA Experience: 1 year
College: South Plains; Houston
Acquired: Signed as a free agent, 2/94

Background: Charles "Bo" Outlaw led the nation in field goal percentage in 1992 and 1993 at the University of Houston, but he was bypassed in both rounds of the 1993 NBA draft. He was tearing up the Continental Basketball Association for the Grand Rapids Hoops before the Clippers signed him to the first of two ten-day contracts in February 1994. Outlaw stuck with the Clippers and wound up starting 14 of his 37 games last season.

Strengths: The 6'8" Outlaw has a serious low-post game. He uses his soft touch inside and effective moves around the basket to convert at an extraordinary percentage. Shooting .587 from the field as an NBA rookie is almost unheard-of, especially for non-centers. Outlaw is also an above-average rebounder and a fine athlete. He blocks shots and works hard at the defensive end.

Weaknesses: Outlaw is undersized for a low-post player, which in all likelihood cost him a spot in the draft. He can't push his man around on most nights. It has not hurt his offensive game as much as it has caused him some defensive match-up problems. Away from the hoop, Outlaw is far less effective. He's a horrible free throw shooter and not much of a dribbler or passer.

Analysis: Outlaw was one of the CBA success stories in 1993-94. He was not given much thought in the draft, but he played his way into the league with a fine start in Grand Rapids and wound up averaging 6.9 points and almost six rebounds per game with the Clippers. His low-post scoring in the big leagues surprised a lot of people. Outlaw was given a chance and took advantage. It appears he'll stick around.

PLAYER SUMMARY

Will	show touch inside
Can't	shoot FTs
Expect	strong rebounding
Don't Expect	raw power
Fantasy Value	$0
Card Value	7-10¢

COLLEGE STATISTICS

		G	FGP	FTP	RPG	PPG
89-90	SP	30	.563	.507	9.6	12.1
90-91	SP	30	.661	.574	10.9	13.2
91-92	HOU	31	.684	.442	8.2	11.9
92-93	HOU	30	.658	.495	10.0	16.2
Totals		121	.640	.503	9.7	13.3

NBA REGULAR-SEASON STATISTICS

			FGs		3-PT FGs		FTs		Rebounds						
	G	MIN	FG	PCT	FG	PCT	FT	PCT	OFF	TOT	AST	STL	BLK	PTS	PPG
93-94 LAC	37	871	98	.587	0	.000	61	.592	81	212	36	36	37	257	6.9
Totals	37	871	98	.587	0	.000	61	.592	81	212	36	36	37	257	6.9

DOUG OVERTON

Team: Washington Bullets
Position: Guard
Height: 6'3" **Weight:** 190
Birthdate: August 3, 1969

NBA Experience: 2 years
College: La Salle
Acquired: Signed as a free agent, 10/92

Background: Overton, a high school teammate of Bo Kimble and the late Hank Gathers at Philadelphia's Dobbins Tech, spent most of his college career at La Salle as a point guard. He was a solid complementary player to Lionel Simmons but struggled after Simmons graduated. Overton was drafted in the second round by Detroit in 1991 and released without playing a game. He averaged 8.1 PPG as a rookie with Washington but slumped to less than half that total last season.

Strengths: Overton can play both guard positions and is capable of scoring at the NBA level. He possesses a pretty decent outside shot with range beyond 20 feet and is an excellent free throw shooter. Overton also keeps his eyes peeled for open teammates and gets the ball to the right people. His Philadelphia years taught him about toughness; he will compete with anyone.

Weaknesses: There were questions about Overton's playmaking ability when he entered the league, and many of those questions remain. Is he a natural point guard? Some say no. He possesses only average quickness and does not penetrate as easily or as often as coaches would like. Though a good shooter, he is prone to prolonged cold spells. He won't come up with a lot of steals or rebounds.

Analysis: Overton is a street-wise player who will stick around in a reserve role. He gives you versatility off the bench, can hit jumpers when open, and does not shy away from a challenge. Some feel he has the potential to be a 3-point specialist, although he has made only four from that range in his career. He underwent thumb surgery late in his rookie year and did not shoot the ball as well last season.

PLAYER SUMMARY

Will	shoot when open
Can't	burn his man
Expect	a competitor
Don't Expect	natural playmaking
Fantasy Value	$0
Card Value	8-15¢

COLLEGE STATISTICS

		G	FGP	FTP	APG	PPG
87-88	LaS	34	.498	.841	2.7	7.8
88-89	LaS	32	.494	.787	7.6	13.2
89-90	LaS	32	.519	.798	6.6	17.2
90-91	LaS	25	.445	.818	5.0	22.3
Totals		123	.486	.814	5.5	14.6

NBA REGULAR-SEASON STATISTICS

				FGs		3-PT FGs		FTs		Rebounds						
		G	MIN	FG	PCT	FG	PCT	FT	PCT	OFF	TOT	AST	STL	BLK	PTS	PPG
92-93	WAS	45	990	152	.471	3	.231	59	.728	25	106	157	31	6	366	8.1
93-94	WAS	61	749	87	.403	1	.091	43	.827	19	69	92	21	1	218	3.6
Totals		106	1739	239	.443	4	.167	102	.767	44	175	249	52	7	584	5.5

BILLY OWENS

Team: Golden State Warriors
Position: Forward/Guard
Height: 6'9" **Weight:** 220
Birthdate: May 1, 1969
NBA Experience: 3 years

College: Syracuse
Acquired: Draft rights traded from Kings for Mitch Richmond, Les Jepsen, and a 1995 2nd-round pick, 11/91

Background: Owens, the 1988 A.P. High School Player of the Year at Carlisle (Pennsylvania) High, was Syracuse's prize recruit. He finished his three-year career ranked among the school's top seven in scoring, rebounds, blocked shots, steals, and assists. With Golden State, Owens was third among rookies in scoring and rebounding in 1991-92 and No. 1 in field goal percentage. He has had surgery on both knees since then, but he returned for a full 1993-94 campaign and was fourth on the Warriors in scoring.

Strengths: Owens brings tremendous versatility to the court. He can play every position but center, passes the ball well, rebounds, runs the floor, and has great quickness. He's a strong finisher, can break his man down off the dribble, and can also score with wing jumpers. He shoots for a high percentage. Owens is a scorer but will also play some defense and block a few shots.

Weaknesses: Owens has limited range and has never been a good free throw shooter. In fact, shooting jumpers is not the best part of his offensive game. He does not possess 3-point range. Owens is turnover-prone and gets called for aggressive fouls. His knees will remain a concern, although they seem to be holding up.

Analysis: Owens roared back last season and answered a lot of questions about the health of his knees. He enjoyed career highs in several categories, fit in well with Chris Webber and Latrell Sprewell, and still scored 15 PPG. The Warriors are loaded with young stars, and Owens must be counted among them.

PLAYER SUMMARY

Will....................play multiple positions
Can't.................................bury his FTs
Expect...........................about 15 PPG
Don't Expect ....3-point range
Fantasy Value.............................$30-35
Card Value.................................12-25¢

COLLEGE STATISTICS

		G	FGP	FTP	RPG	PPG
88-89	SYR	38	.521	.648	6.9	13.0
89-90	SYR	33	.486	.722	8.4	18.2
90-91	SYR	32	.509	.674	11.6	23.3
Totals		103	.505	.682	8.8	17.7

NBA REGULAR-SEASON STATISTICS

				FGs		3-PT FGs		FTs		Rebounds						
		G	MIN	FG	PCT	FG	PCT	FT	PCT	OFF	TOT	AST	STL	BLK	PTS	PPG
91-92	GS	80	2510	468	.525	1	.111	204	.654	243	639	188	90	65	1141	14.3
92-93	GS	37	1201	247	.501	1	.091	117	.639	108	264	144	35	28	612	16.5
93-94	GS	79	2738	492	.507	3	.200	199	.610	230	640	326	83	60	1186	15.0
Totals		196	6449	1207	.513	5	.143	520	.633	581	1543	658	208	153	2939	15.0

ROBERT PACK

Team: Denver Nuggets
Position: Guard
Height: 6'2" **Weight:** 180
Birthdate: February 3, 1969

NBA Experience: 3 years
College: Tyler; Southern Cal.
Acquired: Traded from Trail Blazers for a 1993 2nd-round pick, 10/92

Background: Pack totaled 319 assists in just two years at Southern Cal. He joined former USC stars Gus Williams, Jacque Hill, and Larry Friend when he recorded back-to-back years of 100 or more assists. Pack was not drafted but was signed by Portland and dished out nearly two APG in 1991-92. He has been a valuable reserve for the Nuggets in the past two seasons, leading the team in per-game assists last year.

Strengths: Pack has proven to be more than capable as a back-up point guard and can also play the two spot. He is an accomplished distributor who can score on drives to the basket or with the occasional jump shot. He has averaged around 10 PPG in limited playing time as a Nugget. He has very good quickness, strength, and leaping ability and applies himself at the defensive end.

Weaknesses: Pack is not regarded as a pure shooter and his range is limited. The 3-point area is in another county as far as he is concerned. His play is hot-and-cold and he is not great fundamentally. He takes a few too many chances defensively and will get out of control at times. He commits far too many turnovers.

Analysis: Pack deserves a lot of credit for making a very good Portland team as an undrafted rookie and then making an impact with Denver. The Nuggets looked elsewhere before last season but wound up re-signing Pack early in the campaign. He was one of the big reasons why Denver upset top-seeded Seattle in last year's playoffs. Pack scored 21 points in the decisive Game 5.

PLAYER SUMMARY	
Will	drive and dish
Can't	shoot the 3
Expect	quality minutes
Don't Expect	many starts
Fantasy Value	$2-4
Card Value	5-10¢

COLLEGE STATISTICS

		G	FGP	FTP	APG	PPG
1989-90	USC	28	.472	.677	5.9	12.1
1990-91	USC	29	.480	.794	5.3	14.7
Totals		57	.476	.742	5.6	13.4

NBA REGULAR-SEASON STATISTICS

				FGs		3-PT FGs		FTs		Rebounds						
		G	MIN	FG	PCT	FG	PCT	FT	PCT	OFF	TOT	AST	STL	BLK	PTS	PPG
91-92	POR	72	894	115	.423	0	.000	102	.803	32	97	140	40	4	332	4.6
92-93	DEN	77	1579	285	.470	1	.125	239	.768	52	160	335	81	10	810	10.5
93-94	DEN	66	1382	223	.443	6	.207	179	.758	25	123	356	81	9	631	9.6
Totals		215	3855	623	.451	7	.149	520	.772	109	380	831	202	23	1773	8.2

ROBERT PARISH

Team: Charlotte Hornets
Position: Center
Height: 7'0" **Weight:** 230
Birthdate: August 30, 1953

NBA Experience: 18 years
College: Centenary
Acquired: Signed as a free agent, 7/94

Background: The best player in Centenary history, "Chief" enjoyed four solid seasons with Golden State before his career blossomed in Boston. He played on championship Celtic teams in 1981, '84, and '86. The oldest player in the league at 40 last season, he still figured among Boston's top scorers and rebounders. He signed with Charlotte as a free agent over the summer.

Strengths: Parish is a superb leader who still rebounds, scores, and blocks shots. His high-arching jumper still finds the net. He has more than 22,000 career points, 13,000 rebounds, 1,400 games, and 2,200 blocks. Parish is second to Kareem Abdul-Jabbar in games played.

Weaknesses: Parish, the league's oldest player, is no longer effective for long chunks of minutes. He does not have the first step he used to.

Analysis: After 14 years of glory with the Celtics, Parish will now back up Alonzo Mourning in Charlotte. The Hornets couldn't have found a better tutor. Parish is headed for the Hall of Fame the first year he's eligible.

PLAYER SUMMARY

Will	lead by example
Can't	turn back the clock
Expect	Hall of Fame induction
Don't Expect	two more years
Fantasy Value	$1-3
Card Value	8-15¢

COLLEGE STATISTICS

		G	FGP	FTP	RPG	PPG
72-73	CENT	27	.579	.610	18.7	23.0
73-74	CENT	25	.523	.628	15.3	19.9
74-75	CENT	29	.560	.661	15.4	18.9
75-76	CENT	27	.589	.694	18.0	24.8
Totals		108	.564	.655	16.9	21.6

NBA REGULAR-SEASON STATISTICS

				FGs		3-PT FGs		FTs		Rebounds						
		G	MIN	FG	PCT	FG	PCT	FT	PCT	OFF	TOT	AST	STL	BLK	PTS	PPG
76-77	GS	77	1384	288	.503	0	.000	121	.708	201	543	74	55	94	697	9.1
77-78	GS	82	1969	430	.472	0	.000	165	.625	211	679	95	79	123	1025	12.5
78-79	GS	76	2411	554	.499	0	.000	196	.698	265	916	115	100	217	1304	17.2
79-80	GS	72	2119	510	.507	0	.000	203	.715	257	793	122	58	115	1223	17.0
80-81	BOS	82	2298	635	.545	0	.000	282	.710	245	777	144	81	214	1552	18.9
81-82	BOS	80	2534	669	.542	0	.000	252	.710	288	866	140	68	192	1590	19.9
82-83	BOS	78	2459	619	.550	0	.000	271	.698	260	827	141	79	148	1509	19.3
83-84	BOS	80	2867	623	.542	0	.000	274	.745	243	857	139	55	116	1520	19.0
84-85	BOS	79	2850	551	.542	0	.000	292	.743	263	840	125	56	101	1394	17.6
85-86	BOS	81	2567	530	.549	0	.000	245	.731	246	770	145	65	116	1305	16.1
86-87	BOS	80	2995	588	.556	0	.000	227	.735	254	851	173	64	144	1403	17.5
87-88	BOS	74	2312	442	.589	0	.000	177	.734	173	628	115	55	84	1061	14.3
88-89	BOS	80	2840	596	.570	0	.000	294	.719	342	996	175	79	116	1486	18.6
89-90	BOS	79	2396	505	.580	0	.000	233	.747	259	796	103	38	69	1243	15.7
90-91	BOS	81	2441	485	.598	0	.000	237	.767	271	856	66	66	103	1207	14.9
91-92	BOS	79	2285	468	.535	0	.000	179	.772	219	705	70	68	97	1115	14.1
92-93	BOS	79	2146	416	.535	0	.000	162	.689	246	740	61	57	107	994	12.6
93-94	BOS	74	1987	356	.491	0	.000	154	.740	141	542	82	42	96	866	11.7
Totals		1413	42860	9265	.540	0	.000	3964	.722	4384	13982	2085	1165	2252	22494	15.9

GARY PAYTON

Team: Seattle SuperSonics
Position: Guard
Height: 6'4" **Weight:** 190
Birthdate: July 23, 1968

NBA Experience: 4 years
College: Oregon St.
Acquired: 1st-round pick in 1990 draft
(2nd overall)

Background: Payton was an All-American as a senior at Oregon State, where he set a school scoring record, ended his career second on the NCAA assists list, and set a Pac-10 record with 100 steals in his final season. He has started all but seven games of his first four seasons and has led Seattle in assists each year. Last season, he helped the Sonics to the best record in the league and earned MVP consideration.

Strengths: Payton has lived up to his defensive reputation and can now be considered one of the premier all-around point guards in the game. He hounds the ball, makes his opponent work for everything he gets, and is among the better thieves in basketball. He stands tall at the point, where he handles the ball expertly, gets good penetration, and is a fine finisher. He makes things happen and has improved his scoring average each season to its current 16-plus PPG.

Weaknesses: A noted trash talker, Payton tends to make opponents want to cram the ball down his throat. He is a dreadful free throw shooter and his comfort zone does not extend to the 3-point arc. Shooting is simply not Payton's forte, especially off the dribble.

Analysis: Payton talks a big game but he also plays one. He's a natural point guard who penetrates, hits open teammates, handles the ball, and shuts down his man on defense. He has also become a primary scoring threat and one of the leaders of a team that looks like a perennial championship contender. He loves the game and plays to win every night.

PLAYER SUMMARY	
Will	.....swipe the ball
Can't	..............keep quiet
Expect	.........playmaking, defense
Don't Expect	......less than 12 PPG
Fantasy Value	.........................$25-30
Card Value	...............................12-20¢

COLLEGE STATISTICS

		G	FGP	FTP	APG	PPG
86-87	OSU	30	.459	.671	7.6	12.5
87-88	OSU	31	.489	.699	7.4	14.5
88-89	OSU	30	.475	.677	8.1	20.1
89-90	OSU	29	.504	.690	8.1	25.7
Totals		120	.485	.684	7.8	18.1

NBA REGULAR-SEASON STATISTICS

		G	MIN	FGs FG	FGs PCT	3-PT FGs FG	3-PT FGs PCT	FTs FT	FTs PCT	Rebounds OFF	Rebounds TOT	AST	STL	BLK	PTS	PPG
90-91	SEA	82	2244	259	.450	1	.077	69	.711	108	243	528	165	15	588	7.2
91-92	SEA	81	2549	331	.451	3	.130	99	.669	123	295	506	147	21	764	9.4
92-93	SEA	82	2548	476	.494	7	.206	151	.770	95	281	399	177	21	1110	13.5
93-94	SEA	82	2881	584	.504	15	.278	166	.595	105	269	494	188	19	1349	16.5
Totals		327	10222	1650	.481	26	.210	485	.674	431	1088	1927	677	76	3811	11.7

ANTHONY PEELER

Team: Los Angeles Lakers
Position: Guard
Height: 6'4" **Weight:** 212
Birthdate: November 25, 1969

NBA Experience: 2 years
College: Missouri
Acquired: 1st-round pick in 1992 draft
(15th overall)

Background: Perhaps the most heralded recruit in Missouri history, Peeler lived up to expectations despite an inability to stay out of trouble. He was named Big Eight Player of the Year after averaging 23.4 PPG, 5.5 RPG, and 3.9 APG as a senior. He notched more than 100 assists every season. His checkered off-court record includes a conviction on a felony weapons charge. His troubles dropped him to the 15th spot in the 1992 draft. He enjoyed a fine rookie year before leg injuries caused him to miss more than half of last season.

Strengths: A tremendous athlete, Peeler was drafted by the Texas Rangers in 1988 as a left-handed pitcher/outfielder. He can play both guard positions and is capable of getting to the basket or pulling up for perimeter jumpers. Peeler has 3-point range and thrives in the open court. He competes, has a great feel for the game, and gets his teammates involved with above-average passing skills.

Weaknesses: Peeler's off-court troubles and recent injury woes have been the main setbacks in his basketball career. On the hardwood, he could stand to apply himself more on defense and on the boards. His shooting is streaky and his overall play has been inconsistent to date, even when healthy. He needs to recognize good shots and avoid the others.

Analysis: Assuming Peeler continues to stay out of trouble and can return healthy, the Lakers appear to have made a steal with their No. 15 choice. Peeler made an immediate impact and would have led the team in scoring last season were it not for his extended stints on the injured list. He's a player with loads of natural ability and the potential to become a star.

PLAYER SUMMARY

Will ....run the court
Can't ....control the boards
Expect ....15 PPG
Don't Expect ....steady shooting
Fantasy Value...............................$9-11
Card Value ....12-20¢

COLLEGE STATISTICS

		G	FGP	FTP	RPG	PPG
88-89	MO	36	.504	.754	3.7	10.1
89-90	MO	31	.446	.769	5.4	16.8
90-91	MO	21	.475	.768	6.2	19.4
91-92	MO	29	.459	.806	5.5	23.4
Totals		117	.466	.779	5.1	16.8

NBA REGULAR-SEASON STATISTICS

				FGs		3-PT FGs		FTs		Rebounds						
		G	MIN	FG	PCT	FG	PCT	FT	PCT	OFF	TOT	AST	STL	BLK	PTS	PPG
92-93	LAL	77	1656	297	.468	46	.390	162	.786	64	179	166	60	14	802	10.4
93-94	LAL	30	923	176	.430	14	.222	57	.803	48	109	94	43	8	423	14.1
Totals		107	2579	473	.453	60	.331	219	.791	112	288	260	103	22	1225	11.4

MIKE PEPLOWSKI

Team: Sacramento Kings
Position: Center
Height: 6'11" **Weight:** 270
Birthdate: October 15, 1970

NBA Experience: 1 year
College: Michigan St.
Acquired: 2nd-round pick in 1993 draft (52nd overall)

Background: Peplowski overcame serious knee surgery to carve out a successful college career at Michigan State. He represented the U.S. in the Pan-Am Games in 1991 and was an All-Big Ten choice in 1992. He graduated with the second-highest field goal percentage in Spartan history. Peplowski was drafted in the second round by Sacramento and averaged about three rebounds in a little over ten minutes per game during his 1993-94 rookie season.

Strengths: A big, strong plugger, Peplowski does the dirty work, whether it's setting forceful picks, grabbing rebounds, or giving hard fouls. He managed to foul out twice last season in limited floor time. He can be effective around the basket and rarely takes a bad shot. His work ethic and determination can hardly be called into question. Tell him to do something and he'll do it.

Weaknesses: Peplowski does not have the makings of a standout pro player. His ankles and knees have bothered him and he does not boast much athletic ability to begin with. He's a plodder in transition and lacks explosiveness, to put it kindly. His perimeter defense is weak, his range limited to the paint area, and his free throw shooting atrocious. Peplowski has a long way to go.

Analysis: Peplowski was never a lock to make Sacramento's roster, but he worked his way onto the team and even drew a handful of starts when the Kings ran into injury problems. His job for most of the year was to provide hard fouls, interior defense, and rebounds while seeing action for a few minutes at a time He did so successfully. His limited offense and lack of speed make him unlikely to earn a better role at this level.

PLAYER SUMMARY

Will ....give hard fouls
Can't....................................win a race
Expect....................reserve rebounding
Don't Expect ....acrobatics
Fantasy Value $0
Card Value ....7-12¢

COLLEGE STATISTICS

		G	FGP	FTP	RPG	PPG
89-90	MSU	28	.546	.628	5.8	5.3
90-91	MSU	30	.627	.680	6.9	7.7
91-92	MSU	30	.632	.688	8.6	13.3
92-93	MSU	28	.639	.667	10.0	14.5
Totals		116	.620	.670	7.8	10.2

NBA REGULAR-SEASON STATISTICS

			FGs		3-PT FGs		FTs		Rebounds						
	G	MIN	FG	PCT	FG	PCT	FT	PCT	OFF	TOT	AST	STL	BLK	PTS	PPG
93-94 SAC	55	667	76	.539	0	.000	24	.545	49	169	24	17	25	176	3.2
Totals	55	667	76	.539	0	.000	24	.545	49	169	24	17	25	176	3.2

WILL PERDUE

Team: Chicago Bulls
Position: Center
Height: 7'0"　**Weight:** 240
Birthdate: August 29, 1965

NBA Experience: 6 years
College: Vanderbilt
Acquired: 1st-round pick in 1988 draft
(11th overall)

Background: As a senior at Vanderbilt, Perdue led the league in rebounding and was named Southeastern Conference Player of the Year. Drafted by the Bulls in 1988, he played less than any other first-round pick as a rookie. Perdue has never averaged as many as five PPG in six pro seasons. He spent two separate stints on the injured list last year with a broken finger, and his scoring dipped below three PPG.

Strengths: Perdue has made strides since his discouraging rookie season. Although he's a mediocre shooter and a generally poor offensive player, he stays active and can get to the boards. He's a better passer than Bill Cartwright, and his defense is probably his best asset. He knows his limitations and does not try to exceed them.

Weaknesses: A gifted athlete Perdue is not. He doesn't jump well at all and he's even worse at anticipating the ball. He has convinced everyone in the league that he will never be an offensive threat. His best shot is the "Per-dunk." You want the ball in his hands as few times as possible during an offensive possession.

Analysis: Perdue is popular among Chicago fans, even though his physical limitations will probably prevent him from ever being more than a fill-in center. He had his moments while Chicago cruised to three straight NBA championships, but he certainly wasn't a big reason for the Bulls' success. Perdue is a role-player at best.

PLAYER SUMMARY	
Will	play defense
Can't	score 5 PPG
Expect	limited minutes
Don't Expect	athletic ability
Fantasy Value	$0
Card Value	5-10¢

COLLEGE STATISTICS

		G	FGP	FTP	RPG	PPG
83-84	VAND	17	.467	.444	2.2	2.7
85-86	VAND	22	.585	.438	2.8	3.5
86-87	VAND	34	.599	.618	8.7	17.4
87-88	VAND	31	.634	.673	10.1	18.3
Totals		104	.606	.620	6.8	12.3

NBA REGULAR-SEASON STATISTICS

				FGs		3-PT FGs		FTs		Rebounds						
		G	MIN	FG	PCT	FG	PCT	FT	PCT	OFF	TOT	AST	STL	BLK	PTS	PPG
88-89	CHI	30	190	29	.403	0	.000	8	.571	18	45	11	4	6	66	2.2
89-90	CHI	77	884	111	.414	0	.000	72	.692	88	214	46	19	26	294	3.8
90-91	CHI	74	972	116	.494	0	.000	75	.670	122	336	47	23	57	307	4.1
91-92	CHI	77	1007	152	.547	1	.500	45	.495	108	312	80	16	43	350	4.5
92-93	CHI	72	998	137	.557	0	.000	67	.604	103	287	74	22	47	341	4.7
93-94	CHI	43	397	47	.420	0	.000	23	.719	40	126	34	8	11	117	2.7
Totals		373	4448	592	.489	1	.083	290	.625	479	1320	292	92	190	1475	4.0

SAM PERKINS

Team: Seattle SuperSonics
Position: Forward/Center
Height: 6'9" **Weight:** 250
Birthdate: June 14, 1961
NBA Experience: 10 years

College: North Carolina
Acquired: Traded from Lakers for Benoit Benjamin and draft rights to Doug Christie, 2/93

Background: Perkins was a three-time All-American at North Carolina, where he earned an NCAA title in 1982 and won the Lapchick Award as the nation's outstanding senior in 1984. In six years with Dallas, he became the club's all-time leader in rebounds. Perkins signed with the Lakers in 1990 and was traded to Seattle in 1992-93. Early last season, he netted his 10,000th career point.

Strengths: Perkins provides veteran leadership and versatility on the front line. He scores from both the post and the perimeter. He's a good free throw shooter and hits 3-pointers like few players his size. He led the Sonics in that category last season. He plays defense, rebounds, and plays an intelligent brand of ball.

Weaknesses: Some have called Perkins an underachiever, although many forwards would love to put up the numbers he has during his career. He has shot better than 50 percent just once in his career. His scoring average last season was the worst since his rookie year.

Analysis: Perkins has given the Sonics veteran leadership and steady scoring from both inside and long range. He tied an NBA record in a game early last season by making all seven of his 3-point attempts. He has been good for about 12 PPG on a Seattle team that rates among the best in the NBA.

PLAYER SUMMARY

Will......................score inside and out
Can't ....be left open
Expect ....leadership
Don't Expect......50-percent shooting
Fantasy Value..............................$4-6
Card Value ....7-10¢

COLLEGE STATISTICS

		G	FGP	FTP	RPG	PPG
80-81	NC	37	.626	.741	7.8	14.9
81-82	NC	32	.578	.768	7.8	14.3
82-83	NC	35	.527	.819	9.4	16.9
83-84	NC	31	.589	.856	9.6	17.6
Totals		135	.576	.796	8.6	15.9

NBA REGULAR-SEASON STATISTICS

		G	MIN	FGs FG	FGs PCT	3-PT FGs FG	3-PT FGs PCT	FTs FT	FTs PCT	Rebounds OFF	Rebounds TOT	AST	STL	BLK	PTS	PPG
84-85	DAL	82	2317	347	.471	9	.250	200	.820	189	605	135	63	63	903	11.0
85-86	DAL	80	2626	458	.503	11	.333	307	.814	195	685	153	75	94	1234	15.4
86-87	DAL	80	2687	461	.482	19	.352	245	.828	197	616	146	109	77	1186	14.8
87-88	DAL	75	2499	394	.450	5	.167	273	.822	201	601	118	74	54	1066	14.2
88-89	DAL	78	2860	445	.464	7	.184	274	.833	235	688	127	76	92	1171	15.0
89-90	DAL	76	2668	435	.493	6	.214	330	.778	209	572	175	88	64	1206	15.9
90-91	LAL	73	2504	368	.495	18	.281	229	.821	167	538	108	64	78	983	13.5
91-92	LAL	63	2332	361	.450	15	.217	304	.817	192	556	141	64	62	1041	16.5
92-93	LAL/SEA	79	2351	381	.477	24	.338	250	.820	163	524	156	60	82	1036	13.1
93-94	SEA	81	2170	341	.438	99	.367	218	.801	120	366	111	67	31	999	12.3
Totals		767	25014	3991	.473	213	.307	2630	.814	1868	5751	1370	740	697	10825	14.1

TIM PERRY

Team: Philadelphia 76ers
Position: Forward
Height: 6'9" **Weight:** 220
Birthdate: June 4, 1965
NBA Experience: 6 years

College: Temple
Acquired: Traded from Suns with Jeff
Hornacek and Andrew Lang for
Charles Barkley, 6/92

Background: Perry was named Atlantic 10 Player of the Year as a senior at
Temple, where he finished as the school's career leader in blocked shots.
Although he was taken seventh in the 1988 draft, he spent his first three years
coming off the Suns' bench. He started in 1991-92 and had his best year before
being traded to the 76ers in the Charles Barkley deal. He has averaged nine
PPG in his two years in Philly.

Strengths: Defense and rebounding are the best aspects of Perry's game. He
skies over opponents, blocks shots, works hard around the basket, and has good
instincts for the ball. He has developed his offensive game, which now includes
the 3-point shot and a decent half-hook in the paint. He loves to run and once
scored 31 points last season.

Weaknesses: Perry will never rank among the top scoring big men in the league.
His perimeter jumper is inconsistent and his field goal accuracy very low. His free
throw shooting is nightmarish. Perry is not a skilled ball-handler or passer. His
numbers would be a lot better if his mind were always in the game.

Analysis: Perry has been an interesting if unspectacular player. He made 15
3-pointers in his first five years, then tossed in 73 last season and hit them for a
pretty good percentage. If the rest of his game could develop that same
consistency, Perry would become a more productive player. The Sixers are
holding out hope.

PLAYER SUMMARY	
Will	challenge shots
Can't	shoot FTs
Expect	surprising range
Don't Expect	stardom
Fantasy Value	$2-4
Card Value	5-10¢

COLLEGE STATISTICS

		G	FGP	FTP	RPG	PPG
84-85	TEMP	30	.414	.500	3.9	2.3
85-86	TEMP	31	.566	.575	9.5	11.6
86-87	TEMP	36	.514	.620	8.6	12.9
87-88	TEMP	33	.585	.637	8.0	14.5
Totals		130	.544	.605	7.6	10.5

NBA REGULAR-SEASON STATISTICS

		G	MIN	FGs FG	FGs PCT	3-PT FGs FG	FGs PCT	FTs FT	FTs PCT	Rebounds OFF	Rebounds TOT	AST	STL	BLK	PTS	PPG
88-89	PHO	62	614	108	.537	1	.250	40	.615	61	132	18	19	32	257	4.1
89-90	PHO	60	612	100	.513	1	1.000	53	.589	79	152	17	21	22	254	4.2
90-91	PHO	46	587	75	.521	0	.000	43	.614	53	126	27	23	43	193	4.2
91-92	PHO	80	2483	413	.523	3	.375	153	.712	204	551	134	44	116	982	12.3
92-93	PHI	81	2104	287	.468	10	.204	147	.710	154	409	126	40	91	731	9.0
93-94	PHI	80	2336	272	.435	73	.365	102	.580	117	404	94	60	82	719	9.0
Totals		409	8736	1255	.489	88	.330	538	.654	668	1774	416	207	386	3136	7.7

CHUCK PERSON

Team: San Antonio Spurs
Position: Forward
Height: 6'8" **Weight:** 225
Birthdate: June 27, 1964

NBA Experience: 8 years
College: Auburn
Acquired: Signed as a free agent, 8/94

Background: The all-time leading scorer in Auburn history when he graduated from college, Person immediately made his mark on the NBA with a Rookie of the Year season in 1986-87. In six seasons, he became Indiana's all-time leading NBA scorer. He set a league record for 3-pointers in a playoff game with seven in 1991. He was dealt to Minnesota before the 1992-93 season and slipped some over the last two years. The T'Wolves dumped him last summer, and he was picked up by San Antonio.

Strengths: Person has been one of those rare players who can take over games by himself. When his team needs a bucket, he craves the ball. He can score in the post or from behind the 3-point line, and is a threat to do so whenever the ball is in his hands. He handles the ball and distributes.

Weaknesses: Person often tries to do too much by himself, a large reason he has seen more time on the bench of late. His mouth has also gotten him into trouble, whether shooting it off at opponents or teammates. When his man scores, Person almost always tries to outdo him on the other end.

Analysis: Person can be a dominating all-around player who has won ballgames with his shooting, passing, and even his defense. During his stay in Minnesota, however, he was an inconsistent shooter who put up big numbers one night and next to nothing the next. "The Rifleman" has enjoyed better days.

PLAYER SUMMARY	
Will	score in spurts
Can't	regain consistency
Expect	double-figure scoring
Don't Expect	silence
Fantasy Value	$3-5
Card Value	7-12¢

COLLEGE STATISTICS

		G	FGP	FTP	RPG	PPG
82-83	AUB	28	.541	.758	4.6	9.3
83-84	AUB	31	.543	.728	8.0	19.1
84-85	AUB	34	.544	.738	8.9	22.0
85-86	AUB	33	.519	.804	7.9	21.5
Totals		126	.536	.757	7.5	18.3

NBA REGULAR-SEASON STATISTICS

		G	MIN	FGs FG	FGs PCT	3-PT FGs FG	3-PT FGs PCT	FTs FT	FTs PCT	Rebounds OFF	Rebounds TOT	AST	STL	BLK	PTS	PPG
86-87	IND	82	2956	635	.468	49	.355	222	.747	168	677	295	90	16	1541	18.8
87-88	IND	79	2807	575	.459	59	.333	132	.670	171	536	309	73	8	1341	17.0
88-89	IND	80	3012	711	.489	63	.307	243	.792	144	516	289	83	18	1728	21.6
89-90	IND	77	2714	605	.487	94	.372	211	.781	126	445	230	53	20	1515	19.7
90-91	IND	80	2566	620	.504	69	.340	165	.721	121	417	238	56	17	1474	18.4
91-92	IND	81	2923	616	.480	132	.373	133	.675	114	426	382	68	18	1497	18.5
92-93	MIN	78	2985	541	.433	118	.355	109	.649	98	433	343	67	30	1309	16.8
93-94	MIN	77	2029	356	.422	100	.368	82	.759	55	253	185	45	12	894	11.6
Totals		634	21992	4659	.470	684	.354	1297	.732	997	3703	2271	535	139	11299	17.8

BOBBY PHILLS

Team: Cleveland Cavaliers
Position: Guard
Height: 6'5" **Weight:** 217
Birthdate: December 20, 1969

NBA Experience: 3 years
College: Southern
Acquired: Signed as a free agent, 3/92

Background: Phills, the son of a college dean, stayed home in Baton Rouge, Louisiana, to play at Southern U. He blossomed after a quiet freshman season and wound up launching 788 3-point attempts during his career, making 4.4 treys per game as a senior. Milwaukee took him in the 1991 draft, but Phills was released and the Cavaliers signed him. He played only 204 minutes in his first two seasons, then became a 53-game starter in 1993-94.

Strengths: Phills is much more than a gunner. He is a capable player in many aspects of the game. He brings a nice combination of strength and quickness to the floor and can get to the hole as well as he shoots jumpers. Phills is a good ball-handler and an above-average rebounder from the backcourt. He has the potential to become a solid defensive player and 3-point threat.

Weaknesses: There is little that Phills is unable to do, but his play has been up-and-down during his early pro seasons. He has been streaky with his jump shot and made just one of 12 3-point attempts last year. Phills is also inconsistent on the defensive end. Quick guards give him trouble, yet he's too small to be very effective at forward.

Analysis: After a very slow start to his pro career, Phills seems to have found a home and a role with Cleveland. He averaged 8.3 points per contest last season while cracking the starting lineup on a perennial playoff team. He needs to become more consistent in most aspects of the game, but he has the skills and the desire to stick around.

PLAYER SUMMARY

Will ....rebound
Can't ....avoid streaks
Expect ....all-around ability
Don't Expect ....great consistency
Fantasy Value $0
Card Value ....7-10¢

COLLEGE STATISTICS

		G	FGP	FTP	RPG	PPG
87-88	SOUT	23	.491	.714	1.8	3.7
88-89	SOUT	31	.431	.733	4.6	13.5
89-90	SOUT	31	.451	.657	4.3	20.1
90-91	SOUT	28	.407	.720	4.7	28.4
Totals		113	.413	.710	4.0	17.0

NBA REGULAR-SEASON STATISTICS

				FGs		3-PT FGs		FTs		Rebounds						
		G	MIN	FG	PCT	FG	PCT	FT	PCT	OFF	TOT	AST	STL	BLK	PTS	PPG
91-92	CLE	10	65	12	.429	0	.000	7	.636	4	8	4	3	1	31	3.1
92-93	CLE	31	139	38	.463	2	.400	15	.600	6	17	10	10	2	93	3.0
93-94	CLE	72	1531	242	.471	1	.083	113	.720	71	212	133	67	12	598	8.3
Totals		113	1735	292	.468	3	.158	135	.699	81	237	147	80	15	722	6.4

RICKY PIERCE

Team: Golden State Warriors
Position: Guard
Height: 6'4" **Weight:** 215
Birthdate: August 19, 1959
NBA Experience: 12 years

College: Rice
Acquired: Traded from SuperSonics with draft rights to Carlos Rogers and two 1995 2nd-round picks for Sarunas Marciulionis and Byron Houston, 7/94

Background: Pierce led Rice in scoring and rebounding for three straight years. He played single seasons in Detroit and San Diego, then became one of the NBA's most celebrated bench players in Milwaukee. He won the Sixth Man Award in 1986-87 and 1989-90. Pierce played in his first All-Star Game after a trade to Seattle in 1990-91. He led the Sonics in scoring for two years but injuries slowed him last season. He was dealt to Golden State in July.

Strengths: Pierce has been one of the league's best pure shooters. His strong upper body helps him draw fouls on his way to the hoop. He's one of the NBA's all-time clutch scorers and rarely misses a free throw.

Weaknesses: Most talk of holes in Pierce's game starts and ends with defense. He lacks the lateral quickness and often the interest required to be a stopper. Bone spurs have not made him any faster.

Analysis: Pierce has thrived both as a starter and a reserve in his 12 NBA seasons. He is one of the top free throw shooters in league history and has more than 12,000 career points to his credit. He can still score in the clutch and provides a wealth of experience.

PLAYER SUMMARY	
Will	hit clutch shots
Can't	shut down his man
Expect	great FT shooting
Don't Expect	explosiveness
Fantasy Value	$2-4
Card Value	5-10¢

COLLEGE STATISTICS

		G	FGP	FTP	RPG	PPG
79-80	RICE	26	.480	.718	8.2	19.2
80-81	RICE	26	.518	.706	7.0	20.9
81-82	RICE	30	.511	.794	7.5	26.8
Totals		82	.504	.751	7.6	22.5

NBA REGULAR-SEASON STATISTICS

				FGs		3-PT FGs		FTs		Rebounds						
		G	MIN	FG	PCT	FG	PCT	FT	PCT	OFF	TOT	AST	STL	BLK	PTS	PPG
82-83	DET	39	265	33	.375	1	.143	18	.563	15	35	14	8	4	85	2.2
83-84	SD	69	1280	268	.470	0	.000	149	.861	59	135	60	27	13	685	9.9
84-85	MIL	44	882	165	.537	1	.250	102	.823	49	117	94	34	5	433	9.8
85-86	MIL	81	2147	429	.538	3	.130	266	.858	94	231	177	83	6	1127	13.9
86-87	MIL	79	2505	575	.534	3	.107	387	.880	117	266	144	64	24	1540	19.5
87-88	MIL	37	965	248	.510	3	.214	107	.877	30	83	73	21	7	606	16.4
88-89	MIL	75	2078	527	.518	8	.222	255	.859	82	197	156	77	19	1317	17.6
89-90	MIL	59	1709	503	.510	46	.346	307	.839	64	167	133	50	7	1359	23.0
90-91	MIL/SEA	78	2167	561	.485	46	.397	430	.913	67	191	168	60	13	1598	20.5
91-92	SEA	78	2658	620	.475	33	.268	417	.916	93	233	241	86	20	1690	21.7
92-93	SEA	77	2218	524	.489	42	.372	313	.889	58	192	220	100	7	1403	18.2
93-94	SEA	51	1022	272	.471	6	.188	189	.896	29	83	91	42	5	739	14.5
Totals		767	19896	4725	.500	192	.301	2940	.877	757	1930	1571	652	130	12582	16.4

ED PINCKNEY

Team: Milwaukee Bucks
Position: Forward
Height: 6'9" **Weight:** 215
Birthdate: March 27, 1963
NBA Experience: 9 years

College: Villanova
Acquired: Traded from Celtics with draft rights to Andrei Fetisov for Blue Edwards and Derek Strong, 6/94

Background: The highlight of Pinckney's basketball career was leading Villanova to a national title in 1985 and being named tourney MVP. He spent two years with Phoenix and a year and a half with Sacramento before Boston acquired him in 1989. His best year with the Celtics was the 1991-92 season, when he averaged 7.6 PPG. Pinckney was traded to Milwaukee in June.

Strengths: Pinckney provides strong rebounding on both ends, good defense, and some occasional offense when called upon. He's a nice finisher on the fastbreak and can also rise over his defender for mid-range jumpers. He possesses a soft touch. He does not take many ill-advised shots.

Weaknesses: "Easy Ed" has never really mastered the kind of low-post moves that would help him become a productive scorer. He relies on offensive boards for many of his points. He's not much of a passer or ball-handler and his range is limited. Arthroscopic knee surgery sidelined him for 75 games in 1992-93.

Analysis: Pinckney bounced back from knee surgery and started 35 games last season, sharing the power-forward post with rookie Dino Radja. Pinckney finished third on the Celtics in rebounds but averaged only 5.2 PPG. He is a steady complementary player who provides defense and rebounding, though he offers nothing spectacular at the offensive end.

PLAYER SUMMARY	
Will	hit the boards
Can't	shoot with range
Expect	defensive effort
Don't Expect	10 PPG
Fantasy Value	$2-4
Card Value	5-8¢

COLLEGE STATISTICS

		G	FGP	FTP	RPG	PPG
81-82	VILL	32	.640	.714	7.8	14.2
82-83	VILL	31	.568	.760	9.7	12.5
83-84	VILL	31	.604	.694	7.9	15.4
84-85	VILL	35	.600	.730	8.9	15.6
Totals		129	.604	.723	8.6	14.5

NBA REGULAR-SEASON STATISTICS

		G	MIN	FGs		3-PT FGs		FTs		Rebounds		AST	STL	BLK	PTS	PPG
				FG	PCT	FG	PCT	FT	PCT	OFF	TOT					
85-86	PHO	80	1602	255	.558	0	.000	171	.673	95	308	90	71	37	681	8.5
86-87	PHO	80	2250	290	.584	0	.000	257	.739	179	580	116	86	54	837	10.5
87-88	SAC	79	1177	179	.522	0	.000	133	.747	94	230	66	39	32	491	6.2
88-89	SAC/BOS	80	2012	319	.513	0	.000	280	.800	166	449	118	83	66	918	11.5
89-90	BOS	77	1082	135	.542	0	.000	92	.773	93	225	68	34	42	362	4.7
90-91	BOS	70	1165	131	.539	0	.000	104	.897	155	341	45	61	43	366	5.2
91-92	BOS	81	1917	203	.537	0	.000	207	.812	252	564	62	70	56	613	7.6
92-93	BOS	7	151	10	.417	0	.000	12	.923	14	43	1	4	7	32	4.6
93-94	BOS	76	1524	151	.522	0	.000	92	.736	160	478	62	58	44	394	5.2
Totals		630	12880	1673	.539	0	.000	1348	.767	1208	3218	628	506	381	4694	7.5

SCOTTIE PIPPEN

Team: Chicago Bulls
Position: Forward
Height: 6'7" **Weight:** 225
Birthdate: September 25, 1965
NBA Experience: 7 years
College: Central Arkansas

Acquired: Draft rights traded from SuperSonics for draft rights to Olden Polynice, a 1989 2nd-round pick, and the option to exchange 1989 1st-round picks, 6/87

Background: An NAIA All-American as a senior at Central Arkansas, Pippen arrived in Chicago in the 1987 draft. He improved his all-around game every year and helped the Bulls to the 1991-93 NBA championships. He has led all NBA forwards in assists over the last three years and was the league's No. 8 scorer last season. Pippen has four All-Star Games under his belt and played on the 1992 U.S. Olympic team.

Strengths: The acrobatic Pippen has countless moves to the basket and is an electrifying finisher. He is a fine perimeter shooter with 3-point range. His long arms and quick hands regularly rank him among the league leaders in steals, and he also hits the boards. Pippen is the best passing forward in the game and one of the league's top all-around talents, both offensively and defensively.

Weaknesses: Pippen's biggest weakness is probably his free throw shooting. He was also embroiled in controversy throughout last season. In the playoffs against the Knicks, he refused to re-enter a game.

Analysis: Pippen became an All-Star and All-Defensive Team player with Michael Jordan as a teammate, and there were some who wondered how he would fare after Jordan retired before last season. Pippen responded by turning in a season worthy of MVP consideration. He scored a career-high 22 PPG and finished second in the league in steals. He's become a franchise player.

PLAYER SUMMARY

Will ....thrive in transition
Can't...............................be left open
Expect ....20-plus PPG
Don't Expect ....great FT shooting
Fantasy Value $85-90
Card Value ....15-30¢

COLLEGE STATISTICS

		G	FGP	FTP	RPG	PPG
83-84	CARK	20	.456	.684	3.0	4.3
84-85	CARK	19	.564	.676	9.2	18.5
85-86	CARK	29	.556	.686	9.2	19.8
86-87	CARK	25	.592	.719	10.0	23.6
Totals		93	.563	.695	8.1	17.2

NBA REGULAR-SEASON STATISTICS

				FGs		3-PT FGs		FTs		Rebounds						
		G	MIN	FG	PCT	FG	PCT	FT	PCT	OFF	TOT	AST	STL	BLK	PTS	PPG
87-88	CHI	79	1650	261	.463	4	.174	99	.576	115	298	169	91	52	625	7.9
88-89	CHI	73	2413	413	.476	21	.273	201	.668	138	445	256	139	61	1048	14.4
89-90	CHI	82	3148	562	.489	28	.250	199	.675	150	547	444	211	101	1351	16.5
90-91	CHI	82	3014	600	.520	21	.309	240	.706	163	595	511	193	93	1461	17.8
91-92	CHI	82	3164	687	.506	16	.200	330	.760	185	630	572	155	93	1720	21.0
92-93	CHI	81	3123	628	.473	22	.237	232	.663	203	621	507	173	73	1510	18.6
93-94	CHI	72	2759	627	.491	63	.320	270	.660	173	629	403	211	58	1587	22.0
Totals		551	19271	3778	.491	175	.269	1571	.683	1127	3765	2862	1173	531	9302	16.9

OLDEN POLYNICE

Team: Sacramento Kings
Position: Center
Height: 7'0" **Weight:** 250
Birthdate: November 21, 1964
NBA Experience: 7 years

College: Virginia
Acquired: Traded from Pistons for Pete Chilcutt, a 1994 2nd-round pick, and a conditional 1st-round pick, 2/94

Background: Polynice led Virginia in scoring and rebounding for two seasons and was a three-year leader in field goal accuracy. He was a back-up center with the Sonics until a trade with the L.A. Clippers in 1990-91 allowed him to start. He was traded to Detroit in June 1992 and to Sacramento in February of last season. He finished fifth in the league in rebounding in 1993-94 with 11.9 caroms per contest.

Strengths: Rebounding, defense, and hard work have earned Polynice respect. He can bang with big men yet is quick enough to get out and harass smaller players on the perimeter. He loves crashing the boards. He shoots for a high percentage and scored a career-high 11.6 PPG last season.

Weaknesses: Polynice has a limited offensive arsenal and relies on rebounds for several of his points. He is a poor ball-handler and perimeter shooter and his free throw shooting is atrocious. Teams have not thought enough of his talents as a starter to keep Polynice around for long.

Analysis: Polynice, who once went on a brief hunger strike for starving people in his native Haiti, provides a lot of the physical things you want in a center. He is a terrific rebounder who works hard and can score some. He will never be one of the top centers in the league, but there's always a market for what he does.

PLAYER SUMMARY	
Will	rebound, defend
Can't	make his FTs
Expect	10-plus RPG
Don't Expect	sweet jumpers
Fantasy Value	$5-7
Card Value	5-10¢

COLLEGE STATISTICS

		G	FGP	FTP	RPG	PPG
83-84	VA	33	.551	.588	5.6	7.7
84-85	VA	32	.603	.599	7.6	13.0
85-86	VA	30	.572	.637	8.0	16.1
Totals		95	.578	.612	7.0	12.1

NBA REGULAR-SEASON STATISTICS

		G	MIN	FGs		3-PT FGs		FTs		Rebounds		AST	STL	BLK	PTS	PPG
				FG	PCT	FG	PCT	FT	PCT	OFF	TOT					
87-88	SEA	82	1080	118	.465	0	.000	101	.639	122	330	33	32	26	337	4.1
88-89	SEA	80	835	91	.506	0	.000	51	.593	98	206	21	37	30	233	2.9
89-90	SEA	79	1085	156	.540	1	.500	47	.475	128	300	15	25	21	360	4.6
90-91	SEA/LAC	79	2092	316	.560	0	.000	146	.579	220	553	42	43	32	778	9.8
91-92	LAC	76	1834	244	.519	0	.000	125	.622	195	536	46	45	20	613	8.1
92-93	DET	67	1299	210	.490	0	.000	66	.465	181	418	29	31	21	486	7.3
93-94	DET/SAC	68	2402	346	.523	0	.000	97	.508	299	809	41	42	67	789	11.6
Totals		531	10627	1481	.520	1	.091	633	.561	1243	3152	227	255	217	3596	6.8

TERRY PORTER

Team: Portland Trail Blazers
Position: Guard
Height: 6'3" **Weight:** 195
Birthdate: April 8, 1963

NBA Experience: 9 years
College: Wisconsin-Stevens Point
Acquired: 1st-round pick in 1985 draft
(24th overall)

Background: Porter was an NAIA All-American as a junior and senior at Wisconsin-Stevens Point, where his shooting accuracy was remarkable for a guard. He improved his scoring average in each of his pro seasons before peaking in 1989-90, when he led the Trail Blazers to the NBA Finals. He is Portland's all-time assists king, a two-time All-Star, and the team's annual leader in 3-pointers.

Strengths: Porter boasts deadly shooting skills and unlimited range. He loves taking the big shot and he can stick it off the dribble. He is good with both hands and uses his strength well on penetration moves and defense. Porter can play both guard positions and provides veteran leadership.

Weaknesses: Porter does not possess blinding speed and is not among the most creative guards in the league. He is no longer the best playmaker on his team and was limited to 34 starts during the 1993-94 season. Quicker point guards can give him trouble.

Analysis: Porter is not your prototypical lead guard or the game's top shooting guard, but he can get the job done at both positions. His 3-point shooting can turn games around in a hurry, whether he starts or comes off the bench. He connected on 39 percent of his long-range shots last season.

PLAYER SUMMARY

Will ....score from anywhere
Can't ....burn you with speed
Expect............................instant offense
Don't Expect ....full-time starting
Fantasy Value $6-8
Card Value ....7-12¢

COLLEGE STATISTICS

		G	FGP	FTP	APG	PPG
81-82	WSP	25	.368	.692	0.8	2.0
82-83	WSP	30	.611	.697	5.2	11.4
83-84	WSP	32	.622	.830	4.2	18.8
84-85	WSP	30	.575	.834	4.3	19.7
Totals		117	.589	.796	3.8	13.5

NBA REGULAR-SEASON STATISTICS

				FGs		3-PT FGs		FTs		Rebounds							
		G	MIN	FG	PCT	FG	PCT	FT	PCT	OFF	TOT	AST	STL	BLK	PTS	PPG
85-86	POR	79	1214	212	.474	13	.310	125	.806	35	117	198	81	1	562	7.1
86-87	POR	80	2714	376	.488	13	.217	280	.838	70	337	715	159	9	1045	13.1
87-88	POR	82	2991	462	.519	24	.348	274	.846	65	378	831	150	16	1222	14.9
88-89	POR	81	3102	540	.471	79	.361	272	.840	85	367	770	146	8	1431	17.7
89-90	POR	80	2781	448	.462	89	.374	421	.892	59	272	726	151	4	1406	17.6
90-91	POR	81	2665	486	.515	130	.415	279	.823	52	282	649	158	12	1381	17.0
91-92	POR	82	2784	521	.461	128	.395	315	.856	51	255	477	127	12	1485	18.1
92-93	POR	81	2883	503	.454	143	.414	327	.843	58	316	419	101	10	1476	18.2
93-94	POR	77	2074	348	.416	110	.390	204	.872	45	215	401	79	18	1010	13.1
Totals		723	23208	3896	.473	729	.385	2497	.850	520	2539	5186	1152	90	11018	15.2

BRENT PRICE

Team: Washington Bullets
Position: Guard
Height: 6'1" **Weight:** 185
Birthdate: December 9, 1968

NBA Experience: 2 years
College: South Carolina; Oklahoma
Acquired: 2nd-round pick in 1992
draft (32nd overall)

Background: The younger brother of Cleveland guard Mark Price, Brent became a first-team All-Big Eight selection as a senior at Oklahoma after starting his career at South Carolina. He paced the Sooners in steals, assists, and 3-pointers in his final college season. He scored 56 points against Loyola Marymount as a junior. A second-round selection of Washington, Price has seen spot starting duty over his first two seasons and averaged 6.2 PPG in 1993-94.

Strengths: Although not nearly on the same level as his big brother, Brent Price owns some of the same skills. He has the makings of a fine 3-point and free throw shooter, having hit 50 of 150 long-range attempts last year. He has a quick release and also handles the ball well, finds open men, and works extremely hard. He does little that will hurt his team.

Weaknesses: While Price does little to hurt his own squad, he does not do enough to hurt the opposition. He is a good passer but is not an accomplished drive-and-dish player who makes things happen. He played mostly shooting guard in college. He does not have the same ability as his brother to get his shot off with defenders in his face. He also has some defensive limitations.

Analysis: Brent Price will not soon become the best basketball player in his family. While he resembles his big brother on some counts, he is not nearly as comfortable creating offense from the point-guard position. He also has a long way to go before he approaches Mark's ability to rack up points against NBA defenders. He is, however, a promising shooter and passer who wants to make it at this level.

PLAYER SUMMARY	
Will	find open men
Can't	outscore his brother
Expect	3-point shooting
Don't Expect	great playmaking
Fantasy Value	$1
Card Value	7-12¢

COLLEGE STATISTICS

		G	FGP	FTP	APG	PPG
87-88	SC	29	.460	.857	2.7	10.7
88-89	SC	30	.490	.844	4.3	14.4
90-91	OKLA	35	.416	.838	5.5	17.5
91-92	OKLA	30	.465	.798	6.2	18.7
Totals		124	.454	.828	4.7	15.5

NBA REGULAR-SEASON STATISTICS

		G	MIN	FGs FG	FGs PCT	3-PT FGs FG	3-PT FGs PCT	FTs FT	FTs PCT	Rebounds OFF	Rebounds TOT	AST	STL	BLK	PTS	PPG
92-93	WAS	68	859	100	.358	8	.167	54	.794	28	103	154	56	3	262	3.9
93-94	WAS	65	1035	141	.433	50	.333	68	.782	31	90	213	55	2	400	6.2
Totals		133	1894	241	.398	58	.293	122	.787	59	193	367	111	5	662	5.0

MARK PRICE

Team: Cleveland Cavaliers
Position: Guard
Height: 6'0" **Weight:** 178
Birthdate: February 16, 1964
NBA Experience: 8 years

College: Georgia Tech
Acquired: Draft rights traded from
Mavericks for a 1989 2nd-round pick
and cash, 6/86

Background: Price, Georgia Tech's second all-time leading scorer when he graduated in 1986, was drafted by Dallas and immediately traded to the Cavs. An emergency appendectomy cut short his rookie season, but he went on to become an NBA All-Star two years later. He tore the anterior cruciate ligament in his knee in 1990-91 but has played in the All-Star Game all three years since and was a Dream Team II player.

Strengths: Price is one of the most dangerous shooters in the game, ranking among the all-time leaders from 3-point range and having won the last two Long Distance Shootout titles on All-Star Weekend. He also owns the highest career free throw average of all time. He is deceivingly quick, which allows him to create his own shots or get to the hoop. He's a splendid passer and an underrated defender.

Weaknesses: Price does not have good size, and is therefore not much of a rebounder. Bigger guards can shoot over him.

Analysis: Price just might be the best point guard in the NBA. He owns an All-Star Game record of six 3-pointers and could finish his career as the best free throw shooter in league history. His leadership and superstar abilities continue to earn Price All-NBA recognition, although he is not the flamboyant type. He is an avid church singer and charity supporter.

PLAYER SUMMARY	
Will	lead by example
Can't	be left open
Expect	an All-Star regular
Don't Expect	slam dunks
Fantasy Value	$25-30
Card Value	10-20¢

COLLEGE STATISTICS

		G	FGP	FTP	APG	PPG
82-83	GT	28	.435	.877	3.3	20.3
83-84	GT	29	.509	.824	4.2	15.6
84-85	GT	35	.483	.840	4.3	16.7
85-86	GT	34	.528	.855	4.4	17.4
Totals		126	.487	.850	4.0	17.4

NBA REGULAR-SEASON STATISTICS

				FGs		3-PT FGs		FTs		Rebounds						
		G	MIN	FG	PCT	FG	PCT	FT	PCT	OFF	TOT	AST	STL	BLK	PTS	PPG
86-87	CLE	67	1217	173	.408	23	.329	95	.833	33	117	202	43	4	464	6.9
87-88	CLE	80	2626	493	.506	72	.486	221	.877	54	180	480	99	12	1279	16.0
88-89	CLE	75	2728	529	.526	93	.441	263	.901	48	226	631	115	7	1414	18.9
89-90	CLE	73	2706	489	.459	152	.406	300	.888	66	251	666	114	5	1430	19.6
90-91	CLE	16	571	97	.497	18	.340	59	.952	8	45	166	42	2	271	16.9
91-92	CLE	72	2138	438	.488	101	.387	270	.947	38	173	535	94	12	1247	17.3
92-93	CLE	75	2380	477	.484	122	.416	289	.948	37	201	602	89	11	1365	18.2
93-94	CLE	76	2386	480	.478	118	.397	238	.888	39	228	589	103	11	1316	17.3
Totals		534	16752	3176	.485	699	.409	1735	.906	323	1421	3871	699	64	8786	16.5

DINO RADJA

Team: Boston Celtics
Position: Forward
Height: 6'11" **Weight:** 225
Birthdate: April 24, 1967

NBA Experience: 1 year
College: None
Acquired: 2nd-round pick in 1989 draft (40th overall)

Background: The Celtics had to wait four years for Radja, who continued playing basketball in Europe despite being taken in the second round of the 1989 draft. He won a silver medal with Croatia in the 1992 Olympics and averaged 21.5 points and 10.2 rebounds per game for Virtus Roma of the Italian 1A League in his final campaign overseas. He made an immediate impact as a rookie, finishing second on the team in scoring and first in rebounds. He was No. 5 in scoring and No. 4 in rebounding among all first-year players.

Strengths: Radja started for most of last season and proved to be a better offensive player than many power forwards. He owns a good touch from the perimeter and some aggressive moves in the post. He can also get out and score in transition. Only 13 players in the NBA shot for a higher percentage last season than Radja, who also rebounds and has good court sense.

Weaknesses: The one flaw that stands out is common to many European imports—defense. Radja is willing to work on that end of the court and will block some shots, but he also commits a lot of fouls and does not have great footwork. He is still learning. Considered soft and spoiled by many scouts, Radja has answered his critics.

Analysis: Once considered the second-best player in Europe (behind Toni Kukoc), Radja surprised a lot of people with his smooth transition to the NBA. He was named NBA Rookie of the Month for November, played in the Schick Rookie Game on All-Star Weekend, and became only the sixth Celtic rookie to score more than 1,000 points in a season. Four of the other five are in the Hall of Fame and the other is Larry Bird.

PLAYER SUMMARY	
Will	score, rebound
Can't	avoid fouling
Expect	continued improvement
Don't Expect	a stopper
Fantasy Value	$11-14
Card Value	20-30¢

COLLEGE STATISTICS

—DID NOT PLAY—

NBA REGULAR-SEASON STATISTICS

			FGs		3-PT FGs		FTs		Rebounds						
	G	MIN	FG	PCT	FG	PCT	FT	PCT	OFF	TOT	AST	STL	BLK	PTS	PPG
93-94 BOS	80	2303	491	.521	0	.000	226	.751	191	577	114	70	67	1208	15.1
Totals	80	2303	491	.521	0	.000	226	.751	191	577	114	70	67	1208	15.1

J.R. REID

Team: San Antonio Spurs
Position: Forward
Height: 6'9" **Weight:** 260
Birthdate: March 31, 1968
NBA Experience: 5 years

College: North Carolina
Acquired: Traded from Hornets for Sidney Green, a 1993 1st-round pick, and a 1996 2nd-round pick, 12/92

Background: Coming out of high school in 1986, Reid was the No. 1-ranked player in America. A 1988 U.S. Olympian, he was a consensus All-American as a sophomore at North Carolina. He was forced to play out of position at center in all 82 games as a Charlotte rookie and was named second-team All-Rookie. After scoring about 11 PPG in his first three years, he has dropped into single digits with San Antonio after a 1992 trade.

Strengths: Reid possesses a soft shooting touch from up to 15 feet and a nice offensive game when facing the bucket. He can use his size, strength, and speed to beat opposing forwards off the dribble and get to the hoop. He's a decent low-post defender who can attack the boards when he puts his mind to it. His per-minute scoring is high.

Weaknesses: Reid's biggest problems have to do with his inconsistency. He'll score 20 points one night and three the next. He has a limited offensive repertoire and would rather shoot jumpers than muscle in the paint. Reid's intensity has been questioned. His dribbling is below average and he rarely passes once he gets the ball.

Analysis: This one-time can't-miss superstar has been a disappointment. Reid simply does not possess the complete game required to be a star. He spent most of last season in a reserve position with the Spurs and averaged less than 20 minutes per contest. He will likely spend the rest of his career as a role-player.

PLAYER SUMMARY	
Will	score in spurts
Can't	fulfill his potential
Expect	reserve minutes
Don't Expect	consistent intensity
Fantasy Value	$1-3
Card Value	5-10¢

COLLEGE STATISTICS

		G	FGP	FTP	RPG	PPG
86-87	NC	36	.584	.653	7.4	14.7
87-88	NC	33	.607	.680	8.9	18.0
88-89	NC	27	.614	.669	6.3	15.9
Totals		96	.601	.668	7.6	16.2

NBA REGULAR-SEASON STATISTICS

		G	MIN	FGs FG	FGs PCT	3-PT FGs FG	3-PT FGs PCT	FTs FT	FTs PCT	Rebounds OFF	Rebounds TOT	AST	STL	BLK	PTS	PPG
89-90	CHA	82	2757	358	.440	0	.000	192	.664	199	691	101	92	54	908	11.1
90-91	CHA	80	2467	360	.466	0	.000	182	.703	154	502	89	87	47	902	11.3
91-92	CHA	51	1257	213	.490	0	.000	134	.705	96	317	81	49	23	560	11.0
92-93	CHA/SA	83	1887	283	.476	0	.000	214	.764	120	456	80	47	31	780	9.4
93-94	SA	70	1344	260	.491	0	.000	107	.699	91	220	73	43	25	627	9.0
Totals		366	9712	1474	.468	0	.000	829	.708	660	2186	424	318	180	3777	10.3

GLEN RICE

Team: Miami Heat
Position: Forward/Guard
Height: 6'7" **Weight:** 220
Birthdate: May 28, 1967

NBA Experience: 5 years
College: Michigan
Acquired: 1st-round pick in 1989 draft
(4th overall)

Background: Rice led Michigan to a national title in 1989 while averaging nearly 31 PPG in NCAA tourney play. He finished his college career as the leading scorer in Big Ten history. After being chosen second-team All-Rookie in 1989-90, Rice has improved nearly every phase of his game. Twice he has finished among the league's top ten in scoring, including 1993-94, and he annually hits more than 130 3-pointers.

Strengths: Rice is one of the top shooters and scorers in the game. He can play small forward or big guard, although he is most comfortable from behind the 3-point arc. Rice complements his perimeter prowess with effective drives to the bucket. He ranks among the top free throw shooters in the NBA, is a good rebounder, and led Miami to its first playoff appearance last season.

Weaknesses: Rice is not a great ball-handler and his assist-to-turnover ratio will not set the league on fire. Quick players cause him problems on defense, where he possesses the athletic ability to be a much more dominant player. He often becomes too attached to the long-range shot.

Analysis: Rice has made everyone forget his miserable rookie season, in which he was out of shape and overweight. He appears to be a step away from All-Star caliber. Playing in an All-Star Game is a lifelong dream of his, and it could be fulfilled in the near future. His shooting and scoring speak for themselves, and his work ethic and leadership have helped the Heat reach the postseason.

PLAYER SUMMARY	
Will	shoot the lights out
Can't	star on defense
Expect	an All-Star appearance
Don't Expect	less than 20 PPG
Fantasy Value	$30-35
Card Value	8-15¢

COLLEGE STATISTICS

		G	FGP	FTP	RPG	PPG
85-86	MICH	32	.550	.600	3.0	7.0
86-87	MICH	32	.562	.787	9.2	16.9
87-88	MICH	33	.571	.806	7.2	22.1
88-89	MICH	37	.577	.832	6.3	25.6
Totals		134	.569	.797	6.4	18.2

NBA REGULAR-SEASON STATISTICS

				FGs		3-PT FGs		FTs		Rebounds						
		G	MIN	FG	PCT	FG	PCT	FT	PCT	OFF	TOT	AST	STL	BLK	PTS	PPG
89-90	MIA	77	2311	470	.439	17	.246	91	.734	100	352	138	67	27	1048	13.6
90-91	MIA	77	2646	550	.461	71	.386	171	.818	85	381	189	101	26	1342	17.4
91-92	MIA	79	3007	672	.469	155	.391	266	.836	84	394	184	90	35	1765	22.3
92-93	MIA	82	3082	582	.440	148	.383	242	.820	92	424	180	92	25	1554	19.0
93-94	MIA	81	2999	663	.467	132	.382	250	.880	76	434	184	110	32	1708	21.1
Totals		396	14045	2937	.456	523	.379	1020	.829	437	1985	875	460	145	7417	18.7

POOH RICHARDSON

Team: Los Angeles Clippers
Position: Guard
Height: 6'1" **Weight:** 180
Birthdate: May 14, 1966
NBA Experience: 5 years

College: UCLA
Acquired: Traded from Pacers with Malik Sealy and draft rights to Eric Piatkowski for Mark Jackson and draft rights to Greg Minor, 6/94

Background: Richardson was a four-year starter and three-time All-Pac-10 star at UCLA, where he set a conference record for assists. His pro career in Minnesota was marred by demands to be traded, but he started every game in his last two seasons there. Richardson spent two years with Indiana, though calf and shoulder injuries held him to 37 games last season. He was traded again, to the Clippers, over the summer.

Strengths: Richardson is a pure point guard who involves his teammates and runs the offense. He penetrates, handles the ball, and hits open men with crisp passes. His assist-to-turnover ratio is solid. Richardson is splendid in transition, is a respectable shooter with range, and can score points in bunches.

Weaknesses: Richardson was not a healthy Pacer. A torn calf muscle first hampered him in the 1993 playoffs and it bothered him for most of last season before he separated a shoulder in April. He was also known as a chronic complainer in Minnesota. Pooh is not a great free throw shooter and his 3-point shooting has plunged.

Analysis: Richardson has all the tools to be a quality point guard, but a lack of consistency plagued him in Minnesota and injuries hampered his production as a Pacer. When he is in the lineup, he has to be respected as both a scorer and playmaker who has a good feel for the game. L.A. is holding out high hopes for a healthy return.

PLAYER SUMMARY

Will	run the offense
Can't	avoid the injured list
Expect	10-plus PPG
Don't Expect	many treys
Fantasy Value	$7-9
Card Value	8-12¢

COLLEGE STATISTICS

		G	FGP	FTP	APG	PPG
85-86	UCLA	29	.492	.689	6.2	10.6
86-87	UCLA	32	.527	.582	6.5	10.5
87-88	UCLA	30	.470	.667	7.0	11.6
88-89	UCLA	31	.555	.562	7.6	15.2
Totals		122	.513	.624	6.8	12.0

NBA REGULAR-SEASON STATISTICS

				FGs		3-PT FGs		FTs		Rebounds						
		G	MIN	FG	PCT	FG	PCT	FT	PCT	OFF	TOT	AST	STL	BLK	PTS	PPG
89-90	MIN	82	2581	426	.461	23	.277	63	.589	55	217	554	133	25	938	11.4
90-91	MIN	82	3154	635	.470	42	.328	89	.539	82	286	734	131	13	1401	17.1
91-92	MIN	82	2922	587	.466	53	.342	123	.691	91	301	685	119	25	1350	16.5
92-93	IND	74	2396	337	.479	3	.103	92	.742	63	267	573	94	12	769	10.4
93-94	IND	37	1022	160	.452	3	.250	47	.610	28	110	237	32	3	370	10.0
Totals		357	12075	2145	.467	124	.305	414	.636	319	1181	2783	509	78	4828	13.5

MITCH RICHMOND

Team: Sacramento Kings
Position: Guard
Height: 6'5" **Weight:** 215
Birthdate: June 30, 1965
NBA Experience: 6 years

College: Moberly Area; Kansas St.
Acquired: Traded from Warriors with Les Jepsen and a 1995 2nd-round pick for draft rights to Billy Owens, 11/91

Background: Richmond was a junior college All-American before he spent two years at Kansas State, where he set a single-season record for points. He was a near-unanimous choice for Rookie of the Year in 1989. He improved on his 22-PPG rookie scoring over the next two years and was traded to Sacramento on the eve of the 1991-92 opener. Richmond played in his first All-Star Game last season after a thumb injury kept him from doing so in 1993.

Strengths: Look up "pure scorer" in the dictionary and it should mention Richmond. He nails jumpers with men all over him, hits 3-pointers, and drives through traffic without fear. When he sets his muscular frame in the post, he is almost impossible for smaller defenders to stop. He runs the floor and goes to the glass. He is a good passer who involves his teammates.

Weaknesses: Richmond commits a fair amount of turnovers and fouls and he does not possess blinding speed. There is nothing great about his defense.

Analysis: Richmond has averaged more than 21 PPG in all six of his NBA seasons, an amazing feat. Last season, he ranked seventh in the league in scoring at 23.4 PPG and in 3-point field goal percentage at .407. He finally made a much-deserved All-Star appearance, and it is not likely to be his last. Richmond is not only a great scorer, but a team player as well. His skills would draw more attention on another team.

PLAYER SUMMARY

Will ....score from all over
Can't.............................win with Kings
Expect ....22-plus PPG
Don't Expect..............blinding speed
Fantasy Value $30-35
Card Value ....10-20¢

COLLEGE STATISTICS

		G	FGP	FTP	RPG	PPG
84-85	MA	40	.480	.647	4.6	10.4
85-86	MA	38	.478	.689	6.6	16.0
86-87	KSU	30	.447	.761	5.7	18.6
87-88	KSU	34	.514	.775	6.3	22.6
Totals		142	.481	.732	5.8	16.5

NBA REGULAR-SEASON STATISTICS

		G	MIN	FGs FG	FGs PCT	3-PT FGs FG	3-PT FGs PCT	FTs FT	FTs PCT	Rebounds OFF	Rebounds TOT	AST	STL	BLK	PTS	PPG
88-89	GS	79	2717	649	.468	33	.367	410	.810	158	468	334	82	13	1741	22.0
89-90	GS	78	2799	640	.497	34	.358	406	.866	98	360	223	98	24	1720	22.1
90-91	GS	77	3027	703	.494	40	.348	394	.847	147	452	238	126	34	1840	23.9
91-92	SAC	80	3095	685	.468	103	.384	330	.813	62	319	411	92	34	1803	22.5
92-93	SAC	45	1728	371	.474	48	.369	197	.845	18	154	221	53	9	987	21.9
93-94	SAC	78	2897	635	.445	127	.407	426	.834	70	286	313	103	17	1823	23.4
Totals		437	16263	3683	.474	385	.381	2163	.835	553	2039	1740	554	131	9914	22.7

ISAIAH RIDER

Team: Minnesota Timberwolves
Position: Guard
Height: 6'5" **Weight:** 215
Birthdate: March 12, 1971

NBA Experience: 1 year
College: Nevada-Las Vegas
Acquired: 1st-round pick in 1993 draft
(5th overall)

Background: Upon graduating from an Alameda high school in California, Rider committed to Kansas State but failed to qualify academically. He transferred to a junior college in Kansas, then to a junior college in California, and finally to UNLV. Rider ranked second nationally in scoring in 1992-93 with 29.1 PPG. He was called J.R. in college but announced his preference for Isaiah before his NBA rookie season, in which he finished third among first-year players with 16.6 points per game.

Strengths: Rider is an explosive athlete who plays with great intensity and confidence. He can post up, can shoot from the perimeter, and is regarded as the most acrobatic slam-dunker in basketball. He guaranteed a victory in the 1994 Slam Dunk Contest and won with his "East Bay Funk" dunk. He also won a national slam-dunk contest in college. Rider makes his free throws and shoots with 3-point range. He'll also get to the glass.

Weaknesses: Rider is still fine-tuning some of the little things that make great basketball players. His ball-handling and passing both need work. While he hustles on both ends, he still needs to learn position defense and rebounding. He collected more turnovers than assists last season. All in all, there's nothing major to slow him.

Analysis: Rider is a tremendous talent who has uncanny confidence to go along with it. He gets the idea no one can stop him when he gets the ball in his hands, and much of the time he is correct. Certainly few can stop him when he's hovering above the rim. He became a starter one month into his rookie year and could easily become a 20-PPG scorer.

PLAYER SUMMARY	
Will	play above the rim
Can't	run the point
Expect	acrobatic slams
Don't Expect	tentativeness
Fantasy Value	$12-15
Card Value	50¢-$1.00

COLLEGE STATISTICS

		G	FGP	FTP	RPG	PPG
91-92	UNLV	27	.490	.747	5.2	20.7
92-93	UNLV	28	.515	.826	8.9	29.1
Totals		55	.505	.805	7.1	24.9

NBA REGULAR-SEASON STATISTICS

			FGs		3-PT FGs		FTs		Rebounds						
	G	MIN	FG	PCT	FG	PCT	FT	PCT	OFF	TOT	AST	STL	BLK	PTS	PPG
93-94 MIN	79	2415	522	.468	54	.360	215	.811	118	315	202	54	28	1313	16.6
Totals	79	2415	522	.468	54	.360	215	.811	118	315	202	54	28	1313	16.6

DOC RIVERS

Team: New York Knicks
Position: Guard
Height: 6'4" **Weight:** 185
Birthdate: October 13, 1961

NBA Experience: 11 years
College: Marquette
Acquired: Traded from Clippers in three-team, multi-player deal, 9/92

Background: A Marquette product, Rivers spent eight years with Atlanta. He was an All-Star in 1988-89, though a herniated disc limited him in 1989-90. It was the first time in his career that he did not lead the Hawks in assists or steals. He spent a year with the Clippers and then was dealt to the Knicks before the 1992-93 season. He suffered a season-ending knee injury in December 1993.

Strengths: Rivers does nothing flashy; he just gets the job done. He's a world-class citizen who plays defense, delivers the ball, scores with drives and jumpers, and provides great leadership. Rivers has high-scoring ability and 3-point range.

Weaknesses: Knee surgery is likely to rob Rivers of some of his effectiveness at both ends. He was slipping a notch before the injury. Rivers has seen a decline in his shooting, scoring, and defensive abilities in recent years.

Analysis: Rivers is the guy you want on your side in a tough battle. In his first year as a Knick, he played through a broken nose, sprained wrist, sore back, cut chin requiring stitches, strained knee, and busted teeth. If only he could attack the knee injury the same way. Rivers has lost his starting job in New York to Derek Harper and probably will never be a starter again.

PLAYER SUMMARY

Will ....battle
Can't.................regain quickness
Expect ....veteran leadership
Don't Expect ....10 PPG
Fantasy Value..........................$1
Card Value ....5-10¢

COLLEGE STATISTICS

		G	FGP	FTP	APG	PPG
80-81	MARQ	31	.553	.588	3.6	14.0
81-82	MARQ	29	.453	.648	5.9	14.3
82-83	MARQ	29	.437	.611	4.3	13.2
Totals		89	.478	.615	4.6	13.9

NBA REGULAR-SEASON STATISTICS

				FGs		3-PT FGs		FTs		Rebounds						
		G	MIN	FG	PCT	FG	PCT	FT	PCT	OFF	TOT	AST	STL	BLK	PTS	PPG
83-84	ATL	81	1938	250	.462	2	.167	255	.785	72	220	314	127	30	757	9.3
84-85	ATL	69	2126	334	.476	15	.417	291	.770	66	214	410	163	53	974	14.1
85-86	ATL	53	1571	220	.474	0	.000	172	.608	49	162	443	120	13	612	11.5
86-87	ATL	82	2590	342	.451	4	.190	365	.828	83	299	823	171	30	1053	12.8
87-88	ATL	80	2502	403	.453	9	.273	319	.758	83	366	747	140	41	1134	14.2
88-89	ATL	76	2462	371	.455	43	.347	247	.861	89	286	525	181	40	1032	13.6
89-90	ATL	48	1526	218	.454	24	.364	138	.812	47	200	264	116	22	598	12.5
90-91	ATL	79	2586	444	.435	88	.336	221	.844	47	253	340	148	47	1197	15.2
91-92	LAC	59	1657	226	.424	26	.283	163	.832	23	147	233	111	19	641	10.9
92-93	NY	77	1886	216	.437	39	.317	133	.821	26	192	405	123	9	604	7.8
93-94	NY	19	499	55	.433	19	.365	14	.636	4	39	100	25	5	143	7.5
Totals		723	21343	3079	.451	269	.321	2318	.787	589	2378	4604	1425	309	8745	12.1

STANLEY ROBERTS

Team: Los Angeles Clippers
Position: Center
Height: 7'0" **Weight:** 295
Birthdate: February 7, 1970

NBA Experience: 3 years
College: Louisiana St.
Acquired: Traded from Magic in three-team, multi-player deal, 9/92

Background: Roberts teamed with Shaquille O'Neal for the 1989-90 season at LSU, but academic problems plagued Roberts and he signed with a professional team in Spain. Though his rookie year with Orlando began with jokes about his weight, he ended up averaging 10.4 PPG. He was traded to the Clippers before the 1992-93 campaign and averaged 11.3 PPG and 6.2 RPG as a starting center. A ruptured Achilles tendon ended his 1993-94 season after 14 games.

Strengths: Roberts can be an offensive force around the basket. He has a decent turnaround jumper, is virtually impossible to budge once he gets position on the interior, and owns a very soft inside shooting touch despite his bulk. Roberts finished 13th in the league in blocked shots two years ago and swatted nearly two per game last season. He can also be very effective on the boards.

Weaknesses: Weight and foul trouble have long been the biggest problems for Roberts, who has reported as large as 320 pounds. Fat jokes have followed him. Roberts led the league in personal fouls (332) and disqualifications (15) two years ago. He fouled out twice in just 14 games last year. He does not run the floor well and his passing and free throw shooting are among the most embarrassing in the league.

Analysis: At his best, Roberts can be dominant offensively. Working against him, however, are his weight, his inconsistency, and his time spent on the bench because of foul trouble. Injuries will probably continue to plague Roberts unless he makes a commitment to stay in shape. The Clippers have found no one better to start in the pivot despite all his troubles.

PLAYER SUMMARY

Will ....score inside
Can't ....sink his FTs
Expect ....rebounds, blocks
Don't Expect................crisp passing
Fantasy Value $5-7
Card Value ....5-10¢

COLLEGE STATISTICS

		G	FGP	FTP	RPG	PPG
89-90	LSU	32	.576	.460	9.8	14.1
Totals		32	.576	.460	9.8	14.1

NBA REGULAR-SEASON STATISTICS

				FGs		3-PT FGs		FTs		Rebounds						
		G	MIN	FG	PCT	FG	PCT	FT	PCT	OFF	TOT	AST	STL	BLK	PTS	PPG
91-92	ORL	55	1118	236	.529	0	.000	101	.515	113	336	39	22	83	573	10.4
92-93	LAC	77	1816	375	.527	0	.000	120	.488	181	478	59	34	141	870	11.3
93-94	LAC	14	350	43	.430	0	.000	18	.409	27	93	11	6	25	104	7.4
Totals		146	3284	654	.520	0	.000	239	.492	321	907	109	62	249	1547	10.6

ALVIN ROBERTSON

Team: Denver Nuggets
Position: Guard
Height: 6'4" **Weight:** 208
Birthdate: July 22, 1962
NBA Experience: 9 years

College: Crowder; Arkansas
Acquired: Traded from Pistons with a
1995 2nd-round pick for Mark Macon
and Marcus Liberty, 11/93

Background: Following a memorable career at Arkansas, Robertson was a
member of the 1984 U.S. Olympic team. A four-time NBA All-Star, he was named
NBA Defensive Player of the Year in 1986. He spent five years with San Antonio
before being traded to the Bucks in 1989. He has led the league in steals three
times. He's been with Detroit and Denver over the last two years but spent
1993-94 on the injured list.

Strengths: Robertson creates offense with his tough defense. His on-the-ball
defense and quick hands have earned him a reputation as a professional thief.
Strong and competitive, he slashes his way inside for a lot of his points and
rebounds. He has 3-point range.

Weaknesses: Robertson is an inconsistent perimeter shooter. Opposing guards
would rather leave him open than allow him to drive. He is not as quick as he
used to be and he rubbed some folks the wrong way in Detroit.

Analysis: Robertson started last season on Detroit's suspended list and watched
it from Denver's injured list. When healthy and on top of his game, he is capable
of disrupting opposing offenses by shutting down guards of all speeds and sizes.
He is more likely to come off the bench than to start during his final few seasons.

PLAYER SUMMARY	
Will	hustle on defense
Can't	score in bunches
Expect	combative style
Don't Expect	more All-Star trips
Fantasy Value	$1-3
Card Value	5-10¢

COLLEGE STATISTICS

		G	FGP	FTP	RPG	PPG
80-81	CJC	34	.572	.652	8.4	18.0
81-82	ARK	28	.528	.603	2.2	7.3
82-83	ARK	28	.548	.661	4.9	14.2
83-84	ARK	32	.499	.670	5.5	15.5
Totals		122	.540	.655	5.4	14.0

NBA REGULAR-SEASON STATISTICS

				FGs		3-PT FGs		FTs		Rebounds						
		G	MIN	FG	PCT	FG	PCT	FT	PCT	OFF	TOT	AST	STL	BLK	PTS	PPG
84-85	SA	79	1685	299	.498	4	.364	124	.734	116	265	275	127	24	726	9.2
85-86	SA	82	2878	562	.514	8	.276	260	.795	184	516	448	301	40	1392	17.0
86-87	SA	81	2697	589	.466	13	.271	244	.753	186	424	421	260	35	1435	17.7
87-88	SA	82	2978	655	.465	27	.284	273	.748	165	498	557	243	69	1610	19.6
88-89	SA	65	2287	465	.483	9	.200	183	.723	157	384	393	197	36	1122	17.3
89-90	MIL	81	2599	476	.503	4	.154	197	.741	230	559	445	207	17	1153	14.2
90-91	MIL	81	2598	438	.485	23	.365	199	.757	191	459	444	246	16	1098	13.6
91-92	MIL	82	2463	396	.430	67	.319	151	.763	175	350	360	210	32	1010	12.3
92-93	MIL/DET	69	2006	247	.458	40	.328	84	.656	107	269	263	155	18	618	9.0
Totals		702	22191	4127	.478	195	.300	1715	.748	1511	3724	3606	1946	287	10164	14.5

CLIFFORD ROBINSON

Team: Portland Trail Blazers
Position: Forward
Height: 6'10" **Weight:** 225
Birthdate: December 16, 1966

NBA Experience: 5 years
College: Connecticut
Acquired: 2nd-round pick in 1989 draft (36th overall)

Background: Robinson led Connecticut in scoring for three consecutive seasons. Bypassed until the second round of the 1989 draft, he has never missed a game in his five years and has improved his scoring every season. His strong bench play won Robinson the league's Sixth Man Award for 1992-93. He became a Portland starter last season, played in his first All-Star Game, and averaged 20.1 PPG.

Strengths: Explosive athletic ability, versatility, and the ability to light up the scoreboard make Robinson an invaluable player. He is an elusive driver who can put the ball on the floor and get to the hoop for dazzling finishes. Robinson, who can play four positions, is a tremendous open-court player, an intimidating shot-blocker, and an above-average rebounder. He can shoot with 3-point range.

Weaknesses: Robinson is better at recording turnovers than assists and is still prone to spells of cold shooting. He has had some off-court incidents, including speeding tickets over the last two seasons for driving 110 and 89 mph. His on-court play can also become out of control at times. He must stay away from the wild shots.

Analysis: Robinson has simply become too good a player to begin games on the bench. He beat out such players as Clyde Drexler and Rod Strickland for the Portland scoring lead last season, which says volumes about his ability. When running the court and attacking the basket, Robinson can score with the best of forwards. His 1994 All-Star showing was much deserved.

PLAYER SUMMARY	
Will	attack the hoop
Can't	drive 55
Expect	explosive scoring
Don't Expect	50-percent shooting
Fantasy Value	$25-30
Card Value	7-12¢

COLLEGE STATISTICS

		G	FGP	FTP	RPG	PPG
85-86	CONN	28	.366	.610	3.1	5.6
86-87	CONN	16	.420	.570	7.4	18.1
87-88	CONN	34	.479	.655	6.9	17.6
88-89	CONN	31	.470	.684	7.4	20.0
Totals		109	.452	.644	6.1	15.3

NBA REGULAR-SEASON STATISTICS

				FGs		3-PT FGs		FTs		Rebounds						
		G	MIN	FG	PCT	FG	PCT	FT	PCT	OFF	TOT	AST	STL	BLK	PTS	PPG
89-90	POR	82	1565	298	.397	12	.273	138	.550	110	308	72	53	53	746	9.1
90-91	POR	82	1940	373	.463	6	.316	205	.653	123	349	151	78	76	957	11.7
91-92	POR	82	2124	398	.466	1	.091	219	.664	140	416	137	85	107	1016	12.4
92-93	POR	82	2575	632	.473	19	.247	287	.690	165	542	182	98	163	1570	19.1
93-94	POR	82	2853	641	.457	13	.245	352	.765	164	550	159	118	111	1647	20.1
Totals		410	11057	2342	.455	51	.250	1201	.678	702	2165	701	432	510	5936	14.5

DAVID ROBINSON

Team: San Antonio Spurs
Position: Center
Height: 7'1"   **Weight:** 235
Birthdate: August 6, 1965

NBA Experience: 5 years
College: Navy
Acquired: 1st-round pick in 1987 draft
(1st overall)

Background: As a senior at Navy, Robinson led the nation in blocked shots and was college basketball's consensus Player of the Year. He set NCAA records for blocks in a game and a season. After a two-year stint in the Navy, he exploded onto the pro scene in 1989-90, winning Rookie of the Year honors by a unanimous vote. He was named 1991-92 Defensive Player of the Year, won gold in the 1992 Olympics, has played in the last four All-Star Games, and won his first NBA scoring title last season.

Strengths: Robinson is simply dominant in most aspects of the game. His quickness allows him to explode to the hoop with unstoppable low-post spin moves. He can stick jumpers or swing the ball back outside, as evidenced by his high assist numbers. He clears the boards, runs the break as well as any center, and dominates on defense. He is the best thief among the league's centers. He's also a class act off the court.

Weaknesses: Some used to question Robinson's intensity, but he has definitely kicked it up a notch. He has not led the Spurs to much playoff success, although he personally has performed well in the postseason.

Analysis: Michael Jordan's retirement opened the door for a new NBA scoring champ, and Mr. Robinson clinched it with a 71-point game on the last day of the season. The gifted Robinson is a force who will contend for MVP honors annually in the years to come. Very few players—even ones his size—play at his remarkable level.

PLAYER SUMMARY	
Will	dominate games
Can't	be single-teamed
Expect	a Hall of Fame career
Don't Expect	many "off" nights
Fantasy Value	$85-90
Card Value	25-75¢

COLLEGE STATISTICS

		G	FGP	FTP	RPG	PPG
83-84	NAVY	28	.623	.575	4.0	7.6
84-85	NAVY	32	.644	.626	11.6	23.6
85-86	NAVY	35	.607	.628	13.0	22.7
86-87	NAVY	32	.591	.637	11.8	28.2
Totals		127	.613	.627	10.3	21.0

NBA REGULAR-SEASON STATISTICS

				FGs		3-PT FGs		FTs		Rebounds						
		G	MIN	FG	PCT	FG	PCT	FT	PCT	OFF	TOT	AST	STL	BLK	PTS	PPG
89-90	SA	82	3002	690	.531	0	.000	613	.732	303	983	164	138	319	1993	24.3
90-91	SA	82	3095	754	.552	1	.143	592	.762	335	1063	208	127	320	2101	25.6
91-92	SA	68	2564	592	.551	1	.125	393	.701	261	829	181	158	305	1578	23.2
92-93	SA	82	3211	676	.501	3	.176	561	.732	229	956	301	127	264	1916	23.4
93-94	SA	80	3241	840	.507	10	.345	693	.749	241	855	381	139	265	2383	29.8
Totals		394	15113	3552	.527	15	.238	2852	.738	1369	4686	1235	689	1473	9971	25.3

JAMES ROBINSON

Team: Portland Trail Blazers
Position: Guard
Height: 6'2" **Weight:** 180
Birthdate: August 31, 1970

NBA Experience: 1 year
College: Alabama
Acquired: 1st-round pick in 1993 draft
(21st overall)

Background: Robinson scored 40 PPG as a senior at Murrah High School in Mississippi. He was a marquee recruit for Alabama but sat out his first year because of a questionable ACT score. He eventually was given four full years of eligibility. He became the first freshman to lead the Tide in scoring since 1953 and, after three seasons, was drafted by Portland. Robinson saw action in 58 games last season.

Strengths: A top-flight athlete, Robinson explodes to the basket in transition, finishes with gusto, and can be a fine one-on-one player. He once set a Mississippi high school record in the 300-meter hurdles and won the slam-dunk competition at the McDonald's All-America Game. Robinson shoots with NBA 3-point range and knows how to get open. His athleticism makes him potentially strong as a defensive player.

Weaknesses: Robinson is a classic "tweener." His questionable decision-making keeps him from being an effective point guard, yet he is awfully small to be a standout at the two spot. He plays out of control at times and some would say his substantial ego obscures the team concept. He shot a miserable .365 from the field as a rookie, though his 3-point shooting was encouraging. He's no help on the boards.

Analysis: Robinson got somewhat lost in the shuffle with the Blazers, who had a roster full of veteran guards. As the vets begin to wear down or move on, he will probably get his chance. To make the most of it, Robinson must improve on his decision-making and become a much more consistent player in all respects. He does have the makings of a fine 3-point shooter, but his play inside the arc is cause for concern.

PLAYER SUMMARY	
Will	shoot the 3
Can't	rebound
Expect	reserve minutes
Don't Expect	a true point guard
Fantasy Value	$0
Card Value	7-12¢

COLLEGE STATISTICS

		G	FGP	FTP	APG	PPG
90-91	ALA	33	.470	.699	1.2	16.8
91-92	ALA	34	.445	.712	2.2	19.4
92-93	ALA	29	.420	.682	2.3	20.6
Totals		96	.444	.695	1.9	18.9

NBA REGULAR-SEASON STATISTICS

	G	MIN	FGs FG	PCT	3-PT FGs FG	PCT	FTs FT	PCT	Rebounds OFF	TOT	AST	STL	BLK	PTS	PPG
93-94 POR	58	673	104	.365	23	.315	45	.672	34	78	68	30	15	276	4.8
Totals	58	673	104	.365	23	.315	45	.672	34	78	68	30	15	276	4.8

RUMEAL ROBINSON

Unrestricted Free Agent
Last Team: Charlotte Hornets
Position: Guard
Height: 6'2" **Weight:** 195
Birthdate: November 13, 1966

NBA Experience: 4 years
College: Michigan
Acquired: Traded from Nets for
Johnny Newman, 12/93

Background: The hero of Michigan's 1989 NCAA championship team as a junior, Robinson had a forgettable NBA rookie year in Atlanta. He led the team in assists in his second season and has since played in New Jersey and Charlotte. After his trade to the Hornets in December 1993 for Johnny Newman, Robinson missed more than half of last season because of a foot injury. He averaged only 4.2 PPG and was let go after the season.

Strengths: Robinson has an NBA body and is willing to use it. He's strong, physical, and not afraid to challenge larger players on his way to the bucket. He always looks to score and plays with intensity. Robinson hustles and can be dangerous in the open court. He has 3-point ability, a good feel for the game, and the desire to improve.

Weaknesses: Becoming a more traditional-style point guard is something Robinson has struggled with. He still looks to finish his own plays before looking to set up teammates. He is not a reliable outside shooter, which is perhaps the biggest reason he has spent a great deal of time on three NBA benches. He shot less than 40 percent last season and is also horrible from the free throw line.

Analysis: Robinson had his good days in Atlanta and was once named NBA Player of the Week with New Jersey. His stop in Charlotte was not as successful. He labored on the bench for all but about ten minutes per game and spent much of last season on the injured list. Without consistent minutes, Robinson has had trouble improving.

PLAYER SUMMARY	
Will	challenge
Can't	gain steady minutes
Expect	hustle
Don't Expect	good shooting
Fantasy Value	$1-3
Card Value	7-12¢

COLLEGE STATISTICS

		G	FGP	FTP	APG	PPG
87-88	MICH	33	.553	.667	4.8	9.7
88-89	MICH	37	.557	.656	6.3	14.9
89-90	MICH	30	.490	.676	6.1	19.2
Totals		100	.528	.666	5.8	14.5

NBA REGULAR-SEASON STATISTICS

				FGs		3-PT FGs		FTs		Rebounds						
		G	MIN	FG	PCT	FG	PCT	FT	PCT	OFF	TOT	AST	STL	BLK	PTS	PPG
90-91	ATL	47	674	108	.446	2	.182	47	.587	20	71	132	32	8	265	5.6
91-92	ATL	81	2220	423	.456	34	.327	175	.636	64	219	446	105	24	1055	13.0
92-93	NJ	80	1585	270	.423	20	.357	112	.574	49	159	323	96	12	672	8.4
93-94	NJ/CHA	31	396	55	.362	8	.400	13	.448	6	32	63	18	3	131	4.2
Totals		239	4875	856	.437	64	.335	347	.599	139	481	964	251	47	2123	8.9

DENNIS RODMAN

Team: San Antonio Spurs
Position: Forward
Height: 6'8" **Weight:** 210
Birthdate: May 13, 1961
NBA Experience: 8 years

College: Cooke County;
S.E. Oklahoma St.
Acquired: Traded from Pistons with
Isaiah Morris for Sean Elliott and David
Wood, 10/93

Background: Only 5'11" as a high school senior, Rodman went to work as an airport laborer. An incredible nine-inch growth spurt convinced him to give basketball a try. He was a three-time NAIA All-American at S.E. Oklahoma State. He played in two All-Star Games with Detroit and was the Defensive Player of the Year in 1989-90 and 1990-91. His 18.7 RPG in 1991-92 was the highest average since Wilt Chamberlain had 19.2 in 1971-72. Rodman has led the league in rebounding three years in a row.

Strengths: No forward in recent history has been as dominant defensively and on the boards as Rodman. He's so versatile, he can cover centers or point guards. "Worm" smothers opponents with quickness, speed, and strength. He's an always-moving thorn in every opponent's side.

Weaknesses: Rodman is not in the NBA for his scoring. He can stick an occasional 3-pointer, but his sub-60-percent free throw shooting illustrates his lack of touch. He has been a public-relations nightmare off the court, including a bizarre weapons incident two years ago.

Analysis: Rodman might be the hardest-working player in the NBA, yet he hates to practice, has arrived late for games, and is generally a pain off the court. He performs on game nights, however, and might be the most intriguing player in the game today. He has hauled down 5,000-plus rebounds over the last four years.

PLAYER SUMMARY	
Will	dominate on defense
Can't	score regularly
Expect	17-18 RPG
Don't Expect	P.R. campaigns
Fantasy Value	$9-11
Card Value	8-15¢

COLLEGE STATISTICS

		G	FGP	FTP	RPG	PPG
82-83	CCJ	16	.616	.582	13.3	17.6
83-84	SOS	30	.618	.655	13.1	26.0
84-85	SOS	32	.648	.566	15.9	26.8
85-86	SOS	34	.645	.655	17.8	24.4
Totals		112	.635	.620	15.3	24.5

NBA REGULAR-SEASON STATISTICS

				FGs		3-PT FGs		FTs		Rebounds						
		G	MIN	FG	PCT	FG	PCT	FT	PCT	OFF	TOT	AST	STL	BLK	PTS	PPG
86-87	DET	77	1155	213	.545	0	.000	74	.587	163	332	56	38	48	500	6.5
87-88	DET	82	2147	398	.561	5	.294	152	.535	318	715	110	75	45	953	11.6
88-89	DET	82	2208	316	.595	6	.231	97	.626	327	772	99	55	76	735	9.0
89-90	DET	82	2377	288	.581	1	.111	142	.654	336	792	72	52	60	719	8.8
90-91	DET	82	2747	276	.493	6	.200	111	.631	361	1026	85	65	55	669	8.2
91-92	DET	82	3301	342	.539	32	.317	84	.600	523	1530	191	68	70	800	9.8
92-93	DET	62	2410	183	.427	15	.205	87	.534	367	1132	102	48	45	468	7.5
93-94	SA	79	2989	156	.534	5	.208	53	.520	453	1367	184	52	32	370	4.7
Totals		628	19334	2172	.537	70	.249	800	.587	2848	7666	899	453	431	5214	8.3

RODNEY ROGERS

Team: Denver Nuggets
Position: Forward
Height: 6'7" **Weight:** 250
Birthdate: June 20, 1971

NBA Experience: 1 year
College: Wake Forest
Acquired: 1st-round pick in 1993 draft
(9th overall)

Background: Rogers earned second-team all-conference honors as a freshman at Wake Forest and went on to become 1992-93 Player of the Year in the ACC. An early entrant into the NBA draft, Rogers slipped to the ninth pick in 1993 because of concerns about his weight. He started 14 games as a rookie with Denver last season and averaged 8.1 PPG, mostly while backing up Reggie Williams at small forward.

Strengths: The muscular Rogers calls himself a cross between Charles Barkley and Karl Malone. He is a strong rebounder and inside player who doesn't back down from contact. He occasionally will pop out and hit a jump shot, and he can shoot them with NBA 3-point range. He made 35 of 92 treys as a rookie. Rogers rates average or above average as a ball-handler and he can play both forward positions.

Weaknesses: Rogers is not tall enough to score in close against the league's bigger players. His future is probably at the three spot, for which he could use a more reliable outside shot. He was not the most committed or talented defender among the rookie class last season, although he will block a few shots. He struggled from the free throw line and did not dazzle anyone with his passing.

Analysis: Rogers would have gone higher in the draft had his weight not ballooned to 260. He started his rookie year at 255 and improved his conditioning as the season wore on. He provides muscle on the front line and has also shown the ability to pull his arsenal outside with some degree of effectiveness. He's no Barkley or Malone, but look for continued improvement from Rogers as he gets more games under his belt.

PLAYER SUMMARY	
Will	go to the boards
Can't	sky over big men
Expect	further strides
Don't Expect	great passing
Fantasy Value	$1-3
Card Value	15-30¢

COLLEGE STATISTICS

		G	FGP	FTP	RPG	PPG
90-91	WF	30	.570	.669	7.9	16.3
91-92	WF	29	.614	.683	8.5	20.5
92-93	WF	30	.555	.717	7.4	21.2
Totals		89	.579	.694	7.9	19.3

NBA REGULAR-SEASON STATISTICS

				FGs		3-PT FGs		FTs		Rebounds						
		G	MIN	FG	PCT	FG	PCT	FT	PCT	OFF	TOT	AST	STL	BLK	PTS	PPG
93-94	DEN	79	1406	239	.439	35	.380	127	.672	90	226	101	63	48	640	8.1
Totals		79	1406	239	.439	35	.380	127	.672	90	226	101	63	48	640	8.1

SEAN ROOKS

Team: Dallas Mavericks
Position: Center/Forward
Height: 6'10" **Weight:** 260
Birthdate: September 9, 1969

NBA Experience: 2 years
College: Arizona
Acquired: 2nd-round pick in 1992 draft (30th overall)

Background: After joining Brian Williams and Ed Stokes on the "Tucson Skyline," Rooks led Arizona in scoring and was second in rebounding as a senior. He was a first-team All-Pac-10 selection and finished his career fifth on the Wildcats' career scoring list. A second-round choice of Dallas in 1992, Rooks played well in a summer league and became an instant rookie starter at center. His numbers declined last year, as he missed 35 games because of injuries.

Strengths: Rooks has good size and some skills to match. He has a wide body and has demonstrated a pretty good low-post repertoire, yet he also has the touch to slide out of the lane and knock down mid-range jumpers. Rooks owns good hands and a nice feel for the game. He'll block shots. Coaches have been impressed with his willingness to work and desire to prove himself.

Weaknesses: Rooks has a reputation for inconsistency that dates back to college. He has a tendency to disappear when his head's not in the game. Although he has helped the Mavericks on the boards, Rooks should be a more dominant rebounder and a better defender considering his size. He is not much of a passer and injuries slowed his progress last season.

Analysis: "Wookie," nicknamed after the Star Wars character, has fared pretty well when healthy. He started last season on the injured list with a left foot injury, but he came back and played well enough to be considered a large part of the Mavericks' future. He is not talented enough to revive the slumbering team himself, but he is a potentially productive player in the middle. He has shown glimpses of very strong play.

PLAYER SUMMARY	
Will	look to score
Can't	save the Mavericks
Expect	double-digit points
Don't Expect	great consistency
Fantasy Value	$5-7
Card Value	8-15¢

COLLEGE STATISTICS

		G	FGP	FTP	RPG	PPG
88-89	ARIZ	32	.598	.615	2.8	5.6
89-90	ARIZ	31	.532	.708	4.9	12.7
90-91	ARIZ	35	.562	.658	5.7	11.9
91-92	ARIZ	31	.560	.651	6.9	16.3
Totals		129	.558	.664	5.0	11.6

NBA REGULAR-SEASON STATISTICS

		G	MIN	FGs		3-PT FGs		FTs		Rebounds		AST	STL	BLK	PTS	PPG
				FG	PCT	FG	PCT	FT	PCT	OFF	TOT					
92-93	DAL	72	2087	368	.493	0	.000	234	.602	196	536	95	38	81	970	13.5
93-94	DAL	47	1255	193	.491	0	.000	150	.714	84	259	49	21	44	536	11.4
Totals		119	3342	561	.492	0	.000	384	.641	280	795	144	59	125	1506	12.7

DONALD ROYAL

Team: Orlando Magic
Position: Forward
Height: 6'8" **Weight:** 215
Birthdate: May 2, 1966

NBA Experience: 4 years
College: Notre Dame
Acquired: Signed as a free agent, 8/92

Background: Royal averaged 15.8 PPG and 7.0 RPG during his senior year at Notre Dame, after which he was a third-round draft choice of Cleveland in 1987. He spent his first two pro seasons in the CBA, then played his first NBA ball with Minnesota in 1989-90. He left the T'Wolves for Israel and averaged 20 PPG and eight RPG for Macabbi Tel Aviv. He played with San Antonio for a year and has been an Orlando reserve over the last two seasons.

Strengths: Royal makes a living with the drive. He is a slashing penetrator who knows no fear when it comes to taking the ball to the hole. He can finish his own plays and he makes numerous trips to the free throw line, where he has shot well in the past. Royal is a good defensive player who runs the floor and plays with enthusiasm.

Weaknesses: Royal's drives would be even more effective if he could make defenders respect his jump shot. It's flat and Royal does not shoot it with much range. He has attempted only six 3-pointers in his NBA career. Other than penetrating, his offensive game has a number of holes. He is no better than average as a ball-handler and passer.

Analysis: Most players hate defending a driver like Royal because they know he'll make them work. He has improved his shooting and there was never a question about his work habits. He hustles at both ends of the court and has improved his game tremendously since college. Expect to see more of him in future years.

PLAYER SUMMARY

Will ....get to the line
Can't ....shoot 3-pointers
Expect ....driving, defense
Don't Expect ....perimeter punch
Fantasy Value.............................$1
Card Value ....5-10¢

COLLEGE STATISTICS

		G	FGP	FTP	RPG	PPG
83-84	ND	31	.594	.622	2.3	3.4
84-85	ND	30	.497	.782	5.5	9.1
85-86	ND	28	.583	.766	4.9	10.6
86-87	ND	28	.576	.820	7.0	15.8
Totals		117	.560	.780	4.9	9.5

NBA REGULAR-SEASON STATISTICS

				FGs		3-PT FGs		FTs		Rebounds						
		G	MIN	FG	PCT	FG	PCT	FT	PCT	OFF	TOT	AST	STL	BLK	PTS	PPG
89-90	MIN	66	746	117	.459	0	.000	153	.777	69	137	43	32	8	387	5.9
91-92	SA	60	718	80	.449	0	.000	92	.692	65	124	34	25	7	252	4.2
92-93	ORL	77	1636	194	.496	0	.000	318	.815	116	295	80	36	25	706	9.2
93-94	ORL	74	1357	174	.501	0	.000	199	.740	94	248	61	50	16	547	7.4
Totals		277	4457	565	.482	0	.000	762	.770	344	804	218	143	56	1892	6.8

BRYON RUSSELL

Team: Utah Jazz
Position: Forward
Height: 6'7" **Weight:** 225
Birthdate: December 31, 1970

NBA Experience: 1 year
College: Long Beach St.
Acquired: 2nd-round pick in 1993 draft (45th overall)

Background: Russell sat out a year of basketball at Long Beach State to become academically eligible, then steadily progressed the next three seasons while teaming with fellow 1993 second-round pick Lucious Harris. Russell paced the 49ers in rebounding and blocked shots as a senior and was second on the team in steals. Considered a surprise draft choice by the Jazz, he wound up starting 48 games as a rookie and averaged better than a steal per game.

Strengths: Russell is active, does the dirty work defensively and on the boards, and has intangibles that helped him surprise a lot of people as a first-year NBA player. He's tough and physical and isn't afraid to wrestle with bigger players. Fifteen-foot jump shots are well within his range. He shot for a pretty high percentage as a rookie, showed good defensive instincts for the ball, and played hard every night.

Weaknesses: Russell is not a talented offensive player compared to most other NBA forwards. He does not put the ball on the floor with great confidence, will not rack up the assists, and is prone to poor offensive decision-making. For example, he tried 22 treys last season and hit two. He is also a poor free throw shooter. He's more of a complementary player than a potential standout.

Analysis: Give Russell great credit for his rookie performance. Many expected him to land in the CBA to hone his offensive abilities and skills on the perimeter. However, his aggressive defense and willingness to bang not only kept him around, but earned him a starting job on a talented Utah team for most of the season. His work habits and toughness have served him well.

PLAYER SUMMARY	
Will	swipe the ball
Can't	nail 3-pointers
Expect	aggressive defense
Don't Expect	10 PPG
Fantasy Value	$0
Card Value	7-12¢

COLLEGE STATISTICS

		G	FGP	FTP	RPG	PPG
90-91	LBS	28	.430	.652	5.8	7.9
91-92	LBS	26	.555	.656	7.4	13.9
92-93	LBS	32	.537	.727	6.7	13.2
Totals		86	.513	.683	6.6	11.7

NBA REGULAR-SEASON STATISTICS

			FGs		3-PT FGs		FTs		Rebounds						
	G	MIN	FG	PCT	FG	PCT	FT	PCT	OFF	TOT	AST	STL	BLK	PTS	PPG
93-94 UTA	67	1121	135	.484	2	.091	62	.614	61	181	54	68	19	334	5.0
Totals	67	1121	135	.484	2	.091	62	.614	61	181	54	68	19	334	5.0

JOHN SALLEY

Team: Miami Heat
Position: Forward/Center
Height: 6'11" **Weight:** 240
Birthdate: May 16, 1964
NBA Experience: 8 years

College: Georgia Tech
Acquired: Traded from Pistons for draft rights to Isaiah Morris and a 1993 1st-round pick, 9/92

Background: "Spider" was Georgia Tech's all-time leader in blocked shots before being selected by the Pistons (along with Dennis Rodman) in the 1986 draft. He's been talented but inconsistent for much of his career, though he came up big in the playoffs with Detroit, where he won two NBA championship rings. Salley scored a career-high 9.5 PPG in 1991-92 before signing with Miami, where he's been a part-time starter.

Strengths: Salley is one of the more effective shot-blocking forwards in the league, as his size and quick feet make him tough to shoot around. His post-up game features a nifty hook shot along with his favorite, the spin move. He runs the floor and goes to the glass.

Weaknesses: Salley has been famous for thinking more about his contract than his game. He has never been very consistent, even in his best seasons. Sometimes he's just not there. He is not a great shooter or set-up man on the perimeter and his low-post game lacks one key ingredient—power. Salley picks up a lot of fouls.

Analysis: Salley is an aspiring comedian who has worked night-club gigs. Some would argue that he should spend his free time working on his game. He was once considered a good bet to become a star player, but now he is a marginal Miami starter whose best attribute is shot-blocking.

PLAYER SUMMARY	
Will	swat shots
Can't	overpower defenders
Expect	size, quickness
Don't Expect	nightly intensity
Fantasy Value	$1-3
Card Value	5-10¢

COLLEGE STATISTICS

		G	FGP	FTP	RPG	PPG
82-83	GT	27	.502	.637	5.7	11.5
83-84	GT	29	.589	.674	5.8	11.8
84-85	GT	35	.627	.636	7.1	14.0
85-86	GT	34	.606	.594	6.7	13.1
Totals		125	.587	.633	6.4	12.7

NBA REGULAR-SEASON STATISTICS

		G	MIN	FGs FG	FGs PCT	3-PT FGs FG	3-PT FGs PCT	FTs FT	FTs PCT	Rebounds OFF	Rebounds TOT	AST	STL	BLK	PTS	PPG
86-87	DET	82	1463	163	.562	0	.000	105	.614	108	296	54	44	125	431	5.3
87-88	DET	82	2003	258	.566	0	.000	185	.709	166	402	113	53	137	701	8.5
88-89	DET	67	1458	166	.498	0	.000	135	.692	134	335	75	40	72	467	7.0
89-90	DET	82	1914	209	.512	1	.250	174	.713	154	439	67	51	153	593	7.2
90-91	DET	74	1649	179	.475	0	.000	186	.727	137	327	70	52	112	544	7.4
91-92	DET	72	1774	249	.512	0	.000	186	.715	106	296	116	49	110	684	9.5
92-93	MIA	51	1422	154	.502	0	.000	115	.799	113	313	83	32	70	423	8.3
93-94	MIA	76	1910	208	.477	2	.667	164	.729	132	407	135	56	78	582	7.7
Totals		586	13593	1586	.513	3	.214	1250	.712	1050	2815	713	377	857	4425	7.6

DETLEF SCHREMPF

Team: Seattle SuperSonics
Position: Forward
Height: 6'10" **Weight:** 230
Birthdate: January 21, 1963
NBA Experience: 9 years

College: Washington
Acquired: Traded from Pacers for Derrick McKey and Gerald Paddio, 11/93

Background: A graduate of the University of Washington, Schrempf spent the first three-plus years of his NBA career in Dallas. In 1989, he was traded to Indiana, where his game began to flourish. He won the NBA Sixth Man Award in 1991 and 1992 and was second in 1990. He began starting in 1992-93 and was traded before the 1993-94 season to Seattle, where he averaged 15 PPG.

Strengths: Schrempf is one of the league's most complete and versatile players. He's a superb ball-handler, shooter, and passer, and he can drive the lane or shoot from the outside. Either way, he scores. He's also great on the break, with the ability to start and/or finish plays. He plays strong defense and rebounds with the best of forwards.

Weaknesses: One of the few weaknesses in Schrempf's game is his tendency to spend too much time pleading his case to the refs. He hits less than a third of his 3-point tries, but not much less.

Analysis: Schrempf can do it all, a fact that was recognized in 1993 when he received a much-deserved All-Star invitation. He was simply too valuable to have continued as a Sixth Man candidate. The Sonics appear to have gotten the better deal in the Schrempf-for-Derrick McKey trade. Schrempf helped them to the league's best record.

PLAYER SUMMARY

Will ....handle the ball
Can't ....let bad calls lie
Expect ....all-around ability
Don't Expect...........less than 15 PPG
Fantasy Value $25-30
Card Value ....10-20¢

COLLEGE STATISTICS

		G	FGP	FTP	RPG	PPG
81-82	WASH	28	.452	.553	2.0	3.3
82-83	WASH	31	.466	.717	6.8	10.6
83-84	WASH	31	.539	.736	7.4	16.8
84-85	WASH	32	.558	.714	8.0	15.8
Totals		122	.521	.708	6.2	11.9

NBA REGULAR-SEASON STATISTICS

		G	MIN	FGs		3-PT FGs		FTs		Rebounds						
				FG	PCT	FG	PCT	FT	PCT	OFF	TOT	AST	STL	BLK	PTS	PPG
85-86	DAL	64	969	142	.451	3	.429	110	.724	70	198	88	23	10	397	6.2
86-87	DAL	81	1711	265	.472	33	.478	193	.742	87	303	161	50	16	756	9.3
87-88	DAL	82	1587	246	.456	5	.156	201	.756	102	279	159	42	32	698	8.5
88-89	DAL/IND	69	1850	274	.474	7	.200	273	.780	126	395	179	53	19	828	12.0
89-90	IND	78	2573	424	.516	17	.354	402	.820	149	620	247	59	16	1267	16.2
90-91	IND	82	2632	432	.520	15	.375	441	.818	178	660	301	58	22	1320	16.1
91-92	IND	80	2605	496	.536	23	.324	365	.828	202	770	312	62	37	1380	17.3
92-93	IND	82	3098	517	.476	8	.154	525	.804	210	780	493	79	27	1567	19.1
93-94	SEA	81	2728	445	.493	22	.324	300	.769	144	454	275	73	9	1212	15.0
Totals		699	19753	3241	.494	133	.315	2810	.794	1268	4459	2215	499	188	9425	13.5

BYRON SCOTT

Unrestricted Free Agent
Last Team: Indiana Pacers
Position: Guard
Height: 6'4" **Weight:** 200
Birthdate: March 28, 1961

NBA Experience: 11 years
College: Arizona St.
Acquired: Signed as a free agent, 8/93

Background: In three years, Scott became Arizona State's career scoring leader. He worked his way into the Lakers' starting lineup as a rookie and broke Michael Cooper's team record for career 3-pointers. Scott helped the Lakers to three NBA championships in the 1980s. He was a free-agent signee of the Pacers last season but became a free agent again after the campaign.

Strengths: Scott is a classic spot-up shooter who is deadly when he gets his feet together. He has great range and does not mind taking the pressure shot. He has made plenty of them. He gave the Pacers some of the leadership they needed.

Weaknesses: Scott no longer shoots and scores like he once did. His 10.4 PPG last season was a career low. He is not as adept at creating his own shot as he is at coming off a screen. He's average, at best, with the dribble. In fact, perimeter shooting is his only real strength.

Analysis: It was strange seeing Scott in Pacer blue last season, but by year's end his leadership and clutch shooting had helped Indiana to its best-ever run through the postseason. Scott is not the player he once was, but he can still score in double digits.

PLAYER SUMMARY	
Will	hit clutch shots
Can't	create like Magic
Expect	offensive leadership
Don't Expect	15 PPG
Fantasy Value	$1
Card Value	7-10¢

COLLEGE STATISTICS

		G	FGP	FTP	RPG	PPG
79-80	ASU	29	.500	.733	2.7	13.6
80-81	ASU	28	.505	.693	3.8	16.6
82-83	ASU	33	.513	.782	5.4	21.6
Totals		90	.507	.747	4.0	17.5

NBA REGULAR-SEASON STATISTICS

		G	MIN	FGs FG	FGs PCT	3-PT FGs FG	3-PT FGs PCT	FTs FT	FTs PCT	Rebounds OFF	Rebounds TOT	AST	STL	BLK	PTS	PPG
83-84	LAL	74	1637	334	.484	8	.235	112	.806	50	164	177	81	19	788	10.6
84-85	LAL	81	2305	541	.539	26	.433	187	.820	57	210	244	100	17	1295	16.0
85-86	LAL	76	2190	507	.513	22	.361	138	.784	55	189	164	85	15	1174	15.4
86-87	LAL	82	2729	554	.489	65	.436	224	.892	63	286	281	125	18	1397	17.0
87-88	LAL	81	3048	710	.527	62	.346	272	.858	76	333	335	155	27	1754	21.7
88-89	LAL	74	2605	588	.491	77	.399	195	.863	72	302	231	114	27	1448	19.6
89-90	LAL	77	2593	472	.470	93	.423	160	.766	51	242	274	77	31	1197	15.5
90-91	LAL	82	2630	501	.477	71	.324	118	.797	54	246	177	95	21	1191	14.5
91-92	LAL	82	2679	460	.458	54	.344	244	.838	74	310	226	105	28	1218	14.9
92-93	LAL	58	1677	296	.449	44	.326	156	.848	27	134	157	55	13	792	13.7
93-94	IND	67	1197	256	.467	27	.365	157	.805	19	110	133	62	9	696	10.4
Totals		834	25290	5219	.491	549	.371	1963	.630	598	2526	2399	1054	225	12950	15.5

DENNIS SCOTT

Team: Orlando Magic
Position: Forward
Height: 6'8" **Weight:** 230
Birthdate: September 5, 1968

NBA Experience: 4 years
College: Georgia Tech
Acquired: 1st-round pick in 1990 draft
(4th overall)

Background: Scott led Georgia Tech to the NCAA Final Four as a senior. That year, he recorded the highest single-season point total in Atlantic Coast Conference history and was named ACC Player of the Year. He earned All-Rookie honors in 1990-91, posting the third-highest scoring average among first-year players and setting a rookie record for 3-pointers. He played only 72 games over his second two years because of right knee surgery, Achilles tendinitis, and a strained calf. He averaged a career-low 12.8 PPG in 82 games last season.

Strengths: Scott has range even beyond the 3-point line and boasts one of the sweetest strokes in the game. He once made nine 3-pointers in a game and hit treys at a .399 clip last season. He has the potential to be a big-time scorer. His size serves him well on the perimeter and in the post. He is also a solid passer and ball-handler.

Weaknesses: Scott does not possess great quickness, which hurts him most on defense. He has the potential to be a better rebounder. He too often stays glued to the perimeter. His history of leg injuries must be watched. He shot for a poor percentage from inside the arc last season.

Analysis: Scott is one of the reasons Orlando is a team on the rise. With Shaquille O'Neal in the middle, you need sweet shooters like Scott on the perimeter. The emergence of rookie guard Anfernee Hardaway had much to do with the decline in Scott's point total, but he will continue to play a big role as the Magic continues to grow.

PLAYER SUMMARY

Will	drill the trey
Can't	outscore Shaq
Expect	12-plus PPG
Don't Expect	open shots
Fantasy Value	$5-7
Card Value	10-20¢

COLLEGE STATISTICS

		G	FGP	FTP	RPG	PPG
87-88	GT	32	.440	.655	5.0	15.5
88-89	GT	32	.443	.814	4.1	20.3
89-90	GT	35	.465	.793	6.6	27.7
Totals		99	.452	.777	5.3	21.4

NBA REGULAR-SEASON STATISTICS

				FGs		3-PT FGs		FTs		Rebounds						
		G	MIN	FG	PCT	FG	PCT	FT	PCT	OFF	TOT	AST	STL	BLK	PTS	PPG
90-91	ORL	82	2336	503	.425	125	.374	153	.750	62	235	134	62	25	1284	15.7
91-92	ORL	18	608	133	.402	29	.326	64	.901	14	66	35	20	9	359	19.9
92-93	ORL	54	1759	329	.431	108	.403	92	.786	38	186	136	57	18	858	15.9
93-94	ORL	82	2283	384	.405	155	.399	123	.774	54	218	216	81	32	1046	12.8
Totals		236	6986	1349	.418	417	.386	432	.784	168	705	521	220	84	3547	15.0

MALIK SEALY

Team: Los Angeles Clippers
Position: Forward/Guard
Height: 6'8" **Weight:** 185
Birthdate: February 1, 1970
NBA Experience: 2 years

College: St. John's
Acquired: Traded from Pacers with Pooh Richardson and draft rights to Eric Piatkowski for Mark Jackson and draft rights to Greg Minor, 6/94

Background: Sealy starred at Tolentine High in the Bronx. He led all Big East players in scoring as a senior (22.6 PPG) at hometown St. John's while earning his second straight spot on the all-conference first team. He finished his college career as St. John's' all-time steals leader and finished second to Chris Mullin in scoring. The 14th pick in the 1992 draft, Sealy played minimally with the Pacers for two years before being traded to the Clippers this past June.

Strengths: Sealy brings unlimited energy to the floor. He thrives in a running game, can play both big guard and small forward, and is tougher than he appears. Blessed with great quickness, Sealy has the potential to be a disruptive defensive player in a fullcourt attack. He also looks to score, moves well without the basketball, and does not shy away from pressure shots. He does have 3-point range.

Weaknesses: Sealy has never been a pure shooter, and his first two seasons in a Pacer uniform did nothing to change that. While he will attempt an occasional 3-pointer, he really should be sticking within about 16 feet of the bucket. Sealy is also a poor free throw shooter as well as a below-average passer and ball-handler. He must learn to become more involved in the offense.

Analysis: Some of the greatest exposure Sealy has gained as a pro came when he lost his playbook on a 1993 playoff trip to New York; a radio station broadcast some of the scouting capsules out of it. He has displayed brief flashes of potential as a scorer, once hitting for 27 points in a game last season. He needs to see action in more than 58 or 43 games a season to develop consistency.

PLAYER SUMMARY	
Will	run the court
Can't	shoot reliably
Expect	unlimited energy
Don't Expect	consistency
Fantasy Value	$6-8
Card Value	8-15¢

COLLEGE STATISTICS

		G	FGP	FTP	RPG	PPG
88-89	STJ	31	.489	.558	6.4	12.9
89-90	STJ	34	.525	.746	6.9	18.1
90-91	STJ	32	.492	.743	7.7	22.1
91-92	STJ	30	.472	.793	6.8	22.6
Totals		127	.494	.729	6.9	18.9

NBA REGULAR-SEASON STATISTICS

			FGs		3-PT FGs		FTs		Rebounds						
	G	MIN	FG	PCT	FG	PCT	FT	PCT	OFF	TOT	AST	STL	BLK	PTS	PPG
92-93 IND	58	672	136	.426	7	.226	51	.689	60	112	47	36	7	330	5.7
93-94 IND	43	623	111	.405	4	.250	59	.678	43	118	48	31	8	285	6.6
Totals	101	1295	247	.417	11	.234	110	.683	103	230	95	67	15	615	6.1

RONY SEIKALY

Team: Miami Heat
Position: Center
Height: 6'11" **Weight:** 252
Birthdate: May 10, 1965

NBA Experience: 6 years
College: Syracuse
Acquired: 1st-round pick in 1988 draft (9th overall)

Background: A native of Greece, Seikaly was one of Syracuse's all-time great big men. He was inconsistent as a rookie with Miami in 1988-89 but was chosen as the NBA's Most Improved Player in 1989-90. He averaged a career-high 17.1 PPG in 1992-93 and hasn't been below 15.1 PPG since his rookie campaign. Seikaly annually ranks among the league's top rebounders. He averaged 10.3 RPG last season.

Strengths: Seikaly is one of the most talented and productive rebounders in the league. He grabbed 34 in a game against Washington two years ago, more than the Bullets nabbed as a team. He has good quickness, speed, jumping ability, and confidence. He combines finesse with physical play and gets to the line frequently. He's a fine shot-blocker and low-post defender.

Weaknesses: Seikaly is not one of the league's better-passing big men, and his turnover total (more than 600 over the past three years) results largely from putting the ball on the floor too often. He draws far too many fouls, getting disqualified from eight games in 1993-94. His scoring also dropped last season.

Analysis: Seikaly is one of the cornerstones of a Miami club that has become a playoff team since his arrival. When he sets his mind to dominating the boards, he is completely capable of doing so. He is certainly not the best NBA center in the state of Florida, but there are more than a few teams who would love to have Seikaly in their starting lineup.

PLAYER SUMMARY

Will ....hoard rebounds
Can't ....avoid fouling
Expect ....10-plus RPG
Don't Expect ....ball-handling
Fantasy Value $20-25
Card Value ....8-15¢

COLLEGE STATISTICS

		G	FGP	FTP	RPG	PPG
84-85	SYR	31	.542	.558	6.4	8.1
85-86	SYR	32	.547	.563	7.8	10.1
86-87	SYR	38	.568	.600	8.2	15.1
87-88	SYR	35	.566	.568	9.6	16.3
Totals		136	.560	.576	8.0	12.6

NBA REGULAR-SEASON STATISTICS

				FGs		3-PT FGs		FTs		Rebounds						
		G	MIN	FG	PCT	FG	PCT	FT	PCT	OFF	TOT	AST	STL	BLK	PTS	PPG
88-89	MIA	78	1962	333	.448	1	.250	181	.511	204	549	55	46	96	848	10.9
89-90	MIA	74	2409	486	.502	0	.000	256	.594	253	766	78	78	124	1228	16.6
90-91	MIA	64	2171	395	.481	2	.333	258	.619	207	709	95	51	86	1050	16.4
91-92	MIA	79	2800	463	.489	0	.000	370	.733	307	934	109	40	121	1296	16.4
92-93	MIA	72	2456	417	.480	1	.125	397	.735	259	846	100	38	83	1232	17.1
93-94	MIA	72	2410	392	.488	0	.000	304	.720	244	740	136	59	100	1088	15.1
Totals		439	14208	2486	.483	4	.167	1766	.662	1474	4544	573	312	610	6742	15.4

BRIAN SHAW

Unrestricted Free Agent
Last Team: Miami Heat
Position: Guard
Height: 6'6" **Weight:** 194
Birthdate: March 22, 1966

NBA Experience: 5 years
College: St. Mary's (CA); Cal.-Santa Barbara
Acquired: Traded from Celtics for Sherman Douglas, 1/92

Background: Shaw, the Pacific Coast Athletic Association Player of the Year as a senior at Cal.-Santa Barbara, was a second-team All-Rookie performer with the Celtics in 1988-89. He spent the 1989-90 season in the Italian League. He returned to Boston in 1990-91 and rated 14th in the NBA in assists. Shaw was traded to Miami for Sherman Douglas in 1991-92 and became a free agent after the 1993-94 campaign.

Strengths: Shaw brings good size and rebounding to the backcourt and has the versatility to play both point guard and off guard. He played forward in college and can post up smaller defenders. He's at his best in transition, has some quick moves to the hoop, and can handle and pass the ball. Over the last two years, he has become a 3-point threat.

Weaknesses: Sorely lacking the defensive skills the Celtics wanted from him, Shaw is often unwilling and not very able at that end. Offensively, the 3-pointer is his best weapon. He is not a consistent shooter with a man in his face, will not score a lot from inside the arc, and is not among the more creative guards.

Analysis: Shaw needed to develop an offensive weapon he could rely on, and the 3-point shot has been to his liking. He once made an NBA-record ten 3-pointers (in 15 attempts) in a game two seasons ago. In his first three years, he had made only eight 3's total. Shaw started 52 games for the playoff-qualifying Heat last season.

PLAYER SUMMARY	
Will	shoot with range
Can't	star on defense
Expect	an up-tempo player
Don't Expect	big scoring
Fantasy Value	$2-4
Card Value	7-12¢

COLLEGE STATISTICS

		G	FGP	FTP	RPG	PPG
83-84	SM	14	.361	.737	0.9	2.9
84-85	SM	27	.402	.724	5.3	9.4
86-87	CSB	29	.434	.712	7.7	10.9
87-88	CSB	30	.466	.740	8.7	13.3
Totals		100	.434	.728	6.4	10.1

NBA REGULAR-SEASON STATISTICS

		G	MIN	FGs FG	FGs PCT	3-PT FGs FG	3-PT FGs PCT	FTs FT	FTs PCT	Rebounds OFF	Rebounds TOT	AST	STL	BLK	PTS	PPG
88-89	BOS	82	2301	297	.433	0	.000	109	.826	119	376	472	78	27	703	8.6
90-91	BOS	79	2772	442	.469	3	.111	204	.819	104	370	602	105	34	1091	13.8
91-92	BOS/MIA	63	1423	209	.407	5	.217	72	.791	50	204	250	57	22	495	7.9
92-93	MIA	68	1603	197	.393	43	.331	61	.782	70	257	235	48	19	498	7.3
93-94	MIA	77	2037	278	.417	73	.338	64	.719	104	350	385	71	21	693	9.0
Totals		369	10136	1423	.430	124	.303	510	.798	447	1557	1944	359	123	3480	9.4

LIONEL SIMMONS

Team: Sacramento Kings
Position: Forward
Height: 6'7" **Weight:** 210
Birthdate: November 14, 1968

NBA Experience: 4 years
College: La Salle
Acquired: 1st-round pick in 1990 draft
(7th overall)

Background: Simmons, who won the Wooden Award in 1990 as college basketball's Player of the Year, finished his career at La Salle third on the all-time NCAA scoring list. He became the first player in college history to amass more than 3,000 points and 1,100 rebounds. He finished second to Derrick Coleman in the 1990-91 Rookie of the Year balloting. After three years over the 17-PPG mark, Simmons slumped to 15.1 PPG last season.

Strengths: Simmons is an amazingly versatile player. He scores in the high teens, cleans the boards, plays defense, and is a smooth passer from the wing. He understands the game and makes his teammates better. He possesses an enormous quantity of athletic ability, but his great work ethic and willingness to leave it all on the floor have just as much to do with his success. You know he will earn a full day's pay.

Weaknesses: While Simmons is a scorer, he is by no means a shooter. His mid-range jump shot is unreliable and he does not have 3-point range (he averages less than three 3-pointers per season). His field goal percentage is low because of his inconsistency from the outside. He also commits his share of personal fouls and turnovers.

Analysis: Simmons does a little bit of everything. He has been as valuable to the Kings as any player has been to his team in the last few seasons. He is not yet All-Star caliber, but he is head and shoulders above where many projected he would be as an NBA player.

PLAYER SUMMARY	
Will	make others better
Can't	shoot consistently
Expect	15-plus PPG
Don't Expect	3-pointers
Fantasy Value	$17-20
Card Value	8-15¢

COLLEGE STATISTICS

		G	FGP	FTP	RPG	PPG
86-87	LaS	33	.526	.763	9.8	20.3
87-88	LaS	34	.485	.757	11.4	23.3
88-89	LaS	32	.487	.711	11.4	28.4
89-90	LaS	32	.513	.661	11.1	26.5
Totals		131	.501	.722	10.9	24.6

NBA REGULAR-SEASON STATISTICS

		G	MIN	FGs FG	FGs PCT	3-PT FGs FG	3-PT FGs PCT	FTs FT	FTs PCT	Rebounds OFF	Rebounds TOT	AST	STL	BLK	PTS	PPG
90-91	SAC	79	2978	549	.422	3	.273	320	.736	193	697	315	113	85	1421	18.0
91-92	SAC	78	2895	527	.454	1	.200	281	.770	149	634	337	135	132	1336	17.1
92-93	SAC	69	2502	468	.444	1	.091	298	.819	156	495	312	95	38	1235	17.9
93-94	SAC	75	2702	436	.438	6	.353	251	.777	168	562	305	104	50	1129	15.1
Totals		301	11077	1980	.439	11	.250	1150	.773	666	2388	1269	447	305	5121	17.0

SCOTT SKILES

Team: Washington Bullets
Position: Guard
Height: 6'1" **Weight:** 180
Birthdate: March 5, 1964
NBA Experience: 8 years

College: Michigan St.
Acquired: Traded from Magic with a 1996 1st-round pick for a 1996 2nd-round pick, 7/94

Background: Skiles was an All-America performer as a senior at Michigan State, finishing second in the nation in scoring and setting school records for points, assists, steals, and free throw accuracy. However, he also earned a reputation for off-court trouble and spent time in jail. He was an NBA back-up for four years before coming into his own with Orlando in 1990-91, when he set a league record with 30 assists in a game. He was traded to Washington last summer.

Strengths: They do not come any more competitive than Skiles, who simply despises losing. He knows how to run an offense and find open men. He penetrates and passes with precision, shoots the 3-pointer, and is almost automatic from the free throw line. He plays both guard spots.

Weaknesses: Skiles is not quick enough to keep opposing point guards from driving and is not big enough to keep from being posted up. He's not able to pressure the ball fullcourt and does not rank with the ball-handling wizards of the game. He's not a great athlete.

Analysis: Skiles is as tough as nails and brings that competitive nature to the arena. He is the consummate playmaker who has rated as high as third in the league in assists. Last year, he shared starting time with shooting guard Dennis Scott, yet Skiles finished fifth in the league in 3-point percentage.

PLAYER SUMMARY	
Will	play two positions
Can't	stand losing
Expect	hot shooting
Don't Expect	great defense
Fantasy Value	$7-9
Card Value	7-12¢

COLLEGE STATISTICS

		G	FGP	FTP	APG	PPG
82-83	MSU	30	.493	.831	4.9	12.5
83-84	MSU	28	.480	.832	4.6	14.5
84-85	MSU	29	.505	.789	5.8	17.7
85-86	MSU	31	.554	.900	6.3	27.4
Totals		118	.516	.850	5.4	18.2

NBA REGULAR-SEASON STATISTICS

		G	MIN	FGs FG	FGs PCT	3-PT FGs FG	3-PT FGs PCT	FTs FT	FTs PCT	Rebounds OFF	Rebounds TOT	AST	STL	BLK	PTS	PPG
86-87	MIL	13	205	18	.290	3	.214	10	.833	6	26	45	5	1	49	3.8
87-88	IND	51	760	86	.411	6	.300	45	.833	11	66	180	22	3	223	4.4
88-89	IND	80	1571	198	.448	20	.267	130	.903	21	149	390	64	2	546	6.8
89-90	ORL	70	1460	190	.409	52	.394	104	.874	23	159	334	36	4	536	7.7
90-91	ORL	79	2714	462	.445	93	.408	340	.902	57	270	660	89	4	1357	17.2
91-92	ORL	75	2377	359	.414	91	.364	248	.895	36	202	544	74	5	1057	14.1
92-93	ORL	78	3086	416	.467	80	.340	289	.892	52	290	735	86	2	1201	15.4
93-94	ORL	82	2303	276	.429	68	.412	195	.878	42	189	503	47	2	815	9.9
Totals		528	14476	2005	.434	413	.369	1361	.890	248	1351	3391	423	23	5784	11.0

CHARLES SMITH

Team: New York Knicks
Position: Forward/Center
Height: 6'10" **Weight:** 244
Birthdate: July 16, 1965

NBA Experience: 6 years
College: Pittsburgh
Acquired: Traded from Clippers in three-team, multi-player deal, 9/92

Background: Smith, the Big East Player of the Year as a senior, left Pitt with the school's career records for points and blocked shots. He earned All-Rookie honors with the Clippers in 1988-89 and ranked among the league leaders in scoring, rebounding, and blocked shots over the next two years. A right knee injury limited him in 1991-92, after which he was traded to the Knicks. He has struggled for much of his time with New York and underwent surgery on his right knee last season.

Strengths: Smith is a versatile athlete who can play all three frontcourt positions. He plays bigger than his size, yet he runs the floor and can handle the ball like a smaller man. He is a combination of power and finesse on offense, with range up to the 3-point arc. He has a wide wingspan.

Weaknesses: Smith has been booed by New York fans because of his inconsistency. He's there one night, gone the next. He too often settles for outside shots and does not pass well out of double-teams. His shooting percentage suffers for it. Some have questioned his feel for the game. He should be a better rebounder.

Analysis: Smith has a lot of talent. For the better part of the last two years, however, the consensus was that he was not using it. The two worst scoring years of his career have come in a Knick uniform, and he has not rebounded or defended well enough to make up for the lack of offensive production.

PLAYER SUMMARY

Will.....................play three positions
Can't.......................win over N.Y. fans
Expect ....natural ability
Don't Expect ....consistent play
Fantasy Value $3-5
Card Value ....7-12¢

COLLEGE STATISTICS

		G	FGP	FTP	RPG	PPG
84-85	PITT	29	.502	.706	8.0	15.0
85-86	PITT	29	.404	.762	8.1	15.9
86-87	PITT	33	.550	.735	8.5	17.0
87-88	PITT	31	.558	.764	7.7	18.9
Totals		122	.500	.753	8.1	16.8

NBA REGULAR-SEASON STATISTICS

		G	MIN	FGs FG	FGs PCT	3-PT FGs FG	3-PT FGs PCT	FTs FT	FTs PCT	Rebounds OFF	Rebounds TOT	AST	STL	BLK	PTS	PPG
88-89	LAC	71	2161	435	.495	0	.000	285	.725	173	465	103	68	89	1155	16.3
89-90	LAC	78	2732	595	.520	1	.083	454	.794	177	524	114	86	119	1645	21.1
90-91	LAC	74	2703	548	.469	0	.000	384	.793	216	608	134	81	145	1480	20.0
91-92	LAC	49	1310	251	.466	0	.000	212	.785	95	301	56	41	98	714	14.6
92-93	NY	81	2172	358	.469	0	.000	287	.782	170	432	142	48	96	1003	12.4
93-94	NY	43	1105	176	.443	8	.500	87	.719	66	165	50	26	45	447	10.4
Totals		396	12183	2363	.483	9	.196	1709	.774	897	2495	599	350	592	6444	16.3

CHRIS SMITH

Team: Minnesota Timberwolves
Position: Guard
Height: 6'3" **Weight:** 191
Birthdate: May 17, 1970

NBA Experience: 2 years
College: Connecticut
Acquired: 2nd-round pick in 1992
draft (34th overall)

Background: Smith became the first player in University of Connecticut history to surpass the 2,000-point barrier. He finished his career as the Huskies' all-time leader in 3-pointers made and attempted. Smith was a first-team All-Big East selection as a senior after leading the league at 21.2 PPG. A second-round pick of the Timberwolves, he has played in 80 games in each of his two seasons and averaged 5.9 PPG last season.

Strengths: Smith is a splendid athlete with great quickness. He handles the ball well, can penetrate, and brings a scorer's mentality to the point-guard post. Smith has a nifty crossover dribble that he can use to get his own shots, and he does possess 3-point ability. He filled in for Micheal Williams as a starter for 16 games last season and fared quite well at finding the open man. He is also willing to expend energy on defense.

Weaknesses: Smith has been called a shooting guard in a point guard's body, although he is learning to be a much better distributor. He still does not always make the right pass, however, and he has not shot the ball consistently enough to make up for that deficiency. Smith is not much help on the boards and is not the thief he was expected to be.

Analysis: There are certainly worse ball-handlers and penetrators playing point guard in the NBA, which is to say Smith's critics may have been off the mark. He is a hard worker who wants to make a name for himself, and he's made steady progress since entering the league two years ago. It looks like he will continue to improve in the seasons to come.

PLAYER SUMMARY	
Will	hustle at both ends
Can't	keep to the perimeter
Expect	improvement
Don't Expect	loads of steals
Fantasy Value	$1
Card Value	7-12¢

COLLEGE STATISTICS

		G	FGP	FTP	RPG	PPG
88-89	CONN	29	.405	.565	2.8	9.9
89-90	CONN	37	.417	.811	2.5	17.2
90-91	CONN	31	.439	.719	2.9	18.9
91-92	CONN	30	.415	.800	3.3	21.2
Totals		127	.421	.761	2.9	16.9

NBA REGULAR-SEASON STATISTICS

		G	MIN	FGs		3-PT FGs		FTs		Rebounds		AST	STL	BLK	PTS	PPG
				FG	PCT	FG	PCT	FT	PCT	OFF	TOT					
92-93	MIN	80	1266	125	.433	2	.143	95	.792	32	96	196	48	16	347	4.3
93-94	MIN	80	1617	184	.435	10	.256	95	.674	15	122	285	38	18	473	5.9
Totals		160	2883	309	.434	12	.226	190	.728	47	218	481	86	34	820	5.1

DOUG SMITH

Team: Dallas Mavericks
Position: Forward
Height: 6'10" **Weight:** 240
Birthdate: September 17, 1969

NBA Experience: 3 years
College: Missouri
Acquired: 1st-round pick in 1991 draft
(6th overall)

Background: Smith went from Detroit's MacKenzie High to immediate stardom at Missouri. He starred as the Tigers went 94-35 in his four seasons. He was drafted sixth overall by Dallas, and after a contract holdout he averaged 8.8 PPG and was among the rookie leaders with 5.1 RPG. He raised his scoring average to 10.4 PPG in his second season before returning to the 8.8-PPG mark during the 1993-94 campaign.

Strengths: Smith runs the floor as well as any player his size and dunks with authority. He is a good ball-handler and passer for a big man, with above-average awareness and instincts. Rebounding is probably his biggest asset, and he has the ability to go coast-to-coast. He has a decent mid-range jumper and is a very good free throw shooter. He has improved his defense.

Weaknesses: Smith does not have the low-post game to be a big-time player in the NBA. His around-the-basket moves are limited and predictable and his shooting percentage is frighteningly low for a big man. He has played overweight at times and must make a commitment to conditioning. Smith ranks among the league leaders in personal fouls.

Analysis: One has to wonder whether Smith will ever be able to live up to his status as a No. 6 overall draft choice. He can be a very exciting player in the open court and has some natural ability, but so far he has not been the scorer and rebounder the Mavericks expected him to be. He has started only about half the games he has played over the last two seasons.

PLAYER SUMMARY

Will ....run the floor
Can't......................dominate inside
Expect.............decent rebounding
Don't Expect ....stardom
Fantasy Value.................................$1
Card Value ....7-12¢

COLLEGE STATISTICS

		G	FGP	FTP	RPG	PPG
87-88	MO	30	.504	.640	6.6	11.3
88-89	MO	36	.477	.736	6.9	13.9
89-90	MO	32	.563	.714	9.2	19.8
90-91	MO	30	.497	.821	10.4	23.6
Totals		128	.510	.747	8.2	17.1

NBA REGULAR-SEASON STATISTICS

		G	MIN	FGs FG	FGs PCT	3-PT FGs FG	3-PT FGs PCT	FTs FT	FTs PCT	Rebounds OFF	Rebounds TOT	AST	STL	BLK	PTS	PPG
91-92	DAL	76	1707	291	.415	0	.000	89	.736	129	391	129	62	34	671	8.8
92-93	DAL	61	1524	289	.434	0	.000	56	.757	96	328	104	48	52	634	10.4
93-94	DAL	79	1684	295	.435	2	.222	106	.835	114	349	119	82	38	698	8.8
Totals		216	4915	875	.428	2	.083	251	.780	339	1068	352	192	124	2003	9.3

KENNY SMITH

Team: Houston Rockets
Position: Guard
Height: 6'3" **Weight:** 170
Birthdate: March 8, 1965
NBA Experience: 7 years

College: North Carolina
Acquired: Traded from Hawks with Roy Marble for Tim McCormick and John Lucas, 9/90

Background: Smith established all-time school records for assists and steals at North Carolina, where he was named All-Atlantic Coast Conference as a senior. He averaged double figures in scoring in his first three NBA seasons with Sacramento and Atlanta, but he did not truly shine until a trade brought him to Houston for the 1990-91 campaign. Smith led the Rockets in assists for three straight years before last season.

Strengths: Smith can play both guard positions at a high level. He shoots well enough at off guard and, at the point, is a cat-quick penetrator who gets the ball into the right hands while scoring double figures himself. He led all guards in field goal percentage two years ago, boasts 3-point range, and is a very good free throw shooter. He's a team leader and a class act.

Weaknesses: Smith's scoring average has declined in each of the past three seasons, and he lost playing time to rookie Sam Cassell in last year's playoffs. He is not a great defensive player and does not come up with many steals or rebounds. He seems to put more effort and focus into his offensive game.

Analysis: Smith is not the most dazzling guard in the league and will not likely play in the All-Star Game before his career is finished. But his game is more complete than most gave him credit for in his pre-Houston days. His backcourt play and leadership are big reasons for Houston's success.

PLAYER SUMMARY	
Will	score, distribute
Can't	shine on defense
Expect	classy leadership
Don't Expect	20 PPG
Fantasy Value	$8-10
Card Value	5-10¢

COLLEGE STATISTICS

		G	FGP	FTP	APG	PPG
83-84	NC	23	.519	.800	5.0	9.1
84-85	NC	36	.518	.860	6.5	12.3
85-86	NC	34	.516	.808	6.2	12.0
86-87	NC	34	.502	.807	6.1	16.9
Totals		127	.512	.823	6.0	12.9

NBA REGULAR-SEASON STATISTICS

				FGs		3-PT FGs		FTs		Rebounds						
		G	MIN	FG	PCT	FG	PCT	FT	PCT	OFF	TOT	AST	STL	BLK	PTS	PPG
87-88	SAC	61	2170	331	.477	12	.308	167	.819	40	138	434	92	8	841	13.8
88-89	SAC	81	3145	547	.462	46	.359	263	.737	49	226	621	102	7	1403	17.3
89-90	SAC/ATL	79	2421	378	.466	26	.313	161	.821	18	157	445	79	8	943	11.9
90-91	HOU	78	2699	522	.520	49	.363	287	.844	36	163	554	106	11	1380	17.7
91-92	HOU	81	2735	432	.475	54	.394	219	.866	34	177	562	104	7	1137	14.0
92-93	HOU	82	2422	387	.520	96	.438	195	.878	28	160	446	80	7	1065	13.0
93-94	HOU	78	2209	341	.480	89	.405	135	.871	24	138	327	59	4	906	11.6
Totals		540	17801	2938	.485	372	.387	1427	.826	229	1159	3389	622	52	7675	14.2

LaBRADFORD SMITH

Team: Sacramento Kings
Position: Guard
Height: 6'3" **Weight:** 205
Birthdate: April 3, 1969

NBA Experience: 3 years
College: Louisville
Acquired: Signed as a free agent, 12/93

Background: Smith was expected to be the next Darrell Griffith at Louisville, and while he never lived up to those expectations, he had a solid, sometimes spectacular, four years with the Cardinals. He set a school record for assists and was one of the top free throw shooters in college basketball history. He was drafted 19th by Washington in 1991, but he was released after two-plus seasons and 38 starts. Sacramento signed Smith in December 1993.

Strengths: Smith's greatest asset is his athletic ability. He has high-jumped 6'10" and was drafted by the Toronto Blue Jays as a pitching prospect. Combined with his good size, his leaping ability allows him to challenge (and dunk over) bigger people. He can penetrate, play both guard spots, and score from both inside and outside. He has 3-point range.

Weaknesses: Inconsistency caused the Bullets to give up on Smith. While he can fill both guard positions, his ball-handling and playmaking skills do not match up with those of the league's better point guards. Moreover, he has not shown steady enough shooting ability to tear it up at two guard. He has carried a little extra weight at times and it has hampered his effectiveness.

Analysis: It has been said that Smith is more athlete than basketball player, and that might be true. However, with a little more commitment to the court, Smith could be a fairly productive NBA player. He'll have a big game one night and scramble for a bucket the next. Smith has too much athletic ability to stay attached to the bench. He'll be given every opportunity.

PLAYER SUMMARY	
Will	dunk on the break
Can't	distribute
Expect	big nights
Don't Expect	consistent effort
Fantasy Value	$0
Card Value	5-10¢

COLLEGE STATISTICS

		G	FGP	FTP	RPG	PPG
87-88	LOU	35	.477	.905	2.5	12.7
88-89	LOU	33	.465	.868	2.3	11.9
89-90	LOU	35	.497	.860	3.3	13.5
90-91	LOU	30	.482	.825	3.7	16.6
Totals		133	.481	.866	2.9	13.6

NBA REGULAR-SEASON STATISTICS

				FGs		3-PT FGs		FTs		Rebounds						
		G	MIN	FG	PCT	FG	PCT	FT	PCT	OFF	TOT	AST	STL	BLK	PTS	PPG
91-92	WAS	48	708	100	.407	2	.095	45	.804	30	81	99	44	1	247	5.1
92-93	WAS	69	1546	261	.458	8	.348	109	.858	26	106	186	58	9	639	9.3
93-94	WAS/SAC	66	877	124	.405	21	.350	63	.750	34	84	109	40	5	332	5.0
Totals		183	3131	485	.432	31	.298	217	.813	90	271	394	142	15	1218	6.7

STEVE SMITH

Team: Miami Heat
Position: Guard
Height: 6'7"　**Weight:** 208
Birthdate: March 31, 1969

NBA Experience: 3 years
College: Michigan St.
Acquired: 1st-round pick in 1991 draft (5th overall)

Background: A Detroit product, Smith surpassed Scott Skiles as Michigan State's all-time leading scorer. He led the Big Ten in scoring as a junior and senior and set a conference record by hitting 45 consecutive free throws. He got off to an All-Rookie start with Miami before tearing cartilage in his right knee in January 1992. He underwent a second arthroscopic surgery the next year, but he improved his scoring average to 17.3 PPG last season.

Strengths: Not unlike another Spartan product named Magic Johnson, Smith brings great size and court sense to the point-guard spot. He owns extraordinary passing ability and always spots the open man. Smith is an athletic rebounder from the backcourt, has great leaping ability, and hits jumpers with 3-point range. He is one of the game's best post-up guards and free throw shooters.

Weaknesses: Smith is a below-average defensive player, just as he was in college. He's slight in build and can be out-quicked by opposing point guards. He likes to talk trash on the court. At times, that's a strength. His right knee will continue to be a concern. He also fouled out of six games last season—a high number for a guard.

Analysis: Smith's abilities earned him a spot on Dream Team II, and he is probably close to his first trip to the All-Star Game. He does most everything with an air of confidence, and he does most everything well. Whether it's scoring, shooting, passing, or rebounding, he can take over games. He's fun to watch, unless you're on the opposing team.

PLAYER SUMMARY

Will ....spot open men
Can't ....muscle his man
Expect ....an All-Star invite
Don't Expect......a lack of confidence
Fantasy Value $25-30
Card Value ....15-25¢

COLLEGE STATISTICS

		G	FGP	FTP	APG	PPG
87-88	MSU	28	.466	.758	4.0	10.7
88-89	MSU	33	.478	.763	6.9	17.7
89-90	MSU	31	.526	.695	7.0	20.2
90-91	MSU	30	.474	.802	6.1	25.1
Totals		122	.487	.756	6.1	18.5

NBA REGULAR-SEASON STATISTICS

				FGs	3-PT FGs		FTs		Rebounds						
		G	MIN	FG	PCT	FG	PCT	FT	PCT	OFF	TOT	AST	STL	BLK	PTS	PPG
91-92	MIA	61	1806	297	.454	40	.320	95	.748	81	188	278	59	19	729	12.0
92-93	MIA	48	1610	279	.451	53	.402	155	.787	56	197	267	50	16	766	16.0
93-94	MIA	78	2776	491	.456	91	.347	273	.835	156	352	394	84	35	1346	17.3
Totals		187	6192	1067	.454	184	.355	523	.803	293	737	939	193	70	2841	15.2

TONY SMITH

Team: Los Angeles Lakers
Position: Guard
Height: 6'4" **Weight:** 205
Birthdate: June 14, 1968

NBA Experience: 4 years
College: Marquette
Acquired: 2nd-round pick in 1990 draft (51st overall)

Background: As a senior, Smith set Marquette single-season records for points and scoring average, earning All-Midwestern Collegiate Conference honors. He climbed to second on the all-time school assists list. Smith has spent his first four pro seasons primarily as a back-up point guard, including a stint behind Magic Johnson. He made a career-high 31 starts last season and has upped his scoring every year.

Strengths: A big scorer in college, Smith has been somewhat of a defensive specialist with the Lakers. He first proved himself as such against Michael Jordan in the 1991 NBA Finals. He has good size, speed, and quickness to stick with his man, whether guarding a one or a two. Smith can also play both guard spots on offense and has become a scoring threat.

Weaknesses: Smith is not a natural point guard in the first place, and he is not nearly the playmaker a team likes to have running the show. He finished only fifth on the Lakers in assists last season. Smith is not a great outside shooter and has not fared well from beyond the 3-point arc. Some would call him a "tweener" who has yet to find a real niche.

Analysis: Smith is not one of the top young prospects on a Laker team stocked with youth, but he has shown he is capable of contributing. He was a better defender than most expected when he came into the league and he is gradually becoming more confident with the ball in his hands. His offense will get a boost if he can become more consistent from the perimeter.

PLAYER SUMMARY

Will	bear down defensively
Can't	rely on his range
Expect	quality minutes
Don't Expect	full-time starting
Fantasy Value	$1
Card Value	5-10¢

COLLEGE STATISTICS

		G	FGP	FTP	APG	PPG
86-87	MARQ	29	.534	.753	2.1	8.1
87-88	MARQ	28	.523	.739	2.9	13.1
88-89	MARQ	28	.556	.730	5.6	14.2
89-90	MARQ	29	.495	.856	5.8	23.8
Totals		114	.521	.785	4.1	14.8

NBA REGULAR-SEASON STATISTICS

		G	MIN	FGs FG	FGs PCT	3-PT FGs FG	3-PT FGs PCT	FTs FT	FTs PCT	Rebounds OFF	Rebounds TOT	AST	STL	BLK	PTS	PPG
90-91	LAL	64	695	97	.441	0	.000	40	.702	24	71	135	28	12	234	3.7
91-92	LAL	63	820	113	.399	0	.000	49	.653	31	76	109	39	8	275	4.4
92-93	LAL	55	752	133	.484	2	.182	62	.756	46	87	63	50	7	330	6.0
93-94	LAL	73	1617	272	.441	16	.320	85	.714	106	195	148	59	14	645	8.8
Totals		255	3884	615	.441	18	.228	236	.709	207	429	455	176	41	1484	5.8

RIK SMITS

Team: Indiana Pacers
Position: Center
Height: 7'4" **Weight:** 265
Birthdate: August 23, 1966

NBA Experience: 6 years
College: Marist
Acquired: 1st-round pick in 1988 draft
(2nd overall)

Background: Smits, a two-time East Coast Athletic Conference Player of the Year at Marist, was the second overall selection in the 1988 draft. He was named to the NBA All-Rookie Team. He led the NBA in disqualifications his first two years but ranked among the leaders in field goal percentage as well. He averaged a career-high 15.7 PPG last season but failed to block 100 shots for the second time in his career.

Strengths: At 7'4", Smits amazingly has the coordination, mobility, and soft touch of a small forward. He can shoot from 15 feet and in, go right or left, and is confident with either hand on hook shots in the lane. He shoots for a high percentage. Smits has the height and anticipation to reject a lot of shots.

Weaknesses: Smits has not always asserted himself, and thus has not reached his potential. He lacks the upper-body strength to keep from being pushed around inside. His rebounding remains an embarrassment for a player with his height (6.2 a game last year). He has been slowed by tendinitis in both knees and he led the league with 11 foul-outs last season.

Analysis: Smits has many gifts you would not expect from someone his size, but he will never become one of the premier centers in the game. He plays frighteningly well at times, but he also has too many games where the energy level is simply not there. When he plays well, the Pacers can stack up with the league's best.

PLAYER SUMMARY	
Will	score inside
Can't	reach Ewing's level
Expect	great games
Don't Expect	nightly intensity
Fantasy Value	$16-19
Card Value	5-10¢

COLLEGE STATISTICS

		G	FGP	FTP	RPG	PPG
84-85	MAR	29	.567	.577	5.6	11.2
85-86	MAR	30	.622	.681	8.1	17.7
86-87	MAR	21	.609	.722	8.1	20.1
87-88	MAR	27	.623	.735	8.7	24.7
Totals		107	.609	.693	7.6	18.2

NBA REGULAR-SEASON STATISTICS

		G	MIN	FGs		3-PT FGs		FTs		Rebounds		AST	STL	BLK	PTS	PPG
				FG	PCT	FG	PCT	FT	PCT	OFF	TOT					
88-89	IND	82	2041	386	.517	0	.000	184	.722	185	500	70	37	151	956	11.7
89-90	IND	82	2404	515	.533	0	.000	241	.811	135	512	142	45	169	1271	15.5
90-91	IND	76	1690	342	.485	0	.000	144	.762	116	357	84	24	111	828	10.9
91-92	IND	74	1772	436	.510	0	.000	152	.788	124	417	116	29	100	1024	13.8
92-93	IND	81	2072	494	.486	0	.000	167	.732	126	432	121	27	75	1155	14.3
93-94	IND	78	2113	493	.534	0	.000	238	.793	135	483	156	49	82	1224	15.7
Totals		473	12092	2666	.511	0	.000	1126	.770	821	2701	689	211	688	6458	13.7

ELMORE SPENCER

Team: Los Angeles Clippers
Position: Center
Height: 7'0" **Weight:** 270
Birthdate: December 6, 1969
NBA Experience: 2 years

College: Georgia; Connors St.; Nevada-Las Vegas
Acquired: 1st-round pick in 1992 draft (25th overall)

Background: Spencer averaged 12.0 PPG as a redshirt freshman at Georgia before breaking his foot 11 games into the season. He spent the next year as the nation's hottest junior college prospect while leading Connors State (Oklahoma) to the national title. In two years at Nevada-Las Vegas, Spencer set a school record for career blocked shots. He was drafted 25th by the Clippers, and after averaging less than seven minutes per game as a rookie, he became a starter last season.

Strengths: Spencer is a fine shot-blocker, finishing among the league's top 15 in that category last season. He offers great size and a decent feel for the game. He has a soft touch inside, moves well for a big man, and is regarded as a good rebounder and passer. He plays hard and with enthusiasm. Spencer does not try to do more than he is capable of on offense.

Weaknesses: Spencer's high field goal percentage results from dunks and put-backs, not from a vast repertoire of inside moves. Spencer will make only a little more than half of his free throws and does little from the perimeter. He commits a lot of fouls and turns the ball over more than twice as often as he gets credit for an assist. He is far from consistent.

Analysis: Spencer was handed the Clippers' starting center position because of Stanley Roberts's extended stay on the injured list. He responded by leading the team in blocked shots and improving his scoring average to 8.9 PPG. On most every other team, however, Spencer would be no more than a reserve who could intimidate on the defensive end. He has a lot to learn.

PLAYER SUMMARY	
Will	swat shots
Can't	shoot FTs
Expect	defensive intimidation
Don't Expect	perimeter ability
Fantasy Value	$1-3
Card Value	8-12¢

COLLEGE STATISTICS

		G	FGP	FTP	RPG	PPG
88-89	GEOR	11	.641	.500	5.3	12.0
90-91	UNLV	31	.522	.471	4.0	6.4
91-92	UNLV	28	.637	.546	8.1	14.8
Totals		70	.603	.516	5.9	10.6

NBA REGULAR-SEASON STATISTICS

			FGs		3-PT FGs		FTs		Rebounds						
	G	MIN	FG	PCT	FG	PCT	FT	PCT	OFF	TOT	AST	STL	BLK	PTS	PPG
92-93 LAC	44	280	44	.537	0	.000	16	.500	17	62	8	8	18	104	2.4
93-94 LAC	76	1930	288	.533	0	.000	97	.599	96	415	75	30	127	673	8.9
Totals	120	2210	332	.534	0	.000	113	.582	113	477	83	38	145	777	6.5

FELTON SPENCER

Team: Utah Jazz
Position: Center
Height: 7'0" **Weight:** 265
Birthdate: January 5, 1968

NBA Experience: 4 years
College: Louisville
Acquired: Traded from Timberwolves for Mike Brown, 6/93

Background: Spencer ended his career at Louisville as the school's all-time leader in field goal percentage; he was third in the nation in that category in 1989-90. As a senior, he was one of college basketball's most improved players. He took second-team NBA All-Rookie honors in 1990-91 after setting Minnesota records for rebounds and blocks. After two mediocre seasons, a trade sent him to Utah, where he averaged a career-high 8.6 PPG last year.

Strengths: Spencer loves contact, has good size, and works hard. He is very strong and is solid on the boards. He was seventh in the league in offensive rebounds as a rookie and second on the Jazz in rebounding last season. Spencer is also a more-than-capable defender who can block shots. He plays within himself on offense and shoots for a decent percentage.

Weaknesses: Spencer is not the kind of center who can carry a team. His range is limited to the paint and he is horrible from the free throw line. He ranks among the worst passing big men in basketball, averaging about one assist every two games. He is slow on his feet and has fouled out of 15 games in the last two seasons. Spencer is not very consistent.

Analysis: Utah needed someone to replace Mark Eaton at center, and at times Spencer was capable of handling the job. He is not nearly the shot-blocker Eaton was (who is?), but he scored more than he had during his Minnesota days and helped out with rebounds and low-post defense. However, he is not among the better starting centers.

PLAYER SUMMARY

Will....................................use his body
Can't................outscore the Mailman
Expect ....defense, rebounds
Don't Expect ....crisp passes
Fantasy Value $1-3
Card Value ....8-12¢

COLLEGE STATISTICS

		G	FGP	FTP	RPG	PPG
86-87	LOU	31	.551	.492	2.7	3.8
87-88	LOU	35	.592	.640	4.2	7.4
88-89	LOU	33	.607	.733	5.1	8.2
89-90	LOU	35	.681	.716	8.5	14.9
Totals		134	.628	.676	5.2	8.7

NBA REGULAR-SEASON STATISTICS

		G	MIN	FGs		3-PT FGs		FTs		Rebounds		AST	STL	BLK	PTS	PPG
				FG	PCT	FG	PCT	FT	PCT	OFF	TOT					
90-91	MIN	81	2099	195	.512	0	.000	182	.722	272	641	25	48	121	572	7.1
91-92	MIN	61	1481	141	.426	0	.000	123	.691	167	435	53	27	79	405	6.6
92-93	MIN	71	1296	105	.465	0	.000	83	.654	134	324	17	23	66	293	4.1
93-94	UTA	79	2210	256	.505	0	.000	165	.607	235	658	43	41	67	677	8.6
Totals		292	7086	697	.482	0	.000	553	.667	808	2058	138	139	333	1947	6.7

LATRELL SPREWELL

Team: Golden State Warriors
Position: Guard
Height: 6'5" **Weight:** 190
Birthdate: September 8, 1970

NBA Experience: 2 years
College: Three Rivers; Alabama
Acquired: 1st-round pick in 1992 draft (24th overall)

Background: Though not recruited by a Division I school, Sprewell was a first-team All-SEC choice at Alabama and also made the all-defensive team as a senior, when he averaged 17.8 points, 5.2 rebounds, and 1.8 steals per contest. He broke Derrick McKey's school record for minutes in a season. He was drafted 24th by Golden State, made the All-Rookie second team, and became a star last season. Sprewell played in the 1994 All-Star Game and was 11th in the league in scoring and ninth in steals. He also made the All-NBA first team.

Strengths: Sprewell is a high-energy player who excels on both ends. He is a legitimate stopper who has long arms to go along with great quickness and instincts. He can run and jump with virtually anyone in the league and matches up at three positions. Sprewell is also a big-time scorer with a nice jumper, 3-point range, and the ability to get to the hole. He passes, rebounds, and has a great attitude.

Weaknesses: Sprewell has turned the ball over more than 200 times in each of his first two seasons, although he can be excused because he is on the court more than anyone in the league. His overall field goal percentage could stand to improve, and he must learn to be more patient with the ball.

Analysis: Sprewell, who did not play organized basketball until his senior year of high school, has taken his game to a new level every season. He was among the most improved players in the league last year after a fine rookie campaign. His 3,533 minutes played last season were the most since Leonard "Truck" Robinson's 3,638 in 1977-78. That shows how valuable Sprewell is to his team.

PLAYER SUMMARY	
Will	star at both ends
Can't	keep turnovers down
Expect	a rising superstar
Don't Expect	bench minutes
Fantasy Value	$35-40
Card Value	30-75¢

COLLEGE STATISTICS

		G	FGP	FTP	RPG	PPG
90-91	ALA	33	.511	.690	5.0	8.9
91-92	ALA	35	.493	.771	5.2	17.8
Totals		68	.499	.740	5.1	13.5

NBA REGULAR-SEASON STATISTICS

				FGs		3-PT FGs		FTs		Rebounds						
		G	MIN	FG	PCT	FG	PCT	FT	PCT	OFF	TOT	AST	STL	BLK	PTS	PPG
92-93	GS	77	2741	449	.464	73	.369	211	.746	79	271	295	126	52	1182	15.4
93-94	GS	82	3533	613	.433	141	.361	353	.774	80	401	385	180	76	1720	21.0
Totals		159	6274	1062	.445	214	.363	564	.763	159	672	680	306	128	2902	18.3

JOHN STARKS

Team: New York Knicks
Position: Guard
Height: 6'5" **Weight:** 185
Birthdate: August 10, 1965
NBA Experience: 5 years

College: Northern Oklahoma;
Oklahoma St.
Acquired: Signed as a free agent,
10/90

Background: Starks is a product of four colleges in four years, including Oklahoma State as a senior (1987-88). He signed on with Golden State as a free agent but a back injury ended his rookie season prematurely. He became a CBA All-Star with Cedar Rapids and also played for Memphis in the WBL before making the Knicks' roster in 1990. Starks has finished second on the team in scoring two years in a row.

Strengths: Starks jump-starts the Knicks with his competitive fire, long-range shooting, and outstanding defense. He has made 315 3-pointers over the last three years and tied a record with seven in one half last season. He penetrates and finds open men. Starks wreaks havoc defensively with his supreme quickness and get-out-of-my-face attitude.

Weaknesses: Starks has become known for his flagrant fouls. He commits nearly as many personal fouls as his team's bruising big men and has earned a reputation as a hot head. He can also play out of control at times and is prone to launching wild shots.

Analysis: Starks, who worked at a grocery store before gaining success in pro basketball, has been a sparkplug for the Knicks. Only Patrick Ewing scores more in New York. Starks makes an impact with his shooting, defense, and will to win. He's the kind of player you want on your side. Left knee surgery cost him the final few weeks of last season, though he came back for the playoffs.

PLAYER SUMMARY

Will ....ignite his team
Can't ....avoid confrontations
Expect....................energetic defense
Don't Expect.........tentative shooting
Fantasy Value $14-17
Card Value ....12-20¢

COLLEGE STATISTICS

		G	FGP	FTP	RPG	PPG
84-85	NOK	14	.463	.774	2.4	11.1
87-88	OSU	30	.497	.838	4.7	15.4
Totals		44	.487	.820	4.0	14.0

NBA REGULAR-SEASON STATISTICS

				FGs		3-PT FGs		FTs		Rebounds						
		G	MIN	FG	PCT	FG	PCT	FT	PCT	OFF	TOT	AST	STL	BLK	PTS	PPG
88-89	GS	36	316	51	.408	10	.385	34	.654	15	41	27	23	3	146	4.1
90-91	NY	61	1173	180	.439	27	.290	79	.752	30	131	204	59	17	466	7.6
91-92	NY	82	2118	405	.449	94	.348	235	.778	45	191	276	103	18	1139	13.9
92-93	NY	80	2477	513	.428	108	.321	263	.795	54	204	404	91	12	1397	17.5
93-94	NY	59	2057	410	.420	113	.335	187	.754	37	185	348	95	6	1120	19.0
Totals		318	8141	1559	.431	352	.331	798	.769	181	752	1259	371	56	4268	13.4

LARRY STEWART

Team: Washington Bullets
Position: Forward
Height: 6'8" **Weight:** 230
Birthdate: September 21, 1968

NBA Experience: 3 years
College: Coppin St.
Acquired: Signed as a free agent, 9/91

Background: Stewart attended Dobbins Tech, the same Philadelphia high school that produced Lionel Simmons, Hank Gathers, and Bo Kimble. He was a two-time Mid-Eastern Athletic Conference Player of the Year and finished his career as Coppin State's all-time rebounding king. Not drafted in 1991, he earned second-team All-Rookie honors with the Bullets and played in 81 games the next year. Early last season, Stewart broke his right foot and played in just three 1993-94 games.

Strengths: Stewart is a great athlete who supplements his natural ability with tremendous desire. He's not afraid to battle in the paint against much bigger players. He is especially productive on the offensive glass and in transition. He doesn't take bad shots and shows nice touch around the bucket. He shot .543 from the field in 1992-93.

Weaknesses: A little undersized to be playing in the paint, Stewart is not able to overpower players like he did in college. He does not shoot with enough range or handle the ball well enough to make a living on the perimeter. He turns it over more often than he gets an assist. Stewart is no better than average as a rebounder.

Analysis: Stewart will not be a star, but his first two seasons in the league caused many to wonder why he was not drafted. His work ethic is contagious and made him a favorite of coach Wes Unseld. Besides the foot injury, Stewart was shot and stabbed in a robbery attempt last January, but those injuries weren't as serious as they sound. Physically, he should be all right.

PLAYER SUMMARY

Will ....battle bigger players
Can't ....shoot with range
Expect ....tremendous desire
Don't Expect ....pinpoint passing
Fantasy Value...................................$1
Card Value ....5-10¢

COLLEGE STATISTICS

		G	FGP	FTP	RPG	PPG
88-89	CSC	28	.659	.691	10.0	17.6
89-90	CSC	33	.645	.701	11.2	18.7
90-91	CSC	30	.635	.785	13.4	23.9
Totals		91	.646	.737	11.6	20.0

NBA REGULAR-SEASON STATISTICS

				FGs		3-PT FGs		FTs		Rebounds						
		G	MIN	FG	PCT	FG	PCT	FT	PCT	OFF	TOT	AST	STL	BLK	PTS	PPG
91-92	WAS	76	2229	303	.514	0	.000	188	.807	186	449	120	51	44	794	10.4
92-93	WAS	81	1823	306	.543	0	.000	184	.727	154	383	146	47	29	796	9.8
93-94	WAS	3	35	3	.375	0	.000	7	.700	1	7	2	2	1	13	4.3
Totals		160	4087	612	.527	0	.000	379	.764	341	839	268	100	74	1603	10.0

BRYANT STITH

Team: Denver Nuggets
Position: Guard
Height: 6'5" **Weight:** 210
Birthdate: December 10, 1970

NBA Experience: 2 years
College: Virginia
Acquired: 1st-round pick in 1992 draft
(13th overall)

Background: Without much national fanfare, Stith was named All-ACC three consecutive seasons and led Virginia to the 1992 NIT championship as tournament MVP. He finished his career as the Cavaliers' all-time leader in scoring, minutes, and free throws made. The MVP of the 1992 pre-draft Orlando Classic, he was taken 13th overall by Denver. A broken foot and broken hand limited his rookie season to 39 games, but he started all 82 last year and averaged 12.5 PPG.

Strengths: Stith is a smart player who does a little bit of everything. He is a streak shooter with pretty good range who also rebounds, passes, and hustles on defense. He has great anticipation and comes up with a lot of steals. Coaches also love the intangibles he brings to the floor. He moves well without the ball, plays with toughness, and converts his free throws. You won't out-work him.

Weaknesses: While Stith seems to present the total package, he does not stand out in any one aspect of the game. He'll get mired in his share of shooting slumps and has not demonstrated NBA 3-point range. Nothing about his game is flashy. He has not startled NBA defenders with his ball-handling, passing, or quickness. The same goes for his defense.

Analysis: Stith broke his right foot early in his rookie season—when he landed on teammate Dikembe Mutombo's foot—and then ended the year early when he broke his hand. In his first full season, he made up for lost time. The 1993-94 campaign saw him come into his own as an 82-game starter and double-figure scorer. He appears to have a bright future as a solid all-around talent.

PLAYER SUMMARY	
Will	come up with steals
Can't	hit the NBA trey
Expect	all-around ability
Don't Expect	flashy play
Fantasy Value	$10-13
Card Value	10-20¢

COLLEGE STATISTICS

		G	FGP	FTP	RPG	PPG
88-89	VA	33	.548	.769	6.5	15.5
89-90	VA	32	.481	.777	6.9	20.8
90-91	VA	33	.471	.791	6.2	19.8
91-92	VA	33	.452	.815	6.6	20.7
Totals		131	.483	.789	6.6	19.2

NBA REGULAR-SEASON STATISTICS

				FGs		3-PT FGs		FTs		Rebounds						
		G	MIN	FG	PCT	FG	PCT	FT	PCT	OFF	TOT	AST	STL	BLK	PTS	PPG
92-93	DEN	39	865	124	.446	0	.000	99	.832	39	124	49	24	5	347	8.9
93-94	DEN	82	2853	365	.450	2	.222	291	.829	119	349	199	116	16	1023	12.5
Totals		121	3718	489	.449	2	.154	390	.830	158	473	248	140	21	1370	11.3

JOHN STOCKTON

Team: Utah Jazz
Position: Guard
Height: 6'1" **Weight:** 175
Birthdate: March 26, 1962

NBA Experience: 10 years
College: Gonzaga
Acquired: 1st-round pick in 1984 draft (16th overall)

Background: Stockton led the West Coast Athletic Conference in points as a senior at Gonzaga, and in assists and steals for three years. He has shattered NBA assists records in ten years with Utah. He holds the single-season assists record and has led the league seven straight times. He has played in six consecutive All-Star Games and was a 1992 Olympic gold-medalist.

Strengths: Stockton is the best playmaker in basketball. He is quick and masterful with the ball, with an uncanny ability to take it to the hole and create easy shots for teammates. He has topped 1,000 assists in a season six times in the last seven years. He hits leaners in the lane as well as 3-pointers. Stockton plays good defense and makes few mistakes.

Weaknesses: About the only thing Stockton does not do is crash the boards, but he's not asked to. Larger opponents can shoot over him.

Analysis: Stockton is one of the premier guards in the league—and certainly its best distributor. He makes everyone on his team look better and he has made himself look pretty good along the way. Last year, he became the third player to record 9,000 career assists, topped the 2,000-career steals plateau, and led all guards in field goal percentage.

PLAYER SUMMARY	
Will	drive and dish
Can't	slam dunk
Expect	Hall of Fame induction
Don't Expect	mistakes
Fantasy Value	$35-40
Card Value	20-35¢

COLLEGE STATISTICS

		G	FGP	FTP	APG	PPG
80-81	GONZ	25	.578	.743	1.4	3.1
81-82	GONZ	27	.576	.676	5.0	11.2
82-83	GONZ	27	.518	.791	6.8	13.9
83-84	GONZ	28	.577	.692	7.2	20.9
Totals		107	.559	.719	5.2	12.5

NBA REGULAR-SEASON STATISTICS

		G	MIN	FGs FG	FGs PCT	3-PT FGs FG	3-PT FGs PCT	FTs FT	FTs PCT	Rebounds OFF	Rebounds TOT	AST	STL	BLK	PTS	PPG
84-85	UTA	82	1490	157	.471	2	.182	142	.736	26	105	415	109	11	458	5.6
85-86	UTA	82	1935	228	.489	2	.133	172	.839	33	179	610	157	10	630	7.7
86-87	UTA	82	1858	231	.499	7	.184	179	.782	32	151	670	177	14	648	7.9
87-88	UTA	82	2842	454	.574	24	.358	272	.840	54	237	1128	242	16	1204	14.7
88-89	UTA	82	3171	497	.538	16	.242	390	.863	83	248	1118	263	14	1400	17.1
89-90	UTA	78	2915	472	.514	47	.416	354	.819	57	206	1134	207	18	1345	17.2
90-91	UTA	82	3103	496	.507	58	.345	363	.836	46	237	1164	234	16	1413	17.2
91-92	UTA	82	3002	453	.482	83	.407	308	.842	68	270	1126	244	22	1297	15.8
92-93	UTA	82	2863	437	.486	72	.385	293	.798	64	237	987	199	21	1239	15.1
93-94	UTA	82	2969	458	.528	48	.322	272	.805	72	258	1031	199	22	1236	15.1
Totals		816	26148	3883	.512	359	.353	2745	.822	535	2128	9383	2031	164	10870	13.3

ROD STRICKLAND

Team: Portland Trail Blazers
Position: Guard
Height: 6'3" **Weight:** 185
Birthdate: July 11, 1966

NBA Experience: 6 years
College: DePaul
Acquired: Signed as a free agent, 7/92

Background: Strickland left DePaul for the pros a year early, but not before he led the Blue Demons in scoring, assists, and steals as a junior and climbed among the school's career leaders in each category. He was a back-up point guard with New York as a rookie before becoming a starter in San Antonio. He led the Spurs in assists for two years, then signed as a free agent with Portland in 1992. His scoring shot up to 17.2 PPG last season.

Strengths: Strickland was sixth in the league with 9.0 APG last season. Few players penetrate as easily and frequently as Strickland, whose nifty ball-handling and great quickness allow him to get past even the best defenders. He hits acrobatic shots off his drives and is a first-rate distributor. Strickland is outstanding in transition and can play solid defense.

Weaknesses: Strickland has had some off-court slip-ups and earned a reputation as a troublemaker in New York and San Antonio. He has improved his jumper dramatically, but it is not the strongest part of his game. He is not a 3-point threat.

Analysis: Strickland, who seems to have shed his label as a troublemaker, replaced Terry Porter as the starting point guard for most of last season. His scoring and passing skills complement one another and his quickness gives opponents fits. He has to rate among the better lead guards in the league from a talent standpoint.

PLAYER SUMMARY	
Will	drive and dish
Can't	shoot 3-pointers
Expect	9 APG
Don't Expect	an outside gunner
Fantasy Value	$35-40
Card Value	5-10¢

COLLEGE STATISTICS

		G	FGP	FTP	APG	PPG
85-86	DeP	31	.497	.675	5.1	14.1
86-87	DeP	30	.582	.606	6.5	16.3
87-88	DeP	26	.528	.606	7.8	20.0
Totals		87	.534	.626	6.4	16.6

NBA REGULAR-SEASON STATISTICS

		G	MIN	FGs FG	FGs PCT	3-PT FGs FG	3-PT FGs PCT	FTs FT	FTs PCT	Rebounds OFF	Rebounds TOT	AST	STL	BLK	PTS	PPG
88-89	NY	81	1358	265	.467	19	.322	172	.745	51	160	319	98	3	721	8.9
89-90	NY/SA	82	2140	343	.454	8	.267	174	.626	90	259	468	127	14	868	10.6
90-91	SA	58	2076	314	.482	11	.333	161	.763	57	219	463	117	11	800	13.8
91-92	SA	57	2053	300	.455	5	.333	182	.687	92	265	491	118	17	787	13.8
92-93	POR	78	2474	396	.485	4	.133	273	.717	120	337	559	131	24	1069	13.7
93-94	POR	82	2889	528	.483	2	.200	353	.749	122	370	740	147	24	1411	17.2
Totals		438	12990	2146	.472	49	.277	1315	.716	532	1610	3040	738	93	5656	12.9

DEREK STRONG

Team: Boston Celtics
Position: Forward
Height: 6'8" **Weight:** 220
Birthdate: February 9, 1968
NBA Experience: 3 years

College: Xavier
Acquired: Traded from Bucks with Blue Edwards for Ed Pinckney and draft rights to Andrei Fetisov, 6/94

Background: Strong played with Tyrone Hill as a collegian at Xavier (Ohio), where he averaged 9.9 RPG as a senior. He was drafted late in the second round by Philadelphia in 1990. After failing to make it with the 76ers, he played one game while on a ten-day contract with Washington in 1991-92 and was the CBA MVP and Newcomer of the Year in 1992-93, which he finished with Milwaukee. Strong played 67 games with the Bucks last season, then was traded in June to Boston.

Strengths: Strong lives up to his name on the boards. No matter what position you line him up in, he will rebound. Strong also has the potential to become a fine defensive player at the NBA level. He does not shy away from a challenge and has good athletic skills. He is a decent face-up shooter and he runs the floor with abandon.

Weaknesses: Strong has struggled to make the transition from low-post collegian to perimeter professional. He played mostly center and power forward at Xavier but is undersized for the four spot in the NBA. For that reason, he probably will never match his CBA success at this level. His shooting is streaky and he is not a great passer or ball-handler.

Analysis: Strong needed a year of seasoning at the CBA level and came back to the NBA a much-improved player. He made 11 starts for the Bucks last season and averaged 6.6 points and more than four rebounds per game. He does not have the tools to become a star in the big leagues, but he's good enough to see some action at two positions.

PLAYER SUMMARY

Will ....rebound
Can't...........................dominate inside
Expect ....streak shooting
Don't Expect ....ball-handling
Fantasy Value.....................................$0
Card Value ....8-15¢

COLLEGE STATISTICS

		G	FGP	FTP	RPG	PPG
87-88	XAV	30	.569	.718	7.1	10.6
88-89	XAV	33	.617	.817	8.0	15.3
89-90	XAV	33	.533	.839	9.9	14.2
Totals		96	.573	.802	8.4	13.4

NBA REGULAR-SEASON STATISTICS

		G	MIN	FG	FG PCT	3-PT FG	3-PT PCT	FT	FT PCT	OFF	TOT	AST	STL	BLK	PTS	PPG
91-92	WAS	1	12	0	.000	0	.000	3	.750	1	5	1	0	0	3	3.0
92-93	MIL	23	339	42	.457	4	.500	68	.800	40	115	14	11	1	156	6.8
93-94	MIL	67	1131	141	.413	3	.231	159	.772	109	281	48	38	14	444	6.6
Totals		91	1482	183	.419	7	.333	230	.780	150	401	63	49	15	603	6.6

LaSALLE THOMPSON

Team: Indiana Pacers
Position: Forward
Height: 6'10" **Weight:** 260
Birthdate: June 23, 1961
NBA Experience: 12 years

College: Texas
Acquired: Traded from Kings with Randy Wittman for Wayman Tisdale and a future 2nd-round pick, 2/89

Background: Thompson left Texas after his junior year and was drafted No. 5 overall by Kansas City in 1982. He spent more than six seasons with the Kings in K.C. and Sacramento and ranked among the franchise's all-time leaders in games, rebounds, blocked shots, and field goal percentage. Since Indiana acquired him in 1989, his production has steadily declined.

Strengths: Thompson's primary strength is crashing the boards. The former NCAA rebounding champ has a massive frame, huge hands, and good timing. Thompson is a strong low-post defender who can play power forward or center.

Weaknesses: Tendinitis in his right knee limited Thompson to 30 games last season and has cast doubt upon his future. He was never quick as it was. The biggest knock on Thompson throughout his career has been his inconsistency from one night to the next. He's not much of a scorer.

Analysis: Thompson has made a decent NBA living with his rebounding, interior defense, and ability to fill in at two positions. However, his aching knees and low scoring output do not bode well for his future. His days as a regular contributor appear over.

PLAYER SUMMARY	
Will	play two positions
Can't	burn the nets
Expect	defense, rebounding
Don't Expect	starts
Fantasy Value	$0
Card Value	5-10¢

COLLEGE STATISTICS

		G	FGP	FTP	RPG	PPG
79-80	TEX	30	.558	.748	9.7	12.8
80-81	TEX	30	.572	.728	12.3	19.2
81-82	TEX	27	.528	.677	13.5	18.6
Totals		87	.553	.713	11.8	16.8

NBA REGULAR-SEASON STATISTICS

		G	MIN	FGs FG	FGs PCT	3-PT FGs FG	3-PT FGs PCT	FTs FT	FTs PCT	Rebounds OFF	Rebounds TOT	AST	STL	BLK	PTS	PPG
82-83	KC	71	987	147	.512	0	.000	89	.650	133	375	33	40	61	383	5.4
83-84	KC	80	1915	333	.523	0	.000	160	.717	260	709	86	71	145	826	10.3
84-85	KC	82	2458	369	.531	0	.000	227	.721	274	854	130	98	128	965	11.8
85-86	SAC	80	2377	411	.518	0	.000	202	.732	252	770	168	71	109	1024	12.8
86-87	SAC	82	2166	362	.481	0	.000	188	.737	237	687	122	69	126	912	11.1
87-88	SAC	69	1257	215	.471	2	.400	118	.720	138	427	68	54	73	550	8.0
88-89	SAC/IND	76	2329	416	.489	0	.000	227	.808	224	718	81	79	94	1059	13.9
89-90	IND	82	2126	223	.473	1	.200	107	.799	175	630	106	65	71	554	6.8
90-91	IND	82	1946	276	.488	1	.200	72	.692	154	563	147	63	63	625	7.6
91-92	IND	80	1299	168	.468	0	.000	58	.817	98	381	102	52	34	394	4.9
92-93	IND	63	730	104	.488	0	.000	29	.744	55	178	34	29	24	237	3.8
93-94	IND	30	282	27	.351	0	.000	16	.533	26	75	16	10	8	70	2.3
Totals		877	19872	3051	.496	4	.154	1493	.736	2026	6367	1093	701	936	7599	8.7

OTIS THORPE

Team: Houston Rockets
Position: Forward
Height: 6'10" **Weight:** 245
Birthdate: August 5, 1962
NBA Experience: 10 years

College: Providence
Acquired: Traded from Kings for Rodney McCray and Jim Petersen, 10/88

Background: Thorpe left Providence with the all-time Big East record for rebounds and was a consensus all-conference selection as a senior. He started his pro career with the Kings and has spent the last six years in Houston. He played in the 1992 All-Star Game and has played all 82 games in eight of his ten seasons. Thorpe annually ranks among the league's most accurate field goal shooters.

Strengths: Thorpe has over 7,000 career rebounds and is especially productive on the offensive glass. He uses his muscular frame to bang in the post. The same goes for his interior defense. Thorpe runs the floor, handles the ball, dunks, and does not take unwise shots.

Weaknesses: Thorpe is not among the most polished low-post players in the league. He gets his points off the pick-and-roll and by going to the offensive boards. He also commits a lot of fouls and is a shaky free throw shooter.

Analysis: You know what you'll get from Thorpe on a nightly basis. He'll score in double figures, ignite the transition game, and battle on the boards for ten rebounds an outing. You can also count on good defense and a great attitude. Underrated, he's been one of the better power forwards in the league for the past few years.

PLAYER SUMMARY	
Will	come to play
Can't	shoot FTs
Expect	10 RPG
Don't Expect	weak defense
Fantasy Value	$13-16
Card Value	7-12¢

COLLEGE STATISTICS

		G	FGP	FTP	RPG	PPG
80-81	PROV	26	.515	.658	5.3	9.6
81-82	PROV	27	.541	.661	8.0	14.1
82-83	PROV	31	.636	.659	8.0	16.1
83-84	PROV	29	.580	.653	10.3	17.1
Totals		113	.575	.653	8.0	14.4

NBA REGULAR-SEASON STATISTICS

				FGs		3-PT FGs		FTs		Rebounds						
		G	MIN	FG	PCT	FG	PCT	FT	PCT	OFF	TOT	AST	STL	BLK	PTS	PPG
84-85	KC	82	1918	411	.600	0	.000	230	.620	187	556	111	34	37	1052	12.8
85-86	SAC	75	1675	289	.587	0	.000	164	.661	137	420	84	35	34	742	9.9
86-87	SAC	82	2956	567	.540	0	.000	413	.761	259	819	201	46	60	1547	18.9
87-88	SAC	82	3072	622	.507	0	.000	460	.755	279	837	266	62	56	1704	20.8
88-89	HOU	82	3135	521	.542	0	.000	328	.729	272	787	202	82	37	1370	16.7
89-90	HOU	82	2947	547	.548	0	.000	307	.688	258	734	261	66	24	1401	17.1
90-91	HOU	82	3039	549	.556	3	.429	334	.696	287	846	197	73	20	1435	17.5
91-92	HOU	82	3056	558	.592	0	.000	304	.657	285	862	250	52	37	1420	17.3
92-93	HOU	72	2357	385	.558	0	.000	153	.598	219	589	181	43	19	923	12.8
93-94	HOU	82	2909	449	.561	0	.000	251	.657	271	870	189	66	28	1149	14.0
Totals		803	27064	4898	.554	3	.073	2944	.693	2454	7320	1942	559	352	12743	15.9

SEDALE THREATT

Team: Los Angeles Lakers
Position: Guard
Height: 6'2" **Weight:** 185
Birthdate: September 10, 1961
NBA Experience: 11 years

College: West Virginia Tech
Acquired: Traded from SuperSonics for 1994, 1995, and 1996 2nd-round picks, 10/91

Background: Threatt was an NAIA All-American at West Virginia Tech, where he finished his career as the school's all-time scoring leader. Originally a sixth-round draft pick by Philadelphia, he played six NBA seasons before becoming a double-digit scorer over the last five years with Seattle and the Lakers. He led the Lakers in steals last season and made 20 starts.

Strengths: Threatt is a pure shooter. He is at his best when spotting up off the break, and he rarely misses a free throw. He has developed into a capable floor leader. Threatt knows where to put the ball and is an expert pickpocket. He can defend virtually any guard.

Weaknesses: Threatt does not shoot well from beyond the 3-point arc. He also does not dribble and shoot as well as he catches and shoots. He's probably better at off guard than at the point.

Analysis: Threatt did an admirable job trying to replace Magic Johnson as the Lakers' point guard, but now he's best used as an offensive sparkplug off the bench. He can score points in a hurry and can handle both guard spots. He's also become valuable as a leader on a young Laker team.

PLAYER SUMMARY

Will	hit spot-up jumpers
Can't	thrive from the arc
Expect	backcourt versatility
Don't Expect	missed FTs
Fantasy Value	$2-4
Card Value	5-10¢

COLLEGE STATISTICS

		G	FGP	FTP	APG	PPG
79-80	WVAT	28	.481	.714	3.9	17.8
80-81	WVAT	31	.452	.712	5.7	17.7
81-82	WVAT	34	.500	.729	5.9	22.2
82-83	WVAT	27	.557	.732	6.7	25.5
Totals		120	.498	.724	5.5	20.7

NBA REGULAR-SEASON STATISTICS

		G	MIN	FGs FG	FGs PCT	3-PT FGs FG	3-PT FGs PCT	FTs FT	FTs PCT	Rebounds OFF	Rebounds TOT	AST	STL	BLK	PTS	PPG
83-84	PHI	45	464	62	.419	1	.125	23	.821	17	40	41	13	2	148	3.3
84-85	PHI	82	1304	188	.452	4	.182	66	.733	21	99	175	80	16	446	5.4
85-86	PHI	70	1754	310	.453	1	.042	75	.833	21	121	193	93	5	696	9.9
86-87	PHI/CHI	68	1446	239	.448	7	.219	95	.798	26	108	259	74	13	580	8.5
87-88	CHI/SEA	71	1055	216	.508	3	.111	57	.803	23	88	160	60	8	492	6.9
88-89	SEA	63	1220	235	.494	11	.367	63	.818	31	117	238	83	4	544	8.6
89-90	SEA	65	1481	303	.506	8	.250	130	.828	43	115	216	65	8	744	11.4
90-91	SEA	80	2066	433	.519	10	.286	137	.792	25	99	273	113	8	1013	12.7
91-92	LAL	82	3070	509	.489	20	.323	202	.831	43	253	593	168	16	1240	15.1
92-93	LAL	82	2893	522	.508	14	.264	177	.823	47	273	564	142	11	1235	15.1
93-94	LAL	81	2278	411	.482	5	.152	138	.890	28	153	344	110	19	965	11.9
Totals		789	19031	3428	.487	84	.235	1163	.820	325	1466	3056	1001	110	8103	10.3

WAYMAN TISDALE

Unrestricted Free Agent
Last Team: Sacramento Kings
Position: Forward
Height: 6'9" **Weight:** 260
Birthdate: June 9, 1964

NBA Experience: 9 years
College: Oklahoma
Acquired: Traded from Pacers with a 1990 2nd-round pick for LaSalle Thompson and Randy Wittman, 2/89

Background: At Oklahoma, Tisdale became the first player in college basketball history to be named first-team All-America in his first three seasons. He led the 1984 gold-medal-winning U.S. Olympic team in rebounds and finished his college career with 17 school records. He was an All-Rookie honoree with Indiana before becoming a top scorer in Sacramento. Tisdale, who has averaged 16-17 PPG the last three years, became a free agent this past summer.

Strengths: Tisdale is an accomplished low-post scorer who gets his shots off despite his relatively small size. His offensive arsenal includes a variety of twisting moves in the lane and a consistent short-range jumper. He once averaged 22.3 PPG and is also strong on the boards.

Weaknesses: Defense has never been Tisdale's forte. His size does not serve him well and he expends a lot of energy on offense. He does not pass well out of double-teams and does not have great range. He has fouled out of 12 games over the last two years.

Analysis: Tisdale is a solid scorer and rebounder who was immensely valuable to the Kings, but the All-Star future some had planned for him does not appear to be in the cards. Tisdale will get his points inside and will shoot for a high percentage.

PLAYER SUMMARY	
Will	score inside
Can't	avoid fouling
Expect	16-17 PPG
Don't Expect	a stopper
Fantasy Value	$8-10
Card Value	7-12¢

COLLEGE STATISTICS

		G	FGP	FTP	RPG	PPG
82-83	OKLA	33	.580	.635	10.3	24.5
83-84	OKLA	34	.577	.640	9.7	27.0
84-85	OKLA	37	.578	.703	10.2	25.2
Totals		104	.578	.661	10.1	25.6

NBA REGULAR-SEASON STATISTICS

				FGs		3-PT FGs		FTs		Rebounds						
		G	MIN	FG	PCT	FG	PCT	FT	PCT	OFF	TOT	AST	STL	BLK	PTS	PPG
85-86	IND	81	2277	516	.515	0	.000	160	.684	191	584	79	32	44	1192	14.7
86-87	IND	81	2159	458	.513	0	.000	258	.709	217	475	117	50	26	1174	14.5
87-88	IND	79	2378	511	.512	0	.000	246	.783	168	491	103	54	34	1268	16.1
88-89	IND/SAC	79	2434	532	.514	0	.000	317	.773	187	609	128	55	52	1381	17.5
89-90	SAC	79	2937	726	.525	0	.000	306	.783	185	595	108	54	54	1758	22.3
90-91	SAC	33	1116	262	.483	0	.000	136	.800	75	253	66	23	28	660	20.0
91-92	SAC	72	2521	522	.500	0	.000	151	.763	135	469	106	55	79	1195	16.6
92-93	SAC	76	2283	544	.509	0	.000	175	.758	127	500	108	52	47	1263	16.6
93-94	SAC	79	2557	552	.501	0	.000	215	.808	159	560	139	37	52	1319	16.7
Totals		659	20662	4623	.510	0	.000	1964	.762	1444	4536	954	412	416	11210	17.0

JEFF TURNER

Team: Orlando Magic
Position: Forward
Height: 6'9" **Weight:** 240
Birthdate: April 9, 1962

NBA Experience: 8 years
College: Vanderbilt
Acquired: Signed as a free agent, 7/89

Background: Turner was a two-time SEC All-Academic selection at Vanderbilt and played for the 1984 gold-medal-winning U.S. Olympic team. He saw limited action with New Jersey in his first three pro seasons before opting to play in Europe for two years. Turner returned to the NBA with Orlando, where he has been a part-time starter over the past five years. He averaged 6.6 PPG last year before knee surgery ended his season in April.

Strengths: A perimeter-oriented forward, Turner has a soft touch with his lefty jump shot and can stroke it with 3-point range. He uses his head, is usually in the right spot, and does not try to do more than he is capable of offensively. You know what you'll get from Turner.

Weaknesses: Turner does little offensively other than shoot. He cannot put the ball on the floor and does not possess an inside game to bail him out. He lacks quickness for the perimeter and muscle for the paint. The same dilemma haunts him on defense. His knee could be a concern.

Analysis: Turner had become a contributing starter on a playoff team last year before knee surgery ended his hopes of postseason action. He is the kind of player who won't hurt his team, and he can hit jumpers when open. He works hard and does what's asked of him. He doesn't mind a supporting role, and that's what he'll get.

PLAYER SUMMARY

Will	hit open jumpers
Can't	dazzle with moves
Expect	3-point range
Don't Expect	10 PPG
Fantasy Value	$0
Card Value	5-8¢

COLLEGE STATISTICS

		G	FGP	FTP	RPG	PPG
80-81	VAND	28	.417	.645	3.0	3.6
81-82	VAND	27	.524	.732	5.4	9.3
82-83	VAND	33	.492	.765	5.5	13.2
83-84	VAND	29	.533	.843	7.3	16.8
Totals		117	.506	.772	5.3	10.9

NBA REGULAR-SEASON STATISTICS

		G	MIN	FGs FG	FGs PCT	3-PT FGs FG	3-PT FGs PCT	FTs FT	FTs PCT	Rebounds OFF	Rebounds TOT	AST	STL	BLK	PTS	PPG
84-85	NJ	72	1429	171	.454	0	.000	79	.859	88	218	108	29	7	421	5.8
85-86	NJ	53	650	84	.491	0	.000	58	.744	45	137	14	21	3	226	4.3
86-87	NJ	76	1003	151	.465	0	.000	76	.731	80	197	60	33	13	378	5.0
89-90	ORL	60	1105	132	.429	2	.200	42	.778	52	227	53	23	12	308	5.1
90-91	ORL	71	1683	259	.487	6	.400	85	.759	108	363	97	29	10	609	8.6
91-92	ORL	75	1591	225	.451	1	.125	79	.693	62	246	92	24	16	530	7.1
92-93	ORL	75	1479	231	.529	10	.588	56	.800	74	252	107	19	9	528	7.0
93-94	ORL	68	1536	199	.467	18	.327	35	.778	79	271	60	23	11	451	6.6
Totals		550	10476	1452	.472	37	.336	510	.762	588	1911	591	201	81	3451	6.3

NICK VAN EXEL

Team: Los Angeles Lakers
Position: Guard
Height: 6'1" **Weight:** 171
Birthdate: November 27, 1971

NBA Experience: 1 year
College: Cincinnati
Acquired: 2nd-round pick in 1993 draft (37th overall)

Background: After spending his first two years at a junior college, Van Exel was the ringleader of a Cincinnati Bearcats team that advanced to the Final Four in 1992 and the regional finals in 1993. He was expected to be a first-round draft choice but fell out of favor with scouts, who questioned his attitude. Nevertheless, he was second among all rookies in assists during the 1993-94 season with 5.8 per game for the Lakers. Van Exel started 80 games and averaged 13.6 points per game.

Strengths: Van Exel's game starts with great quickness. He handles the ball extremely well at high speeds and is adept at running an offense. He can also play some shooting guard in addition to the point. He covers 3-point distance fluidly with his jumper and made 123 of his 364 attempts last season. Van Exel uses his wheels on the defensive end, where he has the makings of a top-notch pickpocket.

Weaknesses: A streak shooter, Van Exel is prone to extended cold spells and does not stop shooting when he's in them. He converted less than 40 percent of his field goal tries as a rookie. Some have said his attitude has alienated some people, although it did not seem to cause problems with the Lakers. Van Exel is slight in build and can be backed into the post defensively.

Analysis: Cincinnati coach Bob Huggins predicted there would be some teams who regretted bypassing Van Exel in the first round of the draft, and he was right. Only Anfernee Hardaway was a better rookie distributor last season and some considered Van Exel the most consistent player on the Lakers. If he can develop more consistency, he'll continue to make a name for himself.

PLAYER SUMMARY	
Will	out-quick his man
Can't	dominate physically
Expect	improving defense
Don't Expect	50-percent shooting
Fantasy Value	$6-8
Card Value	35-75¢

COLLEGE STATISTICS

		G	FGP	FTP	APG	PPG
91-92	CINC	34	.446	.673	2.9	12.3
92-93	CINC	31	.386	.725	4.5	18.3
Totals		65	.409	.701	3.6	15.2

NBA REGULAR-SEASON STATISTICS

			FGs		3-PT FGs		FTs		Rebounds						
	G	MIN	FG	PCT	FG	PCT	FT	PCT	OFF	TOT	AST	STL	BLK	PTS	PPG
93-94 LAL	81	2700	413	.394	123	.338	150	.781	47	238	466	85	8	1099	13.6
Totals	81	2700	413	.394	123	.338	150	.781	47	238	466	85	8	1099	13.6

LOY VAUGHT

Team: Los Angeles Clippers
Position: Forward
Height: 6'9" **Weight:** 240
Birthdate: February 27, 1967

NBA Experience: 4 years
College: Michigan
Acquired: 1st-round pick in 1990 draft
(13th overall)

Background: Vaught led the Big Ten in field goal percentage as a junior and senior and was the first Michigan player since Roy Tarpley to average double-figure points and rebounds. He also led the conference in rebounding as a senior. He has improved his scoring by about two PPG every year since averaging 5.5 PPG as a Clipper rookie. His shooting percentage has also climbed to .537, sixth in the league last year.

Strengths: Vaught rarely puts up a bad shot and has become a double-figure scorer. He approaches basketball in workmanlike fashion. Coaches love his desire to hit the boards at both ends. Equally impressive is his muscular frame. He gets up and down the floor, finishes plays, and hits the jumper from medium range with regularity. Few expected this much offense from him.

Weaknesses: Vaught does nothing that a fan would deem spectacular. He does not pass or handle the ball well, amassing a higher number of turnovers than assists over his four-year pro career. Many of his points come from close range after rebounds. He is not a shut-down defender or intimidating shot-blocker.

Analysis: Vaught says he admires players who do the dirty work but do not get a lot of credit, and that is exactly how he plays. He was expected to be a strong NBA rebounder and has not disappointed in that area, leading the Clippers last season with 8.7 boards per game. He has also come a long way with his offensive game, striking for nearly 12 PPG last season in an expanded role. He comes to play every night.

PLAYER SUMMARY

Will ....work tirelessly
Can't ....pass well
Expect ....strong rebounding
Don't Expect ....the spectacular
Fantasy Value $7-9
Card Value ....5-10¢

COLLEGE STATISTICS

		G	FGP	FTP	RPG	PPG
86-87	MICH	32	.557	.500	3.9	4.6
87-88	MICH	34	.621	.724	4.4	10.5
88-89	MICH	37	.661	.778	8.0	12.6
89-90	MICH	31	.595	.804	11.2	15.5
Totals		134	.617	.752	6.8	10.8

NBA REGULAR-SEASON STATISTICS

				FGs		3-PT FGs		FTs		Rebounds						
		G	MIN	FG	PCT	FG	PCT	FT	PCT	OFF	TOT	AST	STL	BLK	PTS	PPG
90-91	LAC	73	1178	175	.487	0	.000	49	.662	124	349	40	20	23	399	5.5
91-92	LAC	79	1687	271	.492	4	.800	55	.797	160	512	71	37	31	601	7.6
92-93	LAC	79	1653	313	.508	1	.250	116	.748	164	492	54	55	39	743	9.4
93-94	LAC	75	2118	373	.537	0	.000	131	.720	218	656	74	76	22	877	11.7
Totals		306	6636	1132	.510	5	.313	351	.731	666	2009	239	188	115	2620	8.6

KENNY WALKER

Unrestricted Free Agent
Last Team: Washington Bullets
Position: Forward
Height: 6'8" **Weight:** 217
Birthdate: August 18, 1964

NBA Experience: 6 years
College: Kentucky
Acquired: Signed as a free agent, 10/93

Background: An All-American at Kentucky in 1985-86, Walker finished his career third on the all-time Wildcat scoring list. He won the NBA Slam Dunk Contest in 1989 after averaging more than ten PPG in his first two NBA seasons. He was released by the Knicks after five years and played two seasons overseas. Walker signed with the Bullets last fall and became a free agent after the season.

Strengths: A great leaper with speed and quickness, "Sky Walker" plays above the rim. He takes high-percentage shots and is capable of being a force on the boards. Walker puts out a whole-hearted effort on defense, blocks shots, and is tough to beat off the dribble.

Weaknesses: Walker has been called a power forward in a small forward's body. He does not handle the ball well, does not create off the dribble, and possesses neither a great jump shot nor great range. His entire offensive game has tailed off since his first two seasons. Walker is not physical enough to match up defensively with bigger power forwards.

Analysis: Walker is a spirited reserve who ignites a team with his defense and ability to finish. However, he is nowhere near the player the Knicks anticipated when they drafted him with the fifth overall pick. Walker has also been somewhat injury-plagued during his career. He missed time last season with a fractured right cheekbone.

PLAYER SUMMARY	
Will	dunk over people
Can't	match college scoring
Expect	fine finishes
Don't Expect	10 PPG
Fantasy Value	$0
Card Value	7-10¢

COLLEGE STATISTICS

		G	FGP	FTP	RPG	PPG
82-83	KEN	31	.611	.662	4.9	7.3
83-84	KEN	34	.555	.734	5.9	12.4
84-85	KEN	31	.559	.768	10.2	22.9
85-86	KEN	36	.582	.764	7.7	20.0
Totals		132	.571	.750	7.1	15.8

NBA REGULAR-SEASON STATISTICS

				FGs		3-PT FGs		FTs		Rebounds						
		G	MIN	FG	PCT	FG	PCT	FT	PCT	OFF	TOT	AST	STL	BLK	PTS	PPG
86-87	NY	68	1719	285	.491	0	.000	140	.757	118	338	75	49	49	710	10.4
87-88	NY	82	2139	344	.473	0	.000	138	.775	192	389	86	63	59	826	10.1
88-89	NY	79	1163	174	.489	5	.250	66	.776	101	230	36	41	45	419	5.3
89-90	NY	68	1595	204	.531	2	.400	125	.723	131	343	49	33	52	535	7.9
90-91	NY	54	771	83	.435	0	.000	64	.780	63	157	13	18	30	230	4.3
93-94	WAS	73	1397	132	.482	0	.000	87	.696	118	289	33	26	59	351	4.8
Totals		424	8784	1222	.486	7	.206	620	.749	723	1746	292	230	294	3071	7.2

REX WALTERS

Team: New Jersey Nets
Position: Guard
Height: 6'4" **Weight:** 190
Birthdate: March 12, 1970

NBA Experience: 1 year
College: Northwestern; Kansas
Acquired: 1st-round pick in 1993 draft
(16th overall)

Background: Walters was ignored by Kansas University as a high school senior, but he transferred there after a strong sophomore campaign at Northwestern. He teamed with Adonis Jordan in 1991-92 to form a dynamic college backcourt. Walters was a two-time All-Big Eight choice and played in the Final Four as a senior. He was drafted 16th by New Jersey in 1993 and played in 48 games last season, scoring 3.4 PPG.

Strengths: Walters is a fine outside shooter with a quick release and fantastic range. He converted half of his 28 3-point attempts as a rookie. He is also a top-notch free throw shooter who will hit at least eight out of ten from the line. He's left-handed, which makes him tricky to guard, and he plays the game with fire. Walters has a great work ethic and energy to burn.

Weaknesses: Walters does not have the size or speed to get to the hole and finish like he did in college, at least not on a regular basis. He's not going to get his shot off with people in his face as well as he can burn the nets off screens or with pull-up jumpers. Walters is combative, but he has a long way to go with his defensive game. His match-ups are almost always quicker than he is. He's not big enough to be a regular two guard.

Analysis: Walters did not play nearly as much as the Nets had hoped, although he did have some encouraging efforts late in his rookie season. There is no doubt about his range and shooting ability, which will be enough to get him minutes. The rest of his game must show significant improvement, however, and some people question how far his abilities can take him.

PLAYER SUMMARY

Will ....knock down treys
Can't ....star on defense
Expect.......................competitive fire
Don't Expect.............great quickness
Fantasy Value..................................$0
Card Value ....12-20¢

COLLEGE STATISTICS

		G	FGP	FTP	APG	PPG
88-89	NW	24	.378	.917	1.4	2.1
89-90	NW	28	.503	.794	4.5	17.6
91-92	KAN	32	.525	.827	3.9	16.0
92-93	KAN	36	.490	.873	4.3	15.3
Totals		120	.500	.837	3.6	13.4

NBA REGULAR-SEASON STATISTICS

			FGs		3-PT FGs		FTs		Rebounds						
	G	MIN	FG	PCT	FG	PCT	FT	PCT	OFF	TOT	AST	STL	BLK	PTS	PPG
93-94 NJ	48	386	60	.522	14	.500	28	.824	6	38	71	15	3	162	3.4
Totals	48	386	60	.522	14	.500	28	.824	6	38	71	15	3	162	3.4

CLARENCE WEATHERSPOON

Team: Philadelphia 76ers
Position: Forward
Height: 6'6" **Weight:** 245
Birthdate: September 8, 1970

NBA Experience: 2 years
College: Southern Mississippi
Acquired: 1st-round pick in 1992 draft (9th overall)

Background: Weatherspoon attended Motley High in Crawford, Mississippi, the same school that produced NFL star Jerry Rice. "Spoon" finished his college career as the all-time Southern Mississippi leader in scoring, rebounding, and blocked shots, and he joined football star Ray Guy when his USM jersey was retired. Weatherspoon, drafted ninth in 1992, was a second-team All-Rookie choice for Philadelphia. He has started all 164 games in two seasons, and he led the 76ers in scoring and rebounding last year.

Strengths: Weatherspoon has been compared to Charles Barkley, and not without foundation. He has the same powerful build and leaping ability, plays hard at both ends, and can dominate the backboards. Weatherspoon can face the basket and shoot or post up his man, and he has used those skills to become Philadelphia's top scorer. He is agile, runs well, and finishes with a flourish. He also blocks shots and is a team player.

Weaknesses: Spoon is no Sir Charles when it comes to breaking down defenders off the dribble. Weatherspoon needs to expand his array of moves to the hoop and continue to improve his jump shot to keep defenders close. Weatherspoon is a solid defender in the post but becomes less effective on the perimeter. He's not a good free throw shooter.

Analysis: While Weatherspoon has not been able to steer the 76ers to the playoffs like Barkley once did, he has accomplished just about everything else in his first two years. He scores, rebounds, plays defense, and works his tail off. Weatherspoon is a star in the making, and a player you'll hear a lot more about if Philadelphia can climb back into the NBA playoff picture.

PLAYER SUMMARY

Will	score, rebound
Can't	win games alone
Expect	10-plus RPG
Don't Expect	3-pointers
Fantasy Value	$45-50
Card Value	10-20¢

COLLEGE STATISTICS

		G	FGP	FTP	RPG	PPG
88-89	SMU	27	.545	.590	10.7	14.7
89-90	SMU	32	.605	.691	11.6	17.8
90-91	SMU	29	.589	.745	12.2	17.8
91-92	SMU	29	.563	.675	10.5	22.3
Totals		117	.576	.677	11.3	18.7

NBA REGULAR-SEASON STATISTICS

		G	MIN	FGs		3-PT FGs		FTs		Rebounds		AST	STL	BLK	PTS	PPG
				FG	PCT	FG	PCT	FT	PCT	OFF	TOT					
92-93	PHI	82	2654	494	.469	1	.250	291	.713	179	589	147	85	67	1280	15.6
93-94	PHI	82	3147	602	.483	4	.235	298	.693	254	832	192	100	116	1506	18.4
Totals		164	5801	1096	.477	5	.238	589	.703	433	1421	339	185	183	2786	17.0

SPUD WEBB

Team: Sacramento Kings
Position: Guard
Height: 5'7" **Weight:** 135
Birthdate: July 13, 1963
NBA Experience: 9 years

College: Midland; North Carolina St.
Acquired: Traded from Hawks with a 1994 2nd-round pick for Travis Mays, 7/91

Background: After pacing North Carolina State in assists for two straight seasons, Webb was drafted by Detroit in 1985 and signed as a free agent with Atlanta three months later. As a Hawks rookie, he won the NBA's Slam Dunk Contest. Webb led Atlanta in assists in 1990-91, then was traded to Sacramento for Travis Mays. He has averaged about seven APG in each of his first three years with the Kings.

Strengths: Webb overcomes his small stature by playing big. Almost everything he does starts with his incredible quickness. He is capable of making jumpers with 3-point range, hits his free throws, and has scored in double figures the last four years. He's a great leaper who finishes breaks with slams. Webb has led the Kings in assists the last three seasons.

Weaknesses: For obvious reasons, Webb is always going to be susceptible to being posted up and shot over by bigger players. He's also no Magic Johnson when it comes to seeing the court. He's a better spot-up shooter than he is off the dribble.

Analysis: Webb is a fan favorite who has run the Sacramento offense for the last three years. He was losing time to rookie Bobby Hurley last season, but Hurley's serious auto accident kept Webb in the starter's role for most of the year.

PLAYER SUMMARY

Will	finish with dunks
Can't	see over his man
Expect	10-plus PPG
Don't Expect	a slow pace
Fantasy Value	$6-8
Card Value	7-12¢

COLLEGE STATISTICS

		G	FGP	FTP	APG	PPG
81-82	MID	38	.515	.781	—	20.8
82-83	MID	35	.445	.774	—	14.6
83-84	NCST	33	.459	.761	6.0	9.8
84-85	NCST	33	.481	.761	5.3	11.1
Totals		139	.479	.773	5.7	14.3

NBA REGULAR-SEASON STATISTICS

				FGs		3-PT FGs		FTs		Rebounds						
		G	MIN	FG	PCT	FG	PCT	FT	PCT	OFF	TOT	AST	STL	BLK	PTS	PPG
85-86	ATL	79	1229	199	.483	2	.182	216	.785	27	123	337	82	5	616	7.8
86-87	ATL	33	532	71	.438	1	.167	80	.762	6	60	167	34	2	223	6.8
87-88	ATL	82	1347	191	.475	1	.053	107	.817	16	146	337	63	11	490	6.0
88-89	ATL	81	1219	133	.459	1	.045	52	.867	21	123	477	70	6	751	9.2
89-90	ATL	82	2184	294	.477	1	.053	162	.871	38	201	477	105	12	1003	13.4
90-91	ATL	75	2197	359	.447	54	.321	231	.868	41	174	417	118	6	1231	16.0
91-92	SAC	77	2724	448	.445	73	.367	262	.859	30	223	547	125	24	1231	14.5
92-93	SAC	69	2335	342	.433	37	.274	279	.851	44	193	481	104	6	1000	14.5
93-94	SAC	79	2567	373	.460	55	.335	204	.813	44	222	528	93	23	1005	12.7
Totals		657	16334	2410	.456	225	.303	1593	.835	267	1465	3575	794	95	6638	10.1

CHRIS WEBBER

Team: Golden State Warriors
Position: Forward/Center
Height: 6'10" **Weight:** 260
Birthdate: March 1, 1973
NBA Experience: 1 year

College: Michigan
Acquired: Draft rights traded from Magic for draft rights to Anfernee Hardaway and 1996, 1998, and 2000 1st-round picks, 6/93

Background: The cornerstone of Michigan's Fab Five 1991 recruiting class, Webber led the Wolverines to back-to-back appearances in the NCAA championship game. He was the first player selected to the Final Four all-tournament team as a freshman and sophomore. The No. 1 overall pick in 1993, he was acquired by Golden State in a draft-day trade with Orlando. Webber was named Rookie of the Year in 1993-94 after finishing first in rebounding and second in scoring among all first-year players.

Strengths: Webber has been a dominant inside player at every level. His strength and quickness give him a great edge around the basket, and he runs the floor like a guard. Webber has soft but strong hands and employs a variety of moves to put the ball in the basket. He was fourth in the league in field goal percentage last season. Webber blocks shots, rebounds with the best of forwards, and knows how to win.

Weaknesses: While Webber has the ball-handling to survive on the perimeter, he does not have the jump shot. He missed all 14 of his 3-point attempts during his rookie season. He is a horrible free throw shooter and commits a lot of fouls.

Analysis: Webber was destined to be an NBA star from the time he was a Detroit Country Day prep All-American. After missing all but two preseason games because of an appendectomy and the first two regular-season games with an ankle sprain, he took the league by storm. He's a joy to watch, has a great head on his shoulders, and can seemingly achieve whatever he desires. He'll be one of the league's feature attractions for years to come.

PLAYER SUMMARY	
Will	dominate inside
Can't	hit his FTs
Expect	an All-Star regular
Don't Expect	lack of confidence
Fantasy Value	$40-45
Card Value	$1.00-2.50

COLLEGE STATISTICS

		G	FGP	FTP	RPG	PPG
91-92	MICH	34	.556	.496	10.0	15.5
92-93	MICH	36	.619	.552	10.1	19.2
Totals		70	.589	.530	10.0	17.4

NBA REGULAR-SEASON STATISTICS

			FGs		3-PT FGs		FTs		Rebounds						
	G	MIN	FG	PCT	FG	PCT	FT	PCT	OFF	TOT	AST	STL	BLK	PTS	PPG
93-94 GS	76	2438	572	.552	0	.000	189	.532	305	694	272	93	164	1333	17.5
Totals	76	2438	572	.552	0	.000	189	.532	305	694	272	93	164	1333	17.5

BILL WENNINGTON

Unrestricted Free Agent
Last Team: Chicago Bulls
Position: Center
Height: 7'0" **Weight:** 260
Birthdate: April 26, 1963

NBA Experience: 7 years
College: St. John's
Acquired: Signed as a free agent, 9/93

Background: Wennington improved his scoring and rebounding numbers in each of his four years at St. John's, where he teamed with Walter Berry and Chris Mullin. The Montreal native spent his first five pro seasons in a reserve role with Dallas before stints with Sacramento and in the Italian League. Chicago brought him back to America for 1993-94.

Strengths: Wennington has good size but has always had the ability to pull his offensive game away from the basket. He is an accurate jump-shooter from medium range. He also runs the floor well for a center, rebounds, and is willing to fill whatever role he is given. He's a team player all the way.

Weaknesses: For low-post play, Wennington is not your man on either end of the court. He is more comfortable facing the bucket on offense and he possesses neither the size nor the know-how to wear down his man with strong defense. He's below average in many respects for a seven-footer, including rebounding and shot-blocking.

Analysis: The Bulls got some surprisingly solid play out of Wennington last season, including some strong minutes in the playoffs. The big Canadian averaged a career-high 7.1 PPG after a year overseas. A free agent after last season, he entered the summer looking for an offer. He'll come off the bench wherever he winds up.

PLAYER SUMMARY	
Will	face the bucket
Can't	control the paint
Expect	reserve minutes
Don't Expect	selfish play
Fantasy Value	$0
Card Value	5-8¢

COLLEGE STATISTICS

		G	FGP	FTP	RPG	PPG
81-82	STJ	30	.435	.676	4.2	3.2
82-83	STJ	33	.605	.698	4.4	5.5
83-84	STJ	26	.593	.675	5.7	11.7
84-85	STJ	35	.602	.816	6.4	12.5
Totals		124	.579	.738	5.2	8.2

NBA REGULAR-SEASON STATISTICS

		G	MIN	FGs FG	FGs PCT	3-PT FGs FG	3-PT FGs PCT	Fts FT	Fts PCT	Rebounds OFF	Rebounds TOT	AST	STL	BLK	PTS	PPG
85-86	DAL	56	562	72	.471	0	.000	45	.726	32	132	21	11	22	189	3.4
86-87	DAL	58	560	56	.424	0	.000	45	.750	53	129	24	13	10	157	2.7
87-88	DAL	30	125	25	.510	1	.500	12	.632	14	39	4	5	9	63	2.1
88-89	DAL	65	1074	119	.433	1	.111	61	.744	82	286	46	16	35	300	4.6
89-90	DAL	60	814	105	.449	0	.000	60	.800	64	198	42	20	21	270	4.5
90-91	SAC	77	1455	181	.436	1	.200	74	.787	101	340	69	46	59	437	5.7
93-94	CHI	76	1371	235	.488	0	.000	72	.818	117	353	70	43	29	542	7.1
Totals		422	5961	793	.456	3	.107	369	.769	463	1477	275	154	185	1958	4.6

DOUG WEST

Team: Minnesota Timberwolves
Position: Guard
Height: 6'6" **Weight:** 200
Birthdate: May 27, 1967

NBA Experience: 5 years
College: Villanova
Acquired: 2nd-round pick in 1989 draft (38th overall)

Background: West was a four-year starter at Villanova, finishing his career third on the school's all-time scoring list. He served as a reserve for Minnesota in each of his first two NBA seasons before being promoted to the starting lineup in 1991-92. He led the Timberwolves in scoring during the 1992-93 season, averaging a career-high 19.3 PPG. The lone holdover from Minnesota's inaugural 1989-90 campaign, he scored 14.7 PPG last season.

Strengths: West is an explosive player with a sweet jumper and good size for the big-guard spot. His shooting percentage is above average for a backcourt player. The athletic West is a fabulous finisher who can take it in traffic for jams. He owns excellent court sense and knows where to deliver the ball. His defense and free throw shooting are solid.

Weaknesses: West does not have the range of most of the league's big guards, as he is out of his element from beyond the 3-point arc. He has the potential to be a much better rebounder than he is. West turns the ball over almost as often as he gets credit for an assist, and he commits a large number of fouls.

Analysis: Compared to where he was a few years ago, West has to be considered one of the most improved players in the league over the last three seasons. He has gone from a reserve on a bad team to one of its most valuable performers. He gives the Timberwolves shooting, scoring, and defense, although he can hardly save the franchise from futility by himself.

PLAYER SUMMARY	
Will	hit from mid-range
Can't	avoid fouling
Expect	a crowd-pleaser
Don't Expect	3-point greatness
Fantasy Value	$10-12
Card Value	5-10¢

COLLEGE STATISTICS

		G	FGP	FTP	RPG	PPG
85-86	VILL	37	.515	.682	3.7	10.2
86-87	VILL	31	.479	.729	4.9	15.2
87-88	VILL	37	.497	.724	4.9	15.8
88-89	VILL	33	.463	.720	4.9	18.4
Totals		138	.486	.716	4.6	14.8

NBA REGULAR-SEASON STATISTICS

		G	MIN	FGs FG	FGs PCT	3-PT FGs FG	3-PT FGs PCT	FTs FT	FTs PCT	Rebounds OFF	Rebounds TOT	AST	STL	BLK	PTS	PPG
89-90	MIN	52	378	53	.393	3	.273	26	.813	24	70	18	10	6	135	2.6
90-91	MIN	75	824	118	.480	0	.000	58	.690	56	136	48	35	23	294	3.9
91-92	MIN	80	2540	463	.518	4	.174	186	.805	107	257	281	66	26	1116	13.9
92-93	MIN	80	3104	646	.517	2	.087	249	.841	89	247	235	85	21	1543	19.3
93-94	MIN	72	2182	434	.487	1	.125	187	.810	61	231	172	65	24	1056	14.7
Totals		359	9028	1714	.502	10	.152	706	.808	337	941	754	261	100	4144	11.5

MARK WEST

Team: Detroit Pistons
Position: Center
Height: 6'10" **Weight:** 246
Birthdate: November 5, 1960

NBA Experience: 11 years
College: Old Dominion
Acquired: Traded from Suns for 1996 and 1999 2nd-round picks, 8/94

Background: West ended his college career at Old Dominion as the third-leading shot-blocker in NCAA history. He was cast off by Dallas and Milwaukee in his first two seasons before landing with Cleveland in 1984-85. A 1988 trade to Phoenix gave him a chance to start. West led the league in field goal accuracy in 1989-90. He started 50 games last season, his 11th in the league, before being traded to Detroit over the summer.

Strengths: West is a workhorse, a capable shot-blocker, and a strong interior defender. He hits the boards and rarely takes a bad shot. He hasn't shot below 54 percent since his rookie year. His 501 consecutive games played is second to A.C. Green among active players.

Weaknesses: Foul trouble follows West. He is not much of an offensive threat and averaged only 4.7 PPG last season, his lowest since his first three years in the league. West can't dribble or pass and he's a poor free throw shooter.

Analysis: West is an old pro who helps his team with defense and hard work. He has stayed amazingly healthy during his career. Offensively, however, the declining West is a weak link. He'll play a lot with the Pistons, but only because they don't have a true starting center.

PLAYER SUMMARY

Will	block shots
Can't	score in an empty gym
Expect	a workhorse
Don't Expect	missed shots
Fantasy Value	$0
Card Value	5-8¢

COLLEGE STATISTICS

		G	FGP	FTP	RPG	PPG
79-80	OD	30	.475	.370	7.1	4.8
80-81	OD	28	.527	.578	10.3	10.9
81-82	OD	30	.610	.531	10.0	15.7
82-83	OD	29	.569	.491	10.8	14.4
Totals		117	.559	.514	9.5	11.4

NBA REGULAR-SEASON STATISTICS

		G	MIN	FGs FG	FGs PCT	3-PT FGs FG	3-PT FGs PCT	FTs FT	FTs PCT	Rebounds OFF	Rebounds TOT	AST	STL	BLK	PTS	PPG
83-84	DAL	34	202	15	.357	0	.000	7	.318	19	46	13	1	15	37	1.1
84-85	MIL/CLE	66	888	106	.546	0	.000	43	.494	90	251	15	13	49	255	3.9
85-86	CLE	67	1172	113	.541	0	.000	54	.524	97	322	20	27	62	280	4.2
86-87	CLE	78	1333	209	.543	0	.000	89	.514	126	339	41	22	81	507	6.5
87-88	CLE/PHO	83	2098	316	.551	0	.000	170	.596	165	523	74	47	147	802	9.7
88-89	PHO	82	2019	243	.653	0	.000	108	.535	167	551	39	35	187	594	7.2
89-90	PHO	82	2399	331	.625	0	.000	199	.691	212	728	45	36	184	861	10.5
90-91	PHO	82	1957	247	.647	0	.000	135	.637	171	564	37	32	161	629	7.7
91-92	PHO	82	1436	196	.632	0	.000	109	.655	134	372	22	14	81	501	6.1
92-93	PHO	82	1558	175	.614	0	.000	86	.518	153	458	29	16	103	436	5.3
93-94	PHO	82	1236	162	.566	0	.000	58	.500	112	295	33	31	109	382	4.7
Totals		820	16298	2113	.592	0	.000	1058	.582	1446	4449	368	274	1179	5284	6.4

ENNIS WHATLEY

Unrestricted Free Agent
Last Team: Atlanta Hawks
Position: Guard
Height: 6'3" **Weight:** 180

Birthdate: August 11, 1962
NBA Experience: 8 years
College: Alabama
Acquired: Signed as a free agent, 9/93

Background: Whatley enjoyed a fine two-year career at Alabama and was drafted 13th by the Kings in 1983, but he played his first two seasons with Chicago after a trade. Whatley has since played with Cleveland, Washington, San Antonio, Atlanta, the Clippers, Portland, and two CBA teams, and he spent the 1992-93 season in Israel. The 1993-94 season marked his second stint with the Hawks.

Strengths: Whatley must be admired for his perseverance. He has never played with the same team for more then two consecutive seasons yet he is still in the NBA after more than a decade of travel. Passing the ball is what puts bread on his table. He knows how to run an offense.

Weaknesses: Whatley is a marginal talent at the NBA level, or he would have found a more permanent home by now. He seems to be a last resort for teams in need of a guard. Whatley does nothing spectacular, does little scoring, and is a hit-or-miss defensive player. He's one-of-23 on 3-pointers for his career.

Analysis: Whatley is nothing if not a world traveler. He's played his eight NBA seasons with seven different teams, including two stops each in both Atlanta and Washington. He was named Import Player of the Year in Israel two years ago and played his first 82-game season last year with Atlanta.

PLAYER SUMMARY	
Will	distribute
Can't	unpack his bags
Expect	perseverance
Don't Expect	10 PPG
Fantasy Value	$0
Card Value	7-10¢

COLLEGE STATISTICS

		G	FGP	FTP	RPG	PPG
81-82	ALA	31	.495	.721	2.5	12.1
82-83	ALA	32	.500	.771	4.0	15.2
Totals		63	.498	.748	3.2	13.7

NBA REGULAR-SEASON STATISTICS

		G	MIN	FGs FG	FGs PCT	3-PT FGs FG	3-PT FGs PCT	FTs FT	FTs PCT	Rebounds OFF	Rebounds TOT	AST	STL	BLK	PTS	PPG
83-84	CHI	80	2159	261	.469	0	.000	146	.730	63	197	662	119	17	668	8.4
84-85	CHI	70	1385	140	.447	1	.111	68	.791	34	101	381	66	10	349	5.0
85-86	CLE/WAS/SA	14	107	15	.429	0	.000	5	.500	4	14	23	5	1	35	2.5
86-87	WAS	73	1816	246	.478	0	.000	126	.764	58	194	392	92	10	618	8.5
87-88	ATL	5	24	4	.444	0	.000	3	.750	0	4	2	2	0	11	2.2
88-89	LAC	8	90	12	.364	0	.000	10	.909	2	16	22	7	1	34	4.3
91-92	POR	23	209	21	.412	0	.000	27	.871	6	21	34	14	3	69	3.0
93-94	ATL	82	1004	120	.508	0	.000	52	.788	22	99	181	59	2	292	3.6
Totals		355	6794	819	.469	1	.043	437	.763	189	646	1697	364	44	2076	5.8

RANDY WHITE

Team: Dallas Mavericks
Position: Forward
Height: 6'8" **Weight:** 240
Birthdate: November 4, 1967

NBA Experience: 5 years
College: Louisiana Tech
Acquired: 1st-round pick in 1989 draft
(8th overall)

Background: White was named American South Player of the Year as a senior at Louisiana Tech, where he drew comparisons to former Bulldog standout Karl Malone. Those comparisons ceased in White's rookie year with Dallas, as he did not get off the bench for 26 of the last 55 games. He climbed to a career-high 9.7 PPG during 1992-93, but he underwent surgery in both knees after that year and spent most of last season on the injured list.

Strengths: White is strong, has athletic skills, and is a good rebounder. A former college center, he is willing to bang inside with the big guys. He runs the floor aggressively, scores off the offensive glass, and finishes on the break. He has displayed shot-blocking potential.

Weaknesses: It hasn't gone as planned for Dallas with this former inside player, even before his knee injuries. White considers himself a good outside shooter, yet he has been no such thing. He can be called a center in a small forward's body. Defensively, White is not quick enough to guard explosive forwards, and that does not take into account the step he's lost after two knee surgeries.

Analysis: White played with his back to the basket in college and has done little as a pro to prove he can be an effective face-up player. He'll have to make a huge recovery to save his NBA career. Torn cartilage in one knee and a calcium deposit in the other forced him to undergo the scope, and last season both knees continued to give him trouble.

PLAYER SUMMARY	
Will	run the floor
Can't	trade in his knees
Expect	a comeback attempt
Don't Expect	much quickness
Fantasy Value	$0
Card Value	5-10¢

COLLEGE STATISTICS

		G	FGP	FTP	RPG	PPG
85-86	LAT	34	.520	.667	4.6	9.2
86-87	LAT	30	.575	.677	6.5	12.6
87-88	LAT	31	.638	.640	11.6	18.6
88-89	LAT	32	.600	.747	10.5	21.2
Totals		127	.592	.689	8.3	15.3

NBA REGULAR-SEASON STATISTICS

		G	MIN	FGs FG	FGs PCT	3-PT FGs FG	3-PT FGs PCT	FTs FT	FTs PCT	Rebounds OFF	Rebounds TOT	AST	STL	BLK	PTS	PPG
89-90	DAL	55	707	93	.369	1	.071	50	.562	78	173	21	24	6	237	4.3
90-91	DAL	79	1901	265	.398	6	.162	159	.707	173	504	63	81	44	695	8.8
91-92	DAL	65	1021	145	.380	4	.148	124	.765	96	236	31	31	22	418	6.4
92-93	DAL	64	1433	235	.435	10	.238	138	.750	154	370	49	63	45	618	9.7
93-94	DAL	18	320	45	.402	6	.300	19	.576	30	83	11	10	10	115	6.4
Totals		281	5382	783	.401	27	.193	490	.707	531	1366	175	209	127	2083	7.4

DOMINIQUE WILKINS

Team: Boston Celtics
Position: Forward
Height: 6'8" **Weight:** 218
Birthdate: January 12, 1960

NBA Experience: 12 years
College: Georgia
Acquired: Signed as a free agent, 7/94

Background: Born in France while his father was stationed in the Air Force, Wilkins became an All-American at Georgia in 1982. He led the NBA in scoring in 1985-86 and has been named to the All-Star Game nine times. 'Nique's 1991-92 season was cut nearly in half by a ruptured Achilles tendon, but he has bounced back with a flourish. He scored 26 PPG during a 1993-94 season that saw him traded from Atlanta to the Clippers. He signed with Boston in July.

Strengths: The 11th NBA player to reach 23,000 career points, Wilkins has the ability to take over games. He has made himself a great outside shooter with 3-point range. "The Human Highlight Film" can still dunk with as much authority as anyone. He's a fine rebounder and an underrated team player.

Weaknesses: Wilkins has a weak left hand. 'Nique has never been a great defensive player even though he has had the athletic skills to reach such heights.

Analysis: Wilkins gained notoriety as a tremendous one-on-one player and has since added to his repertoire. He left Atlanta as the Hawks' all-time scoring leader last season after a February trade for Danny Manning. He will be the primary scorer on the Celtics, although it looks like he will never win an NBA title.

PLAYER SUMMARY	
Will	contend for scoring title
Can't	be left open
Expect	Hall of Fame induction
Don't Expect	less than 25 PPG
Fantasy Value	$18-21
Card Value	12-25¢

COLLEGE STATISTICS

		G	FGP	FTP	RPG	PPG
79-80	GA	16	.525	.730	6.5	18.6
80-81	GA	31	.533	.752	7.5	23.6
81-82	GA	31	.529	.644	8.1	21.3
Totals		78	.530	.699	7.5	21.6

NBA REGULAR-SEASON STATISTICS

		G	MIN	FGs FG	FGs PCT	3-PT FGs FG	3-PT FGs PCT	FTs FT	FTs PCT	Rebounds OFF	Rebounds TOT	AST	STL	BLK	PTS	PPG
82-83	ATL	82	2697	601	.493	2	.182	230	.682	226	478	129	84	63	1434	17.5
83-84	ATL	81	2961	684	.479	0	.000	382	.770	254	582	126	117	87	1750	21.6
84-85	ATL	81	3023	853	.451	25	.309	486	.806	226	557	200	135	54	2217	27.4
85-86	ATL	78	3049	888	.468	13	.186	577	.818	261	618	206	138	49	2366	30.3
86-87	ATL	79	2969	828	.463	31	.292	607	.818	210	494	261	117	51	2294	29.0
87-88	ATL	78	2948	909	.464	38	.295	541	.826	211	502	224	103	47	2397	30.7
88-89	ATL	80	2997	814	.464	29	.276	442	.844	256	553	211	117	52	2099	26.2
89-90	ATL	80	2888	810	.484	59	.322	459	.807	217	521	200	126	47	2138	26.7
90-91	ATL	81	3078	770	.470	85	.341	476	.829	261	732	265	123	65	2101	25.9
91-92	ATL	42	1601	424	.464	37	.289	294	.835	103	295	158	52	24	1179	28.1
92-93	ATL	71	2647	741	.468	120	.380	519	.828	187	482	227	70	27	2121	29.9
93-94	ATL/LAC	74	2635	698	.440	85	.288	442	.847	182	481	169	92	30	1923	26.0
Totals		907	33493	9020	.467	524	.311	5455	.813	2594	6295	2376	1274	596	24019	26.5

GERALD WILKINS

Team: Cleveland Cavaliers
Position: Guard
Height: 6'6" **Weight:** 210
Birthdate: September 11, 1963
NBA Experience: 9 years

College: Moberly Area; Tennessee-Chattanooga
Acquired: Signed as a free agent, 10/92

Background: Dominique's little brother, Gerald slam-dunked his way to three outstanding collegiate seasons at Tennessee-Chattanooga. A durable veteran, he has logged 80 or more games in eight of his nine pro campaigns. He spent his first seven seasons with the Knicks before Cleveland picked him up in 1992-93. Wilkins scored 14.3 PPG last season—near his career average.

Strengths: Wilkins is a fine defensive player because of his quickness, strength, leaping ability, and long arms. He also has some of his big brother's offensive explosiveness, although Gerald is not nearly as consistent as Dominique. He drives the entire lane with a single stride and is a dangerous 3-point shooter.

Weaknesses: Wilkins is a streaky shooter. He's capable of shooting the lights out one night and going 1-for-12 the next. He has tended toward the dramatic during his career instead of making sound decisions with the ball, although he has improved in that area.

Analysis: Few players defended Michael Jordan better than Wilkins, who is respected league-wide as a stopper. He puts his heart and soul into playing defense and makes it tough on his man. Wilkins is also capable of taking over games in transition or from the perimeter, even with a man in his face. But it's his durability and defense that make him the player he has become.

PLAYER SUMMARY	
Will	get in your face
Can't	outscore his brother
Expect	defense, streak shooting
Don't Expect	great consistency
Fantasy Value	$5-7
Card Value	7-10¢

COLLEGE STATISTICS

		G	FGP	FTP	RPG	PPG
81-82	MA	39	.551	.770	5.9	18.5
82-83	T-C	30	.483	.661	3.8	12.6
83-84	T-C	23	.542	.695	4.0	17.3
84-85	T-C	32	.519	.632	4.6	21.0
Totals		124	.526	.685	4.7	17.5

NBA REGULAR-SEASON STATISTICS

		G	MIN	FGs FG	FGs PCT	3-PT FGs FG	3-PT FGs PCT	FTs FT	FTs PCT	Rebounds OFF	Rebounds TOT	AST	STL	BLK	PTS	PPG
85-86	NY	81	2025	437	.468	7	.280	132	.557	92	208	161	68	9	1013	12.5
86-87	NY	80	2758	633	.486	26	.351	235	.701	120	294	354	88	18	1527	19.1
87-88	NY	81	2703	591	.446	39	.302	191	.786	106	270	326	90	22	1412	17.4
88-89	NY	81	2414	462	.451	51	.297	186	.756	95	244	274	115	22	1161	14.3
89-90	NY	82	2609	472	.457	39	.312	208	.803	133	371	330	95	21	1191	14.5
90-91	NY	68	2164	380	.473	9	.209	169	.820	78	207	275	82	23	938	13.8
91-92	NY	82	2344	431	.447	38	.352	116	.730	74	206	219	76	17	1016	12.4
92-93	CLE	80	2079	361	.453	16	.276	152	.840	74	214	183	78	18	890	11.1
93-94	CLE	82	2768	446	.457	84	.396	194	.776	106	303	255	105	38	1170	14.3
Totals		717	21864	4213	.460	309	.327	1583	.748	878	2317	2377	797	188	10318	14.4

BRIAN WILLIAMS

Team: Denver Nuggets
Position: Forward/Center
Height: 6'11" **Weight:** 242
Birthdate: April 6, 1969
NBA Experience: 3 years

College: Maryland; Arizona
Acquired: Traded from Magic for Todd Lichti, Anthony Cook, and a 1994 2nd-round pick, 8/93

Background: Williams, who played at three different high schools, had a terrific freshman season at Maryland but then transferred to Arizona. The Wildcats went 53-14 in his two seasons there. Drafted tenth by Orlando, Williams played in only 48 outings as a rookie. He missed most of the next season because of a bout with clinical depression and a broken hand. He was traded to Denver in August 1993 and saw his first full season, averaging 5.6 RPG and 8.0 PPG.

Strengths: Williams has an abundance of physical gifts. He is quick, jumps well, and runs the floor like a small forward. He's a promising shot-blocker and rebounder with huge hands and good fundamentals in his low-post defense. He also owns a soft touch in the paint as well as the ability to step outside and can 15-foot jumpers.

Weaknesses: Several concerns have surfaced regarding Williams in his first few years. His inconsistency dates back to college, but his rough bout with his emotions during the 1992-93 season was a much larger issue. On the floor, Williams's biggest drawback is his unwillingness to give up the ball once he touches it. He's not a good free throw shooter either.

Analysis: Consider last year a rookie season for Williams. In his first full slate of games, he provided rebounding and shot-blocking off the bench while contributing eight PPG and shooting a very promising .541 from the field. He also played a big part as Denver upset No. 1-seeded Seattle in the first round of the NBA playoffs. He seems to be over his off-court problems and has a bright future ahead of him.

PLAYER SUMMARY	
Will	rebound, defend
Can't	give up the ball
Expect	more than 1 BPG
Don't Expect	stardom
Fantasy Value	$6-8
Card Value	8-15¢

COLLEGE STATISTICS

		G	FGP	FTP	RPG	PPG
87-88	MD	29	.600	.671	6.1	12.5
89-90	ARIZ	32	.553	.727	5.7	10.6
90-91	ARIZ	35	.619	.673	7.8	14.0
Totals		96	.594	.691	6.6	12.4

NBA REGULAR-SEASON STATISTICS

				FGs		3-PT FGs		FTs		Rebounds						
		G	MIN	FG	PCT	FG	PCT	FT	PCT	OFF	TOT	AST	STL	BLK	PTS	PPG
91-92	ORL	48	905	171	.528	0	.000	95	.669	115	272	33	41	53	437	9.1
92-93	ORL	21	240	40	.513	0	.000	16	.800	24	56	5	14	17	96	4.6
93-94	DEN	80	1507	251	.541	0	.000	137	.649	138	446	50	49	87	639	8.0
Totals		149	2652	462	.533	0	.000	248	.665	277	774	88	104	157	1172	7.9

BUCK WILLIAMS

Team: Portland Trail Blazers
Position: Forward
Height: 6'8" **Weight:** 225
Birthdate: March 8, 1960

NBA Experience: 13 years
College: Maryland
Acquired: Traded from Nets for Sam Bowie and a 1989 1st-round pick, 6/89

Background: Williams turned pro after his junior season at Maryland, was named 1982 NBA Rookie of the Year, and played in three All-Star Games as a Net. He helped lead Portland to the championship series after the 1989-90 and 1991-92 seasons and won the NBA's field goal-percentage crown in 1990-91 and 1991-92. The durable Williams played in his 1,000th career game last season.

Strengths: Williams's calling card is rebounding, and he also ranks among the best low-post defenders. Offensively, he converts short jumpers and hooks and never takes a bad shot. He has never shot less than 51 percent from the field. Williams brings a great attitude to work.

Weaknesses: Williams is a below-average passer and does not handle the ball well in the open court. He is a poor free throw shooter and does not score like he used to.

Analysis: Williams, one of the hardest-working men the game has known, continues to lead by example. He has missed five games over the last five years and his businesslike approach is contagious. He is approaching 15,000 career points and has over 11,000 career rebounds to his credit.

PLAYER SUMMARY	
Will	clear the boards
Can't	hit with range
Expect	Hall of Fame induction
Don't Expect	missed starts
Fantasy Value	$3-5
Card Value	5-10¢

COLLEGE STATISTICS

		G	FGP	FTP	RPG	PPG
78-79	MD	30	.583	.550	10.8	10.0
79-80	MD	24	.606	.664	10.1	15.5
80-81	MD	31	.647	.637	11.7	15.5
Totals		85	.615	.623	10.9	13.6

NBA REGULAR-SEASON STATISTICS

				FGs		3-PT FGs		FTs		Rebounds						
		G	MIN	FG	PCT	FG	PCT	FT	PCT	OFF	TOT	AST	STL	BLK	PTS	PPG
81-82	NJ	82	2825	513	.582	0	.000	242	.624	347	1005	107	84	84	1268	15.5
82-83	NJ	82	2961	536	.588	0	.000	324	.620	365	1027	125	91	110	1396	17.0
83-84	NJ	81	3003	495	.535	0	.000	284	.570	355	1000	130	81	125	1274	15.7
84-85	NJ	82	3182	577	.530	1	.250	336	.625	323	1005	167	63	110	1491	18.2
85-86	NJ	82	3070	500	.523	0	.000	301	.676	329	986	131	73	96	1301	15.9
86-87	NJ	82	2976	521	.557	0	.000	430	.731	322	1023	129	78	91	1472	18.0
87-88	NJ	70	2637	466	.560	1	1.000	346	.668	298	834	109	68	44	1279	18.3
88-89	NJ	74	2446	373	.531	0	.000	213	.666	249	696	78	61	36	959	13.0
89-90	POR	82	2801	413	.548	0	.000	288	.706	250	800	116	69	39	1114	13.6
90-91	POR	80	2582	358	.602	0	.000	217	.705	227	751	97	47	47	933	11.7
91-92	POR	80	2519	340	.604	0	.000	221	.754	260	704	108	62	41	901	11.3
92-93	POR	82	2498	270	.511	0	.000	138	.645	232	690	75	81	61	678	8.3
93-94	POR	81	2636	291	.555	0	.000	201	.679	315	843	80	58	47	783	9.7
Totals		1040	36136	5653	.554	2	.083	3541	.663	3872	11364	1452	916	931	14849	14.3

JAYSON WILLIAMS

Team: New Jersey Nets
Position: Forward
Height: 6'10" **Weight:** 245
Birthdate: February 22, 1968

NBA Experience: 4 years
College: St. John's
Acquired: Traded from 76ers for conditional draft picks, 10/92

Background: After guiding St. John's to an NIT title in 1989 as a junior (he was tourney MVP), Williams broke his foot halfway through his senior season. He was drafted by Phoenix in 1990 but was traded to the 76ers four months later. He missed 132 games over his first three seasons, mostly because of injuries. With New Jersey last season, he finally played almost a full schedule. Chuck Daly used him for about 12 minutes a game.

Strengths: Williams has shown signs of being a productive offensive player. He can get his points by posting up, dropping short- to medium-range jump shots, or by converting offensive rebounds. He has a big-league body, save for its history of injuries. Williams is blessed with good athletic skills for his size.

Weaknesses: Injuries have seriously hurt the progress Williams has managed to make. He also takes terrible shots and his field goal percentage reflects it. He too often settles for jumpers, and his outside shooting is far from reliable. On the defensive end, he has never showed much promise. He should block more shots and grab more rebounds than he does. Some have questioned his maturity and work ethic.

Analysis: Williams finally played 70 games last season, but he did not show the kind of form one might expect from a first-rounder in his fourth year in the league. He scored less than five PPG and was horribly inconsistent. In addition to his other problems, Williams seems to have no luck. Hours after coming off the injured list in 1992-93, he broke an ankle while lifting weights in his home.

PLAYER SUMMARY	
Will	hit short jumpers
Can't	shoot for percentage
Expect	occasional surges
Don't Expect	good fortune
Fantasy Value	$0
Card Value	7-12¢

COLLEGE STATISTICS

		G	FGP	FTP	RPG	PPG
87-88	STJ	28	.513	.600	5.1	9.9
88-89	STJ	31	.573	.702	7.9	19.5
89-90	STJ	13	.534	.613	7.8	14.6
Totals		72	.550	.652	6.8	14.9

NBA REGULAR-SEASON STATISTICS

		G	MIN	FGs		3-PT FGs		Fts		Rebounds		AST	STL	BLK	PTS	PPG
				FG	PCT	FG	PCT	FT	PCT	OFF	TOT					
90-91	PHI	52	508	72	.447	1	.500	37	.661	41	111	16	9	6	182	3.5
91-92	PHI	50	646	75	.364	0	.000	56	.636	62	145	12	20	20	206	4.1
92-93	NJ	12	139	21	.457	0	.000	7	.389	22	41	0	4	4	49	4.1
93-94	NJ	70	877	125	.427	0	.000	72	.605	109	263	26	17	36	322	4.6
Totals		184	2170	293	.415	1	.500	172	.612	234	560	54	50	66	759	4.1

JOHN WILLIAMS

Team: Cleveland Cavaliers
Position: Forward/Center
Height: 6'11" **Weight:** 245
Birthdate: August 9, 1962

NBA Experience: 8 years
College: Tulane
Acquired: 2nd-round pick in 1985
draft (45th overall)

Background: Williams's involvement in an alleged point-fixing scandal at Tulane rocked the college basketball world in the mid-1980s. Despite the controversy, he paced the Green Wave in scoring three of his four seasons. Williams was named to the NBA All-Rookie Team in 1987. He went from being one of the league's top sixth men to a starter with the Cavs last season, although nagging injuries have slowed him at times.

Strengths: Williams can shoot, go hard to the basket, draw fouls, block shots, crash the boards, and muscle people off the ball. His ability to play shut-down defense at multiple positions may be his greatest asset. Williams has thrived as a starter and a reserve. He gives his team a lift with his aggressive, unselfish play.

Weaknesses: Passing and ball-handling aren't his best skills, and his left hand is a little shaky. "Hot Rod" also picks up his share of fouls. His late-season and playoff injury problems hurt the Cavs last season.

Analysis: Williams makes almost $4 million a year and works to earn every penny. He is a force in the paint on both ends, runs the floor, and can stick 15-footers in streaks. He has averaged between 11 and 14 PPG each of the last four years and earned a spot in the starting lineup last season. Look for him to post bigger numbers in that role.

PLAYER SUMMARY	
Will	block shots
Can't	handle the ball
Expect	interior defense
Don't Expect	less than 11 PPG
Fantasy Value	$13-16
Card Value	7-12¢

COLLEGE STATISTICS

		G	FGP	FTP	RPG	PPG
81-82	TUL	28	.584	.662	7.2	14.8
82-83	TUL	31	.476	.756	5.4	12.4
83-84	TUL	28	.569	.761	7.9	19.4
84-85	TUL	28	.566	.774	7.8	17.8
Totals		115	.549	.731	7.0	16.0

NBA REGULAR-SEASON STATISTICS

		G	MIN	FGs FG	FGs PCT	3-PT FGs FG	3-PT FGs PCT	FTs FT	FTs PCT	Rebounds OFF	Rebounds TOT	AST	STL	BLK	PTS	PPG
86-87	CLE	80	2714	435	.485	0	.000	298	.745	222	629	154	58	167	1168	14.6
87-88	CLE	77	2106	316	.477	0	.000	211	.756	159	506	103	61	145	843	10.9
88-89	CLE	82	2125	356	.509	1	.250	235	.748	173	477	108	77	134	948	11.6
89-90	CLE	82	2776	528	.493	0	.000	325	.739	220	663	168	86	167	1381	16.8
90-91	CLE	43	1293	199	.463	0	.000	107	.652	111	290	100	36	69	505	11.7
91-92	CLE	80	2432	341	.503	0	.000	270	.752	228	607	196	60	182	952	11.9
92-93	CLE	67	2055	263	.470	0	.000	212	.716	127	415	152	48	105	738	11.0
93-94	CLE	76	2660	394	.478	0	.000	252	.728	207	575	193	78	130	1040	13.7
Totals		587	18161	2832	.486	1	.091	1910	.735	1447	4162	1174	504	1099	7575	12.9

JOHN WILLIAMS

Unrestricted Free Agent
Last Team: Los Angeles Clippers
Position: Forward
Height: 6'9" **Weight:** 300
Birthdate: October 26, 1966

NBA Experience: 7 years
College: Louisiana St.
Acquired: Traded from Bullets for William Bedford and draft rights to Don MacLean, 10/92

Background: A product of the streets of Los Angeles, Williams played only two years of college ball at LSU. He was the SEC's top freshman in 1984-85 and a unanimous All-SEC pick in 1985-86. Eighteen games into the 1989-90 campaign, Williams severely injured his right knee and hasn't been the same since. He spent the 1991-92 season on the Bullets' suspended list after he reported to camp weighing 305 pounds. He started the 1993-94 season on the Clippers' suspended list and was let go after the season.

Strengths: Williams remains a bundle of potential, albeit an enormous bundle. When playing well, he can handle the ball, run the floor, go hard to the glass, and shoot a smooth mid-range jumper. His big, quick hands can make him deceivingly tough defensively. At his best, he's a rare mix of finesse and power.

Weaknesses: Enigma. Head case. Pain in the rear. Williams wore out his welcome in Washington and did not bounce back in his hometown. Williams has yet to show a willingness to keep his weight below the 300 mark regularly. He has been horribly inconsistent throughout his career.

Analysis: Somewhere inside the body of Williams is a player with good skills. Don't count on that player ever emerging, however, because "Hot Plate" seems to have buried himself under a thick layer of flesh and inconsistency.

PLAYER SUMMARY	
Will	show some touch
Can't	control his weight
Expect	horrible inconsistency
Don't Expect	productivity
Fantasy Value	$0
Card Value	7-12¢

COLLEGE STATISTICS

		G	FGP	FTP	RPG	PPG
84-85	LSU	29	.534	.765	6.6	13.4
85-86	LSU	37	.498	.774	8.5	17.8
Totals		66	.511	.771	7.6	15.8

NBA REGULAR-SEASON STATISTICS

		G	MIN	FGs FG	FGs PCT	3-PT FGs FG	3-PT FGs PCT	FTs FT	FTs PCT	Rebounds OFF	Rebounds TOT	AST	STL	BLK	PTS	PPG
86-87	WAS	78	1773	283	.454	8	.222	144	.646	130	366	191	129	30	718	9.2
87-88	WAS	82	2428	427	.469	5	.132	188	.734	127	444	232	117	34	1047	12.8
88-89	WAS	82	2413	438	.466	19	.268	225	.776	158	573	356	142	70	1120	13.7
89-90	WAS	18	632	130	.474	2	.111	65	.774	27	136	84	21	9	327	18.2
90-91	WAS	33	941	164	.417	10	.244	73	.753	42	177	133	39	6	411	12.5
92-93	LAC	74	1638	205	.430	12	.226	70	.543	88	316	142	83	23	492	6.6
93-94	LAC	34	725	81	.431	5	.250	24	.667	37	127	97	25	10	191	5.6
Totals		401	10550	1728	.454	61	.220	789	.708	749	2367	1235	556	182	4306	10.7

KENNY WILLIAMS

Unrestricted Free Agent
Last Team: Indiana Pacers
Position: Forward
Height: 6'9" **Weight:** 205
Birthdate: June 9, 1969

NBA Experience: 4 years
College: Barton County
Acquired: 2nd-round pick in 1990 draft (46th overall)

Background: Recognized as one of the top five high school players in America in 1988, Williams was recruited by North Carolina but never enrolled due to poor grades. He played one year of junior college ball at Barton County Community College in Kansas. Indiana was impressed enough with his camp showings to select him in 1990. He has seen limited minutes, but in 1993-94 Williams averaged a career-high 6.3 PPG. He became a free agent after the season.

Strengths: Williams plays above the rim. He's an excellent athlete who can run the floor all day long, has a quick first step, and knows how to get to the hoop. Williams passes and jumps exceptionally well and he's pretty solid defensively. He can block shots and rebound, especially on the offensive glass. His work ethic and attitude can't be questioned.

Weaknesses: Williams is a big forward playing in a small forward's body. He is more effective as an inside player than on the perimeter but lacks the size to dominate in the paint. His field goal percentage is boosted by "garbage buckets." Although he plays hard and has enjoyed some fine games, he has not been consistent enough to earn a lot of playing time.

Analysis: Williams, who remains a step behind in experience and solid fundamentals, has played a little more in the last two seasons. Last year was his best in several categories. In his lone start of the season, he led the Pacers to a victory over Phoenix with 18 points, 11 rebounds, and a career-high seven assists. He's capable of those kinds of games and should continue to improve.

PLAYER SUMMARY	
Will	run all night
Can't	rely on jumpers
Expect	further improvement
Don't Expect	many starts
Fantasy Value	$0
Card Value	5-10¢

COLLEGE STATISTICS

		G	FGP	FTP	RPG	PPG
88-89	BC	31	—	—	9.0	20.5
Totals		31	—	—	9.0	20.5

NBA REGULAR-SEASON STATISTICS

		G	MIN	FGs FG	FGs PCT	3-PT FGs FG	3-PT FGs PCT	FTs FT	FTs PCT	Rebounds OFF	Rebounds TOT	AST	STL	BLK	PTS	PPG
90-91	IND	75	527	93	.520	0	.000	34	.680	56	131	31	11	31	220	2.9
91-92	IND	60	565	113	.518	0	.000	26	.605	64	129	40	20	41	252	4.2
92-93	IND	57	844	150	.532	0	.000	48	.706	102	228	38	21	45	348	6.1
93-94	IND	68	982	191	.488	0	.000	45	.703	93	205	52	24	49	427	6.3
Totals		260	2918	547	.511	0	.000	153	.680	315	693	161	76	166	1247	4.8

LORENZO WILLIAMS

Team: Dallas Mavericks
Position: Forward/Center
Height: 6'9″ **Weight:** 200
Birthdate: July 15, 1969

NBA Experience: 2 years
College: Polk; Stetson
Acquired: Signed as a free agent, 2/94

Background: Williams played two seasons at Polk Community College in Florida before becoming the all-time Trans America Athletic Conference leader in blocked shots at Stetson. His average of 10.1 RPG as a senior was an all-time Hatter record. Williams was not drafted in 1991 and played in the USBL, CBA, and the now-defunct Global Basketball Association before playing an NBA game. He has played with three different teams in each of his two NBA seasons.

Strengths: Williams is an accomplished rebounder and shot-blocker who can get the job done at any level. He averaged 5.7 RPG last season despite playing less than 20 minutes per outing. He has blocked almost one shot per game during his 65 NBA contests. He has great timing, runs the floor, and works hard at the defensive end. He has put countless hours into getting a shot in the big leagues.

Weaknesses: Williams has some glaring offensive deficiencies. He does not own a vast array of low-post moves nor the strength to power for inside buckets. On top of that, he is a poor perimeter shooter who makes fewer than half of his free throw attempts. For those reasons, he will never score a lot of points in the NBA. He could stand to become more consistent in his decision-making.

Analysis: Williams has been on a whirlwind basketball tour through four different leagues and has served brief NBA stints with Charlotte (twice), Orlando (twice), Boston, and finally Dallas, where he signed for the remainder of the season and the 1994-95 campaign. To stay on the team, he'll have to continue rebounding and blocking shots while showing at least some ability to score.

PLAYER SUMMARY

Will ....hit the boards
Can't ....make his FTs
Expect ....a block a night
Don't Expect..........explosive scoring
Fantasy Value.................................$0
Card Value ....5-10¢

COLLEGE STATISTICS

		G	FGP	FTP	RPG	PPG
89-90	STET	32	.520	.295	8.4	7.8
90-91	STET	31	.540	.667	10.1	9.2
Totals		63	.530	.484	9.2	8.5

NBA REGULAR-SEASON STATISTICS

	G	MIN	FGs FG	FGs PCT	3-PT FGs FG	3-PT FGs PCT	FTs FT	FTs PCT	Rebounds OFF	Rebounds TOT	AST	STL	BLK	PTS	PPG
92-93 CHA/ORL/BOS	27	179	17	.472	0	.000	2	.286	17	55	5	5	17	36	1.3
93-94 ORL/CHA/DAL	38	716	49	.445	0	.000	12	.429	95	217	25	18	46	110	2.9
Totals	65	895	66	.452	0	.000	14	.400	112	272	30	23	63	146	2.2

MICHEAL WILLIAMS

Team: Minnesota Timberwolves
Position: Guard
Height: 6'2" **Weight:** 175
Birthdate: July 23, 1966
NBA Experience: 6 years

College: Baylor
Acquired: Traded from Pacers with Chuck Person for Pooh Richardson and Sam Mitchell, 9/92

Background: Williams, a two-time all-league selection at Baylor, has played for a slew of pro teams. A member of Detroit's championship team in 1988-89, he spent the following season with Phoenix, Dallas, Charlotte, and the CBA's Rapid City Thrillers. He was signed by Indiana and became one of the league's top thieves. He was traded to Minnesota before the 1992-93 campaign and has led the team in assists and steals in both seasons there.

Strengths: Williams has emerged in the NBA with his blistering speed, quick hands, and improved playmaking. He possesses a lightning-quick first step and an above-average pull-up jumper. He has been a hustling defender who comes up with a lot of steals. He made a league-record 97 consecutive free throws before missing one early last season.

Weaknesses: Williams is not the defensive player his numbers say he is. He gets beaten routinely by his man and comes up with steals because he gambles for them. He's no longer one of the best in the league in that category. Williams is not a consistent outside shooter and there are a lot more effective set-up men in the game.

Analysis: Williams might not be a star, but it's a credit to him that he has become a starting point guard who scores, distributes, and thrives at a fast pace. Perhaps the biggest knock on him is that the Timberwolves have not improved much since he has been running the show. He is hardly the only one to blame.

PLAYER SUMMARY	
Will	get to the hoop
Can't	shut down his man
Expect	great quickness
Don't Expect	many missed FTs
Fantasy Value	$16-19
Card Value	5-10¢

COLLEGE STATISTICS

		G	FGP	FTP	APG	PPG
84-85	BAY	28	.487	.793	2.4	14.6
85-86	BAY	22	.462	.806	2.7	13.0
86-87	BAY	31	.475	.714	5.1	17.2
87-88	BAY	34	.505	.697	5.4	18.4
Totals		115	.485	.738	4.0	16.1

NBA REGULAR-SEASON STATISTICS

				FGs		3-PT FGs		FTs		Rebounds						
		G	MIN	FG	PCT	FG	PCT	FT	PCT	OFF	TOT	AST	STL	BLK	PTS	PPG
88-89	DET	49	358	47	.364	2	.222	31	.660	9	27	70	13	3	127	2.6
89-90	PHO/CHA	28	329	60	.504	0	.000	36	.783	12	32	81	22	1	156	5.6
90-91	IND	73	1706	261	.499	1	.143	290	.879	49	176	348	150	17	813	11.1
91-92	IND	79	2750	404	.490	8	.242	372	.871	73	282	647	233	22	1188	15.0
92-93	MIN	76	2661	353	.446	26	.243	419	.907	84	273	661	165	23	1151	15.1
93-94	MIN	71	2206	314	.457	10	.222	333	.839	67	221	512	118	24	971	13.7
Totals		376	10010	1439	.468	47	.230	1481	.867	294	1011	2319	701	90	4406	11.7

REGGIE WILLIAMS

Team: Denver Nuggets   **NBA Experience:** 7 years
Position: Forward/Guard   **College:** Georgetown
Height: 6'7" **Weight:** 195   **Acquired:** Signed as a free agent,
Birthdate: March 5, 1964   1/91

Background: As a senior at Georgetown, Williams was an All-American and Big East Player of the Year. He was named NCAA Tournament MVP when the Hoyas won the title in 1984. He was a letdown with the Clippers, Cleveland, and San Antonio and was released by the Spurs in 1990-91. After being signed by Denver, Williams was one of the most improved players in the league in 1991-92. He has averaged at least 13 PPG in three-plus years with the Nuggets.

Strengths: Williams knocks down jumpers with 3-point range and brings a scorer's mentality to the court. After his first few years, no one would have believed he could thrive as a shooter. He also rebounds, comes up with steals, runs the floor, finds open men, and has a quick first step to the hoop.

Weaknesses: Williams lacks consistency in his play. He is a below-average ball-handler and his 3-point percentage has taken a big drop in the last two years. He also posted his worst field goal percentage as a Nugget last year after three years of much-improved gunning.

Analysis: Williams's career has been a great roller-coaster ride. Projected as a star coming out of college, he was a first-rate flop for three-plus years before finding new life in the Rockies. He could stand to be more consistent, but he has to be admired for the lows he has overcome during his career.

PLAYER SUMMARY	
Will	fire from long range
Can't	dazzle with his dribble
Expect	streak shooting
Don't Expect	much consistency
Fantasy Value	$9-11
Card Value	7-12¢

COLLEGE STATISTICS

		G	FGP	FTP	RPG	PPG
83-84	GEOR	37	.433	.768	3.5	9.1
84-85	GEOR	35	.506	.755	5.7	11.9
85-86	GEOR	32	.528	.732	8.2	17.6
86-87	GEOR	34	.482	.804	8.6	23.6
Totals		138	.490	.768	6.4	15.3

NBA REGULAR-SEASON STATISTICS

		G	MIN	FGs		3-PT FGs		FTs		Rebounds		AST	STL	BLK	PTS	PPG
				FG	PCT	FG	PCT	FT	PCT	OFF	TOT					
87-88	LAC	35	857	152	.356	13	.224	48	.727	55	118	58	29	21	365	10.4
88-89	LAC	63	1303	260	.438	30	.288	92	.754	70	179	103	81	29	642	10.2
89-90	LAC/CLE/SA															
		47	743	131	.388	6	.162	52	.765	28	83	53	32	14	320	6.8
90-91	SA/DEN	73	1896	384	.449	57	.363	166	.843	133	306	133	113	41	991	13.6
91-92	DEN	81	2623	601	.471	56	.359	216	.803	145	405	235	148	68	1474	18.2
92-93	DEN	79	2722	535	.458	33	.270	238	.804	132	428	295	126	76	1341	17.0
93-94	DEN	82	2654	418	.412	64	.278	165	.733	98	392	300	117	66	1065	13.0
Totals		460	12798	2481	.437	259	.300	977	.786	661	1911	1177	646	315	6198	13.5

SCOTT WILLIAMS

Team: Philadelphia 76ers
Position: Center/Forward
Height: 6'10" **Weight:** 230
Birthdate: March 21, 1968

NBA Experience: 4 years
College: North Carolina
Acquired: Signed as a free agent, 7/94

Background: Williams was Dean Smith's first West Coast recruit. Though personal tragedy affected his early development, Williams paced Carolina in rebounding and blocked shots as a senior. After being bypassed in the 1990 NBA draft, Williams was signed by the Bulls as a free agent. He was the only rookie on the 1991 championship squad and helped produce two subsequent Chicago titles. He missed most of last year with a knee injury and then signed with Philadelphia after the season.

Strengths: Williams provides size, rebounding, shot-blocking ability, and low-post defense. He is quick for his size, is agile, and possesses a nice touch within 12-15 feet of the bucket. He gets a lot of points off put-backs. Williams has big, strong hands and an above-average feel for the game. He's improved his scoring every campaign.

Weaknesses: Williams has yet to develop a wide range of effective post moves or the confidence to attack the hoop against the league's more talented big men. His shooting stroke is far from reliable, as a check of his free throw percentage will confirm. He has been plagued by shoulder and knee injuries. He did not play until February of last season.

Analysis: Williams has spent most of his career as part of a four-headed center situation in Chicago, although he will likely play both power forward and center with the Sixers. He signed a huge multi-million-dollar contract with Philly and now must deal with the burden of living up to that pact. He'll need to put a few more points on the board.

PLAYER SUMMARY	
Will	block shots
Can't	rely on jumpers
Expect	adequate defense
Don't Expect	lots of scoring
Fantasy Value	$4-6
Card Value	5-10¢

COLLEGE STATISTICS

		G	FGP	FTP	RPG	PPG
86-87	NC	36	.497	.558	4.2	5.5
87-88	NC	34	.572	.673	6.4	12.8
88-89	NC	35	.556	.654	7.3	11.4
89-90	NC	33	.554	.615	7.3	14.5
Totals		138	.551	.636	6.2	10.9

NBA REGULAR-SEASON STATISTICS

			FGs		3-PT FGs		FTs		Rebounds						
	G	MIN	FG	PCT	FG	PCT	FT	PCT	OFF	TOT	AST	STL	BLK	PTS	PPG
90-91 CHI	51	337	53	.510	1	.500	20	.714	42	98	16	12	13	127	2.5
91-92 CHI	63	690	83	.483	0	.000	48	.649	90	247	50	13	36	214	3.4
92-93 CHI	71	1369	166	.466	0	.000	90	.714	168	451	68	55	66	422	5.9
93-94 CHI	38	638	114	.483	1	.200	60	.612	69	181	39	16	21	289	7.6
Totals	223	3034	416	.479	2	.118	218	.669	369	977	173	96	136	1052	4.7

WALT WILLIAMS

Team: Sacramento Kings
Position: Guard/Forward
Height: 6'8" **Weight:** 230
Birthdate: April 16, 1970

NBA Experience: 2 years
College: Maryland
Acquired: 1st-round pick in 1992 draft (7th overall)

Background: Williams, the Washington, D.C.-area prep Player of the Year in 1988, broke Len Bias's Maryland record for points in a season as a senior. He averaged 26.8 points, 5.6 rebounds, 3.6 assists, and 2.1 steals per outing in his final season, then was drafted seventh in 1992 by Sacramento. Williams earned second-team NBA All-Rookie honors in 1992-93, averaging 17.0 PPG, before dropping to 11.2 PPG last season.

Strengths: Williams has to be regarded as one of the more versatile players around. By late December of his rookie season, he had seen action at all five positions. He is a promising scorer with creative moves, a quick release, 3-point range, and a post-up game. There is very little Williams is unable to do offensively. He is both productive and exciting on that end of the court.

Weaknesses: There are serious doubts about the shooting touch of Williams, who converted just 39 percent of his field goals last season. His 3-point percentage is also well below par. Williams plays defense like a lot of scorers, which is to say his interests and abilities are elsewhere. He has fouled out 12 times in 116 pro games. While possessing great versatility, Williams is not a great pure athlete.

Analysis: Williams has had much to overcome during his first two seasons. A broken finger and right leg injury have kept him from playing a full schedule, and he had to cope with the death of his father to cancer two years ago. His rookie year was fabulous under those circumstances, but last season was a disappointment. He must develop some consistency with his jumper and play some defense if he hopes to become a star like his idol, George Gervin.

PLAYER SUMMARY	
Will	play multiple positions
Can't	star on defense
Expect	improved scoring
Don't Expect	steady shooting
Fantasy Value	$7-9
Card Value	12-25¢

COLLEGE STATISTICS

		G	FGP	FTP	RPG	PPG
88-89	MD	26	.441	.623	3.5	7.3
89-90	MD	33	.483	.776	4.2	12.7
90-91	MD	17	.449	.837	5.1	18.7
91-92	MD	29	.472	.758	5.6	26.8
Totals		105	.466	.762	4.6	16.2

NBA REGULAR-SEASON STATISTICS

		G	MIN	FGs		3-PT FGs		FTs		Rebounds		AST	STL	BLK	PTS	PPG
				FG	PCT	FG	PCT	FT	PCT	OFF	TOT					
92-93	SAC	59	1673	358	.435	61	.319	224	.742	115	265	178	66	29	1001	17.0
93-94	SAC	57	1356	226	.390	38	.288	148	.635	71	235	132	52	23	638	11.2
Totals		116	3029	584	.416	99	.307	372	.695	186	500	310	118	52	1639	14.1

KEVIN WILLIS

Team: Atlanta Hawks
Position: Forward/Center
Height: 7'0" **Weight:** 235
Birthdate: September 6, 1962

NBA Experience: 9 years
College: Michigan St.
Acquired: 1st-round pick in 1984 draft
(11th overall)

Background: Willis led the Big Ten in rebounding and field goal percentage as a junior at Michigan State, where he received all-conference mention as a senior. He has played nine pro seasons with Atlanta, sitting out in 1988-89 with a broken left foot. He dedicated himself to rebounding in 1991-92, played in his first All-Star Game, and has been among the league's top five rebounders ever since.

Strengths: Willis is a strong rebounder and a productive low-post scorer. Even his teammates clear out of the way when he attacks the glass. He averaged a career-high 19.1 PPG last season with a steady medium-range jumper and nifty hook shot. He runs the floor well for a seven-footer and has become a well-rounded player.

Weaknesses: Willis is not an accomplished passer, ball-handler, or free throw shooter. He has been accused of making poor offensive decisions throughout his career, but he has come a long way in that area in the last few years. He should swat more shots than he does.

Analysis: Willis was one of the most improved players in the league three years ago, and now he is firmly established as one of the go-to guys on an Atlanta team that posted the best record in the Eastern Conference last season. He enjoyed his best offensive season, surpassed the 10,000-point mark, and remains a force on the boards.

PLAYER SUMMARY	
Will	score in the post
Can't	dominate on defense
Expect	12-plus RPG
Don't Expect	a shy shooter
Fantasy Value	$30-35
Card Value	5-10¢

COLLEGE STATISTICS

		G	FGP	FTP	RPG	PPG
81-82	MSU	27	.474	.567	4.2	6.0
82-83	MSU	27	.596	.514	9.6	13.3
83-84	MSU	25	.492	.661	7.7	11.0
Totals		79	.530	.579	7.1	10.1

NBA REGULAR-SEASON STATISTICS

				FGs		3-PT FGs		FTs		Rebounds						
		G	MIN	FG	PCT	FG	PCT	FT	PCT	OFF	TOT	AST	STL	BLK	PTS	PPG
84-85	ATL	82	1785	322	.467	2	.222	119	.657	177	522	36	31	49	765	9.3
85-86	ATL	82	2300	419	.517	0	.000	172	.654	243	704	45	66	44	1010	12.3
86-87	ATL	81	2626	538	.536	1	.250	227	.709	321	849	62	65	61	1304	16.1
87-88	ATL	75	2091	356	.518	0	.000	159	.649	235	547	28	68	42	871	11.6
89-90	ATL	81	2273	418	.519	2	.286	168	.683	253	645	57	63	47	1006	12.4
90-91	ATL	80	2373	444	.504	4	.400	159	.668	259	704	99	60	40	1051	13.1
91-92	ATL	81	2962	591	.483	6	.162	292	.804	418	1258	173	72	54	1480	18.3
92-93	ATL	80	2878	616	.506	7	.241	196	.653	335	1028	165	68	41	1435	17.9
93-94	ATL	80	2867	627	.499	9	.375	268	.713	335	963	150	79	38	1531	19.1
Totals		722	22155	4331	.505	31	.242	1760	.695	2576	7220	815	572	416	10453	14.5

TREVOR WILSON

Team: Sacramento Kings
Position: Forward
Height: 6'7" **Weight:** 210
Birthdate: March 16, 1968

NBA Experience: 2 years
College: UCLA
Acquired: Signed as a free agent, 12/93

Background: Wilson was a three-time All-Pac-10 honoree at UCLA, where he earned All-America recognition after averaging 17.2 PPG and 9.1 RPG as a senior. He finished his career behind only Lew Alcindor and Reggie Miller on the all-time Bruin scoring list. He played 25 games as a rookie with Atlanta before spending two years in Spain. Wilson returned last season with the Lakers and Sacramento.

Strengths: Wilson is an excellent athlete who gets up and down the floor like a guard. He looks to score and can be very good in that category. He has good quickness to get to the hoop, and he also uses his strong legs to attack the boards. Wilson is a solid rebounder at both ends. He grabbed ten-plus rebounds ten times in 57 games during the 1993-94 season.

Weaknesses: Wilson is too small to enjoy a productive career at power forward and does not have the range or consistency with his shooting to thrive as a small forward at the NBA level. His ball-handling is also suspect for a perimeter player. He posted far more turnovers than he did assists last season. A check of his free throw shooting says much about his touch with the basketball.

Analysis: Two years in Spain did wonders for Wilson, though not enough to stop the Lakers from letting him go in December 1993. Wilson averaged 21 points and 7.5 rebounds a game during his second year in Spain and played well on the Lakers' 1993 summer-league team, earning another NBA shot. Wilson is a superb athlete and has enjoyed some nice games, but he will be battling again for his roster spot in 1994-95.

PLAYER SUMMARY	
Will	run the floor
Can't	shoot FTs
Expect	rebounding
Don't Expect	offensive range
Fantasy Value	$1
Card Value	7-12¢

COLLEGE STATISTICS

		G	FGP	FTP	RPG	PPG
86-87	UCLA	32	.445	.726	4.8	6.2
87-88	UCLA	30	.521	.621	9.4	15.4
88-89	UCLA	31	.501	.576	8.7	18.4
89-90	UCLA	33	.495	.507	9.1	17.2
Totals		126	.498	.587	7.9	14.3

NBA REGULAR-SEASON STATISTICS

		G	MIN	FGs FG	FGs PCT	3-PT FGs FG	3-PT FGs PCT	FTs FT	FTs PCT	Rebounds OFF	Rebounds TOT	AST	STL	BLK	PTS	PPG
90-91	ATL	25	162	21	.300	0	.000	13	.500	16	40	11	5	1	55	2.2
93-94	LAL/SAC	57	1221	187	.482	0	.000	92	.554	120	273	72	38	11	466	8.2
Totals		82	1383	208	.454	0	.000	105	.547	136	313	83	43	12	521	6.4

DAVID WINGATE

Team: Charlotte Hornets
Position: Guard
Height: 6'5" **Weight:** 185
Birthdate: December 15, 1963

NBA Experience: 8 years
College: Georgetown
Acquired: Signed as a free agent, 11/92

Background: Wingate was a member of the great Georgetown teams of the mid-1980s. He was drafted by Philadelphia and played three years with the 76ers. He also spent two years in San Antonio, including a period in which the Spurs placed him on the suspended list following two off-court legal incidents. Charges were dropped, but the Spurs waived him. Wingate started with Washington in 1991-92 and in Charlotte for much of the last two seasons.

Strengths: Wingate is a certified stopper. He is quick, stays in front of his man, and goes after the ball. He can defend ones and twos effectively. He has greatly improved his shooting and is a reliable ball-handler and passer. He also rebounds well from the backcourt and is a strong finisher.

Weaknesses: Wingate is not a confident scorer, which makes him unique for a starting off guard. Many of his points come in transition. Very few of them come from 3-point range (nine treys over the last six years). Surgery on his left knee kept him out until January of last season.

Analysis: Wingate has enjoyed fine seasons with Washington and Charlotte. He can be effective starting or coming off the bench and has done more of the former than the latter with the Hornets. He won't wear out the scoring column like most shooting guards, but he'll make sure his man doesn't burn the nets either.

PLAYER SUMMARY

Will..........................thrive on defense
Can't..................................rely on range
Expect ....a certified stopper
Don't Expect ....10 PPG
Fantasy Value...............................$0
Card Value ....5-10¢

COLLEGE STATISTICS

		G	FGP	FTP	RPG	PPG
82-83	GEOR	32	.445	.702	3.0	12.0
83-84	GEOR	37	.435	.721	3.6	11.2
84-85	GEOR	38	.484	.689	3.6	12.4
85-86	GEOR	32	.497	.755	4.0	15.9
Totals		139	.467	.719	3.6	12.8

NBA REGULAR-SEASON STATISTICS

				FGs		3-PT FGs		FTs		Rebounds						
		G	MIN	FG	PCT	FG	PCT	FT	PCT	OFF	TOT	AST	STL	BLK	PTS	PPG
86-87	PHI	77	1612	259	.430	13	.250	149	.741	70	156	155	93	19	680	8.8
87-88	PHI	61	1609	218	.400	10	.250	99	.750	44	101	119	47	22	545	8.9
88-89	PHI	33	372	54	.470	2	.333	27	.794	12	37	73	9	2	137	4.2
89-90	SA	78	1856	220	.448	0	.000	87	.777	62	195	208	89	18	527	6.8
90-91	SA	25	563	53	.384	1	.111	29	.707	24	75	46	19	5	136	5.4
91-92	WAS	81	2127	266	.465	1	.056	105	.719	80	269	247	123	21	638	7.9
92-93	CHA	72	1471	180	.536	1	.167	79	.738	49	174	183	66	9	440	6.1
93-94	CHA	50	1005	136	.481	4	.333	34	.667	30	134	104	42	6	310	6.2
Totals		477	10425	1386	.450	32	.205	609	.739	371	1141	1135	488	102	3413	7.2

DAVID WOOD

Unrestricted Free Agent
Last Team: Detroit Pistons
Position: Forward
Height: 6'9" **Weight:** 235
Birthdate: November 11, 1964

NBA Experience: 4 years
College: Skagit Valley; Nevada-Reno
Acquired: Traded from Spurs with Sean Elliott for Dennis Rodman and Isaiah Morris, 10/93

Background: Wood was a center at Nevada-Reno, where he transferred after beginning his college career at Skagit Valley Junior College. He played two games for Chicago in 1988-89 but spent most of his first three years in the CBA and Europe. Wood played all 82 games with Houston in 1990-91, returned to Spain in 1991-92, and has since played single years for the Spurs and Pistons. He became a free agent after last season.

Strengths: Wood does little that stands out to the casual observer, but he plays the game with a lot of heart and helps his teammates look better. He hustles, makes sound decisions, plays defense, rebounds, and is not afraid to mix it up. He is a very good 3-point marksman when he gets a good look at the basket. He made 22 of 49 last year.

Weaknesses: Offense has not been Wood's ticket back to the NBA. He does not create his own shot or shoot well on the move, he has a slow release, and he does not use his dribble effectively. He is not as capable as a perimeter defender as he is in the post. Wood lacks the physical gifts like quickness, speed, and leaping ability.

Analysis: The Pistons obtained Wood from the Spurs in the Dennis Rodman deal, and they got a guy who is not afraid to do the dirty work on the court. Unfortunately, Wood is sorely lacking in natural talent. He will never score 15 PPG as he did in Spain, although he will come to work every night and sink some 3-pointers.

PLAYER SUMMARY

Will ....hit from the arc
Can't ....burn his man
Expect......................sound decisions
Don't Expect ....the spectacular
Fantasy Value $0
Card Value ....5-10¢

COLLEGE STATISTICS

		G	FGP	FTP	RPG	PPG
83-84	SV	29	.546	.704	7.3	9.7
84-85	SV	26	.609	.719	11.6	18.2
86-87	N-R	28	.511	.662	6.0	9.0
87-88	N-R	30	.472	.726	9.4	12.1
Totals		113	.538	.709	8.5	12.1

NBA REGULAR-SEASON STATISTICS

		G	MIN	FGs FG	FGs PCT	3-PT FGs FG	3-PT FGs PCT	FTs FT	FTs PCT	Rebounds OFF	Rebounds TOT	AST	STL	BLK	PTS	PPG
88-89	CHI	2	2	0	.000	0	.000	0	.000	0	0	0	0	0	0	0.0
90-91	HOU	82	1421	148	.424	28	.311	108	.812	107	246	94	58	16	432	5.3
92-93	SA	64	598	52	.444	5	.238	46	.836	38	97	34	13	12	155	2.4
93-94	DET	78	1182	119	.459	22	.449	62	.756	104	239	51	39	19	322	4.1
Totals		226	3203	319	.440	55	.344	216	.800	249	582	179	110	47	909	4.0

ORLANDO WOOLRIDGE

Unrestricted Free Agent
Last Team: Philadelphia 76ers
Position: Forward
Height: 6'9" **Weight:** 215
Birthdate: December 16, 1959

NBA Experience: 13 years
College: Notre Dame
Acquired: Signed as a free agent, 11/93

Background: Woolridge ranked third in the nation in field goal percentage as a Notre Dame senior. He averaged more than 20 PPG for three straight NBA years with Chicago and New Jersey. He entered drug treatment in February 1988, and he returned with the Lakers in 1989-90. He was in the hunt for the 1991 scoring crown with Denver, finishing with 25.1 PPG. He's since played in Detroit, Milwaukee, and Philadelphia, although the Sixers let him go in July.

Strengths: Woolridge remains an explosive scorer with more than 13,000 points to his credit. Few are willing to stand in front of his muscular frame. He runs the floor well, can knock down jumpers, and will block a few shots.

Weaknesses: Woolridge has been pegged as a player who cares more about points than wins. He has never been known as a great defender or rebounder.

Analysis: Woolridge is a natural scorer who has beaten countless defenders off the dribble and still hits for a dozen points a night. However, every new team he has joined in his career has fared worse than it did the season before. That's seven teams and counting.

PLAYER SUMMARY

Will ....get his points
Can't ....star on defense
Expect...12 PPG
Don't Expect ....a team player
Fantasy Value $1-3
Card Value ....5-10¢

COLLEGE STATISTICS

		G	FGP	FTP	RPG	PPG
77-78	ND	24	.526	.485	2.1	4.1
78-79	ND	30	.573	.732	4.8	11.0
79-80	ND	27	.585	.692	6.9	12.2
80-81	ND	28	.650	.667	6.0	14.4
Totals		109	.595	.669	5.0	10.6

NBA REGULAR-SEASON STATISTICS

		G	MIN	FGs FG	FGs PCT	3-PT FGs FG	3-PT FGs PCT	FTs FT	FTs PCT	Rebounds OFF	Rebounds TOT	AST	STL	BLK	PTS	PPG
81-82	CHI	75	1188	202	.513	0	.000	144	.699	82	227	81	23	24	548	7.3
82-83	CHI	57	1627	361	.580	0	.000	217	.638	122	298	97	38	44	939	16.5
83-84	CHI	75	2544	570	.525	1	.500	303	.715	130	369	136	71	60	1444	19.3
84-85	CHI	77	2816	679	.554	0	.000	409	.785	158	435	135	58	38	1767	22.9
85-86	CHI	70	2248	540	.495	4	.174	364	.788	150	350	213	49	47	1448	20.7
86-87	NJ	75	2638	556	.521	1	.125	438	.777	118	367	261	54	86	1551	20.7
87-88	NJ	19	622	110	.445	0	.000	92	.708	31	91	71	13	20	312	16.4
88-89	LAL	74	1491	231	.468	0	.000	253	.738	81	270	58	30	65	715	9.7
89-90	LAL	62	1421	306	.556	0	.000	176	.733	49	185	96	39	46	788	12.7
90-91	DEN	53	1823	490	.498	0	.000	350	.797	141	361	119	69	23	1330	25.1
91-92	DET	82	2113	452	.498	1	.111	241	.683	109	260	88	41	33	1146	14.0
92-93	DET/MIL	58	1555	289	.482	0	.000	120	.678	87	185	115	27	27	698	12.0
93-94	PHI	74	1955	364	.471	1	.071	208	.689	103	298	139	41	56	937	12.7
Totals		851	24041	5150	.513	8	.091	3315	.737	1361	3696	1609	553	569	13623	16.0

HAYWOODE WORKMAN

Team: Indiana Pacers
Position: Guard
Height: 6'3" **Weight:** 180
Birthdate: January 23, 1966
NBA Experience: 3 years

College: Winston-Salem St.;
Oral Roberts
Acquired: Signed as a free agent,
8/93

Background: A three-year starter at Oral Roberts after starting his college career at Winston-Salem State, Workman posted averages of 17.9 points and 5.2 rebounds per game for the Monarchs. He was drafted in the second round by Atlanta in 1989 but played just six games with the Hawks. He was named to the CBA All-Rookie team, then played 73 games for the Bullets before spending two years in the Italian League. He signed with Indiana last season and wound up making 52 starts.

Strengths: Workman has demonstrated the ability to be a quality NBA point man. He drives and dishes, handles the ball well, sets up the offense, and leads the fastbreak. He led the Pacers in assists and finished among the league's top 20 with 6.2 per game. Workman puts forth a strong defensive effort and comes up with steals and rebounds.

Weaknesses: Workman is not the type of point guard who will keep the opposition on its toes with his scoring ability. He looks more to pass than he does to shoot and his perimeter stroke comes and goes. He does not attack the basket enough to spend much time at the line. He seems to play in streaks.

Analysis: Signed by Indiana to be the team's third point guard, Workman wound up starting more games than Pooh Richardson and Vern Fleming combined. He also helped the Pacers to their best-ever playoff run. His two seasons in Italy's premier league helped him immensely. Workman barely missed two triple-doubles last season and gave some clutch performances.

PLAYER SUMMARY	
Will	run the offense
Can't	burn the nets
Expect	assists, steals
Don't Expect	20-point nights
Fantasy Value	$1-3
Card Value	7-12¢

COLLEGE STATISTICS

		G	FGP	FTP	RPG	PPG
84-85	WSS	25	.457	.589	3.0	10.3
86-87	OR	28	.365	.796	3.3	13.8
87-88	OR	29	.415	.755	6.0	19.4
88-89	OR	28	.483	.815	6.1	19.9
Totals		110	.430	.754	4.7	16.0

NBA REGULAR-SEASON STATISTICS

				FGs		3-PT FGs		FTs		Rebounds						
		G	MIN	FG	PCT	FG	PCT	FT	PCT	OFF	TOT	AST	STL	BLK	PTS	PPG
89-90	ATL	6	16	2	.667	0	.000	2	1.000	0	3	2	3	0	6	1.0
90-91	WAS	73	2034	234	.454	12	.240	101	.759	51	242	353	87	7	581	8.0
93-94	IND	65	1714	195	.424	18	.321	93	.802	32	204	404	85	4	501	7.7
Totals		144	3764	431	.441	30	.283	196	.781	83	449	759	175	11	1088	7.6

JAMES WORTHY

Team: Los Angeles Lakers
Position: Forward
Height: 6'9" **Weight:** 225
Birthdate: February 27, 1961

NBA Experience: 12 years
College: North Carolina
Acquired: 1st-round pick in 1982 draft
(1st overall)

Background: Worthy passed up his senior year at North Carolina after leading the Tar Heels to the 1982 NCAA title. He was named MVP of the Final Four after his All-America junior campaign. The top overall draft choice in 1982, Worthy won NBA titles with the Lakers in 1985, 1987, and 1988 and was named MVP of the 1988 Finals. A seven-time All-Star, he averaged a career-low 10.2 PPG last season.

Strengths: Worthy can still put the ball in the hoop if you let him get loose. His baseline spin move can still be effective and usually ends with a patented one-handed dunk. Worthy passes well and is a team leader with loads of championship experience.

Weaknesses: Worthy's knees have caused him to lose a step and have made him almost completely ineffective as a rebounder. He has not been the same player in any respect since undergoing knee surgery in 1992.

Analysis: After a brilliant run that included three championships and seven All-Star Games, Worthy spent all but two games of last season as a reserve. "Big Game James" can still light up the scoreboard when healthy, but his biggest asset at this late stage in his career is his leadership.

PLAYER SUMMARY

Will.............................lead by example
Can't ....regain young legs
Expect ....reserve scoring
Don't Expect ....rebounding
Fantasy Value $0
Card Value ....8-15¢

COLLEGE STATISTICS

		G	FGP	FTP	RPG	PPG
79-80	NC	14	.587	.600	7.4	12.5
80-81	NC	36	.500	.640	8.4	14.2
81-82	NC	34	.573	.674	6.3	15.6
Totals		84	.541	.652	7.4	14.5

NBA REGULAR-SEASON STATISTICS

				FGs		3-PT FGs		FTs		Rebounds						
		G	MIN	FG	PCT	FG	PCT	FT	PCT	OFF	TOT	AST	STL	BLK	PTS	PPG
82-83	LAL	77	1970	447	.579	1	.250	138	.624	157	399	132	91	64	1033	13.4
83-84	LAL	82	2415	495	.556	0	.000	195	.759	157	515	207	77	70	1185	14.5
84-85	LAL	80	2696	610	.572	0	.000	190	.776	169	511	201	87	67	1410	17.6
85-86	LAL	75	2454	629	.579	0	.000	242	.771	136	387	201	82	77	1500	20.0
86-87	LAL	82	2819	651	.539	0	.000	292	.751	158	466	226	108	83	1594	19.4
87-88	LAL	75	2655	617	.531	2	.125	242	.796	129	374	289	72	55	1478	19.7
88-89	LAL	81	2960	702	.548	2	.087	251	.782	169	489	288	99	49	1685	20.5
89-90	LAL	80	2960	711	.548	15	.306	248	.782	160	478	288	99	49	1685	21.1
90-91	LAL	78	3008	716	.492	26	.289	212	.797	107	356	275	104	35	1670	21.4
91-92	LAL	54	2108	450	.447	9	.209	166	.814	98	305	252	76	23	1075	19.9
92-93	LAL	82	2359	510	.447	30	.270	171	.810	73	247	278	92	27	1221	14.9
93-94	LAL	80	1597	340	.406	32	.288	100	.741	48	181	154	45	18	812	10.1
Totals		926	30001	6878	.521	117	.241	2447	.769	1561	4708	2791	1041	624	16320	17.6

LUTHER WRIGHT

Team: Utah Jazz
Position: Center
Height: 7'2" **Weight:** 280
Birthdate: September 22, 1971

NBA Experience: 1 year
College: Seton Hall
Acquired: 1st-round pick in 1993 draft
(18th overall)

Background: Wright starred at Elizabeth High School in New Jersey and was a much-ballyhooed recruit, but his college career was brief and disappointing. Wright had to sit out his freshman year for academic reasons, then did little to distinguish himself in two subsequent seasons. He was overweight most of the time. He was drafted in the first round by Utah in 1993, but he played in only 15 games and was involved in a bizarre incident symptomatic of an attention disorder.

Strengths: Wright is a huge man with impressive basketball skills and vast potential. He catches the ball easily and has displayed some wonderful offensive skills. His repertoire includes soft hook shots, turnaround jumpers, and fine passing ability for a big man. He was unselfish, almost to a fault, during his college career. He has potential as a rebounder and shot-blocker.

Weaknesses: Wright is a project with ground to make up both on and off the court. Recall, he did not play much in college and averaged in single digits in scoring both years. He also encountered more than his share of weight problems. He was found in his car by Utah police under strange circumstances last season, a sign of his off-court problems. In 15 games last year, he scored 19 points and did not get an assist.

Analysis: Utah took a gamble on Wright, and thus far he has paid no dividends. The Jazz decided to give him some time to straighten out his personal troubles in January of last season, placing him on the injured list for the rest of the campaign. Whether Wright is successful in getting his life under control remains to be seen. His immaturity, both on and off the court, could spell trouble.

PLAYER SUMMARY

Will	take up space
Can't	achieve potential
Expect	the unexpected
Don't Expect	maturity
Fantasy Value	$0
Card Value	10-20¢

COLLEGE STATISTICS

		G	FGP	FTP	RPG	PPG
91-92	SH	30	.517	.625	2.8	4.8
92-93	SH	34	.525	.654	7.5	9.0
Totals		64	.522	.644	5.3	7.1

NBA REGULAR-SEASON STATISTICS

			FGs		3-PT FGs		FTs		Rebounds						
	G	MIN	FG	PCT	FG	PCT	FT	PCT	OFF	TOT	AST	STL	BLK	PTS	PPG
93-94 UTA	15	92	8	.348	0	.000	3	.750	6	10	0	1	2	19	1.3
Totals	15	92	8	.348	0	.000	3	.750	6	10	0	1	2	19	1.3

1994 NBA DRAFT

Player	College	Team
1) Glenn Robinson	Purdue	Milwaukee
2) Jason Kidd	California	Dallas
3) Grant Hill	Duke	Detroit
4) Donyell Marshall	Connecticut	Minnesota
5) Juwan Howard	Michigan	Washington
6) Sharone Wright	Clemson	Philadelphia
7) Lamond Murray	California	L.A. Clippers
8) Brian Grant	Xavier	Sacramento
9) Eric Montross	North Carolina	Boston
10) Eddie Jones	Temple	L.A. Lakers
11) Carlos Rogers	Tennessee St.	Seattle
12) Khalid Reeves	Arizona	Miami
13) Jalen Rose	Michigan	Denver
14) Yinka Dare	George Washington	New Jersey
15) Eric Piatkowski	Nebraska	Indiana
16) Clifford Rozier	Louisville	Golden State
17) Aaron McKie	Temple	Portland
18) Eric Mobley	Pittsburgh	Milwaukee
19) Tony Dumas	Missouri-Kansas City	Dallas
20) B.J. Tyler	Texas	Philadelphia
21) Dickey Simpkins	Providence	Chicago
22) Bill Curley	Boston College	San Antonio
23) Wesley Person	Auburn	Phoenix
24) Monty Williams	Notre Dame	New York
25) Greg Minor	Louisville	L.A. Clippers
26) Charlie Ward	Florida St.	New York
27) Brooks Thompson	Oklahoma St.	Orlando

Player	College	Team
28) Deon Thomas	Illinois	Dallas
29) Antonio Lang	Duke	Phoenix
30) Howard Eisley	Boston College	Minnesota
31) Rodney Dent	Kentucky	Orlando
32) Jim McIlvaine	Marquette	Washington
33) Derrick Alston	Duquesne	Philadelphia
34) Gaylon Nickerson	N.W. Oklahoma St.	Atlanta
35) Michael Smith	Providence	Sacramento
36) Andrei Fetisov	Russia	Boston
37) Dontonio Wingfield	Cincinnati	Seattle
38) Darrin Hancock	Kansas	Charlotte
39) Anthony Miller	Michigan St.	Golden State
40) Jeff Webster	Oklahoma	Miami
41) William Njoku	Canada	Indiana
42) Gary Collier	Tulsa	Cleveland
43) Shawnelle Scott	St. John's	Portland
44) Damon Bailey	Indiana	Indiana
45) Dwayne Morton	Louisville	Golden State
46) Voshon Lenard	Minnesota	Milwaukee
47) Jamie Watson	South Carolina	Utah
48) Jevon Crudup	Missouri	Detroit
49) Kris Bruton	Benedict	Chicago
50) Charles Claxton	Georgia	Phoenix
51) Lawrence Funderburke	Ohio St.	Sacramento
52) Anthony Goldwire	Houston	Phoenix
53) Albert Burditt	Texas	Houston
54) Zeljko Rebraca	Yugoslavia	Seattle

BILL CURLEY

Team: Detroit Pistons
Position: Forward/Center
Height: 6′9″
Weight: 220
Birthdate: May 29, 1972

College: Boston College
Acquired: Draft rights traded from
Spurs with a 1997 2nd-round pick for
Sean Elliott, 7/94

Background: Curley earned his stripes with a brilliant run in the 1994 NCAA
Tournament, which ended with a loss to Florida in the East Regional final. Earlier,
he outplayed and out-muscled North Carolina's front line in a victory against the
Tar Heels, and he was a big factor in the Eagles' defeat of Indiana. Curley, a two-
time All-Big East selection, ranks second on Boston College's all-time lists for
scoring and rebounding. He also finished fifth in career shooting accuracy.

Strengths: The prototypical blue-collar player, Curley brings his lunch bucket
and works all night long. Team-oriented, he shares the ball and doesn't bother
himself with statistics. His well-rounded offensive game includes the 15-foot
jumper, the lefty jump hook, and the dribble-drive from the baseline. Scouts like
the way he crashes the offensive boards and finishes plays. He's an excellent
free throw shooter.

Weaknesses: Curley's not a great athlete, nor is he a skilled basketball
technician. Lacking range on his shot, he never made a 20-footer in his college
career. His vertical leap was measured at 22 inches, worst among all participants
at the Phoenix Desert Classic.

Analysis: Curley, who was drafted 22nd overall by San Antonio, was
subsequently traded to Detroit for Sean Elliott. It seems like a bummer of a deal
for the Pistons, as Curley doesn't have Elliott's talent. Cynics would compare him
to Danny Ferry or, worse, to Mark Randall. Nevertheless, Curley will see plenty of
minutes with the talent-poor Pistons.

PLAYER SUMMARY

Will ....bump and grind
Can't ....lead the break
Expect ....a role player
Don't Expect ....finesse
Fantasy Value...............................$1-3
Card Value ....20-35¢

COLLEGE HIGHLIGHTS

- NCAA East Region All-Tournament team, 1994
- All-Big East, 1993 and 1994
- Second-team All-Big East, 1992
- Big East Rookie of the Year, 1991

COLLEGE STATISTICS

		G	FGs FG	FGs PCT	3-PT FGs FG	3-PT FGs PCT	FTs FT	FTs PCT	REB	AST	STL	BLK	PTS	PPG
90-91	BC	30	141	.542	0	.000	96	.691	206	38	36	6	378	12.6
91-92	BC	31	187	.577	0	.000	178	.774	250	29	26	25	552	17.8
92-93	BC	31	181	.580	0	.000	129	.849	235	37	32	29	491	15.8
93-94	BC	34	233	.557	0	.000	215	.793	305	54	27	28	681	20.0
Totals		126	742	.565	0	.000	618	.780	996	158	121	88	2102	16.7

YINKA DARE

Team: New Jersey Nets
Position: Center
Height: 7'1"
Weight: 265

Birthdate: October 10, 1972
College: George Washington
Acquired: 1st-round pick in 1994 draft (14th overall)

Background: A relative newcomer, the Nigerian-born Dare began playing organized basketball in 1991-92 at Milford Academy in Connecticut, and he spent only two seasons at George Washington before entering the draft. He led the Colonials to NCAA Tournament bids both years, and he paced the Atlantic 10 in rebounding and blocked shots as a freshman. He was criticized for leaving school early, yet some scouts thought he was wasting his time on a team that refused to share the ball with him.

Strengths: Dare has all the physical tools: size, agility, speed, quickness, and strength. He didn't display all those qualities in college, but he tested well with NBA teams before the draft. A smart and confident player, he has the potential to develop into a Dikembe Mutombo type, only with a better offensive game. He shows a nice righty jump hook and good instincts on the offensive glass.

Weaknesses: Raw fundamentally, Dare needs lots of repetitions with his offensive moves, as well as schooling on defensive footwork and positioning. His foul-line stroke needs a big upgrade. He carried too much weight in the postseason, causing some NBA teams to question his work ethic. We won't say his passing needs improvement, but he registered only three assists during his entire freshman season.

Analysis: Conventional wisdom said New Jersey would draft a shooting guard such as Aaron McKie, but the Nets found Dare too intriguing to pass up. He figures to be the eventual replacement for Benoit Benjamin, but that transition should take at least a year, if not two. Adding uncertainty to Dare's situation is new Nets boss Butch Beard, who's making his debut as an NBA head coach.

PLAYER SUMMARY	
Will	block shots
Can't	make his FTs
Expect	a good career
Don't Expect	sudden impact
Fantasy Value	$0
Card Value	20-35¢

COLLEGE HIGHLIGHTS
- *Sports Illustrated* Freshman of the Year, 1993
- A.P. honorable-mention All-American, 1993
- Atlantic 10 Rookie of the Year, 1993
- Second-team All-Atlantic 10, 1994

COLLEGE STATISTICS

			FGs		3-PT FGs		FTs							
		G	FG	PCT	FG	PCT	FT	PCT	REB	AST	STL	BLK	PTS	PPG
92-93	GW	30	140	.551	0	.000	86	.473	308	3	17	84	366	12.2
93-94	GW	30	178	.538	0	.000	107	.585	309	18	20	56	463	15.4
Totals		60	318	.544	0	.000	193	.529	617	21	37	140	829	13.8

TONY DUMAS

Team: Dallas Mavericks
Position: Guard
Height: 6'5"
Weight: 190

Birthdate: August 25, 1972
College: Missouri-Kansas City
Acquired: 1st-round pick in 1994 draft (19th overall)

Background: Dumas put up big-time numbers for Missouri-Kansas City, leading the Kangaroos in scoring as a sophomore, junior, and senior and setting school career records for points and rebounds. Ranking eighth nationally in scoring in 1993-94, he lit up Texas Tech for 44 points and Colorado for 43 in back-to-back games. Though he shot poorly at the postseason Phoenix and Chicago camps, he wowed scouts with his measurables and raw potential.

Strengths: A stone scorer, Dumas displays good jump-shooting form, a quick release, and the ability to get to the basket with his dribble and draw fouls. He led the nation in free throw attempts (292) in 1993-94. He's a superb athlete with the speed and hops to be a big factor finishing plays on the break. He has the tools to be more than adequate defensively, getting in his man's face or denying the ball on the wing.

Weaknesses: While he has no glaring weaknesses, Dumas must get stronger and improve his handle in the open court. He could stand to be more selective as a shooter. He must prove he can adjust to rigorous competition after playing for a small NCAA independent.

Analysis: After selecting point guard Jason Kidd earlier in the first round, Dallas selected a shooting-guard prospect in Dumas, who apparently will take Tim Legler's roster spot and compete with Lucious Harris for back-up minutes behind Jim Jackson. Dumas should make the team but will have to scramble for playing time. With the huge jump in competition, it will take him a long while to adjust to the NBA.

PLAYER SUMMARY	
Will	run and gun
Can't	be selective
Expect	a high flyer
Don't Expect	any guarantees
Fantasy Value	$0
Card Value	15-30¢

COLLEGE HIGHLIGHTS
- River City Classic MVP, 1992
- Golden Harvest Classic All-Tournament team, 1993

COLLEGE STATISTICS

			FGs		3-PT FGs		FTs							
		G	FG	PCT	FG	PCT	FT	PCT	REB	AST	STL	BLK	PTS	PPG
90-91	MKC	29	177	.499	19	.279	89	.754	134	87	29	9	462	15.9
91-92	MKC	28	200	.521	39	.500	162	.775	128	72	28	7	601	21.5
92-93	MKC	27	238	.489	45	.354	122	.718	148	98	36	14	643	23.8
93-94	MKC	29	229	.421	74	.361	221	.757	166	87	49	19	753	26.0
Totals		113	844	.477	177	.370	594	.753	576	344	142	49	2459	21.8

BRIAN GRANT

Team: Sacramento Kings
Position: Forward
Height: 6'9"
Weight: 254

Birthdate: March 5, 1972
College: Xavier (Ohio)
Acquired: 1st-round pick in 1994 draft (8th overall)

Background: Recruited without much fanfare from Georgetown (Ohio) High School, Grant signed with Xavier in Cincinnati and made an instant impact. He capped his freshman season with 16 points and 12 rebounds against UConn in the NCAA Tournament, finished second nationally in field goal accuracy (.654) as a junior, and joined Tyrone Hill as the only players to lead the Musketeers in rebounding four seasons. He was a two-time Player of the Year in the Midwestern Collegiate Conference.

Strengths: A steady, tenacious player, Grant makes his living within 12 feet of the basket, both offensively and defensively. He establishes solid position for rebounds, jumps pretty well, and goes after every carom with both hands. He steadily expanded his offensive repertoire and became proficient at shooting close-in jump shots as a senior. Like most Xavier players, he has a good all-around game.

Weaknesses: Grant won't flourish in the NBA until he develops a consistent jump shot from the foul line and corner. Until he does, the league's bigger power forwards will sit on him in the post and neutralize his offense. Also, he needs to smooth his stroke at the foul line.

Analysis: Brian Who? That was the question asked by casual fans when Sacramento selected Grant in the draft. However, he looks like a good choice, considering the Kings' weakness up front and the loss of Wayman Tisdale to free agency. He should be a steady, solid professional. Look for him to move into the starting lineup sometime during his rookie season.

PLAYER SUMMARY	
Will	play with leverage
Can't	shoot with range
Expect	a solid rebounder
Don't Expect	much sizzle
Fantasy Value	$3-5
Card Value	30-50¢

COLLEGE HIGHLIGHTS

- MCC Player of the Year, 1993 and 1994
- A.P. honorable-mention All-American, 1993
- Second-team All-MCC, 1991 and 1992

COLLEGE STATISTICS

			FGs		3-PT FGs		FTs		REB	AST	STL	BLK	PTS	PPG
		G	FG	PCT	FG	PCT	FT	PCT						
90-91	XAV	32	135	.572	0	.000	100	.694	273	20	29	25	370	11.6
91-92	XAV	26	117	.576	0	.000	74	.583	237	23	19	26	308	11.8
92-93	XAV	30	223	.654	0	.000	110	.692	283	46	23	29	556	18.5
93-94	XAV	29	181	.559	1	.333	122	.713	287	47	27	47	485	16.7
Totals		117	656	.594	1	.333	406	.676	1080	136	98	127	1719	14.7

GRANT HILL

Team: Detroit Pistons
Position: Forward
Height: 6'8"
Weight: 225

Birthdate: October 5, 1972
College: Duke
Acquired: 1st-round pick in 1994 draft (3rd overall)

Background: Hill, along with current NBA players Christian Laettner and Bobby Hurley, formed the core of back-to-back national championship teams at Duke in 1991 and 1992. Hill averaged double figures in scoring in each of his four seasons and became the first ACC player with 1,900 points, 700 rebounds, 400 assists, 200 steals, and 100 blocks. He was a consensus All-American in 1993-94 and held Glenn Robinson to 13 points in Duke's victory over Purdue in the 1994 NCAA Tournament.

Strengths: Hill has above-average abilities in every facet of the game. Tremendously versatile, he can play any of three positions (point, shooting guard, small forward) and create mismatches at each. He flourishes in a team concept but can take over a game in the late stages. Defensively, he's one of the best prospects to come into the NBA in recent years. When the Pistons need a stop, he'll get it for them. He's been through the wars and has great maturity.

Weaknesses: There's little not to like about Hill's game. Some people have criticized his shooting, but it's more than adequate from 15 to 20 feet out. Others have pointed to a perceived lack of assertiveness.

Analysis: The Pistons got a break when Hill, who refused to visit Dallas prior to the draft, was available with the third pick. Detroit coach Don Chaney predicted that Hill could have the same kind of impact that Isiah Thomas had after entering the NBA 13 years ago. He'll get most of his minutes at small forward, but he also should see time behind Joe Dumars at shooting guard and Lindsey Hunter at point guard.

PLAYER SUMMARY	
Will	play both ends
Can't	stand losing
Expect	an eventual All-Star
Don't Expect	a Bad Boy
Fantasy Value	$15-18
Card Value	$2.50-5.00

COLLEGE HIGHLIGHTS
- Consensus All-American, 1994
- ACC Player of the Year, 1994
- Henry Iba Corinthian Award winner, 1993
- UPI second-team All-American, 1992 and 1993

COLLEGE STATISTICS

			FGs		3-PT FGs		FTs							
		G	FG	PCT	FG	PCT	FT	PCT	REB	AST	STL	BLK	PTS	PPG
90-91	DUKE	36	160	.516	1	.500	81	.609	183	79	51	30	402	11.2
91-92	DUKE	33	182	.611	0	.000	99	.733	187	134	39	27	463	14.0
92-93	DUKE	26	185	.578	4	.286	94	.746	166	72	64	36	468	18.0
93-94	DUKE	34	218	.462	39	.390	116	.703	233	176	64	40	591	17.4
Totals		129	745	.532	44	.376	390	.698	769	461	218	133	1924	14.9

JUWAN HOWARD

Team: Washington Bullets
Position: Forward
Height: 6'9"
Weight: 250

Birthdate: February 7, 1973
College: Michigan
Acquired: 1st-round pick in 1994 draft
(5th overall)

Background: Howard was the key recruit in Michigan's heralded Fab Five class of 1991; when he signed, the other four (Chris Webber, Jalen Rose, Jimmy King, Ray Jackson) fell in line. Overshadowed by Webber his first two seasons, Howard stepped up last year, boosting his scoring average by 6.2 points and leading the Wolverines in rebounding. His pro stock skyrocketed after a brilliant NCAA Tournament performance, culminated by a 30-point, 13-rebound effort against Arkansas.

Strengths: A blue-collar worker, Howard shows up at both ends of the court. Coaches love his win-at-all-costs approach to the game. He makes the 15-footer from the corner or the foul line, makes plays as a trailer on the break, and rebounds tenaciously. He runs fairly well and has sure hands, and he holds up well defensively against power forwards. His post skills are especially well-refined for someone his age.

Weaknesses: Howard lacks the spring to play above the rim and the ball-handling skills to do much in the open court. He could stand to add some wrinkles to his back-to-the-basket game. Measuring 6'9", he's not particularly big for a power forward by NBA standards and isn't a shot-blocker.

Analysis: The Bullets would have preferred Jason Kidd, though Howard should be a nice consolation prize. He augments a frontcourt that also includes Tom Gugliotta and Don MacLean. Washington is desperate for a center and Howard has all the skills to play the position, but he's just a couple inches too short. Howard should have a solid, if unspectacular, pro career.

PLAYER SUMMARY	
Will	stick the 15-footer
Can't	make the 3
Expect	a rock-solid pro
Don't Expect	a high-flyer
Fantasy Value	$11-14
Card Value	75¢-$1.25

COLLEGE HIGHLIGHTS
- A.P. third-team All-American, 1994
- All-Big Ten, 1994
- NCAA Midwest Region MVP, 1994
- A.P. honorable-mention All-American, 1993

COLLEGE STATISTICS

			FGs		3-PT FGs		FTs							
		G	FG	PCT	FG	PCT	FT	PCT	REB	AST	STL	BLK	PTS	PPG
91-92	MICH	34	150	.450	0	.000	77	.688	212	62	15	21	377	11.1
92-93	MICH	36	206	.506	0	.000	112	.700	267	69	21	14	524	14.6
93-94	MICH	30	261	.557	1	.143	102	.675	266	71	44	21	625	20.8
Totals		100	617	.510	1	.091	291	.688	745	202	80	56	1526	15.3

EDDIE JONES

Team: Los Angeles Lakers
Position: Guard/Forward
Height: 6'6"
Weight: 190

Birthdate: October 20, 1971
College: Temple
Acquired: 1st-round pick in 1994 draft
(10th overall)

Background: Forced to sit out his freshman season at Temple for academic reasons, Jones eased into his career as the Owls' sixth man, then moved into the starting lineup for his junior and senior seasons. The best player in the Atlantic 10 last year, he scored 24 points in a loss to Indiana in the NCAA Tournament. He ranks third on Temple's all-time steals list (197), fourth in blocked shots (107), and sixth in 3-pointers (141).

Strengths: There probably isn't a scout alive who hasn't referred to Jones as a "greyhound" at least once. He flies upcourt, fills a lane on the break, and dunks with style. His actions are smooth and he's a superb leaper. He compensates for his smallish stature with a quick release on his shot. Well-schooled defensively by Temple coach John Chaney, Jones has the long arms and necessary quickness to survive against NBA shooting guards.

Weaknesses: A wing player at Temple, Jones will have to play shooting guard in the NBA. He needs to refine his ball-handling skills and could stand to add some meat to his bones. Few non-point guards can make a living in the NBA at 190 pounds. Adept at shooting on the move, Jones must improve as a spot-up jump-shooter. His free throw shooting leaves a lot to be desired.

Analysis: The Lakers have loaded up on big guards in recent years, adding Jones to a lineup that already includes Anthony Peeler and Doug Christie. New coach Del Harris may use Jones or Christie at small forward. Jones probably won't crack the starting lineup as a rookie, although the people ahead of him aren't a whole lot better.

PLAYER SUMMARY	
Will	finish plays
Can't	muscle up
Expect	a greyhound
Don't Expect	a pit bull
Fantasy Value	$1-3
Card Value	50-75¢

COLLEGE HIGHLIGHTS
- A.P. honorable-mention All-American, 1994
- Atlantic 10 Player of the Year, 1994
- All-Atlantic 10, 1994
- Third-team All-Atlantic 10, 1993

COLLEGE STATISTICS

		G	FGs FG	FGs PCT	3-PT FGs FG	3-PT FGs PCT	FTs FT	FTs PCT	REB	AST	STL	BLK	PTS	PPG
91-92	TEMP	29	122	.437	47	.351	41	.547	119	30	57	19	332	11.4
92-93	TEMP	32	212	.458	49	.348	70	.604	225	56	70	42	543	17.0
93-94	TEMP	31	231	.471	45	.352	88	.662	210	58	70	46	595	19.2
Totals		92	565	.458	141	.350	199	.614	554	144	197	107	1470	16.0

JASON KIDD

Team: Dallas Mavericks
Position: Guard
Height: 6'4"
Weight: 205

Birthdate: March 23, 1973
College: California
Acquired: 1st-round pick in 1994 draft
(2nd overall)

Background: The object of an intense recruiting war, Kidd spurned Kentucky and Kansas, among others, to stay close to his Oakland, California, home for college. As a freshman, he led the country in steals per game, finished sixth in assists, and led Cal to an upset of Duke in the NCAA Tournament. Last season, while leading the nation in assists, he became the Golden Bears' first All-American since 1968 and first-ever Pac-10 Player of the Year. He forfeited two years of eligibility to enter the draft.

Strengths: Kidd has patterned his game after his idol, Magic Johnson. Like Magic, Kidd has tremendous playmaking skills and an overwhelming will to win. He controls a game's tempo at both ends of the court, breaks down defenses off the dribble, and delivers the ball on a dime. He patrols the passing lanes on defense, always willing to take a chance, and is exceptionally strong for the point-guard position.

Weaknesses: His only potentially fatal flaw is a jump shot that lacks consistency and range. Also, he tends to violate conventional basketball wisdom by leaving his feet without a plan, though he usually finds someone to pass to. Questions of character surfaced before the draft because of off-court scrapes, including leaving the scene of an auto accident.

Analysis: Dallas solidified its backcourt with the addition of Kidd, who'll replace Fat Lever at the point and alleviate pressure on shooting guard Jim Jackson, who led the NBA in turnovers last season. Kidd will make the Mavericks better, but he won't be a great player until he expands his offensive game. Expect him to accomplish that feat in time.

PLAYER SUMMARY	
Will	draw and dish
Can't	stroke the trey
Expect	a leader
Don't Expect	the next Magic
Fantasy Value	$12-15
Card Value	$2.50-5.00

COLLEGE HIGHLIGHTS

- A.P. All-American, 1994
- Pac-10 Player of the Year, 1994
- Naismith Award finalist, 1994
- Pac-10 Freshman of the Year, 1993

COLLEGE STATISTICS

			FGs		3-PT FGs		FTs		REB	AST	STL	BLK	PTS	PPG
		G	FG	PCT	FG	PCT	FT	PCT						
92-93	CAL	29	133	.463	24	.286	88	.657	142	222	110	8	378	13.0
93-94	CAL	30	166	.472	51	.362	117	.692	207	272	94	9	500	16.7
Totals		59	299	.468	75	.333	205	.677	349	494	204	17	878	14.9

DONYELL MARSHALL

Team: Minnesota Timberwolves
Position: Forward
Height: 6'9"
Weight: 218

Birthdate: May 18, 1973
College: Connecticut
Acquired: 1st-round pick in 1994 draft (4th overall)

Background: Though he weighed only 175 pounds as a high school senior in Reading, Pennsylvania, Marshall was the most heralded recruit in UConn history. He didn't disappoint, leading the Huskies to two NCAA Tournament bids and the 1994 Big East championship. He averaged 2.7 blocks for his career, most in school history, and last season set a Big East scoring record. He was runner-up to Glenn Robinson for most Player of the Year awards. He forfeited a year's eligibility to enter the draft.

Strengths: Marshall has the skills to flourish at either forward spot. He's a superb shot-blocker with long arms and impeccable timing. He handles the ball very well for a big man, runs the floor easily, and finishes plays at the basket. He rates as an above-average rebounder. Scouts like his ever-expanding offensive game; he can make the 20-footer facing the basket or beat bigger people with quickness in the post.

Weaknesses: Marshall has gained 43 pounds over the past three-plus years, but he still needs more bulk. He was criticized for drifting into cruise control earlier in his career, but he seemed to show more emotion last season. Though generally a good big-game player, he missed crucial free throws in the 1994 NCAA Tournament.

Analysis: Given a year or two to adjust, Marshall should prove to be Minnesota's best draft pick ever—not bad considering Christian Laettner and Isaiah Rider are former T'Wolves picks. He'll play plenty as a rookie and should score in the high teens. Minnesota eased its logjam at small forward when it sent Chuck Person packing in July.

PLAYER SUMMARY	
Will	run and jump
Can't	miss as a pro
Expect	a terrific shot-blocker
Don't Expect	another loudmouth
Fantasy Value	$10-13
Card Value	75¢-$1.25

COLLEGE HIGHLIGHTS
- Consensus All-American, 1994
- Big East Player of the Year, 1994
- Big East All-Tournament team, 1994
- Big East All-Rookie team, 1992

COLLEGE STATISTICS

			FGs		3-PT FGs		FTs							
		G	FG	PCT	FG	PCT	FT	PCT	REB	AST	STL	BLK	PTS	PPG
91-92	CONN	30	125	.424	15	.242	69	.742	183	45	31	78	334	11.1
92-93	CONN	27	166	.500	20	.370	107	.829	210	30	39	56	459	17.0
93-94	CONN	34	307	.512	41	.311	200	.752	302	56	43	111	855	25.1
Totals		91	598	.487	76	.307	376	.771	695	131	113	245	1648	18.1

AARON McKIE

Team: Portland Trail Blazers
Position: Guard
Height: 6'5"
Weight: 209

Birthdate: October 2, 1972
College: Temple
Acquired: 1st-round pick in 1994 draft
(17th overall)

Background: A product of Philadelphia's Simon Gratz High School, McKie stayed home to attend Temple. McKie, whose father died when he was eight and whose mother left a few years later, was forced to the sidelines for academic reasons as a freshman. After that, he had a bang-up career. Among former Owls who played three years, only Guy Rodgers scored more points than McKie, who started all 92 games and scored in double-figures 80 times. While teaming with fellow first-round pick Eddie Jones, McKie led Temple in rebounding from his shooting-guard position in 1993-94.

Strengths: McKie has the right combination of size and aggressiveness to flourish defensively in the NBA. He's a good rebounder for a guard and is 80-percent accurate from the free throw line. A workhorse, he averaged a withering 39.2 minutes per game as a senior. Though not a good shooter, he knows how to score. Scouts love his makeup and work ethic.

Weaknesses: While he'll score 20 points on occasion, McKie gets poor grades for shot selection and consistency, though there's nothing wrong with his shot mechanically. He tends to disappear for long stretches at a time. Like many Temple products, he hasn't developed a sound all-around game. His ball-handling, passing, and decision-making all need work.

Analysis: Clyde Drexler and Terry Porter are getting old, and Tracy Murray and James Robinson have limitations, so Portland zeroed in on a potential replacement at shooting guard. Though he looks like a two-year project, McKie could have an outstanding career if he puts his offensive house in order.

```
PLAYER SUMMARY
Will....................................play defense
Can't.............................shoot straight
Expect ..................a future in Portland
Don't Expect .....much P.T. in 1994-95
Fantasy Value......................................$0
Card Value................................15-30¢
```

COLLEGE HIGHLIGHTS
• A.P. honorable-mention All-American, 1993 and 1994
• Atlantic 10 Player of the Year, 1993
• All-Atlantic 10, 1993 and 1994

COLLEGE STATISTICS

| | | | FGs | | 3-PT FGs | | FTs | | | | | | | |
		G	FG	PCT	FG	PCT	FT	PCT	REB	AST	STL	BLK	PTS	PPG
91-92	TEMP	28	130	.433	42	.321	86	.754	167	94	62	6	388	13.9
92-93	TEMP	33	240	.432	77	.393	123	.789	195	109	76	7	680	20.6
93-94	TEMP	31	193	.401	59	.371	137	.816	224	98	58	10	582	18.8
Totals		92	563	.421	178	.366	346	.790	586	301	196	23	1650	17.9

GREG MINOR

Team: Indiana Pacers
Position: Forward/Guard
Height: 6'6"
Weight: 210
Birthdate: September 18, 1971

College: Louisville
Acquired: Draft rights traded from Clippers with Mark Jackson for Pooh Richardson, Malik Sealy, and draft rights to Eric Piatkowski, 6/94

Background: Unheralded upon his arrival at Louisville, Minor was allowed to grow while players such as Dwayne Morton and Clifford Rozier (who were also drafted in 1994) got the headlines. After sitting out his freshman season to become academically eligible, he led the Cardinals in rebounding as a sophomore, minutes as a junior, and steals as a senior. He then vaulted into the first round of the draft with bang-up work at the postseason Portsmouth Invitational and Phoenix Desert Classic.

Strengths: Scouts consider Minor an outstanding role player who knows how to play and knows how to win. Capable at small forward or shooting guard, he's tough mentally and physically, can guard the opponent's best player, and rebounds aggressively. He's willing to score in the flow of the action, taking whatever offense comes his way. He's successful on a high percentage of his field goal attempts and makes big plays in the clutch.

Weaknesses: While he lacks any one skill that can carry him in the NBA, Minor has no significant weaknesses. His game suffers on the rare occasions when he forces his shots.

Analysis: Drafted by the Clippers with the 25th selection, Minor was dealt to the Pacers, who felt he was a better option than Malik Sealy or Eric Piatkowski as Derrick McKey's back-up at small forward. Additional minutes for Minor were made available when Kenny Williams left as a free agent. He looks like a good pick-up for Indiana.

PLAYER SUMMARY

Will ....play both ends
Can't ....block shots
Expect ....a legit player
Don't Expect ....the main man
Fantasy Value $0
Card Value ....10-20¢

COLLEGE HIGHLIGHTS

• All-Metro, 1994
• Desert Classic All-Tournament team, 1994
• Portsmouth Invitational All-Tournament team, 1994
• Second-team All-Metro, 1993

COLLEGE STATISTICS

| | | FGs | | 3-PT FGs | | FTs | | | | | | | |
| | | FG | PCT | FG | PCT | FT | PCT | REB | AST | STL | BLK | PTS | PPG |
		G											
91-92	LOU	30	113	.473	10	.233	55	.733	154	55	39	5	291	9.7
92-93	LOU	31	156	.527	42	.433	84	.750	170	87	32	12	438	14.1
93-94	LOU	34	179	.513	42	.353	70	.729	209	86	57	16	470	13.8
Totals		95	448	.507	94	.363	209	.739	533	228	128	33	1199	12.6

ERIC MOBLEY

Team: Milwaukee Bucks
Position: Center
Height: 6'11"
Weight: 250

Birthdate: February 1, 1970
College: Allegany; Pittsburgh
Acquired: 1st-round pick in 1994 draft
(18th overall)

Background: Mobley, a heavily recruited prep phenom from New Rochelle, New York, was diverted to Allegany Community College in Maryland as a freshman, then sat out the 1990-91 season to become eligible at Pittsburgh. Progress came slowly, as he scored in double figures just seven times as a sophomore and averaged 10.4 points as a junior. He appeared in the best shape of his career at the Desert Classic after his senior season and played well enough to merit first-round status.

Strengths: Mobley is a legitimate center, a scarce commodity in the 1994 draft. A very good athlete for a big man, he is strong and agile and runs the court well. While not a leaper, he has good shot-blocking ability. Offensively, he's adequate from inside ten feet using an array of jump hooks and power moves. He's a physical rebounder and defender.

Weaknesses: Though a good all-around player, Mobley has no one skill that can carry him in the NBA. Most in need of work is his offense, especially from outside the paint. He isn't a good perimeter shooter, as his career free throw percentage (48.6) attests.

Analysis: After taking Glenn Robinson to fill the small-forward slot, Milwaukee used its second first-round pick on Mobley, who adds the rebounding and shot-blocking dimensions the Bucks have lacked recently. But which Mobley will show up in Milwaukee—the legitimate big man from the Desert Classic or the invisible man from Pittsburgh? If it's the former, the Bucks will have found themselves a serviceable center.

PLAYER SUMMARY	
Will	patrol the middle
Can't	make FTs
Expect	a banger
Don't Expect	much offense
Fantasy Value	$0
Card Value	20-35¢

COLLEGE HIGHLIGHTS
• Third-team All-Big East, 1994
• Desert Classic All-Tournament team, 1994

COLLEGE STATISTICS

		G	FGs FG	FGs PCT	3-PT FGs FG	3-PT FGs PCT	FTs FT	FTs PCT	REB	AST	STL	BLK	PTS	PPG
89-90	ALL	23	163	.674	0	.000	52	.547	241	43	—	—	378	16.4
91-92	PITT	33	99	.559	0	.000	41	.410	153	19	12	57	239	7.2
92-93	PITT	28	117	.542	0	.000	57	.553	209	50	8	52	291	10.4
93-94	PITT	27	155	.568	0	.000	60	.492	237	55	20	75	370	13.7
Pitt. Totals		88	371	.557	0	.000	158	.486	599	124	40	184	900	10.2

ERIC MONTROSS

Team: Boston Celtics
Position: Center
Height: 7'0"
Weight: 275

Birthdate: September 23, 1971
College: North Carolina
Acquired: 1st-round pick in 1994 draft (9th overall)

Background: From Indianapolis, Montross raised a stink in the Hoosier state when he chose North Carolina instead of Indiana for his college ball. He played well as a junior, leading the Tar Heels to a national-championship victory against Michigan (for whom his father played). His performance dipped a bit last season, as did his standing in the eyes of NBA scouts, yet he was still the third senior selected in the 1994 draft.

Strengths: Montross does the things a center is supposed to, such as rebound, take up space in the paint, and help out defensively. Once he gets set on the blocks, you can't move him. He displays good touch on his jumper from 15 feet and in, has soft mitts, and can score with either hand from close range. Strong and tough, he refuses to be bullied by cheap-shot artists. He has a wealth of experience against good competition. Unlike most centers drafted, he is not a project.

Weaknesses: Though a quality college player, Montross may lack the skills for regular NBA duty. What's more, he's too stiff athletically to keep up with quick players. He has a slow release on his jump hook, inviting blocked shots, and struggles to convert at the foul line.

Analysis: Disillusioned with 1993 first-round pick Acie Earl, the Celtics chose another center in hopes of finding a replacement for Robert Parish. Montross would be an ideal back-up on a good team; on the Celtics, he might start if Pervis Ellison isn't healthy. Montross will win wrestling matches inside but will suffer embarrassment at the hands of the Olajuwons and Robinsons of the NBA.

PLAYER SUMMARY

Will ....bump and grind
Can't..............................be intimidated
Expect ....a space-eater
Don't Expect...................a sky-walker
Fantasy Value...............................$2-4
Card Value ....60¢-$1.00

COLLEGE HIGHLIGHTS

- *Basketball Weekly* All-American, 1994
- A.P. second-team All-American, 1993 and 1994
- Final Four All-Tournament team, 1993
- NCAA East Region All-Tournament team, 1993

COLLEGE STATISTICS

		G	FGs FG	PCT	3-PT FGs FG	PCT	FTs FT	PCT	REB	AST	STL	BLK	PTS	PPG
90-91	NC	35	81	.587	0	.000	41	.612	148	11	6	30	203	5.8
91-92	NC	31	140	.574	0	.000	68	.624	218	18	17	30	348	11.2
92-93	NC	38	222	.615	0	.000	156	.684	290	28	22	47	600	15.8
93-94	NC	35	183	.560	0	.000	110	.558	285	29	18	62	476	13.6
Totals		139	626	.585	0	.000	375	.624	941	86	63	169	1627	11.7

LAMOND MURRAY

Team: Los Angeles Clippers
Position: Forward
Height: 6'7"
Weight: 220

Birthdate: April 20, 1973
College: California
Acquired: 1st-round pick in 1994 draft
(7th overall)

Background: Murray teamed with fellow lottery pick Jason Kidd to form the nation's most dynamic duo, yet their presence wasn't enough to get Cal past Wisconsin-Green Bay in the 1994 NCAA Tournament. Murray led the Pac-10 in scoring in 1993-94 and broke Kevin Johnson's career scoring record at California. He scored 28 points vs. Duke and 23 vs. Kansas in the 1993 NCAAs. Like cousin Tracy Murray of the Portland Trail Blazers, Murray left school early to join the NBA.

Strengths: Other than Glenn Robinson, Murray is the closest thing to a scoring machine in the 1994 draft class. He can break down a defense with his dribble and finish plays inside, and he's nearly automatic shooting the wing or baseline jump shot. He gets a ton of points filling a lane on the break. Though he averaged less than two assists per game in college, he is a savvy, creative passer and has a great feel for the game.

Weaknesses: When Cal wasn't pressing and scrambling on defense, it used a lot of zone, so scouts aren't sure how Murray will hold up as a man-to-man defender. He needs to expand his range a little in order to make the NBA 3-pointer. He has no glaring weaknesses.

Analysis: The Clippers, sporting an all-new look for 1994-95, will lean on Murray for scoring. He could be one of the most productive rookies because he'll get every opportunity to play. The Clippers traded Danny Manning last season and his replacement, Dominique Wilkins, was lost to free agency, leaving only Malik Sealy and fellow rookie Eric Piatkowski to compete with Murray at small forward. Murray will likely wind up the winner of the starting job.

PLAYER SUMMARY	
Will	fill it up
Can't	play above the rim
Expect	a nifty passer
Don't Expect	a defensive stopper
Fantasy Value	$4-6
Card Value	50-75¢

COLLEGE HIGHLIGHTS
• John Wooden Award finalist, 1994
• All-Pac-10, 1993 and 1994
• Team USA member, 1993
• Pac-10 All-Freshman team, 1992

COLLEGE STATISTICS

			FGs		3-PT FGs		FTs							
		G	FG	PCT	FG	PCT	FT	PCT	REB	AST	STL	BLK	PTS	PPG
91-92	CAL	28	152	.474	17	.304	66	.710	171	56	34	19	387	13.8
92-93	CAL	30	230	.517	36	.364	76	.628	189	41	32	25	572	19.1
93-94	CAL	30	262	.476	46	.331	159	.764	236	63	44	31	729	24.3
Totals		88	644	.489	99	.337	301	.713	596	160	110	75	1688	19.2

WESLEY PERSON

Team: Phoenix Suns
Position: Guard/Forward
Height: 6'6"
Weight: 195

Birthdate: March 28, 1971
College: Auburn
Acquired: 1st-round pick in 1994 draft
(23rd overall)

Background: The brother of former NBA All-Star Chuck Person, Wesley ended up at Auburn as the Tigers' recruiting pipeline was drying and suffered with some bad teams. He finished his career as the school's third all-time leading scorer, behind his brother and former NBA player Mike Mitchell. He cost himself potential millions when he skipped the postseason NBA camps. Projected to go anywhere from 10th to 16th in the draft, he slipped to 23rd as big guards Jalen Rose, Eric Piatkowski, Aaron McKie, and Tony Dumas were selected before him.

Strengths: Person was the best pure shooter in the draft. Scouts compare him to Reggie Miller, though he doesn't have Miller's lightning-quick release. Person has textbook form, sweet touch, and NBA trey range. A class act, he doesn't toot his own horn the way his brother Chuck does. He plays physical defense, is quick enough to be a positive factor in presses and traps, and rebounds well for someone his size.

Weaknesses: Person must answer questions about his ball-handling skills and floor game after playing mostly forward at Auburn. Is he a guard? Can he create shots for himself and others? Otherwise, he has no burning weaknesses.

Analysis: Phoenix added another weapon to its NBA-leading scoring attack in Person, who probably won't see time at small forward now that the Suns have signed Danny Manning. Person's minutes will come at big guard, backing up Dan Majerle. Person needs extensive playing time to establish himself, but he won't find it in Phoenix.

PLAYER SUMMARY

Will	stroke it good
Can't	guard the jets
Expect	a scorer
Don't Expect	false bravado
Fantasy Value	$0
Card Value	25-50¢

COLLEGE HIGHLIGHTS

- A.P. honorable-mention All-American, 1994
- All-SEC, 1993 and 1994
- *Basketball Weekly* Freshman All-American, 1991

COLLEGE STATISTICS

			FGs		3-PT FGs		FTs							
		G	FG	PCT	FG	PCT	FT	PCT	REB	AST	STL	BLK	PTS	PPG
90-91	AUB	26	153	.471	42	.356	52	.765	147	48	35	31	400	15.4
91-92	AUB	27	208	.506	69	.489	53	.726	183	55	28	29	538	19.9
92-93	AUB	27	194	.556	58	.464	61	.772	192	102	21	17	507	18.8
93-94	AUB	28	217	.484	93	.443	94	.734	179	79	28	11	621	22.2
Totals		108	772	.497	262	.441	260	.747	701	284	112	88	2066	19.1

ERIC PIATKOWSKI

Team: Los Angeles Clippers
Position: Guard/Forward
Height: 6'7"
Weight: 215
Birthdate: September 30, 1970

College: Nebraska
Acquired: Draft rights traded from Pacers with Pooh Richardson and Malik Sealy for Mark Jackson and draft rights to Greg Minor, 6/94

Background: A rapidly maturing player, Piatkowski helped himself immensely with inspired play in front of NBA scouts at the Desert Classic, where he won MVP honors. He began his career at Nebraska with a redshirt season before gradually working his way into a prominent role. Nicknamed the "Polish Rifle," he made a Cornhuskers-record 202 3-pointers and scored 1,934 points, second most in school history. He was drafted 15th overall by Indiana.

Strengths: Piatkowski has big-time shooting skills. Of all the players available in the 1994 draft, only Auburn's Wesley Person has a better stroke. Piatkowski will have no problem with the NBA 3-pointer. What's more, he handles the ball well enough to get his own shot from the small-forward position. Defensively, he does a good job denying the ball on the wing.

Weaknesses: While he handles the rock well for a forward, he probably isn't quite good enough in that department to play shooting guard for long stretches. Likewise, he will have trouble defending the NBA's quicker guards. He has no overwhelming deficiencies.

Analysis: The Clippers acted quickly to fill voids at shooting guard and small forward with the draft-day acquisitions of Lamond Murray and Piatkowski. However, both players are probably best suited for the forward spot, at least early in their careers. If new coach Bill Fitch elects to go up-tempo, Piatkowski could play a major role as an instant-offense player off the bench. He looks to have a good NBA future.

PLAYER SUMMARY	
Will	stroke it good
Can't	defend quickness
Expect	a quality pro
Don't Expect	an attitude
Fantasy Value	$1-3
Card Value	15-30¢

COLLEGE HIGHLIGHTS
- A.P. honorable-mention All-American, 1994
- All-Big Eight, 1993 and 1994
- Big Eight Tournament MVP, 1994
- Desert Classic MVP, 1994

COLLEGE STATISTICS

			FGs		3-PT FGs		FTs							
		G	FG	PCT	FG	PCT	FT	PCT	REB	AST	STL	BLK	PTS	PPG
90-91	NEBR	34	128	.465	44	.346	72	.837	125	68	22	18	372	10.9
91-92	NEBR	29	144	.426	47	.346	79	.725	184	97	21	18	414	14.3
92-93	NEBR	30	178	.485	48	.372	98	.760	171	75	30	8	502	16.7
93-94	NEBR	30	226	.496	63	.366	131	.794	189	82	46	20	646	21.5
Totals		123	676	.471	202	.358	380	.777	669	322	119	64	1934	15.7

KHALID REEVES

Team: Miami Heat
Position: Guard
Height: 6'3"
Weight: 207

Birthdate: July 15, 1972
College: Arizona
Acquired: 1st-round pick in 1994 draft
(12th overall)

Background: A high-profile recruit form New York's Christ the King High School, Reeves chose Arizona, where he was regarded as an underachiever his first three seasons. That changed in 1993-94, as he nearly doubled his scoring average to 24.2 PPG (20th in the country) and propelled the Wildcats to the Final Four. Along the way, he scored 40 points against Michigan and averaged 27.4 points in five NCAA Tournament games. He was one of the stars of the postseason Phoenix Desert Classic.

Strengths: Scouts have compared Reeves to Joe Dumars. He can play both guard spots, break down a defense off the dribble, and create a shot for himself or a teammate. He displays excellent strength when he penetrates, which helps him draw fouls. Reeves is deadly accurate from 12 to 18 feet.

Weaknesses: Reeves has a wealth of talent, but perhaps not the drive to be a star. He appears bored by the game at times. In addition, he's too small—he measured less than 6'2" at the NBA's Chicago cattle call—to deny most shooting guards their points. He rarely had to guard the opponent's best player at Arizona.

Analysis: With free agency looming for Brian Shaw, the Heat needed a guard with playmaking skills. Reeves, though primarily a shooting guard, can survive for brief stretches at the point. Look for him as a back-up at both positions, spelling Steve Smith, Bimbo Coles, and Harold Miner. He could develop into an outstanding NBA player, although he'll have to improve defensively to become another Dumars.

PLAYER SUMMARY

Will ....score in bunches
Can't ....guard the jets
Expect ....a penetrator
Don't Expect ....a bust
Fantasy Value...............................$3-5
Card Value ....40-75¢

COLLEGE HIGHLIGHTS

- John Wooden All-American, 1994
- A.P. second-team All-American, 1994
- Desert Classic All-Tournament team, 1994
- NCAA West Region MVP, 1994

COLLEGE STATISTICS

			FGs		3-PT FGs		FTs							
		G	FG	PCT	FG	PCT	FT	PCT	REB	AST	STL	BLK	PTS	PPG
90-91	ARIZ	35	104	.454	31	.463	78	.690	82	103	36	6	317	9.1
91-92	ARIZ	30	148	.476	44	.370	78	.788	95	110	50	2	418	13.9
92-93	ARIZ	28	118	.498	26	.329	80	.727	97	80	37	1	342	12.2
93-94	ARIZ	35	276	.483	85	.379	211	.799	150	103	64	4	848	24.2
Totals		128	646	.479	186	.380	477	.763	424	396	187	13	1925	15.0

GLENN ROBINSON

Team: Milwaukee Bucks
Position: Forward
Height: 6'8"
Weight: 230

Birthdate: January 10, 1973
College: Purdue
Acquired: 1st-round pick in 1994 draft
(1st overall)

Background: After sitting out his freshman season to become academically eligible, the former prep phenom from Gary, Indiana, made a sudden impact at Purdue, ranking ninth nationally in scoring in 1992-93. Last season, he became the first Big Ten player to top the country in scoring since Purdue's Dave Shellhase in 1966. He was everybody's pick as the college game's Player of the Year. Robinson, also known as "Big Dog," skipped his senior season after receiving assurances that he would be the first player chosen in the draft.

Strengths: Scoring is the name of Robinson's game. He has textbook shooting form and range extending to near the NBA 3-point line. He's a superb finisher on the fastbreak, displays good strength in the paint, and is willing to work for rebounds. He handles the ball well for a forward and will share it with teammates. As scouts say, he knows how to play.

Weaknesses: A poor defensive player, Robinson lacks lateral mobility and figures to struggle against the NBA's quick small forwards. He can't be moved to power forward because, at slightly less than 6'8", he's not big enough. Though he can score in bunches, he needs to refine his post game.

Analysis: Milwaukee wasted little time clearing its small-forward slot, trading Ken Norman to Atlanta and Blue Edwards to Boston. Robinson will start immediately and give the Bucks a boost offensively, but his presence forces Vin Baker—also best suited for small forward—to either power forward or center. Robinson will be a great pro, with the ability to score at least 25 points per game. However, the Larry Bird comparisons may be a little premature, as Robinson still has a little learning to do.

PLAYER SUMMARY

Will ....be the main man
Can't ....guard anybody
Expect............................an instant star
Don't Expect.........................Larry Bird
Fantasy Value............................$35-40
Card Value $3.00-6.00

COLLEGE HIGHLIGHTS

- Consensus All-American, 1994
- A.P. national Player of the Year, 1994
- John Wooden Award winner, 1994
- James Naismith Award winner, 1994

COLLEGE STATISTICS

			FGs		3-PT FGs		FTs							
		G	FG	PCT	FG	PCT	FT	PCT	REB	AST	STL	BLK	PTS	PPG
92-93	PURD	28	246	.474	32	.400	152	.741	258	49	57	34	676	24.1
93-94	PURD	34	368	.483	79	.380	215	.796	344	66	56	31	1030	30.3
Totals		62	614	.479	111	.385	367	.773	602	115	113	65	1706	27.5

CARLOS ROGERS

Team: Golden State Warriors
Position: Forward
Height: 6'11" **Weight:** 220
Birthdate: February 6, 1971
College: Arkansas-Little Rock;
Tennessee St.

Acquired: Draft rights traded from
SuperSonics with Ricky Pierce and a
1995 2nd-round pick for Byron
Houston and Sarunas Marciulionis,
7/94

Background: Rogers sat out his freshman season at Arkansas-Little Rock to become academically eligible, played one season, then sat out another after transferring to Tennessee State, where he was a two-time Ohio Valley Player of the Year. He was the only player in 1993-94 to finish in the top 15 nationally in scoring, rebounding, field goal accuracy, and blocked shots. Rogers was drafted 11th overall before being traded to Golden State.

Strengths: A good athlete, Rogers passes and dribbles well for a power forward, runs the court like a small forward, has good timing, and jumps quickly. He's a constant factor on the offensive boards, getting a lot of dunks on effort plays. Quick feet and good anticipation serve him well on defense. He reminds a lot of people of Vin Baker.

Weaknesses: Though a good scorer, Rogers lacks touch and range on his shot, tending to fire it with a flat trajectory. He tries to do too much with the ball at times, which results in silly turnovers. Also, he needs to add bulk to survive the 82-game NBA grind, especially if he's used mostly at power forward. His free throw shooting needs considerable improvement.

Analysis: Aware that several teams coveted Rogers, Seattle grabbed him after attempts to deal the No. 11 pick to Chicago—as part of a Shawn Kemp-for-Scottie Pippen blockbuster—fell through. Rogers should eventually be a good fit for Golden State as Chris Webber's back-up. Also capable for short spurts at small forward, he has a chance to be a good complementary NBA player.

PLAYER SUMMARY	
Will	reject shots
Can't	pound inside
Expect	a thoroughbred
Don't Expect	a marksman
Fantasy Value	$0
Card Value	25-50¢

COLLEGE HIGHLIGHTS
- A.P. honorable-mention All-American, 1994
- OVC Player of the Year, 1993 and 1994
- All-OVC, 1993 and 1994

COLLEGE STATISTICS

			FGs		3-PT FGs		FTs							
		G	FG	PCT	FG	PCT	FT	PCT	REB	AST	STL	BLK	PTS	PPG
90-91	ALR	19	64	.508	0	.000	31	.554	132	22	11	38	159	8.4
92-93	TSU	29	239	.621	0	.000	111	.624	339	30	19	93	589	20.3
93-94	TSU	31	288	.614	4	.308	179	.649	358	47	21	9	759	24.5
Totals		79	591	.603	4	.250	321	.629	829	99	51	224	1507	19.1

JALEN ROSE

Team: Denver Nuggets
Position: Guard
Height: 6'8"
Weight: 210

Birthdate: January 20, 1973
College: Michigan
Acquired: 1st-round pick in 1994 draft
(13th overall)

Background: Rose was the third of the Fab Five (Chris Webber, Juwan Howard) to be selected in the first round of the NBA draft. He had a memorable three-year career for Michigan, playing in two NCAA championship games. At his best in big games, he scored 25 points vs. Kansas as a sophomore and 31 against Duke as a junior. He and Gary Grant are the only Michigan players with 1,500 points, 400 rebounds, 300 assists, and 100 steals. Rose forfeited his senior season to enter the draft.

Strengths: A vastly improved player in 1993-94, Rose displayed the maturity and consistency that eluded him his first two seasons. He has great basketball instincts, slithery moves in traffic, and a knack for scoring despite unorthodox shooting mechanics. Ball-handling is one of his strengths, as is the ability to see the floor and make the telling pass. He has played in a slew of big games and has usually come out on the winning end.

Weaknesses: His offense won't be a problem in the NBA, but his defense might. He's not quick enough to defend at the point and not physical enough to handle most small forwards. A 6'8" point guard in college, he's without a true position in the NBA. He doesn't have a consistent enough shot to thrive at shooting guard.

Analysis: The Nuggets, building patiently through the draft, added a key player in Rose, who gives them flexibility. He's likely to come off the bench as a rookie, subbing for Bryant Stith in the backcourt and Reggie Williams and Rodney Rogers up front. His defensive shortcomings will be minimized by the presence of Dikembe Mutombo in the middle of the defense.

PLAYER SUMMARY

Will ....play with attitude
Can't ....defend consistently
Expect....................................a solid pro
Don't Expect ....a point guard
Fantasy Value.....................................$1
Card Value. ....75¢-$1.25

COLLEGE HIGHLIGHTS

- John Wooden All-American, 1994
- All-Big Ten, 1994
- A.P. second-team All-American, 1994
- A.P. honorable-mention All-American, 1992

COLLEGE STATISTICS

		G	FGs FG	FGs PCT	3-PT FGs FG	3-PT FGs PCT	FTs FT	FTs PCT	REB	AST	STL	BLK	PTS	PPG
91-92	MICH	34	206	.486	36	.324	149	.756	146	135	38	8	597	17.6
92-93	MICH	36	203	.446	33	.320	116	.720	150	140	43	15	555	15.4
93-94	MICH	32	220	.461	55	.355	141	.734	181	126	38	6	636	19.9
Totals		102	629	.464	124	.336	406	.738	477	401	119	29	1788	17.5

CLIFFORD ROZIER

Team: Golden State Warriors
Position: Center/Forward
Height: 6′9″
Weight: 235

Birthdate: October 31, 1972
College: North Carolina; Louisville
Acquired: 1st-round pick in 1994 draft (16th overall)

Background: Considered a blue-chip recruit out of Bradenton, Florida, Rozier signed with North Carolina, but after a nondescript freshman season, he transferred to Louisville. He led the Metro Conference in rebounding as a sophomore and field goal percentage as a junior, and he set an NCAA single-game accuracy mark by going 15 for 15 against Eastern Kentucky in December 1993. He bypassed his final season of eligibility to enter the draft.

Strengths: Rozier has an NBA body, augmented by good athleticism. He throws his weight around on defense and gets his share of rebounds. He's an effective box-to-box scorer. His .618 field goal percentage as a senior means he'll likely stay above the 50-percent mark in the pros.

Weaknesses: Rozier played poorly at the end of his junior season—making a total of two field goals in two NCAA tourney games—and was fortunate to be drafted as high as he was. He struggles to score when guarded by a big man, usually resorting to a bad, off-balance shot. A center in college, he'll have to play power forward in the NBA, which compounds the problem. He lacks consistency on the boards, judgment as a passer, and a clue at the foul line. He doesn't run well either.

Analysis: The Warriors ignored Rozier's faults in their desperate search for a big man to team with Chris Webber. Rozier can go toe-to-toe with the NBA's strongmen, but he doesn't fit as a center—and neither does Webber. Look for Rozier to play sparingly as a rookie, or even turn to Europe if he can't agree to a contract with Golden State. Eric Mobley probably would have been a better selection for the Warriors.

PLAYER SUMMARY

Will ....tease
Can't...............................run the floor
Expect..a trick
Don't Expect ....a treat
Fantasy Value....................................$0
Card Value ....25-40¢

COLLEGE HIGHLIGHTS

• A.P. All-American, 1994
• Metro Player of the Year, 1993 and 1994
• All-Metro, 1993 and 1994
• Metro Tournament MVP, 1994

COLLEGE STATISTICS

			FGs		3-PT FGs		FTs							
		G	FG	PCT	FG	PCT	FT	PCT	REB	AST	STL	BLK	PTS	PPG
90-91	NC	34	64	.471	0	.000	39	.565	101	18	12	17	167	4.9
92-93	LOU	31	192	.561	0	.000	104	.568	338	62	36	41	488	15.7
93-94	LOU	34	247	.618	0	.000	122	.545	377	53	30	76	616	18.1
Totals		99	503	.573	0	.000	265	.557	816	133	78	134	1271	12.8

DICKEY SIMPKINS

Team: Chicago Bulls
Position: Forward/Center
Height: 6'9"
Weight: 250

Birthdate: April 6, 1972
College: Providence
Acquired: 1st-round pick in 1994 draft (21st overall)

Background: A largely anonymous player at Providence, Simpkins became a first-round pick after inspired work at the postseason Portsmouth Invitational and Phoenix Desert Classic. He averaged 20.5 points and 12.5 rebounds at Portsmouth and 17.3 points at Phoenix, compared with his career college numbers of 9.8 points and 6.3 rebounds. At Providence, he played alongside Michael Smith, a second-round draft pick of the Sacramento Kings.

Strengths: A fine all-around player with NBA size and strength, Simpkins has a good understanding of defense. He is exceptionally strong guarding the post and is adept at taking away passing angles. Though not a leaper, he blocks a lot of shots. He shows a soft touch and some offensive tricks around the basket. He seems to be on the upward path of his learning curve, which bodes well for his future in the NBA.

Weaknesses: First and foremost, Simpkins must play with more fire and aggressiveness. He looked placid next to the ultra-intense Smith. Like most young big men, he needs to expand his offensive repertoire, learning to face the basket and score and to pass out of the double-team.

Analysis: The Bulls, expecting to lose Scott Williams and/or Horace Grant via free agency, selected Simpkins as a potential contributor at power forward. Though he played mostly center in college, Simpkins should have little problem adapting to the four spot. Now that Williams and Grant are indeed gone, Simpkins will make the team and vie with 1993 rookie Corie Blount for playing time. He might end up in the starting lineup.

PLAYER SUMMARY

Will.............................make the team
Can't ....fill it up
Expect ....good skills
Don't Expect ....a rah-rah guy
Fantasy Value...............................$1-3
Card Value ....10-20¢

COLLEGE HIGHLIGHTS

- Desert Classic All-Tournament team, 1994
- Portsmouth Invitational All-Tournament team, 1994
- Big East All-Tournament team, 1993 and 1994

COLLEGE STATISTICS

		G	FGs FG	FGs PCT	3-PT FGs FG	3-PT FGs PCT	FTs FT	FTs PCT	REB	AST	STL	BLK	PTS	PPG
90-91	PROV	32	90	.492	4	.400	67	.609	211	33	24	31	251	7.8
91-92	PROV	30	89	.492	1	.250	90	.703	174	37	14	26	269	9.0
92-93	PROV	33	122	.450	1	.333	106	.596	216	41	25	18	351	10.6
93-94	PROV	30	129	.516	3	.333	94	.686	189	38	22	21	355	11.8
Totals		125	430	.486	9	.346	357	.645	790	149	85	96	1226	9.8

BROOKS THOMPSON

Team: Orlando Magic
Position: Guard
Height: 6'4"
Weight: 195

Birthdate: July 19, 1970
College: Texas A&M; Oklahoma St.
Acquired: 1st-round pick in 1994 draft
(27th overall)

Background: Thompson, a left-hander from Littleton, Colorado, split his college ball between Texas A&M and Oklahoma State, setting 3-point shooting records at both schools. All told, he made 270 treys in four seasons. He increased his scoring average and free throw accuracy each year. He helped OSU to a second-place finish in the Big Eight as a senior while leading the Cowboys in scoring and assists (5.7). He ranked seventh nationally last year in 3-point percentage (47.2).

Strengths: Primarily a shooting guard, Thompson showed at the Chicago pre-draft camp that he has the ball-handling and playmaking skills to merit back-up minutes at the point. His greatest asset is his jump shot, which is a weapon from NBA trey range. He displays good toughness and leadership attributes.

Weaknesses: Though he has a nice shooting stroke, Thompson tends to line-drive the ball at times. His shot selection also needs refinement; he won't be allowed to launch at will in the NBA. He figures to be vulnerable against quickness if asked to play the point. He gets into trouble when he tries to force the action, rather than letting the game come to him.

Analysis: Orlando spent the last pick of the first round on Thompson, who will probably make the team since the club traded point guard Scott Skiles. If he stays with the Magic, Thompson will play only a minor role, as Thompson probably can't play the point and the club already has long-range gunners Dennis Scott and Nick Anderson. His role could expand if he's dealt to a team that needs scoring off the bench.

PLAYER SUMMARY	
Will	bomb away
Can't	crash the boards
Expect	a shooter
Don't Expect	a savior
Fantasy Value	$0
Card Value	10-20¢

COLLEGE HIGHLIGHTS

- All-Big Eight, 1994
- All-Big Eight Tournament, 1994
- Honorable-mention All-Big Eight, 1993

COLLEGE STATISTICS

			FGs		3-PT FGs		FTs							
		G	FG	PCT	FG	PCT	FT	PCT	REB	AST	STL	BLK	PTS	PPG
89-90	TAM	31	95	.377	43	.321	25	.641	73	69	39	1	258	8.3
90-91	TAM	29	150	.470	57	.388	64	.744	91	165	60	3	421	14.5
92-93	OSU	29	140	.456	60	.373	83	.755	113	144	70	3	423	14.6
93-94	OSU	34	179	.446	110	.472	105	.790	137	195	99	3	573	16.9
Totals		123	564	.441	270	.400	277	.753	414	573	268	10	1675	13.6

B.J. TYLER

Team: Philadelphia 76ers
Position: Guard
Height: 6'1"
Weight: 185

Birthdate: April 30, 1971
College: DePaul; Texas
Acquired: 1st-round pick in 1994 draft (20th overall)

Background: Though he prepped in Port Arthur, Texas, Tyler chose to attend DePaul. But after a dismal freshman season, he returned home to play for the Longhorns. He was limited to 13 games his junior season because of a broken foot and was suspended from the SWC Tournament for failing a drug test. He spent time in John Lucas's clinic for drug abuse, though Lucas insisted Tyler was merely treated for depression. He trails only Johnny Moore on Texas' all-time assists list.

Strengths: Tyler has more quickness than any other player selected in the 1994 draft. He can get up and down the floor with the greyhounds, create an opening to get his own shot, and get in his man's face defensively. He has fast hands and the ability to shoot gaps for steals. He also possesses good shooting range and a scorer's mentality. He's never lacking in confidence.

Weaknesses: A smallish 6'1", Tyler has no chance to play shooting guard in the NBA and lacks the playmaking mentality to thrive as a point guard. A selfish player, he looks for his own offense far too much. He needs to sublimate his ego and work on developing a floor game, or else he'll join Lance Blanks, Travis Mays, and Joey Wright as NBA busts from Texas.

Analysis: Philadelphia's selection of Tyler was no surprise considering his relationship with new 76ers coach/G.M. John Lucas. What's more, the Sixers needed a point guard after discovering last season that Dana Barros wasn't a playmaker. Tyler will make the team and could work his way into a rotation that should also include Barros and Johnny Dawkins.

PLAYER SUMMARY

Will ....fire it up
Can't ....find a position
Expect ....a roadrunner
Don't Expect.....................a sure thing
Fantasy Value...........................$1-3
Card Value ....15-30¢

COLLEGE HIGHLIGHTS

• A.P. third-team All-American, 1994
• SWC Player of the Year, 1994
• SWC Classic MVP, 1994
• SWC All-Defensive team, 1994

COLLEGE STATISTICS

			FGs		3-PT FGs		FTs							
		G	FG	PCT	FG	PCT	FT	PCT	REB	AST	STL	BLK	PTS	PPG
89-90	DeP	17	18	.333	3	.167	11	.786	15	36	17	2	50	2.9
91-92	TEX	35	217	.435	84	.365	122	.792	99	229	82	7	640	18.3
92-93	TEX	13	78	.446	33	.355	36	.632	49	79	32	2	225	17.3
93-94	TEX	28	213	.443	99	.374	112	.727	94	175	87	7	637	22.8
Totals		93	526	.434	219	.362	281	.745	257	519	218	18	1552	16.7

CHARLIE WARD

Team: New York Knicks
Position: Guard
Height: 6'2"
Weight: 190

Birthdate: October 12, 1970
College: Florida St.
Acquired: 1st-round pick in 1994 draft (26th overall)

Background: A renowned two-sport star, Ward won college football's Heisman Trophy as a Florida State senior, then turned his attention to basketball where, among other things, he scored 19 points against Duke. He played only one full basketball season yet became the Seminoles' all-time steals leader. After being snubbed in the NFL draft, he ruled out football as a career option, thus boosting his status as a first-round pick in the NBA draft. His stock soared with solid showings at the Phoenix and Chicago pre-draft camps.

Strengths: Ward rates highly as an athlete and off the charts in terms of intangibles. He exudes leadership and character and commands respect from opponents. Though lacking refined techniques, he has good skills, plays with quickness, and gets the ball to the right people. Scouts say he'll have no trouble with the physical grind of the NBA.

Weaknesses: Most of Ward's rough spots can be smoothed with experience and repetition. His one glaring weakness is lack of explosiveness as a penetrator, whether it's for a shot or a pass. His stroke needs work, as evidenced by his 36.5-percent aim in 1993-94.

Analysis: The Knicks added Ward to their crowded picture at point guard. Already onboard on draft day were Derek Harper, Doc Rivers, and Greg Anthony. Harper and Rivers are short-timers, and Anthony has been inconsistent, so Ward will be given a long look to see if he can be the eventual starter. He won't play much as a rookie, but he should feel right at home with the linebacking corps that is the New York Knicks.

PLAYER SUMMARY	
Will	run the offense
Can't	cash the trey
Expect	a two-year project
Don't Expect	pigskin plans
Fantasy Value	$0
Card Value	$1.00-3.00

COLLEGE HIGHLIGHTS
• Sullivan Award winner, 1994
• Heisman Trophy winner, 1993
• Second-team All-ACC Tournament, 1993
• Metro All-Freshman team, 1991

COLLEGE STATISTICS

		G	FGs FG	FGs PCT	3-PT FGs FG	3-PT FGs PCT	FTs FT	FTs PCT	REB	AST	STL	BLK	PTS	PPG
90-91	FSU	30	81	.455	15	.313	62	.713	89	103	71	8	239	8.0
91-92	FSU	28	72	.497	22	.458	35	.530	90	122	75	6	201	7.2
92-93	FSU	17	49	.462	16	.320	18	.667	45	93	48	5	132	7.8
93-94	FSU	16	61	.365	21	.253	25	.625	62	78	44	2	168	10.5
Totals		91	263	.441	74	.323	140	.636	286	396	238	21	740	8.1

MONTY WILLIAMS

Team: New York Knicks
Position: Forward
Height: 6'8"
Weight: 225

Birthdate: October 8, 1971
College: Notre Dame
Acquired: 1st-round pick in 1994 draft
(24th overall)

Background: A fabulously talented player, Williams was forced to miss the 1990-91 and 1991-92 seasons at Notre Dame after being diagnosed with thickening of the muscle between the chambers of the heart. Cleared to play in September 1992, he returned to lead the Irish in scoring and rebounding that season. His ascent continued as a senior when he scored 30 points vs. Boston College and Bill Curley, 31 vs. Providence and Dickey Simpkins, and 34 vs. Duke and Grant Hill.

Strengths: Williams brings an accomplished all-around game to the small-forward position, and he has the versatility to swing to shooting guard for brief periods of time. More of a scorer than a shooter, he handles the ball adroitly and can create his own shot. A good, albeit slender, athlete, Williams has easy moves and a soft touch. He does a good job of drawing contact and getting to the foul line.

Weaknesses: The only significant negative is his heart condition, which scared off several NBA teams with better drafting positions than the Knicks. Doctors don't foresee any problems, but some teams didn't want to take the chance after the heart-related deaths of Hank Gathers and Reggie Lewis. Williams needs to retool his stroke at the line after dipping below 70 percent as a senior.

Analysis: New York, unhappy with the production it received from small forwards Charles Smith and Anthony Mason in 1993-94, took a chance on Williams, who has the potential to be an NBA starter, health allowing. It's doubtful he'll play much as a rookie, however, especially come playoff time, as Pat Riley prefers a reliable eight-man rotation.

PLAYER SUMMARY	
Will	excite the masses
Can't	slug it out
Expect	a good pro
Don't Expect	any guarantees
Fantasy Value	$2-4
Card Value	50-75¢

COLLEGE HIGHLIGHTS
- A.P. honorable-mention All-American, 1994
- World Under-22 Championship team member, 1993

COLLEGE STATISTICS

			FGs		3-PT FGs		FTs							
		G	FG	PCT	FG	PCT	FT	PCT	REB	AST	STL	BLK	PTS	PPG
89-90	ND	29	83	.483	2	.200	54	.740	108	31	15	16	222	7.7
92-93	ND	27	177	.461	25	.338	121	.791	251	39	31	19	500	18.5
93-94	ND	29	237	.511	32	.410	143	.698	239	68	41	15	649	22.4
Totals		85	497	.487	59	.364	318	.738	598	138	87	50	1371	16.1

SHARONE WRIGHT

Team: Philadelphia 76ers
Position: Forward/Center
Height: 6'11"
Weight: 260

Birthdate: January 30, 1973
College: Clemson
Acquired: 1st-round pick in 1994 draft
(6th overall)

Background: Wright is the latest in a long line of standouts, including Norm Nixon and Jeff Malone, from Southwest High School in Macon, Georgia. He had a good, if largely unnoticed, career at Clemson, where he was the only ACC player to average a double-double each of the past two seasons. He finished second in the nation in blocked shots as a sophomore with 4.1 per game. Last year, he ranked 15th nationally in blocked shots (2.9 per game) and 19th in rebounding (10.6). He forfeited his senior season to enter the 1994 draft.

Strengths: Wright has the ideal body to be a power forward/back-up center in the NBA. He displays outstanding strength, a good work ethic, and the willingness to mix it up underneath the basket. His forte is rebounding, but he's also an accomplished shot-blocker. He tends to play best against top competition.

Weaknesses: Other than power lay-ups and dunks, Wright lacks a low-post repertoire. He's sorely in need of some moves with his back to the basket, and he needs to expand his shooting range beyond ten feet. He tends to carry too much weight, and he had some bad games against inferior competition in college. Six-point nights were far too common.

Analysis: The Sixers are touting him as "The Wright Stuff" and are planning to start him at power forward, enabling Clarence Weatherspoon to develop at small forward and easing the inside load on center Shawn Bradley. Some scouts question Wright's future as a starter, but they agree he can be a good rebounding specialist in the NBA. A Weatherspoon/Wright/Bradley front line gives the Sixers great hope for the future.

PLAYER SUMMARY

Will ....mix it up inside
Can't ....score consistently
Expect ....a deluxe rebounder
Don't Expect.............a sudden impact
Fantasy Value................................$2-4
Card Value ....60¢-$1.00

COLLEGE HIGHLIGHTS

- A.P. honorable-mention All-American, 1994
- Third-team All-ACC, 1993

COLLEGE STATISTICS

			FGs		3-PT FGs		FTs							
		G	FG	PCT	FG	PCT	FT	PCT	REB	AST	STL	BLK	PTS	PPG
91-92	CLEM	28	137	.498	0	.000	63	.563	227	11	23	63	337	12.0
92-93	CLEM	30	178	.567	0	.000	93	.669	314	26	22	124	449	15.0
93-94	CLEM	34	186	.525	0	.000	150	.644	362	41	24	99	522	15.4
Totals		92	501	.531	0	.000	306	.632	903	78	69	286	1308	14.2

DERRICK ALSTON

Team: Philadelphia 76ers
Position: Forward
Height: 6'11" **Weight:** 225
Birthdate: August 20, 1972
College: Duquesne
Acquired: 2nd-round pick in 1994 draft
(33rd overall)

PLAYER SUMMARY	
Will	run and jump
Can't	mix it up
Expect	blocked shots
Don't Expect	a total player
Fantasy	$0 Card 20-35¢

Background: Last year, Alston quietly became the first player to lead the Atlantic 10 in scoring and field goal accuracy in the same season. He scored in double figures in 97 of 114 career games and ranks second in Duquesne annals with 1,903 points.

Strengths: An excellent shot-blocker with long arms and good mobility, Alston has been compared to Chicago's Corie Blount, but with a better offensive game. He has a consistent jump shot facing the basket and good instincts for the game.

Weaknesses: Long and lean, he's not ready physically for the NBA grind. A center most of the time in college, he needs to learn a new position (power forward) and expand his offensive package with his back to the basket.

Analysis: Alston entered a crowded picture at power forward. Fellow Sixer rookie Sharone Wright will get most of the playing time, with Tim Perry and Scott Williams also available. Alston might be better off taking a job in Europe for a year or two.

COLLEGE STATISTICS

		G	FGP	FTP	RPG	APG	PPG
90-91	DUQ	28	.536	.598	6.3	1.3	11.3
91-92	DUQ	28	.556	.526	8.0	1.5	13.9
92-93	DUQ	28	.563	.574	9.3	1.1	19.9
93-94	DUQ	30	.578	.601	7.3	1.4	21.3
Totals		114	.561	.576	7.7	1.3	16.7

ADRIAN AUTRY

Team: Unsigned
Position: Guard
Height: 6'4" **Weight:** 207
Birthdate: February 28, 1972
College: Syracuse

PLAYER SUMMARY	
Will	score in quantity
Can't	do it every night
Expect	no guarantees
Don't Expect	Adrian Dantley
Fantasy	$0 Card 10-25¢

Background: Autry, a four-year starter at Syracuse, and Sherman Douglas are the only Orangemen players to tally 1,500 points and 600 assists, and Autry is the only player to lead Syracuse in assists for four seasons. Against Missouri in the 1994 NCAA Tournament, he tied his career high with 31 points, all in the second half and overtime.

Strengths: Though not quick, Autry handles the ball deftly and penetrates well. He has a wide body, which helps him get his shot close to the basket. His outside shooting improved considerably last year. He's a legitimate point guard.

Weaknesses: Autry tends to blow hot and cold with his offensive game. He tried too hard to impress in the postseason camps, forcing plays and using poor judgment. His quickness needs improvement; dropping a few pounds could be the solution.

Analysis: Though scouts considered Autry a good sleeper pick, no team selected him in the draft. He's a boom-or-bust prospect who could develop into a quality NBA point guard or get flushed from the league in a New York minute.

COLLEGE STATISTICS

		G	FGP	FTP	RPG	APG	PPG
90-91	SYR	31	.402	.705	2.5	5.3	9.7
91-92	SYR	31	.367	.703	4.1	4.0	11.0
92-93	SYR	29	.432	.798	3.7	5.6	13.7
93-94	SYR	30	.449	.784	6.0	6.1	16.2
Totals		121	.416	.748	4.1	5.2	12.7

DAMON BAILEY

Team: Indiana Pacers
Position: Guard
Height: 6'3" **Weight:** 201
Birthdate: October 21, 1971
College: Indiana
Acquired: 2nd-round pick in 1994 draft
(44th overall)

PLAYER SUMMARY	
Will .... drill the 15-footer
Can't .... make the NBA trey
Expect .... a struggle to stick
Don't Expect .... Thurl Bailey
Fantasy .... $0   Card ...... 25-50¢

Background: An Indiana high school legend, Bailey persevered through college despite unrealistic expectations from Indiana's zealous fans. He salvaged his career with a good senior season in which he earned All-Big Ten acclaim and led the Hoosiers in scoring and assists.

Strengths: Bailey's savvy tends to compensate for his ordinary athleticism. He honed his shooting stroke to near perfection in 1993-94. He plays well in transition, either getting his shot or setting up others.

Weaknesses: Bailey has several faults. He's never been a true point guard and is a little undersized for shooting guard. He can't beat many people one-on-one and is a step slow defensively. While a good shooter, he lacks range.

Analysis: The Pacers don't have an opening for Bailey, but they might in a year or two when Byron Scott and perhaps Vern Fleming retire. Bailey's best chance is to try the CBA for a couple years to see how he adapts to a system other than Bob Knight's.

COLLEGE STATISTICS

		G	FGP	FTP	RPG	APG	PPG
90-91	IND	33	.506	.692	2.9	2.9	11.4
91-92	IND	34	.497	.765	3.6	3.1	12.4
92-93	IND	35	.459	.728	3.3	4.1	10.1
93-94	IND	30	.481	.802	4.3	4.3	19.6
Totals		132	.485	.754	3.5	3.6	13.2

JAMES BLACKWELL

Team: Unsigned
Position: Guard
Height: 6'0" **Weight:** 190
Birthdate: February 25, 1968
College: Dartmouth

PLAYER SUMMARY	
Will .... share the ball
Can't .... shoot straight
Expect .... a struggle to stick
Don't Expect .. much P.T. in 1994-95
Fantasy .... $0   Card .... N/A

Background: Undrafted out of Dartmouth of the Ivy League in 1991, Blackwell has been kicking around the WBL and CBA. He played for three different CBA clubs in 1993-94 and earned second-team all-league honors with averages of 15.4 points and 7.4 assists per game. He was one of Boston's final training-camp cuts in 1993.

Strengths: A fierce competitor, Blackwell can run a team on offense and put outstanding pressure on the ball defensively. He has average or above-average point-guard skills in all areas except shooting. Strength and toughness are his best assets.

Weaknesses: Blackwell's inability to score is holding him back. He has a bad-looking shot and poor release mechanics. When he's missing, he's missing badly.

Analysis: Blackwell was close to making the NBA in 1993-94 and should be close again. He's not as good a playmaker as some other fringe point guards (such as Chris Corchiani, who beat him out in Boston), but he's better defensively than most. He played with Seattle's team in the Utah summer league.

COLLEGE STATISTICS

		G	FGP	FTP	RPG	APG	PPG
87-88	DART	25	.415	.660	1.5	2.1	4.6
88-89	DART	24	.470	.772	2.7	4.8	11.4
89-90	DART	16	.458	.816	4.1	3.6	13.1
90-91	DART	26	.419	.770	3.0	4.5	19.3
Totals		91	.437	.765	2.7	3.7	12.1

KRIS BRUTON

Team: Chicago Bulls
Position: Guard
Height: 6'5" **Weight:** 190
Birthdate: January 10, 1971
College: Benedict
Acquired: 2nd-round pick in 1994 draft
(49th overall)

PLAYER SUMMARY	
Will	fly to the rack
Can't	stroke it well
Expect	a sky-walker
Don't Expect	a finished product
Fantasy	$0 Card ......10-15¢

Background: Other than foreigners, Bruton was the most obscure selection in the 1994 draft. He played at Benedict College, a tiny school in South Carolina, where he averaged nearly a double-double as a senior while shooting 60 percent from the field. He shined at the Chicago pre-draft camp.

Strengths: A terrific long-term prospect, Bruton has good speed and quickness, live legs, and a lengthy wingspan. He can be a positive factor on the fastbreak and in pressing defenses.

Weaknesses: Bruton isn't close to being ready to play in the NBA. He's inconsistent with his shot, lacking a smooth release and good overall technique. Primarily a shooting guard, he might be able to play some small forward eventually, but only if he adds some meat to his bones.

Analysis: Seeking to overhaul its roster, Chicago took a chance on Bruton. The Bulls have nothing to lose by bringing him to camp, and could discover they have a project worth keeping. Bruton could make the team only because six Chicago players were unrestricted free agents this summer.

COLLEGE STATISTICS

	G	FGP	FTP	RPG	APG	PPG
93-94 BEN	30	.603	.610	9.9	1.6	20.4
Totals	30	.603	.610	9.9	1.6	20.4

ALBERT BURDITT

Team: Houston Rockets
Position: Forward
Height: 6'7" **Weight:** 230
Birthdate: May 15, 1972
College: Texas
Acquired: 2nd-round pick in 1994 draft
(53rd overall)

PLAYER SUMMARY	
Will	swat a few shots
Can't	intimidate
Expect	a quick exit
Don't Expect	any 3-pointers
Fantasy	$0 Card ......10-15¢

Background: A shot-blocking specialist early in his career at Texas, Burditt matured into a good all-around talent, becoming the first player in school history with 1,000 points, 800 rebounds, 200 blocks, and 150 steals. He was named SWC Defensive Player of the Year for 1993-94.

Strengths: Burditt is an excellent shot-blocker and rebounder for his size. A good athlete, he can beat most power forwards down the court for easy baskets.

Weaknesses: At 6'7", Burditt is too short to survive inside in the NBA. Texas played up-tempo, so he wasn't required to hunker down in the trenches at either end. He lacks any significant skill to carry him in the big leagues.

Analysis: Burditt has little chance of making the roster of the world champions. Blocking Burditt's path are Otis Thorpe, Matt Bullard, and Carl Herrera. The Rockets would have preferred point guard Anthony Goldwire, who was selected by Phoenix one pick ahead of Burditt.

COLLEGE STATISTICS

		G	FGP	FTP	RPG	APG	PPG
90-91	TEX	32	.506	.429	4.0	0.5	3.2
91-92	TEX	35	.559	.671	8.7	0.8	6.9
92-93	TEX	12	.540	.607	14.1	1.4	14.9
93-94	TEX	34	.590	.614	8.6	1.1	15.7
Totals		113	.564	.607	7.9	0.9	9.4

GARY COLLIER

Team: Cleveland Cavaliers
Position: Guard
Height: 6'4" **Weight:** 195
Birthdate: October 8, 1971
College: Tulsa
Acquired: 2nd-round pick in 1994 draft (42nd overall)

PLAYER SUMMARY	
Will	fill it up
Can't	run and jump
Expect	a player
Don't Expect	anything now
Fantasy	$0 Card ....10-15¢

Background: Collier emerged suddenly as a sophomore at Tulsa and continued to increase his productivity each year. The first Tulsa player with 1,500 points and 500 rebounds, he lifted the Golden Hurricane to the Sweet 16 of the 1994 NCAA Tournament, averaging 31.3 points in three games.

Strengths: Collier is a solid offensive player who tends to lull his opponent to sleep before erupting for big numbers. Scouts compare him to Jeff Malone, another steady mid-range jump-shooter. Collier has a stout work ethic and thrives in money games.

Weaknesses: Because he's subpar athletically, Collier can be beaten by quickness when he's playing defense. He won't beat his man up and down the court in a push game either.

Analysis: Cleveland used its only pick in the draft on Collier, who has a good chance to stick as a back-up shooting guard. The Cavs appear ready to move John Battle, and Bobby Phills isn't a pure two man. Gerald Wilkins returns as the starter.

COLLEGE STATISTICS

		G	FGP	FTP	RPG	APG	PPG
90-91	TULS	26	.517	.800	1.7	0.2	2.5
91-92	TULS	30	.467	.797	5.6	0.8	13.4
92-93	TULS	29	.535	.679	5.7	1.4	15.0
93-94	TULS	31	.518	.773	6.7	2.4	22.9
Totals		116	.509	.755	5.1	1.3	13.9

JEVON CRUDUP

Team: Detroit Pistons
Position: Forward
Height: 6'9" **Weight:** 230
Birthdate: April 27, 1972
College: Missouri
Acquired: 2nd-round pick in 1994 draft (48th overall)

PLAYER SUMMARY	
Will	do the dirty work
Can't	light it up
Expect	a mauler
Don't Expect	a slacker
Fantasy	$0 Card ....15-25¢

Background: Crudup finished his career among Missouri's top ten in scoring, rebounding, blocks, and steals. Doug Smith, Steve Stipanovich, and Crudup are the only Missouri players to achieve 1,400 points, 800 rebounds, and 100 blocks in a career.

Strengths: Sculpted with muscles on top of muscles, Crudup has a prototypical NBA body. He's physical, rebounds with effort, and runs the court well. Defensively, he lays his body on people and makes them work for their points. He does the little things that help a team win.

Weaknesses: Crudup's offensive game isn't on the same level as his defense. He has bad hands, which limit him to putbacks and short stuff around the hoop. He struggles to convert from the free throw line.

Analysis: Detroit, which reeled in Grant Hill in the first round, could find room for Crudup as the third-string power forward behind Terry Mills and Pete Chilcutt. That assumes the Pistons part company with Cadillac Anderson, as expected.

COLLEGE STATISTICS

		G	FGP	FTP	RPG	APG	PPG
90-91	MISS	15	.526	.571	7.1	1.3	12.0
91-92	MISS	30	.507	.676	8.2	1.8	15.3
92-93	MISS	33	.501	.504	8.3	1.2	13.6
93-94	MISS	31	.484	.643	8.0	1.4	13.2
Totals		109	.502	.607	8.0	1.4	13.7

RODNEY DENT

Team: Orlando Magic
Position: Center
Height: 6'10" **Weight:** 256
Birthdate: December 25, 1970
College: Odessa; Kentucky
Acquired: 2nd-round pick in 1994 draft
(31st overall)

PLAYER SUMMARY	
Will	reject shots
Can't	make FTs
Expect	a project
Don't Expect	a stiff
Fantasy	$0 Card ......15-25¢

Background: Dent spent two seasons at junior college power Odessa College before enrolling at Kentucky. His senior season ended prematurely when he suffered a serious injury to his left knee in January. Never a big-time scorer, he averaged 12.8 points at Odessa and 7.4 at Kentucky.

Strengths: Dent displayed good athleticism before his injury. When healthy, he can run, jump, and beat other big men with quickness. He's a very good shot-blocker.

Weaknesses: Dent risked his future by coming back too quickly after surgery. While quick in the post, he's a bit thin and lacks the strength to push NBA centers off the blocks. He has questionable hands and his offensive game needs a lot of work.

Analysis: Dent might have been selected in the first round if not for questions about his knee. He luckily landed with the Magic, who don't have a back-up for Shaquille O'Neal. Dent won't have to play a lot of minutes, which should allow him to progress at an easy pace.

COLLEGE STATISTICS

		G	FGP	FTP	RPG	APG	PPG
89-90	ODES	31	.538	.640	7.9	0.3	13.1
90-91	ODES	32	.671	.688	8.0	0.3	12.5
92-93	KENT	34	.578	.532	5.1	0.5	6.4
93-94	KENT	11	.676	.556	4.5	0.2	10.5
Ken. Totals		45	.608	.541	5.2	0.4	7.4

HOWARD EISLEY

Team: Minnesota Timberwolves
Position: Guard
Height: 6'3" **Weight:** 180
Birthdate: December 4, 1972
College: Boston College
Acquired: 2nd-round pick in 1994 draft
(30th overall)

PLAYER SUMMARY	
Will	make the team
Can't	create consistently
Expect	a bulldog
Don't Expect	a waterbug
Fantasy	$0 Card ......10-15¢

Background: After playing with Jalen Rose and Voshon Lenard for Detroit's Southwestern High, Eisley went to Boston College, where he led the Eagles in assists four consecutive seasons. He averaged 16.3 points in the 1994 NCAA Tournament as B.C. advanced to the East Regional final.

Strengths: Still improving, Eisley has a chance to be a quality NBA point guard. He's tough and tenacious defensively and has grown into a good offensive player. His range extends to near the NBA 3-point arc. Pressure doesn't seem to faze him.

Weaknesses: Scouts consider him more of a scorer than a pure playmaker. He lacks the quickness to explode by defenders with his dribble. Otherwise, he has no damning faults.

Analysis: Minnesota acted wisely by selecting Eisley. He gives them a player to compete with, and perhaps beat out, back-up point guard Chris Smith. If Eisley works out as expected, the Timberwolves will have flexibility for trades.

COLLEGE STATISTICS

		G	FGP	FTP	RPG	APG	PPG
90-91	BC	30	.360	.750	2.6	3.3	9.9
91-92	BC	31	.488	.746	3.6	4.4	11.6
92-93	BC	31	.443	.834	3.5	4.9	13.7
93-94	BC	34	.476	.790	3.4	4.6	16.0
Totals		126	.444	.784	3.3	4.3	12.9

ANDREI FETISOV

Team: Milwaukee Bucks
Position: Forward
Height: 6'10" **Weight:** 215
College: None
Acquired: Draft rights traded from Celtics with Ed Pinckney for Blue Edwards and Derek Strong, 6/94

PLAYER SUMMARY	
Will	hit the jumper
Can't	defend inside
Expect	a string bean
Don't Expect	anything now
Fantasy	$0 Card	N/A

Background: Fetisov, from St. Petersburg, Russia, played professionally for Forum Valladolid of the Spanish League in 1993-94, averaging 13.4 points and 7.2 rebounds while shooting 32.7 percent from 3-point range. Previously, he played for the Russian team that finished second in the 1993 European championships.

Strengths: While he stands 6'10", Fetisov is viewed by scouts as a small forward who prefers taking jump shots to mixing it up underneath. He moves well with or without the ball and has excellent range. He blocks a few shots and gets his share of rebounds.

Weaknesses: Similar to Vin Baker in size, but more like Matt Bullard talent-wise, Fetisov needs to add meat to his rail-thin body. He's weak above the waist and lacks an advanced post game.

Analysis: The Bucks received the rights to Fetisov, the 36th pick, in a deal with Boston that also netted Ed Pinckney. Fetisov could surface one day in the NBA, but probably not in 1994-95. More likely, he'll stay in Spain for a while. He's not ready for the rigors of 82 games against the best players in the world.

COLLEGE STATISTICS

—DID NOT PLAY—

LAWRENCE FUNDERBURKE

Team: Sacramento Kings
Position: Forward
Height: 6'9" **Weight:** 230
Birthdate: December 15, 1970
College: Indiana; Ohio St.
Acquired: 2nd-round pick in 1994 draft (51st overall)

PLAYER SUMMARY	
Will	go to the glass
Can't	maintain focus
Expect	some skills
Don't Expect	a keeper
Fantasy	$0 Card	20-40¢

Background: Funderburke went to Indiana as a freshman, but a year later he was back in his hometown playing for the Buckeyes. He led Ohio State in field goal percentage and was named third-team All-Big Ten each of his three seasons. He had surgery on both knees before his senior year.

Strengths: A versatile, lefty power forward, Funderburke has the skills to take his man outside, then beat him with the dribble. He's a decent shooter when given time to set himself, though his overall shooting must improve. He has long arms, good timing, and savvy as a rebounder.

Weaknesses: Funderburke needs to smooth wrinkles on his shot, expand his perimeter game, and shed the controversy that dogged him most of his college career.

Analysis: With earlier selections in the 1994 draft, the Kings took Brian Grant and Michael Smith. If Funderburke sticks, it will be as the 12th man. More likely, he will get his pro indoctrination in the CBA.

COLLEGE STATISTICS

		G	FGP	FTP	RPG	APG	PPG
89-90	IND	6	.491	.519	6.7	1.3	11.7
91-92	OSU	23	.548	.654	6.5	0.8	12.2
92-93	OSU	28	.533	.622	6.8	1.2	16.3
93-94	OSU	29	.545	.594	6.6	1.0	15.2
Totals		86	.538	.613	6.6	1.0	14.5

CHAD GALLAGHER

Team: Unsigned
Position: Forward
Height: 6'10" **Weight:** 245
Birthdate: May 30, 1969
College: Creighton

PLAYER SUMMARY	
Will	contribute now
Can't	own the boards
Expect	a decent player
Don't Expect	an intimidator
Fantasy	$0 Card	N/A

Background: Drafted by Phoenix in 1991, Gallagher has been hanging around the fringes for three seasons. He gained an invitation to this year's Chicago pre-draft camp, where he performed well enough to perhaps earn an NBA roster spot in 1994-95. As a collegian, he helped lead Creighton to a pair of NCAA Tournament bids.

Strengths: Gallagher possesses a competent offensive game. He has good hands, a nice touch for a big man, and a good sense for making plays. He can hit the corner and foul-line jumpers consistently.

Weaknesses: After adding bulk to his upper body the past couple years, Gallagher should be able to mix it up on the boards, though he won't be a great rebounder because he lacks explosiveness. Not a pure power forward, he plays more like Jeff Turner than Charles Oakley.

Analysis: Gallagher was scouting around for a job after the Chicago camp. He has a shot to stick if he picks his spot intelligently. Scouts say he could survive with about half the teams in the NBA.

COLLEGE STATISTICS

	G	FGP	FTP	RPG	APG	PPG
87-88 CRE	32	.521	.600	5.3	0.6	11.4
88-89 CRE	27	.564	.667	6.6	0.9	15.3
89-90 CRE	33	.549	.707	8.1	1.4	17.7
90-91 CRE	32	.566	.806	8.8	1.3	19.4
Totals	124	.551	.720	7.2	1.0	16.0

ANTHONY GOLDWIRE

Team: Phoenix Suns
Position: Guard
Height: 6'1" **Weight:** 182
Birthdate: September 6, 1971
College: Pensacola; Houston
Acquired: 2nd-round pick in 1994 draft (52nd overall)

PLAYER SUMMARY	
Will	press the pace
Can't	work the paint
Expect	a fire hydrant
Don't Expect	sudden impact
Fantasy	$0 Card	10-15¢

Background: After two years at Pensacola J.C. in his home state of Florida, Goldwire went to Houston, where he made second-team All-SWC both seasons. He ranks ninth on the Cougars' all-time assists list and fifth in free throw accuracy. He scored 35 points vs. Purdue as a senior.

Strengths: A compact point guard, Goldwire is strong and quick. He's an above-average shooter. He fits best in a push game, where he can put his running and gunning skills to good use.

Weaknesses: Goldwire's size will limit him to point guard in the NBA, yet he lacks top-flight playmaking skills. He must improve at running a team in a patterned offense and creating shots for others off the dribble.

Analysis: Phoenix had a lot of point guards on its summer roster. Kevin Johnson is the starter, with Frank Johnson, Elliot Perry, Duane Cooper, and Goldwire expected to compete for one or two back-up positions. Most likely, Goldwire will begin his pro career in the bushes.

COLLEGE STATISTICS

	G	FGP	FTP	RPG	APG	PPG
90-91 PENS	30	.449	.808	3.0	5.6	10.2
91-92 PENS	31	.431	.762	4.1	7.8	15.4
92-93 HOUS	30	.444	.785	3.1	5.7	14.2
93-94 HOUS	27	.393	.807	3.7	6.1	17.1
Hou. Totals	57	.417	.796	3.4	5.9	15.6

DARRIN HANCOCK

Team: Charlotte Hornets
Position: Guard/Forward
Height: 6'6" **Weight:** 205
Birthdate: November 3, 1971
College: Garden City; Kansas
Acquired: 2nd-round pick in 1994 draft (38th overall)

PLAYER SUMMARY	
Will	.................................dazzle
Can't	..................hit from downtown
Expect	.......................a high-wire act
Don't Expect	................much polish
Fantasy	............$0 Card......10-15¢

Background: Hancock moved from Garden City Community College to Kansas to a pro team in France in the space of four years. He averaged 7.5 points as the starting small forward for the Jayhawks in 1992-93, his only season of Division I play. In 1993-94, he played for Maurienne in France's B league, the equivalent of the NCAA's Division II, averaging 17.3 points.

Strengths: Hancock and B.J. Tyler were the fastest players in the 1994 draft class. Hancock outruns people on the break, can handle the ball in the open court, and finishes with gusto. He has all the tools to be a first-rate defensive player, either at small forward or shooting guard.

Weaknesses: He's not a good shooter, either from the line or the field. Scouts question his aptitude for the game.

Analysis: Charlotte, which traded its first-round pick, was left to take Hancock in the second round. He has a chance to stick because the Hornets are in dire need of defensive help and have an opening with the departure of Eddie Johnson. On the other hand, Hancock is very similar to reserve swing man David Wingate, but not as good.

COLLEGE STATISTICS

		G	FGP	FTP	RPG	APG	PPG
92-93	KANS	34	.542	.658	4.5	1.4	7.5
Totals		34	.542	.658	4.5	1.4	7.5

ASKIA JONES

Team: Unsigned
Position: Guard
Height: 6'5" **Weight:** 205
Birthdate: December 3, 1971
College: Kansas St.

PLAYER SUMMARY	
Will	......................hit the jump shot
Can't	..............................run all night
Expect	...........................a specialist
Don't Expect	..........Caldwell Jones
Fantasy	............$0 Card..........N/A

Background: Jones, the son of former NBA player Wali Jones, is the third-leading scorer in K-State history, one point behind Rolando Blackman. He scored a Big Eight-record 62 points vs. Fresno State in the 1994 NIT quarterfinals, and he was named MVP at the postseason Portsmouth Invitational after scoring 30 points in the championship game.

Strengths: Jones lost much of his athleticism when he suffered an ankle injury that forced him to miss the 1990-91 season, yet he remains a terrific stand-still shooter with expansive range. He has good size and strength.

Weaknesses: Though he's deadly accurate from the field, Jones needs room to get off his shot. That means he needs to improve his quickness and dribbling. Playing more forward than guard in college, he didn't get to handle the ball much.

Analysis: As one scout said, "He has a shot because he has a shot." Jones's shooting skills could land him a reserve job in the NBA. His father works for the Miami Heat, so they should be one of several teams willing to give him a tryout.

COLLEGE STATISTICS

		G	FGP	FTP	RPG	APG	PPG
89-90	KSU	31	.412	.648	2.7	1.5	7.9
91-92	KSU	30	.445	.800	4.3	2.3	15.5
92-93	KSU	30	.417	.750	4.1	2.9	13.2
93-94	KSU	33	.426	.825	3.8	2.0	22.1
Totals		124	.426	.782	3.7	2.2	14.8

ARTURAS KARNISHOVAS

Team: Unsigned
Position: Forward/Guard
Height: 6'8" **Weight:** 220
Birthdate: April 27, 1971
College: Seton Hall

PLAYER SUMMARY	
Will	knock it down
Can't	outrun his man
Expect	a specialist
Don't Expect	anything now
Fantasy	$0 Card .....10-25¢

Background: A four-year starter at Seton Hall, Karnishovas helped the Pirates to NCAA Tournament bids each season. He led the Big East in free throw accuracy in 1993-94 and made 69 of 180 3-point attempts. At age 21, he started for the Lithuanian national team that won the bronze medal at the 1992 Olympics.

Strengths: Karnishovas has plenty of skills and a great feel for the game. Though he shot just 39 percent from the field as a senior, he has a sweet shooting stroke and 20-foot range. Scouts have called him a poor man's Kiki Vandeweghe.

Weaknesses: The biggest questions with Karnishovas are whether he's strong enough and quick enough to play in the NBA. He struggles against good man-to-man defenders. A below-average penetrator, he needs to diversify his game.

Analysis: Expected to go early in the second round, Karnishovas slid out of the draft after playing poorly in the NBA's postseason camps. He played with Milwaukee's summer-league team and has a chance with the roster-thin Bucks.

COLLEGE STATISTICS

		G	FGP	FTP	RPG	APG	PPG
90-91	SH	33	.414	.844	4.6	1.2	7.3
91-92	SH	26	.434	.729	4.2	1.2	8.5
92-93	SH	34	.508	.832	6.6	1.7	14.6
93-94	SH	30	.390	.816	6.8	1.9	18.3
Totals		123	.436	.810	5.6	1.5	12.3

ANTONIO LANG

Team: Phoenix Suns
Position: Forward/Guard
Height: 6'8" **Weight:** 201
Birthdate: May 15, 1972
College: Duke
Acquired: 2nd-round pick in 1994 draft (29th overall)

PLAYER SUMMARY	
Will	run and dunk
Can't	muscle up
Expect	a struggle
Don't Expect	much P.T.
Fantasy	$0 Card .....20-35¢

Background: A former high school All-American, Lang saw his pro stock drop at Duke, where he was stuck behind Grant Hill as a freshman and sophomore. Nevertheless, he contributed to two national championship teams and made third-team All-ACC as a senior.

Strengths: Running, jumping, and finishing are Lang's strong suits. He defends with quickness, technique, and desire. Versatile, he can play small forward or shooting guard.

Weaknesses: Lang has a bad body by NBA standards. His lack of strength poses problems defensively, even against guards. A poor shooter, he never made a 3-pointer in four seasons at Duke. He needs to expand his floor game and hit the weight room or he'll be flushed out of the league in a hurry.

Analysis: Lang has a remote chance of making the Phoenix team. The Suns are loaded at the two and three spots, with Dan Majerle, Danny Manning, Danny Ainge, Cedric Ceballos, and Wesley Person on the summer roster.

COLLEGE STATISTICS

		G	FGP	FTP	RPG	APG	PPG
90-91	DUKE	36	.606	.526	2.6	0.2	4.3
91-92	DUKE	34	.562	.657	4.1	0.7	6.4
92-93	DUKE	31	.523	.655	5.5	0.8	6.9
93-94	DUKE	34	.588	.724	5.4	1.0	12.5
Totals		135	.570	.659	4.3	0.7	7.5

BILLY McCAFFREY

Team: Unsigned
Position: Guard
Height: 6'4" **Weight:** 184
Birthdate: May 30, 1971
College: Duke; Vanderbilt

PLAYER SUMMARY	
Will	share the ball
Can't	shadow the jets
Expect	good fundamentals
Don't Expect	a sure thing
Fantasy	$0 Card	10-25¢

Background: In two seasons at Vanderbilt, McCaffrey amassed 1,359 points, second most in school history. He began his career at Duke, where he played in two Final Fours. He transferred so he could play point guard after being stuck behind Bobby Hurley at Duke.

Strengths: McCaffrey has some guard skills that could translate to the NBA. He can get on a roll with his jump shot, and he has the savvy to run a team from the point. He knows how to draw fouls and is a terrific free throw shooter.

Weaknesses: McCaffrey has a long way to go to become an acceptable pro. He has a slow release and comes off picks slowly. He's not good going to his left. He can't handle a quick opponent at either end.

Analysis: McCaffrey would have been drafted had he come out after his junior year, but he really slipped as a senior. He no longer looks like a poor man's Jeff Hornacek in the eyes of scouts. He'll get looked at by NBA teams, but he probably will have to bounce around the minor leagues before he has a shot to stick.

COLLEGE STATISTICS

	G	FGP	FTP	RPG	APG	PPG
89-90 DUKE	38	.450	.793	0.7	0.9	6.6
90-91 DUKE	38	.481	.832	1.8	1.9	11.6
92-93 VAND	34	.553	.870	2.6	3.6	20.6
93-94 VAND	32	.456	.889	2.6	4.2	20.6
Totals	142	.490	.857	1.9	2.5	14.4

JIM McILVAINE

Team: Washington Bullets
Position: Center
Height: 7'0" **Weight:** 240
Birthdate: July 30, 1972
College: Marquette
Acquired: 2nd-round pick in 1994 draft (32nd overall)

PLAYER SUMMARY	
Will	swat shots
Can't	do anything else
Expect	a back-up
Don't Expect	a bruiser
Fantasy	$0 Card	15-25¢

Background: McIlvaine copped the Great Midwest Player of the Year award as a senior, leading the nation with 4.3 BPG. He finished his career with nearly as many blocks (399, fifth most in NCAA history) as field goals (467). His draft stock dipped when he declined invitations to the NBA's postseason camps to concentrate on his schoolwork.

Strengths: McIlvaine has one skill—the ability to block and alter shots—that can carry him in the NBA. He seemed to improve slightly on offense last season, having introduced a jump hook to his repertoire.

Weaknesses: He has no upper body to speak of and figures to get shoved aside by the NBA's brutish big men. Lacking a good post game, he will struggle to score. His entire game needs work.

Analysis: McIlvaine was passed over by teams that were desperate for center help, such as Dallas and Milwaukee. With Kevin Duckworth in the doghouse, the Bullets might have some minutes available.

COLLEGE STATISTICS

	G	FGP	FTP	RPG	APG	PPG
90-91 MARQ	28	.579	.598	4.7	0.5	8.0
91-92 MARQ	29	.545	.754	4.6	0.6	10.3
92-93 MARQ	28	.578	.714	4.8	0.8	11.0
93-94 MARQ	33	.528	.665	8.3	1.3	13.6
Totals	118	.552	.687	5.7	0.8	10.8

ANTHONY MILLER

Team: Los Angeles Lakers
Position: Forward
Height: 6'9" **Weight:** 255
Birthdate: October 22, 1971
College: Michigan St.
Acquired: Draft rights traded from Warriors for a 1995 2nd-round pick, 6/94

PLAYER SUMMARY	
Will	rebound
Can't	stroke it
Expect	a mauler
Don't Expect	a shot-blocker
Fantasy	$0 Card .....10-15¢

Background: A late-bloomer, Miller had a good senior season at Michigan State after spending his freshman year on the sidelines for academic reasons and his sophomore and junior campaigns as a back-up for Mike Peplowski. Miller finished third nationally in field goal percentage (65.1) in 1993-94. He excelled at the Chicago pre-draft camp.

Strengths: Miller is big and strong and has a decent touch in close. He accepted the challenge of getting in shape to salvage a shot at an NBA career. He's a good interior defender who's willing to mix it up.

Weaknesses: Though he's a massive man, Miller is an average rebounder at best. A one-dimensional offensive player, he gets most of his points within five feet of the basket. He's inept at the foul line.

Analysis: Drafted 39th overall by the Warriors, Miller was immediately dealt to the Lakers, who need a big body to help Vlade Divac and Elden Campbell on the boards. He has perhaps a 50-50 chance to make the team.

COLLEGE STATISTICS

		G	FGP	FTP	RPG	APG	PPG
91-92	MSU	30	.539	.625	5.2	0.8	7.2
92-93	MSU	27	.613	.542	5.1	0.4	6.6
93-94	MSU	32	.651	.574	9.0	0.9	12.6
Totals		89	.609	.583	6.5	0.7	8.9

DWAYNE MORTON

Team: Golden State Warriors
Position: Guard/Forward
Height: 6'6" **Weight:** 190
Birthdate: August 8, 1971
College: Louisville
Acquired: 2nd-round pick in 1994 draft (45th overall)

PLAYER SUMMARY	
Will	shake the rafters
Can't	man the trenches
Expect	a CBA stalwart
Don't Expect	a complete player
Fantasy	$0 Card .....15-25¢

Background: Kentucky's Mr. Basketball as a prep in Louisville, Morton was labeled a can't-miss All-American. While he had a good college career (cut short a year because of academics), he never became a dominant player. He is Louisville's career leader in 3-point accuracy (.461).

Strengths: Morton has the look of a raw Latrell Sprewell, which no doubt attracted the Warriors to him. Like Sprewell, he has superb quickness, can run all day, and has the attributes of a defensive stopper.

Weaknesses: Morton improved very little in four years at Louisville. His jump shot is erratic. He seems to have a poor feel for the game and, like other Cardinal wing men, hasn't had a chance to develop his floor game. He's too thin to play small forward in the NBA.

Analysis: Considering Golden State's riches in the backcourt (Sprewell, Ricky Pierce, Tim Hardaway, even Chris Mullin on occasion), it's hard to imagine Morton making the team. He needs to go to a lesser league and commit himself to improving his game.

COLLEGE STATISTICS

		G	FGP	FTP	RPG	APG	PPG
91-92	LOU	30	.578	.672	3.7	1.2	13.6
92-93	LOU	31	.531	.738	4.7	2.2	16.1
93-94	LOU	34	.480	.720	4.2	2.1	15.3
Totals		95	.524	.711	4.2	1.9	15.0

GAYLON NICKERSON

Team: Atlanta Hawks
Position: Guard
Height: 6′3″ **Weight:** 190
Birthdate: February 5, 1969
College: Wichita St.; Butler C.C.;
Kansas St; N.W. Oklahoma St.
Acquired: 2nd-round pick in 1994 draft
(34th overall)

PLAYER SUMMARY	
Will	rock the Omni
Can't	run a team
Expect	a sparkplug
Don't Expect	a distributor
Fantasy	$0 Card ....20-35¢

Background: Nickerson bounced around so much in college, playing for four different schools, that scouts never got a good fix on his abilities. That changed when he played well at the pre-draft Portsmouth Invitational.

Strengths: The physical package is all there: long arms, size, quickness, and leaping ability. Though not a pure playmaker, he can beat the press with his dribble and create offense in a push game. An emotional player, he reminds scouts of John Starks.

Weaknesses: He played point guard in the pre-draft camps but lacks the instincts for setting up plays for other people. His jumper needs some work. He needs to settle into a situation and be given a chance to grow.

Analysis: The Hawks, with their only selection in the draft, took a shot on Nickerson, who has a chance to develop into a good combination guard, capable of scoring by taking the ball to the basket. He figures to make the team.

COLLEGE STATISTICS

		G	FGP	FTP	RPG	APG	PPG
89-90	WSU	29	.448	.625	5.0	2.2	10.3
91-92	KSU	30	.399	.649	4.3	2.9	9.4
93-94	NWOK	31	.478	.786	5.7	4.9	21.7
Totals		90	.447	.720	5.0	3.4	13.9

WILLIAM NJOKU

Team: Indiana Pacers
Position: Forward
Height: 6′9″ **Weight:** 215
Birthdate: March 5, 1972
College: St. Mary's (Canada)
Acquired: 2nd-round pick in 1994 draft
(41st overall)

PLAYER SUMMARY	
Will	make the jumper
Can't	bump and grind
Expect	a trip abroad
Don't Expect	an impact
Fantasy	$0 Card ....10-15¢

Background: Considered the best college player in Canada in 1993-94, Njoku averaged 25.2 points, 9.1 rebounds, and 3.6 blocks for St. Mary's in Nova Scotia. Though born in Ghana, he has lived in Canada most of his life.

Strengths: Very athletic for a tall man, Njoku runs well and is beginning to fill out physically. A versatile player, he could eventually find work at either small forward or power forward. He has 3-point range, adequate ball-handling skills, and a good sense for the game.

Weaknesses: The level of competition in Canadian colleges is akin to lower-level NCAA Division I, so Njoku hasn't gone head-to-head with many talented players. He needs to add bulk to his 215-pound frame.

Analysis: Though it had no roster spot for Njoku, Indiana drafted him with designs on stashing him overseas, preferably in Spain or Italy, for a couple years. A similar strategy worked with Antonio Davis.

COLLEGE STATISTICS

		G	FGP	FTP	RPG	APG	PPG
90-91	STM	20	.517	.630	8.9	1.0	15.6
91-92	STM	20	.538	.731	9.9	1.3	18.3
92-93	STM	20	.558	.807	9.7	1.0	25.3
93-94	STM	19	.488	.773	9.1	1.4	25.2
Totals		79	.525	.743	9.4	1.2	21.0

ZELJKO REBRACA

Team: Minnesota Timberwolves
Position: Center
Height: 6'11"　**Weight:** 198
Birthdate: April 9, 1973
College: None
Acquired: Draft rights traded from SuperSonics for a 1996 2nd-round pick, 6/94

PLAYER SUMMARY	
Will	stick the "J"
Can't	hold the post
Expect	a string bean
Don't Expect	to see him soon
Fantasy	$0　Card	N/A

Background: A native Serb, Rebraca has played the past four seasons for Partizan Belgrade of the Yugoslavian League. He was named league MVP after the 1993-94 season, in which he averaged 14.4 points and 6.6 rebounds per game. He shot 75.5 percent from the field.

Strengths: Scouts say Rebraca is fairly mobile and a good shooter. More a perimeter player than a banger, he can play either power forward or small forward. He will block a few shots as a help-side defender.

Weaknesses: Though he has played professionally for four years, Rebraca is still young (21) and inexperienced. The regular season in the Yugoslavian League lasts just 22 games. He is far too thin to withstand an NBA season. His assist total (eight all season) indicates his floor game needs work.

Analysis: The last player selected in the 1994 draft, Rebraca was dealt to Minnesota on draft day. The Timberwolves have needed a center badly ever since entering the NBA in 1989. However, Rebraca won't be the answer anytime soon. He'll probably stay in Europe for the next few seasons, with Minnesota retaining his rights.

COLLEGE STATISTICS

—DID NOT PLAY—

SHAWNELLE SCOTT

Team: Portland Trail Blazers
Position: Forward/Center
Height: 6'11"　**Weight:** 260
Birthdate: June 16, 1972
College: St. John's
Acquired: 2nd-round pick in 1994 draft (43rd overall)

PLAYER SUMMARY	
Will	plug away
Can't	shake and bake
Expect	a CBA detour
Don't Expect	Shawnelle Kemp
Fantasy	$0　Card	10-15¢

Background: Scott was reared in the Bronx and played college ball at St. John's. While he had a largely disappointing career with the Redmen, he was playing well as a senior before suffering a torn ligament in his right thumb.

Strengths: Scott has some skills, including a nice touch around the basket. He has the body to play center in the NBA, runs the court easily, and doesn't let himself get pushed around. He plays hard and grabs his share of rebounds.

Weaknesses: He may not have any one asset that can carry him in the big leagues. As one scout said, "He doesn't really do anything." He's far too inconsistent to please most NBA people, who say he needs more maturity and focus. He's a poor free throw shooter.

Analysis: Though Scott has NBA skills, he has little chance to make Portland's roster, which is chock full of big bodies. He needs to go to the CBA for a couple years and figure out what the game is all about.

COLLEGE STATISTICS

		G	FGP	FTP	RPG	APG	PPG
90-91	STJ	32	.500	.529	3.6	0.2	5.2
91-92	STJ	30	.505	.605	5.6	0.6	9.0
92-93	STJ	29	.585	.517	7.8	1.1	13.7
93-94	STJ	22	.530	.590	9.2	1.3	16.0
Totals		113	.536	.561	6.3	0.8	10.5

MICHAEL SMITH

Team: Sacramento Kings
Position: Forward
Height: 6'7" **Weight:** 233
Birthdate: March 28, 1972
College: Providence
Acquired: 2nd-round pick in 1994 draft (35th overall)

PLAYER SUMMARY	
Will	do the dirty work
Can't	hit the trey
Expect	a masher
Don't Expect	finesse
Fantasy	$0 Card	10-20¢

Background: After attending Dunbar High, the same Baltimore school that produced Reggie Lewis, David Wingate, and Muggsy Bogues, Smith went to Providence, where he sat out his freshman season for academic reasons. He proceeded to lead the Big East in boards the next three years.

Strengths: Best described as a blue-collar worker, Smith is big and mobile and has a motor that never stops. Rebounding and defense are his strong suits; he overpowers people with effort around the basket.

Weaknesses: Smith's offensive game leaves a lot to be desired. He shoots his foul shots left-handed and his field goal attempts right-handed, indicating confusion about how to score. He's too small to be a pure NBA power forward.

Analysis: Sacramento drafted two college power forwards in 1993 and three more (Smith, Brian Grant, Lawrence Funderburke) in '94, yet Smith should make the team because he can swing to small forward for defensive purposes and get some of the rebounds the Kings are desperate for.

COLLEGE STATISTICS

	G	FGP	FTP	RPG	APG	PPG
91-92 PROV	31	.495	.579	10.3	1.3	10.7
92-93 PROV	33	.556	.546	11.4	1.2	11.8
93-94 PROV	30	.605	.714	11.5	0.8	12.9
Totals	94	.554	.600	11.0	1.1	11.8

ZAN TABAK

Team: Houston Rockets
Position: Center/Forward
Height: 7'0" **Weight:** 245
Birthdate: June 15, 1970
College: None
Acquired: 2nd-round pick in 1991 draft (51st overall)

PLAYER SUMMARY	
Will	swat shots
Can't	power inside
Expect	a shot to stick
Don't Expect	ESPN highlights
Fantasy	$0 Card	N/A

Background: Tabak was considered a borderline prospect when he was drafted by Houston in 1991. At the time, he was under contract with POP 84 Split, a team in the Yugoslavian League. Last year, he played for Olympia Milano in Italy's A1 league, averaging 15.1 points and 10.3 rebounds.

Strengths: Though nothing special offensively, Tabak runs the court well, which allows him to be a factor as a trailer on the break. He also can score on jump hooks around the basket. His greatest strength is the ability to block shots. He has gained valuable experience playing in Europe.

Weaknesses: Tabak was too weak to make the Rockets when he was drafted in 1991, but he apparently has added enough muscle to have a chance in 1994-95. He lacks range with his shot and won't dazzle anyone with his floor game.

Analysis: Houston may finally receive a return on its investment in Tabak. Scouts say he's a better player than Eric Riley and Richard Petruska, who were at the end of the Rockets' bench in 1993-94. Hakeem Olajuwon averaged 41 minutes per game last year, so there won't be many minutes for Tabak if he sticks.

COLLEGE STATISTICS

—DID NOT PLAY—

DEON THOMAS

Team: Dallas Mavericks
Position: Forward
Height: 6'8" **Weight:** 242
Birthdate: February 24, 1971
College: Illinois
Acquired: 2nd-round pick in 1994 draft
(28th overall)

PLAYER SUMMARY	
Will	bang
Can't	create
Expect	a struggle to stick
Don't Expect	Neon Deon
Fantasy	$0 Card ......15-25¢

Background: Thomas holds Illini records for scoring and blocks, while ranking second in rebounds and field goal accuracy. He's one of three players in college history to shoot better than 60 percent while making at least 800 field goals.

Strengths: Thomas has a pro body and plays hard, crashing the boards at both ends of the court and riding his man defensively. He can make the 12-foot jumper when left unattended.

Weaknesses: A phenomenal high school player, Thomas improved very little in college. His post-up game isn't good enough to carry him in the NBA, and he lacks the ball-handling skills to work outside. He's essentially a man without a position.

Analysis: No team needs physical players more than Dallas, so Thomas should make the roster, though he's no lock. The Mavericks' power-forward picture could get crowded if Terry Davis returns to join holdovers Doug Smith and Popeye Jones.

COLLEGE STATISTICS

	G	FGP	FTP	RPG	APG	PPG
90-91	ILL	30	.577	.643	6.8	0.6	15.1
91-92	ILL	28	.585	.661	6.9	0.7	19.4
92-93	ILL	32	.606	.646	8.0	1.2	18.3
93-94	ILL	28	.633	.693	6.9	1.5	19.6
Totals		118	.601	.661	7.2	1.0	18.0

KENDRICK WARREN

Team: Unsigned
Position: Forward
Height: 6'8" **Weight:** 225
Birthdate: May 27, 1971
College: Virginia Commonwealth

PLAYER SUMMARY	
Will	slam it down
Can't	face and shoot
Expect	a CBA look-see
Don't Expect	polish
Fantasy	$0 Card ....N/A

Background: Warren is one of five players in Metro Conference history to amass 1,500 points, 600 rebounds, 150 blocks, 150 assists, and 100 steals; the others are NBA talents Clarence Weatherspoon, Pervis Ellison, Hot Rod Williams, and Keith Lee. Warren averaged a double-double in 1993-94 while increasing his career dunk total to 207.

Strengths: As his high dunk total attests, Warren is a tough customer around the basket. A great athlete, he runs the court easily and finishes well on the break.

Weaknesses: Considered one of the top ten high school players in 1989-90, Warren never refined his game in four years of college. Scouts give him poor grades for shooting, ball-handling, and defense. He's too small for power forward and not skilled enough for small forward.

Analysis: Warren was touted as a potential first-round pick. But after missing all but two minutes of the postseason Desert Classic because of an injury, he slid all the way out of the draft. He'll end up in someone's camp but seems destined for the minor leagues.

COLLEGE STATISTICS

	G	FGP	FTP	RPG	APG	PPG
90-91	VCU	31	.541	.506	8.5	1.6	15.7
91-92	VCU	29	.543	.508	9.5	2.1	19.0
92-93	VCU	19	.502	.522	9.1	1.9	17.6
93-94	VCU	27	.533	.477	12.4	2.0	18.0
Totals		106	.532	.500	9.9	1.9	17.5

JAMIE WATSON

Team: Utah Jazz
Position: Guard/Forward
Height: 6'7" **Weight:** 190
Birthdate: February 23, 1972
College: South Carolina
Acquired: 2nd-round pick in 1994 draft
(47th overall)

PLAYER SUMMARY	
Will	battle in camp
Can't	bury FTs
Expect	a greyhound
Don't Expect	a teacher's pet
Fantasy	$0 Card ...... 10-15¢

Background: A fairly obscure player by SEC standards, Watson led South Carolina in scoring his junior and senior seasons. He had problems with former Gamecocks coach George Felton, reportedly leading a rebellion that ended with Felton's dismissal in 1993.

Strengths: Watson meets NBA standards for athleticism. Built to play either small forward or big guard, he'll likely settle into the backcourt. He does most everything well, from scoring to defending to rebounding.

Weaknesses: Watson never shot better than 46 percent from the field or 67 percent from the line in any season at South Carolina. His ball-handling and playmaking skills are raw.

Analysis: With its only selection in either round, Utah grabbed what could be the 1994 draft's best sleeper pick. No one, including those in the Jazz's front office, knows how good Watson can be. Utah needs a fifth guard, so he has a good chance to stick.

COLLEGE STATISTICS

		G	FGP	FTP	RPG	APG	PPG
90-91	SC	33	.420	.568	2.5	2.3	6.0
91-92	SC	28	.440	.524	4.5	2.9	7.5
92-93	SC	27	.461	.642	5.0	2.7	14.7
93-94	SC	27	.459	.674	7.0	2.4	18.1
Totals		115	.449	.630	4.7	2.6	11.3

JEFF WEBSTER

Team: Miami Heat
Position: Forward
Height: 6'7" **Weight:** 232
Birthdate: February 19, 1971
College: Oklahoma
Acquired: 2nd-round pick in 1994 draft
(40th overall)

PLAYER SUMMARY	
Will	catch and shoot
Can't	nail the 3
Expect	a specialist
Don't Expect	a sudden impact
Fantasy	$0 Card ...... 10-15¢

Background: Only Wayman Tisdale and Tim McCalister amassed more points in Oklahoma history than Webster, a small forward who led the Big Eight in scoring (23.7) as a senior. He had 30 points vs. Duke as a freshman and 25 against the Blue Devils as a junior.

Strengths: A scorer first and foremost, Webster has a soft shooting touch and a dependable jumper from 15 to 18 feet out. He makes a lot of off-balance and on-the-move shots.

Weaknesses: Scouts rate him average or worse in all areas except scoring. Moreover, he made only six college 3-pointers. His greatest flaw is his ball-handling, which prevents him from penetrating and creating opportunities.

Analysis: Looking to make some changes on its bench, Miami took a flyer on Webster. He probably won't make the team but could end up in the NBA as an off-the-bench scorer in a year or two. He needs to expand his range and work on his floor game.

COLLEGE STATISTICS

		G	FGP	FTP	RPG	APG	PPG
90-91	OKLA	35	.565	.802	5.5	0.2	18.3
91-92	OKLA	30	.521	.788	6.2	0.6	14.4
92-93	OKLA	32	.491	.740	5.8	0.5	16.5
93-94	OKLA	28	.514	.776	7.8	0.7	23.7
Totals		125	.523	.778	6.2	0.5	18.1

DONTONIO WINGFIELD

Team: Seattle SuperSonics
Position: Forward
Height: 6'8" **Weight:** 246
Birthdate: June 23, 1974
College: Cincinnati
Acquired: 2nd-round pick in 1994 draft (37th overall)

PLAYER SUMMARY	
Will	throw it down
Can't	toe the line
Expect	a stud
Don't Expect	a star
Fantasy	$0 Card	15-30¢

Background: A prep sensation from Albany, Georgia, Wingfield was considered one of Bob Huggins's marquee recruits at Cincinnati, but he stayed only one season before entering the NBA draft. He ranked second in the Great Midwest in rebounding and 3-point marksmanship (.404) in 1993-94. Draft experts had him going in the first round, yet he slid to the tenth pick in the second round because of questions about his off-the-court behavior.

Strengths: A top-of-the-line athlete, Wingfield has the necessary strength, speed, and leaping ability to play in the NBA. He's a consistent scorer from the perimeter.

Weaknesses: Inexperience and lack of maturity could hold him back. He hasn't put his skills together and learned how to play the game yet. He needs to concentrate on a post game instead of launching a jump shot every time he touches the ball. Also, his intensity must improve.

Analysis: Seattle doesn't need Wingfield, but it could stash him as the 12th man for a year or two and see if he's worth keeping. Considered a head case, he should feel right at home in the Sonic circus.

COLLEGE STATISTICS

	G	FGP	FTP	RPG	APG	PPG
93-94 CINC	29	.422	.669	9.0	2.0	16.0
Totals	29	.422	.669	9.0	2.0	16.0

OTHER TOP NONDRAFTED PLAYERS

Abdul Fox

Rhode Island, 6'6", 180

A small forward in college, Fox has a chance to make the conversion to NBA shooting guard. He has good size, long arms, and a nice offensive repertoire. Capable of going on a scoring binge, he can get streaky hot with his jump shot or penetrate to the basket and finish plays with dunks. He lacks sound judgment, however, and tends to lose control.

Sam Mitchell

Cleveland St., 6'9", 240

A big, strong power forward with good skills, Mitchell attracted a lot of interest from NBA teams after the draft. He gives a team versatility because he can make plays facing the basket. He needs to keep his weight under control. Originally a Michigan recruit, he transferred to Cleveland State when the Fab Five came to Ann Arbor.

Warren Peebles

Virginia Union, 6'2", 190

Rated a borderline second-round draft pick, Peebles is a skilled combination guard who eventually could be good enough to run a team. He's strong and physical and a good jump-shooter. He was an All-American at Division II Virginia Union, which also produced Charles Oakley, A.J. English, and others. He'll get a long look.

Stevin Smith

Arizona St., 6'2", 208

Considered a top-flight prospect entering his senior season, Smith blew hot and cold, following one good half of play with a bad one. He then was horrible in the postseason Desert Classic. He plays too wildly to please most scouts and is more of a shooting guard than a point man. However, he does possess great strength and explosiveness.

NBA Team Overviews

This section evaluates all 27 NBA teams, sectioning them off by their divisions. For each team, you'll find:

- the club's address and phone number
- arena information
- a listing of the team's owner, general manager (or equivalent thereof), and coaches
- the head coach's record (lifetime and with team)
- a review of the team's history
- team finishes over the last seven years
- a review of the team's 1993-94 season
- the club's 1994-95 roster
- a preview of the 1994-95 season

The team rosters include players who were drafted in June. The rosters list each player's 1993-94 statistics. Stats include games (G), points per game (PPG), rebounds per game (RPG), and assists per game (APG). The category "Exp." (experience) indicates the number of years the player has played in the NBA.

Each 1994-95 season preview tips off with an "opening line," which looks at the players the team lost and those that are coming in. The preview then examines the team at each position, including guard, forward, center, and coaching. "Analysis" evaluates the team's strengths and weaknesses and puts it all into perspective. The preview ends with a prediction, stating where the club is likely to finish within its division.

BOSTON CELTICS

Home: Boston Garden
Capacity: 14,890
Year Built: 1928

Address:
151 Merrimac St.
Boston, MA 02114
(617) 523-6050

Chairman of the Board: Don F. Gaston
General Manager: Jan Volk
Head Coach: Chris Ford
Assistant Coach: Don Casey
Assistant Coach: Jon Jennings
Assistant Coach: Dennis Johnson

Coach Chris Ford			
	W	L	Pct.
NBA Record	187	141	.570
W/Celtics	187	141	.570
1993-94 Record	32	50	.390

Celtics History

The history of the Boston Celtics drips with tradition. The Celtics have won 16 world championships and must be listed with baseball's Yankees, football's Packers, and hockey's Canadiens among the greatest teams in sports history.

Boston began as a member of the old BAA in 1946-47 and joined the NBA at its inception. Red Auerbach took over as coach of the team in 1950-51 and began assembling the pieces of the Celtic machine. He started with guard Bob Cousy (perhaps the best ever on the fastbreak), added Bill Sharman, and in 1956 bagged the big one—Bill Russell.

Boston won its first championship in 1956-57, then won every title from 1958-59 through 1965-66, thoroughly dominating pro basketball. Russell, famous for his battles with Wilt Chamberlain, redefined post defense. His supporting cast included Sam and K.C. Jones, Tom Heinsohn, Frank Ramsey, and John Havlicek.

Auerbach moved to the front office in 1966 and Russell took over as player/coach, but the Celtics didn't falter, winning championships in 1968 and '69. Heinsohn assumed control of the bench in 1969 and won titles in 1974 and '76 with stars like Havlicek, center Dave Cowens, and guard Jo Jo White.

The Celtics' modern era dawned in 1979, when the team drafted forward Larry Bird. Behind Bird and frontcourt partners Robert Parish and Kevin McHale, Boston shared the 1980s' spotlight with the Los Angeles Lakers, taking world championships in 1981, '84, and '86.

Last Seven Years

Season	W	L	Pct.	Place	Playoffs	Coach
1987-88	57	25	.695	First	L-East Finals	K.C. Jones
1988-89	42	40	.512	Third	L-Round 1	Jimmy Rodgers
1989-90	52	30	.634	Second	L-Round 1	Jimmy Rodgers
1990-91	56	26	.683	First	L-East Semis	Chris Ford
1991-92	51	31	.622	First	L-East Semis	Chris Ford
1992-93	48	34	.585	Second	L-Round 1	Chris Ford
1993-94	32	50	.390	Fifth	DNQ	Chris Ford

1993-94 Review

The preseason death of star guard (and captain) Reggie Lewis rocked the Celtics and triggered a tailspin from which Boston could not recover. Not only did the Celts miss Lewis's tremendous scoring skills and strong leadership, but they also had to think the franchise was somewhat jinxed, with Lewis joining Len Bias (1986) as deceased team members.

Lewis's death, coupled with the retirement of Kevin McHale after the 1993 season, left the team essentially rudderless in the NBA's Atlantic Division. The Celtics sank to the back of the pack quickly, and any success they had during the season served to dim their lottery hopes, rather than elevate them into contention.

There were few bright spots. Rookie Dino Radja (15.1 PPG, 7.2 RPG), whose NBA debut received considerably less fanfare than that of countryman Toni Kukoc (Chicago), outplayed his Croatian counterpart and proved that a little Celtic magic still exists in the personnel department. Other than Radja, however, no one really distinguished himself. The Celtics shot a poor 47.2 percent as a team and had no one to depend on to score in crucial situations.

Guards Dee Brown (15.5 PPG) and Sherman Douglas (13.3 PPG) had their moments, but neither could dominate a game. Kevin Gamble (11.5 PPG) and Xavier McDaniel (11.3 PPG) were role-players filling starting positions by default. Again, neither was a go-to guy. Ancient Robert Parish (11.7 PPG, 7.3 RPG), whose stately demeanor could not mask a dwindling game, could no longer bang with the NBA's big men on a regular basis.

Parish's back-up, rookie Acie Earl, struggled mightily on offense. Forward Rick Fox continued to show a complete game in bursts, and veteran power man Ed Pinckney enjoyed a relatively pain-free season but posted unimpressive statistics (5.2 PPG, 6.3 RPG).

1994-95 Roster

No.	Player	Pos.	Ht.	Wt.	Exp.	College	G	RPG	APG	PPG
							|——1993-94——|			
4	Alaa Abdelnaby	F	6'10"	240	4	Duke	13	3.5	0.2	4.9
7	Dee Brown	G	6'1"	161	4	Jacksonville	77	3.9	4.5	15.5
12	Chris Corchiani	G	6'1"	186	3	N. Carolina St.	51	0.9	1.7	2.3
20	Sherman Douglas	G	6'1"	180	5	Syracuse	78	2.5	8.8	13.3
55	Acie Earl	C/F	6'10"	240	1	Iowa	74	3.3	0.2	5.5
—	Blue Edwards	F	6'5"	200	5	East Carolina	82	4.0	2.1	11.6
—	Pervis Ellison	F/C	6'10"	225	5	Louisville	47	5.1	1.5	7.3
44	Rick Fox	F/G	6'7"	231	3	North Carolina	82	4.3	2.6	10.8
31	Xavier McDaniel	F	6'7"	205	9	Wichita St.	82	4.9	1.5	11.3
—	Eric Montross	C	7'0"	275	R	North Carolina	—	—	—	—
27	Jimmy Oliver	G/F	6'5"	208	2	Purdue	44	1.0	0.8	4.9
40	Dino Radja	F	6'11"	225	1	Croatia	80	7.2	1.4	15.1
—	Derek Strong	F	6'8"	220	3	Xavier	67	4.2	0.7	6.6
50	Matt Wenstrom	C	7'1"	250	1	North Carolina	11	1.1	0.0	1.6
—	Dominique Wilkins	F	6'8"	215	12	Georgia	74	6.5	2.3	26.0

Boston Celtics
1994-95 Season Preview

Opening Line: Who says you can't make changes anymore because of the salary cap? The Celtics wheeled and dealed all summer, turning a going-nowhere unit into one with considerable promise. Boston signed big-name free agents Dominique Wilkins and Pervis Ellison, drafted North Carolina center Eric Montross, and traded Ed Pinckney and draft pick Andrei Fetisov for Derek Strong and Blue Edwards. Robert Parish and Kevin Gamble left as free agents.

Guard: The combination of Dee Brown and Sherman Douglas looks good on paper but misfires some on the court. Brown's 15.5 PPG led the Celtics last year, but he's not a feared offensive player. His range is limited and knee problems have taken a few inches off his vertical leap. Douglas is often erratic, though he can deliver the ball to open players. Swing man Edwards, who uses his athletic ability to get to the hoop, could earn the starting two job by midseason. Rick Fox is another athletic swing man who will likely lose minutes to newcomers Edwards and Wilkins. Both Brown and Douglas can play the point, meaning there are a lot of options here.

Forward: While the NBA world focused on Toni Kukoc's arrival last year, Dino Radja slipped into Boston and made an immediate impact at power forward. Radja isn't particularly fast, and he was an old rookie (26), but he can score, grab rebounds, and has the classic European sense for the game. Wilkins is the big-time scorer the Celtics have desperately needed. He'll score 25 PPG and fill the leadership role vacated by the loss of Parish. Xavier McDaniel still possesses big-time scoring skills off the bench, but the "X-Man" is 31 and slowing down some. Alaa Abdelnaby can contribute some low-post offense when healthy. Strong is a banger with limited offensive skills.

Center: The aged Parish is gone, leaving the Celtic center position wide-open. Though a little undersized for the pivot, Ellison can be a terrific shot-blocker, rebounder, and scorer when healthy, which isn't often. Montross is big and effective around the basket but slow and ineffective outside the lane. He'll never be a star, but he'll be solid. Second-year man Acie Earl appears to be a long-term project.

Coaching: Ford's affable style remains popular with the players, and he can't be blamed for the franchise's slide. Still, when a team goes bad, somebody has to take a hit. Last year, it was front-office man Dave Gavitt. If things don't improve this year, Ford could go. Ford is assisted by Don Casey, Jon Jennings, and possible replacement Dennis Johnson.

Analysis: The Celtics have about 11 legitimate NBA players on their roster, which few teams can boast nowadays. Moreover, the team again has a true superstar in Wilkins. He should be able to help the club reach the playoffs. Boston could actually become an Eastern Conference contender if Ellison plays like he did in 1991-92, but that might be a little too much to ask.

Prediction: Third place, Atlantic Division

MIAMI HEAT

Home: Miami Arena
Capacity: 15,200
Year Built: 1988

Owner: Harris Hudson
Managing General Partner:
Harris Hudson
Head Coach: Kevin Loughery
Assistant Coach: Alvin Gentry

Address:
Miami Arena
Miami, FL 33136
(305) 577-4328

Coach Kevin Loughery			
	W	L	Pct.
NBA Record	457	633	.419
W/Heat	116	130	.472
1993-94 Record	42	40	.512

Heat History

In its first three years of existence, Miami won 57 games—combined. But the Heat finally rose in 1991-92, becoming the first of the league's recent expansion teams to make the playoffs.

The city was awarded a franchise in April 1987 and entered the league in 1988-89 under the direction of coach Ron Rothstein. The team had few recognizable players at its inception, but it certainly had some ownership clout in the form of Billy Cunningham, the head coach of the 1982-83 world champion Philadelphia 76ers.

The Heat stumbled to a 15-67 record in its inaugural campaign, relying on rookies Rony Seikaly and Kevin Edwards and a collection of NBA castaways. The following year brought rookies Glen Rice and Sherman Douglas to the Heat, but only three more wins.

Miami fans got to vent their frustrations on a new rival—the expansion Orlando Magic; and the arrival of the 1990 All-Star Game in Miami helped perk up the season. However, the team struggled through another bad campaign in 1990-91, going 24-58. In May 1991, Rothstein resigned under pressure.

New coach Kevin Loughery arrived in 1991-92 and all of a sudden the Heat came alive. With the help of rookie guard Steve Smith, Seikaly in the middle, and an improved Rice, Miami snuck into the playoffs. Once there, however, they were quickly swept by the world champion Chicago Bulls. Despite its young nucleus, the team has not improved much because of injuries and a lack of a physical presence.

Last Six Years

Season	W	L	Pct.	Place	Playoffs	Coach
1988-89	15	67	.183	Sixth	DNQ	Ron Rothstein
1989-90	18	64	.220	Fifth	DNQ	Ron Rothstein
1990-91	24	58	.293	Sixth	DNQ	Ron Rothstein
1991-92	38	44	.463	Fourth	L-Round 1	Kevin Loughery
1992-93	36	46	.439	Fifth	DNQ	Kevin Loughery
1993-94	42	40	.512	Fourth	L-Round 1	Kevin Loughery

1993-94 Review

One year after the club's injury-plagued 1992-93 season, the Heat was back in the postseason. But although the team's five-game loss to top-seeded Atlanta in the opening round was valiant and certainly spirited, Miami closed the season as somewhat of a curiosity.

The Heat boasted some of the league's top young talent—particularly at the guard and small-forward spots—but the team was maddeningly inconsistent. Perhaps it was a result of its thin frontcourt, or maybe a reflection of coach Kevin Loughery, who spent most of the year fighting for his job. The Heat finished the season 42-40, just ahead of Charlotte for the last playoff spot. Miami lacked depth and scoring pop up front and maturity all around. The result was a season of short spurts of success, with little sustained excellence. Despite outscoring its opponents by 219 points, the Heat was just two games over .500.

The good news for Miami was a full, healthy season enjoyed by point guard Steve Smith (17.3 PPG), who had struggled with a bad knee for two years. At 6'7", Smith provided match-up problems for foes and was able to mix a solid outside game with the ability to take it to the basket. His back-up, Bimbo Coles (7.7 PPG), had another solid season.

Small forward Glen Rice (21.1 PPG, 5.4 RPG) again led the team in scoring but spent most of his time away from the paint. Loughery divided the two-guard responsibilities between Brian Shaw (9.0 PPG) and second-year man Harold Miner (10.5 PPG). Miner dazzled offensively, but Shaw was more of a 3-point threat and contributed some rebounds. Neither of the two excelled on the defensive end.

Center Rony Seikaly (15.1 PPG, 10.3 RPG) again proved that hard work and a few solid inside moves could result in a good year, but his numbers dropped from 1992-93 and he continued to go it alone on the boards. Neither Grant Long (11.4 PPG, 7.2 RPG) nor John Salley (7.7 PPG, 5.4 RPG) was a front-line NBA power forward, and back-up center Matt Geiger (7.2 PPG, 4.2 RPG) was an adequate, but hardly imposing, reserve pivot man.

1994-95 Roster

No.	Player	Pos.	Ht.	Wt.	Exp.	College	G	RPG	APG	PPG
34	Willie Burton	G/F	6'8"	219	4	Minnesota	53	2.6	0.7	7.0
12	Bimbo Coles	G	6'2"	185	4	Virginia Tech	76	2.1	3.5	7.7
52	Matt Geiger	C	7'0"	245	2	Georgia Tech	72	4.2	0.4	7.2
33	Alec Kessler	F/C	6'11"	240	4	Georgia	15	0.7	0.1	2.2
43	Grant Long	F	6'8"	248	6	E. Michigan	69	7.2	2.5	11.4
32	Harold Miner	G	6'4"	215	2	Southern Cal.	63	2.5	1.5	10.5
—	Khalid Reeves	G	6'3"	207	R	Arizona	—	—	—	—
41	Glen Rice	G/F	6'7"	220	5	Michigan	81	5.4	2.3	21.1
22	John Salley	F/C	6'11"	250	8	Georgia Tech	76	5.4	1.8	7.7
4	Rony Seikaly	C	6'11"	252	6	Syracuse	72	10.3	1.9	15.1
3	Steve Smith	G	6'7"	213	3	Michigan St.	78	4.5	5.1	17.3
—	Jeff Webster	F	6'7"	232	R	Oklahoma	—	—	—	—

Miami Heat
1994-95 Season Preview

Opening Line: The Heat came mighty close to bumping off the Hawks during last year's playoffs but remain largely the same team that has hung around the bottom of the Eastern Conference playoff ladder for the past three years. The addition of Arizona guard Khalid Reeves in the draft bolsters the team's depth at the crowded backcourt positions, but the Heat needs more inside pop to compete with the top teams in the league.

Guard: Now that he appears healthy, point man Steve Smith is ready to mature into one of the NBA's best. His main attributes are his size, strength, and overall athletic ability. It's unknown whether Harold Miner will ever become the player Miami thought he would be two years ago. Miner scored like a demon in college, often spectacularly, but his defensive skills are lax and he needs to improve his shooting range. Reeves was a strong collegiate scorer with some point-guard skills. Bimbo Coles can do a little bit of everything in the backcourt and is a valuable back-up.

Forward: Glen Rice's production fell off some last year, but he remains one of the league's pure gunners. Rice has huge range, can get his shot off well, and has nights when no one can stop him. He is more of a swing man than a strongman. Grant Long continues to produce adequately at the power-forward spot, but don't ever expect All-Star numbers from him. John Salley remains a disappointment. Salley's a quality shot-blocker, but he wasn't worth a first-round pick. Willie Burton continues to be nagged by injuries and personal problems and hasn't blossomed into the contributor Miami expected.

Center: Rony Seikaly continues to do a creditable job. His resume is well known: He can shoot inside or out and heads to the boards with vigor, but he lacks the big-time height and size to dominate. Back-up Matt Geiger has the size and strength but lacks Seikaly's mobility.

Coaching: Kevin Loughery's affable demeanor and long-time status in the league probably saved his job following last season. His career sub-.500 won-loss record couldn't have. This is an important year for him, because Charlotte and Orlando are threatening to whip past their expansion partner. Alvin Gentry assists him.

Analysis: Miami has teased us for three years, looking ready to move ahead at times and stuck in neutral during other instances. The cast remains the same for this season, and other than some more production from Smith and the possible maturation of Miner, little progress appears imminent. Miami needs more beef on the front line and has to develop a better bench. The playoffs are a distinct possibility, but don't look for too much beyond that. This looks like another .500 ballclub.

Prediction: Fourth place, Atlantic Division

NEW JERSEY NETS

Home: Meadowlands Arena
Capacity: 20,029
Year Built: 1981

Address:
Meadowlands Arena
East Rutherford, NJ 07073
(201) 935-8888

Chairman of the Board: Alan L. Aufzien
Executive V.P./General Manager:
Willis Reed
Head Coach: Butch Beard
Assistant Coach: Jerry Eaves
Assistant Coach: Paul Silas

Coach Butch Beard			
	W	L	Pct.
NBA Record	0	0	.000
W/Nets	0	0	.000
1993-94 Record	0	0	.000

Nets History

Basketball fans can choose from two images of the Nets. The first comes from the mid-1970s, back in the days of the ABA, when the club was still based on Long Island. Back then, the team featured skywalking forward Julius Erving, the man who carried the Nets to the 1976 league title. The second image is that of the late '80s/early '90s club, one that posted six straight depressing seasons in the New Jersey Meadowlands.

The franchise was born in 1967 as the New Jersey Americans, a charter member of the ABA. The team moved to Long Island the next year, became the New York Nets, and acquired high-scoring Rick Barry for the 1970-71 season. The Nets made it to the ABA Finals the next year, but they lost Barry to the NBA. Erving came aboard in 1973-74 and led the team to the league title in 1975-76. When the Nets became one of four teams to merge with the NBA, they appeared to be in great shape.

Then the problems started. Erving had a contract dispute with owner Roy Boe, who sold him to Philadelphia. The Nets made the playoffs six of the next ten years but won only one series, beating Philadelphia in 1983-84. That team featured a fine frontcourt of Buck Williams, Albert King, and Darryl Dawkins.

The years 1986-91 were dismal, as management made poor draft decisions. The Nets have improved in the last three years, thanks to forward Derrick Coleman and guard Kenny Anderson, but haven't done much better than .500.

Last Seven Years

Season	W	L	Pct.	Place	Playoffs	Coach
1987-88	19	63	.232	Fifth	DNQ	D. Wohl/B. MacKinnon/ W. Reed
1988-89	26	56	.317	Fifth	DNQ	Willis Reed
1989-90	17	65	.207	Sixth	DNQ	Bill Fitch
1990-91	26	56	.317	Fifth	DNQ	Bill Fitch
1991-92	40	42	.488	Third	L-Round 1	Bill Fitch
1992-93	43	39	.524	Third	L-Round 1	Chuck Daly
1993-94	45	37	.549	Third	L-Round 1	Chuck Daly

1993-94 Review

If the Nets thought the beginning of the 1993-94 season would end the problems brought on by a tragic and tumultuous off-season, they were wrong. Though nothing during the 82-game season could approach the magnitude of guard Drazen Petrovic's death, enough happened to keep New Jersey in the headlines for the wrong things. The result was a seventh-place finish in the Eastern Conference and a quick playoff exit courtesy of the hated Knicks.

The team's problems, however, started well before the last week in April. The previous off-season featured Petrovic's untimely death on the German Autobahn, speculation about coach Chuck Daly's resignation, and the questionable trade of center Sam Bowie to the Lakers for enigmatic underachiever Benoit Benjamin.

Trouble began when talented power forward Derrick Coleman began grousing about his contract. The ensuing media circus produced a hefty payday for the inconsistent star, but it couldn't have helped the Nets, who were trying to integrate several new faces into the lineup. Despite Daly's championship pedigree, the Nets remained one of the toughest franchises to coach.

Coleman (20.2 PPG, 11.3 RPG) was an All-Star, but he was also prone to disappearing during key stretches. Point guard Kenny Anderson (18.8 PPG, 9.6 APG), the team's other budding superstar, also made it to the All-Star Game but showed his inexperience with an awful playoff performance. Anderson's backcourt mate, Kevin Edwards (14.0 PPG), didn't approach Petrovic's contributions, but he was steady. The same could be said for veteran forward Armon Gilliam (11.8 PPG, 6.1 RPG) and surprising rookie frontcourt performer P.J. Brown (5.7 PPG, 6.2 RPG).

Moody Chris Morris (10.9 PPG) battled injuries much of the year, and Benjamin (9.3 PPG, 6.5 RPG) was hardly the answer in the middle, despite a reunion with his college coach, Nets G.M. Willis Reed. Reserve swing man Johnny Newman (10.3 PPG) shot as often as he could, and though forward Jayson Williams remained healthy for a change, his attitude was still on the injured list.

1994-95 Roster

No.	Player	Pos.	Ht.	Wt.	Exp.	College	G	RPG	APG	PPG
7	Kenny Anderson	G	6'1"	168	3	Georgia Tech	82	3.9	9.6	18.8
00	Benoit Benjamin	C	7'0"	265	9	Creighton	77	6.5	0.6	9.3
42	P.J. Brown	F/C	6'11"	240	1	Louisiana Tech	79	6.2	1.2	5.7
44	Derrick Coleman	F	6'10"	258	4	Syracuse	77	11.3	3.4	20.2
—	Yinka Dare	C	7'1"	265	R	G. Washington	—	—	—	—
21	Kevin Edwards	G	6'3"	210	6	DePaul	82	3.4	2.8	14.0
43	Armon Gilliam	F	6'9"	250	7	UNLV	82	6.1	0.8	11.8
4	Rick Mahorn	F	6'10"	260	13	Hampton Inst.	28	1.9	0.2	2.1
34	Chris Morris	F	6'8"	220	6	Auburn	50	4.6	1.7	10.9
33	Dwayne Schintzius	C	7'2"	285	4	Florida	30	3.0	0.4	2.3
2	Rex Walters	G	6'4"	190	1	Kansas	48	0.8	1.5	3.4
1	David Wesley	G	6'0"	190	1	Baylor	60	0.7	2.1	3.1
55	Jayson Williams	F	6'10"	245	4	St. John's	70	3.8	0.4	4.6

New Jersey Nets
1994-95 Season Preview

Opening Line: So, this is what it has come to in the Jersey swamps. Chuck Daly leaves town, and the team toys with the idea of changing its name to something more exciting and marketable. How fitting. While the Knicks win fans with good play, the Nets try gimmicks. New coach Butch Beard comes from the college ranks and inherits a curious collection of superstars and question marks. The draft didn't do much to clear the air, since New Jersey grabbed hulking center Yinka Dare of George Washington, who could be excellent or monumentally disappointing.

Guard: There is no doubt that Kenny Anderson has moved into the NBA's top echelon of point guards. Although his outside shooting remains suspect, Anderson is a blur off the dribble and a marvel in the open court. Kevin Edwards is not Drazen Petrovic, but he did produce pretty good numbers at the two spot last year. Edwards is best at taking the ball to the basket. Second-year man Rex Walters can shoot, but he needs to learn more about playing the pro game.

Forward: He may not make the NBA's Congeniality Team, but Derrick Coleman continues to post big numbers at power forward. Sure, he still takes some ridiculous shots, and there are nights when he just doesn't show up, but Coleman is still one of the premier talents at the four spot. Chris Morris is back at the small-forward position, so expect more rapid-fire shooting (and scoring). Expect big offense out of Armon Gilliam too, along with productive rebounding. Just don't expect him to pass or play defense. P.J. Brown surprised many people last year by playing all three frontcourt spots reasonably well. If he can improve his shooting, he'll be a good one. Johnny Newman was an unrestricted free agent this summer. Jayson Williams continues to disappoint.

Center: One year after he traded for enigmatic Benoit Benjamin, G.M. Willis Reed selected Dare, who has a great body and gobs of potential but has played only three years of organized ball in this country and has been criticized for the same lack of work ethic as Benjamin. Add in career problem child Dwayne Schintzius and the Nets may have the league's worst aggregate attitude in the pivot.

Coaching: Beard was an assistant in the NBA before achieving reasonable success at Howard. His biggest challenge with New Jersey is getting the Nets to play defense—Daly found out how tough that was—and keeping the big egos from rotting away the team. He's assisted by Jerry Eaves and Paul Silas.

Analysis: If Dare is a legitimate big man, the Nets will become one of the league's top teams in three years or so. If he is another giant package of unrealized potential, expect the franchise to continue to wallow around .500. Anderson and Coleman are stars, but the rest of the team's identity is difficult to measure. Once again, Reed has taken a chance. Things worked out with Anderson. They had better with Dare.

Prediction: Fifth place, Atlantic Division

NEW YORK KNICKS

Home: Madison Square Garden
Capacity: 19,763
Year Built: 1968

Address:
Two Pennsylvania Plaza
New York, NY 10121
(212) 465-6471

Governor: Stanley R. Jaffe
General Manager: Ernie Grunfeld
Head Coach: Pat Riley
Assistant Coach: Jeff Van Gundy

Coach Pat Riley			
	W	L	Pct.
NBA Record	701	272	.720
W/Knicks	168	78	.683
1993-94 Record	57	25	.695

Knicks History

Despite playing in the nation's media capital, the Knicks have spent much of their existence in the shadow of their rival to the north—Boston.

Soon after the franchise's inception as a BAA member, the Knicks made trips to the NBA Finals—in 1951, '52, and '53. Hall of Fame coach Joe Lapchick melded forward Carl Braun with Harry Gallatin, Dick McGuire, and Nat "Sweetwater" Clifton and reached the playoffs nine consecutive years (1947-55).

The following ten years were not so kind. The Knicks wandered through six coaches and made the playoffs only once—1958-59. But fortunes changed quickly when Red Holzman took over in 1967-68. The Knicks built a powerhouse on the backs of center Willis Reed, forwards Bill Bradley and Dave DeBusschere, and guards Walt "Clyde" Frazier and Dick Barnett. In 1969-70, they defeated the Lakers in seven games for the title.

Jerry Lucas replaced Reed in the middle, and flashy Earl Monroe joined Frazier to form one of the game's best-ever backcourts. Together, they won the NBA championship in 1973.

The subsequent 20 seasons have featured only modest success. High-scoring Bernard King provided some thrills in the mid-1980s, and star center Patrick Ewing sparked the team to the Atlantic Division title in 1988-89. New coach Pat Riley has won three straight division titles but has fallen short in his quest for an NBA championship.

Last Seven Years

Season	W	L	Pct.	Place	Playoffs	Coach
1987-88	38	44	.463	Second	L-Round 1	Rick Pitino
1988-89	52	30	.634	First	L-East Semis	Rick Pitino
1989-90	45	37	.549	Third	L-East Semis	Stu Jackson
1990-91	39	43	.476	Third	L-Round 1	Stu Jackson/ John MacLeod
1991-92	51	31	.622	First	L-East Semis	Pat Riley
1992-93	60	22	.732	First	L-East Finals	Pat Riley
1993-94	57	25	.695	First	L-NBA Finals	Pat Riley

1993-94 Review

Basketball purists may have heaved a huge sigh of relief when the Knicks fell to Houston in Game 7 of the NBA Finals, but even the staunchest New York hater had to admire the overwhelming effort and commitment exhibited by Pat Riley's team. Several clubs had more pure talent than the Knicks, but none had the intense desire to win and compete, which began with Riley and trickled down through the entire team.

Granted, New York did take its defensive intensity and desire to win to an ugly and brutal extreme, but the Knicks achieved considerable success. Center Patrick Ewing (24.5 PPG, 11.2 RPG) was again the key, assuming the role as No. 1 option on offense and then anchoring the defense from the pivot spot. Many believed that New York's failure to win the title was a blotch on Ewing's record and showed an inability to win the big one, but he was strong all year and had tremendous performances in the Knicks' Game 7 survivals against Chicago and Indiana.

Mercurial off guard John Starks (19.0 PPG) overcame a midseason knee injury to provide New York with a strong outside option, and he should be remembered for his strong play throughout the entire year. The midyear acquisition of Derek Harper (9.6 PPG) from the Mavericks was just as important as any contributions from Ewing and Starks, because it solidified the point spot in the wake of Doc Rivers's early knee injury. Harper played great defense, ran the show, and scored more and more as he became comfortable with the Knicks.

Back-up man Greg Anthony calmed down some, but he and second-year shooting guard Hubert Davis (11.0 PPG) were unreliable in the clutch. Up front, veteran power forward Charles Oakley (11.8 PPG, 11.8 RPG) continued his role as chief rebounder and enforcer, and he also expanded his offensive game considerably. Small forward Charles Smith (10.4 PPG) remained an enigma, scoring well some nights and disappearing others. There was no mistaking Anthony Mason (7.2 PPG, 5.8 RPG), however. He was the guy banging, bouncing, and pushing opponents around.

1994-95 Roster

No.	Player	Pos.	Ht.	Wt.	Exp.	College	G	1993-94 RPG	APG	PPG
50	Greg Anthony	G	6'2"	185	3	UNLV	80	2.4	4.6	7.8
20	Rolando Blackman	G	6'6"	206	13	Kansas St.	55	1.7	1.4	7.3
4	Anthony Bonner	F	6'8"	225	4	St. Louis	73	4.7	1.2	5.1
44	Hubert Davis	G	6'5"	183	2	North Carolina	56	1.2	2.9	11.0
33	Patrick Ewing	C	7'0"	240	9	Georgetown	79	11.2	2.3	24.5
11	Derek Harper	G	6'4"	206	11	Illinois	82	1.7	4.1	9.6
14	Anthony Mason	F	6'7"	250	5	Tennessee St.	73	5.8	2.1	7.2
34	Charles Oakley	F	6'9"	245	9	Virginia Union	82	11.8	2.7	11.8
25	Doc Rivers	G	6'4"	185	11	Marquette	19	2.1	5.3	7.5
54	Charles Smith	F	6'10"	244	6	Pittsburgh	43	3.8	1.2	10.4
3	John Starks	G	6'5"	185	5	Oklahoma St.	59	3.1	5.9	19.0
—	Charlie Ward	G	6'2"	190	R	Florida St.	—	—	—	—
—	Monty Williams	F	6'8"	225	R	Notre Dame	—	—	—	—

New York Knicks
1994-95 Season Preview

Opening Line: The Knicks came within a game of the NBA championship last year and return enough talent to be one of the main contenders for the title this season. New York's defensive philosophy has served it well during the past few seasons, but the Finals loss to Houston demonstrated the team's lack of offensive pop. If New York is to win a championship, it must match its aggressive defense with an equally effective offense. Drafting Notre Dame scorer Monty Williams and Florida State point man Charlie Ward could help.

Guard: Derek Harper's arrival last year gave the Knicks a complete floor leader who could shoot, play defense, pass, and run a team. Back-up Greg Anthony is an adequate reserve who needs substantial work on his shot and still needs to rein in his flamboyance. He'll be challenged by Ward, who is small but knows how to win. John Starks was expected to join the league's elite in 1993-94, but he was felled by injury and inconsistency. To ascend to the perennial All-Star status that could await him, Starks needs to produce at the same level every night. Third-year man Hubert Davis has impressed fans with his sweet outside shooting.

Forward: The Knicks boast one of the league's toughest, strongest—and offensively desolate—forward lines. Power forward Charles Oakley can move mountains, but his offensive game disintegrates outside the paint. Anthony Mason comes off the bench snarling, but he knocks down opponents far better than he does jumpers. Anthony Bonner is another hard worker who can rebound, finish on the break, and bounce away enemies. Three man Charles Smith looks like he could be a major offensive force in the NBA, but his demeanor, lack of confidence, and bouts with disinterest limit him as well. The key is Williams, who can score in droves but has a poor medical history (heart problems). If healthy, he'll help considerably.

Center: Though Patrick Ewing is still seeking the NBA title that would legitimize his superstardom, he continues to be a substantial presence in the middle for New York. Ewing can shoot inside or out, play solid post defense, and swat enemy shots from the weak side. Ancient Herb Williams became an unrestricted free agent this summer.

Coaching: Pat Riley continues to preach the defensive gospel in New York, and it's hard to believe that he once unleashed the Lakers on opponents at warp speed. Anyone who can reinvent himself that thoroughly deserves tremendous credit. His 701-272 career record says it all. He's assisted by Jeff Van Gundy.

Analysis: The Knicks could have won the title in 1993-94 and are legitimate threats this year. However, the NBA is becoming less tolerant of their brutal tactics and could clamp down harder this season. The Knicks will have to fend off an emerging Orlando team to win the Atlantic Division.

Prediction: Second place, Atlantic Division

ORLANDO MAGIC

Home: Orlando Arena
Capacity: 15,291
Year Built: 1989

Address:
Orlando Arena
One Magic Place
Orlando, FL 32801
(407) 649-3200

Chairman: Rich DeVos
General Manager: Pat Williams
Head Coach: Brian Hill
Assistant Coach: Bob Hill
Assistant Coach: Tree Rollins

Coach Brian Hill			
	W	L	Pct.
NBA Record	50	32	.610
W/Magic	50	32	.610
1993-94 Record	50	32	.610

Magic History

It's surprising that the Magic is not owned by a consortium of Mickey Mouse, Donald Duck, and Pluto. After all, the team has worked hard to tie itself to the Disney World image of Orlando. When the team presented its franchise application check to David Stern on July 2, 1986, it also handed the NBA commissioner a set of Mickey Mouse ears.

Magic fans have ridden a roller coaster of emotions over the last five years. After a predictably dreadful 18-64 debut in 1989-90, the Magic improved to 31-51 in 1990-91. Injuries ruined the 1991-92 season, but center Shaquille O'Neal brought glittering new magic to Orlando in 1992-93.

Orlando's inaugural season was noteworthy for style, as the Magic unveiled their classy pinstriped uniforms. Coach Matt Guokas blended expansion-draft acquisitions Reggie Theus, Sam Vincent, Otis Smith, and Scott Skiles with rookie Nick Anderson into a team that was exciting, though not very successful.

Things perked up in 1990-91. Orlando drafted sharp-shooter Dennis Scott, and Skiles developed into one of the league's top point guards. Orlando played .500 ball after the All-Star break and had a 24-17 home record. However, Skiles fizzled out in 1991-92 and Scott missed most of the year with an injury. With little other talent, Orlando finished the year as the East's worst team.

With the No. 1 pick in the 1992 draft, the Magic grabbed O'Neal, a mega-superstar who improved the club by 20 games in 1992-93. Orlando missed the 1993 playoffs by a tie-breaker but amazingly won the pre-draft lottery again. The team drafted Chris Webber, traded him for rookie Anfernee Hardaway, and dreamed of bright days ahead.

Last Five Years

Season	W	L	Pct.	Place	Playoffs	Coach
1989-90	18	64	.220	Seventh	DNQ	Matt Guokas
1990-91	31	51	.378	Fourth	DNQ	Matt Guokas
1991-92	21	61	.256	Seventh	DNQ	Matt Guokas
1992-93	41	41	.500	Fourth	DNQ	Matt Guokas
1993-94	50	32	.610	Second	L-Round 1	Brian Hill

1993-94 Review

Shaqmania continued to rule the NBA's marketing world during the 1993-94 season, and the Magic's large, multi-national conglomerate of a center actually stepped up his game to a level near his business dealings.

Despite being criticized for his heavy off-season schedule, Shaquille O'Neal helped lift the Magic to a franchise-record 50 wins and its first-ever playoff appearance. Unfortunately for Central Florida residents, the postseason stay was abbreviated, as Orlando became Indiana's first-ever NBA playoff victim—in a three-game sweep, no less.

Even with the embarrassing postseason performance, the Magic's 1993-94 experience was a positive one. O'Neal (29.3 PPG, 13.2 RPG) continued his emergence as a dominant pivot man, finishing second in the league in scoring and rebounding and leading everyone in shooting percentage (59.9 percent).

Shaq, though, had plenty of help. Rookie point guard Anfernee Hardaway (16.0 PPG, 6.6 APG) grew quickly into the position and showed flashes of future stardom. Hardaway was often a magician with the ball and displayed considerable ability to create his own shot.

The Magic had considerable firepower besides its two talented youngsters. Forward Nick Anderson (15.8 PPG, 5.9 RPG) enjoyed a healthy season and produced consistently, while Dennis Scott (12.8 PPG, 39.9 percent from 3-point range) continued to be a dangerous bombardier. Veteran Scott Skiles received the Good Soldier Award for volunteering to surrender his starting point-guard job to Hardaway in the interest of team harmony.

If only the frontcourt situation could have been so settled. Midseason acquisition Anthony Avent (5.3 PPG, 4.6 RPG) struggled in his complementary role at power forward, while Jeff Turner (6.6 PPG) continued to be a 6'9" jump-shooter before tearing a knee ligament late in the season. Reserve swing man Donald Royal (7.4 PPG) provided considerable spark off the bench, particularly on defense, while Larry Krystkowiak contributed up front in a reserve role.

1994-95 Roster

No.	Player	Pos.	Ht.	Wt.	Exp.	College	G	RPG	APG	PPG
25	Nick Anderson	G/F	6'6"	220	5	Illinois	81	5.9	3.6	15.8
00	Anthony Avent	F	6'10"	235	2	Seton Hall	74	4.6	0.9	5.3
14	Anthony Bowie	G	6'6"	200	5	Oklahoma	70	1.7	1.5	4.6
24	Rodney Dent	C	6'10"	256	R	Kentucky	—	—	—	—
—	Horace Grant	F	6'10"	235	7	Clemson	70	11.0	3.4	15.1
43	Geert Hammink	F/C	7'0"	262	1	Louisiana St.	1	1.0	1.0	2.0
1	Anfernee Hardaway	G/F	6'7"	200	1	Memphis St.	82	5.4	6.6	16.0
34	Greg Kite	C/F	6'11"	263	11	Brigham Young	29	2.4	0.1	1.2
32	Shaquille O'Neal	C	7'1"	301	2	Louisiana St.	81	13.2	2.4	29.3
5	Donald Royal	F	6'8"	210	4	Notre Dame	74	3.4	0.8	7.4
3	Dennis Scott	G/F	6'8"	229	4	Georgia Tech	82	2.7	2.6	12.8
—	Brooks Thompson	G	6'4"	195	R	Oklahoma St.	—	—	—	—
55	Keith Tower	F/C	6'11"	250	1	Notre Dame	11	0.5	0.1	0.7
31	Jeff Turner	F	6'9"	240	8	Vanderbilt	68	4.0	0.9	6.6

Orlando Magic
1994-95 Season Preview

Opening Line: The Magic may have two of the league's most exciting young players and some sporty uniforms, but they still don't have an NBA playoff series win. Indiana's sweep of the Magic in last year's first round proved a longtime NBA corollary: Hype doesn't win titles. The Magic looks to take a mighty step forward this year after signing All-Star power forward Horace Grant.

Guard: Anfernee Hardaway's first year as an NBA point guard featured plenty of highlights and quite a few struggles—just about normal for a rookie starter. A tremendous passer with great instincts, Hardaway is a dangerous combination of size and speed. Star shooter Dennis Scott continues to confound those who think the limits of his range have been exhausted. Anybody who can nail 40 percent of 388 treys is a dangerous weapon. Anthony Bowie is another guy who can light it up, as can first-round pick Brooks Thompson. Orlando had to trade Scott Skiles to make room for Grant's salary. The team will miss his backcourt leadership.

Forward: Scott's partner in long-distance bombing is three man Nick Anderson, who—when healthy—can score inside or out. Anderson can grab about six boards a night, drive well, and even snatch a few steals. Grant brings outstanding defense, rebounding, and championship experience to the power-forward position. Anthony Avent brings size at 6'10", but he has a limited offensive game and is soft against the tougher power men. Second-round draft pick Rodney Dent can bang, provided his knee is healthy. Jeff Turner is little more than a 6'9" jump-shooter. Donald Royal is a fierce defender at small forward and is an excellent inside scorer.

Center: A nimble 7'1", 303 pounds, Shaquille O'Neal is a rare blend of speed and size. Though Shaq has been criticized for having little offensive prowess outside of the monster dunk, he doesn't always need much more, since few NBA centers can stop him from barreling hoopward. Still, the man needs to improve his free throw shooting—as well as his passing when opponents surround him with three defenders. Orlando is in desperate need of a back-up center, as Greg Kite is ready for the retirement home.

Coaching: You can't criticize Brian Hill's first year in Orlando. He took the team to a franchise-record 50 wins and its first-ever playoff berth, all while fostering the development of several young players. His next step is some postseason success, something this diligent coach should produce. He is assisted by Bob Hill and Tree Rollins.

Analysis: To many fans, the Magic is little more than Shaq's Traveling All-Star Show, and the big fella does pack arenas and sell products at record rates. But Orlando has a chance to be more. Hardaway is a star in training, and Anderson and Scott bring big-time scoring punch to the equation. Grant fills the team's desperate need for a power forward. Depth is a slight problem, but no one in the East has a better starting lineup.

Prediction: First place, Atlantic Division

PHILADELPHIA 76ERS

Home: The Spectrum
Capacity: 18,168
Year Built: 1967

Address:
Veterans Stadium
P.O. Box 25040
Philadelphia, PA 19147
(215) 339-7600

Owner: Harold Katz
General Manager: John Lucas
Head Coach: John Lucas
Assistant Coach: Ron Adams
Assistant Coach: Tom Thibodeau
Assistant Coach: Maurice Cheeks

Coach John Lucas			
	W	L	Pct.
NBA Record	94	49	.657
W/76ers	0	0	.000
1993-94 Record	55	27	.671

Sixers History

The 76ers own the distinction of having the Alpha and Omega of NBA basketball history. The 1966-67 Sixers thrashed the league with a 68-13 record and a world title. On the other hand, the 1972-73 Sixers stumbled to the worst-ever mark of 9-73.

The Sixers began in 1949-50 as the Syracuse Nationals and reached the first NBA Finals series, losing in six games to Minneapolis. Hall of Fame center Dolph Schayes was the big gun on both that team and the 1953-54 squad that fell again in the NBA Finals, this time to the Lakers.

The team moved to Philadelphia in 1963-64 and acquired Wilt Chamberlain in a trade in early 1965. They moved onto a level with the dominating Boston Celtics and began to challenge them for league supremacy. In fact, the Nationals/Sixers have met the Celtics in 17 playoff series, winning seven. Philadelphia beat Boston in the 1967 East finals on the way to the NBA title.

The Sixers nosedived in the early 1970s, but the arrival of coach Gene Shue and ABA imports George McGinnis and Julius Erving signaled a renaissance. Philadelphia advanced to the NBA Finals in 1976-77 but lost to Portland. Similar excursions were made in 1979-80 and 1981-82, thanks to Erving, Bobby Jones, Maurice Cheeks, and Andrew Toney.

Moses Malone arrived for the 1982-83 season, and the Sixers blitzed to another NBA title. In 1984, Philly drafted super-forward Charles Barkley, who led the team to the 1989-90 Atlantic Division title.

Last Seven Years

Season	W	L	Pct.	Place	Playoffs	Coach
1987-88	36	46	.439	Fourth	DNQ	Matt Guokas/Jim Lynam
1988-89	46	36	.561	Second	L-Round 1	Jim Lynam
1989-90	53	29	.646	First	L-East Semis	Jim Lynam
1990-91	44	38	.537	Second	L-East Semis	Jim Lynam
1991-92	35	47	.427	Fifth	DNQ	Jim Lynam
1992-93	26	56	.317	Sixth	DNQ	Doug Moe/Fred Carter
1993-94	25	57	.305	Sixth	DNQ	Fred Carter

1993-94 Review

After one season of the Shawn Bradley Rebuilding Project, the Sixers resembled the same cast of sad-sack characters that stumbled to a dismal lottery finish in 1992-93. Philadelphia lost one more game in 1993-94 than it did the previous season, and it stumbled home with an abundance of questions.

The largest question, of course, was Bradley, who began the season as a lost, 7'6" fawn but matured into a contributor by mid-year, only to have his progress aborted by a freak dislocated left kneecap in February. As Bradley developed, so did the Sixers, who overcame a dreary start to stand at 20-26 when the big guy went down.

However, following Bradley's injury, the Sixers slid into a dismal 1-25 funk. Even when healthy, Bradley (10.3 PPG, 6.2 RPG) lacked the strength and power—not to mention a consistent low-post move—to be a big-time NBA center. While the Sixer brass stressed patience with the praying mantis-framed rookie, little optimism surrounded the rest of the team.

Second-year forward Clarence Weatherspoon (18.4 PPG, 10.1 RPG) was the exception. Weatherspoon improved his shooting range and continued his strong inside play from the three spot. But that was about it for highlights. The Sixers dished talented lead guard Jeff Hornacek to Utah in midseason for a much-needed first-round draft pick and machine-gunning two guard Jeff Malone, who staged a scoring duel down the stretch with ancient forward Orlando Woolridge (12.7 PPG).

It's not like anybody else was ready to step up. Point guard Dana Barros wore down quickly after a quick start, although he did show some 3-point shooting skills. Forward Tim Perry—the last remaining player from the awful Charles Barkley trade—was inconsistent and overmatched, while veteran point guard Johnny Dawkins appeared in desperate need of a new address.

Rookie power forward Warren Kidd was unpolished and ineffective, and journeyman center Eric Leckner tried hard in Bradley's absence but couldn't deliver. Moses Malone's cranky back reduced him to a bit player at center, while rookie guard Greg Graham was rarely a factor.

1994-95 Roster

No.	Player	Pos.	Ht.	Wt.	Exp.	College	——1993-94——		
							G	RPG	APG	PPG
—	Derrick Alston	F	6'11"	225	R	Duquesne	—	—	—	—
3	Dana Barros	G	5'11"	163	5	Boston College	81	2.4	5.2	13.3
76	Shawn Bradley	C	7'6"	248	1	Brigham Young	49	6.2	2.0	10.3
12	Johnny Dawkins	G	6'2"	170	8	Duke	72	1.7	3.7	6.6
20	Greg Graham	G	6'4"	174	1	Indiana	70	1.2	0.9	4.8
25	Jeff Malone	G	6'4"	205	11	Mississippi St.	77	2.6	1.6	16.4
23	Tim Perry	F	6'9"	220	6	Temple	80	5.1	1.2	9.0
—	B.J. Tyler	G	6'1"	185	R	Texas	—	—	—	—
35	C. Weatherspoon	F	6'7"	240	2	S. Mississippi	82	10.1	2.3	18.4
—	Scott Williams	C	6'10"	230	4	North Carolina	38	4.8	1.0	7.6
—	Sharone Wright	F/C	6'11"	260	R	Clemson	—	—	—	—

Philadelphia 76ers
1994-95 Season Preview

Opening Line: The Sixers enter the 1994-95 season with their fourth coach in as many years. John Lucas steps into the coaching and G.M. spots and must find a way to build a winner around 7'6" question mark Shawn Bradley. Acquiring hulking center/forward Sharone Wright, quick point man B.J. Tyler, and 6'11" shooter Derrick Alston on draft day can only help the Sixers' shallow rotation. Free agent pick-up Scott Williams replaces free agent departees Orlando Woolridge and Warren Kidd.

Guard: The Sixer backcourt is in shambles. In less than six months, the team replaced a pair of outstanding off guards—Hersey Hawkins and Jeff Hornacek—with Jeff Malone and Greg Graham. Malone is a shot-a-minute gunner who plays little defense and is reluctant to pass the ball. Graham is a second-year project with an erratic shooting touch. Point man Dana Barros wore down considerably as last season plodded on and is still more of a small-fry two man. Though Tyler is lightning-quick and can score some, he has a history of personal problems and inconsistent play. Veteran Johnny Dawkins's bad knee prevents him from moving, shooting, and driving the way he did in the late 1980s.

Forward: Clarence Weatherspoon has matured into a legitimate small-forward star in just two seasons. 'Spoon has improved his shooting range, can get double-figure rebounds every other night, and is an intense competitor. Wright played center in college but will be moved to the four spot this year. He must rebound, play defense, and score some. Wright is capable of all three if he stays in shape. Williams is an active player who will rebound and play defense. Alston is a thin shooter with little ability to go inside. Somebody told Tim Perry that he was a 3-point shooter last year instead of a journeyman forward.

Center: Before he hurt his knee in mid-February, Bradley was actually improving. But he still has an overwhelming amount of work to do. The Sixers tried to put more weight on his broom-handle frame during the off-season and even brought in Kareem Abdul-Jabbar to teach Bradley the sky-hook. Eric Leckner was traded to Detroit in July.

Coaching: Lucas did a great job with San Antonio, blending a strange aggregation into a contender. But he didn't win in the playoffs, so his departure may not hurt the Spurs that much. Of course, in Philadelphia, he doesn't need to worry about the playoffs. Lucas is a good motivator with faith in his players and the willingness to let them develop. He is assisted by Maurice Cheeks, Ron Adams, and Tom Thibodeau.

Analysis: The Sixers remain a long way from the playoffs, despite three consecutive trips to the lottery. The backcourt is a mess and the frontcourt is progressing slowly. Lucas may galvanize the young players into a hungry unit, but he can't mask the lack of talent. Philly fans are already looking forward to the 1995 draft.

Prediction: Seventh place, Atlantic Division

WASHINGTON BULLETS

Home: USAir Arena
Capacity: 18,756
Year Built: 1973

Address:
USAir Arena
Landover, MD 20785
(301) 773-2255

Chairman of the Board: Abe Pollin
V.P./General Manager: John Nash
Head Coach: Jim Lynam
Assistant Coach: Bob Staak
Assistant Coach: Derek Smith

Coach Jim Lynam			
	W	L	Pct.
NBA Record	246	264	.482
W/Bullets	0	0	.000
1993-94 Record	0	0	.000

Bullets History

The Bullets' greatest years came in the 1970s, but the franchise rolled off the assembly line in 1961-62 as the Chicago Packers. In 1963, it blew the Windy City, moved to Baltimore, and adopted its current nickname.

In 1964-65, the Bullets advanced to the Western finals behind center Walt Bellamy and forward Bailey Howell. Prior to the 1968-69 season, Baltimore drafted huge Wes Unseld, and he went on to win the MVP Award in his first season. Unseld teamed with bruising Gus Johnson and slick Earl "The Pearl" Monroe to help the Bullets win the Eastern Division.

The Bullets made their first trip to the NBA Finals in 1970-71, but they were dispatched in four games by Milwaukee. They made it back in 1974-75, this time as Washington, but Golden State swept them 4-0. Dick Motta took over the Bullets in 1976-77 and led them to the Finals the following year. This time, Unseld, Elvin Hayes, Bob Dandridge, and company whipped Seattle in seven games. The Sonics got revenge in the Finals the next year, winning in five games and closing out the Bullets' big decade.

The 1980s featured some talented players (Jeff Ruland, Rick Mahorn, Greg Ballard, Jeff Malone) but few highlights. The Bullets won just one playoff series during the whole decade, and by its end they were a lottery team. Unseld took over as coach in 1987-88 but—outside of Bernard King and then Pervis Ellison—has had little to work with. Injuries and thin talent have stymied his efforts.

Last Seven Years

Season	W	L	Pct.	Place	Playoffs	Coach
1987-88	38	44	.463	Second	L-Round 1	K. Loughery/W. Unseld
1988-89	40	42	.488	Fourth	DNQ	Wes Unseld
1989-90	31	51	.378	Fourth	DNQ	Wes Unseld
1990-91	30	52	.366	Fourth	DNQ	Wes Unseld
1991-92	25	57	.305	Sixth	DNQ	Wes Unseld
1992-93	22	60	.268	Seventh	DNQ	Wes Unseld
1993-94	24	58	.234	Seventh	DNQ	Wes Unseld

1993-94 Review

In the end, Wes Unseld was nothing if not consistent. The man who meant so much to the Bullets during his playing career closed out his coaching tenure in the nation's capital by coaxing only 24 wins out of his team—about the same as his five previous seasons. When he resigned following their last game of 1993-94, a win over Charlotte, balloons and confetti dropped from the USAir Arena ceiling. It was tough to tell whether the Bullet brass was paying tribute to their former hero or celebrating his departure.

You can't fault Unseld completely for Washington's slow slip into the NBA's dregs. Poor personnel moves like the preseason trade of talented forward Harvey Grant to Portland for overrated center Kevin Duckworth gave him little with which to work. The Bullets were especially bad defensively, yielding 107.7 points per game.

There were a few highlights last season, most notably the development of second-year forward Don MacLean (18.2 PPG, 6.2 RPG) into a solid small forward. Fellow soph Tom Gugliotta (17.1 PPG, 9.3 RPG) was again an all-around contributor at the other forward spot and should be an All-Star within a season or two.

The middle was another story. Duckworth was a colossal bust, and Pervis Ellison's cranky knees limited him to just 47 games of action. Gheorghe Muresan, the 7'7" Romanian curiosity, was slow and awkward, to be sure, but he contributed much more than anyone thought he could and displayed some effective moves in the low post. Veteran Kenny Walker had a healthy season for a change and provided an occasional spark off the bench at forward.

The Bullets' backcourt play was inconsistent. Shooter Rex Chapman (18.2 PPG) played 60 games at the two spot and led the team in scoring, while rookies Calbert Cheaney (12.0 PPG) and Mitchell Butler (6.9 PPG) showed flashes of future success. Point guard Michael Adams (12.1 PPG, 6.9 APG) threw up shots at random, while reserves Brent Price and Doug Overton showed none of the consistency needed to run an NBA team every night.

1994-95 Roster

No.	Player	Pos.	Ht.	Wt.	Exp.	College	G	RPG	APG	PPG
									1993-94	
32	Mitchell Butler	G	6'5"	210	1	UCLA	75	3.0	1.0	6.9
3	Rex Chapman	G	6'4"	195	6	Kentucky	60	2.4	3.1	18.2
40	Calbert Cheaney	F/G	6'7"	215	1	Indiana	65	2.9	1.9	12.0
00	Kevin Duckworth	C	7'0"	275	8	E. Illinois	69	4.7	0.8	6.6
24	Tom Gugliotta	F	6'10"	240	2	N. Carolina St.	78	9.3	3.5	17.1
—	Juwan Howard	F	6'9"	250	R	Michigan	—	—	—	—
34	Don MacLean	F	6'10"	235	2	UCLA	75	6.2	2.1	18.2
—	Jim McIlvaine	C	7'0"	240	R	Marquette	—	—	—	—
77	Gheorghe Muresan	C	7'7"	315	1	Cluj	54	3.6	0.3	5.6
14	Doug Overton	G	6'3"	190	2	La Salle	61	1.1	1.5	3.6
20	Brent Price	G	6'1"	185	2	Oklahoma	65	1.4	3.3	6.2
—	Scott Skiles	G	6'1"	180	8	Michigan St.	82	2.3	6.1	9.9
33	Larry Stewart	F	6'8"	230	3	Coppin St.	3	2.3	0.7	4.3

Washington Bullets
1994-95 Season Preview

Opening Line: Loyal franchise soldier Wes Unseld has been pushed off the sidelines and behind a desk, but don't blame him for the Bullets' current sad status. Nobody could have won with those guys, and that includes Jim Lynam, who comes to Washington to help old pal John Nash try to resurrect the good times. First-round pick Juwan Howard of Michigan should help at the power-forward spot. Washington replaced point guard Michael Adams with Scott Skiles but lost oft-injured center Pervis Ellison to free agency.

Guard: Apparently tired of seeing their point guard, Adams, launch 3's all night, the Bullets will turn to Skiles, a hard-nosed, veteran distributor. Fans should see an improvement. We can't be too sure about Rex Chapman, who has missed significant parts of the past three seasons. Chapman did shoot it well last year and has great physical tools, but he must stay healthy over an entire season to prove his worth. Mitchell Butler has promise and can score well off the dribble, but his shooting range must expand. Brent Price is a slower version of his brother, and one can never tell what Doug Overton will do next at the point.

Forward: Tom Gugliotta brings a tremendous collection of skills to the four spot. He can shoot from far out, bang well inside, and grab a bunch of rebounds. Don MacLean's sophomore year featured the kind of shooting Washington expected when it acquired him two years back. Second-year man Calbert Cheaney was playing well until a freak ankle injury sidelined him last season. He should get more and more time this year and blossom into a good NBA scorer. He could find himself at off guard. Adding Howard to this mix gives the Bullets a good frontcourt collection. He scores well from the post, hits the 15-footer, and was a quiet leader at Michigan.

Center: After watching Kevin Duckworth for a year, Bullets fans were probably ready to kill Nash for dealing Harvey Grant to Portland for the portly center. Duckworth is slow, soft, and often disinterested. Reserve Gheorghe Muresan (7'7") is slow but displayed a surprising touch around the basket. Second-round pick Jim McIlvaine blocked a ton of shots in college but has an immature offensive game.

Coaching: Lynam won the Atlantic Division while coaching the Sixers, but that was a long time ago and it was accomplished with Charles Barkley. Lynam knows the game, can teach well, and doesn't take much grief from players. Expect the Bullets to provide maximum effort every night. He is assisted by Bob Staak and Derek Smith.

Analysis: The Bullets find themselves well below the Eastern Conference playoff teams, and the climb will take some time. The last three drafts have produced some quality frontcourt players, but the guard line still needs help and the pivot position must be addressed. Lynam will keep the team competitive in most games, but effort isn't enough in this league.

Prediction: Sixth place, Atlantic Division

ATLANTA HAWKS

Home: The Omni
Capacity: 16,510
Year Built: 1972

Address:
One CNN Center
Suite 405, South Tower
Atlanta, GA 30303
(404) 827-3800

Owner: Ted Turner
V.P./General Manager: Pete Babcock
Head Coach: Lenny Wilkens
Assistant Coach: Dick Helm
Assistant Coach: Brian Winters

Coach Lenny Wilkens			
	W	L	Pct.
NBA Record	926	917	.502
W/Hawks	57	25	.695
1993-94 Record	57	25	.695

Hawks History

Few teams have had as many different addresses as the Hawks. Before settling in Georgia, the franchise roamed the Midwest, calling Moline, Rock Island, Davenport, Milwaukee, and St. Louis home.

An original member of the NBA, the franchise was first known as the Tri-City (Moline, Rock Island, and Davenport) Blackhawks. Two years later, it moved to Milwaukee and shortened its nickname to its current form. Though active off the court, it wasn't until the team drafted Bob Pettit in 1954 that it started to show some life on it.

The Hawks moved to St. Louis in 1955, won consecutive Western Conference championships from 1957-61, and defeated Boston in 1958 for the franchise's lone NBA title. Pettit, Cliff Hagan, Ed Macauley, Charlie Share, and Slater Martin formed the nucleus of those teams. In the title win over Boston, Pettit played with his broken left wrist in a cast, and Share played with his busted jaw wired shut.

The 1960s featured talented players like Lou Hudson, Joe Caldwell, and Zelmo Beatty, but the Hawks could not get back to the NBA Finals. The team moved to Atlanta for the 1968-69 season and staggered through the next decade as a .500 team.

Things started to change in 1982, when Atlanta drafted exciting forward Dominique Wilkins. The Hawks won the NBA Central Division title in 1986-87 and recorded a franchise-record 57 wins. The team hovered around .500 in the early 1990s before a sudden rebirth under new coach Lenny Wilkens in 1993-94.

Last Seven Years

Season	W	L	Pct.	Place	Playoffs	Coach
1987-88	50	32	.610	Second	L-East Semis	Mike Fratello
1988-89	52	30	.634	Third	L-Round 1	Mike Fratello
1989-90	41	41	.500	Sixth	DNQ	Mike Fratello
1990-91	43	39	.524	Fourth	L-Round 1	Bob Weiss
1991-92	38	44	.463	Fifth	DNQ	Bob Weiss
1992-93	43	39	.524	Fourth	L-Round 1	Bob Weiss
1993-94	57	25	.695	First	L-East Semis	Lenny Wilkens

1993-94 Review

If Lenny Wilkens did one thing with the Hawks in 1993-94, he introduced them to the concept of defense. After several somewhat successful seasons with the Cavaliers, Wilkens moved south and took on the challenge of converting the Hawks from a selfish group of underachievers into contenders. He succeeded.

Atlanta allowed only 96.2 PPG, a drop of 12 from the previous season. The change in philosophy earned the Hawks a Central Division title and the best record in the Eastern Conference. It also helped them win a playoff series—a gruesome, fight-filled affair with Miami—for the first time since 1988. However, against Indiana in the Eastern semis, Atlanta reverted to form and fell apart, unable to match the Pacers' mix of inside bashing and outside gunning.

A controversial midseason trade that exiled high-scoring fan favorite Dominique Wilkins to the Clippers for free agent-to-be Danny Manning (20.6 PPG, 6.8 RPG) gave Atlanta more frontcourt pop but robbed it of an outside threat, something that proved fatal in the playoffs. Manning produced, but he disappeared for stretches during the postseason.

Manning's frontcourt mate, Kevin Willis (19.1 PPG, 12.0 RPG), dominated the boards and had his best scoring season as a professional. Center Jon Koncak (4.2 PPG, 4.5 RPG) showed some flashes of aggressive play, but he remained a below-average pivot man.

There was nothing sub-standard, however, about point guard Mookie Blaylock (13.8 PPG, 9.7 APG, 2.62 SPG), who finished third in the league in both steals and assists and was a tremendous starting point for the Hawks. Stacey Augmon's production (14.8 PPG, 4.8 RPG) continued to rise, although he was not a true two guard, and veteran Craig Ehlo (10.0 PPG), a longtime Wilkens favorite in Cleveland, added some punch off the bench.

Center Andrew Lang (6.1 PPG, 3.8 RPG) added pivot defense in place of Blair Rasmussen, who missed the whole season with a bad back. Duane Ferrell (7.1 PPG) and Adam Keefe (4.3 PPG, 3.2 RPG) were below-average forward reserves.

1994-95 Roster

No.	Player	Pos.	Ht.	Wt.	Exp.	College	1993-94			
							G	RPG	APG	PPG
2	Stacey Augmon	G/F	6'8"	205	3	UNLV	82	4.8	2.3	14.8
10	Mookie Blaylock	G	6'1"	185	5	Oklahoma	81	5.2	9.7	13.8
34	Doug Edwards	F	6'7"	235	1	Florida St.	16	1.1	0.5	2.7
3	Craig Ehlo	G/F	6'7"	205	11	Washington St.	82	3.4	3.3	10.0
25	Snoopy Graham	F	6'6"	200	3	Ohio	21	0.6	0.6	2.8
31	Adam Keefe	F	6'9"	241	2	Stanford	63	3.2	0.5	4.3
32	Jon Koncak	C	7'0"	250	9	Southern Meth.	82	4.5	1.2	4.2
28	Andrew Lang	C	6'11"	250	6	Arkansas	82	3.8	0.6	6.1
—	Jim Les	G	5'11"	175	6	Bradley	18	0.7	2.2	2.5
—	Gaylon Nickerson	G	6'3"	190	R	N.W. Okla. St.	—	—	—	—
—	Ken Norman	F	6'9"	223	7	Illinois	82	6.1	2.7	11.9
41	Blair Rasmussen	C	7'0"	250	9	Oregon	—	—	—	—
42	Kevin Willis	F/C	7'0"	240	9	Michigan St.	80	12.0	1.9	19.1

Atlanta Hawks
1994-95 Season Preview

Opening Line: The Hawks posted the best record in the Eastern Conference last season but self-destructed once the playoffs came around, nearly losing to eighth-seeded Miami and then falling fast to Indiana. The arrival of Lenny Wilkens on the bench has improved the Hawks' overall team defense, but now someone must save the team's offense, as high-scoring Danny Manning has left as a free agent. Forward Ken Norman, acquired in an off-season trade, is a modest addition.

Guard: Mookie Blaylock has become one of the NBA's most effective point guards—an outstanding distributor, floor leader, and defensive force. Now if Blaylock could shoot it better, he'd become one of the game's elite. Though Stacey Augmon continues to start at the two spot, he is really a small forward. That is part of Atlanta's problem. For while Augmon plays great defense and finishes well on the break, he cannot bomb from long distance, something Indiana exploited in the playoffs. Reserve Craig Ehlo, a longtime Wilkens favorite, shoots well from the outside but is a step slow. Back-up point man Ennis Whatley (a free agent this summer) gets the ball into the right hands.

Forward: Power forward Kevin Willis can be counted on for double-figure rebounds, at least one monster dunk, and plenty of facial expressions every game. Norman will score and rebound, but he isn't much of a defender and has been unhappy with the Clippers and Bucks, his previous two stops. Duane Ferrell is active around the basket, while Adam Keefe takes up space and can shoot it a little in close. Snoopy Graham and sophomore Doug Edwards will earn more minutes this year because of the loss of Manning.

Center: Jon Koncak was worth about 40 percent of his big contract last season. The big guy makes his presence felt defensively, but his scoring and rebounding numbers are atrocious. Andrew Lang is an excellent back-up center. He's a solid defensive presence and has a little touch around the basket.

Coaching: Wilkens has turned Atlanta into a great defensive team, but he still has trouble in the playoffs (he has posted losing records in nine of his last ten trips). Wilkens-coached teams win in the regular season but seem to lack a killer instinct during the postseason. Nonetheless, he has helped the Hawk franchise immensely. He is assisted by Dick Helm and Brian Winters.

Analysis: In the wide-open Central Division, the Hawks still have a remote chance to win the title. But without a real scorer at small forward and a stronger presence in the middle, they are ill-equipped to play with the stronger halfcourt teams. Willis, Blaylock, and Augmon form a solid nucleus, but Atlanta needs more to contend for the title. The signing of Ron Harper, whom the Hawks were eyeing late in the summer, would be a welcome addition.

Prediction: Third place, Central Division

CHARLOTTE HORNETS

Home: Charlotte Coliseum
Capacity: 23,698
Year Built: 1988

Address:
Hive Drive
Charlotte, NC 28217
(704) 357-0252

Owner: George Shinn
Director of Player Personnel:
Dave Twardzik
Head Coach: Allan Bristow
Assistant Coach: Bill Hanzlik
Assistant Coach: T.R. Dunn

Coach Allan Bristow			
	W	L	Pct.
NBA Record	116	130	.472
W/Hornets	116	130	.472
1993-94 Record	41	41	.500

Hornets History

They've always loved college basketball down on Tobacco Road, so it was natural for the NBA to try and tap into that market. Huge crowds have filled Charlotte Coliseum to back the Hornets since their inception. In the first three years, the level of play was below the high expectations of spoiled Carolina fans. However, the club has improved significantly over the last two seasons.

The city was awarded a franchise in April 1987, and it created an immediate stir by commissioning renowned clothing designer Alexander Julian to create the uniforms. The Hornets may have looked sharp in their teal-and-blue pinstriped duds, but their 20-62 record in 1988-89, their initial season, wasn't as fashionable. Among the highlights of that first season was the play of veteran Kelly Tripucka and exciting guards Muggsy Bogues and Rex Chapman.

Charlotte took a step backward in 1989-90, winning only 19 games, and coach Dick Harter was replaced by Gene Littles. Rookie J.R. Reid, a star at North Carolina, was a crowd favorite, though his 6'9" frame seemed too small for the center spot.

Littles boosted the team's production to 26 wins in 1990-91, as rookie guard Kendall Gill showed flashes of a brilliant future. In 1991-92, Allan Bristow took over as coach and the team added thunder-dunking rookie Larry Johnson, who helped improve the team by five games. With the addition of yet another stellar rookie—tenacious center Alonzo Mourning—Charlotte took a monster step in 1992-93, knocking off Boston in the first round of the playoffs.

Last Six Years

Season	W	L	Pct.	Place	Playoffs	Coach
1988-89	20	62	.244	Sixth	DNQ	Dick Harter
1989-90	19	63	.232	Seventh	DNQ	Dick Harter/Gene Littles
1990-91	26	56	.317	Seventh	DNQ	Gene Littles
1991-92	31	51	.378	Sixth	DNQ	Allan Bristow
1992-93	44	38	.537	Third	L-East Semis	Allan Bristow
1993-94	41	41	.500	Fifth	DNQ	Allan Bristow

1993-94 Review

The folks at NBA Properties will be happy to hear that the Hornets' disappointing 41-41 1993-94 record will do little to deter the smashing sales performance of the team's teal-colored products.

Charlotte may have slipped considerably from its exciting playoff performance of the previous year, but the young Hornets had a legitimate excuse for their troubles. Unlike some teams—see Clippers and Lakers—that slid out of the postseason because of insufficient talent or motivation, Charlotte found itself watching the playoffs because of injuries to stars Larry Johnson and Alonzo Mourning.

The unfortunate medical mishaps may have ruined 1993-94 at the Hive, but they only interrupted what will surely be a climb into NBA contention. Though Mourning (21.5 PPG, 10.2 RPG) was again a fearsome presence in the middle, he played only 60 games. And Johnson (16.4 PPG, 8.8 RPG) saw his numbers drop through 51 contests as his back never fully healed. With Mourning and Johnson out, the Hornets were truly lost, despite some fairly impressive performances by the supporting cast.

Guard Hersey Hawkins (14.4 PPG), acquired before the season from Philadelphia, was a consistent scorer, and reserve gunner Dell Curry (16.3 PPG) continued to prove his worth as one of the league's top long-range bombers. Point guard was again a good-news/bad-news proposition in Charlotte. Tiny Muggsy Bogues (10.8 PPG, 10.1 APG) was second in the NBA in assists and improved his shooting percentage (47.1 percent) considerably, but his 5'3" frame was hardly suited for the league's bang-bang defensive style.

Veteran forwards Frank Brickowski (13.2 PPG) and Eddie Johnson (11.5 PPG) provided some offensive pop while Mourning and Johnson rehabbed, and Kenny Gattison continued to provide a solid reserve presence underneath. One of the bigger disappointments of the season was rookie forward Scott Burrell, who was felled by a variety of injuries and never got a chance to mesh his considerable open-court talents with the Hornets' up-tempo style.

1994-95 Roster

| No. | Player | Pos. | Ht. | Wt. | Exp. | College | —1993-94— | | |
							G	RPG	APG	PPG
—	Michael Adams	G	5'10"	175	9	Boston College	70	2.6	6.9	12.1
25	Tony Bennett	G	6'0"	175	2	Wis.-Green Bay	74	1.2	2.2	3.4
1	Muggsy Bogues	G	5'3"	140	7	Wake Forest	77	4.1	10.1	10.8
24	Scott Burrell	G/F	6'7"	218	1	Connecticut	51	2.6	1.2	4.8
30	Dell Curry	G	6'5"	200	8	Virginia Tech	82	3.2	2.7	16.3
43	LeRon Ellis	C	6'10"	240	2	Syracuse	50	3.8	0.5	4.4
44	Kenny Gattison	F	6'8"	252	7	Old Dominion	77	4.7	1.2	7.7
32	Darrin Hancock	G/F	6'6"	205	R	Kansas	—	—	—	—
3	Hersey Hawkins	G	6'3"	190	6	Bradley	82	4.6	2.6	14.4
2	Larry Johnson	F	6'7"	250	3	UNLV	51	8.8	3.6	16.4
33	Alonzo Mourning	C	6'10"	240	2	Georgetown	60	10.2	1.4	21.5
—	Robert Parish	C	7'0"	230	18	Centenary	74	7.3	1.1	11.7
11	David Wingate	G/F	6'5"	185	8	Georgetown	50	2.7	2.1	6.2

Charlotte Hornets
1994-95 Season Preview

Opening Line: Charlotte fans should consider 1993-94 merely an unfortunate detour on the road to contention. The young, brash Hornets were plagued by injuries last year and fell into the lottery morass. Now, with stars Larry Johnson and Alonzo Mourning 100 percent again, Charlotte can continue its climb toward the top of the Central Division and beyond. Newcomers Robert Parish and Michael Adams are welcome additions.

Guard: The Hersey Hawkins/Dell Curry two-guard tandem gives the Hornets significant firepower. Curry is one of the league's top-flight bombardiers. Hawkins lacks the range of Curry, but he is no less dangerous. Muggsy Bogues continues to be one of the league's quickest players and most productive assist men. Despite the obvious disadvantages of being 5'3", Bogues piles up steals every night and is an all-around pest. Adams—a veteran, trey-shooting point guard—will challenge Bogues for the starting job. David Wingate has the defensive talent but lacks an offensive game, and Tony Bennett is a mediocre point reserve. Wingate also plays small forward.

Forward: It seems fitting that Larry Johnson's endorsement alter-ego is a grandmother, since the star forward's aching back forced him to spend plenty of time in a rocking chair last year. When healthy, Johnson can overwhelm teams inside and out, on the break and in halfcourt sets. The problem comes at the other forward spot. Kenny Gattison can hardly be considered a premier power forward. Gattison is an adequate scorer with limited range. The Hornets need an injury-free year from second-year man Scott Burrell, whose excellent athletic skills make him a natural for the team's up-tempo style.

Center: Like L.J., only injuries can prevent Mourning from joining the NBA's dominant players at his position. An intimidator with a mean streak, Mourning can score from the low post and step outside to nail the jumper. His warrior mentality is what sets him apart. Parish is the perfect back-up, offering quality minutes and championship experience.

Coaching: You can't blame Allan Bristow for Charlotte's problems last year, but you can bet he'll be a target if the Hornets underachieve this season. Many wonder whether he can instill the type of defensive attitude into this team so that it can thrive during the playoffs. He enters the season in one of the more tenuous positions among NBA coaches. Bill Hanzlik and T.R. Dunn assist him.

Analysis: Last year at this time, all anybody could talk about was how the Hornets were a team of the future. Now, North Carolinians are hoping the poor 1993-94 season was merely an injury-induced fluke. Mourning and Johnson are a strong foundation, and the Hawkins/Curry/Bogues/Adams backcourt is one of the deepest in the league. Parish is the veteran leader they need. Expect a challenge for the Central title and some significant playoff progress.

Prediction: First place, Central Division

CHICAGO BULLS

Home: United Center
Capacity: 21,500
Year Built: 1994

Address:
1901 W. Madison
Chicago, IL 60612
(312) 455-4000

Chairman: Jerry Reinsdorf
V.P./Basketball Operations:
Jerry Krause
Head Coach: Phil Jackson
Assistant Coach: Jimmy Rodgers
Assistant Coach: Jim Cleamons
Assistant Coach: Tex Winter

Coach Phil Jackson			
	W	L	Pct.
NBA Record	295	115	.720
W/Bulls	295	115	.720
1993-94 Record	55	27	.671

Bulls History

The Bulls were defined in the early 1990s by the atmospheric antics of all-world Michael Jordan, but the team's 28-year history has not always been so spectacular. Until 1991, Chicago never advanced to the NBA Finals.

Chicago joined the league in 1966 as a lone expansion club. After four losing seasons, the Bulls enjoyed regular-season success during their next five. Coach Dick Motta pulled together Chet Walker, Bob Love, Jerry Sloan, and Norm Van Lier to form a quick team that advanced to the West finals in 1973-74, losing in four games to Milwaukee. The following year, the Bulls acquired Nate Thurmond from Golden State and won the Midwest Division, only to drop a disappointing 4-3 decision to the Warriors in the West finals.

Chicago managed only two winning seasons during the next 12 and won just one playoff series, but the Bulls' fortunes changed radically in 1984 when they selected Jordan with the third pick in the draft. Almost instantly, Jordan became an ambassador for basketball everywhere.

By 1987, the results matched the enthusiasm. Chicago surrounded Jordan with young talents like Scottie Pippen, John Paxson, and Horace Grant and advanced to the Eastern Conference finals in 1988-89 and 1989-90, losing both times to Detroit. The Bulls matured in 1990-91 and knocked off the L.A. Lakers in the NBA Finals. In 1991-92, Chicago defeated Portland for its second world crown, then, in 1992-93, three-peated with a win over Phoenix.

Last Seven Years

Season	W	L	Pct.	Place	Playoffs	Coach
1987-88	50	32	.610	Second	L-East Semis	Doug Collins
1988-89	47	35	.573	Fifth	L-East Finals	Doug Collins
1989-90	55	27	.671	Second	L-East Finals	Phil Jackson
1990-91	61	21	.744	First	NBA Champs	Phil Jackson
1991-92	67	15	.817	First	NBA Champs	Phil Jackson
1992-93	57	25	.695	First	NBA Champs	Phil Jackson
1993-94	55	27	.671	Second	L-East Semis	Phil Jackson

1993-94 Review

Could there have been a crazier, more difficult season in pro basketball than the one endured by players, coaches, management, and fans of the Bulls? Before training camp even began, the defending three-time NBA champions bid a stunned farewell to basketball's greatest player ever. Michael Jordan's departure reduced the Bulls from a dynasty to a questionable contender with more than a few questions.

Would Scottie Pippen be able to take over the main role? Could the Bulls thrive in crucial situations without their leader and consummate clutch performer? Would Phil Jackson be able to cobble together a playoff squad from a few remaining stars and the likes of Pete Myers, Steve Kerr, and Bill Wennington? And how would celebrated Croatian import Toni Kukoc blend with his new teammates?

By season's end, Chicago had answered the questions—and they did so rather emphatically. The Bulls won 55 regular-season games, relying on Pippen, ball movement, and strong team defense. Pippen (22.0 PPG, 8.7 RPG) was marvelous, earning first-team All-NBA honors and providing strong leadership—until the playoffs, that is. He refused to re-enter Game 4 of the Eastern Conference semifinals against New York (won by the Knicks in seven games) because he wouldn't get the last shot.

Plenty of other Bulls had a great year. Power forward Horace Grant (15.1 PPG, 11.0 RPG) was a marvel during what turned out to be his last year in Chicago, and point guard B.J. Armstrong (14.8 PPG, 44.4 3-point FGP) continued his maturation into one of the best at his position. Kukoc (10.9 PPG) struggled with the long year and physical play but won several games with last-second shots.

The combination of Kerr (8.6 PPG) and Myers (7.9 PPG) came nowhere near Jordan's level, but it was effective at times. Scott Williams (7.6 PPG) missed half the season with injuries and was inconsistent at power forward when healthy. Ancient Bill Cartwright (5.6 PPG) also suffered through an injury-plagued year and made noise about retiring, while Wennington (7.1 PPG, 4.6 RPG) and midseason acquisition Luc Longley (6.9 PPG, 5.7 RPG) were productive pivot reserves.

1994-95 Roster

No.	Player	Pos.	Ht.	Wt.	Exp.	College	G	RPG	APG	PPG
								—1993-94—		
10	B.J. Armstrong	G	6'2"	185	5	Iowa	82	2.1	3.9	14.8
44	Corie Blount	F/C	6'10"	242	1	Cincinnati	67	2.9	0.8	3.0
—	Kris Bruton	G	6'5"	190	R	Benedict	—	—	—	—
3	Jo Jo English	G	6'4"	195	2	South Carolina	36	1.3	1.1	3.6
7	Toni Kukoc	F/G	6'11"	230	1	Croatia	75	4.0	3.4	10.9
13	Luc Longley	C	7'2"	265	3	New Mexico	76	5.7	1.4	6.9
32	Will Perdue	C	7'0"	240	6	Vanderbilt	43	2.9	0.8	2.7
33	Scottie Pippen	F	6'7"	225	7	Cent. Arkansas	72	8.7	5.6	22.0
—	Dickey Simpkins	F/C	6'9"	250	R	Providence	—	—	—	—

Chicago Bulls
1994-95 Season Preview

Opening Line: Year Two A.M. (After Michael) begins with a definite air of uncertainty surrounding the Bulls. Their 1993-94 run to 55 wins was unexpected and will be impossible to repeat. That's because All-Star power forward Horace Grant and reserve forward Scott Williams have left as free agents. Providence rookie forward Dickey Simpkins will hardly fill their shoes.

Guard: B.J. Armstrong has developed into a top-notch NBA point guard. He's a vigilant defender and one of the league's top 3-point shooters. He also can run the Bulls' complicated triangle sets quite well. There's trouble at the two spot, where Pete Myers would make a good back-up but is hardly a solid starter. Myers is athletic and sound on the break, but his shooting range is limited. Jo Jo English isn't much more accomplished. Steve Kerr does little more than drain the 3-pointer, although he's one of the best in the league in that department. Veteran John Paxson has announced his retirement.

Forward: Scottie Pippen's infamous pout against the Knicks will dog him forever. He can rationalize it all he wants, but the temper tantrum bothered management so much that they considered trading him in the off-season. Pippen did it all last season, shooting from way out, driving to the hoop, handling the ball, and banging the boards. If his demeanor were as solid as his game is diverse, he'd be a megastar. Bulls fans hope Toni Kukoc will settle down this year and play consistent ball. The Croatian import was tired by the end of last season and his play reflected it. He'll likely come off the bench again this year, despite the loss of Grant. Corie Blount provides some bulk and punch at the four spot. He could win the starting power-forward job by default. Simpkins can score and rebound from the four position.

Center: Call it a four-headed monster. Bill Cartwright is prehistoric, Luc Longley is erratic, Bill Wennington is limited, and Will Perdue is awkward. Together, they comprise 24 fouls a game and a pretty fair NBA pivot man. Wennington and Cartwright (as well as Myers and Kerr) were unrestricted free agents this summer, but all were expected to re-sign with the Bulls.

Coaching: When someone figures out how Jackson won 55 games and almost made it to the Eastern Conference finals, let us know. Anyone who doubts this eclectic free spirit's ability to flat-out coach should have been convinced in 1993-94. Jackson is imaginative, has superior motivational skills, and just knows how to win. He's assisted by Tex Winter, Jim Cleamons, and Jimmy Rodgers.

Analysis: Like the Pistons before them, the Bulls are beginning to crumble. You can't lose players like Jordan and Grant and expect to remain a contender. The front office realizes this and it looks like it might disassemble the club and rebuild. It appears the Bulls are ready to trade Pippen for a younger talent and perhaps a draft pick.

Prediction: Fifth place, Central Division

CLEVELAND CAVALIERS

Home: Gateway Arena
Capacity: 20,750
Year Built: 1994

Address:
100 Gateway Plaza
Cleveland, OH 44115
(216) 659-9100

Chairman of the Board: Gordon Gund
Executive V.P./General Manager:
Wayne Embry
Head Coach: Mike Fratello
Assistant Coach: Richie Adubato
Assistant Coach: Ron Rothstein
Assistant Coach: Jim Boylan

Coach Mike Fratello			
	W	L	Pct.
NBA Record	371	288	.563
W/Cavaliers	47	35	.573
1993-94 Record	47	35	.573

Cavaliers History

Since their debut in 1970, the Cavaliers have been one of the NBA's most disappointing teams, winning only one playoff series in their first 21 years. In their early years, the Cavs didn't have many marquee players—the result of some poor drafting and questionable trades during the 1970s. Things changed in the late 1980s thanks to smarter drafting and the stewardship of coach Lenny Wilkens.

The early years were tough, as Cleveland spent its first four seasons in the Central basement. In 1975-76, coach Bill Fitch was rewarded for his patience with a division title, as well as the team's first playoff series win. They beat Washington in seven games in the Eastern Conference semis.

Center Jim Chones, forwards Campy Russell and Jim Brewer, and guard Bobby "Bingo" Smith were the main performers on that team, but the good times ended soon thereafter. Cleveland qualified for the playoffs the next two seasons but made it back only once (1984-85) in the ensuing nine years.

In 1986, the Cavs began their renaissance by drafting center Brad Daugherty. Daugherty, guards Ron Harper and Mark Price, and forward Larry Nance led the Cavs to a 42-40 record in 1987-88 and a 57-25 mark the next year. After two disappointing seasons, Cleveland put it together again in 1991-92. The Cavaliers went 57-25 and roared to the conference finals, where they lost to Chicago in six games. They again lost to the Bulls in the 1993 and 1994 playoffs.

Last Seven Years

Season	W	L	Pct.	Place	Playoffs	Coach
1987-88	42	40	.512	Fourth	L-Round 1	Lenny Wilkens
1988-89	57	25	.695	Second	L-Round 1	Lenny Wilkens
1989-90	42	40	.512	Fourth	L-Round 1	Lenny Wilkens
1990-91	33	49	.402	Sixth	DNQ	Lenny Wilkens
1991-92	57	25	.695	Second	L-East Finals	Lenny Wilkens
1992-93	54	28	.659	Second	L-East Semis	Lenny Wilkens
1993-94	47	35	.573	Third	L-Round 1	Mike Fratello

1993-94 Review

As the 1993-94 season wore on, first-year Cavaliers coach Mike Fratello had to be wondering whether someone at NBC had put a hex on him for leaving his analyst's job. Injuries to key performers conspired to derail any periodic momentum Cleveland could build and reduced the Cavs to an average first-round playoff opponent. Cleveland's quick exit against Chicago—who else?—was hardly the way Fratello thought the season would go.

Renowned for his ability to instill toughness into teams, the fiery Fratello was expected to make the soft underachievers realize their potential. Although Cleveland led the NBA with just 13.9 turnovers per game, the Cavs had trouble with close games, finishing just 1-10 in contests decided by three points or less. Neither Fratello nor his players could be blamed for Cleveland's 47-35 season, its worst since 1990-91, a similarly injury-ravaged season.

When playoff time came around, the Cavalier inactive list was filled with All-Stars. Center Brad Daugherty (17.0 PPG, 10.2 RPG) was felled by a herniated disk in his back and played just 50 pain-filled games. Power forward Larry Nance (11.2 PPG) made just 33 appearances, thanks to cartilage damage in his knee. Forward John Williams (13.7 PPG, 7.6 RPG) made it through the regular season just fine but broke a bone in his hand before the Bulls series. And guard John Battle dislocated his elbow at midseason and was done for the year.

Cleveland's preferred starting lineup played just seven games together. That left point guard Mark Price (17.3 PPG, 7.8 APG, 39.7 3-point FGP) and veteran Gerald Wilkins (14.3 PPG) as the team leaders, and the two produced admirably. There just wasn't enough help, though Williams came up big during the regular season, as did forward Tyrone Hill (10.6 PPG, 8.8 RPG).

Point guard Terrell Brandon (8.3 PPG) continued to wait patiently for his turn to lead the team, and CBA veteran Bobby Phills (8.3 PPG) filled in adequately up front. Enigmatic Danny Ferry (5.0 PPG) had his worst season in the NBA.

1994-95 Roster

No.	Player	Pos.	Ht.	Wt.	Exp.	College	G	1993-94 RPG	APG	PPG
16	Gary Alexander	F	6'7"	240	1	South Florida	11	1.4	0.2	1.7
10	John Battle	G	6'2"	190	9	Rutgers	51	0.8	1.6	6.6
11	Terrell Brandon	G	6'0"	180	3	Oregon	73	2.2	3.8	8.3
—	Michael Cage	C/F	6'9"	240	10	San Diego St.	82	5.4	0.5	4.6
—	Gary Collier	G	6'4"	195	R	Tulsa	—	—	—	—
43	Brad Daugherty	C	7'0"	263	8	North Carolina	50	10.2	3.0	17.0
35	Danny Ferry	F	6'10"	245	4	Duke	70	2.0	1.1	5.0
54	Jay Guidinger	C	6'10"	255	2	Minn.-Duluth	32	1.0	0.1	1.5
32	Tyrone Hill	F	6'9"	245	4	Xavier (OH)	57	8.8	0.8	10.6
12	Gerald Madkins	G	6'4"	200	1	UCLA	22	0.5	0.9	1.6
24	Chris Mills	F	6'6"	216	1	Arizona	79	5.1	1.6	9.4
14	Bobby Phills	G	6'5"	217	3	Southern	72	2.9	1.8	8.3
25	Mark Price	G	6'0"	178	8	Georgia Tech	76	3.0	7.8	17.3
21	Gerald Wilkins	G	6'6"	210	9	Tenn.-Chattan.	82	3.7	3.1	14.3
18	John Williams	F/C	6'11"	245	8	Tulane	76	7.6	2.5	13.7

Cleveland Cavaliers
1994-95 Season Preview

Opening Line: Mike Fratello left the comfort of the NBC analyst chair for this? The Czar of the Telestrator's first year in Cavland was haunted by injuries—not the best thing to happen to a squad with an aging nucleus. Cleveland moves into a new, downtown arena this season, and Fratello must hope the evil spirits that sabotaged last season won't follow. Second-round pick Gary Collier, a guard from Tulsa, comes along for the ride, as does free agent pick-up Michael Cage.

Guard: Mark Price's numbers fell off a little last season, but he remains one of the league's top pure point guards. He can penetrate and pass and is a highly accurate 3-point shooter. His back-up, Terrell Brandon, continues to wait patiently for his shot at running the team, although he might not ever get it if his shooting doesn't improve. Veteran Gerald Wilkins isn't going to pile up the points, but he doesn't have to in the Cavs' balanced set. An above-average outside shooter, Wilkins also shuts down opposing big guards. John Battle and Bobby Phills can both provide a spark in relief at the two spot. The athletic Collier will be hard-pressed to find playing time.

Forward: The Cavs boast one of the league's most versatile rotations here. The aging Larry Nance can still score and rebound—not to mention fire down a monster dunk or two. If he re-signs with the Cavs, he'll team with John "Hot Rod" Williams to form an athletic frontcourt combination. The veteran Cage is still a warrior on the boards. Promising second-year man Chris Mills needs to improve his shooting and grow stronger, but he has NBA tools. Tyrone Hill, a solid pick-up last year, is a tremendous rebounder. Danny Ferry moves closer to the end of the bench with each passing season.

Center: Health permitting, Brad Daugherty will continue to be one of the league's better centers. Unspectacular and soft-spoken, Daugherty has a soft shooting touch, a good body, and the ability to grab ten boards a game. His defense, however, remains soft. Daugherty doesn't block that many shots and doesn't have the aggressive attitude of the upper-echelon big men.

Coaching: Fratello never took Atlanta too far in the playoffs, but few can dispute his ability to motivate a team. He may be just what the Cavs need to propel them past the early rounds of the playoffs, even though last year's injury epidemic didn't allow him to prove it. Former NBA head coaches Ron Rothstein and Richie Adubato, as well as Jim Boylan, are Fratello's assistants.

Analysis: The Cavaliers continue to tread water in the Eastern Conference, teasing with their potential but never delivering more than an early playoff exit. One of these years, the entire starting lineup will retire and Cleveland will have to start over again. The Cavs still have enough talent to play with any team during the regular season, but they have yet to translate that into the postseason. It may sound monotonous, but this could be the year. Then again....

Prediction: Fourth place, Central Division

DETROIT PISTONS

Home: The Palace
Capacity: 21,454
Year Built: 1988

Managing Partner: William Davidson
Director of Player Personnel:
Bill McKinney
Head Coach: Don Chaney
Assistant Coach: Brendan Malone
Assistant Coach: Walt Perrin

Address:
The Palace
Two Championship Dr.
Auburn Hills, MI 48326
(313) 377-0100

Coach Don Chaney			
	W	L	Pct.
NBA Record	237	328	.419
W/Pistons	20	62	.244
1993-94 Record	20	62	.244

Pistons History

Any discussion of Pistons history is bound to be a little heavy on the "Bad Boy" years. After three fruitless decades, the Pistons won back-to-back NBA titles in 1988-89 and 1989-90.

The franchise was established in Fort Wayne, Indiana, in 1941 as a member of the old National Basketball League. It joined the BAA in 1948 and became a charter NBA club in 1949. The Fort Wayne Pistons, led by high-scoring George Yardley, advanced to the NBA Finals twice during the 1950s, losing to Syracuse in 1954-55 and Philadelphia in 1955-56.

The Pistons moved to Detroit in 1957 but began to falter, finishing below .500 for the next 13 seasons. Detroit made some news during the period, naming 24-year-old Dave DeBusschere player/coach in 1964 and drafting hot-shot guard Dave Bing in 1966. Things got a little better in the mid-1970s. Detroit posted a 52-30 record in 1973-74, due largely to the play of Bing and center Bob Lanier. But the Pistons were eliminated in the Western semis and had to wait another nine seasons for a strong team.

That came in 1983-84 when Chuck Daly took over as coach. Daly, building his team around point guard Isiah Thomas, won the Central Division title in 1987-88. They advanced to the NBA Finals that season, losing to Los Angeles in seven games. Thomas, Bill Laimbeer, Dennis Rodman, and Joe Dumars were not denied the next two years, sweeping the Lakers in 1988-89 and whipping Portland in 1989-90.

Last Seven Years

Season	W	L	Pct.	Place	Playoffs	Coach
1987-88	54	28	.650	First	L-NBA Finals	Chuck Daly
1988-89	63	19	.768	First	NBA Champs	Chuck Daly
1989-90	59	23	.720	First	NBA Champs	Chuck Daly
1990-91	50	32	.610	Second	L-East Finals	Chuck Daly
1991-92	48	34	.585	Third	L-Round 1	Chuck Daly
1992-93	40	42	.488	Sixth	DNQ	Ron Rothstein
1993-94	20	62	.244	Sixth	DNQ	Don Chaney

1993-94 Review

Isiah Thomas picked a perfect time to quit. Having seen the bleak Piston future, Zeke decided to take the lifetime-achievement payoff and polish his championship rings, rather than take part in the considerable rebuilding necessary in the Motor City. Thomas joined former Bad Boy Bill Laimbeer on the retirement ledger, with Laimbeer choosing to bow out after just one month.

The Pistons were bad from the start and spent the season challenging Milwaukee for the Eastern Conference's worst record. Give Detroit credit, however, for recognizing the value of not over-extending itself. By finishing the year with 13 straight losses, the Pistons finished tied with the Bucks and Minnesota for the second-worst record in the NBA. Their commitment to youth had dual benefits, helping secure solid lottery status this year while also giving playing time to 1993's first-round picks.

Detroit's problem was pretty obvious: The team couldn't score. The Pistons averaged only 96.9 points per game, third worst in the league. Outside of veteran sniper Joe Dumars (20.4 PPG) and improving forward Terry Mills (17.3 PPG, 8.4 RPG), Detroit lacked any consistent point production. Even the acquisition of forward Sean Elliott (12.1 PPG) from San Antonio prior to the season (for Dennis Rodman) could not jump-start the sagging offense.

Detroit's pivot picture was no better. Mills and erratic Cadillac Anderson (6.4 PPG, 7.4 RPG) were hardly enough in the middle after a midseason trade sent Olden Polynice—a relentless rebounder and hard-working defender—to Sacramento for big man Pete Chilcutt and draft picks.

With Thomas gone and Dumars concluding his ninth season, the Pistons auditioned a pair of rookies in the backcourt, but with predictable results. Point man Lindsey Hunter (10.3 PPG, 4.8 APG) distributed the ball well and proved he could play some pretty good defense, although he shot just 37.5 percent from the field. Shooter Allan Houston struggled from the field (40.5 percent) and was not prone to passing too much. Veteran Mark Macon, acquired in mid-year from Denver, was hardly an example to the youngsters, thanks to his 37.5-percent shooting.

1994-95 Roster

No.	Player	Pos.	Ht.	Wt.	Exp.	College	—1993-94— G	RPG	APG	PPG
33	Greg Anderson	F/C	6'10"	230	6	Houston	77	7.4	0.7	6.4
34	Pete Chilcutt	F/C	6'10"	232	3	North Carolina	76	4.9	1.1	5.9
—	Jevon Crudup	F	6'9"	230	R	Missouri	—	—	—	—
—	Bill Curley	F	6'9"	220	R	Boston College	—	—	—	—
4	Joe Dumars	G	6'3"	195	9	McNeese St.	69	2.2	3.8	20.4
—	Grant Hill	F	6'8"	225	R	Duke	—	—	—	—
20	Allan Houston	G	6'6"	200	1	Tennessee	79	1.5	1.3	8.5
1	Lindsey Hunter	G	6'2"	195	1	Jackson St.	82	2.3	4.8	10.3
—	Eric Leckner	C	6'11"	265	5	Wyoming	71	4.0	1.2	5.1
2	Mark Macon	G	6'5"	200	3	Temple	42	1.0	1.2	3.9
6	Terry Mills	F	6'10"	250	4	Michigan	80	8.4	2.2	17.3
—	Mark West	C	6'10"	246	11	Old Dominion	82	3.6	0.4	4.7

Detroit Pistons
1994-95 Season Preview

Opening Line: A cynic might say that the one-time Bad Boys are now just merely bad. But help is on the way. The addition of Duke star Grant Hill with the third pick in the draft helps bolster the Piston offense, which was abysmal last season, and second-round pick Jevon Crudup of Missouri could be a steal at power forward. The retirement of Isiah Thomas will give Lindsey Hunter a chance to improve, and the additions of centers Mark West and Eric Leckner will at least plug a hole in the middle. However, Detroit's trade of Sean Elliott for rookie Bill Curley seems to be a step backward.

Guard: The retirement of Thomas leaves a gaping hole in the Piston backcourt, from the production and leadership standpoints, and Hunter has much growing to do before he can come close to Thomas's production. Hunter has all the tools you look for in a point guard but is far too inconsistent. Two man Joe Dumars remains one of the best in the game, a classy sniper with excellent defensive instincts. Unfortunately, second-year pro Allan Houston has a long way to go as his back-up. He was inconsistent and overmatched at times last year. Reserve Mark Macon excels on the defensive end.

Forward: Mills has developed into a solid power man. His main problem is that the Pistons simply have no one to help him underneath. Cadillac Anderson is not a true NBA center, and that means Mills has to spend a lot of time in the pivot. Hill will start immediately at small forward. The Blue Devil has excellent ball-handling skills, plays tremendous defense, is an outstanding athlete, and knows how to win. Expect Curley to work his tail off inside but don't expect too much else. He's probably too slow to be effective in the NBA. Crudup has a good body and the ability to score inside and rebound.

Center: Don't look for any offense out of this pivot trio. West, acquired from Phoenix, may have the highest field goal percentage of any active NBA player, but his only strengths are shot-blocking and rebounding. Leckner, acquired from Philadelphia, is a willing, rough-hewn competitor with limited abilities. Pete Chilcutt is a soft, perimeter-style replacement.

Coaching: Don Chaney didn't get it done in Houston when he had Hakeem Olajuwon, so it's not exactly a given that he'll revitalize the Pistons. His players-first style of coaching will help the transition period, but he needs to get the Pistons into the playoffs quickly to keep his job. He's assisted by Brendan Malone and Walt Perrin.

Analysis: The addition of Hill will help, but it won't offset the leadership vacuum Thomas's departure creates. The Pistons are still at least a year away from playoff contention and need several untested players to come through before they can creep out of the lottery. The scoreboard should get more of a workout this year, but don't expect more than 30 wins.

Prediction: Seventh place, Central Division

INDIANA PACERS

Home: Market Square Arena
Capacity: 16,530
Year Built: 1974

Address:
300 E. Market St.
Indianapolis, IN 46204
(317) 263-2100

Owners: Melvin Simon, Herbert Simon
President: Don Walsh
Head Coach: Larry Brown
Assistant Coach: Gar Heard
Assistant Coach: Bill Blair
Assistant Coach: Billy King

Coach Larry Brown			
	W	L	Pct.
NBA Record	481	377	.561
W/Pacers	47	35	.573
1993-94 Record	47	35	.573

Pacers History

If there could be such a thing as the "Boston Celtics of the ABA," it definitely would have been the Indiana Pacers. The Pacers won three ABA titles and finished second twice between 1968-69 and 1974-75.

The Pacers were sorry to see the old league die. Since joining the NBA, the Pacers have been nearly moribund, reaching the playoffs only seven times during their 18 years in the league. Despite playing in a basketball-crazed state, the Pacers did not win an NBA playoff series before last year.

But the old days were something in Indianapolis. Led by Mel Daniels, a 6'9" bull of a center, the early Pacers featured a lineup that was equal to many NBA teams. Guard Freddie Lewis and forward Roger Brown were deadly scorers, and power forward Bob Netolicky was a bruiser. In 1971, Indiana signed forward George McGinnis from Indiana University. It later added guard Bill Keller and forward Billy Knight to a potent rotation.

Yet the same penchant for accumulating talented personnel did not carry over to Indiana's years in the NBA. The Pacers have had only three winning seasons since the merger, and in recent years they became known for their perennial mediocrity. Indiana had the offense in recent seasons—from long-range bombers Chuck Person and Reggie Miller to do-everything forward Detlef Schrempf—but it lacked the strong defense, team chemistry, and mental toughness to excel in the playoffs.

Last Seven Years

Season	W	L	Pct.	Place	Playoffs	Coach
1987-88	38	44	.463	Sixth	DNQ	Jack Ramsay
1988-89	28	54	.341	Sixth	DNQ	J. Ramsay/G. Irvine/ D. Versace
1989-90	42	40	.512	Fourth	L-Round 1	Dick Versace
1990-91	41	41	.500	Fifth	L-Round 1	Dick Versace/Bob Hill
1991-92	40	42	.488	Fourth	L-Round 1	Bob Hill
1992-93	41	41	.500	Fifth	L-Round 1	Bob Hill
1993-94	47	35	.573	Third	L-East Finals	Larry Brown

1993-94 Review

It took Pacers fans just one season to see why all those teams had wanted Larry Brown to coach them over the years. Brown came to Speedway City with a reputation for impatience and a proclivity toward leaving town, but he transformed the previously mediocre franchise into an Eastern Conference finalist. Brown's demanding tactics turned a collection of underachieving holdovers and a few key newcomers into a relentless group that played aggressive defense and made 48.6 percent of its shots (second in the NBA).

After winning their final eight regular-season games to finish with a club-record 47 wins, the Pacers dispatched Orlando for the franchise's first playoff-series victory. They then toppled Atlanta before falling in a thrilling seventh game to New York in the Eastern finals.

It started with Reggie Miller (19.9 PPG, 42.1 3-point FGP), the team's outrageous machine-gunning two guard who was a marvel throughout the playoffs. His fourth-quarter salvo in Game 5 against the Knicks (and New York fan Spike Lee) will be remembered as one of the great performances in recent playoff history. He and much-improved center Rik Smits (15.7 PPG, 6.2 RPG) provided a solid inside-outside scoring punch.

Forward Derrick McKey (12.0 PPG, 5.3 RPG)—acquired before the season in a controversial trade for Detlef Schrempf—did a little of everything, particularly on the defensive end. When the Pacers had to get rough, they did it with emerging power forward Dale Davis (11.7 PPG, 10.9 RPG), who could get nasty with any of the position's elite. Husky rookie Antonio Davis (7.7 PPG, 6.2 RPG), a surprise from the Italian League, also provided some muscle.

Point guard Haywoode Workman (7.7 PPG, 6.2 APG), another Italian import, impressed with defense and passing to take over the starting job from Pooh Richardson at midseason. Veteran Laker castoff Byron Scott (10.4 PPG) proved he still had some scoring pop—as well as some much-needed leadership ability. Reserve point guard Vern Fleming (6.5 PPG) was his usual, steady self.

1994-95 Roster

No.	Player	Pos.	Ht.	Wt.	Exp.	College	1993-94 G	RPG	APG	PPG
—	Damon Bailey	G	6'3"	201	R	Indiana	—	—	—	—
33	Antonio Davis	F/C	6'9"	230	1	Texas-El Paso	81	6.2	0.7	7.7
32	Dale Davis	F	6'11"	230	3	Clemson	66	10.9	1.5	11.7
10	Vern Fleming	G	6'5"	185	10	Georgia	55	2.2	3.1	6.5
43	Scott Haskin	F	6'11"	250	1	Oregon St.	27	2.0	0.2	2.0
—	Mark Jackson	G	6'1"	180	7	St. John's	79	4.4	8.6	10.9
9	Derrick McKey	F	6'10"	225	7	Alabama	76	5.3	4.3	12.0
31	Reggie Miller	G	6'7"	185	7	UCLA	79	2.7	3.1	19.9
—	Greg Minor	F/G	6'6"	210	R	Louisville	—	—	—	—
5	Sam Mitchell	F	6'7"	210	5	Mercer	75	2.5	0.9	4.8
—	William Njoku	F	6'9"	215	R	St. Mary's	—	—	—	—
45	Rik Smits	C	7'4"	265	6	Marist	78	6.2	2.0	15.7
41	LaSalle Thompson	F/C	6'10"	260	12	Texas	30	2.5	0.5	2.3
3	Haywoode Workman	G	6'3"	180	3	Oral Roberts	65	3.1	6.2	7.7

Indiana Pacers
1994-95 Season Preview

Opening Line: Emboldened by last year's fantastic playoff run, Indiana is primed to challenge for the Central Division title. If coach Larry Brown stays around—and he hasn't made any noise about leaving—the Pacers have the kind of youthful talent that could eventually win it all in the newly wide-open NBA. Adding a real point guard in Mark Jackson as well as first-round swing man Greg Minor of Louisville should help the team's offense immensely.

Guard: If there are people out there who still don't believe Reggie Miller is the best pure shooter in the NBA, please replay the fourth quarter of Game 5 against the Knicks. Miller's range extends to Terre Haute, and his ability to rub his man off the staggered screen—the Pacers' trademark—creates a myriad of scoring chances. Jackson will get him the ball and rejuvenate the stagnant Pacer break. He can even score a little. Haywoode Workman is a revelation at the point. He's a throwback to the times when playmakers simply dribbled, passed, and played defense. Veteran Vern Fleming is a solid back-up at the point. Byron Scott will provide experience, savvy, and streak shooting—if he re-signs. Expect Minor, an all-around talent, to be worked in slowly.

Forward: Few teams in the league can unleash a trio of strong, tall bangers like the Pacers can. If any of them could score consistently, Indiana would be nearly unstoppable. Derrick McKey settled into Brown's defensive-oriented system well and scored just enough to be considered a three man. Dale Davis has matured into the power-forward spot and is among the top five pure rebounders at his position. Last year's surprise, European expatriate Antonio Davis, has a big-time physique, a major appetite under the boards, and a minimalist offensive game. Sam Mitchell and Kenny Williams are adequate reserves.

Center: Rik Smits dropped 20 pounds and all of a sudden he became a big-time low-post scorer. You figure it out. The Dutch Boy still isn't a terror on the boards, and he won't block too many shots, but with McKey and the Davises around him, he doesn't have to. Smits finally became the center Indiana needed in 1993-94, and he teams with Miller to give the Pacers a solid inside-outside tandem.

Coaching: Nobody ever doubted Larry Brown's ability to coach. The man has thrived wherever he has gone—pro or college. The question is whether he'll stay, due to admitted impatience. Brown is good friends with Indiana president Donnie Walsh, and that should keep him around for a while. Veteran assistant Bill Blair, Gar Heard, and Billy King comprise Brown's staff.

Analysis: Last season wasn't a fluke. The Pacers are talented, play great defense, and have a mastermind on the bench in Brown. They do need a little more offensive pop, particularly up front, if they are going to challenge for the championship again. Nevertheless, Indiana is well-positioned for the next couple seasons.

Prediction: Second place, Central Division

MILWAUKEE BUCKS

Home: Bradley Center
Capacity: 18,633
Year Built: 1988

Address:
Bradley Center
1001 N. Fourth St.
Milwaukee, WI 53203
(414) 227-0500

Owner: Herb Kohl
Director of Player Personnel: Lee Rose
Head Coach: Mike Dunleavy
Assistant Coach: Frank Hamblen
Assistant Coach: Jim Eyen
Assistant Coach: Butch Carter

Coach Mike Dunleavy			
	W	L	Pct.
NBA Record	149	179	.454
W/Bucks	48	116	.293
1993-94 Record	20	62	.244

Bucks History

In their first 23 years of existence (through 1990-91), the Bucks missed out on postseason play only four times. But despite that gleaming record, the franchise's glory period is long past.

Milwaukee stumbled through its rookie season in 1968-69, but the Bucks won the coin toss with Phoenix for the rights to UCLA star Lew Alcindor. The Bucks signed the big rookie and embarked on a five-year run of success. In 1969-70, Milwaukee reached the Eastern finals, and the arrival of guard Oscar Robertson during the off-season was the final piece in coach Larry Costello's puzzle. In 1970-71, Alcindor, Robertson, Bob Dandridge, Greg Smith, and Jon McGlocklin led the Bucks to a 66-16 record and the NBA championship.

Alcindor changed his name to Kareem Abdul-Jabbar, and in 1973-74 the Bucks made it back to the title series. However, they lost to Boston in seven games. Jabbar was dealt to Los Angeles for four players following the 1974-75 season, and the Bucks floundered for the next four years, finishing over the .500 mark just once.

Don Nelson took over as coach in 1976-77 and directed the team back into the playoffs on a regular basis. But although the nucleus of Sidney Moncrief, Junior Bridgeman, Marques Johnson, and Terry Cummings was strong enough to win 50-plus games each year from 1980-81 to 1986-87, the Bucks couldn't get back to the NBA Finals. The club had grown too old by the early 1990s and began a rebuilding program.

Last Seven Years

Season	W	L	Pct.	Place	Playoffs	Coach
1987-88	42	40	.512	Fourth	L-Round 1	Del Harris
1988-89	49	33	.598	Fourth	L-East Semis	Del Harris
1989-90	44	38	.537	Third	L-Round 1	Del Harris
1990-91	48	34	.585	Third	L-Round 1	Del Harris
1991-92	31	51	.378	Sixth	DNQ	Del Harris/Frank Hamblen
1992-93	28	54	.341	Seventh	DNQ	Mike Dunleavy
1993-94	20	62	.244	Sixth	DNQ	Mike Dunleavy

1993-94 Review

If the Bucks don't get it going soon, the key members of their youth movement will be eligible for social security. Milwaukee slogged through another year with the league's youngest roster, managing just 20 wins.

The Bucks had considerable trouble scoring last year and were beaten frequently on the boards—a testimony to their lack of power players up front. Milwaukee lacked depth at all positions and had few players on the roster who could be considered future All-Stars.

There were a few bright spots, most notably 6'11" rookie Vin Baker (13.5 PPG, 7.6 RPG), who had a solid season despite being forced to play out of position in the pivot for much of the year. Baker was named to the All-Rookie Team—quite an accomplishment for a guy who came into the league after spending four years at Hartford as a jump-shooting three man.

Point guard Eric Murdock (15.3 PPG, 6.7 APG, 2.4 SPG) continued to thrive in a starting role, leading the team in scoring and finishing fifth in the league in steals. Second-year man Todd Day (12.7 PPG) continued to have trouble shooting from the two spot, making just 41.5 percent of his shots from the field and only 22.2 percent from beyond the 3-point line.

Free-agent forward Ken Norman (11.9 PPG, 6.1 RPG) had his lowest scoring output since his rookie season and spent part of the year expressing his dissatisfaction about being stuck with Milwaukee. Hey, it was your decision, Ken. Forward partner Blue Edwards (11.6 PPG, 4.0 RPG) followed up his breakthrough 1992-93 campaign with diminished production, although he was a durable starter.

The bench was weak, as forward Derek Strong (6.6 PPG), guards Jon Barry (6.2 PPG, 41.4 FGP) and Lee Mayberry (5.3 PPG, 41.5 FGP), and veteran center Brad Lohaus (4.0 PPG) provided little off the pine. The best news in Milwaukee came in May, when the Bucks won the draft lottery and the right to draft Glenn Robinson.

1994-95 Roster

| No. | Player | Pos. | Ht. | Wt. | Exp. | College | 1993-94 | | |
							G	RPG	APG	PPG
42	Vin Baker	F/C	6'11"	250	1	Hartford	82	7.6	2.0	13.5
17	Jon Barry	G	6'5"	204	2	Georgia Tech	72	2.0	2.3	6.2
—	Marty Conlon	F/C	6'11"	245	3	Providence	30	4.6	1.1	7.8
00	Anthony Cook	F/C	6'9"	240	3	Arizona	25	2.2	0.2	2.5
40	Joe Courtney	F	6'9"	235	2	S. Mississippi	52	1.1	0.3	3.2
10	Todd Day	G/F	6'7"	200	2	Arkansas	76	4.1	1.8	12.7
—	Andrei Fetisov	F	6'10"	215	R	None	—	—	—	—
—	Roy Hinson	F/C	6'9"	215	8	Rutgers	—	—	—	—
54	Brad Lohaus	F/C	6'11"	238	7	Iowa	67	2.2	0.9	4.0
11	Lee Mayberry	G	6'1"	172	2	Arkansas	82	1.2	2.6	5.3
—	Eric Mobley	C	6'11"	250	R	Pittsburgh	—	—	—	—
5	Eric Murdock	G	6'1"	200	3	Providence	82	3.2	6.7	15.3
—	Ed Pinckney	F	6'9"	215	9	Villanova	76	6.3	0.8	5.2
13	Glenn Robinson	F	6'8"	230	R	Purdue	—	—	—	—

Milwaukee Bucks
1994-95 Season Preview

Opening Line: The rebuilding program continues in Cheesetown, with the latest cog being rookie forward Glenn "Big Dog" Robinson. The Bucks chose Robinson, a big-time scorer from Purdue, with the first pick in the 1994 draft and can't wait to unleash him on the rest of the NBA. Milwaukee also drafted center Eric Mobley from Pittsburgh and guard Voshon Lenard from Minnesota—although Lenard decided to return to school. Ken Norman, Blue Edwards, and Derek Strong were traded for Ed Pinckney, Roy Hinson, and Russian draft pick Andrei Fetisov.

Guard: Eric Murdock brings quickness, strong defense, and pretty good shooting range to the Buck offense. He's not the biggest guy in the world, but he's durable and well-conditioned. Third-year man Todd Day is still erratic at the two spot and must improve his dismal shooting percentage if he wants to start. His former Arkansas backcourt mate, point man Lee Mayberry, has also struggled with the pro game and is a below-average shooter, although he can distribute it well. Jon Barry has good size but can't shoot like his famous dad.

Forward: The addition of Robinson, whose blend of power and finesse make him a tremendous inside-outside scoring threat, gives the Bucks true hope for the future. Robinson will probably play the three spot, although his strength will allow him to spend some time at power forward. By sending Ken Norman south, the Bucks cleared room under the salary cap and also freed themselves from a disgruntled player. Pinckney is an aging veteran who knows how to play defense and rebound. Anthony Cook, Roy Hinson, Joe Courtney, and Marty Conlon are all lucky to be on an NBA roster.

Center: When Vin Baker was shooting the lights out at Hartford, he couldn't have dreamed he'd be playing center in the NBA, but he actually acquitted himself well in the middle during his rookie season. Baker is obviously out of place in the pivot, but he showed the ability to score inside, rebound, and even block some shots. If Mobley can play defense and rebound, Baker would be a solid four guy. Veteran Brad Lohaus is an extremely limited post reserve.

Coaching: That NBA Finals appearance with the Lakers is getting older and older for Dunleavy. He said the rebuilding process would take time, but the addition of Robinson will elevate expectations. Dunleavy is patient and smart, but he had better win soon. He is assisted by Frank Hamblen, Jim Eyen, and Butch Carter.

Analysis: Adding Robinson will boost ticket sales, help the staggering Buck offense, and bolster the team's rebounding. But it won't make up for a serious lack of power in the middle or a shaky two-guard situation. The Bucks will put an improved team on the court this season, but they'll be fodder for stronger, better defensive teams in the league. The playoffs are still a long way off.

Prediction: Sixth place, Central Division

DALLAS MAVERICKS

Home: Reunion Arena
Capacity: 17,502
Year Built: 1980

Address:
777 Sports St.
Dallas, TX 75207
(214) 748-1808

Owner: Donald Carter
General Manager: Norm Sonju
Head Coach: Dick Motta
Assistant Coach: Brad Davis
Assistant Coach: Kip Motta

Coach Dick Motta			
	W	L	Pct.
NBA Record	912	933	.494
W/Mavericks	246	307	.465
1993-94 Record	0	0	.000

Mavericks History

Most NBA franchises start out bad and then get better. The Mavericks started out surprisingly well but have since gone down the tubes.

Dallas entered the league in 1980 and soon made its mark. In the 1981 draft, the Mavs selected Mark Aguirre, Rolando Blackman, and Jay Vincent. In 1983, they brought in standout guards Dale Ellis and Derek Harper. That high-scoring nucleus, coached by Dick Motta, won 43 games in 1983-84, finishing second in the Midwest and advancing to the West semifinals.

Dallas won the Midwest in 1986-87, buoyed by the addition of mammoth center James Donaldson and rookie forward Roy Tarpley, but the Mavs bowed out in the first round of the playoffs. The excitement really ran high the next season. Motta was replaced by former Phoenix coach John MacLeod, and Dallas stretched eventual champion Los Angeles to seven games in the Western finals.

Things started to sour in 1988-89. Aguirre was traded in midseason to Detroit for the mercurial Adrian Dantley, and Tarpley played only 19 games due to alcohol-abuse problems. The Mavericks fell to 38-44 in 1988-89, and though they rebounded to 47-35 the next season, MacLeod was fired and Dallas lost in the first round of the 1990 playoffs.

The last four seasons have been disastrous. The downfall was triggered by a lifetime ban on Tarpley, but injuries, bad trades, and dissension have also crippled the Mavericks. In 1992-93 and 1993-94, they fielded two of the poorest teams in NBA history.

Last Seven Years

Season	W	L	Pct.	Place	Playoffs	Coach
1987-88	53	29	.646	Second	L-West Finals	John MacLeod
1988-89	38	44	.463	Fourth	DNQ	John MacLeod
1989-90	47	35	.573	Third	L-Round 1	John MacLeod/R. Adubato
1990-91	28	54	.341	Sixth	DNQ	Richie Adubato
1991-92	22	60	.268	Fifth	DNQ	Richie Adubato
1992-93	11	71	.134	Sixth	DNQ	Richie Adubato/Gar Heard
1993-94	13	69	.159	Sixth	DNQ	Quinn Buckner

1993-94 Review

Last year, the Mavericks were able to claim that they finally won more regular-season games than the Cowboys. The Mavs' 13 wins topped the Cowpokes' 12. Of course, the footballers won three more in the playoffs, a place the Mavs haven't been since 1990.

Despite the arrival of new coach Quinn Buckner and talented rookie forward Jamal Mashburn—not to mention a full year of service from guard Jim Jackson—the Mavericks were awful. About the happiest guy in Maverickland was veteran guard Derek Harper, who was traded to the contending New York Knicks at midseason for Tony Campbell.

That didn't help Buckner, whose first year out of the NBC studios was not pleasant. A disciplinarian who no doubt took copious notes while playing for Indiana martinet Bobby Knight, Buckner made few friends among the players, and his poor record led to his dismissal at season's end. His patterned offense and propensity for yanking players after the slightest mistakes resembled a college philosophy rather than a pro outlook.

Buckner clashed early with the talented Mashburn, who needed a visit from his college coach, Rick Pitino, to settle him down. Mashburn scored enough (19.2 PPG), but his rebounding was off (4.5) and his shooting percentage (40.6) was weak. Still, he and the versatile Jackson were a pretty good Maverick nucleus. Jackson (19.2 PPG) was not without fault himself, shooting poorly from the field (44.5 percent) and committing a pile of turnovers.

Center Sean Rooks missed half the season with injuries and was soft inside, as was perennially disappointing forward Doug Smith (8.8 PPG). Rookie Popeye Jones was a strong rebounder (7.5 RPG) but an unpolished offensive performer at forward, and swing man Tim Legler (8.3 PPG) provided some pop off the bench. Veteran point guard Fat Lever, his knees ravaged by multiple injuries, was a shell of his former self, and Campbell (8.8 PPG), arguably the unluckiest man in the NBA, never stopped shooting.

1994-95 Roster

No.	Player	Pos.	Ht.	Wt.	Exp.	College	1993-94			
							G	RPG	APG	PPG
43	Terry Davis	F/C	6'10"	250	5	Virginia Union	15	4.9	0.4	3.7
7	Tony Dumas	G	6'5"	190	R	Missouri-K.C.	—	—	—	—
30	Lucious Harris	G	6'5"	190	1	Long Beach St.	77	2.0	1.4	5.4
35	Donald Hodge	C	7'0"	240	3	Temple	50	1.9	0.6	2.7
24	Jimmy Jackson	G	6'6"	220	2	Ohio St.	82	4.7	4.6	19.2
54	Popeye Jones	F	6'8"	250	1	Murray St.	81	7.5	1.2	5.8
5	Jason Kidd	G	6'4"	205	R	California	—	—	—	—
23	Tim Legler	G	6'4"	200	4	La Salle	79	1.6	1.5	8.3
32	Jamal Mashburn	F	6'8"	240	1	Kentucky	79	4.5	3.4	19.2
45	Sean Rooks	C/F	6'10"	260	2	Arizona	47	5.5	1.0	11.4
34	Doug Smith	F	6'10"	238	3	Missouri	79	4.4	1.5	8.8
25	Deon Thomas	F	6'8"	242	R	Illinois	—	—	—	—
33	Randy White	F	6'8"	238	5	Louisiana Tech	18	4.6	0.6	6.4
44	Lorenzo Williams	F/C	6'9"	200	2	Stetson	38	5.7	0.7	2.9

Dallas Mavericks
1994-95 Season Preview

Opening Line: Dick Motta returns to the bench in Reunion Arena and probably won't believe what he sees. The Mavs were serious title contenders when he was coach and won 55 games in his final year. All that did was get him fired. A performance like that this season would elevate him to the Dallas sporting Valhalla. At least Motta will like his draft picks: Jason Kidd of California, Tony Dumas of Missouri-Kansas City, and Deon Thomas of Illinois.

Guard: Kidd has a chance to be a dominant player. He has good size and fantastic defensive instincts. Kidd was a passing wizard at California and should put people in the seats in Dallas. He does, however, need some serious work on his shot. Jimmy Jackson is glad to have Kidd beside him. Jackson, who led the league in turnovers last year, can now concentrate on what he does best—put the ball in the hole. Fat Lever had his first healthy season in a while last year and should be a valuable mentor for Kidd (if he re-signs). Lucious Harris and Tim Legler can shoot the ball extremely well—just not at the NBA level. Dumas's forte is scoring, particularly off the dribble,

Forward: Jamal Mashburn is a two guard caught in a small forward's body. Mashburn launched 299 treys last season, not to mention another 1,000 or so shots. Mash plays little defense and hardly rebounds as well as his chiseled 6'8" frame would indicate. Tony Campbell, another full-time shooter, may leave the team as a free agent. Motta would love to see Terry Davis come all the way back from the automobile accident that shattered his elbow following the 1992-93 season. Davis played in 15 games last year and could be a solid power forward for the Mavs. Second-year man Popeye Jones is another big-time boarder who needs to extend his shooting range. Doug Smith shoots poorly and isn't as good a rebounder as he should be. Thomas could be a valuable reserve at power forward.

Center: What a mess. The Mavs hope Sean Rooks will develop into a productive pivot man, but he is inconsistent and often disinterested—a pity given his size and natural quickness. Greg Dreiling and Donald Hodge back him up, but job auditions are being held nightly.

Coaching: The decision to pull Motta off the scrap heap of discarded coaches smacks of nostalgia, but the guy can run a team. You won't hear any of the carping that was present last year when Quinn Buckner tried to be Bobby Knight. Motta won't take any guff. He's assisted by Brad Davis and Kip Motta.

Analysis: Things can't get any worse for the Mavs, and with Motta around, the scenario should improve. Kidd will struggle at times during his rookie year, but he has tremendous ability and should help Mashburn and Jackson grow. The four and five spots, however, aren't so settled. If Davis is healthy and Rooks consistent, the Mavs will be pretty good, but don't expect much from either at this point. The playoffs are probably not a realistic goal.

Prediction: Fifth place, Midwest Division

DENVER NUGGETS

Home: McNichols Sports Arena
Capacity: 17,022
Year Built: 1975

Address:
1635 Clay St.
Denver, CO 80204
(303) 893-6700

Owner: COMSAT Denver, Inc.
General Manager: Bernie Bickerstaff
Head Coach: Dan Issel
Assistant Coach: Gene Littles
Assistant Coach: Mike Evans

Coach Dan Issel			
	W	L	Pct.
NBA Record	78	86	.476
W/Nuggets	78	86	.476
1993-94 Record	42	40	.512

Nuggets History

The Nuggets were one of the rarities of the old ABA—a team that stayed in the same place throughout the league's tumultuous nine-year history. A charter ABA member, the Denver Rockets were one of the league's strongest franchises.

Early on, Rocket fans were thrilled by the high-flying exploits of forward Spencer Haywood, who led Denver to the Western Conference finals in 1969-70, where it lost to Los Angeles. But Haywood soon left and the franchise's fortunes dimmed until 1974, when G.M. Carl Scheer and coach Larry Brown came to the Rockies from the Carolina Cougars.

Scheer immediately changed the team nickname to the Nuggets. Denver won 65 games in 1974-75 but lost in the Western finals to Indiana. The next season, the Nuggets acquired star guard David Thompson and made it to the league championship series.

The Nuggets were one of four ABA teams to merge with the NBA in 1976, and they won the Midwest Division in their first two seasons. Denver won Midwest titles in 1984-85 and 1987-88 under Doug Moe and made it to the Western finals in 1985, but they failed in their bid for the elusive NBA championship.

Following the 1989-90 season, Denver fired Moe and hired Paul Westhead. Westhead's high-octane running game didn't bring too many results, as Denver registered the league's worst record in 1990-91. Young stars like Dikembe Mutombo and Mahmoud Abdul-Rauf have helped the team take a healthy step forward each of the last three seasons.

Last Seven Years

Season	W	L	Pct.	Place	Playoffs	Coach
1987-88	54	28	.659	First	L-West Semis	Doug Moe
1988-89	44	38	.537	Third	L-Round 1	Doug Moe
1989-90	43	39	.524	Fourth	L-Round 1	Doug Moe
1990-91	20	62	.244	Seventh	DNQ	Paul Westhead
1991-92	24	58	.293	Fourth	DNQ	Paul Westhead
1992-93	36	46	.439	Fourth	DNQ	Dan Issel
1993-94	42	40	.512	Fourth	L-West Semis	Dan Issel

1993-94 Review

You might say that the Nugget train arrived in the playoff station a year early. Denver inherited the final Western Conference playoff spot in 1993-94, using youth and a few choice veterans to forge a 42-40 record. Denver then stunned top-seeded Seattle in the first round of the playoffs—the first eighth seed ever to accomplish that feat—and then nearly overcame a 3-0 hole before succumbing in seven games to Utah in the Western semis.

Coach Dan Issel's Nuggets did it with defense, combining an aggressive perimeter game with the intimidating interior presence of center Dikembe Mutombo. The Nuggets allowed only 98.8 PPG, tenth in the league, and were second in defensive field goal percentage, forcing teams to make only 43.8 percent of their shots.

Mutombo (12.0 PPG, 11.8 RPG, 4.1 BPG) led the NBA in blocked shots and continued to develop as one of the league's best defensive pivot men. Mutombo's offensive skills still need to develop, but so do most of his mates'.

The Nuggets scored just 100.3 PPG and lacked a big-time scorer. Neither of the team's shooters, three man Reggie Williams (13.0 PPG, 41.2 FGP) nor off guard Bryant Stith (12.5 PPG, 45.0 FGP), was capable of lighting up an opponent every night. When they were combined with power forward LaPhonso Ellis's limited perimeter game, the Nuggets' problems became evident.

Nevertheless, the team made terrific strides, a fact highlighted by the strong play of point guard Mahmoud Abdul-Rauf (18.0 PPG, 4.5 APG). Reserve Robert Pack (9.6 PPG, 5.4 APG) was the only true point man the team had and logged more assists per game than Abdul-Rauf in half the minutes.

Rookie forward Rodney Rogers (8.1 PPG) never became comfortable with his role; he would start one night and barely get off the bench the next. Center/power forward Brian Williams (8.0 PPG, 5.6 RPG) overcame the physical and emotional problems he had in Orlando to post a solid season, and Tom Hammonds was an adequate reserve at the four spot.

1994-95 Roster

No.	Player	Pos.	Ht.	Wt.	Exp.	College	G	RPG	APG	PPG
							|—1993-94—|			
3	M. Abdul-Rauf	G	6'1"	162	4	Louisiana St.	80	2.1	4.5	18.0
43	Kevin Brooks	F	6'8"	200	3	S.W. Louisiana	34	0.6	0.1	2.5
20	LaPhonso Ellis	F	6'8"	240	2	Notre Dame	79	8.6	2.1	15.4
21	Tom Hammonds	F	6'9"	225	5	Georgia Tech	74	2.7	0.5	4.1
4	Darnell Mee	G	6'5"	177	1	W. Kentucky	38	0.9	0.4	1.9
55	Dikembe Mutombo	C	7'2"	250	3	Georgetown	82	11.8	1.5	12.0
14	Robert Pack	G	6'2"	190	3	Southern Cal.	66	1.9	5.4	9.6
42	Mark Randall	F	6'9"	235	3	Kansas	28	0.8	0.4	2.1
7	Alvin Robertson	G	6'4"	208	10	Arkansas	—	—	—	—
54	Rodney Rogers	F	6'7"	250	1	Wake Forest	79	2.9	1.3	8.1
5	Jalen Rose	G	6'8"	210	R	Michigan	—	—	—	—
23	Bryant Stith	G	6'5"	208	2	Virginia	82	4.3	2.4	12.5
8	Brian Williams	F	6'11"	250	3	Arizona	80	5.6	0.6	8.0
34	Reggie Williams	F/G	6'7"	195	7	Georgetown	82	4.8	3.7	13.0

Denver Nuggets
1994-95 Season Preview

Opening Line: Denver must now figure out how to top the 1993-94 campaign, when it upset Seattle and came within one game of dispatching Utah. Coach Dan Issel played it cool throughout last year's playoffs, emphasizing the "we're just happy to be here" attitude. This year, the Nuggets and their fans will be happy with only continued playoff advancement, which will come if the team can score more. First-round draft pick Jalen Rose, a noted scorer, joins the young cast.

Guard: Mahmoud Abdul-Rauf is a good NBA guard, but it's tough to classify him as a point man and he's too small to be a full-time two guard. Abdul-Rauf is more of a scorer than a floor general, although he can do some of the penetrating and dishing stuff too. His back-up, hyperkinetic Robert Pack, is more of a true point, but his level of play varies dramatically—sometimes in the same game. That's why the Nuggets drafted Rose. They hope he can rein in his flamboyant personality and run a team at 6'8". He has skills but may be better suited for a swing-man role. Bryant Stith has a two-guard's game but is unable to score much from downtown.

Forward: LaPhonso Ellis is quickly establishing himself as a solid power forward. He is athletic and quite capable in the open floor, and his rebounding numbers could soon hit ten a game. Now, about that shooting range: Ellis must make the 15-footer consistently if he wants to join the elite. Reggie Williams can shoot (and shoot and shoot), but his accuracy is questionable and his defense nonexistent. Second-year man Rodney Rogers still doesn't know whether he's a three or four man. Brian Williams, on the other hand, became a valuable contributor at the four and five spots last year, and his big body is a valuable asset off the bench. Tom Hammonds is best used close to the basket.

Center: Dikembe Mutombo will never be the first option for any team on offense, but he certainly has the last word on defense. Mutombo led the NBA in blocked shots last year and is developing into a Russellesque blend of rebounding and defense.

Coaching: Issel is the perfect man for a young team. He commands respect because of his NBA success and knows how to stroke his players' developing egos. The real challenge comes now that the team is establishing itself as a playoff participant. How well he squires the Nuggets from the bottom of the playoff ladder to the top will ultimately determine his coaching success or failure. Mike Evans and former Hornets head coach Gene Littles assist him.

Analysis: Last year was a great one for the Nuggets and 1994-95 can bring even better tidings, provided Denver can find clear-cut roles for its out-of-position players and put a few more points on the board. The Nuggets are truly a Western Conference team on the rise, but there is a lot of traffic ahead of them and more work to do.

Prediction: Third place, Midwest Division

HOUSTON ROCKETS

Home: The Summit
Capacity: 16,279
Year Built: 1975

Address:
10 Greenway Plaza East
P.O. Box 272349
Houston, TX 77277
(713) 627-0600

Owner: Les Alexander
General Manager: Bob Weinhauer
Head Coach: Rudy Tomjanovich
Assistant Coach: Bill Berry
Assistant Coach: Carroll Dawson
Assistant Coach: Larry Smith

Coach Rudy Tomjanovich			
	W	L	Pct.
NBA Record	129	65	.665
W/Rockets	129	65	.665
1993-94 Record	58	24	.707

Rockets History

Throughout their 27 seasons in San Diego and Houston, the Rockets have featured some of the NBA's finest big men. The tradition began during the team's second year when it drafted Elvin Hayes. Behind Hayes, the league's leading scorer and Rookie of the Year, San Diego advanced to the 1968-69 Western Conference semis, losing to Atlanta.

The Rockets moved to Houston in 1971, but Hayes spent only one season there before being dealt to Baltimore. Houston then built its team around considerably shorter players such as 5'11" guard Calvin Murphy and forwards Mike Newlin and Rudy Tomjanovich.

Star center No. 2 came in 1976, when Moses Malone moved over from the defunct ABA. Houston won the Central Division crown in 1976-77 and advanced to the NBA Finals in 1980-81, losing in six games to Boston. In 1983, the Rockets drafted 7'4" Ralph Sampson from Virginia; one year later, they selected the dominating Akeem Olajuwon. In 1985-86, Houston made it back to the NBA Finals behind its "Twin Towers," only to lose to Boston in six.

Trouble hit the next season. Injuries crippled Sampson's career and coach Bill Fitch was fired following the 1987-88 season. Don Chaney took over in 1988-89, and though the Rockets showed some spunk in 1990-91, they again fizzled in the playoffs. Houston won its division under Tomjanovich in 1992-93, but it lost in the West semis. True success didn't come until 1993-94, when Olajuwon carried Houston to its first NBA championship.

Last Seven Years

Season	W	L	Pct.	Place	Playoffs	Coach
1987-88	46	36	.561	Fourth	L-Round 1	Bill Fitch
1988-89	45	37	.549	Second	L-Round 1	Don Chaney
1989-90	41	41	.500	Fifth	L-Round 1	Don Chaney
1990-91	52	30	.634	Third	L-Round 1	Don Chaney
1991-92	42	40	.512	Third	DNQ	D. Chaney/R. Tomjanovich
1992-93	55	27	.671	First	L-West Semis	Rudy Tomjanovich
1993-94	58	24	.707	First	NBA Champs	Rudy Tomjanovich

1993-94 Review

To many, the Rockets' 1994 NBA championship was a triumph of good over evil. By bringing the first-ever major title to the sports-crazed Texas town, Rudy Tomjanovich's team prevailed over the New York Knicks and the rough-and-tumble style of play that many felt was tarnishing the NBA's image. The Rockets came back from a 2-0 deficit in the second round against Phoenix and then subdued Utah and New York for the crown.

Houston's title was also an exclamation point to the outstanding career of center Hakeem Olajuwon, who became the first person in league history to win the MVP, NBA Finals MVP, and Defensive Player of the Year Awards in the same season. The Dream (27.3 PPG, 11.9 RPG, 3.7 BPG) was outstanding in every area of the game and stepped into the role of the league's top player left vacant by Michael Jordan.

Olajuwon's sparkling array of moves was nearly unstoppable on the offensive end, and his excellent pivot principles anchored Houston's solid defense. He did, however, have plenty of help. Power forward Otis Thorpe (14.0 PPG, 10.6 RPG) was again a rock, particularly on the boards, and second-year man Robert Horry (9.9 PPG) continued his development into a solid NBA performer.

Point guard Kenny Smith (11.6 PPG) led the Houston 3-point brigade, which set NBA records for attempts and attempts made. But Smith disappeared at times, a trait that led to the discovery of rookie Sam Cassell (6.7 PPG), who blossomed into a smooth, clutch performer during the playoffs. Two man Vernon Maxwell lived up to his "Mad Max" reputation by alternating periods of unbelievable marksmanship with wildness and loss of control.

Reserve forward Mario Elie scored well off the bench and provided a tough defensive presence, while Carl Herrera was effective inside and out. Matt Bullard scored from the perimeter, and back-up point man Scott Brooks spelled Smith well, although he lost his job to Cassell late in the year.

1994-95 Roster

| No. | Player | Pos. | Ht. | Wt. | Exp. | College | —1993-94— | | |
							G	RPG	APG	PPG
1	Scott Brooks	G	5'11"	165	6	Cal.-Irvine	73	1.4	2.0	5.2
—	Albert Burditt	F	6'7"	230	R	Texas	—	—	—	—
10	Sam Cassell	G	6'3"	195	1	Florida St.	66	2.0	2.9	6.7
35	Earl Cureton	F	6'9"	215	11	Detroit	2	6.0	0.0	2.0
17	Mario Elie	G	6'5"	210	4	American Inter.	67	2.7	3.1	9.3
7	Carl Herrera	F	6'9"	225	3	Houston	75	3.8	0.5	4.7
25	Robert Horry	F	6'9"	220	2	Alabama	81	5.4	2.9	9.9
21	Chris Jent	F	6'7"	220	1	Ohio St.	3	5.0	2.3	10.3
11	Vernon Maxwell	G	6'4"	190	6	Florida	75	3.1	5.1	13.6
34	Hakeem Olajuwon	C	7'0"	255	10	Houston	80	11.9	3.6	27.3
3	Richard Petruska	C/F	6'10"	260	1	UCLA	22	1.4	0.0	2.4
42	Eric Riley	C	7'0"	245	1	Michigan	47	1.3	0.2	1.9
20	Larry Robinson	G/F	6'5"	180	4	Centenary	6	1.7	1.0	4.2
30	Kenny Smith	G	6'3"	170	7	North Carolina	78	1.8	4.2	11.6
33	Otis Thorpe	F	6'10"	246	10	Providence	82	10.6	2.3	14.0

Houston Rockets
1994-95 Season Preview

Opening Line: Anyone who claims they expected the Rockets to begin the 1994-95 season as defending NBA champions is lying. Houston entered last season with a promising nucleus and substantial talent, but Phoenix, Seattle, and even San Antonio were perceived as sturdier contenders. Surprise! Now, the Rockets will try the repeat, which is a realistic goal in the new dynasty-less NBA.

Guard: When in control and concentrating, Vernon Maxwell is a top-flight bomber and a dangerous scorer. But Mad Max's emotions are always simmering, and an eruption can come at any time. Point man Kenny Smith can shoot the open 3 and is a solid defender and floor leader, but consistency is a problem. That's why the Rockets drafted Sam Cassell last year, and the rookie showed the ability to play both guard positions with verve and flash. Veteran swing man Mario Elie can score in a hurry, and waterbug Scott Brooks is an experienced point man, although he's a little undersized.

Forward: It's hard to comprehend that the Rockets were going to dish Robert Horry to Detroit for Sean Elliott. Horry may have been inconsistent last year, but he has a good pro body at the three spot, 3-point range, and a bright future. He and venerable power man Otis Thorpe provide a tremendous frontcourt complement to Hakeem Olajuwon. Nobody will ever call Thorpe a polished offensive player, but his defense and rebounding are superior. Carl Herrera is an emerging reserve, although his shooting could improve some and his defense needs work. Matt Bullard is a 6'10" jump-shooter, something that kept him from seeing serious minutes against the rugged Knicks.

Center: With Michael Jordan toiling in the bush leagues, Olajuwon filled the superstar breech and took home the NBA's MVP Award last year. Olajuwon remains one of the game's most creative post players, with an array of unstoppable jumpers, quick baseline moves, and powerful dunks and follow-ups. Moreover, he's the best defensive player in the league, as he swats away shots like there's no tomorrow. Veteran Earl Cureton can provide short bursts of excitement and productivity. Second-year man Eric Riley needs to get stronger.

Coaching: The Rockets shot—and made—more 3-pointers last year than any other team in history and played the kind of physical halfcourt defense generally found in the Eastern Conference. Credit coach Rudy Tomjanovich with that strategy, along with keeping the team together when the Rockets fell behind Phoenix 2-0 at home in the Western semis. He is assisted by Carroll Dawson, Bill Berry, and Larry Smith.

Analysis: As long as Olajuwon remains a dominant force, the Rockets will be contenders, particularly with Tomjanovich making such good use of the big guy's supporting cast. The Rockets should win the Midwest Division again this year and launch a serious defense of their title, but their reign is a fragile one, especially given the talent in the rest of the Western Conference.

Prediction: First place, Midwest Division

MINNESOTA TIMBERWOLVES

Home: Target Center
Capacity: 19,006
Year Built: 1990

Address:
Target Center
600 First Ave. North
Minneapolis, MN 55403
(612) 673-1600

Owner: Glen Taylor
General Manager: Jack McCloskey
Head Coach: TBA
Assistant Coaches: TBA

Timberwolves History

After five years in the NBA, Minnesota finds itself right where it started—at the bottom rung of the ladder.

The Timberwolves first took to the court in 1989-90, and the initial year's results were predictable—22-60. Ironically, the poor record did nothing to stem the enthusiasm of the Twin Cities faithful, who packed the Metrodome with 26,000-plus fans per night, establishing an NBA season attendance record.

The team featured some bright spots that first year. Forward Tony Campbell emerged as a top scoring threat, and rookie guard Pooh Richardson was an adroit playmaker and scorer. Under defensive-minded coach Bill Musselman, the T'Wolves were one of the league's best at maintaining tempo and stopping opponents from scoring.

For 1990-91, Minnesota added 7'0" center Felton Spencer and forward Gerald Glass, and they moved into the brand new Target Center in downtown Minneapolis. The team improved to 29-53, good for fifth in the Midwest Division. But despite the seven-game improvement, Musselman got the axe and was replaced by Jimmy Rodgers.

The change did nothing to help the team, as the 1991-92 T'Wolves finished with the league's worst record. After the season, Minnesota drafted Christian Laettner and landed standouts Chuck Person and Micheal Williams in a trade for Richardson and Sam Mitchell. Nevertheless, the 1992-93 club still lacked the talent to win 20 games. In midseason, Rodgers was replaced by the young Sidney Lowe.

Last Five Years

Season	W	L	Pct.	Place	Playoffs	Coach
1989-90	22	60	.268	Sixth	DNQ	Bill Musselman
1990-91	29	53	.354	Fifth	DNQ	Bill Musselman
1991-92	15	67	.183	Sixth	DNQ	Jimmy Rodgers
1992-93	19	63	.232	Fifth	DNQ	J. Rodgers/S. Lowe
1993-94	20	62	.244	Fifth	DNQ	Sidney Lowe

1993-94 Review

The good times just kept on rolling in the Land of 10,000 Lakes during the 1993-94 season. While the NBA waited to see if the team was actually going to stay in Minnesota's Target Center or move to Nashville or anywhere else, the Timberhound players continued to complain about playing time, practice schedules, and anything else that occurred to them.

Coach Sidney Lowe's first full season with the team provided another chapter in the history of the worst recent expansion franchise. Minnesota skulked to a 20-62 record—a one-win improvement over 1992-93's desultory performance. Some things never change, like the Timberwolves' woeful offense, which produced more points than only one other team—Dallas.

The Timberwolves did have the dubious distinction of tying the Clippers for the most turnovers per game (18.0), a tribute to their selfish play. Christian Laettner (16.8 PPG, 8.6 RPG) was the top fumbler with 3.7 each night. The petulant second-year forward with the monster attitude posted steady numbers while leading the team in minutes, but his misunderstood-guy routine continued to grate on the rest of the league.

Rookie guard Isaiah (don't call me J.R.) Rider (16.6 PPG) had a solid debut but spent much of the season clamoring for more minutes, even though he averaged 30.5 per game. His wrist probably needed the rest, however, since he led the team in shots launched. Nonetheless, Rider teamed with veteran Doug West (14.7 PPG) to give Minnesota plenty of punch from the two spot. Point guard Micheal Williams (13.7 PPG, 7.2 APG) was adequate, while gunner Chuck Person (11.6 PPG) had his worst season in the league, shooting just 42.2 percent from the field.

The pivot was another big problem for the Wolves. Tired of underachieving Luc Longley, they traded him for Stacey King, another inconsistent center. Preseason acquisition Mike Brown (3.6 PPG, 5.5 RPG) was hardly inspiring off the bench. Veteran Thurl Bailey (7.4 PPG) was steady as a reserve forward, while Chris Smith (5.9 PPG) provided average depth at point guard.

1994-95 Roster

No.	Player	Pos.	Ht.	Wt.	Exp.	College	G	RPG	APG	PPG
								1993-94		
40	Mike Brown	F/C	6'10"	260	8	G. Washington	82	5.5	0.9	3.6
23	Brian Davis	G/F	6'7"	215	1	Duke	68	0.8	0.3	1.9
—	Howard Eisley	G	6'3"	180	R	Boston College	—	—	—	—
51	Andres Guibert	F/C	6'10"	242	1	Cuba	5	3.2	0.4	3.0
7	Stanley Jackson	G	6'3"	185	1	Alabama-Birm.	17	1.6	0.9	2.2
21	Stacey King	F/C	6'11"	250	4	Oklahoma	49	4.9	1.2	7.9
32	Christian Laettner	F	6'11"	235	2	Duke	70	8.6	4.4	16.8
—	Donyell Marshall	F	6'9"	218	R	Connecticut	—	—	—	—
25	Marlon Maxey	F	6'8"	250	2	Texas-El Paso	55	3.6	0.2	4.5
34	Isaiah Rider	G/F	6'5"	215	1	UNLV	79	4.0	2.6	16.6
3	Chris Smith	G	6'3"	190	2	Connecticut	80	1.5	3.6	5.9
5	Doug West	G	6'6"	200	5	Villanova	72	3.2	2.4	14.7
24	Micheal Williams	G	6'2"	175	6	Baylor	71	3.1	7.2	13.7

Minnesota Timberwolves
1994-95 Season Preview

Opening Line: The citizens of Minnesota fought hard to keep their Wolves from heading down the Mississippi to New Orleans, and one can only wonder why. Since its inception, the franchise has floundered, combining poor personnel decisions with rancid on-court play. The selections of Connecticut forward Donyell Marshall and Boston College guard Howard Eisley in this year's draft will help some, but the Wolves enter the 1994-95 season with little hope of making the playoffs.

Guard: If the T'Wolves were a college team, they could go with a three-guard rotation and both Doug West and Isaiah Rider would be happy. Instead, the team is stuck with two shooting guards and must use them together—with Rider in the three position. Rider is a big-time scorer who wants to shoot every time he touches the ball, and West is a maturing two man who also isn't shy about launching the rock. That leaves veteran point man Micheal Williams to decide who gets the ball. Williams can deliver it and even make a shot or two if he ever gets the ball back. Chris Smith is an athletic back-up point, but he needs help with his shot. Eisley shot the trey well in college, and he possesses the ball-handling and defensive skills to handle the point too.

Forward: Besides his immature attitude and foul mouth, Christian Laettner needs to improve his shooting percentage and cut down on the turnovers. Still, he and Marshall have the potential to be a great forward tandem. Marshall can shoot the trey, excel on the break, score in the low post, and block shots with his long arms. He received an undeserved reputation as a big-game choker after his performance against Florida in the NCAA tourney, but Marshall is a legitimate star-in-waiting. Veteran Thurl Bailey (who may leave as a free agent) is an unheralded back-up at either position. Ditto for young Marlon Maxey, a big body who can play defense. Minnesota bought out Chuck Person's contract.

Center: This is one of the NBA's premier black holes. Mike Brown has limited mobility and few offensive skills. Stacey King can score but is not a defensive presence. He has never lived up to his considerable potential.

Coaching: New owner Glen Taylor let the axe fly in August, as he fired head coach Sidney Lowe and assistants Jim Brewer and Chuck Davisson. As September approached, no replacements had been named.

Analysis: The NBA may have forced the Timberwolves to stay in Minnesota, but it can't do anything about getting the squad into the playoffs, short of a Marshall Plan-type bailout, and maybe that's why they chose Donyell. Minnesota has a big hole in the middle, could use a better point guard, and is packed with volatile personalities. Other than that, everything is fine.

Prediction: Sixth place, Midwest Division

SAN ANTONIO SPURS

Home: Alamodome
Capacity: 20,500
Year Built: 1993

Address:
100 Montana St.
San Antonio, TX 78203
(210) 554-7700

Chairman of the Board: Robert McDermott
General Manager: Gregg Popovich
Head Coach: TBA
Assistant Coaches: TBA

Spurs History

This Texas franchise was born in Dallas in 1967 as a charter member of the ABA. Its name? The Dallas Chaparrals. The stay in Dallas was a haphazard one, featuring six coaches in six years, low attendance, and little playoff success.

Angelo Drossos moved the club to the home of the Alamo in 1973, and the team was renamed the Spurs. It was an exciting squad that fans embraced immediately. The Spurs had 50-plus-win seasons in 1974-75 and 1975-76 and moved into the NBA at full gallop.

Led by unstoppable guard George Gervin, mammoth center Artis Gilmore, and a talented supporting cast that included Johnny Moore, Larry Kenon, and James Silas, the Spurs won two Central and three Midwest Division championships in six years. Gervin was the NBA scoring champ four times. However, San Antonio could not make it to the NBA Finals, as it fell in the conference finals three times.

The Spurs' nucleus began to age in the mid-1980s, and the team fell from its lofty status. But the collapse did lead to something worthwhile. In 1987, the Spurs drafted David Robinson of Navy. The team continued to sag in the next two seasons while Robinson completed his military obligation, but he joined the Spurs in 1989-90.

Robinson immediately emerged as one of the NBA's best centers. He teamed with Terry Cummings and Sean Elliott to help San Antonio win the Midwest title in both 1989-90 and 1990-91. Despite fine records over the last five years, the Spurs haven't been able to reach the conference finals.

Last Seven Years

Season	W	L	Pct.	Place	Playoffs	Coach
1987-88	31	51	.378	Fifth	L-Round 1	Bob Weiss
1988-89	21	61	.256	Fifth	DNQ	Larry Brown
1989-90	56	26	.683	First	L-West Semis	Larry Brown
1990-91	55	27	.671	First	L-Round 1	Larry Brown
1991-92	47	35	.573	Second	L-Round 1	Larry Brown/Bob Bass
1992-93	49	33	.598	Second	L-West Semis	J. Tarkanian/J. Lucas
1993-94	55	27	.671	Second	L-Round 1	John Lucas

1993-94 Review

Following its surprising first-round playoff elimination by the Utah Jazz, San Antonio was able to reflect upon its first season in the Alamodome as one that included the superlative, the outrageous, and the disappointing. The Spurs waged a season-long battle with the Houston Rockets for Midwest supremacy, falling three games short but still putting together the Western Conference's fourth-best record.

Along the way, San Antonio fans were able to chart the remarkable season of center David Robinson (29.8 PPG, 10.7 RPG), who clearly took charge of the team and warranted serious consideration for the MVP trophy. His 71-point outburst against the Clippers on the final day of the year also secured him the NBA scoring title, much to the chagrin of Shaquille O'Neal.

The outrageous Dennis Rodman made his presence felt in San Antonio the moment he was acquired from Detroit. From his multi-hued hairstyles and nine tattoos to his complete indifference toward scoring (he led the NBA with 17.3 RPG, but scored just 4.7 PPG), Rodman was a curiosity at times, a warrior at others, and a pain in the neck just about all season. His unwarranted cheap shots at Utah's John Stockton, Karl Malone, and Tom Chambers in the playoffs cast a pall over the whole franchise and gained Rodman a heap of criticism.

What really hurt San Antonio was its point-guard situation. Neither Negele Knight (9.2 PPG) nor Vinny Del Negro (10.0 PPG, 4.2 APG) established himself as a clear quarterback, and the Spurs' offense sputtered because of it. Sure, Dale Ellis (15.2 PPG, 49.4 FGP) and Willie Anderson (11.9 PPG) scored their points at the two and three spots, but the Spurs lacked continuity on offense, particularly when Robinson wasn't on the court.

J.R. Reid (9.0 PPG, 3.1 RPG) was an adequate frontcourt reserve, and veteran frontcourt man Terry Cummings made it through the season on a rehabilitated knee. But reserve power forward Antoine Carr played in only 34 games, and mercurial guard Lloyd Daniels shot just 37.6 percent from the floor.

1994-95 Roster

No.	Player	Pos.	Ht.	Wt.	Exp.	College	G	RPG	APG	PPG
								—1993-94—		
40	Willie Anderson	G/F	6'8"	200	6	Georgia	80	3.0	4.3	11.9
34	Terry Cummings	F	6'9"	245	12	DePaul	59	5.0	0.8	7.3
24	Lloyd Daniels	G	6'7"	205	2	None	65	1.7	1.4	5.7
15	Vinny Del Negro	G	6'4"	200	4	N. Carolina St.	77	2.1	4.2	10.0
—	Sean Elliott	F	6'8"	215	5	Arizona	73	3.6	2.7	12.1
3	Dale Ellis	G	6'7"	215	11	Tennessee	77	3.3	1.0	15.2
—	Avery Johnson	G	5'11"	175	6	Southern	82	2.1	5.3	10.9
32	Negele Knight	G	6'1"	182	4	Dayton	65	1.6	3.0	9.2
—	Moses Malone	C	6'10"	255	18	None	55	4.1	0.6	5.3
—	Chuck Person	F	6'8"	225	8	Auburn	77	3.3	2.4	11.6
7	J.R. Reid	F/C	6'9"	265	5	North Carolina	70	3.1	1.0	9.0
50	David Robinson	C	7'1"	235	5	Navy	80	10.7	4.8	29.8
10	Dennis Rodman	F	6'8"	210	8	S.E. Okla. St.	79	17.3	2.3	4.7
20	Chris Whitney	G	6'0"	171	1	Clemson	40	0.7	1.3	1.8

San Antonio Spurs
1994-95 Season Preview

Opening Line: The Spurs enter 1994-95 with more questions than easy answers. The defection of dynamic coach John Lucas and a roster that relies too heavily on its superstar—center David Robinson—make San Antonio a team in danger of losing touch with the Western Conference big boys. The trade of draft pick Bill Curley to Detroit for former Spurs forward Sean Elliott was a positive move. The pick-up of another big-name forward, Chuck Person, indicates that the team wants to trade bad boy Dennis Rodman.

Guard: No one has ever doubted Dale Ellis's ability to score. His numbers may have been down last year, but his shooting percentage was high, even with a slew of 3-pointers. The point-guard situation is not so settled. The Spurs would love to have Negele Knight take over the spot, but he is erratic and more suited for scoring. Vinny Del Negro is a capable floor leader, but he'll never remind anyone of John Stockton. Vagabond Avery Johnson is quick and can dish it, but his shooting is shaky. Lloyd Daniels continues to soar in small bursts and confound the rest of the time. He may struggle without Lucas's steady hand.

Forward: Rodman is the league's best pure rebounder and one of its greatest defenders. Unfortunately, he has severely limited offensive skills and a personality that makes nitroglycerin seem stable. Management can't tolerate him much longer. Small forward Elliott struggled during his year in Detroit, but a return to the Western Conference—and its wide-open style of ball—could be just what he needs. Willie Anderson is an accomplished scorer, although he is too thin (6'8", 200) to be a valuable inside player. Person is another little forward who assaults foes with long bombs and verbal garbage. J.R. Reid is a valuable inside scorer and banger who's best suited to coming off the bench. Terry Cummings is at the end of a great career.

Center: David Robinson just keeps getting better. The big guy led the NBA in scoring last year and continues to dazzle with his unique blend of low-post dominance and open-court capabilities. The Admiral is one of the best shot-blockers in the league and has a strong enough character to steer the ship. Ancient Moses Malone will back him up.

Coaching: As of late August, the Spurs had yet to name a successor to Lucas, which further added to the uncertainty that surrounded the team.

Analysis: Lucas helped resurrect the Spurs, and with him gone to Philadelphia, San Antonio becomes a curious club. There is enough talent to contend for the Midwest Division championship, but with volatile personalities like Rodman and Daniels on the team, there is potential for disaster. Robinson can be counted on for superlative performances every night, but nothing else is a given with San Antonio.

Prediction: Fourth place, Midwest Division

UTAH JAZZ

Home: Delta Center
Capacity: 19,911
Year Built: 1991

Owner: Larry H. Miller
General Manager: Tim Howells
Head Coach: Jerry Sloan
Assistant Coach: Phil Johnson
Assistant Coach: Gordon Chiesa
Assistant Coach: David Fredman

Address:
Delta Center
301 W. South Temple
Salt Lake City, UT 84101
(801) 325-2500

Coach Jerry Sloan			
	W	L	Pct.
NBA Record	398	292	.577
W/Jazz	304	171	.640
1993-94 Record	53	29	.646

Jazz History

About the last city you'd expect to find a team named the Jazz would be in puritan Salt Lake City, Utah. However, the name comes with an easy explanation. When the franchise was born back in 1974, its hometown was New Orleans, a jazzy place if ever there was one. When it moved west in 1979, it decided to hold on to the name.

The early days did have their moments. In the mid-1970s, Louisiana native "Pistol" Pete Maravich lit up the Bayou, scoring baskets in bushels and once torching the Knicks for 68 points. Maravich's knee went out in 1977-78 and, despite the emergence of all-world rebounder Leonard "Truck" Robinson, the Jazz limped along.

Coach Frank Layden was hired in 1981-82 and immediately became popular for his sense of humor and regular-guy charm. The Jazz captured the Midwest Division crown in 1983-84 and advanced to the conference semifinals, relying on league scoring leader Adrian Dantley, quick backcourt men Darrell Griffith and Ricky Green, and mammoth, 7'4" center Mark Eaton.

The Jazz selected power forward Karl Malone in the 1985 draft, and he was an immediate sensation, teaming with assist machine John Stockton to form a solid nucleus. Utah won the 1988-89 Midwest title under new coach Jerry Sloan but fell in the first round of the playoffs. Utah advanced to the conference semis in 1990-91, and in 1991-92 the Jazz fell to Portland in the West finals.

Last Seven Years

Season	W	L	Pct.	Place	Playoffs	Coach
1987-88	47	35	.573	Third	L-West Semis	Frank Layden
1988-89	51	31	.622	First	L-Round 1	Frank Layden/Jerry Sloan
1989-90	55	27	.671	Second	L-Round 1	Jerry Sloan
1990-91	54	28	.659	Second	L-West Semis	Jerry Sloan
1991-92	55	27	.671	First	L-West Finals	Jerry Sloan
1992-93	47	35	.573	Third	L-Round 1	Jerry Sloan
1993-94	53	29	.646	Third	L-West Finals	Jerry Sloan

1993-94 Review

If the Jazz was finally going to make it to the NBA Finals, 1993-94 was the year. It wasn't necessarily a case of exceptional balance and talent—Utah may never have that—but rather a case of being in the right place at the right time. With San Antonio's Dennis Rodman suspended, the Jazz was able to roll over the Spurs in the playoffs. Then in Round 2, they got to play Denver, which had ousted No. 1-seeded Seattle in Round 1. Utah beat the Nuggets in seven games before falling to Houston in five.

During the season, the Jazz posted a record of 53-29, winning six more games than the previous year. The acquisition of multi-talented backcourt man Jeff Hornacek for gunning guard Jeff Malone and a draft pick from the 76ers proved to be a wise move. Still, Utah finished third in the Midwest Division and appeared to be falling behind the Rockets and Spurs.

As usual, the all-galaxy tandem of power forward Karl Malone (25.2 PPG, 11.5 RPG) and point guard John Stockton (15.1 PPG, 12.6 APG, 2.4 SPG) powered the Jazz, with both players rejuvenated after the 1992-93 whirlwind that included various Dream Team responsibilities. Malone and Stockton worked their games every way imaginable and were again the team's soul. As was proven during the previous six years, though, two superstars do not a title contender make.

Hornacek (15.9 PPG) was a valuable acquisition, both for his long-range bombing and his ability to handle the ball. He, Stockton, and Jay Humphries (7.5 PPG, 2.9 APG) gave the Jazz a solid backcourt rotation. But, as usual, frontcourt players not named Malone were a problem. Center Mark Eaton missed the whole year with a bad back, leaving an eager but overmatched Felton Spencer (8.6 PPG, 8.3 RPG) as the main man in the middle. Free-agent acquisition Tom Chambers (11.2 PPG) provided his customary instant offense—and little else—while the small-forward trio of David Benoit (6.5 PPG), rookie Bryon Russell (5.0 PPG, 2.7 RPG), and Tyrone Corbin (8.0 PPG, 4.7 RPG) was adequate but not championship caliber.

1994-95 Roster

| No. | Player | Pos. | Ht. | Wt. | Exp. | College | 1993-94 | | |
							G	RPG	APG	PPG
21	David Benoit	F	6'8"	220	3	Alabama	55	4.7	0.4	6.5
20	Walter Bond	G	6'5"	200	2	Minnesota	56	1.1	0.6	3.1
23	Tyrone Corbin	F	6'6"	222	9	DePaul	82	4.7	1.5	8.0
25	John Crotty	G	6'1"	185	2	Virginia	45	0.7	1.7	2.9
14	Jeff Hornacek	G	6'4"	190	8	Iowa St.	80	3.5	5.2	15.9
43	Stephen Howard	F	6'9"	230	2	DePaul	9	1.8	0.1	3.4
6	Jay Humphries	G	6'3"	185	10	Colorado	75	1.7	2.9	7.5
32	Karl Malone	F	6'9"	256	9	Louisiana Tech	82	11.5	4.0	25.2
34	Bryon Russell	F	6'7"	225	1	Long Beach St.	67	2.7	0.8	5.0
50	Felton Spencer	C	7'0"	265	4	Louisville	79	8.3	0.5	8.6
12	John Stockton	G	6'1"	175	10	Gonzaga	82	3.2	12.6	15.1
—	Jamie Watson	G/F	6'7"	190	R	South Carolina	—	—	—	—
44	Luther Wright	C	7'2"	280	1	Seton Hall	15	0.7	0.0	1.3

Utah Jazz
1994-95 Season Preview

Opening Line: Things returned to usual in Rocky Mountain country last year, with the Jazz heading back to the Western finals—and losing. Utah again showed that it has enough talent to reach a certain level but not the necessary ingredients to go past that plateau. And so it is for 1994-95. The Jazz will look pretty much like it did last spring, as the team did not have a first-round pick and did not make a deal. Tom Chambers was let go.

Guard: The Jazz stole Jeff Hornacek from Philadelphia last year for gunner Jeff Malone. Hornacek can play the one or two spot, is an excellent spot-up jump-shooter, and can penetrate as well as most point guards. He teams with John Stockton, who remains the NBA's preeminent point man, working the Jazz's give-and-go series perfectly with the Mailman. He'll become the NBA's all-time assist leader this year. Back-up Jay Humphries can swing between both guard spots, making the Jazz even more versatile at the position. Deep reserves John Crotty and Walter Bond are average shooters, with Crotty better suited to handling the basketball.

Forward: It doesn't get any better than Karl Malone at power forward. The guy remains among the league's top scorers and rebounders every year and is an outstanding money player. The problem comes at the three spot, where Tyrone Corbin, David Benoit, and Bryon Russell staged a season-long bout for the starting job—with no clear-cut winner. Corbin, perhaps the best of the bunch, operates well inside. Benoit has oodles of potential but continues to shoot like a shot-putter. Second-year man Russell could blossom into a starter if he could gain some more consistency.

Center: Sure, Felton Spencer remains slow and plodding and you'll never see him finishing on the break, but Spencer is a major space-eater with some offensive ability. Second-year man Luther Wright is still very much a project—and a question mark due to a chemical imbalance/attention deficit-induced trip to the injured list.

Coaching: Last year at this time, Jerry Sloan appeared to be in a little trouble. But the Jazz's rebound to the Western finals will keep him on the bench for another season. Sloan continues to crank out 50-win seasons, which is all you could expect from him considering his club's limitations. Sloan is assisted by Gordon Chiesa, David Fredman, and Phil Johnson.

Analysis: The Jazz remains among the ten or so best teams in the NBA and should challenge Houston and San Antonio for the Midwest title—again. But the seven-game near-miss against Denver in the Western semis and the graying beards on Stockton and Malone prove that this team's window of opportunity for title contention is closing fast. A full season of Hornacek and Stockton in the backcourt will make a difference, but the Jazz are still too inconsistent at the small-forward and center positions to win a title.

Prediction: Second place, Midwest Division

GOLDEN STATE WARRIORS

Home: Oakland Coliseum Arena
Capacity: 15,025
Year Built: 1966

Address:
Oakland Coliseum Arena
Oakland, CA 94621
(510) 638-6300

Chairman: Jim Fitzgerald
General Manager: Don Nelson
Head Coach: Don Nelson
Assistant Coach: Donn Nelson
Assistant Coach: Paul Pressey

Coach Don Nelson			
	W	L	Pct.
NBA Record	803	573	.584
W/Warriors	263	229	.535
1993-94 Record	50	32	.610

Warriors History

Present-day Warrior fans may find it difficult to identify with the team's East Coast roots. For 16 seasons, the Philadelphia Warriors enjoyed success in the old BAA and as a charter member of the NBA. Philadelphia won the first BAA championship in 1946-47 behind scoring machine Joe Fulks.

The Warriors advanced to the BAA finals in 1948, losing to Baltimore. But they defeated Fort Wayne in 1956 to win the NBA title behind Paul Arizin, Neil Johnston, and Tom Gola. In 1959, Wilt Chamberlain joined the team and was an immediate sensation, winning the MVP Award in his rookie season. The team moved to San Francisco in 1962 and lost to Boston in the NBA Finals in 1963-64. The Warriors traded Chamberlain to the new Philadelphia 76ers in 1964-65, then lost to the Sixers in the NBA Finals two years later.

The Warriors changed their name to Golden State in 1971 and moved across the bay to Oakland, where the championship drought continued until 1974-75. That year, coach Al Attles incorporated a ten-man rotation around Rick Barry and took the Warriors to the NBA title.

The Warriors didn't rebound again until 1988, when Don Nelson took over as coach. Using a small lineup built around Chris Mullin and Mitch Richmond, the Warriors made it to the Western semis in 1988-89. Point guard Tim Hardaway was added for the 1989-90 season, and in 1990-91 Golden State again advanced to the West semis, losing to the Los Angeles Lakers. Fifty-win seasons in 1991-92 and 1993-94 led to little playoff success.

Last Seven Years

Season	W	L	Pct.	Place	Playoffs	Coach
1987-88	20	62	.244	Fifth	DNQ	George Karl/Ed Gregory
1988-89	43	39	.524	Fourth	L-West Semis	Don Nelson
1989-90	37	45	.451	Fifth	DNQ	Don Nelson
1990-91	44	38	.537	Fourth	L-West Semis	Don Nelson
1991-92	55	27	.671	Second	L-Round 1	Don Nelson
1992-93	34	48	.415	Sixth	DNQ	Don Nelson
1993-94	50	32	.610	Third	L-Round 1	Don Nelson

1993-94 Review

The cover of the 1994-95 Golden State media guide should feature coach Don Nelson in a wizard's outfit, because folks around the league are still trying to figure out how he kept the Warriors competitive last year with two major contributors out for the year with knee injuries.

The off-season losses of guards Tim Hardaway and Sarunas Marciulionis cast a funk over the franchise, but Nelson was able to coax 50 wins and a surprising third-place finish out of the squad. Though Golden State made a hasty, first-round playoff exit against Phoenix, it could look back on the year as a successful one and view 1994-95 with great expectations.

The Warriors continued their high-scoring ways, averaging 107.9 PPG, second in the NBA. It all started with second-year guard Latrell Sprewell (21.0 PPG), who matured from a rookie curiosity into a bona-fide sensation. The man who came into the league with a reputation as a one-dimensional defensive specialist proved he could score, and—later in the year—handle the point-guard position. He and Rookie of the Year Chris Webber (17.5 PPG, 9.1 RPG) helped offset the huge holes caused by Hardaway's and Marciulionis's absences and kept the Warriors clicking.

They had plenty of help, of course. Veteran Chris Mullin came back from a hand injury to score 16.8 PPG, getting stronger as the season wore on. Forward Billy Owens (15.0 PPG, 8.1 RPG, 4.1 APG) was his usual multi-faceted self, and Avery Johnson brought some consistency to the point-guard position.

As usual, the Warriors were weak in the middle, which had as much to do with their 106.1 PPG surrendered as the team's up-tempo style. Victor Alexander (8.7 PPG, 4.5 RPG) and Chris Gatling (8.2 PPG, 4.8 RPG) simply won't lead anyone to a championship, and their ineffectiveness forced Nelson to play Webber at center more than he should have. Tiny Keith Jennings (5.7 PPG) provided some excitement at the point and on the fastbreak, and Jeff Grayer (6.8 PPG) shot 52.6 percent from the field as a reserve swing man.

1994-95 Roster

No.	Player	Pos.	Ht.	Wt.	Exp.	College	1993-94 G	RPG	APG	PPG
52	Victor Alexander	C/F	6'9"	265	3	Iowa St.	69	4.5	1.0	8.7
25	Chris Gatling	F/C	6'10"	225	3	Old Dominion	82	4.8	0.5	8.2
44	Jeff Grayer	G/F	6'5"	210	6	Iowa St.	67	2.9	0.9	6.8
10	Tim Hardaway	G	6'0"	195	4	Texas-El Paso	—	—	—	—
2	Keith Jennings	G	5'7"	160	2	E. Tenn. St.	76	1.2	2.9	5.7
—	Dwayne Morton	G/F	6'6"	190	R	Louisville	—	—	—	—
17	Chris Mullin	F	6'7"	215	9	St. John's	62	5.6	5.1	16.8
30	Billy Owens	F/G	6'9"	220	3	Syracuse	79	8.1	4.1	15.0
—	Ricky Pierce	G	6'4"	215	12	Rice	51	1.6	1.8	14.5
—	Carlos Rogers	F	6'11"	220	R	Tennessee St.	—	—	—	—
44	Clifford Rozier	C/F	6'9"	235	R	Louisville	—	—	—	—
15	Latrell Sprewell	G	6'5"	190	2	Alabama	82	4.9	4.7	21.0
4	Chris Webber	F/C	6'9"	245	1	Michigan	76	9.1	3.6	17.5

Golden State Warriors
1994-95 Season Preview

Opening Line: No one would have been surprised if Don Nelson had executed a perfect swan dive off the Golden Gate Bridge last season. For the second consecutive year, key injuries conspired against his Warriors and threatened to turn another promising campaign into a lottery debacle. Nellie rescued Golden State last year, and with his young team a year older—and healthier—1994-95 should be even better. The exciting Warriors added some size, as they drafted Clifford Rozier of Louisville and acquired 6'11" Carlos Rogers of Tennessee State from Seattle, along with aging gunner Ricky Pierce.

Guard: If Tim Hardaway's knee is healed completely, he'll be one of basketball's best point men. He can score, break down a defender, and lead the break with aplomb. Teaming him with Latrell Sprewell in the same backcourt would be outrageous. During his two years in the NBA, Sprewell has become one of the league's rising stars, a tremendous blend of scoring, defense, and confidence. Adding Pierce, a classy long-range bomber, to that mix turbocharges the Warriors even further. Keith Jennings offers great quickness and long-range bombs, but his 5'7" size limits him. Free agent Avery Johnson was not re-signed.

Forward: Okay, so Chris Webber can't shoot too well from beyond ten feet. The guy can get to the basket, and when he does, he's nearly unstoppable. He's a top-flight power man destined for greatness. Chris Mullin rebounded slowly from his broken thumb last year but should be at full speed this season, bringing outstanding shooting range and tremendous scoring instincts to the three spot. Billy Owens, who shoots it well, grabs plenty of boards, and can pass, will be a potent weapon off the bench. Rozier's stock fell during last year's NCAA tourney, but he can score inside and has a good body—something the Warriors need. Veteran Jeff Grayer scores instantly off the bench.

Center: All together, now: If only Golden State had a real center. Victor Alexander and Chris Gatling are big, but each would be better suited as a power forward. Nelson put Webber in the middle at times but that isn't a long-term solution. Rogers has the height for the position, but at 220 pounds he is better suited for the wing.

Coaching: Despite his well-publicized run-in with Webber, Nelson remains one of the league's top bench men. His go-go style is exciting and productive, and he's worked magic with undersized, injury-plagued teams. He is assisted by son Donn Nelson and Paul Pressey.

Analysis: A season ticket to the Warriors will again provide six months of ooohs and ahhhs, but without a substantial pivot presence, fans won't be able to see their favorites last too long in the playoffs. A healthy Warrior club could average 120 points a game—really. But some bulk and power is needed with that finesse and flash, particularly in the newly pumped-up NBA.

Prediction: Third place, Pacific Division

LOS ANGELES CLIPPERS

Home: L.A. Memorial Sports Arena
Capacity: 16,005
Year Built: 1959

Address:
3939 S. Figueroa St.
Los Angeles, CA 90037
(213) 748-8000

Owner: Donald T. Sterling
Executive V.P./General Manager: Elgin Baylor
Head Coach: Bill Fitch
Assistant Coaches: TBA

Coach Bill Fitch			
	W	L	Pct.
NBA Record	845	877	.491
W/Clippers	0	0	.000
1993-94 Record	0	0	.000

Clippers History

Despite brief success in the mid-1970s and playoff appearances in 1991-92 and 1992-93, the Clippers have been one of the league's weakest and most poorly managed teams.

Born the Buffalo Braves in 1970, the team flourished briefly under the direction of Jack Ramsay. The Braves crept above the .500 mark (42-40) in 1973-74, behind NBA scoring leader Bob McAdoo, slick playmaker Ernie DiGregorio, and sharp-shooting forward Jim McMillian. The Braves improved to 49-33 the next season with MVP McAdoo again leading the way. Washington bounced the Braves from the 1975 Eastern semifinals, but the Braves persevered and whipped Philadelphia in the first round of the 1976 playoffs before succumbing to Boston in the semis.

Thus ended the good times for Braves/Clippers fans. Prior to the 1978-79 season, Braves owner John Y. Brown traded the team to Irving Levin in return for control of the Celtics. Levin moved the club to San Diego, renamed it the Clippers, and watched it register an abysmal 17-65 mark in 1981-82. The Clippers moved north to L.A. for the 1984-85 season and were an immediate poor cousin to the flourishing Lakers.

Though they won 30-plus games in 1984-85 and 1985-86, the Clippers embarked on three straight miserable seasons, with the lowlight being a 12-70 mark in 1986-87. Despite young talent such as Ron Harper and Danny Manning, the Clippers failed to rise above mediocrity in the late '80s and early '90s.

Last Seven Years

Season	W	L	Pct.	Place	Playoffs	Coach
1987-88	17	65	.207	Sixth	DNQ	Gene Shue
1988-89	21	61	.256	Seventh	DNQ	Gene Shue/Don Casey
1989-90	30	52	.366	Sixth	DNQ	Don Casey
1990-91	31	51	.378	Sixth	DNQ	Mike Schuler
1991-92	45	37	.549	Fifth	L-Round 1	Mike Schuler/Mack Calvin/ Larry Brown
1992-93	41	41	.500	Fourth	L-Round 1	Larry Brown
1993-94	27	55	.329	Seventh	DNQ	Bob Weiss

1993-94 Review

After all the problems the Clippers endured prior to the 1993-94 season, fans, players, and management had to believe that once the games started, things would settle down. Wrong. L.A.'s miseries only grew after the season began, and the franchise that had seemed ready to shed its laughingstock status back in 1991-92 settled back among the NBA's lesser lights and provided enough chuckles to fill an episode of "Seinfeld."

Under coach Bob Weiss, the Clips deteriorated into a defenseless Pacific patsy. It wasn't all Weiss's fault. The preseason exit of free-agent forward Ken Norman to Milwaukee and the midseason trade of Danny Manning to Atlanta for one-dimensional gunner Dominique Wilkins drained L.A. of its core. By season's end, only guard Ron Harper—who jogged his way through another productive (20.1 PPG) but uninspired season—remained from the promising nucleus that had generated hope.

While the Orlando Magic squawked that the Clippers allowed David Robinson to win the scoring title with a 71-point outburst on the season's final day, the complaining was unjustified. Several NBA stars could have lit up the Clips in a similar manner during 1993-94 had they wished. Simply put, the Clippers were the NBA's worst defensive team. L.A. allowed a league-high 108.7 PPG.

That didn't matter to Wilkins, who went on a scoring binge after joining the Clippers and finished fourth in the league with 26.0 PPG. After Wilkins and Harper, there was little offensive production in L.A. Power forward Loy Vaught (11.7 PPG, 8.7 RPG) had another quietly effective year, while point guard Mark Jackson (10.9 PPG, 8.6 APG) was among the league leaders in assists.

Center Elmore Spencer (8.9 PPG, 5.5 RPG) was mediocre in the middle, and veteran Gary Grant (7.5 PPG) provided adequate depth in the backcourt. After that, it was a grab bag of outcasts and misfits—and a little bad luck. Corpulent center Stanley Roberts missed all but 14 games with a torn Achilles tendon, while chunky forward John Williams was injured and overweight.

1994-95 Roster

No.	Player	Pos.	Ht.	Wt.	Exp.	College	G	1993-94 RPG	APG	PPG
24	Terry Dehere	G	6'3"	190	1	Seton Hall	64	1.1	1.2	5.3
30	Harold Ellis	G	6'5"	220	1	Morehouse	49	3.1	0.6	8.7
23	Gary Grant	G	6'3"	195	6	Michigan	78	1.8	3.7	7.5
42	Bob Martin	C	7'0"	255	1	Minnesota	53	2.2	0.3	2.1
—	Tony Massenburg	F	6'9"	245	3	Maryland	—	—	—	—
—	Lamond Murray	F	6'7"	220	R	California	—	—	—	—
6	Bo Outlaw	F	6'8"	210	1	Houston	37	5.7	1.0	6.9
—	Eric Piatkowski	G/F	6'7"	215	R	Nebraska	—	—	—	—
—	Pooh Richardson	G	6'1"	180	5	UCLA	37	3.0	6.4	10.0
53	Stanley Roberts	C	7'0"	290	3	Louisiana St.	14	6.6	0.8	7.4
—	Malik Sealy	F	6'8"	192	2	St. John's	43	2.7	1.1	6.6
27	Elmore Spencer	C	7'0"	270	2	UNLV	76	5.5	1.0	8.9
35	Loy Vaught	F	6'9"	240	4	Michigan	75	8.7	1.0	11.7
14	Randy Woods	G	6'0"	190	2	La Salle	40	0.7	1.8	3.6

Los Angeles Clippers
1994-95 Season Preview

Opening Line: What can you say about this franchise? Just three years ago, things looked so bright. And now...well, get out the lifeboats. Free agent defections (most recently Dominique Wilkins), a new coach (Bill Fitch), and the same malaise that has characterized the franchise will make for another disappointing season. Some draft-day wheeling and dealing brought a cast of new players to Clipland, including rookie forward Lamond Murray of California, shooter Eric Piatkowski of Nebraska, and former Pacers Malik Sealy and Pooh Richardson.

Guard: Richardson returns to the site of his excellent college career (UCLA) to run L.A.'s offense. Richardson is fantastic in the open court but can be an erratic shooter. Though he has the classic point-guard skills, he needs an attitude improvement. The Clips hope to pair Pooh with high-scoring Ron Harper, but—as of late August—Harper was peddling his wares as a free agent. League scouts think Piatkowski could be a tremendous find. He has unbelievable shooting range, can pass, and understands the game. But is he quick enough to guard anybody? Gary Grant will back up Richardson and will make the Pooh Bear look positively consistent by comparison. Second-year man Terry Dehere has great shooting range but is extremely erratic.

Forward: Murray enters the league with polished scoring skills, a great body, some great college numbers, and a propensity for disappearing in big games. He fills L.A.'s huge scoring need but will require time to develop consistency. Quiet Loy Vaught is a rebounding machine at the four spot and is a deadly finisher inside the paint. It's too bad he's buried in Clipland. Don't expect too much from Sealy, although he will get a chance to play more in L.A. His shooting needs substantial work, and his lithe frame is not suited for frontcourt rough stuff. Charles Outlaw has potential to be a solid inside force.

Center: Stanley Roberts is a huge man with surprising offensive skills around the basket. Injuries, weight, and foul trouble have plagued him. Elmore Spencer is slow, overweight, and overmatched against 90 percent of the pivot men he faces. LeRon Ellis can score well inside but is too thin to hang with the big boys.

Coaching: Bill Fitch, who has coached more games than anyone in NBA history, becomes the Clippers' 15th coach in the last 18 years. Fitch, 60, lost control of his players in New Jersey in 1991-92. It's surprising he's still interested in coaching.

Analysis: The Clippers appear committed to a youth movement, and that means a few more trips to the draft lottery are in order before the playoffs become a reality again. L.A. is betting heavily on Murray and Richardson to be productive right away, and hoping that Piatkowski and Sealy can join Vaught as solid complementary pieces. Even if all that happens, the immediate future looks bleak for the Clippers—as usual.

Prediction: Seventh place, Pacific Division

LOS ANGELES LAKERS

Home: The Great Western Forum
Capacity: 17,505
Year Built: 1967

Address:
3900 W. Manchester Blvd.
P.O. Box 10
Inglewood, CA 90306
(310) 419-3100

Owner: Dr. Jerry Buss
General Manager: Mitch Kupchak
Head Coach: Del Harris
Assistant Coach: Bill Bertka
Assistant Coach: Michael Cooper
Assistant Coach: Larry Drew

Coach Del Harris			
	W	L	Pct.
NBA Record	332	341	.493
W/Lakers	0	0	.000
1993-94 Record	0	0	.000

Lakers History

No team has equaled the tradition and success of the Boston Celtics, but the Lakers have come close. During the franchise's 45 years of existence, it has put a dazzling array of talent onto NBA courts. Along the way, it has won 11 world championships.

The Laker magic began in Minneapolis and was built around 6'10" center George Mikan, clearly the premier player of his day. With Mikan, Bob Pollard, Vern Mikkelsen, and Slater Martin, the Minneapolis Lakers won five titles in six years from 1949-54. In 1960, the team moved to Los Angeles, keeping its Minnesota-style nickname. But the early years in L.A. led to heartbreak, as the Lakers lost in the NBA Finals to the Celtics six times, despite the heroics of guard Jerry West and forward Elgin Baylor.

Even the arrival of Wilt Chamberlain in 1968-69 couldn't stop the string of runner-up finishes. The Lakers dropped the 1968-69 series to the Celtics and the 1969-70 title series to the Knicks. The Lakers gained revenge two years later by going 69-13 (including a 33-game winning streak) and beating New York 4-1 in the Finals.

Kareem Abdul-Jabbar continued the tradition of Hall of Fame pivot men for the Lakers when he was acquired from Milwaukee in 1975. But it wasn't until Magic Johnson was drafted in 1979 that the Lakers truly began to shine. The team won five titles in the 1980s, including two over Boston, and assumed the "Showtime" image that predominated its home city.

Last Seven Years

Season	W	L	Pct.	Place	Playoffs	Coach
1987-88	62	20	.756	First	NBA Champs	Pat Riley
1988-89	57	25	.695	First	L-NBA Finals	Pat Riley
1989-90	63	19	.768	First	L-West Semis	Pat Riley
1990-91	58	24	.707	Second	L-NBA Finals	Mike Dunleavy
1991-92	43	39	.524	Sixth	L-Round 1	Mike Dunleavy
1992-93	39	43	.476	Fifth	L-Round 1	Randy Pfund
1993-94	33	49	.402	Fifth	DNQ	R. Pfund/M. Johnson

1993-94 Review

The 1993-94 Lakers proved that a little Magic doesn't necessarily go a long way. The team's 16-game experiment with former superstar Magic Johnson as coach was unable to salvage the season, as the team finished 33-49 and missed the playoffs for the first time since 1976.

The arrival of Magic, who assumed the team's reins as a favor to Lakers owner Jerry Buss, energized the team briefly as L.A. won four of its first five games under his stewardship to inch closer to Denver in the playoff derby. But a ten-game losing skein at season's end trashed any postseason dreams and left a sour taste in Johnson's mouth. He announced he would not return to the bench for 1994-95.

The 1993-94 Lakers lacked the talent, work habits, and hard-earned pride that had served them so well during the 1980s. The presence of forwards James Worthy and Kurt Rambis was merely for show, as the veterans of the Showtime Era were relegated to bench duty. Injuries sidelined promising second-year guard Anthony Peeler (stress fracture) and back-up center Sam Bowie (knee) for more than half the season, but Laker fans couldn't blame injuries too much for their team's slide. Good, old-fashioned ineptness and disinterest were the main culprits.

Center Vlade Divac (14.2 PPG, 10.8 RPG) enjoyed a healthy season and was a bright spot for L.A., as were rookies Nick Van Exel (13.6 PPG, 5.8 APG) and George Lynch (9.6 PPG, 5.8 RPG). Van Exel, a machine-gunning point man from Cincinnati, just missed the NBA record for 3-pointers by a rookie. Lynch, a stoic product of the Dean Smith system, logged considerable time at small forward.

Power forward Elden Campbell (12.3 PPG, 6.8 RPG) continued to tease the Lakers with his inconsistent play, although his production did increase somewhat under Magic's stern hand. Second-year man Doug Christie (10.3 PPG) was inconsistent at the three spot, but veteran Sedale Threatt proved to be a solid back-up to Van Exel at the point.

1994-95 Roster

No.	Player	Pos.	Ht.	Wt.	Exp.	College	G	RPG	APG	PPG
								|—1993-94—|		
31	Sam Bowie	C	7'1"	263	9	Kentucky	25	5.2	1.9	8.9
41	Elden Campbell	F/C	6'11"	250	4	Clemson	76	6.8	1.1	12.3
8	Doug Christie	G/F	6'6"	205	1	Pepperdine	65	3.6	2.1	10.3
12	Vlade Divac	C	7'1"	260	5	Serbia	79	10.8	3.9	14.2
40	Antonio Harvey	C/F	6'11"	225	1	Pfeiffer	27	2.2	0.2	2.6
—	Eddie Jones	G/F	6'6"	190	R	Temple	—	—	—	—
23	Reggie Jordan	G	6'4"	200	1	New Mexico St.	23	2.9	1.1	5.4
24	George Lynch	F	6'8"	220	1	North Carolina	71	5.8	1.4	9.6
—	Anthony Miller	F	6'9"	255	R	Michigan St.	—	—	—	—
1	Anthony Peeler	G	6'4"	212	2	Missouri	30	3.6	3.1	14.1
34	Tony Smith	G	6'4"	205	4	Marquette	73	2.7	2.0	8.8
3	Sedale Threatt	G	6'2"	185	11	W. Virg. Tech	81	1.9	4.2	11.9
9	Nick Van Exel	G	6'1"	171	1	Cincinnati	81	2.9	5.8	13.6
42	James Worthy	F	6'9"	225	12	North Carolina	80	2.3	1.9	10.1

Los Angeles Lakers
1994-95 Season Preview

Opening Line: NBA commissioner David Stern may have loved the fact that Magic Johnson volunteered to close the 1993-94 season as L.A.'s head coach, but Magic wasn't too thrilled about trying to prepare today's players for battle. So, the Lakers open the 1994-95 season with Del Harris at the helm and will try to resume the business of catching up to the rest of the Pacific Division. First-round pick Eddie Jones of Temple is a positive but hardly earth-shattering acquisition.

Guard: Nick Van Exel developed from a questionable draft pick last season into an unpredictable, exciting point guard. When he's focused and in control, Van Exel can blast past defenders, nail the 3-pointer, and run the team. His emergence puts Sedale Threatt back in the reserve point role, where the veteran is especially productive. Figure Jones for the starting two-guard spot. He can run, jump, and shoot and had one of the quickest first steps to the basket in all of college basketball last year. Anthony Peeler will put up a pretty good fight for the position, but unless he nails more of his shots and can improve his range, he'll be Jones's understudy by January. Tony Smith does a little of everything off the bench.

Forward: Though the team has some recognizable names up front, none has distinguished himself during the past few seasons. Doug Christie has all the physical tools to be a strong swing man, but injuries and rotten shooting have hindered him from developing. James Worthy is at the end of a marvelous career and can only be counted on for small periods of production. Second-year man George Lynch is a strong rebounder with limited offensive skills away from the basket. Trying to figure out power forward Elden Campbell could tax the most patient of people. He has great physical tools but continues to infuriate the Lakers with his lackadaisical attitude.

Center: Now that his back is healthy, Vlade Divac has become a solid NBA center. He rebounds well, can pass, and has a nice shooting touch. He'll never dominate, but he is certainly a plus in the middle. If Sam Bowie is ever healthy again, he'll provide much of the same. Of course, given Bowie's checkered medical history, that is one big "if."

Coaching: Harris has developed a reputation for teaching defense, something that will help a team that allowed opponents to make 47.6 percent of their shots last year. Harris had moderate success with the Milwaukee Bucks in the late 1980s but shouldn't be viewed as the franchise savior. He'll be assisted by Bill Bertka, Larry Drew, and Michael Cooper.

Analysis: The Lakers are a long way from their Showtime days. While the rest of the Pacific Division has been infused with young superstars, Team Hollywood ironically lacks a marquee player. Jones is a solid acquisition, but the Lakers have questions at nearly every position and need a couple more impact players before they can contend again.

Prediction: Fifth place, Pacific Division

PHOENIX SUNS

Home: America West Arena
Capacity: 19,100
Year Built: 1992

Address:
201 E. Jefferson St.
Phoenix, AZ 85004
(602) 379-7900

Chief Executive Officer: Jerry Colangelo
V.P./Player Personnel:
Dick Van Arsdale
Head Coach: Paul Westphal
Assistant Coach: Scotty Robertson
Assistant Coach: Lionel Hollins

Coach Paul Westphal			
	W	L	Pct.
NBA Record	118	46	720
W/Suns	118	46	720
1993-94 Record	56	26	.683

Suns History

If there is one team in the NBA synonymous with the term "near miss," it is the Suns. Throughout its 26-year history, Phoenix has missed out on superstars and championships by the narrowest of margins.

The team's destiny was shaped by a coin toss following the 1968-69 season, when the Suns lost the draft rights to Lew Alcindor to the Milwaukee Bucks. Instead, the Suns chose journeyman-to-be Neal Walk and continued a seven-year run of mediocrity. Players like Connie Hawkins and Dick Van Arsdale made things exciting, but the Suns could only make the playoffs once during the period.

The next close call came during the 1976 playoffs, when underdog Phoenix advanced to the NBA Finals against Boston. With the series tied 2-2, the Suns lost Game 5 in a triple-overtime heart-stopper, 128-126. In 1978-79, center Alvan Adams, forward Truck Robinson, and superb guard Paul Westphal formed a solid nucleus that again fell just short, losing to Seattle in a seven-game Western Conference finals.

The Suns enjoyed some success in the early 1980s and won the Pacific Division in 1980-81. They dropped off in the middle of the decade but picked up the slack again in the late 1980s. Tom Chambers, Kevin Johnson, and Dan Majerle led Phoenix to four straight 50-plus-win seasons. The addition of Charles Barkley pushed Phoenix past the 60-win plateau in 1992-93, and they made it all the way to the NBA Finals before losing to Chicago.

Last Seven Years

Season	W	L	Pct.	Place	Playoffs	Coach
1987-88	28	54	.341	Fourth	DNQ	John Wetzel
1988-89	55	27	.671	Second	L-West Finals	Cotton Fitzsimmons
1989-90	54	28	.659	Third	L-West Finals	Cotton Fitzsimmons
1990-91	55	27	.671	Third	L-Round 1	Cotton Fitzsimmons
1991-92	53	29	.646	Third	L-West Semis	Cotton Fitzsimmons
1992-93	62	20	.756	First	L-NBA Finals	Paul Westphal
1993-94	56	26	.683	Second	L-West Semis	Paul Westphal

1993-94 Review

One year after the Suns seemed so close to winning their first-ever NBA championship, uncertainty ruled the team's future. Phoenix's surprising Western Conference semifinal exit, courtesy of Houston, raised questions about whether the team's window of opportunity had been shut.

Coach Paul Westphal coaxed an injury-riddled team to 56 wins, but Phoenix was unable to dominate its Western foes like it had in 1992-93. The largest dose of doubt came from forward Charles Barkley, who was hobbled by a bad back throughout most of the season and was visibly incapacitated during the playoffs. As always, half a Barkley (21.6 PPG, 11.2 RPG in 65 games) was worth two of most everyone else.

As was the case in 1992-93, the Phoenix backcourt was strong and explosive. Point guard Kevin Johnson (20.0 PPG, 9.5 APG) missed 15 games, as usual, but he was marvelous during the playoffs, picking up much of the slack when Barkley couldn't get it done. Dan Majerle (16.5 PPG) became obsessed with the downtown shot, setting an NBA record for 3-pointers (192). Veteran Danny Ainge (8.9 PPG) had his lowest point production in a decade, and began to show his age in the playoffs, while Frank Johnson (4.6 PPG) was a fine back-up point.

The off-season acquisition of power forward A.C. Green (14.7 PPG, 9.2 RPG) helped the Suns' interior game substantially, and second-year center Oliver Miller (9.2 PPG, 6.9. RPG) continued his development in the middle. Cedric Ceballos (19.1 PPG) missed 29 games with injuries but was a strong scoring threat at forward, picking up where the suspended Richard Dumas (substance abuse) left off last year. Veteran Mark West was a dependable force on defense in the pivot, and Joe Kleine (3.9 PPG) gave Westphal six fouls and some banging underneath.

1994-95 Roster

No.	Player	Pos.	Ht.	Wt.	Exp.	College	G	RPG	APG	PPG
							|—1993-94—|			
22	Danny Ainge	G	6'5"	185	13	Brigham Young	68	1.9	2.6	8.9
34	Charles Barkley	F	6'6"	250	10	Auburn	65	11.2	4.6	21.6
23	Cedric Ceballos	F	6'7"	225	4	Cal. St. Fuller.	53	6.5	1.7	19.1
11	Duane Cooper	G	6'1"	185	2	Southern Cal.	23	0.4	1.2	2.1
21	Richard Dumas	F	6'7"	210	1	Oklahoma St.	—	—	—	—
—	Anthony Goldwire	G	6'1"	182	R	Houston	—	—	—	—
45	A.C. Green	F	6'9"	224	9	Oregon St.	82	9.2	1.7	14.7
7	Kevin Johnson	G	6'1"	190	7	California	67	2.5	9.5	20.0
35	Joe Kleine	C	7'0"	271	9	Arkansas	74	2.6	0.6	3.9
—	Antonio Lang	F/G	6'8"	201	R	Duke	—	—	—	—
27	Malcolm Mackey	F/C	6'10"	248	1	Georgia Tech	22	1.1	0.0	1.5
9	Dan Majerle	G/F	6'6"	220	6	Cent. Michigan	80	4.4	3.8	16.5
—	Danny Manning	F	6'10"	234	6	Kansas	68	6.8	3.8	20.6
25	Oliver Miller	C/F	6'9"	280	2	Arkansas	69	6.9	3.5	9.2
0	Jerrod Mustaf	F	6'10"	244	4	Maryland	33	1.7	0.2	2.2
2	Elliot Perry	G	6'0"	160	2	Memphis St.	27	1.4	4.6	3.9
—	Wesley Person	G/F	6'6"	195	R	Auburn	—	—	—	—

Phoenix Suns
1994-95 Season Preview

Opening Line: Suns management is praising the heavens after signing Danny Manning this summer. The team told the star forward that, because of the salary cap, they didn't have much money to offer him, but he wanted to play in Phoenix anyway. He'll team with Charles Barkley, whose effectiveness could be reduced by age and a career of banging. The Suns had a good draft, swiping accomplished scorer Wesley Person of Auburn late in the first round and adding Duke forward Antonio Lang early in the second.

Guard: All-Star Kevin Johnson will continue to fuel the aggressive Phoenix attack by blasting to the hoop and either scoring or dishing. Backcourt mate Dan Majerle has completed the transition from kamikaze pilot to bombardier and will again be one of the league's top 3-point marksmen. Majerle can still rumble through the lane with regularity. Veteran back-up Danny Ainge can still shoot it, but he's slowing down some. He and ancient Frank Johnson (who may leave as a free agent) form a geriatric reserve backcourt that could use an injection of new life. That should come courtesy of Person, who has his brother's ability to score but not his affinity for bad behavior. He could be a steal.

Forward: The addition of Manning, a multi-talented All-Star, gives Phoenix perhaps the greatest forward corps in the history of basketball. Manning is a wonderful team player who also scores 20 PPG. When injury-free, Barkley is still an unstoppable blend of talent and will. Stoic A.C. Green can play either forward position and brings defense, rebounding, and a selfless persona to a team with plenty of offensive personality. Emerging Cedric Ceballos is an accomplished scorer inside the lane and excellent on the break. Richard Dumas, an explosive small forward, is on the suspended list because of drug problems. Lang is wondering where he's going to play.

Center: Oliver Miller offers a deadly shooting touch in close, excellent shot-blocking ability, and good rebounding skills. Still, Miller's big body could use some more hardening and stamina. Phoenix had to dump Mark West to make room for Manning, leaving bruiser Joe Kleine as the only back-up.

Coaching: Westphal's quiet manner was praised when he brought Phoenix to the brink of the title in 1992-93, but his methods were questioned some last year when the Suns blew a 2-0 lead against Houston. Still, he knows how to handle players and metes out playing time according to talent and attitude—a good philosophy. He is assisted by Lionel Hollins and Scotty Robertson.

Analysis: The Suns enter 1994-95 as the team to beat in the NBA. They have an All-Star at every position except center, plus a pair of reserve forwards that would start for most teams. If Barkley's out of the lineup, the Suns will still be an excellent team. With him, they will dominate.

Prediction: First place, Pacific Division

PORTLAND TRAIL BLAZERS

Home: Memorial Coliseum
Capacity: 12,888
Year Built: 1960

Address:
700 N.E. Multnomah St.
Suite 600
Portland, OR 97232
(503) 234-9291

Chairman: Paul Allen
General Manager: Bob Whitsitt
Head Coach: P.J. Carlesimo
Assistant Coach: Rick Carlisle
Assistant Coach: Dick Harter

Coach P.J. Carlesimo			
	W	L	Pct.
NBA Record	0	0	.000
W/Blazers	0	0	.000
1993-94 Record	0	0	.000

Trail Blazers History

Few teams in sports can boast of fan loyalty the way Portland can. The Blazers have sold out Memorial Coliseum more than 700 consecutive times, believed to be a record for any sport.

Portland was a typical expansion team in the early 1970s, losing far more often than it won and shuttling players and coaches in and out. Early stars included Geoff Petrie, Sidney Wicks, and future Blazers coach Rick Adelman.

Things began to change in 1974 when the Blazers drafted UCLA center Bill Walton. Two years later, Jack Ramsay became coach and led the team to its only NBA title. With Walton serving as a do-everything high-post in Ramsay's motion offense, Portland upset Philadelphia in the 1977 Finals 4-2. Bob Gross, Maurice Lucas, Dave Twardzik, and Lionel Hollins comprised the rest of that starting unit.

The Blazers appeared primed to repeat in 1977-78, but Walton injured his foot and Portland was eliminated by Seattle in the West semifinals. Walton never returned to form, and the Blazers fell behind Los Angeles and Seattle as the top team in the Pacific Division.

In the 1980s, management drafted star guards Clyde Drexler and Terry Porter, and in 1989 Portland traded for rebounding forward Buck Williams. The Blazers had world-championship talent, but they couldn't quite win the big one. Portland fell to Detroit in the 1990 NBA Finals, lost to the Lakers in the 1991 West finals, and fell to Chicago in the 1992 NBA Finals.

Last Seven Years

Season	W	L	Pct.	Place	Playoffs	Coach
1987-88	53	29	.646	Second	L-Round 1	Mike Schuler
1988-89	39	43	.476	Fifth	L-Round 1	M. Schuler/R. Adelman
1989-90	59	23	.720	Second	L-NBA Finals	Rick Adelman
1990-91	63	19	.768	First	L-West Finals	Rick Adelman
1991-92	57	25	.695	First	L-NBA Finals	Rick Adelman
1992-93	51	31	.622	Third	L-Round 1	Rick Adelman
1993-94	47	35	.573	Fourth	L-Round 1	Rick Adelman

1993-94 Review

The window of championship opportunity that seemed so wide open earlier this decade has finally slammed shut in the City of Roses. Portland's first-round loss to Houston was the team's second straight speedy postseason exit and exposed the aging Blazers as a team in serious need of some new legs. Though Portland had some injury trouble, most notably center Chris Dudley's broken ankle, its fourth-place Pacific finish was the result of a nucleus that had clearly seen better days. The Blazers failed to win 50 games for the first time since 1988-89 and were never a threat to Seattle or Phoenix.

Shooting guard Clyde Drexler (19.2 PPG) was healthy and productive most of the year, but the legendary bounce had been mostly drained from his achy legs. Drexler shot just 42.8 percent from the field and spent a lot of time bombing away from the perimeter—with poor results. Veteran power forward Buck Williams (9.7 PPG, 10.4 RPG) continued to be a force on the backboards, but at age 34, his days of dominating younger four men were over.

Dudley, acquired as a free agent before the season to give Portland a sturdy defensive presence in the middle, played only six regular-season games before succumbing to injury. Emerging star Clifford Robinson was then called upon to play in the middle—not his best position. Despite the relocation, Robinson (20.1 PPG, 6.7 RPG) was a force, scoring from everywhere while making his presence felt at the defensive end.

Harvey Grant (10.4 PPG), stolen from Washington for Kevin Duckworth, was adequate at small forward, but his production fell significantly as he tried to fit in with the rest of the Blazers' high scorers. Once known for an awful attitude, point guard Rod Strickland (17.2 PPG, 9.0 APG) took over the lead-guard spot from Terry Porter (13.1 PPG, 5.2 APG) and emerged as one of the conference's best. Reserve forward Tracy Murray led the league in 3-point shooting (.459), while Jerome Kersey continued to digress. Rebounding specialist Mark Bryant was a solid interior fill-in.

1994-95 Roster

No.	Player	Pos.	Ht.	Wt.	Exp.	College	G	RPG	APG	PPG
								——1993-94——		
2	Mark Bryant	F	6'9"	245	6	Seton Hall	79	4.0	0.5	5.6
22	Clyde Drexler	G	6'7"	222	11	Houston	68	6.5	4.9	19.2
44	Harvey Grant	F	6'9"	235	6	Oklahoma	77	4.6	1.4	10.4
25	Jerome Kersey	F	6'7"	225	10	Longwood	78	4.2	1.0	6.5
—	Aaron McKie	G	6'5"	209	R	Temple	—	—	—	—
31	Tracy Murray	G/F	6'8"	225	2	UCLA	66	1.7	0.5	6.6
30	Terry Porter	G	6'3"	195	9	Wis.-Stevens Pt.	77	2.8	5.2	13.1
3	Clifford Robinson	F/C	6'10"	225	5	Connecticut	82	6.7	1.9	20.1
26	James Robinson	G	6'2"	180	1	Alabama	58	1.3	1.2	4.8
—	Shawnelle Scott	F/C	6'11"	260	R	St. John's	—	—	—	—
1	Rod Strickland	G	6'3"	185	6	DePaul	82	4.5	9.0	17.2
52	Buck Williams	F	6'8"	225	13	Maryland	81	10.4	1.0	9.7
6	Joe Wolf	F/C	6'11"	230	7	North Carolina	—	—	—	—

Portland Trail Blazers
1994-95 Season Preview

Opening Line: Though the Blazer lineup has undergone some changes from the unit that challenged for the NBA title in the early 1990s, Portland remains a team caught in neutral, unable to reinvent itself to catch the Western Conference's new powers. To inject some new life, Portland's management hired former Seton Hall whiz P.J. Carlesimo to handle the coaching chores. He and draft pick Aaron McKie of Temple begin the process of rebirth.

Guard: Once a loose-cannon point guard, Rod Strickland has become a sturdy starter who can score, distribute, and thrill. His emergence has relegated Terry Porter to the bench but has helped the overall Blazer rotation. Porter can still shoot well from 3-point range and knows how to run a team, but he is losing steam and struggles from inside the arc. Clyde Drexler's aging knees have limited his playing time and offensive repertoire. Once known as "The Glide," Drexler now is content to launch treys, unable to swoop through defenses anymore. Expect Carlesimo to groom McKie, a solid player with an NBA-type body and questionable long-range shooting ability, as Drexler's replacement. James "Hollywood" Robinson is a wild second-year player whose minutes will slip at two guard.

Forward: Venerable Buck Williams continues to rebound, make lay-ups, and play solid baseline defense, but his age and limited mobility make him fodder for Pacific power forwards like Shawn Kemp and Chris Webber. Harvey Grant endured off-season wrist surgery that will hamper him early on, meaning Jerome Kersey might have to man the three spot this fall. Kersey was once a big-league small forward, but his game has deteriorated year after year. Tracy Murray is purely a downtown shooter, albeit a darn good one.

Center: Clifford Robinson has moved into the starting pivot position and delivered. Hardly a prototype center because of his size (6'10", 225) and better suited for Williams's four spot—when he retires—Robinson is mobile, active, and able to put 20 points on the board. The Blazers would love to have a healthy Chris Dudley in the middle for his defense and rebounding. Big Mark Bryant is an effective banger in reserve.

Coaching: Carlesimo transformed the Hall from a tiny New Jersey patsy to a national power, using his considerable knowledge of the game and his intensity. He is qualified to coach in the NBA, but is his high-strung personality suited for the grind? Carlesimo knows how to motivate younger players, but Portland's vets may not go for his approach. He's assisted by Rick Carlisle and Dick Harter.

Analysis: Portland is at a crucial time in its history. The Blazers need McKie to develop at off guard and Dudley to be a legitimate pivot man—something he hasn't ever been—if they are to contend. That's asking a lot. The Blazers won't stink up the joint, but they won't approach the Pacific's top guns either.

Prediction: Fourth place, Pacific Division

SACRAMENTO KINGS

Home: ARCO Arena
Capacity: 17,317
Year Built: 1988

Address:
One Sports Parkway
Sacramento, CA 95834
(916) 928-0000

Managing General Partner: Jim Thomas
General Manager: Geoff Petrie
Head Coach: Garry St. Jean
Assistant Coach: Mike Schuler
Assistant Coach: Eddie Jordan
Assistant Coach: Mike Bratz

Coach Garry St. Jean			
	W	L	Pct.
NBA Record	53	111	.323
W/Kings	53	111	.323
1993-94 Record	28	54	.341

Kings History

Like the sun rises in the East and sets in the West, so has the Royals/Kings franchise. The Rochester (New York) Royals, a charter member of the NBA, won the franchise's only league title in 1950-51. But cross-country franchise moves, ending in Sacramento, have only led to futility.

That Rochester championship team featured a slick backcourt of Bob Davies, Bobby Wanzer, and Red Holzman, with Arnie Risen in the middle. Rochester advanced to the West finals in 1951-52, but it lost to Minneapolis. The Royals made the playoffs only once from 1956-61, though they featured a potent forecourt of Maurice Stokes, Jack Twyman, and Clyde Lovellette.

The team moved to Cincinnati for the 1957-58 season and added exciting rookie Oscar Robertson in 1960. The Royals advanced to the Eastern finals in 1962-63 and 1963-64, thanks to Robertson, Twyman, and 1963-64 Rookie of the Year Jerry Lucas, but the success was short-lived. The team didn't have a winning season from 1966-67 to 1973-74 and moved again in 1972, splitting time between Kansas City and Omaha as the Kings.

In 1974-75, the team won 44 games and featured brilliant point guard Nate "Tiny" Archibald. The 1980-81 edition lost to Houston in the conference finals. The most recent move came in 1985, when the franchise landed in Sacramento. Aside from a brief playoff appearance that season, the club has been a perennial lottery team ever since.

Last Seven Years

Season	W	L	Pct.	Place	Playoffs	Coach
1987-88	24	58	.293	Sixth	DNQ	B. Russell/J. Reynolds
1988-89	27	55	.329	Sixth	DNQ	Jerry Reynolds
1989-90	23	59	.280	Seventh	DNQ	J. Reynolds/D. Motta
1990-91	25	57	.305	Seventh	DNQ	Dick Motta
1991-92	29	53	.347	Seventh	DNQ	Dick Motta/Rex Hughes
1992-93	25	57	.305	Seventh	DNQ	Garry St. Jean
1993-94	28	54	.341	Sixth	DNQ	Garry St. Jean

1993-94 Review

After four consecutive dead-last finishes in the NBA's Pacific Division, the 1993-94 Kings won 28 games and moved into sixth. You'll have to pardon the residents of California's capital for not popping champagne corks. It was another one of those years in Sacramento, in which a thin roster and untimely injuries conspired to keep the team among the league's worst.

The Kings qualified for another draft lottery and showed few signs of becoming a playoff contender any time soon. That could change if the team would stay healthy for a full season. Last year, Walt Williams and rookie point man Bobby Hurley were sidelined for extended periods. Hurley's injuries were particularly disconcerting. He lasted just 19 games before a horrible automobile accident put his basketball career in jeopardy. His misfortune cast an early pall over the team.

As usual, the Kings were miserable defensively, allowing the third-most points in the NBA. And coach Garry St. Jean's up-tempo offense wasn't much better, producing just 101.1 PPG and 45.2-percent aggregate shooting. There were a few highlights, most notably Mitch Richmond (23.4 PPG), who rebounded from his broken thumb to assert himself as one of the league's best guards. Forwards Wayman Tisdale (16.7 PPG, 7.1 RPG) and Lionel Simmons (15.1 PPG, 7.5 RPG) were solid, and midseason acquisition Olden Polynice (11.6 PPG, 11.9 RPG) was his usual rebounding self in the pivot.

Spud Webb (12.7 PPG, 6.7 APG) was adequate at the point, but the Kings lacked depth. Williams proved he could do a lot of things pretty well but nothing spectacular before exiting with a severely sprained ankle.

Trevor Wilson (8.2 PPG) and CBA pick-up Andre Spencer (5.7 PPG) were hardly stalwarts at forward, and Randy Brown (4.5 PPG) was a mediocre reserve guard. Causwell (4.4 PPG) was again felled by injuries and missed half the season, and rookie center Mike Peplowski simply took up space.

1994-95 Roster

| | | | | | | | —1993-94— | | |
No.	Player	Pos.	Ht.	Wt.	Exp.	College	G	RPG	APG	PPG
7	Frank Brickowski	F/C	6'10"	250	10	Penn St.	71	5.7	3.1	13.2
3	Randy Brown	G	6'3"	190	3	New Mexico St.	61	1.8	2.2	4.5
34	Duane Causwell	C	7'0"	240	4	Temple	41	4.5	0.3	4.4
—	Brian Grant	F	6'9"	254	R	Xavier	—	—	—	—
—	L. Funderburke	F	6'9"	230	R	Ohio St.	—	—	—	—
7	Bobby Hurley	G	6'0"	165	1	Duke	19	1.8	6.1	7.1
54	Mike Peplowski	C	6'11"	270	1	Michigan St.	55	3.1	0.4	3.2
0	Olden Polynice	C	7'0"	250	7	Virginia	68	11.9	0.6	11.6
2	Mitch Richmond	G	6'5"	215	6	Kansas St.	78	3.7	4.0	23.4
22	Lionel Simmons	F	6'7"	210	4	La Salle	75	7.5	4.1	15.1
15	LaBradford Smith	G	6'3"	205	3	Louisville	66	1.3	1.7	5.0
—	Michael Smith	F	6'7"	233	R	Providence	—	—	—	—
20	Andre Spencer	F	6'6"	220	2	N. Arizona	28	2.6	0.8	5.7
4	Spud Webb	G	5'7"	135	9	N. Carolina St.	79	2.8	6.7	12.7
42	Walt Williams	G/F	6'8"	230	2	Maryland	57	4.1	2.3	11.2
21	Trevor Wilson	F	6'8"	215	2	UCLA	57	4.8	1.3	8.2

Sacramento Kings
1994-95 Season Preview

Opening Line: If any rebuilding process can be described as brick-by-brick, it is Sacramento's. Each year, the Kings make little, if any, tangible progress in the Pacific Division, and this season should be no exception. A healthy Bobby Hurley will help at point guard, and the addition of forwards Brian Grant of Xavier, Michael Smith of Providence, and Lawrence Funderburke of Ohio State should beef up the Kings' inside presence. Free-agent forward Frank Brickowski will also help up front.

Guard: The horrible auto accident derailed Hurley's NBA development almost at its outset. Though doctors expect a full recovery, there are still many questions about the Duke product, particularly his size, strength, and shooting ability. There are no questions about his backcourt mate, Mitch Richmond. A luminous presence amidst Sacramento's mediocrity, Richmond is an outstanding pure shooter with a tremendous ability to get to the basket. If Hurley isn't 100 percent, veteran Spud Webb, who handled last year's demotion with class, will run the team. The book on Webb is well-worn. He's small, quick, and fair with the shot. He's a defensive liability but knows how to run a team. Reserve Randy Brown is a tough defender with limited range and an affinity for fouling opponents.

Forward: What do you do with Walt Williams? At 6'8", he's not a real guard; and because of his thin frame, he isn't particularly suited for forward. Williams is a classic 'tweener who brings excellent skills but a poor shooting touch to several positions. Veteran three man Lionel Simmons can shoot, although his numbers fell somewhat last year. The veteran Brickowski can hold his own at power forward, while three man Trevor Wilson can fill it up in a hurry off the bench. Grant is an interesting prospect who should score and rebound pretty well, while Smith and Funderburke add bulk at the four spot.

Center: Adding Olden Polynice was a great stopgap move for the Kings, but he is not a long-term solution. Polynice is a ferocious rebounder and strong defender, but he doesn't score as well as you'd like. Duane Causwell has gone from prospect to bust. Second-year man Mike Peplowski takes up a bunch of space but is awfully slow.

Coaching: Garry St. Jean still can't get the Kings to play defense. Opponents shot 47.9 percent against Sacramento last year and scored 106.9 PPG. Maybe the guy should attend a Pat Riley clinic or something, because a few more years like 1993-94 and St. Jean's going to be looking for work. He's assisted by Mike Bratz, Eddie Jordan, and Mike Schuler.

Analysis: The Kings could break the 30-win barrier this year, but don't expect them to leave it in their rear-view mirrors. Sacramento needs to play better defense, improve its point-guard play, and establish a strong presence in the middle. History indicates that any progress they make will be minimal.

Prediction: Sixth place, Pacific Division

SEATTLE SUPERSONICS

Home: The Coliseum
Capacity: 14,252
Year Built: 1962

Address:
190 Queen Anne Ave. N.
Suite 200
Seattle, WA 98109
(206) 281-5800

Owner: Barry Ackerley
President/G.M.: Wally Walker
Head Coach: George Karl
Assistant Coach: Bob Kloppenburg
Assistant Coach: Tim Grgurich

Coach George Karl			
	W	L	Pct.
NBA Record	264	237	.527
W/Sonics	145	61	.704
1993-94 Record	63	19	.768

SuperSonics History

Prior to Seattle's resurgence in the 1990s, there was only one Sonic boom. It came in the late 1970s.

Seattle's 1977-78 team featured rookie center Jack Sikma, rebounding machine Paul Silas, and the guard triumvirate of Gus Johnson, Dennis Johnson, and "Downtown" Fred Brown. They fell in seven games to Washington in the NBA Finals. The team was not denied the following season. The Sonics soared to the Pacific Division championship and dispatched Los Angeles and Phoenix in the playoffs. The Sonics won the title in five games over the Bullets.

That two-year period stands in stark contrast to the team's early years. Born in 1967, the team failed to qualify for the playoffs for seven seasons and boasted few stars other than powerful Bob Rule and highly talented but enigmatic Spencer Haywood. Seattle made it to the Western semifinals in 1974-75 and 1975-76, setting the stage for its runs to the Finals.

After a 56-26 season in 1979-80, the Sonics wallowed through a decade of mediocrity. The 1986-87 season was a stunner, however. Despite finishing with a losing record, the Sonics advanced to the Western finals, thanks to the high-scoring trio of Xavier McDaniel, Dale Ellis, and Tom Chambers. A new cast of characters emerged in the early 1990s, headed by Shawn Kemp and Gary Payton and coached by George Karl. They roared to the 1993 Western finals, where they lost to Phoenix in seven games.

Last Seven Years

Season	W	L	Pct.	Place	Playoffs	Coach
1987-88	44	38	.537	Third	L-Round 1	Bernie Bickerstaff
1988-89	47	35	.573	Third	L-West Semis	Bernie Bickerstaff
1989-90	41	41	.500	Fourth	DNQ	Bernie Bickerstaff
1990-91	41	41	.500	Fifth	L-Round 1	K.C. Jones
1991-92	47	35	.573	Fourth	L-West Semis	K.C. Jones/George Karl
1992-93	55	27	.671	Second	L-West Finals	George Karl
1993-94	63	19	.768	First	L-Round 1	George Karl

1993-94 Review

What was supposed to be a season of success and celebration in Seattle was quickly reduced to one of ignominy, depression, and despair. The Sonics, proud holders of the NBA's best record (63-19), were humiliated in the first round of the playoffs by the upstart Denver Nuggets. By losing in five games, the brash Sonics became the first-ever top-seeded team to lose to an eighth seed.

Seattle had rolled to the gaudy regular-season mark on the strength of its diverse ten-man rotation, a smothering fullcourt defense, and a mix-and-match passel of veterans and youngsters united in their ability to talk junk and overwhelm opponents. In the wake of the first-round loss, some cracks were evident in Seattle's alleged invincibility.

Despite the collection of talent, the Sonics had no go-to guy. And while their defense forced a league-leading 20.3 turnovers per game, it wasn't as effective in halfcourt sets as in the open court. Coach George Karl may have deflected criticism about his style with the 63 wins from November-April, but three losses in May resurrected questions about his capabilities.

Still, it was a great regular-season ride. Emerging power forward Shawn Kemp (18.1 PPG, 10.8 RPG) moved one step closer to superstardom with his athletic inside game, while trash-spewing point guard Gary Payton (16.5 PPG, 6.0 APG) triggered the Sonic defensive assault with his relentless pressure. Talent abounded everywhere else.

Off-season acquisition Kendall Gill (14.1 PPG) teamed with veteran Ricky Pierce (14.5 PPG) to give Seattle a tremendous combination at two guard, while Nate McMillan brought an excellent floor game to the reserve point spot. Multi-talented forward Detlef Schrempf (15.0 PPG, 5.6 RPG, 3.4 APG), acquired just before the season for Derrick McKey, had another tremendous season.

Swing man Vincent Askew (9.1 PPG) provided instant pop off the bench, while veteran forward/center Sam Perkins (12.3 PPG, 4.5 RPG) was a steadying influence on and off the court. Powerful Michael Cage (5.4 RPG) continued to be a force on the boards.

1994-95 Roster

No.	Player	Pos.	Ht.	Wt.	Exp.	College	1993-94		
							G	RPG	APG	PPG
17	Vincent Askew	G	6'6"	226	5	Memphis St.	80	2.3	2.4	9.1
13	Kendall Gill	G	6'5"	200	4	Illinois	79	3.4	3.5	14.1
21	Byron Houston	F	6'5"	250	2	Oklahoma St.	71	2.7	0.5	2.8
50	Ervin Johnson	C	6'11"	242	1	New Orleans	45	2.6	0.2	2.6
40	Shawn Kemp	F	6'10"	245	5	None	79	10.8	2.6	18.1
35	Chris King	F	6'8"	215	1	Wake Forest	15	1.0	0.7	3.7
—	S. Marciulionis	G	6'5"	215	4	Lithuania	—	—	—	—
10	Nate McMillan	G/F	6'5"	197	8	N. Carolina St.	73	3.9	5.3	6.0
20	Gary Payton	G	6'4"	190	4	Oregon St.	82	3.3	6.0	16.5
4	Sam Perkins	F/C	6'9"	257	10	North Carolina	81	4.5	1.4	12.3
—	Zeljko Rebraca	C	6'11"	198	R	Serbia	—	—	—	—
11	Detlef Schrempf	F	6'10"	230	9	Washington	81	5.6	3.4	15.0
—	Dontonio Wingfield	F	6'8"	246	R	Cincinnati	—	—	—	—

Seattle SuperSonics
1994-95 Season Preview

Opening Line: Sifting through the rubble of the Sonics' humiliating first-round playoff departure was not an easy task. Rising again will be even tougher. According to whom one believed, the 1993-94 Sonics were done in by arrogance, the inability to play halfcourt basketball, poor coaching, or all of the above. Convincing this team of talented, albeit egotistical, players that the future is still bright may prove daunting. To facilitate its rebound, Seattle was active this summer, acquiring Sarunas Marciulionis and Byron Houston from Golden State for Ricky Pierce and rookie Carlos Rogers.

Guard: Gary Payton has matured into an All-Star-calibre point guard. Supremely talented offensively and defensively, Payton is tarnished only by his propensity for talking trash. Kendall Gill is a multi-talented off guard, but he is not the kind of bomber this team needs. If his knee and back are healthy, Marciulionis will provide plenty of scoring and lots of hustle. Nate McMillan is a top-flight point reserve who shoots it well from downtown and is a demon on defense.

Forward: Few teams can boast the collection of frontcourt talent Seattle has. Shawn Kemp has blossomed from man-child to all man, and his power game makes him one of the league's premier four men. Detlef Schrempf just does everything well—from scoring to rebounding to passing—and is an unselfish complement to his big-ego teammates. Vincent Askew is capable of scoring points in bunches. Houston is undersized at 6'5", but he can rebound and should be an asset in Seattle's pressure defense. Veteran Michael Cage was not re-signed, but powerful rookie Dontonio Wingfield has promise.

Center: In an age of giant, low-post monsters, Sam Perkins hardly fits the bill, with his propensity for lurking along the perimeter. But the veteran can go inside, score with either hand, grab enough rebounds, and play some solid defense. What the Sonics could use is a quality back-up. Second-year man Ervin Johnson is thin and progressing slowly.

Coaching: Karl has been praised and ridiculed for his job in Seattle. Some still believe he has the ability to take the Sonics to the title, while others point at his checkered past and wonder. If he is to be successful, though, he must exercise a little more control over the players and prepare them better for the rigors of postseason play. He is assisted by Tim Grgurich and Bob Kloppenburg.

Analysis: Last year's quick exit could be a tremendous learning experience for Seattle. If this talented team concentrates and plays hard against every playoff opponent, whether it's the Nuggets or Knicks, it will succeed. The talent is there, and there is still time to achieve plenty. It's all up to the Sonics. Kemp, Payton, and Gill are all big-time talents with long, productive careers ahead of them. What they need most is guidance and a system that allows them to adapt to teams that slow things down.

Prediction: Second place, Pacific Division

N B A Awards and Records

This section showcases the NBA's champions, award-winners, and record-setters—as well as a history of No. 1 draft picks. Here is a breakdown of what you'll find:

- World Champions

- Most Valuable Players
- Rookies of the Year
- Most Improved Players
- NBA Finals MVPs
- Defensive Players of the Year
- Sixth Man Award winners
- Coaches of the Year

- All-NBA Teams
- All-Rookie Teams
- All-Defensive Teams

- All-Star Game results

- career leaders
- active career leaders
- regular-season records
- game records
- team records—season
- team records—game
- playoff records—career
- playoff records—series
- playoff records—game
- playoff records—team

- history of No. 1 draft picks

WORLD CHAMPIONS

	CHAMPION	FINALIST	RESULT		CHAMPION	FINALIST	RESULT
1946-47	Philadelphia	Chicago	4-1	1970-71	Milwaukee	Baltimore	4-0
1947-48	Baltimore	Philadelphia	4-2	1971-72	Los Angeles	New York	4-1
1948-49	Minneapolis	Washington	4-2	1972-73	New York	Los Angeles	4-1
1949-50	Minneapolis	Syracuse	4-2	1973-74	Boston	Milwaukee	4-3
1950-51	Rochester	New York	4-3	1974-75	Golden State	Washington	4-0
1951-52	Minneapolis	New York	4-3	1975-76	Boston	Phoenix	4-2
1952-53	Minneapolis	New York	4-1	1976-77	Portland	Philadelphia	4-2
1953-54	Minneapolis	Syracuse	4-3	1977-78	Washington	Seattle	4-3
1954-55	Syracuse	Fort Wayne	4-3	1978-79	Seattle	Washington	4-1
1955-56	Philadelphia	Fort Wayne	4-1	1979-80	Los Angeles	Philadelphia	4-2
1956-57	Boston	St. Louis	4-3	1980-81	Boston	Houston	4-2
1957-58	St. Louis	Boston	4-2	1981-82	Los Angeles	Philadelphia	4-2
1958-59	Boston	Minneapolis	4-0	1982-83	Philadelphia	Los Angeles	4-0
1959-60	Boston	St. Louis	4-3	1983-84	Boston	Los Angeles	4-3
1960-61	Boston	St. Louis	4-1	1984-85	L.A. Lakers	Boston	4-2
1961-62	Boston	Los Angeles	4-3	1985-86	Boston	Houston	4-2
1962-63	Boston	Los Angeles	4-2	1986-87	L.A. Lakers	Boston	4-2
1963-64	Boston	San Francisco	4-1	1987-88	L.A. Lakers	Detroit	4-3
1964-65	Boston	Los Angeles	4-1	1988-89	Detroit	L.A. Lakers	4-0
1965-66	Boston	Los Angeles	4-3	1989-90	Detroit	Portland	4-1
1966-67	Philadelphia	San Francisco	4-2	1990-91	Chicago	L.A. Lakers	4-1
1967-68	Boston	Los Angeles	4-2	1991-92	Chicago	Portland	4-2
1968-69	Boston	Los Angeles	4-3	1992-93	Chicago	Phoenix	4-2
1969-70	New York	Los Angeles	4-3	1993-94	Houston	New York	4-3

MOST VALUABLE PLAYERS

	PLAYER	PPG		PLAYER	PPG
1955-56	Bob Pettit, St. Louis	25.7	1975-76	Kareem Abdul-Jabbar, L.A.	27.7
1956-57	Bob Cousy, Boston	20.6	1976-77	Kareem Abdul-Jabbar, L.A.	26.2
1957-58	Bill Russell, Boston	16.6	1977-78	Bill Walton, Portland	18.9
1958-59	Bob Pettit, St. Louis	29.2	1978-79	Moses Malone, Houston	24.8
1959-60	Wilt Chamberlain, Phil.	37.6	1979-80	Kareem Abdul-Jabbar, L.A.	24.8
1960-61	Bill Russell, Boston	16.9	1980-81	Julius Erving, Philadelphia	24.6
1961-62	Bill Russell, Boston	18.9	1981-82	Moses Malone, Houston	31.1
1962-63	Bill Russell, Boston	16.8	1982-83	Moses Malone, Philadelphia	24.5
1963-64	Oscar Robertson, Cincinnati	31.4	1983-84	Larry Bird, Boston	24.2
1964-65	Bill Russell, Boston	14.1	1984-85	Larry Bird, Boston	28.7
1965-66	Wilt Chamberlain, Phil.	33.5	1985-86	Larry Bird, Boston	25.8
1966-67	Wilt Chamberlain, Phil.	24.1	1986-87	Magic Johnson, L.A. Lakers	23.9
1967-68	Wilt Chamberlain, Phil.	24.3	1987-88	Michael Jordan, Chicago	35.0
1968-69	Wes Unseld, Baltimore	13.8	1988-89	Magic Johnson, L.A. Lakers	22.5
1969-70	Willis Reed, New York	21.7	1989-90	Magic Johnson, L.A. Lakers	22.3
1970-71	Lew Alcindor, Milwaukee	31.7	1990-91	Michael Jordan, Chicago	31.5
1971-72	Kareem Abdul-Jabbar, Mil.	34.8	1991-92	Michael Jordan, Chicago	30.1
1972-73	Dave Cowens, Boston	20.5	1992-93	Charles Barkley, Phoenix	25.6
1973-74	Kareem Abdul-Jabbar, Mil.	27.0	1993-94	Hakeem Olajuwon, Houston	27.3
1974-75	Bob McAdoo, Buffalo	34.5			

ROOKIES OF THE YEAR

1952-53	Don Meineke, Fort Wayne	1973-74	Ernie DiGregorio, Buffalo
1953-54	Ray Felix, Baltimore	1974-75	Keith Wilkes, Golden State
1954-55	Bob Pettit, Milwaukee	1975-76	Alvan Adams, Phoenix
1955-56	Maurice Stokes, Rochester	1976-77	Adrian Dantley, Buffalo
1956-57	Tom Heinsohn, Boston	1977-78	Walter Davis, Phoenix
1957-58	Woody Sauldsberry, Philadelphia	1978-79	Phil Ford, Kansas City
1958-59	Elgin Baylor, Minneapolis	1979-80	Larry Bird, Boston
1959-60	Wilt Chamberlain, Philadelphia	1980-81	Darrell Griffith, Utah
1960-61	Oscar Robertson, Cincinnati	1981-82	Buck Williams, New Jersey
1961-62	Walt Bellamy, Chicago	1982-83	Terry Cummings, San Diego
1962-63	Terry Dischinger, Chicago	1983-84	Ralph Sampson, Houston
1963-64	Jerry Lucas, Cincinnati	1984-85	Michael Jordan, Chicago
1964-65	Willis Reed, New York	1985-86	Patrick Ewing, New York
1965-66	Rick Barry, San Francisco	1986-87	Chuck Person, Indiana
1966-67	Dave Bing, Detroit	1987-88	Mark Jackson, New York
1967-68	Earl Monroe, Baltimore	1988-89	Mitch Richmond, Golden State
1968-69	Wes Unseld, Baltimore	1989-90	David Robinson, San Antonio
1969-70	Lew Alcindor, Milwaukee	1990-91	Derrick Coleman, New Jersey
1970-71	Dave Cowens, Boston	1991-92	Larry Johnson, Charlotte
	Geoff Petrie, Portland	1992-93	Shaquille O'Neal, Orlando
1971-72	Sidney Wicks, Portland	1993-94	Chris Webber, Golden State
1972-73	Bob McAdoo, Buffalo		

MOST IMPROVED PLAYERS

1985-86	Alvin Robertson, San Antonio	1990-91	Scott Skiles, Orlando
1986-87	Dale Ellis, Seattle	1991-92	Pervis Ellison, Washington
1987-88	Kevin Duckworth, Portland	1992-93	Chris Jackson, Denver
1988-89	Kevin Johnson, Phoenix	1993-94	Don MacLean, Washington
1989-90	Rony Seikaly, Miami		

NBA FINALS MVPS

1969	Jerry West, Los Angeles	1982	Magic Johnson, Los Angeles
1970	Willis Reed, New York	1983	Moses Malone, Philadelphia
1971	Lew Alcindor, Milwaukee	1984	Larry Bird, Boston
1972	Wilt Chamberlain, Los Angeles	1985	Kareem Abdul-Jabbar, L.A. Lakers
1973	Willis Reed, New York	1986	Larry Bird, Boston
1974	John Havlicek, Boston	1987	Magic Johnson, L.A. Lakers
1975	Rick Barry, Golden State	1988	James Worthy, L.A. Lakers
1976	Jo Jo White, Boston	1989	Joe Dumars, Detroit
1977	Bill Walton, Portland	1990	Isiah Thomas, Detroit
1978	Wes Unseld, Washington	1991	Michael Jordan, Chicago
1979	Dennis Johnson, Seattle	1992	Michael Jordan, Chicago
1980	Magic Johnson, Los Angeles	1993	Michael Jordan, Chicago
1981	Cedric Maxwell, Boston	1994	Hakeem Olajuwon, Houston

DEFENSIVE PLAYERS OF THE YEAR

1982-83	Sidney Moncrief, Milwaukee	1988-89	Mark Eaton, Utah
1983-84	Sidney Moncrief, Milwaukee	1989-90	Dennis Rodman, Detroit
1984-85	Mark Eaton, Utah	1990-91	Dennis Rodman, Detroit
1985-86	Alvin Robertson, San Antonio	1991-92	David Robinson, San Antonio
1986-87	Michael Cooper, L.A. Lakers	1992-93	Hakeem Olajuwon, Houston
1987-88	Michael Jordan, Chicago	1993-94	Hakeem Olajuwon, Houston

SIXTH MAN AWARD WINNERS

1982-83	Bobby Jones, Philadelphia	1988-89	Eddie Johnson, Phoenix
1983-84	Kevin McHale, Boston	1989-90	Ricky Pierce, Milwaukee
1984-85	Kevin McHale, Boston	1990-91	Detlef Schrempf, Indiana
1985-86	Bill Walton, Boston	1991-92	Detlef Schrempf, Indiana
1986-87	Ricky Pierce, Milwaukee	1992-93	Cliff Robinson, Portland
1987-88	Roy Tarpley, Dallas	1993-94	Dell Curry, Charlotte

COACHES OF THE YEAR

1962-63	Harry Gallatin, St. Louis	1978-79	Cotton Fitzsimmons, Kansas City
1963-64	Alex Hannum, San Francisco	1979-80	Bill Fitch, Boston
1964-65	Red Auerbach, Boston	1980-81	Jack McKinney, Indiana
1965-66	Dolph Schayes, Philadelphia	1981-82	Gene Shue, Washington
1966-67	Johnny Kerr, Chicago	1982-83	Don Nelson, Milwaukee
1967-68	Richie Guerin, St. Louis	1983-84	Frank Layden, Utah
1968-69	Gene Shue, Baltimore	1984-85	Don Nelson, Milwaukee
1969-70	Red Holzman, New York	1985-86	Mike Fratello, Atlanta
1970-71	Dick Motta, Chicago	1986-87	Mike Schuler, Portland
1971-72	Bill Sharman, Los Angeles	1987-88	Doug Moe, Denver
1972-73	Tom Heinsohn, Boston	1988-89	Cotton Fitzsimmons, Phoenix
1973-74	Ray Scott, Detroit	1989-90	Pat Riley, L.A. Lakers
1974-75	Phil Johnson, K.C.-Omaha	1990-91	Don Chaney, Houston
1975-76	Bill Fitch, Cleveland	1991-92	Don Nelson, Golden State
1976-77	Tom Nissalke, Houston	1992-93	Pat Riley, New York
1977-78	Hubie Brown, Atlanta	1993-94	Lenny Wilkens, Atlanta

ALL-NBA TEAMS

1946-47
Joe Fulks, PHI
Bob Feerick, WAS
Stan Miasek, DET
Bones McKinney, WAS
Max Zaslofsky, CHI

1947-48
Joe Fulks, PHI
Max Zaslofsky, CHI
Ed Sadowski, BOS
Howie Dallmar, PHI
Bob Feerick, WAS

1948-49
George Mikan, MIN
Joe Fulks, PHI
Bob Davies, ROC
Max Zaslofsky, CHI
Jim Pollard, MIN

1949-50
George Mikan, MIN
Jim Pollard, MIN
Alex Groza, IND
Bob Davies, ROC
Max Zaslofsky, CHI

1950-51
George Mikan, MIN
Alex Groza, IND
Ed Macauley, BOS
Bob Davies, ROC
Ralph Beard, IND

1951-52
George Mikan, MIN
Ed Macauley, BOS
Paul Arizin, PHI
Bob Cousy, BOS
Bob Davies, ROC
Dolph Schayes, SYR

1952-53
George Mikan, MIN
Bob Cousy, BOS
Neil Johnston, PHI
Ed Macauley, BOS
Dolph Schayes, SYR

1953-54
Bob Cousy, BOS
Neil Johnston, PHI

George Mikan, MIN
Dolph Schayes, SYR
Harry Gallatin, NY

1954-55
Neil Johnston, PHI
Bob Cousy, BOS
Dolph Schayes, SYR
Bob Pettit, MIL
Larry Foust, FW

1955-56
Bob Pettit, STL
Paul Arizin, PHI
Neil Johnston, PHI
Bob Cousy, BOS
Bill Sharman, BOS

1956-57
Paul Arizin, PHI
Dolph Schayes, SYR
Bob Pettit, STL
Bob Cousy, BOS
Bill Sharman, BOS

1957-58
Dolph Schayes, SYR
George Yardley, DET
Bob Pettit, STL
Bob Cousy, BOS
Bill Sharman, BOS

1958-59
Bob Pettit, STL
Elgin Baylor, MIN
Bill Russell, BOS
Bob Cousy, BOS
Bill Sharman, BOS

1959-60
Bob Pettit, STL
Elgin Baylor, MIN
Wilt Chamberlain, PHI
Bob Cousy, BOS
Gene Shue, DET

1960-61
Elgin Baylor, LA
Bob Pettit, STL
Wilt Chamberlain, PHI
Bob Cousy, BOS
Oscar Robertson, CIN

1961-62
Bob Pettit, STL
Elgin Baylor, LA
Wilt Chamberlain, PHI
Jerry West, LA
Oscar Robertson, CIN

1962-63
Elgin Baylor, LA
Bob Pettit, STL
Bill Russell, BOS
Oscar Robertson, CIN
Jerry West, LA

1963-64
Bob Pettit, STL
Elgin Baylor, LA
Wilt Chamberlain, SF
Oscar Robertson, CIN
Jerry West, LA

1964-65
Elgin Baylor, LA
Jerry Lucas, CIN
Bill Russell, BOS
Oscar Robertson, CIN
Jerry West, LA

1965-66
Rick Barry, SF
Jerry Lucas, CIN
Wilt Chamberlain, PHI
Oscar Robertson, CIN
Jerry West, LA

1966-67
Rick Barry, SF
Elgin Baylor, LA
Wilt Chamberlain, PHI
Jerry West, LA
Oscar Robertson, CIN

1967-68
Elgin Baylor, LA
Jerry Lucas, CIN
Wilt Chamberlain, PHI
Dave Bing, DET
Oscar Robertson, CIN

1968-69
Billy Cunningham, PHI
Elgin Baylor, LA
Wes Unseld, BAL

Earl Monroe, BAL
Oscar Robertson, CIN

1969-70
Billy Cunningham, PHI
Connie Hawkins, PHO
Willis Reed, NY
Jerry West, LA
Walt Frazier, NY

1970-71
John Havlicek, BOS
Billy Cunningham, PHI
Lew Alcindor, MIL
Jerry West, LA
Dave Bing, DET

1971-72
John Havlicek, BOS
Spencer Haywood, SEA
Kareem Abdul-Jabbar, MIL
Jerry West, LA
Walt Frazier, NY

1972-73
John Havlicek, BOS
Spencer Haywood, SEA
Kareem Abdul-Jabbar, MIL
Nate Archibald, KCO
Jerry West, LA

1973-74
John Havlicek, BOS
Rick Barry, GS
Kareem Abdul-Jabbar, MIL
Walt Frazier, NY
Gail Goodrich, LA

1974-75
Rick Barry, GS
Elvin Hayes, WAS
Bob McAdoo, BUF
Nate Archibald, KCO
Walt Frazier, NY

1975-76
Rick Barry, GS
George McGinnis, PHI
Kareem Abdul-Jabbar, LA
Nate Archibald, KC
Pete Maravich, NO

1976-77
Elvin Hayes, WAS
David Thompson, DEN

Kareem Abdul-Jabbar, LA
Pete Maravich, NO
Paul Westphal, PHO

1977-78
Truck Robinson, NO
Julius Erving, PHI
Bill Walton, POR
George Gervin, SA
David Thompson, DEN

1978-79
Marques Johnson, MIL
Elvin Hayes, WAS
Moses Malone, HOU
George Gervin, SA
Paul Westphal, PHO

1979-80
Julius Erving, PHI
Larry Bird, BOS
Kareem Abdul-Jabbar, LA
George Gervin, SA
Paul Westphal, PHO

1980-81
Julius Erving, PHI
Larry Bird, BOS
Kareem Abdul-Jabbar, LA
George Gervin, SA
Dennis Johnson, PHO

1981-82
Larry Bird, BOS
Julius Erving, PHI
Moses Malone, HOU
George Gervin, SA
Gus Williams, SEA

1982-83
Larry Bird, BOS
Julius Erving, PHI
Moses Malone, PHI
Magic Johnson, LA
Sidney Moncrief, MIL

1983-84
Larry Bird, BOS
Bernard King, NY
Kareem Abdul-Jabbar, LA
Magic Johnson, LA
Isiah Thomas, DET

1984-85
Larry Bird, BOS
Bernard King, NY
Moses Malone, PHI
Magic Johnson, LAL
Isiah Thomas, DET

1985-86
Larry Bird, BOS
Dominique Wilkins, ATL
Kareem Abdul-Jabbar, LAL
Magic Johnson, LAL
Isiah Thomas, DET

1986-87
Larry Bird, BOS
Kevin McHale, BOS
Akeem Olajuwon, HOU
Magic Johnson, LAL
Michael Jordan, CHI

1987-88
Larry Bird, BOS
Charles Barkley, PHI
Akeem Olajuwon, HOU
Michael Jordan, CHI
Magic Johnson, LAL

1988-89
Karl Malone, UTA
Charles Barkley, PHI
Akeem Olajuwon, HOU
Magic Johnson, LAL
Michael Jordan, CHI

1989-90
Karl Malone, UTA
Charles Barkley, PHI
Patrick Ewing, NY
Magic Johnson, LAL
Michael Jordan, CHI

1990-91
Karl Malone, UTA
Charles Barkley, PHI
David Robinson, SA
Michael Jordan, CHI
Magic Johnson, LAL

1991-92
Karl Malone, UTA
Chris Mullin, GS
David Robinson, SA
Michael Jordan, CHI
Clyde Drexler, POR

1992-93
Charles Barkley, PHO
Karl Malone, UTA
Hakeem Olajuwon, HOU
Michael Jordan, CHI
Mark Price, CLE

1993-94

FIRST
Scottie Pippen, CHI
Karl Malone, UTA
Hakeem Olajuwon, HOU
John Stockton, UTA
Latrell Sprewell, GS

SECOND
Shawn Kemp, SEA
Charles Barkley, PHO
David Robinson, SA
Mitch Richmond, SAC
Kevin Johnson, PHO

ALL-ROOKIE TEAMS

1962-63
Terry Dischinger, CHI
Chet Walker, SYR
Zelmo Beaty, STL
John Havlicek, BOS
Dave DeBusschere, DET

1963-64
Jerry Lucas, CIN
Gus Johnson, BAL
Nate Thurmond, SF
Art Heyman, NY
Rod Thorn, BAL

1964-65
Willis Reed, NY
Jim Barnes, NY
Howard Komives, NY
Lucious Jackson, PHI
Wally Jones, BAL
Joe Caldwell, DET

1965-66
Rick Barry, SF
Billy Cunningham, PHI
Tom Van Arsdale, DET
Dick Van Arsdale, NY
Fred Hetzel, SF

1966-67
Lou Hudson, STL
Jack Marin, BAL
Erwin Mueller, CHI
Cazzie Russell, NY
Dave Bing, DET

1967-68
Earl Monroe, BAL
Bob Rule, SEA
Walt Frazier, NY
Al Tucker, SEA
Phil Jackson, NY

1968-69
Wes Unseld, BAL
Elvin Hayes, SD
Bill Hewitt, LA
Art Harris, SEA
Gary Gregor, PHO

1969-70
Lew Alcindor, MIL
Bob Dandridge, MIL
Jo Jo White, BOS
Mike Davis, BAL
Dick Garrett, LA

1970-71
Geoff Petrie, POR
Dave Cowens, BOS
Pete Maravich, ATL
Calvin Murphy, SD
Bob Lanier, DET

1971-72
Elmore Smith, BUF
Sidney Wicks, POR
Austin Carr, CLE
Phil Chenier, BAL
Clifford Ray, CHI

1972-73
Bob McAdoo, BUF
Lloyd Neal, POR
Fred Boyd, PHI
Dwight Davis, CLE
Jim Price, LA

1973-74
Ernie DiGregorio, BUF
Ron Behagen, KCO
Mike Bantom, PHO
John Brown, ATL
Nick Weatherspoon, CAP

1974-75
Keith Wilkes, GS
John Drew, ATL
Scott Wedman, KCO
Tom Burleson, SEA
Brian Winters, LA

1975-76
Alvan Adams, PHO
Gus Williams, GS
Joe Meriweather, HOU
John Shumate, PHO/BUF
Lionel Hollins, POR

1976-77
Adrian Dantley, BUF
Scott May, CHI
Mitch Kupchak, WAS
John Lucas, HOU
Ron Lee, PHO

1977-78
Walter Davis, PHO
Marques Johnson, MIL
Bernard King, NJ
Jack Sikma, SEA
Norm Nixon, LA

1978-79
Phil Ford, KC
Mychal Thompson, POR
Ron Brewer, POR
Reggie Theus, CHI
Terry Tyler, DET

1979-80
Larry Bird, BOS
Magic Johnson, LA
Bill Cartwright, NY
Calvin Natt, POR
David Greenwood, CHI

1980-81
Joe Barry Carroll, GS
Darrell Griffith, UTA
Larry Smith, GS
Kevin McHale, BOS
Kelvin Ransey, POR

1981-82
Kelly Tripucka, DET
Jay Vincent, DAL
Isiah Thomas, DET
Buck Williams, NJ
Jeff Ruland, WAS

1982-83
Terry Cummings, SD
Clark Kellogg, IND
Dominique Wilkins, ATL
James Worthy, LA
Quintin Dailey, CHI

1983-84
Ralph Sampson, HOU
Steve Stipanovich, IND
Byron Scott, LA
Jeff Malone, WAS
Thurl Bailey, UTA
Darrell Walker, NY

1984-85
Michael Jordan, CHI
Akeem Olajuwon, HOU
Sam Bowie, POR
Charles Barkley, PHI
Sam Perkins, DAL

1985-86
Xavier McDaniel, SEA
Patrick Ewing, NY
Karl Malone, UTA
Joe Dumars, DET
Charles Oakley, CHI

1986-87
Brad Daugherty, CLE
Ron Harper, CLE
Chuck Person, IND
Roy Tarpley, DAL
John Williams, CLE

1987-88
Mark Jackson, NY
Armon Gilliam, PHO
Kenny Smith, SAC
Greg Anderson, SA
Derrick McKey, SEA

1988-89
Mitch Richmond, GS
Willie Anderson, SA
Hersey Hawkins, PHI
Rik Smits, IND
Charles Smith, LAC

1989-90
David Robinson, SA
Tim Hardaway, GS
Vlade Divac, LAL
Sherman Douglas, MIA
Pooh Richardson, MIN

1990-91
Derrick Coleman, NJ
Lionel Simmons, SAC
Dee Brown, BOS
Kendall Gill, CHA
Dennis Scott, ORL

1991-92
Larry Johnson, CHA
Dikembe Mutombo, DEN
Billy Owens, GS
Steve Smith, MIA
Stacey Augmon, ATL

1992-93
Shaquille O'Neal, ORL
Alonzo Mourning, CHA
Christian Laettner, MIN
Tom Gugliotta, WAS
LaPhonso Ellis, DEN

1993-94

FIRST
Chris Webber, GS
Anfernee Hardaway, ORL
Vin Baker, MIL
Jamal Mashburn, DAL
Isaiah Rider, MIN

SECOND
Dino Radja, BOS
Nick Van Exel, LAL
Shawn Bradley, PHI
Toni Kukoc, CHI
Lindsey Hunter, DET

ALL-DEFENSIVE TEAMS

1968-69
Dave DeBusschere, NY
Nate Thurmond, SF
Bill Russell, BOS
Walt Frazier, NY
Jerry Sloan, CHI

1969-70
Dave DeBusschere, NY
Gus Johnson, BAL
Willis Reed, NY
Walt Frazier, NY
Jerry West, LA

1970-71
Dave DeBusschere, NY
Gus Johnson, BAL

Nate Thurmond, SF
Walt Frazier, NY
Jerry West, LA

1971-72
Dave DeBusschere, NY
John Havlicek, BOS
Wilt Chamberlain, LA
Jerry West, LA
Walt Frazier, NY
Jerry Sloan, CHI

1972-73
Dave DeBusschere, NY
John Havlicek, BOS
Wilt Chamberlain, LA

Jerry West, LA
Walt Frazier, NY

1973-74
Dave DeBusschere, NY
John Havlicek, BOS
Kareem Abdul-Jabbar, MIL
Norm Van Lier, CHI
Walt Frazier, NY
Jerry Sloan, CHI

1974-75
John Havlicek, BOS
Paul Silas, BOS
Kareem Abdul-Jabbar, MIL
Jerry Sloan, CHI
Walt Frazier, NY

1975-76
Paul Silas, BOS
John Havlicek, BOS
Dave Cowens, BOS
Norm Van Lier, CHI
Don Watts, SEA

1976-77
Bobby Jones, DEN
E.C. Coleman, NO
Bill Walton, POR
Don Buse, IND
Norm Van Lier, CHI

1977-78
Bobby Jones, DEN
Maurice Lucas, POR
Bill Walton, POR
Lionel Hollins, POR
Don Buse, PHO

1978-79
Bobby Jones, PHI
Bobby Dandridge, WAS
Kareem Abdul-Jabbar, LA
Dennis Johnson, SEA
Don Buse, PHO

1979-80
Bobby Jones, PHI
Dan Roundfield, ATL
Kareem Abdul-Jabbar, LA
Dennis Johnson, SEA
Don Buse, PHO
Micheal Ray Richardson, NY

1980-81
Bobby Jones, PHI
Caldwell Jones, PHI
Kareem Abdul-Jabbar, LA
Dennis Johnson, PHO
Micheal Ray Richardson, NY

1981-82
Bobby Jones, PHI
Dan Roundfield, ATL
Caldwell Jones, PHI
Michael Cooper, LA
Dennis Johnson, PHO

1982-83
Bobby Jones, PHI
Dan Roundfield, ATL
Moses Malone, PHI
Sidney Moncrief, MIL
Dennis Johnson, PHO
Maurice Cheeks, PHI

1983-84
Bobby Jones, PHI
Michael Cooper, LA
Tree Rollins, ATL
Maurice Cheeks, PHI
Sidney Moncrief, MIL

1984-85
Sidney Moncrief, MIL
Paul Pressey, MIL
Mark Eaton, UTA
Michael Cooper, LAL
Maurice Cheeks, PHI

1985-86
Paul Pressey, MIL
Kevin McHale, BOS
Mark Eaton, UTA
Sidney Moncrief, MIL
Maurice Cheeks, PHI

1986-87
Kevin McHale, BOS
Michael Cooper, LAL
Akeem Olajuwon, HOU
Alvin Robertson, SA
Dennis Johnson, BOS

1987-88
Kevin McHale, BOS
Rodney McCray, HOU
Akeem Olajuwon, HOU
Michael Cooper, LAL
Michael Jordan, CHI

1988-89
Dennis Rodman, DET
Larry Nance, CLE
Mark Eaton, UTA
Michael Jordan, CHI
Joe Dumars, DET

1989-90
Dennis Rodman, DET
Buck Williams, POR
Akeem Olajuwon, HOU
Michael Jordan, CHI
Joe Dumars, DET

1990-91
Dennis Rodman, DET
Buck Williams, POR
David Robinson, SA
Michael Jordan, CHI
Alvin Robertson, MIL

1991-92
Dennis Rodman, DET
Scottie Pippen, CHI
David Robinson, SA
Michael Jordan, CHI
Joe Dumars, DET

1992-93
Dennis Rodman, DET
Scottie Pippen, CHI
Hakeem Olajuwon, HOU
Michael Jordan, CHI
Joe Dumars, DET

1993-94
FIRST
Scottie Pippen, CHI
Charles Oakley, NY
Hakeem Olajuwon, HOU
Gary Payton, SEA
Mookie Blaylock, ATL

SECOND
Dennis Rodman, SA
Horace Grant, CHI
David Robinson, SA
Nate McMillan, SEA
Latrell Sprewell, GS

ALL-STAR GAMES

	RESULT	SITE	MVP
1950-51	East 111, West 94	Boston	Ed Macauley, Boston
1951-52	East 108, West 91	Boston	Paul Arizin, Philadelphia
1952-53	West 79, East 75	Fort Wayne	George Mikan, Minneapolis
1953-54	East 98, West 93 (OT)	New York	Bob Cousy, Boston
1954-55	East 100, West 91	New York	Bill Sharman, Boston
1955-56	West 108, East 94	Rochester	Bob Pettit, St. Louis
1956-57	East 109, West 97	Boston	Bob Cousy, Boston
1957-58	East 130, West 118	St. Louis	Bob Pettit, St. Louis
1958-59	West 124, East 108	Detroit	E. Baylor, Minn./B. Pettit, St. L.
1959-60	East 125, West 115	Philadelphia	Wilt Chamberlain, Philadelphia
1960-61	West 153, East 131	Syracuse	Oscar Robertson, Cincinnati
1961-62	West 150, East 130	St. Louis	Bob Pettit, St. Louis
1962-63	East 115, West 108	Los Angeles	Bill Russell, Boston
1963-64	East 111, West 107	Boston	Oscar Robertson, Cincinnati
1964-65	East 124, West 123	St. Louis	Jerry Lucas, Cincinnati
1965-66	East 137, West 94	Cincinnati	Adrian Smith, Cincinnati
1966-67	West 135, East 120	San Francisco	Rick Barry, San Francisco
1967-68	East 144, West 124	New York	Hal Greer, Philadelphia
1968-69	East 123, West 112	Baltimore	Oscar Robertson, Cincinnati
1969-70	East 142, West 135	Philadelphia	Willis Reed, New York
1970-71	West 108, East 107	San Diego	Lenny Wilkens, Seattle
1971-72	West 112, East 110	Los Angeles	Jerry West, Los Angeles
1972-73	East 104, West 84	Chicago	Dave Cowens, Boston
1973-74	West 134, East 123	Seattle	Bob Lanier, Detroit
1974-75	East 108, West 102	Phoenix	Walt Frazier, New York
1975-76	East 123, West 109	Philadelphia	Dave Bing, Washington
1976-77	West 125, East 124	Milwaukee	Julius Erving, Philadelphia
1977-78	East 133, West 125	Atlanta	Randy Smith, Buffalo
1978-79	West 134, East 129	Detroit	David Thompson, Denver
1979-80	East 144, West 135 (OT)	Washington	George Gervin, San Antonio
1980-81	East 123, West 120	Cleveland	Nate Archibald, Boston
1981-82	East 120, West 118	E. Rutherford	Larry Bird, Boston
1982-83	East 132, West 123	Los Angeles	Julius Erving, Philadelphia
1983-84	East 154, West 145 (OT)	Denver	Isiah Thomas, Detroit
1984-85	West 140, East 129	Indianapolis	Ralph Sampson, Houston
1985-86	East 139, West 132	Dallas	Isiah Thomas, Detroit
1986-87	West 154, East 149 (OT)	Seattle	Tom Chambers, Seattle
1987-88	East 138, West 133	Chicago	Michael Jordan, Chicago
1988-89	West 143, East 134	Houston	Karl Malone, Utah
1989-90	East 130, West 113	Miami	Magic Johnson, L.A. Lakers
1990-91	East 116, West 114	Charlotte	Charles Barkley, Philadelphia
1991-92	West 153, East 113	Orlando	Magic Johnson, L.A. Lakers
1992-93	West 135, East 132 (OT)	Utah	Karl Malone, Utah/ John Stockton, Utah
1993-94	East 127, West 118	Minneapolis	Scottie Pippen, Chicago

CAREER LEADERS

(Players active at the close of 1993-94
are listed in bold)

POINTS

Kareem Abdul-Jabbar	38,387
Wilt Chamberlain	31,419
Moses Malone	**27,360**
Elvin Hayes	27,313
Oscar Robertson	26,710
John Havlicek	26,395
Alex English	25,613
Jerry West	25,192
Dominique Wilkins	**24,019**
Adrian Dantley	23,177
Elgin Baylor	23,149
Robert Parish	**22,494**
Larry Bird	21,791
Hal Greer	21,586
Michael Jordan	21,541
Walt Bellamy	20,941
Bob Pettit	20,880
George Gervin	20,708
Bernard King	19,655
Tom Chambers	**19,521**
Walter Davis	19,521

GAMES

Kareem Abdul-Jabbar	1,560
Robert Parish	**1,413**
Moses Malone	**1,312**
Elvin Hayes	1,303
John Havlicek	1,270
Paul Silas	1,254
Alex English	1,193
Hal Greer	1,122
James Edwards	**1,112**
Jack Sikma	1,107

MINUTES

Kareem Abdul-Jabbar	57,446
Elvin Hayes	50,000
Wilt Chamberlain	47,859
John Havlicek	46,471
Moses Malone	**44,922**
Oscar Robertson	43,886
Robert Parish	**42,860**
Bill Russell	40,726
Hal Greer	39,788
Walt Bellamy	38,940

SCORING AVERAGE

(Minimum 400 Games or 10,000 Points)

Michael Jordan	32.3
Wilt Chamberlain	30.1
Elgin Baylor	27.4
Jerry West	27.0
Dominique Wilkins	**26.5**
Bob Pettit	26.4
George Gervin	26.2
Karl Malone	**26.0**
Oscar Robertson	25.7
Kareem Abdul-Jabbar	24.6

REBOUNDS

Wilt Chamberlain	23,924
Bill Russell	21,620
Kareem Abdul-Jabbar	17,440
Elvin Hayes	16,279
Moses Malone	**16,166**
Nate Thurmond	14,464
Walt Bellamy	14,241
Robert Parish	**13,982**
Wes Unseld	13,769
Jerry Lucas	12,942

ASSISTS

Magic Johnson	9,921
Oscar Robertson	9,887
John Stockton	**9,383**
Isiah Thomas	**9,061**
Maurice Cheeks	7,392
Lenny Wilkens	7,211
Bob Cousy	6,955
Guy Rodgers	6,917
Nate Archibald	6,476
John Lucas	6,454

STEALS

Maurice Cheeks	2,310
John Stockton	**2,031**
Alvin Robertson	**1,946**
Isiah Thomas	**1,861**
Michael Jordan	1,815
Clyde Drexler	**1,721**
Magic Johnson	1,698
Lafayette Lever	**1,666**
Gus Williams	1,638
Larry Bird	1,556

BLOCKED SHOTS

Kareem Abdul-Jabbar	3,189
Mark Eaton	3,064
Hakeem Olajuwon	2,741
Tree Rollins	2,506
Robert Parish	2,252
George T. Johnson	2,082
Manute Bol	2,077
Larry Nance	2,027
Patrick Ewing	1,984
Elvin Hayes	1,771

PERSONAL FOULS

Kareem Abdul-Jabbar	4,657
Elvin Hayes	4,193
Robert Parish	4,191
James Edwards	3,937
Jack Sikma	3,879
Hal Greer	3,855
Dolph Schayes	3,664
Bill Laimbeer	3,633
Tom Chambers	3,553
Walt Bellamy	3,536

DISQUALIFICATIONS

Vern Mikkelsen	127
Walter Dukes	121
Charlie Share	105
Paul Arizin	101
Darryl Dawkins	100
James Edwards	95
Tom Gola	94
Tom Sanders	94
Steve Johnson	92
Tree Rollins	92

FIELD GOALS ATTEMPTED

Kareem Abdul-Jabbar	28,307
Elvin Hayes	24,272
John Havlicek	23,930
Wilt Chamberlain	23,497
Alex English	21,036
Elgin Baylor	20,171
Oscar Robertson	19,620
Dominique Wilkins	19,335
Moses Malone	19,190
Jerry West	19,032

FIELD GOALS MADE

Kareem Abdul-Jabbar	15,837
Wilt Chamberlain	12,681
Elvin Hayes	10,976
Alex English	10,659
John Havlicek	10,513
Oscar Robertson	9,508

Moses Malone	9,422
Robert Parish	9,265
Dominique Wilkins	9,020
Jerry West	9,016

FIELD GOAL PCT.
(Minimum 2,000 FGM)

Artis Gilmore	.599
Mark West	.592
Steve Johnson	.572
Darryl Dawkins	.572
James Donaldson	.571
Jeff Ruland	.564
Charles Barkley	.562
Kareem Abdul-Jabbar	.559
Kevin McHale	.554
Otis Thorpe	.554

FREE THROWS ATTEMPTED

Wilt Chamberlain	11,862
Moses Malone	11,058
Kareem Abdul-Jabbar	9,304
Oscar Robertson	9,185
Jerry West	8,801
Adrian Dantley	8,351
Dolph Schayes	8,273
Bob Pettit	8,119
Walt Bellamy	8,088
Elvin Hayes	7,999

FREE THROWS MADE

Moses Malone	8,509
Oscar Robertson	7,694
Jerry West	7,160
Dolph Schayes	6,979
Adrian Dantley	6,832
Kareem Abdul-Jabbar	6,712
Bob Pettit	6,182
Wilt Chamberlain	6,057
Elgin Baylor	5,763
Dominique Wilkins	5,455

FREE THROW PCT.
(Minimum 1,200 FTM)

Mark Price	.906
Rick Barry	.900
Calvin Murphy	.892
Scott Skiles	.890
Larry Bird	.886
Bill Sharman	.883
Ricky Pierce	.877
Reggie Miller	.877
Kiki Vandeweghe	.872
Jeff Malone	.871

3-PT. FIELD GOALS ATTEMPTED

Michael Adams	2,735
Dale Ellis	2,520
Danny Ainge	2,437
Reggie Miller	2,152
Vernon Maxwell	1,981
Derek Harper	1,952
Chuck Person	1,934
Terry Porter	1,892
Larry Bird	1,727
Mark Price	1,707

3-PT. FIELD GOALS MADE

Dale Ellis	1,013
Danny Ainge	924
Michael Adams	906
Reggie Miller	840
Terry Porter	729
Mark Price	699
Chuck Person	684
Derek Harper	681
Larry Bird	649
Vernon Maxwell	634

3-PT. FIELD GOAL PCT.
(Minimum 100 Made)

Steve Kerr	.445
B.J. Armstrong	.443
Drazen Petrovic	.437
Mark Price	.409
Trent Tucker	.408
Jim Les	.405
Mike Iuzzolino	.404
Dale Ellis	.402
Craig Hodges	.400
Dana Barros	.398

MOST VICTORIES, COACH

Red Auerbach	938
Lenny Wilkens	926
Jack Ramsay	864
Dick Motta	856
Bill Fitch	845
Cotton Fitzsimmons	805
Don Nelson	803
Gene Shue	784
John MacLeod	707
Pat Riley	701

ACTIVE CAREER LEADERS

(Includes players active at the close
of the 1993-94 season)

POINTS

Moses Malone	27,360
Dominique Wilkins	24,019
Robert Parish	22,494
Tom Chambers	19,521
Karl Malone	19,050
Isiah Thomas	18,822
Hakeem Olajuwon	17,899
Eddie Johnson	17,658
Rolando Blackman	17,623
Charles Barkley	17,530

GAMES

Robert Parish	1,413
Moses Malone	1,312
James Edwards	1,112
Tree Rollins	1,105
Buck Williams	1,040
Tom Chambers	1,013
Eddie Johnson	1,007
Rolando Blackman	980
Isiah Thomas	979
Danny Ainge	968

MINUTES

Moses Malone	44,922
Robert Parish	42,860
Buck Williams	36,136
Isiah Thomas	35,516
Dominique Wilkins	33,493
Tom Chambers	32,589
Rolando Blackman	32,087
Larry Nance	30,697
James Worthy	30,001
Eddie Johnson	29,181

SCORING AVERAGE
(Minimum 400 Games or 10,000 Points)

Dominique Wilkins	26.5
Karl Malone	26.0
Patrick Ewing	23.8
Hakeem Olajuwon	23.7
Charles Barkley	23.6
Mitch Richmond	22.7
Chris Mullin	21.9
Moses Malone	20.9
Clyde Drexler	20.7
Terry Cummings	20.1

REBOUNDS

Moses Malone	16,166
Robert Parish	13,982
Buck Williams	11,364
Hakeem Olajuwon	9,464
Charles Barkley	8,734
Karl Malone	8,058
Charles Oakley	7,685
Dennis Rodman	7,666
Larry Nance	7,352
Otis Thorpe	7,320

ASSISTS

John Stockton	9,383
Isiah Thomas	9,061
Terry Porter	5,186
Sleepy Floyd	5,049
Derek Harper	5,026
Kevin Johnson	4,912
Muggsy Bogues	4,794
Clyde Drexler	4,725
Lafayette Lever	4,696
Mark Jackson	4,639

STEALS

John Stockton	2,031
Alvin Robertson	1,946
Isiah Thomas	1,861
Clyde Drexler	1,721
Lafayette Lever	1,666
Derek Harper	1,539
Hakeem Olajuwon	1,448
Doc Rivers	1,425
Dominique Wilkins	1,274
Charles Barkley	1,227

BLOCKED SHOTS

Mark Eaton	3,064
Hakeem Olajuwon	2,741
Tree Rollins	2,506
Robert Parish	2,252
Manute Bol	2,077
Larry Nance	2,027
Patrick Ewing	1,984
Moses Malone	1,730
Herb Williams	1,511
David Robinson	1,473

PERSONAL FOULS

Robert Parish	4,191
James Edwards	3,937
Tom Chambers	3,553
Buck Williams	3,529
Tree Rollins	3,314
Rick Mahorn	3,155
Moses Malone	3,061
Dan Schayes	2,985
Isiah Thomas	2,971
Mark Eaton	2,955

DISQUALIFICATIONS

James Edwards	95
Tree Rollins	92
Robert Parish	86
Tom Chambers	74
Rick Mahorn	74
Hakeem Olajuwon	71
Frank Brickowski	61
Dan Schayes	60
LaSalle Thompson	56
Shawn Kemp	53

FIELD GOALS ATTEMPTED

Dominique Wilkins	19,335
Moses Malone	19,190
Robert Parish	17,167
Isiah Thomas	15,904
Tom Chambers	15,289
Eddie Johnson	15,006
Terry Cummings	14,232
Jeff Malone	14,197
Rolando Blackman	13,969
Hakeem Olajuwon	13,761

FIELD GOALS MADE

Moses Malone	9,422
Robert Parish	9,265
Dominique Wilkins	9,020
Isiah Thomas	7,194
Tom Chambers	7,174
Eddie Johnson	7,154
Hakeem Olajuwon	7,107
Karl Malone	7,027
Terry Cummings	6,934
Rolando Blackman	6,887

FIELD GOAL PCT.
(Minimum 2,000 FGM)

Mark West	.592
Charles Barkley	.562
Otis Thorpe	.554
Buck Williams	.554
Larry Nance	.546
Robert Parish	.540
Dennis Rodman	.537
Brad Daugherty	.532
Horace Grant	.530
David Robinson	.527

FREE THROWS ATTEMPTED

Moses Malone	11,058
Karl Malone	6,890
Dominique Wilkins	6,706
Charles Barkley	6,381
Tom Chambers	6,133
Robert Parish	5,491
Buck Williams	5,337
Isiah Thomas	5,316
Hakeem Olajuwon	5,212
James Edwards	4,623

FREE THROWS MADE

Moses Malone	8,509
Dominique Wilkins	5,455
Karl Malone	4,956
Tom Chambers	4,952
Charles Barkley	4,683
Isiah Thomas	4,036
Robert Parish	3,964
Hakeem Olajuwon	3,675
Rolando Blackman	3,620
Clyde Drexler	3,591

FREE THROW PCT.
(Minimum 1,200 FTM)

Mark Price	.906
Scott Skiles	.890
Ricky Pierce	.877
Reggie Miller	.877
Jeff Malone	.871
Hersey Hawkins	.867
Micheal Williams	.867
Chris Mullin	.862
Jeff Hornacek	.860
Michael Adams	.850

3-PT. FIELD GOALS ATTEMPTED

Michael Adams	2,735
Dale Ellis	2,520
Danny Ainge	2,437
Reggie Miller	2,152
Vernon Maxwell	1,981

Derek Harper	1,952
Chuck Person	1,934
Terry Porter	1,892
Mark Price	1,707
Dominique Wilkins	1,684

3-PT. FIELD GOALS MADE

Dale Ellis	1,013
Danny Ainge	924
Michael Adams	906
Reggie Miller	840
Terry Porter	729
Mark Price	699
Chuck Person	684
Derek Harper	681
Vernon Maxwell	634
Hersey Hawkins	554

3-PT. FIELD GOAL PCT.
(Minimum 100 Made)

Steve Kerr	.445
B.J. Armstrong	.443
Mark Price	.409
Jim Les	.405
Dale Ellis	.402
Dana Barros	.398
Hersey Hawkins	.394
Reggie Miller	.390
Kenny Smith	.387
Dennis Scott	.386

MOST VICTORIES, COACH

Lenny Wilkens	926
Don Nelson	803
Pat Riley	701
Chuck Daly	564
Larry Brown	481
Kevin Loughery	457
Jerry Sloan	398
Mike Fratello	371
Phil Jackson	295
Rick Adelman	291

REGULAR-SEASON RECORDS

MINUTES
(First Kept in 1951-52)

3,882	Wilt Chamberlain, PHI	1961-62
3,836	Wilt Chamberlain, PHI	1967-68
3,806	Wilt Chamberlain, SF	1962-63
3,773	Wilt Chamberlain, PHI	1960-61
3,737	Wilt Chamberlain, PHI	1965-66
3,698	John Havlicek, BOS	1971-72
3,689	Wilt Chamberlain, SF	1963-64
3,682	Wilt Chamberlain, PHI	1966-67
3,681	Nate Archibald, KCO	1972-73
3,678	John Havlicek, BOS	1970-71

POINTS

4,029	Wilt Chamberlain, PHI	1961-62
3,586	Wilt Chamberlain, SF	1962-63
3,041	Michael Jordan, CHI	1986-87
3,033	Wilt Chamberlain, PHI	1960-61
2,948	Wilt Chamberlain, SF	1963-64
2,868	Michael Jordan, CHI	1987-88
2,831	Bob McAdoo, BUF	1974-75
2,822	Kareem Abdul-Jabbar, MIL	1971-72
2,775	Rick Barry, SF	1966-67
2,753	Michael Jordan, CHI	1989-90

SCORING AVERAGE
(Minimum 70 Games or 1,400 Points)

50.4	Wilt Chamberlain, PHI	1961-62
44.8	Wilt Chamberlain, SF	1962-63
38.4	Wilt Chamberlain, PHI	1960-61
37.6	Wilt Chamberlain, PHI	1959-60
37.1	Michael Jordan, CHI	1986-87
36.9	Wilt Chamberlain, SF	1963-64
35.6	Rick Barry, SF	1966-67
35.0	Michael Jordan, CHI	1987-88
34.8	Kareem Abdul-Jabbar, MIL	1971-72
34.7	Wilt Chamberlain, SF/PHI	1964-65

REBOUNDS
(First Kept in 1950-51)

2,149	Wilt Chamberlain, PHI	1960-61
2,052	Wilt Chamberlain, PHI	1961-62
1,957	Wilt Chamberlain, PHI	1966-67
1,952	Wilt Chamberlain, PHI	1967-68
1,946	Wilt Chamberlain, SF	1962-63
1,943	Wilt Chamberlain, PHI	1965-66
1,941	Wilt Chamberlain, PHI	1959-60
1,930	Bill Russell, BOS	1963-64
1,878	Bill Russell, BOS	1964-65
1,868	Bill Russell, BOS	1960-61

ASSISTS

1,164	John Stockton, UTA	1990-91
1,134	John Stockton, UTA	1989-90
1,128	John Stockton, UTA	1987-88
1,126	John Stockton, UTA	1991-92
1,123	Isiah Thomas, DET	1984-85
1,118	John Stockton, UTA	1988-89
1,099	Kevin Porter, DET	1978-79
1,031	John Stockton, UTA	1993-94
991	Kevin Johnson, PHO	1988-89
989	Magic Johnson, LAL	1990-91

STEALS
(First Kept in 1973-74)

301	Alvin Robertson, SA	1985-86
281	Don Buse, IND	1976-77
265	Micheal Richardson, NY	1979-80
263	John Stockton, UTA	1988-89
261	Slick Watts, SEA	1975-76
260	Alvin Robertson, SA	1986-87
259	Michael Jordan, CHI	1987-88
246	Alvin Robertson, MIL	1990-91
244	John Stockton, UTA	1991-92
243	Micheal Richardson, NJ	1984-85
243	Alvin Robertson, SA	1987-88

BLOCKED SHOTS
(First Kept in 1973-74)

456	Mark Eaton, UTA	1984-85
397	Manute Bol, WAS	1985-86
393	Elmore Smith, LA	1973-74
376	Akeem Olajuwon, HOU	1989-90
369	Mark Eaton, UTA	1985-86
351	Mark Eaton, UTA	1982-83
345	Manute Bol, GS	1988-89
343	Tree Rollins, ATL	1982-83
342	Hakeem Olajuwon, HOU	1992-93
338	Kareem Abdul-Jabbar, LA	1975-76

PERSONAL FOULS

386	Darryl Dawkins, NJ	1983-84
382	Darryl Dawkins, NJ	1982-83
372	Steve Johnson, KC	1981-82
367	Bill Robinzine, KC	1978-79
366	Bill Bridges, STL	1967-68
363	Lonnie Shelton, NY	1976-77
363	James Edwards, IND	1978-79
361	Kevin Kunnert, HOU	1976-77
358	Dan Roundfield, ATL	1978-79
358	Rick Mahorn, WAS	1983-84

DISQUALIFICATIONS
(First Kept in 1950-51)

26	Don Meineke, FTW	1952-53
25	Steve Johnson, KC	1981-82
23	Darryl Dawkins, NJ	1982-83
22	Walter Dukes, DET	1958-59
22	Darryl Dawkins, NJ	1983-84
21	Joe Meriweather, ATL	1976-77
20	Joe Fulks, PHI	1952-53
20	Vern Mikkelsen, MIN	1957-58
20	Walter Dukes, DET	1959-60
20	Walter Dukes, DET	1961-62
20	George Johnson, NJ	1977-78

FIELD GOALS ATTEMPTED

3,159	Wilt Chamberlain, PHI	1961-62
2,770	Wilt Chamberlain, SF	1962-63
2,457	Wilt Chamberlain, PHI	1960-61
2,311	Wilt Chamberlain, PHI	1959-60
2,298	Wilt Chamberlain, SF	1963-64
2,279	Michael Jordan, CHI	1986-87

2,273 .....Elgin Baylor, LA..................1962-63
2,217 .....Rick Barry, GS....................1974-75
2,215 .....Elvin Hayes, SD..................1970-71
2,166 .....Elgin Baylor, LA..................1960-61

FIELD GOALS MADE

1,597 ......Wilt Chamberlain, PHI 1961-62
1,463 ......Wilt Chamberlain, SF.........1962-63
1,251 ......Wilt Chamberlain, PHI 1960-61
1,204 ......Wilt Chamberlain, SF.........1963-64
1,159 ......Kareem Abdul-Jabbar, MIL.1971-72
1,098 .....Michael Jordan, CHI 1986-87
1,095 .....Bob McAdoo, BUF...............1974-75
1,074 .....Wilt Chamberlain, PHI 1965-66
1,069 .....Michael Jordan, CHI 1987-88
1,065 .....Wilt Chamberlain, PHI 1959-60

FIELD GOAL PCT.
(Minimum 300 FGM)

.727 ......Wilt Chamberlain, LA...........1972-73
.683 ......Wilt Chamberlain, PHI 1966-67
.670 ....Artis Gilmore, CHI...............1980-81
.652 ....Artis Gilmore, CHI...............1981-82
.649 ......Wilt Chamberlain, LA...........1971-72
.637 ....James Donaldson, LAC........1984-85
.632 ....Steve Johnson, SA 1985-86
.626 ....Artis Gilmore, SA 1982-83
.625 ....Mark West, PHO 1989-90
.623 ....Artis Gilmore, SA 1984-85

FREE THROWS ATTEMPTED

1,363 ......Wilt Chamberlain, PHI 1961-62
1,113 ......Wilt Chamberlain, SF.........1962-63
1,054 ......Wilt Chamberlain, PHI 1960-61
1,016 ......Wilt Chamberlain, SF.........1963-64
991......Wilt Chamberlain, SF..............1959-60
977......Jerry West, LA 1965-66
976......Wilt Chamberlain, PHI 1965-66
972......Michael Jordan, CHI 1986-87
951......Charles Barkley, PHI 1987-88
946......Adrian Dantley, UTA..............1983-84

FREE THROWS MADE

840 ....Jerry West, LA......................1965-66
835 ....Wilt Chamberlain, PHI 1961-62
833 ....Michael Jordan, CHI 1986-87
813 ....Adrian Dantley, UTA.............1983-84
800 ....Oscar Robertson, CIN 1963-64
753 ....Rick Barry, SF 1966-67
742 ....Oscar Robertson, CIN 1965-66
737 ....Moses Malone, PHI 1984-85
736 ....Oscar Robertson, CIN 1966-67
723 ....Michael Jordan, CHI 1987-88

FREE THROW PCT.
(Minimum 125 FTM)

.958 ......Calvin Murphy, HOU............1980-81
.956 ....Mahmoud Abdul-Rauf, DEN.1993-94
.948 ....Mark Price, CLE 1992-93
.947 ....Mark Price, CLE 1991-92
.947 ....Rick Barry, HOU 1978-79
.945 ....Ernie DiGregorio, BUF.........1976-77
.935 ....Chris Jackson, DEN 1992-93
.935 ....Ricky Sobers, CHI 1980-81
.935 ....Rick Barry, HOU 1979-80
.932 ....Bill Sharman, BOS................1958-59

3-PT. FIELD GOALS ATTEMPTED
(Rule went into effect in 1979-80)

564 ....Michael Adams, DEN 1990-91
510 ....Vernon Maxwell, HOU 1990-91
503 ....Dan Majerle, PHO 1993-94
473 ....Vernon Maxwell, HOU 1991-92
466 ....Michael Adams, DEN 1988-89
438 ....Dan Majerle, PHO 1992-93
432 ....Michael Adams, DEN 1989-90
419 ....Reggie Miller, IND 1992-93
403 ....Vernon Maxwell, HOU 1993-94
396 ....Glen Rice, MIA 1991-92

3-PT. FIELD GOALS MADE

192 ....Dan Majerle, PHO................1993-94
172 ....Vernon Maxwell, HOU 1990-91
167 ....Michael Adams, DEN...........1990-91
167 ....Dan Majerle, PHO................1992-93
167 ....Reggie Miller, IND................1992-93
166 ....Michael Adams, DEN...........1988-89
162 ....Dale Ellis, SEA....................1988-89
162 ....Vernon Maxwell, HOU 1991-92
158 ....Michael Adams, DEN...........1989-90
155 ....Glen Rice, MIA 1991-92
155 ....Dennis Scott, ORL 1993-94

3-PT. FIELD GOAL PCT.
(Minimum 50 Made)

.507 ....Steve Kerr, CLE 1989-90
.491 ....Craig Hodges, MIL/PHO 1987-88
.486........Mark Price, CLE 1987-88
.481........Craig Hodges, CHI 1989-90
.478........Dale Ellis, SEA 1988-89
.461........Jim Les, SAC 1990-91
.459........Tracy Murray, POR 1993-94
.453........B.J. Armstrong, CHI 1992-93
.451........Chris Mullin, GS 1992-93
.451........Craig Hodges, MIL 1985-86
.449........Drazen Petrovic, NJ 1992-93

GAME RECORDS

POINTS
100 ...Wilt Chamberlain, PHI vs. NY, March 2, 1962
78 .....Wilt Chamberlain, PHI vs. LA, Dec. 8, 1961 (3 OT)
73 .....Wilt Chamberlain, PHI vs. CHI, Jan. 13, 1962
73 .....Wilt Chamberlain, SF vs. NY, Nov. 6, 1962
73 .....David Thompson, DEN vs. DET, April 9, 1978
72 .....Wilt Chamberlain, SF vs. LA, Nov. 3, 1962
71 .....Elgin Baylor, LA vs. NY, Nov. 15, 1960
71 .....David Robinson, SA vs. LAC, Apr. 24, 1994
70 .....Wilt Chamberlain, SF vs. SYR, March 10, 1963
69 .....Michael Jordan, CHI vs. CLE, March 28, 1990 (OT)
68 .....Wilt Chamberlain, PHI vs. CHI, Dec. 16, 1967
68 .....Pete Maravich, NO vs. NY, Feb. 25, 1977

REBOUNDS
55 .....Wilt Chamberlain, PHI vs. BOS, Nov. 24, 1960
51 .....Bill Russell, BOS vs. SYR, Feb. 5, 1960
49 .....Bill Russell, BOS vs. PHI, Nov. 16, 1957
49 .....Bill Russell, BOS vs. DET, March 11, 1965
45 .....Wilt Chamberlain, PHI vs. SYR, Feb. 6, 1960
45 .....Wilt Chamberlain, PHI vs. LA, Jan. 21, 1961

ASSISTS
30 .....Scott Skiles, ORL vs. DEN, Dec. 30, 1990
29 .....Kevin Porter, NJ vs. HOU, Feb. 24, 1978
28 .....Bob Cousy, BOS vs. MIN, Feb. 27, 1959
28 .....Guy Rodgers, SF vs. STL, March 14, 1963
28 .....John Stockton, UTA vs. SA, Jan. 15, 1991

STEALS
11 .....Larry Kenon, SA vs. KC, Dec. 26, 1976
10 .....Jerry West, LA vs. SEA, Dec. 7, 1973
10 .....Larry Steele, POR vs. L.A., Nov. 16, 1974
10 .....Fred Brown, SEA vs. PHI, Dec. 3, 1976
10 .....Gus Williams, SEA vs. NJ, Feb. 22, 1978
10 .....Eddie Jordan, NJ vs. PHI, March 23, 1979
10 .....Johnny Moore, SA vs. IND, March 6, 1985
10 .....Fat Lever, DEN vs. IND, March 9, 1985
10 ......Clyde Drexler, POR vs. MIL, Jan. 10, 1986
10 .....Alvin Robertson, SA vs. PHO, Feb. 18, 1986

10 .....Ron Harper, CLE vs. PHI, March 10, 1987
10 .....Michael Jordan, CHI vs. NJ, Jan. 29, 1988
10 .....Alvin Robertson, SA vs. HOU, Jan. 11, 1989 (OT)
10 .....Alvin Robertson, MIL vs. UTA, Nov. 19, 1990
10 .....Kevin Johnson, PHO vs. WAS, Dec. 9, 1993

BLOCKED SHOTS
17 .....Elmore Smith, LA vs. POR, Oct. 28, 1973
15 .....Manute Bol, WAS vs. ATL, Jan. 25, 1986
15 .....Manute Bol, WAS vs. IND, Feb. 26, 1987
15 .....Shaquille O'Neal, ORL vs. NJ, Nov. 20, 1993
14 .....Elmore Smith, LA vs. DET, Oct. 26, 1973
14 .....Elmore Smith, LA vs. HOU, Nov. 4, 1973
14 .....Mark Eaton, UTA vs. POR, Jan. 18, 1985
14 .....Mark Eaton, UTA vs. SA, Feb. 18, 1989

FIELD GOALS ATTEMPTED
63 .....Wilt Chamberlain, PHI vs. NY, March 2, 1962
62 .....Wilt Chamberlain, PHI vs. LA, Dec. 8, 1961 (3 OT)
60 .....Wilt Chamberlain, SF vs. CIN, Oct. 28, 1962 (OT)
58 .....Wilt Chamberlain, SF vs. PHI, Nov. 26, 1964

FIELD GOALS MADE
36 .....Wilt Chamberlain, PHI vs. NY, March 2, 1962
31 .....Wilt Chamberlain, PHI vs. LA, Dec. 8, 1961 (3 OT)
30 .....Wilt Chamberlain, PHI vs. CHI, Dec. 16, 1967
30 .....Rick Barry, GS vs. POR, March 26, 1974
29 .....Wilt Chamberlain, PHI vs. CHI, Jan. 13, 1962
29 .....Wilt Chamberlain, SF vs. LA, Nov. 3, 1962
29 .....Wilt Chamberlain, SF vs. NY, Nov. 16, 1962
29 .....Wilt Chamberlain, LA vs. PHO, Feb. 9, 1969

FIELD GOAL PCT.
(Minimum 15 Attempts)
1.000.Wilt Chamberlain, PHI vs. BAL, Feb. 24, 1967 (18/18)
1.000.Wilt Chamberlain, PHI vs. BAL, March 19, 1967 (16/16)

1.000.Wilt Chamberlain, PHI vs. LA, Jan. 20, 1967 (15/15)

.947..Wilt Chamberlain, SF vs. NY, Nov. 27, 1963 (18/19)

.941..Wilt Chamberlain, PHI vs. BAL, Nov. 25, 1966 (16/17)

FREE THROWS ATTEMPTED

34 .....Wilt Chamberlain, PHI vs. STL, Feb. 22, 1962

32 .....Wilt Chamberlain, PHI vs. NY, March 2, 1962

31 .....Adrian Dantley, UTA vs. DEN, Nov. 25, 1983

29 .....Lloyd Free, SD vs. ATL, Jan. 13, 1979

29 .....Adrian Dantley, UTA vs. DAL, Oct. 31, 1980

29 .....Adrian Dantley, UTA vs. HOU, Jan. 4, 1984

FREE THROWS MADE

28 .....Wilt Chamberlain, PHI vs. NY, March 2, 1962

28 .....Adrian Dantley, UTA vs. HOU, Jan. 4, 1984

27 .....Adrian Dantley, UTA vs. DEN, Nov. 25, 1983

26 .....Adrian Dantley, UTA vs. DAL, Oct. 31, 1980

26 .....Michael Jordan, CHI vs. NJ, Feb. 26, 1987

FREE THROW PCT.
(Most with No Misses)

1.000..Dominique Wilkins, ATL vs. CHI, Dec. 8, 1992 (23/23)

1.000..Bob Pettit, STL vs. BOS, Nov. 22, 1961 (19/19)

1.000..Bill Cartwright, NY vs. KC, Nov. 17, 1981 (19/19)

1.000..Adrian Dantley, DET vs. CHI, Dec. 15, 1987 (19/19) (OT)

3-PT. FIELD GOALS ATTEMPTED

20 .....Michael Adams, DEN vs. LAC, April 12, 1991

19 .....Dennis Scott, ORL vs. MIL, April 13, 1993

16 .....Michael Adams, DEN vs. MIL, March 23, 1991 (OT)

16 .....Nick Van Exel, LAL vs. UTA, Apr. 24, 1994

3-PT. FIELD GOALS MADE

10 .....Brian Shaw, MIA vs. MIL, April 8, 1993

9 ....Dale Ellis, SEA vs. LAC, April 20, 1990

9 ....Michael Adams, DEN vs. LAC, April 12, 1991

9 ....Dennis Scott, ORL vs. MIL, April 13, 1993

TEAM RECORDS—SEASON

HIGHEST WINNING PCT.

.841 .....69-13 Los Angeles, 1971-72

.840 .....68-13 Philadelphia, 1966-67

.829 .....68-14 Boston, 1972-73

LOWEST WINNING PCT.

.110 ..... 9-73 Philadelphia, 1972-73

.125 ..... 6-42 Providence, 1947-48

.134 .....11-71 Dallas, 1992-93

HIGHEST WINNING PCT., HOME

.976 .....40-1 Boston, 1985-86

.971 .....33-1 Rochester, 1949-50

.969 .....31-1 Syracuse, 1949-50

HIGHEST WINNING PCT., ROAD

.816 .....31-7 Los Angeles, 1971-72

.800 .....32-8 Boston, 1972-73

.780 .....32-9 Boston, 1974-75

CONSECUTIVE WINS

33 ....Los Angeles, Nov. 5, 1971-Jan. 7, 1972

20 ....Milwaukee, Feb. 6-March 8, 1971

20 ....Washington, March 13-Dec. 4, 1948 (overlapping seasons)

CONSECUTIVE WINS
(Start of Season)

15 ....Washington, Nov. 3-Dec. 4, 1948

14 ....Boston, Oct. 22-Nov. 27, 1957

12 ....Seattle, Oct. 29-Nov. 19, 1982

CONSECUTIVE LOSSES

24 ....Cleveland, March 19-Nov. 5, 1982 (overlapping seasons)

21 ....Detroit, March 7-Oct. 22, 1980 (overlapping seasons)

20 ....Philadelphia, Jan. 9-Feb. 11, 1973

20 ....Dallas, Nov. 13-Dec. 22, 1993

CONSECUTIVE WINS, HOME
38 ....Boston, Dec. 10, 1985-Nov. 28, 1986
           (overlapping seasons)
36 ....Philadelphia, Jan. 14, 1966-Jan. 20,
           1967 (overlapping seasons)
34 ....Portland, March 5, 1977-Feb. 3, 1978
           (overlapping seasons)

CONSECUTIVE WINS, ROAD
16 ....Los Angeles, Nov. 6, 1971-Jan. 7, 1972
12 ....New York, Oct. 14-Dec. 10, 1969
12 ....Los Angeles, Oct. 15-Dec. 20, 1972

HIGHEST SCORING AVERAGE
126.5 ...Denver, 1981-82
125.4 ...Philadelphia, 1961-62
125.2 ...Philadelphia, 1966-67

LOWEST SCORING AVERAGE
(Since 1954-55, first year of the 24-second
clock)
87.4 .....Milwaukee, 1954-55
90.8 .....Rochester, 1954-55
91.1 .....Syracuse, 1954-55

FEWEST POINTS ALLOWED PER GAME
(Since 1954-55, first year of the 24-second
clock)
89.9 .....Syracuse, 1954-55
90.0 .....Ft. Wayne, 1954-55
90.4 .....Milwaukee, 1954-55

MOST POINTS ALLOWED PER GAME
130.8 ...Denver, 1990-91
126.0 ...Denver, 1981-82
125.1 ...Seattle, 1967-68

TEAM RECORDS—GAME

MOST POINTS
186 ......Detroit vs. Denver, Dec. 13, 1983
           (3 OT)
184 ......Denver vs. Detroit, Dec. 13, 1983
           (3 OT)
173 ......Boston vs. Minneapolis, Feb. 27, 1959
173 ......Phoenix vs. Denver, Nov. 10, 1990
171 ......San Antonio vs. Milwaukee, March 6,
           1982 (3 OT)
169 ......Philadelphia vs. New York, March 2,
           1962

FEWEST POINTS
(Since 1954-55, first year of the 24-second
clock)
57 ....Milwaukee vs. Boston, Feb. 27, 1955
59 ....Sacramento vs. Charlotte, Jan. 10, 1991
61 ....New York vs. Detroit, April 12, 1992
61 ....Indiana vs. Cleveland, March 22, 1994

MOST POINTS, BOTH TEAMS
370 ...Detroit (186) vs. Denver (184), Dec. 13,
        1983 (3 OT)
337 ...San Antonio (171) vs. Milwaukee (166),
        March 6, 1982 (3 OT)
318 ...Denver (163) vs. San Antonio (155), Jan.
        11, 1984

316 ...Philadelphia (169) vs. New York (147),
        March 2, 1962
316 ...Cincinnati (165) vs. San Diego (151),
        March 12, 1970
316 ...Phoenix (173) vs. Denver (143), Nov. 10,
        1990

FEWEST POINTS, BOTH TEAMS
(Since 1954-55, first year of the 24-second
clock)
119 ...Milwaukee (57) vs. Boston (62), Feb. 27,
        1955
133 ...New York (61) vs. Detroit (72), April 12,
        1992
135 ...Syracuse (66) vs. Ft. Wayne (69), Jan. 25,
        1955

LARGEST MARGIN OF VICTORY
68 .....Cleveland (148) vs. Miami (80), Dec. 17,
        1991
63 .....Los Angeles (162) vs. Golden State (99),
        March 19, 1972
62 .....Syracuse (162) vs. New York (100), Dec.
        25, 1960
59 .....Golden State (150) vs. Indiana (91),
        March 19, 1977
59 .....Milwaukee (143) vs. Detroit (84), Dec. 26,
        1978

PLAYOFF RECORDS—CAREER

POINTS
5,762 ...Kareem Abdul-Jabbar
4,457 ...Jerry West
3,897 ...Larry Bird

SCORING AVERAGE
(Minimum 25 Games)
34.7 .....Michael Jordan
29.1 .....Jerry West
27.3 .....Karl Malone

REBOUNDS
4,104 ...Bill Russell
3,913 ...Wilt Chamberlain
2,481 ...Kareem Abdul-Jabbar

REBOUNDS PER GAME
(Minimum 25 Games)
24.9 .....Bill Russell
24.5 ....Wilt Chamberlain
14.9 .....Wes Unseld

ASSISTS
2,320 ...Magic Johnson
1,062 ...Larry Bird
1,006 ...Dennis Johnson

ASSISTS PER GAME
(Minimum 25 Games)
12.5 .....Magic Johnson
11.1 ....John Stockton
 8.9......Isiah Thomas

PLAYOFF RECORDS—SERIES

POINTS
2-Game Series
68 ....Bob McAdoo, NY vs. CLE, 1978

3-Game Series
135 ......Michael Jordan, CHI vs. MIA, 1992

4-Game Series
150 ......Akeem Olajuwon, HOU vs. DAL, 1988

5-Game Series
226 ......Michael Jordan, CHI vs. CLE, 1988

6-Game Series
278 ......Jerry West, LA vs. BAL, 1965

7-Game Series
284 ......Elgin Baylor, LA vs. BOS, 1962

REBOUNDS
2-Game Series
41 ....Moses Malone, HOU vs. ATL, 1979

3-Game Series
84 ....Bill Russell, BOS vs. SYR, 1957

4-Game Series
118 ......Bill Russell, BOS vs. MIN, 1959

5-Game Series
160 ......Wilt Chamberlain, PHI vs. BOS, 1967

6-Game Series
171 ......Wilt Chamberlain, PHI vs. SF, 1967

7-Game Series
220 ......Wilt Chamberlain, PHI vs. BOS, 1965

ASSISTS
2-Game Series
20 ....Frank Johnson, WAS vs. NJ, 1982

3-Game Series
48 ....Magic Johnson, LAL vs. SA, 1986

4-Game Series
57 ....Magic Johnson, LAL vs. PHO, 1989

5-Game Series
85 ....Magic Johnson, LAL vs. POR, 1985

6-Game Series
90 ....Johnny Moore, SA vs. LA, 1983

7-Game Series
115 ......John Stockton, UTA vs. LAL, 1988

PLAYOFF RECORDS—GAME

POINTS
63.....Michael Jordan, CHI vs. BOS, April 20, 1986 (2 OT)
61.....Elgin Baylor, LA vs. BOS, April 14, 1962
56.....Wilt Chamberlain, PHI vs. SYR, March 22, 1962
56.....Michael Jordan, CHI vs. MIA, Apr. 29, 1992
56......Charles Barkley, PHO vs. GS, May 4, 1994

REBOUNDS
41.....Wilt Chamberlain, PHI vs. BOS, April 5, 1967
40.....Bill Russell, BOS vs. PHI, March 23, 1958
40.....Bill Russell, BOS vs. STL, March 29, 1960
40.....Bill Russell, BOS vs. LA, April 18, 1962 (OT)

ASSISTS
24......Magic Johnson, LA vs. PHO, May 15, 1984
24.....John Stockton, UTA vs. LAL, May 17, 1988
23.....Magic Johnson, LAL vs. POR, May 3, 1985

STEALS
8.......Rick Barry, GS vs. SEA, April 14, 1975
8.......Lionel Hollins, POR vs. LA, May 8, 1977
8.......Maurice Cheeks, PHI vs. NJ, April 11, 1979
8.......Craig Hodges, MIL vs. PHI, May 9, 1986
8.......Tim Hardaway, GS vs. LAL, May 8, 1991

BLOCKED SHOTS
10.....Mark Eaton, UTA vs. HOU, April 26, 1985
10.....Akeem Olajuwon, HOU vs. LAL, April 29, 1990

PLAYOFF RECORDS—TEAM

CONSECUTIVE GAMES WON
13.....L.A. Lakers, 1988-89
12.....Detroit, 1989-90
9.....Los Angeles, 1982
9.....Chicago, 1992-93

CONSECUTIVE GAMES LOST
11.....Baltimore, 1965-66 and 1969-70
11.....Denver, 1988-90 and 1994
10.....New Jersey, 1984-86 and 1992

CONSECUTIVE SERIES WON
18.....Boston, 1959-1967
13.....Chicago, 1991-94
11.....L.A. Lakers, 1987-89

MOST POINTS, GAME
157...Boston vs. New York, April 28, 1990
156...Milwaukee vs. Philadelphia, March 30, 1970
153...L.A. Lakers vs. Denver, May 22, 1985
153...Portland vs. Phoenix, May 11, 1992 (2 OT)

FEWEST POINTS, GAME
(Since 1954-55, first year of the 24-second clock)
68.....New York vs. Indiana, May 28, 1994
69.....Indiana vs. Atlanta, May 12, 1994

70.....Golden State vs. Los Angeles, April 21, 1973
70.....Seattle vs. Houston, April 23, 1982

MOST POINTS, BOTH TEAMS, GAME
304...Portland (153) vs. Phoenix (151), May 11, 1992 (2 OT)
285...San Antonio (152) vs. Denver (133), April 26, 1983
285...Boston (157) vs. New York (128), April 28, 1990

FEWEST POINTS, BOTH TEAMS, GAME
145...Syracuse (71) vs. Ft. Wayne (74), March 24, 1956
156...New York (68) vs. Indiana (88), May 28, 1994
157...Kansas City (76) vs. Phoenix (81), April 17, 1981
157...Detroit (78) vs. Boston (79), May 30, 1988

LARGEST MARGIN OF VICTORY, GAME
58.....Minneapolis (133) vs. St. Louis (75), March 19, 1956
56.....Los Angeles (126) vs. Golden State (70), April 21, 1973
50.....Milwaukee (136) vs. San Francisco (86), April 4, 1971

NBA FIRST-ROUND PICKS
(Since 1970)

ATLANTA HAWKS

1994	(no 1st-round pick)
1993	Doug Edwards, Florida St.
1992	Adam Keefe, Stanford
1991	Stacey Augmon, UNLV
	Anthony Avent, Seton Hall
1990	Rumeal Robinson, Michigan
1989	Roy Marble, Iowa
1988	(no 1st-round pick)
1987	Dallas Comegys, DePaul
1986	Billy Thompson, Louisville
1985	Jon Koncak, Southern Methodist
1984	Kevin Willis, Michigan St.
1983	(no 1st-round pick)
1982	Keith Edmonson, Purdue
1981	Al Wood, N. Carolina
1980	Don Collins, Washington St.
1979	(no 1st-round pick)
1978	Butch Lee, Marquette
	Jack Givens, Kentucky
1977	Tree Rollins, Clemson
1976	Armond Hill, Princeton
1975	David Thompson, N. Carolina St.
	Marvin Webster, Morgan St.
1974	Tom Henderson, Hawaii
	Mike Sojourner, Utah
1973	Dwight Jones, Houston
	John Brown, Missouri
1972	(no 1st-round pick)
1971	George Trapp, Long Beach St.
1970	Pete Maravich, Louisiana St.
	John Vallely, UCLA

BOSTON CELTICS

1994	Eric Montross, N. Carolina
1993	Acie Earl, Iowa
1992	Jon Barry, Georgia Tech
1991	Rick Fox, N. Carolina
1990	Dee Brown, Jacksonville
1989	Michael Smith, Brigham Young
1988	Brian Shaw, Cal.-Santa Barbara
1987	Reggie Lewis, Northeastern
1986	Len Bias, Maryland
1985	Sam Vincent, Michigan St.
1984	Michael Young, Houston
1983	Greg Kite, Brigham Young
1982	Darren Tillis, Cleveland St.
1981	Charles Bradley, Wyoming
1980	Kevin McHale, Minnesota
1979	(no 1st-round pick)
1978	Larry Bird, Indiana St.
	Freeman Williams, Portland St.
1977	Cedric Maxwell, N.C.-Charlotte
1976	Norm Cook, Kansas
1975	Tom Boswell, S. Carolina
1974	Glenn McDonald, Long Beach St.

1973	Steve Downing, Indiana
1972	Paul Westphal, Southern Cal.
1971	Clarence Glover, Western Kentucky
1970	Dave Cowens, Florida St.

CHARLOTTE HORNETS

1994	(no 1st-round pick)
1993	Greg Graham, Indiana
	Scott Burrell, Connecticut
1992	Alonzo Mourning, Georgetown
1991	Larry Johnson, UNLV
1990	Kendall Gill, Illinois
1989	J.R. Reid, N. Carolina
1988	Rex Chapman, Kentucky

CHICAGO BULLS

1994	Dickey Simpkins, Providence
1993	Corie Blount, Cincinnati
1992	Byron Houston, Oklahoma St.
1991	Mark Randall, Kansas
1990	(no 1st-round pick)
1989	Stacey King, Oklahoma
	B.J. Armstrong, Iowa
	Jeff Sanders, Georgia Southern
1988	Will Perdue, Vanderbilt
1987	Olden Polynice, Virginia
	Horace Grant, Clemson
1986	Brad Sellers, Ohio St.
1985	Keith Lee, Memphis St.
1984	Michael Jordan, N. Carolina
1983	Sidney Green, UNLV
1982	Quintin Dailey, San Francisco
1981	Orlando Woolridge, Notre Dame
1980	Kelvin Ransey, Ohio St.
1979	David Greenwood, UCLA
1978	Reggie Theus, UNLV
1977	Tate Armstrong, Duke
1976	Scott May, Indiana
1975	(no 1st-round pick)
1974	Maurice Lucas, Marquette
	Cliff Pondexter, Long Beach St.
1973	Kevin Kunnert, Iowa
1972	Ralph Simpson, Michigan St.
1971	Kennedy McIntosh, E. Michigan
1970	Jimmy Collins, New Mexico St.

CLEVELAND CAVALIERS

1994	(no 1st-round pick)
1993	Chris Mills, Arizona
1992	(no 1st-round pick)
1991	Terrell Brandon, Oregon
1990	(no 1st-round pick)
1989	John Morton, Seton Hall
1988	Randolph Keys, Southern Miss.
1987	Kevin Johnson, California
1986	Brad Daugherty, N. Carolina
	Ron Harper, Miami (OH)

1985	Charles Oakley, Virginia Union
1984	Tim McCormick, Michigan
1983	Roy Hinson, Rutgers
	Stewart Granger, Villanova
1982	John Bagley, Boston College
1981	(no 1st-round pick)
1980	Chad Kinch, N.C.-Charlotte
1979	(no 1st-round pick)
1978	Mike Mitchell, Auburn
1977	(no 1st-round pick)
1976	Chuckie Williams, Kansas St.
1975	John Lambert, Southern Cal.
1974	Campy Russell, Michigan
1973	Jim Brewer, Minnesota
1972	Dwight Davis, Houston
1971	Austin Carr, Notre Dame
1970	John Johnson, Iowa

DALLAS MAVERICKS

1994	Jason Kidd, California
	Tony Dumas, Missouri-K.C.
1993	Jamal Mashburn, Kentucky
1992	Jim Jackson, Ohio St.
1991	Doug Smith, Missouri
1990	(no 1st-round pick)
1989	Randy White, Louisiana Tech
1988	(no 1st-round pick)
1987	Jim Farmer, Alabama
1986	Roy Tarpley, Michigan
1985	Detlef Schrempf, Washington
	Bill Wennington, St. John's
	Uwe Blab, Indiana
1984	Sam Perkins, N. Carolina
	Terence Stansbury, Temple
1983	Dale Ellis, Tennessee
	Derek Harper, Illinois
1982	Bill Garnett, Wyoming
1981	Mark Aguirre, DePaul
	Rolando Blackman, Kansas St.
1980	Kiki Vandeweghe, UCLA

DENVER NUGGETS

1994	Jalen Rose, Michigan
1993	Rodney Rogers, Wake Forest
1992	LaPhonso Ellis, Notre Dame
	Bryant Stith, Virginia
1991	Dikembe Mutombo, Georgetown
	Mark Macon, Temple
1990	Chris Jackson, Louisiana St.
1989	Todd Lichti, Stanford
1988	Jerome Lane, Pittsburgh
1987	(no 1st-round pick)
1986	Maurice Martin, St. Joseph's
	Mark Alarie, Duke
1985	Blair Rasmussen, Oregon
1984	(no 1st-round pick)
1983	Howard Carter, Louisiana St.
1982	Rob Williams, Houston
1981	(no 1st-round pick)
1980	James Ray, Jacksonville

	Carl Nicks, Indiana St.
1979	(no 1st-round pick)
1978	Rod Griffin, Wake Forest
	Mike Evans, Kansas St.
1977	Tom LaGarde, N. Carolina
	Anthony Roberts, Oral Roberts
1976	(no 1st-round pick)

DETROIT PISTONS

1994	Grant Hill, Duke
1993	Lindsey Hunter, Jackson St.
	Allan Houston, Tennessee
1992	Don MacLean, UCLA
1991	(no 1st-round pick)
1990	Lance Blanks, Texas
1989	Kenny Battle, Illinois
1988	(no 1st-round pick)
1987	(no 1st-round pick)
1986	John Salley, Georgia Tech
1985	Joe Dumars, McNeese St.
1984	Tony Campbell, Ohio St.
1983	Antoine Carr, Wichita St.
1982	Cliff Levingston, Wichita St.
	Ricky Pierce, Rice
1981	Isiah Thomas, Indiana
	Kelly Tripucka, Notre Dame
1980	Larry Drew, Missouri
1979	Greg Kelser, Michigan St.
	Roy Hamilton, UCLA
	Phil Hubbard, Michigan
1978	(no 1st-round pick)
1977	(no 1st-round pick)
1976	Leon Douglas, Alabama
1975	(no 1st-round pick)
1974	Al Eberhard, Missouri
1973	(no 1st-round pick)
1972	Bob Nash, Hawaii
1971	Curtis Rowe, UCLA
1970	Bob Lanier, St. Bonaventure

GOLDEN ST. WARRIORS

1994	Clifford Rozier, Louisville
1993	Anfernee Hardaway, Memphis St.
1992	Latrell Sprewell, Alabama
1991	Chris Gatling, Old Dominion
	Victor Alexander, Iowa St.
	Shaun Vandiver, Colorado
1990	Tyrone Hill, Xavier
1989	Tim Hardaway, Texas-El Paso
1988	Mitch Richmond, Kansas St.
1987	Tellis Frank, Western Kentucky
1986	Chris Washburn, N. Carolina St.
1985	Chris Mullin, St. John's
1984	(no 1st-round pick)
1983	Russell Cross, Purdue
1982	Lester Conner, Oregon St.
1981	(no 1st-round pick)
1980	Joe Barry Carroll, Purdue
	Rickey Brown, Mississippi St.
1979	(no 1st-round pick)

1978	Purvis Short, Jackson St.
	Raymond Townsend, UCLA
1977	Rickey Green, Michigan
	Wesley Cox, Louisville
1976	Robert Parish, Centenary
	Sonny Parker, Texas A&M
1975	Joe Bryant, La Salle
1974	Jamaal Wilkes, UCLA
1973	Kevin Joyce, S. Carolina
1972	(no 1st-round pick)
1971	Darnell Hillman, San Jose St.
1970	(no 1st-round pick)

HOUSTON ROCKETS

1994	(no 1st-round pick)
1993	Sam Cassell, Florida St.
1992	Robert Horry, Alabama
1991	John Turner, Phillips
1990	Alec Kessler, Georgia
1989	(no 1st-round pick)
1988	Derrick Chievous, Missouri
1987	(no 1st-round pick)
1986	Buck Johnson, Alabama
1985	Steve Harris, Tulsa
1984	Akeem Olajuwon, Houston
1983	Ralph Sampson, Virginia
	Rodney McCray, Louisville
1982	Terry Teagle, Baylor
1981	(no 1st-round pick)
1980	(no 1st-round pick)
1979	Lee Johnson, E. Texas St.
1978	(no 1st-round pick)
1977	(no 1st-round pick)
1976	John Lucas, Maryland
1975	Joe Meriweather, Southern Illinois
1974	Bobby Jones, N. Carolina
1973	Ed Ratleff, Long Beach St.
1972	(no 1st-round pick)
1971	Cliff Meely, Colorado
1970	Rudy Tomjanovich, Michigan

INDIANA PACERS

1994	Eric Piatkowski, Nebraska
1993	Scott Haskin, Oregon St.
1992	Malik Sealy, St. John's
1991	Dale Davis, Clemson
1990	(no 1st-round pick)
1989	George McCloud, Florida St.
1988	Rik Smits, Marist
1987	Reggie Miller, UCLA
1986	Chuck Person, Auburn
1985	Wayman Tisdale, Oklahoma
1984	Vern Fleming, Georgia
1983	Steve Stipanovich, Missouri
	Mitchell Wiggins, Florida St.
1982	Clark Kellogg, Ohio St.
1981	Herb Williams, Ohio St.
1980	(no 1st-round pick)
1979	Dudley Bradley, N. Carolina
1978	Rick Robey, Kentucky

1977	(no 1st-round pick)
1976	(no 1st-round pick)

LOS ANGELES CLIPPERS

1994	Lamond Murray, California
	Greg Minor, Louisville
1993	Terry Dehere, Seton Hall
1992	Randy Woods, La Salle
	Elmore Spencer, UNLV
1991	LeRon Ellis, Syracuse
1990	Bo Kimble, Loyola Marymount
	Loy Vaught, Michigan
1989	Danny Ferry, Duke
1988	Danny Manning, Kansas
	Hersey Hawkins, Bradley
1987	Reggie Williams, Georgetown
	Joe Wolf, N. Carolina
	Ken Norman, Illinois
1986	(no 1st-round pick)
1985	Benoit Benjamin, Creighton
1984	Lancaster Gordon, Louisville
	Michael Cage, San Diego St.
1983	Byron Scott, Arizona St.
1982	Terry Cummings, DePaul
1981	Tom Chambers, Utah
1980	Michael Brooks, La Salle
1979	(no 1st-round pick)
1978	(no 1st-round pick)
1977	(no 1st-round pick)
1976	Adrian Dantley, Notre Dame
1975	(no 1st-round pick)
1974	Tom McMillen, Maryland
1973	Ernie DiGregorio, Providence
1972	Bob McAdoo, N. Carolina
1971	Elmore Smith, Kentucky St.
1970	John Hummer, Princeton

LOS ANGELES LAKERS

1994	Eddie Jones, Temple
1993	George Lynch, North Carolina
1992	Anthony Peeler, Missouri
1991	(no 1st-round pick)
1990	Elden Campbell, Clemson
1989	Vlade Divac, Yugoslavia
1988	David Rivers, Notre Dame
1987	(no 1st-round pick)
1986	Ken Barlow, Notre Dame
1985	A.C. Green, Oregon St.
1984	Earl Jones, District of Columbia
1983	(no 1st-round pick)
1982	James Worthy, N. Carolina
1981	Mike McGee, Michigan
1980	(no 1st-round pick)
1979	Earvin Johnson, Michigan St.
	Brad Holland, UCLA
1978	(no 1st-round pick)
1977	Ken Carr, N. Carolina St.
	Brad Davis, Maryland
	Norm Nixon, Duquesne
1976	(no 1st-round pick)

1975 David Meyers, UCLA
Junior Bridgeman, Louisville
1974 Brian Winters, S. Carolina
1973 Kermit Washington, American
1972 Travis Grant, Kentucky St.
1971 Jim Cleamons, Ohio St.
1970 Jim McMillian, Columbia

MIAMI HEAT
1994 Khalid Reeves, Arizona
1993 (no 1st-round pick)
1992 Harold Miner, Southern Cal.
1991 Steve Smith, Michigan St.
1990 Willie Burton, Minnesota
Dave Jamerson, Ohio
1989 Glen Rice, Michigan
1988 Rony Seikaly, Syracuse
Kevin Edwards, DePaul

MILWAUKEE BUCKS
1994 Glenn Robinson, Purdue
Eric Mobley, Pittsburgh
1993 Vin Baker, Hartford
1992 Todd Day, Arkansas
Lee Mayberry, Arkansas
1991 Kevin Brooks, S.W. Louisiana
1990 Terry Mills, Michigan
1989 (no 1st-round pick)
1988 Jeff Grayer, Iowa St.
1987 (no 1st-round pick)
1986 Scott Skiles, Michigan St.
1985 Jerry Reynolds, Louisiana St.
1984 Kenny Fields, UCLA
1983 Randy Breuer, Minnesota
1982 Paul Pressey, Tulsa
1981 Alton Lister, Arizona St.
1980 (no 1st-round pick)
1979 Sidney Moncrief, Arkansas
1978 George Johnson, St. John's
1977 Kent Benson, Indiana
Marques Johnson, UCLA
Ernie Grunfeld, Tennessee
1976 Quinn Buckner, Indiana
1975 (no 1st-round pick)
1974 Gary Brokaw, Notre Dame
1973 Swen Nater, UCLA
1972 Russell Lee, Marshall
Julius Erving, Massachusetts
1971 Collis Jones, Notre Dame
1970 Gary Freeman, Oregon St.

MINNESOTA TIMBERWOLVES
1994 Donyell Marshall, Connecticut
1993 Isaiah (J.R.) Rider, UNLV
1992 Christian Laettner, Duke
1991 Luc Longley, New Mexico
1990 Felton Spencer, Louisville
Gerald Glass, Mississippi
1989 Pooh Richardson, UCLA

NEW JERSEY NETS
1994 Yinka Dare, G. Washington
1993 Rex Walters, Kansas
1992 (no 1st-round pick)
1991 Kenny Anderson, Georgia Tech
1990 Derrick Coleman, Syracuse
Tate George, Connecticut
1989 Mookie Blaylock, Oklahoma
1988 Chris Morris, Auburn
1987 Dennis Hopson, Ohio St.
1986 Dwayne Washington, Syracuse
1985 (no 1st-round pick)
1984 Jeff Turner, Vanderbilt
1983 (no 1st-round pick)
1982 Sleepy Floyd, Georgetown
Eddie Phillips, Alabama
1981 Buck Williams, Maryland
Albert King, Maryland
Ray Tolbert, Indiana
1980 Mike O'Koren, N. Carolina
Mike Gminski, Duke
1979 Calvin Natt, N.E. Louisiana
Cliff Robinson, Southern Cal.
1978 Winford Boynes, San Francisco
1977 Bernard King, Tennessee
1976 (no 1st-round pick)

NEW YORK KNICKS
1994 Monty Williams, Notre Dame
Charlie Ward, Florida St.
1993 (no 1st-round pick)
1992 Hubert Davis, North Carolina
1991 Greg Anthony, UNLV
1990 Jerrod Mustaf, Maryland
1989 (no 1st-round pick)
1988 Rod Strickland, DePaul
1987 Mark Jackson, St. John's
1986 Kenny Walker, Kentucky
1985 Patrick Ewing, Georgetown
1984 (no 1st-round pick)
1983 Darrell Walker, Arkansas
1982 Trent Tucker, Minnesota
1981 (no 1st-round pick)
1980 Mike Woodson, Indiana
1979 Bill Cartwright, San Francisco
Larry Demic, Arizona
Sly Williams, Rhode Island
1978 Micheal Ray Richardson, Montana
1977 Ray Williams, Minnesota
1976 (no 1st-round pick)
1975 Eugene Short, Jackson St.
1974 (no 1st-round pick)
1973 Mel Davis, St. John's
1972 Tom Riker, S. Carolina
1971 Dean Meminger, Marquette
1970 Mike Price, Illinois

ORLANDO MAGIC
1994 Brooks Thompson, Oklahoma St.
1993 Chris Webber, Michigan

Geert Hammink, Louisiana St.
1992 Shaquille O'Neal, Louisiana St.
1991 Brian Williams, Arizona
Stanley Roberts, Louisiana St.
1990 Dennis Scott, Georgia Tech
1989 Nick Anderson, Illinois

PHILADELPHIA 76ERS

1994 Sharone Wright, Clemson
B.J. Tyler, Texas
1993 Shawn Bradley, Brigham Young
1992 Clarence Weatherspoon, S. Miss.
1991 (no 1st-round pick)
1990 (no 1st-round pick)
1989 Kenny Payne, Louisville
1988 Charles Smith, Pittsburgh
1987 Chris Welp, Washington
1986 (no 1st-round pick)
1985 Terry Catledge, S. Alabama
1984 Charles Barkley, Auburn
Leon Wood, Fullerton St.
Tom Sewell, Lamar
1983 Leo Rautins, Syracuse
1982 Mark McNamara, California
1981 Franklin Edwards, Cleveland St.
1980 Andrew Toney, S.W. Louisiana
Monti Davis, Tennessee St.
1979 Jim Spanarkel, Duke
1978 (no 1st-round pick)
1977 Glenn Mosley, Seton Hall
1976 Terry Furlow, Michigan St.
1975 Darryl Dawkins, Evans High School
1974 Marvin Barnes, Providence
1973 Doug Collins, Illinois St.
Raymond Lewis, Los Angeles St.
1972 Fred Boyd, Oregon St.
1971 Dana Lewis, Tulsa
1970 Al Henry, Wisconsin

PHOENIX SUNS

1994 Wesley Person, Auburn
1993 Malcolm Mackey, Georgia Tech
1992 Oliver Miller, Arkansas
1991 (no 1st-round pick)
1990 Jayson Williams, St. John's
1989 Anthony Cook, Arizona
1988 Tim Perry, Temple
Dan Majerle, Central Michigan
1987 Armon Gilliam, UNLV
1986 William Bedford, Memphis St.
1985 Ed Pinckney, Villanova
1984 Jay Humphries, Colorado
1983 (no 1st-round pick)
1982 David Thirdkill, Bradley
1981 Larry Nance, Clemson
1980 (no 1st-round pick)
1979 Kyle Macy, Kentucky
1978 Marty Byrnes, Syracuse
1977 Walter Davis, N. Carolina
1976 Ron Lee, Oregon

1975 Alvan Adams, Oklahoma
Ricky Sobers, UNLV
1974 John Shumate, Notre Dame
1973 Mike Bantom, St. Joseph's
1972 Corky Calhoun, Pennsylvania
1971 John Roche, S. Carolina
1970 Greg Howard, New Mexico

PORTLAND TRAIL BLAZERS

1994 Aaron McKie, Temple
1993 James Robinson, Alabama
1992 Dave Johnson, Syracuse
1991 (no 1st-round pick)
1990 Alaa Abdelnaby, Duke
1989 Byron Irvin, Missouri
1988 Mark Bryant, Seton Hall
1987 Ronnie Murphy, Jacksonville
1986 Walter Berry, St. John's
Arvidas Sabonis, Soviet Union
1985 Terry Porter, Wisc.-Stevens Point
1984 Sam Bowie, Kentucky
Bernard Thompson, Fresno St.
1983 Clyde Drexler, Houston
1982 Lafayette Lever, Arizona St.
1981 Jeff Lamp, Virginia
Darnell Valentine, Kansas
1980 Ronnie Lester, Iowa
1979 Jim Paxson, Dayton
1978 Mychal Thompson, Minnesota
Ron Brewer, Arkansas
1977 Rich Laurel, Hofstra
1976 Wally Walker, Virginia
1975 Lionel Hollins, Arizona St.
1974 Bill Walton, UCLA
1973 Barry Parkhill, Virginia
1972 LaRue Martin, Loyola (IL)
1971 Sidney Wicks, UCLA
1970 Geoff Petrie, Princeton

SACRAMENTO KINGS

1994 Brian Grant, Xavier
1993 Bobby Hurley, Duke
1992 Walt Williams, Maryland
1991 Billy Owens, Syracuse
Pete Chilcutt, N. Carolina
1990 Lionel Simmons, La Salle
Travis Mays, Texas
Duane Causwell, Temple
Anthony Bonner, St. Louis
1989 Pervis Ellison, Louisville
1988 Ricky Berry, San Jose St.
1987 Kenny Smith, N. Carolina
1986 Harold Pressley, Villanova
1985 Joe Kleine, Arkansas
1984 Otis Thorpe, Providence
1983 Ennis Whatley, Alabama
1982 LaSalle Thompson, Texas
Brook Steppe, Georgia Tech
1981 Steve Johnson, Oregon St.
Kevin Loder, Alabama St.

1980	Hawkeye Whitney, N. Carolina St.
1979	Reggie King, Alabama
1978	Phil Ford, N. Carolina
1977	Otis Birdsong, Houston
1976	Richard Washington, UCLA
1975	Bill Robinzine, DePaul
	Bob Bigelow, Pennsylvania
1974	Scott Wedman, Colorado
1973	Ron Behagen, Minnesota
1972	(no 1st-round pick)
1971	Ken Durrett, La Salle
1970	Sam Lacey, New Mexico St.

SAN ANTONIO SPURS

1994	Bill Curley, Boston College
1993	(no 1st-round pick)
1992	Tracy Murray, UCLA
1991	(no 1st-round pick)
1990	Dwayne Schintzius, Florida
1989	Sean Elliott, Arizona
1988	Willie Anderson, Georgia
1987	David Robinson, Navy
	Greg Anderson, Houston
1986	Johnny Dawkins, Duke
1985	Alfredrick Hughes, Loyola (IL)
1984	Alvin Robertson, Arkansas
1983	John Paxson, Notre Dame
1982	(no 1st-round pick)
1981	(no 1st-round pick)
1980	Reggie Johnson, Tennessee
1979	Wiley Peck, Mississippi St.
1978	Frankie Sanders, Southern
1977	(no 1st-round pick)
1976	(no 1st-round pick)

SEATTLE SUPERSONICS

1994	Carlos Rogers, Tennessee St.
1993	Ervin Johnson, New Orleans
1992	Doug Christie, Pepperdine
1991	Rich King, Nebraska
1990	Gary Payton, Oregon St.
1989	Dana Barros, Boston College
	Shawn Kemp, Trinity J.C.
1988	Gary Grant, Michigan
1987	Scottie Pippen, Central Arkansas
	Derrick McKey, Alabama
1986	(no 1st-round pick)
1985	Xavier McDaniel, Wichita St.
1984	(no 1st-round pick)
1983	Jon Sundvold, Missouri
1982	(no 1st-round pick)
1981	Danny Vranes, Utah
1980	Bill Hanzlik, Notre Dame
1979	James Bailey, Rutgers
	Vinnie Johnson, Baylor
1978	(no 1st-round pick)
1977	Jack Sikma, Illinois Wesleyan
1976	Bob Wilkerson, Indiana
1975	Frank Oleynick, Seattle
1974	Tom Burleson, N. Carolina St.

1973	Mike Green, Louisiana Tech
1972	Bud Stallworth, Kansas
1971	Fred Brown, Iowa
1970	Jim Ard, Cincinnati

UTAH JAZZ

1994	(no 1st-round pick)
1993	Luther Wright, Seton Hall
1992	(no 1st-round pick)
1991	Eric Murdock, Providence
1990	(no 1st-round pick)
1989	Blue Edwards, E. Carolina
1988	Eric Leckner, Wyoming
1987	Jose Ortiz, Oregon St.
1986	Dell Curry, Virginia Tech
1985	Karl Malone, Louisiana Tech
1984	John Stockton, Gonzaga
1983	Thurl Bailey, N. Carolina St.
1982	Dominique Wilkins, Georgia
1981	Danny Schayes, Syracuse
1980	Darrell Griffith, Louisville
	John Duren, Georgetown
1979	Larry Knight, Loyola (IL)
1978	James Hardy, San Francisco
1977	(no 1st-round pick)
1976	(no 1st-round pick)
1975	Rich Kelley, Stanford
1974	(no 1st-round pick)

WASHINGTON BULLETS

1994	Juwan Howard, Michigan
1993	Calbert Cheaney, Indiana
1992	Tom Gugliotta, N. Carolina St.
1991	LaBradford Smith, Louisville
1990	(no 1st-round pick)
1989	Tom Hammonds, Georgia Tech
1988	Harvey Grant, Oklahoma
1987	Muggsy Bogues, Wake Forest
1986	John Williams, Louisiana St.
	Anthony Jones, UNLV
1985	Kenny Green, Wake Forest
1984	Melvin Turpin, Kentucky
1983	Jeff Malone, Mississippi St.
	Randy Wittman, Indiana
1982	(no 1st-round pick)
1981	Frank Johnson, Wake Forest
1980	Wes Matthews, Wisconsin
1979	(no 1st-round pick)
1978	Roger Phegley, Bradley
	Dave Corzine, DePaul
1977	Greg Ballard, Oregon
	Bo Ellis, Marquette
1976	Mitch Kupchak, N. Carolina
	Larry Wright, Grambling
1975	Kevin Grevey, Kentucky
1974	Len Elmore, Maryland
1973	Nick Weatherspoon, Illinois
1972	(no 1st-round pick)
1971	Stan Love, Oregon
1970	George Johnson, Stephen F. Austin

N B A Year-By-Year Results

This section lists the final standings of every NBA season since its inception in 1946-47. Actually, in its first three years of existence, the league was called the BAA (Basketball Association of America), but it is still considered part of NBA history.

This section also includes league leaders in every major category since 1946-47. In its first four years of existence, the league kept track of only four statistics—scoring, assists, field goal percentage, and free throw percentage. In 1950-51, it began keeping track of rebounds. In 1973-74, the league added blocked shots and steals to the stat sheets. In 1979-80, the 3-point shot arrived in the NBA.

Because most statistical categories are based on averages, the NBA has had to establish qualifying criteria (e.g., a player can only qualify for the scoring championship if he appears in at least 70 games). Through the years, the league has frequently changed its qualifying criteria. These are the standards that players have had to meet in order to qualify:

Scoring
1946-47 to 1968-69: Based on total points, not on an average.
1969-70 to 1973-74: Minimum 70 games.
1974-75 to present: Minimum 70 games or 1,400 points.

Rebounds
1950-51 to 1968-69: Based on total rebounds, not on an average.
1969-70 to 1973-74: Minimum 70 games.
1974-75 to present: Minimum 70 games or 800 rebounds.

Assists
1946-47 to 1968-69: Based on total assists, not on an average.
1969-70 to 1973-74: Minimum 70 games.
1974-75 to present: Minimum 70 games or 400 assists.

Steals
1973-74: Minimum 70 games.
1974-75 to present: Minimum 70 games or 125 steals.

Blocked Shots
1973-74: Minimum 70 games.
1974-75 to present: Minimum 70 games or 100 blocks.

Field Goal Pct.
Over the years, the NBA has changed the qualifications for field goal percentage 14 times. Since 1974-75, a player has needed to make 300 field goals in order to qualify.

Free Throw Pct.
Since its inception, the league has changed the qualifications for free throw percentage 13 times. Since 1974-75, a player has needed to make 125 free throws in order to qualify.

3-Point Field Goal Pct.
1979-80 to 1989-90: Minimum 25 3-point field goals made.
1990-91 to present: Minimum 50 3-point field goals made.

Besides standings and statistics, this section contains results of every playoff series of every season. The last year of this section, 1993-94, has been expanded to include more statistical information.

1946-47
FINAL STANDINGS

Eastern Division

	W	L	PCT.	GB
Washington	49	11	.817	
Philadelphia	35	25	.583	14
New York	33	27	.550	16
Providence	28	32	.467	21
Toronto	22	38	.367	27
Boston	22	38	.367	27

Western Division

	W	L	PCT.	GB
Chicago	39	22	.639	
St. Louis	38	23	.623	1
Cleveland	30	30	.500	8.5
Detroit	20	40	.333	18.5
Pittsburgh	15	45	.250	23.5

POINTS

	AVG.	NO.
J. Fulks, PHI	23.2	1389
B. Feerick, WAS	16.3	926
S. Miasek, DET	14.9	895
E. Sadowski, TOR/CLE	16.5	877
M. Zaslofsky, CHI	14.4	877
E. Calverley, PRO	14.3	845
C. Halbert, CHI	12.7	773
J. Logan, STL	12.6	770
L. Mogus, CLE/TOR	13.0	753
C. Gunther, PIT	14.1	734
D. Martin, PRO	12.2	733
F. Scolari, WAS	12.6	728
H. Beenders, PRO	12.3	713
J. Janisch, DET	11.6	697
H. McKinney, WAS	12.0	695
E. Shannon, PRO	12.1	687
M. Riebe, CLE	12.1	663
M. McCarron, TOR	10.8	649
F. Baumholtz, CLE	14.0	631
D. Carlson, CHI	10.7	630

ASSISTS

	AVG.	NO.
E. Calverley, PRO	3.4	202
K. Sailors, CLE	2.3	134
O. Schectman, NY	2.0	109
H. Dallmar, PHI	1.7	104
M. Rottner, CHI	1.7	93
S. Miasek, DET	1.6	93

E. Shannon, PRO	1.5	84
L. Mogus, CLE/TOR	1.4	84
J. Logan, STL	1.3	78
B. Feerick, WAS	1.3	69

FIELD GOAL PCT.

Bob Feerick, WAS	.401
Ed Sadowski, TOR/CLE	.369
Earl Shannon, PRO	.339
Coulby Gunther, PIT	.336
Max Zaslofsky, CHI	.329
Don Carlson, CHI	.322
Connie Simmons, BOS	.320
John Norlander, WAS	.319
Ken Sailors, CLE	.309
Mel Riebe, CLE	.307

FREE THROW PCT.

Fred Scolari, WAS	.811
Tony Kapper, PIT/BOS	.795
Stan Stutz, NY	.782
Bob Feerick, WAS	.762
John Logan, STL	.748
Max Zaslofsky, CHI	.737
Joe Fulks, PHI	.730
Leo Mogus, CLE/TOR	.723
George Mearns, PRO	.720
Tony Jaros, CHI	.707

QUARTERFINALS

Philadelphia 73, St. Louis 68
St. Louis 73, Philadelphia 51
Philadelphia 75, St. Louis 59

Cleveland 77, New York 51
New York 86, Cleveland 74
New York 93, Cleveland 71

SEMIFINALS

Chicago 81, Washington 65
Chicago 69, Washington 53
Chicago 67, Washington 55
Washington 76, Chicago 69
Washington 67, Chicago 55
Chicago 66, Washington 61

Philadelphia 82, New York 70
Philadelphia 72, New York 53

BAA FINALS

Philadelphia 84, Chicago 71
Philadelphia 85, Chicago 74
Philadelphia 75, Chicago 72
Chicago 74, Philadelphia 73
Philadelphia 83, Chicago 80

1947-48
FINAL STANDINGS

Eastern Division

	W	L	PCT.	GB
Philadelphia	27	21	.563	
New York	26	22	.542	1
Boston	20	28	.417	7
Providence	6	42	.125	21

Western Division

	W	L	PCT.	GB
St. Louis	29	19	.604	
Baltimore	28	20	.583	1
Chicago	28	20	.583	1
Washington	28	20	.583	1

POINTS	AVG.	NO.
M. Zaslofsky, CHI	21.0	1007
J. Fulks, PHI	22.1	949
E. Sadowski, BOS	19.4	910
B. Feerick, WAS	16.1	775
S. Miasek, CHI	14.9	716
C. Braun, NY	14.3	671
J. Logan, STL	13.4	644
J. Palmer, NY	13.0	622
R. Rocha, STL	12.7	611
F. Scolari, WAS	12.5	589
H. Dallmar, PHI	12.2	587
K. Hermsen, BAL	12.0	575
E. Calverley, PRO	11.9	559
J. Reiser, BAL	11.5	541
B. Smawley, STL	11.1	535
K. Sailors, PRO	11.9	524
G. Nostrand, PRO	11.6	521
M. Bloom, BAL/BOS	10.6	508
D. Holub, NY	10.5	504
B. Jeannette, BAL	10.7	491

ASSISTS	AVG.	NO.
H. Dallmar, PHI	2.5	120
E. Calverley, PRO	2.5	119
J. Seminoff, CHI	1.8	89
C. Gilmur, CHI	1.6	77
A. Phillip, CHI	2.3	74
E. Sadowski, BOS	1.6	74

	AVG.	NO.
B. Jeannette, BAL	1.5	70
J. Logan, STL	1.3	62
C. Braun, NY	1.3	61
S. Mariaschin, BOS	1.4	60

FIELD GOAL PCT.

Bob Feerick, WAS	.340
Ed Sadowski, BOS	.323
Carl Braun, NY	.323
Max Zaslofsky, CHI	.323
Chick Reiser, BAL	.322
John Palmer, NY	.315
Red Rocha, STL	.314
Mel Riebe, BOS	.309
Belus Smawley, STL	.308
Stan Miasek, CHI	.303

FREE THROW PCT.

Bob Feerick, WAS	.788
Max Zaslofsky, CHI	.784
Joe Fulks, PHI	.762
Buddy Jeannette, BAL	.758
Howie Dallmar, PHI	.744
John Palmer, NY	.744
John Logan, STL	.743
John Norlander, WAS	.742
Chick Reiser, BAL	.741
Fred Scolari, WAS	.732

QUARTERFINALS

Baltimore 85, New York 81
New York 79, Baltimore 69
Baltimore 84, New York 77

Chicago 79, Boston 72
Boston 81, Chicago 77
Chicago 81, Boston 74

SEMIFINALS

St. Louis 60, Philadelphia 58
Philadelphia 65, St. Louis 64
Philadelphia 84, St. Louis 56
St. Louis 56, Philadelphia 51
St. Louis 69, Philadelphia 62
Philadelphia 84, St. Louis 61
Philadelphia 85, St. Louis 46

Baltimore 73, Chicago 67
Baltimore 89, Chicago 72

BAA FINALS

Philadelphia 71, Baltimore 60
Baltimore 66, Philadelphia 63
Baltimore 72, Philadelphia 70
Baltimore 78, Philadelphia 75
Baltimore 91, Baltimore 82
Baltimore 88, Philadelphia 73

1948-49
FINAL STANDINGS

Eastern Division

	W	L	PCT.	GB
Washington	38	22	.633	
New York	32	28	.533	6
Baltimore	29	31	.483	9
Philadelphia	28	32	.467	10
Boston	25	35	.417	13
Providence	12	48	.200	26

Western Division

	W	L	PCT.	GB
Rochester	45	15	.750	
Minneapolis	44	16	.733	1
Chicago	38	22	.633	7
St. Louis	29	31	.483	16
Fort Wayne	22	38	.367	23
Indianapolis	18	42	.300	27

POINTS

	AVG.	NO.
G. Mikan, MIN	28.3	1698
J. Fulks, PHI	26.0	1560
M. Zaslofsky, CHI	20.6	1197
A. Risen, ROC	16.6	995
E. Sadowski, PHI	15.3	920
B. Smawley, STL	15.5	914
B. Davies, ROC	15.1	904
K. Sailors, PRO	15.8	899
C. Braun, NY	14.2	810
J. Logan, STL	14.1	803
J. Pollard, MIN	14.8	784
C. Simmons, BAL	13.0	779
R. Lumpp, IND/NY	12.7	777
B. Feerick, WAS	13.0	752
H. Shannon, PRO	13.4	736
H. McKinney, WAS	12.7	723
A. Phillip, CHI	12.0	718
J. Palmer, NY	12.3	714
K. Hermsen, WAS	11.8	708
W. Budko, BAL	11.5	692

ASSISTS

	AVG.	NO.
B. Davies, ROC	5.4	321
A. Phillip, CHI	5.3	319
J. Logan, STL	4.8	276
E. Calverley, PRO	4.3	251
G. Senesky, PHI	3.9	233
J. Seminoff, BOS	3.9	229

G. Mikan, MIN	3.6	218
K. Sailors, PRO	3.7	209
B. Feerick, WAS	3.2	188
B. Wanzer, ROC	3.1	186

FIELD GOAL PCT.

Arnie Risen, ROC	.423
George Mikan, MIN	.416
Ed Sadowski, PHI	.405
Jim Pollard, MIN	.396
Red Rocha, STL	.389
Bob Wanzer, ROC	.379
Connie Simmons, BAL	.377
Herm Schaefer, MIN	.374
Belus Smawley, STL	.372
Howie Shannon, PRO	.364

FREE THROW PCT.

Bob Feerick, WAS	.859
Max Zaslofsky, CHI	.840
Bob Wanzer, ROC	.823
Herm Schaefer, MIN	.817
Howie Shannon, PRO	.804
Harold Tidrick, IND/BAL	.800
John Logan, STL	.791
John Pelkington, FTW/BAL	.790
Walter Budko, BAL	.790
Joe Fulks, PHI	.787

EAST SEMIFINALS

Washington 92, Phil. 70
Washington 80, Phil. 78

Baltimore 82, New York 81
New York 84, Baltimore 74
New York 103, Balt. 99 (OT)

EAST FINALS

Washington 77, New York 71
New York 86, Wash. 84 (OT)
Washington 84, New York 76

WEST SEMIFINALS

Rochester 93, St. Louis 64
Rochester 66, St. Louis 64

Minneapolis 84, Chicago 77
Minneapolis 101, Chicago 85

WEST FINALS

Minneapolis 80, Rochester 79
Minneapolis 67, Rochester 55

BAA FINALS

Minneapolis 88, Washington 84
Minneapolis 76, Washington 62
Minneapolis 94, Washington 74
Washington 83, Minneapolis 71
Washington 74, Minneapolis 65
Minneapolis 77, Washington 56

1949-50
FINAL STANDINGS

Eastern Division

	W	L	PCT.	GB
Syracuse	51	13	.797	
New York	40	28	.588	13
Washington	32	36	.471	21
Philadelphia	26	42	.382	27
Baltimore	25	43	.368	28
Boston	22	46	.324	31

Western Division

	W	L	PCT.	GB
Indianapolis	39	25	.609	
Anderson	37	27	.578	2
Tri-Cities	29	35	.453	10
Sheboygan	22	40	.355	16
Waterloo	19	43	.306	19
Denver	11	51	.177	27

Central Division

	W	L	PCT.	GB
Minneapolis	51	17	.750	
Rochester	51	17	.750	
Fort Wayne	40	28	.588	11
Chicago	40	28	.588	11
St. Louis	26	42	.382	25

POINTS

	AVG.	NO.
G. Mikan, MIN	27.4	1865
A. Groza, IND	23.4	1496
F. Brian, AND	17.8	1138
M. Zaslofsky, CHI	16.4	1115
E. Macauley, STL	16.1	1081
D. Schayes, SYR	16.8	1072
C. Braun, NY	15.4	1031
K. Sailors, DEN	17.3	987
J. Pollard, MIN	14.7	973
F. Schaus, FTW	14.3	972
J. Fulks, PHI	14.2	965
R. Beard, IND	14.9	895
B. Davies, ROC	14.0	895
D. Mehen, WAT	14.4	892
J. Nichols, WAS/TC	13.1	879
E. Sadowski, PHI/BAL	12.6	872
P. Hoffman, BAL	14.4	866
F. Scolari, WAS	13.0	860
V. Gardner, PHI	13.5	853
B. Smawley, STL	13.7	834

ASSISTS

	AVG.	NO.
D. McGuire, NY	5.7	386
A. Phillip, CHI	5.8	377
B. Davies, ROC	4.6	294
A. Cervi, SYR	4.7	264
G. Senesky, PHI	3.9	264

D. Schayes, SYR	4.0	259
J. Pollard, MIN	3.8	252
J. Seminoff, BOS	3.8	249
C. Braun, NY	3.7	247
J. Logan, STL	3.9	240

FIELD GOAL PCT.

Alex Groza, IND	.478
Dick Mehen, WAT	.420
Bob Wanzer, ROC	.414
George Mikan, MIN	.407
John Hargis, AND	.405
Red Rocha, STL	.405
Vern Mikkelsen, MIN	.399
Ed Macauley, STL	.398
Jack Toomay, DEN	.397
Harry Gallatin, NY	.396

FREE THROW PCT.

Max Zaslofsky, CHI	.843
Chick Reiser, WAS	.835
Al Cervi, SYR	.829
Belus Smawley, STL	.828
Frank Brian, AND	.824
Fred Scolari, WAS	.822
Fred Schaus, FTW	.818
Leo Kubiak, WAT	.814
Bob Wanzer, ROC	.806
John Logan, STL	.783

EAST SEMIFINALS
Syracuse 2, Philadelphia 0
New York 2, Washington 0

EAST FINALS
Syracuse 2, New York 1

CENTRAL SEMIFINALS
Minneapolis 2, Chicago 0
Fort Wayne 2, Rochester 0

CENTRAL FINALS
Minneapolis 2, Fort Wayne 0

WEST SEMIFINALS
Indianapolis 2, Sheboygan 1
Anderson 2, Tri-Cities 1

WEST FINALS
Anderson 2, Indianapolis 1

NBA SEMIFINALS
Minneapolis 2, Anderson 0

NBA FINALS
Minneapolis 68, Syracuse 66
Syracuse 91, Minneapolis 85
Minneapolis 91, Syracuse 77
Minneapolis 77, Syracuse 69
Syracuse 83, Minneapolis 76
Minneapolis 110, Syracuse 95

1950-51
FINAL STANDINGS

Eastern Division

	W	L	PCT.	GB
Philadelphia	40	26	.606	
Boston	39	30	.565	2.5
New York	36	30	.545	4
Syracuse	32	34	.485	8
Baltimore	24	42	.364	16
Washington*	10	25	.286	14.5

*Folded on Jan. 9, 1951

Western Division

	W	L	PCT.	GB
Minneapolis	44	24	.647	
Rochester	41	27	.603	3
Fort Wayne	32	36	.471	12
Indianapolis	31	37	.456	13
Tri-Cities	25	43	.368	19

POINTS

	AVG.	NO.
G. Mikan, MIN	28.4	1932
A. Groza, IND	21.7	1429
E. Macauley, BOS	20.4	1384
J. Fulks, PHI	18.7	1236
F. Brian, TC	16.8	1144
P. Arizin, PHI	17.2	1121
D. Schayes, SYR	17.0	1121
R. Beard, IND	16.8	1111
B. Cousy, BOS	15.6	1078
A. Risen, ROC	16.3	1077
D. Eddleman, TC	15.3	1040
F. Schaus, FTW	15.1	1028
V. Boryla, NY	14.9	982
B. Davies, ROC	13.5	955
L. Foust, FTW	13.5	915
V. Mikkelsen, MIN	14.1	904
F. Scolari, WAS/SYR	13.4	883
K. Murray, BAL/FTW	12.9	850
G. Ratkovicz, SYR	12.9	849
H. Gallatin, NY	12.8	845

REBOUNDS

	AVG.	NO.
D. Schayes, SYR	16.4	1080
G. Mikan, MIN	14.1	958
H. Gallatin, NY	12.1	800
A. Risen, ROC	12.0	795
A. Groza, IND	10.7	709
L. Foust, FTW	10.0	681
V. Mikkelsen, MIN	10.2	655
P. Arizin, PHI	9.8	640
E. Macauley, BOS	9.1	616
J. Coleman, ROC	8.7	584

ASSISTS

	AVG.	NO.
A. Phillip, PHI	6.3	414
D. McGuire, NY	6.3	400
G. Senesky, PHI	5.3	342
B. Cousy, BOS	4.9	341
R. Beard, IND	4.8	318
B. Davies, ROC	4.6	287
F. Brian, TC	3.9	266
F. Scolari, WAS/SYR	3.9	255
E. Macauley, BOS	3.7	252
D. Schayes, SYR	3.8	251

FIELD GOAL PCT.

Alex Groza, IND	.470
Ed Macauley, BOS	.466
George Mikan, MIN	.428
Jack Coleman, ROC	.421
Harry Gallatin, NY	.416
George Ratkovicz, SYR	.415
Paul Arizin, PHI	.407
Vince Boryla, NY	.406
Vern Mikkelsen, MIN	.402
Robert Wanzer, ROC	.401

FREE THROW PCT.

Joe Fulks, PHI	.855
Belus Smawley, SYR/BAL	.850
Bob Wanzer, ROC	.850
Fred Scolari, WAS/SYR	.843
Vince Boryla, NY	.837
Fred Schaus, FTW	.835
Sonny Hertzberg, BOS	.826
Frank Brian, TC	.823

EAST SEMIFINALS

Syracuse 91, Phil. 89 (OT)
Syracuse 90, Philadelphia 78

New York 83, Boston 69
New York 92, Boston 78

EAST FINALS

New York 103, Syracuse 92
Syracuse 102, New York 80
New York 97, Syracuse 75
Syracuse 90, New York 83
New York 83, Syracuse 81

WEST SEMIFINALS

Minneapolis 95, Indian. 81
Indianapolis 108, Minn. 88
Minneapolis 85, Indian. 80

Rochester 110, Fort Wayne 81
Fort Wayne 83, Rochester 78
Rochester 97, Fort Wayne 78

WEST FINALS

Minneapolis 76, Rochester 73
Rochester 70, Minneapolis 66
Rochester 83, Minneapolis 70
Rochester 80, Minneapolis 75

NBA FINALS

Rochester 92, New York 65
Rochester 99, New York 84
Rochester 78, New York 71
New York 79, Rochester 73
New York 92, Rochester 89
New York 80, Rochester 73
Rochester 79, New York 75

1951-52
FINAL STANDINGS

Eastern Division

	W	L	PCT.	GB
Syracuse	40	26	.606	
Boston	39	27	.591	1
New York	37	29	.561	3
Philadelphia	33	33	.500	7
Boston	20	46	.303	20

Western Division

	W	L	PCT.	GB
Rochester	41	25	.621	
Minneapolis	40	26	.606	1
Indianapolis	34	32	.515	7
Fort Wayne	29	37	.439	12
Milwaukee	17	49	.258	24

POINTS	AVG.	NO.
P. Arizin, PHI	25.4	1674
G. Mikan, MIN	23.8	1523
B. Cousy, BOS	21.7	1433
E. Macauley, BOS	19.2	1264
B. Davies, ROC	16.2	1052
F. Brian, FTW	15.9	1051
L. Foust, FTW	15.9	1047
B. Wanzer, ROC	15.7	1033
A. Risen, ROC	15.6	1032
V. Mikkelsen, MIN	15.3	1009
J. Pollard, MIN	15.5	1005
F. Scolari, BAL	14.6	933
M. Zaslofsky, NY	14.1	931
J. Fulks, PHI	15.1	922
J. Graboski, IND	13.7	904
F. Schaus, FTW	14.1	872
D. Schayes, SYR	13.8	868
R. Rocha, SYR	12.9	854
L. Barnhorst, IND	12.4	820
A. Phillip, PHI	12.0	790

REBOUNDS	AVG.	NO.
L. Foust, FTW	13.3	880
M. Hutchins, MIL	13.3	880
G. Mikan, MIN	13.5	866
A. Risen, ROC	12.7	841
D. Schayes, SYR	12.3	773
P. Arizin, PHI	11.3	745
N. Clifton, NY	11.8	731
J. Coleman, ROC	10.5	692
V. Mikkelsen, MIN	10.3	681
H. Gallatin, NY	10.0	661

ASSISTS	AVG.	NO.
A. Phillip, PHI	8.2	539
B. Cousy, BOS	6.7	441
B. Davies, ROC	6.0	390
D. McGuire, NY	6.1	388
F. Scolari, BAL	4.7	303
G. Senesky, PHI	4.9	280
B. Wanzer, ROC	4.0	262
L. Barnhorst, IND	3.9	255
S. Martin, MIN	3.8	249
F. Schaus, FTW	4.0	247

FIELD GOAL PCT.	
Paul Arizin, PHI	.448
Harry Gallatin, NY	.442
Ed Macauley, BOS	.432
Bob Wanzer, ROC	.425
Vern Mikkelsen, MIN	.419
Jack Coleman, ROC	.415
George King, SYR	.406
Paul Walther, IND	.401
Red Rocha, SYR	.401
Bob Lavoy, IND	.397

FREE THROW PCT.	
Bob Wanzer, ROC	.904
Al Cervi, SYR	.883
Bill Sharman, BOS	.859
Frank Brian, FTW	.848
Fred Scolari, BAL	.835
Fred Schaus, FTW	.833
Joe Fulks, PHI	.825
Bill Tosheff, IND	.824

EAST SEMIFINALS
Syracuse 102, Phil. 83
Philadelphia 100, Syrac. 95
Syracuse 84, Phil. 78

Boston 105, New York 94
New York 101, Boston 97
New York 88, Boston 87 (2OT)

EAST FINALS
New York 87, Syracuse 85
Syracuse 102, New York 92
New York 99, Syracuse 92
New York 100, Syracuse 93

WEST SEMIFINALS
Rochester 95, Fort Wayne 78
Rochester 92, Fort Wayne 86

Minneapolis 78, Indian. 70
Minneapolis 94, Indian. 87

WEST FINALS
Rochester 88, Minn. 78
Minneapolis 83, Roch. 78
Minneapolis 77, Roch. 67
Minneapolis 82, Roch. 80

NBA FINALS
Minneapolis 83, N.Y. 79 (OT)
New York 80, Minneapolis 72
Minneapolis 82, New York 77
New York 90, Minn. 89 (OT)
Minneapolis 102, New York 89
New York 76, Minneapolis 68
Minneapolis 82, New York 65

1952-53
FINAL STANDINGS

Eastern Division

	W	L	PCT.	GB
New York	47	23	.671	
Syracuse	47	24	.662	.5
Boston	46	25	.648	1.5
Baltimore	16	54	.229	31
Philadelphia	12	57	.174	34.5

Western Division

	W	L	PCT.	GB
Minneapolis	48	22	.686	
Rochester	44	26	.629	4
Fort Wayne	36	33	.522	11.5
Indianapolis	28	43	.394	20.5
Milwaukee	27	44	.380	21.5

POINTS

	AVG.	NO.
N. Johnston, PHI	22.3	1564
G. Mikan, MIN	20.6	1442
B. Cousy, BOS	19.8	1407
E. Macauley, BOS	20.3	1402
D. Schayes, SYR	17.8	1262
B. Sharman, BOS	16.2	1147
J. Nichols, MIL	15.8	1090
V. Mikkelsen, MIN	15.0	1047
D. Davies, ROC	15.6	1029
B. Wanzer, ROC	14.6	1020
C. Braun, NY	14.0	977
L. Barnhorst, IND	13.6	967
L. Foust, FTW	14.3	958
P. Seymour, SYR	14.2	952
D. Barksdale, BAL	13.8	899
J. Graboski, IND	13.0	894
A. Risen, ROC	13.0	884
H. Gallatin, NY	12.4	865
J. Pollard, MIN	13.0	859
J. Fulks, PHI	11.9	832

REBOUNDS

	AVG.	NO.
G. Mikan, MIN	14.4	1007
N. Johnston, PHI	13.9	979
D. Schayes, SYR	13.0	920
H. Gallatin, NY	13.1	916
M. Hutchins, MIL	11.2	793
J. Coleman, ROC	11.1	774
L. Foust, FTW	11.5	769
N. Clifton, NY	10.9	761
A. Risen, ROC	11.0	745
J. Graboski, IND	10.0	687

ASSISTS

	AVG.	NO.
B. Cousy, BOS	7.7	547
A. Phillip, PHI/FTW	5.7	397
G. King, SYR	5.1	364
D. McGuire, NY	4.9	296
P. Seymour, SYR	4.4	294
B. Davies, ROC	4.2	280
E. Macauley, BOS	4.1	280
L. Barnhorst, IND	3.9	277
G. Senesky, PHI	3.8	264
B. Wanzer, ROC	3.6	252

FIELD GOAL PCT.

Neil Johnston, PHI	.45242
Ed Macauley, BOS	.45236
Harry Gallatin, NY	.444
Bill Sharman, BOS	.436
Vern Mikkelsen, MIN	.435
Ernie Vandeweghe, NY	.435
Jack Coleman, ROC	.420
Slater Martin, MIN	.410
Bob Lavoy, IND	.402
George King, SYR	.402

FREE THROW PCT.

Bill Sharman, BOS	.850
Fred Scolari, FTW	.844
Dolph Schayes, SYR	.827
Carl Braun, NY	.825
Fred Schaus, FTW	.821
Odie Spears, ROC	.819
Paul Seymour, SYR	.817
Bob Cousy, BOS	.816

EAST SEMIFINALS

New York 80, Baltimore 62
New York 90, Baltimore 81

Boston 87, Syracuse 81
Boston 111, Syr. 105 (4OT)

EAST FINALS

New York 95, Boston 91
Boston 86, New York 70
New York 101, Boston 82
New York 82, Boston 75

WEST SEMIFINALS

Minneapolis 85, Indian. 69
Minneapolis 81, Indian. 79

Fort Wayne 84, Rochester 77
Rochester 83, Fort Wayne 71
Fort Wayne 67, Rochester 65

WEST FINALS

Minneapolis 83, Fort Wayne 73
Minneapolis 82, Fort Wayne 75
Fort Wayne 98, Minneapolis 95
Fort Wayne 85, Minneapolis 82
Minneapolis 74, Fort Wayne 58

NBA FINALS

New York 96, Minneapolis 88
Minneapolis 73, New York 71
Minneapolis 90, New York 75
Minneapolis 71, New York 69
Minneapolis 91, New York 84

1953-54
FINAL STANDINGS

Eastern Division

	W	L	PCT.	GB
New York	44	28	.611	
Boston	42	30	.583	2
Syracuse	42	30	.583	2
Philadelphia	29	43	.403	15
Baltimore	16	56	.222	28

Western Division

	W	L	PCT.	GB
Minneapolis	46	26	.639	
Rochester	44	28	.611	2
Fort Wayne	40	32	.556	6
Milwaukee	21	51	.292	25

POINTS

	AVG.	NO.
N. Johnston, PHI	24.4	1759
B. Cousy, BOS	19.2	1383
E. Macauley, BOS	18.9	1344
G. Mikan, MIN	18.1	1306
R. Felix, BAL	17.6	1269
D. Schayes, SYR	17.1	1228
B. Sharman, BOS	16.0	1155
L. Foust, FTW	15.1	1090
C. Braun, NY	14.8	1062
B. Wanzer, ROC	13.3	958
H. Gallatin, NY	13.2	949
A. Risen, ROC	13.2	949
J. Graboski, PHI	13.3	944
P. Seymour, SYR	13.1	931
B. Davies, ROC	12.3	887
J. Pollard, MIN	11.7	831
G. King, SYR	11.3	817
M. Zaslofsky, FTW	12.5	811
V. Mikkelsen, MIN	11.1	797
D. Sunderlage, MIL	11.2	760

REBOUNDS

	AVG.	NO.
H. Gallatin, NY	15.3	1098
G. Mikan, MIN	14.3	1028
L. Foust, FTW	13.4	967
R. Felix, BAL	13.3	958
D. Schayes, SYR	12.1	870
N. Johnston, PHI	11.1	797
A. Risen, ROC	10.1	728
M. Hutchins, FTW	9.7	695
L. Hitch, MIL	9.6	691
J. Graboski, PHI	9.4	670

ASSISTS

	AVG.	NO.
B. Cousy, BOS	7.2	518
A. Phillip, FTW	6.3	449
P. Seymour, SYR	5.1	364
D. McGuire, NY	5.2	354
B. Davies, ROC	4.5	323
J. George, PHI	4.4	312
P. Hoffman, BAL	4.0	285
G. King, SYR	3.8	272
E. Macauley, BOS	3.8	271
D. Finn, PHI	3.9	265

FIELD GOAL PCT.

Ed Macauley, BOS	.486
Bill Sharman, BOS	.450
Neil Johnston, PHI	.449
Clyde Lovellette, MIN	.423
Ray Felix, BAL	.411
Larry Foust, FTW	.409
Eddie Miller, BAL	.407
Jack Coleman, ROC	.405
Harry Gallatin, NY	.404
Mel Hutchins, FTW	.401

FREE THROW PCT.

Bill Sharman, BOS	.844
Dolph Schayes, SYR	.827
Carl Braun, NY	.825
Paul Seymour, SYR	.813
Bob Zawoluk, PHI	.809
Bob Cousy, BOS	.787
Harry Gallatin, NY	.784
George Mikan, MIN	.777

EAST ROUND ROBIN

Boston 93, New York 71
Syracuse 96, Boston 95 (OT)
Syracuse 75, New York 68
Boston 79, New York 78
Syracuse 103, New York 99
Syracuse 98, Boston 85

EAST FINALS

Syracuse 109, Boston 104
Syracuse 83, Boston 76

WEST ROUND ROBIN

Rochester 82, Fort Wayne 75
Minneapolis 109, Rochester 88
Minneapolis 90, Fort Wayne 85
Minneapolis 78, Fort Wayne 73
Rochester 89, Fort Wayne 71

WEST FINALS

Minneapolis 89, Rochester 76
Rochester 74, Minneapolis 73
Minneapolis 82, Rochester 72

NBA FINALS

Minneapolis 79, Syracuse 68
Syracuse 62, Minneapolis 60
Minneapolis 81, Syracuse 67
Syracuse 80, Minneapolis 69
Minneapolis 84, Syracuse 73
Syracuse 65, Minneapolis 63
Minneapolis 87, Syracuse 80

1954-55
FINAL STANDINGS

Eastern Division

	W	L	PCT.	GB
Syracuse	43	29	.597	
New York	38	34	.528	5
Boston	36	36	.500	7
Philadelphia	33	39	.458	10

Western Division

	W	L	PCT.	GB
Fort Wayne	43	29	.597	
Minneapolis	40	32	.556	3
Rochester	29	43	.403	14
Milwaukee	26	46	.361	17

POINTS

	AVG.	NO.
N. Johnston, PHI	22.7	1631
P. Arizin, PHI	21.0	1512
B. Cousy, BOS	21.2	1504
B. Pettit, MIL	20.4	1466
F. Selvy, BAL/MIL	19.0	1348
D. Schayes, SYR	18.8	1333
V. Mikkelsen, MIN	18.4	1327
C. Lovellette, MIN	18.7	1311
B. Sharman, BOS	18.4	1253
E. Macauley, BOS	17.6	1248
L. Foust, FTW	17.0	1189
C. Braun, NY	15.1	1074
H. Gallatin, NY	14.6	1053
P. Seymour, SYR	14.6	1050
R. Felix, NY	14.4	1038
G. Yardley, FTW	17.3	1036
J. Baechtold, NY	13.9	1003
S. Martin, MIN	13.6	976
J. Graboski, PHI	13.6	954
N. Clifton, NY	13.1	944

REBOUNDS

	AVG.	NO.
N. Johnston, PHI	15.1	1085
H. Gallatin, NY	13.8	995
B. Pettit, MIL	13.8	994
D. Schayes, SYR	12.3	887
R. Felix, NY	11.4	818
C. Lovellette, MIN	11.5	802
J. Coleman, ROC	10.1	729
V. Mikkelsen, MIN	10.2	722
A. Risen, ROC	10.2	703
L. Foust, FTW	10.0	700

ASSISTS

	AVG.	NO.
B. Cousy, BOS	7.8	557
D. McGuire, NY	7.6	542
A. Phillip, FTW	7.7	491
P. Seymour, SYR	6.7	483
S. Martin, MIN	5.9	427
J. George, PHI	5.3	359
G. King, SYR	4.9	331
B. Sharman, BOS	4.1	280
E. Macauley, BOS	3.9	275
C. Braun, NY	3.9	274

FIELD GOAL PCT.

Larry Foust, FTW	.487
Jack Coleman, ROC	.462
Neil Johnston, PHI	.440
Ray Felix, NY	.438
Clyde Lovellette, MIN	.435
Bill Sharman, BOS	.427
Ed Macauley, BOS	.424
Vern Mikkelsen, MIN	.422
John Kerr, SYR	.419
George Yardley, FTW	.418

FREE THROW PCT.

Bill Sharman, BOS	.897
Frank Brian, FTW	.851
Dolph Schayes, SYR	.833
Dick Schnittker, MIN	.823
Jim Baechtold, NY	.823
Harry Gallatin, NY	.814
Odie Spears, ROC	.812
Paul Seymour, SYR	.811

EAST SEMIFINALS
Boston 122, New York 101
New York 102, Boston 95
Boston 116, New York 109

EAST FINALS
Syracuse 110, Boston 100
Syracuse 116, Boston 110
Boston 100, Syracuse 97 (OT)
Syracuse 110, Boston 94

WEST SEMIFINALS
Minneapolis 82, Rochester 78
Rochester 94, Minneapolis 92
Minneapolis 119, Roch. 110

WEST FINALS
Fort Wayne 96, Minneapolis 79
Fort Wayne 98, Minn. 97 (OT)
Minneapolis 99, F.W. 91 (OT)
Fort Wayne 105, Minn. 96

NBA FINALS
Syracuse 86, Fort Wayne 82
Syracuse 87, Fort Wayne 84
Fort Wayne 96, Syracuse 89
Fort Wayne 109, Syracuse 102
Fort Wayne 74, Syracuse 71
Syracuse 109, Fort Wayne 104
Syracuse 92, Fort Wayne 91

1955-56
FINAL STANDINGS

Eastern Division

	W	L	PCT.	GB
Philadelphia	45	27	.625	
Boston	39	33	.542	6
Syracuse	35	37	.486	10
New York	35	37	.486	10

Western Division

	W	L	PCT.	GB
Fort Wayne	37	35	.514	
Minneapolis	33	39	.458	4
St. Louis	33	39	.458	4
Rochester	31	41	.431	6

POINTS

	AVG.	NO.
B. Pettit, STL	25.7	1849
P. Arizin, PHI	24.2	1741
N. Johnston, PHI	22.1	1547
C. Lovellette, MIN	21.5	1526
D. Schayes, SYR	20.4	1472
B. Sharman, BOS	19.9	1434
B. Cousy, BOS	18.8	1356
E. Macauley, BOS	17.5	1240
G. Yardley, FTW	17.4	1233
L. Foust, FTW	16.2	1166
M. Stokes, ROC	16.8	1125
C. Braun, NY	15.4	1112
J. Twyman, ROC	14.4	1038
J. Graboski, PHI	14.4	1034
H. Gallatin, NY	13.9	1002
J. George, PHI	13.9	1000
C. Share, STL	13.6	976
V. Mikkelsen, MIN	13.4	962
J. Kerr, SYR	13.3	961
J. Coleman, ROC/STL	12.8	957

REBOUNDS

	AVG.	NO.
B. Pettit, STL	16.2	1164
M. Stokes, ROC	16.3	1094
C. Lovellette, MIN	14.0	992
D. Schayes, SYR	12.4	891
N. Johnston, PHI	12.5	872
C. Share, STL	10.8	774
H. Gallatin, NY	10.3	740
J. Coleman, ROC/STL	9.2	688
G. Yardley, FTW	9.7	686
L. Foust, FTW	9.0	648

ASSISTS

	AVG.	NO.
B. Cousy, BOS	8.9	642
J. George, PHI	6.3	457
S. Martin, MIN	6.2	445
A. Phillip, FTW	5.9	410
G. King, SYR	5.7	410
T. Gola, PHI	5.9	404
D. McGuire, NY	5.8	362
B. Sharman, BOS	4.7	339
M. Stokes, ROC	4.9	328
C. Braun, NY	4.1	298

FIELD GOAL PCT.

Neil Johnston, PHI	.457
Paul Arizin, PHI	.448
Larry Foust, FTW	.447
Ken Sears, NY	.438
Bill Sharman, BOS	.438
Clyde Lovellette, MIN	.434
Charles Share, STL	.430
Bob Houbregs, FTW	.430
Bob Pettit, STL	.429
Mel Hutchins, FTW	.425

FREE THROW PCT.

Bill Sharman, BOS	.867
Dolph Schayes, SYR	.858
Dick Schnittker, MIN	.856
Bob Cousy, BOS	.844
Carl Braun, NY	.838
Slater Martin, MIN	.833
Paul Arizin, PHI	.810
Vern Mikkelsen, MIN	.804

EAST SEMIFINALS

Boston 110, Syracuse 93
Syracuse 101, Boston 98
Syracuse 102, Boston 97

EAST FINALS

Philadelphia 109, Syracuse 87
Syracuse 122, Phil. 118
Philadelphia 119, Syracuse 96
Syracuse 108, Phil. 104
Philadelphia 109, Syrac. 104

WEST SEMIFINALS

St. Louis 116, Minneapolis 115
Minneapolis 133, St. Louis 75
St. Louis 116, Minneapolis 115

WEST FINALS

St. Louis 86, Fort Wayne 85
St. Louis 84, Fort Wayne 74
Fort Wayne 107, St. Louis 84
Fort Wayne 93, St. Louis 84
Fort Wayne 102, St. Louis 97

NBA FINALS

Philadelphia 98, Fort Wayne 94
Fort Wayne 84, Philadelphia 83
Philadelphia 100, Fort W. 96
Philadelphia 107, Fort W. 105
Philadelphia 99, Fort Wayne 88

1956-57
FINAL STANDINGS

Eastern Division

	W	L	PCT.	GB
Boston	44	28	.611	
Syracuse	38	34	.528	6
Philadelphia	37	35	.514	7
New York	36	36	.500	8

Western Division

	W	L	PCT.	GB
St. Louis	34	38	.472	
Minneapolis	34	38	.472	
Fort Wayne	34	38	.472	
Rochester	31	41	.431	3

POINTS

	AVG.	NO.
P. Arizin, PHI	25.6	1817
B. Pettit, STL	24.7	1755
D. Schayes, SYR	22.5	1617
N. Johnston, PHI	22.8	1575
G. Yardley, FTW	21.5	1547
C. Lovellette, MIN	20.8	1434
B. Sharman, BOS	21.1	1413
B. Cousy, BOS	20.6	1319
E. Macauley, STL	16.5	1187
D. Garmaker, MIN	16.3	1177
J. Twyman, ROC	16.3	1174
T. Heinsohn, BOS	16.2	1163
M. Stokes, ROC	15.6	1124
H. Gallatin, NY	15.0	1079
K. Sears, NY	14.8	1069
J. Graboski, PHI	14.3	1032
C. Braun, NY	13.9	1001
V. Mikkelsen, MIN	13.7	986
E. Conlin, SYR	13.4	953
J. Kerr, SYR	12.4	891

REBOUNDS

	AVG.	NO.
M. Stokes, ROC	17.4	1256
B. Pettit, STL	14.6	1037
D. Schayes, SYR	14.0	1008
B. Russell, BOS	19.6	943
C. Lovellette, MIN	13.5	932
N. Johnston, PHI	12.4	855
J. Kerr, SYR	11.2	807
W. Dukes, MIN	11.2	794
G. Yardley, FTW	10.5	755
J. Loscutoff, BOS	10.4	730

ASSISTS

	AVG.	NO.
B. Cousy, BOS	7.5	478
J. McMahon, STL	5.1	367
M. Stokes, ROC	4.6	331
J. George, PHI	4.6	307
S. Martin, NY/STL	4.1	269
C. Braun, NY	3.6	256
G. Shue, FTW	3.3	238
B. Sharman, BOS	3.5	236
L. Costello, PHI	3.3	236
D. Schayes, SYR	3.2	229

FIELD GOAL PCT.

Neil Johnston, PHI	.447
Charles Share, STL	.439
Jack Twyman, ROC	.439
Bob Houbregs, FTW	.432
Bill Russell, BOS	.427
Clyde Lovellette, MIN	.426
Paul Arizin, PHI	.422
Ed Macauley, STL	.419
Ken Sears, NY	.418
Ray Felix, NY	.416

FREE THROW PCT.

Bill Sharman, BOS	.905
Dolph Schayes, SYR	.904
Dick Garmaker, MIN	.839
Paul Arizin, PHI	.829
Neil Johnston, PHI	.826
Bob Cousy, BOS	.821
Carl Braun, NY	.809
Vern Mikkelsen, MIN	.807

EAST SEMIFINALS

Syracuse 103, Philadelphia 96
Syracuse 91, Philadelphia 80

EAST FINALS

Boston 108, Syracuse 90
Boston 120, Syracuse 105
Boston 83, Syracuse 80

WEST SEMIFINALS

Minneapolis 131, Fort W. 127
Minneapolis 110, Fort W. 108

WEST FINALS

St. Louis 118, Minneapolis 109
St. Louis 106, Minneapolis 104
St. Louis 143, Minn. 135 (2OT)

NBA FINALS

St. Louis 125, Boston 123 (OT)
Boston 119, St. Louis 99
St. Louis 100, Boston 98
Boston 123, St. Louis 118
Boston 124, St. Louis 109
St. Louis 96, Boston 94
Boston 125, St. L. 123 (2OT)

1957-58
FINAL STANDINGS

Eastern Division

	W	L	PCT.	GB
Boston	49	23	.681	
Syracuse	41	31	.569	8
Philadelphia	37	35	.514	12
New York	35	37	.486	14

Western Division

	W	L	PCT.	GB
St. Louis	41	31	.569	
Detroit	33	39	.458	8
Cincinnati	33	39	.458	8
Minneapolis	19	53	.264	22

POINTS

	AVG.	NO.
G. Yardley, DET	27.8	2001
D. Schayes, SYR	24.9	1791
B. Pettit, STL	24.6	1719
C. Lovellete, CIN	23.4	1659
P. Arizin, PHI	20.7	1406
B. Sharman, BOS	22.3	1402
C. Hagan, STL	19.9	1391
N. Johnston, PHI	19.5	1388
K. Sears, NY	18.6	1342
V. Mikkelsen, MIN	17.3	1248
J. Twyman, CIN	17.2	1237
T. Heinsohn, BOS	17.8	1230
W. Naulls, NY	18.1	1228
L. Foust, MIN	16.8	1210
C. Braun, NY	16.5	1173
B. Cousy, BOS	18.0	1167
B. Russell, BOS	16.6	1142
F. Ramsey, BOS	16.5	1137
D. Garmaker, MIN	16.1	1094
J. Kerr, SYR	15.2	1094

REBOUNDS

	AVG.	NO.
B. Russell, BOS	22.7	1564
B. Pettit, STL	17.4	1216
M. Stokes, CIN	18.1	1142
D. Schayes, SYR	14.2	1022
J. Kerr, SYR	13.4	963
W. Dukes, DET	13.3	954
L. Foust, MIN	12.2	876
C. Lovellette, CIN	12.1	862
V. Mikkelsen, MIN	11.2	805
W. Naulls, NY	11.8	799

ASSISTS

	AVG.	NO.
B. Cousy, BOS	7.1	463
D. McGuire, DET	6.6	454
M. Stokes, CIN	6.4	403
C. Braun, NY	5.5	393
G. King, CIN	5.3	337
J. McMahon, STL	4.6	333
T. Gola, PHI	5.5	327
R. Guerin, NY	5.0	317
L. Costello, SYR	4.4	317
J. George, CIN	3.3	234

FIELD GOAL PCT.

Jack Twyman, CIN	.452
Cliff Hagan, STL	.443
Bill Russell, BOS	.442
Ray Felix, NY	.442
Clyde Lovellette, CIN	.441
Ken Sears, NY	.439
Neil Johnston, PHI	.429
Ed Macauley, STL	.428
Larry Costello, SYR	.426
Bill Sharman, BOS	.424

FREE THROW PCT.

Dolph Schayes, SYR	.904
Bill Sharman, BOS	.893
Bob Cousy, BOS	.850
Carl Braun, NY	.849
Dick Schnittker, MIN	.848
Larry Costello, SYR	.847
Gene Shue, DET	.844
Willie Naulls, NY	.826

EAST SEMIFINALS

Syracuse 86, Philadelphia 82
Philadelphia 95, Syracuse 93
Philadelphia 101, Syracuse 88

EAST FINALS

Boston 107, Philadelphia 98
Boston 109, Philadelphia 87
Boston 106, Philadelphia 92
Philadelphia 111, Boston 97
Boston 93, Philadelphia 88

WEST SEMIFINALS

Detroit 100, Cincinnati 93
Detroit 124, Cincinnati 104

WEST FINALS

St. Louis 114, Detroit 111
St. Louis 99, Detroit 96
Detroit 109, St. Louis 89
St. Louis 145, Detroit 101
St. Louis 120, Detroit 96

NBA FINALS

St. Louis 104, Boston 102
Boston 136, St. Louis 112
St. Louis 111, Boston 108
Boston 109, St. Louis 98
St. Louis 102, Boston 100
St. Louis 110, Boston 109

1958-59
FINAL STANDINGS

Eastern Division

	W	L	PCT.	GB
Boston	52	20	.722	
New York	40	32	.556	12
Syracuse	35	37	.486	17
Philadelphia	32	40	.444	20

Western Division

	W	L	PCT.	GB
St. Louis	49	23	.681	
Minneapolis	33	39	.458	16
Detroit	28	44	.389	21
Cincinnati	19	53	.264	30

POINTS

	AVG.	NO.
B. Pettit, STL	29.2	2105
J. Twyman, CIN	25.8	1857
P. Arizin, PHI	26.4	1851
E. Baylor, MIN	24.9	1742
C. Hagan, STL	23.7	1707
D. Schayes, SYR	21.3	1534
K. Sears, NY	21.0	1488
B. Sharman, BOS	20.4	1466
B. Cousy, BOS	20.0	1297
R. Guerin, NY	18.2	1291
J. Kerr, SYR	17.8	1285
G. Shue, DET	17.6	1266
T. Heinsohn, BOS	18.8	1242
G. Yardley, DET/SYR	19.8	1209
B. Russell, BOS	16.7	1168
W. Sauldsberry, PHI	15.4	1112
L. Costello, SYR	15.8	1108
F. Ramsey, BOS	15.4	1107
W. Naulls, NY	15.7	1068
J. Graboski, PHI	14.7	1058

REBOUNDS

	AVG.	NO.
B. Russell, BOS	23.0	1612
B. Pettit, STL	16.4	1182
E. Baylor, MIN	15.0	1050
J. Kerr, SYR	14.0	1008
D. Schayes, SYR	13.4	962
W. Dukes, DET	13.3	958
W. Sauldsberry, PHI	11.5	826
C. Hagan, STL	10.9	783
J. Graboski, PHI	10.4	751
W. Naulls, NY	10.6	723

ASSISTS

	AVG.	NO.
B. Cousy, BOS	8.6	557
D. McGuire, DET	6.2	443
L. Costello, SYR	5.4	379
R. Guerin, NY	5.1	364
C. Braun, NY	4.8	349
S. Martin, NY	4.7	336
J. McMahon, STL	4.1	298
B. Sharman, BOS	4.1	292
E. Baylor, MIN	4.1	287
T. Gola, PHI	4.2	269

FIELD GOAL PCT.

Ken Sears, NY	.490
Bill Russell, BOS	.457
Cliff Hagan, STL	.456
Clyde Lovellette, STL	.454
Hal Greer, SYR	.454
John Kerr, SYR	.441
Bob Pettit, STL	.438
Larry Costello, SYR	.437
Sam Jones, BOS	.434
Paul Arizin, PHI	.431

FREE THROW PCT.

Bill Sharman, BOS	.932
Dolph Schayes, SYR	.864
Ken Sears, NY	.861
Bob Cousy, BOS	.855
Willie Naulls, NY	.830
Clyde Lovellette, STL	.820
Paul Arizin, PHI	.813
Vern Mikkelsen, MIN	.806

EAST SEMIFINALS

Syracuse 129, New York 123
Syracuse 131, New York 115

EAST FINALS

Boston 131, Syracuse 109
Syracuse 120, Boston 118
Boston 133, Syracuse 111
Syracuse 119, Boston 107
Boston 129, Syracuse 108
Syracuse 133, Boston 121
Boston 130, Syracuse 125

WEST SEMIFINALS

Minneapolis 92, Detroit 89
Detroit 117, Minneapolis 103
Minneapolis 129, Detroit 102

WEST FINALS

St. Louis 124, Minneapolis 90
Minneapolis 106, St. Louis 98
St. Louis 127, Minneapolis 97
Minneapolis 108, St. Louis 98
Minneapolis 98, St. L. 97 (OT)
Minneapolis 106, St. Louis 104

NBA FINALS

Boston 118, Minneapolis 115
Boston 128, Minneapolis 108
Boston 123, Minneapolis 120
Boston 118, Minneapolis 113

1959-60
FINAL STANDINGS

Eastern Division

	W	L	PCT.	GB
Boston	59	16	.787	
Philadelphia	49	26	.653	10
Syracuse	45	30	.600	14
New York	27	48	.360	32

Western Division

	W	L	PCT.	GB
St. Louis	46	29	.613	
Detroit	30	45	.400	16
Minneapolis	25	50	.333	21
Cincinnati	19	56	.253	27

POINTS

	AVG.	NO.
W. Chamberlain, PHI	37.6	2707
J. Twyman, CIN	31.2	2338
E. Baylor, MIN	29.6	2074
B. Pettit, STL	26.1	1882
C. Hagan, STL	24.8	1859
G. Shue, DET	22.8	1712
D. Schayes, SYR	22.5	1689
T. Heinsohn, BOS	21.7	1629
R. Guerin, NY	21.8	1615
P. Arizin, PHI	22.3	1606
G. Yardley, SYR	20.2	1473
B. Cousy, BOS	19.4	1455
C. Lovellette, STL	20.8	1416
W. Naulls, NY	21.4	1388
B. Sharman, BOS	19.3	1370
B. Russell, BOS	18.2	1350
B. Howell, DET	17.8	1332
K. Sears, NY	18.5	1187
T. Gola, PHI	15.0	1122
F. Ramsey, BOS	15.3	1117

REBOUNDS

	AVG.	NO.
W. Chamberlain, PHI	27.0	1941
B. Russell, BOS	24.0	1778
B. Pettit, STL	17.0	1221
E. Baylor, MIN	16.4	1150
D. Schayes, SYR	12.8	959
W. Naulls, NY	14.2	921
J. Kerr, SYR	12.2	913
W. Dukes, DET	13.4	883
K. Sears, NY	13.7	876
C. Hagan, STL	10.7	803

ASSISTS

	AVG.	NO.
B. Cousy, BOS	9.5	715
G. Rodgers, PHI	7.1	482
R. Guerin, NY	6.3	468
L. Costello, SYR	6.3	449
T. Gola, PHI	5.5	409
D. McGuire, DET	5.3	358
R. Hundley, MIN	4.6	338
S. Martin, STL	5.2	330
J. McCarthy, STL	4.4	328
C. Hagan, STL	4.0	299

FIELD GOAL PCT.

Ken Sears, NY	.477
Hal Greer, SYR	.476
Clyde Lovellette, STL	.468
Bill Russell, BOS	.467
Cliff Hagan, STL	.464
W. Chamberlain, PHI	.461
Bill Sharman, BOS	.456
Bailey Howell, DET	.456
Sam Jones, BOS	.454
George Yardley, SYR	.453

FREE THROW PCT.

Dolph Schayes, SYR	.893
Gene Shue, DET	.872
Ken Sears, NY	.868
Bill Sharman, BOS	.866
Larry Costello, SYR	.862
Willie Naulls, NY	.836
Clyde Lovellette, STL	.821
George Yardley, SYR	.816

EAST SEMIFINALS

Philadelphia 115, Syracuse 92
Syracuse 125, Phil. 119
Philadelphia 132, Syrac. 112

EAST FINALS

Boston 111, Philadelphia 105
Philadelphia 115, Boston 110
Boston 120, Philadelphia 90
Boston 112, Philadelphia 104
Philadelphia 128, Boston 107
Boston 119, Philadelphia 117

WEST SEMIFINALS

Minneapolis 113, Detroit 112
Minneapolis 114, Detroit 99

WEST FINALS

St. Louis 112, Minneapolis 99
Minneapolis 120, St. Louis 113
St. Louis 93, Minneapolis 89
Minneapolis 103, St. Louis 101
Minn. 117, St. L. 110 (OT)
St. Louis 117, Minneapolis 96
St. Louis 97, Minneapolis 86

NBA FINALS

Boston 140, St. Louis 122
St. Louis 113, Boston 103
Boston 102, St. Louis 86
St. Louis 106, Boston 96
Boston 127, St. Louis 102
St. Louis 105, Boston 102
Boston 122, St. Louis 103

1960-61
FINAL STANDINGS

Eastern Division

	W	L	PCT.	GB
Boston	57	22	.722	
Philadelphia	46	33	.582	11
Syracuse	38	41	.481	19
New York	21	58	.266	36

Western Division

	W	L	PCT.	GB
St. Louis	51	28	.646	
Los Angeles	36	43	.456	15
Detroit	34	45	.430	17
Cincinnati	33	46	.418	18

POINTS

	AVG.	NO.
W. Chamberlain, PHI.	38.4	3033
E. Baylor, LA	34.8	2538
O. Robertson, CIN	30.5	2165
B. Pettit, STL	27.9	2120
J. Twyman, CIN	25.3	1997
D. Schayes, SYR	23.6	1868
W. Naulls, NY	23.4	1846
P. Arizin, PHI	23.2	1832
B. Howell, DET	23.6	1815
G. Shue, DET	22.6	1765
R. Guerin, NY	21.8	1720
C. Hagan, STL	21.9	1705
T. Heinsohn, BOS	21.3	1579
H. Greer, SYR	19.6	1551
C. Lovellette, STL	22.0	1471
J. West, LA	17.6	1389
B. Cousy, BOS	18.1	1378
B. Russell, BOS	16.9	1322
D. Barnett, SYR	16.9	1320
F. Ramsey, BOS	15.1	1191

REBOUNDS

	AVG.	NO.
W. Chamberlain, PHI.	27.2	2149
B. Russell, BOS	23.9	1868
B. Pettit, STL	20.3	1540
E. Baylor, LA	19.8	1447
B. Howell, DET	14.4	1111
W. Naulls, NY	13.4	1055
W. Dukes, DET	14.1	1028
D. Schayes, SYR	12.2	960
J. Kerr, SYR	12.0	951
W. Embry, CIN	10.9	864

ASSISTS

	AVG.	NO.
O. Robertson, CIN	9.7	690
G. Rodgers, PHI	8.7	677
B. Cousy, BOS	7.7	587
G. Shue, DET	6.8	530
R. Guerin, NY	6.4	503
J. McCarthy, STL	5.4	430
L. Costello, SYR	5.5	413
C. Hagan, STL	4.9	381
E. Baylor, LA	5.1	371
R. Hundley, LA	4.4	350

FIELD GOAL PCT.

W. Chamberlain, PHI	.509
Jack Twyman, CIN	.488
Larry Costello, SYR	.482
Oscar Robertson, CIN	.473
Barney Cable, SYR	.472
Bailey Howell, DET	.469
Clyde Lovellette, STL	.453
Dick Barnett, SYR	.452
Wayne Embry, CIN	.451
Hal Greer, SYR	.451

FREE THROW PCT.

Bill Sharman, BOS	.921
Dolph Schayes, SYR	.868
Gene Shue, DET	.856
Frank Ramsey, BOS	.833
Paul Arizin, PHI	.833
Dave Gambee, SYR	.831
Clyde Lovellette, STL	.830
Ken Sears, NY	.830

EAST SEMIFINALS

Syracuse 115, Phil. 107
Syracuse 115, Phil. 114
Syracuse 106, Phil. 103

EAST FINALS

Boston 128, Syracuse 115
Syracuse 115, Boston 98
Boston 133, Syracuse 110
Boston 120, Syracuse 107
Boston 123, Syracuse 101

WEST SEMIFINALS

Los Angeles 120, Detroit 102
Los Angeles 120, Detroit 118
Detroit 124, Los Angeles 113
Detroit 123, Los Angeles 114
Los Angeles 137, Detroit 120

WEST FINALS

Los Angeles 122, St. Louis 118
St. Louis 121, Los Angeles 106
Los Angeles 118, St. Louis 112
St. Louis 118, Los Angeles 117
Los Angeles 121, St. Louis 112
St. Louis 114, L.A. 113 (OT)
St. Louis 105, Los Angeles 103

NBA FINALS

Boston 129, St. Louis 95
Boston 116, St. Louis 108
St. Louis 124, Boston 120
Boston 119, St. Louis 104
Boston 121, St. Louis 112

1961-62
FINAL STANDINGS

Eastern Division

	W	L	PCT.	GB
Boston	60	20	.750	
Philadelphia	49	31	.613	11
Syracuse	41	39	.513	19
New York	29	51	.363	31

Western Division

	W	L	PCT.	GB
Los Angeles	54	26	.675	
Cincinnati	43	37	.538	11
Detroit	37	43	.463	17
St. Louis	29	51	.363	25
Chicago	18	62	.225	36

POINTS

	AVG.	NO.
W. Chamberlain, PHI.	50.4	4029
W. Bellamy, CHI	31.6	2495
O. Robertson, CIN	30.8	2432
B. Pettit, STL	31.1	2429
J. West, LA	30.8	2310
R. Guerin, NY	29.5	2303
W. Naulls, NY	25.0	1877
E. Baylor, LA	38.3	1836
J. Twyman, CIN	22.9	1831
C. Hagan, STL	22.9	1764
T. Heinsohn, BOS	22.1	1742
P. Arizin, PHI	21.9	1706
H. Greer, SYR	22.8	1619
B. Howell, DET	19.9	1576
G. Shue, DET	19.0	1522
W. Embry, CIN	19.8	1484
B. Russell, BOS	18.9	1436
S. Jones, BOS	18.4	1435
R. LaRusso, LA	17.2	1374
D. Gambee, SYR	16.7	1338

REBOUNDS

	AVG.	NO.
W. Chamberlain, PHI.	25.7	2052
B. Russell, BOS	23.6	1790
W. Bellamy, CHI	19.0	1500
B. Pettit, STL	18.7	1459
J. Kerr, SYR	14.7	1176
J. Green, NY	13.3	1066
B. Howell, DET	12.6	996
O. Robertson, CIN	12.5	985
W. Embry, CIN	13.0	977
E. Baylor, LA	18.6	892

ASSISTS

	AVG.	NO.
O. Robertson, CIN	11.4	899
G. Rodgers, PHI	7.9	663
B. Cousy, BOS	7.8	584
R. Guerin, NY	6.9	539
G. Shue, DET	5.8	465
J. West, LA	5.4	402
F. Selvy, LA	4.8	381
B. Leonard, CHI	5.4	378
C. Hagan, STL	4.8	370
A. Bockhorn, CIN	4.6	366

FIELD GOAL PCT.

Walt Bellamy, CHI	.519
W. Chamberlain, PHI.	.506
Jack Twyman, CIN	.479
Oscar Robertson, CIN	.478
Al Attles, PHI	.474
Larry Foust, STL	.471
Clyde Lovellette, STL	.471
Cliff Hagan, STL	.470
Wayne Embry, CIN	.466
Rudy LaRusso, LA	.466

FREE THROW PCT.

Dolph Schayes, SYR	.896
Willie Naulls, NY	.842
Larry Costello, SYR	.837
Frank Ramsey, BOS	.825
Cliff Hagan, STL	.825
Tom Meschery, PHI	.824
Richie Guerin, NY	.820
Hal Greer, SYR	.819

EAST SEMIFINALS

Philadelphia 110, Syrac. 103
Philadelphia 97, Syracuse 82
Syracuse 101, Phil. 100
Syracuse 106, Philadelphia 99
Philadelphia 121, Syrac. 104

EAST FINALS

Boston 117, Philadelphia 89
Philadelphia 113, Boston 106
Boston 129, Philadelphia 114
Philadelphia 110, Boston 106
Boston 119, Philadelphia 104
Philadelphia 109, Boston 99
Boston 109, Philadelphia 107

WEST SEMIFINALS

Detroit 123, Cincinnati 122
Cincinnati 129, Detroit 107
Detroit 118, Cincinnati 107
Detroit 112, Cincinnati 111

WEST FINALS

Los Angeles 132 Detroit 108
Los Angeles 127, Detroit 112
Los Angeles 111, Detroit 106
Detroit 118, Los Angeles 117
Detroit 132, Los Angeles 125
Los Angeles 123, Detroit 117

NBA FINALS

Boston 122, Los Angeles 108
Los Angeles 129, Boston 122
Los Angeles 117, Boston 115
Boston 115, Los Angeles 103
Los Angeles 126, Boston 121
Boston 119, Los Angeles 105
Boston 110, L.A. 107 (OT)

1962-63
FINAL STANDINGS

Eastern Division

	W	L	PCT.	GB
Boston	58	22	.725	
Syracuse	48	32	.600	10
Cincinnati	42	38	.525	16
New York	21	59	.263	37

Western Division

	W	L	PCT.	GB
Los Angeles	53	27	.663	
St. Louis	48	32	.600	5
Detroit	34	46	.425	19
San Francisco	31	49	.388	22
Chicago	25	55	.313	28

POINTS

	AVG.	NO.
W. Chamberlain, SF	44.8	3586
E. Baylor, LA	34.0	2719
O. Robertson, CIN	28.3	2264
B. Pettit, STL	28.4	2241
W. Bellamy, CHI	27.9	2233
B. Howell, DET	22.7	1793
R. Guerin, NY	21.5	1701
J. Twyman, CIN	19.8	1586
H. Greer, SYR	19.5	1562
D. Ohl, DET	19.3	1547
S. Jones, BOS	19.7	1499
J. West, LA	27.1	1489
L. Shaffer, SYR	18.6	1488
T. Dischinger, CHI	25.5	1452
J. Green, NY	18.1	1444
T. Heinsohn, BOS	18.9	1440
D. Barnett, LA	18.0	1437
W. Embry, CIN	18.6	1411
B. Russell, BOS	16.8	1309
J. Kerr, SYR	15.7	1255

REBOUNDS

	AVG.	NO.
W. Chamberlain, SF	24.3	1946
B. Russell, BOS	23.0	1843
W. Bellamy, CHI	16.4	1309
B. Pettit, STL	15.1	1191
E. Baylor, LA	14.3	1146
J. Kerr, SYR	13.1	1049
J. Green, NY	12.1	964
W. Embry, CIN	12.3	936
B. Howell, DET	11.5	910
B. Boozer, CIN	11.1	878

ASSISTS

	AVG.	NO.
G. Rodgers, SF	10.4	825
O. Robertson, CIN	9.5	758
B. Cousy, BOS	6.8	515
S. Green, CHI	5.8	422
E. Baylor, LA	4.8	386
L. Wilkens, STL	5.1	381
B. Russell, BOS	4.5	348
R. Guerin, NY	4.4	348
L. Costello, SYR	4.3	334
J. Barnhill, STL	4.2	322

FIELD GOAL PCT.

W. Chamberlain, SF	.528
Walt Bellamy, CHI	.527
Oscar Robertson, CIN	.518
Bailey Howell, DET	.516
Terry Dischinger, CHI	.512
Dave Budd, NY	.502
Jack Twyman, CIN	.480
Al Attles, SF	.478
Sam Jones, BOS	.476
John Kerr, SYR	.474

FREE THROW PCT.

Larry Costello, SYR	.881
Richie Guerin, NY	.848
Elgin Baylor, LA	.837
Tom Heinsohn, BOS	.835
Hal Greer, SYR	.834
Frank Ramsey, BOS	.816
Dick Barnett, LA	.815
Adrian Smith, CIN	.811

EAST SEMIFINALS

Syracuse 123, Cincinnati 120
Cincinnati 133, Syracuse 115
Syracuse 121, Cincinnati 117
Cincinnati 125, Syracuse 118
Cincinnati 131, Syrac. 127 (OT)

EAST FINALS

Cincinnati 135, Boston 132
Boston 125, Cincinnati 102
Cincinnati 121, Boston 116
Boston 128, Cincinnati 110
Boston 125, Cincinnati 120
Cincinnati 109, Boston 99
Boston 142, Cincinnati 131

WEST SEMIFINALS

St. Louis 118, Detroit 99
St. Louis 122, Detroit 108
Detroit 107, St. Louis 103
St. Louis 104, Detroit 100

WEST FINALS

Los Angeles 112, St. Louis 104
Los Angeles 101, St. Louis 99
St. Louis 125, Los Angeles 112
St. Louis 124, Los Angeles 114
Los Angeles 123, St. Louis 100
St. Louis 121, Los Angeles 113
Los Angeles 115, St. Louis 100

NBA FINALS

Boston 117, Los Angeles 114
Boston 113, Los Angeles 106
Los Angeles 119, Boston 99
Boston 108, Los Angeles 105
Los Angeles 126, Boston 119
Boston 112, Los Angeles 109

1963-64
FINAL STANDINGS

Eastern Division

	W	L	PCT.	GB
Boston	59	21	.738	
Cincinnati	55	25	.688	4
Philadelphia	34	46	.425	25
New York	22	58	.275	37

Western Division

	W	L	PCT.	GB
San Francisco	48	32	.600	
St. Louis	46	34	.575	2
Los Angeles	42	38	.525	6
Baltimore	31	49	.388	17
Detroit	23	57	.288	25

POINTS

	AVG.	NO.
W. Chamberlain, SF	36.9	2948
O. Robertson, CIN	31.4	2480
B. Pettit, ST	27.4	2190
W. Bellamy, BAL	27.0	2159
J. West, LA	28.7	2064
E. Baylor, LA	25.4	1983
H. Greer, PHI	23.3	1865
B. Howell, DET	21.6	1666
T. Dischinger, BAL	20.8	1662
J. Havlicek, BOS	19.9	1595
S. Jones, BOS	19.4	1473
D. Barnett, LA	18.4	1433
C. Hagan, STL	18.4	1413
R. Scott, DET	17.6	1406
J. Lucas, CIN	17.7	1400
W. Embry, CIN	17.3	1383
G. Johnson, BAL	17.3	1352
L. Chappell, PHI/NY	17.1	1350
J. Kerr, PHI	16.8	1340
C. Walker, PHI	17.3	1314

REBOUNDS

	AVG.	NO.
B. Russell, BOS	24.7	1930
W. Chamberlain, SF	22.3	1787
J. Lucas, CIN	17.4	1375
W. Bellamy, BAL	17.0	1361
B. Pettit, STL	15.3	1224
R. Scott, DET	13.5	1078
G. Johnson, BAL	13.6	1064
J. Kerr, PHI	12.7	1018
E. Baylor, LA	12.0	936
W. Embry, CIN	11.6	925

ASSISTS

	AVG.	NO.
O. Robertson, CIN	11.0	868
G. Rodgers, SF	7.0	556
K. Jones, BOS	5.1	407
J. West, LA	5.6	403
W. Chamberlain, SF	5.0	403
R. Guerin, NY/STL	4.7	375
H. Greer, PHI	4.7	374
B. Russell, BOS	4.7	370
L. Wilkens, STL	4.6	359
J. Egan, DET/NY	5.4	358

FIELD GOAL PCT.

Jerry Lucas, CIN	.527
W. Chamberlain, SF	.524
Walt Bellamy, BAL	.513
Terry Dischinger, BAL	.496
Bill McGill, NY	.487
Jerry West, LA	.484
Oscar Robertson, CIN	.483
Bailey Howell, DET	.472
John Green, NY	.470
Bob Pettit, STL	.463

FREE THROW PCT.

Oscar Robertson, CIN	.853
Jerry West, LA	.832
Hal Greer, PHI	.829
Tom Heinsohn, BOS	.827
Richie Guerin, NY/STL	.818
Cliff Hagan, STL	.813
Bailey Howell, DET	.809
Elgin Baylor, LA	.804

EAST SEMIFINALS

Cincinnati 127, Phil. 102
Philadelphia 122, Cinc. 114
Cincinnati 101, Philadelphia 89
Philadelphia 129, Cinc. 120
Cincinnati 130, Phil. 124

EAST FINALS

Boston 103, Cincinnati 87
Boston 101, Cincinnati 90
Boston 102, Cincinnati 92
Cincinnati 102, Boston 93
Boston 109, Cincinnati 95

WEST SEMIFINALS

St. Louis 115, Los Angeles 104
St. Louis 106, Los Angeles 90
Los Angeles 107, St. Louis 105
Los Angeles 97, St. Louis 88
St. Louis 121, Los Angeles 108

WEST FINALS

St. Louis 116, San Fran. 111
San Francisco 120, St. L. 85
St. Louis 113, San Fran. 109
San Francisco 111, St. L. 109
San Francisco 121, St. L. 97
St. Louis 123, S.F. 95
San Francisco 105, St. L. 95

NBA FINALS

Boston 108, San Francisco 96
Boston 124, San Francisco 101
San Francisco 115, Boston 91
Boston 98, San Francisco 95
Boston 105, San Francisco 99

1964-65
FINAL STANDINGS

Eastern Division

	W	L	PCT.	GB
Boston	62	18	.715	
Cincinnati	48	32	.600	14
Philadelphia	40	40	.500	22
New York	31	49	.388	31

Western Division

	W	L	PCT.	GB
Los Angeles	49	31	.613	
St. Louis	45	35	.563	4
Baltimore	37	43	.463	12
Detroit	31	49	.388	18
San Francisco	17	63	.213	32

POINTS

	AVG.	NO.
W. Chamber., SF/PHI	34.7	2534
J. West, LA	31.0	2292
O. Robertson, CIN	30.4	2279
S. Jones, BOS	25.9	2070
E. Baylor, LA	27.1	2009
W. Bellamy, BAL	24.8	1981
W. Reed, NY	19.5	1560
B. Howell, BAL	19.2	1534
T. Dischinger, DET	18.2	1456
D. Ohl, BAL	18.4	1420
G. Johnson, BAL	18.6	1415
J. Lucas, CIN	21.4	1414
H. Greer, PHI	20.2	1413
J. Havlicek, BOS	18.3	1375
Z. Beaty, STL	16.9	1351
D. DeBusschere, DET	16.7	1322
L. Wilkens, STL	16.5	1284
N. Thurmond, SF	16.5	1273
A. Smith, CIN	15.1	1210
J. Barnes, NY	15.5	1159

REBOUNDS

	AVG.	NO.
B. Russell, BOS	24.1	1878
W. Chamber., SF/PHI	22.9	1673
N. Thurmond, SF	18.1	1395
J. Lucas, CIN	20.0	1321
W. Reed, NY	14.7	1175
W. Bellamy, BAL	14.6	1166
G. Johnson, BAL	13.0	988
L. Jackson, PHI	12.9	969
Z. Beaty, STL	12.1	966
E. Baylor, LA	12.8	950

ASSISTS

	AVG.	NO.
O. Robertson, CIN	11.5	861
G. Rodgers, SF	7.3	565
K. Jones, BOS	5.6	437
L. Wilkens, STL	5.5	431
B. Russell, BOS	5.3	410
J. West, LA	4.9	364
H. Greer, PHI	4.5	313
K. Loughery, BAL	3.7	296
E. Baylor, LA	3.8	280
L. Costello, PHI	4.3	275

FIELD GOAL PCT.

W. Chamberlain, SF/PHI	.510
Walt Bellamy, BAL	.509
Jerry Lucas, CIN	.498
Jerry West, LA	.497
Bailey Howell, BAL	.495
Terry Dischinger, DET	.493
John Egan, NY	.488
Zelmo Beaty, STL	.482
Oscar Robertson, CIN	.480
Paul Neumann, PHI/SF	.473

FREE THROW PCT.

Larry Costello, PHI	.877
Oscar Robertson, CIN	.839
Howard Komives, NY	.835
Adrian Smith, CIN	.830
Jerry West, LA	.821
Sam Jones, BOS	.820
Bob Pettit, STL	.820
Jerry Lucas, CIN	.814

EAST SEMIFINALS
Philadelphia 119, Cinc. 117(OT)
Cincinnati 121, Phil. 120
Philadelphia 108, Cincinnati 94
Philadelphia 119, Cinc. 112

EAST FINALS
Boston 108, Philadelphia 98
Philadelphia 109, Boston 103
Boston 112, Philadelphia 94
Philadelphia 134, Bos. 131 (OT)
Boston 114, Philadelphia 108
Philadelphia 112, Boston 106
Boston 110, Philadelphia 109

WEST SEMIFINALS
Baltimore 108, St. Louis 105
St. Louis 129, Baltimore 105
Baltimore 131, St. Louis 99
Baltimore 109, St. Louis 103

WEST FINALS
Los Angeles 121, Balt. 115
Los Angeles 118, Balt. 115
Baltimore 122, L.A. 115
Baltimore 114, L.A. 112
Los Angeles 120, Balt. 112
Los Angeles 117, Balt. 115

NBA FINALS
Boston 142, Los Angeles 110
Boston 129, Los Angeles 123
Los Angeles 126, Boston 105
Boston 112, Los Angeles 99
Boston 129, Los Angeles 96

1965-66
FINAL STANDINGS

Eastern Division

	W	L	PCT.	GB
Philadelphia	55	25	.688	
Boston	54	26	.675	1
Cincinnati	45	35	.563	10
New York	30	50	.375	25

Western Division

	W	L	PCT.	GB
Los Angeles	45	35	.563	
Baltimore	38	42	.475	7
St. Louis	36	44	.450	9
San Francisco	35	45	.438	10
Detroit	22	58	.275	23

POINTS

	AVG.	NO.
W. Chamberlain, PHI	33.5	2649
J. West, LA	31.3	2476
O. Robertson, CIN	31.3	2378
R. Barry, SF	25.7	2059
W. Bellamy, BAL/NY	22.8	1820
H. Greer, PHI	22.7	1819
D. Barnett, NY	23.1	1729
J. Lucas, CIN	21.5	1697
Z. Beaty, STL	20.7	1656
S. Jones, BOS	23.5	1577
E. Miles, DET	19.6	1566
D. Ohl, BAL	20.6	1502
A. Smith, CIN	18.4	1470
G. Rodgers, SF	18.6	1468
R. Scott, DET	17.9	1411
B. Howell, BAL	17.3	1364
K. Loughery, BAL	18.2	1349
J. Havlicek, BOS	18.8	1334
D. DeBusschere, DET	16.4	1297
L. Wilkens, STL	18.0	1244

REBOUNDS

	AVG.	NO.
W. Chamberlain, PHI	24.6	1943
B. Russell, BOS	22.8	1779
J. Lucas, CIN	21.1	1668
N. Thurmond, SF	18.0	1312
W. Bellamy, BAL/NY	15.7	1254
Z. Beaty, STL	13.6	1086
B. Bridges, STL	12.2	951
D. DeBusschere, DET	11.6	916
W. Reed, NY	11.6	883
R. Barry, SF	10.6	850

ASSISTS

	AVG.	NO.
O. Robertson, CIN	11.1	847
G. Rodgers, SF	10.7	846
K. Jones, BOS	6.3	503
J. West, LA	6.1	480
L. Wilkens, STL	6.2	429
H. Komives, NY	5.3	425
W. Chamberlain, PHI	5.2	414
W. Hazzard, LA	4.9	393
R. Guerin, STL	4.9	388
H. Greer, PHI	4.8	384

FIELD GOAL PCT.

W. Chamberlain, PHI	.540
John Green, NY/BAL	.536
Walt Bellamy, BAL/NY	.506
Al Attles, SF	.503
Happy Hairston, CIN	.489
Bailey Howell, BAL	.488
Bob Boozer, LA	.484
Oscar Robertson, CIN	.475
Zelmo Beaty, STL	.473
Jerry West, LA	.473

FREE THROW PCT.

Larry Siegfried, BOS	.881
Rick Barry, SF	.862
Howard Komives, NY	.861
Jerry West, LA	.860
Adrian Smith, CIN	.850
Oscar Robertson, CIN	.842
Paul Neumann, SF	.836
Kevin Loughery, BAL	.830

EAST SEMIFINALS

Cincinnati 107, Boston 103
Boston 132, Cincinnati 125
Cincinnati 113, Boston 107
Boston 120, Cincinnati 103
Boston 112, Cincinnati 103

EAST FINALS

Boston 115, Philadelphia 96
Boston 114, Philadelphia 93
Philadelphia 111, Boston 105
Boston 114, Phil. 110 (OT)
Boston 120, Philadelphia 112

WEST SEMIFINALS

St. Louis 113, Baltimore 111
St. Louis 105, Baltimore 100
St. Louis 121, Baltimore 112

WEST FINALS

Los Angeles 129, St. Louis 106
Los Angeles 125, St. Louis 116
St. Louis 120, Los Angeles 113
Los Angeles 107, St. Louis 95
St. Louis 112, Los Angeles 100
St. Louis 131, Los Angeles 127
Los Angeles 130, St. Louis 121

NBA FINALS

Los Angeles 133, Bos. 129 (OT)
Boston 129, Los Angeles 109
Boston 120, Los Angeles 106
Boston 122, Los Angeles 117
Los Angeles 121, Boston 117
Los Angeles 123, Boston 115
Boston 95, Los Angeles 93

1966-67
FINAL STANDINGS

Eastern Division

	W	L	PCT.	GB
Philadelphia	68	13	.840	
Boston	60	21	.741	8
Cincinnati	39	42	.481	29
New York	36	45	.444	32
Baltimore	20	61	.247	48

Western Division

	W	L	PCT.	GB
San Francisco	44	37	.543	
St. Louis	39	42	.481	5
Los Angeles	36	45	.444	8
Chicago	33	48	.407	11
Detroit	30	51	.370	14

POINTS

	AVG.	NO.
R. Barry, SF	35.6	2775
O. Robertson, CIN	30.5	2412
W. Chamberlain, PHI	24.1	1956
J. West, LA	28.7	1892
E. Baylor, LA	26.6	1862
H. Greer, PHI	22.1	1765
J. Havlicek, BOS	21.4	1733
W. Reed, NY	20.9	1628
B. Howell, BOS	20.0	1621
D. Bing, DET	20.0	1601
S. Jones, BOS	22.1	1594
C. Walker, PHI	19.3	1567
G. Johnson, BAL	20.7	1511
W. Bellamy, NY	19.0	1499
B. Cunningham, PHI	18.5	1495
L. Hudson, STL	18.4	1471
G. Rodgers, CHI	18.0	1459
J. Lucas, CIN	17.8	1438
B. Boozer, CHI	18.0	1436
E. Miles, DET	17.6	1425

REBOUNDS

	AVG.	NO.
W. Chamberlain, PHI	24.2	1957
B. Russell, BOS	21.0	1700
J. Lucas, CIN	19.1	1547
N. Thurmond, SF	21.3	1382
B. Bridges, STL	15.1	1190
W. Reed, NY	14.6	1136
D. Imhoff, LA	13.3	1080
W. Bellamy, NY	13.5	1064
L. Ellis, BAL	12.0	970
D. DeBusschere, DET	11.8	924

ASSISTS

	AVG.	NO.
G. Rodgers, CHI	11.2	908
O. Robertson, CIN	10.7	845
W. Chamberlain, PHI	7.8	630
B. Russell, BOS	5.8	472
J. West, LA	6.8	447
L. Wilkens, STL	5.7	442
H. Komives, NY	6.2	401
K. Jones, BOS	5.0	389
R. Guerin, STL	4.4	345
P. Neumann, SF	4.4	342

FIELD GOAL PCT.

W. Chamberlain, PHI	.683
Walt Bellamy, NY	.521
Bailey Howell, BOS	.512
Oscar Robertson, CIN	.493
Willis Reed, NY	.490
Chet Walker, PHI	.488
Bob Boozer, CHI	.487
Tom Hawkins, LA	.481
Happy Hairston, CIN	.479
Dick Barnett, NY	.478

FREE THROW PCT.

Adrian Smith, CIN	.903
Rick Barry, SF	.884
Jerry West, LA	.878
Oscar Robertson, CIN	.873
Sam Jones, BOS	.857
Larry Siegfried, BOS	.847
Wally Jones, PHI	.838
John Havlicek, BOS	.828

EAST SEMIFINALS
Philadelphia 3, Cincinnati 1
Boston 3, New York 1

EAST FINALS
Philadelphia 127, Boston 113
Philadelphia 107, Boston 102
Philadelphia 115, Boston 104
Boston 121, Philadelphia 117
Philadelphia 140, Boston 116

WEST SEMIFINALS
San Francisco 3, L.A. 0
St. Louis 3, Chicago 0

WEST FINALS
San Francisco 117, St. L. 115
San Francisco 143, St. L. 136
St. Louis 115, S.F. 109
St. Louis 109, S.F. 104
San Francisco 123, St. L. 102
San Francisco 112, St. L. 107

NBA FINALS
Phil. 141, S.F. 135 (OT)
Philadelphia 126, S.F. 95
San Francisco 130, Phil. 124
Philadelphia 122, S.F. 108
San Francisco 117, Phil. 109
Philadelphia 125, S.F. 122

1967-68
FINAL STANDINGS

Eastern Division

	W	L	PCT.	GB
Philadelphia	62	20	.756	
Boston	54	28	.659	8
New York	43	39	.524	19
Detroit	40	42	.488	22
Cincinnati	39	43	.476	23
Baltimore	36	46	.439	26

Western Division

	W	L	PCT.	GB
St. Louis	56	26	.683	
Los Angeles	52	30	.634	4
San Francisco	43	39	.524	13
Chicago	29	53	.354	27
Seattle	23	59	.280	33
San Diego	15	67	.183	41

POINTS

	AVG.	NO.
D. Bing, DET	27.1	2142
E. Baylor, LA	26.0	2002
W. Chamberlain, PHI	24.3	1992
E. Monroe, BAL	24.3	1991
H. Greer, PHI	24.1	1976
O. Robertson, CIN	29.2	1896
W. Hazzard, SEA	23.9	1894
J. Lucas, CIN	21.4	1760
Z. Beaty, STL	21.1	1733
R. LaRusso, SF	21.8	1726
J. Havlicek, BOS	20.7	1700
W. Reed, NY	20.8	1685
B. Boozer, CHI	21.5	1655
L. Wilkens, STL	20.0	1638
B. Howell, BOS	19.8	1621
A. Clark, LA	19.9	1612
S. Jones, BOS	21.3	1553
J. Mullins, SF	18.9	1493
B. Rule, SEA	18.1	1484
C. Walker, PHI	17.9	1465

REBOUNDS

	AVG.	NO.
W. Chamberlain, PHI	23.8	1952
J. Lucas, CIN	19.0	1560
B. Russell, BOS	18.6	1451
C. Lee, SF	13.9	1141
N. Thurmond, SF	22.0	1121
R. Scott, BAL	13.7	1111
B. Bridges, STL	13.4	1102
D. DeBusschere, DET	13.5	1081
W. Reed, NY	13.2	1073
W. Bellamy, NY	11.7	961

ASSISTS

	AVG.	NO.
W. Chamberlain, PHI	8.6	702
L. Wilkens, STL	8.3	679
O. Robertson, CIN	9.7	633
D. Bing, DET	6.4	509
W. Hazzard, SEA	6.2	493
A. Williams, SD	4.9	391
A. Attles, SF	5.8	390
J. Havlicek, BOS	4.7	384
G. Rodgers, CHI/CIN	4.8	380
H. Greer, PHI	4.5	372

FIELD GOAL PCT.

W. Chamberlain, PHI	.595
Walt Bellamy, NY	.541
Jerry Lucas, CIN	.519
Jerry West, LA	.514
Len Chappell, CIN/DET	.513
Oscar Robertson, CIN	.500
Tom Hawkins, LA	.499
Terry Dischinger, DET	.494
Don Nelson, BOS	.494
Henry Finkel, SD	.492

FREE THROW PCT.

Oscar Robertson, CIN	.873
Larry Siegfried, BOS	.868
Dave Gambee, SD	.847
Fred Hetzel, SF	.833
Adrian Smith, CIN	.829
Sam Jones, BOS	.827
Flynn Robinson, CIN/CHI	.821
John Havlicek, BOS	.812

EAST SEMIFINALS

Philadelphia 4, New York 2
Boston 4, Detroit 2

EAST FINALS

Boston 127, Philadelphia 118
Philadelphia 115, Boston 106
Philadelphia 122, Boston 114
Philadelphia 110, Boston 105
Boston 122, Philadelphia 104
Boston 114, Philadelphia 106
Boston 100, Philadelphia 96

WEST SEMIFINALS

San Francisco 4, St. Louis 2
Los Angeles 4, Chicago 1

WEST FINALS

Los Angeles 133, S.F. 105
Los Angeles 115, S.F. 112
Los Angeles 128, S.F. 124
Los Angeles 106, S.F. 100

NBA FINALS

Boston 107, Los Angeles 101
Los Angeles 123, Boston 113
Boston 127, Los Angeles 119
Los Angeles 119, Boston 105
Boston 120, L.A. 117 (OT)
Boston 124, Los Angeles 109

1968-69
FINAL STANDINGS

Eastern Division

	W	L	PCT.	GB
Baltimore	57	25	.695	
Philadelphia	55	27	.671	2
New York	54	28	.659	3
Boston	48	34	.585	9
Cincinnati	41	41	.500	16
Detroit	32	50	.390	25
Milwaukee	27	55	.329	30

Western Division

	W	L	PCT.	GB
Los Angeles	55	27	.671	
Atlanta	48	34	.585	7
San Francisco	41	41	.500	14
San Diego	37	45	.451	18
Chicago	33	49	.402	22
Seattle	30	52	.366	25
Phoenix	16	66	.195	39

POINTS

	AVG.	NO.
E. Hayes, SD	28.4	2327
E. Monroe, BAL	25.8	2065
B. Cunningham, PHI	24.8	2034
B. Rule, SEA	24.0	1965
O. Robertson, CIN	24.7	1955
G. Goodrich, PHO	23.8	1931
H. Greer, PHI	23.1	1896
E. Baylor, LA	24.8	1881
L. Wilkens, SEA	22.4	1835
D. Kojis, SD	22.5	1820
K. Loughery, BAL	22.6	1806
D. Bing, DET	23.4	1800
J. Mullins, SF	22.8	1775
J. Havlicek, BOS	21.6	1771
L. Hudson, ATL	21.9	1770
W. Reed, NY	21.1	1733
B. Boozer, CHI	21.7	1716
D. Van Arsdale, PHO	21.0	1678
W. Chamberlain, LA	20.5	1664
F. Robinson, CHI/MIL	20.0	1662

REBOUNDS

	AVG.	NO.
W. Chamberlain, LA	21.1	1712
W. Unseld, BAL	18.2	1491
B. Russell, BOS	19.3	1484
E. Hayes, SD	17.1	1406
N. Thurmond, SF	19.7	1402
J. Lucas, CIN	18.4	1360
W. Reed, NY	14.5	1191
B. Bridges, ATL	14.2	1132
W. Bellamy, NY/DET	12.5	1101
B. Cunningham, PHI	12.8	1050

ASSISTS

	AVG.	NO.
O. Robertson, CIN	9.8	772
L. Wilkens, SEA	8.2	674
W. Frazier, NY	7.9	635
G. Rodgers, MIL	6.9	561
D. Bing, DET	7.1	546
A. Williams, SD	6.6	524
G. Goodrich, PHO	6.4	518
W. Hazzard, ATL	5.9	474
J. Havlicek, BOS	5.4	441
J. West, LA	6.9	423

FIELD GOAL PCT.

W. Chamberlain, LA	.583
Jerry Lucas, CIN	.551
Willis Reed, NY	.521
Terry Dischinger, DET	.515
Walt Bellamy, NY/DET	.510
Joe Caldwell, ATL	.507
Walt Frazier, NY	.505
Tom Hawkins, LA	.499
Lou Hudson, ATL	.492
Jon McGlocklin, MIL	.487

FREE THROW PCT.

Larry Siegfried, BOS	.864
Jeff Mullins, SF	.843
Jon McGlocklin, MIL	.842
Flynn Robinson, CHI/MIL	.839
Oscar Robertson, CIN	.838
Fred Hetzel, MIL/CIN	.838
Jack Marin, BAL	.830
Jerry West, LA	.821

EAST SEMIFINALS

New York 4, Baltimore 0
Boston 4, Philadelphia 1

EAST FINALS

Boston 108, New York 100
Boston 112, New York 97
New York 101, Boston 91
Boston 97, New York 96
New York 112, Boston 104
Boston 106, New York 105

WEST SEMIFINALS

Los Angeles 4, San Fran. 2
Atlanta 4, San Diego 2

WEST FINALS

Los Angeles 95, Atlanta 93
Los Angeles 104, Atlanta 102
Atlanta 99, Los Angeles 86
Los Angeles 100, Atlanta 85
Los Angeles 104, Atlanta 96

NBA FINALS

Los Angeles 120, Boston 118
Los Angeles 118, Boston 112
Boston 111, Los Angeles 105
Boston 89, Los Angeles 88
Los Angeles 117, Boston 104
Boston 99, Los Angeles 90
Boston 108, Los Angeles 106

1969-70
FINAL STANDINGS

Eastern Division

	W	L	PCT.	GB
New York	60	22	.732	
Milwaukee	56	26	.683	4
Baltimore	50	32	.610	10
Philadelphia	42	40	.512	18
Cincinnati	36	46	.439	24
Boston	34	48	.415	26
Detroit	31	51	.378	29

Western Division

	W	L	PCT.	GB
Atlanta	48	34	.585	
Los Angeles	46	36	.561	2
Chicago	39	43	.476	9
Phoenix	39	43	.476	9
Seattle	36	46	.439	12
San Francisco	30	52	.366	18
San Diego	27	55	.329	21

SCORING

Jerry West, LA	31.2
Lew Alcindor, MIL	28.8
Elvin Hayes, SD	27.5
Billy Cunningham, PHI	26.1
Lou Hudson, ATL	25.4
Connie Hawkins, PHO	24.6
Bob Rule, SEA	24.6
John Havlicek, BOS	24.2
Earl Monroe, BAL	23.4
Dave Bing, DET	22.9
Tom Van Arsdale, CIN	22.8
Jeff Mullins, SF	22.1
Hal Greer, PHI	22.0
Flynn Robinson, MIL	21.8
Willis Reed, NY	21.7
Chet Walker, CHI	21.5
Dick Van Arsdale, PHO	21.3
Joe Caldwell, ATL	21.1
Bob Love, CHI	21.0
Walt Frazier, NY	20.9

REBOUNDS

Elvin Hayes, SD	16.9
Wes Unseld, BAL	16.7
Lew Alcindor, MIL	14.5
Bill Bridges, ATL	14.4
Gus Johnson, BAL	13.9
Willis Reed, NY	13.9
Billy Cunningham, PHI	13.6
Tom Boerwinkle, CHI	12.5
Paul Silas, PHO	11.7
Clyde Lee, SF	11.3

ASSISTS

Len Wilkens, SEA	9.1
Walt Frazier, NY	8.2
Clem Haskins, CHI	7.6
Jerry West, LA	7.5
Gail Goodrich, PHO	7.5
Walt Hazzard, ATL	6.8
John Havlicek, BOS	6.8
Art Williams, SD	6.3
Norm Van Lier, CIN	6.2
Dave Bing, DET	6.0

FIELD GOAL PCT.

Johnny Green, CIN	.559
Darrall Imhoff, PHI	.540
Lou Hudson, ATL	.531
Jon McGlocklin, MIL	.530
Dick Snyder, SEA	.528
Jim Fox, PHO	.524
Lew Alcindor, MIL	.518
Wes Unseld, BAL	.518
Walt Frazier, NY	.518
Dick Van Arsdale, PHO	.508

FREE THROW PCT.

Flynn Robinson, MIL	.898
Chet Walker, CHI	.850
Jeff Mullins, SF	.847
John Havlicek, BOS	.844
Bob Love, CHI	.842
Earl Monroe, BAL	.830
Lou Hudson, ATL	.824
Jerry West, LA	.824

EAST SEMIFINALS

New York 4, Baltimore 3
Milwaukee 4, Philadelphia 1

EAST FINALS

New York 110, Milwaukee 102
New York 112, Milwaukee 111
Milwaukee 101, New York 96
New York 117, Milwaukee 105
New York 132, Milwaukee 96

WEST SEMIFINALS

Atlanta 4, Chicago 1
Los Angeles 4, Phoenix 3

WEST FINALS

Los Angeles 119, Atlanta 115
Los Angeles 105, Atlanta 94
Los Angeles 115, Atl. 114 (OT)
Los Angeles 133, Atlanta 114

NBA FINALS

New York 124, L.A. 112
Los Angeles 105, N.Y. 103
New York 111, L.A. 108 (OT)
Los Angeles 121, N.Y. 115 (OT)
New York 107, L.A. 100
Los Angeles 135, N.Y. 113
New York 113, L.A. 99

1970-71
FINAL STANDINGS

Eastern Conference
Atlantic Division

	W	L	PCT.	GB
New York	52	30	.634	
Philadelphia	47	35	.573	5
Boston	44	38	.537	8
Buffalo	22	60	.268	30

Central Division

	W	L	PCT.	GB
Baltimore	42	40	.512	
Atlanta	36	46	.439	6
Cincinnati	33	49	.402	9
Cleveland	15	67	.183	27

Western Conference
Midwest Division

	W	L	PCT.	GB
Milwaukee	66	16	.805	
Chicago	51	31	.622	15
Phoenix	48	34	.585	18
Detroit	45	37	.549	21

Pacific Division

	W	L	PCT.	GB
Los Angeles	48	34	.585	
San Francisco	41	41	.500	7
San Diego	40	42	.488	8
Seattle	38	44	.463	10
Portland	29	53	.354	19

SCORING
Lew Alcindor, MIL 31.7
John Havlicek, BOS 28.9
Elvin Hayes, SD 28.7
Dave Bing, DET 27.0
Lou Hudson, ATL 26.8
Bob Love, CHI....................25.2
Geoff Petrie, POR..............24.8
Pete Maravich, ATL 23.2
Billy Cunningham, PHI......23.0
Tom Van Arsdale, CIN......22.9
Chet Walker, CHI 22.0
Dick Van Arsdale, PHO.....21.9
Walt Frazier, NY................21.7
Earl Monroe, BAL..............21.4
Jo Jo White, BOS...............21.3
Archie Clark, PHI 21.3
Willis Reed, NY 20.9
Connie Hawkins, PHO 20.9
Jeff Mullins, SF 20.8

REBOUNDS
W. Chamberlain, LA...........18.2
Wes Unseld, BAL...............16.9
Elvin Hayes, SD 16.6
Lew Alcindor, MIL 16.0
Jerry Lucas, SF 15.8
Bill Bridges, ATL 15.0
Dave Cowens, BOS...........15.0
Tom Boerwinkle, CHI.........13.8
Nate Thurmond, SF 13.8
Willis Reed, NY 13.7

ASSISTS
Norm Van Lier, CIN...........10.1
Len Wilkens, SEA............... 9.2
Oscar Robertson, MIL 8.2
John Havlicek, BOS 7.5
Walt Frazier, NY 6.7
Walt Hazzard, ATL 6.3
Ron Williams, SF............... 5.9
Nate Archibald, CIN........... 5.5
Archie Clark, PHI 5.4
Dave Bing, DET 5.0

FIELD GOAL PCT.
Johnny Green, CIN.............587
Lew Alcindor, MIL..............577
W. Chamberlain, LA 545
Jon McGlocklin, MIL 535
Dick Snyder, SEA..............531
Greg Smith, MIL 512
Bob Dandridge, MIL 509
Wes Unseld, BAL...............501
Jerry Lucas, SF 498

FREE THROW PCT.
Chet Walker, CHI 859
Oscar Robertson, MIL 850
Ron Williams, SF...............844
Jeff Mullins, SF..................844
Dick Snyder, SEA..............837
Stan McKenzie, POR 836
Jerry West, LA...................832
Jimmy Walker, DET...........831

EAST SEMIFINALS
New York 4, Atlanta 1
Baltimore 4, Philadelphia 3

EAST FINALS
New York 112, Baltimore 111
New York 107, Baltimore 88
Baltimore 114, New York 88
Baltimore 101, New York 80
New York 89, Baltimore 84
Baltimore 113, New York 96
Baltimore 93, New York 91

WEST SEMIFINALS
Milwaukee 4, San Francisco 1
Los Angeles 4, Chicago 3

WEST FINALS
Milwaukee 106, L.A. 85
Milwaukee 91, Los Angeles 73
Los Angeles 118, Milw. 107
Milwaukee 117, L.A. 94
Milwaukee 116, L.A. 98

NBA FINALS
Milwaukee 98, Baltimore 88
Milwaukee 102, Baltimore 83
Milwaukee 107, Baltimore 99
Milwaukee 118, Baltimore 106

1971-72
FINAL STANDINGS

Eastern Conference

Atlantic Division

	W	L	PCT.	GB
Boston	56	26	.683	
New York	48	34	.585	8
Philadelphia	30	52	.366	26
Buffalo	22	60	.268	34

Central Division

	W	L	PCT.	GB
Baltimore	38	44	.463	
Atlanta	36	46	.439	2
Cincinnati	30	52	.366	8
Cleveland	23	59	.280	15

Western Conference

Midwest Division

	W	L	PCT.	GB
Milwaukee	63	19	.768	
Chicago	57	25	.695	6
Phoenix	49	33	.598	14
Detroit	26	56	.317	37

Pacific Division

	W	L	PCT.	GB
Los Angeles	69	13	.841	
Golden State	51	31	.622	18
Seattle	47	35	.573	22
Houston	34	48	.415	35
Portland	18	64	.220	51

SCORING

K. Abdul-Jabbar, MIL	34.8
Nate Archibald, CIN	28.2
John Havlicek, BOS	27.5
Spencer Haywood, SEA	26.2
Gail Goodrich, LA	25.9
Bob Love, CHI	25.8
Jerry West, LA	25.8
Bob Lanier, DET	25.7
Archie Clark, BAL	25.2
Elvin Hayes, HOU	25.2
Lou Hudson, ATL	24.7
Sidney Wicks, POR	24.5
Billy Cunningham, PHI	23.3
Walt Frazier, NY	23.2
Jo Jo White, BOS	23.1
Jack Marin, BAL	22.3
Chet Walker, CHI	22.0
Jeff Mullins, GS	21.5
Nate Thurmond, GS	21.4
Cazzie Russell, GS	21.4

REBOUNDS

W. Chamberlain, LA	19.2
Wes Unseld, BAL	17.6
K. Abdul-Jabbar, MIL	16.6
Nate Thurmond, GS	16.1
Dave Cowens, BOS	15.2
Elmore Smith, BUF	15.2
Elvin Hayes, HOU	14.6
Clyde Lee, GS	14.5
Bob Lanier, DET	14.2

ASSISTS

Jerry West, LA	9.7
Len Wilkens, SEA	9.6
Nate Archibald, CIN	9.2
Archie Clark, BAL	8.0
John Havlicek, BOS	7.5
Norm Van Lier, CIN/CHI	6.9
Billy Cunningham, PHI	5.9
Jeff Mullins, GS	5.9
Walt Frazier, NY	5.8
Walt Hazzard, BUF	5.6

FIELD GOAL PCT.

W. Chamberlain, LA	.649
K. Abdul-Jabbar, MIL	.574
Walt Bellamy, ATL	.545
Dick Snyder, SEA	.529
Jerry Lucas, NY	.512
Walt Frazier, NY	.512
Jon McGlocklin, MIL	.510
Chet Walker, CHI	.505
Lucius Allen, MIL	.505

FREE THROW PCT.

Jack Marin, BAL	.894
Calvin Murphy, HOU	.890
Gail Goodrich, LA	.850
Chet Walker, CHI	.847
Dick Van Arsdale, PHO	.845
Stu Lantz, HOU	.838
John Havlicek, BOS	.834
Cazzie Russell, GS	.833

EAST SEMIFINALS

Boston 4, Atlanta 2
New York 4, Baltimore 2

EAST FINALS

New York 116, Boston 94
New York 106, Boston 105
Boston 115, New York 109
New York 116, Boston 98
New York 111, Boston 103

WEST SEMIFINALS

Los Angeles 4, Chicago 0
Milwaukee 4, Golden St. 1

WEST FINALS

Milwaukee 93, Los Angeles 72
Los Angeles 135, Milw. 134
Los Angeles 108, Milw. 105
Milwaukee 114, L.A. 88
Los Angeles 115, Milw. 90
Los Angeles 104, Milw. 100

NBA FINALS

New York 114, Los Angeles 92
Los Angeles 106, New York 92
Los Angeles 107, New York 96
Los Angeles 116, N.Y. 111 (OT)
Los Angeles 114, N.Y. 100

1972-73
FINAL STANDINGS

Eastern Conference
Atlantic Division

	W	L	PCT.	GB
Boston	68	14	.829	
New York	57	25	.695	11
Buffalo	21	61	.256	47
Philadelphia	9	73	.110	59

Central Division

	W	L	PCT.	GB
Baltimore	52	30	.634	
Atlanta	46	36	.561	6
Houston	33	49	.402	19
Cleveland	32	50	.390	20

Western Conference
Midwest Division

	W	L	PCT.	GB
Milwaukee	60	22	.732	
Chicago	51	31	.622	9
Detroit	40	42	.488	20
K.C.-Omaha	36	46	.439	24

Pacific Division

	W	L	PCT.	GB
Los Angeles	60	22	.732	
Golden State	47	35	.573	13
Phoenix	38	44	.463	22
Seattle	26	56	.317	34
Portland	21	61	.256	39

SCORING

Nate Archibald, KCO	34.0
K. Abdul-Jabbar, MIL	30.2
Spencer Haywood, SEA	29.2
Lou Hudson, ATL	27.1
Pete Maravich, ATL	26.1
Charlie Scott, PHO	25.3
Geoff Petrie, POR	24.9
Gail Goodrich, LA	23.9
Sidney Wicks, POR	23.8
Bob Lanier, DET	23.8
John Havlicek, BOS	23.8
Bob Love, CHI	23.1
Dave Bing, DET	22.4
Rick Barry, GS	22.3
Elvin Hayes, BAL	21.2
Walt Frazier, NY	21.1
Austin Carr, CLE	20.5
Dave Cowens, BOS	20.5
Len Wilkens, CLE	20.5

REBOUNDS

W. Chamberlain, LA	18.6
Nate Thurmond, GS	17.1
Dave Cowens, BOS	16.2
K. Abdul-Jabbar, MIL	16.1
Wes Unseld, BAL	15.9
Bob Lanier, DET	14.9
Elvin Hayes, BAL	14.5
Walt Bellamy, ATL	13.0
Paul Silas, BOS	13.0
Spencer Haywood, SEA	12.9

ASSISTS

Nate Archibald, KCO	11.4
Len Wilkens, CLE	8.4
Dave Bing, DET	7.8
Oscar Robertson, MIL.	7.5
Norm Van Lier, CHI	7.1
Pete Maravich, ATL	6.9
John Havlicek, BOS	6.6
Herm Gilliam, ATL	6.3
Charlie Scott, PHO	6.1
Jo Jo White, BOS	6.1

FIELD GOAL PCT.

W. Chamberlain, LA	.727
Matt Guokas, KCO	.570
K. Abdul-Jabbar, MIL	.554
Curtis Rowe, DET	.519
Jim Fox, SEA	.515
Jerry Lucas, NY	.513
Mike Riordan, BAL	.510
Archie Clark, BAL	.507
Bob Kauffman, BUF	.505

FREE THROW PCT.

Rick Barry, GS	.902
Calvin Murphy, HOU	.888
Mike Newlin, HOU	.886
Jimmy Walker, HOU	.884
Bill Bradley, NY	.871
Cazzie Russell, GS	.864
Dick Snyder, SEA	.861
Dick Van Arsdale, PHO	.859

EAST SEMIFINALS
Boston 4, Atlanta 2
New York 4, Baltimore 1

EAST FINALS
Boston 134, New York 108
New York 129, Boston 96
New York 98, Boston 91
New York 117, Bost. 110 (2OT)
Boston 98, New York 97
Boston 110, New York 100
New York 94, Boston 78

WEST SEMIFINALS
Los Angeles 4, Chicago 3
Golden St. 4, Milwaukee 2

WEST FINALS
Los Angeles 101, G.S. 99
Los Angeles 104, G.S. 93
Los Angeles 126, G.S. 70
Golden St. 117, L.A. 109
Los Angeles 128, G.S. 118

NBA FINALS
Los Angeles 115, N.Y. 112
New York 99, Los Angeles 95
New York 87, Los Angeles 83
New York 103, Los Angeles 98
New York 102, Los Angeles 93

1973-74
FINAL STANDINGS

Eastern Conference
Atlantic Division

	W	L	PCT.	GB
Boston	56	26	.683	
New York	49	33	.598	7
Buffalo	42	40	.512	14
Philadelphia	25	57	.305	31

Central Division

	W	L	PCT.	GB
Capital	47	35	.573	
Atlanta	35	47	.427	12
Houston	32	50	.390	15
Cleveland	29	53	.354	18

Western Conference
Midwest Division

	W	L	PCT.	GB
Milwaukee	59	23	.720	
Chicago	54	28	.659	5
Detroit	52	30	.634	7
K.C.-Omaha	33	49	.402	26

Pacific Division

	W	L	PCT.	GB
Los Angeles	47	35	.573	
Golden State	44	38	.537	3
Seattle	36	46	.439	11
Phoenix	30	52	.366	17
Portland	27	55	.329	20

SCORING
Bob McAdoo, BUF 30.6
Pete Maravich, ATL 27.7
K. Abdul-Jabbar, MIL 27.0
Gail Goodrich, LA............25.3
Rick Barry, GS 25.1
Rudy Tomjanovich, HOU ..24.5
Geoff Petrie, POR 24.3
Spencer Haywood, SEA ..23.5
John Havlicek, BOS 22.6
Bob Lanier, DET 22.5

REBOUNDS
Elvin Hayes, CAP.............18.1
Dave Cowens, BOS.........15.7
Bob McAdoo, BUF 15.1
K. Abdul-Jabbar, MIL 14.5
Happy Hairston, LA.........13.5
Spencer Haywood, SEA ..13.4
Sam Lacey, KCO 13.4
Bob Lanier, DET 13.3
Clifford Ray, CHI.............12.2

ASSISTS
Ernie DiGregorio, BUF 8.2
Calvin Murphy, HOU 7.4
Len Wilkens, CLE............. 7.1
Walt Frazier, NY 6.9
Dave Bing, DET................ 6.9
Norm Van Lier, CHI 6.9
Oscar Robertson, MIL. 6.4
Rick Barry, GS.................. 6.1

STEALS
Larry Steele, POR.............2.68
Steve Mix, PHI 2.59
Randy Smith, BUF 2.48
Jerry Sloan, CHI...............2.38
Rick Barry, GS 2.11
Phil Chenier, CAP.............2.04

BLOCKED SHOTS
Elmore Smith, LA..............4.85
K. Abdul-Jabbar, MIL 3.49
Bob McAdoo, BUF 3.32
Bob Lanier, DET 3.04
Elvin Hayes, CAP..............2.96
Garfield Heard, BUF 2.84

FIELD GOAL PCT.
Bob McAdoo, BUF 547
K. Abdul-Jabbar, MIL.........539
Rudy Tomjanovich, HOU.. .536
Calvin Murphy, HOU .... .522
Butch Beard, GS .... .512
Clifford Ray, CHI .... .511

FREE THROW PCT.
Ernie DiGregorio, BUF ..... .902
Rick Barry, GS................. .899
Jeff Mullins, GS .... .875
Chet Walker, CHI............. .875
Bill Bradley, NY............... .874
Calvin Murphy, HOU .... .868

EAST SEMIFINALS
Boston 4, Buffalo 2
New York 4, Capital 3

EAST FINALS
Boston 113, New York 88
Boston 111, New York 99
New York 103, Boston 100
Boston 98, New York 91
Boston 105, New York 94

WEST SEMIFINALS
Milwaukee 4, Los Angeles 1
Chicago 4, Detroit 3

WEST FINALS
Milwaukee 101, Chicago 85
Milwaukee 113, Chicago 111
Milwaukee 113, Chicago 90
Milwaukee 115, Chicago 99

NBA FINALS
Boston 98, Milwaukee 83
Milwaukee 105, Bos. 96 (OT)
Boston 95, Milwaukee 83
Milwaukee 97, Boston 89
Boston 96, Milwaukee 87
Milwaukee 102, Bos. 101 (2OT)
Boston 102, Milwaukee 87

1974-75
FINAL STANDINGS

Eastern Conference
Atlantic Division

	W	L	PCT.	GB
Boston	60	22	.732	
Buffalo	49	33	.598	11
New York	40	42	.488	20
Philadelphia	34	48	.415	26

Central Division

	W	L	PCT.	GB
Washington	60	22	.732	
Houston	41	41	.500	19
Cleveland	40	42	.488	20
Atlanta	31	61	.378	29
New Orleans	23	59	.280	37

Western Conference
Midwest Division

	W	L	PCT.	GB
Chicago	47	35	.573	
K.C.-Omaha	44	38	.537	3
Detroit	40	42	.488	7
Milwaukee	38	44	.463	9

Pacific Division

	W	L	PCT.	GB
Golden State	48	34	.585	
Seattle	43	39	.524	5
Portland	38	44	.463	10
Phoenix	32	50	.390	16
Los Angeles	30	52	.366	18

SCORING
Bob McAdoo, BUF 34.5
Rick Barry, GS 30.6
K. Abdul-Jabbar, MIL 30.0
Nate Archibald, KCO.........26.5
Charlie Scott, PHO............24.3
Bob Lanier, DET 24.0
Elvin Hayes, WAS............23.0
Gail Goodrich, LA.............22.6
Spencer Haywood, SEA ...22.4
Fred Carter, PHI................21.9

REBOUNDS
Wes Unseld, WAS 14.8
Dave Cowens, BOS..........14.7
Sam Lacey, KCO 14.2
Bob McAdoo, BUF 14.1
K. Abdul-Jabbar, MIL 14.0
Happy Hairston, LA...........12.8
Paul Silas, BOS 12.5
Elvin Hayes, WAS.............12.2
Bob Lanier, DET 12.0

ASSISTS
Kevin Porter, WAS 8.0
Dave Bing, DET................. 7.7
Nate Archibald, KCO 6.8
Randy Smith, BUF............. 6.5
Pete Maravich, NO 6.2
Rick Barry, GS.................. 6.2
Slick Watts, SEA 6.1

STEALS
Rick Barry, GS 2.85
Walt Frazier, NY...............2.44
Larry Steele, POR.............2.41
Slick Watts, SEA 2.32
Fred Brown, SEA 2.31
Phil Chenier, WAS 2.29

BLOCKED SHOTS
K. Abdul-Jabbar, MIL 3.26
Elmore Smith, LA..............2.92
Nate Thurmond, CHI..........2.44
Elvin Hayes, WAS.............2.28
Bob Lanier, DET 2.26
Bob McAdoo, BUF 2.12

FIELD GOAL PCT.
Don Nelson, BOS .... .539
Butch Beard, GS .... .528
Rudy Tomjanovich, HOU.. .525
K. Abdul-Jabbar, MIL........ .513
Bob McAdoo, BUF............ .512
Kevin Kunnert, HOU .... .512

FREE THROW PCT.
Rick Barry, GS.................. .904
Calvin Murphy, HOU .... .883
Bill Bradley, NY................ .873
Nate Archibald, KCO......... .872
Jim Price, LA/MIL .... .871
John Havlicek, BOS .... .870

EAST FIRST ROUND
Houston 2, New York 1

EAST SEMIFINALS
Washington 4, Buffalo 3
Boston 4, Houston 1

EAST FINALS
Washington 4, Boston 2

WEST FIRST ROUND
Seattle 2, Detroit 1

WEST SEMIFINALS
Golden St. 4, Seattle 2
Chicago 4, K.C.-Omaha 2

WEST FINALS
Golden St. 4, Chicago 3

NBA FINALS
Golden St. 101, Washington 95
Golden St. 92, Washington 91
Golden St. 109, Wash. 101
Golden St. 96, Washington 95

1975-76
FINAL STANDINGS

Eastern Conference
Atlantic Division

	W	L	PCT.	GB
Boston	54	28	.659	
Buffalo	46	36	.561	8
Philadelphia	46	36	.561	8
New York	38	44	.463	16

Central Division

	W	L	PCT.	GB
Cleveland	49	33	.598	
Washington	48	34	.585	1
Houston	40	42	.488	9
New Orleans	38	44	.463	11
Atlanta	29	53	.354	20

Western Conference
Midwest Division

	W	L	PCT.	GB
Milwaukee	38	44	.463	
Detroit	36	46	.439	2
Kansas City	31	51	.378	7
Chicago	24	58	.293	14

Pacific Division

	W	L	PCT.	GB
Golden State	59	23	.720	
Seattle	43	39	.524	16
Phoenix	42	40	.512	17
Los Angeles	40	42	.488	19
Portland	37	45	.451	22

SCORING
Bob McAdoo, BUF 31.1
K. Abdul-Jabbar, LA..........27.7
Pete Maravich, NO............25.9
Nate Archibald, KC 24.8
Fred Brown, SEA 23.1
George McGinnis, PHI 23.0
Randy Smith, BUF 21.8
John Drew, ATL 21.6
Bob Dandridge, MIL 21.5
Rick Barry, GS 21.0

REBOUNDS
K. Abdul-Jabbar, LA..........16.9
Dave Cowens, BOS 16.0
Wes Unseld, WAS 13.3
Paul Silas, BOS 12.7
Sam Lacey, KC 12.6
George McGinnis, PHI 12.6
Bob McAdoo, BUF 12.4
Elmore Smith, MIL 11.4
Spencer Haywood, NY......11.3

ASSISTS
Slick Watts, SEA 8.1
Nate Archibald, KC 7.9
Calvin Murphy, HOU 7.3
Norm Van Lier, CHI 6.6
Rick Barry, GS.................. 6.1
Dave Bing, WAS............... 6.0
Randy Smith, BUF 5.9

STEALS
Slick Watts, SEA 3.18
George McGinnis, PHI 2.57
Paul Westphal, PHO 2.56
Rick Barry, GS 2.49
Chris Ford, DET 2.17
Larry Steele, POR.............2.10

BLOCKED SHOTS
K. Abdul-Jabbar, LA..........4.12
Elmore Smith, MIL 3.05
Elvin Hayes, WAS.............2.53
Harvey Catchings, PHI......2.19
George Johnson, GS 2.12
Bob McAdoo, BUF 2.05

FIELD GOAL PCT.
Wes Unseld, WAS .... .56085
John Shumate, BUF ..... .56081
Jim McMillian, BUF .... .536
Bob Lanier, DET.............. .532
K. Abdul-Jabbar, LA .... .529
Elmore Smith, MIL........... .518

FREE THROW PCT.
Rick Barry, GS.................. .923
Calvin Murphy, HOU .... .907
Cazzie Russell, LA .... .892
Bill Bradley, NY .... .878
Fred Brown, SEA............. .869
Mike Newlin, HOU .... .865

EAST FIRST ROUND
Buffalo 2, Philadelphia 1

EAST SEMIFINALS
Boston 4, Buffalo 2
Cleveland 4, Washington 3

EAST FINALS
Boston 4, Cleveland 2

WEST FIRST ROUND
Detroit 2, Milwaukee 1

WEST SEMIFINALS
Golden St. 4, Detroit 2
Phoenix 4, Seattle 2

WEST FINALS
Phoenix 4, Golden St. 3

NBA FINALS
Boston 98, Phoenix 87
Boston 105, Phoenix 90
Phoenix 105, Boston 98
Phoenix 109, Boston 107
Boston 128, Phoe. 126 (3OT)
Boston 87, Phoenix 80

1976-77
FINAL STANDINGS

Eastern Conference
Atlantic Division

	W	L	PCT.	GB
Philadelphia	50	32	.610	
Boston	44	38	.537	6
N.Y. Knicks	40	42	.488	10
Buffalo	30	52	.366	20
N.Y. Nets	22	60	.288	28

Central Division

	W	L	PCT.	GB
Houston	49	33	.598	
Washington	48	34	.585	1
San Antonio	44	38	.537	5
Cleveland	43	39	.524	6
New Orleans	35	47	.427	14
Atlanta	31	51	.378	18

Western Conference
Midwest Division

	W	L	PCT.	GB
Denver	50	32	.610	
Detroit	44	38	.537	6
Chicago	44	38	.537	6
Kansas City	40	42	.488	10
Indiana	36	46	.439	14
Milwaukee	30	52	.366	20

Pacific Division

	W	L	PCT.	GB
Los Angeles	53	29	.646	
Portland	49	33	.598	4
Golden State	46	36	.561	7
Seattle	40	42	.488	13
Phoenix	34	48	.415	19

SCORING
Pete Maravich, NO...........31.1
Billy Knight, IND............26.6
K. Abdul-Jabbar, LA.......26.2
David Thompson, DEN.....25.9
Bob McAdoo, BUF/NYK....25.8
Bob Lanier, DET 25.3
John Drew, ATL...............24.2
Elvin Hayes, WAS...........23.7
George Gervin, SA..........23.1
Dan Issel, DEN 22.3

REBOUNDS
Bill Walton, POR 14.4
K. Abdul-Jabbar, LA.......13.3
Moses Malone, BUF/HOU ...13.1
Artis Gilmore, CHI 13.0
Bob McAdoo, BUF/NYK....12.9
Elvin Hayes, WAS...........12.5
Swen Nater, MIL.............12.0
George McGinnis, PHI.....11.5

ASSISTS
Don Buse, IND 8.5
Slick Watts, SEA 8.0
Norm Van Lier, CHI 7.8
Kevin Porter, DET 7.3
Tom Henderson, ATL/WAS... 6.9
Rick Barry, GS................. 6.0
Jo Jo White, BOS 6.0

STEALS
Don Buse, IND 3.47
Brian Taylor, KC.............2.76
Slick Watts, SEA.............2.71
Quinn Buckner, MIL 2.43
Mike Gale, SA 2.33
Bobby Jones, DEN...........2.27

BLOCKED SHOTS
Bill Walton, POR 3.25
K. Abdul-Jabbar, LA.........3.18
Elvin Hayes, WAS............2.68
Artis Gilmore, CHI 2.48
Caldwell Jones, PHI.........2.44
George Johnson, GS/BUF ...2.27

FIELD GOAL PCT.
K. Abdul-Jabbar, LA .... .579
Mitch Kupchak, WAS........ .572
Bobby Jones, DEN .... .570
George Gervin, SA........... .544
Bob Lanier, DET.............. .534
Bob Gross, POR............... .529

FREE THROW PCT.
Ernie DiGregorio, BUF ..... .945
Rick Barry, GS................. .916
Calvin Murphy, HOU .... .886
Mike Newlin, HOU .... .885
Fred Brown, SEA............. .884

EAST FIRST ROUND
Washington 2, Cleveland 1
Boston 2, San Antonio 0

EAST SEMIFINALS
Philadelphia 4, Boston 3
Houston 4, Washington 2

EAST FINALS
Philadelphia 4, Houston 2

WEST FIRST ROUND
Portland 2, Chicago 1
Golden St. 2, Detroit 1

WEST SEMIFINALS
Los Angeles 4, Golden St. 3
Portland 4, Denver 2

WEST FINALS
Portland 4, Los Angeles 0

NBA FINALS
Philadelphia 107, Portland 101
Philadelphia 107, Portland 89
Portland 129, Philadelphia 107
Portland 130, Philadelphia 98
Portland 110, Philadelphia 104
Portland 109, Philadelphia 107

1977-78
FINAL STANDINGS

Eastern Conference
Atlantic Division

	W	L	PCT.	GB
Philadelphia	55	27	.671	
New York	43	39	.524	12
Boston	32	50	.390	23
Buffalo	27	55	.329	28
New Jersey	24	58	.293	31

Central Division

	W	L	PCT.	GB
San Antonio	52	30	.634	
Washington	44	38	.537	8
Cleveland	43	39	.524	9
Atlanta	41	41	.500	11
New Orleans	39	43	.476	13
Houston	28	54	.341	24

Western Conference
Midwest Division

	W	L	PCT.	GB
Denver	48	34	.585	
Milwaukee	44	38	.537	4
Chicago	40	42	.488	8
Detroit	38	44	.463	10
Indiana	31	51	.378	17
Kansas City	31	51	.378	17

Pacific Division

	W	L	PCT.	GB
Portland	58	24	.707	
Phoenix	49	33	.598	9
Seattle	47	35	.573	11
Los Angeles	45	37	.549	13
Golden State	43	39	.524	15

SCORING
George Gervin, SA..........27.22
David Thompson, DEN 27.15
Bob McAdoo, NY 26.5
K. Abdul-Jabbar, LA 25.8
Calvin Murphy, HOU 25.6
Paul Westphal, PHO 25.2
Randy Smith, BUF 24.6
Bob Lanier, DET 24.5
Walter Davis, PHO 24.2
Bernard King, NJ.............24.2

REBOUNDS
Truck Robinson, NO 15.7
Moses Malone, HOU 15.0
Dave Cowens, BOS 14.0
Elvin Hayes, WAS............13.3
Swen Nater, BUF 13.2
Artis Gilmore, CHI 13.1
K. Abdul-Jabbar, LA 12.9
Bob McAdoo, NY 12.8

ASSISTS
Kevin Porter, DET/NJ..........10.2
John Lucas, HOU 9.4
Ricky Sobers, IND 7.4
Norm Nixon, LA 6.8
Norm Van Lier, CHI 6.8
Henry Bibby, PHI.............. 5.7

STEALS
Ron Lee, PHO.................2.74
Gus Williams, SEA...........2.34
Quinn Buckner, MIL 2.29
Mike Gale, SA 2.27
Don Buse, PHO 2.26
Foots Walker, CLE............2.17

BLOCKED SHOTS
George Johnson, NJ.........3.38
K. Abdul-Jabbar, LA 2.98
Tree Rollins, ATL 2.73
Bill Walton, POR..............2.52
Billy Paultz, SA................2.43
Artis Gilmore, CHI 2.21

FIELD GOAL PCT.
Bobby Jones, DEN .... .578
Darryl Dawkins, PHI .... .575
Artis Gilmore, CHI .... .559
K. Abdul-Jabbar, LA .... .550
Alex English, MIL.............. .542

FREE THROW PCT.
Rick Barry, GS................. .924
Calvin Murphy, HOU .... .918
Fred Brown, SEA.............. .898
Mike Newlin, HOU .... .874
Scott Wedman, KC........... .870

EAST FIRST ROUND
Washington 2, Atlanta 0
New York 2, Cleveland 0

EAST SEMIFINALS
Philadelphia 4, New York 0
Washington 4, San Antonio 2

EAST FINALS
Washington 4, Philadelphia 2

WEST FIRST ROUND
Seattle 2, Los Angeles 1
Milwaukee 2, Phoenix 0

WEST SEMIFINALS
Seattle 4, Portland 2
Denver 4, Milwaukee 3

WEST FINALS
Seattle 4, Denver 2

NBA FINALS
Seattle 106, Washington 102
Washington 106, Seattle 98
Seattle 93, Washington 92
Washington 120, Seat. 116(OT)
Seattle 98, Washington 94
Washington 117, Seattle 82
Washington 105, Seattle 99

1978-79
FINAL STANDINGS

Eastern Conference
Atlantic Division

	W	L	PCT.	GB
Washington	54	28	.659	
Philadelphia	47	35	.573	7
New Jersey	37	45	.451	17
New York	31	51	.378	23
Boston	29	53	.354	25

Western Conference
Midwest Division

	W	L	PCT.	GB
Kansas City	48	34	.585	
Denver	47	35	.573	1
Indiana	38	44	.463	10
Milwaukee	38	44	.463	10
Chicago	31	51	.378	17

Central Division

	W	L	PCT.	GB
San Antonio	48	34	.585	
Houston	47	35	.573	1
Atlanta	46	36	.561	2
Cleveland	30	52	.366	18
Detroit	30	52	.366	18
New Orleans	26	56	.317	22

Pacific Division

	W	L	PCT.	GB
Seattle	52	30	.634	
Phoenix	50	32	.610	2
Los Angeles	47	35	.573	5
Portland	45	37	.549	7
San Diego	43	39	.524	9
Golden State	38	44	.463	14

SCORING
George Gervin, SA............29.6
Lloyd Free, SD 28.8
Marques Johnson, MIL 25.6
Bob McAdoo, NY/BOS 24.8
Moses Malone, HOU.........24.8
David Thompson, DEN 24.0
Paul Westphal, PHO.........24.0
K. Abdul-Jabbar, LA..........23.8
Artis Gilmore, CHI.............23.7
Walter Davis, PHO............23.6

REBOUNDS
Moses Malone, HOU.........17.6
Rich Kelley, NO.................12.8
K. Abdul-Jabbar, LA..........12.8
Artis Gilmore, CHI.............12.7
Jack Sikma, SEA 12.4
Elvin Hayes, WAS.............12.1
Robert Parish, GS.............12.1

ASSISTS
Kevin Porter, DET.............13.4
John Lucas, GS.................. 9.3
Norm Nixon, LA 9.0
Phil Ford, KC 8.6
Paul Westphal, PHO 6.5
Rick Barry, HOU 6.3

STEALS
M.L. Carr, DET..................2.46
Ed Jordan, NJ 2.45
Norm Nixon, LA................2.45
Foots Walker, CLE 2.36
Phil Ford, KC....................2.20
Randy Smith, SD 2.16

BLOCKED SHOTS
K. Abdul-Jabbar, LA 3.95
George Johnson, NJ..........3.24
Tree Rollins, ATL 3.14
Robert Parish, GS.............2.86
Terry Tyler, DET 2.45

FIELD GOAL PCT.
Cedric Maxwell, BOS .... .584
K. Abdul-Jabbar, LA........... .577
Wes Unseld, WAS............. .577
Artis Gilmore, CHI .... .575
Swen Nater, SD................ .569

FREE THROW PCT.
Rick Barry, HOU .... .947
Calvin Murphy, HOU .... .928
Fred Brown, SEA.............. .888
Robert Smith, DEN............ .883
Ricky Sobers, IND .... .882

EAST FIRST ROUND
Philadelphia 2, New Jersey 0
Atlanta 2, Houston 0

EAST SEMIFINALS
Washington 4, Atlanta 3
San Antonio 4, Philadelphia 3

EAST FINALS
Washington 4, San Antonio 3

WEST FIRST ROUND
Phoenix 2, Portland 1
Los Angeles 2, Denver 1

WEST SEMIFINALS
Seattle 4, Los Angeles 1
Phoenix 4, Kansas City 1

WEST FINALS
Seattle 4, Phoenix 3

NBA FINALS
Washington 99, Seattle 97
Seattle 92, Washington 82
Seattle 105, Washington 95
Seattle 114, Wash. 112 (OT)
Seattle 97, Washington 93

1979-80
FINAL STANDINGS

Eastern Conference
Atlantic Division

	W	L	PCT.	GB
Boston	61	21	.744	
Philadelphia	59	23	.720	2
Washington	39	43	.476	22
New York	39	43	.476	22
New Jersey	34	48	.415	27

Central Division

	W	L	PCT.	GB
Atlanta	50	32	.610	
Houston	41	41	.500	9
San Antonio	41	41	.500	9
Indiana	37	45	.451	13
Cleveland	37	45	.451	13
Detroit	16	66	.195	34

Western Conference
Midwest Division

	W	L	PCT.	GB
Milwaukee	49	33	.598	
Kansas City	47	35	.573	2
Denver	30	52	.366	19
Chicago	30	52	.366	19
Utah	24	58	.293	25

Pacific Division

	W	L	PCT.	GB
Los Angeles	60	22	.732	
Seattle	56	26	.683	4
Phoenix	55	27	.671	5
Portland	38	44	.463	22
San Diego	35	47	.427	25
Golden State	24	58	.293	36

SCORING
George Gervin, SA............33.1
Lloyd Free, SD.................30.2
Adrian Dantley, UTA 28.0
Julius Erving, PHI..............26.9
Moses Malone, HOU.........25.8
K. Abdul-Jabbar, LA..........24.8
Dan Issel, DEN................23.8
Elvin Hayes, WAS............23.0
Otis Birdsong, KC 22.7
Mike Mitchell, CLE 22.2

REBOUNDS
Swen Nater, SD 15.0
Moses Malone, HOU........14.5
Wes Unseld, WAS 13.3
Caldwell Jones, PHI..........11.9
Jack Sikma, SEA 11.1

ASSISTS
Micheal Richardson, NY ...10.1
Nate Archibald, BOS 8.4
Foots Walker, CLE 8.0
Norm Nixon, LA 7.8
John Lucas, GS................ 7.5

STEALS
Micheal Richardson, NY ...3.23
Ed Jordan, NJ 2.72

Dudley Bradley, IND 2.57
Gus Williams, SEA 2.44
Magic Johnson, LA 2.43

BLOCKED SHOTS
K. Abdul-Jabbar, LA..........3.41
George Johnson, NJ.........3.19
Tree Rollins, ATL 2.98
Terry Tyler, DET 2.68
Elvin Hayes, WAS............2.33

FIELD GOAL PCT.
Cedric Maxwell, BOS .... .609
K. Abdul-Jabbar, LA...........604
Artis Gilmore, CHI .... .595
Adrian Dantley, UTA......... .576
Tom Boswell, DEN/UTA .... .564

FREE THROW PCT.
Rick Barry, HOU .... .935
Calvin Murphy, HOU .... .897
Ron Boone, UTA .... .893
Paul Silas, SA.................. .887

3-PT. FIELD GOAL PCT.
Fred Brown, SEA.............. .443
Chris Ford, BOS .... .427
Larry Bird, BOS .... .406
John Roche, DEN............. .380

EAST FIRST ROUND
Philadelphia 2, Washington 0
Houston 2, San Antonio 1

EAST SEMIFINALS
Boston 4, Houston 0
Philadelphia 4, Atlanta 1

EAST FINALS
Philadelphia 4, Boston 1

WEST FIRST ROUND
Seattle 2, Portland 1
Phoenix 2, Kansas City 1

WEST SEMIFINALS
Los Angeles 4, Phoenix 1
Seattle 4, Milwaukee 3

WEST FINALS
Los Angeles 4, Seattle 1

NBA FINALS
Los Angeles 109, Phil. 102
Philadelphia 107, L.A. 104
Los Angeles 111, Phil. 101
Philadelphia 105, L.A. 102
Los Angeles 108, Phil. 103
Los Angeles 123, Phil. 107

1980-81
FINAL STANDINGS

Eastern Conference
Atlantic Division

	W	L	PCT.	GB
Boston	62	20	.756	
Philadelphia	62	20	.756	
New York	50	32	.610	12
Washington	39	43	.476	23
New Jersey	24	58	.293	38

Central Division

	W	L	PCT.	GB
Milwaukee	60	22	.732	
Chicago	45	37	.549	15
Indiana	44	38	.537	16
Atlanta	31	51	.378	29
Cleveland	28	54	.341	32
Detroit	21	61	.256	39

Western Conference
Midwest Division

	W	L	PCT.	GB
San Antonio	52	30	.634	
Kansas City	40	42	.488	12
Houston	40	42	.488	12
Denver	37	45	.451	15
Utah	28	54	.341	24
Dallas	15	67	.183	37

Pacific Division

	W	L	PCT.	GB
Phoenix	57	25	.695	
Los Angeles	54	28	.659	3
Portland	45	37	.549	12
Golden State	39	43	.476	18
San Diego	36	46	.439	21
Seattle	34	48	.415	23

SCORING
Adrian Dantley, UTA 30.7
Moses Malone, HOU.........27.8
George Gervin, SA............27.1
K. Abdul-Jabbar, LA..........26.2
David Thompson, DEN 25.5
Otis Birdsong, KC 24.6
Julius Erving, PHI..............24.6
Mike Mitchell, CLE 24.5
Lloyd Free, GS..................24.1
Alex English, DEN.............23.8

REBOUNDS
Moses Malone, HOU........14.8
Swen Nater, SD 12.4
Larry Smith, GS 12.1
Larry Bird, BOS................10.9
Jack Sikma, SEA 10.4

ASSISTS
Kevin Porter, WAS 9.1
Norm Nixon, LA 8.8
Phil Ford, KC 8.8
Micheal Richardson, NY.... 7.9
Nate Archibald, BOS 7.7

STEALS
Magic Johnson, LA 3.43
Micheal Richardson, NY ...2.94

Quinn Buckner, MIL 2.40
Maurice Cheeks, PHI.......2.38
Ray Williams, NY 2.34

BLOCKED SHOTS
George Johnson, SA........3.39
Tree Rollins, ATL 2.93
K. Abdul-Jabbar, LA..........2.85
Robert Parish, BOS 2.61
Artis Gilmore, CHI 2.41

FIELD GOAL PCT.
Artis Gilmore, CHI ...... .670
Darryl Dawkins, PHI .... .607
Cedric Maxwell, BOS .... .588
Bernard King, GS .... .588
K. Abdul-Jabbar, LA .... .574

FREE THROW PCT.
Calvin Murphy, HOU .... .958
Ricky Sobers, CHI .... .935
Mike Newlin, NJ................ .888
Jim Spanarkel, DAL.......... .887

3-PT. FIELD GOAL PCT.
Brian Taylor, SD .... .383
Freeman Williams, SD...... .340
Joe Hassett, DAL/GS......... .340
Mike Bratz, CLE .... .337

EAST FIRST ROUND
Philadelphia 2, Indiana 0
Chicago 2, New York 0

EAST SEMIFINALS
Boston 4, Chicago 0
Philadelphia 4, Milwaukee 3

EAST FINALS
Boston 4, Philadelphia 3

WEST FIRST ROUND
Houston 2, Los Angeles 1
Kansas City 2, Portland 1

WEST SEMIFINALS
Kansas City 4, Phoenix 3
Houston 4, San Antonio 3

WEST FINALS
Houston 4, Kansas City 1

NBA FINALS
Boston 98, Houston 95
Houston 92, Boston 90
Boston 94, Houston 71
Houston 91, Boston 86
Boston 109, Houston 80
Boston 102, Houston 91

1981-82
FINAL STANDINGS

Eastern Conference
Atlantic Division

	W	L	PCT.	GB
Boston	63	19	.768	
Philadelphia	58	24	.707	5
New Jersey	44	38	.537	19
Washington	43	39	.524	20
New York	33	49	.402	30

Central Division

	W	L	PCT.	GB
Milwaukee	55	27	.671	
Atlanta	42	40	.512	13
Detroit	39	43	.476	16
Indiana	35	47	.427	20
Chicago	34	48	.415	21
Cleveland	15	67	.183	40

Western Conference
Midwest Division

	W	L	PCT.	GB
San Antonio	48	34	.585	
Denver	46	36	.561	2
Houston	46	36	.561	2
Kansas City	30	52	.366	18
Dallas	28	54	.341	20
Utah	25	57	.305	23

Pacific Division

	W	L	PCT.	GB
Los Angeles	57	25	.695	
Seattle	52	30	.634	5
Phoenix	46	36	.561	11
Golden State	45	37	.549	12
Portland	42	40	.512	15
San Diego	17	65	.207	40

SCORING
George Gervin, SA............32.3
Moses Malone, HOU.........31.1
Adrian Dantley, UTA 30.3
Alex English, DEN............25.4
Julius Erving, PHI.............24.4
K. Abdul-Jabbar, LA.........23.9
Gus Williams, SEA...........23.4
Bernard King, GS.............23.2
World B. Free, GS............22.9
Larry Bird, BOS...............22.9

REBOUNDS
Moses Malone, HOU.........14.7
Jack Sikma, SEA 12.7
Buck Williams, NJ 12.3
Mychal Thompson, POR.....11.7
Maurice Lucas, NY............11.3

ASSISTS
Johnny Moore, SA............. 9.6
Magic Johnson, LA............ 9.5
Maurice Cheeks, PHI......... 8.4
Nate Archibald, BOS 8.0
Norm Nixon, LA 8.0

STEALS
Magic Johnson, LA 2.67
Maurice Cheeks, PHI.......2.65

Micheal Richardson, NY ...2.60
Quinn Buckner, MIL...........2.49
Ray Williams, NJ...............2.43

BLOCKED SHOTS
George Johnson, SA..........3.12
Tree Rollins, ATL 2.84
K. Abdul-Jabbar, LA 2.72
Artis Gilmore, CHI 2.70
Robert Parish, BOS 2.40

FIELD GOAL PCT.
Artis Gilmore, CHI 652
Steve Johnson, KC............613
Buck Williams, NJ.............582
K. Abdul-Jabbar, LA 579
Calvin Natt, POR 576

FREE THROW PCT.
Kyle Macy, PHO................899
Charlie Criss, SD..............887
John Long, DET 865
George Gervin, SA............864

3-PT. FIELD GOAL PCT.
Campy Russell, NY 439
Andrew Toney, PHI 424
Kyle Macy, PHO 390
Brian Winters, MIL 387

EAST FIRST ROUND
Philadelphia 2, Atlanta 0
Washington 2, New Jersey 0

EAST SEMIFINALS
Boston 4, Washington 1
Philadelphia 4, Milwaukee 2

EAST FINALS
Philadelphia 4, Boston 3

WEST FIRST ROUND
Seattle 2, Houston 1
Phoenix 2, Denver 1

WEST SEMIFINALS
Los Angeles 4, Phoenix 0
San Antonio 4, Seattle 1

WEST FINALS
Los Angeles 4, San Antonio 0

NBA FINALS
Los Angeles 124, Phil. 117
Philadelphia 110, L.A. 94
Los Angeles 129, Phil. 108
Los Angeles 111, Phil. 101
Philadelphia 135, L.A. 102
Los Angeles 114, Phil. 104

1982-83
FINAL STANDINGS

Eastern Conference
Atlantic Division

	W	L	PCT.	GB
Philadelphia	65	17	.793	
Boston	56	26	.683	9
New Jersey	49	33	.598	16
New York	44	38	.537	21
Washington	42	40	.512	23

Central Division

	W	L	PCT.	GB
Milwaukee	51	31	.622	
Atlanta	43	39	.524	8
Detroit	37	45	.451	14
Chicago	28	54	.341	23
Cleveland	23	59	.280	28
Indiana	20	62	.244	31

Western Conference
Midwest Division

	W	L	PCT.	GB
San Antonio	53	29	.646	
Denver	45	37	.549	8
Kansas City	45	37	.549	8
Dallas	38	44	.463	15
Utah	30	52	.366	23
Houston	14	68	.171	39

Pacific Division

	W	L	PCT.	GB
Los Angeles	58	24	.707	
Phoenix	53	29	.646	5
Seattle	48	34	.585	10
Portland	46	36	.561	12
Golden State	30	52	.366	28
San Diego	25	57	.305	33

SCORING
Alex English, DEN	28.4
Kiki Vandeweghe, DEN	26.7
Kelly Tripucka, DET	26.5
George Gervin, SA	26.2
Moses Malone, PHI	24.5
Mark Aguirre, DAL	24.4
Joe Barry Carroll, GS	24.1
World B. Free, GS/CLE	23.9
Reggie Theus, CHI	23.8
Terry Cummings, SD	23.7

REBOUNDS
Moses Malone, PHI	15.3
Buck Williams, NJ	12.5
Bill Laimbeer, DET	12.1
Artis Gilmore, SA	12.0
Jack Sikma, SEA	11.4

ASSISTS
Magic Johnson, LA	10.5
Johnny Moore, SA	9.8
Rickey Green, UTA	8.9
Larry Drew, KC	8.1
Frank Johnson, WAS	8.1

STEALS
Micheal Richardson, GS/NJ	2.84
Rickey Green, UTA	2.82

Johnny Moore, SA	2.52
Isiah Thomas, DET	2.46
Darwin Cook, NJ	2.37

BLOCKED SHOTS
Tree Rollins, ATL	4.29
Bill Walton, POR	3.61
Mark Eaton, UTA	3.40
Larry Nance, PHO	2.65
Artis Gilmore, CHI	2.34

FIELD GOAL PCT.
Artis Gilmore, SA	.626
Steve Johnson, KC	.624
Darryl Dawkins, NJ	.599
K. Abdul-Jabbar, LA	.588
Buck Williams, NJ	.588

FREE THROW PCT.
Calvin Murphy, HOU	.920
Kiki Vandeweghe, DEN	.875
Kyle Macy, PHO	872
George Gervin, SA	.853

3-PT. FIELD GOAL PCT.
Mike Dunleavy, SA	.345
Isiah Thomas, DET	.288
Darrell Griffith, UTA	.288
Allen Leavell, HOU	.240

EAST FIRST ROUND
Boston 2, Atlanta 1
New York 2, New Jersey 0

EAST SEMIFINALS
Philadelphia 4, New York 0
Milwaukee 4, Boston 0

EAST FINALS
Philadelphia 4, Milwaukee 1

WEST FIRST ROUND
Denver 2, Phoenix 1
Portland 2, Seattle 0

WEST SEMIFINALS
Los Angeles 4, Portland 1
San Antonio 4, Denver 1

WEST FINALS
Los Angeles 4, San Antonio 2

NBA FINALS
Philadelphia 113, L.A. 107
Philadelphia 103, L.A. 93
Philadelphia 111, L.A. 94
Philadelphia 115, L.A. 108

1983-84
FINAL STANDINGS

Eastern Conference
Atlantic Division

	W	L	PCT.	GB
Boston	62	20	.756	
Philadelphia	52	30	.634	10
New York	47	35	.573	15
New Jersey	45	37	.549	17
Washington	35	47	.427	27

Central Division

	W	L	PCT.	GB
Milwaukee	50	32	.610	
Detroit	49	33	.598	1
Atlanta	40	42	.488	10
Cleveland	28	54	.341	22
Chicago	27	55	.329	23
Indiana	26	56	.317	24

Western Conference
Midwest Division

	W	L	PCT.	GB
Utah	45	37	.549	
Dallas	43	39	.524	2
Denver	38	44	.463	7
Kansas City	38	44	.463	7
San Antonio	37	45	.451	8
Houston	29	53	.354	16

Pacific Division

	W	L	PCT.	GB
Los Angeles	54	28	.659	
Portland	48	34	.585	6
Seattle	42	40	.512	12
Phoenix	41	41	.500	13
Golden State	37	45	.451	17
San Diego	30	52	.366	24

SCORING
Adrian Dantley, UTA 30.6
Mark Aguirre, DAL 29.5
Kiki Vandeweghe, DEN....29.4
Alex English, DEN..............26.4
Bernard King, NY..............26.3
George Gervin, SA............25.9
Larry Bird, BOS.................24.2
Mike Mitchell, SA...............23.3
Terry Cummings, SD 22.9
Purvis Short, GS................22.8

REBOUNDS
Moses Malone, PHI............13.4
Buck Williams, NJ 12.3
Jeff Ruland, WAS..............12.3
Bill Laimbeer, DET.............12.2
Ralph Sampson, HOU 11.1

ASSISTS
Magic Johnson, LA 13.1
Norm Nixon, SD.................11.1
Isiah Thomas, DET.............11.1
John Lucas, SA..................10.7
Johnny Moore, SA.............. 9.6

STEALS
Rickey Green, UTA............2.65
Isiah Thomas, DET 2.49

Gus Williams, SEA.............2.36
Maurice Cheeks, PHI..........2.28
Magic Johnson, LA 2.24

BLOCKED SHOTS
Mark Eaton, UTA 4.28
Tree Rollins, ATL 3.60
Ralph Sampson, HOU 2.40
Larry Nance, PHO.............2.11
Artis Gilmore, SA 2.06

FIELD GOAL PCT.
Artis Gilmore, SA...............631
James Donaldson, SD......596
Mike McGee, LA................594
Darryl Dawkins, NJ............593
Calvin Natt, POR 583

FREE THROW PCT.
Larry Bird, BOS 888
John Long, DET.................884
Bill Laimbeer, DET 866
Walter Davis, PHO 863

3-PT. FIELD GOAL PCT.
Darrell Griffith, UTA 361
Mike Evans, DEN 360
Johnny Moore, SA.............322
Michael Cooper, LA 314

EAST FIRST ROUND
Boston 3, Washington 1
Milwaukee 3, Atlanta 2
New Jersey 3 Philadelphia 2
New York 3, Detroit 2

EAST SEMIFINALS
Boston 4, New York 3
Milwaukee 4, New Jersey 2

EAST FINALS
Boston 4, Milwaukee 1

WEST FIRST ROUND
Los Angeles 3, Kansas City 0
Utah 3, Denver 2
Phoenix 3, Portland 2
Dallas 3, Seattle 2

WEST SEMIFINALS
Los Angeles 4, Dallas 1
Phoenix 4, Utah 2

WEST FINALS
Los Angeles 4, Phoenix 2

NBA FINALS
Los Angeles 115, Boston 109
Boston 124, L.A. 121 (OT)
Los Angeles 137, Boston 104
Boston 129, L.A. 125 (OT)
Boston 121, Los Angeles 103
Los Angeles 119, Boston 108
Boston 111, Los Angeles 102

1984-85
FINAL STANDINGS

Eastern Conference
Atlantic Division

	W	L	PCT.	GB
Boston	63	19	.768	
Philadelphia	58	24	.707	5
New Jersey	42	40	.512	21
Washington	40	42	.488	23
New York	24	58	.293	39

Central Division

	W	L	PCT.	GB
Milwaukee	59	23	.720	
Detroit	46	36	.561	13
Chicago	38	44	.463	21
Cleveland	36	46	.439	23
Atlanta	34	48	.415	25
Indiana	22	60	.268	37

Western Conference
Midwest Division

	W	L	PCT.	GB
Denver	52	30	.634	
Houston	48	34	.585	4
Dallas	44	38	.537	8
San Antonio	41	41	.500	11
Utah	41	41	.500	11
Kansas City	31	51	.378	21

Pacific Division

	W	L	PCT.	GB
L.A. Lakers	62	20	.756	
Portland	42	40	.512	20
Phoenix	36	46	.439	26
L.A. Clippers	31	51	.378	31
Seattle	31	51	.378	31
Golden State	22	60	.268	40

SCORING
Bernard King, NY 32.9
Larry Bird, BOS................28.7
Michael Jordan, CHI 28.2
Purvis Short, GS 28.0
Alex English, DEN.............27.9
Dominique Wilkins, ATL....27.4
Adrian Dantley, UTA 26.6
Mark Aguirre, DAL............25.7
Moses Malone, PHI...........24.6
Terry Cummings, MIL 23.6

REBOUNDS
Moses Malone, PHI...........13.1
Bill Laimbeer, DET 12.4
Buck Williams, NJ 12.3
Akeem Olajuwon, HOU......11.9
Mark Eaton, UTA 11.3

ASSISTS
Isiah Thomas, DET 13.9
Magic Johnson, LAL 12.6
Johnny Moore, SA 10.0
Norm Nixon, LAC 8.8
John Bagley, CLE.............. 8.6

STEALS
Micheal Richardson, NJ 2.96
Johnny Moore, SA 2.79

Lafayette Lever, DEN..........2.46
Michael Jordan, CHI 2.39
Doc Rivers, ATL.................2.36

BLOCKED SHOTS
Mark Eaton, UTA 5.56
Akeem Olajuwon, HOU.......2.68
Sam Bowie, POR 2.67
Wayne Cooper, DEN 2.46
Tree Rollins, ATL................2.39

FIELD GOAL PCT.
James Donaldson, LAC..... .637
Artis Gilmore, SA............... .623
Otis Thorpe, KC................. .600
K. Abdul-Jabbar, LAL......... .599
Larry Nance, PHO .... .587

FREE THROW PCT.
Kyle Macy, PHO .... .907
Kiki Vandeweghe, POR.... .896
Brad Davis, DAL................ .888
Kelly Tripucka, DET.......... .885

3-PT. FIELD GOAL PCT.
Byron Scott, LAL .... .433
Larry Bird, BOS................. .427
Brad Davis, DAL................ .409
Trent Tucker, NY .... .403

EAST FIRST ROUND
Boston 3, Cleveland 1
Milwaukee 3, Chicago 1
Philadelphia 3, Washington 1
Detroit 3, New Jersey 0

EAST SEMIFINALS
Boston 4, Detroit 2
Philadelphia 4, Milwaukee 0

EAST FINALS
Boston 4, Philadelphia 1

WEST FIRST ROUND
L.A. Lakers 3, Phoenix 0
Denver 3, San Antonio 2
Utah 3, Houston 2
Portland 3, Dallas 1

WEST SEMIFINALS
L.A. Lakers 4, Portland 1
Denver 4, Utah 1

WEST FINALS
L.A. Lakers 4, Denver 1

NBA FINALS
Boston 148, L.A. Lakers 114
L.A. Lakers 109, Boston 102
L.A. Lakers 136, Boston 111
Boston 107, L.A. Lakers 105
L.A. Lakers 120, Boston 111
L.A. Lakers 111, Boston 100

1985-86
FINAL STANDINGS

Eastern Conference
Atlantic Division

	W	L	PCT.	GB
Boston	67	15	.817	
Philadelphia	54	28	.659	13
Washington	39	43	.476	28
New Jersey	39	43	.476	28
New York	23	59	.280	44

Central Division

	W	L	PCT.	GB
Milwaukee	57	25	.695	
Atlanta	50	32	.610	7
Detroit	46	36	.561	11
Chicago	30	52	.366	27
Cleveland	29	53	.354	28
Indiana	26	56	.317	31

Western Conference
Midwest Division

	W	L	PCT.	GB
Houston	51	31	.622	
Denver	47	35	.573	4
Dallas	44	38	.537	7
Utah	42	40	.512	9
Sacramento	37	45	.451	14
San Antonio	35	47	.427	16

Pacific Division

	W	L	PCT.	GB
L.A. Lakers	62	20	.756	
Portland	40	42	.488	22
L.A. Clippers	32	50	.390	30
Phoenix	32	50	.390	30
Seattle	31	51	.378	31
Golden State	30	52	.366	32

SCORING
Dominique Wilkins, ATL....30.3
Adrian Dantley, UTA 29.8
Alex English, DEN............29.8
Larry Bird, BOS................25.8
Purvis Short, GS 25.5
Kiki Vandeweghe, POR 24.8
Moses Malone, PHI..........23.8
Akeem Olajuwon, HOU......23.5
Mike Mitchell, SA 23.4
World B. Free, CLE...........23.4

REBOUNDS
Bill Laimbeer, DET 13.1
Charles Barkley, PHI.........12.8
Buck Williams, NJ 12.0
Moses Malone, PHI...........11.8
Ralph Sampson, HOU 11.1

ASSISTS
Magic Johnson, LAL 12.6
Isiah Thomas, DET 10.8
Reggie Theus, SAC............ 9.6
John Bagley, CLE.............. 9.4
Maurice Cheeks, PHI 9.2

STEALS
Alvin Robertson, SA..........3.67
Micheal Richardson, NJ....2.66

Clyde Drexler, POR 2.63
Maurice Cheeks, PHI........2.52
Lafayette Lever, DEN.......2.28

BLOCKED SHOTS
Manute Bol, WAS..............4.96
Mark Eaton, UTA..............4.61
Akeem Olajuwon, HOU......3.40
Wayne Cooper, DEN 2.91
Benoit Benjamin, LAC......2.61

FIELD GOAL PCT.
Steve Johnson, SA .... .632
Artis Gilmore, SA .... .618
Larry Nance, PHO............ .581
James Worthy, LAL........... .579
Kevin McHale, BOS .... .574

FREE THROW PCT.
Larry Bird, BOS.............. .8963
Chris Mullin, GS .... .8957
Mike Gminski, NJ .... .893
Jim Paxson, POR............. .889

3-PT. FIELD GOAL PCT.
Craig Hodges, MIL .... .4506
Trent Tucker, NY .... .4505
Ernie Grunfeld, NY .... .426
Larry Bird, BOS................ .423

EAST FIRST ROUND
Boston 3, Chicago 0
Milwaukee 3, New Jersey 0
Philadelphia 3, Washington 2
Atlanta 3, Detroit 1

EAST SEMIFINALS
Boston 4, Atlanta 1
Milwaukee 4, Philadelphia 3

EAST FINALS
Boston 4, Milwaukee 0

WEST FIRST ROUND
L.A. Lakers 3, San Antonio 0
Houston 3, Sacramento 0
Denver 3, Portland 1
Dallas 3, Utah 1

WEST SEMIFINALS
L.A. Lakers 4, Dallas 2
Houston 4, Denver 2

WEST FINALS
Houston 4, L.A. Lakers 1

NBA FINALS
Boston 112, Houston 100
Boston 117, Houston 95
Houston 106, Boston 104
Houston 106, Boston 103
Houston 111, Boston 96
Boston 114, Houston 97

1986-87
FINAL STANDINGS

Eastern Conference
Atlantic Division

	W	L	PCT.	GB
Boston	59	23	.720	
Philadelphia	45	37	.549	14
Washington	42	40	.512	17
New Jersey	24	58	.293	35
New York	24	58	.293	35

Central Division

	W	L	PCT.	GB
Atlanta	57	25	.695	
Detroit	52	30	.634	5
Milwaukee	50	32	.610	7
Indiana	41	41	.500	16
Chicago	40	42	.488	17
Cleveland	31	51	.378	26

Western Conference
Midwest Division

	W	L	PCT.	GB
Dallas	55	27	.671	
Utah	44	38	.537	11
Houston	42	40	.512	13
Denver	37	45	.451	18
Sacramento	29	53	.354	26
San Antonio	28	54	.341	27

Pacific Division

	W	L	PCT.	GB
L.A. Lakers	65	17	.793	
Portland	49	33	.598	16
Golden State	42	40	.512	23
Seattle	39	43	.476	26
Phoenix	36	46	.439	29
L.A. Clippers	12	70	.146	53

SCORING
Michael Jordan, CHI 37.1
Dominique Wilkins, ATL....29.0
Alex English, DEN.............28.6
Larry Bird, BOS.................28.1
Kiki Vandeweghe, POR 26.9
Kevin McHale, BOS 26.1
Mark Aguirre, DAL 25.7
Dale Ellis, SEA..................24.9
Moses Malone, WAS 24.1
Magic Johnson, LAL 23.9

REBOUNDS
Charles Barkley, PHI.........14.6
Charles Oakley, CHI 13.1
Buck Williams, NJ 12.5
James Donaldson, DAL 11.9
Bill Laimbeer, DET 11.6

ASSISTS
Magic Johnson, LAL 12.2
Sleepy Floyd, GS...............10.3
Isiah Thomas, DET 10.0
Doc Rivers, ATL.................10.0
Terry Porter, POR 8.9

STEALS
Alvin Robertson, SA...........3.21
Michael Jordan, CHI 2.88

Maurice Cheeks, PHI........2.65
Ron Harper, CLE 2.55
Clyde Drexler, POR 2.49

BLOCKED SHOTS
Mark Eaton, UTA 4.06
Manute Bol, WAS..............3.68
Akeem Olajuwon, HOU......3.39
Benoit Benjamin, LAC.......2.60
Alton Lister, SEA...............2.40

FIELD GOAL PCT.
Kevin McHale, BOS........... .604
Artis Gilmore, SA............... .597
Charles Barkley, PHI .... .594
James Donaldson, DAL..... .586
K. Abdul-Jabbar, LAL .... .564

FREE THROW PCT.
Larry Bird, BOS .... .910
Danny Ainge, BOS .... .897
Bill Laimbeer, DET .... .894
Byron Scott, LAL .... .892

3-PT. FIELD GOAL PCT.
Kiki Vandeweghe, POR..... .481
Detlef Schrempf, DAL....... .478
Danny Ainge, BOS .... .443
Byron Scott, LAL .... .436

EAST FIRST ROUND
Boston 3, Chicago 0
Atlanta 3, Indiana 1
Detroit 3, Washington 0
Milwaukee 3, Philadelphia 2

EAST SEMIFINALS
Boston 4, Milwaukee 3
Detroit 4, Atlanta 1

EAST FINALS
Boston 4, Detroit 3

WEST FIRST ROUND
L.A. Lakers 3, Denver 0
Seattle 3, Dallas 1
Houston 3, Portland 1
Golden St. 3, Utah 2

WEST SEMIFINALS
L.A. Lakers 4, Golden St. 1
Seattle 4, Houston 2

WEST FINALS
L.A. Lakers 4, Seattle 0

NBA FINALS
L.A. Lakers 126, Boston 113
L.A. Lakers 141, Boston 122
Boston 109, L.A. Lakers 103
L.A. Lakers 107, Boston 106
Boston 123, L.A. Lakers 108
L.A. Lakers 106, Boston 93

1987-88 FINAL STANDINGS

Eastern Conference
Atlantic Division

	W	L	PCT.	GB
Boston	57	25	.695	
Washington	38	44	.463	19
New York	38	44	.463	19
Philadelphia	36	46	.439	21
New Jersey	19	63	.232	38

Central Division

	W	L	PCT.	GB
Detroit	54	28	.659	
Atlanta	50	32	.610	4
Chicago	50	32	.610	4
Cleveland	42	40	.512	12
Milwaukee	42	40	.512	12
Indiana	38	44	.463	16

Western Conference
Midwest Division

	W	L	PCT.	GB
Denver	54	28	.659	
Dallas	53	29	.646	1
Utah	47	35	.573	7
Houston	46	36	.561	8
San Antonio	31	51	.378	23
Sacramento	24	58	.293	30

Pacific Division

	W	L	PCT.	GB
L.A. Lakers	62	20	.756	
Portland	53	29	.646	9
Seattle	44	38	.537	18
Phoenix	28	54	.341	34
Golden State	20	62	.244	42
L.A. Clippers	17	65	.207	45

SCORING
Michael Jordan, CHI 35.0
Dominique Wilkins, ATL...30.7
Larry Bird, BOS 29.9
Charles Barkley, PHI........28.3
Karl Malone, UTA.............27.7
Clyde Drexler, POR 27.0
Dale Ellis, SEA................25.8
Mark Aguirre, DAL 25.1
Alex English, DEN............25.0
Akeem Olajuwon, HOU ... 22.8

REBOUNDS
Michael Cage, LAC 13.03
Charles Oakley, CHI 13.00
Akeem Olajuwon, HOU....12.1
Karl Malone, UTA.............12.0
Buck Williams, NJ 11.9

ASSISTS
John Stockton, UTA.........13.8
Magic Johnson, LAL 11.9
Mark Jackson, NY............10.6
Terry Porter, POR 10.1
Doc Rivers, ATL 9.3

STEALS
Michael Jordan, CHI 3.16
Alvin Robertson, SA..........2.96

John Stockton, UTA..........2.95
Lafayette Lever, DEN.........2.72
Clyde Drexler, POR 2.51

BLOCKED SHOTS
Mark Eaton, UTA 3.71
Benoit Benjamin, LAC.......3.41
Patrick Ewing, NY 2.99
Akeem Olajuwon, HOU....2.71
Manute Bol, WAS.............2.70

FIELD GOAL PCT.
Kevin McHale, BOS........... .604
Robert Parish, BOS........... .589
Charles Barkley, PHI .... .587
John Stockton, UTA.......... .574
Walter Berry, SA............... .563

FREE THROW PCT.
Jack Sikma, MIL .... .922
Larry Bird, BOS .... .916
John Long, IND .... .907
Mike Gminski, NJ/PHI .... .906

3-PT. FIELD GOAL PCT.
Craig Hodges, MIL/PHO .... .491
Mark Price, CLE .... .486
John Long, IND .... .442
G. Henderson, NY/PHI .... .423

EAST FIRST ROUND
Boston 3, New York 1
Detroit 3, Washington 2
Atlanta 3, Milwaukee 2
Chicago 3, Cleveland 2

EAST SEMIFINALS
Boston 4, Atlanta 3
Detroit 4, Chicago 1

EAST FINALS
Detroit 4, Boston 2

WEST FIRST ROUND
L.A. Lakers 3, San Antonio 0
Denver 3, Seattle 2
Utah 3, Portland 1
Dallas 3, Houston 1

WEST SEMIFINALS
L.A. Lakers 4, Utah 3
Dallas 4, Denver 2

WEST FINALS
L.A. Lakers 4, Dallas 3

NBA FINALS
Detroit 105, L.A. Lakers 93
L.A. Lakers 108, Detroit 96
L.A. Lakers 99, Detroit 86
Detroit 111, L.A. Lakers 86
Detroit 104, L.A. Lakers 94
L.A. Lakers 103, Detroit 102
L.A. Lakers 108, Detroit 105

1988-89 FINAL STANDINGS

Eastern Conference
Atlantic Division

	W	L	PCT.	GB
New York	52	30	.634	
Philadelphia	46	36	.561	6
Boston	42	40	.512	10
Washington	40	42	.488	12
New Jersey	26	56	.317	26
Charlotte	20	62	.244	32

Central Division

	W	L	PCT.	GB
Detroit	63	19	.768	
Cleveland	57	25	.695	6
Atlanta	52	30	.634	11
Milwaukee	49	33	.598	14
Chicago	47	35	.573	16
Indiana	28	54	.341	35

Western Conference
Midwest Division

	W	L	PCT.	GB
Utah	51	31	.622	
Houston	45	37	.549	6
Denver	44	38	.537	7
Dallas	38	44	.463	13
San Antonio	21	61	.256	30
Miami	15	67	.183	36

Pacific Division

	W	L	PCT.	GB
L.A. Lakers	57	25	.695	
Phoenix	55	27	.671	2
Seattle	47	35	.573	10
Golden State	43	39	.524	14
Portland	39	43	.476	18
Sacramento	27	55	.329	30
L.A. Clippers	21	61	.256	36

SCORING
Michael Jordan, CHI 32.5
Karl Malone, UTA...............29.1
Dale Ellis, SEA...................27.5
Clyde Drexler, POR 27.2
Chris Mullin, GS.................26.5
Alex English, DEN..............26.5
Dominique Wilkins, ATL......26.2
Charles Barkley, PHI...........25.8
Tom Chambers, PHO 25.7
Akeem Olajuwon, HOU.....24.8

REBOUNDS
Akeem Olajuwon, HOU.....13.5
Charles Barkley, PHI.........12.5
Robert Parish, BOS 12.5
Moses Malone, ATL...........11.8
Karl Malone, UTA...............10.7

ASSISTS
John Stockton, UTA............13.6
Magic Johnson, LAL 12.8
Kevin Johnson, PHO..........12.2
Terry Porter, POR 9.5
Nate McMillan, SEA 9.3

STEALS
John Stockton, UTA............3.21
Alvin Robertson, SA...........3.03

Michael Jordan, CHI 2.89
Lafayette Lever, DEN..........2.75
Clyde Drexler, POR 2.73

BLOCKED SHOTS
Manute Bol, GS.................4.31
Mark Eaton, UTA................3.84
Patrick Ewing, NY 3.51
Akeem Olajuwon, HOU....3.44
Larry Nance, CLE 2.82

FIELD GOAL PCT.
Dennis Rodman, DET .... .595
Charles Barkley, PHI.......... .579
Robert Parish, BOS........... .570
Patrick Ewing, BOS........... .567
James Worthy, LAL .... .548

FREE THROW PCT.
Magic Johnson, LAL.......... .911
Jack Sikma, MIL................ .905
Scott Skiles, IND .... .903
Mark Price, CLE .... .901

3-PT. FIELD GOAL PCT.
Jon Sundvold, MIA .... .522
Dale Ellis, SEA .... .478
Mark Price, CLE .... .441
Hersey Hawkins, PHI .... .428

EAST FIRST ROUND
Detroit 3, Boston 0
New York 3, Philadelphia 0
Chicago 3, Cleveland 2
Milwaukee 3, Atlanta 2

EAST SEMIFINALS
Detroit 4, Milwaukee 0
Chicago 4, New York 2

EAST FINALS
Detroit 4, Chicago 2

WEST FIRST ROUND
L.A. Lakers 3, Portland 0
Golden St. 3, Utah 0
Phoenix 3, Denver 0
Seattle 3, Houston 1

WEST SEMIFINALS
L.A. Lakers 4, Seattle 0
Phoenix 4, Golden St. 1

WEST FINALS
L.A. Lakers 4, Phoenix 0

NBA FINALS
Detroit 109, L.A. Lakers 97
Detroit 108, L.A. Lakers 105
Detroit 114, L.A. Lakers 110
Detroit 105, L.A. Lakers 97

1989-90 FINAL STANDINGS

Eastern Conference

Atlantic Division

	W	L	PCT.	GB
Philadelphia	53	29	.646	
Boston	52	30	.634	1
New York	45	37	.549	8
Washington	31	51	.378	22
Miami	18	64	.220	35
New Jersey	17	65	.207	36

Central Division

	W	L	PCT.	GB
Detroit	59	23	.720	
Chicago	55	27	.671	4
Milwaukee	44	38	.537	15
Cleveland	42	40	.512	17
Indiana	42	40	.512	17
Atlanta	41	41	.500	18
Orlando	18	64	.220	41

Western Conference

Midwest Division

	W	L	PCT.	GB
San Antonio	56	26	.683	
Utah	55	27	.671	1
Dallas	47	35	.573	9
Denver	43	39	.524	13
Houston	41	41	.500	15
Minnesota	22	60	.268	34
Charlotte	19	63	.232	37

Pacific Division

	W	L	PCT.	GB
L.A. Lakers	63	19	.768	
Portland	59	23	.720	4
Phoenix	54	28	.659	9
Seattle	41	41	.500	22
Golden State	37	45	.451	26
L.A. Clippers	30	52	.366	33
Sacramento	23	59	.280	40

SCORING

Michael Jordan, CHI	33.6
Karl Malone, UTA	31.0
Patrick Ewing, NY	28.6
Tom Chambers, PHO	27.2
Dominique Wilkins, ATL	26.7
Charles Barkley, PHI	25.2
Chris Mullin, GS	25.1
Reggie Miller, IND	24.6
Akeem Olajuwon, HOU	24.3
David Robinson, SA	24.3

REBOUNDS

Akeem Olajuwon, HOU	14.0
David Robinson, SA	12.0
Charles Barkley, PHI	11.5
Karl Malone, UTA	11.1
Patrick Ewing, NY	10.9

ASSISTS

John Stockton, UTA	14.5
Magic Johnson, LAL	11.5
Kevin Johnson, PHO	11.4
Tyrone Bogues, CHA	10.7

STEALS

Michael Jordan, CHI	2.77
John Stockton, UTA	2.65
Scottie Pippen, CHI	2.57
Alvin Robertson, MIL	2.56
Derek Harper, DAL	2.28

BLOCKED SHOTS

Akeem Olajuwon, HOU	4.59
Patrick Ewing, NY	3.99
David Robinson, SA	3.89
Manute Bol, GS	3.17
Benoit Benjamin, LAC	2.63

FIELD GOAL PCT.

Mark West, PHO	.625
Charles Barkley, PHI	.600
Robert Parish, BOS	.580
Karl Malone, UTA	.562

FREE THROW PCT.

Larry Bird, BOS	.930
Eddie Johnson, PHO	.917
Walter Davis, DEN	.912
Joe Dumars, DET	.900

3-PT. FIELD GOAL PCT.

Steve Kerr, CLE	.507
Craig Hodges, CHI	.481
Drazen Petrovic, POR	.459
Jon Sundvold, MIA	.440

EAST FIRST ROUND

Detroit 3, Indiana 0
Philadelphia 3, Cleveland 2
Chicago 3, Milwaukee 1
New York 3, Boston 2

EAST SEMIFINALS

Detroit 4, New York 1
Chicago 4, Philadelphia 1

EAST FINALS

Detroit 4, Chicago 3

WEST FIRST ROUND

L.A. Lakers 3, Houston 1
San Antonio 3, Denver 0
Portland 3, Dallas 0
Phoenix 3, Utah 2

WEST SEMIFINALS

Phoenix 4, L.A. Lakers 1
Portland 4, San Antonio 3

WEST FINALS

Portland 4, Phoenix 2

NBA FINALS

Detroit 105, Portland 99
Portland 106, Detroit 105 (OT)
Detroit 121, Portland 106
Detroit 112, Portland 109
Detroit 92, Portland 90

1990-91 FINAL STANDINGS

Eastern Conference

Atlantic Division

	W	L	PCT.	GB
Boston	56	26	.683	
Philadelphia	44	38	.537	12
New York	39	43	.476	17
Washington	30	52	.366	26
New Jersey	26	56	.317	30
Miami	24	58	.293	32

Central Division

	W	L	PCT.	GB
Chicago	61	21	.744	
Detroit	50	32	.610	11
Milwaukee	48	34	.585	13
Atlanta	43	39	.524	18
Indiana	41	41	.500	20
Cleveland	33	49	.402	28
Charlotte	26	56	.317	35

Western Conference

Midwest Division

	W	L	PCT.	GB
San Antonio	55	27	.671	
Utah	54	28	.659	1
Houston	52	30	.634	3
Orlando	31	51	.378	24
Minnesota	29	53	.354	26
Dallas	28	54	.341	27
Denver	20	62	.244	35

Pacific Division

	W	L	PCT.	GB
Portland	63	19	.768	
L.A. Lakers	58	24	.707	5
Phoenix	55	27	.671	8
Golden State	44	38	.537	19
Seattle	41	41	.500	22
L.A. Clippers	31	51	.378	32
Sacramento	25	57	.305	38

SCORING
Michael Jordan, CHI..........31.5
Karl Malone, UTA..............29.0
Bernard King, WAS 28.4
Charles Barkley, PHI 27.6
Patrick Ewing, NY..............26.6
Michael Adams, DEN 26.5
Dominique Wilkins, ATL 25.9
Chris Mullin, GS 25.7
David Robinson, SA 25.6
Mitch Richmond, GS 23.9

REBOUNDS
David Robinson, SA 13.0
Dennis Rodman, DET 12.5
Charles Oakley, NY............12.1
Karl Malone, UTA 11.8
Patrick Ewing, NY..............11.2

ASSISTS
John Stockton, UTA 14.2
Magic Johnson, LAL...........12.5
Michael Adams, DEN 10.5
Kevin Johnson, PHO..........10.1

STEALS
Alvin Robertson, MIL.........3.04
John Stockton, UTA 2.85

Michael Jordan, CHI...........2.72
Tim Hardaway, GS 2.61
Scottie Pippen, CHI 2.35

BLOCKED SHOTS
Hakeem Olajuwon, HOU ...3.95
David Robinson, SA 3.90
Patrick Ewing, NY..............3.19
Manute Bol, PHI 3.01
Chris Dudley, NJ 2.51

FIELD GOAL PCT.
Buck Williams, POR 602
Robert Parish, BOS 598
Kevin Gamble, BOS 587
Charles Barkley, PHI 570

FREE THROW PCT.
Reggie Miller, IND 918
Jeff Malone, UTA................917
Ricky Pierce, MIL/SEA.........913
Kelly Tripucka, CHA 910

3-PT. FIELD GOAL PCT.
Jim Les, SAC.....................461
Trent Tucker, NY 418
Jeff Hornacek, PHO 418
Terry Porter, POR 415

EAST FIRST ROUND
Chicago 3, New York 0
Boston 3, Indiana 2
Detroit 3, Atlanta 2
Philadelphia 3, Milwaukee 0

EAST SEMIFINALS
Chicago 4, Philadelphia 1
Detroit 4, Boston 2

EAST FINALS
Chicago 4, Detroit 0

WEST FIRST ROUND
Portland 3, Seattle 2
Golden St. 3, San Antonio 1
L.A. Lakers 3, Houston 0
Utah 3, Phoenix 1

WEST SEMIFINALS
Portland 4, Utah 1
L.A. Lakers 4, Golden St. 1

WEST FINALS
L.A. Lakers 4, Portland 2

NBA FINALS
L.A. Lakers 93, Chicago 91
Chicago 107, L.A. Lakers 86
Chicago 104, L.A. 96 (OT)
Chicago 97, L.A. Lakers 82
Chicago 108, L.A. Lakers 101

1991-92 FINAL STANDINGS

Eastern Conference
Atlantic Division

	W	L	PCT.	GB
Boston	51	31	.622	
New York	51	31	.622	
New Jersey	40	42	.488	11
Miami	38	44	.463	13
Philadelphia	35	47	.427	16
Washington	25	57	.305	26
Orlando	21	61	.256	30

Central Division

	W	L	PCT.	GB
Chicago	67	15	.817	
Cleveland	57	25	.695	10
Detroit	48	34	.585	19
Indiana	40	42	.488	27
Atlanta	38	44	.463	29
Charlotte	31	51	.378	36
Milwaukee	31	51	.378	36

Western Conference
Midwest Division

	W	L	PCT.	GB
Utah	55	27	.671	
San Antonio	47	35	.573	8
Houston	42	40	.512	13
Denver	24	58	.293	31
Dallas	22	60	.268	33
Minnesota	15	67	.183	40

Pacific Division

	W	L	PCT.	GB
Portland	57	25	.695	
Golden State	55	27	.671	2
Phoenix	53	29	.646	4
Seattle	47	35	.573	10
L.A. Clippers	45	37	.549	12
L.A. Lakers	43	39	.524	14
Sacramento	29	53	.347	28

SCORING
Michael Jordan, CHI 30.1
Karl Malone, UTA 28.0
Chris Mullin, GS................25.6
Clyde Drexler, POR 25.0
Patrick Ewing, NY 24.0
Tim Hardaway, GS 23.4
David Robinson, SA 23.2
Charles Barkley, PHI 23.1
Mitch Richmond, SAC.......22.5
Glen Rice, MIA 22.3

REBOUNDS
Dennis Rodman, DET.......18.7
Kevin Willis, ATL...............15.5
Dikembe Mutombo, DEN ..12.3
David Robinson, SA 12.2
Hakeem Olajuwon, HOU ..12.1

ASSISTS
John Stockton, UTA 13.7
Kevin Johnson, PHO 10.7
Tim Hardaway, GS 10.0
Muggsy Bogues, CHA 9.1

STEALS
John Stockton, UTA 2.98
Micheal Williams, IND.......2.95

Alvin Robertson, MIL 2.56
Mookie Blaylock, NJ 2.36
David Robinson, SA 2.32

BLOCKED SHOTS
David Robinson, SA 4.49
Hakeem Olajuwon, HOU ..4.34
Larry Nance, CLE 3.00
Patrick Ewing, NY 2.99
Dikembe Mutombo, DEN ..2.96

FIELD GOAL PCT.
Buck Williams, POR...........604
Otis Thorpe, HOU 592
Horace Grant, CHI 578
Brad Daugherty, CLE ...... .570

FREE THROW PCT.
Mark Price, CLE 947
Larry Bird, BOS..................926
Ricky Pierce, SEA.............916
Rolando Blackman, DAL...898

3-PT. FIELD GOAL PCT.
Dana Barros, SEA .... .446
Drazen Petrovic, NJ......... .444
Jeff Hornacek, PHO......... .439
Mike Iuzzolino, DAL .... .434

EAST FIRST ROUND
Chicago 3, Miami 0
Boston 3, Indiana 1
Cleveland 3, New Jersey 1
New York 3, Detroit 2

EAST SEMIFINALS
Chicago 4, New York 3
Cleveland 4, Boston 3

EAST FINALS
Chicago 4, Cleveland 2

WEST FIRST ROUND
Portland 3, L.A. Lakers 1
Utah 3, L.A. Clippers 2
Seattle 3, Golden St. 1
Phoenix 3, San Antonio 0

WEST SEMIFINALS
Portland 4, Phoenix 1
Utah 4, Seattle 1

WEST FINALS
Portland 4, Utah 2

NBA FINALS
Chicago 122, Portland 89
Portland 115, Chi. 104 (OT)
Chicago 94, Portland 84
Portland 93, Chicago 88
Chicago 119, Portland 106
Chicago 97, Portland 93

1992-93 FINAL STANDINGS

Eastern Conference

Atlantic Division

	W	L	PCT.	GB
New York	60	22	.732	
Boston	48	34	.585	12
New Jersey	43	39	.524	17
Orlando	41	41	.500	19
Miami	36	46	.439	24
Philadelphia	26	56	.317	34
Washington	22	60	.268	38

Central Division

	W	L	PCT.	GB
Chicago	57	25	.695	
Cleveland	54	28	.659	3
Charlotte	44	38	.537	13
Atlanta	43	39	.524	14
Indiana	41	41	.500	16
Detroit	40	42	.488	17
Milwaukee	28	54	.341	29

Western Conference

Midwest Division

	W	L	PCT.	GB
Houston	55	27	.671	
San Antonio	49	33	.598	6
Utah	47	35	.573	8
Denver	36	46	.439	19
Minnesota	19	63	.232	36
Dallas	11	71	.134	44

Pacific Division

	W	L	PCT.	GB
Phoenix	62	20	.756	
Seattle	55	27	.671	7
Portland	51	31	.622	11
L.A. Clippers	41	41	.500	21
L.A. Lakers	39	43	.476	23
Golden State	34	48	.415	28
Sacramento	25	57	.305	37

SCORING
Michael Jordan, CHI 32.6
Dominique Wilkins, ATL...29.9
Karl Malone, UTA 27.0
Hakeem Olajuwon, HOU ..26.1
Charles Barkley, PHO......25.6
Patrick Ewing, NY 24.2
Joe Dumars, DET 23.5
Shaquille O'Neal, ORL......23.4
David Robinson, SA..........23.4
Danny Manning, LAC.......22.8

REBOUNDS
Dennis Rodman, DET.......18.3
Shaquille O'Neal, ORL......13.9
Dikembe Mutombo, DEN ..13.0
Hakeem Olajuwon, HOU ..13.0
Kevin Willis, ATL...............12.9

ASSISTS
John Stockton, UTA..........12.0
Tim Hardaway, GS 10.6
Scott Skiles, ORL...............9.4
Mark Jackson, LAC 8.8

STEALS
Michael Jordan, CHI 2.83
Mookie Blaylock, ATL 2.54

John Stockton, UTA..........2.43
Nate McMillan, SEA.........2.37
Alvin Robertson, MIL/DET....2.25

BLOCKED SHOTS
Hakeem Olajuwon, HOU ..4.17
Shaquille O'Neal, ORL......3.53
Dikembe Mutombo, DEN ..3.50
Alonzo Mourning, CHA 3.47
David Robinson, SA..........3.22

FIELD GOAL PCT.
Cedric Ceballos, PHO...... .576
Brad Daugherty, CLE ...... .571
Dale Davis, IND .... .568
Shaquille O'Neal, ORL .... .562

FREE THROW PCT.
Mark Price, CLE .... .948
Chris Jackson, DEN .... .935
Eddie Johnson, SEA......... .911
Micheal Williams, MIN .... .907

3-PT. FIELD GOAL PCT.
B.J. Armstrong, CHI .... .453
Chris Mullin, GS .... .451
Drazen Petrovic, NJ .... .449
Kenny Smith, HOU .... .438

EAST FIRST ROUND
New York 3, Indiana 1
Chicago 3, Atlanta 0
Cleveland 3, New Jersey 2
Charlotte 3, Boston 1

EAST SEMIFINALS
New York 4, Charlotte 1
Chicago 4, Cleveland 0

EAST FINALS
Chicago 4, New York 2

WEST FIRST ROUND
Phoenix 3, L.A. Lakers 2
Houston 3, L.A. Clippers 2
Seattle 3, Utah 2
San Antonio 3, Portland 1

WEST SEMIFINALS
Seattle 4, Houston 3
Phoenix 4, San Antonio 2

WEST FINALS
Phoenix 4, Seattle 3

NBA FINALS
Chicago 100, Phoenix 92
Chicago 111, Phoenix 108
Phoenix 129, Chic. 121 (3OT)
Chicago 111, Phoenix 105
Phoenix 108, Chicago 98
Chicago 99, Phoenix 98

1993-94 FINAL STANDINGS

Eastern Conference
Atlantic Division

	W	L	PCT.	GB
New York	57	25	.695	
Orlando	50	32	.610	7
New Jersey	45	37	.549	12
Miami	42	40	.512	15
Boston	32	50	.390	25
Philadelphia	25	57	.305	32
Washington	24	58	.234	33

Central Division

	W	L	PCT.	GB
Atlanta	57	25	.695	
Chicago	55	27	.671	2
Indiana	47	35	.573	10
Cleveland	47	35	.573	10
Charlotte	41	41	.500	16
Detroit	20	62	.244	37
Milwaukee	20	62	.244	37

Western Conference
Midwest Division

	W	L	PCT.	GB
Houston	58	24	.707	
San Antonio	55	27	.671	3
Utah	53	29	.646	5
Denver	42	40	.512	16
Minnesota	20	62	.244	38
Dallas	13	69	.159	45

Pacific Division

	W	L	PCT.	GB
Seattle	63	19	.768	
Phoenix	56	26	.683	7
Golden State	50	32	.610	13
Portland	47	35	.573	16
L.A. Lakers	33	49	.402	30
Sacramento	28	54	.341	35
L.A. Clippers	27	55	.329	36

SCORING

David Robinson, SA	29.8
Shaquille O'Neal, ORL	29.3
Hakeem Olajuwon, HOU	27.3
D. Wilkins, ATL/LAC	26.0
Karl Malone, UTA	25.2
Patrick Ewing, NY	24.5
Mitch Richmond, SAC	23.4
Scottie Pippen, CHI	22.0
Charles Barkley, PHO	21.6
Glen Rice, MIA	21.1
Latrell Sprewell, GS	21.0
Danny Manning, LAC/ATL	20.6
Joe Dumars, DET	20.4
Derrick Coleman, NJ	20.2
Ron Harper, LAC	20.1
Cliff Robinson, POR	20.2
Reggie Miller, IND	19.9
Jimmy Jackson, DAL	19.2

REBOUNDS

Dennis Rodman, SA	17.3
Shaquille O'Neal, ORL	13.2
Kevin Willis, ATL	12.0
Hakeem Olajuwon, HOU	11.9
Olden Polynice, DET/SAC	11.9
Dikembe Mutombo, DEN	11.8
Charles Oakley, NY	11.8
Karl Malone, UTA	11.5

ASSISTS

John Stockton, UTA	12.6
Muggsy Bogues, CHA	10.1
Mookie Blaylock, ATL	9.7
Kenny Anderson, NJ	9.6
Kevin Johnson, PHO	9.5
Rod Strickland, POR	9.0
Sherman Douglas, BOS	8.8
Mark Jackson, LAC	8.6

STEALS

Nate McMillan, SEA	2.96
Scottie Pippen, CHI	2.93
Mookie Blaylock, ATL	2.62
John Stockton, UTA	2.43
Eric Murdock, MIL	2.40
Anfernee Hardaway, ORL	2.32
Gary Payton, SEA	2.29
Tom Gugliotta, WAS	2.21

BLOCKED SHOTS

Dikembe Mutombo, DEN	4.10
Hakeem Olajuwon, HOU	3.71
David Robinson, SA	3.31
Alonzo Mourning, CHA	3.13
Shawn Bradley, PHI	3.00
Shaquille O'Neal, ORL	2.85
Patrick Ewing, NY	2.75
Oliver Miller, PHO	2.26

FIELD GOAL PCT.

Shaquille O'Neal, ORL	.599
Dikembe Mutombo, DEN	.569
Otis Thorpe, HOU	.561
Chris Webber, GS	.552
Shawn Kemp, SEA	.538
Loy Vaught, LAC	.537
Cedric Ceballos, PHO	.535
Rik Smits, IND	.534

FREE THROW PCT.

M. Abdul-Rauf, DEN	.956
Reggie Miller, IND	.908
Ricky Pierce, SEA	.896
Sedale Threatt, LAL	.890
Mark Price, CLE	.888
Glen Rice, MIA	.880
Jeff Hornacek, PHI/UTA	.878
Scott Skiles, ORL	.878

3-PT. FIELD GOAL PCT.

Tracy Murray, POR	.459
B.J. Armstrong, CHI	.444
Reggie Miller, IND	.421
Steve Kerr, CHI	.419
Scott Skiles, ORL	.412
Eric Murdock, MIL	.411
Mitch Richmond, SAC	.407
Kenny Smith, HOU	.405

1993-94 HOME-AWAY RECORDS

	HOME	AWAY	TOTAL		HOME	AWAY	TOTAL
Seattle	37-4	26-15	63-19	Denver	28-13	14-27	42-40
Atlanta	36-5	21-20	57-25	Charlotte	28-13	13-28	41-41
Phoenix	36-5	20-21	56-26	Miami	22-19	20-21	42-40
Houston	35-6	23-18	58-24	L.A. Lakers	21-20	12-29	33-49
Utah	33-8	20-21	53-29	Sacramento	20-21	8-33	28-54
New York	32-9	25-16	57-25	Boston	18-23	14-27	32-50
San Antonio	32-9	23-18	55-27	L.A. Clippers	17-24	10-31	27-55
Chicago	31-10	24-17	55-27	Washington	17-24	7-34	24-58
Orlando	31-10	19-22	50-32	Philadelphia	15-26	10-31	25-57
Cleveland	31-10	16-25	47-35	Minnesota	13-28	7-34	20-62
Portland	30-11	17-24	47-35	Milwaukee	11-30	9-32	20-62
Golden St.	29-12	21-20	50-32	Detroit	10-31	10-31	20-62
Indiana	29-12	18-23	47-35	Dallas	6-35	7-34	13-69
New Jersey	29-12	16-25	45-37				

1994 PLAYOFFS

EAST FIRST ROUND
Miami 93, Atlanta 88
Atlanta 104, Miami 86
Miami 90, Atlanta 86
Atlanta 103, Miami 89
Atlanta 102, Miami 91

New York 91, New Jersey 80
New York 90, New Jersey 81
New Jersey 93, N.Y. 92 (OT)
New York 102, New Jersey 92

Chicago 104, Cleveland 96
Chicago 105, Cleveland 96
Chicago 95, Cleveland 92 (OT)

Indiana 89, Orlando 88
Indiana 103, Orlando 101
Indiana 99, Orlando 86

EAST SEMIFINALS
New York 90, Chicago 86
New York 96, Chicago 91
Chicago 104, New York 102
Chicago 95, New York 83
New York 87, Chicago 86
Chicago 93, New York 79
New York 87, Chicago 77

Indiana 96, Atlanta 85
Atlanta 92, Indiana 69
Indiana 101, Atlanta 81
Indiana 102, Atlanta 86

Atlanta 88, Indiana 76
Indiana 98, Atlanta 79

EAST FINALS
New York 100, Indiana 89
New York 89, Indiana 78
Indiana 88, New York 68
Indiana 83, New York 77
Indiana 93, New York 86
New York 98, Indiana 91
New York 94, Indiana 90

WEST FIRST ROUND
Seattle 106, Denver 82
Seattle 97, Denver 87
Denver 110, Seattle 93
Denver 94, Seattle 85 (OT)
Denver 98, Seattle 94 (OT)

Houston 114, Portland 104
Houston 115, Portland 104
Portland 118, Houston 115
Houston 92, Portland 89

Phoenix 111, Golden St. 104
Phoenix 117, Golden St. 111
Phoenix 140, Golden St. 133

San Antonio 106, Utah 89
Utah 96, San Antonio 84
Utah 105, San Antonio 72
Utah 95, San Antonio 90

WEST SEMIFINALS
Phoenix 91, Houston 87
Phoenix 124, Hou. 117 (OT)
Houston 118, Phoenix 102
Houston 107, Phoenix 96
Houston 107, Phoenix 96
Phoenix 103, Houston 86
Houston 104, Phoenix 94

Utah 100, Denver 91
Utah 104, Denver 94
Utah 111, Denver 109 (OT)
Denver 83, Utah 82
Denver 109, Utah 101 (2OT)
Denver 94, Utah 91
Utah 91, Denver 81

WEST FINALS
Houston 100, Utah 88
Houston 104, Utah 99
Utah 95, Houston 86
Houston 80, Utah 78
Houston 94, Utah 83

NBA FINALS
Houston 85, New York 78
New York 91, Houston 83
Houston 93, New York 89
New York 91, Houston 82
New York 91, Houston 84
Houston 86, New York 84
Houston 90, New York 84

1993-94 OFFENSIVE TEAM STATISTICS

TEAM	FIELD GOALS			FREE THROWS			REBOUNDS			MISCELLANEOUS						SCORING	
	ATT	FGs	PCT	ATT	FTs	PCT	OFF	DEF	TOT	AST	PFs	DQ	STL	TO	BLK	PTS	AVG
Phoenix	7080	3429	.484	2301	1674	.728	1220	2453	3673	2261	1639	8	745	1305	460	8876	108.2
Golden State	7145	3512	.492	2304	1529	.664	1183	2396	3579	2198	1789	18	804	1433	511	8844	107.9
Portland	7427	3371	.454	2396	1781	.743	1302	2460	3762	2070	1827	5	744	1210	409	8795	107.3
Charlotte	7100	3382	.476	2135	1632	.764	1019	2475	3494	2214	1747	17	724	1266	394	8732	106.5
Seattle	6901	3338	.484	2374	1769	.745	1148	2233	3381	2112	1914	16	1053	1262	365	8687	105.9
Orlando	6883	3341	.485	2346	1590	.678	1177	2356	3533	2070	1713	10	683	1327	456	8666	105.7
Miami	6896	3197	.464	2223	1744	.785	1235	2407	3642	1856	2024	26	643	1315	374	8475	103.4
New Jersey	7115	3169	.445	2495	1900	.762	1300	2556	3856	1900	1693	9	696	1196	576	8461	103.2
L.A. Clippers	7163	3343	.467	2128	1509	.709	1120	2410	3530	2169	1769	18	807	1474	421	8447	103.0
Utah	6729	3207	.477	2379	1761	.740	1059	2385	3444	2179	1988	13	751	1191	364	8354	101.9
Atlanta	7039	3247	.461	2070	1556	.752	1250	2423	3673	2056	1625	5	915	1252	449	8318	101.4
Cleveland	6731	3133	.465	2254	1736	.770	1090	2353	3443	2049	1701	15	705	1136	426	8296	101.2
Houston	6733	3197	.475	1978	1469	.743	926	2619	3545	2087	1646	7	717	1338	485	8292	101.1
Sacramento	7027	3179	.452	2292	1676	.731	1122	2349	3471	2029	1979	27	669	1333	355	8291	101.1
Indiana	6516	3167	.486	2387	1762	.738	1130	2409	3539	2055	1974	19	706	1440	457	8280	101.0
Boston	7057	3333	.472	2003	1463	.730	1037	2380	3417	1928	1849	19	674	1242	440	8267	100.8
L.A. Lakers	7316	3291	.450	1967	1410	.717	1260	2204	3464	1983	1877	13	751	1197	461	8233	100.4
Washington	6826	3193	.468	2162	1618	.748	1071	2189	3260	1823	1715	9	701	1403	321	8229	100.4
Denver	6781	3156	.465	2423	1739	.718	1105	2557	3662	1763	1926	19	679	1422	686	8221	100.3
San Antonio	6688	3178	.475	2151	1597	.742	1189	2597	3786	1896	1662	4	561	1198	456	8202	100.0
New York	6735	3098	.460	2097	1564	.746	1175	2542	3717	2067	2001	23	752	1360	385	8076	98.5
Philadelphia	6819	3103	.455	2112	1509	.714	1012	2394	3406	1827	1488	7	663	1368	525	8033	98.0
Chicago	6815	3245	.476	1859	1310	.705	1143	2391	3534	2102	1750	11	740	1306	354	8033	98.0
Detroit	7017	3169	.452	1715	1253	.731	1027	2320	3347	1767	1935	23	602	1236	309	7949	96.9
Milwaukee	6807	3044	.447	2181	1530	.702	1126	2154	3280	1946	1821	19	800	1343	407	7949	96.9
Minnesota	6535	2985	.457	2303	1777	.772	990	2343	3333	1967	2016	20	600	1478	440	7930	96.7
Dallas	7070	3055	.432	1942	1450	.747	1271	2150	3421	1629	2007	13	767	1393	299	7801	95.1

1993-94 DEFENSIVE TEAM STATISTICS

TEAM	FIELD GOALS			FREE THROWS			REBOUNDS			MISCELLANEOUS						SCORING		
	ATT	FGs	PCT	ATT	FTs	PCT	OFF	DEF	TOT	AST	PFs	DQ	STL	TO	BLK	PTS	AVG	DIF
New York	6451	2783	.431	2341	1684	.719	1016	2245	3261	1677	1897	22	677	1420	333	7503	91.5	+7.0
San Antonio	6880	3066	.446	1875	1349	.719	1089	2153	3242	1769	1916	16	632	1020	346	7771	94.9	+3.1
Chicago	6542	3029	.463	1987	1470	.740	985	2240	3225	1840	1725	13	730	1335	374	7780	94.9	+3.1
Atlanta	6954	3163	.455	1732	1285	.742	1157	2358	3515	1897	1722	13	641	1465	338	7886	96.2	+5.3
Houston	7166	3152	.440	1871	1377	.736	1134	2438	3572	1901	1743	13	767	1221	312	7925	96.6	+4.3
Seattle	6459	2928	.453	2374	1760	.741	1084	2191	3275	1808	1884	8	686	1666	421	7942	96.9	+4.0
Cleveland	6741	3131	.464	1967	1446	.735	1059	2335	3394	2006	1797	12	628	1293	461	7966	97.1	+4.0
Indiana	6614	2978	.450	2422	1768	.730	1132	2153	3285	1902	1986	23	826	1340	389	7997	97.5	+3.5
Utah	6641	2973	.448	2444	1773	.725	1100	2327	3427	1806	1922	15	593	1318	459	8008	97.7	+4.2
Denver	7000	3065	.438	2349	1761	.750	1118	2331	3449	1745	1957	18	725	1245	502	8099	98.8	+1.5
Miami	6641	3036	.457	2527	1889	.748	1284	2533	3817	1821	1946	23	689	1314	438	8256	100.7	+2.7
New Jersey	7125	3266	.458	2038	1514	.743	1142	2528	3670	1919	1901	25	715	1248	582	8281	101.0	+2.2
Orlando	7125	3263	.458	2047	1525	.745	1197	2305	3502	2103	1844	16	756	1228	442	8347	101.8	+3.9
Phoenix	7135	3379	.474	1998	1438	.720	1086	2247	3333	2154	1870	16	748	1254	437	8479	103.4	+4.8
Milwaukee	6625	3255	.491	2284	1684	.737	1086	2495	3581	2092	1777	13	768	1416	420	8480	103.4	-6.5
Minnesota	6874	3244	.472	2451	1783	.727	1102	2296	3398	2108	1855	21	824	1164	549	8498	103.6	-6.9
Dallas	6508	3212	.494	2498	1841	.737	1101	2503	3604	1970	1649	7	782	1428	507	8514	103.8	-8.7
Portland	7057	3311	.469	2216	1661	.750	1016	2481	3497	2094	1944	15	654	1391	393	8579	104.6	+2.6
L.A. Lakers	7008	3337	.476	2346	1683	.717	1284	2533	3817	2163	1659	10	664	1344	427	8585	104.7	-4.3
Detroit	6878	3255	.473	2451	1805	.736	1191	2590	3781	2097	1602	9	721	1169	368	8587	104.7	-7.8
Boston	7034	3357	.477	2218	1673	.754	1131	2508	3639	2089	1738	12	690	1273	414	8618	105.1	-4.3
Philadelphia	7338	3549	.484	1774	1297	.744	1202	2607	3809	2357	1729	10	806	1190	385	8658	105.6	-7.6
Golden State	7332	3428	.468	2108	1540	.731	1324	2408	3732	2184	1870	18	842	1426	408	8701	106.1	+1.7
Charlotte	7359	3463	.471	2036	1507	.740	1287	2467	3684	2116	1761	12	629	1260	430	8707	106.7	+0.2
Sacramento	7017	3360	.479	2448	1767	.722	1189	2574	3763	2052	1895	14	746	1341	498	8764	106.9	-5.8
Washington	7026	3569	.508	1996	1444	.723	1119	2362	3481	2113	1823	8	815	1291	470	8834	107.7	-7.4
L.A. Clippers	7421	3512	.473	2209	1584	.717	1348	2568	3916	2220	1788	11	898	1364	476	8916	108.7	-5.7

1994 NBA FINALS COMPOSITE BOX

New York	G	AVG MIN	FGs FG-ATT	PCT	FTs FT-ATT	PCT	REB	AST	STL	BLK	TOT PTS	AVG PTS
Patrick Ewing	7	44.0	58-160	.363	15-21	.714	87	12	9	30	132	18.9
John Starks	7	41.9	39-106	.368	30-39	.769	22	41	11	1	124	17.7
Derek Harper	7	38.0	42-90	.467	14-17	.824	21	42	17	1	115	16.4
Charles Oakley	7	40.7	31-64	.484	15-18	.833	83	17	8	1	77	11.0
Charles Smith	7	26.7	26-59	.441	13-19	.684	30	12	4	7	65	9.3
Anthony Mason	7	29.3	22-47	.468	16-25	.640	48	9	5	0	60	8.6
Greg Anthony	7	11.4	10-31	.323	2-2	1.00	6	17	3	1	23	3.3
Anthony Bonner	2	5.5	2-2	1.00	0-1	.000	2	0	0	0	4	2.0
Hubert Davis	5	7.6	2-10	.200	3-6	.500	2	2	0	1	8	1.6
Herb Williams	4	1.8	0-1	.000	0-0	.000	0	0	0	1	0	0.0
Totals	**7**	**48.0**	**232-570**	**.407**	**108-148**	**.730**	**301**	**152**	**57**	**43**	**608**	**86.9**

3-PT. FGP—36-105, .343 (Harper 17-39, Starks 16-50, Davis 1-1, Ewing 1-5, Anthony 1-8, Smith 0-2).

Houston	G	AVG MIN	FGs FG-ATT	PCT	FTs FT-ATT	PCT	REB	AST	STL	BLK	TOT PTS	AVG PTS
Hakeem Olajuwon	7	43.1	75-150	.500	37-43	.860	64	25	11	27	188	26.9
Vernon Maxwell	7	37.7	35-96	.365	15-22	.682	23	20	4	0	94	13.4
Robert Horry	7	37.9	24-74	.324	13-21	.619	43	26	9	4	72	10.3
Sam Cassell	7	22.6	19-45	.422	25-27	.926	22	20	9	2	70	10.0
Otis Thorpe	7	39.6	27-52	.519	11-22	.500	79	23	6	0	65	9.3
Carl Herrera	7	17.3	22-38	.579	6-8	.750	25	3	3	1	50	7.1
Kenny Smith	7	25.4	14-36	.389	6-6	1.00	10	22	5	0	39	5.6
Matt Bullard	2	13.5	2-10	.200	2-4	.500	6	0	1	1	8	4.0
Mario Elie	7	11.3	5-20	.250	5-6	.833	7	7	2	1	17	2.4
Earl Cureton	1	2.0	0-0	.000	0-0	.000	0	0	0	0	0	0.0
Chris Jent	3	2.3	0-2	.000	0-0	.000	1	0	0	0	0	0.0
Totals	**7**	**48.0**	**223-523**	**.426**	**120-159**	**.755**	**280**	**146**	**50**	**36**	**603**	**86.1**

3-PT. FGP—37-121, .306 (Horry 11-36, Maxwell 9-40, Cassell 7-16, Smith 5-14, Elie 2-5, Bullard 2-7, Olajuwon 1-1, Jent 0-2).

1993-94 MOST VALUABLE PLAYER VOTING

H. Olajuwon, HOU (66)	889	Shawn Kemp, SEA	17	Dennis Rodman, SA	1
D. Robinson, SA (24)	730	Karl Malone, UTA	17	Kevin Willis, ATL	1
S. Pippen, CHI (7)	390	Mark Price, CLE	7	Mookie Blaylock, ATL	1
S. O'Neal, ORL (3)	289	Charles Barkley, PHO	5	D. Wilkins, ATL/LAC	1
P. Ewing, NY (1)	255	Latrell Sprewell, GS	1	John Stockton, UTA	1
Gary Payton, SEA	20	Kevin Johnson, PHO	1		

* 1st-place votes in parentheses.

DEFENSIVE PLAYER OF THE YEAR		SIXTH MAN AWARD		ROOKIE OF THE YEAR	
H. Olajuwon, HOU	23	Dell Curry, CHA	46	Chris Webber, GS	53
David Robinson, SA	22	Nate McMillan, SEA	37	A. Hardaway, ORL	47
D. Mutombo, DEN	19	Craig Ehlo, ATL	7	Jamal Mashburn, DAL	1
Scottie Pippen, CHI	11	Ricky Pierce, SEA	3		
Gary Payton, SEA	9	Armon Gilliam, NJ	2	COACH OF THE YEAR	
Dennis Rodman, SA	8	Dennis Rodman, SA	1	Lenny Wilkens, ATL	71
Mookie Blaylock, ATL	3	Johnny Newman, NJ	1	Phil Jackson, CHI	16
Nate McMillan, SEA	3	Steve Kerr, CHI	1	George Karl, SEA	8
Charles Oakley, NY	2	Anthony Mason, NY	1	R. Tomjanovich, HOU	3
Horace Grant, CHI	1	Mario Elie, HOU	1	Don Nelson, GS	1
		Orlando Woolridge, PHI	1	Pat Riley, NY	1
				Chuck Daly, NJ	1

1994-95 N B A Schedule

Below is the NBA schedule for the 1994-95 season. All game times listed are local (except November 4 and 5 Japan games, which are Eastern). TNT telecasts are denoted by a "•", TBS games by a "+", and NBC games by a "#". The symbol "@" indicates more games that NBC may telecast; the network will make its decision at a later date.

Fri Nov 4
NY at Bos, 7:30
Mil at Phi, 7:30
Orl at Was, 7:30
Ind at Atl, 7:30
LAL at Det, 8:00
•Cha at Chi, 7:00
NJ at Hou, 7:30
GS at SA, 7:30
Min at Den, 7:00
Mia at Uta, 7:00
•Por at LAC (Japan) 11:00
Pho at Sac, 7:30

Sat Nov 5
Phi at Orl, 7:30
Cle at Cha, 7:30
Det at Atl, 7:30
Bos at Ind, 7:30
Was at Chi, 7:30
LAL at Mil, 7:30
Hou at Min, 7:00
NJ at Dal, 7:30
GS at Den, 7:00
LAC at Por (Japan), 10:00
Uta at Sea, 7:00

Sun Nov 6
Mia at Pho, 7:00

Mon Nov 7
Phi at Chi, 7:30
NJ at SA, 7:30
Atl at Uta, 7:00

Tue Nov 8
LAL at NY, 7:30
•Hou at Cle, 8:00
Min at Det, 7:30
Den at Dal, 7:30
Mia at GS, 7:30

Wed Nov 9
Chi at NJ, 7:30
Was at Phi, 7:30
Orl at Cha, 7:30
Hou at Ind, 6:00
LAL at Min, 7:30
Uta at SA, 7:30
Atl at Pho, 7:00
Sac at Sea, 7:00

Thu Nov 10
+Orl at NY, 8:00
Mil at Cle, 7:30
Ind at Det, 7:30
Atl at LAC, 7:30
Por at Sac, 7:30

Fri Nov 11
Hou at Bos, 7:30
Dal at Phi, 7:30
NJ at Was, 7:30
•Cha at Mil, 7:00
Chi at Min, 7:00
GS at Uta, 7:00
Den at LAL, 7:30
Pho at Sea, 7:00

Sat Nov 12
Hou at NJ, 8:00
Orl at Phi, 7:30
Was at Mia, 8:00
Det at Cha, 7:30
Ind at Cle, 7:30
Dal at Chi, 7:30
Bos at Min, 7:00
NY at SA, 7:30
Uta at Den, 7:00
Pho at LAC (Anah), 7:30
LAL at GS, 7:30
Atl at Sac, 7:30

Sun Nov 13
LAC at Sea, 6:00

Mon Nov 14
NY at Uta, 7:00

Tue Nov 15
Sea at NJ, 7:30
Was at Orl, 7:30
Dal at Mia, 7:30
Bos at Atl, 7:30
Cha at Cle, 7:30
Phi at Det, 7:30
Ind at Mil, 7:30
Sac at Hou, 7:30
•SA at Den, 6:00
LAL at LAC, 7:30
Min at GS, 7:30
Pho at Por, 7:00

Wed Nov 16
Sea at Bos, 7:30
Mia at Phi, 7:30
Chi at SA, 7:30
Min at Pho, 7:00
NY at LAL, 7:30

Thu Nov 17
Was at NJ, 7:30
LAC at Cha, 7:30
Sac at Dal, 7:30
+Chi at Hou, 7:00
Det at Den, 7:00
NY at GS, 7:30
Cle at Por, 7:00

Fri Nov 18
LAC at Phi, 7:30
NJ at Orl, 7:30
Bos at Mia, 7:30
Mil at Atl, 7:30
•Sea at Ind, 8:00
Det at Uta, 7:00
Por at Pho, 7:00
Cle at LAL, 7:30

Sat Nov 19
Atl at NY, 8:30

Bos at Was, 7:30
Ind at Cha, 7:30
Sea at Mil, 7:30
SA at Min, 7:00
Chi at Dal, 7:30
Hou at Den, 7:00
Uta at GS, 7:30

Sun Nov 20
LAC at NJ, 7:00
Cle at Sac, 6:00
Det at Por, 7:00

Mon Nov 21
SA at NY, 7:30
Mia at Orl, 7:30
Pho at Uta, 7:30

Tue Nov 22
Mil at Bos (Hart), 7:30
•GS at Cha, 8:00
Phi at Atl, 7:30
Min at Cle, 7:30
Por at Hou, 7:30
Chi at LAC, 7:30
NJ at Sea, 7:00

Wed Nov 23
Cha at Bos, 7:30
Hou at Orl, 7:30
Cle at Mia, 7:30
Mil at Det, 7:30
Atl at Min, 7:00
Por at SA, 7:30
Chi at Den, 7:00
Sea at Uta, 7:30
LAC at Pho, 7:00
Dal at LAL, 7:30
NJ at Sac, 7:30

Thu Nov 24
+GS at Ind, 8:00

Fri Nov 25
Orl at Bos, 7:30
Cle at Was (Balt), 7:30
LAL at Atl, 7:30
Mia at Det, 8:00
Mil at Ind, 7:30
Phi at Min, 7:00
Por at Dal, 7:30
Sea at SA, 7:30
Chi at Uta, 7:00
NJ at LAC, 3:00
Den at Sac, 7:00

Sat Nov 26
Cha at NY, 1:00
Bos at Phi, 7:30
LAL at Was, 7:30
GS at Cle, 7:30
Orl at Mil, 7:30
Sea at Hou, 7:30
Dal at Den, 7:00
SA at Pho, 7:00

Sun Nov 27
GS at Det, 7:00
NJ at Pho, 7:00
Uta at Sac, 6:00
Ind at Por, 7:00

Mon Nov 28
Min at SA, 7:30
Ind at Sea, 7:00

Tue Nov 29
LAL at NJ, 7:30
NY at Was, 7:30
Sac at Mia, 7:30
Cha at Atl, 7:30
Pho at Mil, 7:30
Min at Dal, 7:30
Den at Hou, 7:30
LAC at GS, 7:30
Uta at Por, 7:00

Wed Nov 30
Det at Bos, 7:30
Sac at Orl, 7:30
Mia at Cha, 7:30
LAL at Cle, 7:30
+Pho at Chi, 7:00
SA at Sea, 7:00

Thu Dec 1
Cle at Mil, 7:30

Den at Dal, 7:30
Min at Uta, 7:00
Ind at LAC, 7:30
Hou at GS, 7:30

Fri Dec 2
Pho at Bos, 7:30
Sac at Phi, 7:30
Det at Was, 7:30
●NY at Orl, 8:00
NJ at Mia, 7:30
Atl at Chi, 7:30
Hou at LAL, 7:30
SA at Por, 7:00

Sat Dec 3
Was at NY, 7:30
Sac at NJ, 8:00
Orl at Atl, 7:30
Phi at Cle, 7:30
Pho at Det, 7:30
Bos at Chi, 7:30
Uta at Dal, 7:30
Cha at Den, 7:00
Min at LAC, 7:30
Ind at GS, 7:30
Mil at Sea, 7:00

Sun Dec 4
Mil at Por, 7:00

Mon Dec 5
NY at Phi, 7:30
NJ at Chi, 7:30
Cha at LAC, 7:30

Tue Dec 6
Bos at NY, 7:30
Atl at NJ, 7:30
Pho at Was, 7:30
Orl at Cle, 7:30
Det at Ind, 7:30
Den at Min, 7:00
Dal at SA, 7:30
Cha at Uta, 7:00
GS at LAL, 7:30
Mil at Sac, 7:30
●Hou at Sea, 5:00

Wed Dec 7
Atl at Bos, 7:30
Cle at Orl, 7:30
Phi at Mia, 7:30
Mil at LAC, 7:30

Thu Dec 8
Pho at NJ, 7:30
Was at Dal, 7:30
+Cha at Hou, 7:00
Uta at SA, 7:30
Sea at Sac, 7:30

Fri Dec 9
Cle at Bos, 7:30
Ind at Phi, 7:30
Orl at Mia, 7:30
NY at Atl, 7:30
●Chi at Det, 8:00
LAC at LAL, 7:30
GS at Por, 7:00

Sat Dec 10
Phi at NY, 7:30
Bos at NJ, 7:30
Atl at Orl, 7:30
Det at Cle, 7:30
Mia at Ind, 7:30
Chi at Mil, 7:30
Pho at Min, 7:00
Cha at Dal, 7:30
SA at Hou, 7:30
Was at Den, 7:00
LAL at Uta, 7:00
Sea at LAC, 7:30
GS at Sac, 7:30

Sun Dec 11
Sac at Por, 7:00

Mon Dec 12
Den at Bos, 7:30
Mia at NY, 7:30
Orl at NJ, 7:30
Was at SA, 7:30
Por at Uta, 7:00
GS at Pho, 7:00

Tue Dec 13
Mia at Phi, 7:30
Mil at Cha, 7:30
Min at Atl, 7:30
Ind at Cle, 7:30
Det at Chi, 7:30
●LAL at Dal, 7:00
Was at Hou, 7:30
Sac at GS, 7:30

Wed Dec 14
Cle at NJ, 7:30
Den at Orl, 7:30

Cha at Det, 7:30
Atl at Ind, 7:30
Phi at Mil, 7:30
Uta at Min, 7:00
Bos at SA, 7:30
Sea at Pho, 7:00
LAC at Por, 7:00

Thu Dec 15
Uta at Was, 7:30
+Den at Mia, 8:00
Bos at Dal, 7:30
LAL at Hou, 7:30
GS at LAC (Anah), 7:30
NY at Sac, 7:30
Por at Sea, 7:00

Fri Dec 16
Cle at Phi, 7:30
Chi at Atl, 7:30
Cha at Ind, 7:30
NJ at Min, 7:00
●NY at Pho, 6:00
●Orl at GS, 7:30

Sat Dec 17
Det at Phi, 7:30
Min at Was, 7:30
Atl at Mia, 7:30
Den at Cha, 7:30
Uta at Chi, 7:30
Bos at Hou, 7:30
LAL at SA, 7:30
Sac at Pho, 7:00
Dal at LAC (Anah), 7:30
Orl at Sea, 7:00

Sun Dec 18
Mia at NJ, 7:30
Uta at Mil, 6:00
NY at Por, 5:00

Mon Dec 19
Cle at Chi, 7:30
Bos at Den, 7:00
Was at Pho, 7:00

Tue Dec 20
●NJ at NY, 8:00
Uta at Phi, 7:30
Ind at Cha, 7:30
Mil at Atl, 7:30
Min at LAL, 7:30

Dal at GS, 7:30
Was at Sac, 7:30
Orl at Por, 7:00
LAC at Sea, 7:00

Wed Dec 21
Det at NJ, 7:30
Mil at Mia, 7:30
Chi at Ind, 7:30
SA at Den, 7:00
Orl at LAC, 7:30

Thu Dec 22
Cle at NY, 7:30
Phi at Cha, 7:30
Uta at Atl, 7:30
+Pho at Hou, 7:00
Was at GS, 7:30
Min at Sac, 7:30
Dal at Sea, 7:00

Fri Dec 23
Phi at Bos, 7:30
Mil at Orl, 7:30
Cha at Mia, 7:30
NJ at Cle, 7:30
Atl at Det, 8:00
●Ind at Chi, 7:00
Hou at SA, 7:30
Den at Pho, 7:00
Was at LAC, 7:30
Sac at LAL, 7:30
Dal at Por, 7:00

Sun Dec 25
#Sea at Den, 2:00
#NY at Chi, 5:30

Mon Dec 26
Orl at Was, 7:30
Hou at Mia, 7:30
Bos at Cle, 1:00
NJ at Mil, 7:30
LAC at Min, 7:00
Dal at Pho, 7:00
Phi at Por, 7:00
Sac at Sea, 7:00

Tue Dec 27
NY at NJ, 7:30
Mia at Orl, 7:30
Mil at Det, 7:30
LAC at Chi, 7:30
Pho at Dal, 7:30
Atl at Hou, 7:30

Cha at SA, 7:30
Ind at Den, 7:00
LAL at GS, 7:30
Por at Sac, 7:30

Wed Dec 28
Chi at Bos, 7:30
Det at NY, 7:30
Was at Cle, 7:30
Ind at Uta, 7:00
Phi at Sea, 7:00

Thu Dec 29
LAC at Mia, 7:30
+Orl at Cha, 8:00
SA at Atl, 7:30
GS at Hou, 7:30
Sea at LAL, 7:30
Den at Por, 7:00

Fri Dec 30
SA at Was, 7:30
LAC at Orl, 7:30
Atl at Cle, 7:30
Bos at Det, 8:00
NJ at Ind, 7:30
Mia at Chi, 7:30
Cha at Mil, 7:30
NY at Min, 7:30
GS at Dal, 7:30
Por at Den, 7:00
Hou at Uta, 7:00
LAL at Pho, 7:00
Phi at Sac, 7:30

Tue Jan 3
Ind at NJ, 7:30
Sea at Was, 7:30
Por at Atl, 7:30
Den at Min, 7:00
Hou at Dal, 7:30
Mil at Uta, 7:30
Det at LAL, 7:30
SA at GS, 7:30
●Pho at Sac, 5:00

Wed Jan 4
Mia at Bos, 7:30
Atl at NY, 7:30
NJ at Orl, 7:30
Por at Cha, 7:30
Sea at Cle, 7:30
Was at Ind, 7:30
Den at Chi, 7:30
Phi at Pho, 7:00

Thu Jan 5
Min at Mia, 7:30
Dal at Hou, 7:30
+SA at Uta, 6:00
Phi at LAC, 7:30
Mil at GS, 7:30
Det at Sac, 7:30

Fri Jan 6
Por at Bos, 7:30
Cha at NJ, 7:30
Min at Orl, 7:30
Was at Atl, 7:30
NY at Cle, 7:30
●Sea at Chi, 7:00
Ind at Dal, 7:30
Mil at LAL, 7:30

Sat Jan 7
Por at Was, 7:30
Bos at Cha, 7:30
NJ at Atl, 7:30
Chi at Cle, 7:30
Ind at Hou, 7:30
Pho at Den, 7:00
Phi at Uta, 7:00
SA at LAC, 7:30
Mia at Sac, 7:30

Sun Jan 8
Min at NY, 6:00
Orl at Det, 7:00
Mil at Den, 7:00
Mia at LAL, 6:30

Mon Jan 9
Was at Bos, 7:30
Dal at Uta, 7:00
Mil at Pho, 7:00
LAL at Por, 7:00

Tue Jan 10
●Ind at NY, 8:00
Atl at Was, 7:30
Cha at Cle, 7:30
NJ at Det, 7:30
Orl at Chi, 7:30
Sac at Min, 7:00
LAC at SA, 7:30
Sea at GS, 7:30

Wed Jan 11
Ind at Bos, 7:30
Chi at Phi, 7:30
Det at Orl, 7:30

Min at Cha, 7:30
Sac at Mil, 7:30
LAC at Dal, 7:30
Mia at Hou, 7:30
Den at Uta, 7:00
Pho at LAL, 7:30
GS at Por, 7:00

Thu Jan 12
+Mia at SA, 7:00
Dal at Den, 7:00
Cle at Pho, 7:00

Fri Jan 13
●Uta at Bos, 8:00
NJ at Phi, 7:30
Ind at Was, 7:30
Orl at Atl, 7:30
Sac at Chi, 7:30
NY at Mil, 7:30
Det at Min, 7:00
SA at Hou, 7:30
GS at LAL, 7:30
LAC at Sea, 7:00

Sat Jan 14
Uta at NY, 7:30
Min at NJ, 7:30
Phi at Orl, 7:30
Chi at Cha, 7:30
Was at Det, 7:30
Mil at Ind, 7:30
Mia at Dal, 7:30
Hou at Den, 7:00
Pho at LAC, 7:30
Cle at GS, 7:30

Sun Jan 15
Sac at Bos, 7:00
Dal at SA, 6:00
Por at Sea, 6:00

Mon Jan 16
NJ at NY, 1:00
Det at Phi, 2:00
Chi at Was, 1:00
Mia at Atl, 3:30
Uta at Ind, 6:00
Hou at Min, 7:00
LAC at LAL, 1:30
Den at GS, 2:00

Tue Jan 17
SA at Bos, 7:30
Cha at Orl, 7:30

●Den at Pho, 7:00
Por at Sac, 7:30
Cle at Sea, 7:00

Wed Jan 18
Bos at Mia, 7:30
SA at Cha, 7:30
Phi at Atl, 7:30
Uta at Det, 7:30
LAL at Ind, 7:30
Mil at Chi, 7:30
Orl at Dal, 7:30
Cle at LAC, 7:30

Thu Jan 19
Was at Mil, 7:30
Sea at Min, 7:00
+NY at Hou, 7:00
GS at Sac, 7:30
Pho at Por, 7:00

Fri Jan 20
LAL at Bos, 7:30
Phi at Was (Balt),
  7:30
SA at Mia, 7:30
NJ at Cha, 7:30
Hou at Det, 8:00
Atl at Ind, 7:30
Min at Chi, 7:30
NY at Dal, 7:30
●Orl at Den, 6:00
Cle at Uta, 7:00
Por at LAC, 7:30

Sat Jan 21
LAL at Phi, 7:30
Bos at Atl, 7:30
Det at Mil, 7:30
Sea at Dal, 7:30
Cle at Den, 7:00
Sac at LAC (Anah),
  7:30

Sun Jan 22
Was at NJ, 2:00
NY at Mia, 7:30
SA at Ind, 2:30
#Hou at Chi, 12:00
Cha at Min, 2:30
#Orl at Pho, 1:30
Sac at Por, 7:00

Mon Jan 23
LAL at Cha, 7:30
LAC at Cle, 7:30
Dal at Uta, 7:00

Tue Jan 24
Por at NY, 7:30
Bos at Orl, 7:30
Ind at Mia, 7:30
Phi at Det, 7:30
●SA at Chi, 7:00
Hou at Mil, 7:30
Pho at Min, 7:00
NJ at GS, 7:30
Dal at Sac, 7:30
Den at Sea, 7:00

Wed Jan 25
LAC at Bos, 7:30
Mil at Phi, 7:30
Atl at Cha, 7:30
Sac at Uta, 7:00
NJ at LAL, 7:30

Thu Jan 26
LAC at NY, 7:30
GS at Was, 7:30
+Chi at Orl, 8:00
Cle at Atl, 7:30
Por at Det, 7:30
Pho at Ind, 7:30
Hou at SA, 7:30
Uta at Sea, 7:00

Fri Jan 27
GS at Bos, 7:30
Pho at Phi, 7:30
●NY at Cha, 8:00
Por at Cle, 7:30
Mia at Mil, 7:30
Min at Dal, 7:30
NJ at Den, 7:00

Sat Jan 28
LAC at Was, 7:30
Mil at Orl, 7:30
Cha at Atl, 7:30
Mia at Det, 7:30
Phi at Ind, 7:30
Sac at Dal, 7:30
Min at Hou, 7:30
Den at SA, 7:30
NJ at Uta, 7:00
LAL at Sea, 12:30

Sun Jan 29
#Pho at NY, 12:00
#GS at Chi, 1:30

Mon Jan 30
Sea at Phi, 7:30
Atl at Mia, 7:30
Pho at Cle, 7:30
LAC at Det, 7:30
Min at Uta, 7:00
NJ at Por, 7:00

Tue Jan 31
GS at NY, 7:30
●Cha at Was, 8:00
Dal at Mil, 7:30
Den at Hou, 7:30
Chi at LAL, 7:30
SA at Sac, 7:30

Wed Feb 1
Cha at Bos, 7:30
Mil at NJ, 7:30
Was at Phi, 7:30
Det at Mia, 7:30
GS at Atl, 7:30
Cle at Ind, 7:30
Dal at Min, 7:30
Den at Uta, 7:00
LAL at Pho, 7:00
SA at Por, 7:00

Thu Feb 2
+Sea at Orl, 8:00
Cle at Det, 7:30
Uta at Hou, 7:30
Chi at Sac, 7:30

Fri Feb 3
NY at Phi, 7:30
Mia at Was, 7:30
Mil at Cha, 7:30
●Sea at Atl, 8:00
Orl at Ind, 7:30
Por at Min, 7:00
SA at Dal, 7:30
●Chi at Pho, 8:30
Den at LAL, 7:30
LAC at GS, 7:30

Sat Feb 4
Bos at NJ, 8:00
Ind at Cle, 7:30
Atl at Det, 7:30
Phi at Mil, 7:30

Uta at Dal, 7:30
Sac at SA, 7:30
LAL at LAC, 7:30

Sun Feb 5
Min at Bos, 7:00
#NY at Orl, 1:00
Sea at Mia, 1:00
Was at Cha, 2:00
#Hou at Pho, 1:30
Chi at GS, 5:00

Mon Feb 6
Det at NJ, 7:30
Atl at Phi, 7:30
Hou at Por, 7:00

Tue Feb 7
Mil at NY, 7:30
Ind at Cha, 7:30
Phi at Cle, 7:30
●GS at Min, 7:00
Pho at Dal, 7:30
LAL at Den, 7:00
Uta at LAC, 7:30
SA at Sea, 7:00

Wed Feb 8
Cle at Bos, 7:30
Dal at Orl, 7:30
Was at Mia, 7:30
NJ at Atl, 7:30
Cha at Det, 7:30
NY at Ind, 7:30
Min at Mil, 7:30
Pho at Uta, 7:00
SA at LAL, 7:30
Hou at Sac, 7:30
Chi at Por, 7:00

Thu Feb 9
+GS at Den, 6:00
Hou at LAC, 7:30
Chi at Sea, 7:00

Sun Feb 12
#All-Star Game
  (Pho), 4:00

Tue Feb 14
Cha at NJ, 7:30
Ind at Orl, 7:30
Mil at Mia, 7:30
NY at Det, 7:30
Was at Min, 7:00

Por at Dal, 7:30
LAC at Hou, 7:30
●Uta at SA, 7:00
Atl at Den, 7:00
Bos at Sac, 7:30
GS at Sea, 7:00

Wed Feb 15
Min at Phi, 7:30
Orl at Cle, 7:30
Det at Ind, 7:30
Was at Chi, 7:30
Por at Pho, 7:00
Sea at LAL, 7:30
Bos at GS, 7:30

Thu Feb 16
Den at NJ, 7:30
NY at Mia, 7:30
+Hou at Cha, 8:00
Cle at Mil, 7:30
SA at Uta, 7:00
LAL at Sac, 7:30

Fri Feb 17
Mia at NY, 7:30
Hou at Was, 7:30
Phi at Orl, 7:30
Det at Chi, 7:30
Ind at Min, 7:00
Atl at Dal, 7:30
●GS at Pho, 6:00
Bos at LAC, 7:30
Sea at Por, 7:00

Sat Feb 18
Cle at NJ, 7:30
Den at Phi, 7:30
Det at Cha, 7:30
Chi at Mil, 7:30
Atl at SA, 7:30
Bos at Uta, 7:00
Sea at GS, 7:30
LAC at Sac, 7:30

Sun Feb 19
#Hou at NY, 1:00
Den at Was, 6:00
Mia at Ind, 2:30
Orl at Min, 2:30
Uta at Pho, 7:00
Por at LAL, 6:30

Mon Feb 20
Chi at Cha, 7:30

Mia at Cle, 6:00
Sac at Det, 7:30
Orl at Mil, 7:30
Phi at GS, 7:30
LAL at Sea, 7:00

Tue Feb 21
Cle at NY, 7:30
Dal at Was, 7:30
Chi at Atl, 7:30
●SA at Hou, 7:00
LAC at Den, 7:30
Bos at Pho, 7:00
Min at Por, 7:00

Wed Feb 22
Ind at NJ, 7:30
Sac at Cha, 7:30
Was at Mil, 7:30
Pho at SA, 7:30
LAC at Uta, 7:00
Phi at LAL, 7:30
Por at GS, 7:30
Min at Sea, 7:00

Thu Feb 23
Orl at Bos (Hart), 7:30
Sac at NY, 7:30
Dal at Atl, 7:30
Det at Hou, 7:30
+Phi at Den, 6:00

Fri Feb 24
Dal at NJ, 7:30
Atl at Was (Balt), 7:30
Bos at Orl, 7:30
●Chi at Mia, 8:00
Ind at Mil, 7:30
Det at SA, 7:30
LAC at Pho, 7:00
Cha at LAL, 7:30
Uta at Por, 7:00
Den at Sea, 7:00

Sat Feb 25
Sac at Was, 7:30
NJ at Cle, 7:30
GS at Hou, 7:30
LAL at LAC, 7:30

Sun Feb 26
Phi at NY, 6:00
#Chi at Orl, 1:00

Dal at Ind, 2:30
Mia at Min, 2:30
GS at SA, 6:00
@Uta at Den, 1:30
@Cha at Pho, 1:30

Mon Feb 27
Ind at Bos, 7:30
Sac at Atl, 7:30
Mil at Det, 7:30
NJ at Chi, 7:30
Cle at Hou, 7:30
Uta at LAL, 7:30
LAC at Por, 7:00
Cha at Sea, 7:00

Tue Feb 28
Phi at Was, 7:30
●NY at Orl, 8:00
Mia at Mil, 7:30
Hou at Dal, 7:30
Cle at SA, 7:30
Min at Den, 7:00
Pho at LAC, 7:30

Wed Mar 1
Was at Bos, 7:30
Ind at Det, 7:30
Mia at Chi, 7:30
Pho at LAL, 7:30
Uta at GS, 7:30
Min at Sac, 7:30

Thu Mar 2
+Chi at NY, 7:30
Atl at Mil, 7:30
Cle at Dal, 7:30
+Orl at Hou, 8:30
Sea at LAC (Anah), 7:30
Cha at Por, 7:00

Fri Mar 3
Mil at Bos, 7:30
Phi at NJ, 7:30
Ind at Was, 7:30
Det at Atl, 7:30
Hou at Min, 7:00
Orl at SA, 7:30
Mia at Den, 7:00
●Sea at Pho, 6:00
Sac at LAL, 7:30
Cha at GS, 7:30

Sat Mar 4
Chi at Phi, 7:30
NY at Cle, 7:30
Bos at Ind, 7:30
Det at Dal, 7:30
Por at Uta, 1:30
Den at LAC, 7:30

Sun Mar 5
@Mil at NJ, 1:00
Atl at Orl, 7:30
Was at Mia, 1:00
@Hou at SA, 12:00
Min at LAL, 6:30
#Pho at GS, 12:30
Cha at Sac, 6:00

Mon Mar 6
Por at Chi, 7:30
Min at LAC, 7:30
GS at Sea, 7:00

Tue Mar 7
Bos at NY, 7:30
LAL at Mia, 7:30
Det at Cle, 7:30
Por at Mil, 7:30
Den at Dal, 7:30
●Pho at Hou, 7:00
Ind at SA, 7:30
Uta at Sac, 7:30

Wed Mar 8
NY at Bos, 7:30
NJ at Phi, 7:30
Det at Was, 7:30
LAL at Orl, 7:30
Den at Atl, 7:30
Sea at Min, 7:00
Dal at Uta, 7:30
LAC at GS, 7:30

Thu Mar 9
Por at Mia, 7:30
Sea at Cha, 7:30
+SA at Cle, 8:00
Ind at Sac, 7:30

Fri Mar 10
NJ at Bos, 7:30
SA at Phi, 7:30
Mil at Was (Balt), 7:30
Por at Orl, 7:30

NY at Atl, 7:30
Den at Det, 8:00
Cle at Chi, 7:30
LAL at Min, 7:00
Sac at Uta, 7:00
Ind at Pho, 7:00
GS at LAC, 7:30

Sat Mar 11
Sea at NY, 8:30
NJ at Was, 7:30
Mia at Cha, 7:30
LAL at Chi, 7:30
Dal at Hou, 7:30

Sun Mar 12
Atl at Bos, 2:30
Cle at Phi, 1:00
#SA at Orl, 12:00
Uta at Mia, 6:00
Sea at Det, 7:00
Den at Mil, 1:30
Por at Min, 2:30
GS at Pho, 7:00
Sac at LAC, 3:00

Mon Mar 13
Was at Cha, 7:30
●Hou at Atl, 8:00
Ind at LAL, 7:30
Dal at GS, 7:30

Tue Mar 14
●Den at NY, 8:00
Hou at Phi, 7:30
Chi at Was, 7:30
Uta at Orl, 7:30
Cha at Mil, 7:30
Min at SA, 7:30
Det at Pho, 7:00
Dal at Sac, 7:30
Mia at Por, 7:00
Bos at Sea, 7:00

Wed Mar 15
Orl at NJ, 7:30
Mil at Ind, 7:30
Atl at Chi, 7:30
Det at LAC, 7:30
LAL at GS, 7:30

Thu Mar 16
+Pho at Cha, 8:00
Uta at Cle, 7:30

Min at Hou, 7:30
Phi at SA, 7:30
Sac at Den, 7:00
Bos at Por, 7:00
Mia at Sea, 7:00

Fri Mar 17
Uta at NJ, 7:30
NY at Was, 7:30
Orl at Ind, 7:30
Mil at Chi, 7:30
Cle at Min, 7:00
Phi at Dal, 7:30
Mia at LAC, 7:30
Bos at LAL, 7:30
GS at Sac, 7:30

Sat Mar 18
NJ at NY, 7:30
Pho at Atl, 7:30
Dal at SA, 7:30
Por at Den, 7:00
Det at Sea, 12:30

Sun Mar 19
Cle at Was, 1:00
Pho at Mia, 6:00
@Uta at Cha, 12:00
@Chi at Ind, 12:00
Bos at Mil, 1:30
LAC at Min, 2:30
Phi at Hou, 2:30
Sac at LAL, 6:30
Det at GS, 5:00

Mon Mar 20
LAC at Atl, 7:30
Dal at Cle, 7:30
Sea at SA, 7:30
Den at Sac, 7:30

Tue Mar 21
Cha at NY, 7:30
●Pho at Orl, 8:00
Ind at Mia, 7:30
NJ at Det, 7:30
GS at Mil, 7:30
Sea at Hou, 7:30
Was at Por, 7:00

Wed Mar 22
Chi at Bos, 7:30
SA at NJ, 7:30
GS at Phi, 7:30

Mia at Atl, 7:30
Sac at Cle, 7:30
LAC at Ind, 7:30
Dal at Min, 7:00
Den at Uta, 7:00
Por at LAL, 7:30

Thu Mar 23
+Cha at Orl, 8:00
Dal at Det, 7:30
LAC at Mil, 7:30
Uta at Hou, 7:30
NY at Den, 7:00
Was at Sea, 7:00

Fri Mar 24
Bos at Phi, 7:30
GS at Mia, 7:30
Atl at Cle, 7:30
Sac at Ind, 7:30
Orl at Chi, 7:30
SA at Min, 7:00
Hou at Pho, 7:00
Was at LAL, 7:30
Sea at Por, 7:00

Sat Mar 25
Ind at Phi, 7:30
NJ at Mia, 7:30
Cle at Cha, 7:30
Chi at Atl, 7:30
Bos at Det, 7:30
SA at Mil, 7:30
Uta at Dal, 7:30
NY at LAC, 7:30

Sun Mar 26
#GS at Orl, 12:00
Sac at Min, 2:30
Hou at LAL, 6:30
Den at Por, 5:00
NY at Sea, 6:00

Mon Mar 27
SA at Det, 7:30
NJ at Ind, 7:30
LAC at Den, 7:00
Was at Uta, 7:00

Tue Mar 28
●Chi at NY, 8:00
GS at NJ, 7:30
Bos at Mia, 7:30
Mil at Dal, 7:30

LAL at Hou, 7:30
Uta at Pho, 7:00
Orl at Sac, 7:30
Atl at Por, 7:00

Wed Mar 29
Cha at Phi, 7:30
Mia at Was, 7:30
NY at Det, 7:30
Cle at Ind, 7:30
LAL at SA, 7:30
Min at Sea, 7:00

Thu Mar 30
Por at NJ, 7:30
Dal at Cha, 7:30
Bos at Chi, 7:30
Hou at LAC, 7:30
+Atl at GS, 5:00
Pho at Sac, 7:30

Fri Mar 31
Mia at Bos, 7:30
Dal at NY, 7:30
Por at Phi, 7:30
Was at Cle, 7:30
Den at Ind, 7:30
Mil at SA, 7:30
●Orl at Uta, 6:00
Min at Pho, 7:00
Atl at LAL, 7:30
Sac at Sea, 7:00

Sat Apr 1
Was at Det, 7:30
Phi at Chi, 7:30
Mil at Hou, 7:30
Uta at LAC (Anah),
7:30
Min at GS, 7:30

Sun Apr 2
Dal at Bos, 4:00
@NY at NJ, 1:30
Cha at Mia, 6:00
Den at Cle, 4:00
Por at Ind, 2:30
@Pho at SA, 12:30
Orl at LAL, 6:30
Atl at Sea, 1:00

Tue Apr 4
Ind at NY, 7:30
Phi at Mia, 7:30

Bos at Cle, 7:30
LAL at Den, 7:00
Sea at Uta, 7:00
SA at LAC, 7:30
●Pho at GS, 6:00
Hou at Sac, 7:30
Min at Por, 7:00

Wed Apr 5
Chi at NJ, 7:30
Det at Orl, 7:30
Phi at Cha, 7:30
Cle at Atl, 7:30
Was at Ind, 7:30
NY at Mil, 7:30
LAL at Dal, 7:30

Thu Apr 6
+Sea at Den, 6:00
Hou at GS, 7:30
SA at Sac, 7:30

Fri Apr 7
Phi at Bos, 7:30
Cha at Was, 7:30
●Ind at Atl, 8:00
Orl at Det, 8:00
Cle at Chi, 7:30
NJ at Mil, 7:30
Min at Dal, 7:30
Uta at LAL, 7:30
Hou at Por, 7:00

Sat Apr 8
Det at NY, 8:30
Mia at NJ, 7:30
Orl at Phi, 7:30
Sea at Dal, 7:30
SA at GS, 7:30
LAC at Sac, 7:30

Sun Apr 9
Bos at Was, 1:00
@Chi at Cle, 1:00
@Cha at Ind, 12:00
@Atl at Mil, 12:00

@Hou at Den, 1:30
SA at LAL, 6:30
@Pho at Por, 12:30

Mon Apr 10
Bos at Cha, 7:30
Den at Min, 7:00
GS at Dal, 7:30

Tue Apr 11
Mia at NY, 7:30
Atl at Phi, 7:30
Cle at Orl, 7:30
Ind at Chi, 7:30
Det at Mil, 7:30
Dal at Hou, 7:30
Por at SA, 7:30
LAL at Uta, 7:00
Sac at LAC, 7:30
●Pho at Sea, 6:00

Wed Apr 12
NJ at Cha, 7:30
Was at Atl, 7:30
Chi at Det, 7:30
GS at Min, 7:00
SA at Pho, 7:00
LAL at Sac, 7:30

Thu Apr 13
Orl at Bos, 7:30
Was at NY, 7:30
NJ at Phi, 7:30
Cle at Mia, 7:30
Por at Hou, 7:30
+GS at Uta, 6:00
Den at LAC, 7:30
Dal at Sea, 7:00

Fri Apr 14
Atl at Cle, 7:30
Cha at Det, 8:00
●NY at Ind, 7:00
Mil at Min, 7:00
Sac at SA, 7:30
Pho at Den, 7:00

Sat Apr 15
Det at Bos (Hart),
  7:30
Phi at NJ, 7:30
Mil at Was, 7:30
@Orl at Mia, 3:30
Sac at Hou, 7:30
LAC at Uta, 7:00
LAL at Pho, 7:00
@Sea at GS, 12:30
Dal at Por, 7:00

Sun Apr 16
@Atl at Cha, 3:00
Min at Ind, 2:30
#NY at Chi, 4:30
@SA at Den, 1:00
Dal at LAL, 6:30

Mon Apr 17
NJ at Bos, 7:30
Mil at NY, 7:30
Cha at Phi, 7:30
Was at Orl, 7:30
Chi at Mia, 7:30
LAC at Hou, 7:30
Por at Sea, 7:00

Tue Apr 18
Cle at Det, 7:30
Uta at Min, 7:00
LAC at Dal, 7:30
●Den at SA, 7:00
Sac at Pho, 7:00
Sea at LAL, 7:30
Por at GS, 7:30

Wed Apr 19
Atl at NJ, 7:30
Orl at Was, 7:30
Mia at Cle, 7:30
Phi at Ind, 7:30
Bos at Mil, 7:30
Min at Den, 7:00
Hou at Uta, 7:00

Thu Apr 20
+NY at Cha, 8:00
Det at Chi, 7:30
SA at Dal, 7:30
Sac at GS, 7:30
LAL at Por, 7:00
Hou at Sea, 7:00

Fri Apr 21
NY at Bos, 7:30
Was at NJ, 7:30
Mia at Phi, 7:30
●Ind at Orl, 8:00
Det at Atl, 7:30
Mil at Cle, 7:30
LAC at SA, 7:30
Min at Uta, 7:00
Dal at Pho, 7:00
Sea at Sac, 7:30

Sat Apr 22
@Cha at Chi, 2:30
Por at LAL, 7:30
@Den at GS, 12:30

Sun Apr 23
#Orl at NY, 1:00
Bos at NJ, 6:00
Phi at Was, 1:00
Det at Mia, 6:00
@Cle at Cha, 3:30
@Atl at Ind, 2:30
Chi at Mil, 1:30
SA at Min, 2:30
@Uta at Hou, 2:30
Sac at Den, 7:00
@Sea at Pho, 12:30
Dal at LAC, 3:00
GS at Por, 7:00

BASKETBALL HALL OF FAME

This section honors the 200 people and four teams that are enshrined in the Naismith Memorial Basketball Hall of Fame in Springfield, Mass-achusetts. Like the Hall of Fame, this section is divided into five categories: players, coaches, contributors, referees, and teams. The section includes bios on each member of the Hall. At the end of each bio is a date in parentheses; this is the year the member was enshrined into the Hall.

Abbreviations include BAA (Basketball Association of America), NBL (National Basketball League), ABA (American Basketball Association), and AAU (American Athletic Union). Others include NAIA (National Association of Intercollegiate Athlet-ics), NIT (National Invitational Tournament), NABC (National Association of Basketball Coaches), and USBWA (United States Basketball Writers Association).

PLAYERS

NATE ARCHIBALD

Guard: Small in stature at 6'1", "Tiny" Archibald was a giant on the court. After starring at Texas-El Paso, he began his pro career in Cincinnati in 1970-71. In 1972-73, he led the NBA in assists (11.4) and scoring (34.0). In 1980-81, he helped the Celtics win the NBA title. Archibald played in six All-Star Games and was league MVP in 1981. (1991)

PAUL ARIZIN

Forward: A star at Villanova, where he was college Player of the Year in 1950, the sharp-shooting Arizin averaged better than 22 PPG over his ten-year NBA ca-reer in Philadelphia. Known for his deadly jump shot, Arizin led the league in scoring in 1952 and '57 and led the Warriors to the NBA title in 1956. He retired with 16,266 points and ten All-Star Game ap-pearances. (1977)

TOM BARLOW

Forward: In the early years of this cen-tury, when the Eastern League was popu-lar, "Babe" Barlow was among the game's most exciting players. A pro at age 16,

Babe enjoyed 20 seasons of roundball (from 1912-32). Barlow was known as much for his defensive skills as for his scoring. (1980)

RICK BARRY

Forward: One of the game's most accu-rate shooters, Barry starred at Miami of Florida. In 1965, Rick led the NCAA with an average of 37.4 PPG. As a pro, he played in both the ABA and NBA and is the only player to lead both leagues in scoring. His career NBA free throw pct. was .900, a record that held until 1992-93. In 1975, he led the Golden State Warriors to the NBA title. (1986)

ELGIN BAYLOR

Forward: Baylor was considered the most devastating, artistic forward of his era. After a spectacular college career in which he led Seattle to the NCAA finals in 1958, Baylor debuted in the NBA in 1958-59. He averaged 24.9 PPG as a rookie with Minneapolis and won Rookie of the Year honors. Over his 14-year career, he averaged 27.4 points per game. (1976)

JOHNNY BECKMAN

Forward: From 1910 until the 1940s, Beckman was often called the Babe Ruth of basketball. A star in the Interstate, New York State, and Eastern Leagues, Beckman eventually joined the Original Celtics. As their captain, he led them to some of their greatest years. (1972)

WALT BELLAMY

Center: After playing for Indiana University and the 1960 gold-medal-winning Olympic team, Bellamy became NBA Rookie of the Year with the 1962 Chicago Packers, averaging 31.6 PPG and 19.0 RPG. He played 14 NBA seasons with six different teams, averaging 20.1 PPG and 13.7 RPG. (1993)

SERGEI BELOV

Guard: Belov was considered a basketball magician who could score at will. The 6'3" guard led the Russian national team to four European and two world championships. In the Olympics, he helped the Soviet national team to one gold medal (1972) and three bronze medals. (1992)

CAROL BLAZEJOWSKI

Guard: Only Pete Maravich scored more points in college than Blazejowski. At 5'10", the "Blaze" totaled 3,199 points during her career (31.7 PPG) at New Jersey's Montclair State College. She was the first recipient of the Wade Trophy and was a three-time All-American. (1994)

BENNIE BORGMANN

Guard: Though only 5'8", Borgmann was one of the most popular touring pros on the East Coast in the early years. His pro career spanned over 2,500 games in various Eastern leagues. It wasn't unusual for Borgmann to score half of his team's points during any given game. He later coached both at the college and professional level. (1961)

BILL BRADLEY

Forward: "Dollar Bill" Bradley was an intelligent player with a graceful, deadly shooting touch. As a three-time All-American at Princeton, he averaged 30 PPG and was the 1965 college Player of the Year. In 1964, he helped the U.S. win the Olympic gold medal. A Rhodes Scholar, Bradley played ten seasons with the New York Knicks, amassing 9,217 points, 2,533 assists, and two NBA championship rings. He is currently a U.S. senator in New Jersey. (1982)

JOE BRENNAN

Forward: "Poison Joe" Brennan enjoyed a 17-year pro career, starting at age 19 when he joined the Brooklyn Visitation and led them to their greatest years. In 1950, the New York Basketball Old-Timers voted Brennan second only to Johnny Beckman as the greatest player of his era. (1974)

AL CERVI

Guard: An outstanding clutch performer, Cervi was an immediate star with the NBL's Buffalo Bisons. His pro career was interrupted by a five-year stint in World War II, but he resumed his career in 1945, playing for the Rochester Royals. In 1948, he became a player/coach for the Syracuse Nats. He was named Coach of the Year five times in the next eight seasons. (1984)

WILT CHAMBERLAIN

Center: At 7'1", Wilt "The Stilt" Chamberlain was an awesome, dominant figure on the court. After two All-America years at Kansas, Wilt spent a year with the Harlem Globetrotters before entering the NBA in 1959. In just his first year, he was named the NBA's MVP. During 14 years, he was the league MVP four times (1960, 1966-68). He still holds NBA records for career rebounds (23,924), season scoring average (50.4 in 1961-62), and most points in a game (100). He won world titles with Philadelphia (1967) and Los Angeles ('72). (1978)

CHARLES COOPER

Center: In his day, "Tarzan" Cooper was a giant among men. The 6'4", 214-pound Cooper was a consistent winner for 20 years of pro basketball. In 11 years with the New York Renaissance, his teams compiled a record of 1,303-203. In 1932-33, the club won 88 straight games. He has been called the greatest center of his day. (1976)

BOB COUSY

Guard: At 6'1", Cousy made his name as the most sensational passer the game had ever known. After three All-America years at Holy Cross, "Mr. Basketball" joined the Boston Celtics in 1950. Eventually, he led them to six NBA titles, including five in a row (1959-63). He led the league in assists for eight straight years (1953-60) and played in 13 consecutive All-Star Games. (1970)

DAVE COWENS

Center: Cowens was a tough, physical player. "The Redhead" starred at Florida State, where he averaged 19 points and 17 rebounds per game. In his first NBA season with Boston, he was Co-Rookie of the Year. In ten seasons with the Celtics, he won two championships (1974 and '76) and was player/coach for a year. In his career, Cowens averaged 17.6 PPG and collected 10,444 rebounds. (1991)

BILLY CUNNINGHAM

Guard: A scrappy playmaker at North Carolina, Cunningham debuted with the 76ers in 1965. In 11 pro seasons (including two with the ABA Carolina Cougars), Cunningham made the All-NBA first team three times and was named ABA MVP in 1973. In 770 pro games, he averaged 21.8 PPG. He became the 76ers' coach in 1978, bringing them a 454-196 record over eight seasons, including a league title in 1983. (1985)

BOB DAVIES

Guard: Davies has been called the "first superstar of modern pro basketball." A two-time All-American at Seton Hall, Davies turned pro in 1945 with Rochester. In ten BAA and NBA seasons, he was all-league seven times. He led the Royals to league titles in 1946, '47, and '51. His patented behind-the-back dribble made him popular with fans. (1969)

FORREST DeBERNARDI

Forward/Guard/Center: DeBernardi's career revolved around AAU tournaments. He was an AAU All-American in 1921, '22, and '23 and won four AAU titles. In 11 AAU tournaments, "De" was all-tournament seven times. He starred at three different positions. (1961)

DAVE DeBUSSCHERE

Forward: DeBusschere was one of the game's great defensive forwards. After three All-America years at the University of Detroit, DeBusschere debuted with his hometown Pistons in 1962. Two years later, at age 24, he became the Pistons' player/coach. He was traded to the Knicks in 1969 and helped them to two championships (1970 and '73). In 875 games, he amassed 14,053 points and 9,618 rebounds. (1982)

DUTCH DEHNERT

Guard: Without Henry "Dutch" Dehnert, there might never have been a three-second rule in basketball. Back in the 1920s, playing for the powerful Celtics, Dehnert inadvertently invented pivot play when he routinely stationed himself at the foul line to relay passes back and forth to weaving teammates. Though he didn't play either high school or college ball, Dehnert honed his skills in Eastern pro leagues. (1968)

PAUL ENDACOTT

Guard: Endacott attended Kansas, where he achieved status as "the greatest player ever coached" by Kansas' Phog Allen. Endacott was selected as Player of the Year in 1923. In 1969, he received the Sportsmen's World Award in basketball, because his "exemplary personal conduct has made him an outstanding inspiration for youth to emulate." (1971)

JULIUS ERVING

Forward: An extraordinary leaper, the spectacular Dr. J. had the ability to change directions in mid-air. The Massachusetts alum brought attention to the ABA, where he averaged 28.7 PPG and 12.1 RPG in five seasons. With the NBA's 76ers, he was named to 11 All-Star Games, averaged 22.0 PPG, and led his 1983 team to the world title. He's one of three ABA/NBA players to reach 30,000 points. (1993)

BUD FOSTER

Guard: Harold "Bud" Foster, a star player in college, also excelled as a coach. As a senior at Wisconsin in 1930, he earned All-America honors. Foster played briefly as a pro before embarking on a glorious 25-year career as a coach. He guided Wisconsin to three Big Ten titles and the NCAA championship (1941). (1964)

WALT FRAZIER

Guard: A smooth guard known for sleek passing and laser-accurate shooting, "Clyde" Frazier played 13 seasons in the NBA, including ten with the New York Knicks. Frazier helped the Knicks to league titles in 1970 and 1973, played in seven All-Star Games, was a celebrated defensive wizard, and finished his career with an average of 18.9 PPG. (1986)

MARTY FRIEDMAN

Guard: A turn-of-the-century hero, Max "Marty" Friedman was one of a pair of hoops stars known as the "Heavenly Twins" (his counterpart was Barney Sedran). Friedman was one of the great defensive players of his era. He played in six Eastern leagues and, in 1915, helped Carbondale win 35 straight games. He later won accolades as well as championships as a coach. (1971)

JOE FULKS

Forward: "Jumping Joe" Fulks was one of the first scoring superstars of the BAA and NBA. An ambidextrous jump-shot artist, Fulks shocked the BAA in 1946-47 by scoring 23.2 points per game for Philadelphia. Two years later, he averaged 26.0 PPG and was named *The Sporting News* Athlete of the Year for 1949. (1977)

LADDIE GALE

Forward: Lauren "Laddie" Gale's excellence on the court helped bring recognition to the basketball programs in the Pacific Northwest. Gale was an All-American at Oregon, and in 1939 he led his school to the NCAA title. Gale played professionally and was also a successful coach. (1976)

HARRY GALLATIN

Center: A large center for his time (6'6"), Harry "The Horse" Gallatin was the centerpiece of the New York Knicks for nine years. Gallatin established a consecutive-games-played record (746) that included regular-season, playoff, All-Star, and exhibition contests. In 1953-54, he led the NBA in rebounds (1,098). He later went on to a successful coaching career at the pro and college levels. (1991)

WILLIAM GATES

Guard: In 1938, "Pop" Gates led Benjamin Franklin (New York) to a high school title. In 1939, he helped the New York Renaissance to 68 straight victories and a World Professional Championship.

Throughout his 12-year career, he played for many outstanding teams, including the Harlem Globetrotters, where he was a player/coach from 1950-55. (1988)

TOM GOLA
Forward: Gola combined outstanding scoring prowess with defensive wizardry to become one of the most respected all-around players in the game. At La Salle in the mid-1950s, Gola was a four-year All-American, averaging 21 points and 20 rebounds per game. He played ten years professionally with Philadelphia, San Francisco, and New York, scoring 7,871 points. He was often high in assists and rebounds. (1975)

HAL GREER
Guard: Greer was the first black scholarship athlete to attend Marshall (1955-59) and earned All-America status in 1958. He played five years with the Syracuse Nationals before joining the powerful Philadelphia 76ers for another ten seasons. He recorded 21,586 career points, was named to ten All-Star Games, and won a world title in 1967. (1981)

ROBERT GRUENIG
Center: A 6'8" center with a shooter's touch, "Ace" Gruenig was a brilliant AAU performer. He shined in the AAU from 1931 until he retired in the late 1940s. From 1937-48, he was the annual choice as first-team all-tournament center. In 1943, he received the Los Angeles Sports Award Medallion as the nation's greatest player. (1963)

CLIFF HAGAN
Forward: At Kentucky, Hagan was a two-time All-American (1952 and '54) who led his Wildcats to an NCAA title in 1951 and a perfect 25-0 record in 1954. During ten years in the NBA with the St. Louis Hawks, he scored 13,447 points, relying heavily on his amazingly accurate hook shot. He appeared in four All-Star Games and helped the Hawks win the league title in 1958. He also played three years in the ABA, serving as player/coach for the Dallas Chaparrals. (1977)

VICTOR HANSON
Guard: Hanson starred at Syracuse in basketball, football, and baseball. He was a three-time All-American in hoops (1925-27), winning a national championship in 1926. In his senior campaign, Hanson was the college Player of the Year. He later played pro ball with the Cleveland Rosenblums, and he also played minor-league baseball in the New York Yankees' farm system. (1960)

LUSIA HARRIS
Center: During her career at Delta State, the 6'3" Harris became one of women's basketball's early superstars. She finished her career with 2,981 points (25.9 PPG) and 1,662 rebounds (14.4 RPG). Harris was a three-time All-American and won three national titles (1975-77). She also played on the 1976 Olympic team. (1992)

JOHN HAVLICEK
Forward: After leading Ohio State to three NCAA finals and one championship, "Hondo" Havlicek embarked on a 16-year NBA career with Boston. Havlicek began as the Celts' sixth man, ultimately earned a starting spot, and was later named team captain. In his career, he scored 26,395 points, appeared in 13 All-Star Games, and was an eight-time member of the NBA All-Defensive Team. (1983)

CONNIE HAWKINS
Forward: Hawkins, similar in style to Julius Erving, left Iowa during his freshman year and played two years with the Harlem Globetrotters (1964-66). In the ABA's inaugural season, he was named league MVP after leading Pittsburgh to the title. Hawkins played seven NBA sea-

sons with Phoenix, Los Angeles, and Atlanta, averaging 16.5 PPG and 7.9 RPG. (1992)

ELVIN HAYES

Forward: The 6'9" Hayes used strength, speed, and grace to achieve amazing results. At Houston, "The Big E." was a three-time All-American and 1968 college Player of the Year. Hayes led the NBA in scoring as a rookie and went on to play 16 years with San Diego, the Bullets, and Houston. In 1977-78, he led the Bullets to the NBA title. He played exactly 50,000 NBA minutes—second most in league history. He scored 27,313 points. (1989)

TOMMY HEINSOHN

Forward: A two-time All-American at Holy Cross, Heinsohn became the NBA Rookie of the Year for Boston in 1957 and started for the champion Celtics for the next eight seasons. Heinsohn, who was named to six All-Star Games, averaged 18.6 PPG over his career. In 1970, he took over as coach. He guided Boston to a 427-263 record and two NBA titles. (1985)

NAT HOLMAN

Guard: Holman, who gained fame as coach of the City College of New York Beavers, was also a player of note from 1916-33. Holman joined the Original Celtics in 1920, stayed nine seasons, and was one of their greatest players, exploiting his skills as a passer, shooter, and strategist. In 1933, he retired from playing to concentrate on coaching. In 1950, his Beavers won both the NIT and NCAA titles, which no team had ever done before. (1964)

BOB HOUBREGS

Center: Houbregs was an All-American with Washington in 1953, leading the Huskies to a third-place finish in the '53 NCAA Tournament. Houbregs held the second-highest scoring average in NCAA Tournament history (34.8 PPG) before being drafted by Milwaukee. He played five years in the NBA and later served as G.M. of the Seattle SuperSonics from 1970-73. (1986)

CHUCK HYATT

Forward: One of the finest amateur players of the century, Hyatt starred at the University of Pittsburgh from 1927-30 and was a three-time All-American. He was the top scorer in the nation in 1930. The Panthers were 60-7 during Hyatt's career, winning national titles in 1928 and '30. He later joined the Phillips 66 Oilers and became a legend of the AAU circuit. (1959)

DAN ISSEL

Forward: After averaging 25.8 PPG in college at Kentucky, Issel continued to smoke the nets in the ABA (six years, 25.6 PPG) and the NBA (nine years, all with Denver, 20.4 PPG). Though a solid rebounder, Issel will forever be known for his scoring, as he tallied 27,482 points in his pro career. He became coach of the Nuggets in 1992-93. (1993)

HARRY JEANNETTE

Guard: From 1938-48, "Buddy" Jeannette was regarded as basketball's top backcourt player. He was adept at passing, clutch shooting, and defense. Jeannette garnered four MVP Awards in the NBL and ABL and played on five championship teams. He also coached for Georgetown and in the NBA (Baltimore). (1994)

WILLIAM JOHNSON

Center: Tall and lanky, "Skinny" Johnson was a dominant center for Kansas from 1930-33. He guided his squad to a record of 42-11 and three Big Six championships. In 1934, as an AAU star, he was the top scorer in the Missouri Valley. In 1975, he was named an All-Time Great in Oklahoma, his home state. (1976)

NEIL JOHNSTON

Center: After two years at Ohio State, the 6'8" Johnston tried his luck as a pitcher, signing a pro baseball contract. A sore arm turned him back to basketball, where he joined the Philadelphia Warriors in 1951. In eight seasons, he led the NBA in scoring and field goal percentage three times, led in rebounding once, and helped the Warriors win the title in 1956. A knee injury ended his playing career, but he stayed in the game as a coach, a scout, and an athletic director. (1989)

K.C. JONES

Guard: After starring in college at San Francisco, Jones joined the Boston Celtics in 1958 and stayed for nine years, where he was a dependable guard on their great teams. As a coach, Jones won more than 500 NBA games, including 308 with the Celts. He was involved in 11 titles in Boston—eight as a player, one as an assistant coach, and two as head coach (1984 and '86). (1988)

SAM JONES

Guard: After playing brilliantly at tiny North Carolina College, Jones cracked the Celtics lineup in 1958 and became part of ten championship teams. He led the club in scoring three times and averaged 25.9 PPG in 1964-65. His patented jump shot off the glass was feared around the NBA. (1983)

EDWARD KRAUSE

Center: A star at Notre Dame in the early 1930s, Krause was a three-time All-American in two sports—basketball and football. At 6'3", 215 pounds, he was considered the first "agile" center. "Moose" later played professionally in the Midwest and New England before returning to the college scene as a coach and athletic director. (1975)

BOB KURLAND

Center: The first of the truly great seven-foot centers, Kurland carved out one of the most impressive amateur careers ever. At Oklahoma State, he led his squad to NCAA titles in 1945 and '46, leading the nation in scoring the latter year. He later played six seasons of AAU ball with the Phillips 66 Oilers, where he was All-AAU each year and an Olympian in 1948 and '52. (1961)

BOB LANIER

Center: A two-time All-American at St. Bonaventure, Lanier debuted with Detroit in 1970. A strong, no-nonsense center, Lanier played in eight All-Star Games and tallied 19,248 points and 9,698 rebounds in his career. In each of Lanier's five seasons in Milwaukee, the Bucks won the Central Division title. (1992)

JOE LAPCHICK

Center: The son of immigrants, Lapchick began playing professional basketball at age 17 without a high school education. The 6'5" center played in several leagues and centered the Original Celtics from 1923-27. Later, he became a great coach, leading St. John's to four NIT titles. He also coached the New York Knicks for nine seasons. (1966)

CLYDE LOVELLETTE

Center: Lovellette was a winner wherever he played. As a college star at Kansas, he was a three-time All-American (1950-52) and the Big Seven scoring champion each year. In 1952, he led the nation in scoring and guided the Jayhawks to the NCAA title. He played for the 1952 gold-medal Olympic team before starting an 11-year NBA career. He played with the champion Minneapolis Lakers in 1954 and later won titles with the 1963 and '64 Boston Celtics. (1987)

JERRY LUCAS

Forward: A fine shooter, passer, and defensive ace, Lucas was a two-time college Player of the Year at Ohio State, where his team captured an NCAA title. He also helped the U.S. win the gold in the 1960 Olympics. In 1963-64 with Cincinnati, Lucas was the NBA's Rookie of the Year. He went on to play in seven All-Star Games and was part of the New York Knicks' 1973 championship team. He finished his career with 14,053 points and 12,942 rebounds. (1979)

HANK LUISETTI

Forward: Luisetti was a revolutionary who broke old standards by developing a one-handed shot. In three seasons at Stanford, Hank led his squad to successive Pacific Coast Conference titles. An All-American in 1937 and '38, Luisetti was the first college player ever to score 50 points in a game. He later starred on the AAU scene. (1959)

ED MACAULEY

Forward: "Easy Ed" Macauley was a four-time All-American at St. Louis (1946-49). In 1947, he led the nation with a .524 shooting percentage, and he was MVP of the NIT the following year. Macauley played ten NBA seasons, earning seven All-Star Game appearances and netting 11,234 career points. (1960)

PETE MARAVICH

Forward: Maravich, one of the greatest gunners in history, shattered many NCAA records, including highest career scoring average (44.2). Maravich starred at Louisiana State, earning three All-America berths and college Player of the Year honors in 1970. "Pistol Pete" played NBA ball with Atlanta, the Jazz, and Boston. In 658 NBA games, he averaged 24.2 PPG. In 1976-77, he led the league in scoring with a 31.1 average. (1986)

SLATER MARTIN

Guard: At 5'10", "Dugie" Martin was the first "small superstar" of the NBA, playing in the 1950s. After three outstanding years at Texas, Martin joined the NBA. He played for four league championship teams in Minneapolis before moving to St. Louis, where he helped the Hawks win the 1958 title. In 11 seasons, he tallied 3,160 assists and earned a reputation as a defensive genius. (1981)

BRANCH McCRACKEN

Forward: McCracken starred for three years at Indiana University, winning the conference MVP Award in 1928. During his career, he scored nearly one-third of all the points recorded by the Hoosiers. He later had great success as a coach, winning four Big Ten and two NCAA titles at Indiana. (1960)

JACK McCRACKEN

Center: A two-time All-American at N.W. Missouri State (1931-32), McCracken was known for his outstanding passing and domination of the backboards. As a star of the AAU circuit, he was an eight-time All-American between 1932 and 1945 and won two AAU championships. (1962)

BOBBY McDERMOTT

Forward: McDermott turned pro as a teenager and played for 17 years. He was a seven-time NBL All-Star, won five straight MVP Awards, and led the league twice in scoring. He was a champion with Brooklyn, Fort Wayne, Chicago, and the Original Celtics. (1987)

DICK McGUIRE

Guard: McGuire, an All-American at St. John's, helped the New York Knicks to three straight NBA Finals (1951-53). Though he averaged just 8.0 PPG in 11 NBA seasons with New York and Detroit, McGuire made seven All-Star Games thanks to his point-guard skills. (1993)

ANN MEYERS

Guard: Meyers, of UCLA, was women's basketball's first four-time All-American. She also helped the 1976 Olympic team to a silver medal. In 1979, Meyers became the first and only woman to sign with an NBA club (Indiana Pacers), although she didn't make the team. (1993)

GEORGE MIKAN

Center: The game's first dominating big man, the 6'10" Mikan was a three-time NBA scoring leader and played in the first four NBA All-Star Games. Previously, he was a three-time All-American at DePaul and twice was named college Player of the Year (1945 and '46), leading the nation in scoring in both of those years. Mikan played on five NBA title teams in Minneapolis. (1959)

EARL MONROE

Guard: Earl "The Pearl" Monroe's slick ball-handling and dead-eye shooting made him a prolific scorer and crowd-pleaser. A two-time All-American at Winston-Salem State, he was drafted by Baltimore and was the NBA Rookie of the Year in 1968. He spent 13 years in the NBA and helped the New York Knicks win the 1973 league title. An amazing clutch player, Monroe set an NBA record for most points (13) in a single overtime period. (1989)

CALVIN MURPHY

Guard: The 5'9" Murphy was a brilliant free throw shooter, canning 78 straight with Houston in 1980-81, the year he shot a record .958 overall. The mighty mite averaged 33.1 PPG as a three-time All-American at Niagara. He scored 17.9 per game in his 13 NBA seasons, all with the Rockets. (1993)

STRETCH MURPHY

Center: Murphy was one of the most feared big men of his time, as he helped Purdue to a Big Ten title in 1928. A two-time All-American, Murphy set a Western Conference and Big Ten scoring mark when he netted 143 points in 1929. In his senior year, 1930, he captained Purdue to an undefeated record. (1960)

PAT PAGE

Forward: An outstanding defensive player and a star in three sports, Page led his University of Chicago squad to Western Conference titles in 1907, 1909 (when they were undefeated), and 1910. In 1910, Page was named college Player of the Year. He later coached at Chicago, Butler, and the College of Idaho. (1962)

BOB PETTIT

Forward: A three-time All-American at Louisiana State (1952-54), Pettit played ten NBA seasons with the St. Louis Hawks. He was named NBA MVP in 1956 and '59. He led the Hawks to the league title in 1958. He finished as the greatest scorer in league history with 20,880 points. (1970)

ANDY PHILLIP

Guard: One of the stars of the University of Illinois' "Whiz Kids," Phillip set Big Ten scoring marks in 1942 and '43 and once scored 40 points in a game. Phillip's college career was disrupted by three years in World War II. However, he returned to Illinois and enjoyed an All-America year in 1947. He later played in the BAA and NBA for more than a decade. (1961)

JIM POLLARD

Forward: After earning All-America status at Stanford, Pollard entered the military, where he was a Service All-Star. He led Stanford to an NCAA championship in 1942 and later starred in the AAU circuit, winning MVP honors in 1947 and '48. He joined the Minneapolis Lakers in 1949 and helped them to five league championships. (1977)

FRANK RAMSEY

Guard: A two-time All-American while playing at Kentucky (1952 and '54), Ramsey joined the Boston Celtics and revolutionized the game by "inventing" the sixth-man position. Ramsey won seven titles in nine NBA seasons. He was called "the most versatile player in the NBA" by his longtime coach, Red Auerbach. (1981)

WILLIS REED

Center: One of the most intense competitors of his time, Reed began as a two-time All-American at Grambling. In ten pro seasons with the New York Knicks, he won two NBA titles (1970 and '73), was Rookie of the Year (1964-65), and played in seven All-Star Games. He averaged 18.7 PPG in his career and grabbed 8,414 boards. (1981)

OSCAR ROBERTSON

Guard: One of the greatest all-around players ever, "The Big O," starred at the University of Cincinnati, where he was a two-time college Player of the Year and a three-time scoring leader among major-college players. As a pro for Cincinnati, he was league MVP in 1964. Later, he led the Milwaukee Bucks to the 1971 NBA title. He finished his career with 26,710 points (25.7 PPG) and set an NBA record with 9,887 assists. (1979)

JOHN ROOSMA

Forward: Roosma made his mark on the game as a member of the U.S. Army squad. In his Army career, he scored more than 1,000 points, including 354 in one season. Roosma, whose Army team went 70-3 during his tenure, served in the military for 30 years and retired as an Army colonel in 1956. (1961)

BILL RUSSELL

Center: Russell reigns as one of the great winners and rebounders of all time. As a collegian, he was Player of the Year in 1956 for San Francisco and also led his school to two NCAA titles. He then led the U.S. to gold in the 1956 Olympic Games. As a pro, he helped the Celtics to eight straight NBA crowns (1959-66) and 11 in 13 years. He collected 21,620 rebounds, averaged 15.1 PPG, and was league MVP five times. As player/coach, he led the Celts to titles in 1968 and '69. (1974)

HONEY RUSSELL

Guard: A great defensive player, John "Honey" Russell played against the best players in virtually every professional league during his 28-year career. He led the Cleveland Rosenblums to five straight titles (1925-29) and later coached his alma mater, Seton Hall, to nearly 300 victories, including a string of 44 straight. In 1946-47, he became the first coach of the NBA Boston Celtics. (1964)

DOLPH SCHAYES

Forward: Schayes played his college ball at New York University, where he was an All-American in 1948. In 15 seasons with the Syracuse Nationals, he was one of the game's great scorers, chalking up 19,249 points (18.2 per game). From February 1952 to December 1961, he played in a record 765 straight games. Later, he was named Coach of the Year in 1966 when he guided the Philadelphia 76ers to a division title. (1972)

ERNEST SCHMIDT

Forward: Schmidt was known as "One Grand Schmidt" after scoring 1,000 career points in his Kansas State Teachers College days. He was a four-time conference all-star in the early 1930s and was widely recognized as the greatest player ever to come out of the Missouri Valley. Later, he suited up for three seasons on the AAU circuit, playing for Denver and Reno. (1973)

JOHN SCHOMMER

Center: A star in basketball, football, baseball, and track, Schommer led the Chicago Maroon basketball squad to three straight Big Ten titles (1907-09) and was the conference scoring leader all three years. He also enjoyed a 47-year career as athletic director, coach, and teacher at Illinois Institute of Technology. In 1949, the Helms Foundation named him a center on its All-Time All-America Team. (1959)

BARNEY SEDRAN

Guard: At 5'4", Sedran proved that size truly wasn't everything. Despite being banished from high school basketball, Sedran starred at City College of New York and was his team's leading scorer three years in a row. Upon his graduation in 1911, he embarked on a 15-year pro career that included ten championships. He helped Carbondale to 35 straight victories in 1914-15 and later was a coach for another 20 years. (1962)

JULIANA SEMENOVA

Center: The Soviet seven-footer dominated her international opponents, winning two Olympic gold medals (1976 and 1980) and three world championship golds. Semenova never lost a game in 18 years of international competition. (1993)

BILL SHARMAN

Guard: After two All-America years at Southern California, the sharp-shooting Sharman enjoyed an 11-year stint in the NBA, where he played on four championship Boston Celtics teams in the 1950s and early 1960s. Sharman's secret weapon was free throw shooting. His career 88-percent mark is among the best ever. After retiring with 12,665 points, he won titles as a coach in the ABA and NBA. (1975)

CHRISTIAN STEINMETZ

Guard: The "father of Wisconsin basketball," Christian Steinmetz turned basketball into a recognized sport at the University of Wisconsin. As a senior in 1905, he set school scoring records (some of which would stand for the next 50 years) including most points in a game (50) and most points in a season (462). (1961)

JOHN THOMPSON

Guard: A star at Montana State, John "Cat" Thompson was selected to All-Rocky Mountain Conference teams for four years in a row. In 1929, they were the Helms national champions and the Cat was named Player of the Year. Thompson eventually became a coach, where he remained for 14 years. (1962)

NATE THURMOND

Center: An All-American at Bowling Green, Thurmond was a defensive genius with strong shooting skills. In his 14-year NBA career, he averaged 15 points and 15 rebounds per game. In a 1974 game, he became the first to record a "quadruple-double." Playing for several NBA teams, Thurmond was named to seven All-Star Games. (1984)

JACK TWYMAN

Forward: An All-American at Cincinnati, Jack Twyman joined the Rochester Royals in 1955-56. In 11 NBA seasons, he scored 15,840 points. A durable forward with precision shooting skills, Twyman played 823 games (including a stretch of 609 consecutively) and averaged 19.2 PPG. He also played on six All-Star teams. (1982)

WES UNSELD

Center: After an explosive career at Louisville, where he was an All-American in 1967 and '68, Unseld entered the NBA with an equally loud bang in 1968-69, when he was the NBA's MVP for the Baltimore Bullets. Unseld led the Bullets to an NBA title in 1978. In his career, he averaged 14 boards a game and played in five All-Star Games. He also served as coach of the Washington Bullets. (1987)

FUZZY VANDIVIER

Guard: Robert "Fuzzy" Vandivier became one of the greatest players in the history of Indiana basketball. He took his perennial-champion Franklin High School team directly to Franklin College in 1922 and helped establish a legendary squad. He is a member of the All-Time All-Star Five of Indiana. (1974)

ED WACHTER

Center: As a turn-of-the-century player, Wachter starred on nearly every team in the Eastern circuit. He was an annual scoring champion and a member of more title-winning clubs than anyone else of his time. Later, as a coach at Harvard, he founded the New England Basketball Association and struggled to gain national uniformity of rules and regulations. (1961)

BILL WALTON

Center: The big redhead carried UCLA to an 86-4 record and two NCAA titles (1972-73), earning college Player of the Year awards from 1972-74. Though he sat out four different NBA seasons because of injuries, he helped both Portland (1977) and Boston (1986) to NBA titles. Walton was named league MVP in 1977-78 with Portland. (1993)

BOBBY WANZER

Guard: An All-American at Seton Hall in 1946, Wanzer played for ten seasons with the Rochester Royals. He was the NBA's MVP in 1952-53, two years after helping the Royals win the 1951 NBA title. An outstanding shooter, Wanzer led the league in free throw accuracy (90 percent) in 1951-52. Later, he coached the Royals for three years. (1986)

JERRY WEST

Guard: One of the greatest high-pressure performers of all time, Jerry West earned his nickname "Mr. Clutch" during 14 seasons with the Los Angeles Lakers. A two-time All-American while at West Virginia, West averaged 27.0 PPG in the NBA. He was also named to 14 All-Star Games and helped the Lakers win the 1972 NBA title. (1979)

NERA WHITE

Center: The 6'1" White was one of the most complete female players of all time. From 1955-69, she led a team sponsored by Nashville Business College to ten AAU national championships. She was named the AAU tournament's MVP ten times and an AAU All-American 15 years in a row. In 1957-58, White led the U.S. to the world championship. (1992)

LENNY WILKENS

Guard: A leader and a winner, Lenny Wilkens enjoyed success at every level of the game. As an All-American at Providence College, he was the 1960 NIT MVP. Wilkens, a 6'1" guard, went on to play 15 seasons in the NBA, averaging 16.5 PPG and making nine All-Star appearances. He later coached the Seattle SuperSonics, one of his former teams, to the 1979 NBA championship. As an NBA coach, he has won over 900 games. (1988)

JOHN WOODEN

Forward: Before becoming one of basketball's greatest coaches, Wooden was an outstanding player in his own right. A three-time All-American at Purdue (1930-32) and college Player of the Year (1932), he set a Big Ten scoring record in his senior year and led his team to the national title. Wooden later starred as a pro for Indianapolis' Kautsky Grocers, where he once hit 138 straight free throws. (1960)

COACHES

PHOG ALLEN

Forrest "Phog" Allen was one of the game's greatest coaches. In his nearly 40 years of coaching, much of it at his alma mater (Kansas), Allen's teams won 31 championships, three national titles, and 746 games. He co-founded the National Association of Basketball Coaches in 1927. (1959)

HAROLD ANDERSON

Anderson earned 11 letters in three sports before turning to coaching at age 23. After nine years coaching high school ball, he moved to the University of Toledo in 1934. There, he went 142-41. In over 20 years at Bowling Green, he made several trips to NCAA Tournaments and NITs. His coaching record was 504-226. (1984)

RED AUERBACH

Called by many "the greatest coach in the history of the NBA," Red Auerbach is the only coach ever to win more than 1,000 games in pro basketball. A player at George Washington, Auerbach joined the burgeoning NBA as a coach in 1946. He took the job at Boston in 1950 and led the Celtics to nine NBA titles, including eight straight from 1959-66. He has been a part of the Celtic front office ever since. (1968)

SAM BARRY

A graduate of Wisconsin, Justin "Sam" Barry coached at Iowa for seven years, where he won the Big Ten title in 1923 and shared it in 1926. His greatest years came when he moved to Southern California, where he coached for 17 years. There, he won three conference titles and seven division titles. (1978)

ERNEST BLOOD

From 1906-15, Blood's Potsdam (New York) High School squad never lost a game. From 1915-24 at Passaic (New Jersey) High School, his team won 200 games, lost just once, and claimed seven state titles. He later coached at St. Benedict's Prep, winning another five state crowns. He also coached at West Point and Clarkson. (1960)

HOWARD CANN

A three-sport athlete while at New York University, Cann led NYU to the 1920 AAU title. He was a shot-putter on the 1920 Olympic team before becoming a coach at NYU for 35 years. His record was 409-232, which included an undefeated season in 1933-34. (1967)

H. CLIFFORD CARLSON

Two years after earning a medical degree, Dr. Carlson began coaching the University of Pittsburgh and remained a coach for more than 30 years. He led Pitt to a pair of national championships (1928 and '30) and is credited with inventing the "Figure Eight" offense. Carlson was a founder of the National Association of Basketball Coaches. (1959)

LOU CARNESECCA

Carnesecca took each of his St. John's teams to a postseason tournament (18 NCAAs, six NITs). Carnesecca, who won his 500th collegiate game in 1991, earned national Coach of the Year honors in both 1983 and '85. He also coached the ABA's New York Nets from 1970-73. (1992)

BEN CARNEVALE

A graduate of New York University, Bernard Carnevale became a great teacher and coach. He earned his greatest honors during a 20-year stay with the U.S. Naval Academy, where he coached the Middies to 257 wins between 1946 and 1966. He also managed the 1968 U.S. Olympic team. (1969)

EVERETT CASE

A graduate of Wisconsin, Case enjoyed a 40-year coaching career. In 21 years of high school coaching, he won 467 games and four Indiana state championships. He later went to coach at North Carolina State (1946-65), where he won 377 games and six straight Southern Conference titles. He finished his career with 844 wins and 258 losses. (1981)

DENNY CRUM

Crum has coached at Louisville for 23 years, taking his Cardinals to six Final Fours and two NCAA championships (1980 and 1986). In compiling his 546-198 record, he became the second-fastest college coach to win 500 games. Crum was named college Coach of the Year three times. (1994)

CHUCK DALY

Daly gained recent notoriety for coaching the 1992 U.S. Olympic Dream Team, but before that he led Detroit to two NBA championships (1989 and 1990). During his 12 years as an NBA coach, Daly amassed a 564-379 record and a splendid 74-48 record in the playoffs. (1994)

EVERETT DEAN

An All-American at Indiana in 1921, Dean went to Carleton College after graduation and coached his way to a 48-4 record. He returned to Indiana and won 163 games over the next 14 years. He joined Stanford as a coach in 1938 and led the school to the 1942 NCAA title. He retired from coaching in 1955. (1966)

ED DIDDLE

Diddle was a successful high school coach before joining Western Kentucky in 1922. He stayed at WKU for the next 42 years, guiding the famous "fastbreak" Hilltoppers to 32 conference championships. He also took them to three NCAA Tournaments and eight NITs. Diddle was the first man in history to coach 1,000 games at the same school. (1971)

BRUCE DRAKE

A college star while attending Oklahoma, Drake later coached the Sooners, starting in 1939. In 17 years, his club won 200 games and captured six Big Six or Big Seven titles. Drake also served as chairman of the National Rules Committee and president of the NABC. (1972)

CLARENCE GAINES

In 1947, "Big House" Gaines was named athletic director and head coach of all sports at Winston-Salem State College. Five decades later, he was still at Winston-Salem and had become only the second college basketball coach to win 800 games. In 1967, his Rams, led by future NBA superstar Earl Monroe, won the NCAA College Division title. (1981)

JACK GARDNER

James "Jack" Gardner is the only college coach to lead two different universities to the Final Four twice apiece. At Kansas State, he won three Big Seven titles and made it to the Final Four in 1948 and 1951. At Utah, Gardner guided his ballclub to the 1961 and 1966 Final Four. In 36 years, he posted a 70-percent winning mark and 649 victories. (1983)

SLATS GILL

An All-American at Oregon State, Amory "Slats" Gill eventually coached his alma mater for 35 years, until 1964. His Beavers won 599 games, five Pacific Coast Conference titles, and nine Northern Division titles. Under Gill, the Beavers were ranked in the top five nationally in 1947, '49, and '55. (1967)

MARV HARSHMAN

Harshman captured 13 letters at Pacific Lutheran and was a two-time All-American in basketball. He began his coaching career in the mid-1940s at Lutheran, then coached at Washington State and Washington during the next four decades. His teams won a total of 642 games. (1984)

EDDIE HICKEY

Besides being a prolific writer and researcher, Hickey was a successful coach. He enjoyed success at three universities—Creighton, St. Louis (where he won the 1948 NIT title), and Marquette (where he was named USBWA Coach of the Year in 1959). Over 35 years, his teams won 436 games. (1978)

HOWARD HOBSON

Hobson was the first coach to win major championships on the West Coast and the East Coast. "Hobby" took Oregon to three conference titles (1937-39) and the first NCAA crown (1939), and he later guided Yale to five Big Three titles. His basketball teams won 400 games during his 28-year tenure. Hobson used his vast intellect to advance the game strategically and tactically. (1965)

RED HOLZMAN

Holzman was a collegiate star at the City College of New York, where he was a two-time All-American. Later, during his eight years as a player with NBL Rochester, he guided the club to the 1951 league title. He coached the New York Knicks for 14 years, winning NBA titles in 1970 and '73. He was the NBA's Coach of the Year in 1970. (1985)

HENRY IBA

Iba took over at Oklahoma State in 1934 and led the Aggies to 14 Missouri Valley championships, the 1965 Big Eight crown, and the 1945 and '46 NCAA titles. Iba also coached the U.S. Olympic team to gold medals in 1964 and 1968. He won 767 Division I games—third on the all-time list. (1968)

DOGGIE JULIAN

An accomplished athlete who played pro baseball and football, Alvin "Doggie" Julian became a solid coach for 41 years. His basketball teams won 381 games and made several trips to NCAA Tournaments and NITs. In 1947, his Holy Cross club won the NCAA crown. At Dartmouth, his squad was a three-time Ivy League champ (1956, '58, and '59). (1967)

FRANK KEANEY

Keaney was instrumental in changing the face of basketball at the University of Rhode Island. Named athletic director at the school in 1920, Keaney instituted the fastbreak, "point-per-minute" offense that eventually led his teams to 403 victories over 27 seasons. (1960)

GEORGE KEOGAN

Keogan took over as coach of Notre Dame in 1923 and led the Fighting Irish to 327 wins in the next two decades. During one stretch, his team lost only five of 61 games. His greatest claim to fame was creating a shifting man-to-man defense. (1961)

BOB KNIGHT

His practices may come under fire, but no one has ever questioned Knight's ability to get the most from his players. He has coached 22 years at Indiana, where he has won three NCAA championships (1976, '81, and '87) and has never had a losing season. Knight also coached successfully at Army, where he led the Cadets to a 102-52 record over six years. He is a three-time USBWA Coach of the Year. (1991)

WARD LAMBERT

A trained chemist, Ward "Piggy" Lambert also coached at Purdue, where he won 11 Big Ten titles and 371 games over 30 years. Among his more famous players were Charlie Murphy and John Wooden, both of whom executed Lambert's fast-break style to near perfection. (1960)

HARRY LITWACK

Litwack coached 21 years at Temple, his alma mater. At Temple, Litwack earned the reputation for "doing more with less than any coach in basketball history." Litwack's Owls won 373 games (losing 193) and went to 13 postseason tournaments. In 1969, they captured the NIT title. (1975)

KENNETH LOEFFLER

Loeffler played and coached the game and also earned a degree in law. He led La Salle to the 1952 NIT title and the 1954 NCAA crown. He guided the NBA St. Louis Bombers to a 1948 division title. Loeffler also coached at Yale and Texas A&M. (1964)

DUTCH LONBORG

A star at Kansas, Arthur "Dutch" Lonborg took to coaching in 1922. Dutch won 323 games at McPherson College, Washburn, and Northwestern. Later, he served as chairman of the NCAA Tournament committee and the U.S. Olympic basketball committee, and was manager of the 1960 U.S. Olympic team. (1972)

ARAD McCUTCHAN

A graduate of Evansville College, Mc-Cutchan returned to his alma mater in 1946 and began a remarkable coaching career. He won five NCAA College Division championships and 514 games. In 1964 and '65, Arad was NCAA College Division Coach of the Year. McCutchan is one of only two college basketball coaches to win five NCAA titles. (1980)

AL McGUIRE

In his last game as a coach, McGuire led Marquette to the 1977 NCAA championship. It capped off a 13-year career at Marquette that saw him go 295-80.

McGuire won the 1970 NIT and went 28-1 in 1970-71. He won Coach of the Year honors in both 1971 and '74. (1992)

FRANK McGUIRE

McGuire is the only coach to win at least 100 games at three different colleges: St. John's (103), North Carolina (164), and South Carolina (283). He is also the only coach to reach the NCAA finals at two schools, winning it all with the 32-0 North Carolina Tar Heels in 1957, and losing it with St. John's in '52. McGuire also coached a season in the NBA, leading the 1962 Philadelphia Warriors to 49 wins. (1976)

JOHN McLENDON

McLendon began his long coaching career while still a student at Kansas. He coached high school, college, AAU, and pro basketball, winning 522 total games. He was the first coach to win three straight national titles, as he led Tennessee State to NAIA crowns in 1957-59. He also coached the Denver Rockets of the fledgling ABA. (1978)

WALTER MEANWELL

A doctor of public health medicine, Dr. Meanwell coached basketball at Wisconsin for two decades and also coached Missouri for a couple years. During that time, he won 290 games and six conference titles. He later authored a book (with Knute Rockne) on training, conditioning, and injury care. (1959)

RAY MEYER

A coaching legend at DePaul, Meyer started out as captain of the Notre Dame basketball team. He eventually spent 42 years as leader of the Blue Demons (1943-84), guiding them to 724 victories and 22 NCAA and National Invitation Tournaments. His Demons captured the NIT title in 1945. (1978)

RALPH MILLER

A star player under Phog Allen at Kansas, "Cappy" Miller began a 38-year college coaching career in 1951. He coached at Wichita State (13 years), Iowa (six years), and Oregon State (19 years). He enjoyed 33 winning seasons and was the USBWA Coach of the Year in 1981 and '82. In all, his teams won 657 games. (1987)

PETE NEWELL

A 1939 graduate of Loyola, Newell coached at the University of San Francisco, Michigan State, and Cal.-Berkeley. As a coach, Newell won the 1949 NIT title with USF, the 1959 NCAA crown with Cal.-Berkeley, and the 1960 Olympic gold medal. In 1960, he was elected USBWA Coach of the Year. Newell's instructional programs have helped develop countless NBA stars. (1978)

JACK RAMSAY

Not only did Ramsay win 864 NBA games (third most in history), but he also won 234 college games at St. Joseph's (PA). Ramsay's NBA stops included Philadelphia, Buffalo, Portland, and Indiana. His Trail Blazers made the playoffs nine times in ten years and won the 1977 NBA title. (1992)

CESARE RUBINI

Rubini's name is synonymous with Italian basketball. In 37 years as both player and coach, Rubini won 15 Italian basketball championships—five as a player and ten as coach. Rubini has been president of the World Association of Basketball Coaches since 1979. (1994)

ADOLPH RUPP

After a championship career at Kansas, Rupp coached Kentucky from 1931-72 and became the winningest coach in college history. Along the way, he won 875 games. His teams advanced to 24 Southeast Conference titles, won four NCAA

crowns, and nabbed one NIT title. He was co-coach of the 1948 gold-medal Olympic team. (1968)

LEONARD SACHS

Sachs became the coach at Loyola of Chicago in 1924. Over the next 19 years, his teams won 224 games. His use of the 2-2-1 zone defense, in which the center was used as a blocker, was responsible for a growing trend toward big men in the game. (1961)

EVERETT SHELTON

A coach and clinician, Shelton won 850 games in his 46-year career. Shelton coached two national title-winning teams—the AAU Denver Safeways in 1937 and the NCAA-champion Wyoming team in 1943. He was a successful teaching coach in high school, college, and amateur basketball. (1979)

DEAN SMITH

A successful player in Phog Allen's program at Kansas, Smith became coach of North Carolina in 1962. He's still there. Smith has won 802 games, has a winning percentage of .777, and has appeared in an all-time record 23 NCAA Tournaments. He won the NCAA championship in 1982 and 1993 and copped a gold medal in the 1976 Olympics. (1982)

FRED TAYLOR

The Ohio-born Taylor starred on Ohio State's 1950 Big Ten championship team. After a brief pro baseball career in the Washington Senators' system, Taylor eventually became head coach of Ohio State in 1959. Over the next 18 years, the Buckeyes won 297 games, took the 1960 NCAA title, and were runners-up in 1961 and '62. He was named USBWA Coach of the Year in both 1961 and '62. (1985)

MARGARET WADE

Wade coached girls high school basketball in Mississippi, going 453-89 over 19 years. She returned to her alma mater, Delta State, in 1973 and led it to three straight national championships. Wade retired in 1979 with a career record of 633-117. (1984)

STANLEY WATTS

A graduate of Brigham Young, Watts became coach of the BYU varsity in 1949. During his 23 years in that post, the Cougars won 433 games and two NIT crowns (1951 and '66). In 1972, he left coaching to become BYU's athletic director. (1985)

JOHN WOODEN

One of the greatest coaches of all time, Wooden coached 13 years of ball in high schools and at Indiana State before arriving at UCLA in 1948. From 1964-75, UCLA won ten NCAA titles, including seven straight from 1967-73. He was UPI Coach of the Year six times. Wooden is the only person to be voted into the Hall of Fame twice—as both a player and a coach. (1972)

PHIL WOOLPERT

Woolpert's University of San Francisco team won national titles in 1955 and '56, winning 60 games in a row. Woolpert won UPI Coach of the Year honors both years. In 1955, he became the youngest coach ever to win an NCAA title. (1992)

CONTRIBUTORS

SENDA ABBOTT

Senda Berenson Abbott read of the "invention" of basketball by Dr. James Naismith, contacted him, and subsequently adapted a set of rules for women. Abbott's guidelines remained in effect for 75 years. (1984)

CLAIR BEE

A coach for 29 years, Bee's Long Island University teams (1931-51) won an astonishing 95 percent of their games. In 1939, they won the NIT. Bee later coached Baltimore in the NBA (1952-54) and was the inventor of the 1-3-1 zone defense. Bee wrote more than 20 sports books. (1967)

WALTER BROWN

In 1946, Brown spearheaded the movement to organize the BAA. As president of the Boston Garden Arena Corp., he was able to house one of the first BAA teams—the Celtics. From 1961-64, Brown served as chairman of the Basketball Hall of Fame's board of trustees. (1965)

JOHN BUNN

An all-around athlete at Kansas, Bunn coached 25 years at Stanford, Springfield, and Colorado State, winning 321 games in his career. Bunn wrote several textbooks on basketball. (1964)

BOB DOUGLAS

Douglas organized the famous all-black Renaissance Five in 1922. A road club facing racism wherever they went, the Rens won 2,318 games in 22 years, including 88 straight in 1933, another 128 total in 1934, and the World Professional Championship in 1939. (1971)

AL DUER

Duer helped establish the NAIA, formerly the National Association of Intercollegiate Basketball. He served as its executive secretary from 1949-1971. He supervised the 1955 tournament, which was the first national basketball tourney to include black institutions. (1981)

CLIFFORD FAGAN

Fagan became executive director of the National Federation of High School Athletic Associations in 1959. He held the post for 18 years and expanded the organization to include all 50 states. He also was co-editor of *Basketball Rules Simplified.* (1983)

HARRY FISHER

As a player, Fisher led Columbia to undefeated seasons in 1904 and '05. He also coached for 11 years at Columbia. Later, Fisher was hand-picked by General Douglas MacArthur to guide the U.S. Military Academy. He led the Academy to a 46-5 record. (1973)

LARRY FLEISHER

Fleisher founded and led the National Basketball Players Association from 1962-88. Schooled at Harvard Law, Fleisher introduced collective bargaining to pro sports. He helped players obtain benefits such as pension plans and minimum-salary levels. Fleisher also helped establish free agency in sports. (1991)

EDDIE GOTTLIEB

A Russian-born immigrant and an adroit promoter, Gottlieb helped organize the BAA in 1946. He coached the Philadelphia team that won the first BAA title (1947). Gottlieb served as chairman of the NBA Rules Committee for 25 years. (1971)

LUTHER GULICK

As physical training chairman at Springfield College in Massachusetts, Dr. Gulick asked James Naismith to create "an indoor game." The game Naismith created, of course, was basketball. Gulick helped create the Public School League of New York City, the Camp Fire Girls, and the Boy Scouts of America. (1959)

LESTER HARRISON

As owner of the Rochester Royals for 13 years, Harrison won an NBL title in 1946 and an NBA crown in 1951. Harrison was a proponent of the time clock and many other game innovations. (1979)

FERENC HEPP

Dr. Hepp was the first director of Hungary's National School of Physical Education and Sports. Hepp was associated with basketball in Hungary from the 1930s on, and he wrote an important multi-language dictionary of basketball terminology. (1980)

EDWARD HICKOX

Hickox spent four decades as a coach and was the first executive secretary of the NABC. He served as president from 1944-46. Hickox also was a resident historian for two decades. (1959)

TONY HINKLE

Paul "Tony" Hinkle coached Butler University in his native Indiana, where he won 560 games and a national title in 1929. He became known as the "dean of Indiana coaches;" at one point, 55 of his charges held coaching positions in Indiana. (1965)

NED IRISH

Irish was a master promoter who, as basketball director at Madison Square Garden, instituted college doubleheaders. In 1946, he helped organize the BAA and also formed the New York Knickerbockers. (1964)

R. WILLIAM JONES

Jones was a British subject born and educated in Rome, Italy. In 1929, he brought basketball to Switzerland, and soon he co-founded the International Amateur Basketball Federation. Jones helped spread the game to 130 countries. (1964)

J. WALTER KENNEDY

Kennedy served as NBA commissioner from 1963-75. Under Kennedy's caring and watchful leadership, the NBA boomed in TV revenue, in attendance, and in the number of teams competing. (1980)

EMIL LISTON

Besides coaching Baker University for 25 years, Liston organized the National Association of Intercollegiate Basketball and became its director in 1940. It has since grown to 500 members and is now known as the National Association of Intercollegiate Athletics. (1974)

BILL MOKRAY

A superstar among basketball publicists, Mokray spent 21 years with the Boston Celtics. He compiled statistics for the *Converse Basketball Yearbook* and edited an award-winning basketball encyclopedia in 1963. (1965)

RALPH MORGAN

As a student at Pennsylvania, Morgan called for the formation of the Collegiate Basketball Rules Committee. He remained on the committee for more than a quarter-century. In 1910, at age 26, he formed the Eastern Intercollegiate Basketball League, currently known as the Ivy League. (1959)

FRANK MORGENWECK

"Pop" Morgenweck began his pro basketball career in 1901 as a 26-year-old manager in the NBL. In 1925, his Kingston (New York) squad played a six-game championship series with the New York Celtics, splitting it 3-3. From 1912 to his retirement in 1931, Morgenweck won various championship titles. (1962)

JAMES NAISMITH

Naismith is recognized as the "father of basketball." While serving as an instructor at the Springfield, Massachusetts, YMCA in 1891, Prof. Naismith searched for an indoor game that his boys could enjoy during the winter. He asked a custodian to nail two peach baskets to the gymnasium balcony, and the rest is history. (1959)

JOHN O'BRIEN

Besides playing pro basketball, O'Brien formed the Metropolitan Basketball League in 1921. He served as president and treasurer of the MBL for seven years. He then reorganized the American Basketball League and served as president until 1953. (1961)

LARRY O'BRIEN

O'Brien spent many years in politics as advisor to Presidents John Kennedy and Lyndon Johnson. He was named commissioner of the NBA in 1975. During his nine-year tenure, a collective-bargaining agreement was reached and the league expanded to 23 teams. (1991)

HAROLD OLSEN

Olsen coached for 23 years at Ohio State, winning five conference titles. Later, as chairman of the National Rules Committee, he helped pass the adoption of the ten-second rule. In 1938-39, he chaired the NABC study of an NCAA Tournament, which became a huge success. (1959)

MAURICE PODOLOFF

Born in Russia, Podoloff assumed the leadership of the BAA in June 1946. Through his sensitivity and high standards, he was able to lead a merger between the BAA and the NBL, thus creating the NBA in 1949. He served as NBA president and, in 1954, secured the league's first TV contract. (1973)

HENRY PORTER

Porter invented the "molded" basketball, the fan-shaped backboard, and the 29½-

inch ball. He also wrote a handbook and developed the use of instructional films. (1960)

WILLIAM REID

A 1918 graduate of Colgate, Reid later coached his alma mater to 151 wins. He also served as manager and athletic director at Colgate for 36 years. Reid served as vice-president of the NCAA from 1942-46. (1963)

ELMER RIPLEY

A star pro player in the 1910s, Ripley later coached at Wagner, Yale, Georgetown, Columbia, Notre Dame, John Carroll, West Point, and Regis. He also guided the Harlem Globetrotters (1953-56) and the 1960 Canadian Olympic team. (1972)

LYNN ST. JOHN

St. John served as Ohio State's athletic director from 1915-47. He was chairman of the NCAA Rules Committee for 18 years, and he helped form the National Basketball Committee of United States and Canada. (1962)

ABE SAPERSTEIN

The "father of the Harlem Globetrotters," Saperstein originally was asked to coach the Negro American Legion Team in 1926. It was from this team that the Globetrotters were born. Saperstein served the team as owner, manager, coach, and sometimes player. (1970)

ARTHUR SCHABINGER

A four-sport college star, Schabinger coached two decades and won 80 percent of his games at Ottawa University, Emporia State, and Creighton. Schabinger helped conceive the National Association of Basketball Coaches. (1961)

AMOS ALONZO STAGG

Besides becoming a great college football coach, Stagg played in the first public basketball game, held on March 11, 1892. Stagg also led the University of Chicago's first basketball team, back in 1896. (1959)

EDWARD STEITZ

Steitz coached Springfield College and also served as the school's athletic director. Steitz wrote more than 300 articles and 60 books and conducted hundreds of rules clinics around the world. (1983)

CHUCK TAYLOR

Following an 11-year pro career, Charles Taylor produced the first *Converse Basketball Yearbook* and, in 1931, designed the famous Converse Chuck Taylor basketball sneaker. (1968)

BERTHA TEAGUE

Teague coached girls basketball at Cairo (Oklahoma) High School in 1926, then moved to Byng High and stayed for 42 years (1927-69). Her teams won 38 conference titles and eight state championships, winning 1,152 games while losing 115. (1984)

OSWALD TOWER

Tower remained in basketball for more than 60 years. As a member of the Rules Committee (1910-59), he edited the *Official Guide* from 1915-59 and was the official rules interpreter during the same period. (1959)

ARTHUR TRESTER

Trester was brought in to save the struggling Indiana High School Athletic Association in 1913. Over time, he helped the IHSAA stabilize and grow. In the meantime, he built Indiana's annual basketball tournament, which became known as a model of efficiency. (1961)

CLIFFORD WELLS
A 1920 graduate of Indiana University, Wells won 617 games during 29 years of high school coaching in Indiana. In 1945, he became head coach at Tulane, where he stayed for 18 years. Wells conducted more than 100 clinics worldwide. (1971)

LOU WILKE
Wilke served as president of the National AAU, and he chaired the AAU Basketball Committee for seven terms. He was manager of the 1948 U.S. Olympic basketball team. (1982)

REFEREES

JIM ENRIGHT
During his 24-year career, Enright was a respected referee in the Big Ten, Big Eight, and Missouri Valley. He was also a clinician and a sports writer and served as president of the USBWA in 1967. (1978)

GEORGE HEPBRON
A friend of Dr. James Naismith, Hepbron was a pioneer of basketball rules. Hepbron helped draft the first guide book on how to play the game. He also refereed the first AAU tournament at Bay Ridge Athletic Club. (1960)

GEORGE HOYT
An early pioneer of the game, Hoyt traveled the Northeast introducing the principles of officiating to coaches and referees. He coached many teams and refereed many games during the first half of this century. (1961)

PAT KENNEDY
The colorful Kennedy officiated for 18 years at the high school, college, and pro levels. He was the NBA's supervisor of officials from 1946-50, and he also toured with the Harlem Globetrotters. (1959)

LLOYD LEITH
Leith began a coaching career in 1927 and won 207 games at three California high schools. For 25 years, he was the top referee in the Pacific Coast Conference. He officiated in numerous NCAA Tournaments. (1982)

RED MIHALIK
Mihalik began refereeing in the mid-1930s, and by 1951 he was voted the "best referee in the United States." An official at the amateur, collegiate, and pro levels, Mihalik also refereed at the 1964 and '68 Olympic Games. (1985)

JOHN NUCATOLA
Nucatola played ten years of pro basketball before starting his officiating career. Over the years, he called more than 2,000 games, including games in the NCAA Tournament and NBA. (1977)

ERNEST QUIGLEY
Quigley, a four-sport star at Kansas at the turn of the century, became a multi-sport official too. For three decades, he was a National League umpire, a football official, and a respected basketball ref. (1961)

J. DALLAS SHIRLEY
Shirley presented countless papers and clinics worldwide concerning rules interpretation. He spent 32 years as an official in various college conferences and international tournaments—including the 1960 Olympics. (1979)

DAVID TOBEY

After a successful pro career as a player, Tobey turned to coaching, winning 367 high school games and 348 college games. From 1918-25, he refereed all vital pro games and was considered one of the best. (1961)

DAVID WALSH

Walsh enjoyed a 45-year career as a teacher, coach, and official in high school, college, and pro basketball. Walsh went on to conduct many clinics and rules-interpretation conferences. (1961)

TEAMS

FIRST TEAM

Under the direction of James Naismith, the first game was played in 1891 at the Springfield (Massachusetts) YMCA Training School. The game was played with a peach basket and a soccer ball, and legend has it that only one basket was scored in the contest. (1959)

ORIGINAL CELTICS

Founded by promoters Jim and Tom Furey after World War I, the Original Celtics were a sensational barnstorming team. The Celts were known for their innovative strategies and brilliant passing. Johnny Beckman and Joe Lapchick were among the stars. (1959)

BUFFALO GERMANS

The Germans were a touring team from Buffalo that played from 1895-1929. The Germans played against amateurs and pros and compiled an all-time record of 792-86. At one point, they won 111 straight games. (1961)

NEW YORK RENS

Founded by Bob Douglas in 1922, the all-black Renaissance Five was a brilliant barnstorming club. Though they often encountered racism, the Rens won 2,318 games in 22 years, including 88 straight in 1933. Charles "Tarzan" Cooper starred in the middle. (1963)

100 Top College Stars & 64 Top College Teams

The following two sections evaluate the best players and teams in college basketball. Of the thousands of players in the college ranks, you'll read about the 100 that are expected to make the biggest impact in 1994-95. You'll also find season previews on the top 64 teams in the country.

Each player's scouting report begins with his vital stats, such as school, position, and height. Next comes a four-part evaluation of the player. "Background" reviews the player's career, starting with high school and continuing up through the 1993-94 season. "Strengths" examines his best assets, and "weaknesses" pinpoints his significant flaws. "Analysis" tries to put the player's whole game into perspective.

For a quick rundown on each player, you'll find a "player summary" box. You'll also get the player's career statistics. The stats include games (G), field goal percentage (FGP), free throw percentage (FTP), rebounds per game (RPG), assists per game (APG), and points per game (PPG).

Each of the 64 teams receives a one-page season preview. It begins with the basics, including 1993-94 overall record (this record includes NCAA or NIT games). It also lists the team's record in 1994 tournament play ("NCAAs: 2-1" means the team won two NCAA Tournament games and then lost the third). The coach's career Division I record is also listed.

Each season preview begins with an "opening line," which discusses the players it lost and the newcomers that are coming in. The preview then rates the team at each position—guard, forward, and center. "Analysis" evaluates the team's strengths and weaknesses and puts it all into perspective.

Finally, each preview contains the team's 1994-95 roster, which includes the team's top 12 players. The roster lists each player's 1993-94 statistics. The stats include field goal percentage (FGP), free throw percentage (FTP), 3-point field goals/attempts (3-PT), rebounds per game (RPG), assists per game (APG), and points per game (PPG).

DANYA ABRAMS

School: Boston College
Year: Sophomore
Position: Forward
Height: 6'7" **Weight:** 265
Birthdate: September 7, 1974
Birthplace: Greenburgh, NY

PLAYER SUMMARY	
Will	defend with vigor
Can't	avoid fouls
Expect	offensive rebounds
Don't Expect	soft play

Background: Relatively unheralded upon his arrival at Boston College, Abrams impressed coach Jim O'Brien instantly last year and earned a starting nod alongside four seniors in December. He became the first Eagle since Bill Curley in 1990-91 to be honored on the Big East All-Rookie team.

Strengths: "Meek" is a word not associated with Abrams. A fierce competitor, he uses every one of his 265 pounds to lean on taller foes in the painted area. He is adept at moving opponents farther from the basket than they want to be and keeping them away from the glass.

Weaknesses: Aggressive play leads to fouls, and Abrams needs to learn that there are times to back off. His critics, the most notable of whom is Dean Smith, imply that Abrams's game borders on the dirty. As he matures, look for better discretion in those situations.

Analysis: Few were aware of Abrams nationally until he committed the foul that ended Derrick Phelps's season. Abrams, though, is more than the hatchet man his critics would have you believe he is. There is clearly an edge to his game, but he also is a tireless rebounder with quality scoring skills.

COLLEGE STATISTICS

		G	FGP	FTP	RPG	APG	PPG
93-94	BC	34	.464	.585	7.1	0.7	10.4
Totals		34	.464	.585	7.1	0.7	10.4

CORY ALEXANDER

School: Virginia
Year: Junior
Position: Guard
Height: 6'1" **Weight:** 178
Birthdate: June 22, 1973
Birthplace: Waynesboro, VA

PLAYER SUMMARY	
Will	handle the ball
Can't	play physical
Expect	renewed health
Don't Expect	poor decisions

Background: During his stint at Virginia's Oak Hill Academy, Alexander was rated as one of the nation's top point guards. He became an immediate starter in Charlottesville and held that spot until the season opener last year, when an ankle injury sent him to the sidelines for the season.

Strengths: There were too many times when UVA struggled to get into its offense last year. That won't be a problem with Alexander. He's an adroit ball-handler with excellent court vision. There's been significant improvement in his own shot selection.

Weaknesses: Alexander is not a classic jump-shooter, and on occasion he thinks shot first, pass second. When that happens, Virginia's offense slows. He also must cope with the psychological impact of returning from a nasty ankle injury.

Analysis: Virginia reached the second round of the NCAA Tournament without Alexander, but it was a chore. The Cavaliers simply could not create good scoring opportunities. Alexander will be an enormous help in that area. He is one of the nation's top lead guards and should be eager to prove his worth to NBA scouts.

COLLEGE STATISTICS

		G	FGP	FTP	RPG	APG	PPG
91-92	VIRG	33	.376	.686	3.2	4.4	11.2
92-93	VIRG	31	.453	.705	3.5	4.6	18.8
93-94	VIRG	1	—	—	1.0	2.0	—
Totals		65	.419	.696	3.3	4.5	14.7

JEROME ALLEN

School: Pennsylvania
Year: Senior
Position: Guard
Height: 6'4" **Weight:** 176
Birthdate: January 28, 1973
Birthplace: Philadelphia, PA

PLAYER SUMMARY	
Will	find ways to score
Can't	get any acclaim
Expect	team success
Don't Expect	pure shooting

Background: Allen's decision to attend Penn was a surprise, as he had scholarship offers from larger programs. He chose Penn, though, for its educational possibilities, and made a huge impact. As a sophomore, he was named Ivy League Player of the Year.

Strengths: Some individuals are hard to classify other than to simply label them "a player." Allen is one of those individuals. His is a well-rounded game that isn't characterized by the spectacular. This intelligent guard has terrific instincts and is an exceptional passer. He slashes to the hole and is a strong defender.

Weaknesses: This is not a textbook jump-shooter. Allen can shoot from downtown but is prone to bouts of inconsistency with his long-range shot. If given a choice, defenders will try to keep him from driving at the expense of open jump shots.

Analysis: It is no coincidence that Penn has not lost in Ivy League play since Allen's freshman year. A steady veteran, Allen leads through example. He plays with a passion and savvy that are accompanied by athleticism. He'll be remembered as one of the best ever in the Ivy League.

COLLEGE STATISTICS

	G	FGP	FTP	RPG	APG	PPG
91-92 PENN	26	.411	.684	3.6	3.2	12.2
92-93 PENN	27	.423	.667	4.7	4.9	13.1
93-94 PENN	28	.401	.787	4.5	4.6	14.5
Totals	81	.412	.727	4.3	4.3	13.3

RAY ALLEN

School: Connecticut
Year: Sophomore
Position: Guard/Forward
Height: 6'5" **Weight:** 195
Birthdate: July 20, 1975
Birthplace: Dalzell, SC

PLAYER SUMMARY	
Will	soar for dunks
Can't	swat shots
Expect	more points
Don't Expect	further anonymity

Background: A top-50 recruit, Allen was South Carolina's Mr. Basketball as a senior at Hillcrest High School. He picked UConn over Kentucky and Alabama. Although he never started, Allen was UConn's second-leading scorer and a first-team Freshman All-American choice of *Basketball Times.*

Strengths: This terrific athlete has a well-rounded game. He takes good shots and is a quality shooter from 3-point country. If foes guard him too tightly, he'll explode past them into the lane, where he finishes with authority. A reliable free throw shooter, Allen is pesky defensively.

Weaknesses: Like most young players, Allen's defense could stand some improvement. His enormous athletic skills, though, will one day allow him to be among the Big East's best in that category. At the offensive end, Allen just needs to be a bit more assertive.

Analysis: There was much hoopla about a UConn team that many had pegged for the Final Four, but this man was overlooked to some degree. That will change. All of the ingredients are in place for a breakthrough campaign for Allen. Before he's done in Storrs, Allen may be remembered as one of the school's finest ever.

COLLEGE STATISTICS

	G	FGP	FTP	RPG	APG	PPG
93-94 CONN	34	.510	.792	4.6	1.6	12.6
Totals	34	.510	.792	4.6	1.6	12.6

DEREK ANDERSON

School: Ohio St.
Year: Junior
Position: Forward
Height: 6'6" **Weight:** 185
Birthdate: July 18, 1974
Birthplace: Louisville, KY

PLAYER SUMMARY	
Will	come up with steals
Can't	let injury linger
Expect	daring dunks
Don't Expect	missed FTs

Background: As a senior, Anderson was class president at Doss High School and the runner-up pick as Player of the Year in Kentucky. Anderson accepted the OSU scholarship that became free when Jim Jackson turned pro. He's been a regular starter in college, save for the latter portion of 1993-94 when a leg injury sidelined him.

Strengths: A fabulous first step allows Anderson to catch defenders by surprise. This swing man thrives in open-floor settings, where he can use his multitude of moves to finish a play or to create an opening for a teammate. Anderson is an exceptional passer for a non-point guard and makes the difficult appear easy.

Weaknesses: It remains to be seen just what kind of impact the broken leg suffered in February will have on Anderson. It would be a shame if it inhibits his ability to run the court or soar on dunks.

Analysis: Before being felled at Illinois, Anderson appeared to be reaching his stride as one of the Big Ten's most promising underclassmen. He's got the entire athletic package, and the hope in Columbus is that he'll be ready to go when the new campaign begins.

COLLEGE STATISTICS

	G	FGP	FTP	RPG	APG	PPG
92-93 OSU	22	.456	.809	3.3	2.7	10.2
93-94 OSU	22	.466	.814	4.9	4.9	15.0
Totals	44	.462	.812	4.1	3.8	12.6

COREY BECK

School: Arkansas
Year: Senior
Position: Guard
Height: 6'2" **Weight:** 200
Birthdate: May 27, 1971
Birthplace: Memphis, TN

PLAYER SUMMARY	
Will	defend tenaciously
Can't	attract attention
Expect	constant pressure
Don't Expect	many turnovers

Background: Like many of the national champion Razorbacks, Beck came to the school from Memphis. He prepped at Fairley High School and made his collegiate debut as a sophomore in 1992-93. He started 20 times that season and made his mark as a defensive stopper.

Strengths: Beck is the embodiment of Nolan Richardson's "40 minutes of hell" concept. He is a terror at the defensive end, a physical sort with quickness and a knack for creating turnovers. Few perimeter players rebound like Beck. He also is adept at handling the basketball and directing Arkansas' attack.

Weaknesses: Although a capable scorer, Beck understands that is not his role here. Opposing defenses will back off him beyond the 3-point line because, unlike some of his teammates, he is not a great long-distance shooter.

Analysis: Others get the attention, but Beck is at the heart of Arkansas' success. His grit sets the tone for the Razorbacks, and he is a handful for anyone he guards. He was one of those who made Grant Hill's life difficult in the NCAA title game, and there will be more of that to come in 1994-95.

COLLEGE STATISTICS

	G	FGP	FTP	RPG	APG	PPG
92-93 ARK	30	.496	.672	3.8	3.6	7.0
93-94 ARK	34	.506	.667	3.9	5.0	8.8
Totals	64	.502	.669	3.8	4.3	8.0

MARIO BENNETT

School: Arizona St.
Year: Junior
Position: Center/Forward
Height: 6'9" **Weight:** 225
Birthdate: August 1, 1973
Birthplace: Denton, TX

PLAYER SUMMARY	
Will	dunk with authority
Can't	worry about knee
Expect	greater reliability
Don't Expect	further setbacks

Background: A third-team Freshman All-American pick of *Basketball Times* in 1991-92, Bennett suffered a torn anterior cruciate ligament in his left knee the following summer and missed the entire 1992-93 campaign. He returned last year and was an All-Pac-10 selection.

Strengths: Once a lithe 200-pounder, Bennett has added upper-body strength—and that makes him a presence inside. He can leap and loves to dunk the basketball. You'll not see many wild shots lofted by Bennett. Good hands and quickness make him a handful for plodding centers.

Weaknesses: The knee injury was severe, and for much of 1993-94 Bennett was feeling his way around the Pac-10. He has yet to regain trust in that leg, which is not uncommon with an injury so serious. There's no question he has lost some quickness because of the injury.

Analysis: That Bennett could play as he did last year, essentially on one leg, is a great sign for coach Bill Frieder. No Sun Devil is more important to his club than this man. He provides an interior element that is crucial for any NCAA Tournament contender.

COLLEGE STATISTICS

	G	FGP	FTP	RPG	APG	PPG
91-92 ASU	33	.574	.614	6.8	0.8	12.5
93-94 ASU	21	.593	.508	8.6	1.5	16.2
Totals	54	.583	.563	7.5	1.1	13.9

EDDIE BENTON

School: Vermont
Year: Junior
Position: Guard
Height: 5'11" **Weight:** 170
Birthdate: February 16, 1975
Birthplace: Pittsburgh, PA

PLAYER SUMMARY	
Will	zip around defenders
Can't	block shots
Expect	tons of points
Don't Expect	networks to notice

Background: UMass coach John Calipari tipped off Vermont coach Tom Brennan about Benton, and the results have been outstanding. As a freshman, Benton was an instant hit, emerging as the North Atlantic Conference's Rookie of the Year. He reached the 1,000-point plateau at a younger age than anyone in NCAA history, and he was sixth in NCAA scoring last year.

Strengths: Defenders best bring their track shoes when facing Benton. His acceleration is extraordinary and he shifts gears with the best. An adroit ball-handler, he knows how and when to cut to the goal. If foes back off, he can sting them with accurate jumpers, good to 22 feet.

Weaknesses: Early in his career, Benton eschewed the weight room. But after seeing how it helped him, his dedication to strength training has increased, which is important because he still is too easily pushed around at the defensive end. Taller guards can post him up.

Analysis: In terms of individual production, Benton's first two seasons have been extraordinary. What he needs now, though, is help; Vermont has finished in the bottom half of the NAC in each of his two seasons.

COLLEGE STATISTICS

	G	FGP	FTP	RPG	APG	PPG
92-93 VERM	26	.414	.837	3.0	4.5	23.8
93-94 VERM	26	.385	.833	2.5	3.8	26.4
Totals	52	.398	.835	2.8	4.2	25.1

TRAVIS BEST

School: Georgia Tech
Year: Senior
Position: Guard
Height: 5'11" **Weight:** 180
Birthdate: July 12, 1972
Birthplace: Springfield, MA

PLAYER SUMMARY	
Will	confound defenders
Can't	get a moment's rest
Expect	pro scouts to watch
Don't Expect	many bricks

Background: This left-hander once scorched the nets for 81 points in high school. He signed with Georgia Tech as the heir to Kenny Anderson and has been the starter at point guard from Day One. In the past two years, he has been an All-District choice of the USBWA.

Strengths: While other point guards struggle with the perimeter jumper, Best is smooth. He's got a quick release on his jumper and has the foot speed to separate from defenders. That quickness of foot also allows him to penetrate into the lane. There are few lead guards as bothersome as this man at the defensive end.

Weaknesses: For all that he has accomplished, there are too many peaks and valleys in Best's game. It sometimes seems that if he isn't shooting the ball well, the rest of his game suffers. This may be a result of fatigue, as Best is rarely rested.

Analysis: Best has been one of the premier point guards in America's most storied conference, the ACC. He offers the complete package and now must focus on doing a complete job every night. If that happens, he'll be a legitimate All-American.

COLLEGE STATISTICS

		G	FGP	FTP	RPG	APG	PPG
91-92	GT	35	.449	.735	2.5	5.7	12.3
92-93	GT	30	.472	.752	3.1	5.9	16.3
93-94	GT	29	.462	.866	3.6	5.8	18.3
Totals		94	.461	.794	3.1	5.8	15.4

DONNIE BOYCE

School: Colorado
Year: Senior
Position: Guard
Height: 6'5" **Weight:** 195
Birthdate: September 2, 1973
Birthplace: Chicago, IL

PLAYER SUMMARY	
Will	be overlooked
Can't	score enough to win
Expect	school scoring records
Don't Expect	great ball-handling

Background: A relatively anonymous recruit from Chicago's Proviso East High School, Boyce became an immediate starter at Colorado in 1991. He was a fifth-team Freshman All-American pick of *Basketball Weekly* and has led the Buffaloes in scoring in each of his three seasons.

Strengths: Boyce can get up and go. A quality ball-handler, he uses the dribble to break down defenders and set up face-up jumpers. Contact doesn't scare him and he's an excellent passer, adroit at finding the open man when defenses double-team him. Smaller guards have a hard time dealing with his assortment of gifts.

Weaknesses: Free throw shooting has never been Boyce's forte. He is not a disgrace at the line, but the Buffs need every point they can get. Ball-handling can be a problem against pesky defenders.

Analysis: The woes of Colorado have effectively shielded Boyce from the spotlight, and that's a shame. This is one of the Big Eight's premier players, an athlete who scores with style. Colorado will likely struggle again this year, but it won't be because of this man.

COLLEGE STATISTICS

		G	FGP	FTP	RPG	APG	PPG
91-92	COLO	28	.419	.564	4.8	3.1	14.9
92-93	COLO	27	.455	.639	6.2	3.6	19.1
93-94	COLO	26	.401	.708	6.7	4.5	22.4
Totals		81	.424	.653	5.9	3.7	18.7

RICK BRUNSON

School: Temple
Year: Senior
Position: Guard
Height: 6'3" **Weight:** 190
Birthdate: June 14, 1972
Birthplace: Salem, MA

PLAYER SUMMARY	
Will	be a catalyst
Can't	maintain consistency
Expect	penetration
Don't Expect	any bench time

Background: Brunson was a McDonald's All-American at Salem High School. After a tough freshman year, he pondered a transfer to Boston College but chose to remain at Temple. As a sophomore, he assumed the starting point-guard job and led the Owls to the NCAA West Regional final.

Strengths: When this left-hander gets into the zone, he is nearly unstoppable. He loves to take people off the dribble and get into the lane. A pull-up jumper in traffic is a trademark, and he keeps defenses honest with his 3-point shooting.

Weaknesses: Brunson began his career as a shooting guard and he still commits some awkward turnovers when he works at the point. His passes are sometimes forced, and the decisions he makes aren't the instinctive kind of a veteran point guard.

Analysis: Since arriving at Temple, Brunson has matured from an unreliable off guard to one of the better lead guards in the country. His scoring burden will be heavy since Aaron McKie and Eddie Jones are gone, and it's very possible he'll spend some time back at his old spot. Whatever the position, he'll play a ton of minutes.

COLLEGE STATISTICS

	G	FGP	FTP	RPG	APG	PPG
91-92 TEMP	30	.320	.609	2.6	1.9	4.9
92-93 TEMP	33	.396	.655	3.0	4.5	14.0
93-94 TEMP	31	.370	.647	4.1	4.6	12.4
Totals	94	.374	.642	3.2	3.7	10.6

JUNIOR BURROUGH

School: Virginia
Year: Senior
Position: Forward
Height: 6'8" **Weight:** 248
Birthdate: January 18, 1973
Birthplace: Charlotte, NC

PLAYER SUMMARY	
Will	clean the glass
Can't	thread the needle
Expect	reliable production
Don't Expect	the spectacular

Background: After beginning his high school career in his native West Charlotte, Burrough moved to Oak Hill Academy, where he was rated one of the best power-forward prospects in America. An immediate starter at Virginia, Burrough is on track to finish among UVA's leaders in points, blocked shots, and rebounds.

Strengths: When it comes to the offensive boards, Burrough is relentless. He knows the shooting tendencies of his teammates and understands how to be in position if those attempts go awry. At the defensive end, Burrough uses his strength to push the opposition away from the basket.

Weaknesses: For all of the points he has scored during his stint in Charlottesville, Burrough does not boast a vast offensive repertoire. He has limited range on his jump shot and struggles to find the open man when he gets double-teamed.

Analysis: In quiet fashion, Burrough has enjoyed an impressive career. He knows how to score and has made strides in expanding his game. With a strong off-season effort, he'll be in position to emerge as one of the ACC's best all-around threats.

COLLEGE STATISTICS

	G	FGP	FTP	RPG	APG	PPG
91-92 VIRG	33	.446	.695	5.8	0.2	13.2
92-93 VIRG	31	.438	.638	7.2	0.6	14.6
93-94 VIRG	31	.405	.638	7.0	0.9	15.0
Totals	95	.429	.657	6.7	0.6	14.3

MARCUS CAMBY

School: Massachusetts
Year: Sophomore
Position: Center/Forward
Height: 6'11" **Weight:** 215
Birthdate: March 22, 1974
Birthplace: Hartford, CT

PLAYER SUMMARY	
Will	run like the wind
Can't	add enough strength
Expect	greater consistency
Don't Expect	a true center

Background: After Camby missed much of his junior season in high school, many major programs placed his name on the back burner. UMass didn't, and Camby has rewarded the team nicely. The Freshman of the Year in the Atlantic 10, Camby was also a second-team Freshman All-American pick of *Basketball Times*.

Strengths: At nearly seven feet, Camby has as much foot speed as some guards. Great hands make him a good receiver in the post or on the wing, and he is a fine shooter facing the basket. He is also among the nation's finest shot-blockers, making him an imposing presence at a tender age.

Weaknesses: Camby does not have the type of body to move people around in the paint. He's lithe, and coach John Calipari is eager to see Camby add strength. Stamina can be an issue too, as fatigue can lead to ill-advised fouls.

Analysis: In last year's preseason NIT, Camby announced his arrival with a strong performance against North Carolina, and he was a key factor as UMass rolled to the A-10 crown. As he adds experience, he'll become more consistent. He could become the best player this school has produced since Julius Erving.

COLLEGE STATISTICS

	G	FGP	FTP	RPG	APG	PPG
93-94 MASS	29	.494	.596	6.4	1.2	10.2
Totals	29	.494	.596	6.4	1.2	10.2

JEFF CAPEL

School: Duke
Year: Sophomore
Position: Guard
Height: 6'5" **Weight:** 195
Birthdate: February 12, 1975
Birthplace: Fayetteville, NC

PLAYER SUMMARY	
Will	display versatility
Can't	maintain composure
Expect	more shot attempts
Don't Expect	a sophomore jinx

Background: The son of a coach (his father, Jeff Capel Sr., is head coach at Old Dominion), Jeff Jr. was a hoops prodigy from an early age. In 1993, he was North Carolina's prep Player of the Year and a top-50 recruit. As a freshman, he earned a starting assignment in December and kept it through the NCAA title game.

Strengths: Capel possesses an excellent feel for the game. He understands how to deliver the basketball to his teammates in places they can score with it. In addition, he is a fine shooter in his own right, accurate and dangerous from long range. He's also willing to take the ball to the basket.

Weaknesses: As a freshman, Capel battled bouts of inconsistency. A great game would be followed by a relatively poor outing. Turnovers became a problem against teams that pressured the basketball well; and this year, Grant Hill won't be around to bail him out of those spots.

Analysis: In the NCAA finals, there were times when Capel struggled against Arkansas. However, he never appeared daunted by the failures, and that's a good sign. He has tremendous tools and the knowledge of how to use them.

COLLEGE STATISTICS

	G	FGP	FTP	RPG	APG	PPG
93-94 DUKE	34	.458	.656	2.7	3.2	8.6
Totals	34	.458	.656	2.7	3.2	8.6

RANDOLPH CHILDRESS

School: Wake Forest
Year: Senior
Position: Guard
Height: 6'2" **Weight:** 175
Birthdate: September 21, 1972
Birthplace: Clinton, MD

PLAYER SUMMARY	
Will	score consistently
Can't	satisfy himself
Expect	quiet efficiency
Don't Expect	poor leadership

Background: Billed as one of the top prep point guards in the nation as a senior at Flint Hill Prep, Childress stepped immediately into the lineup at Wake Forest. In June 1991, he suffered a major knee injury that required reconstructive surgery, causing him to miss one full season. In 1993-94, he was an All-Seaboard pick of *Basketball Times*.

Strengths: Childress has a knack for being right in the midst of the action, and that's just fine with coach Dave Odom. He is a very capable ball-handler who knows no fear when driving the lane. His pull-up jumper is superb and he has great range on his shot. He is a take-charge guy.

Weaknesses: While Childress shows no mental scars from the knee surgery, he is probably not as quick as he once was. That can cause problems against some of the elusive guards in the ACC.

Analysis: Overshadowed by Rodney Rogers early in his career, Childress stepped forward last year when the Demon Deacons desperately needed him. He is a fine offensive talent and combines those skills with great confidence and a fierce desire to succeed.

COLLEGE STATISTICS

		G	FGP	FTP	RPG	APG	PPG
90-91	WF	29	.449	.772	2.1	2.2	14.0
92-93	WF	30	.484	.810	2.8	4.2	19.7
93-94	WF	29	.415	.789	3.4	3.9	19.6
Totals		88	.449	.792	2.8	3.5	17.8

ERWIN CLAGGETT

School: St. Louis
Year: Senior
Position: Guard
Height: 6'1" **Weight:** 180
Birthdate: June 3, 1975
Birthplace: Venice, IL

PLAYER SUMMARY	
Will	light up scoreboards
Can't	seem to get mean
Expect	greater visibility
Don't Expect	great ball-handling

Background: This relatively unheralded athlete came to St. Louis from Venice High School, where he was the 1990-91 Metro East Player of the Year. Claggett was a first-team All-Great Midwest pick as both a sophomore and junior. Last year, he was a third-team *Basketball Times* All-American.

Strengths: When it comes to putting the ball in the basket, Claggett's terrific. Among his qualities are a sweet shooting stroke and deft quickness. He'll make you pay if you foul him, and he is a good rebounder for a small guard.

Weaknesses: It's not in Claggett's nature to be mean, and that sometimes causes defensive problems. A touch more tenacity is all he needs because he already has the quickness and desire to hawk the basketball. His ball-handling work needs to be upgraded if he hopes to make a serious push for an NBA job next year.

Analysis: Claggett's pro future is subject to debate because he is not an instinctive point guard and it's hard to be an NBA off guard when you're 6'1". At this level, though, he's outstanding, especially when teamed with backcourt mate H Waldman.

COLLEGE STATISTICS

		G	FGP	FTP	RPG	APG	PPG
91-92	SL	28	.385	.708	2.3	1.9	10.3
92-93	SL	28	.447	.829	3.8	3.8	19.7
93-94	SL	29	.411	.726	3.2	3.7	17.4
Totals		85	.418	.767	3.1	3.1	15.8

CHARLES CLAXTON

School: Georgia
Year: Senior
Position: Center
Height: 7'0" **Weight:** 265
Birthdate: December 13, 1970
Birthplace: St. Thomas, Virgin Islands

PLAYER SUMMARY	
Will	discourage lane drives
Can't	be pushed around
Expect	more consistency
Don't Expect	high FT pct.

Background: The native of St. Thomas spent his prep career at Miami Carol City High School, where he averaged 18 points and 11 rebounds as a senior. He enrolled at Georgia and hit the weight room during a redshirt year. He was on the SEC's All-Freshman team in 1992 but has improved only slightly over the last two years.

Strengths: Very agile for a man his size, Claxton has a fine shooting touch around the basket. He is a presence at the defensive end, blocking shots and altering many more. Contact does not offend him and he plays particularly well against prime-time competition.

Weaknesses: The adjective that best describes Claxton is "raw." One night he looks like a superstar; the next night he's barely visible. He often commits ill-advised fouls, and his free throw shooting is far below par.

Analysis: Claxton declared himself eligible for the 1994 draft, but after being selected 50th overall by Phoenix, he decided to go back to Georgia. It was a wise decision because he's still too raw for the NBA. Rebounding and free throw shooting are areas he can improve upon this year.

COLLEGE STATISTICS

	G	FGP	FTP	RPG	APG	PPG
91-92 GEOR	29	.524	.532	6.6	0.3	9.4
92-93 GEOR	29	.564	.482	6.6	0.4	11.5
93-94 GEOR	30	.530	.423	7.9	0.6	10.9
Totals	88	.540	.475	7.0	0.5	10.6

DAN CROSS

School: Florida
Year: Senior
Position: Guard
Height: 6'3" **Weight:** 193
Birthdate: August 16, 1973
Birthplace: Carbondale, IL

PLAYER SUMMARY	
Will	make crisp passes
Can't	be spotted in a crowd
Expect	All-SEC plaudits
Don't Expect	inconsistency

Background: As a child, Cross emulated Earl "The Pearl" Monroe and became an all-state selection at Carbondale High School. He landed at Florida after considering other SEC schools and earned a starting nod midway through his sophomore season. As a junior, he was a second-team All-Deep South pick of *Basketball Weekly*.

Strengths: An excellent ball-handler, Cross is equally adept at the point- or off-guard spots. He has the quickness to go around people with the basketball and can convert his opportunities in the lane into points. Heavy pressure doesn't faze him, and he'll take the big shot late in a game.

Weaknesses: Cross is rarely spectacular. He doesn't have the style that might draw more attention to him. That's not a major issue for coach Lon Kruger, but it likely costs Cross in the exposure department.

Analysis: Florida's Final Four visit no doubt increased Cross's visibility, and he deserved it because he is one of the more underrated lead guards in the country. Defensively sound, Cross understands how to create shots for his teammates. Opponents also must respect his perimeter shot.

COLLEGE STATISTICS

	G	FGP	FTP	RPG	APG	PPG
91-92 FLOR	33	.456	.651	1.8	2.0	5.6
92-93 FLOR	28	.568	.639	2.3	1.8	5.2
93-94 FLOR	37	.482	.828	3.9	3.9	15.7
Totals	98	.490	.752	2.7	2.7	9.3

KENT CULUKO

School: James Madison
Year: Senior
Position: Guard
Height: 6'4" **Weight:** 190
Birthdate: January 4, 1973
Birthplace: Suffern, NY

PLAYER SUMMARY	
Will	try to draw fouls
Can't	pass up a 3
Expect	All-CAA votes
Don't Expect	many rebounds

Background: Culuko piled up the points at Mahwah High School in New Jersey, scoring 2,780 in his career. Last year, he helped lead James Madison to the NCAA Tournament for the first time in 11 years. He already owns JMU's record for 3-pointers.

Strengths: This man's calling card is his wonderful shooting touch from long range. He catches and releases the ball in one motion, and that makes his shot hard to block. Culuko can also take the ball to the basket, and when he's fouled he makes the opponent pay with an excellent stroke from the free throw line.

Weaknesses: As is the case with most stand-still jump-shooters, Culuko's rhythm can be thrown off if defenses get in his face. If he's forced to dribble before releasing his shot, he is less accurate than if he has the opportunity to set himself.

Analysis: Some guys just know how to shoot, and Culuko is one of them. James Madison advanced to the NCAA Tournament last year when Culuko sank a 3 as time expired in the CAA final. He'll be the biggest factor in their attempt to return to the field of 64.

COLLEGE STATISTICS

		G	FGP	FTP	RPG	APG	PPG
91-92	JM	32	.450	.725	2.0	1.6	13.6
92-93	JM	29	.421	.832	2.0	0.8	11.8
93-94	JM	30	.445	.921	3.6	1.2	16.5
Totals		91	.440	.831	2.5	1.2	14.0

ERICK DAMPIER

School: Mississippi St.
Year: Sophomore
Position: Center
Height: 6'11" **Weight:** 230
Birthdate: July 14, 1974
Birthplace: Jackson, MS

PLAYER SUMMARY	
Will	defend the post
Can't	play with finesse
Expect	authoritative rebounds
Don't Expect	slick passing

Background: This two-time all-state center at Lawrence County High School in Monticello helped lead his club to a three-year record of 103-12. As a senior, he was a *USA Today* honorable-mention All-American. In his first season at Mississippi State, he was an honorable-mention Freshman All-American.

Strengths: Defensive presence is a valued commodity, and Dampier is just that for a resurgent MSU Bulldog squad. He is mobile and relishes the opportunity to hamper his opponent's offensive game. On the backboards, Dampier has good timing and gains good position with a powerful torso.

Weaknesses: Dampier's offensive game still has many rough edges. He lacks finesse at times and needs to focus on developing a signature low-post scoring move. His ball-handling and passing skills need to be upgraded too.

Analysis: Mississippi State enjoyed a revival in 1993-94, and this promising pivot was literally at the center of it all. Dampier is already a tremendous defender, and Bulldog coach Richard Williams hopes to help improve Dampier's offensive skills. Dampier keeps improving, and that's always a good sign for a big man.

COLLEGE STATISTICS

		G	FGP	FTP	RPG	APG	PPG
93-94	MSU	29	.589	.491	8.7	0.8	11.9
Totals		29	.589	.491	8.7	0.8	11.9

ANDREW DeCLERCQ

School: Florida
Year: Senior
Position: Center/Forward
Height: 6'10" **Weight:** 224
Birthdate: February 1, 1973
Birthplace: Detroit, MI

PLAYER SUMMARY	
Will	reject shots
Can't	launch treys
Expect	heady defense
Don't Expect	poor decisions

Background: This engineering major is an excellent student and was sought by Duke and Virginia as well as Florida. He signed with the Gators out of Countryside High School in Clearwater and was a member of the SEC's All-Freshman team in 1991-92.

Strengths: Doing the dirty work is an obligation DeClercq takes very seriously. His hustle is best typified by a play in last year's NCAA regionals when he caught Boston College's Howard Eisley from behind and blocked his shot. He'll take a charge and will steal the ball if an offensive player gets careless. A soft touch allows him to shoot medium-range jumpers accurately.

Weaknesses: Aside from height, DeClercq does not possess overwhelming physical gifts other than his leaping ability. He's not especially quick and lacks muscle in his upper body. Larger players can move him around inside.

Analysis: DeClercq's junior season wasn't his best, at least until NCAA Tournament action got underway. This is a well-rounded athlete who is ideally suited to Lon Kruger's team-oriented approach. His do-anything attitude sets the tone for the Gators.

COLLEGE STATISTICS

	G	FGP	FTP	RPG	APG	PPG
91-92 FLOR	33	.506	.655	6.2	0.8	8.8
92-93 FLOR	28	.567	.584	7.1	0.5	10.5
93-94 FLOR	37	.544	.654	7.9	1.5	8.8
Totals	98	.538	.630	7.1	1.0	9.4

TONY DELK

School: Kentucky
Year: Junior
Position: Guard
Height: 6'1" **Weight:** 185
Birthdate: January 28, 1974
Birthplace: Covington, TN

PLAYER SUMMARY	
Will	stroke the 3
Can't	intimidate defensively
Expect	All-SEC kudos
Don't Expect	slippage

Background: A scoring machine in high school, Delk was rated as the class of 1992's premier 3-point marksman by *Basketball Times*. He served as Dale Brown's back-up in 1992-93 before becoming a starter last year. He was Kentucky's scoring leader.

Strengths: Kentucky coach Rick Pitino loves the 3-pointer, and this man has the green light to launch as many of them as he likes. His stroke is pure. He also possesses sufficient quickness to go around those who get too close on the perimeter.

Weaknesses: Delk's lack of height can be a problem at the off-guard position. Taller guards have no problem looking over him, although Delk does his best to be pesky. His ball-handling is not the best and that's something he'll have to address if he hopes to play in the NBA.

Analysis: As a freshman, Delk looked overmatched when Pitino tried to make him a back-up point guard. Since returning to the off-guard spot, Delk has flourished. He stepped forward as Kentucky's most dangerous offensive weapon last year. This year, he'll be asked to carry a leadership burden as well.

COLLEGE STATISTICS

	G	FGP	FTP	RPG	APG	PPG
92-93 KENT	30	.452	.727	1.9	0.7	4.5
93-94 KENT	34	.455	.639	4.5	1.7	15.6
Totals	64	.454	.660	3.3	1.3	10.9

TIM DUNCAN

School: Wake Forest
Year: Sophomore
Position: Forward
Height: 6'10" **Weight:** 227
Birthdate: May 25, 1976
Birthplace: St. Croix, Virgin Islands

PLAYER SUMMARY	
Will	contest shots
Can't	push people around
Expect	steady progress
Don't Expect	much hoopla

Background: Of the new arrivals at Wake Forest last season, Duncan was paid virtually no heed. Instead, the focus was on Ricardo Peral and Makhtar Ndiaye. Those two never played a minute for Wake Forest, but Duncan emerged as one of the ACC's top freshmen. He started every game and led the Demon Deacons in shots blocked.

Strengths: The most imposing element of Duncan's game at this stage is his explosive leaping ability and timing at the defensive end. Foes must always account for where he is. Unlike some shot-blockers, he is not averse to rebounding either. He runs the floor well.

Weaknesses: In a rugged league like the ACC, Duncan's lack of upper-body strength is a major negative. Stronger centers and forwards are able to move him around. Duncan will never be a giant but a bit of work in the weight room would help.

Analysis: Last year, the Demon Deacons lost Rodney Rogers and two imports they expected to help, yet they managed to reach the NCAA Tournament and win a game. This man was one reason why. He's already a major factor at the defensive end, and his offensive game figures to expand as he adds more post moves.

COLLEGE STATISTICS

	G	FGP	FTP	RPG	APG	PPG
93-94	WF	33	.545	.745	9.6	0.9	9.8
Totals		33	.545	.745	9.6	0.9	9.8

LAZELLE DURDEN

School: Cincinnati
Year: Senior
Position: Guard
Height: 6'2" **Weight:** 175
Birthdate: January 29, 1973
Birthplace: Toledo, OH

PLAYER SUMMARY	
Will	fire away
Can't	do it on defense
Expect	plenty of trifectas
Don't Expect	line-drive shots

Background: Ohio's leading prep scorer in 1990-91 while at Rossford High, Durden was listed as one of *Basketball Times'* top 65 seniors in the nation. After gaining eligibility in 1992-93, Durden started slowly but shot 50 percent from 3-point land in that year's NCAA Tournament.

Strengths: Durden's range runs from the midcourt stripe on in. The owner of a rainbow jumper, he can silence an opposing crowd with a bomb from 25 feet or so. Durden has the foot speed to beat his defender down the floor and the elevation to get the jumper off with a hand in his face.

Weaknesses: "Streaky" is a characteristic of long-range bombers, and Durden can be just that. When he's off, his jumpers can be ugly. The Bearcats place great emphasis on defense and, though he's made strides, Durden is not in the class of former Bearcat great Nick Van Exel in that area.

Analysis: There are some rough edges to Durden's game, but his explosiveness and penetration skills overshadow them. With his speed and quickness, he gives Cincinnati the kind of perimeter edge it must have to succeed without an overwhelming interior presence.

COLLEGE STATISTICS

	G	FGP	FTP	RPG	APG	PPG
92-93	CINC	31	.382	.868	1.0	0.3	5.3
93-94	CINC	25	.436	.778	2.9	1.1	17.8
Totals		56	.421	.809	1.9	0.7	10.9

TYUS EDNEY

School: UCLA
Year: Senior
Position: Guard
Height: 5'10" **Weight:** 145
Birthdate: February 14, 1973
Birthplace: Gardena, CA

PLAYER SUMMARY	
Will	elude defenders
Can't	be trapped
Expect	plenty of assists
Don't Expect	turnovers

Background: Although a star at Long Beach Poly High School, Edney did not carry a national profile entering college. As a rookie, though, he immediately earned a starting berth and was a third-team Freshman All-American. He was an All-Pac-10 pick as a sophomore and junior.

Strengths: Edney's quickness is such that it often leaves defenders looking foolish. Foes must be careful not to get too close or this senior will fly by and into the lane, where he is adept at spotting the open man. Despite the fact that he operates at a fast pace, Edney is under control.

Weaknesses: This slight defender might be the lightest player in major college basketball. That's not a big issue from a stamina standpoint, but it can cause match-up troubles defensively. Edney must be sneaky to avoid post-up situations, where he is overmatched.

Analysis: One of the nation's most underappreciated gems, Edney is one of the few lead guards today who understands how to make use of his great natural quickness. He has developed a reliable jumper to keep foes honest and is a terror on the fastbreak.

COLLEGE STATISTICS

		G	FGP	FTP	RPG	APG	PPG
91-92	UCLA	32	.472	.797	2.1	2.8	5.6
92-93	UCLA	33	.483	.841	3.5	5.6	13.6
93-94	UCLA	28	.466	.820	3.4	5.8	15.4
Totals		93	.474	.825	3.0	4.7	11.4

STEVE EDWARDS

School: Miami (FL)
Year: Junior
Position: Guard
Height: 6'6" **Weight:** 195
Birthdate: March 1, 1973
Birthplace: Miami, FL

PLAYER SUMMARY	
Will	regain scoring touch
Can't	maintain consistency
Expect	plenty of action
Don't Expect	sound fundamentals

Background: One of the most sought-after players ever to come out of the state of Florida, Edwards was an All-Freshman team pick of *Eastern Basketball* in 1992-93, as he led the Hurricanes in scoring.

Strengths: No compass to the goal is needed here. Edwards has quick feet and the ability to slash to the net. He's an adequate ball-handler and can connect on the pull-up jump shot. He is at his best in the open floor, where he can use his array of fakes and hesitation moves to convert.

Weaknesses: After a solid season of shooting as a frosh, Edwards endured some horrific nights last winter. Too many shots were forced against defenses geared to stop him. He must learn how to use screens to free himself from double-teams, and he cannot allow himself to grow frustrated when things don't develop quickly.

Analysis: The past season was not what anyone expected from Edwards. The Hurricanes were shut out in Big East play and this man saw his scoring numbers fall dramatically. The talent is still there and the hope is that an off-season of hard work and newfound resolve will result in an exciting campaign.

COLLEGE STATISTICS

		G	FGP	FTP	RPG	APG	PPG
92-93	MIA	27	.418	.693	3.4	3.9	15.9
93-94	MIA	26	.356	.604	3.4	2.4	8.8
Totals		53	.393	.668	3.4	3.2	12.4

BRIAN EVANS

School: Indiana
Year: Junior
Position: Forward
Height: 6'8" **Weight:** 211
Birthdate: September 13, 1973
Birthplace: Terre Haute, IN

PLAYER SUMMARY	
Will	knock down 3's
Can't	outquick the opposition
Expect	sound defense
Don't Expect	foolish turnovers

Background: Evans completed a somewhat unheralded prep career at Terre Haute South High School. He did earn all-state honors as a senior but wasn't a nationally prominent recruit. He was redshirted during his first year in Bloomington and then became a role-player on the 1992-93 squad. Last year, he emerged as a regular starter.

Strengths: The southpaw has a steady shooting stroke. His mechanics on the release are good and he won't back down from lofting that shot at critical moments. He can decipher a good shot from a bad one and will mix it up on the backboards. On defense, he recognizes when to switch.

Weaknesses: Speed afoot is an item Evans must survive without. Slashing forwards can present problems, although Evans does benefit from the fact that Indiana plays excellent help defense. The speed issue also prevents him from beating quicker players off the dribble.

Analysis: Evans has emerged as one of Indiana's most important performers. Smart and sure, he executes Bob Knight's offense in an efficient manner and toils diligently at the defensive end. He'll be an important team leader.

COLLEGE STATISTICS

		G	FGP	FTP	RPG	APG	PPG
92-93	IND	35	.425	.685	3.9	1.3	5.3
93-94	IND	27	.448	.793	6.8	2.2	11.9
Totals		62	.440	.741	5.2	1.7	8.2

JAMAL FAULKNER

School: Alabama
Year: Senior
Position: Forward
Height: 6'7" **Weight:** 210
Birthdate: July 3, 1971
Birthplace: New York, NY

PLAYER SUMMARY	
Will	use athletic skills
Can't	escape troubled past
Expect	exciting offensive play
Don't Expect	a defensive force

Background: Space does not allow us to fully chart Faulkner's checkered past. Alabama is his second collegiate stop, as he left Arizona State under a cloud. His name is not recalled fondly at Pittsburgh either, where his recruitment helped lead to NCAA sanctions.

Strengths: At every stop, Faulkner has scored. He's a sometimes-brilliant transition player who handles the ball well for a man his size. Faulkner picked up lots of stop-and-go moves from his days in New York City, and he's big enough to lend a hand on the backboards.

Weaknesses: Faulkner does not carry the reputation of being a great defender. In too many situations, he is more concerned with what he can do at the offensive end. Passing is not his best attribute, and his free throw shooting is shaky.

Analysis: Alabama coach David Hobbs took a chance on Faulkner's great tools and was rewarded with a solid season. The forward was content to fit into the Crimson Tide's scheme. If Faulkner continues to be a solid citizen, Alabama will have a fine player on its hands.

COLLEGE STATISTICS

		G	FGP	FTP	RPG	APG	PPG
90-91	ASU	30	.492	.699	6.2	1.2	15.4
91-92	ASU	29	.408	.643	5.6	0.9	12.6
93-94	ALAB	26	.430	.646	6.1	1.9	13.5
Totals		85	.446	.664	6.0	1.3	13.9

ROB FEASTER
School: Holy Cross
Year: Senior
Position: Guard/Forward
Height: 6'5" **Weight:** 205
Birthdate: May 15, 1973
Birthplace: Wilmette, IL

PLAYER SUMMARY	
Will	set school records
Can't	get any air time
Expect	quality shooting
Don't Expect	many headlines

Background: Feaster played in the Chicago Catholic League but was not highly touted, in large part because he played center. At Holy Cross, he made the transition to the perimeter. In 1993-94, he was a third-team All-East pick of *Eastern Basketball.*

Strengths: For a man who finished among the national scoring leaders, Feaster is not a one-dimensional gunner. A fierce competitor, he can score from virtually any spot on the floor. Feaster has range to 3-point land and can score off post-up maneuvers as well. He can rebound too.

Weaknesses: There's wasn't a great deal of experienced help on hand at Holy Cross last winter, which occasionally led Feaster to force shots and passes. His assist-to-turnover ratio could stand improvement, as he must adjust better to the double- and triple-teams that have become a regular obstacle for him to overcome.

Analysis: In a region saturated with big-time programs (Boston College, UMass, UConn), Feaster toils quietly. However, he is a versatile performer who took his game up a notch in 1993-94. A run at the national scoring title is a possibility.

COLLEGE STATISTICS

		G	FGP	FTP	RPG	APG	PPG
91-92	HC	29	.490	.800	3.2	1.4	8.0
92-93	HC	30	.508	.773	5.7	2.5	17.7
93-94	HC	28	.472	.702	6.5	3.5	28.0
Totals		87	.487	.737	5.1	2.5	17.8

MICHAEL FINLEY
School: Wisconsin
Year: Senior
Position: Forward/Guard
Height: 6'7" **Weight:** 200
Birthdate: March 6, 1973
Birthplace: Melrose Park, IL

PLAYER SUMMARY	
Will	not back down
Can't	crunch heavyweights
Expect	greater visibility
Don't Expect	mediocre defense

Background: Like teammate Donnie Boyce, Finley did not carry much of a national profile at Proviso East High School. As a freshman, however, Finley started 28 times and was an honorable-mention All-Big Ten selection. By his junior season, Finley was a second-team All-American selection of *Basketball Times.*

Strengths: A wide assortment of skills highlights Finley's resume. He's got great quickness and runs the floor exceptionally well. His jumper is solid and he has range to 20 feet. An unselfish sort, Finley can find the open man when defenses double-team him. He is a supremely versatile defender, capable of handling all kinds of perimeter foes.

Weaknesses: Finley will never be a poster child for a muscle magazine. His frame is thin, and more physical offensive players are his most difficult defensive challenge.

Analysis: To some extent, Finley has been lost in the shuffle of great Big Ten players during his career, and that's a shame because he is a special player. However, as perhaps the best returning talent in the Big Ten, Finley will receive more recognition this year before moving on.

COLLEGE STATISTICS

		G	FGP	FTP	RPG	APG	PPG
91-92	WISC	31	.453	.742	4.9	2.7	12.3
92-93	WISC	28	.467	.771	5.8	3.1	22.1
93-94	WISC	29	.466	.786	6.7	3.2	20.4
Totals		88	.463	.767	5.8	3.0	18.1

DAMON FLINT

School: Cincinnati
Year: Sophomore
Position: Forward/Guard
Height: 6'5" **Weight:** 191
Birthdate: October 21, 1973
Birthplace: Cincinnati, OH

PLAYER SUMMARY	
Will	leap high
Can't	stop improving
Expect	his star to rise
Don't Expect	weakness

Background: Flint originally said he'd attend OSU but reversed course when it was revealed that OSU committed an NCAA violation during its recruitment of him. Flint played a major role in the Bearcats' Great Midwest Conference Tournament title.

Strengths: Thanks to his great leaping ability, his teammates have dubbed him "Flight No. 3." Flint is versatile and is a good enough ball-handler to work at the point. From that vantage point, he can see over defenses and use his exceptional passing acumen. His long arms and quickness make him a large obstacle in the Bearcats' various traps.

Weaknesses: Any concentration lapse at the defensive end earns Cincinnati players a spot on Bob Huggins's bench, and Flint found himself there on occasion. He let his concentration waver at times. He also must be careful not to force the action when opportunities aren't there.

Analysis: Supremely talented, Flint's fine debut was somewhat overshadowed by that of classmate Dontonio Wingfield. Wingfield declared for the NBA draft, though, so now folks outside the city limits will learn what those in Cincinnati already know: Damon Flint is a rising star.

COLLEGE STATISTICS

	G	FGP	FTP	RPG	APG	PPG
93-94 CINC	32	.375	.588	3.8	2.8	12.6
Totals	32	.375	.588	3.8	2.8	12.6

JAMES FORREST

School: Georgia Tech
Year: Senior
Position: Forward
Height: 6'8" **Weight:** 240
Birthdate: August 13, 1972
Birthplace: Atlanta, GA

PLAYER SUMMARY	
Will	use strength to dominate
Can't	erase shots
Expect	soft jumpers
Don't Expect	long-range accuracy

Background: This native son of Atlanta first got to know Georgia Tech coach Bobby Cremins when he was 12, and the two have gotten along well since. Forrest was an All-American at Southside High School, a Freshman All-American at Tech, and the 1993 ACC Tournament MVP.

Strengths: Billed as a taller Larry Johnson, Forrest hasn't disappointed. Blessed with both raw power and finesse, Forrest operates well in the low post or facing the basket. He is a strong rebounder who knows how to use his body to get position.

Weaknesses: Forrest, who's not a first-rate ball-handler, needs to develop that skill so that he may take foes off the dribble. Perimeter defense can be a problem, especially if the man Forrest is guarding is smaller and quicker. At times he has allowed his weight to become a negative.

Analysis: After a super performance in the 1993 postseason, Forrest seemed poised for a huge year. That didn't really happen, in part because of injuries. With the knowledge that this is his last chance to impress the NBA talent gurus, Forrest will likely step forward with a strong effort.

COLLEGE STATISTICS

		G	FGP	FTP	RPG	APG	PPG
91-92	GT	35	.509	.708	6.4	1.8	13.3
92-93	GT	30	.542	.687	7.5	1.4	19.5
93-94	GT	25	.468	.725	7.9	1.4	19.0
Totals		90	.508	.703	7.2	1.6	17.0

DANIEL FORTSON

School: Cincinnati
Year: Freshman
Position: Forward/Center
Height: 6'9" **Weight:** 230
Birthdate: March 27, 1976
Birthplace: Pittsburgh, PA

PLAYER SUMMARY	
Will	slap shots away
Can't	relax on defense
Expect	him to get to the line
Don't Expect	pure finesse

Background: Fortson's prep career was the source of great controversy, as he was forced to sit out his junior season after transferring to Shaler High School as a sophomore. In his senior campaign, he averaged 29.6 points and 16.1 rebounds en route to earning a spot on the McDonald's All-America team.

Strengths: When he has the basketball in the paint, Fortson understands how to score. He creates room for himself and then uses one of many moves designed to get the basketball to the hole or him to the free throw line. He knows how to rebound, and he's got the timing necessary to deflect shots.

Weaknesses: The year layoff did nothing to help Fortson's game, and it took him a while to scrape the rust away. He will need to adjust to the high-quality man-to-man defense he will be expected to play at Cincinnati. Foot movement and avoiding silly fouls are keys.

Analysis: Dontonio Wingfield stuck around for only one season at Cincinnati, but coach Bobby Huggins seems to have the perfect replacement for him. A natural power forward, Fortson can score inside and isn't prone to taking awkward 3's like Wingfield sometimes did.

JELANI GARDNER

School: California
Year: Freshman
Position: Guard
Height: 6'6" **Weight:** 200
Birthdate: December 26, 1975
Birthplace: Bellflower, CA

PLAYER SUMMARY	
Will	be new Kidd on block
Can't	get started soon enough
Expect	Pac-10 Frosh of the Year
Don't Expect	shaky ball-handling

Background: Perhaps the most coveted guard on the West Coast, Gardner made his mark with strong performances at the summer invitational camps. As a senior at St. Bosco High School, he averaged 25 points and seven assists a game. He was a first-team all-state pick, a McDonald's All-American, and a first-team *USA Today* choice.

Strengths: In the manner of an Anfernee Hardaway, Gardner is a tall guard who is comfortable handling the basketball. He is accustomed to running an offense, and his size advantage over other points allows him to avoid traps and find open mates. Opponents must respect his perimeter shot, which is first-rate.

Weaknesses: After two seasons of watching the exquisite passes of Jason Kidd, Cal's fans will have to adjust to Gardner. He is not the instinctive floor general Kidd was and is much more prone to turnovers than was his predecessor. His defensive effort must be improved upon too.

Analysis: Gardner considered UCLA, Arkansas, and Syracuse before choosing California, and he would have immediately helped all of those programs. His presence at Cal will be significant. He'll see lots of action and should step forward as a candidate for national Freshman of the Year honors.

KIWANE GARRIS

School: Illinois
Year: Sophomore
Position: Guard
Height: 6'2" **Weight:** 176
Birthdate: September 24, 1974
Birthplace: Chicago, IL

PLAYER SUMMARY	
Will	log heavy minutes
Can't	wait to drive
Expect	fewer turnovers
Don't Expect	unreliability

Background: This two-time all-state pick in Illinois was rated as one of the nation's top 30 seniors by *FutureStars*. The Westinghouse High School star admired Kendall Gill and decided to attend Gill's alma mater. As a frosh, Garris was second on the Illini in scoring and was a second-team *Basketball Times* Freshman All-American.

Strengths: Garris has had the basketball in his hands throughout his career and is among the best at handling it. His first step off the dribble is explosive and he gets into the lane in a hurry. Once there, he'll finish with gusto or earn a free throw. At the line, he's a first-class shooter.

Weaknesses: Garris struggled at times last season as he coped with the pressure defenses applied throughout the Big Ten. Sometimes he forced the action and dribbled into traps. As the season went on, though, Garris did a better job of recognizing those traps and his turnovers diminished.

Analysis: This guard was thrust into an arduous situation last year when former starter Rennie Clemons was declared ineligible prior to the season. Garris responded well, however. Now experienced, he'll be one of the Midwest's premier point guards.

COLLEGE STATISTICS

		G	FGP	FTP	RPG	APG	PPG
93-94	ILL	28	.433	.803	3.5	3.8	15.9
Totals		28	.433	.803	3.5	3.8	15.9

RASHARD GRIFFITH

School: Wisconsin
Year: Sophomore
Position: Center
Height: 7'1" **Weight:** 265
Birthdate: October 8, 1974
Birthplace: Chicago, IL

PLAYER SUMMARY	
Will	be a force
Can't	get enough shots
Expect	potent slams
Don't Expect	a long run here

Background: Griffith emerged as one of the nation's foremost prep big men by the time he was a sophomore at Martin Luther King High School. After winning a state championship as a senior, Griffith went to Madison, where he was a consensus Freshman All-American.

Strengths: This youngster had a man-sized body when he was 15, and he's learned how to use his enormous size and strength to his advantage. Good hands allow him to catch the ball well, and he seals defenders off with his body. When he gets the ball in the post, he demands double or triple coverage. He toils diligently on the backboards.

Weaknesses: After the Badgers were eliminated in the NCAA Tournament, Griffith went public with his displeasure at how coach Stu Jackson used him offensively. There may be validity to the argument, but it's a measure of Griffith's immaturity that he aired those thoughts in public.

Analysis: What appeared to be a very encouraging freshman season was tainted by Griffith's postseason pout, which was accompanied by a threat to leave Wisconsin. Ironically, Griffith decided to stay while coach Jackson blew town. Griffith should dominate in 1994-95.

COLLEGE STATISTICS

		G	FGP	FTP	RPG	APG	PPG
93-94	WISC	25	.538	.580	8.5	1.0	13.9
Totals		25	.538	.580	8.5	1.0	13.9

ALFRED GRIGSBY
School: California
Year: Senior
Position: Forward
Height: 6'9" **Weight:** 225
Birthdate: March 7, 1973
Birthplace: Houston, TX

PLAYER SUMMARY	
Will	play a key role
Can't	avoid foul trouble
Expect	reliable interior work
Don't Expect	sweet passes

Background: The state of Texas perennially produces excellent basketball talent, and Grigsby was among the best in the class of 1991. He helped California on the boards and on the scoreboard before missing most of last year because of injury.

Strengths: This is your basic nuts-and-bolts power forward. When the ball is up on the glass, Grigsby goes and gets it. When he recovers the ball, he has enough skill to score or get to the line. He is at his best in the transition game, where he has the speed to run the floor and finish a sequence with a thunderclap dunk.

Weaknesses: An earnest defender, Grigsby has to become more discerning about when and where to foul. Too frequently, he commits a silly foul and finds himself on the bench. He is not an offensive presence from the outside and his free throw shooting should be better.

Analysis: Injuries ruined a promising year at California, and Grigsby was not immune. Still, he is an imposing talent who will be the prime frontcourt scoring option for a revamped Cal offense. Count on some entertaining dunks and steady scoring.

COLLEGE STATISTICS
		G	FGP	FTP	RPG	APG	PPG
91-92	CAL	25	.576	.583	6.2	0.8	10.2
92-93	CAL	29	.598	.648	5.8	0.6	10.0
93-94	CAL	3	.545	.500	3.7	0.7	5.3
Totals		57	.586	.615	6.2	0.7	9.2

ZENDON HAMILTON
School: St. John's
Year: Freshman
Position: Forward/Center
Height: 6'11" **Weight:** 225
Birthplace: Floral Park, NY

PLAYER SUMMARY	
Will	zip down the floor
Can't	push people around
Expect	double-figure scoring
Don't Expect	physical domination

Background: Van Coleman's *FutureStars* listed Hamilton as the nation's top center in the prep class of 1994. As a senior at Sewhanhaka High School, he averaged 32 points, 15 rebounds, four steals, and three assists per outing and was named a McDonald's All-American.

Strengths: Hamilton gets to the spot as quickly as any big man in the country. Few centers can keep pace with him running the court, and he can finish plays on the fastbreak. Facing the basket, he has a soft shooting touch and good springs to ensure that his shot is not blocked.

Weaknesses: At 225 pounds, Hamilton is bound to be pushed around on his first run through the Big East Conference. His thin frame leaves him vulnerable to wide-body types under the glass. He also must learn the nuances of playing effective interior defense at the collegiate level.

Analysis: He wasn't quite as sought after as his pal—and now teammate—Felipe Lopez, but make no mistake, this is a blue-chip prospect, one of the ten best prepsters in the class of '94. This explosive scorer will put points on the board at St. John's, and he offers a nice complement to the gifted Lopez.

OTHELLA HARRINGTON

School: Georgetown
Year: Junior
Position: Center
Height: 6'10" **Weight:** 236
Birthplace: Jackson, MS

PLAYER SUMMARY	
Will	attract defenders
Can't	find room to operate
Expect	sound defense
Don't Expect	outside shooting

Analysis: The most coveted prospect in the class of 1996, Harrington was *Basketball Times'* national Player of the Year as a senior at Murrah High School. At Georgetown, Harrington gained recognition as national Freshman of the Year. He was a first-team All-Seaboard choice of *Basketball Times* in 1993-94.

Strengths: In an era when big men cringe at being labeled a center, Harrington embraces the term. He's a throwback who loves working with his back to the basket and finding a way to score. Physical activity does not daunt him, and rebounding is one of his fortes.

Weaknesses: Because Georgetown's outside shooting has been so atrocious during Harrington's career, it's hard to know whether he turns the ball over too much because there are no passing lanes or because he lacks passing skills. Foul trouble can occasionally be a problem.

Analysis: After a superb freshman campaign, Harrington did not take the step forward many expected. However, he is an enormous talent with an excellent work ethic who benefits from summer practices with Alonzo Mourning and Patrick Ewing. Expect him to take that forward step this year.

COLLEGE STATISTICS

	G	FGP	FTP	RPG	APG	PPG
92-93 GEOR	33	.573	.746	8.8	1.0	16.8
93-94 GEOR	31	.551	.733	8.0	1.2	14.7
Totals	64	.563	.739	8.4	1.1	15.8

ALAN HENDERSON

School: Indiana
Year: Senior
Position: Forward
Height: 6'9" **Weight:** 214
Birthdate: December 12, 1972
Birthplace: Indianapolis, IN

PLAYER SUMMARY	
Will	make soft jumpers
Can't	relax for a moment
Expect	a preseason All-American
Don't Expect	single coverage

Background: Henderson came to Bloomington with a strong academic and athletic record. He made 26 starts as a freshman and was enjoying a superb sophomore season before a knee injury sidelined him. Upon his return, he became a *Basketball Times* second-team All-American.

Strengths: A wide array of offensive moves is Henderson's signature. He is an excellent face-up jump-shooter who can also do heavy damage off of offensive rebounds. Never one to force the action, Henderson has an excellent feel for when and how to get his shots. He's a quality defender who adds a shot-blocking dimension.

Weaknesses: In the early stages of 1993-94, Henderson really seemed to struggle with his mobility. By season's end, the leg looked better and the psychological doubts appeared behind him. Elite big men can overpower him at times inside.

Analysis: Henderson worked hard to rehabilitate his knee, and for that reason he was able to enjoy a solid junior season. He is Indiana's best player and the reason the Hoosiers will again be a factor in the national championship hunt.

COLLEGE STATISTICS

		G	FGP	FTP	RPG	APG	PPG
91-92	IND	33	.508	.661	7.2	0.5	11.6
92-93	IND	30	.487	.637	8.1	0.9	11.1
93-94	IND	30	.531	.657	10.3	1.2	17.8
Totals		93	.511	.653	8.5	0.9	13.4

RONNIE HENDERSON

School: Louisiana St.
Year: Sophomore
Position: Guard
Height: 6'4" **Weight:** 190
Birthdate: March 29, 1974
Birthplace: Jackson, MS

PLAYER SUMMARY	
Will	tickle the twine
Can't	wait for help
Expect	rainbow J's
Don't Expect	tenacious defense

Background: A product of the famed program at Murrah High School, Henderson was rated the top off-guard prospect in the nation as a senior by Van Coleman's *FutureStars*. The McDonald's All-American bounced back from a shoulder separation suffered in high school to make a strong debut at LSU.

Strengths: Offense is this man's specialty. Unlimited range is probably too strong an assessment for his shot, but there is little doubt that his stroke is true. He's got a quick release on his jumper and has the explosive burst needed to get to the basket.

Weaknesses: As is the case with a number of high scorers, shot selection is often a problem with Henderson. He can be in such a rush to shoot that he overlooks such things as double-teams and open mates. Consistency was a problem too, and he needs to focus more on stopping folks at the defensive end.

Analysis: No one was hampered more by the knee injury that felled classmate Randy Livingston than this man. Without anyone to set him up, Henderson was forced to create for himself. Still, he was productive; and with Livingston back, he could be ready for a big year.

COLLEGE STATISTICS

		G	FGP	FTP	RPG	APG	PPG
93-94	LSU	27	.378	.711	3.6	1.2	15.9
Totals		27	.378	.711	3.6	1.2	15.9

ODELL HODGE

School: Old Dominion
Year: Junior
Position: Center
Height: 6'9" **Weight:** 260
Birthdate: March 26, 1973
Birthplace: Martinsville, VA

PLAYER SUMMARY	
Will	intimidate shooters
Can't	loft long bombs
Expect	rebounding intensity
Don't Expect	bad shots

Background: No one in the history of Virginia prep basketball scored more points (2,530) than did Hodge. The two-time Virginia AA Player of the Year stepped into the college ranks in 1992-93 and started immediately. He was the CAA Rookie of the Year.

Strengths: This "Big O" is a wide-body, and that affords him great leverage in battles with other big men. Once he establishes position in the low post, it is a major chore to move him. Hodge has excellent hands and a nice touch with the basketball. He also has the leaping ability and timing to rate with the nation's blocked-shot leaders.

Weaknesses: As is the case with many big men, passing is not Hodge's calling card. It's not that he won't surrender the basketball—he will—but he doesn't always find the open man. That can lead to turnovers.

Analysis: He's not a household name and probably won't become one at ODU. However, Hodge is very effective. He is a presence at the defensive end and won't pick up silly fouls. Offensively, he comprehends how and when to use his bulk to create offense. This is a well-rounded, active pivot.

COLLEGE STATISTICS

		G	FGP	FTP	RPG	APG	PPG
92-93	OD	29	.560	.762	9.1	0.7	14.7
93-94	OD	31	.547	.682	9.0	1.4	19.4
Totals		60	.552	.714	9.0	1.1	17.1

FRED HOIBERG

School: Iowa St.
Year: Senior
Position: Guard/Forward
Height: 6'4" **Weight:** 196
Birthdate: October 15, 1972
Birthplace: Ames, IA

PLAYER SUMMARY	
Will ....thrive in the clutch
Can't............return shots to sender
Expect...an Academic All-American
Don't Expect ....passive play

Background: Iowa's Mr. Basketball while a senior at Ames High School in 1991, Hoiberg stayed close to home to attend college. He was the Big Eight Freshman of the Year in 1991-92 and has earned All-Big Eight acclaim the last two seasons.

Strengths: Good grades are not always a barometer of smart decision-making on the basketball floor, but in this case they translate to heady play. Hoiberg doesn't force the issue and is the consummate team player. He hits the 15-foot jump shot and finishes plays in fastbreak situations. He's also an excellent free throw shooter.

Weaknesses: Although not a dominant player, Hoiberg could be more assertive in some scoring situations. Occasionally, he will pass up a shot in favor of a pass to a less talented scorer. Though a willing defender, Hoiberg can be beaten by elusive guards and overpowered by taller forwards.

Analysis: There are some striking parallels between Hoiberg's career and that of former Nebraska star Eric Piatkowski. Hoiberg is not the shooter Piatkowski is, but he has been effective outside the limelight for three seasons. He could be ready for a big finish.

COLLEGE STATISTICS

		G	FGP	FTP	RPG	APG	PPG
91-92	ISU	34	.573	.806	5.3	2.5	12.1
92-93	ISU	31	.550	.816	6.3	3.0	11.6
93-94	ISU	27	.535	.864	6.7	3.6	20.2
Totals		92	.552	.834	6.0	3.0	14.3

JERALD HONEYCUTT

School: Tulane
Year: Sophomore
Position: Forward
Height: 6'9" **Weight:** 210
Birthdate: October 20, 1974
Birthplace: Grambling, LA

PLAYER SUMMARY	
Will ....dunk with verve
Can't ....add enough strength
Expect ....greater consistency
Don't Expect...................it to be dull

Background: Targeted by the prep sleuths as one of the nation's best players in high school, Honeycutt was pursued by many elite programs. Landing Honeycutt was considered a coup for Tulane coach Perry Clark. In his debut season last year, Honeycutt was a second-team Freshman All-American choice of *Basketball Times*.

Strengths: Honeycutt's skills would be extraordinary if he were 6'2". At 6'9", they make him very special. Lithe and quick, Honeycutt runs the floor exceptionally well and is at his best finishing plays on the fastbreak. He can slash to the hole off the dribble and can make enough jump shots to keep defenders honest.

Weaknesses: His flair for the dramatic can sometimes get Honeycutt into trouble. In his effort to make the spectacular, he occasionally overlooks the simpler, more effective play. He is in need of more upper-body strength.

Analysis: Honeycutt's freshman season offered the usual recipe of inexperience, mistakes, and inconsistency. However, it was also filled with enticing suggestions of what the future may hold. This is a marvelously talented wing player with the desire to get better.

COLLEGE STATISTICS

		G	FGP	FTP	RPG	APG	PPG
93-94	TUL	29	.403	.680	6.7	1.9	15.3
Totals		29	.403	.680	6.7	1.9	15.3

RAY JACKSON

School: Michigan
Year: Senior
Position: Forward
Height: 6'6" **Weight:** 225
Birthdate: November 13, 1973
Birthplace: Austin, TX

PLAYER SUMMARY	
Will	sacrifice his body
Can't	escape foul trouble
Expect	aggressive defense
Don't Expect	a lazy effort

Background: This was the Fab Five's answer to Ringo Starr. Although a top-100 player, Jackson did not carry the prep credentials the rest of Michigan's class of 1995 did. Still, it was his insertion into the starting lineup in 1992 that ignited Michigan's first run to the NCAA finals.

Strengths: Jackson's willingness to do the dirty work endeared him to coach Steve Fisher. He has handled Michigan's most difficult defensive assignments and in 1993-94 was asked to play out of position at power forward. Jackson stepped into the void and played well.

Weaknesses: Jackson struggles at times on the offensive end because opponents don't respect his jumper. Against superior foes, Jackson has a disturbing habit of acquiring fouls.

Analysis: No doubt Jackson will relish 1994-95, as he should receive his long-anticipated place in the spotlight. He'll post better offensive numbers, but the critical element will be his concentration. As a senior, Jackson must make better choices about when to attack and when to back off—at both ends of the floor.

COLLEGE STATISTICS

		G	FGP	FTP	RPG	APG	PPG
91-92	MICH	34	.545	.457	3.0	1.7	4.6
92-93	MICH	29	.493	.633	4.1	2.2	9.0
93-94	MICH	31	.491	.682	6.3	2.6	11.4
Totals		94	.502	.621	4.4	2.2	8.2

OTIS JONES

School: Air Force
Year: Senior
Position: Guard
Height: 6'0" **Weight:** 172
Birthdate: June 16, 1972
Birthplace: Selma, AL

PLAYER SUMMARY	
Will	be a catalyst
Can't	be caught
Expect	a run at scoring title
Don't Expect	many to notice

Background: Wasting no time after stepping onto campus at Colorado Springs, Jones was an impact player from the outset. He earned a starting nod as a freshman and led the Falcons in scoring as a sophomore. In each of the last two seasons, he has been named first-team All-WAC.

Strengths: Air Force coach Reggie Minton calls Jones his quarterback, and he is that. He is a fine ball-handler in traffic who can beat his man and create shot opportunities in the lane. An explosive scorer, Jones has nights where he is almost unstoppable offensively.

Weaknesses: Since so much at Air Force rests on his shoulders, Jones is frequently guilty of trying to do too much. He can't do it alone. Forced shots are too common and Jones must learn to trust his peers. His lack of stature creates some defensive woes.

Analysis: The Air Force Academy has had trouble competing in the WAC in recent years. It simply hasn't attracted enough talent like Jones to compete for the league crown. Unfortunately, it doesn't look like Jones will get much help this year either.

COLLEGE STATISTICS

		G	FGP	FTP	RPG	APG	PPG
91-92	AF	29	.440	.806	2.9	2.8	9.0
92-93	AF	27	.404	.798	2.9	2.2	15.2
93-94	AF	26	.447	.770	3.6	2.8	25.5
Totals		82	.431	.786	3.1	2.6	16.3

JIMMY KING

School: Michigan
Year: Senior
Position: Guard
Height: 6'5" **Weight:** 200
Birthdate: August 9, 1973
Birthplace: Plano, TX

PLAYER SUMMARY	
Will	.....be asked for more
Can't	.....rely on athletic ability
Expect	.....more scoring
Don't Expect	.....Fab hoopla

Background: A second-team *Parade* All-American at Plano East High School, King was a member of Michigan's Fab Five recruiting class. He has been an integral part of the Wolverine clubs that have been to two NCAA finals and one regional final.

Strengths: This explosive athlete thrives in a transition game. A great leaper, King is Michigan's top dunker. He's also an underrated defender. With long arms and quick feet, he is a large obstacle for opponents and a versatile tool for coach Steve Fisher.

Weaknesses: Although King has complained that he's been a low-priority option in Michigan's offense, the truth is that he hasn't added much to his offensive game in the past two seasons. He remains prone to streaks of poor perimeter shooting and he seems to lose confidence in his shot quickly. At times, he can be careless with the basketball.

Analysis: King is something of a mystery. He has not tapped into his enormous offensive gifts in the manner many expected he would. Perhaps that is owed to a lack of opportunity. If so, this is his chance to prove himself.

COLLEGE STATISTICS

		G	FGP	FTP	RPG	APG	PPG
91-92	MICH	34	.496	.736	3.3	2.3	9.9
92-93	MICH	36	.509	.648	4.4	3.1	10.8
93-94	MICH	29	.489	.646	3.8	2.6	12.3
Totals		99	.498	.674	3.8	2.7	11.0

KERRY KITTLES

School: Villanova
Year: Junior
Position: Forward
Height: 6'5" **Weight:** 175
Birthdate: June 12, 1974
Birthplace: New Orleans, LA

PLAYER SUMMARY	
Will	.....attract more notice
Can't	.....rely on brawn
Expect	.....further development
Don't Expect	.....many "off" nights

Background: Originally recruited by Rollie Massimino's staff, Kittles came to Villanova from St. Augustine High School. When Massimino exited for UNLV, Kittles found himself playing for a coach, Steve Lappas, he didn't know. He adjusted, though, and was a second-team All-East pick by *Eastern Basketball* as a sophomore.

Strengths: The change in coaches probably helped Kittles. He is a superb athlete who might have become hamstrung in the slow tempo Massimino favored at Villanova. Now he is free to use his quickness and slashing ability to create scoring chances. Fast hands make him a dangerous defender.

Weaknesses: Kittles has been asked to do much for a young Wildcat team, and sometimes that burden seems to wear on him. Additional upper-body strength would probably help him in the stamina department.

Analysis: After taking a major step forward last year, Kittles is poised to become one of the Big East's marquee attractions. The Wildcats surprised a lot of folks with their surge to the NIT title and Kittles was a major reason for that. This first-class scorer should carry Villanova back to the NCAA Tournament.

COLLEGE STATISTICS

		G	FGP	FTP	RPG	APG	PPG
92-93	VILL	27	.482	.673	3.5	2.9	10.9
93-94	VILL	32	.452	.705	6.5	3.4	19.7
Totals		59	.461	.696	5.1	3.2	15.7

TOM KLEINSCHMIDT

School: DePaul
Year: Senior
Position: Guard
Height: 6'5" **Weight:** 210
Birthdate: February 21, 1973
Birthplace: Chicago, IL

PLAYER SUMMARY	
Will	play smart basketball
Can't	rely on quickness
Expect	quality shooting
Don't Expect	selfish play

Background: Kleinschmidt was runner-up for Illinois' Mr. Basketball award in 1990-91. His decision to stay in the area marked a major victory for DePaul coach Joey Meyer, who was trying to reestablish the school's recruiting presence in Chicagoland. Kleinschmidt was a *Basketball Times* All-Midwest choice last year.

Strengths: Kleinschmidt has a wonderful feel for the game. Versatility is a major asset, as he can post up on the box or square up and use his quick-release jumper. He is also a fine ball-handler.

Weaknesses: Kleinschmidt can be taken advantage of at the defensive end. He lacks foot speed and has a tough time with quicker guards who can penetrate. In an effort to make steals, he'll sometimes get caught out of position. There are times when he tries to do too much offensively.

Analysis: This versatile athlete had a standout campaign in 1993-94, although it was largely unnoticed because DePaul failed to make the NCAA Tournament. Simply put, Kleinschmidt needs more help. He's a team-oriented star who needs other weapons to relieve some of the pressure.

COLLEGE STATISTICS

		G	FGP	FTP	RPG	APG	PPG
91-92	DeP	28	.396	.714	2.8	2.1	5.6
92-93	DeP	31	.465	.755	5.4	3.0	17.7
93-94	DeP	26	.487	.718	6.2	4.1	20.5
Totals		85	.464	.734	4.8	3.0	14.6

RAEF LaFRENTZ

School: Kansas
Year: Freshman
Position: Forward/Center
Height: 6'11" **Weight:** 225
Birthdate: May 29, 1976
Birthplace: Monona, IA

PLAYER SUMMARY	
Will	fulfill expectations
Can't	be pushed around
Expect	a strong debut
Don't Expect	poor work habits

Background: Iowa does not have a history of producing great scholastic basketball talent, but this youngster may change that image. As a senior, he averaged 34 points, 16 rebounds, and six blocks per game and shot 74 percent from the field. A McDonald's All-American, he is listed as the No. 1 power-forward prospect in the freshman class by Van Coleman's *FutureStars*.

Strengths: LaFrentz has size and a great understanding of how to use it for one so young. He gets good position and uses an array of hooks and soft jumpers to score around the basket. He'll also effectively grab caroms and keep the opposition away from the glass. Banging big bodies doesn't trouble him.

Weaknesses: The level of defense LaFrentz will be asked to play at Kansas is far more intense than what he knew in high school. His man-to-man defense must be upgraded. He'll also need to learn how to recognize and react to the double-team at the offensive end.

Analysis: The state of Iowa was heartbroken when LaFrentz chose to leave his native area for Kansas. It has been said that LaFrentz's game most resembles that of another player from a Midwestern state not known for its great prep prospects—Kevin McHale of Minnesota.

RUSSELL LARSON

School: Brigham Young
Year: Senior
Position: Forward
Height: 6'10" **Weight:** 215
Birthdate: September 15, 1970
Birthplace: South Weber, UT

PLAYER SUMMARY	
Will	shoot smoothly
Can't	overpower centers
Expect	more double-doubles
Don't Expect	widespread fame

Background: Upon arriving at BYU from Clearfield High School, Larson scored 21 points and grabbed 12 rebounds in his first college start. He was the WAC's Freshman of the Year in 1991 and a first-team All-Far West pick last year by *Basketball Weekly*.

Strengths: Thanks to his height and an arm span that covers more than 86 inches, Larson is a presence at the defensive end. When his team has the ball, he is one of the most efficient post men in the country. He has a good medium-range jump shot and mixes that with an eagerness to grab rebounds.

Weaknesses: Larson is more of a finesse player than a muscle man, and that can be troublesome when the opposition features a powerful big man. He's certainly willing to play the physical game, but at times his build betrays him in those situations.

Analysis: BYU coach Roger Reid was devastated when Shawn Bradley did not return to school after serving his two-year mission. With Bradley, the Cougars might have had a shot at the national title. Larson salved some of those wounds. He's not Bradley, but he's awfully talented.

COLLEGE STATISTICS

		G	FGP	FTP	RPG	APG	PPG
91-92	BYU	32	.540	.816	5.1	0.5	9.9
92-93	BYU	33	.631	.733	4.4	1.0	10.8
93-94	BYU	32	.553	.819	9.1	1.4	19.9
Totals		97	.571	.797	6.2	1.0	13.5

JASON LAWSON

School: Villanova
Year: Sophomore
Position: Center
Height: 6'11" **Weight:** 215
Birthdate: September 2, 1974
Birthplace: Philadelphia, PA

PLAYER SUMMARY	
Will	deflect shots
Can't	resist fouling
Expect	more polish
Don't Expect	stagnant play

Background: The prep class of 1993 in Philadelphia was that city's best in decades, and Lawson was a prominent member of that group. However, the Olney High School star often found himself overshadowed by Rasheed Wallace. Unlike Wallace, Lawson stayed home and became an immediate starter at Villanova.

Strengths: You'll be hard-pressed to find a big man with Lawson's skills. Good hands allow him to make for a good low-post receiver, and he understands how to get his shot off in traffic. On the backboards, Lawson is attentive and willing to mix it up with menacing foes. Those who drive the lane best be wary of his shot-blocking talent.

Weaknesses: A primary off-season goal for Lawson was to hit the weight room. He lacked upper-body strength last year, and that caused foul problems. At the defensive end, Lawson needs to concentrate on moving his feet and not reaching.

Analysis: Lawson received a trial by fire as a freshman and responded admirably. He improved in all facets of his game as the season progressed. Foul trouble became less of a problem, which is a positive sign, because with Lawson, the Wildcats are able to play with anyone.

COLLEGE STATISTICS

		G	FGP	FTP	RPG	APG	PPG
93-94	VILL	32	.523	.583	6.6	1.2	10.1
Totals		32	.523	.583	6.6	1.2	10.1

VOSHON LENARD

School: Minnesota
Year: Senior
Position: Guard
Height: 6'4" **Weight:** 205
Birthdate: May 14, 1973
Birthplace: Detroit, MI

PLAYER SUMMARY	
Will	take the big shot
Can't	maintain consistency
Expect	All-Big Ten honors
Don't Expect	bad defense

Background: Lenard teamed with Jalen Rose to lead Detroit Southwestern to consecutive state titles. Named a *Parade* All-American, Lenard selected Minnesota and started every game in his rookie year. He has earned All-Big Ten consideration each of the past two seasons.

Strengths: Lenard is extremely well-rounded and can score in a variety of manners. His jump shot has nearly limitless range, and he's got the quickness to beat the defense in dribble-drive situations. He is persistent on the defensive end and he loves to make plays at crunch time.

Weaknesses: For all of his success, Lenard hasn't proven that he can consistently play at an All-American level. Too many times, big nights have been followed by mediocre outings. Lenard needs to play well in prime time in order to carry the reputation some of his Big Ten peers do.

Analysis: Lenard declared himself eligible for the 1994 NBA draft, but after being selected 46th overall, he went back to school. A dose more consistency and a major highlight or two could help him become a first-round pick.

COLLEGE STATISTICS

		G	FGP	FTP	RPG	APG	PPG
91-92	MINN	32	.421	.812	3.7	2.7	12.8
92-93	MINN	31	.481	.802	3.6	2.6	17.1
93-94	MINN	33	.472	.844	3.7	2.2	18.9
Totals		96	.461	.820	3.7	2.5	16.3

FELIPE LOPEZ

School: St. John's
Year: Freshman
Position: Guard
Height: 6'5" **Weight:** 178
Birthplace: Santiago, Dominican Republic

PLAYER SUMMARY	
Will	wow crowds
Can't	escape attention
Expect	a frosh All-American
Don't Expect	selfish play

Background: Targeted as a great one at the age of 14, Lopez has established himself as the best freshman prospect in the land. He led Rice High School to a New York state title as a senior, averaging 27 points and ten rebounds per game. He dominated play at the McDonald's All-America Game, pouring in 24 points.

Strengths: Court vision is the quality that most endears Lopez to his teammates. At 6'5", he's a competent enough ball-handler to play point guard. He concentrates on finding the open man; and if defenders ease off him, he can make them pay with a confident jumper. On drives, he explodes to the goal.

Weaknesses: Lopez will face two major challenges as a frosh—one physical, the other mental. He has a thin frame, and that may create a stamina problem for a man expected to carry a heavy workload as a rookie. In addition, the Latin community of New York has made him an icon, and that's a heavy burden for an 18-year-old to carry.

Analysis: They're rolling out the Redmen's carpet for this phenomenal frosh, who's expected to make the same kind of impact on the college game as Chris Webber, Glenn Robinson, and Jason Kidd did in recent years. St. John's coach Brian Mahoney will turn him loose, and it's expected there will be some exciting results.

COREY LOUIS

School: Florida St.
Year: Freshman
Position: Center
Height: 6'10" **Weight:** 220
Birthdate: February 12, 1977
Birthplace: Miami, FL

PLAYER SUMMARY	
Will	clean the glass
Can't	excel on perimeter
Expect	a starting assignment
Don't Expect	a finished product

Background: In recent years, South Florida has begun to produce fine hoops talent to rival its traditional supply of football players. Louis is the latest basketball prodigy. He was a dominant figure at Northwestern High School for the past two seasons, averaging 17.4 points and 14.5 rebounds as a senior.

Strengths: It used to be that big men trailed the play. That's not necessarily so any longer, and Louis is one of the new breed who can get out and run. He is at his best under the boards, using his great leaping ability to grab rebounds. Of all the freshmen in America, Louis might be the best pure shot-blocker.

Weaknesses: Don't expect to see a Rashard Griffith here—Louis is very much a work in progress. His low-post game needs considerable development, as he has no set go-to move. In high school, he largely relied on athletic gifts and grit, and that will have to change at this level.

Analysis: Florida State missed the NCAA Tournament last year largely because it had a weak interior presence after losing Rodney Dobard and Doug Edwards. Louis will help remedy that shortfall. If he can keep out of foul trouble, he will be a defensive force. His offense will take longer to develop.

MATT MALONEY

School: Pennsylvania
Year: Senior
Position: Guard
Height: 6'3" **Weight:** 200
Birthdate: December 6, 1971
Birthplace: Silver Spring, MD

PLAYER SUMMARY	
Will	connect from outside
Can't	post up
Expect	heady quarterbacking
Don't Expect	turnovers

Background: Upon graduation from Haddonfield High School, Maloney found himself listed as one of the nation's top 100 prospects by *FutureStars*. He enrolled at Vanderbilt and spent one season in Nashville before transferring home to Philadelphia.

Strengths: Temple assistant Jim Maloney is Matt's dad, so it is no surprise to learn that the younger Maloney is a shrewd floor general. He handles the basketball and understands how to set up his Quaker teammates in the motion offense. His perimeter jumper must be respected. To lay back is to find yourself counting up the 3's.

Weaknesses: At times, he'll loft ill-advised shots that have little chance of going in. Maloney needs to be a bit more selective in deciding when to launch his shot.

Analysis: The Quakers began their Ivy League dominance when Maloney became eligible. He and Jerome Allen form one of the top backcourts in the East. Penn won the Ivy League's first NCAA Tournament game in more than a decade last year and Maloney had a lot to do with it.

COLLEGE STATISTICS

	G	FGP	FTP	RPG	APG	PPG
90-91 VAND	30	.410	.786	1.5	1.7	4.1
92-93 PENN	27	.412	.776	3.3	3.6	16.3
93-94 PENN	28	.393	.897	2.6	3.8	14.0
Totals	85	.408	.839	2.4	3.0	11.2

CUONZO MARTIN

School: Purdue
Year: Senior
Position: Forward
Height: 6'6" **Weight:** 210
Birthdate: September 23, 1971
Birthplace: East St. Louis, IL

PLAYER SUMMARY	
Will	knock down J's
Can't	continue inconsistency
Expect	stingy defense
Don't Expect	another "Big Dog"

Background: After earning all-state and St. Louis Metro Player of the Year honors in 1990-91, Martin spent a year at New Hampton Prep School before coming to Purdue. As a freshman he made 12 starts, and the following year he was named the youngest captain ever under Gene Keady.

Strengths: During the past two seasons, Martin has made his mark as one of the Big Ten's finest defenders. He has the size to handle forwards and the quickness to chase guards. When his team has the ball, Martin usually takes good shots and makes the extra pass.

Weaknesses: The offensive part of his game comes and goes. At times, Martin can be on fire from long range. On other occasions, his shots clang off the rim. Martin must become a more dependable offensive threat, as the Boilers need a new go-to man.

Analysis: For the past two seasons, Purdue's players have taken pains to tell us they were not a one-man (read Glenn Robinson) unit. Now's their chance to prove it. Martin will be at the forefront of that effort. If he is able to produce, the Boilermakers will remain a factor in the Big Ten race.

COLLEGE STATISTICS

	G	FGP	FTP	RPG	APG	PPG
91-92 PURD	33	.521	.759	3.3	1.5	5.8
92-93 PURD	28	.522	.807	3.7	2.4	11.9
93-94 PURD	34	.463	.735	4.3	1.9	16.3
Totals	95	.491	.765	3.7	1.9	11.3

JERRY McCULLOUGH

School: Pittsburgh
Year: Senior
Position: Guard
Height: 5'11" **Weight:** 175
Birthdate: November 26, 1973
Birthplace: New York, NY

PLAYER SUMMARY	
Will	drive into the lane
Can't	stay under control
Expect	head fakes
Don't Expect	pure shooting

Background: This is your typical inner-city New York guard. McCullough played for New York's famed AAU Gauchos club and caught the eye of a Pittsburgh assistant. After playing behind Sean Miller as a freshman, McCullough got the starting nod each of the past two seasons.

Strengths: A lot of players have a hard time matching McCullough's jetlike quickness when he has the basketball. He is difficult to trap because he's a terrific ball-handler who can dribble himself out of trouble. McCullough is most dangerous when handling the ball on the break.

Weaknesses: McCullough sometimes goes at such a fast pace that he rushes passes. He needs to do a better job of accepting the basic pass and not attempting to make each pass the stuff of highlight reels.

Analysis: A wonderful sophomore year was followed by a competent junior campaign. Unfortunately, McCullough did not display the kind of patience and shooting accuracy former coach Paul Evans would have liked. In a new system that stresses speed and 3's, McCullough will thrive if he improves his consistency.

COLLEGE STATISTICS

	G	FGP	FTP	RPG	APG	PPG
91-92 PITT	33	.386	.629	1.6	2.7	7.4
92-93 PITT	28	.385	.772	3.8	5.6	15.3
93-94 PITT	25	.388	.725	4.0	7.0	13.3
Totals	86	.386	.718	3.0	4.9	11.7

ANTONIO McDYESS

School: Alabama
Year: Sophomore
Position: Forward
Height: 6'9" **Weight:** 215
Birthdate: September 7, 1974
Birthplace: Quitman, MS

PLAYER SUMMARY	
Will ....rebound with verve
Can't ....bury treys
Expect ....regional recognition
Don't Expect......................lazy play

Background: This alumnus of Quitman Consolidated High School was a *Parade* All-American hunted by the top schools in the Southeast. McDyess was impressed by Crimson Tide coach David Hobbs and the school's tradition. He was an honorable-mention Freshman All-American.

Strengths: Though he's an admirer of David Robinson, McDyess's rebounding gifts evoke more images of Dennis Rodman than of Robinson. He has the desire and tenacity to become one of the nation's best in that area. Offensively, McDyess is no slouch. He's got a nice touch around the basket and the power to create space for himself.

Weaknesses: Like most frosh, McDyess was prone to fits of inconsistency last year. With experience, those bouts should become less frequent. As he earns more minutes, teams will try to lure him into foul trouble, and that's something this eager shot-blocker must avoid.

Analysis: The Tide didn't receive much national notoriety last winter, but that could change in 1994-95. McDyess is one of the SEC's fine, young big men, and he'll get a much greater opportunity to thrive this year. One day, Alabama fans might liken him to Robert Horry and Derrick McKey.

COLLEGE STATISTICS

	G	FGP	FTP	RPG	APG	PPG
93-94 ALAB	26	.564	.533	8.1	0.4	11.4
Totals	26	.564	.533	8.1	0.4	11.4

TONY MILLER

School: Marquette
Year: Senior
Position: Guard
Height: 5'11" **Weight:** 190
Birthdate: April 16, 1973
Birthplace: Cleveland, OH

PLAYER SUMMARY	
Will.........................dribble and dish
Can't...............................get noticed
Expect............sound fundamentals
Don't Expect...............fancy moves

Background: Miller led St. Joseph's High School to state football and basketball championships. Most thought he would attend college on a football scholarship (as a quarterback), but the persistence of Marquette coach Kevin O'Neill won out. He's been a three-year starter with the Warriors.

Strengths: When he was a child, Miller was always the smallest guy on the court and the taller players blocked his shots. So Miller learned to set up others first and shoot second. It's a trait that defines his game today. He's also a fierce competitor and the clear captain of a team that reached last year's Sweet 16.

Weaknesses: There isn't a great deal of flash to Miller's game, and that causes people to overlook him when rating the nation's best point guards. He also doesn't shoot as much as some others, and that hurts his standing among stat freaks.

Analysis: New coach Mike Deane will discover what O'Neill implicitly understood: Miller is the heart and soul of the Warriors. Deane has a history of creating offense for his point guards, so it's a good bet that Miller's scoring numbers will improve.

COLLEGE STATISTICS

	G	FGP	FTP	RPG	APG	PPG
91-92 MARQ	29	.353	.513	4.4	7.6	6.4
92-93 MARQ	28	.415	.671	4.1	7.6	8.8
93-94 MARQ	33	.344	.535	4.9	8.3	7.2
Totals	90	.369	.574	4.5	7.9	7.5

LAWRENCE MOTEN

School: Syracuse
Year: Senior
Position: Guard/Forward
Height: 6'5" **Weight:** 185
Birthdate: March 25, 1972
Birthplace: Washington, DC

PLAYER SUMMARY	
Will	score silently
Can't	overpower people
Expect	All-American votes
Don't Expect	loud boasting

Background: A product of Washington, D.C., Moten was a well-decorated prepster at Archbishop Carroll High School before moving on for a year at New Hampton Prep. In 1991-92, he was the consensus pick as the national Freshman of the Year.

Strengths: It is fitting that, as a youngster, Moten's favorite pro athlete was George Gervin. Like the Spurs star, Moten is a quiet assassin. He's quick and is adept at slashing to the goal. As a junior, he played guard regularly after spending much of his first two seasons at small forward. He handled the new assignment with aplomb.

Weaknesses: Moten has been accused of disappearing at times. An unassuming type, Moten needs to demand the ball and take charge of the Orange offense at critical moments.

Analysis: Only Donyell Marshall had a better Big East campaign than Moten. A versatile performer, Moten has the offensive game to make a serious push for All-American honors. He's also a sneaky defender who can step into the passing lanes and create turnovers, which lead to transition scores.

COLLEGE STATISTICS

	G	FGP	FTP	RPG	APG	PPG
91-92 SYR	32	.497	.752	6.0	2.0	18.2
92-93 SYR	29	.473	.652	4.8	2.7	17.9
93-94 SYR	30	.501	.698	4.5	2.2	21.5
Totals	91	.491	.707	5.1	2.3	19.2

CHARLES O'BANNON

School: UCLA
Year: Sophomore
Position: Forward
Height: 6'6" **Weight:** 210
Birthdate: February 22, 1975
Birthplace: Bellflower, CA

PLAYER SUMMARY	
Will	swish shots
Can't	punish physically
Expect	dunking fun
Don't Expect	an incomplete game

Background: A consensus first-team prep All-American at Artesia High School, O'Bannon was sought by the nation's most storied programs. In the end he picked UCLA, the school his father attended. Teamed with brother Ed, Charles was an instant force, earning first-team Freshman All-American plaudits from Basketball Times.

Strengths: This smooth left-hander brings all of the ingredients to the table. He possesses the kind of quickness that can leave defenders gasping for air, and he also has a quality pull-up jumper. O'Bannon has a smooth release on his shot and unleashes it quickly.

Weaknesses: After a superb start last season, O'Bannon faded in the middle portion of the schedule as he struggled to adjust to the longer college slate. That slide coincided with UCLA's second-half slump. He needs to find greater consistency and develop better endurance so there aren't any late-season slumps.

Analysis: It was an outstanding debut for O'Bannon, despite the slide that put UCLA out of the NCAA Tournament in the first round. He and his brother Ed have a unique bond, and that translates into some exciting transition action for Bruin fans.

COLLEGE STATISTICS

	G	FGP	FTP	RPG	APG	PPG
93-94 UCLA	28	.514	.647	6.8	1.6	11.6
Totals	28	.514	.647	6.8	1.6	11.6

ED O'BANNON

School: UCLA
Year: Senior
Position: Forward
Height: 6'8" **Weight:** 215
Birthdate: August 14, 1972
Birthplace: Los Angeles, CA

PLAYER SUMMARY	
Will	slice to the hoop
Can't	be ignored on boards
Expect	national attention
Don't Expect	nasty disposition

Background: The nation's top prep player of 1990, as selected by *Basketball Times*, O'Bannon was felled by a torn anterior cruciate ligament suffered in a 1990 pick-up game. After sitting out the 1990-91 campaign, O'Bannon returned with considerable rust on his game. However, he's been an All-Pac-10 pick each of the past two years.

Strengths: When the action is fast and furious, O'Bannon is at his best. He's got a quick first step and effectively slides to the goal, where he is strong enough to finish plays. Defenses must pay him heed on the glass because he can do damage with put-back scores.

Weaknesses: A pleasant disposition serves O'Bannon well off the floor, but a bit more assertiveness might help on the court. Too often, O'Bannon will go through stretches where he doesn't touch the ball. He needs to become more effective in the halfcourt.

Analysis: After the shocking knee injury that nearly sabotaged his career, O'Bannon has responded with solid numbers to date. To reach the next plateau, he must expand his skills and not be afraid to dominate. All the tools for stardom are still here.

COLLEGE STATISTICS

		G	FGP	FTP	RPG	APG	PPG
91-92	UCLA	23	.416	.630	3.0	0.5	3.6
92-93	UCLA	33	.539	.707	7.0	1.7	16.7
93-94	UCLA	28	.484	.745	8.8	2.1	18.2
Totals		84	.502	.718	6.5	1.5	13.6

GREG OSTERTAG

School: Kansas
Year: Senior
Position: Center
Height: 7'2" **Weight:** 275
Birthdate: March 6, 1973
Birthplace: Dallas, TX

PLAYER SUMMARY	
Will	occupy space
Can't	depend on speed
Expect	solid screens
Don't Expect	fancy fakes

Background: An imposing baseball pitcher in high school, Ostertag developed into the Texas Large Class Player of the Year as a senior at Duncanville High. He signed with Kansas on the first day of the early signing period and led the team in blocks as a freshman. He became a starter last season.

Strengths: His sheer size makes him a considerable obstacle in the paint. Opponents have a hard time getting off shots in the lane when he's on the floor. At the offensive end, he has a soft touch to 12 feet and sets strong picks.

Weaknesses: Ostertag is a plodder. His weight has been a problem at times and that has reduced his stamina and effectiveness. He must avoid reach-in fouls and concentrate on playing good position defense.

Analysis: After displaying early promise as an underclassmen, Ostertag has struggled to take the next step. Inconsistency has plagued him, and that must change as he enters his senior season. Nevertheless, Ostertag has great size, and that element—combined with his soft shooting skills—makes him an intriguing candidate for a big season.

COLLEGE STATISTICS

		G	FGP	FTP	RPG	APG	PPG
91-92	KANS	32	.545	.653	3.5	0.2	4.8
92-93	KANS	29	.517	.600	4.1	0.4	5.3
93-94	KANS	35	.533	.631	8.8	0.3	10.3
Totals		96	.532	.628	5.6	0.3	7.0

RAY OWES

School: Arizona
Year: Senior
Position: Forward
Height: 6'8" **Weight:** 200
Birthdate: December 11, 1972
Birthplace: San Bernardino, CA

PLAYER SUMMARY	
Will	shoot smoothly
Can't	make the no-look pass
Expect	offensive rebounds
Don't Expect	brash talk

Background: Arizona has effectively mined the vast recruiting areas of Southern California during the Lute Olson era, and Owes is a product of that. The alumnus of San Bernardino High School was rated among the nation's top power forwards by Van Coleman's *FutureStars*. As a sophomore, he emerged as a starter.

Strengths: While foes were focused on the theatrics of guards Damon Stoudamire and Khalid Reeves last year, Owes quietly did his job inside. He goes to the boards with a vengeance, and his quickness is a problem for most power forwards. He also has a reliable face-up jumper.

Weaknesses: Owes is undersized for a power forward. He does not have the physique to push and shove with the muscular types who usually patrol the lanes. His passing skills have improved but his passes rarely lead to scores.

Analysis: Against Arkansas in the Final Four, Owes demonstrated the kind of brilliance some prep sleuths envisioned for him. He has gradually improved throughout his career in Tucson and appears ready to shoulder more responsibility.

COLLEGE STATISTICS

		G	FGP	FTP	RPG	APG	PPG
91-92	ARIZ	27	.568	.400	1.7	0.3	2.1
92-93	ARIZ	27	.539	.529	5.1	0.4	7.6
93-94	ARIZ	35	.501	.642	8.1	0.7	12.9
Totals		89	.517	.585	5.3	0.5	8.0

CHEROKEE PARKS

School: Duke
Year: Senior
Position: Center
Height: 6'11" **Weight:** 235
Birthdate: October 11, 1972
Birthplace: Huntington Beach, CA

PLAYER SUMMARY	
Will	drain short jumpers
Can't	let focus lapse
Expect	more leadership
Don't Expect	timid responses

Background: This high school All-American was a high priority for UCLA, but he chose to head to Durham instead. As a freshman, he was Christian Laettner's whipping boy in practice, but by his junior season he was Duke's second-leading scorer and an All-Seaboard choice of *Basketball Times*.

Strengths: Establishing good position is a Parks trademark. He seals defenders off with his body and catches the ball well in traffic. A drop-step move or turnaround jumper usually results in a score. Unlike some big men, Parks is adept at passing out of double-teams.

Weaknesses: A laid-back sort, Parks occasionally lets his concentration wander, particularly when the opposition is weak. Developing a will to dominate would be a major plus.

Analysis: There are some who would say that Parks has not achieved the superstardom envisioned for him in high school. Clearly he has not dominated, yet his stats have shown steady progress. A new season offers him a chance to add the spectacular to a career that has been steady.

COLLEGE STATISTICS

		G	FGP	FTP	RPG	APG	PPG
91-92	DUKE	34	.571	.725	2.4	0.4	5.0
92-93	DUKE	32	.652	.720	6.9	0.4	12.3
93-94	DUKE	34	.536	.772	8.4	0.9	14.4
Totals		100	.582	.745	5.9	0.6	10.5

ANDRAE PATTERSON

School: Indiana
Year: Freshman
Position: Forward
Height: 6'8" **Weight:** 225
Birthplace: Abilene, TX

PLAYER SUMMARY	
Will ....dunk with thunder	
Can't ....be shackled	
Expect ....a starting nod	
Don't Expect ....missed rebounds	

Background: Texas' reputation as a rich recruiting area lured Indiana to the turf for the first time in recent memory. This man was the target, and for good reason. He was a McDonald's All-American last year, and Van Coleman's *FutureStars* listed him as the No. 2 power-forward prospect in the land.

Strengths: Power and athleticism are Patterson's signatures. Not only does he run the floor with grace, but he is explosive around the basket. Strong hands and good lift make him a presence on the backboards. Those skills are augmented by a soft shooting touch that extends to 15 feet.

Weaknesses: As usually happens with standout big men, Patterson was allowed to roam around on defense in search of blocked shots. That won't be tolerated in Bloomington. He'll get lessons in defensive footwork and positioning. Offensively, he must adapt to Indiana's pass-and-cut system, which most big men are unfamiliar with.

Analysis: Indiana enjoyed a stellar recruiting year, and this youngster is its linchpin. Last year, the Hoosiers lacked athleticism in the frontcourt when you got past Alan Henderson, and Patterson will address that need. He'll be a nice frontcourt complement and a future force in the Big Ten.

STEVE PAYNE

School: Ball St.
Year: Senior
Position: Forward
Height: 6'7" **Weight:** 198
Birthdate: June 27, 1972
Birthplace: Chicago, IL

PLAYER SUMMARY	
Will ....sweep rebounds	
Can't ....drain treys	
Expect...............first-team All-MAC	
Don't Expect .....a household name	

Background: In some respects a late bloomer, Payne finished his prep career at Shepard High School with a flourish. He was named to the *Chicago Tribune's* all-state second team. After sitting out for academic reasons as a freshman, Payne was MVP of the Mid-American Conference Tournament as a sophomore.

Strengths: Although thin, Payne is a first-rate rebounder. He is a good leaper and seals his man off well for position under the boards. From an offensive standpoint, he doesn't attempt to do things he cannot. He scores off putbacks and with quick moves around the goal.

Weaknesses: If Payne has aspirations beyond the MAC, he must extend the range on his jumper. At 6'7", he simply cannot survive at power forward at the next level. His ball-handling skills are weak, and he is not a good passer out of the double-team.

Analysis: Some of Payne's thunder in the MAC has been stolen by Gary Trent, but this is a quality player in his own right. He is a defensive presence for a team that prides itself on its effort at that end of the floor. Moreover, he can control the glass.

COLLEGE STATISTICS

		G	FGP	FTP	RPG	APG	PPG
92-93	BSU	34	.595	.669	9.9	0.5	12.4
93-94	BSU	26	.568	.744	11.0	2.0	20.5
Totals		60	.580	.710	10.4	1.1	15.9

TOM PIPKINS

School: Duquesne
Year: Sophomore
Position: Guard
Height: 6'3" **Weight:** 185
Birthdate: June 24, 1975
Birthplace: New Kensington, PA

PLAYER SUMMARY	
Will	score in bunches
Can't	find the spotlight
Expect	first-team All-A-10
Don't Expect	widespread acclaim

Background: Dukes coach John Carroll made recruiting Pipkins a priority and was richly rewarded. Pipkins set a Duquesne record for points by a freshman and was the Atlantic 10's top freshman scorer. He was a third-team *Basketball Times* Freshman All-American.

Strengths: When the Dukes needed a play on the perimeter last year, they turned to this man. He's got quick feet, and his shooting stroke is true. Scoring off the dribble or off a catch matters not to Pipkins, as he's effective doing both. A steady free throw shooter, he can also lend a hand on the backboards.

Weaknesses: The Dukes have used zone defenses at times, and that hasn't helped Pipkins's man-to-man skills. Like many young players, he needs to retain his concentration at the defensive end and take pride in shutting down the opposition. His consistency from the perimeter could stand improvement too.

Analysis: By the time Duquesne reached the NIT, Pipkins was as essential to the team's success as was former Duke star Derrick Alston. Pipkins has the stuff to be a 20-PPG scorer and is one of the East's most dangerous offensive threats.

COLLEGE STATISTICS

	G	FGP	FTP	RPG	APG	PPG
93-94 DUQ	30	.403	.744	4.7	2.7	14.7
Totals	30	.403	.744	4.7	2.7	14.7

THEO RATLIFF

School: Wyoming
Year: Senior
Position: Forward/Center
Height: 6'10" **Weight:** 190
Birthdate: April 17, 1973
Birthplace: Demopolis, AL

PLAYER SUMMARY	
Will	scare penetrators
Can't	stroke sweet J's
Expect	blocked shots title
Don't Expect	huge point totals

Background: Barely a ripple of notice was made when Ratliff committed to Wyoming in 1991. Viewed as an untapped athlete, Ratliff became a defensive factor quickly. As a sophomore, he led the nation in shots blocked. He finished third nationally in that category as a junior.

Strengths: Timing and leaping ability set Ratliff apart at the defensive end. He reads defensive breakdowns well and knows when to leave his man to help his teammates. Although not a great rebounder, Ratliff makes an effort and grabs his share of caroms.

Weaknesses: "Raw" is the word that best sums up Ratliff's offensive package. He runs the floor well and can score some in transition, but his offensive game in the halfcourt is limited. In some respects, he is hindered by a lack of bulk. What he could really use is a signature move or two that he could consistently rely upon.

Analysis: Ratliff has few peers in the middle when it comes to blocking shots. His is an effortless swat that is the backbone of Wyoming's defense. Further development at the offensive end is a must if Ratliff hopes to make it at the next level.

COLLEGE STATISTICS

	G	FGP	FTP	RPG	APG	PPG
91-92 WYO	27	.438	.583	2.0	0.3	1.8
92-93 WYO	28	.538	.517	6.2	0.3	9.2
93-94 WYO	28	.569	.649	7.8	1.0	15.4
Totals	83	.549	.594	5.3	0.5	8.9

BRYANT REEVES

School: Oklahoma St.
Year: Senior
Position: Center
Height: 7'0" **Weight:** 285
Birthdate: June 8, 1973
Birthplace: Fort Smith, AR

PLAYER SUMMARY	
Will	shoot the hook
Can't	catch speedsters
Expect	a big finish
Don't Expect	a cosmopolitan guy

Background: Hailing from tiny Gans, Oklahoma, Reeves has been one of the college game's most endearing stories. His first major trip in a plane came as a freshman, when the Cowboys traveled to New York for the preseason NIT. Reeves was the Big Eight Player of the Year as a sophomore and All-Big Eight last season.

Strengths: Driving the lane and encountering Reeves is akin to running headlong into a tree. Reeves is a huge presence. For a big man, he generally steers clear of foul trouble. On offense, Reeves has a graceful shooting stroke and a collection of basic moves that make him an interior force.

Weaknesses: As a junior, Reeves struggled to cope with defenses designed solely to stop him. He began finding the open man as the season progressed, but it is an area he must continue to improve upon. Pivots who run the floor can beat him to the opposite end.

Analysis: Reeves is not the most naturally gifted center, but he's come a long way in three years under Eddie Sutton. He has thrived against big-time competition and definitely has an NBA future ahead of him.

COLLEGE STATISTICS

		G	FGP	FTP	RPG	APG	PPG
91-92	OSU	36	.521	.633	5.1	0.7	8.1
92-93	OSU	29	.621	.650	10.0	1.2	19.5
93-94	OSU	34	.585	.595	9.7	1.5	21.0
Totals		99	.584	.621	8.1	1.1	15.9

TERRENCE RENCHER

School: Texas
Year: Senior
Position: Guard
Height: 6'3" **Weight:** 180
Birthdate: February 19, 1973
Birthplace: Bronx, NY

PLAYER SUMMARY	
Will	shoot on the move
Can't	slow down
Expect	clear leadership
Don't Expect	to shut him down

Background: The consensus New York City Player of the Year as a senior at St. Raymond's High School, Rencher was coveted by Rutgers and Seton Hall as well as Texas. He was the Southwest Conference Freshman of the Year in 1992 and is the youngest player in Longhorn history to reach the 1,000-point plateau.

Strengths: Texas loves to run the basketball, and that approach suits Rencher. He's a good ball-handler and extremely quick. On the fastbreak, he can hit the pull-up jump shot or knife to the basket. He rebounds well for a guard.

Weaknesses: With things moving so quickly, Rencher sometimes gets lost in the moment. Better control would serve him well. Rencher also needs to work on his 3-point shot; though he's a scorer, he's not a pure shooter.

Analysis: Rencher has been a fixture in Tom Penders's backcourt since his freshman year. However, his consistency has wavered during the past two seasons, in part due to injury. Texas is expecting big things from Rencher with B.J. Tyler gone, and he appears ready for the challenge.

COLLEGE STATISTICS

		G	FGP	FTP	RPG	APG	PPG
91-92	TEX	34	.463	.706	4.3	3.6	19.1
92-93	TEX	24	.381	.713	5.1	3.5	19.6
93-94	TEX	34	.413	.706	5.4	3.1	15.9
Totals		92	.422	.708	4.9	3.4	18.0

SHAWN RESPERT
School: Michigan St.
Year: Senior
Position: Guard
Height: 6'3" **Weight:** 175
Birthdate: February 6, 1972
Birthplace: Detroit, MI

PLAYER SUMMARY	
Will	score in bunches
Can't	direct traffic
Expect	Big Ten scoring title
Don't Expect	single coverage

Background: After having his first season at MSU ruined by a knee injury, Respert emerged as a second-team Freshman All-American pick of *Basketball Weekly* in 1991-92. He has led the Spartans in scoring in each of his three seasons and was second in the Big Ten to Glenn Robinson in that category last season.

Strengths: This man is a point producer. Offering excellent quickness, Respert can score from virtually anywhere on the court. He's a quality shooter from even beyond the 3-point arc. In the open floor, he can handle the ball and finish plays.

Weaknesses: Respert has definite NBA aspirations—he nearly turned pro after his junior season—but if he is to realize those, he must think more like a point guard. He is not an instinctive passer and is unaccustomed to directing the offense.

Analysis: MSU coach Jud Heathcote was 90 percent sure he would lose Respert to the NBA, but he has him back and that's good news for both player and coach. If Respert upgrades his game a notch, he'll be an All-American.

COLLEGE STATISTICS

		G	FGP	FTP	RPG	APG	PPG
90-91	MSU	1	—	—	—	—	—
91-92	MSU	30	.503	.872	2.1	2.1	15.8
92-93	MSU	28	.481	.856	4.0	2.6	20.1
93-94	MSU	32	.484	.840	4.0	2.5	24.3
Totals		91	.487	.852	3.3	2.4	19.9

JOHNNY RHODES
School: Maryland
Year: Junior
Position: Guard
Height: 6'5" **Weight:** 200
Birthdate: September 13, 1972
Birthplace: Washington, DC

PLAYER SUMMARY	
Will	score in bunches
Can't	be ignored
Expect	reliable production
Don't Expect	much bench time

Background: A product of Dunbar High School in Washington, D.C., Rhodes led his team to two city titles before spending a year at Maine Central Institute. As a freshman, he was runner-up in balloting for ACC Rookie of the Year.

Strengths: Asked to carry less of a scoring burden as a sophomore, Rhodes showed that the rest of his game matched his scoring skills. He can pressure the basketball defensively and is a capable passer. Few can match his first step with the basketball, and he can pull up for the short jumper after beating his man.

Weaknesses: With a heavy load of minutes to carry, Rhodes has learned how to pace himself, and that means there are times when he isn't at his best. In those instances, bad shots are sometimes launched and his defense suffers. The hope at Maryland is that a better bench will make the starters more effective.

Analysis: He didn't get the ink he received as a freshman, but Rhodes was no less effective as a sophomore than he was in 1992-93. Blending his skills with talented mates, this all-around talent will be one of the ACC's top performers.

COLLEGE STATISTICS

		G	FGP	FTP	RPG	APG	PPG
92-93	MARY	28	.420	.530	5.2	3.3	14.0
93-94	MARY	30	.419	.623	6.8	4.1	12.5
Totals		58	.419	.575	6.0	3.7	13.2

RODRICK RHODES

School: Kentucky
Year: Junior
Position: Forward
Height: 6'7" **Weight:** 200
Birthdate: September 24, 1973
Birthplace: Jersey City, NJ

PLAYER SUMMARY	
Will	score off putbacks
Can't	rely solely on talent
Expect	improved shooting
Don't Expect	great consistency

Background: This was the most sought-after prep player in the high school class of 1992. The McDonald's All-American finished his career as the all-time leading scorer at St. Anthony's High School, whose hoop alums include Bobby Hurley and Terry Dehere. He was the MVP of the 1993 ECAC Holiday Festival as a freshman.

Strengths: In the transition game, he can be a force. Rhodes has terrific speed and can convert when he has a lane to the basket. Quick hands make him a threat defensively and he has the long arms and body to be a stopper.

Weaknesses: Rhodes lists his favorite hobby as "taking it easy," and there are those who say he takes it easy a little too often. Too often he disappears and lets the other team dictate the action to him. His perimeter-shooting stroke needs a lot of work.

Analysis: The gauntlet lies before Rhodes. Billed as one of America's next great ones, he really hasn't come close to achieving stardom. All the ingredients are there, however. If he can add some strength and improve his shooting consistency, he could still assume the mantle.

COLLEGE STATISTICS

	G	FGP	FTP	RPG	APG	PPG
92-93 KENT	33	.451	.693	2.4	1.8	9.1
93-94 KENT	33	.436	.777	4.1	2.8	14.6
Totals	66	.442	.750	3.3	2.3	11.8

LOU ROE

School: Massachusetts
Year: Senior
Position: Forward
Height: 6'7" **Weight:** 210
Birthdate: July 14, 1972
Birthplace: Atlantic City, NJ

PLAYER SUMMARY	
Will	out-muscle defenders
Can't	hit from downtown
Expect	relentless rebounding
Don't Expect	a lazy attitude

Background: Roe was New Jersey's Player of the Year as a senior at Atlantic City High School. He averaged 20 minutes a game as a freshman and was a first-team All-Atlantic 10 choice as both a sophomore and junior.

Strengths: An impressive work ethic has fueled Roe's ascension to the elite. That trait also makes him a tremendous rebounder. Once his strong hands grip the ball, it is rarely surrendered. He does his best work on the offensive glass and has added some low-post moves to give him greater scoring opportunities.

Weaknesses: Many of Roe's points come off others' misses, as he is not a naturally gifted offensive performer. He has limited shooting range on his jumper and could use a signature move at the offensive end.

Analysis: In the 1990s, the UMass program has been defined by its toughness and unrelenting style. Roe symbolizes that style as well as anyone. He is a fine low-post defender who has improved his offensive game. Further enhancement would make him a serious threat to become A-10 Player of the Year.

COLLEGE STATISTICS

	G	FGP	FTP	RPG	APG	PPG
91-92 MASS	34	.529	.672	6.4	0.9	7.8
92-93 MASS	31	.564	.725	9.2	1.3	13.8
93-94 MASS	35	.505	.667	8.3	1.7	18.6
Totals	100	.528	.684	8.0	1.3	13.5

SHEA SEALS

School: Tulsa
Year: Sophomore
Position: Guard
Height: 6'5" **Weight:** 190
Birthdate: August 26, 1975
Birthplace: Tulsa, OK

PLAYER SUMMARY	
Will	hit area-code J's
Can't	stop rebounding
Expect	MVC Player of the Year
Don't Expect	failure

Background: Oklahoma's High School Player of the Year as a senior at McLain High, Seals chose to stay in town to play his college basketball. He started all but one contest in his debut season and was named a third-team Freshman All-American by *Basketball Times*. In addition, he was the Missouri Valley's Newcomer of the Year.

Strengths: This man's perimeter game is very polished. He is an exceptional shooter from long range, and defenses must acknowledge his prowess. If they come too close, he's got the kind of speed needed to turn the corner and get into the lane. There aren't many guards who contribute on the backboards the way he does.

Weaknesses: It's hard to quibble with Seals's game. There are moments when he's a bit too eager to gamble at the defensive end, and that leads to breakdowns now and again. Also, he'll occasionally launch a bad shot.

Analysis: Largely obscured until the NCAA Tournament, Seals authored one of the best freshman seasons in the nation. There is no reason to think he won't build upon that. He's one of the best players to come into the Missouri Valley Conference during the 1990s.

COLLEGE STATISTICS

	G	FGP	FTP	RPG	APG	PPG
93-94 TULS	28	.426	.748	6.5	3.5	16.8
Totals	28	.426	.748	6.5	3.5	16.8

JESS SETTLES

School: Iowa
Year: Sophomore
Position: Forward
Height: 6'7" **Weight:** 210
Birthdate: July 7, 1974
Birthplace: Winfield, IA

PLAYER SUMMARY	
Will	thrive in the clutch
Can't	avoid fouls
Expect	steady offense
Don't Expect	blocked shots

Background: A fine prep player from a state without a long history of producing them, Settles was a well-regarded prospect when he signed with the Hawkeyes in 1993. He made 27 starts as an Iowa freshman, finished second on the team in scoring, and was an honorable-mention All-Midwest choice of *Basketball Weekly*.

Strengths: This is a versatile forward whose athleticism is a good fit for the up-tempo attack favored by coach Dr. Tom Davis. Settles works for good shots and is among the Big Ten's field goal-percentage leaders. A threat from 3-point range, he is also a sound free throw shooter and rebounder.

Weaknesses: The one negative in Settles's freshman campaign was his propensity for fouling. He committed 80 fouls and was disqualified five times. That must change. Settles must reach less and move his feet more. Also, he must be more careful with the basketball in the transition game.

Analysis: The task before Settles last year was enormous: Step into the power-forward spot previously held down by the late Chris Street, another Iowan. He handled the situation marvelously and is the cornerstone of Iowa's rebuilding efforts.

COLLEGE STATISTICS

	G	FGP	FTP	RPG	APG	PPG
93-94 IOWA	27	.574	.789	7.5	2.3	15.3
Totals	27	.574	.789	7.5	2.3	15.3

DORON SHEFFER

School: Connecticut
Year: Sophomore
Position: Guard
Height: 6'5" **Weight:** 185
Birthdate: March 12, 1972
Birthplace: Ramat Efal, Israel

PLAYER SUMMARY	
Will	keep his cool
Can't	sky high
Expect	pretty passes
Don't Expect	turnovers

Background: The international resume of this man is extensive. Sheffer was a member of the Israeli national team and his teammates included former UConn star Nadav Henefeld. In 1992-93, Sheffer led his club to the Israeli national championship before coming to Connecticut, where he immediately assumed a starting role.

Strengths: There aren't many passers in the nation better than this man. He has superb court vision and finds passing lanes where there seemingly are none. Defenders must respect his shot because he's very effective when he has time to get set. His great feel for the game makes him a defensive nuisance.

Weaknesses: Sheffer needs time to release his jumper, and tall, athletic defenders can be a bother to him. He's not especially quick, and that sometimes causes him problems at the defensive end.

Analysis: Although he has lacked great scoring numbers, Sheffer's value at Connecticut should not be underestimated. His savvy and passing acumen are essential to UConn's high-octane offense, especially in the halfcourt set. It is his creativity that allows his mates to find easy scores.

COLLEGE STATISTICS

	G	FGP	FTP	RPG	APG	PPG
93-94 CONN	34	.505	.735	3.8	4.8	11.9
Totals	34	.505	.735	3.8	4.8	11.9

JOE SMITH

School: Maryland
Year: Sophomore
Position: Center/Forward
Height: 6'9" **Weight:** 220
Birthdate: July 26, 1975
Birthplace: Norfolk, VA

PLAYER SUMMARY	
Will	keep improving
Can't	find time to rest
Expect	stardom
Don't Expect	any letdown

Analysis: While he received some plaudits in high school (such as the MVP trophy at the fabled Boston Shootout in 1993), Smith was not the most ballyhooed of newcomers entering 1993-94. Yet by year's end, Smith was a consensus choice as national Freshman of the Year and first-team All-ACC.

Strengths: A tremendous athlete, Smith runs the floor as well as any big man in the country. He's very quick, and that makes life tough for the larger men who must try to check him. That quickness helps him on the glass. His great leaping ability and timing make him a shot-blocking menace.

Weaknesses: There wasn't much Smith didn't do as a freshman, so he will have to deal with greater defensive scrutiny this season. Passing out of double-teams is something he'll have to work on.

Analysis: No individual was a greater national surprise last year than this man. He opened with a dominating performance against Georgetown and never really slumped. By season's end, he was among the nation's best. The only real fear they have at Maryland is that pro basketball's dollars may lure him before his four years of eligibility are complete. He's that good.

COLLEGE STATISTICS

	G	FGP	FTP	RPG	APG	PPG
93-94 MARY	30	.522	.734	10.7	0.8	19.4
Totals	30	.522	.734	10.7	0.8	19.4

JERRY STACKHOUSE

School: North Carolina
Year: Sophomore
Position: Forward
Height: 6'6" **Weight:** 218
Birthdate: November 5, 1974
Birthplace: Kinston, NC

PLAYER SUMMARY	
Will	up his scoring
Can't	wait to begin
Expect	All-ACC honors
Don't Expect	shaky defense

Background: Chosen by many as national Player of the Year as a high school senior, Stackhouse's arrival in Chapel Hill elicited great expectations. Despite having veterans ahead of him, Stackhouse became a major contributor by season's end. His brightest moment came at the ACC Tournament, where he was named MVP.

Strengths: Billed as the latest great Tar Heel wing player, Stackhouse is as good as advertised. He'll beat people off the dribble and will connect on the jump shot. On the inside, he is equally effective scoring in traffic and assisting on the backboards.

Weaknesses: Friction developed between Carolina's veterans and promising freshmen last season. The veterans felt the rookies, Stackhouse included, were too cocky and impatient. Those vets are gone, but the mental adjustment to coach Dean Smith's structured system is something Stackhouse still must cope with.

Analysis: After sharing minutes with his elders, Stackhouse now has a chance to be what he was prior to arriving in Chapel Hill— the go-to guy. He has all the tools to be a star and the opportunity is now his. Anything less than a berth on the All-ACC team will be a disappointment.

COLLEGE STATISTICS

	G	FGP	FTP	RPG	APG	PPG
93-94 NC	35	.466	.732	5.0	2.0	12.2
Totals	35	.466	.732	5.0	2.0	12.2

KEBU STEWART

School: UNLV
Year: Sophomore
Position: Forward
Height: 6'8" **Weight:** 230
Birthdate: December 19, 1973
Birthplace: Brooklyn, NY

PLAYER SUMMARY	
Will	work down low
Can't	pile up assists
Expect	relentless rebounding
Don't Expect	steady FT shooting

Background: A 1992 graduate of Our Savior Lutheran High School in the Bronx, Stewart averaged 36.2 points and 17.2 rebounds as a senior. Redshirted for the 1992-93 season after signing with UNLV, Stewart made a successful bow in 1993-94. He was among the national leaders in rebounding and placed second in scoring at UNLV.

Strengths: Stewart has an excellent base from which to work. A powerful frame makes him hard to move in the lane, and he has superb ball skills. Near the shadow of the basket, he demands double-team attention. It is also essential that defenses keep him away from the offensive glass. If they don't, he will burn them with putbacks.

Weaknesses: In the area of assists-to-turnovers, Stewart's numbers were awful. Only ten of his passes led to scores in 22 games last winter. He must concentrate on making better passes and reading double-team situations. Aggressive play on his part sometimes leads to foul difficulty.

Analysis: The decline of UNLV's fortunes in the post-Tarkanian era has relegated Stewart and friends to anonymity. The wonderfully gifted Stewart, though, could change that. He is the top returning player in the Big West Conference.

COLLEGE STATISTICS

	G	FGP	FTP	RPG	APG	PPG
93-94 UNLV	22	.493	.614	11.6	0.5	18.9
Totals	22	.493	.614	11.6	0.5	18.9

DAMON STOUDAMIRE

School: Arizona
Year: Senior
Position: Guard
Height: 5'11" **Weight:** 162
Birthdate: September 3, 1973
Birthplace: Portland, OR

PLAYER SUMMARY	
Will	push the basketball
Can't	soar for blocks
Expect	Pac-10 stardom
Don't Expect	a timid athlete

Background: Oregon's 1991 Player of the Year, Stoudamire participated in the U.S. Olympic Festival before enrolling at Arizona. As a rookie, he was the third guard in a three-guard rotation, but he assumed a starting assignment in 1992-93. He's been an All-Pac-10 choice the past two seasons.

Strengths: This southpaw loves having the basketball in his hands. He is most effective in transition, rushing the ball up the floor and finding the open man as defenders scramble to backpedal. Opponents cannot back off too far because Stoudamire can hit the pull-up 3-pointer or take it to the hole. He's also a quick defender.

Weaknesses: Prone to streaks of hot and cold shooting, Stoudamire sometimes fires too rapidly. He needs to concentrate on taking fewer bad shots. Coach Lute Olson would like to get him more rest too.

Analysis: Stoudamire saw his stock soar in the 1994 NCAA Tournament. He directed the Wildcats to the Final Four in Charlotte and made great decisions throughout. His shooting wavered against Arkansas, but that had as much to do with weariness as it did anything else.

COLLEGE STATISTICS

		G	FGP	FTP	RPG	APG	PPG
91-92	ARIZ	30	.455	.771	2.2	2.5	7.2
92-93	ARIZ	28	.438	.791	4.1	5.7	11.0
93-94	ARIZ	35	.448	.800	4.5	5.9	18.3
Totals		93	.447	.792	3.6	4.8	12.5

BOB SURA

School: Florida St.
Year: Senior
Position: Guard
Height: 6'5" **Weight:** 200
Birthdate: March 25, 1973
Birthplace: Wilkes-Barre, PA

PLAYER SUMMARY	
Will	hit the "J" off a screen
Can't	resist drives
Expect	tons of points
Don't Expect	savvy leadership

Background: Pennsylvania's small-school Player of the Year as a senior at GAR Memorial High School, Sura made a huge splash as a frosh at FSU, taking ACC Rookie of the Year honors. He led an NCAA Tournament team in scoring as a sophomore and has been a second-team All-ACC selection each of the past two years.

Strengths: There's no fear here. Sura loves to fly into the lane with his superior jumping ability and can finish the play. He's also a serious threat from long range. The look-away pass is one of his favorite ploys, and he is diligent in his defensive work.

Weaknesses: As a junior, Sura made strides in his decision-making, which is his greatest weakness. There were fewer forced shots and silly fouls. He's still prone to playing out of control, however, and bad passes remain nettlesome.

Analysis: A marked man for the first time in his college career, Sura adjusted last year as the season progressed. He possesses wonderful athletic gifts and will receive greater assistance from the interior of the Seminole lineup. That combination should add up to FSU's return to NCAA play.

COLLEGE STATISTICS

		G	FGP	FTP	RPG	APG	PPG
91-92	FSU	31	.461	.627	3.5	2.5	12.3
92-93	FSU	34	.452	.638	6.1	2.7	19.9
93-94	FSU	27	.469	.664	7.9	4.5	21.2
Totals		92	.460	.640	5.7	3.1	17.7

KELLY THAMES

School: Missouri
Year: Sophomore
Position: Forward
Height: 6'7" **Weight:** 207
Birthdate: April 13, 1975
Birthplace: St. Louis, MO

PLAYER SUMMARY	
Will	be smooth as silk
Can't	stop improving
Expect	a starring role
Don't Expect	a slump

Background: As a senior at Jennings High School, Thames was voted "Mr. Show-Me Basketball" by the Missouri Basketball Coaches Association and Player of the Year by the *St. Louis Post Dispatch.* At Missouri, Thames stepped into a starting role and was a fifth-team Freshman All-American pick of *Basketball Weekly.*

Strengths: An elusive sort, Thames is quick for a tall man and operates with ease in the paint or on the perimeter. He has a quality jump shot with the proper mechanics. On the inside, he gets good position in post-up situations and uses soft hands to snag rebounds. His graceful gait disguises his excellent foot speed.

Weaknesses: The place coach Norm Stewart most wanted Thames to visit this past off-season was the weight room. He needs more upper-body strength, and that will come through lifting and maturity.

Analysis: CBS analyst Al McGuire fell in love with Thames's game during the NCAA Tournament, and it's easy to understand why. He's athletic and quick and plays with a rare style. His complete package of skills will only improve as he adds more years of Big Eight experience to his resume.

COLLEGE STATISTICS

		G	FGP	FTP	RPG	APG	PPG
93-94	MO	32	.514	.729	7.1	1.2	12.2
Totals		32	.514	.729	7.1	1.2	12.2

KURT THOMAS

School: Texas Christian
Year: Senior
Position: Center
Height: 6'9" **Weight:** 230
Birthdate: October 4, 1972
Birthplace: Dallas, TX

PLAYER SUMMARY	
Will	produce inside
Can't	let focus waver
Expect	All-SWC kudos
Don't Expect	great maturity

Background: Thomas's career has been plagued by injuries. As a senior at Dallas Hillcrest High School, he suffered a broken ankle. In college, he redshirted the entire 1992-93 season because of a broken tibia. Last year, he played part of the year with a broken hand and still led TCU in scoring.

Strengths: Blessed with soft hands, Thomas is a quality scorer. He uses a soft jumper to make all kinds of shots around the basket, and he can finish a play with a rim-rattling slam. One of the best rebounders in the Southwest, Thomas does a good bit of damage off of putbacks.

Weaknesses: Maturity was sometimes lacking when he played for former coach Moe Iba. Thomas would often pout when he was removed from the game, and the coaching staff appeared to tread lightly where Thomas was concerned. Increased stamina would be a big plus.

Analysis: Despite some flaws, Thomas was one of the SWC's best players last year. Now, with the accomplished Billy Tubbs coaching him, a big season could be in store. Thomas has the tools and needs only maturity to become a force.

COLLEGE STATISTICS

		G	FGP	FTP	RPG	APG	PPG
90-91	TCU	28	.444	.500	1.1	0.1	1.9
91-92	TCU	21	.487	.667	5.4	1.1	7.1
93-94	TCU	27	.509	.645	9.7	1.9	20.7
Totals		76	.503	.641	5.1	1.0	9.6

SCOTTY THURMAN

School: Arkansas
Year: Junior
Position: Forward
Height: 6'5" **Weight:** 200
Birthdate: November 10, 1974
Birthplace: Ruston, LA

PLAYER SUMMARY	
Will	talk the talk
Can't	forget The Shot
Expect	long-range accuracy
Don't Expect	modesty

Background: As a prep star at Ruston High, Thurman scored 2,475 points—yet there was not a lot of hype attached to his arrival at Arkansas. Attention soon came, though, as Thurman became a Freshman All-American pick of *Basketball Times* while starting 31 times.

Strengths: The kind of shot Thurman sank to beat Duke in the 1994 NCAA finals is his calling card. The self-assured veteran arcs rainbow 3-pointers with impressive accuracy. He's also quick and athletic and willing to pay the price at the defensive end.

Weaknesses: One of the more talkative players in college basketball during games, Thurman's tongue can get him into trouble at times. Off-balance shots are still a little too common. Also, more upper-body strength would allow him to become a force in post-up situations.

Analysis: Thurman is a pure offensive talent. He'll beat defenders off the dribble or—as he did against Antonio Lang at crunch time—from deep outside. The two years' worth of experience he's received at the game's highest levels has helped his maturity. This guy's wearing a championship ring for a reason.

COLLEGE STATISTICS

	G	FGP	FTP	RPG	APG	PPG
92-93 ARK	31	.465	.800	4.4	2.2	17.4
93-94 ARK	34	.469	.732	4.5	3.0	15.9
Totals	65	.467	.765	4.5	2.6	16.6

KAREEM TOWNES

School: La Salle
Year: Senior
Position: Guard
Height: 6'3" **Weight:** 175
Birthdate: February 9, 1973
Birthplace: Philadelphia, PA

PLAYER SUMMARY	
Will	keep scoreboard changing
Can't	pass up a shot
Expect	explosions to the hoop
Don't Expect	quality defense

Background: As a senior at Southern High School, Townes became a gunner of legendary proportions as he averaged 41 PPG. He became an instant starter for coach Speedy Morris at La Salle. In his two seasons of active duty, he's been a first-team All-MCC pick.

Strengths: Blessed with exceptional quickness, Townes can score from virtually any angle. Off the dribble, he is usually too fast for his foe; and when he reaches the lane, he knows how to finish the play. His long-range shot is streaky, but when it's on there aren't many guards who can stop it.

Weaknesses: The quintessential schoolyard player, Townes sometimes seems to think that every possession is an opportunity for him to launch a shot. He needs to play with more control. Defensively, his concentration isn't always what it should be.

Analysis: Townes has posted some remarkable numbers at both the high school and collegiate level, but Morris was unhappy with how last season went. He'd be much happier if Townes focused less on scoring and improved the rest of his game, for he is already one of the nation's most explosive scorers.

COLLEGE STATISTICS

	G	FGP	FTP	RPG	APG	PPG
92-93 LaS	27	.369	.698	3.5	3.0	22.5
93-94 LaS	27	.374	.772	3.4	2.0	22.9
Totals	54	.372	.735	3.5	2.5	22.7

GARY TRENT

School: Ohio
Year: Junior
Position: Forward
Height: 6'7" **Weight:** 230
Birthdate: September 22, 1974
Birthplace: Columbus, OH

PLAYER SUMMARY	
Will............set the pace in the MAC
Can't..................be seen in prime time
Expect......................great decisions
Don't Expect........poor confidence

Background: Overlooked by some larger schools as a prep senior at Hamilton Township High School, Trent has made those programs rue their oversight. He is a two-time Mid-American Conference Player of the Year as well as a second-team All-Midwest pick of *Basketball Weekly*.

Strengths: The first item about Trent's game that strikes observers is its completeness. He loves to work on the inside, and his first step is explosive. Those who concentrate solely on his inside work, though, best not ignore his jumper—he can drain the 3. This is also a smart player who finds open mates when double-teamed.

Weaknesses: At times, Trent can be drawn into making poor passes when he is trying to match another star's output. While strong, Trent can have trouble when he is matched defensively against quality tall men.

Analysis: Only the most ardent hoop fans are familiar with this youngster, but that may change. Trent is a Big Ten-calibre talent who will continue to haunt an Ohio State program that ignored him when it had its chance. He is the most dominant player to play in the Mid-American Conference since Dan Majerle.

COLLEGE STATISTICS

	G	FGP	FTP	RPG	APG	PPG
92-93 OHIO	27	.651	.696	9.3	1.6	19.0
93-94 OHIO	33	.576	.722	11.4	2.0	25.4
Totals	60	.603	.712	10.5	1.8	22.5

DAVID VAUGHN

School: Memphis St.
Year: Junior
Position: Forward
Height: 6'9" **Weight:** 235
Birthdate: March 23, 1973
Birthplace: Tulsa, OK

PLAYER SUMMARY	
Will..................................hit sweet J's
Can't.................dribble like a guard
Expect ....first-team All-GMC
Don't Expect............further slumps

Background: The nephew of Memphis State coach Larry Finch, Vaughn was named a first-team Freshman All-American by *Basketball Times*. A partially torn anterior cruciate ligament in his left knee ended his 1992-93 season after one game.

Strengths: Vaughn has a wealth of skills for a power player. He's got the requisite bulk to move people around under the basket, and he's got the moves to capitalize when he gets into good position. He can drill the face-up jumper.

Weaknesses: There are moments when Vaughn is too eager to dribble. Until he enhances his ball-handling skills, he should leave the work to guards who are best suited to avoiding traps. Vaughn made too many turnovers last year and not enough quality passes to open men.

Analysis: Few teams underachieved as badly as the Tigers did last year, and Vaughn was partly responsible. There was friction among cocky freshmen, some of it reportedly because the youngsters thought Finch's nephew got preferential treatment. That talk must end so the Tigers can concentrate on using Vaughn's vast skills.

COLLEGE STATISTICS

	G	FGP	FTP	RPG	APG	PPG
91-92 MEMP	34	.513	.761	8.3	0.7	13.4
92-93 MEMP	1	.364	—	8.0	2.0	10.0
93-94 MEMP	28	.496	.757	12.0	1.1	16.6
Totals	63	.502	.758	9.9	0.9	14.8

JACQUE VAUGHN

School: Kansas
Year: Sophomore
Position: Guard
Height: 6'1" **Weight:** 180
Birthdate: February 11, 1975
Birthplace: Pasadena, CA

PLAYER SUMMARY	
Will	make smart passes
Can't	handle tall guards
Expect	strong leadership
Don't Expect	dull plays

Background: The No. 2 point-guard prospect in the prep class of 1993 brought an impressive resume to Lawrence. Vaughn made straight A's throughout high school with the exception of a B+ in a tenth-grade English class. He was the Dial Award winner as the top male prep scholar-athlete in the country. Vaughn was a *Basketball Times* first-team Freshman All-American.

Strengths: Flashy and intelligent, Vaughn is a unique package of speed and smarts. He can turn the corner with the basketball on most defenders and get into the lane, where he loves to create easy shots for his Jayhawk teammates. Vaughn can also pressure the basketball on the perimeter.

Weaknesses: Although he hit a bomb to beat Indiana in December, Vaughn is not a sweet-shooting long-range marksman. Defenses will sag off of him to protect the lane, and that reduces Vaughn's passing options. His jumper must improve.

Analysis: One of the more talented prep prospects, Vaughn delivered as a freshman. He assumed a leadership position on a good Kansas team and helped steer it to the regional semifinals. Vaughn's scoring and assist totals should rise as he grows more acclimated to the college game.

COLLEGE STATISTICS

		G	FGP	FTP	RPG	APG	PPG
93-94	KANS	35	.467	.670	2.5	5.2	7.8
Totals		35	.467	.670	2.5	5.2	7.8

H WALDMAN

School: St. Louis
Year: Senior
Position: Guard
Height: 6'3" **Weight:** 195
Birthdate: January 21, 1972
Birthplace: Las Vegas, NV

PLAYER SUMMARY	
Will	control the tempo
Can't	clean the glass
Expect	crisp passes
Don't Expect	great scoring

Background: For starters, his real name is H because both his father and grandfather were named Herb but his mother didn't care for the name. The Nevada Player of the Year in high school, Waldman signed with UNLV and played two years for the Rebels before transferring when NCAA sanctions took effect.

Strengths: Waldman understands how to create for others. He has a feel for passing lanes and angles, which helps set up easy scores for the likes of Erwin Claggett and the big men inside. A quick first step helps him get past the first wave of defense.

Weaknesses: It's not unusual for a great creator to sometimes get too creative, and that happens with Waldman. On occasion, he attempts to be too fine, and the result is a turnover. At the defensive end, he must stay focused on the job at hand.

Analysis: Don't let the scoring totals fool you. Waldman was sought by the likes of Kentucky and Michigan out of high school for a reason. His exceptional feel for the game and outstanding ball-handling skills help keep the Billikens under control and out of danger against pressing defenses.

COLLEGE STATISTICS

		G	FGP	FTP	RPG	APG	PPG
90-91	UNLV	31	.512	.600	1.0	2.3	2.1
91-92	UNLV	27	.507	.731	1.3	3.0	4.1
93-94	SL	29	.436	.805	2.7	5.2	10.3
Totals		87	.461	.758	1.7	3.5	5.5

JOHN WALLACE

School: Syracuse
Year: Junior
Position: Forward
Height: 6'7" **Weight:** 215
Birthdate: February 9, 1974
Birthplace: Rochester, NY

PLAYER SUMMARY	
Will	collect rebounds
Can't	shoot 3's
Expect	steady scoring
Don't Expect	a physical player

Background: As a senior at Greece-Athena High School, Wallace was a prep All-American, courted by the Eastern powers. He earned a great deal of respect from his Orange mates for choosing the school even though it had just been hit by NCAA penalties. A strong debut earned Wallace second-team Freshman All-American honors from *Basketball Weekly*.

Strengths: There is a knack to great rebounding, and Wallace has it. He isn't especially powerful but he gets good position underneath to grab caroms. Defenders must put a body on him or he will score off putbacks. Soft hands allow him to shoot effectively from 15 feet facing the basket. He's also a willing defender.

Weaknesses: Although a fine rebounder, Wallace is not much of a physical presence inside. Added bulk would enhance his game. He is not a threat to drain 3's.

Analysis: Wallace has patiently waited as most of the plays at Syracuse have been run for Adrian Autry and Lawrence Moten. Autry's gone, so Wallace should get more offensive looks. His offensive skills and ability to run the floor should result in better scoring numbers.

COLLEGE STATISTICS

		G	FGP	FTP	RPG	APG	PPG
92-93	SYR	29	.526	.718	7.6	1.3	11.1
93-94	SYR	30	.566	.761	9.0	1.7	15.0
Totals		59	.547	.746	8.3	1.5	13.1

RASHEED WALLACE

School: North Carolina
Year: Sophomore
Position: Forward/Center
Height: 6'10" **Weight:** 225
Birthdate: September 17, 1974
Birthplace: Philadelphia, PA

PLAYER SUMMARY	
Will	alter shots
Can't	keep quiet
Expect	improved stats
Don't Expect	to be bored

Background: Called the best big man in Philadelphia since the days of Wilt Chamberlain, Wallace was pursued by the most prominent programs in America. As a freshman, Wallace became a starter in February and saw lots of action in NCAA play.

Strengths: Among big men nationally, only Marcus Camby can rival Wallace's speed. The left-hander receives the ball well and will have more room to flash his low-post skills now that Eric Montross and Kevin Salvadori have graduated. Wallace has a great sense of timing at the defensive end and comes from off the ball to swat away shots.

Weaknesses: His penchant for talking trash on the floor was curbed but not eradicated as a freshman. As he matures, that should become less of an issue. One advantage Wallace had last winter was that he never dealt with low-post double-teams. Learning to adapt to those will be a challenge.

Analysis: The fact that Wallace moved ahead of steady veterans like Salvadori in Dean Smith's system—which historically favors seniors—says much about this man's enormous gifts. This season, Wallace will be in the middle from the start, and that will lead to increased scoring and rebounding numbers. The apprenticeship is over.

COLLEGE STATISTICS

		G	FGP	FTP	RPG	APG	PPG
93-94	NC	35	.604	.604	6.6	0.5	9.5
Totals		35	.604	.604	6.6	0.5	9.5

JEROD WARD

School: Michigan
Year: Freshman
Position: Forward
Height: 6'9" **Weight:** 205
Birthdate: May 5, 1976
Birthplace: Clinton, MS

PLAYER SUMMARY	
Will	dominate on the wing
Can't	run through people
Expect	immediate impact
Don't Expect	a disappointment

Background: As is the case with most prep prodigies, Ward first made his mark on the summer camp circuit. In his senior season at Clinton High School, Ward was voted a McDonald's All-American and a first-team *USA Today* All-American. Van Coleman's *FutureStars* lists him as the premier quick-forward prospect in the incoming class of freshmen.

Strengths: The traditionally staid fans at Crisler Arena may have a hard time staying in their seats for this newcomer. Ward has an incredible first step and is a fine ball-handler for a man standing 6'9". He has a height advantage over most of those who must check him, and he uses that to his benefit.

Weaknesses: Ward is not a power player and will take his lumps underneath the basket as a rookie, particularly if he plays alongside classmate Willie Mitchell, another finesse performer. At the defensive end, Ward must concentrate more on sound fundamental play than blocking shots.

Analysis: He kept his suitors in suspense until May, but Ward's choice means Michigan will remain a player in the national championship race. This is a graceful athlete capable of the exceptional, and it would be a shock if he plays all four seasons in Ann Arbor. The NBA is in his future.

CARLIN WARLEY

School: St. Joseph's
Year: Senior
Position: Forward
Height: 6'7" **Weight:** 240
Birthdate: January 6, 1971
Birthplace: Philadelphia, PA

PLAYER SUMMARY	
Will	create room inside
Can't	strike from outside
Expect	crushing picks
Don't Expect	disinterested play

Background: That Warley assaulted Wilt Chamberlain's prep scoring records in high school (he scored 2,358 points) seems appropriate. Chamberlain is his godfather. Warley's father, Ben, played in the NBA. Carlin has enjoyed three productive years at St. Joe's, including 1993-94, when he was a second-team All-Atlantic 10 pick.

Strengths: Brute force is the cornerstone of Warley's game. He's strong and is not afraid to use his power to establish position under the basket. Warley has excellent timing in rebounding situations and has a good sense for where the ball will carom to.

Weaknesses: Away from the basket, Warley is uncomfortable. His face-up jumper is not a strength, as most of his points are the result of putbacks. Often forced to play in the middle, Warley has difficulty with tall, natural centers.

Analysis: Warley was forced to sit out his freshman campaign, but the NCAA decided to give him back his lost season of eligibility. Warley is a warrior whose style punishes the opposition. He was a major reason why St. Joe's survived injuries to remain competitive in 1993-94.

COLLEGE STATISTICS

		G	FGP	FTP	RPG	APG	PPG
91-92	SJ	28	.518	.695	9.0	1.4	11.6
92-93	SJ	29	.496	.652	9.0	1.9	12.0
93-94	SJ	28	.470	.684	11.4	2.0	16.4
Totals		85	.491	.677	9.8	1.7	13.3

DeJUAN WHEAT

School: Louisville
Year: Sophomore
Position: Guard
Height: 6'0" **Weight:** 160
Birthdate: October 14, 1973
Birthplace: Louisville, KY

PLAYER SUMMARY	
Will	drive and dish
Can't	battle the giants
Expect	quality treys
Don't Expect	much relief

Background: Ballard High School has a long history of producing basketball stars who went on to success at Louisville, and Wheat's the latest. As a senior, he averaged 22.8 points per game. After sitting out a season, Wheat was *Basketball Times'* Newcomer of the Year in 1993-94.

Strengths: Forced to step immediately into the lineup in his first season of college basketball, Wheat displayed excellent leadership qualities. He's very quick, can dribble through traffic, and can find the open man on the fastbreak. Defenders can't relax when he's on the perimeter, for he has a good long-range stroke.

Weaknesses: Experienced guards gave Wheat some trouble last season. His thin frame takes a beating over the long haul, and powerful guards can post him up in one-on-one situations. Sometimes he needs to exert more patience when opportunities are unavailable.

Analysis: After Keith LeGree's transfer, point guard was a huge question mark at Louisville entering last season. Wheat solved that problem. He kept improving as the season went along and was among the Metro Conference's elite by March. Greater consistency would add that much more.

COLLEGE STATISTICS

	G	FGP	FTP	RPG	APG	PPG
93-94	LOU	34	.450	.769	2.1	3.2	12.6
Totals		34	.450	.769	2.1	3.2	12.6

DONALD WILLIAMS

School: North Carolina
Year: Senior
Position: Guard
Height: 6'3" **Weight:** 194
Birthdate: February 24, 1973
Birthplace: Raleigh, NC

PLAYER SUMMARY	
Will	stroke the jumper
Can't	maintain his confidence
Expect	a return to form
Don't Expect	perfect health

Background: North Carolina's Player of the Year in high school, Williams signed with the Tar Heels and saw limited action as a freshman. He earned a starting nod as a sophomore and gunned his team to the 1993 national championship, winning the Final Four's Most Outstanding Player Award.

Strengths: When he's right, Williams is one of the best pure shooters in the country. A quick release and steady eye make him deadly from 3-point land. Williams also knows how to find the open man when defenses come too close to him. He has improved his ball-handling.

Weaknesses: Williams seemed to lose confidence after he was hurt in 1993-94. His fabled shooting touch seemed to leave him after his injury, and that had much to do with North Carolina's early departure from last year's NCAA Tournament.

Analysis: Williams won't fondly recall his junior season. It was wrought with injury and self-doubt. Renewed health should give him the jump-start he needs to regain his previous stature. All of the ingredients for a big season are in place if he can avoid the injury bug.

COLLEGE STATISTICS

		G	FGP	FTP	RPG	APG	PPG
91-92	NC	29	.377	.571	0.7	0.6	2.2
92-93	NC	37	.458	.829	1.9	1.2	14.3
93-94	NC	26	.422	.770	2.4	2.2	14.3
Totals		92	.436	.795	1.7	1.3	10.5

ERIC WILLIAMS
School: Providence
Year: Senior
Position: Forward
Height: 6'8" **Weight:** 218
Birthdate: July 17, 1972
Birthplace: Newark, NJ

PLAYER SUMMARY	
Will	lead team in scoring
Can't	rely on outside shot
Expect	success under new coach
Don't Expect	superior passing

Background: This decorated prep athlete at Shabazz High School in Newark was an all-state choice as a senior. He then attended Vincennes Junior College, where he was a first-team junior college All-American as a sophomore. At P.C., he led the club in scoring last year.

Strengths: He's a skilled big man who owns a nifty shooting stroke with range to 15 feet. Williams has the size to work on the interior and is hard to stop when he operates in the painted area. He has good quickness for a man of his stature and can move up and down the floor.

Weaknesses: Perhaps it was because rebounding ace Michael Smith played alongside him, but Williams's rebounding production was not what it should have been last year. He needs to be willing to get his hands dirty, especially on the defensive boards. He should work inside more and not rely so much on the perimeter shot.

Analysis: Williams enjoyed a strong junior season, scoring more points than many would have envisioned. New Friar coach Pete Gillen will ask him to upgrade his defense and rebounding, and he has the tools to do so. Williams will thrive in Gillen's uptempo system.

COLLEGE STATISTICS

	G	FGP	FTP	RPG	APG	PPG
93-94 PROV	30	.508	.660	5.0	1.2	15.7
Totals	30	.508	.660	5.0	1.2	15.7

CORLISS WILLIAMSON
School: Arkansas
Year: Junior
Position: Forward
Height: 6'7" **Weight:** 245
Birthdate: December 4, 1973
Birthplace: Russellville, AR

PLAYER SUMMARY	
Will	resemble Larry Johnson
Can't	miss as a pro
Expect	a first-team All-American
Don't Expect	ill-advised shots

Background: A consensus high school All-American, Williamson might be the best player ever produced in Arkansas. This super-prospect was on the SEC All-Freshman team despite missing 13 games due to injury. He was named to the A.P.'s second-team All-American squad in 1993-94.

Strengths: This is a complete player. Williamson has the size, power, and will to dominate on the interior. He is an excellent receiver in the low post and has superb touch with the basketball. In the past two seasons, he's added range to his jumper. He's a first-rate rebounder.

Weaknesses: Unlike many of his Razorback mates, Williamson is not a threat from 3-point territory. Improvement at the free throw line would help him both now and when he reaches the next level.

Analysis: Arkansas coach Nolan Richardson said prior to last season that he did not anticipate having Williamson for more than three years, and that's not an unrealistic scenario. With his performance in last year's Final Four, Williamson showed that he is one of the nation's great players. He's a sure All-American and a top-five NBA draft choice.

COLLEGE STATISTICS

	G	FGP	FTP	RPG	APG	PPG
92-93 ARK	18	.574	.622	5.1	1.7	14.6
93-94 ARK	34	.626	.700	7.7	2.2	20.4
Totals	52	.611	.675	6.8	2.0	18.4

ALABAMA

Conference: Southeastern   **1993-94 NCAAs:** 1-1
1993-94: 20-10, 2nd SEC West   **Coach:** David Hobbs (36-23)

Opening Line: The top five scorers return from an Alabama team that rebuilt in a hurry in 1993-94. The Crimson Tide not only earned a bid to the NCAA Tournament, but they knocked off a higher-seeded team in the first round ('Bama was a No. 9 seed, Providence a No. 8) before falling to Glenn Robinson and Purdue in Round 2. The Tide players' appetites were merely whetted, as they enter the 1994-95 season with high expectations.

Guard: The team's two major graduation losses are in the backcourt (swing man Shon Peck-Love and guard Walter Pitts), but the cupboard isn't exactly bare. Marvin Orange runs a steady ship at the point, and swing man Artie Griffin—a junior college transfer who led the team in assists and steals last year—is poised for a strong senior season. Eric Washington and sharpshooter Bryan Passink both have valuable experience.

Forward: Former Pac-10 Freshman of the Year Jamal Faulkner settled in nicely for his new team last year, leading the Tide in scoring and finishing third in both rebounds and assists. Jason Caffey and Antonio McDyess also ranked among the top three on the team in scoring and rebounding. McDyess is an excellent defensive player, topping the Tide in blocks and tying for third in steals last year. Swing man Anthony Brown will get his share of minutes.

Center: Roy Rogers rides saddle in the pivot, with help from Wade Kaiser. Neither gets substantial minutes. Rogers can help the team with his shot-blocking.

Analysis: This is a team to watch in the SEC. They can score, defend, and rebound well, and that's a formula for success. Faulkner should go out with a bang, especially with pro scouts watching him closely this year. David Hobbs has done a fine job in his two years at Alabama, but fans will expect a little more from his talented club this season.

1994-95 ROSTER

	POS	HT	YR	FGP	FTP	3-PT	RPG	APG	PPG
Jamal Faulkner	F	6'7"	Sr.	.43	.65	22/77	5.9	1.9	13.5
Jason Caffey	F	6'8"	Sr.	.52	.63	1/2	6.3	0.7	12.8
Antonio McDyess	F/C	6'9"	So.	.56	.53	—	8.1	0.4	11.4
Marvin Orange	G	6'1"	Jr.	.42	.74	58/135	2.1	2.8	10.1
Artie Griffin	G/F	6'4"	Sr.	.40	.66	31/87	2.6	3.0	7.4
Anthony Brown	G/F	6'5"	Jr.	.31	.64	5/33	1.8	0.6	3.6
Eric Washington	G	6'4"	So.	.40	.73	5/28	1.0	0.7	3.5
Bryan Passink	G	6'3"	Jr.	.47	.65	14/35	0.8	0.5	3.4
Roy Rogers	C	6'9"	Jr.	.49	.68	—	2.7	0.1	3.0
Wade Kaiser	C	6'9"	So.	.29	.72	0/1	1.7	0.1	1.8
Terrance Bethel	G	6'0"	Sr.	.38	.71	0/2	0.3	1.0	1.2
Marco Whitfield	G	6'0"	Jr.	—	—	—	—	—	—

ARIZONA

Conference: Pac-10
1993-94: 29-6, 1st Pac-10

1993-94 NCAAs: 4-1
Coach: Lute Olson (458-179)

Opening Line: The Wildcats shook their reputation as NCAA Tournament underachievers by advancing to the Final Four last spring. "En garde" was the rallying cry, thanks to arguably the best guard tandem in all of college basketball—Khalid Reeves and Damon Stoudamire. Reeves is gone this year, but Stoudamire and the rest of the starting lineup return to help Arizona retain its hold over the West Coast.

Guard: It's Stoudamire's team now, and every indication says he's up to the task. His 18.3 PPG last year were the most by a Wildcat junior since Sean Elliott's 19.6 in 1988. He pushes the ball up the floor as well as anyone. Reggie Geary, a human blanket on defense, brings experience and intensity to the backcourt. Joe McLean (6'6") is a Jud Buechler clone who should get more minutes. Frosh Miles Simon is a blue-chipper.

Forward: Ray Owes scored in double figures in 27 games as a junior and was fourth in the Pac-10 in rebounding. Joseph Blair shot 65.5 percent from the field in his last 23 games. They are a formidable duo inside, and Owes isn't afraid to drift out to the 3-point line. Corey Williams can also sink the trey, while 6'9" Ben Davis—an outstanding juco transfer—will add quality depth to the front line.

Center: The Wildcats went with a three-guard lineup last year, but Blair patrols the pivot in a conventional offense. He's an inside banger who knows his shooting range. No one on the roster stands taller than 6'9".

Analysis: It's been the same old same-old in Tucson. Seven of the last nine seasons have resulted in a league title for Arizona, and this year looks no different. This team won't be shy about launching the 3-pointer either, though with Reeves gone, last year's school-record 787 attempts probably won't be matched. Don't be surprised if Owes emerges as an All-Pac-10 performer.

1994-95 ROSTER

	POS	HT	YR	FGP	FTP	3-PT	RPG	APG	PPG
Damon Stoudamire	G	5'11"	Sr.	.45	.80	93/265	4.5	5.9	18.3
Ray Owes	F	6'9"	Sr.	.50	.64	17/53	8.1	0.7	12.9
Joseph Blair	F/C	6'9"	Jr.	.61	.44	0/1	7.2	0.6	10.1
Reggie Geary	G	6'2"	Jr.	.45	.60	27/89	3.7	3.5	7.4
Corey Williams	F	6'7"	Jr.	.49	.62	14/33	2.5	0.5	3.8
Joe McLean	G	6'6"	Jr.	.38	.58	17/60	1.8	0.4	3.1
Jarvis Kelley	F	6'9"	So.	.50	.67	—	1.8	0.1	2.1
Ben Davis	F	6'9"	Jr.	—	—	—	—	—	—
Michael Dickerson	F	6'5"	Fr.	—	—	—	—	—	—
Kelvin Eafon	G	6'1"	Fr.	—	—	—	—	—	—
Donnell Harris	F	6'9"	Fr.	—	—	—	—	—	—
Miles Simon	G	6'4"	Fr.	—	—	—	—	—	—

ARKANSAS

Conference: Southeastern
1993-94: 31-3, 1st SEC West

1993-94 NCAAs: 6-0
Coach: Nolan Richardson (339-112)

Opening Line: What do the Razorbacks do for an encore? After hanging around the tops of the polls for the last several years, Arkansas finally earned top billing in 1993-94, winning its first national championship with a 76-72 triumph over Duke in the NCAA championship game. The scary part is that the top seven players from that season in the sun are back for 1994-95. President Bill Clinton is in Hog Heaven.

Guard: Point guard Corey Beck is the "heart of the team," according to Richardson, and Beck's big-game attitude was in full force while earning All-Final Four recognition. Reserve Al Dillard's range is seemingly limitless, and the team grandpa is never afraid to launch the 3-pointer. Clint McDaniel adds to the embarrassment of riches, having started 13 games last year. McDaniel was brilliant in the NCAA Tournament.

Forward: Junior strongman Corliss Williamson will be a leading candidate—if not *the* leading candidate—for national Player of the Year honors. He's virtually unstoppable with the ball in his hands, and he's developed into a nifty passer too. Scotty Thurman secured a spot in Final Four lore with his decisive 3-pointer in the title game vs. Duke. The long-range bomber extraordinaire is 62 3-pointers away from the school's career record.

Center: Dwight Stewart might not look like an athlete, with his baby face and baby fat, but he can play. He can hit the trey too. Darnell Robinson, one of the best freshman in the SEC last year, adds beef up front.

Analysis: The Razorbacks have something in common with every other national champion in the 1990s: A repeat title seems like a strong possibility. Remember, though, that only Duke followed up on the promise, while UNLV and North Carolina fell short. There are no guarantees. It never hurts, though, to have the leader of the free world in your corner.

1994-95 ROSTER

	POS	HT	YR	FGP	FTP	3-PT	RPG	APG	PPG
Corliss Williamson	F	6'7"	Jr.	.63	.70	—	7.7	2.2	20.4
Scotty Thurman	F	6'6"	Jr.	.47	.73	85/198	4.5	3.0	15.9
Alex Dillard	G	6'1"	Sr.	.40	.79	75/183	1.1	1.4	8.9
Corey Beck	G	6'2"	Sr.	.51	.67	5/11	3.9	5.0	8.8
Clint McDaniel	G	6'4"	Sr.	.41	.75	38/108	2.8	1.9	8.1
Dwight Stewart	C	6'9"	Sr.	.45	.65	37/95	5.0	1.4	8.0
Darnell Robinson	C	6'11"	So.	.46	.58	7/23	4.7	1.9	7.6
Davor Rimac	G	6'7"	Sr.	.46	.79	32/79	1.9	0.9	4.8
Lee Wilson	C	6'11"	So.	.49	.58	—	3.1	0.4	3.4
Reggie Garrett	F	6'4"	Jr.	—	—	—	—	—	—
Kareem Reid	G	5'10"	Fr.	—	—	—	—	—	—
Landis Williams	F	6'7"	Fr.	—	—	—	—	—	—

BOSTON COLLEGE

Conference: Big East   **1993-94 NCAAs:** 3-1
1993-94: 23-11, 3rd Big East   **Coach:** Jim O'Brien (185-178)

Opening Line: B.C. made it to the big time last year—well, at least to the cover of *Sports Illustrated*—when it knocked off North Carolina to advance to the NCAA tourney's Sweet 16. Senior captains Bill Curley, Howard Eisley, and Malcolm Huckaby—as well as senior guard Gerrod Abram—were the driving forces behind the Eagles' climb back to respectability. They will be sorely missed, but the winning attitude they helped establish and a highly touted freshman class should lessen the blow of their graduation.

Guard: Chris Herren is a blue-chip recruit expected to help immediately. As for experience, senior Marc Molinsky has plenty of that, and he finally gets a chance to start after three seasons as a valuable reserve. Molinsky's deadly from behind the 3-point arc.

Forward: Danya Abrams was a Big East All-Rookie selection last year, and he should only get better. A starter in 23 games as a freshman, Abrams is a strong rebounder with good post skills. A stress fracture of the left foot ended Keenan Jourdan's freshman season a bit early, but he showed a fine shooting touch while starting 13 games. Paul Grant, an aggressive rebounder, can play both forward and center. Bevan Thomas is a transfer who sat out last season.

Center: There will be a Curley in the pivot, but it's not Bill (who, as mentioned, has graduated). Bill's little brother Mickey, who isn't so little at 6'9″, is set to carry on the Curley legacy. Bill left mighty big shoes to fill, though. Grant is the only other center on the roster.

Analysis: The talent is there for an upper-division finish in the Big East, and maybe even a run at the league title. One thing's for certain, the Eagles are no longer the lovable losers of the conference. Much depends on how quickly the freshmen adjust to the college game.

1994-95 ROSTER

	POS	HT	YR	FGP	FTP	3-PT	RPG	APG	PPG
Danya Abrams	F	6'7″	So.	.46	.58	—	7.1	0.7	10.4
Marc Molinsky	G	6'5″	Sr.	.41	1.00	33/81	1.6	0.8	4.1
Paul Grant	F/C	6'10″	Jr.	.49	.59	—	2.2	0.3	3.3
Keenan Jourdan	F	6'7″	So.	.56	.45	6/11	2.1	0.5	2.9
Jim Ryan	G	6'1″	Sr.	.65	.80	0/1	0.4	0.3	2.7
Kevin Hrobowski	F	6'6″	Sr.	.43	.60	5/10	2.2	0.5	2.7
Brad Christianson	F	6'7″	So.	.22	.71	0/7	1.2	0.5	1.2
Mickey Curley	C	6'9″	Fr.	—	—	—	—	—	—
Antonio Granger	G	6'5″	Fr.	—	—	—	—	—	—
Chris Herren	G	6'2″	Fr.	—	—	—	—	—	—
Bevan Thomas	F	6'8″	So.	—	—	—	—	—	—
Duane Woodward	G	6'3″	Fr.	—	—	—	—	—	—

BRIGHAM YOUNG

Conference: Western Athletic
1993-94: 22-10, 3rd WAC

1993-94 NIT: 1-1
Coach: Roger Reid (114-48)

Opening Line: It could be said that last year's fifth consecutive 20-plus-win season under Roger Reid's direction was an overachievement for the Cougars, who were expected to struggle after losing Shawn Bradley to the NBA. On the other hand, it could be said that such success was simply the norm for this perennial WAC powerhouse. Either way, results should be pretty similar this time around—better, actually, as eight lettermen return from last year's NIT squad.

Guard: It could be an all-Reid starting backcourt, as coach's sons Randy and Robbie are the only returning guards with starting experience. Randy, a junior who shares the team leadership role with forward Russell Larson, started all 32 games last year, while Robbie started twice. Neither is afraid of the 3-point arc, as they tied for the team lead in attempts (100) with the younger brother connecting on one more (35). Craig Wilcox will again be a key contributor.

Forward: Larson had one of the best scoring seasons ever for a Cougar junior last year, and he has a chance to etch himself forever in BYU lore with a strong senior campaign. He will be the leading candidate for WAC Player of the Year honors. Shane Knight and Mark Durrant aren't spectacular, but they both possess good experience. Returning missionary Justin Weidauer should see time, as should sharpshooter Grant Berges, who redshirted last year.

Center: Kenneth Roberts gained some seasoning last year after returning from a mission. Senior Jay Thompson, Australian Cory Reader, and shot-blocker Bret Jepsen will vie for time.

Analysis: The Cougars are deep and talented, and they have a star player in Larson. Expect to see Brigham Young listed among the top 25 in the polls again, and expect another 20-plus-win season for coach Reid. The Cougars will battle New Mexico for supremacy in the WAC.

1994-95 ROSTER

	POS	HT	YR	FGP	FTP	3-PT	RPG	APG	PPG
Russell Larson	F	6'11"	Sr.	.55	.82	10/35	9.1	1.4	19.9
Kenneth Roberts	F/C	6'8"	Jr.	.58	.80	1/2	6.0	1.9	12.8
Randy Reid	G	6'2"	Jr.	.52	.79	34/100	2.1	2.7	11.8
Shane Knight	F	6'9"	Sr.	.42	.58	30/93	3.8	1.7	7.8
Robbie Reid	G	6'1"	So.	.39	.61	35/100	2.3	2.2	6.8
Mark Durrant	F	6'6"	Sr.	.50	.73	8/25	4.6	2.1	6.4
Craig Wilcox	G/F	6'5"	Sr.	.41	.56	16/59	1.7	1.1	5.5
Jay Thompson	C	6'8"	Sr.	.44	.65	—	1.5	0.2	2.9
Grant Berges	F	6'8"	Fr.	—	—	—	—	—	—
Bret Jepsen	C	6'10"	Fr.	—	—	—	—	—	—
Cory Reader	C	7'0"	Jr.	—	—	—	—	—	—
Justin Weidauer	F	6'7"	So.	—	—	—	—	—	—

CINCINNATI

Conference: Great Midwest   **1993-94 NCAAs:** 0-1
1993-94: 22-10, 4th GMC   **Coach:** Bob Huggins (213-92)

Opening Line: Last season, the Bearcats won their third straight Great Midwest Conference Tournament and made their third straight trip to the NCAA tourney, despite losing five starters from the previous year. This time around, only center Mike Harris has graduated. However, coach Bob Huggins got bad news in April when talented freshman Dontonio Wingfield decided to test the NBA waters.

Guard: Damon Flint handled point-guard duties with aplomb during his freshman season, despite having never played the position before. He'll need to upgrade his field goal percentage. LaZelle Durden is the team's top scoring threat, thanks largely to an accurate 3-point eye. Darnell Burton proved to be a good long-range shooter and prolific in the steals department as a frosh. Marko Wright won the point-guard job as a freshman last year before being sidelined with a foot injury. Cincinnati welcomes transfer Keith LeGree, who was a starting point guard for Louisville.

Forward: Wingfield made a huge impact as a freshman last year, ranking second in the GMC in both rebounding and 3-point shooting. With him, Cincinnati would have been a national powerhouse. Curtis Bostic, the grizzled veteran on the team, is becoming a more fluid offensive player, while Keith Gregor is a defensive stopper. Blue-chipper Bobby Brannen will get plenty of minutes.

Center: Jackson Julson saw mostly spot duty as a frosh, but more will be expected of him in the future. Danny Fortson was a top-ten prep last season who will be expected to contribute immediately. He can score, get to the line, and clean the boards.

Analysis: Some highly touted recruits join a talented, young nucleus, and that spells trouble for the rest of the GMC. Durden, Flint, and Fortson are all marquee attractions. A fourth straight conference tourney title is a strong possibility, even with the loss of Wingfield.

1994-95 ROSTER

	POS	HT	YR	FGP	FTP	3-PT	RPG	APG	PPG
LaZelle Durden	G	6'2"	Sr.	.44	.78	102/244	2.9	1.1	17.8
Damon Flint	G	6'5"	So.	.37	.59	50/175	3.8	2.8	12.6
Darnell Burton	G	6'2"	So.	.39	.77	49/134	2.8	2.2	9.1
Curtis Bostic	F	6'5"	Sr.	.45	.69	1/10	5.3	1.1	8.8
Keith Gregor	F	6'5"	Jr.	.50	.73	1/8	3.7	2.4	6.1
John Jacobs	F	6'7"	Jr.	.46	.45	0/1	3.4	0.7	4.7
Jackson Julson	F/C	6'9"	So.	.47	.74	1/2	1.7	0.3	2.0
Marko Wright	G	6'1"	So.	.39	.75	3/5	0.4	0.8	1.2
Bobby Brannen	F	6'8"	Fr.	—	—	—	—	—	—
Danny Fortson	F/C	6'9"	Fr.	—	—	—	—	—	—
Keith LeGree	G	6'1"	Jr.	—	—	—	—	—	—
Arthur Long	C	6'10"	Jr.	—	—	—	—	—	—

CONNECTICUT

Conference: Big East   **1993-94 NCAAs:** 2-1
1993-94: 29-5, 1st Big East   **Coach:** Jim Calhoun (412-228)

Opening Line: With first-team All-American Donyell Marshall leading the way, the Huskies capped a Big East championship last year with a berth in the NCAA tourney's Sweet 16—UConn's third Sweet 16 appearance in five years. Marshall opted early for the NBA, but everyone else is back. These Huskies will be aiming just as high as last year's team, with the focus this time on team effort rather than the accomplishments of an individual player. Coach Jim Calhoun will distribute the wealth.

Guard: Reigning Big East Rookie of the Year Doron Sheffer of Israel and veteran point guard Kevin Ollie will be backcourt mates again. Sheffer's a good distributor and shooter, and he's adept at picking pockets. Ollie has better than a 2-1 assist-to-turnover ratio for his career. Ray Allen, who was second on the team in scoring last year despite not starting a game, and 3-point ace Brian Fair round out a backcourt that doesn't take a backseat to any in the country.

Forward: Donny Marshall is ready for a big senior season after a breakthrough junior campaign. He was third-team All-Big East last year. It would have been nice to still have the other Don Marshall, Donyell, but without him UConn will need stepped-up effort from defensive specialist Rudy Johnson. Look for some forward play out of the group listed under "Center."

Center: The four-man rotation includes Eric Hayward, Travis Knight, Kirk King, and Boo Willingham. There's experience at this position but it certainly isn't the focal point of the team. Knight is a seven-footer.

Analysis: Boy, this would have been a real powerhouse if the star were back, but even without him this group should be strong. The Huskies will go as far as the talented backcourt takes them. That could very easily be to the Sweet 16, which has become a perennial trip for Calhoun's Huskies.

1994-95 ROSTER

	POS	HT	YR	FGP	FTP	3-PT	RPG	APG	PPG
Ray Allen	G	6'5"	So.	.51	.79	33/82	4.6	1.6	12.6
Donny Marshall	F	6'6"	Sr.	.52	.77	23/64	5.5	1.3	12.4
Doron Sheffer	G	6'5"	So.	.51	.73	50/123	3.8	4.8	11.9
Brian Fair	G	6'3"	Sr.	.47	.69	40/98	1.0	1.0	7.1
Kevin Ollie	G	6'3"	Sr.	.47	.73	2/10	2.4	6.1	6.4
Eric Hayward	F	6'7"	Jr.	.47	.64	—	4.2	0.4	3.4
Travis Knight	C	7'0"	Jr.	.44	.50	—	2.9	0.7	2.5
Kirk King	F	6'8"	So.	.45	.27	—	2.4	0.3	1.5
Rudy Johnson	F	6'6"	Jr.	.38	.53	0/3	1.0	0.3	1.3
Nantambu Willingham	C	6'10"	Sr.	.45	.40	—	1.9	0.2	0.9
Marcus Thomas	G	6'0"	So.	.40	.25	3/8	0.1	0.3	0.6
Uri Cohen-Mintz	F	6'8"	Fr.	—	—	—	—	—	—

DePaul

Conference: Great Midwest   **1993-94 NIT:** 0-1
1993-94: 16-12, T-5th GMC   **Coach:** Joey Meyer (200-106)

Opening Line: DePaul bounced back from a one-year absence from postseason play to earn an NIT berth last year. It was the school's 16th postseason invite in the past 17 seasons. Nine letter-winners are back to make sure this year's postseason invite has four letters (NCAA) rather than three. Things had better get better. How much lower can DePaul sink than not only losing in the first round of the NIT, but to Northwestern, its traditionally lowly crosstown rival?

Guard: Off guard Brandon Cole is an excellent all-around player, but he needs to be more consistent with his shot. His field goal percentage last year was a mere 40.5, considerably lower than the year before. Peter Patton started the last nine games of the season and improved his assist-to-turnover ratio from worse than 1-1 in 1992-93 to nearly 2-1. Lead guard Belefia Parks started 21 games last year, but over the summer he was dismissed from the team for disciplinary reasons. Marcus Singer will provide quality minutes if he finds some consistency with his shot.

Forward: Swing man Tom Kleinschmidt will vie for All-America honors. He doesn't have a classic athletic build, but he does have multi-faceted skills. He's also the team leader. Former prep phenom Will Macon and Brian Currie will be asked to contribute more. Both averaged fewer than five points and 15 minutes per game last year.

Center: Bryant Bowden started four games last year, so he has some seasoning. He must avoid foul trouble, though, as he was second on the team in that department last season.

Analysis: Coach Joey Meyer admitted that his team fell apart at the 3-point line last season, and that the team's ball-handling was not what it should have been. Those will be obvious points of emphasis for the coach. With everybody a year older and wiser, the Blue Demons should ride Kleinschmidt's coattails to contention in the GMC.

1994-95 ROSTER

	POS	HT	YR	FGP	FTP	3-PT	RPG	APG	PPG
Tom Kleinschmidt	G/F	6'5"	Sr.	.49	.72	26/79	6.2	4.1	20.5
Brandon Cole	G	6'0"	Sr.	.40	.83	34/124	4.5	3.2	13.0
Bryant Bowden	F/C	6'8"	Jr.	.46	.79	0/1	4.9	0.4	6.7
Peter Patton	G	6'1"	Jr.	.36	.84	24/71	2.5	3.0	5.4
Will Macon	F	6'7"	Sr.	.41	.62	—	4.5	0.9	4.7
Brian Currie	F	6'7"	Jr.	.56	.53	—	2.7	0.3	3.9
Marcus Singer	G	6'6"	So.	.35	.46	16/55	1.4	0.4	3.3
Dwayne Austin	G	6'1"	So.	.47	.44	1/7	0.4	0.7	1.7
Malik Murray	F	6'8"	Jr.	.67	1.00	—	0.8	0.1	1.0
Jermaine Watts	G	6'1"	Fr.	—	—	—	—	—	—

DUKE

Conference: Atlantic Coast
1993-94: 28-6, 1st ACC

1993-94 NCAAs: 5-1
Coach: Mike Krzyzewski (422-183)

Opening Line: Superstar Grant Hill, Antonio Lang, and Marty Clark graduated this past spring as one of the most successful classes in college basketball history: three NCAA title games, two championships. The thing about Duke is that more history is always waiting to be made. Coach Mike Krzyzewski landed another solid recruiting class to offset his losses, and he politely turned down David Stern's offer to coach in the bigs.

Guard: Chris Collins and Jeff Capel can hold their own with any backcourt in the country, as both are versatile enough to man either guard slot. On offense, both extend their opponents to 3-point distance. Touted recruits Trajan Langdon (a rare Alaskan player) and Steve Wojciechowski will fill in the gaps.

Forward: The Blue Devils are green at the forward posts. Carmen Wallace, Joey Beard, Greg Newton, and Tony Moore spent more time watching than playing last year. Fans expecting another Christian Laettner or Grant Hill will be disappointed. Highly regarded freshman Ricky Price should earn some minutes.

Center: Duke has a dynamic duo in the pivot. Cherokee Parks, who has shown vast improvement in each of his three seasons, should vie for All-America honors. Look for Parks to average close to 20 points per game. Fellow senior Erik Meek is a nice luxury off the bench. Though he doesn't score much, Meek can rebound and do the dirty work well.

Analysis: While this program has its priorities in order—Duke cancelled a summer tour overseas so some players could concentrate on academics—the basketball side of things is never left wanting. Six of the last seven Blue Devil squads made it to the Final Four; so besides talent, this group has tradition in its corner. Add to that the usual craziness in Cameron Indoor Stadium and the results this year should be pretty much the same as usual.

1994-95 ROSTER

	POS	HT	YR	FGP	FTP	3-PT	RPG	APG	PPG
Cherokee Parks	C	6'11"	Sr.	.54	.77	3/17	8.4	0.9	14.4
Chris Collins	G	6'3"	Jr.	.40	.71	76/202	2.0	2.3	10.0
Jeff Capel	G	6'5"	So.	.46	.66	32/76	2.7	3.2	8.6
Erik Meek	C	6'10"	Sr.	.55	.60	—	4.2	0.4	3.5
Kenny Blakeney	G	6'4"	Sr.	.69	.75	2/3	1.1	2.0	3.3
Carmen Wallace	F	6'6"	So.	.56	.57	2/5	0.5	0.1	1.6
Joey Beard	F	6'9"	So.	.50	.70	0/2	0.5	0.2	1.3
Greg Newton	F	6'11"	So.	.36	.54	—	1.3	0.4	1.1
Tony Moore	F	6'8"	Jr.	.60	.64	—	0.8	0.2	1.1
Trajan Langdon	G	6'4"	Fr.	—	—	—	—	—	—
Ricky Price	G/F	6'6"	Fr.	—	—	—	—	—	—
Steve Wojciechowski	G	5'11"	Fr.	—	—	—	—	—	—

EVANSVILLE

Conference: Missouri Valley   **1993-94 NIT:** 0-1
1993-94: 21-10, T-2nd MCC   **Coach:** Jim Crews (169-98)

Opening Line: The Purple Aces won a respectable 21 games last year before falling to Tulane in the first round of the NIT. Evansville moves to a new neighborhood this year, leaving the friendly confines of the Midwestern Collegiate Conference—where the Aces ruled the roost along with Xavier—for the Missouri Valley Conference. Evansville will have to replace three men in the backcourt—Jermaine Ball, Todd Cochenour, and Mark Hisle. Ball's departure was unexpected.

Guard: Brent Kell is a backcourt Ace who does return. Kell was the NCAA leader in 3-point accuracy last season, canning 50 percent of the trifectas he threw up. Depth is the main concern, as there are no other experienced guards on the roster. Toby Madison, a redshirt freshman, and Brian Jackson, a junior college transfer, will likely round out the three-guard rotation.

Forward: Andy Elkins is among the best to ever don a Purple Aces uniform, with a wealth of skills at his disposal. Elkins is a 20-PPG scorer who's particularly deadly from 3-point range. He'll also clean the glass. Tough, strong Reed Jackson is no slouch himself. He'll rip down boards, score, and lead the team in assists. Chris Quinn did nothing but improve as a freshman, so Crews's crew is loaded at the forward posts.

Center: Scott Sparks and Jeff Layden will split duty in the middle. Although neither averaged six points or four rebounds per game last year, both should enjoy more success now that they have gained some experience. Layden is the stronger of the two.

Analysis: Don't be surprised if Evansville throws its own "Welcome to the MVC Party" and walks away with the league trophy. Elkins can carry the team if he has to, but that's not the case. Jackson and Kell also have all-conference potential. It's fun to watch Elkins and Kell pop in 3-pointers as if they were lay-ups.

1994-95 ROSTER

	POS	HT	YR	FGP	FTP	3-PT	RPG	APG	PPG
Andy Elkins	F	6'7"	Sr.	.49	.73	88/192	8.3	2.8	21.5
Reed Jackson	F	6'5"	Sr.	.51	.72	12/41	7.9	4.8	13.5
Brent Kell	G	6'0"	Jr.	.48	.88	62/123	2.0	1.4	11.9
Scott Sparks	C	7'0"	Jr.	.50	.67	—	3.3	0.6	5.8
Toby Madison	G	6'3"	Fr.	.50	.50	2/5	1.0	0.5	5.0
Jeff Layden	C	6'9"	So.	.53	.56	—	3.7	0.5	4.6
Chris Quinn	F	6'5"	So.	.48	.61	1/3	2.1	0.4	4.3
Matt Hopson	G	6'0"	So.	.25	.25	0/3	0.3	0.1	0.3
Curt Begle	F	6'8"	Fr.	—	—	—	—	—	—
Brian Jackson	G	6'1"	Jr.	—	—	—	—	—	—
Darick Loving	G	6'3"	Fr.	—	—	—	—	—	—
Emi Morales	F	6'8"	Fr.	—	—	—	—	—	—

FLORIDA

Conference: Southeastern   **1993-94 NCAAs:** 4-1
1993-94: 29-8, T-1st SEC East   **Coach:** Lon Kruger (208-156)

Opening Line: While the Gators earned a lofty No. 3 seed for the NCAA Tournament last year, they still qualified for Cinderella status by reaching the Final Four. Maybe that had something to do with low preseason expectations (some experts had the Gators pegged for fourth place in the SEC East). However, after tournament victories over James Madison, Pennsylvania, Connecticut, and Boston College, Florida won't be underestimated this year.

Guard: The stellar guard duo of Dan Cross and Craig Brown is minus Brown this year. Half that tandem is still a pretty good deal for Florida, as Cross ranks among the top point guards in the country. He's deadly from beyond the arc, though he needs to cut down on the turnovers. Sophomore Greg Williams got his feet wet last year and will be more active this season. Swing man Jason Anderson brings experience to the table.

Forward: Dametri Hill is a fan favorite in Gainesville, and he asserted himself last year to the tune of 23 double-figure scoring games. He shot 51 percent from the field. Small forward isn't the team's strength, as neither Brian Thompson nor Tony Mickens add much in the way of offense. LeRon Williams, a top-50 recruit, could win the starting job.

Center: Andrew DeClercq is a hustler who gets things done on the court. He's always among the conference leaders in rebounds and blocked shots. A good defender, he's the Gators' top shot-blocker and fairly adept at picking pockets. Svein Dyrkolbotn and John Griffiths provide relief.

Analysis: The Gators graduated only one of their top six scorers, so last year should prove to be no fluke. Brown is a big loss, but Cross and DeClercq have enough horses backing them up to make another run in the NCAA Tournament, though not necessarily to the Final Four. Coach Lon Kruger gets high marks for his rebuilding job.

1994-95 ROSTER

	POS	HT	YR	FGP	FTP	3-PT	RPG	APG	PPG
Dan Cross	G	6'3"	Sr.	.48	.83	55/124	3.9	3.9	15.7
Dametri Hill	C/F	6'7"	Jr.	.51	.66	0/2	4.9	0.6	12.7
Andrew DeClercq	F/C	6'10"	Sr.	.54	.65	1/3	7.9	1.5	8.8
Jason Anderson	G/F	6'5"	Jr.	.44	.62	9/38	3.8	1.5	7.2
Brian Thompson	F	6'6"	Jr.	.41	.48	1/11	3.9	1.3	5.5
Greg Williams	G	6'2"	So.	.29	.78	8/30	0.8	1.1	2.1
Tony Mickens	F	6'5"	Sr.	.26	.53	6/31	1.5	0.9	1.9
Svein Dyrkolbotn	C/F	6'8"	Sr.	.62	.55	—	1.6	0.2	1.8
John Griffiths	C	6'10"	So.	.29	.67	—	1.2	0.1	1.0
Damon Maddox	F	6'8"	Fr.	—	—	—	—	—	—
Dan Williams	G	6'3"	Fr.	—	—	—	—	—	—
LeRon Williams	F	6'7"	Fr.	—	—	—	—	—	—

FLORIDA STATE

Conference: Atlantic Coast   **1993-94 NCAAs/NIT:** Not invited
1993-94: 13-14, T-7th ACC   **Coach:** Pat Kennedy (281-150)

Opening Line: Even with a Heisman Trophy winner on the roster, the Seminoles suffered a disappointing season in 1993-94. Heck, it was such an "off" year that Pat Kennedy was using a four-guard lineup by season's end. Although Charlie Ward graduated, FSU welcomes back some maturing veterans and says hello to some exciting newcomers.

Guard: Bob Sura was the ACC's leading scorer last year and now will vie for All-America honors. He can get to the hole, sink the 3-pointer, and defend tenaciously. Though never known as a leader, Sura must assert himself in that department this year. Point guard James Collins had one of the most impressive freshman seasons in the Kennedy era, ranking third on the team in scoring, assists, and steals. Reinforcements are on the way with blue-chippers LaMarr Greer and Geoff Brower.

Forward: Last year, FSU lost starter Derrick Carroll after five games to shoulder surgery, but he should be back. They'll need him because Maurice Robinson, a part-time starter last year, has transferred. Top-ten freshman Corey Louis, a tremendous rebounder and shot-blocker, should be a big boon up front.

Center: Andre Reid and Kirk Luchman split time in the pivot last year, and they will do so again. Neither is much of an offensive threat, though Reid is a real asset on the glass, particularly the offensive glass. He's got to be more selective with his fouls, though, as he was disqualified from ten games last year.

Analysis: With all the negative headlines the Seminole football team got this past spring, more pressure might be put on the basketball team to boost the school's ego. Nevertheless, the hoopsters should be up to the task. Sura is the marquee talent that every contender needs. They'll be dancing again in Tallahassee come March.

1994-95 ROSTER

	POS	HT	YR	FGP	FTP	3-PT	RPG	APG	PPG
Bob Sura	G/F	6'5"	Sr.	.47	.65	52/164	7.9	4.5	21.2
Derrick Carroll	F	6'6"	So.	.47	—	9/22	3.0	1.0	11.3
James Collins	G	6'4"	So.	.41	.68	39/120	3.9	2.3	11.0
Andre Reid	C	7'0"	Sr.	.47	.56	0/2	6.2	0.5	6.9
Kirk Luchman	F/C	6'10"	So.	.52	.72	—	4.0	0.5	5.8
Scott Shepherd	G	5'11"	Jr.	.38	.86	11/29	1.0	0.8	3.0
Nick Bryant	G	5'8"	Sr.	.25	.88	1/3	0.3	0.8	2.2
David Grabuloff	F	6'7"	So.	.25	.75	0/2	1.0	0.8	0.9
Geoff Brower	G	6'4"	Fr.	—	—	—	—	—	—
LaMarr Greer	G	6'5"	Fr.	—	—	—	—	—	—
Corey Louis	F	6'9"	Fr.	—	—	—	—	—	—
Tim Wooden	F	6'11"	Jr.	—	—	—	—	—	—

GEORGETOWN

Conference: Big East   **1993-94 NCAAs:** 1-1
1993-94: 19-12, T-4th Big East   **Coach:** John Thompson (503-190)

Opening Line: John Thompson enters his 23rd season as coach of the Hoyas with a wide grin on his face. Not only is Thompson's 21st straight postseason appearance virtually assured, but this year's squad possesses the necessary ingredients to be playing in Seattle come April. Spirited lead guard Joey Brown and forwards Robert Churchwell and Duane Spencer must be replaced, but Thompson's got the horses to do it.

Guard: The ongoing development of junior playmaker Eric Micoud will largely determine just how good the Hoyas can be in 1994-95. If eligible, frosh recruit Allen Iverson will be tough to keep on the bench. One of the top prep juniors in the nation in 1992-93 with 31.6 PPG, Iverson was convicted and jailed on three felony counts for his role in a February 14, 1993, bowling alley brawl. George Butler is the Hoyas' primary 3-point threat. Dependable seniors John Jacques and Irvin Church will also see plenty of minutes.

Forward: Although he's not much of a factor on offense, 6'8", 250-pound Don Reid was one of the most improved players in the Big East last year. He's a solid rebounder and shot-blocker. Don't be surprised to see Jahidi White, one of the premier recruits in the country, lead the Hoyas' forwards in scoring by season's end. Spencer left school for family reasons, meaning there will be minutes for Kevin Millen.

Center: Following in the footsteps of Ewing, Mourning, and Mutombo, leading scorer and rebounder Othella Harrington is en route to All-America accolades. A power player with a soft jumper, Harrington can do damage inside and outside.

Analysis: Even without Iverson, Thompson's squad still can compete with anybody. However, unless Butler or someone else scores regularly from the perimeter, opposing defenses will make things tough on Harrington and White by clogging the lane. An eligible Iverson would solve that problem.

1994-95 ROSTER

	POS	HT	YR	FGP	FTP	3-PT	RPG	APG	PPG
Othella Harrington	C	6'10"	Jr.	.55	.73	0/1	8.0	1.2	14.7
George Butler	G	6'2"	Sr.	.40	.77	29/98	2.7	1.4	13.8
Don Reid	F	6'8"	Sr.	.64	.63	—	5.9	0.9	7.7
John Jacques	G	6'3"	Sr.	.33	.73	19/65	1.0	0.7	3.9
Irvin Church	G	6'1"	Sr.	.38	.50	14/39	1.3	0.2	3.7
Eric Micoud	G	6'1"	Jr.	.30	.70	16/60	0.6	0.7	3.1
Kevin Millen	G/F	6'6"	Sr.	.31	.57	11/30	1.8	—	2.5
Dan Kelly	G	6'2"	So.	.40	.75	1/1	0.3	0.8	1.3
Boubacar Aw	F	6'6"	Fr.	—	—	—	—	—	—
Allen Iverson	G	6'0"	Fr.	—	—	—	—	—	—
Jerry Nichols	G/F	6'4"	Fr.	—	—	—	—	—	—
Jahidi White	F/C	6'9"	Fr.	—	—	—	—	—	—

GEORGE WASHINGTON

Conference: Atlantic 10   **1993-94 NCAAs:** 1-1
1993-94: 18-12, T-3rd A-10   **Coach:** Mike Jarvis (175-96)

Opening Line: The loss of Yinka Dare's size (7'1", 265), strength, and defensive presence in the middle devastates the Colonials. Nonetheless, life goes on in the nation's capital following last year's NCAA tourney berth (on the heels of a Sweet 16 finish in 1992-93). Forward Nimbo Hammons and shooting guard Kwame Evans are coach Mike Jarvis's only returning starters.

Guard: The graduation of standout playmaker Alvin Pearsall leaves defensive-minded reserve Omo Moses running this year's squad. The ex-Pitt Panther, who possesses impressive quickness and leaping ability, must become more of a force offensively. Moses's backcourt partner, Evans, provides ample offense with tremendous shooting range. He can also score inside. A thin bench will be led by senior Billy Calloway and frosh Darin Green.

Forward: Hammons ranked second behind Dare in both points and rebounds last winter. Explosive around the basket, he can also step outside and bury the 3 with regularity. Bulky sophomore Ferdinand Williams is expected to join Hammons in the starting lineup. The 6'10", 245-pounder earned some valuable experience last season (ten minutes per night). Seasoned Vaughn Jones will back up Hammons after starting 15 times in 1993-94.

Center: Although seniors Anthony Wise and Daryl Collette are both seven-footers, they're projects at best. Wise is the better player of the two because he's more experienced and has better hands. Look for Williams to move to the low post before the first of the year.

Analysis: While a 20-win season is going to be extremely difficult without Dare and Pearsall, it's possible if Hammons and Evans both step up. Evans needs to play with more intensity at the defensive end. Moses is going to have to contribute more offense too. G.W. should have the manpower to hold its own with everyone in the A-10 besides UMass.

1994-95 ROSTER

	POS	HT	YR	FGP	FTP	3-PT	RPG	APG	PPG
Nimbo Hammons	F	6'5"	Sr.	.39	.71	52/156	5.5	2.3	14.1
Kwame Evans	G	6'6"	Jr.	.38	.72	57/167	4.7	1.7	13.2
Vaughn Jones	F	6'6"	Jr.	.39	.65	1/8	4.8	2.6	7.3
Omo Moses	G	6'2"	Sr.	.32	.71	23/82	2.7	1.5	6.2
Antoine Hart	F	6'8"	Sr.	.50	.57	—	1.4	0.3	1.5
Ferdinand Williams	F	6'10"	So.	.40	.71	—	1.5	0.1	1.2
Billy Calloway	G	6'3"	Sr.	.26	.56	2/9	0.5	0.1	1.1
Anthony Wise	C	7'0"	Sr.	.40	.33	—	0.7	—	0.5
Daryl Collette	C	7'1"	Sr.	.50	—	—	0.4	—	0.2
Darin Green	G/F	6'4"	Fr.	—	—	—	—	—	—
Rasheed Hazzard	G	6'0"	Fr.	—	—	—	—	—	—
Alexander Koul	C	7'1"	So.	—	—	—	—	—	—

GEORGIA

Conference: Southeastern
1993-94: 14-16, 4th SEC East

1993-94 NCAAs/NIT: Not invited
Coach: Hugh Durham (510-301)

Opening Line: The Bulldogs lose just two seniors—starting point guard Bernard Davis and swing man Cleveland Jackson, who never played to his potential. Coach Hugh Durham is thanking his lucky stars that seven-footer Charles Claxton, who had declared himself eligible for the NBA draft, decided to come back to school after being drafted 50th overall. Leading scorer Shandon Anderson also returns, joined by a trio of talented junior college transfers.

Guard: Veterans Ty Wilson and Pertha Robinson will likely begin the season as the starting backcourt, but most of the Bulldogs' new talent is at the guard positions. Tyrone Allick, Georgia's only new recruit, is a cat-quick point guard from the Virgin Islands. J.C. transfers Katu Davis and James Gray will contribute big minutes as they learn Durham's offense.

Forward: Anderson averaged 13.8 PPG last season while splitting time between big guard and small forward. With the influx of backcourt talent for Georgia, Anderson will likely stick with the small-forward spot this year. Carlos Strong will again occupy the power-forward position, but he needs to grab more boards. Swing man Steve Jones and juco transfer Curtis Carrington will also look to find minutes in the frontcourt. Reserve Dathon Brown is no longer on the team.

Center: Claxton, very active for a big man, will rebound and intimidate on the defensive end. He needs to improve his consistency as well as his free throw shooting. Junior Terrell Bell will back up the big guy. Bell is a solid rebounder and a good leaper who can swat shots, but he needs to show some polish on the offensive end.

Analysis: The Bulldogs are loaded at the guard and small-forward spots, making them one of the most athletic teams in the country. With Claxton back in the fold, this team could be in the upper echelon of college basketball. They'll be a favorite to win the Southeastern Conference.

1994-95 ROSTER

	POS	HT	YR	FGP	FTP	3-PT	RPG	APG	PPG
Shandon Anderson	F/G	6'7"	Jr.	.48	.66	6/34	5.6	3.8	13.8
Carlos Strong	F	6'8"	Jr.	.47	.59	0/4	6.1	1.4	11.1
Charles Claxton	C	7'0"	Sr.	.53	.42	—	7.9	0.6	10.9
Ty Wilson	G	6'3"	Sr.	.41	.70	35/86	1.7	1.4	6.0
Steve Jones	F/G	6'6"	Jr.	.60	.82	1/7	2.5	1.2	5.4
Terrell Bell	C/F	6'11"	Jr.	.54	.43	—	3.8	0.2	3.5
Pertha Robinson	G	6'1"	Jr.	.48	.50	11/31	1.3	1.9	2.4
Kris Nordholz	G	5'10"	Jr.	.25	.67	0/2	0.3	1.2	1.3
Tyrone Allick	G	6'2"	Fr.	—	—	—	—	—	—
Curtis Carrington	F	6'5"	Jr.	—	—	—	—	—	—
Katu Davis	G	6'2"	Jr.	—	—	—	—	—	—
James Gray	G	6'3"	Jr.	—	—	—	—	—	—

GEORGIA TECH

Conference: Atlantic Coast   **1993-94 NIT:** 0-1
1993-94: 16-13, 6th ACC   **Coach:** Bobby Cremins (356-218)

Opening Line: Despite the return of four quality starters last year, the incredibly inconsistent Yellow Jackets failed to receive an invite to the NCAA's Big Dance. To make matters worse, they lost to Siena in the opening round of NIT play, 76-68. While Ivano Newbill and Martice Moore must be replaced, Bobby Cremins does welcome back one of the premier inside-outside combinations in the country in seniors James Forrest and Travis Best.

Guard: A capable floor general who can set up an open teammate, score with regularity, and dig in defensively, Best has the potential to be one of the nation's finest all-around guards. Backcourt mate Drew Barry, who missed five games with a cracked bone in his foot last year, can also handle the ball and play tough defense. He'll be asked to score more. Back-ups C.J. Williams and Todd Harlicka attempted a combined 15 shots in 1993-94.

Forward: Muscle-bound Forrest simply wasn't the same player last year after severely spraining his ankle vs. N.C. State on February 26. When healthy, he can hold his own with any power forward in the country at both ends. He's an All-American candidate. Freshmen Mike Maddox and Matt Harpring will have to contribute in a hurry at small forward, since Moore unexpectedly transferred to Colorado in June.

Center: Newbill's seven boards per game will be missed. While Eddie Elisma has reportedly bulked up some from his 6'9", 200-pound frame of a year ago, he still doesn't have the type of body you need to bang in the ACC. He'll rely largely on Forrest and raw frosh Bucky Hodge for support.

Analysis: If Best, Barry, and Forrest can stay healthy for the entire season, the Yellow Jackets will be in position to return to the NCAAs, despite a thin bench. More consistent play out of Best will be the key. At least one of the frosh frontcourters must become a factor—perhaps Maddox.

1994-95 ROSTER

	POS	HT	YR	FGP	FTP	3-PT	RPG	APG	PPG
James Forrest	F	6'8"	Sr.	.47	.72	0/6	7.9	1.4	19.0
Travis Best	G	5'11"	Sr.	.46	.87	49/144	3.6	5.8	18.3
Drew Barry	G	6'5"	Jr.	.42	.78	27/81	3.4	5.9	8.1
Eddie Elisma	F/C	6'9"	So.	.51	.48	1/1	4.4	0.5	5.1
Yann Barbic	G/F	6'6"	So.	.41	.62	4/14	1.4	1.2	2.1
C.J. Williams	G	6'2"	So.	.33	1.00	—	0.9	—	0.9
Todd Harlicka	G	6'2"	So.	.22	—	1/6	0.1	—	0.4
John Kelly	G	5'11"	Jr.	—	—	0/1	—	0.2	—
Matt Harpring	G/F	6'6"	Fr.	—	—	—	—	—	—
Bucky Hodge	F/C	6'9"	Fr.	—	—	—	—	—	—
Michael Maddox	F	6'8"	Fr.	—	—	—	—	—	—

ILLINOIS

Conference: Big Ten   **1993-94 NCAAs:** 0-1
1993-94: 17-11, T-4th Big Ten   **Coach:** Lou Henson (626-306)

Opening Line: Power forward Deon Thomas has left Champaign for the NBA, taking his 20 points and seven rebounds per game with him. Lou Henson's squad still has many weapons, however. Point guard Kiwane Garris was a surprise star as a freshman. If he can sidestep the sophomore jinx, the Illini should find themselves back in the NCAA Tournament.

Guard: Garris returns to lead the Illinois attack this year after averaging 15.9 PPG and amassing 33 steals last season. Junior Richard Keene will play the off-guard position. Keene is a smooth offensive player who shot better from beyond the 3-point arc than from inside it. Keene also led the team in assists. Freshmen Matt Heldman, Bryant Notree, and Kevin Turner will provide back-up help.

Forward: Jerry Hester was a pleasant surprise as a freshman last season, averaging eight points and four boards per game. Robert Bennett will join Hester in the frontcourt. Bennett, a senior, is effective around the basket but will have to step up his game with Thomas gone. Redshirt freshman Brett Robisch is a power forward project at 6'10''. True freshman Jerry Gee is the Illini power forward of the future and will play many minutes this season.

Center: Senior Shelly Clark is the big man in the middle for Illinois. Clark was a bit of a disappointment as a juco transfer last season, but he could blossom now that he's out of the shadow of Thomas. Clark's bulk makes him a banger beneath the boards. Senior Steve Roth is short on talent but big on size and effort.

Analysis: The Fighting Illini barely squeaked into the NCAA tourney last season and have since lost their top player. But Henson's team has an intriguing blend of talented players. If Garris, Keene, and Clark can put up solid numbers and freshman Gee can develop quickly, Illinois will easily improve on last season's 17-11 finish and head back to postseason play.

1994-95 ROSTER

	POS	HT	YR	FGP	FTP	3-PT	RPG	APG	PPG
Kiwane Garris	G	6'2''	So.	.43	.80	29/87	3.5	3.8	15.9
Shelly Clark	C	6'9''	Sr.	.51	.63	—	6.4	1.3	9.5
Jerry Hester	F	6'6''	So.	.41	.73	21/65	4.0	1.5	8.1
Richard Keene	G	6'6''	Jr.	.38	.64	48/113	3.5	4.0	8.0
Robert Bennett	F	6'6''	Sr.	.51	.66	—	3.7	0.4	5.0
Chris Gandy	F	6'9''	So.	.56	.60	1/1	1.9	0.3	3.4
Steve Roth	C	6'10''	Sr.	.56	.50	—	1.6	0.1	1.6
Jerry Gee	F	6'7''	Fr.	—	—	—	—	—	—
Matt Heldman	G	6'0''	Fr.	—	—	—	—	—	—
Bryant Notree	G	6'4''	Fr.	—	—	—	—	—	—
Brett Robisch	F/C	6'10''	Fr.	—	—	—	—	—	—
Kevin Turner	G	6'3''	Fr.	—	—	—	—	—	—

INDIANA

Conference: Big Ten   **1993-94 NCAAs:** 2-1
1993-94: 21-9, 3rd Big Ten   **Coach:** Bob Knight (640-223)

Opening Line: After advancing to the Sweet 16 for the fourth straight year in 1993-94, the Hoosiers were promptly upset by an upstart Boston College team. The good news: Indiana's entire frontcourt returns in 1994-95. The bad: Bob Knight's top three guards do not. How good's the recruiting class? One expert compares forward Andrae Patterson with George McGinnis and swing man Charlie Miller with Calbert Cheaney.

Guard: The graduations of Damon Bailey, Pat Graham, and Todd Leary cost the Hoosiers nearly 40 points of offense per game. Ready or not, sophomores Sherron Wilkerson and Steve Hart will likely be plugged into the starting lineup. True frosh Neil Reed will see plenty of action too. A superb athlete with a scorer's mentality, Wilkerson (injured late last year) will be the key.

Forward: I.U.'s success this winter will hinge largely on the play of Alan Henderson and Brian Evans, one of the premier forward combos in the country. They combined to average 30 points and 17 rebounds per contest last season. While Henderson does a lot of the dirty work inside, Evans is a fine shooter who likes to square up and fire 3's. Patterson, considered by many to be the nation's top power-forward prospect, has the ability to contribute in a hurry.

Center: Understatement of understatements: Knight needs more out of Todd Lindeman in the middle. In 20 minutes per game last year, Lindeman averaged fewer than six points and four rebounds. Richard Mandeville and Robbie Eggers are still developing.

Analysis: If the backcourt and center positions were on par with the forwards, Indiana fans would be booking early-April flights to Seattle. They need not bother. Unless the backcourt comes together more quickly than expected, another Sweet 16 finish is the best the Hoosiers can realistically hope for. This young squad will be better in 1995-96.

1994-95 ROSTER

	POS	HT	YR	FGP	FTP	3-PT	RPG	APG	PPG
Alan Henderson	F	6'9"	Sr.	.53	.66	2/6	10.3	1.2	17.8
Brian Evans	F	6'8"	Jr.	.45	.79	43/94	6.8	2.2	11.9
Todd Lindeman	C	7'0"	Jr.	.55	.60	—	3.9	0.3	5.6
Steve Hart	G	6'3"	So.	.50	.67	4/9	2.0	1.1	3.9
Sherron Wilkerson	G	6'4"	So.	.36	.69	10/34	2.3	2.0	3.2
Richard Mandeville	C	7'0"	So.	.35	.50	—	1.8	0.1	1.1
Pat Knight	G	6'6"	Sr.	.27	.71	1/1	0.7	1.1	0.8
Robbie Eggers	F/C	6'10"	Fr.	—	—	—	—	—	—
Rob Hodgson	F	6'7"	Fr.	—	—	—	—	—	—
Charlie Miller	F/G	6'7"	Fr.	—	—	—	—	—	—
Andrae Patterson	F	6'8"	Fr.	—	—	—	—	—	—
Neil Reed	G	6'3"	Fr.	—	—	—	—	—	—

IOWA

Conference: Big Ten
1993-94: 11-16, T-10th Big Ten
1993-94 NCAAs/NIT: Not invited
Coach: Tom Davis (437-238)

Opening Line: Iowa's challenge this year will be avoiding back-to-back losing seasons. It hasn't happened in Iowa City since 1973-74 and 1974-75, when Dick Schultz and Lute Olson were in charge. Everyone who started a game in 1993-94 returns, except leading scorer James Winters (18 PPG). Nebraska transfer Andre Woolridge is sure to give the backcourt a much-needed boost.

Guard: While Mon'ter Glasper does an adequate job at the point with five-plus assists per game, offense is not his forte. That's okay, though, with shooting guards Jim Bartels and Chris Kingsbury on the roster. They both attempt plenty of 3's. Kingsbury also has experience manning the point. Woolridge's presence and Kevin Skillett's experience means there will be plenty of healthy backcourt competition.

Forward: Jess Settles's development as an up-and-coming star makes the loss of Winters easier to handle. Named 1993-94 Big Ten Rookie of the Year, Settles paced last year's team in rebounds and finished second in scoring. Talented junior Kenyon Murray lines up across from Settles. Highly regarded as a frosh, Murray is on the verge of blossoming into the star everyone expected he'd be when he was recruited.

Center: At times, 6'8" Russ Millard plays like a bona fide seven-footer. Other times, you'd think he was six feet tall. Millard is a good shooter who needs to focus more on his defense, specifically denying opponents' entry passes into the lane. John Carter is a true banger who'll see time at forward and center.

Analysis: Quite simply, the 1993-94 Hawkeyes underachieved. After starting slowly in league play, they were too young and inexperienced to get things turned around by season's end. Although improving your record is an intimidating task in the Big Ten, the Hawkeyes have the manpower to do it. When talk about the nation's most improved teams arises, Iowa should be near the top of the list.

1994-95 ROSTER

	POS	HT	YR	FGP	FTP	3-PT	RPG	APG	PPG
Jess Settles	F	6'7"	So.	.57	.79	16/42	7.5	2.3	15.3
Kenyon Murray	F	6'5"	Jr.	.41	.56	12/56	5.8	2.0	12.3
Jim Bartels	G/F	6'6"	Sr.	.44	.60	49/131	5.5	1.7	11.5
Russ Millard	F/C	6'8"	Jr.	.51	.73	15/49	5.3	1.3	11.2
Chris Kingsbury	G	6'5"	So.	.33	.82	44/137	2.6	1.3	8.2
Mon'ter Glasper	G	6'2"	Jr.	.33	.58	16/51	2.8	5.2	4.8
John Carter	F/C	6'9"	Sr.	.46	.52	—	2.1	0.1	2.5
Kevin Skillett	G	6'3"	Sr.	.30	.65	5/27	1.7	1.9	2.0
Ryan Bowen	F	6'9"	Fr.	—	—	—	—	—	—
James Head	F	6'7"	Fr.	—	—	—	—	—	—
Greg Helmers	C	6'10"	Fr.	—	—	—	—	—	—
Andre Woolridge	G	6'1"	So.	—	—	—	—	—	—

IOWA STATE

Conference: Big Eight   **1993-94 NCAAs/NIT:** Not invited
1993-94: 14-13, T-6th Big Eight   **Coach:** Tim Floyd (161-84)

Opening Line: He was coming, then he wasn't coming, then he was coming again. "He" is Tim Floyd, the former New Orleans basketball coach who takes over the Iowa State helm from Johnny Orr, the winningest coach in ISU history. Floyd inherits the top five scorers from the 1993-94 Cyclones, and loses players who accounted for only a combined 15 starts. This will be a senior-dominated club, which usually means good results.

Guard: Fred "The Mayor" Hoiberg is the heart and soul of this basketball team. Aside from team-captain duties, he's the best Cyclone scorer and passer—and second best to Loren Meyer in rebounding. He logs the most minutes on the court and plays both guard and forward. A couple of 5'11" players will share the point duties again: Jason Kimbrough and Jacy Holloway. They put up similar stats last year, with neither being much of a scoring threat. Derrick Hayes had a fine freshman season.

Forward: Julius Michalik is a wiry big man who can score inside and outside and has a nice touch on his shot. The native Slovakian is a deft ball-handler for his size. He's joined up front by Hurl Beechum, a versatile athlete who can shoot the 3-pointer; James Hamilton, a former MVC Freshman of the Year; and Saun Jackson, a defensive specialist.

Center: Loren Meyer had the highest scoring and rebounding averages on the team last year, though he played just a half-season. He runs the floor well and often finishes the break with thunderous dunks. Meyer can hold his own with just about any center in the country.

Analysis: The nucleus for a Big Eight title run is in place for Floyd, who always seemed to have New Orleans in the NCAA Tournament hunt. There's no question where the leadership will come from—the senior class—so it's just a matter of everyone playing up to their abilities and avoiding injuries.

1994-95 ROSTER

	POS	HT	YR	FGP	FTP	3-PT	RPG	APG	PPG
Loren Meyer	C	6'10"	Sr.	.61	.74	0/0	9.5	1.7	22.3
Fred Hoiberg	G/F	6'4"	Sr.	.53	.86	59/131	6.7	3.6	20.2
Julius Michalik	F	6'11"	Sr.	.58	.86	19/57	5.7	1.9	20.0
Derrick Hayes	G	6'3"	So.	.40	.68	8/31	2.3	1.5	7.3
Hurl Beechum	F	6'5"	Sr.	.41	.75	39/101	2.3	1.3	6.7
James Hamilton	F	6'6"	Sr.	.36	.58	0/2	4.0	1.3	3.9
Jason Kimbrough	G	5'11"	So.	.30	.89	9/37	1.1	3.1	3.7
Saun Jackson	F	6'3"	Sr.	.46	.78	1/5	1.8	0.3	3.1
Jacy Holloway	G	5'11"	So.	.40	.76	5/18	1.3	3.4	2.2
Joe Modderman	F/G	6'8"	So.	.42	.70	9/20	0.8	0.5	2.2
Klay Edwards		6'8"	Fr.	—	—	—	—	—	—
Joe Hebert	G	5'11"	Jr.	—	—	—	—	—	—

JAMES MADISON

Conference: Colonial Athletic   **1993-94 NCAAs:** 0-1
1993-94: 20-10, T-1st Colonial   **Coach:** Lefty Driesell (641-289)

Opening Line: Last spring, for the first time since 1983, the Dukes advanced to the NCAA Tournament after four straight NIT appearances. Although they dropped their first game to Florida (by two points), the invite proved that veteran coach Lefty Driesell's program has finally turned the corner. With practically everyone returning except leading scorer Clayton Ritter, the Dukes are the odds-on favorites to again finish atop the Colonial.

Guard: Diminutive juco transfer Dennis Leonard did a fine job at the point last winter with four assists and nearly nine points per game. In fact, Driesell believes Leonard could have an NBA future with improved defense. Senior Kent Culuko is one of the best long-range shooters at the collegiate level. Incredibly, he shot 224 3's a year ago, making 45 percent. Junior Darren McLinton (10.3 PPG) provides instant offense off the bench.

Forward: Ritter's absence puts a lot of pressure on Louis Rowe. Rowe, the perfect complement to Ritter a year ago, is a fine athlete who can play as many as three positions. Charles Lott will likely share time at the other forward post with heralded recruit Lamont Boozer and juco transfer James Coleman. Driesell is especially high on Boozer.

Center: Junior Kareem Robinson started 14 games in the middle last season. Whether he can become a full-time starter and play 25-plus minutes a game in 1994-95 remains to be seen. Robinson does figure heavily in Driesell's plans.

Analysis: If newcomers like Boozer and Coleman can fit in relatively quickly, the Dukes should be able to open up an early lead in the Colonial. Outrebounded on a regular basis in 1993-94, JMU needs healthier totals out of Robinson, Lott, and Rowe. Culuko is a streak shooter who's worth the price of admission when his shots are falling. His play will ultimately dictate just how far this team goes.

1994-95 ROSTER

	POS	HT	YR	FGP	FTP	3-PT	RPG	APG	PPG
Kent Culuko	G	6'4"	Sr.	.44	.92	101/224	3.6	1.2	16.5
Louis Rowe	F	6'7"	Sr.	.51	.69	13/49	5.0	2.9	14.2
Darren McLinton	G	5'11"	Jr.	.45	.80	42/100	1.7	2.0	10.3
Dennis Leonard	G	5'11"	Sr.	.39	.70	31/86	2.7	3.9	8.8
Kareem Robinson	C	6'8"	Jr.	.59	.28	—	3.2	0.3	4.7
Charles Lott	F	6'8"	So.	.41	.35	3/12	1.8	0.2	2.2
Ryan Culicerto	G	6'4"	So.	.39	.70	3/11	0.7	0.3	1.6
Vladimir Cuk	C	6'9"	Sr.	.25	—	0/1	0.1	—	0.3
Lamont Boozer	F	6'9"	Fr.	—	—	—	—	—	—
Eric Carpenter	F	6'9"	Fr.	—	—	—	—	—	—
James Coleman	F/C	6'9"	Jr.	—	—	—	—	—	—
James Pelham	G	6'2"	Fr.	—	—	—	—	—	—
Heath Smith	F	6'9"	Fr.	—	—	—	—	—	—

KANSAS

Conference: Big Eight   **1993-94 NCAAs:** 2-1
1993-94: 27-8, 3rd Big Eight   **Coach:** Roy Williams (159-45)

Opening Line: Led by seniors Steve Woodberry and Richard Scott, the Jayhawks made it to the Sweet 16 last year before losing to Purdue. It marked the fifth straight year the Jayhawks had won a minimum of 27 games. They're certainly capable of making it six years in a row in 1994-95 as they welcome back three returning starters and five experienced reserves. A talented transfer and a highly regarded frosh join the fray.

Guard: Jacque Vaughn, the Big Eight's 1993-94 Newcomer of the Year, played like a seasoned veteran last winter. The cat-quick playmaker averaged more than five assists per game. Three-point specialist Greg Gurley and California transfer Jerod Haase take over for Woodberry at shooting guard. Diminutive Calvin Rayford (5'7") does a fine job of pushing the ball up the floor.

Forward: Junior small forward Sean Pearson, one of the team's 3-point threats, must become more involved in the Jayhawks' offense after averaging less than eight PPG last season. Pearson's a terrific all-around athlete who played well down the stretch last spring. Kansas will have a size advantage against most teams at big forward with 6'11" Scot Pollard, 6'10" Nick Proud, and 6'11" Raef LaFrentz. LaFrentz, one of the top ten high school seniors in the nation, will contribute immediately.

Center: If imposing senior Greg Ostertag (7'2", 275 pounds) picks up where he left off late last year, he'll be swarmed by NBA scouts. Big, strong, and agile, Ostertag should pay major dividends at both ends. LaFrentz, Pollard, and Proud all have low-post skills too.

Analysis: Never very flashy, the Jayhawks will again rely on a balanced, team-oriented attack that places a high priority on defense. It's Roy Williams's way. Ostertag's ongoing improvement in the middle and Vaughn's leadership should enable the Jayhawks to remain in the thick of the Big Eight race.

1994-95 ROSTER

	POS	HT	YR	FGP	FTP	3-PT	RPG	APG	PPG
Greg Ostertag	C	7'2"	Sr.	.53	.63	0/2	8.8	0.3	10.3
Jacque Vaughn	G	6'0"	So.	.47	.67	28/70	2.5	5.2	7.8
Sean Pearson	F	6'5"	Jr.	.40	.60	37/107	2.8	1.3	7.6
Scot Pollard	C/F	6'11"	So.	.54	.69	—	4.9	0.4	7.5
Greg Gurley	G	6'5"	Sr.	.47	.84	41/91	1.5	0.9	4.9
Nick Proud	C/F	6'10"	So.	.45	.69	—	1.8	0.1	3.2
B.J. Williams	F	6'8"	So.	.51	.37	—	2.5	0.4	2.8
Calvin Rayford	G	5'7"	Sr.	.33	.62	4/18	1.7	3.4	2.3
T.J. Whatley	G	6'4"	Jr.	.18	.55	0/7	0.4	—	0.7
Jerod Haase	G	6'3"	So.	—	—	—	—	—	—
Raef LaFrentz	C/F	6'11"	Fr.	—	—	—	—	—	—
Billy Thomas	G/F	6'4"	Fr.	—	—	—	—	—	—

KANSAS STATE

Conference: Big Eight   **1993-94 NIT:** 3-2
1993-94: 20-14, T-6th Big Eight   **Coach:** Tom Asbury (125-59)

Opening Line: KSU's three leading scorers (Askia Jones, Anthony Beane, and Deryl Cunningham)—as well as its coach, Dana Altman—have all departed from a squad that advanced to the NIT semifinals last March. However, it's not time to push the panic button for new coach Tom Asbury (formerly of Pepperdine). Both starting forwards return, as do key reserves. Moreover, the Wildcats' promising recruits made one recruiting expert's national top-25 list.

Guard: While backing up Beane, junior Brian Gavin showed signs of becoming a key contributor late last year. His playmaking and rebounding are more impressive than his scoring. Juco transfer Elliott Hatcher will push Gavin for the starting job. Belvis Noland, one of the Big Eight's top newcomers in 1993-94, may be switched from small forward to shooting guard to take better advantage of his 3-point range.

Forward: Demond Davis is a relentless defender who didn't miss a start in 1993-94. He sets the tone defensively in the paint. Heralded freshman Mark Young (from Baton Rouge) should be tough to keep out of the starting lineup based on his prep career. Noland will also swing to the frontcourt when needed. Blue-chip freshman Reggie McFerren is academically ineligible.

Center: Senior Hamilton Strickland, the strongest player on the team, has the inside track on the starting low-post job. Greatly improved over the off-season, Strickland is expected to split time with pencil-thin sophomore Kevin Lewis. Very developed offensively, Lewis is the most talented true center to wear a KSU uniform in years.

Analysis: Although it may take the Wildcats some time to jell with a new coach, a new starting backcourt, and five recruits, this will be a team to be reckoned with come February. Someone must establish himself as the team leader, be it lead guards Gavin and Hatcher, or veteran frontcourters Noland and Davis.

1994-95 ROSTER

	POS	HT	YR	FGP	FTP	3-PT	RPG	APG	PPG
Belvis Noland	G/F	6'4"	Sr.	.39	.56	31/105	3.9	1.2	7.5
Demond Davis	G/F	6'4"	Sr.	.36	.57	11/39	6.1	1.3	6.0
Brian Gavin	G	6'1"	Jr.	.38	.50	16/47	1.3	0.8	2.9
Stanley Hamilton	F	6'6"	Sr.	.56	.65	0/1	1.9	0.5	1.8
Kevin Lewis	C	6'10"	So.	.45	.25	0/1	1.3	0.2	1.7
Judd Mourning	G	6'0"	So.	1.00	.75	2/2	0.1	0.6	1.1
Hamilton Strickland	C	6'9"	Sr.	.22	1.00	—	0.5	—	0.5
Michael Bowens	F	6'7"	Fr.	—	—	—	—	—	—
Elliott Hatcher	G	6'0"	Jr.	—	—	—	—	—	—
Ayome May	G	6'4"	Fr.	—	—	—	—	—	—
Aaron Swartzendruber	G	6'2"	Fr.	—	—	—	—	—	—
Mark Young	G/F	6'6"	Fr.	—	—	—	—	—	—

KENTUCKY

Conference: Southeastern   **1993-94 NCAAs:** 1-1
1993-94: 27-7, T-1st SEC East   **Coach:** Rick Pitino (255-112)

Opening Line: Losing in the second round of last spring's NCAA Tournament to Marquette certainly wasn't what coach Rick Pitino had in mind last year. With Kentucky's big people clogged in the middle against the Warriors' tall timbers, the guards needed to strike from the perimeter. They didn't. Floor general Travis Ford—as well as part-time starters Rodney Dent, Jeff Brassow, and Gimel Martinez—must be replaced.

Guard: Sophomore point guard Anthony "Ant" Epps may get the nod as this year's starter. Epps's job will be made easier by the presence of All-SEC candidate Tony Delk. He stepped up his 3-point shooting in 1993-94 and led the Wildcats in scoring with nearly 17 PPG. Depth will be supplied by Jeff Sheppard and Chris Harrison at big guard and star recruit Allen Edwards at the point. Don't be surprised to see Edwards (whose brother Doug plays for the Atlanta Hawks) replace Epps before season's end.

Forward: Consistent junior Jared Prickett (7.0 RPG) is Pitino's kind of player. What he lacks in talent he makes up for with hard work. Junior Rodrick Rhodes is a silky-smooth performer who'd be an All-American if he displayed Prickett's consistency. He did score in double figures in 28 of 33 games last season. Trash-talking frosh Antoine Walker was considered the best prep player in Chicago as a senior.

Center: After Dent went down with a knee injury last January, Andre Riddick and Walter McCarty gained valuable playing time. Riddick started the final 18 games of the 1993-94 campaign, establishing himself as a gifted shot-blocker.

Analysis: No goal's too high for a Pitino-coached team built around talented players like Delk, Rhodes, and Prickett. Lacking overall size and a bona fide go-to guy inside, the Wildcats will again rely on their pressure defense and perimeter shooters. Expect to see them at the top of the polls once again.

1994-95 ROSTER

	POS	HT	YR	FGP	FTP	3-PT	RPG	APG	PPG
Tony Delk	G	6'1"	Jr.	.45	.64	95/254	4.5	1.7	16.6
Rodrick Rhodes	F	6'7"	Jr.	.44	.78	32/117	4.1	2.8	14.6
Jared Prickett	F	6'9"	Jr.	.48	.58	1/14	7.0	2.4	8.2
Andre Riddick	C	6'9"	Sr.	.57	.40	0/3	5.0	0.8	7.9
Walter McCarty	F/C	6'9"	Jr.	.47	.55	19/50	3.9	1.1	5.7
Jeff Sheppard	G	6'4"	So.	.56	.65	7/19	0.8	1.0	3.7
Anthony Epps	G	6'2"	So.	.44	.54	11/28	0.7	1.2	2.0
Chris Harrison	G	6'1"	Sr.	.28	.70	8/31	0.4	0.4	2.0
Allen Edwards	G	6'5"	Fr.	—	—	—	—	—	—
Cameron Mills	G	6'3"	Fr.	—	—	—	—	—	—
Scott Padgett	F	6'8"	Fr.	—	—	—	—	—	—
Antoine Walker	F	6'8"	Fr.	—	—	—	—	—	—

LOUISIANA STATE

Conference: Southeastern   **1993-94 NCAAs/NIT:** Not invited
1993-94: 11-16, 5th SEC West   **Coach:** Dale Brown (414-239)

Opening Line: Despite talent on the roster, LSU came up well short of expectations last year. The Tigers struggled last season due to a mixture of inexperience—no player had more than two seasons of college ball under his belt—and injury. A preseason knee injury to top recruit Randy Livingston seriously hampered LSU's chances for a successful season. Livingston is back but this year's team will have to cope with the unexpected losses of forward Jamie Brandon and guard Brandon Titus.

Guard: The tandem of Livingston and Ronnie Henderson on the court together will be a welcome sight to LSU fans. Livingston should be 100 percent healthy after rehabilitating his torn ACL. Henderson had a rough shooting season as a freshman but still managed to score more than 16 PPG. This duo could quickly become one of the country's best. Livingston's health is critical because of the serious lack of experienced depth.

Forward: Brandon, who led the team in scoring last season, left school this summer, meaning the frontcourt is as bare-bones as the backcourt. Clarence Ceasar is a solid power forward with good rebounding instincts and a knack for collecting steals. Roman Roubtchenko, from the Ukraine, is adjusting slowly to U.S. college basketball.

Center: Senior Glover Jackson has the inside track on the starting center spot, but he could be pushed by a famous progeny. Recruit Adam Walton, son of Bill, doesn't quite have his father's height or flair. Nevertheless, Walton has solid skills and could play his way into the starting lineup pretty soon.

Analysis: Brown has a great pair of guards, but the loss of Brandon leaves some question marks up front. Livingston's health is a critical factor in how the team will fare this season. If he is at the height of his powers, LSU may be able to transcend a depth problem on the front line to become a threat in the SEC.

1994-95 ROSTER

	POS	HT	YR	FGP	FTP	3-PT	RPG	APG	PPG
Ronnie Henderson	G	6'4"	So.	.39	.71	72/223	3.7	1.2	16.5
Clarence Ceasar	F	6'8"	Sr.	.45	.60	46/125	6.4	1.9	14.9
Roman Roubtchenko	F	6'8"	Jr.	.39	.67	7/20	3.1	0.4	3.4
Glover Jackson	C	6'10"	Sr.	.43	.45	—	2.1	0.2	2.3
David Bosley	G	6'0"	So.	.33	.50	2/7	0.5	0.7	1.2
Alonzo Johnson	C	6'10"	Jr.	—	—	—	—	—	—
Randy Livingston	G	6'4"	Fr.	—	—	—	—	—	—
Landers Nolley	G/F	6'7"	Jr.	—	—	—	—	—	—
Tony Pietrowski	G	6'2"	Fr.	—	—	—	—	—	—
Djole Palfi	F	6'9"	Fr.	—	—	—	—	—	—
Garrick Scott	F	6'10"	Jr.	—	—	—	—	—	—
Adam Walton	F/C	6'9"	Fr.	—	—	—	—	—	—

LOUISVILLE

Conference: Metro   **1993-94 NCAAs:** 2-1
1993-94: 28-8, 1st Metro   **Coach:** Denny Crum (546-200)

Opening Line: The Cardinals find their wings clipped following the loss of their top three scorers—Clifford Rozier, Dwayne Morton, and Greg Minor. Coach Denny Crum has assembled a bumper crop of recruits to bolster a squad that doesn't have a single senior. How quickly this youthful squad will become a force in the Metro Conference is a big question.

Guard: The backcourt is the only part of the Cardinals' starting lineup to return intact. Sophomores DeJuan Wheat and Jason Osborne were both tested under fire as freshmen last season, and the experience can only help. Osborne struggled as a shooter, but his 6'8" frame makes him a handful for smaller defenders. Wheat is the only returnee to average double figures in scoring last season. Sharp-shooting Tick Rogers is the first man off the bench.

Forward: Top recruit Samaki Walker will likely move directly into the starting lineup. Walker has the makings of a dominant power forward and could be an instant star. Junior Brian Kiser, a solid outside shooter, is the top candidate for the small-forward spot. Freshman Damion Dantzler will also be called upon to provide quality minutes up front.

Center: Sophomore Matt Simons is the only true center on the Cardinals' roster, but he is a project who may have to battle for significant playing time. Simons is 6'11" but blocked just six shots and grabbed 31 boards in 32 games last year. Sophomore Beau Zach Smith can bang beneath the boards. Louisville's style of play doesn't demand a dominant big man.

Analysis: This year's Cardinal team is stocked with talent. How ready this talent is remains to be seen. If Walker can be an impact rookie and the backcourt remains steady, Crum may have a sleeper team come tourney time. Look for Louisville to rely more than ever on athleticism and the transition game.

1994-95 ROSTER

	POS	HT	YR	FGP	FTP	3-PT	RPG	APG	PPG
DeJuan Wheat	G	6'0"	So.	.45	.77	64/167	2.1	3.2	12.6
Jason Osborne	F/G	6'8"	So.	.39	.56	44/125	6.0	4.1	9.6
Tick Rogers	G	6'5"	Jr.	.47	.52	9/29	2.9	1.2	4.2
Brian Kiser	F	6'7"	Jr.	.43	.68	14/36	1.6	1.0	2.8
Alvin Sims	G/F	6'4"	So.	.35	.52	4/12	1.0	0.4	2.0
Matt Simons	C	6'11"	So.	.53	.50	—	1.0	0.3	1.5
Beau Zach Smith	F/C	6'8"	So.	.38	.73	—	1.2	0.3	1.0
Damion Dantzler	F	6'7"	Fr.	—	—	—	—	—	—
Craig Farmer	G/F	6'5"	Fr.	—	—	—	—	—	—
Eric Johnson	G/F	6'3"	Fr.	—	—	—	—	—	—
Alex Sanders	F	6'7"	Fr.	—	—	—	—	—	—
Samaki Walker	F	6'9"	Fr.	—	—	—	—	—	—

MARQUETTE

Conference: Great Midwest   **1993-94 NCAAs:** 2-1
1993-94: 24-9, 1st GMC   **Coach:** Mike Deane (190-102)

Opening Line: The Warriors stormed to a Great Midwest title last year, then beat S.W. Louisiana and powerful Kentucky in the NCAA Tournament. However, this will be a major transitional season for Marquette. Kevin O'Neil, the Warriors' coach for the past five years, has taken the top job at Tennessee. Can Marquette's success be sustained by his successor, Mike Deane? That will depend upon returnees like Tony Miller, Roney Eford, and Amal McCaskill.

Guard: Miller will hold the point-guard reins again as a senior. The 5'11" floor general has started 90 consecutive games and is the school's all-time assist leader. He may be counted on to score more this season. Sophomore Anthony Pieper is a candidate for the off-guard slot vacated by Robb Logterman. Pieper is the leading scorer in the history of Wisconsin prep basketball, so he knows how to shoot the ball.

Forward: Long-range bomber Eford should shine as a junior. The small forward slumped as a sophomore but could become one of the conference's top players. Faisal Abraham, sparsely used by O'Neill as a freshman, may become a starter this season. Abraham has all the tools. Abel Joseph will also see his minutes increase as a sophomore due to the graduation of Damon Key.

Center: Shot-blocking threat Jim McIlvaine is gone, leaving quite a hole in the center of the Warriors' defense. McCaskill is the top candidate to replace McIlvaine. McCaskill needs to bulk up to take the pounding inside, but his natural athleticism and quickness are assets.

Analysis: The loss of O'Neill as coach and McIlvaine and Key as inside threats will be felt heavily at Marquette. Still, this remains a talented team tested by the competitiveness of the Great Midwest. Miller is a true leader on the floor. If he can rally this team, it could be a sleeper in the postseason.

1994-95 ROSTER

	POS	HT	YR	FGP	FTP	3-PT	RPG	APG	PPG
Roney Eford	F/G	6'6"	Jr.	.42	.69	39/96	6.2	2.3	10.3
Tony Miller	G	5'11"	Sr.	.34	.53	41/120	4.9	8.3	7.2
Amal McCaskill	F/C	6'10"	Jr.	.68	.64	—	3.3	0.5	5.2
Anthony Pieper	G	6'3"	So.	.37	.74	30/93	0.9	1.1	4.9
Chris Crawford	F	6'8"	So.	.36	.69	6/13	0.6	0.2	1.8
Faisal Abraham	F	6'7"	So.	.48	.60	—	1.5	0.2	1.4
Abel Joseph	F	6'8"	So.	.30	—	—	0.6	—	0.8
Dwaine Streater	F/C	6'8"	Jr.	.50	—	—	0.4	—	0.7
Shane Littles	G	6'3"	So.	.25	—	1/4	0.5	0.2	0.5
Aaron Hutchins	G	5'9"	Fr.	—	—	—	—	—	—
Zack McCall	F	6'3"	Fr.	—	—	—	—	—	—
Richard Shaw	F/C	6'11"	Fr.	—	—	—	—	—	—

MARYLAND

Conference: Atlantic Coast
1993-94: 18-12, T-4th ACC

1993-94 NCAAs: 2-1
Coach: Gary Williams (286-197)

Opening Line: A year after their surprising Sweet 16 appearance, the Terrapins are looking for an even bigger season. Coach Gary Williams returns his entire starting lineup—two sophomores and three juniors. At the center of Maryland's attack, literally, is sophomore star Joe Smith, last year's national Freshman of the Year. Smith is surrounded by a talented squad that is both young and experienced.

Guard: The junior tandem of Johnny Rhodes and Duane Simpkins returns to terrorize the ACC again. Rhodes worked hard to improve his game at the offensive end last season and led the team in minutes played. He's also a defensive standout with quick hands and good instincts. Simpkins, a solid point guard, has a steady outside shot. Sophomore Matt Kovarik is a capable back-up at either position.

Forward: Exree Hipp developed into a big-time offensive threat as a sophomore, scoring 35 points in one contest last season. Hipp is also a capable defender but needs to cut down on turnovers. Sophomore Keith Booth plays a mean power forward despite standing just 6'5". Mario Lucas can provide a lift off the bench.

Center: Smith is a natural power forward, but the pivot-poor Terps are happy to use him in the middle. Smith has great physical gifts and the smarts to use them well. He can still get pushed around by heavier opponents, but his jumping ability and quickness make him formidable in the low post. The Terrapins don't have a true center.

Analysis: This team should be a force to be reckoned with in the ACC for the next few years. Smith surprised many teams with his play early as a freshman, and he held up well under the pressure of double- and triple-teams later in the season. Williams's squad thrives on big-game pressure and should find itself in many big games this season.

1994-95 ROSTER

	POS	HT	YR	FGP	FTP	3-PT	RPG	APG	PPG
Joe Smith	F/C	6'10"	So.	.52	.73	2/5	10.7	0.8	19.4
Exree Hipp	F	6'8"	Jr.	.47	.69	31/94	4.0	2.5	13.2
Johnny Rhodes	G	6'4"	Jr.	.42	.62	40/129	6.8	4.1	12.5
Duane Simpkins	G	6'0"	Jr.	.49	.78	38/88	2.6	4.5	11.8
Keith Booth	F	6'5"	So.	.45	.58	11/27	6.1	2.2	10.8
Mario Lucas	F	6'8"	Jr.	.39	.59	3/10	3.6	0.4	5.4
Donny Judd	F	6'5"	Sr.	.42	.67	2/4	0.8	—	2.0
Matt Kovarik	G	6'5"	So.	.42	.79	2/8	1.1	1.1	1.8
Wayne Bristol	G	6'1"	Sr.	.38	.63	4/10	0.8	0.3	1.7
Matt Raydo	G	5'10"	So.	—	.43	0/2	0.3	0.2	0.3
Rodney Elliott	F	6'8"	Fr.	—	—	—	—	—	—
Sarunas Jasikevicius	G	6'4"	Fr.	—	—	—	—	—	—

MASSACHUSETTS

Conference: Atlantic 10
1993-94: 28-7, 1st A-10

1993-94 NCAAs: 1-1
Coach: Jim Calipari (129-64)

Opening Line: The Minutemen made quite a run last year, finishing with the second-most wins in school history before losing in the second round of the NCAAs to Maryland. UMass started last season by knocking off North Carolina and never lost that momentum. Jim Calipari's team includes frontcourt sensations Lou Roe and Marcus Camby. Calipari and his players must now deal with the pressure of being one of the top teams in the country.

Guard: Senior Mike Williams will again start at off guard for the Minutemen. Williams was the team's second-leading scorer last year with 14.6 PPG, but he still needs to work on his outside shot (39.8 percent from the floor last season). Derek Kellogg, also a senior, is an experienced floor general with a reliable stroke from 3-point land. Edgar Padilla and Carmelo Travieso will round out the backcourt rotation.

Forward: Roe came into his own as a junior last season, averaging 18.6 points and 8.3 caroms per game. He has many gifts, including good passing instincts. Dana Dingle returns at the small-forward post after a solid sophomore season in which he improved every aspect of his game. Donta Bright will swing between small forward and big guard, providing scoring punch.

Center: Camby had a fine freshman season, setting a conference record for blocks by a first-year player. If Camby could add more consistency to his game, the 6'11" leaper would become one of the country's top players. Back-up Jeff Meyer is another shot-blocker, and Ted Cottrell will add more depth to the pivot.

Analysis: It is difficult to say whether the Minutemen can repeat their successes of last year. With other teams gunning for them, UMass may find this season a bumpier road to travel. Nevertheless, with players like Camby and Roe and a solid corps of experienced players, Calipari's club will be one of the teams to beat come tourney time.

1994-95 ROSTER

	POS	HT	YR	FGP	FTP	3-PT	RPG	APG	PPG
Lou Roe	F	6'7"	Sr.	.50	.67	4/15	8.3	1.7	18.6
Mike Williams	G	6'2"	Sr.	.40	.64	50/174	3.4	2.9	14.6
Donta Bright	G/F	6'6"	Jr.	.46	.66	5/13	5.8	2.2	10.8
Marcus Camby	C	6'11"	So.	.49	.60	0/4	6.4	1.2	10.2
Dana Dingle	F	6'6"	Jr.	.47	.55	5/9	6.2	1.6	8.0
Derek Kellogg	G	6'3"	Sr.	.38	.60	61/160	3.7	4.2	7.4
Edgar Padilla	G	6'1"	So.	.41	.81	21/68	1.5	2.5	4.5
Carmelo Travieso	G	6'2"	So.	.32	.83	11/41	0.5	0.3	2.3
Jeff Meyer	C	7'2"	Sr.	.50	.53	—	2.1		1.9
Rigoberto Nunez	F	6'7"	Jr.	.35	.31	0/7	1.8	0.3	1.5
Ted Cottrell	C/F	6'9"	Jr.	.48	.29	—	1.2	0.1	1.4
Inus Norville	F	6'9"	Fr.	—	—	—	—	—	—

MEMPHIS STATE

Conference: Great Midwest   **1993-94 NCAAs/NIT:** Not invited
1993-94: 13-16, T-5th GMC   **Coach:** Larry Finch (158-97)

Opening Line: Last year, the Tigers finished below .500 for the first time since the 1980-81 season. But the downswing may not last long for coach Larry Finch's club. Forward Jerrell Horne is the only significant player not returning from last year's team, and all five starters are back. The Tigers also landed a major recruit by persuading hometown hero Lorenzen Wright to stay in Memphis. Three players—Michael Smith, Johnny Miller, and Sidney Coles—transferred.

Guard: Chris Garner and Deuce Ford were the most effective backcourt tandem for Memphis last season, and the sophomore duo will likely start again this season. Garner is small but still an effective defender. Ford had a bad shooting season, hitting just 38.2 percent from the floor. Marcus Nolan and Leon Mitchell also have experience as starters and should push Garner and Ford if they don't show improvement.

Forward: Power forward David Vaughn took steps toward becoming a star last season. He's a powerful inside presence on both ends of the court, as he blocked 107 shots last season while grabbing more than 100 offensive rebounds. Sophomore small forward Cedric Henderson is also an offensive threat as a slasher from the wing. Swing man Rodney Newsom (9.8 PPG) is likely to be the first man off the bench for the Tigers.

Center: Wright will be given every chance to start at center, which allows Vaughn to play big forward rather than the pivot. Wright is an athletic 6'10" center with polished offensive skills and good instincts on defense.

Analysis: Vaughn and Henderson are among the best forward pairs in the country. Still, Finch faces a fistful of questions this season. Can the backcourt provide consistent play? Can Wright be an effective starting center? Does Memphis have enough depth? If the answers to these questions are "yes," the Tigers should roar back above the .500 mark.

1994-95 ROSTER

	POS	HT	YR	FGP	FTP	3-PT	RPG	APG	PPG
David Vaughn	F	6'9"	Jr.	.50	.76	7/21	12.0	1.1	16.6
Cedric Henderson	F	6'6"	So.	.47	.60	18/67	5.1	1.9	13.7
Rodney Newsom	G/F	6'6"	Jr.	.42	.73	46/113	3.3	0.8	9.8
Chris Garner	G	5'10"	So.	.39	.65	13/52	2.8	4.4	6.4
Deuce Ford	G/F	6'6"	So.	.38	.59	13/46	3.2	1.4	5.8
Justin Wimmer	G/F	6'8"	Sr.	.39	.68	16/48	1.9	1.2	5.6
Marcus Nolan	G	6'2"	Sr.	.49	.70	9/24	1.0	1.8	4.8
Leon Mitchell	G	6'3"	Sr.	.59	.50	5/10	2.1	1.5	2.0
Jason Smith	F	6'6"	Jr.	.54	.50	—	1.1	0.2	1.7
Mingo Johnson	G	6'2"	Jr.	—	—	—	—	—	—
Michael Wilson	F	6'7"	Jr.	—	—	—	—	—	—
Lorenzen Wright	C	6'10"	Fr.	—	—	—	—	—	—

MICHIGAN

Conference: Big Ten
1993-94: 24-8, 2nd Big Ten

1993-94 NCAAs: 3-1
Coach: Steve Fisher (123-45)

Opening Line: And then there were two. The three highest-profile members of the Fab Five—Chris Webber, Jalen Rose, and Juwan Howard—have moved on to the NBA, with no NCAA championship to show for their college years. The remaining two, Jimmy King and Ray Jackson, have one final shot at a ring. Don't discount their chances of finally getting one, because coach Steve Fisher has done it again. He's brought in five freshmen who happen to rank as the No. 1 recruiting class in the country.

Guard: King and point guard Dugan Fife return to the starting lineup. King needs to assert himself more as a senior, as he'll likely be the team's No. 1 scoring option. He must regain his 3-point accuracy. Fife is a gutty performer who improved as last season progressed. Talented point guard Bobby Crawford should improve on a disappointing freshman campaign, while freshman Travis Conlan should see plenty of court time.

Forward: Jackson is a given in the starting lineup, but after that the Wolverines have a host of options. Olivier Saint-Jean showed flashes as a frosh last year, and then there are this year's newcomers, all with blue-chip credentials. Jerod Ward, Maceo Baston, Willie Mitchell, and Maurice Taylor are all 6'8" or 6'9", and all averaged 20-plus points and 10-plus rebounds as high school seniors. Ward is the headliner.

Center: Makhtar Ndiaye made an impact after transferring from Wake Forest last January. He doesn't offer much offense, but the Senegal native has a big upside in potential. The freshmen big men will offer help in the pivot.

Analysis: Fisher doesn't rebuild; he reloads. Don't expect much of a drop-off from last year. There is plenty of talent, and King and Jackson know you can be successful with a freshman-flavored roster. The Wolverines will contend for the Big Ten crown and, yes, the national championship.

1994-95 ROSTER

	POS	HT	YR	FGP	FTP	3-PT	RPG	APG	PPG
Jimmy King	G	6'5"	Sr.	.49	.65	29/87	3.8	2.6	12.3
Ray Jackson	F	6'6"	Sr.	.49	.68	7/34	6.3	2.6	11.4
Dugan Fife	G	6'2"	Jr.	.42	.63	48/120	2.7	2.7	6.5
Bobby Crawford	G	6'3"	So.	.43	.57	23/56	1.6	1.0	4.3
Olivier Saint-Jean	F	6'7"	So.	.51	.57	4/14	2.3	0.5	3.6
Leon Derricks	F	6'9"	Jr.	.42	.53	—	2.2	1.1	2.3
Makhtar Ndiaye	C	6'8"	So.	.35	.64	0/5	2.2	0.3	1.7
Maceo Baston	C/F	6'9"	Fr.	—	—	—	—	—	—
Travis Conlan	G	6'4"	Fr.	—	—	—	—	—	—
Willie Mitchell	F/G	6'8"	Fr.	—	—	—	—	—	—
Maurice Taylor	C/F	6'9"	Fr.	—	—	—	—	—	—
Jerod Ward	F/G	6'9"	Fr.	—	—	—	—	—	—

MICHIGAN STATE

Conference: Big Ten   **1993-94 NCAAs:** 1-1
1993-94: 20-12, T-4th Big Ten   **Coach:** Jud Heathcote (398-267)

Opening Line: Well, he's back. Star guard Shawn Respert, that is. Respert has chosen to use his last season of eligibility at Michigan State rather than enter the NBA. Respert's coach, Jud Heathcote, is also likely in his last season as a Spartan. The legendary head-thunker appears to have another middle-of-the-Big Ten-type team on his hands. Junior forward Quinton Brooks is the only returnee besides Respert to average as many as seven points per game.

Guard: With the defection to the NBA of so many high-profile juniors in the Big Ten, conference Player of the Year honors are well within reach for Respert. The 6'3" scoring machine can sink one from nearly any spot on the court. His leadership will be crucial to the Spartans' success. Eric Snow, whose brother won the Butkus Award as an MSU middle linebacker, is back for his senior season at the point. He's a good distributor, but he's still a major liability at the foul line.

Forward: Brooks and Daimon Beathea should get the nod as starters. Brooks will need to become the frontcourt leader. He's a high-percentage shooter who also has the best rebounding credentials of any returnee. Beathea started 18 games last year. Jamie Feick and former Mr. Basketball Jon Garavaglia will be expected to expand their roles this season. Steve Polonowski and swing man Steve Nicodemus also have some experience, although very limited.

Center: The Spartans lack a true center, so one or more of the players mentioned in the forward category, especially Feick, will log time in the pivot.

Analysis: Expect Respert to lead the Big Ten in scoring, and challenge for the national lead. That's about the biggest expectation you should have for this club, which should qualify for the NCAA Tournament but not have a realistic chance of advancing very far. As was the case last year, there is no consistent source of offense other than Respert.

1994-95 ROSTER

	POS	HT	YR	FGP	FTP	3-PT	RPG	APG	PPG
Shawn Respert	G	6'3"	Sr.	.48	.84	92/205	4.0	2.5	24.3
Quinton Brooks	F	6'7"	Jr.	.53	.77	3/10	4.4	0.9	11.3
Eric Snow	G	6'3"	Sr.	.51	.45	13/45	3.5	6.7	6.8
Daimon Beathea	F	6'7"	Jr.	.44	.56	9/21	3.3	1.1	5.0
Jamie Feick	F/C	6'9"	Jr.	.55	.49	0/2	3.3	0.7	3.0
Jon Garavaglia	F	6'9"	So.	.51	.17	0/6	2.0	0.5	2.7
Steve Polonowski	F	6'9"	So.	.32	.80	1/11	1.2	0.1	1.4
Mark Prylow	G	6'3"	Sr.	.27	1.00	3/10	1.0	—	1.0
Steve Nicodemus	G/F	6'4"	Jr.	.43	1.00	1/4	0.3	0.2	0.8
David Hart	G	6'4"	Jr.	.33	.50	0/1	0.4	0.4	0.5
Ray Weathers	G	6'3"	So.	—	—	—	—	—	—
Thomas Kelley	G	6'2"	Fr.	—	—	—	—	—	—

MINNESOTA

Conference: Big Ten   **1993-94 NCAAs:** 1-1
1993-94: 21-12, T-4th Big Ten   **Coach:** Clem Haskins (233-185)

Opening Line: Coach Clem Haskins rejoiced on July 12 when star guard Voshon Lenard, who had left school early for the NBA draft, announced he was coming back to school. The good news made up for the graduations of point guard Arriel McDonald and forward Randy Carter, two of the Big Ten's best at their positions.

Guard: Lenard can do it all at this level, from hitting the trey to blasting to the hole to shutting down his man on defense. More consistency would make him an All-American candidate. Townsend Orr is the team's second-leading returning scorer, and he'll go from first guard off the bench to the starting lineup. Orr can shoot the 3 and is a good distributor. The only other backcourt returnee with significant experience is Ryan Wolf, whose strength is his shooting. Two heralded freshmen, Sam Jacobson and Eric Harris, will be counted upon heavily.

Forward: David Grim, a two-time Academic All-Big Ten selection, can teach you how to put the ball in the basket. Like Lenard and Orr, he has good 3-point range. Jayson Walton hasn't been able to see consistent minutes thus far because of a knee injury, but he has good inside-outside skills. John Thomas showed promise as a true freshman last year.

Center: Chad Kolander, a former Mr. Basketball in Minnesota, has finally become more of a shooter for the Gophers. Always a good defensive player, Kolander will have to deal with higher expectations this year, especially in the rebounding department with Carter's defection. Seven-footer Trevor Winter will see more time as a sophomore.

Analysis: Expect good defense, a positive turnover margin, and all-out hustle— the usual signs of a well-coached team—from Haskins's Gophers. With the return of Lenard, Minnesota can now make a run at the conference title. A trip to the NCAA Tournament is a given.

1994-95 ROSTER

	POS	HT	YR	FGP	FTP	3-PT	RPG	APG	PPG
Voshon Lenard	G	6'4"	Sr.	.47	.84	86/209	3.7	2.2	18.9
Townsend Orr	G	6'1"	Sr.	.48	.74	44/119	3.2	3.3	9.9
Jayson Walton	F	6'6"	Sr.	.41	.66	—	4.5	1.0	7.0
Chad Kolander	F/C	6'9"	Sr.	.46	.63	—	3.9	1.5	6.8
David Grim	F	6'7"	Jr.	.41	.51	28/78	3.3	1.3	6.8
John Thomas	F	6'9"	So.	.39	.43	—	2.5	0.1	2.5
Trevor Winter	C	7'0"	So.	.50	.75	1/1	1.0	0.1	1.6
Ryan Wolf	G	6'3"	Sr.	.25	.79	5/19	0.7	0.4	1.4
Eric Harris	G	6'1"	Fr.	—	—	—	—	—	—
Sam Jacobson	G	6'5"	Fr.	—	—	—	—	—	—
Darrell Whaley	G	6'4"	Fr.	—	—	—	—	—	—

MISSISSIPPI STATE

Conference: Southeastern   **1993-94 NIT:** 0-1
1993-94: 18-11, 3rd SEC West   **Coach:** Richard Williams (116-114)

Opening Line: There weren't many expectations for last year's young Bulldog squad, but Richard Williams got MSU into the postseason for the third time in five years. The Dogs pulled off their surprising campaign thanks to improved post play, a refusal to play dead on the road, solid contributions from the bench, and suffocating defense. Those traits will be evident again, plus this year's team is loaded with senior leadership.

Guard: T.J. Honore gives MSU a quality playmaker and defender at the point, and also a lot of minutes. Marcus Grant, who plays off guard and small forward, is generally responsible for shutting down the opponent's top shooter. Though he doesn't always start or play tons of minutes, Darryl Wilson is far and away the team's best scorer. Aggressive and a quick shooter, Wilson keeps opposing defenses honest.

Forward: Russell Walters is a converted center who has worked hard to adjust to power forward. He's a solid rebounder. At small forward, Brian Price is a steady performer. He does his job in relative anonymity, yet his numbers can't be ignored. Vandale Thomas can also put points on the board, though he needs to improve his shooting.

Center: The biggest starter in MSU history, Erick Dampier made a huge impact as a freshman last year. Expected to contribute immediately on defense, which he did, Dampier surprised even his coach with his 59-percent shooting and 12 PPG. He gets spelled by Bubba Wilson, who has improved noticeably.

Analysis: Last year was no fluke. Goals are higher this year in Starkville, and Mississippi State is a real sleeper to keep an eye on. For the Bulldogs to be a conference title contender, Wilson and Dampier must avoid any sort of second-year letdown.

1994-95 ROSTER

	POS	HT	YR	FGP	FTP	3-PT	RPG	APG	PPG
Darryl Wilson	G	6'1"	Jr.	.42	.81	67/181	3.4	2.5	16.2
Erick Dampier	C	6'11"	So.	.59	.49	—	8.7	0.8	11.9
Marcus Grant	F/G	6'6"	Sr.	.43	.58	37/122	3.4	3.0	9.8
Brian Price	F	6'8"	Sr.	.46	.69	0/3	5.0	1.2	8.4
T.J. Honore	G	6'2"	Sr.	.35	.54	20/90	2.5	4.4	8.1
Vandale Thomas	G/F	6'4"	So.	.38	.73	—	3.5	1.5	7.0
Bubba Wilson	C	6'10"	Jr.	.60	.60	—	3.3	0.2	6.5
Russell Walters	F/C	6'10"	Jr.	.44	.47	0/3	5.6	0.7	6.0
Jay Walton	F	6'7"	Jr.	.40	.67	—	1.1	0.1	1.1
Marcus Bullard	G	6'3"	Fr.	—	—	—	—	—	—
Whit Hughes	G/F	6'5"	Fr.	—	—	—	—	—	—
David Rula	G	6'3"	Fr.	—	—	—	—	—	—

MISSOURI

Conference: Big Eight   **1993-94 NCAAs:** 3-1
1993-94: 28-4, 1st Big Eight   **Coach:** Norm Stewart (640-310)

Opening Line: Jevon Crudup and Melvin Booker took the Tigers on quite a joyride as seniors last year. Missouri entered the 1993-94 season with modest expectations, and left it one game shy of the Final Four. Trouble is, Crudup, Booker, and five other seniors who pushed the Tigers to a No. 1 seed in the NCAAs finished up their eligibility with the loss to Arizona in the Elite Eight. A solution? It might just come in the form of a freshman class *Hoop Scoop* rates as the third best in the country. Norm Stewart's teams always manage to win.

Guard: With the departure of Booker, the biggest need is for a point guard. Kelly Thames and Julian Winfield are both swing-man types. Thames has a quick first step and is a prolific rebounder. Winfield could handle the point. Senior Paul O'Liney, who has travelled a roundabout path to Missouri, has big-time scoring skills. Kendrick Moore, Troy Hudson, and Corey Tate are top 70-type recruits who will make a big impact.

Forward: Marlo Finner and Derek Grimm each started two games last year. Finner's a tenacious inside player, while Grimm has more of a finesse game. Freshman Scott Combs will compete for playing time. One of the seven-foot centers will probably play the four spot.

Center: Sammie and Simeon Haley give new meaning to the term "Twin Towers." The 7'0" juco transfers bring coveted height to the Tiger middle. Freshman Monte Hardge is just as tall, but with a thicker body. Having three seven-footers will help compensate for a lack of experience in the pivot.

Analysis: Don't look for the Tigers to hang around the tops of the polls like last year, but don't expect a complete collapse either. This will be a middle-of-the-pack Big Eight team. However ready the freshman class is to contribute will determine the extent of Mizzou's success.

1994-95 ROSTER

	POS	HT	YR	FGP	FTP	3-PT	RPG	APG	PPG
Kelly Thames	G/F	6'7"	So.	.51	.73	5/15	7.1	1.2	12.2
Paul O'Liney	G	6'2"	Sr.	.38	.75	43/115	2.6	1.7	10.3
Julian Winfield	G/F	6'5"	Jr.	.50	.50	1/3	3.0	1.2	4.3
Marlo Finner	F	6'6"	Sr.	.52	.53	3/12	3.2	0.5	3.5
Derek Grimm	F	6'9"	So.	.50	.63	0/4	1.4	0.1	2.1
Scott Combs	F	6'7"	Fr.	—	—	—	—	—	—
Sammie Haley	F/C	7'0"	Jr.	—	—	—	—	—	—
Simeon Haley	F/C	7'0"	Jr.	—	—	—	—	—	—
Monte Hardge	C	7'0"	Fr.	—	—	—	—	—	—
Troy Hudson	G	6'1"	Fr.	—	—	—	—	—	—
Kendrick Moore	G	6'2"	Fr.	—	—	—	—	—	—
Corey Tate	G/F	6'4"	So.	—	—	—	—	—	—

NAVY

Conference: Patriot League
1993-94: 17-13, T-1st Patriot

1993-94 NCAAs: 0-1
Coach: Don DeVoe (353-260)

Opening Line: The top eight scorers return to a squad that was within four points of No. 1-seeded Missouri in last spring's NCAA Tournament. This year's club is looking to build off the momentum of an 11-3 finish to 1993-94. The Middies play an aggressive man-to-man defense and get contributions from everybody. A couple of Patriot All-Rookie picks, Randy Torgrimson and Brian Walker, weren't even among the team's top five scorers, which says a lot about Navy's depth.

Guard: T.J. Hall went from playing few minutes as a sophomore to scoring nearly 14 PPG last year. He is the barometer of the team's success: When T.J.'s on, so are the Middies; when he's off, Navy has a tough time winning. Walker is the distributor. The Middies went on their late-season run when he was inserted into the starting lineup. Jim Hamilton adds deadly 3-point marksmanship, while Torgrimson and Scott Holden provide solid depth. Hamilton set a school record for treys in 1993-94.

Forward: Wes Cooper is a fine post-up player who always sports a stellar field goal percentage. A strong player, Cooper gets the job done despite a relative lack of height. Larry Green, who can play center or forward, is a gifted leaper.

Center: Navy set a Patriot League record by outrebounding opponents by an average of five per game last year, with junior Alex Kohnen leading the way. He can dominate the glass. Three times last season he grabbed 17 boards.

Analysis: While the Middies wouldn't match up physically with top teams from the super conferences, they're certainly NCAA Tournament material. Don't expect Navy to be shut out when it comes time for all-conference selections, as was the case last year. This year's Middies go into the season having earned significant respect. It's a team that likes to launch the triple but also crashes the boards hard.

1994-95 ROSTER

	POS	HT	YR	FGP	FTP	3-PT	RPG	APG	PPG
T.J. Hall	G	6'3"	Sr.	.45	.74	35/93	3.2	2.3	13.7
Jim Hamilton	G	6'4"	Jr.	.44	.63	76/184	3.4	1.2	11.2
Wes Cooper	F	6'5"	Sr.	.54	.49	—	5.5	0.4	9.6
Alex Kohnen	C	6'11"	Jr.	.50	.60	—	7.3	0.6	8.2
Larry Green	F/C	6'7"	Sr.	.51	.52	0/1	4.2	0.4	7.0
Randy Torgrimson	G	6'0"	So.	.39	.82	29/76	1.8	1.9	6.2
Brian Walker	G	5'8"	So.	.42	.61	4/20	2.8	3.5	5.9
Scott Holden	G	6'2"	So.	.39	.57	14/33	2.0	2.3	5.6
Kico Eaton	G	6'4"	Jr.	.33	.17	2/3	0.5	1.0	2.2
Michael Green	F	6'4"	So.	.50	.50	0/1	1.7	0.5	1.6
Ryan Torgrimson	G	6'0"	Sr.	.50	.72	2/5	0.8	0.7	1.4
Sylvester Joseph	F	6'3"	So.	.29	.27	1/4	0.9	0.1	1.1

NEBRASKA

Conference: Big Eight
1993-94: 20-10, 4th Big Eight

1993-94 NCAAs: 0-1
Coach: Danny Nee (253-170)

Opening Line: After surprisingly winning last year's Big Eight Tournament, Nebraska was bounced by Pennsylvania in the first round of the NCAAs. Atoning for the tourney disappointment will be difficult without high-scoring Eric Piatkowski and starters Bruce Chubick and Jamar Johnson. Head coach Danny Nee brought in a solid recruiting class, which should jell with the key returnees for another strong season.

Guard: Jaron Boone stepped up as a starter last year when Piatkowski slid over from shooting guard to small forward. Boone can also handle the point. Erick Strickland, the best all-around athlete on the roster, can play both backcourt positions as well. Strickland is willing to take chances defensively—he led the club in steals—but his risk-taking also leads to a lot of fouls.

Forward: Explosive Terrance Badgett will likely step into the open small-forward spot. Nee could turn to freshmen Chad Ideus and Andy Markowski to fill the void at power forward if talented Melvin Brooks is forced to play in the pivot. Continually improving Jason Glock, who adopted Chubick's work ethic, should also make more of a contribution this season. Another ballyhooed frosh, 6'7" Chester Surles, can play both small forward and off guard.

Center: Rail-thin Mikki Moore (6'11", 195) wasn't ready for Big Eight action last year, but a summer in the weight room could help him realize his considerable potential. Brooks (6'8") is undersized for the pivot, which could keep Nee from using him there—especially if Moore, 6'11" freshman Leif Nelson, or juco transfer Chris Sallee develop.

Analysis: Just like last year, the Cornhuskers are an athletic club that will give opponents problems in an up-tempo game. Either Boone or Strickland needs to emerge as the go-to player in Piatkowski's absence. And down low, someone's going to have to step up to do the dirty work, which Chubick did last year.

1994-95 ROSTER

	POS	HT	YR	FGP	FTP	3-PT	RPG	APG	PPG
Jaron Boone	G	6'7"	Jr.	.48	.71	35/95	2.6	3.6	12.2
Erick Strickland	G	6'4"	Jr.	.42	.81	41/117	3.4	3.2	10.7
Terrance Badgett	F	6'6"	Jr.	.50	.58	3/19	4.6	1.5	8.6
Melvin Brooks	F/C	6'8"	Sr.	.49	.78	10/25	4.3	1.6	4.8
Jason Glock	G/F	6'5"	Jr.	.51	.88	8/25	1.8	1.2	4.3
Mikki Moore	C	6'11"	So.	.45	.61	0/2	0.9	0.1	2.2
Lee Steinbrook	G	6'2"	Jr.	1.00	.50	1/1	0.8	—	2.0
Chad Ideus	F	6'7"	Fr.	—	—	—	—	—	—
Andy Markowski	F	6'7"	Fr.	—	—	—	—	—	—
Leif Nelson	C	6'11"	Fr.	—	—	—	—	—	—
Chris Sallee	C	6'11"	Jr.	—	—	—	—	—	—
Chester Surles	G/F	6'7"	Fr.	—	—	—	—	—	—

NEVADA-LAS VEGAS

Conference: Big West   **1993-94 NCAAs/NIT:** Not invited
1993-94: 15-13, T-5th Big West   **Coach:** Rollie Massimino (393-262)

Opening Line: It all hit rock bottom for Rollie Massimino in 1993-94. Poor performances by the Runnin' Rebels on the floor translated into poor attendance. Massimino found himself getting booed and harassed, and he even traded verbal barbs with some hecklers after a January loss at the Thomas & Mack Center. Needless to say, three straight years without an NCAA tourney berth has the UNLV faithful restless.

Guard: Off guard Reggie Manuel, known as a defensive stopper for most of his career, showed some offensive flash last year, sporting the Runnin' Rebels' best 3-point numbers. Jermaine "Sunshine" Smith is a strong, athletic performer who's fearless going to the hoop and has no problem guarding taller players. He should take over for Dedan Thomas at the point. Damian Smith is a capable back-up for Manuel.

Forward: Patrick Savoy is electrifying, able to put an emphatic exclamation mark on a fastbreak with an alley-oop jam. The missing link is junior Clayton Johnson. A starter at small forward for the first six games of 1993-94, Johnson—who boasts a 41-inch vertical leap—was lost for the year when he tore his left anterior cruciate ligament. If he comes back at full strength, watch out. Brian Hocevar is a steady player, willing and able to do the dirty work.

Center: With Johnson back, allowing Savoy to play power forward, Kebu Stewart can slide back down to center. All the 6'8", 230-pounder did in his first season of college ball was lead the Big West in both rebounding and scoring. April signees Dennis Jordan and Eric Lee should also make contributions inside.

Analysis: The Rebels have the talent, but probation sanctions and the Vegas atmosphere prevent Massimino from ever fully enjoying himself out in the desert sun. UNLV will have to play every non-conference game on the road this year, so it'll definitely have to earn its trip to the NCAA Tournament.

1994-95 ROSTER

	POS	HT	YR	FGP	FTP	3-PT	RPG	APG	PPG
Kebu Stewart	F/C	6'8"	Jr.	.49	.61	0/1	11.6	0.5	18.9
Reggie Manuel	G	6'3"	Sr.	.42	.80	65/168	3.5	1.7	17.2
Clayton Johnson	F	6'5"	Jr.	.39	.91	6/27	5.0	1.2	11.7
Patrick Savoy	F	6'8"	Sr.	.51	.73	15/45	6.6	0.5	11.5
Lawrence Thomas	G	6'1"	So.	.44	.53	3/7	2.5	2.8	9.8
Jermaine Smith	G	6'2"	So.	.34	.76	24/82	2.9	2.3	8.6
Damian Smith	G	6'2"	Jr.	.36	.71	16/56	0.6	0.6	4.0
Brian Hocevar	F	6'8"	So.	.36	.56	0/1	2.6	0.2	2.5
Mike Curtis	G/F	6'6"	Sr.	.46	.83	0/1	0.5	0.2	1.7
Dennis Jordan	C	6'10"	Jr.	—	—	—	—	—	—
Eric Lee	C	6'10"	Fr.	—	—	—	—	—	—

NEW MEXICO

Conference: Western Athletic   **1993-94 NCAAs:** 0-1
1993-94: 23-8, 1st WAC   **Coach:** Dave Bliss (348-226)

Opening Line: You might not know it, but New Mexico is in esteemed company in the college basketball world. It's one of just four schools—along with Duke, Syracuse, and North Carolina—to post 20 wins in each of the last eight years. Playing home games in The Pit helps. Coach Dave Bliss must replace three starters, including dead-eye shooter Greg Brown.

Guard: Swing man Marlow White isn't gun-shy about firing the 3's, which is what Bliss wants in his up-tempo system. However, Brown's departure could make it tougher for White to get his shots as defenses can now key on him. Charles "Spider" Smith, Bliss's prize recruit of 1993, should step to the fore as a go-to player. The lack of a proven playmaker is the major concern, as Cornelius Ausborne redshirted last year. True freshman Royce Olney, New Mexico's two-time high school Player of the Year at point guard, will get a baptism by fire.

Forward: White will likely swing between shooting guard and small forward. He'll be needed along the front line to pick up the rebounding slack now that Lewis LaMar is gone. Wide-body Brian Hayden can also provide some rebounding punch but is a liability offensively. Spot performer Greg Schornstein gives the Lobos some good height up front. Frosh Clayton Shields and juco import Shawn Simpson should provide much-needed depth.

Center: With a nice touch from 3-point range, Canonchet Neves was the perfect center for Bliss's system. Plugging either Hayden or Schornstein into the position takes away that outside threat. Newcomer Marty Cotwright was one of the best junior college centers last year.

Analysis: Bliss has plugged similar new numbers into the lineup before. But if he can't find someone to ignite the offense in the fashion Brown did, then the 20-win-season streak could be in jeopardy. White and Smith will have to come up with big years.

1994-95 ROSTER

	POS	HT	YR	FGP	FTP	3-PT	RPG	APG	PPG
Marlow White	G/F	6'5"	Sr.	.48	.76	94/237	6.0	2.0	17.0
Charles Smith	G	6'4"	So.	.42	.61	40/119	3.6	2.2	10.1
Brian Hayden	F/C	6'9"	Sr.	.56	.55	—	3.9	0.2	4.4
Rodney Sanders	G	6'3"	Sr.	.31	.50	9/28	0.8	2.4	3.9
Greg Schornstein	F	6'6"	So.	.43	.65	4/11	1.5	0.3	1.7
Eric Thomas	G	6'6"	Sr.	.43	—	1/3	1.0	0.6	1.4
Cornelius Ausborne	G	6'0"	Fr.	—	—	—	—	—	—
Marty Cotwright	F/C	6'9"	Jr.	—	—	—	—	—	—
Steve Lewis	G	6'4"	Jr.	—	—	—	—	—	—
Royce Olney	G	6'2"	Fr.	—	—	—	—	—	—
Clayton Shields	F	6'7"	Fr.	—	—	—	—	—	—
Shawn Simpson	F/C	6'8"	Jr.	—	—	—	—	—	—

NEW MEXICO STATE

Conference: Big West   **1993-94 NCAAs:** 0-1
1993-94: 23-8, 1st Big West   **Coach:** Neil McCarthy (393-187)

Opening Line: After losing only two key players, Neil McCarthy probably doesn't know what to do with himself. Usually, he's scouring the juco ranks in hopes of revamping his ballclub. In 1993-94, the Aggies made it to their fifth consecutive NCAA Tournament despite plugging eight transfers into the lineup. This year, though, it's quality rather than quantity that must be replaced, as NMSU must replace rebounding machine James Dockery and 26-year-old vet D.J. Jackson.

Guard: Skip McCoy and Rodney Walker both were selected to the 1994 Big West All-Tournament team. Though an athletic slasher, Walker had a wretched 3-point percentage for a shooting guard. McCoy is the defensive ace in McCarthy's system, in which he rotates ten players through the lineup for intense, six-minute spurts. Point guard Keith Johnson is an excellent penetrator but not a feared scoring threat. Junior college transfer Troy Brewer will try to provide instant offense off the bench.

Forward: Dockery was the Aggies' best inside presence, both in scoring and rebounding. Jackson decided to test his skills in Europe, leaving the cupboard pretty bare. Versatile Paul Jarrett, the club's best pure shooter, will have to work more on the low blocks this season. Several untested players, including Crafton Ferguson, Daniel Hicks, and Chris Lopez, will play more than they expected.

Center: Undersized yet skilled inside, Johnny Selvie will have to put up some of the statistics that made him one of the top high school and junior college players in the country. He must also cut down on his fouls. Help on the low blocks comes from 6'9" juco import Spelling Davis.

Analysis: Someone will have to step up on the boards in order for the Aggies to continue their high-octane, up-tempo attack, which boasted a Big West-best 81.5 points per game last year. Strong depth and tenacious defense are the things that make this team special.

1994-95 ROSTER

	POS	HT	YR	FGP	FTP	3-PT	RPG	APG	PPG
Thomas Wyatt	G	6'6"	Sr.	.44	.74	17/59	5.2	2.4	10.0
Rodney Walker	G	6'4"	Sr.	.50	.58	10/47	3.2	1.2	9.6
Keith Johnson	G	6'3"	Sr.	.56	.46	0/7	2.6	4.9	7.3
Johnny Selvie	F/C	6'6"	Sr.	.56	.52	—	4.4	0.7	6.9
Paul Jarrett	F	6'8"	Jr.	.39	.69	37/100	2.9	0.9	5.8
Lance Jackson	G	6'0"	Jr.	.34	.69	3/12	1.7	1.5	5.3
Skip McCoy	G	5'10"	Sr.	.38	.52	28/77	1.3	1.1	4.3
Troy Brewer	G	6'2"	Jr.	—	—	—	—	—	—
Spelling Davis	F/C	6'9"	Jr.	—	—	—	—	—	—
Crafton Ferguson	F	6'8"	Jr.	—	—	—	—	—	—
Daniel Hicks	G/F	6'4"	Jr.	—	—	—	—	—	—
Chris Lopez	F	6'5"	So.	—	—	—	—	—	—

NEW ORLEANS

Conference: Sun Belt   **1993-94 NIT:** 1-1
1993-94: 20-10, 3rd Sun Belt   **Coach:** George Price (0-0)

Opening Line: The college basketball world was stunned in late July after hearing that newly appointed New Orleans coach Tommy Joe Eagles, age 45, had collapsed during a basketball game and died. Eagles, the former head coach at Auburn, had replaced Tim Floyd, who had left to coach Iowa State. New coach George "Tic" Price, an assistant coach last year who was promoted in August, will try to hold this team together.

Guard: Dedric Willoughby shook off the effects of a knee injury to post the best statistics of any Sun Belt Conference freshman last year. An outstanding shooter, he'll be the Privateers' unquestioned leader and go-to player. The playmaking skills of sparkplug Gerald Williams, a first-team All-Sun Belt selection last year, will be sorely missed. Jimmie Smith doesn't have Williams's flair but is a hard-nosed performer who rarely makes a mistake.

Forward: Greek import Andrej Zelenbaba has a nice perimeter touch and could function well in an up-tempo system, but he doesn't play with a lot of intensity on the defensive end. Junior Conerly is a strong defender and rebounder but is undersized (6'6") and limited offensively for a power forward. Combined, neither has the experience or presence on both ends to replace the departed Melvin Simon. A juco crop of Jerran Cobb, Bobby Davis, and James Douglas—all 6'5"—will battle for playing time.

Center: Michael McDonald is not an offensive force in the pivot—and he's awful from the line—but New Orleans desperately needs his rebounding and shot-blocking ability. Newcomer Gevon Garner is the only other center on the roster.

Analysis: In order for another postseason appearance to become a reality, the Privateers are going to need some big-time help in the paint and they must also develop some depth. Coach Price has to incorporate new players into a new system. He's fortunate to have Willoughby, who will win a few games on his own.

1994-95 ROSTER

	POS	HT	YR	FGP	FTP	3-PT	RPG	APG	PPG
Dedric Willoughby	G/F	6'2"	So.	.43	.80	44/110	2.1	0.7	9.0
Michael McDonald	C	6'10"	Sr.	.60	.51	—	6.9	0.5	5.7
Andrej Zelenbaba	F	6'8"	Sr.	.43	.89	4/14	1.3	0.5	2.5
Jimmie Smith	G	5'10"	Sr.	.38	.45	0/4	1.2	1.5	1.9
Junior Conerly	F	6'6"	Sr.	.89	—	—	1.2	0.1	1.1
Corey Brown	G	6'4"	Fr.	—	—	—	—	—	—
Jerran Cobb	F	6'5"	Jr.	—	—	—	—	—	—
Bobby Davis	F	6'5"	Jr.	—	—	—	—	—	—
James Douglas	F	6'5"	Jr.	—	—	—	—	—	—
Gevon Garner	C	6'9"	Jr.	—	—	—	—	—	—
Steve Meyer	G	6'3"	Fr.	—	—	—	—	—	—
Andy Seigle	F	6'9"	Jr.	—	—	—	—	—	—

NORTH CAROLINA

Conference: Atlantic Coast   **1993-94 NCAAs:** 1-1
1993-94: 28-7, 2nd ACC   **Coach:** Dean Smith (802-230)

Opening Line: Although North Carolina was expected to repeat as NCAA champ in 1994, all hopes crashed and burned with a stunning second-round upset by Boston College in the NCAA Tournament. Though three starters have departed, it might be a case of addition by substraction as Dean Smith no longer needs to worry about upsetting the team's chemistry when divvying up minutes.

Guard: Lead guard Derrick Phelps will be the toughest piece to replace, as unproven sophomore Jeff McInnis steps into Phelps's starting point-guard spot. Starter Donald Williams is back, but he struggled mightily with his shooting stroke after being the hero of the 1993 Final Four. There's plenty of depth behind Williams at shooting guard with steady Dante Calabria and athletic Larry Davis. Freshman Shammond Williams will back up McInnis.

Forward: Jerry Stackhouse played well at the end of the regular season and has the tools and talents to play both forward spots, although he is most dominant at small forward. After redshirting last year because of the stockpile of talent, Ed Geth—who saw limited mop-up action in 1992-93—gets a shot at the power-forward position.

Center: After playing out of position at power forward last year due to Eric Montross's presence, sophomore Rasheed Wallace now gets the chance to showcase his extraordinary talents. Some added bulk and more maturity could make him a legitimate All-America candidate by season's end. Seven-footer Serge Zwikker is a luxury off the bench.

Analysis: Although slightly inexperienced and thin at forward, the Tar Heels certainly have the talent for another trip to the Final Four. It boils down to leadership and intensity. Both were noticeably absent last year, as UNC didn't get the job done on defense or on the boards. This year, the leadership burden falls squarely on Williams's shoulders.

1994-95 ROSTER

	POS	HT	YR	FGP	FTP	3-PT	RPG	APG	PPG
Donald Williams	G	6'3"	Sr.	.42	.77	42/124	2.4	2.2	14.3
Jerry Stackhouse	F	6'6"	So.	.47	.73	2/20	5.0	2.0	12.2
Rasheed Wallace	C	6'10"	So.	.60	.60	0/1	6.6	0.5	9.5
Dante Calabria	G	6'4"	Jr.	.43	.72	41/118	2.9	2.4	8.1
Jeff McInnis	G	6'4"	So.	.46	.64	27/65	1.7	2.4	5.6
Larry Davis	G	6'3"	Jr.	.67	.80	0/2	0.7	0.5	2.4
Serge Zwikker	C	7'2"	So.	.52	.75	—	0.7	0.1	1.5
Pearce Landry	G	6'5"	Sr.	.43	.83	1/9	0.3	0.5	1.2
Ed Geth	F	6'8"	So.	—	—	—	—	—	—
Pat Sullivan	F	6'8"	Sr.	—	—	—	—	—	—
Ryan Sullivan	G	6'2"	Fr.	—	—	—	—	—	—
Shammond Williams	G	6'2"	Fr.	—	—	—	—	—	—

NORTH CAROLINA-CHARLOTTE

Conference: Metro   **1993-94 NIT:** 0-1
1993-94: 16-13, T-2nd Metro   **Coach:** Jeff Mullins (149-118)

Opening Line: Defensively last year, UNCC held its opponents to 67.4 PPG and under 40-percent shooting from the floor. But the 49ers often broke down offensively, shooting just better than 40 percent. Leading scorer and rebounder Jarvis Lang is one of three starters to return, but what UNCC desperately needs is a playmaker to step forward to keep its offense from stalling.

Guard: Andre Davis, the Metro Conference's Freshman of the Year in 1992-93, missed too many of his 127 3-point attempts last season. If Roderick Howard wants to assume the starting point-guard position, he'll have to play with more intensity on the defensive end. Back-up shooting guard Shanderic Downs should be more consistent as a sophomore after turning the ball over 41 times (compared to 27 assists) last season. Look for versatile junior college import Ponce James to push both Howard and Downs for playing time.

Forward: Although out of position at small forward, converted guard Bob Kummer performed admirably in 1993-94, playing strong defense and ranking second on the club in assists. Lang is immensely talented and powerful close to the basket, although he has a tendency to do too much on his own. Mullins has stocked the position with three standout juco recruits—Quincy Alexander, Roy Wells, and Bruce Patterson—as well as touted prepster DeMarco Johnson.

Center: Capable pivot man Rodney Odom has graduated, but his production should be easily replaced by seven-footer Jermain Parker. Last year, Parker led the club in blocked shots and finished third in rebounding despite playing only 16 minutes per game.

Analysis: By bringing in four juco transfers, Mullins is sending a clear message that he wants to turn things around in a hurry by using experienced players who can contribute immediately. The key will be the emergence of a scorer and playmaker to take some of the pressure off Lang.

1994-95 ROSTER

	POS	HT	YR	FGP	FTP	3-PT	RPG	APG	PPG
Jarvis Lang	F	6'7"	Sr.	.56	.74	0/3	10.1	0.8	16.4
Andre Davis	G	6'1"	Jr.	.34	.75	38/127	2.4	2.1	11.0
Shanderic Downs	G/F	6'4"	So.	.40	.44	35/87	2.6	0.9	6.1
Bobby Kummer	G/F	6'6"	Jr.	.36	.73	25/81	4.6	2.1	5.7
Roderick Howard	G	5'10"	So.	.43	.84	28/70	0.6	1.0	5.4
Jermain Parker	C	7'0"	Sr.	.41	.65	—	5.2	0.5	5.1
Jason Dominick	C	6'10"	So.	—	.33	—	0.9	—	0.3
Quincy Alexander	F	6'8"	Jr.	—	—	—	—	—	—
Ponce James	G	6'2"	Jr.	—	—	—	—	—	—
DeMarco Johnson	F	6'8"	Fr.	—	—	—	—	—	—
Bruce Patterson	G/F	6'4"	Jr.	—	—	—	—	—	—
Roy Wells	F	6'6"	Jr.	—	—	—	—	—	—

OHIO STATE

Conference: Big Ten
1993-94: 13-16, T-8th Big Ten

1993-94 NCAAs/NIT: Not invited
Coach: Randy Ayers (98-52)

Opening Line: Coach Randy Ayers, coming off two sub-par seasons, is starting to feel the heat in Columbus. Help was supposed to be on the way for 1993-94 from prep standout Damon Flint, but recruiting violations sent him to Cincinnati. This year, Ayers lost recruiting wars for local standouts J.J. Lucas—the son of three-time OSU All-American Jerry Lucas—and Samaki Walker. To make matters worse, would-be starter Charles Macon has been ruled academically ineligible and forward Nate Wilbourne decided to transfer.

Guard: The Buckeyes will miss Jamie Skelton's leadership but not his itchy trigger finger. A fearless penetrator, Derek Anderson was easily the club's most consistent performer last year before breaking a leg in February. Flanked by sweet-shooting Greg Simpson, Anderson gives Ayers a major-league duo in the backcourt. Freshmen Carlos Davis and Robert Shelton will provide depth.

Forward: The loss of Macon hurts, as the former Indiana Mr. Basketball was ready to make a significant impact in his junior season. Austin Peay transfer Ricky Yudt, the OVC Freshman of the Year in 1992, will vie for Lawrence Funderburke's old power-forward post. Tweener Rickey Dudley has the strength but not the size to be an effective performer with his back to the basket. There are no other true forwards on the roster.

Center: So far, the Antonio Watson/Gerald Eaker center tandem has occupied space more than anything else. Watson is still trying to shake off the effects of a knee injury two years ago, while Eaker got a baptism by fire in his first year after redshirting in 1992-93. Both need to improve their work on the boards.

Analysis: In Anderson, Simpson, and Yudt, the Buckeyes have three guys who can play with the best in the Big Ten. However, the team's depth is a huge concern; as the school year was approaching, there were only nine players on the roster. Besides bench depth, the Buckeyes need a defensive stopper and rebounding enforcer to step forward. If not, the club will struggle to compete in the Big Ten.

1994-95 ROSTER

	POS	HT	YR	FGP	FTP	3-PT	RPG	APG	PPG
Derek Anderson	G/F	6'6"	Jr.	.47	.81	21/62	4.9	4.9	15.0
Greg Simpson	G	6'1"	Jr.	.48	.71	38/91	3.0	3.4	11.1
Antonio Watson	F/C	6'9"	Sr.	.55	.76	—	3.2	0.5	5.4
Rickey Dudley	F	6'7"	Sr.	.37	.69	—	3.8	0.9	3.5
Gerald Eaker	C	6'11"	So.	.44	.50	—	2.7	0.3	3.3
Doug Etzler	G	6'0"	Sr.	.41	.85	17/34	0.8	1.7	2.6
Carlos Davis	G	6'4"	Fr.	—	—	—	—	—	—
Robert Shelton	G	6'3"	Fr.	—	—	—	—	—	—
Rick Yudt	F	6'7"	Jr.	—	—	—	—	—	—

OKLAHOMA

Conference: Big Eight   **1993-94 NCAAs/NIT:** Not invited
1993-94: 15-13, 5th Big Eight   **Coach:** Kelvin Sampson (103-103)

Opening Line: Say goodbye to Billy Ball in Norman. After 14 seasons, coach Billy Tubbs surprisingly packed his bags for Texas Christian, leaving a rebuilding project for former Washington State head man Kelvin Sampson. Three starters are gone, including standout forward Jeff Webster, which means Sampson will have to rely heavily on the talents of emerging star Ryan Minor in the early going.

Guard: The point-guard spot is firmly in the capable hands of senior John Ontjes, named Big Eight Newcomer of the Year in 1993-94. The juco transfer finished 21st in the nation in assists, although he must do a better job in the turnover department. Now that versatile Pete Lewis is gone, juniors Dion Barnes and Shon Alexander will likely split time at shooting guard. Freshman Prince Fowler could also see significant minutes, spelling Ontjes at point guard.

Forward: Minor inherits the scoring and rebounding burden from Webster and is poised for stardom. Minor still needs to bulk up and show he can play hard on a consistent basis. Senior Calvin Curry was a solid addition as a juco transfer last year, averaging 14.5 points per game. Alexander can swing to small forward, while several untested forwards will battle each other for playing time.

Center: Tubbs opted for a center-by-committee plan last season, and Sampson will likely continue with that philosophy. James Mayden and Jason Yanish hardly strike fear in opposing pivot men, and neither is a shot-blocking presence. Recruit Evan Wiley may need to develop quickly.

Analysis: The lack of a quality big man will keep Tubbs's stamp on the team during Sampson's inaugural campaign, as Tubbs's trademark run-and-gun style of play didn't hinge on an imposing center. If Minor develops into the 20-PPG, ten-RPG star that he should become, Oklahoma will be back in the NCAA Tournament sooner rather than later.

1994-95 ROSTER

	POS	HT	YR	FGP	FTP	3-PT	RPG	APG	PPG
Ryan Minor	F	6'7"	Jr.	.50	.77	30/78	7.4	1.8	16.2
Calvin Curry	G/F	6'7"	Sr.	.39	.60	76/213	5.1	1.8	14.5
John Ontjes	G	6'0"	Sr.	.43	.87	23/61	3.3	6.5	9.7
Dion Barnes	G	6'2"	Jr.	.38	.43	12/45	1.7	1.6	4.9
Jason Yanish	C	6'11"	Jr.	.40	.75	—	2.5	0.4	3.1
Shon Alexander	G/F	6'6"	Jr.	.46	.62	4/12	1.8	0.8	2.8
James Mayden	C	6'10"	Sr.	.30	.52	1/4	2.4	—	1.7
Ernie Abercrombie	F	6'5"	Jr.	—	—	—	—	—	—
Antonio Bobo	F	6'8"	Fr.	—	—	—	—	—	—
Prince Fowler	G	5'11"	Fr.	—	—	—	—	—	—
Maurice McCree	G/F	6'7"	Fr.	—	—	—	—	—	—
Evan Wiley	F/C	6'11"	Fr.	—	—	—	—	—	—

OKLAHOMA STATE

Conference: Big Eight   **1993-94 NCAAs:** 1-1
1993-94: 24-10, 2nd Big Eight   **Coach:** Eddie Sutton (526-199)

Opening Line: After wobbling to an 8-4 start last season, the Cowboys were viewed as underachievers. But Eddie Sutton's team came back to complete a quietly solid year. So much was expected of monster center Bryant "Big Country" Reeves that his fine season (21.0 PPG, 9.7 RPG) was considered a disappointment. Brooks Thompson's outside sniping, which took pressure off Reeves inside, will be sorely missed.

Guard: Assist leaders Thompson and Scott Sutton are gone, leaving a hole at point guard. Randy Rutherford is an off guard who will likely play some point guard this year. Rutherford is a potent outside gunner who should increase his 13.1-PPG average with the ball in his hands on a consistent basis. If Chianti Roberts is to settle in as the other starting guard, he must improve his wretched 3-point and free throw percentages.

Forward: Terry Collins will never be mistaken for a superstar, but the solid senior will either be a starter or the first man off the bench this year because he does the little things coaches love. Scott Pierce will chip in a little, but Sutton will need to find some scoring punch from the forwards. Freshman Jason Skaer could provide some help.

Center: Now a senior, the 7'0", 285-pound Reeves is expected to be one of the top players in the country. The big center is surprisingly fluid for his size and is virtually unstoppable if single-teamed (which won't be often this year). Ben Baum and 7'0" freshman John Nelson will provide depth in the pivot.

Analysis: This team will sink or swim with Reeves, period. He was stung by criticism last year but responded with a strong finish. If Sutton can fashion a supporting cast around Big Country, the Cowboys could challenge for the Big Eight title. With only two double-figure scorers returning, though, OSU may have trouble scoring enough points to beat top teams.

1994-95 ROSTER

	POS	HT	YR	FGP	FTP	3-PT	RPG	APG	PPG
Bryant Reeves	C	7'0"	Sr.	.59	.59	0/1	9.7	1.5	21.0
Randy Rutherford	G	6'3"	Sr.	.44	.84	78/193	4.7	2.8	13.1
Chianti Roberts	G/F	6'5"	So.	.44	.52	10/41	3.0	2.0	4.7
Terry Collins	F	6'6"	Sr.	.51	.54	1/4	1.9	1.0	2.7
Scott Pierce	F	6'8"	Sr.	.49	.50	0/2	2.4	0.7	2.3
Jason Turk	G	6'1"	Jr.	.50	.50	2/3	—	0.3	1.0
Ben Baum	C	6'11"	So.	.33	.70	—	0.5	0.1	0.9
Chad Alexander	G	6'3"	Fr.	—	—	—	—	—	—
Kevin Miles	F	6'9"	So.	—	—	—	—	—	—
John Nelson	C	7'0"	Fr.	—	—	—	—	—	—
Andre Owens	G	5'10"	Jr.	—	—	—	—	—	—
Jason Skaer	F	6'7"	Fr.	—	—	—	—	—	—

OLD DOMINION

Conference: Colonial Athletic   **1993-94 NIT:** 1-1
1993-94: 21-10, T-1st CAA   **Coach:** Jeff Capel (16-14)

Opening Line: Last season, the Monarchs missed the NCAA Tournament on a buzzer-beater by James Madison in the CAA tourney finals. Coach Oliver Purnell subsequently bolted for Dayton, but he didn't leave the cupboard bare, as a pair of future NBA players—center Odell Hodge and forward Petey Sessoms—return for another season. Purnell might just be wishing he was in Norfolk when things get tough in Dayton this winter.

Guard: The tandem of Kevin Swann and Kevin Larkin formed the Colonial Athletic Association's top backcourt last year, but both are gone. Three sophomores—E.J. Sherod, Corey Robinson, and Mark Johnson—will comprise the backcourt rotation for the Monarchs. Sherod is not a scorer and will probably land the starting point-guard spot. Robinson and Johnson have potential to be fine off guards, but both need more seasoning.

Forward: Sessoms's scoring averaged dipped from 16.9 PPG as a sophomore to 16.0 PPG last season, due largely to inconsistency. For stretches, Sessoms was dominant. Maturity will only improve his game, which is fluid and unforced. Small forward Mike Jones is a reliable third option in the offense.

Center: Hodge is a future NBA star at power forward, but the 6'9", 260-pounder will cause havoc in the pivot for Old Dominion for at least one more season. The athletic Hodge led the team in scoring, rebounds, and blocked shots last season. He refined his offensive skills greatly last year. Derrick Parker is a capable, if undersized, back-up.

Analysis: Last season's NIT appearance was a disappointment; they're thinking only NCAAs this year. If the backcourt can contribute some outside scoring punch to open up the floor, Sessoms and Hodge will create points near the basket. It's too bad new coach Jeff Capel couldn't convince his son—Duke's emerging star guard, Jeff Capel Jr.—to switch schools.

1994-95 ROSTER

	POS	HT	YR	FGP	FTP	3-PT	RPG	APG	PPG
Odell Hodge	C/F	6'9"	Jr.	.55	.68	—	9.0	1.4	19.4
Petey Sessoms	F	6'7"	Sr.	.42	.82	90/215	5.6	1.6	16.0
Mike Jones	F	6'5"	Sr.	.41	.79	68/170	5.1	1.7	14.6
David Harvey	F	6'8"	Sr.	.42	.53	0/4	3.5	0.5	4.0
Mark Johnson	G	6'3"	So.	.41	.40	10/28	0.5	0.5	2.4
Mario Mullen	F	6'6"	Jr.	.42	.45	1/2	1.9	0.5	2.3
E.J. Sherod	G	6'4"	So.	.33	.61	3/11	0.9	1.3	2.3
Derrick Parker	C	6'9"	Jr.	.39	.45	—	2.2	0.1	1.8
Corey Robinson	G	6'2"	So.	.38	.58	4/10	0.7	0.4	1.8
Corey Parker	F	6'6"	Jr.	—	—	0/1	0.1	—	—
Brion Dunlap	G	5'11"	Fr.	—	—	—	—	—	—
Duffy Samuels	G	5'9"	Jr.	—	—	—	—	—	—

PENNSYLVANIA

Conference: Ivy League   **1993-94 NCAAs:** 1-1
1993-94: 25-3, 1st Ivy   **Coach:** Fran Dunphy (84-49)

Opening Line: The Quakers return much of the team that upset Nebraska by a 90-80 margin in the first round of the NCAA Tournament last season. Coach Fran Dunphy's team has similarities to other Ivy League teams—a lack of size, for instance—but Pennsylvania breaks the stereotype with an athletic backcourt tandem and an up-tempo style. Guards Matt Maloney and Jerome Allen, now seniors, will try to lead Penn to a third straight undefeated conference season.

Guard: The team's strengths, Maloney and Allen, set themselves apart from other Ivy League guards with their fierce defense. Moreover, both are good shooters and capable playmakers who can create their own shots. Allen was a second-team All-East selection of *Basketball Weekly* last year, while Maloney wasn't far behind. Scott Kegler and Donald Moxley will contribute off the bench.

Forward: Shawn "Dr. Detroit" Trice was the Quakers' fourth-leading scorer last year (8.5 PPG) and also led the squad in rebounds (7.1 RPG). He's especially good on the offensive glass. Eric Moore saw many minutes at center last year and could play some pivot again this season, but he's better suited to the power-forward slot.

Center: If Moore switches to the forward spot, junior Tim Krug will likely inherit the pivot position. Krug is the Quakers' best shot-blocker and also has a nice touch from outside the 3-point line (40.7 percent). Sophomore Nat Graham will also see time at center.

Analysis: The Quakers lost swing man Barry Pierce but are otherwise unscathed by graduation. Although Pennsylvania lacks the size to compete with the nation's top schools on a consistent basis, this is a team you won't want to draw in the first round of the NCAA Tournament. Don't be surprised to see the Quakers hanging around in the 20s of the top-25 rankings. Another Ivy League championship is a lock.

1994-95 ROSTER

	POS	HT	YR	FGP	FTP	3-PT	RPG	APG	PPG
Jerome Allen	G	6'4"	Sr.	.40	.79	50/146	4.5	4.6	14.5
Matt Maloney	G	6'3"	Sr.	.39	.90	66/202	2.6	3.8	14.0
Shawn Trice	F	6'7"	Sr.	.58	.67	0/1	7.1	0.7	8.5
Eric Moore	F/C	6'7"	Sr.	.47	.55	15/41	4.9	1.2	8.1
Tim Krug	F/C	6'8"	Jr.	.51	.52	11/27	3.8	0.6	6.7
Scott Kegler	G	6'6"	Sr.	.44	.82	36/80	1.4	1.1	5.1
Nat Graham	C	6'7"	So.	.32	.46	2/8	1.4	0.4	1.7
Cedric Laster	F	6'5"	Jr.	.24	.50	4/15	0.7	0.2	1.5
Donald Moxley	G	6'2"	Jr.	.23	.53	0/4	1.3	0.3	1.3
Bill Guthrie	F/C	6'9"	Jr.	.35	—	0/2	1.3	0.1	0.9
Jamie Lyren	G	6'3"	So.	.33	.57	1/1	0.4	0.4	0.6
Michael Melcher	F/C	6'8"	Fr.	—	—	—	—	—	—

PENN STATE

Conference: Big Ten   **1993-94 NCAAs/NIT:** Not invited
1993-94: 13-14, T-8th Big Ten   **Coach:** Bruce Parkhill (249-233)

Opening Line: The Nittany Lions weren't tame kittens last season. Coach Bruce Parkhill's team knocked off two ranked clubs and just missed a .500 season and an NIT selection. Entering their third campaign in the Big Ten, the team's taking aim at the NCAA Tournament. With four starters returning, the Nittany Lions may actually have a shot at their goal.

Guard: Starter Michael Jennings is gone, but sophomore point guard Dan Earl should be the cornerstone of the Penn State attack for years to come. Senior swing man Greg Bartram will likely fill the shooting-guard spot, but he needs to further develop his offensive skills against the tough defense of the Big Ten. Donovan Williams and Chris Rogers will be back-ups, with freshman Pete Lisicky waiting in the wings.

Forward: Rahsaan Carlton made the transition from sixth man to starter last season, finishing as the team's second-leading scorer (10.1 PPG). Carlton is a slasher who can also play the perimeter, but he needs to raise the level of his game for the Lions to be a success. Phil "Big House" Williams was an instant success at the power-forward slot and should only improve as a sophomore.

Center: English import John Amaechi is now a senior, and his game has progressed each year. While still rather limited on the offensive end, Amaechi did lead the Lions in scoring last season (16.9 PPG). Amaechi no longer shies away from contact under the boards, as he grabbed 8.9 RPG last year. Michael Joseph is a solid if unspectacular back-up.

Analysis: Buoyed by last year's relative success, the Nittany Lions are ready to rise from the Big Ten's lower reaches. Amaechi is no superstar, but he is solid enough to lead Penn State to a few upsets. If Earl and Phil Williams improve significantly as sophomores, the Lions could manage a small roar.

1994-95 ROSTER

	POS	HT	YR	FGP	FTP	3-PT	RPG	APG	PPG
John Amaechi	C/F	6'10"	Sr.	.51	.70	4/15	8.9	1.5	16.9
Rahsaan Carlton	F	6'6"	Jr.	.44	.73	29/76	3.1	0.4	10.1
Dan Earl	G	6'3"	So.	.39	.65	32/86	2.5	4.2	8.4
Greg Bartram	G/F	6'5"	Sr.	.34	.76	29/83	2.6	1.3	6.4
Phil Williams	F/C	6'8"	So.	.60	.60	—	5.3	0.4	5.4
Donovan Williams	G	6'1"	Sr.	.36	.64	2/10	1.2	1.0	3.4
Michael Joseph	C	6'10"	Sr.	.54	.60	—	1.6	0.2	1.6
Chris Rogers	G	6'0"	Jr.	.50	—	0/1	0.3	—	0.6
Calvin Booth	C	6'11"	Fr.	—	—	—	—	—	—
Pete Lisicky	G	6'4"	Fr.	—	—	—	—	—	—
Damien McKnight	G	6'2"	Fr.	—	—	—	—	—	—
T.J. McNulty	G/F	6'5"	Fr.	—	—	—	—	—	—

PITTSBURGH

Conference: Big East   **1993-94 NCAAs/NIT:** Not invited
1993-94: 13-14, 8th Big East   **Coach:** Ralph Willard (81-41)

Opening Line: The Panthers enter this season with a big hole in the middle of their lineup—a 6'11", 250-pound hole once occupied by the now-departed Eric Mobley. New coach Ralph Willard brings a familiar style to the Big East—the up-tempo, pressing, 3-point attack of former Providence head man Rick Pitino. A new coach and the absence of a go-to man means there will be plenty of opportunities for players to step into the limelight.

Guard: Senior point guard Jerry McCullough assumes the team leadership mantle. McCullough averaged 13.3 PPG and 7.0 APG last season and is a dangerously quick defender. Sophomore Jason Maile will assume off-guard duties. Maile is capable of putting up the numbers, but he's still unproven. Gunner Sotiris Aggelou and point man Andre Alridge will round out the backcourt.

Forward: Orlando Antigua returns at the small-forward spot after averaging 10.7 PPG last season. The senior will bear a greater scoring burden in Willard's attack. Antigua is a smooth ball-handler and deadly in transition, but his outside shot needs work (41 percent last year). Senior Chris Gant worked his way into the starting lineup last year and was the team's second-leading boarder (6.7 RPG). Senior Willie Cauley is good under the boards and has fine range for a power forward.

Center: Senior Jaime Peterson was an effective back-up to Mobley last season. Now, he wins the center spot by default. Peterson is better suited for the power-forward position, but he's the closest thing to a center the Panthers have. This is a weak spot for Pitt.

Analysis: Willard's style of play is perfectly suited for this collection of run-and-gunners. He's also blessed with experience, as his four leading returning scorers are seniors. If Antigua can play up to his prep billing when he was Paul Evans's prize recruit four years ago, then Pitt will make some noise in the Big East .

1994-95 ROSTER

	POS	HT	YR	FGP	FTP	3-PT	RPG	APG	PPG
Jerry McCullough	G	5'11"	Sr.	.39	.73	36/105	4.0	7.0	13.3
Orlando Antigua	F	6'7"	Sr.	.41	.75	47/112	4.4	1.7	10.7
Chris Gant	F	6'7"	Sr.	.44	.78	2/6	6.7	1.1	8.6
Willie Cauley	F	6'7"	Sr.	.46	.49	6/19	3.6	0.9	6.9
Sotiris Aggelou	G	6'3"	So.	.36	.73	26/82	1.9	0.9	6.1
Jaime Peterson	C	6'8"	Sr.	.54	.59	—	3.5	0.5	4.9
Jason Maile	G	6'4"	So.	.36	.54	19/60	1.1	0.8	4.2
Garrick Thomas	G	6'4"	Jr.	.41	.57	14/45	1.9	0.6	3.8
Andre Alridge	G	6'2"	Jr.	.35	.80	3/11	0.7	1.7	1.7
Chad Varga	F	6'6"	So.	—	—	—	—	—	—

PURDUE

Conference: Big Ten
1993-94: 29-5, 1st Big Ten

1993-94 NCAAs: 3-1
Coach: Gene Keady (335-154)

Opening Line: Poor Gene Keady. The Purdue coach loses five players from last year's squad. Well, four players and a basketball godsend—Glenn Robinson. The Big Dog's 30.3 PPG and 10.1 RPG have moved on to the NBA, while Keady must stay behind with a team missing nearly every key component from last year's Big Ten champs. Cuonzo Martin is a star in the making, but he's no Mr. Robinson.

Guard: The starting backcourt of Matt Waddell and Porter Roberts returns intact. Roberts is not much of an outside-shooting threat, but his play at the point improved steadily throughout last season. Waddell is a sharpshooter and solid leader who is limited defensively. Swing man Herb Dove, a senior, will see increased playing time. Freshman Chad Austin has potential.

Forward: Martin will start at the three spot and will also see time at big guard. Martin's improved outside shot was a big plus for the Boilermakers last year; this year, he must become a consistent scorer. Brandon Brantley will be the power forward after playing some center last year. Brantley is a good rebounder with a nice touch around the basket. Small forward Justin Jennings will likely be the first player off the bench.

Center: With the Big Dog gone, attention will now be focused on a guy who is just big. Matt ten Dam, a 7'2", 305-pounder from Holland, is a project with potential. At worst, ten Dam can clog the lane on defense. Look for Brantley to still get major pivot minutes with the graduations of Ian Stanback, Cornelius McNary, and Kenny Williams—Purdue's center by committee.

Analysis: Keady's cupboard isn't exactly bare. There is leadership in the backcourt and solid depth, and Martin is ready to step from Robinson's shadow. He'll be the one they'll now turn to in clutch situations. Despite its losses, Purdue remains a top Big Ten team.

1994-95 ROSTER

	POS	HT	YR	FGP	FTP	3-PT	RPG	APG	PPG
Cuonzo Martin	F/G	6'6"	Sr.	.46	.74	88/196	4.3	1.9	16.3
Matt Waddell	G	6'4"	Sr.	.47	.80	44/105	3.9	4.8	11.3
Porter Roberts	G	6'3"	Jr.	.42	.66	9/32	3.2	4.1	5.3
Brandon Brantley	F/C	6'8"	Jr.	.54	.57	—	4.5	0.4	4.5
Justin Jennings	F	6'6"	Jr.	.55	.61	—	1.8	0.6	4.2
Herb Dove	G	6'5"	Jr.	.49	.60	—	2.5	0.6	3.7
Todd Foster	G	6'1"	Jr.	.36	—	12/40	1.0	0.9	2.1
Chad Austin	G	6'2"	Fr.	—	—	—	—	—	—
Roy Hairston	F	6'8"	Jr.	—	—	—	—	—	—
David Lesmond	F	6'8"	Fr.	—	—	—	—	—	—
Brad Miller	C	6'11"	Fr.	—	—	—	—	—	—
Matt ten Dam	C	7'2"	Fr.	—	—	—	—	—	—

SETON HALL

Conference: Big East   **1993-94 NCAAs:** 0-1
1993-94: 17-13, 7th Big East   **Coach:** George Blaney (394-314)

Opening Line: Last season was odd for Pirate coach P.J. Carlesimo. Not only did Seton Hall win fewer than 20 games for only the second time in six seasons, but the Pirates had to get hot at the end just to make the NCAA Tournament. With Arturas Karnishovas gone, a new group of players must rise to the occasion for Seton Hall to contend in the Big East. Trouble is, P.J.'s now in Portland. The bearded sideline general decided to do what many of his players have been lucky enough to do—join the NBA ranks. Successor George Blaney, a 22-year coach at Holy Cross, is respected among his peers.

Guard: Ironman Bryan Caver is gone from the point, but the return of Danny Hurley—who left school last year while undergoing treatment for depression—should bolster the guard corps. Dwight and Andre Brown (no relation) will share the shooting-guard spot. Dwight is a tough defender with a sweet stroke. Andre needs to improve his shot selection after shooting a woeful 29 percent last year.

Forward: Karnishovas did a number of things for the Pirates and will not be easily replaced. John Leahy and Adrian Griffin are talented players who have the potential to score in double figures. Chris Davis has limited skills but plays with a lot of heart.

Center: Wide-body Darrell Mims is gone, taking his six boards per game with him. Recruit Jacky Kaba could find himself playing big minutes as a true freshman center. Actually, he'll have to play because no one else on the team is taller than 6'7".

Analysis: Blaney may have trouble milking enough points from his lineup, although he's known for getting the most out of his talent. The play of the Browns at guard and the confidence of Hurley at the point should help the Hall reach the NCAA tourney for the fifth consecutive year. The Pirates will probably finish back in the pack in the Big East, however.

1994-95 ROSTER

	POS	HT	YR	FGP	FTP	3-PT	RPG	APG	PPG
Adrian Griffin	F	6'5"	Jr.	.47	.60	2/6	7.8	2.2	9.7
Dwight Brown	G	6'4"	Sr.	.41	.55	34/88	2.0	1.1	7.1
John Leahy	F	6'7"	Sr.	.32	.81	31/110	2.8	1.2	6.0
Andre Brown	G	6'3"	So.	.29	.54	21/73	1.3	1.0	4.3
Danny Hurley	G	6'2"	Jr.	.12	.50	2/9	4.0	3.0	3.5
John Yablonski	G	5'10"	Jr.	.13	1.00	0/2	0.6	0.6	1.1
Chris Davis	F	6'7"	Sr.	.39	.50	—	1.4	0.2	1.0
Roger Ingraham	F	6'7"	Jr.	—	—	—	—	—	—
Jacky Kaba	C	6'10"	Fr.	—	—	—	—	—	—
Levell Sanders	G	6'2"	Fr.	—	—	—	—	—	—
Jearwaun Tuck	G	5'10"	Jr.	—	—	—	—	—	—
Donnell Williams	F	6'7"	Fr.	—	—	—	—	—	—

SOUTHERN CALIFORNIA

Conference: Pac-10   **1993-94 NIT:** 0-1
1993-94: 16-12, 7th Pac-10   **Coach:** George Raveling (336-292)

Opening Line: Coach George Raveling's club climbed into the NIT last year, although their stay was as short as could be as USC lost to Fresno State in overtime in the first round. The Trojans lose second-leading scorer Mark Boyd as well as highly skilled sophomore center Avondre Jones, who left school. Forward Lorenzo Orr is clearly the headliner of this team.

Guard: Junior Burt Harris grew into the starting point-guard spot last year and will reprise his role this season. Harris is a competent long-range shooter who continues to improve his skills as a floor general. Brandon Martin returns as the off guard after a spotty shooting year (41.5 percent). Martin can score in bunches but he needs a lot of shots to do it. Sophomore Claude Green and swing man Stais Boseman will round out the guard rotation.

Forward: Orr didn't quite take his game to the next level last season after a fine NIT performance as a sophomore. This year will give the 6'7" senior a chance to show he can be a star. He will be if he can cut down on turnovers and improve his outside shot. Sophomore Jaha Wilson is a contender for the other forward slot, while swing man Tremayne Anchrum will also see time in the frontcourt.

Center: Fans are mourning the loss of Jones, an athletic 6'11" pivot who was a top-ten recruit. Kirk Homenick, a seven-foot junior, does return, but he doesn't have the skills to match his height. Untested David Crouse will have to contribute something.

Analysis: Raveling hoped his program would become a Pac-10 powerhouse, but the unexpected loss of Jones is a major step backward. Orr will throw down some thunder dunks and put points on the board, but he won't be able to do it alone. A strong interior presence is seriously lacking. Making the NCAA Tournament will be a difficult fight.

1994-95 ROSTER

	POS	HT	YR	FGP	FTP	3-PT	RPG	APG	PPG
Lorenzo Orr	F	6'7"	Sr.	.48	.59	—	6.6	1.6	13.4
Brandon Martin	G	6'4"	Jr.	.42	.75	32/84	2.8	1.3	12.4
Burt Harris	G	5'10"	Jr.	.43	.69	56/144	1.7	3.1	10.3
Tremayne Anchrum	F/G	6'5"	Sr.	.49	.49	17/40	5.4	1.6	6.3
Stais Boseman	G/F	6'4"	So.	.28	.59	12/46	2.1	1.5	4.4
Jaha Wilson	F	6'5"	So.	.41	.60	0/7	3.1	0.6	3.9
Claude Green	G	6'3"	So.	.31	.42	14/50	0.8	0.5	3.7
Kirk Homenick	C	7'0"	Jr.	.30	.58	—	0.9	0.1	0.8
Craig Slaughter	G	6'0"	So.	—	.50	—	—	0.3	0.3
David Crouse	F/C	6'11"	So.	—	—	—	—	—	—
Cameron Murray	G	6'1"	Fr.	—	—	—	—	—	—
Tyson Reuter	G	6'3"	Jr.	—	—	—	—	—	—

STANFORD

Conference: Pac-10   **1993-94 NIT:** 0-1
1993-94: 17-11, T-4th Pac-10   **Coach:** Mike Montgomery (279-168)

Opening Line: The Cardinal fell a win or two short of an NCAA Tournament appearance last season. Coach Mike Montgomery loses two starters—forward Brent Williams and center Jim Morgan—but still has a fairly deep team. Guard Dion Cross (15.1 PPG) is this team's star, but he'll need some help to lead Stanford to the Big Dance.

Guard: Cross is cat-quick and has a sweet outside shot. He struggled against some junk defenses last year, but Cross seems to find a way to get the job done in big games. Point guard Brevin Knight started every game for Stanford last year and is as quick as Cross. Knight's outside shot is so-so, but he can break a defense down off the dribble. Swing man David Harbour is an offensive sparkplug off the bench.

Forward: Senior Andy Poppink returned from a back injury last year to average 12.4 PPG and 7.4 RPG. Poppink will be counted on to maintain or improve those numbers. Junior Darren Allaway and senior Bart Lammersen will vie for the empty power-forward spot. Prized recruit Mark Madsen decided to go on a mission and will thus miss the season.

Center: The loss of Morgan leaves the pivot wide open. Problem is, no one appears ready to fill his shoes. Senior Todd Manley could win the job, but he is unproven as a career back-up. Freshman seven-footer Tim Young could win the starting nod with a strong preseason showing. Lammersen could also help out if need be.

Analysis: Stanford has lacked a quality big man since Adam Keefe left for the NBA. Young could change that, but this team will rise or fall with the talents of guards like Cross this season. The Cardinal was 10-8 in the conference last season, and an improvement on that record should get Montgomery's club into the NCAAs.

1994-95 ROSTER

	POS	HT	YR	FGP	FTP	3-PT	RPG	APG	PPG
Dion Cross	G	6'2"	Jr.	.44	.79	54/128	2.7	1.3	15.1
Andy Poppink	F	6'7"	Sr.	.47	.71	8/23	7.4	1.8	12.4
Brevin Knight	G	5'10"	So.	.35	.76	11/55	3.9	5.4	11.1
David Harbour	G/F	6'3"	Sr.	.37	.60	12/44	2.7	1.5	7.3
Darren Allaway	F	6'8"	Jr.	.55	.41	—	3.7	0.2	4.3
Bart Lammersen	F/C	6'9"	Sr.	.58	.44	—	2.2	0.2	2.2
Todd Manley	F/C	6'9"	Sr.	.67	.42	2/2	0.8	0.4	1.6
Rich Jackson	F	6'6"	So.	.56	1.00	2/3	0.5	0.2	1.1
Warren Gravely	G	6'3"	Sr.	.16	.17	0/10	0.4	0.7	0.3
Kamba Tshionyi	G	6'2"	Fr.	—	—	—	—	—	—
Tim Young	C	7'1"	Fr.	—	—	—	—	—	—

SYRACUSE

Conference: Big East
1993-94: 23-7, 2nd Big East

1993-94 NCAAs: 2-1
Coach: Jim Boeheim (434-140)

Opening Line: Things got back to normal in upstate New York in 1993-94 as Syracuse—after a one-year, NCAA-imposed hiatus from the NCAA Tournament—made its eighth Sweet 16 appearance under head coach Jim Boeheim. Four starters return from last year's club, led by All-America candidate Lawrence Moten.

Guard: The versatile Moten put his slashing and driving abilities on display last season, as he upped his shooting percentage and point production by doing most of his damage going to the basket. Without Adrian Autry beside him, though, Moten is sure to draw more attention from defenses. Autry's back-up, Lazarus Sims, is a good penetrator and distributor but a wretched shooter. This will cause problems for Syracuse, as teams will leave Sims alone and double-team Moten.

Forward: John Wallace, an excellent rebounder and scorer close to the basket, has the tools and moxie to give the Orangemen their most dominating presence at power forward since Derrick Coleman. A more mature Lucious Jackson played under control last season and gave Boeheim a small forward he could rely upon. Sophomore Jim Hayes can grab a few boards off the bench.

Center: Although only 6'8", Otis Hill has a strong upper body and fine leaping ability, which allows him to play much larger than his size—particularly on the defensive end, where he's most effective. Back-up J.B. Reafsnyder has a nice shot from the perimeter, but he must get more physical in the paint.

Analysis: Wallace and Hill give the Orangemen one of the top inside tandems in the country, and a more halfcourt-oriented attack could be in the offing if Moten doesn't get any help in the backcourt. Moten may even handle the ball a lot himself to try to make things happen. A little depth would make the Orangemen Final Four material.

1994-95 ROSTER

	POS	HT	YR	FGP	FTP	3-PT	RPG	APG	PPG
Lawrence Moten	G	6'5"	Sr.	.50	.70	50/176	4.5	2.2	21.5
John Wallace	F	6'7"	Jr.	.57	.76	0/2	9.0	1.7	15.0
Lucious Jackson	F	6'6"	Sr.	.46	.76	29/91	3.8	1.7	10.1
Otis Hill	C	6'8"	So.	.54	.58	—	5.6	1.2	7.9
J.B. Reafsnyder	C	6'10"	Jr.	.41	.60	—	3.2	0.7	3.5
Lazarus Sims	G	6'4"	Jr.	.24	.77	2/16	1.1	1.9	1.3
Elimu Nelson	G	6'2"	Sr.	.21	—	0/4	1.0	0.1	0.7
Jim Hayes	F/C	6'9"	So.	.25	—	—	1.8	0.1	0.4
Mike Begovich	G	5'10"	So.	.25	—	—	0.3	0.2	0.3
James May	G	5'10"	So.	—	—	—	—	—	—
Todd Burgan	G/F	6'6"	Fr.	—	—	—	—	—	—
Bobby Lazor	F	6'6"	Fr.	—	—	—	—	—	—

TEMPLE

Conference: Atlantic 10   **1993-94 NCAAs:** 1-1
1993-94: 23-8, 2nd A-10   **Coach:** John Chaney (276-105)

Opening Line: John Chaney's troops had it backwards in 1993-94. They got off to a fast start (16-2) and then petered out at the finish (second-round exit from the NCAA Tournament). Without superb swing men Eddie Jones and Aaron McKie returning from a team that had little depth to begin with, Temple is certain to struggle at the start of the year.

Guard: Point guard Rick Brunson was the Owls' most complete player in 1993-94. This season, he'll have to be the club's most dominant performer, which means an inconsistent jumper will have to dramatically improve. Chris Ozment and William Rice have both been bit players the last two years, and it remains to be seen whether they're ready for prime-time action. Chaney will give incoming freshman Johnny Miller a good look.

Forward: Jason Ivey and Derrick Battie are solid veterans who do their best work on the boards. The 6'6", 213-pound Ivey has the right size for small forward but usually played at power forward or center the last two years, when Chaney got frustrated by the inconsistent play of Battie and William Cunningham. Battie still needs to develop into an offensive threat and avoid foul trouble. So far, junior Julian King, a true swing man, has been too out of control.

Center: Simply put, the enigmatic Cunningham has to produce. Chaney was banking on that production last year, but Cunningham actually regressed statistically. With no proven outside shooters, the offense will flow through Cunningham first.

Analysis: Two givens: The Owls, mirroring their fiery coach's intensity, will continue to play their tenacious match-up zone defense; also, Chaney will rely basically on a seven-man rotation. With the opposition ganging up on Brunson, Temple will first need to establish an inside scoring presence from Ivey, Battie, and Cunningham in order to be successful.

1994-95 ROSTER

	POS	HT	YR	FGP	FTP	3-PT	RPG	APG	PPG
Rick Brunson	G	6'3"	Sr.	.37	.65	50/167	4.1	4.6	12.4
Derrick Battie	F	6'9"	Jr.	.45	.52	0/2	5.0	0.1	5.9
Jason Ivey	F	6'6"	Jr.	.37	.45	—	5.4	0.3	4.7
William Cunningham	C	6'11"	Jr.	.40	.39	—	4.2	—	1.6
William Rice	F/G	6'6"	Jr.	.64	.17	1/2	0.6	—	0.9
Chris Ozment	G	6'4"	Sr.	.29	.50	2/6	0.9	0.1	0.8
Julian King	G/F	6'5"	Jr.	.33	—	1/1	0.6	0.1	0.3
Marco Van Velsen	F	6'9"	Jr.	—	—	—	0.3	—	—
Levan Alston	G	6'2"	Jr.	—	—	—	—	—	—
Huey Futch	F	6'7"	So.	—	—	—	—	—	—
Johnny Miller	G	6'1"	Fr.	—	—	—	—	—	—
Lynard Stewart	F	6'7"	Fr.	—	—	—	—	—	—

TEXAS

Conference: Southwest
1993-94: 26-8, 1st SWC

1993-94 NCAAs: 1-1
Coach: Tom Penders (348-255)

Opening Line: Tom Penders said he would have his best team at Texas in 1993-94, but few believed him after star point guard B.J. Tyler missed the start of the season, checking himself into the John Lucas Center in Houston for treatment of depression. Well, once Tyler returned to the lineup in mid-December, Penders proved to be prophetic, as the Longhorns claimed the SWC regular-season crown and won their first-ever conference tournament title.

Guard: Stepping into Tyler's role as team leader will be senior Terrence Rencher, who can dish and score equally well but hasn't lived up to the huge expectations levied on him after his standout freshman season. Roderick Anderson, a key contributor last year, inherits the starting point-guard position vacated by Tyler. The Longhorns will need to find an outside-shooting spark off the bench now that Tony Watson has graduated.

Forward: Not having Albert Burditt's presence on the boards is a huge blow, particularly for a team that runs as much as the Longhorns. Tremaine Wingfield and Reggie Freeman both have extensive experience. Wingfield's team-high 61.2 field goal percentage was mainly due to his strong work on the offensive glass. Senior Carl Simpson and junior college transfer Sonny Alvarado look to be the best candidates to assume Burditt's rebounding and shot-blocking chores.

Center: At 6'9", Rich McIver provided a presence in the middle last year, but as far as production goes, he'll have to come up with more than five points and three rebounds per game. Sheldon Quarles is a decent shot-blocker but needs to be more aggressive in the pivot.

Analysis: With the Longhorns' running style, they can easily absorb Tyler's loss in the scoring department. The more pressing need is to find somebody to step into Burditt's role as the rebounder and enforcer. Without much competition, though, this club should coast through the weak SWC.

1994-95 ROSTER

	POS	HT	YR	FGP	FTP	3-PT	RPG	APG	PPG
Terrence Rencher	G	6'3"	Sr.	.41	.71	37/143	5.4	3.1	15.9
Roderick Anderson	G	5'10"	Sr.	.45	.71	35/108	3.2	5.2	12.3
Tremaine Wingfield	F	6'7"	Sr.	.61	.34	0/2	4.4	0.3	6.1
Reggie Freeman	G/F	6'5"	So.	.42	.74	16/56	2.6	0.9	5.3
Rich McIver	C	6'9"	Sr.	.47	.54	—	3.1	0.2	4.6
Carl Simpson	F	6'8"	Sr.	.46	.54	—	2.4	0.3	3.2
Sheldon Quarles	C/F	6'10"	Jr.	.37	.60	0/3	1.0	—	1.6
Tommy Penders	G	6'2"	Sr.	.40	.55	7/15	0.7	0.3	1.5
Sonny Alvarado	F/C	6'8"	Jr.	—	—	—	—	—	—
Carlton Dixon	G	6'5"	Fr.	—	—	—	—	—	—
Nathion Gilmore	F	6'9"	Jr.	—	—	—	—	—	—
Brandy Perryman	G	6'2"	Fr.	—	—	—	—	—	—

TULANE

Conference: Metro   **1993-94 NIT:** 1-1
1993-94: 18-11, T-2nd Metro   **Coach:** Perry Clark (81-66)

Opening Line: After a meteoric rise the previous two seasons, the Green Wave leveled off in 1993-94. A freshman, Jerald Honeycutt, emerged as the club's leading scorer, but the team was lacking in experience, as evidenced by its 5-10 record away from New Orleans. With six of last year's top players returning, though, the Green Wave should be riding high once again in 1994-95.

Guard: Kim Lewis was just a shadow of himself last year after missing the 1992-93 season with a broken leg. LeVeldro Simmons, who split the starting shooting-guard duties with Lewis last season, is the best backcourt performer in Perry Clark's posse. Chris Cameron must improve his 3-point stroke to justify the number of treys he takes. Super-quick Pointer Williams has left school.

Forward: Honeycutt, a silky-smooth wing player who was the most heralded player ever to sign with Tulane, led the team in rebounding as well as scoring last year. Honeycutt also displayed his youth with a team-high 94 turnovers and poor shot selection. Taking over for departed Carlin Hartman at power forward, Rayshard Allen will team with Honeycutt to form one of the best sophomore forward tandems in the country. Correy Childs, a sophomore swing man, should also see plenty of time off the bench.

Center: Depth and experience are noticeably lacking with the graduation of Makeba Perry, who was limited offensively but provided sound rebounding and interior defense. Vershawn Eley has played in only 16 total games his first two seasons. Freshmen David McLeod and Lawrence Nelson will grow up in a hurry.

Analysis: This is a typical Tulane team under Clark—loaded with guards and swing men but lacking an inside punch. Someone will need to emerge in the pivot. Moreover, the Green Wave will need to shoot a lot better from the perimeter—as a team, they shot only .265 from 3-point range last season—in order to make it to the Big Dance in 1995.

1994-95 ROSTER

	POS	HT	YR	FGP	FTP	3-PT	RPG	APG	PPG
Jerald Honeycutt	F	6'9"	So.	.40	.68	37/131	6.7	1.9	15.3
LeVeldro Simmons	G	6'4"	Jr.	.47	.79	18/62	2.7	1.9	12.3
Rayshard Allen	F	6'7"	So.	.55	.61	1/2	5.1	0.7	8.8
Kim Lewis	G	6'4"	Sr.	.42	.73	22/72	3.8	1.8	7.8
Chris Cameron	G	6'4"	So.	.41	.41	14/65	3.0	1.5	5.8
Correy Childs	G/F	6'6"	So.	.46	.67	7/21	1.6	0.5	5.5
Antonio Jackson	G	6'2"	Sr.	.45	.45	0/2	1.6	0.5	1.8
Vershawn Eley	C	6'9"	Jr.	.40	.50	—	1.0	0.2	1.7
Gus Abbott	F	6'9"	Fr.	—	—	—	—	—	—
David McLeod	C	6'11"	Fr.	—	—	—	—	—	—
Lawrence Nelson	C	6'10"	Fr.	—	—	—	—	—	—

UCLA

Conference: Pac-10
1993-94: 21-7, T-2nd Pac-10

1993-94 NCAAs: 0-1
Coach: Jim Harrick (304-150)

Opening Line: After climbing to the top spot in the polls in late January 1994, the Bruins plummeted to No. 17 by the time the NCAA Tournament rolled around, and then were thoroughly embarrassed by Tulsa in the first round. With last year's nucleus back and one of the country's best recruiting classes arriving, coach Jim Harrick is in for his most pressure-filled season in Westwood.

Guard: Diminutive Tyus Edney was the best point guard in the conference last season not named Jason Kidd. With his scoring numbers continuing to increase, he's on the verge of stardom. A suitable replacement must be found for Shon Tarver at shooting guard. Marquis Burns has been impressive from 3-point range, while Kevin Dempsey, another long-range marksman, can easily rotate between shooting guard and small forward. Cameron Dollar will complete his two-year apprenticeship under Edney.

Forward: The "Brothers Rim"—Ed and Charles O'Bannon—are back for their second year as the starting forward tandem. Ed has completely shaken off the effects of the serious knee injury from four years ago, and he upped his rebounding and scoring numbers last season. With loads of offensive talent, Charles needs to improve defensively. Beyond the O'Bannons, the Bruins have no appreciable experience, which opens the way for freshman J.R. Henderson.

Center: George Zidek, a native of Czechoslovakia, surprised many by taking the starting job from Rodney Zimmerman last season. He was among the Pac-10 leaders in field goal percentage and rebounding, although he was constantly in foul trouble. Zidek will be pushed by freshman omm'A Givens, a blue-chipper.

Analysis: Depth was the Bruins ultimate downfall in 1993-94, as evidenced by their late-season swoon. Harrick is hoping his prize recruiting class can fill that void as the season progresses. If not, it will be an even hotter summer in L.A. for Harrick in 1995.

1994-95 ROSTER

	POS	HT	YR	FGP	FTP	3-PT	RPG	APG	PPG
Ed O'Bannon	F	6'8"	Sr.	.48	.74	16/56	8.8	2.1	18.2
Tyus Edney	G	5'10"	Sr.	.47	.82	24/64	3.4	5.8	15.4
Charles O'Bannon	F	6'7"	So.	.51	.65	18/47	6.8	1.6	11.6
George Zidek	C	7'0"	Sr.	.52	.76	0/2	7.0	0.5	11.1
Kevin Dempsey	G/F	6'6"	Jr.	.41	.61	14/40	1.6	1.3	4.6
Cameron Dollar	G	6'1"	So.	.47	.59	4/14	1.5	2.7	3.9
Marquis Burns	G	6'4"	Jr.	.45	.56	9/20	1.9	0.7	2.9
Ike Nwankwo	C	6'11"	So.	.49	.33	—	1.6	0.4	2.3
Toby Bailey	G	6'5"	Fr.	—	—	—	—	—	—
omm'A Givens	C/F	6'10"	Fr.	—	—	—	—	—	—
J.R. Henderson	F	6'9"	Fr.	—	—	—	—	—	—
Kris Johnson	G/F	6'4"	Fr.	—	—	—	—	—	—

VILLANOVA

Conference: Big East   **1993-94 NIT:** 5-0
1993-94: 20-12, T-4th Big East   **Coach:** Steve Lappas (84-93)

Opening Line: How quickly things change. Everyone thought Rollie Massimino got out of Philly at the right time (1992), leaving Steve Lappas with a major mess to clean up. But in 1993-94, Villanova finished strong and won the NIT. The team returns all five starters, led by All-America candidate Kerry Kittles. And the last time we checked on Rollie out in Las Vegas...well, he hadn't exactly made anyone forget about Jerry Tarkanian.

Guard: It's tough to find a deeper backcourt than Kittles, Jonathan Haynes, Alvin Williams, and spot performer Roscoe Harris. Kittles, a swing man who usually is paired with the opposition's small forward, was the school's first All-Big East first-team selection since 1986. Haynes earned All-NIT recognition for his playmaking. Sophomore sparkplug Williams played starter's minutes last season despite never making it out for the opening tip.

Forward: Getting Ron Wilson back for another year at power forward is a bonus, but he may lose some of his minutes to N.C. State transfer Chuck Kornegay, who will be eligible in January. Junior Eric Eberz has a nice shooting stroke for his size, which allows him to heat up quickly. Eberz led the club in 3-point percentage last season.

Center: The Wildcats' play picked up in February with the improvement of freshman center Jason Lawson, who learned how to avoid foul trouble. Lawson finished second in the league in blocked shots and was a monster on the boards in February and March. With Kornegay around, Wilson can easily slide down to center when Lawson needs a breather.

Analysis: While opponents spend their time devising ways to stop Kittles, look for Lawson to emerge as one of the top players in the Big East. A glimpse of that scenario came at the end of last season. With what's returning and the addition of Kornegay, the biggest battle for Lappas will be dividing up the minutes.

1994-95 ROSTER

	POS	HT	YR	FGP	FTP	3-PT	RPG	APG	PPG
Kerry Kittles	G/F	6'5"	Jr.	.45	.71	73/209	6.5	3.4	19.7
Eric Eberz	F	6'7"	Jr.	.45	.75	62/158	4.3	1.4	12.6
Jonathan Haynes	G	6'3"	Sr.	.42	.73	46/129	3.5	5.7	11.7
Jason Lawson	C	6'11"	So.	.52	.58	—	6.6	1.2	10.1
Alvin Williams	G	6'4"	So.	.39	.70	20/51	2.8	2.8	7.9
Ron Wilson	F/C	6'9"	Sr.	.47	.63	—	5.5	0.7	5.9
Roscoe Harris	G	6'4"	Jr.	.36	.78	38/118	1.5	0.9	5.9
Arthur Quarterman	F	6'8"	So.	.29	.50	—	1.9	0.1	1.6
Zeffy Penn	F	6'6"	So.	.25	.58	0/1	1.1	0.3	1.0
Jaime Gregg	F	6'8"	Jr.	.33	.75	1/2	0.2	0.3	1.0
Chuck Kornegay	F	6'9"	So.	.33	—	0/1	—	—	0.2
Adam Shafer	G	6'5"	Fr.	—	—	—	—	—	—

VIRGINIA

Conference: Atlantic Coast   **1993-94 NCAAs:** 1-1
1993-94: 18-13, T-4th ACC   **Coach:** Jeff Jones (80-46)

Opening Line: Their style may not be pleasing to the eye, but the results are. Under Jeff Jones, the Cavaliers have captured an NIT championship and appeared in three NCAA Tournaments by winning with a tough, bump-and-grind, man-to-man defense. Last year, that defense helped compensate for the loss of point guard Cory Alexander to a broken ankle. Jones was feeling pretty good this summer after landing a top-ten recruiting class.

Guard: Freshman Harold Deane filled in admirably for Alexander last season after Alexander suffered his injury in an embarrassing season-opening loss at home to Connecticut (77-36). Deane's tenacious defense fits right in with Jones's philosophy, but Alexander's offensive skills were noticeably absent. Jones will likely find a way to put Deane and Alexander on the floor at the same time. Swing man Jamal Robinson will put a few points on the board.

Forward: Workhorse Junior Burrough took over the team's go-to role in Alexander's absence. His offensive game still needs more polish, particularly from the free throw line, but expect close to 20 points and ten rebounds a game from the big guy. If senior Jason Williford displays the confidence he had in high school, he should be a fine complement to Burrough at small forward. Freshman Norman Nolan will also get a long look.

Center: Yuri Barnes is the typical lunch-pail Cavalier center of the late 1980s and early 1990s. Barnes is a bruising banger who scores on a lot of putbacks. Freshman Chase Metheney—all 7'3" of him—is the Cavs' best prospect in the pivot since Olden Polynice and Ralph Sampson, but he needs some seasoning before making an impact in the ACC.

Analysis: The Cavs topped the ACC in both scoring defense and field goal-percentage defense last season. Look for that trend to continue. With the return of Alexander's savvy and scoring punch, this team will wreak plenty of havoc.

1994-95 ROSTER

	POS	HT	YR	FGP	FTP	3-PT	RPG	APG	PPG
Junior Burrough	F	6'8"	Sr.	.40	.64	12/37	7.0	0.9	15.0
Harold Deane	G	6'1"	So.	.37	.71	51/154	3.5	2.8	12.3
Jason Williford	F/G	6'5"	Sr.	.38	.67	36/93	6.1	2.4	9.8
Yuri Barnes	F/C	6'8"	Sr.	.43	.59	—	6.3	0.5	8.5
Jamal Robinson	G/F	6'6"	So.	.43	.72	18/56	3.1	1.0	7.1
Chris Alexander	F/C	6'8"	Jr.	.44	.60	—	2.5	0.2	1.7
Cory Alexander	G	6'1"	Jr.	—	—	0/2	1.0	2.0	—
Martin Walton	F	6'8"	So.	—	—	—	—	—	—
Chase Metheney	C	7'3"	Fr.	—	—	—	—	—	—
Norman Nolan	F	6'8"	Fr.	—	—	—	—	—	—
Curtis Staples	G	6'2"	Fr.	—	—	—	—	—	—
Maurice Watkins	F/G	6'5"	So.	—	—	—	—	—	—

WAKE FOREST

Conference: Atlantic Coast
1993-94: 21-12, 3rd ACC

1993-94 NCAAs: 1-1
Coach: Dave Odom (128-102)

Opening Line: Last year, the Demon Deacons were able to withstand the early exit of Rodney Rogers to the NBA and the unexpected loss—as well as the controversy surrounding it—of talented freshman Makhtar Ndiaye due to recruiting violations. In leading Wake to an unprecedented fourth straight NCAA Tournament, Dave Odom was selected as ACC Coach of the Year.

Guard: Randolph Childress stands alone as the ACC's best big-game performer. Confident in either going to the hoop or pulling up with the jumper, Childress is far and away the leader of the team. This year, though, Childress won't be buoyed by the 3-point precision of Marc Blucas and steady floor leadership of Charlie Harrison. Wake football quarterback Rusty LaRue figures to move into a starting spot, while junior Barry Canty will see his minutes increase. Three freshmen will battle for playing time.

Forward: The cupboard's particularly bare here. Departed Trelonnie Owens was the club's only true starting forward last year, and Bobby Fitzgibbons—who was expected to return—decided to transfer. Travis Banks played well at the end of last season and will win a starting job by default. Spanish import Ricardo Peral (6'10") will likely take over the power-forward spot. Newcomers Sean Allen and Antonio Jackson are the only other forwards available.

Center: Tim Duncan, who the globetrotting Odom recruited from the Virgin Islands, was a pleasant surprise last season. Duncan's forte is shot-blocking, but his offensive game will be more polished this year, virtually out of necessity since he'll have little help in the paint.

Analysis: Odom proved last year that it's his system just as much as his personnel that has turned Wake into a consistent winner. A stingy defense will keep the Demon Deacons close in games this year, and when it comes time for a big play down the stretch, they can turn to either Childress or Duncan.

1994-95 ROSTER

	POS	HT	YR	FGP	FTP	3-PT	RPG	APG	PPG
Randolph Childress	G	6'2"	Sr.	.41	.79	75/204	3.4	3.9	19.6
Tim Duncan	C	6'10"	So.	.55	.75	1/1	9.6	0.9	9.8
Travis Banks	F	6'6"	Sr.	.44	.68	0/2	4.5	1.0	6.0
Rusty LaRue	G	6'2"	Jr.	.43	.60	36/80	1.5	0.4	4.7
Barry Canty	G	6'5"	Jr.	.26	.50	5/18	0.8	0.5	1.2
Sean Allen	F	6'8"	Jr.	—	—	—	—	—	—
Jerry Braswell	G	6'1"	Fr.	—	—	—	—	—	—
Steven Goolsby	G	6'4"	Fr.	—	—	—	—	—	—
Antonio Jackson	F	6'8"	Fr.	—	—	—	—	—	—
Ricardo Peral	F	6'10"	So.	—	—	—	—	—	—
Tony Rutland	G	6'1"	Fr.	—	—	—	—	—	—

WISCONSIN

Conference: Big Ten   **1993-94 NCAAs:** 1-1
1993-94: 18-11, 7th Big Ten   **Coach:** Stan Van Gundy (0-0)

Opening Line: After building the best Wisconsin basketball program in decades, coach Stu Jackson up and left in July. Though he boasted two of the most talented players in the land—Rashard Griffith and Michael Finley—Jackson just wasn't happy with the traveling lifestyle of college coaching. He took an office job with the expansion Vancouver franchise in the NBA. Former assistant Stan Van Gundy will keep the system running.

Guard: After being plagued by injuries early in 1993-94, Darnell Hoskins backed up star point guard Tracy Webster. Hoskins has displayed some offensive potential, but Webster's presence will be sorely missed on the defensive end, where he ranks as Wisconsin's all-time leader in steals. After ranking second in the Big Ten in 3-point percentage in 1992-93, Andy Kilbride tailed off last season.

Forward: The all-around talent of swing man Michael Finley and Wisconsin's up-tempo attack have been a wonderful fit. With a better supporting cast, Finley wasn't forced to do it all in 1993-94. He will be the conference's marquee player heading into this season. Brian Kelley is a wide body, good for doing some dirty work, while sophomore Jalil Roberts is a Finley clone.

Center: Frustrated with his role in a stagnant halfcourt offense, Griffith actually quit the team last spring and threatened to enter the NBA draft or transfer. His departure would have been devastating to Wisconsin, particularly on the boards and in the blocked-shots department. The lack of a quality back-up is a concern.

Analysis: The Badgers will try to improve their halfcourt offense in order to keep their big fella happy—even though Finley excels in an open-court game. The Badgers will need to develop some depth if they intend to challenge for the Big Ten title. They must also maintain their focus; the team has taken major nosedives at the ends of the last two seasons.

1994-95 ROSTER

	POS	HT	YR	FGP	FTP	3-PT	RPG	APG	PPG
Michael Finley	F	6'6"	Sr.	.47	.79	66/182	6.7	3.2	20.4
Rashard Griffith	C	6'11"	So.	.54	.58	—	8.5	1.0	13.9
Andy Kilbride	G	6'3"	Sr.	.42	.81	54/131	2.6	1.9	7.4
Jalil Roberts	F/G	6'4"	So.	.36	.63	25/81	2.2	0.7	5.5
Brian Kelley	F	6'7"	Sr.	.46	.63	3/10	4.6	0.8	5.3
Howard Moore	F	6'6"	Sr.	.57	.91	—	1.4	0.2	2.8
Darnell Hoskins	G	6'0"	So.	.35	.73	5/23	1.2	2.1	2.7
Chris Conger	G	6'3"	Sr.	.44	—	3/8	0.2	0.2	1.1
Booker Coleman	F	6'8"	Fr.	—	—	—	—	—	—
Sean Daugherty	F	6'10"	Fr.	—	—	—	—	—	—
Sean Mason	G	6'2"	Fr.	—	—	—	—	—	—
Osita Nwachukwu	F	6'8"	Jr.	—	—	—	—	—	—

XAVIER

Conference: Midwestern Collegiate   **1993-94 NIT:** 2-1
1993-94: 22-8, 1st MCC   **Coach:** Skip Prosser (17-13)

Opening Line: Well, Pete Gillen finally did it. After flirting with offers from Virginia, Notre Dame, and Villanova in recent years, Gillen bolted for Providence. Former Musketeer assistant Skip Prosser, who engineered a miraculous one-year, worst-to-first turnaround at Loyola (Maryland), inherits the program he helped build with Gillen.

Guard: Depth abounds in the backcourt. Sherwin Anderson displayed plenty of promise as a freshman with his quickness and creativity. He'll be flanked by seniors Jeff Massey and Michael Hawkins as Prosser figures to continue Gillen's pressing attack, which relies heavily on a three-guard lineup. Hawkins's offensive numbers slipped a bit in 1993-94, but his aggressive, unselfish style is an invaluable asset. Massey was the MCC's Newcomer of the Year last season and owns the club's best shooting stroke from 3-point land. Versatile Kenny Harvey and heralded recruit Brien Hanley will fit well into the rotation.

Forward: Explosive Tyrice Walker will be sorely missed, particularly in the transition game. Burly senior Larry Sykes, noted mostly for his defensive and rebounding prowess early in his career, recorded ten double-figure scoring games in 1993-94 and will be counted on heavily for frontcourt production. Swing man Pete Sears will see most of his action at small forward, while touted frosh T.J. Johnson will also figure into the fray.

Center: There's a huge void in the middle now that two-time MCC Player of the Year Brian Grant has graduated. Without a suitable back-up returning either, Sykes will likely slide over to center in the early going.

Analysis: The Musketeers have the quickness and depth in the backcourt to be a disruptive defensive team. Whether that can translate into offensive production in transition remains to be seen. Without Walker and Grant, Xavier doesn't seem to have the horses in the frontcourt to compete with the country's better teams.

1994-95 ROSTER

	POS	HT	YR	FGP	FTP	3-PT	RPG	APG	PPG
Jeff Massey	G	6'1"	Sr.	.43	.67	53/142	2.1	2.4	12.7
Larry Sykes	F/C	6'9"	Sr.	.50	.53	—	5.7	0.9	8.4
Michael Hawkins	G/F	6'0"	Sr.	.37	.64	37/100	2.1	2.2	6.8
Pete Sears	G/F	6'4"	Sr.	.44	.73	1/7	3.4	0.6	6.5
Sherwin Anderson	G	5'11"	So.	.52	.55	5/13	1.0	1.4	2.6
Ken Harvey	G	6'2"	So.	.29	.78	10/41	0.7	0.8	2.1
DeWaun Rose	F	6'8"	Sr.	.32	.55	1/4	1.2	0.3	1.7
Tyson Brit	G/F	6'3"	So.	.18	.50	1/11	0.7	0.2	0.7
Kevin Carr	F/C	6'8"	Jr.	—	—	—	—	—	—
Brien Hanley	G/F	6'4"	Fr.	—	—	—	—	—	—
T.J. Johnson	F	6'6"	Fr.	—	—	—	—	—	—
Terrance Payne	F	6'7"	Fr.	—	—	—	—	—	—

College Basketball Review

The final section in the book reviews the 1993-94 college basketball season and lists important historical information.

First, you'll find the final 1993-94 standings of 33 conferences in Division I. Their conference records include regular-season conference games only. Their overall records include all postseason tournament games, including conference tournaments, the NCAA, and the NIT. The standings indicate the teams that made the NCAA Tourney (*), those that won their conference tournaments (#), and those that were ineligible for postseason play (@).

The recap of the 1993-94 season also includes the following:

- final A.P. poll and A.P. All-Americans
- Division I statistical leaders
- NCAA Tournament game-by-game results

- NCAA finals boxscore
- NIT results
- women's final CNN/*USA Today* poll
- women's NCAA tourney results

Finally, you'll find Division I historical information, including the following:

- national champions (1901-94)
- Final Four results (1939-94)
- Division I career leaders
- Division I season records
- Division I game records
- winningest Division I teams

The NCAA Tournament didn't begin until 1939. Prior to that, there were no official national champions. However, the Helms Foundation selected national champs retroactively for the years 1901-38. These are the teams that are listed in the national champions chart.

DIVISION I FINAL STANDINGS, 1993-94

Atlantic Coast

	Conference			Overall		
	W	L	PCT.	W	L	PCT.
*Duke	12	4	.750	28	6	.824
*#North Carolina	11	5	.688	28	7	.800
*Wake Forest	9	7	.563	21	12	.636
*Virginia	8	8	.500	18	13	.581
*Maryland	8	8	.500	18	12	.600
Georgia Tech	7	9	.438	16	13	.552
Florida St.	6	10	.375	13	14	.481
Clemson	6	10	.375	18	16	.529
N. Carolina St.	5	11	.313	11	19	.367

Atlantic 10

	Conference			Overall		
	W	L	PCT.	W	L	PCT.
*#Massachusetts	14	2	.875	28	7	.800
*Temple	12	4	.750	23	8	.742
*George Wash.	8	8	.500	18	12	.600
West Virginia	8	8	.500	17	12	.586
Duquesne	8	8	.500	17	13	.567
Rhode Island	7	9	.438	10	17	.407
Rutgers	6	10	.375	11	16	.407
St. Joseph's	5	11	.313	14	14	.500
St. Bonaventure	4	12	.250	10	17	.370

Big East

	Conference			Overall		
	W	L	PCT.	W	L	PCT.
*Connecticut	16	2	.889	29	5	.853
*Syracuse	13	5	.722	23	7	.767
*Boston College	11	7	.611	23	11	.676
*#Providence	10	8	.556	20	10	.667
Villanova	10	8	.556	20	12	.625
*Georgetown	10	8	.556	19	12	.613
*Seton Hall	8	10	.444	17	13	.567
Pittsburgh	7	11	.389	13	14	.481
St. John's	5	13	.278	12	17	.414
Miami (FL)	0	18	.000	7	20	.259

Big Eight

	Conference			Overall		
	W	L	PCT.	W	L	PCT.
*Missouri	14	0	1.00	28	4	.875
*Oklahoma St.	10	4	.714	24	10	.706
*Kansas	9	5	.643	27	8	.771
*#Nebraska	7	7	.500	20	10	.667
Oklahoma	6	8	.429	15	13	.536
Kansas St.	4	10	.286	20	14	.588
Iowa St.	4	10	.286	14	13	.519
Colorado	2	12	.143	10	17	.370

Big Sky

	Conference			Overall		
	W	L	PCT.	W	L	PCT.
Weber St.	10	4	.714	20	10	.667
Idaho St.	10	4	.714	18	9	.667
Idaho	9	5	.643	18	10	.643
Montana St.	8	6	.571	16	11	.593
*#Boise St.	7	7	.500	17	13	.567
Montana	6	8	.429	19	9	.679
Northern Arizona	6	8	.429	13	13	.500
E. Washington	0	14	.000	5	21	.192

Big South

	Conference			Overall		
	W	L	PCT.	W	L	PCT.
Towson St.	16	2	.889	21	9	.700
Campbell	14	4	.778	20	9	.690
Radford	13	5	.722	20	8	.714
*#Liberty	13	5	.722	18	12	.600
N.C.-Greenville	11	7	.611	15	12	.556
Charleston South.	8	10	.444	9	18	.333
Maryl.-Balt. County	6	12	.333	6	21	.222
Winthrop	5	13	.278	4	23	.148
N.C.-Asheville	3	15	.167	3	24	.111
Coastal Carol.	1	17	.056	15	11	.577

Big Ten

	Conference			Overall		
	W	L	PCT.	W	L	PCT.
*Purdue	14	4	.778	29	5	.853
*Michigan	13	5	.722	24	8	.750
*Indiana	12	6	.667	21	9	.700
*Illinois	10	8	.556	17	11	.607
*Minnesota	10	8	.556	21	12	.636
*Michigan St.	10	8	.556	20	12	.625
*Wisconsin	8	10	.444	18	11	.621
Ohio St.	6	12	.333	13	16	.448
Penn St.	6	12	.333	13	14	.481
Northwestern	5	13	.278	15	14	.517
Iowa	5	13	.278	11	16	.407

Big West

	Conference			Overall		
	W	L	PCT.	W	L	PCT.
*#New Mexico St.	12	6	.667	23	8	.742
Utah St.	11	7	.611	14	13	.519
Long Beach St.	11	7	.611	17	10	.630
San Jose St.	11	7	.611	15	12	.556
UNLV	10	8	.556	15	13	.536
Pacific	10	8	.556	17	14	.548
Cal.-Santa Barb.	9	9	.500	13	17	.433
Fullerton St.	6	12	.333	8	19	.296
Nevada	6	12	.333	11	17	.393
Cal.-Irvine	4	14	.222	10	20	.333

Colonial Athletic

	Conference			Overall		
	W	L	PCT.	W	L	PCT.
Old Dominion	10	4	.714	21	10	.677
*#James Madison	10	4	.714	20	10	.667
N.C.-Wilmington	9	5	.643	18	10	.643
Richmond	8	6	.571	14	14	.500
East Carolina	7	7	.500	15	12	.556
George Mason	5	9	.357	10	17	.370
American	5	9	.357	8	19	.296
William & Mary	2	12	.143	4	23	.148

East Coast

	Conference			Overall		
	W	L	PCT.	W	L	PCT.
Troy St.	5	0	1.00	13	14	.481
N.E. Illinois	4	1	.800	17	11	.607
Buffalo	3	2	.600	10	18	.357
Chicago St.	2	3	.400	4	23	.148

	Conference W	L	PCT.	Overall W	L	PCT.
#Hofstra	1	4	.200	9	20	.310
Central Conn. St.	0	5	.000	4	22	.154

Great Midwest

	Conference W	L	PCT.	Overall W	L	PCT.
*Marquette	10	2	.833	24	9	.727
*St. Louis	8	4	.667	23	6	.793
*Alabama-Birm.	8	4	.667	22	8	.733
*#Cincinnati	7	5	.583	22	10	.688
DePaul	4	8	.333	16	12	.571
Memphis St.	4	8	.333	13	16	.448
Dayton	1	11	.083	6	21	.222

Ivy League

	Conference W	L	PCT.	Overall W	L	PCT.
*#Pennsylvania	14	0	1.00	25	3	.893
Princeton	11	3	.786	18	8	.692
Yale	7	7	.500	10	16	.385
Brown	6	8	.429	12	14	.462
Dartmouth	6	8	.429	10	16	.385
Harvard	5	9	.357	9	17	.346
Columbia	4	10	.286	6	20	.231
Cornell	3	11	.214	8	18	.308

Metro

	Conference W	L	PCT.	Overall W	L	PCT.
*#Louisville	10	2	.833	28	8	.778
N.C.-Charlotte	7	5	.583	16	13	.552
Tulane	7	5	.583	18	11	.621
Virginia Tech	6	6	.500	18	10	.643
Virginia Common.	5	7	.417	14	13	.519
S. Mississippi	5	7	.417	15	15	.500
South Florida	2	10	.167	10	17	.370

Metro Atlantic Athletic

	Conference W	L	PCT.	Overall W	L	PCT.
Canisius	12	2	.857	22	7	.759
Siena	10	4	.714	25	8	.758
Manhattan	10	4	.714	19	11	.633
St. Peter's	8	6	.571	14	13	.519
*#Loyola (MD)	6	8	.429	17	13	.567
Fairfield	4	10	.286	8	19	.296
Iona	3	11	.214	7	20	.259
Niagara	3	11	.214	6	21	.222

Mid-American

	Conference W	L	PCT.	Overall W	L	PCT.
*#Ohio	14	4	.778	25	8	.758
Bowling Green	12	6	.667	18	10	.643
Miami (OH)	12	6	.667	19	11	.633
Ball St.	11	7	.611	16	12	.571
Toledo	10	8	.556	15	12	.556
Eastern Michigan	10	8	.556	15	12	.556
Kent St.	8	10	.444	13	14	.481
Western Michigan	7	11	.389	14	14	.500
Central Michigan	4	14	.222	5	21	.192
Akron	2	16	.111	8	18	.308

Mid-Continent

	Conference W	L	PCT.	Overall W	L	PCT.
*#Wis.-Green Bay	15	3	.833	27	7	.794
Valparaiso	14	4	.778	20	8	.714
Illinois-Chicago	14	4	.778	20	9	.690
Cleveland St.	9	9	.500	14	15	.483
Wright St.	9	9	.500	12	18	.400
Eastern Illinois	7	11	.389	12	15	.444
Northern Illinois	7	11	.389	10	17	.370
Wis.-Milwaukee	7	11	.389	10	17	.370
Western Illinois	5	13	.278	7	20	.259
Youngstown St.	3	15	.167	5	21	.192

Mid-Eastern Athletic

	Conference W	L	PCT.	Overall W	L	PCT.
Coppin St.	16	0	1.00	22	8	.733
Maryl.-E. Shore	10	6	.625	16	12	.571
*#N. Carolina A&T	10	6	.625	16	14	.533
S. Carolina St.	10	6	.625	16	13	.552
Bethune-Cookman	8	8	.500	9	18	.333
Howard	7	9	.438	10	17	.370
Delaware St.	5	11	.313	8	19	.296
Morgan St.	4	12	.250	8	21	.276
Florida A&M	2	14	.125	4	23	.148

Midwestern Collegiate

	Conference W	L	PCT.	Overall W	L	PCT.
Xavier (OH)	8	2	.800	22	8	.733
Evansville	6	4	.600	21	11	.656
Butler	6	4	.600	16	13	.552
#Detroit Mercy	5	5	.500	16	13	.552
La Salle	4	6	.400	11	16	.407
Loyola (IL)	1	9	.100	8	19	.296

Missouri Valley

	Conference W	L	PCT.	Overall W	L	PCT.
*#South. Illinois	16	4	.800	23	7	.767
*Tulsa	16	4	.800	23	8	.742
Bradley	15	5	.750	23	8	.742
Illinois St.	12	7	.632	16	11	.593
Northern Iowa	12	8	.600	16	13	.552
S.W. Missou. St.	7	12	.368	12	15	.444
Wichita St.	6	13	.316	9	18	.333
Drake	6	13	.316	11	16	.407
Creighton	3	15	.167	7	22	.241
Indiana St.	3	15	.167	4	22	.154

North Atlantic

	Conference W	L	PCT.	Overall W	L	PCT.
*#Drexel	12	2	.857	25	5	.833
Maine	11	3	.786	20	9	.690
Hartford	9	5	.643	16	12	.571
New Hampshire	8	6	.571	15	13	.536
Delaware	7	7	.500	14	13	.519
Boston	4	10	.286	11	16	.407
Vermont	3	11	.214	12	15	.444
Northeastern	2	12	.143	5	22	.185

COLLEGE BASKETBALL REVIEW

Northeast

	Conference			Overall		
	W	L	PCT.	W	L	PCT.
*#Rider	14	4	.778	21	9	.700
Monmouth	13	5	.722	18	11	.621
Robert Morris	11	7	.611	14	14	.500
Wagner	11	7	.611	16	12	.571
Fairleigh Dickin.	10	8	.556	14	13	.519
Marist	10	8	.556	14	13	.519
Mount St. Mary's	9	9	.500	14	14	.500
St. Francis (NY)	9	9	.500	13	15	.464
LIU-Brooklyn	2	16	.111	3	24	.111
St. Francis (PA)	1	17	.056	1	26	.037

Ohio Valley

	Conference			Overall		
	W	L	PCT.	W	L	PCT.
Murray St.	15	1	.938	23	6	.793
*#Tennessee St.	12	4	.750	19	12	.613
Austin Peay	10	6	.625	11	16	.407
Eastern Kentucky	9	7	.563	13	14	.481
Morehead St.	8	8	.500	14	14	.500
S.E. Missouri St.	5	11	.313	10	17	.370
Tennessee Tech	5	11	.313	10	21	.323
@Middle Tenn. St.	5	11	.313	8	19	.296
Tenn.-Martin	3	13	.188	5	22	.185

Pacific-10

	Conference			Overall		
	W	L	PCT.	W	L	PCT.
*Arizona	14	4	.778	29	6	.829
*UCLA	13	5	.722	21	7	.750
*California	13	5	.722	22	8	.733
*Washington St.	10	8	.556	20	11	.645
Stanford	10	8	.556	17	11	.607
Arizona St.	10	8	.556	15	13	.536
Southern Cal.	9	9	.500	16	12	.571
Oregon	6	12	.333	10	17	.370
Washington	3	15	.167	5	22	.185
Oregon St.	2	16	.111	6	21	.222

Patriot League

	Conference			Overall		
	W	L	PCT.	W	L	PCT.
*#Navy	9	5	.643	17	13	.567
Fordham	9	5	.643	12	15	.444
Colgate	9	5	.643	17	12	.586
Holy Cross	9	5	.643	14	14	.500
Bucknell	6	8	.429	10	17	.370
Lehigh	6	8	.429	10	17	.370
Lafayette	4	10	.286	9	19	.321
Army	4	10	.286	7	20	.259

Southeastern East

	Conference			Overall		
	W	L	PCT.	W	L	PCT.
*Florida	12	4	.750	29	8	.784
*#Kentucky	12	4	.750	27	7	.794
Vanderbilt	9	7	.563	20	12	.625
Georgia	7	9	.438	14	16	.467
South Carolina	4	12	.250	9	19	.321
Tennessee	2	14	.125	5	22	.185

Southeastern West

	Conference			Overall		
	W	L	PCT.	W	L	PCT.
*Arkansas	14	2	.875	31	3	.912
*Alabama	12	4	.750	20	10	.667
Mississippi St.	9	7	.563	18	11	.621
Mississippi	7	9	.438	14	13	.519
Louisiana St.	5	11	.313	11	16	.407
Auburn	3	13	.188	11	17	.393

Southern

	Conference			Overall		
	W	L	PCT.	W	L	PCT.
*#Tenn.-Chattan.	14	4	.778	23	7	.767
Davidson	13	5	.722	22	8	.733
E. Tenn. St.	13	5	.722	16	14	.533
Appalachian St.	12	6	.667	16	11	.593
Georgia Southern	9	9	.500	14	14	.500
Western Carolina	8	10	.444	12	16	.429
Marshall	7	11	.389	9	18	.333
Citadel	6	12	.333	11	16	.407
Furman	6	12	.333	10	18	.357
Virginia Military	2	16	.111	5	23	.179

Southland

	Conference			Overall		
	W	L	PCT.	W	L	PCT.
N.E. Louisiana	15	3	.833	19	9	.679
*#S.W. Texas St.	14	4	.778	25	7	.781
Nicholls St.	12	6	.667	19	9	.679
North Texas	9	9	.500	14	15	.483
McNeese St.	9	9	.500	11	16	.407
Texas-San Ant.	8	10	.444	12	15	.444
Sam Houston St.	7	11	.389	7	20	.259
Stephen Austin	6	12	.333	9	18	.333
Northwestern St.	6	12	.333	11	15	.423
Texas-Arlington	4	14	.222	7	22	.241

Southwest

	Conference			Overall		
	W	L	PCT.	W	L	PCT.
*#Texas	12	2	.857	26	8	.765
Texas A&M	10	4	.714	19	11	.633
Texas Tech	10	4	.714	17	11	.607
Baylor	7	7	.500	16	11	.593
Rice	6	8	.429	15	14	.517
Houston	5	9	.357	8	19	.296
SMU	3	11	.214	6	21	.222
Texas Christian	3	11	.214	7	20	.259

Southwestern Athletic

	Conference			Overall		
	W	L	PCT.	W	L	PCT.
*#Texas Southern	12	2	.857	19	11	.633
Jackson St.	11	3	.786	19	10	.655
Alabama St.	10	4	.714	19	10	.655
Southern-B.R.	8	6	.571	16	11	.593
Missi. Valley St.	6	8	.429	10	17	.370
Grambling St.	4	10	.286	9	18	.333
Alcorn St.	3	11	.214	3	24	.111
Prairie View	2	12	.143	5	22	.185

Sun Belt

	Conference			Overall		
	W	L	PCT.	W	L	PCT.
*West. Kentucky	14	4	.778	20	11	.645
*#S.W. Louisiana	13	5	.722	22	8	.733
New Orleans	12	6	.667	20	10	.667
Jacksonville	11	7	.611	17	11	.607
Arkansas St.	10	8	.556	15	12	.556
South Alabama	9	9	.500	13	14	.481
Texas-Pan Am.	9	9	.500	16	12	.571
Arkan.-Little Rock	6	12	.333	13	15	.464
Lamar	6	12	.333	10	17	.370
Louisiana Tech	0	18	.000	2	25	.074

Trans America Athletic

	Conference			Overall		
	W	L	PCT.	W	L	PCT.
*Charleston (SC)	14	2	.875	24	4	.857
*#Central Florida	11	5	.688	21	9	.700
Stetson	9	7	.563	14	15	.483
Georgia St.	9	7	.563	13	14	.481
Centenary	8	8	.500	16	12	.571
Florida Intl.	7	9	.438	11	16	.407
S.E. Louisiana	7	9	.438	10	17	.370
Samford	4	12	.250	10	18	.357
Mercer	3	13	.188	5	24	.172

West Coast

	Conference			Overall		
	W	L	PCT.	W	L	PCT.
Gonzaga	12	2	.857	22	8	.733
*#Pepperdine	8	6	.571	19	11	.633
San Francisco	8	6	.571	17	11	.607
San Diego	7	7	.500	18	11	.621

Portland	6	8	.429	13	17	.433
Santa Clara	6	8	.429	13	14	.481
St. Mary's	5	9	.357	13	14	.481
Loyola Marymount	4	10	.286	6	21	.222

Western Athletic

	Conference			Overall		
	W	L	PCT.	W	L	PCT.
*New Mexico	14	4	.778	23	8	.742
Fresno St.	13	5	.722	21	11	.656
Brigham Young	12	6	.667	22	10	.688
*#Hawaii	11	7	.611	18	15	.545
Texas-El Paso	8	10	.444	18	12	.600
Colorado St.	8	10	.444	15	13	.536
Utah	8	10	.444	14	14	.500
Wyoming	7	11	.389	14	14	.500
San Diego St.	6	12	.333	12	16	.429
Air Force	3	15	.167	8	18	.308

Division I Independents

	Overall		
	W	L	PCT
Southern Utah St.	16	11	.593
Missouri-Kansas City	12	17	.414
Notre Dame	12	17	.414
Cal. St.-Northridge	8	18	.308
Oral Roberts	6	21	.222
Sacramento St.	1	26	.037

*   Selected to the NCAA Tournament.

\# Won postseason conference tournament. The Big Ten, Ivy League, and Pacific-10 did not hold tournaments.

@ Ineligible for both the NCAA Tournament and NIT.

Final A.P. Poll, 1993-94

	W-L	Points
1) North Carolina (37)	27-6	1,576
2) Arkansas (16)	25-3	1,546
3) Purdue (11)	26-4	1,493
4) Connecticut	27-4	1,400
5) Missouri	25-3	1,352
6) Duke	23-5	1,252
7) Kentucky	26-6	1,236
8) Massachusetts (1)	27-6	1,229
9) Arizona	25-5	1,095
10) Louisville	26-5	1,039
11) Michigan	21-7	996
12) Temple	22-7	840
13) Kansas	25-7	777
14) Florida	25-7	758
15) Syracuse	21-6	743
16) California	22-7	574
17) UCLA	21-6	559
18) Indiana	19-8	396
19) Oklahoma St.	23-9	384
20) Texas	25-7	291
21) Marquette	22-8	265
22) Nebraska	20-9	217
23) Minnesota	20-11	202
24) St. Louis	23-5	192
25) Cincinnati	22-9	188

A.P. ALL-AMERICA TEAM

First Team
*Glenn Robinson, Purdue
Donyell Marshall, Connecticut
Clifford Rozier, Louisville
Grant Hill, Duke
Jason Kidd, California

Second Team
Corliss Williamson, Arkansas
Eric Montross, North Carolina
Khalid Reeves, Arizona St.
Jalen Rose, Michigan
Melvin Booker, Missouri

* Winner of the Naismith Award, Wooden Award, and Rupp Trophy, which recognize the national Player of the Year.

Poll taken prior to the NCAA Tournament and the NIT. Won-loss records reflect performances at the time the poll was taken. First-place votes in parentheses.

DIVISION I LEADERS, 1993-94

SCORING

Glenn Robinson, Purdue	30.3
Rob Feaster, Holy Cross	28.0
Jervaughn Scales, Southern-B.R.	27.1
Frankie King, Western Carolina	26.9
Tucker Neale, Colgate	26.6
Eddie Benton, Vermont	26.4
Doremus Bennerman, Siena	26.0
Tony Dumas, Missouri-K.C.	26.0
Otis Jones, Air Force	25.5
Izett Buchanan, Marist	25.4

REBOUNDS

Jerome Lambert, Baylor	14.8
Jervaughn Scales, Southern-B.R.	14.2
Erik Kubel, Northwestern St.	13.1
Kendrick Warren, Virginia Commonwealth	12.4
Malik Rose, Drexel	12.4
David Vaughn, Memphis St.	12.0
Reggie Jackson, Nicholls St.	12.0
Melvin Simon, New Orleans	11.8
Kebu Stewart, Nevada-Las Vegas	11.6
Carlos Rogers, Tennessee St.	11.5

ASSISTS

Jason Kidd, California	9.1
David Edwards, Texas A&M	8.8
Tony Miller, Marquette	8.3
Eathan O'Bryant, Nevada	8.3
Abdul Abdullah, Providence	8.0
Howard Nathan, N.E. Louisiana	7.8
Orlando Smart, San Francisco	7.6
Dan Pogue, Campbell	7.4
Dedan Thomas, Nevada-Las Vegas	7.3
Nelson Haggerty, Baylor	7.3

STEALS

Shawn Griggs, S.W. Louisiana	4.0
Gerald Walker, San Francisco	3.9
Andre Cradle, LIU-Brooklyn	3.8
Jason Kidd, California	3.1
B.J. Tyler, Texas	3.1
Clarence Ceasar, Louisiana St.	3.0
Greg Black, Texas-Pan American	2.9
Brooks Thompson, Oklahoma St.	2.9
Alex Robertson, Dayton	2.9
LaMarcus Golden, Tennessee	2.9

BLOCKED SHOTS

Grady Livingston, Howard	4.4
Jim McIlvaine, Marquette	4.3
Theo Ratliff, Wyoming	4.1
David Vaughn, Memphis St.	3.8
Tim Duncan, Wake Forest	3.8
Marcus Camby, Massachusetts	3.6
Kevin Cato, South Alabama	3.5
Donyell Marshall, Connecticutt	3.3
Michael McDonald, New Orleans	3.2
Pascal Fleury, Maryland-Balt. County	3.2

FIELD GOAL PCT.

Mike Atkinson, Long Beach St.	69.5
Lynwood Wade, S.W. Texas St.	65.2
Anthony Miller, Michigan St.	65.1
Deon Thomas, Illinois	63.3
Aaron Swinson, Auburn	63.1
Clayton Ritter, James Madison	62.8
Corliss Williamson, Arkansas	62.6
David Ardayfio, Army	62.3
Jimmy Lunsford, Alabama St.	62.0
Clifford Rozier, Louisville	61.8

FREE THROW PCT.

Danny Basile, Marist	94.4
Dandrea Evans, Troy St.	93.5
Casey Schmidt, Valparaiso	92.6
Matthew Hildebrand, Liberty	92.5
Kent Culuko, James Madison	92.1
Ryan Yoder, Colorado St.	91.5
Travis Ford, Kentucky	91.2
Ryan Hoover, Notre Dame	90.5
Marty Cline, Morehead St.	90.1
Randy Tucker, Northern Illinois	89.9

3-PT. FIELD GOAL PCT.

Brent Kell, Evansville	50.4
Brian Santiago, Fresno St.	50.0
Brandon Born, Tenn.-Chattanooga	49.6
Chris Young, Canisius	48.6
Howard Eisley, Boston College	48.4
Marc Blucas, Wake Forest	47.7
Brooks Thompson, Oklahoma St.	47.2
Brooks Barnhard, San Diego	47.2
Bubba Donnelly, Robert Morris	47.1
Scott Neely, Campbell	46.8

SCORING OFFENSE, TEAM

Southern-Baton Rouge	101.0
Troy St.	97.6
Arkansas	93.4
Texas	91.7
Murray St.	90.0
Arizona	89.3
Nicholls St.	89.0
San Francisco	88.9
Oklahoma	88.5
George Mason	88.3

SCORING DEFENSE, TEAM

Princeton	52.3
Temple	54.7
Wisconsin-Green Bay	55.1
Alabama-Birmingham	60.2
Marquette	61.8
S.W. Missouri St.	62.6
Coppin St.	64.1
Pennsylvania	64.3
Pepperdine	64.5
S.W. Texas St.	64.7

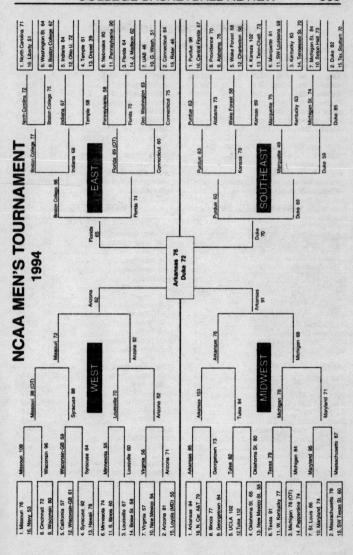

1994 NCAA FINALS BOXSCORE

Arkansas 76, Duke 72

Duke	MIN	FG-A	FT-A	REB	AST	PF	PTS
Hill	38	4-11	3-5	14	6	3	12
Lang	34	6-9	3-3	5	3	5	15
Parks	30	7-10	0-1	7	0	3	14
Capel	35	6-16	0-0	5	4	3	14
Collins	34	4-11	0-0	0	1	1	12
Clark	15	1-6	1-2	1	3	2	3
Meek	14	1-2	0-0	7	0	1	2
Totals	200	29-65	7-11	44	17	18	72

FGP—.446. FTP—.636. 3-PT FGP—7-20, .350
(Collins 4-8, Capel 2-6, Hill 1-4, Clark 0-2).

Arkansas	MIN	FG-A	FT-A	REB	AST	PF	PTS
Williamson	35	10-24	3-5	8	3	3	23
Biley	3	0-0	0-0	0	0	1	0
Stewart	29	3-11	0-0	9	4	3	6
Beck	35	5-11	5-8	10	4	3	15
Thurman	36	6-13	0-0	5	1	2	15
McDaniel	32	2-5	2-4	2	3	2	7
Robinson	12	1-5	0-0	2	0	1	2
Dillard	8	1-5	1-2	1	0	1	4
Rimac	5	0-1	0-0	0	0	0	0
Wilson	5	2-2	0-0	4	0	1	4
Totals	200	30-77	11-19	44	15	17	76

FGP—.390. FTP—.579. 3-PT FGP—5-18, .278
(Thurman 3-5, McDaniel 1-3, Dillard 1-4, Beck 0-1,
Stewart 0-5).

Halftime—Arkansas 34, Duke 33. Attendance—23,674
(Charlotte Coliseum).

1994 NIT RESULTS

First Round
New Orleans 79, Texas A&M 73
Vanderbilt 77, Oklahoma 67
Fresno St. 79, Southern Cal. 76 (OT)
Bradley 66, Murray St. 58
Northwestern 69, DePaul 68
Xavier (OH) 80, Miami (OH) 68
Duquesne 75, N.C.-Charlotte 73
Siena 76, Georgia Tech 68
Tulane 76, Evansville 63
Clemson 96, Southern Miss. 85
Old Dominion 76, Manhattan 74
West Virginia 85, Davidson 69
Gonzaga 80, Stanford 76
Kansas St. 78, Mississippi St. 69
Brigham Young 74, Arizona St. 67
Villanova 103, Canisius 79

Second Round
Clemson 96, West Virginia 79
Vanderbilt 78, New Orleans 59
Villanova 82, Duquesne 66
Xavier 83, Northwestern 79 (OT)
Fresno St. 68, BYU 66
Kansas St. 66, Gonzaga 64
Bradley 79, Old Dominion 75
Siena 89, Tulane 79

Third Round
Villanova 76, Xavier 74
Vanderbilt 89, Clemson 74
Siena 75, Bradley 62
Kansas St. 115, Fresno St. 77

Semifinals
Vanderbilt 82, Kansas St. 76
Villanova 66, Siena 58

Finals
Villanova 80, Vanderbilt 73

WOMEN'S FINAL
CNN/USA TODAY POLL, 1993-94

1) North Carolina (35)	33-2	.875
2) Louisiana Tech	31-4	.840
3) Purdue	29-5	.785
4) Alabama	26-7	.766
5) Tennessee	31-2	.730
6) Penn St.	28-3	.683
7) Connecticut	30-3	.661
8) Stanford	25-6	.600
9) Southern Cal.	26-4	.592
10) Colorado	27-5	.567
11) Texas Tech	28-5	.491
12) Virginia	27-5	.459
13) Vanderbilt	25-8	.434
14) Seton Hall	27-5	.410
15) Iowa	21-7	.344
16) S. Mississippi	26-5	.319
17) Kansas	22-6	.248
18) Montana	25-5	.220
19) Texas A&M	23-8	.194
20) Mississippi	24-9	.182
21) Washington	21-8	.161
22) Clemson	20-10	.123
23) Texas	22-9	.94
24) Florida Inter.	25-4	.82
25) Florida	22-7	.77

Poll taken after the NCAA Tournament. Won-loss
records include tournament results. First-place votes
in parentheses.

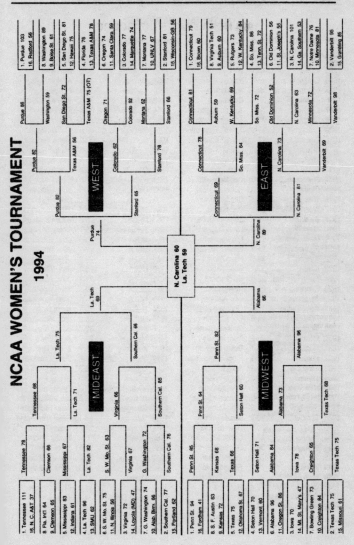

NCAA WOMEN'S TOURNAMENT
1994

NATIONAL CHAMPIONS

YEAR	CHAMPION	RECORD	COACH	YEAR	CHAMPION	RECORD	COACH
1901	Yale	10-4	No coach	1948	Kentucky	36-3	Adolph Rupp
1902	Minnesota	11-0	Louis Cooke	1949	Kentucky	32-2	Adolph Rupp
1903	Yale	15-1	W.H. Murphy	1950	CCNY	24-5	Nat Holman
1904	Columbia	17-1	No coach	1951	Kentucky	32-2	Adolph Rupp
1905	Columbia	19-1	No coach	1952	Kansas	28-3	Phog Allen
1906	Dartmouth	16-2	No coach	1953	Indiana	23-3	Branch McCracken
1907	Chicago	22-2	Joseph Raycroft	1954	La Salle	26-4	Ken Loeffler
1908	Chicago	21-2	Joseph Raycroft	1955	San Francisco	28-1	Phil Woolpert
1909	Chicago	12-0	Joseph Raycroft	1956	San Francisco	29-0	Phil Woolpert
1910	Columbia	11-1	Harry Fisher	1957	North Carolina	32-0	Frank McGuire
1911	St. John's	14-0	Claude Allen	1958	Kentucky	23-6	Adolph Rupp
1912	Wisconsin	15-0	Doc Meanwell	1959	California	25-4	Pete Newell
1913	Navy	9-0	Louis Wenzell	1960	Ohio St.	25-3	Fred Taylor
1914	Wisconsin	15-0	Doc Meanwell	1961	Cincinnati	27-3	Edwin Jucker
1915	Illinois	16-0	Ralph Jones	1962	Cincinnati	29-2	Edwin Jucker
1916	Wisconsin	20-1	Doc Meanwell	1963	Loyola (IL)	29-2	George Ireland
1917	Washington St.	25-1	Doc Bohler	1964	UCLA	30-0	John Wooden
1918	Syracuse	16-1	Edmund Dollard	1965	UCLA	28-2	John Wooden
1919	Minnesota	13-0	Louis Cooke	1966	Texas Western	28-1	Don Haskins
1920	Pennsylvania	22-1	Lon Jourdet	1967	UCLA	30-0	John Wooden
1921	Pennsylvania	21-2	Edward McNichol	1968	UCLA	29-1	John Wooden
1922	Kansas	16-2	Phog Allen	1969	UCLA	29-1	John Wooden
1923	Kansas	17-1	Phog Allen	1970	UCLA	28-2	John Wooden
1924	North Carolina	25-0	Bo Shepard	1971	UCLA	29-1	John Wooden
1925	Princeton	21-2	Al Wittmer	1972	UCLA	30-0	John Wooden
1926	Syracuse	19-1	Lew Andreas	1973	UCLA	30-0	John Wooden
1927	Notre Dame	19-1	George Keogan	1974	N. Carol. St.	30-1	Norm Sloan
1928	Pittsburgh	21-0	Doc Carlson	1975	UCLA	28-3	John Wooden
1929	Montana St.	36-2	Shubert Dyche	1976	Indiana	32-0	Bobby Knight
1930	Pittsburgh	23-2	Doc Carlson	1977	Marquette	25-7	Al McGuire
1931	Northwestern	16-1	Dutch Lonborg	1978	Kentucky	30-2	Joe B. Hall
1932	Purdue	17-1	Piggy Lambert	1979	Michigan St.	26-6	Jud Heathcote
1933	Kentucky	20-3	Adolph Rupp	1980	Louisville	33-3	Denny Crum
1934	Wyoming	26-3	Dutch Witte	1981	Indiana	26-9	Bobby Knight
1935	New York	18-1	Howard Cann	1982	North Carolina	32-2	Dean Smith
1936	Notre Dame	22-2-1	George Keogan	1983	N. Carol. St.	28-8	Jim Valvano
1937	Stanford	25-2	John Bunn	1984	Georgetown	34-3	John Thompson
1938	Temple	23-2	James Usilton	1985	Villanova	25-10	Rollie Massimino
1939	Oregon	29-5	Howard Hobson	1986	Louisville	32-7	Denny Crum
1940	Indiana	20-3	Branch McCracken	1987	Indiana	30-4	Bobby Knight
1941	Wisconsin	20-3	Bud Foster	1988	Kansas	27-11	Larry Brown
1942	Stanford	28-4	Everett Dean	1989	Michigan	30-7	Steve Fisher
1943	Wyoming	31-2	Everett Shelton	1990	UNLV	35-5	Jerry Tarkanian
1944	Utah	22-4	Vadal Peterson	1991	Duke	32-7	Mike Krzyzewski
1945	Oklahoma A&M	27-4	Hank Iba	1992	Duke	34-2	Mike Krzyzewski
1946	Oklahoma A&M	31-2	Hank Iba	1993	North Carolina	34-4	Dean Smith
1947	Holy Cross	27-3	Doggie Julian	1994	Arkansas	31-3	Nolan Richardson

FINAL FOUR RESULTS

YEAR	CHAMPION	FINALS OPP.	SCORE	RUNNER-UP	RUNNER-UP
1939	Oregon	Ohio St.	46-33	Oklahoma	Villanova
1940	Indiana	Kansas	60-42	Duquesne	Southern Cal.
1941	Wisconsin	Washington St.	39-34	Arkansas	Pittsburgh
1942	Stanford	Dartmouth	53-38	Colorado	Kentucky
1943	Wyoming	Georgetown	46-34	DePaul	Texas
1944	Utah	Dartmouth	42-40 (OT)	Iowa St.	Ohio St.
1945	Oklahoma A&M	New York	49-45	Arkansas	Ohio St.
1946	Oklahoma A&M	North Carolina	43-40	Ohio St.	California
1947	Holy Cross	Oklahoma	58-47	Texas	CCNY
1948	Kentucky	Baylor	58-42	Holy Cross	Kansas St.
1949	Kentucky	Oklahoma A&M	46-36	Illinois	Oregon St.
1950	CCNY	Bradley	71-68	N. Carol. St.	Baylor
1951	Kentucky	Kansas St.	68-58	Illinois	Oklahoma A&M
1952	Kansas	St. John's	80-63	Illinois	Santa Clara
1953	Indiana	Kansas	69-68	Washington	Louisiana St.
1954	La Salle	Bradley	92-76	Penn St.	Southern Cal.
1955	San Francisco	La Salle	77-63	Colorado	Iowa
1956	San Francisco	Iowa	83-71	Temple	SMU
1957	North Carolina	Kansas	54-53 (3 OT)	San Francisco	Michigan St.
1958	Kentucky	Seattle	84-72	Temple	Kansas St.
1959	California	West Virginia	71-70	Cincinnati	Louisville
1960	Ohio St.	California	75-55	Cincinnati	New York
1961	Cincinnati	Ohio St.	70-65 (OT)	St. Joe's (PA)	Utah
1962	Cincinnati	Ohio St.	71-59	Wake Forest	UCLA
1963	Loyola (IL)	Cincinnati	60-58 (OT)	Duke	Oregon St.
1964	UCLA	Duke	98-83	Michigan	Kansas St.
1965	UCLA	Michigan	91-80	Princeton	Wichita St.
1966	Texas Western	Kentucky	72-65	Duke	Utah
1967	UCLA	Dayton	79-64	Houston	North Carolina
1968	UCLA	North Carolina	78-55	Ohio St.	Houston
1969	UCLA	Purdue	92-72	Drake	North Carolina
1970	UCLA	Jacksonville	80-69	New Mexico St.	St. Bonaventure
1971	UCLA	Villanova	68-62	W. Kentucky	Kansas
1972	UCLA	Florida St.	81-76	North Carolina	Louisville
1973	UCLA	Memphis St.	87-66	Indiana	Providence
1974	N. Carol. St.	Marquette	76-64	UCLA	Kansas
1975	UCLA	Kentucky	92-85	Louisville	Syracuse
1976	Indiana	Michigan	86-68	UCLA	Rutgers
1977	Marquette	North Carolina	67-59	UNLV	N.C.-Charlotte
1978	Kentucky	Duke	94-88	Arkansas	Notre Dame
1979	Michigan St.	Indiana St.	75-64	DePaul	Pennsylvania
1980	Louisville	UCLA	59-54	Purdue	Iowa
1981	Indiana	North Carolina	63-50	Virginia	Louisiana St.
1982	North Carolina	Georgetown	63-62	Houston	Louisville
1983	N. Carol. St.	Houston	54-52	Georgia	Louisville
1984	Georgetown	Houston	84-75	Kentucky	Virginia
1985	Villanova	Georgetown	66-64	Memphis St.	St. John's
1986	Louisville	Duke	72-69	Kansas	Louisiana St.
1987	Indiana	Syracuse	74-73	Providence	UNLV
1988	Kansas	Oklahoma	83-79	Arizona	Duke
1989	Michigan	Seton Hall	80-79 (OT)	Duke	Illinois
1990	UNLV	Duke	103-73	Arkansas	Georgia Tech
1991	Duke	Kansas	72-65	North Carolina	UNLV
1992	Duke	Michigan	71-51	Indiana	Cincinnati
1993	North Carolina	Michigan	77-71	Kansas	Kentucky
1994	Arkansas	Duke	76-72	Arizona	Florida

DIVISION I CAREER LEADERS

POINTS

3,667	Pete Maravich, Louisiana St.
3,249	Freeman Williams, Portland St.
3,217	Lionel Simmons, La Salle
3,165	Alphonso Ford, Miss. Valley St.
3,066	Harry Kelly, Texas Southern
3,008	Hersey Hawkins, Bradley
2,973	Oscar Robertson, Cincinnati
2,951	Danny Manning, Kansas
2,914	Alfredrick Hughes, Loyola (IL)
2,884	Elvin Hayes, Houston

SCORING AVERAGE

44.2	Pete Maravich, Louisiana St.
34.6	Austin Carr, Notre Dame
33.8	Oscar Robertson, Cincinnati
33.1	Calvin Murphy, Niagara
32.7	Dwight Lamar, S.W. Louisiana
32.5	Frank Selvy, Furman
32.3	Rick Mount, Purdue
32.1	Darrell Floyd, Furman
32.0	Nick Werkman, Seton Hall
31.5	Willie Humes, Idaho St.

REBOUNDS

2,201	Tom Gola, La Salle
2,030	Joe Holup, George Washington
1,916	Charlie Slack, Marshall
1,884	Ed Conlin, Fordham
1,802	Dickie Hemric, Wake Forest
1,751	Paul Silas, Creighton
1,716	Art Quimby, Connecticut
1,688	Jerry Harper, Alabama
1,679	Jeff Cohen, William & Mary
1,675	Steve Hamilton, Morehead St.

ASSISTS

1,076	Bobby Hurley, Duke
1,038	Chris Corchiani, N. Carolina St.
983	Keith Jennings, E. Tennessee St.
960	Sherman Douglas, Syracuse
950	Greg Anthony, Portland & UNLV
939	Gary Payton, Oregon St.
902	Orlando Smart, San Francisco
894	Andre LaFleur, Northeastern
884	Jim Les, Bradley
883	Frank Smith, Old Dominion

STEALS

376	Eric Murdock, Providence
341	Michael Anderson, Drexel
341	Kenny Robertson, Cleveland St.
334	Keith Jennings, E. Tennessee St.
329	Greg Anthony, Portland & UNLV
328	Chris Corchiani, N. Carolina St.
321	Gary Payton, Oregon St.
314	Mark Woods, Wright St.
310	Scott Burrell, Connecticut
304	Elliot Perry, Memphis St.

BLOCKED SHOTS

453	Alonzo Mourning, Georgetown
419	Rodney Blake, St. Joseph's (PA)
412	Shaquille O'Neal, Louisiana St.
409	Kevin Roberson, Vermont
399	Jim McIlvaine, Marquette
392	Tim Perry, Temple
374	Pervis Ellison, Louisville
365	Acie Earl, Iowa
354	Dikembe Mutombo, Georgetown
351	David Robinson, Navy

FIELD GOAL PCT.

69.0	Ricky Nedd, Appalachian St.
68.5	Steve Scheffler, Purdue
67.8	Steve Johnson, Oregon St.
66.8	Murray Brown, Florida St.
66.5	Lee Campbell, S.W. Missouri St.
66.4	Warren Kidd, Middle Tenn. St.
66.2	Joe Senser, West Chester
65.6	Kevin Magee, California-Irvine
65.4	Orlando Phillips, Pepperdine
65.1	Bill Walton, UCLA

FREE THROW PCT.

90.9	Greg Starrick, Kentucky & S. Illinois
90.1	Jack Moore, Nebraska
90.0	Steve Henson, Kansas St.
89.8	Steve Alford, Indiana
89.8	Bob Lloyd, Rutgers
89.5	Jim Barton, Dartmouth
89.2	Tommy Boyer, Arkansas
88.8	Rob Robbins, New Mexico
88.5	Sean Miller, Pittsburgh
88.5	Ron Perry, Holy Cross

3-PT FIELD GOAL PCT.

49.7	Tony Bennett, Wisc.-Green Bay
49.3	Keith Jennings, E. Tennessee St.
47.5	Kirk Manns, Michigan St.
47.2	Tim Locum, Wisconsin
46.6	David Olson, Eastern Illinois
46.0	Sean Jackson, Ohio & Princeton
46.0	Barry Booker, Vanderbilt
45.9	Kevin Booth, Mt. St. Mary's
45.9	Dave Calloway, Monmouth
45.8	Tony Ross, San Diego St.

MOST VICTORIES, COACH

876	Adolph Rupp
802	Dean Smith
767	Hank Iba
759	Ed Diddle
746	Phog Allen
724	Ray Meyer
664	John Wooden
657	Ralph Miller
645	Don Haskins
642	Marv Harshman

DIVISION I SEASON RECORDS

POINTS

1,381	Pete Maravich, Louisiana St.	1970
1,214	Elvin Hayes, Houston	1968
1,209	Frank Selvy, Furman	1954
1,148	Pete Maravich, Louisiana St.	1969
1,138	Pete Maravich, Louisiana St.	1968
1,131	Bo Kimble, Loyola Marymount	1990
1,125	Hersey Hawkins, Bradley	1988
1,106	Austin Carr, Notre Dame	1970
1,101	Austin Carr, Notre Dame	1971
1,090	Otis Birdsong, Houston	1977

SCORING AVERAGE

44.5	Pete Maravich, Louisiana St.	1970
44.2	Pete Maravich, Louisiana St.	1969
43.8	Pete Maravich, Louisiana St.	1968
41.7	Frank Selvy, Furman	1954
40.1	Johnny Neumann, Mississippi	1971
38.8	Freeman Williams, Portland St.	1977
38.8	Billy McGill, Utah	1962
38.2	Calvin Murphy, Niagara	1968
38.1	Austin Carr, Notre Dame	1970
38.0	Austin Carr, Notre Dame	1971

REBOUNDS

734	Walter Dukes, Seton Hall	1953
652	Leroy Wright, Pacific	1959
652	Tom Gola, La Salle	1954
645	Charlie Tyra, Louisville	1956
631	Paul Silas, Creighton	1964
624	Elvin Hayes, Houston	1968
621	Artis Gilmore, Jacksonville	1970
618	Tom Gola, La Salle	1955
612	Ed Conlin, Fordham	1953
611	Art Quimby, Connecticut	1955

ASSISTS

406	Mark Wade, Nevada-Las Vegas	1987
399	Avery Johnson, Southern	1988
373	Anthony Manuel, Bradley	1988
333	Avery Johnson, Southern	1987
328	Mark Jackson, St. John's	1986
326	Sherman Douglas, Syracuse	1989
310	Greg Anthony, Nevada-Las Vegas	1991
310	Sam Crawford, New Mexico St.	1993
309	Reid Gettys, Houston	1984
305	Carl Golston, Loyola (IL)	1985

STEALS

150	Mookie Blaylock, Oklahoma	1988
142	Aldwin Ware, Florida A&M	1988
139	Darron Brittman, Chicago St.	1986
138	Nadav Henefeld, Connecticut	1990
131	Mookie Blaylock, Oklahoma	1989
130	Ronn McMahon, Eastern Washington	1990
124	Marty Johnson, Towson St.	1988

120	Shawn Griggs, S.W. Louisiana	1994
120	Jim Paguaga, St. Francis (NY)	1986
114	Tony Fairley, Charleston So.	1987
112	Scott Burrell, Connecticut	1991

BLOCKED SHOTS

207	David Robinson, Navy	1986
177	Shawn Bradley, Brigham Young	1991
169	Alonzo Mourning, Georgetown	1989
160	Alonzo Mourning, Georgetown	1992
157	Shaquille O'Neal, Louisiana St.	1992
151	Dikembe Mutombo, Georgetown	1991
144	David Robinson, Navy	1987
143	Cedric Lewis, Maryland	1991
142	Jim McIlvaine, Marquette	1994
140	Shaquille O'Neal, Louisiana St.	1991
139	Kevin Roberson, Vermont	1992

FIELD GOAL PCT.

74.6	Steve Johnson, Oregon St.	1981
72.2	Dwayne Davis, Florida	1989
71.3	Keith Walker, Utica	1985
71.0	Steve Johnson, Oregon St.	1980
70.4	Oliver Miller, Arkansas	1991
70.3	Alan Williams, Princeton	1987
70.2	Mark McNamara, California	1982
70.0	Warren Kidd, Middle Tenn. St.	1991
70.0	Pete Freeman, Akron	1991
69.9	Joe Senser, West Chester	1977

FREE THROW PCT.

95.9	Craig Collins, Penn St.	1985
95.0	Rod Foster, UCLA	1982
94.4	Danny Basile, Marist	1994
94.4	Carlos Gibson, Marshall	1978
94.2	Jim Barton, Dartmouth	1986
93.9	Jack Moore, Nebraska	1982
93.5	Dandrea Evans, Troy St.	1994
93.5	Rob Robbins, New Mexico	1990
93.3	Tommy Boyer, Arkansas	1962
93.1	Damon Goodwin, Dayton	1986
92.9	Brian Magid, George Washington	1980
92.9	Mike Joseph, Bucknell	1990

3-PT FIELD GOAL PCT.

63.4	Glenn Tropf, Holy Cross	1988
63.2	Sean Wightman, Western Michigan	1992
59.2	Keith Jennings, E. Tenn. St.	1991
58.5	Dave Calloway, Monmouth	1989
57.3	Steve Kerr, Arizona	1988
57.1	Reginald Jones, Prairie View	1987
56.3	Joel Tribelhorn, Colorado St.	1989
56.0	Mike Joseph, Bucknell	1988
55.7	Christian Laettner, Duke	1992
54.8	Reginald Jones, Prairie View	1988

DIVISION I GAME RECORDS

POINTS

72	Kevin Bradshaw, U.S. Intl. vs. Loyola Mary.	1991
69	Pete Maravich, Louisiana St. vs. Alabama	1970
68	Calvin Murphy, Niagara vs. Syracuse	1968
66	Jay Handlan, Washington & Lee vs. Furman	1951
66	Pete Maravich, Louisiana St. vs. Tulane	1969
66	Anthony Roberts, Oral Rob. vs. N.C. A&T	1977
65	Anthony Roberts, Oral Roberts vs. Oregon	1977
65	Scott Haffner, Evansville vs. Dayton	1989
64	Pete Maravich, Louisiana St. vs. Kentucky	1970
63	Johnny Neumann, Mississippi St. vs. LSU	1971
63	Hersey Hawkins, Bradley vs. Detroit	1988

REBOUNDS

51	Bill Chambers, William & Mary vs. Virginia	1953
43	Charlie Slack, Marshall vs. Morris Harvey	1954
42	Tom Heinsohn, Holy Cross vs. Boston Coll.	1955
40	Art Quimby, Connecticut vs. Boston U.	1955
39	Maurice Stokes, St. Fran. (PA) vs. J. Carroll	1955
39	Dave DeBusschere, Detroit vs. C. Michigan	1960
39	Keith Swagerty, Pacific vs. Cal.-Santa Barb.	1965

ASSISTS

22	Tony Fairley, Charleston So. vs. Arms. St.	1987
22	Avery Johnson, Southern vs. Texas South.	1988
22	Sherman Douglas, Syracuse vs. Providence	1989
21	Mark Wade, Nevada-Las Vegas vs. Navy	1986
21	Kelvin Scarborough, New Mexico vs. Hawaii	1987
21	Anthony Manuel, Bradley vs. Cal.-Irvine	1987
21	Avery Johnson, Southern vs. Alabama St.	1988

STEALS

13	Mookie Blaylock, Oklahoma vs. Centenary	1987
13	Mookie Blaylock, Oklahoma vs. Loyola Mary.	1988
12	Kenny Robertson, Cleveland St. vs. Wagner	1988
12	Terry Evans, Oklahoma vs. Florida A&M	1993
11	Darron Brittman, Chicago St. vs. McKendree	1986
11	Darron Brittman, Chicago St. vs. St. Xavier	1986
11	Marty Johnson, Towson St. vs. Bucknell	1988
11	Aldwin Ware, Florida A&M vs. Tuskegee	1988
11	Mark Macon, Temple vs. Notre Dame	1989
11	Carl Thomas, E. Michigan vs. Chicago St.	1991
11	Ron Arnold, St. Fran. (NY) vs. Mt. St. Mary's	1993

BLOCKED SHOTS

14	David Robinson, Navy vs. N.C.-Wilmington	1986
14	Shawn Bradley, BYU vs. E. Kentucky	1990
13	Kevin Roberson, Vermont vs. New Hamp.	1992
12	David Robinson, Navy vs. James Madison	1986
12	Derrick Lewis, Maryland vs. James Madison	1987
12	Rodney Blake, St. Joseph's (PA) vs. Cle. St.	1987
12	Walter Palmer, Dartmouth vs. Harvard	1988
12	Alan Ogg, Alabama-Birm. vs. Florida A&M	1988
12	Dikembe Mutombo, Georget. vs. St. John's	1989
12	Shaquille O'Neal, LSU vs. Loyola Mary.	1990
12	Cedric Lewis, Maryland vs. South Florida	1991

DIVISION I WINNINGEST TEAMS

ALL-TIME WINS

	YRS	WINS
North Carolina	84	1,598
Kentucky	91	1,587
Kansas	96	1,542
St. John's	87	1,494
Duke	89	1,463
Oregon St.	93	1,421
Temple	98	1,416
Notre Dame	89	1,374
Pennsylvania	93	1,387
Syracuse	93	1,383
Indiana	94	1,350
Washington	92	1,323
UCLA	75	1,315
Western Kentucky	75	1,304
Princeton	94	1,297
Fordham	91	1,287
Purdue	96	1,286
West Virginia	85	1,279
North Carolina St.	82	1,265
Utah	86	1,262
Illinois	89	1,262

ALL-TIME WINNING PCT.

	W	L	T	PCT.
Nevada-Las Vegas	762	240	0	.760
Kentucky	1,588	513	1	.756
North Carolina	1,598	571	0	.737
St. John's	1,494	652	0	.696
UCLA	1,315	584	0	.692
Kansas	1,542	697	0	.689
Syracuse	1,383	651	0	.680
Western Kentucky	1,304	616	0	.679
Duke	1,463	709	0	.674
DePaul	1,150	569	0	.669
Notre Dame	1,374	718	1	.657
Louisville	1,257	662	0	.655
La Salle	1,056	575	0	.647
Indiana	1,350	720	0	.652
Arkansas	1,172	626	0	.652
Temple	1,416	769	0	.648
Weber St.	584	319	0	.647
Illinois	1,262	701	0	.643
Houston	875	486	0	.643
Utah	1,262	711	0	.640